O'Brien & Company
Chartered Accountants,
Crestfield Centre,
Riverstown,
Glanmire.
Co. Cork

July 2003

GW00500751

PH: 021-4823200

FORENSIC ACCOUNTING

UNITED KINGDOM
Sweet & Maxwell Ltd
London

AUSTRALIA
LBC Information Services Ltd
Sydney

CANADA and USA
Carswell
Toronto

NEW ZEALAND
Brooker's
Auckland

SINGAPORE and MALAYSIA
Sweet & Maxwell
Singapore and Kuala Lumpur

Forensic Accounting

Niamh Brennan

BSc, PhD (Warwick), FCA,
Michael MacCormac Professor of Management
University College Dublin

and

John Hennessy

BA, FCA, FCIArb,
Barrister-at-law (King's Inns)

DUBLIN
ROUND HALL SWEET & MAXWELL
2001

Published in 2001 by
Round Hall Ltd
43 Fitzwilliam Place
Dublin 2

Typeset by
Gough Typesetting Services and Keystrokes,
Dublin

Printed by
MPG Books, Cornwall

ISBN 1-85800-203-6

A catalogue record for this book
is available from the British Library.

For Michael and Hugh, Ross & John

N.B.

For Mary

J.H.

FOREWORD

The greatly increased role of accountants as witnesses in our courts is amply demonstrated by the remarkable scope of this admirable work. Not merely are they regularly required in personal injuries actions to deal with difficult questions of loss of earnings and profits: the huge increase in the number of family law and employment cases has inevitably resulted in an ever increasing demand for their services in those areas also. It is now a fact of life that commercial disputes, when they come to the High Court, tend to become extremely complex and protracted and again the role of accountants in dealing with such matters as the appropriate estimation of damages can be very significant.

All this has been accompanied by a vast volume of legislation regulating companies. The statutory functions of accountants as auditors and the many other circumstances in which they may be called upon to give evidence makes it important for them to have a reasonable understanding of the law and how it operates in practice. In the criminal field in Ireland, in contrast to other common law jurisdictions such as the United Kingdom and the United States, prosecutions for major fraud offences are still relatively infrequent. When they do happen, however, the evidence of accountants, both for the prosecution and the defence, is frequently of crucial importance.

I believe that Professor Niamh Brennan and Mr. John Hennessy have rendered the accountancy profession a signal service by producing this enormously comprehensive guide to forensic accounting. While they make it clear that their primary audience is not lawyers, I have no doubt that members of both branches of the legal profession will also find much that is of interest and value to them in this book.

I am sure that the work will receive a warm welcome from the accountancy profession, that it will be extremely useful to both accountants and lawyers in preparing cases for trial and that, in the result, the legal system itself will be the beneficiary of the remarkable industry and wide ranging knowledge of a number of professional disciplines which is reflected throughout the book. I wish it the success that it thoroughly deserves.

Ronan Keane,
Four Courts,
Dublin 7.

October 12, 2001.

PREFACE

"The business of an accountant and auditor is innately unsympathetic, and it is liable to suffer in efficiency when undertaken in a more or less obliging and friendly spirit." (per Meredith J. in the Supreme Court in *Leech v. Stokes Brothers and Pim* [1937] I.R. 787 at 832).

Forensic accounting was a term hardly known 30 years ago, let alone when the learned judge made the somewhat caustic observation quoted above. In many ways his underlying sentiment remains as true today as it was then, insofar as it concerns the independence, objectivity and professional integrity which characterise the good accountant. Those qualities are, in fact, required in even greater measure when an accountant gives evidence as an expert in a legal context. That is because the expert accountant's duty is to the court and not to the party by whom the expert is called to give evidence – a principle easily forgotten but fundamental to the proper functioning of our system of justice.

Although accounts and accountants have been the subject of litigation for as long as there have been courts and commerce, regular involvement of accountants as experts in dispute resolution is a recent phenomenon. A number of factors have contributed to the growing demand for expert accounting assistance. Among them is the huge increase in professional regulations that govern the provision of accounting and auditing services to the community. At the same time, there has been a significant increase in the quantity and complexity of legislation impacting on commercial disputes and on other matters involving accounts and financial analysis. Commercial transactions and financial calculations in the twenty-first century are much more sophisticated and are often not readily understood by non-accountants, including lawyers, judges and juries. As a result, litigation often brings together unfamiliar bedfellows: lawyers with little or no accounting training, and expert accountants with a limited knowledge of the legal system.

This book sets out to help bridge the knowledge gap between lawyers and accountants. It is neither a purely legal work nor an accounting text, but rather has a dual purpose. It attempts to give forensic accountants an understanding of legal principles underlying possible resolution of disputes in which their assistance is likely to be requested, and to provide them with an appreciation of how the legal system works. We hope that lawyers, while not the primary readership for the book, may also find many areas of interest, especially those dealing with accounting technicalities and other considerations underlying the financial calculations performed by accounting experts.

There is no doubt that the role of the forensic accountant will increase in importance in years to come. Not only will forensic accountants continue to provide important assistance in litigation, but the increase in arbitration and other forms of dispute resolution reflects an appreciation that, when expert knowledge is vested in the adjudicator, the process can be fairer, quicker and less costly. In this regard, it should be noted that the Civil Procedure Rules in England provide for the use of a single expert in certain cases instead of an expert on each side. These developments point to the increasing importance of an expert accountant in assisting in the decision-making process as well as in advising the parties to a dispute.

Enactment of the Company Law Enforcement Act 2001 in July 2001 adds a number of important new provisions to Irish company law, many of which will affect the practice of forensic accounting, Although at the time of writing dates have yet to be fixed for the coming in to operation of many of the sections of the Act, including all sections relating to the new corporate enforcement regime, the relevant provisions of the Act have been including and discussed in the text.

The book is divided into five parts. After the introduction in Part I, Part II deals with fraud. This issue is given substantial consideration, as forensic accounting often involves allegations of fraud. The Criminal Justice (Theft and Fraud Offences) Bill 2000 had not been enacted at the time of writing, and relevant provisions of the Bill as initiated are dealt with in the book.

Part III has a strong legal bias and deals with the wide variety of specific situations and contexts in which forensic accountants might be involved – distinguishing between litigation involving individuals and corporate litigation.

Part IV deals with the important issue of the calculation of damages. It describes the legal basis for the award of damages and examines methods used for their calculation. Part V gives an overview of legal procedure and terminology most likely to be encountered by forensic accountants, and includes discussion of injunctions, the laws of evidence, discovery and accountants' reports and evidence in a courtroom setting.

Lord Justice Harman once described accountants as "the witch doctors of the modern world" (*Miles v. Clarke* [1953] 1 W.L.R. 537 at 539). This book examines the truth behind the "magic" to help forensic accountants and their clients to understand the real value that can be added to resolution of disputes when they work together.

Niamh Brennan
John Hennessy
October 1, 2001

ACKNOWLEDGEMENTS

Any book that attempts to summarise in single chapters topics to which other writers have devoted volumes is bound to have limitations. The resulting shortcomings are the responsibility of the authors alone. However, we have had the benefit of the willing assistance of several experts who have given unselfishly of their time and expertise in reviewing specific chapters in draft form and providing invaluable comments and suggestions. For their comments and encouragement we thank Paul Appleby, Frank Brady, Alacoque Condon, Kieran Corrigan, Tom Courtney, Patrick Donnelly, Anne Dunne, Éimear Fisher, Adrian Hardiman, Gerard Hogan, Michael McDowell, Michael Moriarty, Des Peelo, Mark Sanfey and James Skehan. We are particularly indebted to Tom Courtney, who read a preliminary draft of the entire manuscript, for his helpful suggestions on the general structure and focus of the book.

Many others gave generously of their advice and answered our numerous queries and requests including John Bowen-Walsh, Elisha Caulfield, Blanaid Clarke, Brian Daly, Christopher Doyle, Peter Durnin, Tony Eklof, Ruth Fitzgerald, Paul Gibney, Paddy Hunt, Geraldine Hurley, Brian Hutchinson, John Gibson, Ann Lane, Terry McGlynn, Felix McKenna, Sinead McSweeney, Kate Marshall, Declan Maunsell, Damien Moloney, Yvonne Murphy, Liam O'Daly, Christopher O'Toole, Barry Quinlan, Lizanne Senior and Caroline Walsh.

We also thank Henry Murdoch for his diagram on the Irish justice system which he has allowed us to reproduce in Chapter 2.

We gratefully acknowledge the financial assistance received from the Department of Accountancy, UCD to help with proof-reading.

This book took considerably longer to write than originally planned and we thank our Commissioning Editor, Catherine Dolan, for her patience. We also acknowledge the assistance of other Round Hall staff including Barbara Conway, Dave Ellis, Gilbert Gough, Frank Kearney and Terri McDonnell. Last but not least, we owe particular thanks to Elizabeth Senior for her sharp eye, her attention to detail and her willingness to engross herself in the unfamiliar territory of accountancy.

We are delighted that the Chief Justice, Mr Justice Ronan Keane, agreed to provide the foreword to this book and we are grateful to him for his helpful insights and observations.

Without the support, encouragement and patience of our respective spouses, Michael and Mary, it would not have been possible to devote so much time and energy to this project. Our children, Hugh, Ross and John, and Michael, Lena,

Jack, Simon, Harry and Sally, throughout the two years spent writing this book, provided each of us with welcome distractions from the world of forensic accounting. The six Hennessys lost two beloved grandparents, Michael and Grace, in that period and their passing has reminded us of how much we owe to those who nurtured us and those whom we now nurture. Completion of this work allows us to restore our full attention, with renewed enthusiasm, to that

INFORMATION ABOUT THE AUTHORS

Niamh Brennan, BSc, PhD (Warwick), FCA

Prof. Niamh Brennan is Michael MacCormac Professor of Management at University College Dublin. She was awarded a first class honours science degree (Microbiology and Biochemistry) from University College Dublin after which she joined Stokes Kennedy Crowley (now KPMG) where she qualified as a chartered accountant. She then joined the Department of Accountancy, UCD where she teaches financial accounting and financial reporting at both undergraduate and postgraduate levels. She obtained her PhD from the University of Warwick, having been awarded the 1994 Bass Leisure/British Accounting Association doctoral award.

Author/co-author of a number of books on financial reporting, she has also published papers on a variety of topics in leading accounting journals. She is a non-executive director of *Ulster Bank* and *Co-Operation Ireland*, and is a former non-executive director of Bank of Ireland's life assurance subsidiary, *Lifetime Assurance*, and the Irish state forestry company, *Coillte Teoranta*. She has been appointed by the Minister of Agriculture, Food and Rural Development to the Audit Committee of the Department for a three-year term commencing in 2000. She is a past Chairman of the Leinster Society of Chartered Accountants.

She has acted as expert witness in a number of leading cases requiring independent financial expertise.

John Hennessy, BA, FCA, FCIArb, Barrister-at-Law

John Hennessy is a Mathematical Sciences graduate of Trinity College Dublin. He is a Fellow of the Institute of Chartered Accountants in Ireland and of the Chartered Institute of Arbitrators. He also has a BL degree and a Diploma in Legal Studies from the Honorable Society of King's Inns. He is a practising barrister.

John spent 18 years with Arthur Andersen, including six years as a partner in the firm's worldwide partnership. There he provided audit, advisory, forensic accounting and consulting services to clients in a variety of industries including financial services, telecommunications, manufacturing and aviation, and in the public sector. He established the firm's litigation consulting practice in Dublin, providing forensic accounting services to corporate litigants. He has prepared and delivered expert evidence for a variety of clients engaged in litigation and arbitration proceedings.

During his career in the accounting profession John was involved for almost ten years in the development and promulgation of professional standards, principally in the auditing area. He was a founder member and sole Irish representative on the Auditing Practices Board, the body that sets standards for auditors in the UK and Ireland.

He is non-executive Chairman of *CPL Resources plc*, the publicly quoted recruitment and employment services group. He is also a part-time lecturer on the Master of Accounting programme at University College Dublin.

TABLE OF CONTENTS

PART I
INTRODUCTION

PART II
FRAUD

PART III
ROLE OF FORENSIC ACCOUNTANTS

PART IV
FORENSIC ACCOUNTING CALCULATIONS

PART V
PROCEDURAL ASPECTS OF FORENSIC ACCOUNTING

DETAILED TABLE OF CONTENTS

PART II
FRAUD

PART IV
FORENSIC ACCOUNTING CALCULATIONS

TABLE OF CASES

TABLE OF LEGISLATION

UNITED KINGDOM
Table of Statutes

Table of Statutory Instruments

INTERNATIONAL AND EUROPEAN CONVENTIONS

LIST OF TABLES, FIGURES AND CASE HISTORIES

List of Figures throughout Text

List of Cases Histories Throughout Text

TABLE OF ABBREVIATIONS

Abbreviation	Explanation
A.C.	Appeal Cases
A.G.	Attorney General
All E.R.	All England Law Reports
A.L.R.	Australian Law Reports
APB	Auditing Practices Board
A.R.	Alberta Ct. of Appeal
B.C.C.	British Company Law Cases
Bus. L. Rev.	Business Law Review
CAB	Criminal Assets Bureau
Cal. Rptr.	California Reporter (United States)
CCA	Court of Criminal Appeal
Cir.Ct.	Circuit Court
Ch.	Chancery
Ch.D.	Chancery Division
C.L.P.	Commercial Law Practitioner
Crim. L.R.	Criminal Law Reports
DPP	Director of Public Prosecutions
DTI	Department of Trade and Industry (U.K.)
E.G.	Estates Gazette
E.G.L.R.	Estates Gazette Law Reports
E.R.	English Reports
Ex.	Exchequer Reports/Cases
Exch.	Exchequer Reports
Ex. D.	Exchequer Division
Fed. Cas.	Federal Cases (U.S.)
F.C.R.	Federal Court Reports (Australia)
FRS	Financial Reporting Standard
High Ct.	High Court
HL	House of Lords appeals
ibid.	Referring to the same source
ILGS	Index linked government stock
I.L.R.M.	Irish Law Reports Monthly
I.L.T.R.	Irish Law Times Reports
I.R.	Irish Reports
I.T.C.	Irish Tax Cases
I.T.R.	Irish Tax Reports

Abbreviation	Explanation
I.T.L.R.	Irish Times Law Reports
K.B. (or Q.B.)	King's or Queen's Bench
Lloyd's Rep.	Lloyd's List Law Reports
Macq.	Macqueen (Sc.)
No.	Number
N.S.W.L.R.	New South Wales Law Report
N.Z.L.R.	New Zealand Law Reports
Para.	Paragraph
PAYE	Pay-As-You-Earn
P. & C.R.	Property & Compenation Reports
P.I.Q.R.	Personal Injuries and Quantum Reports
Q.B.D.	Queen's Bench Division
R.P.C.	Reports of Patent Cases
R.V.R.	Rating and Valuation Reporter
SAS	Statement of Auditing Standards
S.C.R.	Supreme Court Reports (Canada)
Sup. Ct.	Supreme Court
S.I.	Statutory Instrument
Sol. J.	Solicitor's Journal
S.T.C.	Simon's Tax Cases
T.C.	Tax Cases
U.D.	Unfair Dismissals
VAT	Value-Added-Tax
W.L.R.	Weekly Law Reports

PART I

INTRODUCTION

INTRODUCTION TO FORENSIC ACCOUNTING

CHAPTER 1

INTRODUCTION TO FORENSIC ACCOUNTING

What is forensic accounting?

1–01 The term "forensic accounting" was first used by the Canadian accountant Robert Lindquist to describe the special combination of skills applied in preparing and reviewing financial evidence.[1] Although relatively recent in the accounting profession, the role of a forensic expert in other professions has been in place for many years. Forensic, according to the *Oxford English Dictionary* (full-length version), means: "Pertaining to, connected with, or used in courts of law; suitable or analogous to pleadings in court".[2] It implies an ability to meet the exacting standards of a court of law (thus, forensic science, forensic psychiatry, etc.). Forensic accountants are often referred to as "financial detectives".

1–02 The integration of accounting, auditing and investigative ability and their application to litigation yield the specialty known as forensic accounting. Accordingly, the term "forensic" in the accounting profession deals with the application of financial expertise to financial investigation, to legal problems and disputes and in conflict resolution. Forensic accounting describes expert specialist accounting work performed for court or other legally sensitive purposes. It involves gathering information and providing accounting analysis that is suitable to the court which will assist in discussion, negotiation and, ultimately, dispute resolution. The accounting information may be required for presentation as evidence in a court of law, whether that court is criminal or civil, or in another dispute resolution forum.

1–03 A forensic accountant is one who performs an orderly analysis, investigation, inquiry, test, inspection or examination, or any combination of financial information, in an attempt to assess the merits of a situation, and form an expert opinion.

Forensic accounting differs from traditional accounting work. Forensic accountants look *behind*, rather then merely at, the numbers.[3] Whilst accounting knowledge and expertise is an assumed fundamental, the difference lies in the

---

[1] Johnson, P. "Forensic accounting – a legal support" (1996) C.L.P. 206.
[2] *Oxford English Dictionary* (2nd ed., Oxford University Press, Oxford, 1989), p. 55.
[3] Michael G. Kessler & Associates, Ltd, "Forensic Accounting", www.investigation.com.

expert's experience of working with sensitive evidence, with lawyers, with law enforcement agencies (where required) and with the legal system. Forensic accountants perform their work with a view to its potential use in a legal or quasi-legal environment. Where there is suspicion of fraud, a forensic accountant will question how and why that fraud was committed. Accounting work performed without this focus, and without relevant skills and knowledge, can (completely innocently) significantly impair the value of crucial evidence by failing to link it to relevant matters in dispute.

1–04   Forensic accountants do not win or lose cases on their own – they conduct evaluations, examinations, and inquiries and report the results of their findings in an unbiased, objective and professional manner. This objectivity and independence is a key element of the input of forensic accountants.

1–05   Greater complexity than before marks business dealings in the twenty-first century, and with it come more opportunities for error or wrongdoing. The old model of business, with conventional rules and structures, and with checks and balances, is now outdated. As companies globalise or downsize, restructure, or re-engineer themselves, traditional lines of responsibilities are being blurred. Increased business complexity in a litigious environment has enhanced the need for forensic accountants.

Forensic accounting within the Irish legal system

1–06   Forensic accounting by its nature involves accountants working within the legal system. It would be unrealistic to expect forensic accountants to have a detailed understanding of all legal issues arising in forensic accounting assignments. Nonetheless, some understanding of the legal system will be invaluable to the forensic accountant's appreciation of the part he is to play in the dispute in which he is engaged to advise. Accordingly, this book, while not a legal textbook, attempts to provide accountants with an introduction to legal areas in which forensic accounting has a role to play. Both statute law and case law relevant to forensic accounting is considered.

Services provided by forensic accountants

1–07   Forensic accountants can engage in public practice or be employed by insurance companies, banks, the police, government agencies and other organisations. Clients of forensic accountants include:

– lawyers on behalf of their clients;

– insurance companies;

- insurance claims managers;

- insurance loss adjusters;

- investigators;

- banks;

- management of a client firm *e.g.* audit clients;

- client firm professional advisers, *e.g.* auditors, lawyers;

- prosecuting authorities such as the Director of Public Prosecutions;

- Gardaí;

- regulatory agencies;

- other governmental authorities;

- receivers, liquidators and examiners.

1–08 Forensic accountants are becoming increasingly important in the resolution of disputes. This is because:

- more individuals and companies are turning to the law to resolve disputes;

- the sums of money involved in disputes are increasing in size;

- both business transactions and the legislation applicable to them, including taxation legislation, are becoming increasingly complex; and

- former clients and third parties are suing professional advisers more frequently.

1–09 Forensic accounting covers two broad areas:

- investigative accounting which frequently applies where fraud is alleged; and

- litigation support which the American Institute of Certified Public Accountants describes as "any professional assistance non-lawyers provide to lawyers in the litigation process".[4]

1–10 Transactions and activities involving companies in which a forensic accountant might act are listed in Table 1.1 overleaf.

---

[4] Wagner, M.J. and Frank, P.B., *Technical Consulting Practice Aid No. 7 – Litigation Services* (American Institute of Certified Public Accountants Management Advisory Services, New York, 1986).

Table 1.1: Work of forensic accountants analysed by category

Civil litigation involving individuals	Criminal	Commercial litigation	Corporate cases	Other
Personal injury claims	Management and employee fraud	Breach of contract	Shareholder disputes	Professional negligence
Fatal accident cases	Third party fraud	Breach of warranty	Responsibilities of directors	Non-court investigations
Wrongful dismissal	False accounting	Product liability	Disqualification of directors	Alternative dispute resolution
Discrimination in employment	Computer crime	Insurance claims including stock loss and theft, business interruption and consequential loss	Examinerships	
Matrimonial and separation disputes	Arson for profit	Construction	Insolvency	
Bankruptcy	Tax offences	Patent and copyright claims	Reckless trading	
Taxation disputes	Crimes by shareholders, directors, company officers, auditors	Competition law	Misrepresentation	
	Money laundering	Computer piracy and e-commerce	Partnership disputes	
	Investment fraud	Compulsory acquisition		
	Fraudulent misrepresentation	Taxation disputes		

1–11 Table 1.2 provides examples of forensic accounting assignments.

Table 1.2: Examples of assignments in which forensic accountants have advised

> - Provision of key accounting evidence in criminal actions against company directors, *e.g.* involving fraudulent accounting.
> - Involvement in situations where moneys held in solicitors' client accounts had been misappropriated.
>
> - Co-ordinating the evidence of experts into a single report for the defence of directors accused of PAYE, VAT and accounting frauds, involving an allegation of deliberate transfer of trade into newly created companies.
>
> - Advising in civil and criminal matters involving unauthorised transfers of cash between companies, analysing financial transactions and documenting embezzlement for court exhibits and testimony.

Fraud and investigative accounting

1–12 Forensic accountants become involved in a wide range of investigations, spanning many industries. Investigative accounting usually involves the application of accounting principles and rules to basic financial data with a view to testing the validity of assertions based on accounting information or verifying the accuracy and completeness of financial statements. The level of investigation, possible and necessary, depends on the availability and quality of books and records.

Investigative accounting is used in connection with allegations or suspicions of fraud which could potentially lead to civil, criminal or disciplinary proceedings. For example, where fraud is suspected in a retail business, an investigative accountant may examine business records and compare actual cash takings and profits with those predicted by reference to stock movements and expected margins. Definitions of, and legal aspects of, fraud, together with causes, categorisation, effects and methods of fraud are considered in Chapter 3. The role of company accountants and company auditors in relation to preventing, detecting and reporting fraud is examined in Chapter 4.

The focus of investigative accounting is on accounting issues, but the role of forensic accountants can extend to a more general investigation which includes evidence gathering. Investigative accounting can also extend to forensic audit, which involves examining evidence of an assertion to determine whether it is supported adequately by underlying evidence, usually of an accounting nature. An example is the forensic audit of sales records to verify quantum of commission due under an agency agreement.

1–13 Investigative accounting is often associated with criminal investigations.

Here, the primary concern is to develop evidence around motive, opportunity and benefit.

A typical criminal investigative accounting assignment is an investigation of employee theft. Other examples include insurance fraud, kickbacks and proceeds of crime investigations. Such assignments involve:

–   scrutinising of documents and records in both written and electronic formats;

–   reconstructing a clear and detailed picture of what happened;

–   reviewing the facts;

–   co-ordinating other experts including, for example:

  – private investigators;

  – forensic document examiners;

  – consulting engineers;

–   suggesting possible courses of action;

–   assisting with the protection and recovery of assets, which might include civil action or criminal prosecution.

Table 1.3 below gives examples of the types of investigations in which forensic accountants become involved. Forensic accounting investigations are dealt with in more detail in Chapter 5.

1–14   Forensic investigations into criminal offences can involve assisting the police, the Criminal Assets Bureau, the Director of Public Prosecutions, or other organisations such as the Law Society. A forensic accountant's report is prepared with the objective of presenting relevant and reliable evidence, together with a considered opinion, in a professional and concise manner.

1–15   Business investigations can involve forensic intelligence gathering, funds tracing, asset identification and recovery, and due diligence reviews. Employee fraud investigations often involve procedures to determine the existence, nature and extent of fraud, and may concern the identification of a perpetrator. These investigations often entail interviews with personnel who had access to missing records, funds or other assets and a detailed review of the documentary evidence.

Accounting expertise in litigation and dispute resolution

1–16   There are many circumstances in which accountants may give evidence in court or as participants in other approaches to resolving disputes. It is important that accountants be aware of their role, duties and responsibilities in such contexts. The professional standards and ethical guidelines applying in court situations differ somewhat from those applying in other client assignments. These

Table 1.3: Investigative services provided by forensic accountants

- Arson and fraud investigations for insurance purposes
- Review of suspected fraudulent insurance claims
- Fraud and white-collar crime investigations
- Criminal and civil investigations and actions regarding suspected fraud and financial irregularities, including fraudulent acts, claims, conveyances, embezzlements, defalcations, etc.
- Analysis of transactions and financial information for motive
- Concealment and misrepresentation analysis
- Tax investigations
- Money laundering investigations
- Review of conduct of directors
- Investigations under the Companies Acts and other regulatory investigations
- Fraud and risk management surveys and reports
- Fraud prevention and awareness strategy development
- Fraud detection
- Valuation of losses arising from fraud
- Computer forensics – electronic evidence recovery
- Examination and investigation of financial records and financial data, transaction analysis and tracing
- Investigating and assessing the financial position of individuals or companies
- Pre-litigation investigations
- Reconstruction of accounting and financial records
- Tracing, locating, repatriating and recovering (misappropriated) assets
- Recovery of losses through insurance claims and civil litigation
- Witness location and interviewing
- Locating information and documentation

are discussed in Chapter 6, which ends by considering issues for both the client and the forensic accountant to take into account when agreeing terms of the engagement.

Litigation support

1–17 Litigation support involves the forensic accountant as part of a team providing specialist advice in legal disputes, or where a claim for financial compensation is at issue. Assistance of an accounting nature is provided in both existing and contemplated litigation. Evaluations may be done in preparation for settlement negotiations, mediation, arbitration, and trials, both civil and criminal.

Forensic accountants examine the books and records of individuals and companies in litigation situations to assist lawyers in developing and preparing their case. The forensic accountant usually deals with issues related to the quantification and analysis of economic (*i.e.* monetary/financial) damages. A typical litigation-support assignment would be to calculate the financial loss resulting from a breach of contract. Losses of revenues and profits may have to be measured and valuations of business property or ownership interests may need to be carried out. Forensic accountants also provide input in areas where legal liability is influenced by matters within their field of expertise (*e.g.* the application of accounting standards in assessing whether financial statements have been properly prepared).

1–18   The role of the forensic accountant in litigation support is broader than is often assumed. The view that a forensic accountant only has a role when a case goes to trial is widely held but inaccurate. In fact, most cases do not go to trial and the quality and effectiveness of pre-trial activities is a significant source of opportunity (or danger) for the parties. Forensic accountants can act for plaintiffs or defendants in civil proceedings and for the prosecuting authorities or defendants in criminal cases. Forensic accountants can assist plaintiffs in preparing a claim or, alternatively, materially reduce a claim when acting for defendants.

Expert forensic accountants can advise plaintiffs or defendants from an early stage on the financial aspects of the action. There is little point in reaching the door of the court, with perhaps significant liability for costs, if the value of the case is relatively modest and the case could have been settled sooner. Whether a dispute is settled by negotiation or through the courts, there will almost always be a benefit from authoritative and persuasive evidence based on financial and investigative skills.

1–19   Areas in which forensic accountants provide litigation services were shown in Table 1.1. Forensic accountants can provide assistance in a wide variety of disputes. Some of these are discussed briefly below and many are considered in more detail in later chapters.

Personal injury claims

1–20   Forensic accountants are often asked to quantify the economic (*i.e.* financial) losses arising from personal injuries sustained (including fatal accident cases). The types of case giving rise to such litigation are varied and include motor vehicle accidents, industrial accidents, medical malpractice, etc. Forensic accountants need to be familiar with the law and practice regarding such situations. These are briefly outlined in Chapter 7 (paras **7–03** *et seq.*). The calculation of damages for personal injuries is dealt with in Chapter 16.

Employment disputes

1–21   Employment disputes mainly arise in one of two situations: unfair or wrongful dismissals and allegations of discrimination in employment. The relevant law relating to such litigation is also summarised in Chapter 7 (paras **7–30** *et seq.*). The calculation of economic damages in cases of wrongful dismissal often involves issues similar to those arising in loss-of-earnings calculations in personal injury cases. The financial calculations tend to be based on employment data relating directly to the individual plaintiff employee(s) and/ or derived from national or industry employment data.

Matrimonial disputes

1–22 From a forensic accounting point of view, matrimonial disputes often involve calculation of income, valuation of assets and proposed distribution of matrimonial property. The assets to be valued may be businesses, homes or other assets. Tracing and locating assets may be required in this context. The law relating to separation and divorce is briefly considered in Chapter 7 (paras **7–70** *et seq.*), while Chapter 18 discusses methods of valuing businesses, with some reference to particular valuation issues arising in divorce cases (see paras **18–89** *et seq.*). As divorce has only recently been legislated for in Ireland, practice in this area is at an early stage.

Bankruptcy

1–23 Forensic accountants may occasionally have a role to play in bankruptcy proceedings. Such cases are infrequent, as most individuals conduct their business through companies. The limited role of forensic accountants in bankruptcy cases is considered in Chapter 7 (paras **7–115** *et seq.*).

Criminal cases

1–24 Criminal cases, especially those involving allegations of fraud, may require expert evidence of accountants, who may act for either the prosecution or defence. Prosecution of white-collar crime in Ireland is likely to increase, with the recent appointment of a Director of Corporate Enforcement and with additional legislation dealing with fraud. Cases involving allegations of fraud may involve complex financial transactions which can only be understood with the assistance of expert accountants. Chapter 8 examines criminal law and criminal offences relating to white-collar crime, and under company law. Sundry other criminal offences arising under company law and in cases of money laundering and investment fraud, are considered. Criminal offences under competition law are also included in this chapter.

Commercial disputes

1–25 Commercial cases frequently involve forensic accountants. Such cases can cover a wide variety of legal areas. Some of these are considered in Chapter 9. Examples of assignments involving commercial losses include contract disputes (breach of contract or breach of warranty), product liability claims, insurance claims (*e.g.* business interruptions, property losses, employee dishonesty claims), construction claims, trademark and patent infringements, losses stemming from breach of non-competition agreements and expropriations. Forensic accountants often act in insurance cases, either for the insurance company, the independent loss adjusters or the insured, to assist in calculation of damages or in the settlement of the case. Insurance policies differ significantly as to policy conditions. Accordingly, these assignments involve a detailed review of the policy to investigate coverage issues and the method of calculating loss.

Many such cases require the services of forensic accountants for the purposes of calculating damages (either for the client or to evaluate the other side's calculations), which can be substantial. Services include assessing, investigating and reporting on financial issues, including considering economic matters such as industry trends, trends in employment and the general level of economic activity. The calculation of commercial damages is dealt with in Chapter 17.

Companies and partnerships

1–26   Company and partnership disputes involving shareholders, directors or partners often involve a detailed analysis of numerous years' accounting records to quantify the issues in dispute. For example, a common issue that often arises is the compensation and benefits received by disputing shareholders or partners. Disputes concerning financial matters also arise in insolvencies and examinerships, especially where reckless trading or misrepresentation is alleged. These cases frequently involve forensic accountants. The legal background to such cases is outlined in Chapter 10, which considers the role of forensic accountants in the various contexts discussed.

In such disputes, forensic accountants can also be asked to assist in the valuation of shareholdings and this is covered in Chapter 18.

Taxation

1–27   Most accountants working in the area of taxation act as advisers, and may appear in court (or in front of the Appeal Commissioners) as such. However, forensic accountants have a particular and unique role to play in taxation disputes. This role, and the context in which it is played, is presented in Chapter 11. The role of forensic accountants in tax appeals, in cases of serious tax fraud and in avoidance cases where accounting principles are at issue, is also considered in Chapter 11.

Accountants' liability

1–28   Investigations of the liability of accountants for alleged negligence are often approached from two different but complementary perspectives, these being:

– technical, which seeks to establish whether a breach of generally accepted accounting principles or generally accepted auditing standards of practice has occurred;

– calculation of loss suffered.

This area is covered in Chapter 12.

Company investigations and tribunals of inquiry

1–29 Ireland has seen a significant increase in company investigations and in tribunals of inquiry in recent years. Many of these have involved accountants either as experts or as witnesses of fact. The legal context in which company investigations and tribunals take place is introduced in Chapter 13, with an emphasis on the role of accountants generally, and of forensic accountants in particular.

Alternative dispute resolution

1–30 Because of their familiarity and comfort with legal issues and procedures, some forensic accountants have sought out special training and become involved in alternative dispute resolution (ADR). ADR services include arbitration and mediation services which are designed to help individuals and businesses resolve disputes with minimal disruption and in a timely and cost effective fashion. Forensic accountants can act as experts for parties engaged in ADR or as the provider of the ADR service (*e.g.* as mediator or arbitrator). ADR is discussed more fully in Chapter 14.

Forensic accounting calculations

1–31 Most cases in which forensic accountants act will involve accounting calculations. This is particularly so in cases involving awards for damages. Part IV of the book deals with such calculations. Forensic accountants must have some familiarity with the law of damages and this is summarised at the start of Part IV in Chapter 15. The chapter considers when damages arise, the various types of damages (not all of which involve accounting calculations) and the legal principles applying to recovery of damages. Of particular importance for forensic accounting calculations is mitigation of damages.

1–32 Chapters 16 and 17 examine calculation of personal injury and commercial damages respectively, and outline some accounting principles applying to such calculations. Both chapters consider methods of calculating damages, factors influencing the calculations and the effect of taxation on the calculation of damages.

Many disputes involve valuation of businesses. Chapter 18 discusses various methods of valuation and the factors affecting business values. In particular, approaches to valuing private companies are discussed, together with some evidence from reported cases on approaches taken by the courts to such private company valuations.

1–33 Part IV concludes by considering the effect of the time value of money on amounts of damages. Given the length of time for some cases to come to court, together with the award of damages in respect of lengthy future periods, monetary amounts frequently need to be adjusted to their present values for plaintiffs to be fairly compensated. Chapter 19 discusses some of the approaches taken to discounting awards for damages, and to calculating awards of interest on damages.

Procedural aspects of forensic accounting

1–34 It is important for forensic accountants to have an overall understanding of the legal environment in which their expert evidence will be presented. Part V deals with procedural aspects of forensic accounting and concentrates on the more common elements of legal procedure that are relevant to the work of the forensic accountant.

Overview of civil and criminal procedure

1–35 In particular, Chapter 20 outlines procedure in a civil case and in a criminal case. The glossary in Appendix 3 defines common accounting and legal terms that might be relevant to forensic accounting cases.

Injunctions

1–36 The topic of injunctions is included in Chapter 21 of this book for two reasons. First, injunctions are powerful legal weapons in disputes. Many disputes, especially commercial cases, never proceed beyond the determination of injunctive proceedings. Thus, the injunction hearing may be the start and end of a commercial case. Accountants involved in legal disputes (especially commercial litigation) should be aware of the potential uses of injunctions.

Second, injunctive relief is only available where damages would not be an adequate remedy to "right the wrong" that has been committed. Because the issue of the adequacy of damages is so central to the determination of whether an injunction will be granted, and because the court will consider the financial implications of various possible scenarios, the value of forensic accounting expertise to such proceedings is clear.

Evidence

1–37 Chapter 22 outlines the laws of evidence, discovery and interrogatories. Many of these provisions will apply to forensic accounting evidence and a familiarity with them will be of assistance to those involved in giving such evidence. Chapter 23 examines procedural issues applying specifically to forensic accountants both in preparing their reports and thereafter in giving expert evidence in court.

Retaining forensic accountants

1–38   Forensic accountants are often retained to analyse, interpret, summarise and present complex financial and business-related issues in a manner that is both understandable and properly supported. A party's legal advisers initially determines the need for financial/business expertise; the forensic accountant is then consulted. Activities to which the forensic accountant might contribute during a case, either acting for plaintiff or defendant, are shown in Table 1.4 on page 19.

1–39   The point at which forensic accountants become involved varies from case to case. In some cases, the solicitor may involve forensic accountants at the initial stages. In other situations, forensic accountants may only be called on when the case is finally due to go to court after years of out-of-court preparation and negotiation. Ideally, forensic accountants should be retained as early as possible in order to obtain maximum benefit. The assistance that a forensic accountant can provide early in the process can be significant in reducing the overall cost and maximising the benefit. If retained early, forensic accountants can help to focus the case on significant matters, to identify additional areas of damages, to assist with settlement negotiations and to provide a preliminary assessment of the quantum of damages. Forensic accountants are usually independent of the dispute. The regular accountant, financial adviser or auditor of a firm or individual involved in a dispute might be regarded as having a conflict of interest arising from his existing relationship.

1–40   It is important that the solicitor retain the forensic accountant, and that, as far as possible, correspondence to and from the forensic accountant be with the solicitor. This may help to protect certain correspondence relating to the dispute by way of privilege. However, regulations currently applying to High Court proceedings in Ireland involving personal injuries require reports by experts on which a party to litigation intends to rely to be exchanged by the parties in advance of trial (see paras **22–51 to 22–52**). Normally, there will be a number of drafts of these reports. Drafts must be presented for review to clients to ensure they are factually accurate. Disagreements between clients and advisers may be highlighted when different drafts of expert reports are compared.

1–41   Relatively straightforward cases may involve meetings and interviews (consultations) to obtain the necessary information. More complex cases may involve a review of large volumes of legal correspondence, of previous hearings and injunctions and of detailed financial records. If the forensic accountant is being engaged as an expert witness then he should be given access to all of the relevant documentation. If restrictions are imposed upon the scope of the investigation, there is potential for an adverse impact upon the comprehensiveness and validity of the findings. In such circumstances, the forensic accountant should consider carefully whether to accept the engagement. On the other hand, when all relevant information is provided, an enhanced quality of information is generated by the forensic accountant and is available for use in disputes and dispute resolution. This will lead to better communication and greater chances for successful resolution of disputes, to increased probabilities for favourable settlements, and to preservation or recovery of assets.

1–42   A crucial factor in the role played by the forensic accountant in providing litigation support is the nature of the report and/or evidence to be given. The facts of the particular case, together with the approach being adopted by the legal team, determine what is required from the forensic accountant. The forensic accountant can prepare a definitive report based on matters of fact he investigated. In preparing his report, the forensic accountant will use professional judgment to arrive at and express his opinion on the facts. In this sense, the report may combine issues both of fact and of opinion. However, the added value provided by the forensic accountant is derived from his considered professional opinion.

1–43   Opinion reports by their nature are subjective and rely on the professional judgment of the forensic accountant. In order to support such opinions, it is necessary for the forensic accountant to be able to demonstrate in court the adequacy and completeness of the work undertaken in forming that opinion. The other side in the litigation may also use a forensic accountant in an effort to undermine the validity of the opinion.

Accountants as witnesses

1–44   In a court of law, accountants may be asked or required to give evidence in one of two situations: as witnesses of fact or as expert witnesses. It is important that accountants understand the distinction between these two situations and provide their evidence accordingly. There are significant differences in position, function and potential pitfalls between an expert accountant called as such without prior involvement in the actual facts giving rise to litigation, and an accountant who was auditor, adviser or employee before the litigation started. This is discussed below, and again in paras **6-31** *et seq.*

Accountants as witnesses of fact

1–45   As a general rule, evidence in court proceedings is limited to statements of facts observed by witnesses, and witnesses are not permitted to express opinions or draw inferences from the facts. The basis for this rule of evidence is that to allow such opinions or inferences to be stated by a witness would be to undermine the role of the judge or jury as the finder of fact.

Accountants appearing in court as witnesses of fact are not acting as forensic accountants. Instead, they are assisting the court in its quest to ascertain the

Table 1.4: Work of forensic accountants in a legal context

Alternative dispute resolution (see Chapter 14)
- Arbitration of disputes and dispute resolution
- Advising in pre-hearing negotiations
- Mediation and negotiation

Pre-trial (see Chapters 6 and 23)
- Reviewing relevant documentation, forming an initial assessment of the financial aspects of a case, identifying areas of loss
- Briefing the legal team on the financial aspects and intricacies of the case
- Assisting with settlement discussions and negotiations
- Advising on the merits of case, pre-trial strategies and on case strategy
- Suggesting sources of evidence
- Discovery assistance – identifying documentation necessary to support or refute a claim
- Reviewing the documentation provided by the other side to assess its completeness and its implications, and providing input to any necessary application for discovery of documents or interrogatories
- Document management
- Assisting in preparing interrogatories
- Reviewing and critiquing the opposing expert's report, reporting on its strengths and weaknesses
- Preparing and developing financial exhibits for trial
- Co-ordinating other experts and investigators

Accounting calculations (see Part IV, Chapters 16–19)
- Earnings losses calculation
- Business economic loss calculation
- Share valuations

Exhibits and evidence for trial (see Chapters 6 and 23)
- Assessment of, and quantifying economic damages – actual or potential losses or damages
- Claims analysis
- Preparation of expert reports, reviews and evidence for use either in negotiation or in litigation in accordance with agreed terms of reference

During trial (see Chapters 6 and 23)
- Attending at trial to hear all relevant evidence, including that of the opposing expert
- Anticipation of the other party's case
- Preparing questions to be used in cross-examination at trial
- Advising on cross-examination of the opposing expert
- Assessment of opposing experts and witnesses
- Expert witness testimony – giving oral evidence in direct examination and cross-examination by the opposing side

true facts of the situation. For example, where a fraud on a company is alleged, the company's accountant, acting as a witness of fact, may tender evidence as to the effect of the fraud on the company's financial position, the extent to which the company's books and records reveal that cash or other assets have been misappropriated, or the manner in which the company's control systems were overridden.

In presenting evidence of facts, the accountant will have to consider several issues with which a forensic accountant acting in the same proceedings need not concern himself. These may include:

– possibility of personal liability for losses if the accountant was a director or shadow director of the company at the relevant time;

– any other conflicts of interest arising;

– possibility that a forensic accountant engaged by the opposing side may give expert evidence adverse to him as company accountant, such as a view that proper books of account were not maintained by the company;

– need to engage an expert on his own behalf; and

– possibility that his own evidence might serve to incriminate the accountant himself, and the consequent possible need to invoke a privilege against self-incrimination by declining to give evidence on certain matters.

It is clear that the role of the accountant as witness of fact, and the matters that he may consider, differ significantly from those of the forensic accountant acting as an expert.

Accountants as expert witnesses

1–46   A significant exception to the rule that witnesses may not give opinion evidence is that expert witnesses are permitted to state their opinions on matters within their area of expertise. This exception affords to accountants, and to other experts, a different status to that enjoyed by other witnesses. It is important to note that a court will only allow expert opinion if, on the facts, alleged or proven, the judge or jury cannot reasonably form their own conclusions without expert help. This reinforces the role of the judge or jury as the finder of fact.

Where the court has determined that expert assistance is required, it must then be satisfied that the professional tendered by a party is an appropriate expert for the purposes of the case. In order to be treated as an expert witness by a court, an accountant or other professional, unless already well known to the court, must establish his relevant credentials and expertise in evidence. This is normally done at the commencement of the expert's evidence and the onus rests with the party calling the expert to satisfy the court as to their relevant expertise.

Skills required of forensic accountants

1–47   Many cases turn out to be more complex than they might seem at first. Forensic accountants need to delve beneath the surface, beyond the obvious, applying intuition, critical analysis and a perceptive understanding of human behaviour to obtain a true picture of key events, transactions and business dealings. Skills required of the forensic accountant include how to conduct investigations, financial analyses and other accounting procedures at a level acceptable to the legal system. As forensic accounting assignments are related to judicial or quasi-judicial dispute resolution, forensic accountants require a basic understanding of applicable law, including the law of evidence and legal procedure. The most competently conducted investigation is of no value should the evidence gathered be ruled to be inadmissible, or the expert accounting witness be found to fall short in respect of the requirements of expertise, credibility or independence.

1–48 Among the benefits to be derived from the involvement of a skilled forensic accountant are specialist knowledge, independence, objectivity and experience in negotiating and in giving evidence. The practical and in-depth analysis that a forensic accountant will bring to a case can uncover trends, patterns and other factors that bring to light relevant financial issues. A capable forensic accountant should have the following qualities:

– relevant knowledge of business and of how a wrong is committed;

– knowledge of investigative techniques and an appropriate level of relevant experience;

– experience of computerised applications to assist in the analysis and presentation of financial evidence;

– ability to research relevant literature, publications and statistics to provide reliable and independently verifiable information in his area of expertise;

– organisational ability to collect data and to exercise proper control over large volumes of documentary evidence;

– analytical skills to interpret financial information and identify financial issues;

– knowledge of legal aspects such as basic rules of evidence (covered in Chapter 22) relating to admissibility of evidence and the drawing of inferences;

– understanding of what needs to be proved so that only relevant and reliable evidence is documented in reports, letters and affidavits and is compiled in a concise, logical and persuasive manner;

– ability to overcome obstacles – rarely will all necessary financial information be readily available;

– ability to work as part of a team with witnesses of fact, solicitors, barristers, other experts and the authorities as appropriate. Although the expert's opinion is an independent one, he must be able to understand how it fits into the structure and logic of the case;

– sound professional judgment;

– independence, objectivity and integrity;

– effective communication and writing skills and an ability to present findings clearly in the form of written reports;

– ability to consider alternatives and to be aware of the potential shortcomings of a case, which can be useful in preparing for cross-examination;

– ability to give oral evidence with confidence, to tell a story clearly, succinctly and simply, to present visual aids in the form of exhibits and collections of documents to support trial evidence and to stand up to cross-examination in a court of law, without displaying sarcasm or other non-professional behaviour which could taint the expert's opinion.

Concluding comment

1–49   As the scale, volume and complexity of litigation continue to increase, the opportunities for forensic accountants to provide value-added services to litigators, and for the resolution of disputes to benefit from their involvement, continue to multiply. However, it must be remembered that expert evidence is admissible in court as an exception to the general rule against opinion evidence, and judges are in no way obliged to permit such evidence to be given if they feel it is unnecessary. It is therefore essential that forensic accountants uphold the highest professional standards in all aspects of their work before offering themselves to a court dealing with a dispute.

THE LEGAL SYSTEM IN IRELAND

CHAPTER 2

THE LEGAL SYSTEM IN IRELAND

Introduction

2–01   This chapter provides a brief and inevitably incomplete description of the Irish legal system. Its purpose is to give an overview of the manner in which disputes find their way to resolution through the legal system. It therefore describes the context within which accounting experts find themselves contributing to the resolution of disputes. It is important for forensic accountants to appreciate how their contribution fits into the wider legal process. However, readers should note that many finer points of detail concerning the Irish legal system and its workings have been sacrificed in the interests of brevity and clarity.[1]

A common law system

2–02   Like the United Kingdom, the United States, Australia, Canada, New Zealand and other jurisdictions, Ireland is a common law country. This fact needs some elucidation.

Long before statutes were derived, the customary and often unwritten law forbade certain activities. Murder, rape, arson and cheat (in the sense of depriving someone of his property by deception) are all common law crimes and also civil (*i.e.* non-criminal) wrongs or "torts" ("tort" is a Norman French word meaning a wrong).

When statutes – written laws passed by parliament and formally proclaimed by the sovereign head of state – became commonplace, they supplemented rather than replaced common law. For example, the factual constituents of the crime of murder are laid down by common law but the mental element required has long been defined by statute.

Today, much criminal law, contract, tort and other areas are common law based, while other areas such as road traffic law and company law are statute-based. But there are no watertight compartments: a common law subject will

---

[1] Useful additional general introductions to the legal system in Ireland can be found in Delany, V.T.H. and Lysaght, C. (ed), *The Administration of Justice in Ireland* (4th ed., Institute of Public Administration, Dublin, 1975); Doolan, B. *Principles of Irish Law* (5th ed., Gill & Macmillan, Dublin, 1999); Byrne, R. and McCutcheon, J.P. *The Irish Legal System* (3rd ed., Butterworths, Dublin, 1996).

have important statutory provisions, *e.g.* the Defamation Act 1961, while the enforcement of road traffic law or company law will vitally involve the law of evidence with its deep common law roots.

2–03 Common law is judge-made law, the product of judicial development of existing precedents. A leading twentieth century example of this process is the law of negligence. The concepts of a "duty" owed to one's "neighbour" not to injure him as a result of the "foreseeable" consequences of one's actions, was almost entirely developed in this way, incrementally since the 1930s. The extension of the net of professional negligence from doctors to architects, bankers, builders and accountants happened in the same way. There have been parallel advances, and some retreats, in other areas.

Common law jurisprudence may be contrasted with the civil law or code-based approach. This approach derives remotely from Ancient Rome, but more immediately from the Code Napoleon, devised by that Emperor and enforced on the lands he conquered in the early nineteenth century. The word "civil" in this context is a reference to the Roman "civilians" or secular lawyers, not to civil versus criminal.

Code-based systems have the virtue of certainty and precision but the drawback of inflexibility. Common law is almost infinitely flexible and can, within broad limits, be developed by the upper judiciary. Flexibility like this is purchased at the price of some uncertainty, but this is small in extent at any particular time. Because of their law-making role (limited though it is), the status of judges tends to be high in common law systems.

Constitutions

2–04 Common law systems trace their remote origin to England. Over the centuries, there have been divergences from the British model. The most momentous of these was the adoption by the American rebels of the 1780s of a detailed written constitution. They then developed an entirely new form of common law system. Ireland's 1937 Constitution, like many others throughout the world, is influenced by the United States example.

Common law respected customary rights and prohibitions, but held that, in the last resort, all power derived from the king, who could change any law at will. In the seventeenth century, this power became attributed to the King-in-Parliament and later, in practice, to parliament itself. British theorists only speak of the "Sovereignty of Parliament". Consistent with this theory, neither English nor United Kingdom law ever had a written constitution.

2–05 Ireland, by contrast, since independence has been a constitutional entity. All power is seen as deriving from the people, according to rules they have expressed in the Constitution. That document lays down rules distributing this derived power amongst the three branches of government – legislative, executive and judicial – and establishes rules for its exercise by each branch. Very significantly, the Constitution also defines the rights of citizens individually and in groups. This may be done in a very detailed way (*e.g.* concerning the protection of citizens' liberty by "habeas corpus") or by the use of general language, for example in providing instances, but not a comprehensive list, of the citizen's personal rights. This has allowed the courts to proclaim additional rights, made relevant by new circumstances. The rights to travel, to matrimonial privacy, to tax equity, to bodily integrity and to privacy are in this category.

2–06 Constitutional rights have been identified, expounded and given practical application by the courts very consistently in the years since about 1965. For the practical purposes of a forensic accountant, this is particularly significant in relation to procedures. If information or admissions adverse to a person – which may lead to his dismissal or imprisonment, for example – are to be obtained, they must meet the stringent criteria of the courts as to admissibility. When an investigation is well advanced and a definite suspect is in view, the forensic accountant will normally take legal advice on this matter. But much earlier stages of an investigation may throw up issues affecting admissibility. The forensic accountant, accordingly, must himself possess a good sense of the requirement of common law and constitutional justice in relation to evidence – gathering.

Hierarchy of laws

2–07 As is the case with all common law legal systems, Irish law does not comprise a single set of rules or principles that can be identified, written down and followed. Instead, our body of law has evolved over many centuries from a variety of sources resulting in a legal framework that is never entirely clear, is constantly changing and developing, and often gives rise to conflicts within itself. Ultimately, such conflicts must be resolved either by the courts or by the legislature through the enactment of unequivocal legislation. Even then, decisions of the courts and legislation can be subject to challenge.

2–08 To allow a course to be plotted through the maze that is the legal system, it is useful to construct a hierarchy of laws to demonstrate the relative persuasiveness of rules and principles derived from the various possible sources. As with all analysis of matters legal, to be brief and clear can only be done at the cost of absolute precision. Nevertheless, a broad hierarchy of sources of Irish law, from highest to lowest, is as follows:

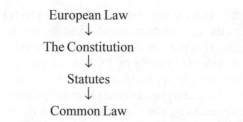

European Law
↓
The Constitution
↓
Statutes
↓
Common Law

2–09 The Irish Constitution, *Bunreacht na hÉireann*, was adopted by the people of Ireland in 1937 and has been amended on several occasions since. It forms the bedrock of our laws, setting out, among many other things, the principles with which all laws must comply. In particular, Article 15 of the Constitution vests the sole and exclusive power of making laws for the State in the Houses of the Oireachtas. The Constitution also states that "[t]he Oireachtas shall not enact any law which is in any respect repugnant to this Constitution" and that laws repugnant to the Constitution are invalid. These provisions make it clear that, where the Constitution and statute law conflict, the Constitution prevails.

2–10 However, another provision of the Constitution has the effect of placing the Constitution itself to a limited extent second in the hierarchy of laws described above. This provision is contained in Article 29 of the Constitution and results from our membership of the European Community. The relevant provision reads as follows:

> "No provision of this Constitution invalidates laws enacted, acts done or measures adopted by the State necessitated by the obligations of membership of the Communities or prevents laws enacted, acts done or measures adopted by the Communities, or institutions thereof, from having the force of law in the State."

Litigants who feel that a domestic law, or the finding of a domestic court, is in conflict with a European law operative in the State can find fertile ground in this provision, first in the Irish courts and, ultimately in the European Court of Justice.

2–11 Common law or judge-made law, as it is often known, represents the accumulated wisdom of the courts of the State, and of their predecessors. Irish courts will follow precedents established by an equal or higher court in matters where there is no statutory authority. For instance, where the High Court makes a decision on a point of law, this must be followed where the identical point arises, by all lower courts in subsequent cases and usually by the High Court itself in such circumstances. The Supreme Court on appeal, the legislature through a new statute, the people through a constitutional amendment and/or the European Court of Justice can overrule this precedent. The Supreme Court has reserved to itself the right to overrule its own previous decisions in particular circumstances.

As a result, the importance of legal precedent cannot be overestimated. Despite the explosion in legislation in recent years, many areas of the law remain unregulated by statute, leaving it to the judiciary to interpret the law in the context of the particular facts presented in a case. Nevertheless, it should not be forgotten that Irish statutes that are not repugnant to the Constitution take precedence over common law.

The system – generally adversarial, not inquisitorial

2–12 It is essential first to understand that Irish civil litigation and alternative dispute resolution proceedings are generally adversarial in nature. The practical effect of this is that parties in dispute must each present their case before a court or other decision-making body (*e.g.* an arbitrator). Criminal proceedings are accusatorial in nature and require the prosecuting authorities to prove their case to a high standard.

Presentation of cases is usually done by lawyers. Lawyers lead evidence, which may include oral testimony, documents and other items, and can include the evidence of experts engaged on their clients' behalf. They will also cross-examine witnesses called by the other parties. Essentially, the role of the lawyers is to present to the court their client's version of the facts, together with the relevant legal principles and precedents on which the court's decision should be based. Having heard the evidence, including any expert testimony, and legal submissions of the parties, the court makes a determination on the issues in dispute. This will usually involve the court in making findings of fact in respect of disputed matters, and in applying to those facts the relevant law as interpreted by the court.

2–13 Although the majority of situations in which accounting experts find themselves involve adversarial dispute resolution, certain matters are resolved through inquisitorial fact-finding processes which fall outside the administration of justice. Best known of these is the tribunal of inquiry, the purpose of which is to ascertain facts rather than to apportion culpability or to punish. Accounting expertise can be very useful in assisting in the determination of matters of fact. Accountants can also become involved in other non-adversarial processes such as mediation, which is designed to move the parties to agreement rather than to find in favour of one or the other.

Lawyers and courts in Ireland

Lawyers' functions

2–14   The Irish legal profession comprises two types of lawyers – solicitors and barristers – who work in a variety of courts.

Solicitors

2–15   The principal responsibilities of the solicitor in relation to litigation are to obtain the facts initially and advise the client, to administer the progress of the case from the taking of initial instructions to the hearing of the action, and to brief and liaise with counsel. In essence, the solicitor runs the case from its beginning until it is heard or settled. This can involve very significant amounts of correspondence and meetings, including instructing and receiving reports from experts. It also involves the preparation of the case for hearing, including the organisation of the witnesses and documents needed for trial.

Solicitors have a right of audience in all courts and this is used most frequently in the District Court, where most proceedings are handled by solicitors. Barristers are normally briefed to conduct cases in the higher courts.

Barristers

2–16   Barristers are instructed by solicitors to prepare a case for trial and to represent their client's interests at the hearing of the action. They generally draft the principal court documents necessary for the case and provide advice or opinions on legal matters relevant to the case. Barristers often represent clients in settlement negotiations.

Traditionally, barristers were prohibited from accepting instructions from anyone other than a solicitor. In recent years, and following a report of the Fair Trade Commission in 1990,[2] this prohibition has been relaxed and barristers can now be instructed directly by members of certain other professions, including accountants, in non-court matters. This is known as direct professional access.

2–17   Senior Counsel are barristers of considerable experience and expertise who have been called to the inner bar by the Chief Justice. Barristers who are not Senior Counsel are referred to as junior counsel.

The courts

2–18   Article 34 of the Constitution states: "Justice shall be administered in courts established by law by judges appointed in the manner provided by this Constitution, and, save in such special and limited cases as may be prescribed by law, shall be administered in public."

---

[2] Fair Trade Commission, *Annual Report 1990*.

Figure 2.1[3] overleaf summarises the variety of ways in which a dispute can find its way into the legal system and the various fora in which the outcome of the dispute can be determined, either at first instance or following an appeal.

District Court

2-19   The District Court is a court of summary jurisdiction. This means that, under the Constitution, it is empowered to hear and determine minor (and certain other) criminal offences without a jury. There is no definition of "minor offences" in either the Constitution or statute, and the courts have therefore developed a framework within which such offences can be distinguished from more serious offences.

Although no precise formula has been developed, the courts have indicated that one significant factor in deciding whether an offence is minor is the severity of the punishment specified by law. As a result, statutes creating offences triable summarily generally limit the penalties to levels likely to indicate that the offence is minor. Indictable offences are offences that are not minor and, subject to certain exceptions, cannot be tried summarily. This means that such offences must be tried on indictment, *i.e.* before a judge and jury.

The District Court hears all criminal cases triable summarily and certain criminal cases triable on indictment and civil cases where the amount claimed does not exceed £5,000.

The District Court is presided over by a District Judge, sitting alone, who is addressed as "Judge". The jurisdiction of any District Court is limited by reference to the district and area in which the court is located.

Circuit Court

2-20   The Circuit Court is the venue for criminal trials on indictment, except for trials of certain charges (including murder and rape) which are reserved for the Central Criminal Court, and except for matters referred to the Special Criminal Court. A judge and jury hear criminal trials in the Circuit Criminal Court.

Civil claims in excess of £5,000 but not more than £30,000 are heard by a judge sitting alone in the Circuit Court. Changes in Court jurisdication due to take effect on January 1, 2002 include a significant increase in the upper limit of £30,000 to €100,000. Appeals arising from decisions of the District Court are heard *de novo* (*i.e.* the case is heard in full again as if for the first time) in the Circuit Court by a judge sitting alone.

As is the case for the District Court, the jurisdiction of a Circuit Court is limited by reference to the geographical location of the court. For this purpose, the State is divided into eight circuits: Dublin, Cork, Northern, Eastern, South

---

[3] Murdoch, H., *Murdoch's Dictionary of Irish Law* (3rd ed., Topaz Publications, Dublin 2000).

Figure 2.1: Irish Justice System 2000

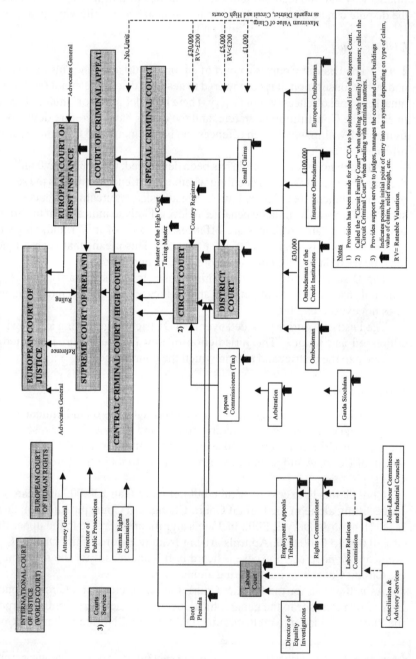

Notes

1) Provision has been made for the CCA to be subsumed into the Supreme Court.
2) Called the "Circuit Family Court" when dealing with family law matters; called the "Circuit Criminal Court" when dealing with criminal matters.
3) Provides support service to judges, manages the courts and court buildings

▲ Indicates possible initial point of entry into the system depending on type of claim, value of claim, relief sought, etc.

RV= Rateable Valuation.

Maximum Value of Claim as regards District, Circuit and High Courts

No Limit
£30,000 RV>£200
£5,000 RV<£200
£1,000

£100,000
£30,000

East, South West, Midland and Western. Judges of the Circuit Court are addressed as "My Lord" or "Your Lordship".

High Court

2–21   The High Court hears civil cases where the amount claimed exceeds the upper limit of the Circuit Court Jurisdiction. Most civil cases are heard before a judge sitting alone, although certain matters (including defamation proceedings) are heard by a judge and jury. The High Court also sits as an appeal court in civil matters. Decisions of the Circuit Court in such matters can be appealed to the High Court where a full *de novo* rehearing takes place. When sitting as a criminal court, the High Court is known as the Central Criminal Court.

In addition, the High Court will hear and determine points of law referred to it from the District Court. The process of referring a point of law to a higher court is referred to as a "case stated".

The Constitution accords to the High Court full original jurisdiction to hear all matters, "whether of law or fact, civil or criminal", at first instance. Although much of this jurisdiction is conferred on lower courts, consideration of the constitutionality of a law cannot be undertaken by a lower court. High Court judges are usually addressed as "My Lord", although certain lady judges are believed to prefer to be addressed as "Judge".

Special Criminal Court

2–22   This court is used to hear certain specified ("scheduled") criminal offences and also other criminal offences where, in the particular case, the Director of Public Prosecutions has certified that the ordinary courts are inadequate to secure the effective administration of justice and the preservation of public peace and order. The Special Criminal Court normally comprises three judges (one from each of the High, Circuit and District Courts), and has been used in recent years to hear, among other cases, certain terrorist-related and drug-related murder trials.

Court of Criminal Appeal

2–23   Decisions of the Circuit Criminal Court, the Central Criminal Court and the Special Criminal Court can be appealed to the Court of Criminal Appeal. This court is the final arbiter of criminal proceedings, subject only to the possibility of further appeal to the Supreme Court, for which leave must be obtained, in cases where a point of law of exceptional public importance is involved. The Court of Criminal Appeal can hear appeals against both conviction and sentence.

The Court of Criminal Appeal sits as a three-judge court, usually with one Supreme Court judge and two High Court judges. Recent legislation envisages the abolition of this court with its functions being taken over by the Supreme Court.

Supreme Court

2–24 The highest court in the land is the Supreme Court, which is the court of final appeal and hears appeals on points of law from decisions of the High Court. The court also hears appeals by way of case stated from the Circuit Court on points of law. At present there are eight Supreme Court judges, including the Chief Justice, and the court normally sits as a five-judge court or a three-judge court – or, indeed, as both simultaneously. In 2001 the Supreme Court sat for the first time as a court of seven. Except for decisions on the constitutionality of legislation, when a single judgment of the court is read, each judge on the court will normally express his or her view on the case. Where judges differ in their views, the majority prevails. As for the High Court, Supreme Court judges are addressed as "My Lord".

Criminal cases and civil cases

2–25 The two principal branches of Irish law are the civil law and the criminal law. Although they overlap to the extent that many crimes can constitute civil wrongs and vice versa, two sets of characteristics distinguish civil and criminal cases from each other.

The parties

2–26 The first of these distinguishing characteristics is that the parties to the actions differ. Most criminal cases are prosecuted on behalf of the State, normally by the Director of Public Prosecutions (the "DPP"). The objective of such cases is to establish the person or persons who have committed a breach of a specific law with a view to having them convicted of the crime and sentenced accordingly. The party taking the case is described as the prosecution and the accused person is called the defendant or the accused. In essence, criminal proceedings are taken in order to prove a wrong against society and to punish it.

2–27 Civil cases, on the other hand, are fought between two or more parties with a view to resolving a private dispute between them in favour of one or more of the parties. The party instituting the proceedings is called the plaintiff and the party against whom the plaintiff is proceeding is the defendant.

The two most common causes of action in civil proceedings are torts and breaches of contract. They each have different characteristics and the time-limits within which proceedings must be initiated vary depending on the nature of the wrong.

2–28 A tort is a private or civil wrong or injury, other than a breach of contract, inflicted by one person on another, compensatable by damages. In general, actions in tort cannot be commenced more than six years after the cause of action arises.

However, where a claim for damages for negligence, nuisance or breach of duty includes a claim for damages for personal injury, the time-limit is three years from the date of the occurrence of the cause of action or, if later, from the date the injured person (or, if that person is deceased, his or her personal representative) first became aware of the significance of the injury, its cause, the identify of the person who caused it and, if the defendant is to be a different person, the identity of and reason for proceeding against the defendant. This later date is known as the "date of knowledge". The time-limit for actions taken on an instrument executed under seal and for actions (other than by the State) to recover land is 12 years.

2–29 An action in contract will most often arise from a breach of an expressed or implied term in a contract. However, disputes over contracts can also arise due to mistake on the part of one or both parties entering into the contract, misrepresentation by one party to another or duress exerted by one party over another. Contracts can also fall foul of other rules rendering them illegal (*e.g.* contracts to commit a crime or otherwise contrary to public policy) or void (*e.g.* contracts in restraint of trade). The law of equity can also intervene in a contract (*e.g.* where there is undue influence by one party over another). It is clear that contracts represent fertile ground for those who specialise in the resolution of disputes.

In general, actions arising under contract cannot be commenced more than six years after the cause of action arises.

Standard of proof in criminal and civil cases

2–30 The second distinguishing feature between civil and criminal matters is the standard of proof required. In criminal cases, the prosecution is required to prove its case "beyond a reasonable doubt". This is a high standard reflecting the fact that all persons are regarded as innocent until proven guilty. The plaintiff in a civil case is required to prove his case "on the balance of probabilities", *i.e.* he must satisfy the court that it is more likely than not that his version of events is the true version.

Jurisdiction in criminal and civil cases

2–31 The venue for the hearing of a case is determined by a number of factors. In criminal cases in particular, the determination of the appropriate court is a very technical subject. In summary:

(1) Minor criminal cases are heard in the District Court before a judge alone.

(2) Most serious criminal cases are heard in the Circuit Criminal Court before a judge and jury.

(3) Certain specific serious offences (including murder, rape, treason and piracy) are heard in the Central Criminal Court (the name given to the High Court when hearing criminal matters) before a judge and jury.

(4) Certain specific serious criminal cases can be heard in the Special Criminal Court before three judges – in practice only cases involving terrorism or gross intimidation are certified for hearing in this court.

(5) District Court criminal decisions can be appealed for full rehearing in the Circuit Criminal Court before a judge sitting alone.

(6) Decisions of the Circuit Criminal Court, the Central Criminal Court and the Special Criminal Court can be appealed to the Court of Criminal Appeal.

(7) Specific points of law can be referred from the District Court to the High Court and from the Circuit Court to the Supreme Court – this is known as a "case stated".

2–32 Civil cases commence in either the District Court, the Circuit Court or the High Court, depending generally on the significance of the dispute as measured by the amount of damages claimed or, if property is involved, the rateable valuation of the property concerned. With certain specific exceptions, a judge sitting alone hears civil cases. Appeals are generally to the next highest court, with the Supreme Court being the ultimate arbiter of matters on appeal in the State.

It should be noted that litigants also have recourse to the courts of the European Community, which have the power to apply principles of European law, which take precedence over national law, to domestic disputes.

Procedure in criminal cases

2–33 Criminal cases normally commence when the Gardaí believe that an individual has committed an offence, *i.e.* breached a provision of a statute that carries a penalty when breached. For lesser offences, the individual will be sent a summons requiring him to appear at a sitting of the District Court to answer the charge. The summons must set out the alleged offence in detail and specify the date, time and venue of the court hearing.

2–34 For more serious offences, the suspected offender will usually be arrested and questioned by the Gardaí. In such cases the decision as to whether to prosecute is taken by the Director of Public Prosecutions based on the information gathered by the Gardaí.

The Director of Public Prosecutions must prosecute all criminal offences except minor ones. Non-minor prosecutions are referred to as "indictable".

2–35 Any person may *institute* a prosecution for most indictable offences and carry it through the "preliminary examination"[4] in the District Court. At the end of this procedure, the District Judge decides whether the prosecution has shown sufficient evidence to put the defendant on trial, and if so sends him forward to a higher court for trial.

If this happens in a private prosecution, the private prosecutor can do no more. Only the DPP can conduct a prosecution on indictment. If the case is to continue, one or other of these officials must take it over.

Private prosecutions for indictable offences are rare, but fraud is one area in which they sometimes occur.

2–36 Many offences with which a forensic accountant is likely to be concerned are commenced on the complaint of an allegedly defrauded person or company. In practice, these will be serious offences, triable on indictment. Often the complaint will be made after the discovery of defalcation by the complainant's own accountant or by a forensic accountant consulted when suspicion arises.

It is essential to bear in mind, however, that unlike civil proceedings, criminal proceedings cannot be dropped or discontinued at the option of the complainant. Often, an individual or a company may be gravely embarrassed at the public revelation of exactly how they were defrauded, because it will reveal foolishness, greed or slipshod procedures on their part. But once a complaint of a criminal offence has been made, what happens afterwards is a matter entirely for the authorities.

2–37 In all criminal prosecutions, the *onus* of proof is on the prosecution. The standard of proof is proof beyond reasonable doubt. This applies to the general issue of guilt, and to all subsidiary issues.

In financial cases, there is unlikely to be significant eyewitness testimony. The general context will be established by direct evidence, but the essential elements of fraud will often rely on a proper trail. Usually this will be circumstantial evidence from a legal viewpoint: that is, a body of evidence whose components are mutually re-enforcing and from which the guilt of the accused may be inferred.

The requirements of proof beyond reasonable doubt demand that such circumstantial evidence must not merely be consistent with the guilt of the accused, but inconsistent with any other reasonable explanation.

2–38 Once a decision to prosecute in respect of an indictable offence has been made, the accused person will normally appear before a District Judge and be formally charged. Certain indictable offences can be tried summarily in the District Court provided:

---

[4] The preliminary examination procedure has been abolished with effect from October 1, 2001 by Part III of the Criminal Justice Act 1999.

- the District Judge concludes that the matter is minor;

- the accused person is advised of his right to a trial before judge and jury and waives that right; and

- in certain cases, the DPP consents to a summary trial.

Otherwise the District Judge conducts the preliminary examination[5] before sending the case forward for trial. The District Judge will also decide on:

- whether bail should be allowed; or

- whether the accused should be remanded to prison; and

- any application for legal aid.

2–39 When the accused person is brought before the trial court, the indictment is formally read. The indictment is a formal written description of the details of the offence or offences with which the accused person is charged. The hearing at which it is formally read is called the arraignment. Following the reading of the indictment, the accused person is asked to plead guilty or not guilty. If the plea is "guilty" at the arraignment or at the hearing of the criminal case, the judge will proceed to sentencing. If the plea is "not guilty", the case proceeds. Following the empanelling of the jury, the prosecution's case is heard first, followed by the defence, although the defendant is not obliged to give evidence. Where there is a jury, the jury decides all matters of fact. The judge directs the jury on matters of law and on the legal weight of the evidence. On a conviction, the judge passes sentence, which may involve a prison term, a fine, community service or a combination.

Procedure in civil cases

2–40 Civil cases normally begin when an individual or organisation decides to seek redress through the courts for a wrong allegedly committed by another party or parties. Often, other attempts at resolving the issue will have been made before the decision is made to resort to litigation.

Proceedings are commenced when the aggrieved party – the plaintiff – issues and serves on the other party – the defendant – a document setting out the relief claimed. The Statute of Limitations 1957 and the Statute of Limitations (Amendment) Act 1991, and certain other statutes, establish time-limits within which cases must be commenced before becoming "statute-barred".

2–41 Usually, but not always, the plaintiff will be seeking monetary damages as compensation for the alleged wrong. As pointed out above, the amount of

---

[5] The preliminary examination procedure has been abolished with effect from October 1, 2001 by Part III of the Criminal Justice Act 1999.

damages claimed will determine the court in which the proceedings are commenced, and this in turn determines the type of document used to initiate the case. Once the plaintiff's claim has been formally communicated to the defendant by the service on him of the document containing the details of the claim, the defendant is afforded a period of time in which to respond formally to the claim. Depending on its content, this response may elicit further formal communication from the plaintiff. The documents passing to and fro in this manner are collectively referred to as the pleadings.

2–42 Once pleadings have been exchanged (and often before this), both sides will begin to assemble evidence to support their cases. The nature of the necessary evidence will depend on the facts of the case and the basis for the claim. For instance, if a self-employed individual is injured in a car accident and loses time at work and business as a result, evidence will be needed of the circumstances of the accident (to establish liability), of the nature and severity of the injuries (to support a claim for damages for pain and suffering) and of the business and profits lost as a result of the accident (to support a claim for lost earnings). Expert evidence may well be needed in all of these areas, for instance from an engineer in respect of the cause of the accident, from one or several doctors in respect of the injuries and the medical prognosis, and from an accountant and an actuary in respect of lost earnings.

2–43 Gathering of evidence will often include discovery and inspection of relevant documents by both sides. For instance, if the plaintiff's claim includes loss of profits, the defendant may seek discovery of accounting and tax records relevant to the plaintiff's calculation of the loss. This process of discovery usually involves both sides swearing affidavits listing all relevant documents that are or have been in their custody, power or possession, and distinguishing between those documents which can be made available and those that cannot. The latter category includes documents no longer in the custody, power or possession of the party, and documents in respect of which a claim of privilege is being made. The documents most commonly withheld from discovery on foot of a claim of privilege are those that are confidential communications between a party and that party's legal advisers. Experts will generally be involved in the inspection of discovered documents and will take account in their reports of what emerges from the discovery and inspection process.

2–44 Most civil cases settle before trial. Experts can play a significant role in moving a case towards settlement by providing an objective and independent view of important aspects of liability and/or quantum in the case and of the strengths and weaknesses of the case. Where a case does not settle, it is set down for trial. At the hearing, the plaintiff's evidence is heard first and the defendant's counsel can cross-examine the plaintiff's witnesses on this evidence. Following the presentation of the plaintiff's case, the defendant's evidence is presented and the plaintiff's counsel can cross-examine. In both cases, counsel can re-examine his own witness on any new matter arising during cross-examination. Table 2.1 summarises the sequence of events in a civil case involving expert evidence.

Table 2.1: Sequence of events in civil cases

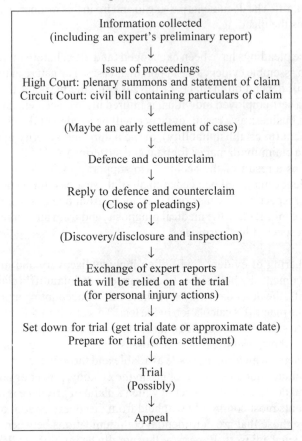

Information collected
(including an expert's preliminary report)
↓
Issue of proceedings
High Court: plenary summons and statement of claim
Circuit Court: civil bill containing particulars of claim
↓
(Maybe an early settlement of case)
↓
Defence and counterclaim
↓
Reply to defence and counterclaim
(Close of pleadings)
↓
(Discovery/disclosure and inspection)
↓
Exchange of expert reports
that will be relied on at the trial
(for personal injury actions)
↓
Set down for trial (get trial date or approximate date)
Prepare for trial (often settlement)
↓
Trial
(Possibly)
↓
Appeal

Alternative dispute resolution

2–45 Recent years have seen an increasing number of disputes being referred by agreement for resolution in fora other than the courts. Alternative dispute resolution is regarded in some situations as being cheaper and quicker than litigation. In disputes involving highly technical areas, it can also be an advantage for the parties to be able to select or agree on individuals with the necessary specialist knowledge, experience and expertise to help them resolve the matters at issue. The most commonly used methods of alternative dispute resolution are mediation and arbitration. This topic is covered in more detail in Chapter 14.

Other administrative and adjudicative bodies

2–46 Certain other bodies exist, or are established from time to time, to hear and determine disputes or make findings of fact. These include:

- Employment Appeals Tribunal, which hears and determines claims by employees that they have been unfairly dismissed by an employer.
- Ombudsman, who investigates poor administration in the public service and makes non-binding recommendations.
- Coroners' Courts, which conduct public inquests into unexplained deaths and make findings.
- Oireachtas committees, which conduct hearings and make reports.
- An Bord Pleanála, which hears and determines appeals from decisions of planning authorities.
- Appeal Commissioners, which hear and determine appeals from tax assessments raised by inspectors of taxes.
- Tribunals of inquiry, which inquire into specific events and make findings of fact – this is dealt with in Chapter 13.

Costs

2–47 Costs of litigation can be viewed from two perspectives: the client perspective and the perspective of the provider of the service (*e.g.* the forensic accountant). This section discusses legal costs from the point of view of the client, or more accurately from the point of view of who pays the cost. Charging and collecting accountants' fees are discussed in paras **6–80** *et seq.*and paras **6.89** *et seq.*

2–48 Costs of litigation can be high and courts have considerable discretion in determining who pays. The Legal Aid Board is the source of payment of the experts' fees where the expert has acted for a legally assisted party. The concept behind the provision of legal aid by the State to individuals is that, where there is a significant risk that justice may not be done unless assistance is provided to a party to the proceedings, then, as part of the cost of justice and the rule of law, the State ought to provide the necessary assistance.

Order for costs

2–49 At the end of civil proceedings, the judge will usually make an order for costs. Where no order for costs is made, each party bears its own costs. Where there are court hearings (*e.g.* motions) prior to the full hearing of the substantive proceedings, the judge will often make an order reserving the issue of the costs of the earlier proceedings to the trial judge. This allows the judge who determines the full action, and who is therefore in the best position to judge the merits of each aspect of the case, to decide, based on the outcome of the case, who should pay the costs of the various prior proceedings.

The order for costs that follows the hearing of the substantive proceedings will usually specify which party is to pay the other party's costs. In the majority of cases, the paying party is the losing party and the receiving party is the winning party. In the event of an appeal, a stay on the order for costs is usually made pending the outcome of the appeal. Again, an order for costs will follow the decision by the appeal court.

The order for costs will include not only payment of legal fees, but also any reasonable disbursements incurred in the conduct of the case. This will include the fees of any experts instructed in the case.

2–50	Whether the expert represented the winning or losing party dictates who will ultimately bear the cost of the expert's fees. Regardless of who has to foot the bill, the responsibility and obligation for payment of the expert's fees normally lies with the instructing solicitors. The fact that the expert's client (the winning side in the case) has an order for costs payable by the losing party does not shift the obligation to pay the expert from the winning client's solicitor to the losing party, notwithstanding the order for costs. Liability for the payment of an expert's fees will always remain with the party who has contracted with the expert – usually the solicitor. The entitlement to payment is contractual and is not dictated by the amount recoverable on taxation.

Costs in criminal cases

2–51	Where legal aid is available in a criminal case, the costs of both sides (the prosecution and the defence) are borne by the State. Where no legal aid is available, generally each side bears its own costs. However, in certain cases where the accused person is acquitted, the court can award costs against the State, *i.e.* the State can be required to pay the accused person's costs.

Criminal legal aid[6, 7]

2–52	Legal aid in criminal cases has been a feature of the Irish legal system for some decades (see also para **20–78**). Although severely limited initially, it became more widely available on the enactment of the Criminal Justice (Legal

---

[6] This summary of the criminal legal aid scheme has been adapted from Criminal Legal Aid Review Committee, *First Report An Examination of the Feasibility of Introducing a Public Defender System for Ireland* (Government Publications, Dublin, October 1999).
[7] The authors acknowledge the assistance of Éimear Fisher of the Department of Justice, Equality and Law Reform in drafting this section.

Aid) Act 1962 which came into operation on April 1, 1965. The Act made State assistance available in respect of all serious crimes where the court came to the view that the defendant was of insufficient means to afford the necessary legal assistance himself. In the case of *State (Healy) v. Donoghue*[8] the Supreme Court held that accused persons must be informed by the court of their right to apply for legal aid.

2–53   Under the Act, legal aid is provided free to persons whose means are insufficient to enable them to pay for legal representation in criminal cases, provided certain conditions are met. The Criminal Justice (Legal Aid) Regulations 1965[9] lays down conditions for the operation of the legal aid scheme. These regulations set out the fees and expenses (including reasonable disbursements) payable to solicitors and counsel. In addition, the regulations provide for the payment of certain expenses of defence witnesses (such as forensic accountants).

Application for legal aid may be made to the court orally or in writing by the applicant or his legal representative. The court must be satisfied that the applicant is a person of insufficient means and, in addition, that by reason of the "gravity of the charge" or "exceptional circumstances" it is essential in the interest of justice that the applicant should have legal aid in the preparation and conduct of his case. Where the charge is one of murder or where an appeal is one from the Court of Criminal Appeal to the Supreme Court, legal aid will be granted once the court is satisfied that the applicant is a person of insufficient means (the accused may be required to complete a statement of means for this purpose).

2–54   In other cases, legal aid separate to that covered by the 1962 Act is available to applicants for judicial review in connection with criminal matters, under what is known as the Attorney General's scheme (see also para **20–78**).

Reclaiming costs

2–55   The amounts payable in respect of criminal legal aid for various services are set out in statutory instruments made pursuant to section 10 of the 1962 Act. The Department of Justice, Equality and Law Reform administers the criminal legal aid system. In order for expert witness fees to be paid, the Department requires the claimant (*e.g.* a forensic accountant who has acted as an expert witness for the defence in a fraud case) to partially complete a Form L.A. 5 which is also partially completed by the solicitor and certified by an officer of the court. Payment of fees is made upon receipt of this completed form in the Department. This form is reproduced in Table 2.2 below.

---

[8] [1976] I.R. 325.
[9] S.I. No. 12 of 1965.

Table 2.2: Reclaiming costs in criminal legally-aided cases

FORM L.A. 5

CRIMINAL JUSTICE (LEGAL AID) ACT, 1962
CRIMINAL JUSTICE (LEGAL AID) REGULATIONS, 1965

CLAIM FOR FEE FOR MEDICAL OR TECHNICAL REPORT NECESSARILY REQUIRED FOR USE BY THE DEFENCE IN A CASE IN RELATION TO WHICH A CERTIFICATE FOR FREE LEGAL AID HAS BEEN GRANTED

PART I	(to be completed by the person who prepared the Report) 1. Name: .... 2. Address: .... 3. Professional or technical qualifications: .... 4. Subject matter of Report: .... 5. Outline of work involved in preparing Report: .... 6. Length of Report (approx. number of words): .... 7. Date on which Report submitted: .... 8. Fee claimed: .... Signed: .... Date: ....
PART II	(to be completed by the Solicitor assigned under the certificate for free legal aid) The certificate for free legal aid relating to the case in which the Report referred to in PART I was prepared, was granted by the (a) .... Court at (b) .... on .... 19 .... The Report was required for use by the defence because (c) .... I certify that the information given at items 1 to 4 and at items 6 and 7 of PART I is correct. Signed: .... Name of Solicitor's firm: .... Address of Solicitor's Office: .... Date .... Solicitor's ref. No. ....
AH1789	

2–56 Regulation 11(1)(c) of the Criminal Justice (Legal Aid) Regulations 1965, as amended by Regulation 6 of the Criminal Justice (Legal Aid) (Amendment) Regulations 1978,[10] provides for parity of payment between professional witnesses who appear for the prosecution and defence. It states:

[10] S.I. No. 33 of 1978.

"The fees and expenses of witnesses (other than those referred to in paragraph (b) of this Regulation) holding a professional qualification attending on behalf of the defence (in obedience to a summons or in compliance with a request (being a request which in the opinion of the court was reasonable)) to give professional evidence at the hearing of a case in relation to which a certificate for free legal aid has been granted shall be payable under the Act at a rate corresponding to the rate for the time being at which fees and expenses to such witnesses summoned and attending on behalf of the prosecution to give professional evidence at the hearing or at similar hearings are paid."

Professional expert witnesses may be asked to provide a breakdown of hours in respect of consultations, court attendance and preparation of reports.

2–57 In deciding whether a claim is reasonable, the Department of Justice, Equality and Law Reform considers the fees paid under the parity rule as set out in Regulation 11(1)(c) of the Criminal Justice (Legal Aid) Regulations 1965. In the event that the prosecution has not retained a similar expert witness, the Department takes cognisance of the rates of fee paid by the Legal Aid Authorities of Northern Ireland, Scotland and England/Wales. It is, of course, open to an expert witness, through his/her solicitor, to inquire as to the level of fees paid by the Department.

Costs in civil cases

2–58 The general rule in civil cases is that "costs follow the event", *i.e.* that the losing party pays both his own costs and those of the winning party. An exception to this rule can arise when an award of damages is such that, while the claim succeeded, it could have been heard in a lower court. In these circumstances, the award of costs can be restricted to the costs that would have been incurred had the claim been heard in the lower court. In general, judges have significant discretion in deciding on the award of costs in civil cases.

2–59 The Rules of the Superior Courts make provision for the right to costs, and the award of costs in any proceeding is at the discretion of the court. Once costs have been awarded, the parties are free to agree the amount of costs not already measured.

Civil legal aid[11]

2–60 In certain circumstances, the State meets the costs of the plaintiff's and/ or the defendant's legal representation under the Civil Legal Aid Act 1995. The purpose of the scheme is to make the services of solicitors and, where necessary, barristers available to persons of modest means at little cost.

---

[11] The authors are grateful to Frank Brady, Director of the Legal Aid Board for his comments on this section.

Legal aid for civil cases has not been available for as long as criminal legal aid, despite various attempts to introduce it. Following criticism by the European Court of Human Rights and the receipt of recommendations from a government-appointed committee set up to review the position, a non-statutory scheme was established and run by the Legal Aid Board in 1979. This scheme was underfunded for a number of years and was subject to further criticism. Against this background, civil legal aid was finally put on a statutory basis with the passing of the Civil Legal Aid Act 1995. A newly constituted Board administers the statutory scheme. Where legal aid is available, it can cover witness expenses and the costs of obtaining reports.

2–61 Section 24 of the Civil Legal Aid Act 1995 provides that the purpose of the scheme is to enable any person whose means are within the limits specified in the scheme to obtain legal service in a situation where:

– a reasonably prudent person whose means were outside those limits would be likely to seek such services at his own expense, if his means were such that the cost involved, while representing a financial obstacle to him, would not be such as to impose undue financial hardship; and

– a competent lawyer would be likely to advise him to obtain such services.

2–62 The Act provides that a legal aid certificate must be granted in respect of proceedings in the court of lowest jurisdiction. Under the Civil Legal Aid Regulations 1996,[12] the solicitor must first apply for a legal aid certificate setting out the necessary information required to allow the Legal Aid Board to consider the application. The certificate, if granted, will specify, *inter alia*, whether, and to what extent, the fees or expenses of any expert or any witness may be paid. Normally, when the Board is authorising the engaging of an expert witness, such as a forensic accountant, an estimate of costs is obtained in advance together with details of the work to be undertaken. The expert is notified of the fee the Board is willing to pay, which takes account of the time to be spent on the case, any reports to be prepared and court attendance. If an expert is instructed in a legal aid case, and the certificate does not confirm that the expert's fees and expenses will be paid, legal aid will not be payable in respect of the expert's work. If a legally-aided party incurs costs without the authority of the Legal Aid Board, then the Board will not pay those costs.

2–63 Certain types of claim are specifically excluded from eligibility for civil legal aid. It is not possible to obtain legal aid in respect of the following proceedings:

– defamation;

---

[12] S.I. No. 273 of 1996.

– disputes concerning rights and interests in and over land;

– civil matters within the jurisdiction of the District Court (Small Claims Procedure) Rules 1993;

– licensing;

– conveyancing (save in connection with a matter in which legal aid or advice has already been given);

– election petitions;

– proceedings taken in a representative or fiduciary or official capacity which may be more conveniently funded in the opinion of the Board;

– cases taken by or on behalf of a group of persons;

– a criminal law matter (apart from certain legal services to a rape victim).

2–64 There are some exceptions to allow for disputes concerning rights and interests in and over land, which arise in the context of matrimonial proceedings, or proceedings by formerly engaged couples. Provision is also made for an exception in the case of proceedings taken on behalf of someone suffering from an infirmity of the mind or body, where the proceedings relate to the applicant's home and where not to grant legal aid would cause hardship to the applicant. Certain probate work may also be undertaken in limited circumstances. There is a similar exception in respect of licensing matters where not the granting of a licence would cause hardship to the applicant, and in respect of conveyancing matters in connection with a matter in which legal aid or advice has already been given.

2–65 Legal aid is delivered almost exclusively through law centres by full-time salaried solicitors. Since 1993, private solicitors have been engaged in barring, maintenance and custody cases in the District Court to complement the law centre service. In practice, law centres provide an almost exclusive family law service and have developed a recognised expertise in this area. In addition, the Board set up a specialised legal service for asylum seekers – the Refugee Legal Service.

Access to legal advice and aid

2–66 Section 26 of the Civil Legal Aid Act 1995 provides that a person may apply for legal aid or advice through any law centre irrespective of his place of residence. The section goes on to say that any law centre may provide legal aid or advice to more than one party to a dispute, provided that each party is represented by a separate solicitor and, where appropriate, separate barrister.

The basic eligibility requirement for legal aid under the Act is essentially that the applicant must satisfy a means test and must also have a case with a reasonable chance of success. The means test is designed to cover low income groups such as social welfare recipients but also persons of moderate incomes who can afford to contribute a portion, but not the full cost, of the legal services provided to them. Financial eligibility is determined by reference to assessment provisions set out in the regulations. The assessment involves computation of disposable income, disposable capital and the determination of contributions payable. The means test is performed at the law centre and an appointment is allocated to the person seeking advice. Applications for legal aid can be determined within the law centre for certain District Court family law matters, but must be determined by the Legal Aid Board head office for other matters.

Taxation of costs

2–67   Where, following the making of an order for costs requiring one party to pay the costs of the other, the parties are unable to agree an appropriate level of costs between them, the matter will be sent for adjudication to the Taxing Master in the High Court, or the county registrar in the Circuit Court. The process of measuring reasonable costs conducted by the Taxing Master is called "taxation", and his determinations can be appealed to the High Court. Recent cases in which the court has changed the taxed costs include *Commissioner of Irish Lights v. Maxwell*[13] and *Best v. Wellcome Foundation Ltd (No. 3)*.[14] In *Dunne v. Fox*,[15] the Taxing Master's decision was upheld by the High Court.

2–68   On taxation of costs, the Taxing Master or, on appeal the court, may decide that the expert's fees are excessive or unreasonable and disallow a portion of the fees claimed. Although the losing side does not have to pay the expert's full fees, it should not follow that the expert is out of pocket. The expert's entitlement to the full fee is contractual, and is not dictated by the amount recovered on taxation. Usually the expert will agree with the instructing solicitor to act on, say, an hourly rate basis. The expert will have invoiced the solicitor for an amount commensurate with the number of hours actually worked and not commensurate with the number of hours actually allowed by the court on taxation. This is subject to the agreement made at the outset between the solicitor and the expert. This is discussed further in the context of engagement letters in para **6.80** *et seq.*

2–69   If parties fail to agree costs and the matter is referred to the Taxing Master or the county registrar, recoverable costs will be measured on a "party and party" basis, *i.e.* those costs necessary for the conduct of the action. The process of taxation, which is independent of the parties, is based on experience

---

[13] [1997] 3 I.R. 474.
[14] [1996] 3 I.R. 378.
[15] [1999] 1 I.R. 283.

of appropriate costs in a variety of cases and knowledge of court decisions on the matter of costs. The Taxing Master has wide discretion in performing a taxation of costs, and can summon witnesses and examine them on oath as necessary.

2–70 Taxing Masters are frequently asked to tax the costs of expert witnesses and there is a growing body of case law on the subject. Flynn and Halpin review much of this case law and conclude that:

> "On a party and party taxation, the Taxing Master must firstly be satisfied that the expert or experts were necessary and required and when he is satisfied that they were needed he then approaches the question of what the appropriate fee is, having regard to the circumstances and the nature of the case."[16]

It is clear that each case is decided on its own merits within a broad set of principles. Experts would be well advised to ensure that their invoices are as detailed as possible, allowing the Taxing Master to gain a full appreciation of the nature and extent of their work. They should also be prepared to appear before the Taxing Master to explain their services in further detail, if asked to do so.

2–71 Common reasons why expert fees are reduced on taxation are as follows:

- failure to keep proper records;
- failure to delegate less complex aspects of the expert's work to junior staff;
- instruction of an inappropriate expert or an expert in the wrong location;
- time and work spent on matters and issues which do not form part of the expert's evidence;
- amendments required to the draft report arising from the expert's own actions and errors;
- expert's charging rates regarded as too high;
- unreasonable time spent by the expert on the work;
- expert fees claimed as costs previously included as a specific head of damage within the settlement;
- expert's fee irrecoverable under legal aid.

2–72 Experts can take a number of steps to minimise the risk of courts reducing their charges. On taxation, courts are required to inquire as to the reasonableness of experts' fees. There is usually no evidence before the Taxing Master as to the

---

[16]Flynn, J.T. and Halpin, T., *Taxation of Costs* (Blackhall Publishing, Dublin, 1999), p. 639.

reasonableness of the invoice other than the invoice itself. It is rare for the court to require attendance of the expert at the hearing. Consequently, the detailed content of the invoice is very important. Large proportions of costs may be disallowed by the Taxing Master due to the inadequacy of the invoice submitted by the expert. The expert should ensure that his invoice or account clearly details the work undertaken, the time spent on each element of the work, by whom and when. The total charge should be set out showing how it is computed.

Halpin and Flynn[17] provide useful guidance on the detailed records to be kept in cases that would assist in the costs being allowed in taxation. They quote the Taxing Master's comments in *Superwood Holdings plc v. Sun Alliance & London Insurance plc* on records that should be kept for taxation purposes:

> "Had a time-record been kept, it would have been helpful in determining the physical input into the case and the actual cost thereunder. Therefore, the best and most accurate way to establish exactly and precisely how much to charge a client for work is to determine how much time it took to finish or complete that work, having regard to the calibre of the personnel, dictated by the nature of the work, coupled with the other elements of the instruction fee ... The instruction fee is dependent upon the actual work that is done and, as such, incorporates all factors, both tangible and intangible. Time should be justifiably spent on a case and any time that is abnormal, excessive or improper should be disallowed on taxation, whether it be on a party and party or a solicitor-and-client basis. This case was at the outset envisaged to take some time both in preparation and in the course of the hearing. Therefore, given the amount of estimated damages, it was incumbent upon the solicitor to record the work in some sort of a concrete manner".[18]

Reference was made in the *Superwood* case to the necessity of not only recording the amount of time spent, but also the work done in that time, as quoted by Payne J. in *Re Kingsley*,[19] where he stated:

> ". . . I ought to add that this case illustrates the dangers which are present if reliance is placed on a modern system of recording, without at the same time retaining the old and well-tried practice of keeping attendance notes showing briefly the time taken and the purport of the work done by day. It may be that this case will invite attention to the importance of appreciating the limits to which the computer system can be used in cases where taxation of costs must follow litigation and to the necessity of preserving as well the use of the traditional systems".[20]

---

[17]Halpin, T. and Flynn, J., "Taxing times" *Law Society Gazette*, January/February 2000 (www.lawsociety.ie/janfeb2kGaz.htm#tax).

[18]Ruling of the Taxing Master, December 17, 1997, as quoted by Flynn J.T. and Halpin, T. in *Taxation of Costs* (Blackhall Publishing, Dublin, 1999), p. 281.

[19][1978] 122 S.J. 457.

[20]Ruling of the Taxing Master, December 17, 1997, as quoted by Flynn J.T. and Halpin, T. in *Taxation of Costs* (Blackhall Publishing, Dublin, 1999), p. 282.

Concluding comment

2–73 The manner in which justice is administered in Ireland can sometimes seem complicated and quite obscure. This is, at least in part, because practice and procedure in the courts have developed in a somewhat unstructured way over a lengthy period. Nevertheless, in general the courts are efficient, effective and fair and, importantly, transparent to those who care to look. Given that most courts are freely open to the public, it is perhaps surprising how few citizens take the time to visit and observe our legal system in action. Certainly, those hoping to participate in the system, including forensic accountants, would be well advised to spend some time in court. The best way to understand the system, and to be prepared for its idiosyncrasies, is to experience it first hand.

Part II

FRAUD

WHAT IS FRAUD?

CHAPTER 3

WHAT IS FRAUD?

3–01 This chapter provides a brief introduction to various aspects of fraud. It is not an exhaustive consideration of the topic.[1] Chapter 8 further considers fraud in that it deals with the criminal offences which largely concern fraudulent behaviour.

Introduction

3–02 Fraud involves direct or intentional misrepresentation or omission of a material fact.[2] The term "fraud" is used extensively in litigation in both civil and criminal cases. Fraud is an element of many criminal offences and civil wrongs and consequently there is no offence of fraud *per se*. Instead, the law makes provision for offences and wrongs committed fraudulently or involving an element of fraud.

Normally the law punishes offences and wrongs that involve fraud more heavily than those that do not. For example, penalties for offences resulting in underpayment of taxes are doubled in many cases where fraud is involved.[3] Thus, the word "fraud" is commonly used as an umbrella term to cover a multitude of offences which may differ markedly in size, varying from very small (*e.g.* false expense claim) to very large (*e.g.* fictitious overseas subsidiary).

Motivations for fraud are various. Opportunities for fraud can depend on the control environment in the organisation. The work environment has a significant effect on the likelihood of fraud. Hiring of honest staff, valuing honesty highly in the corporate culture, treating staff fairly and having high codes of

---

[1] Readers are referred to Bologna, G.J. and Lindquist, R.J., *Fraud Auditing and Forensic Accounting: New Tools and Techniques* (2nd ed., John Wiley & Sons, Inc, New York, 1995); Comer, M.J., *Corporate Fraud* (3rd ed., Gower Publishing Ltd., Aldershot, 1998); and Davies, D., *Fraud Watch* (2nd ed., ABG Professional Information, London, 2000). In addition, a useful chapter on fraud and embezzlement is included in Parker, T.R., "White collar crime: fraud and embezzlement" in *Litigation Services Handbook. The Role of the Accountant as Expert* (2nd ed., Weil, R.L., Wagner, M.J. and Frank, P.B. (eds), John Wiley & Sons, Inc., New York, 1995), Chap. 23.

[2] Spielman, J.A., "Accountant's liability" in *Litigation Services Handbook. The Role of the Accountant as Expert*, (2nd ed., Weil, R.L., Wagner, M.J. and Frank, P.B. (eds), John Wiley & Sons, Inc., New York, 1995), p. 12.4.

[3] See, for example, s. 1053 of the Taxes Consolidation Act 1997.

58 *Forensic Accounting*

ethics all help to prevent fraud. Regular monitoring and enforcement of internal controls will assist prevention of fraud. These issues are considered in more detail in Chapter 4.

Relevance to forensic accounting

3–03 Fraud is an area of civil and criminal law in which forensic accountants are very likely to be involved. Fraud is a legal concept. It is not the job of forensic accountants to determine whether a fraud has taken place. This can only be decided ultimately by a court. However, forensic accountants often play a central role in the gathering and presentation of evidence where a fraud may have taken place. It is therefore important that forensic accountants have an understanding of both the legal considerations and the types and methods of fraud. This chapter attempts to fulfil that need.

Definitions of fraud

3–04 No statutory definition of fraud exists. Instead, the legislature intentionally leaves this question of interpretation to the courts. Huntington and Davies[4] point out:

> "English law does not define fraud. However, Buckley J's description in *Re London and Globe Finance Ltd*[5] encapsulates the two key elements: 'to defraud is to deprive by deceit'".

In fact, Buckley J. described fraud in the context of deceit and a fuller extract from his judgment provides a better appreciation of the meaning of fraud. He said:

> "To deceive is, I apprehend, to induce a man to believe that a thing is true which is false, and which the person practising the deceit knows or believes to be false. To defraud is to deprive by deceit: it is by deceit to induce a man to act to his injury. More tersely it may be put, that to deceive is by falsehood to induce a state of mind; to defraud is by deceit to induce a course of action."[6]

3–05 In this regard, the recently published Criminal Justice (Theft and Fraud Offences) Bill 2000 is of interest. In this Bill, it is proposed to enact a statutory definition of "deception" as follows:

> "For the purposes of this Act a person deceives if he or she—
> (a) creates or reinforces a false impression, including a false impression as to law, value or intention or other state of mind,

---

[4] Huntington, I. and Davies, D., *Fraud Watch: A Guide for Business* (1st ed., Accountancy Books, London, 1994), p. 3.
[5] *Re London and Globe Finance Corporation Ltd* [1903] 1 Ch. 728.
[6] *ibid.* at 732–733.

(b)   prevents another person from acquiring information which would affect that person's judgement of a transaction, or

(c)   fails to correct a false impression which the deceiver previously created or reinforced or which the deceiver knows to be influencing another to whom he or she stands in a fiduciary or confidential relationship,

and references to deception shall be construed accordingly."[7]

Although there may be some difficulties with this proposed definition which may be ironed out before the Bill is enacted, it represents an interesting and welcome attempt to place some boundaries around the meaning of the concept of deception, which itself is a close cousin of fraud. Aspects of the Bill are also discussed in Chapter 8 on crime.

3–06   Huntington and Davies[8] considered that any fraud would have two essential elements. There must be: (i) an attempt at concealment or deception; and (ii) there must have been some loss in the form of deprivation of funds or assets. In practice, it can be difficult to establish that there has been a cover-up, even when there is good reason to believe that there has been some dishonesty. On other occasions, deception will be obvious but it will not be easy to show that it has direct financial consequences.

3–07   The definitions of fraud vary – five alternative definitions are summarised in Table 3.1. French's definition of fraud is in line with Huntington and Davies.[9] However, Comer's definition would seem to be a somewhat wider interpretation of the meaning of the word "fraud". The Auditing Practices Board's definition of fraud in *Statement of Auditing Standards* (SAS) 110 *Fraud and Error* adds the intentional misstatement of financial statements to the definition. SAS 110 also points out: "It is for the court to determine in a particular instance whether fraud has occurred."[10] This is important – until a case is proven, one is dealing only with suspicions and allegations of fraud.

3–08   Several statutory definitions in Irish law, while not defining the term "fraud", include references to it, thus throwing further light on its meaning. Among these is the statutory definition of "larceny" contained in the Larceny Act 1916. This lengthy definition, which still forms the basis of Irish criminal law in the areas of stealing, burglary and robbery, includes the following:

"A person steals who, without the consent of the owner, fraudulently and without

---

[7] Criminal Justice (Theft and Fraud Offences) Bill 2000, s. 2(2).
[8] Huntington, I. and Davies, D., *Fraud Watch: A Guide for Business* (1st ed., Accountancy Books, London, 1994), p. 3.
[9] *ibid.*
[10] Auditing Practices Board, *Statement of Auditing Standards 110: Fraud and Error* (Auditing Practices Board, London, 1995), para. 3.

Table 3.1: Definitions of fraud

Definition	Source
"Deception, either by stating what is false or by suppressing what is true, in order to induce a person to give up something of value."	French[11]
"Any behaviour by which one person intends to gain a dishonest advantage over another."	Comer[12]
"The use of deception with the intention of obtaining advantage, avoiding an obligation or causing loss to a third party."	HM Treasury, *Fraud Report*[13]
"... 'fraud' comprises both the use of deception to obtain an unjust or illegal financial advantage and intentional misrepresentations affecting the financial statements by one or more individuals among management, employees, or third parties. Fraud may involve • falsification or alteration of accounting records or other documents, • misappropriation of assets or theft, • suppression or omission of the effects of transactions from records or documents, • recording of transactions without substance, • intentional misapplication of accounting policies, or • wilful misrepresentation of transactions or of the entity's state of affairs."	Auditing Practices Board[14]
"Fraud is the dishonest obtaining of a benefit by a person from another person, or the dishonest exposing by one person of another person to risk or possible risk, in circumstances where, but for the dishonesty, the obtaining of the benefit or the exposure to the risk would be lawful."	MacGregor and Hobbs[15]

a claim of right made in good faith, takes and carries away anything capable of being stolen with intent at the time of such taking permanently to deprive the owner thereof ...".[16]

Several commentators have expressed discomfort with the inclusion of the concept of fraud in the statutory definition of the offence of larceny.[17] This discomfort has centred on the assertions that the word "fraudulently" adds no additional meaning not already encapsulated by the phrase "without a claim of

---

[11] French, D., *Dictionary of Accounting Terms* (Institute of Chartered Accountants in England and Wales, 1985), p. 128.

[12] Comer, M.J., *Corporate Fraud* (3rd ed., Gower Publishing Ltd, Aldershot, 1998), p. 624.

[13] HM Treasury, *Fraud Report 1994–95* (HM Treasury, London, 1995).

[14] Auditing Practices Board, *Statement of Auditing Standards 110: Fraud and Error* (Auditing Practices Board, London, 1995), para. 4.

[15] MacGregor, G. and Hobbs, I., *Expert Accounting Evidence: A Guide for Litigation Support* (Accountancy Books, London, 1998), p. 409.

[16] Larcency Act 1916, s. 1(1).

[17] See, *e.g.* Charleton, P., McDermott P.A. and Bolger, M., *Criminal Law* (Butterworths, Dublin, 1999), pp. 798–799.

right made in good faith" and that there are situations where an action not involving fraudulent intent nevertheless should be regarded as larceny. However, as long as the word remains in the definition, the courts will attempt, as they have attempted, to ensure that fraudulent intent remains an ingredient of the offence.[18]

3–09 The definition of larceny, and the whole of the 1916 Act, will be superseded if and when the Criminal Justice (Theft and Fraud Offences) Bill 2000 becomes law. This Bill introduces a new, simpler definition of theft that omits any reference to fraud but includes in section 4(1) a reference to dishonesty, as follows:

> "Subject to section 5, a person is guilty of theft if he or she dishonestly appropriates property without the consent of its owner and with the intention of depriving its owner of it."

3–10 The actual identification of a transaction as a "fraud" adds to the problem of its definition. Levi[19] has pointed out:

> ". . . fraud does present some special problems, because it offers the possibility of inducing into the victim an erroneous interpretation of what has happened. The victim may believe that he or she has been unfortunate or has made a commercial misjudgment: capitalism, after all, is taking risks and profiting or losing by one's risk-taking. Victims may even remain unaware that they had lost money at all."

3–11 The classification of an action as being fraudulent may depend on the motivation behind it (*e.g.* was it deliberate or accidental?). Burns[20] asks "[a]t what point does sharp practice become fraud?". This seems to imply that the dividing line between the two, in certain circumstances, may be fine. Oakes and Standish[21] considered that:

> "As fraud is the product of deception, it follows that estimation of its incidence is subject to significant error, with the true but unknown extent of fraud greater than detected fraud. In turn, detected fraud is greater than the extent of successful criminal prosecutions and civil damages for fraud, where the difference comprises fraud events on which companies take no action toward prosecution or recovery, and of unsuccessful actions. Detected fraud events within companies not followed by prosecution or recovery actions may nevertheless provoke dismissal or diminished career prospects."

---

[18] See, *e.g. R. v. Williams* [1953] 1 Q.B. 660.
[19] Levi, M., *Regulating Fraud: White-collar Crime and the Criminal Process* (Tavistock Publications, London, 1987) p. 27.
[20] Burns, S. "Easy money" *Accountancy,* August 1998, p. 38.
[21] Oakes, R. and Standish, P., "Organisational values as contingent variables in fraud" (Paper presented at the British Accounting Association National Conference, Cardiff Business School, March 1996), p.2.

3–12 Higson[22] has also pointed to the difficulties arising from the absence of a definition of fraud, pointing out that the imprecision of the term may limit its usefulness in drafting any future legislation.

Legal perspectives on fraud

3–13 Fraud is not a legal term of art and is therefore ascribed its ordinary meaning by courts. As already pointed out, there is no all-embracing offence of fraud. Thus, it is not in itself a criminal offence to commit a fraud on a person. However, the words "defraud" and "fraudulently" are used in both common law and statutory offences, with the result that certain acts of fraud are offences. Such offences are referred to in 44 Acts of the Oireachtas in the years 1990 to 2000 alone (see Table 3.2). In addition, several other Acts, while not using the term "fraud", create offences arising from behaviour of a fraudulent nature.

Table 3.2: 1990–2000 statutes creating offences involving fraud

1. An Bord Bia Act 1994	25. Investor Compensation Act 1998
2. Central Bank Act 1997	26. Larceny Act 1990
3. Civil Legal Aid Act 1995	27. Merchant Shipping Act 1992
4. Companies Act 1990	28. Merchant Shipping (Salvage and Wreck) Act 1993
5. Companies (Amendment) Act 1990	29. Metrology Act 1996
6. Control of Horses Act 1996	30. Milk (Regulation of Supply) Act 1994
7. Credit Union Act 1997	31. National Beef Assurance Scheme Act 2000
8. Criminal Justice Act 1994	32. National Standards Authority of Ireland Act 1996
9. Electoral Act 1992	33. Netting of Financial Contracts Act 1995
10. Electronic Commerce Act 2000	34. Patents Act 1992
11. European Parliament Elections Act 1997	35. Pensions (Amendment) Act 1996
12. Europol Act 1997	36. Powers of Attorney Act 1996
13. Family Law Act 1995	37. Radiological Protection Act 1991
14. Finance Act 1991	38. Refugee Act 1996
15. Finance (No. 2) Act 1992	39. Solicitors (Amendment) Act 1994
16. Finance Act 1994	40. Stamp Duties Consolidation Act 1999
17. Finance Act 1996	41. Stock Exchange Act 1995
18. Finance Act 1999	42. Taxes Consolidation Act 1997
19. Finance (No. 2) Act 2000	43. Trade Marks Act 1996
20. Firearms (Firearm Certificates for Non-Residents) Act 2000	44. Waiver of Certain Tax, Interest and Penalties Act 1993
21. Fisheries (Amendment) Act 2000	
22. Industrial Development Act 1993	
23. Investment Intermediaries Act 1995	
24. Investment Limited Partnerships Act 1994	

Note: Although fraud is mentioned in a number of statutes not listed above, the above Acts create offences that involve fraud.

[22] Higson, A., *Why is Management Reticent to Report Fraud? An Exploratory Study* (Fraud Advisory Panel, London, 1999).

It can readily be seen from the above analysis that fraud is a pervasive element in criminal law, and many criminal offences are created by statute in terms that envisage the commission of the offences with or without fraudulent intent.

3–14   A specific act of fraud may be a criminal offence, a civil wrong or provide grounds for rescinding a contract. As already stated, criminal fraud requires proof of an intentional deception. Civil fraud requires that the victim suffers damage. Fraud in the inducement of a contract may render the contract voidable.[23] Fraud is relevant in the following legal situations, *inter alia*:

- Civil cases, *e.g.* tort of deceit (see paras **3–21** *et seq.*), fraudulent misrepresentation (see paras **10–79** *et seq.*).

- Company law offences involving fraud, including fraudulent trading (see paras **8–55** *et seq.*), fraudulent preference, offences involving fraud by officers of a company in liquidation.

- Revenue offences involving fraud.

- Fraud by a debtor in bankruptcy.

- Specific criminal offences involving fraud, *e.g.* larceny (see para. **8–11**), embezzlement (see paras. **8–12** *et seq.*), cheating, damage with intent to defraud, fraudulent conversion (see paras. **8–20** *et seq.*), conspiracy to defraud (see paras **8–34** *et seq.*), obtaining credit by fraud, obtaining by false pretences (see paras. **8–26** *et seq.*), forgery with intent to defraud, making fraudulent entries in books of account, false accounting (see paras. **8–35** *et seq.*).

3–15   The civil wrong of fraudulent misrepresentation involves the following elements[24]:

- A false representation or a wilful omission made regarding a material fact.

- The defendant reasonably knew the misrepresentation was false.

- The defendant intended for the misrepresentation to be acted upon.

- Believing it to be accurate, the victim (plaintiff) took some action or relied on the misrepresentation.

- The victim was damaged in some way, usually monetarily, as a result of the misrepresentation.

---

[23] Bologna, G.J. and Lindquist, R.J., *Fraud Auditing and Forensic Accounting: New Tools and Techniques* (2nd ed., John Wiley & Sons Inc., New York, 1995), p. 3.
[24] Edelhertz, H., *The Nature, Impact and Prosecution of White Collar Crime*, U.S. Government Printing Office, 1970, as quoted in *Litigation Services Handbook. The Role of the Accountant as Expert,* (2nd ed., Weil, R. L., Wagner, M.J. and Frank, P.B. (eds), John Wiley & Sons, Inc., New York, 1995), p. 23.2.

3–16   According to Edelhertz,[25] criminal fraud has five principal components, common to virtually every white-collar crime:

– Intent to commit a wrongful act or to achieve a purpose inconsistent with the law or public policy.

– The disguise of the purpose.

– Offender's reliance on the victim's ignorance or carelessness.

– Victim's voluntary action to assist the offender.

– Concealment of the crime.

3–17   A narrower form of criminal fraud is larceny which has the additional elements of:

– Taking another's money or property.

– Taking it against the will, or without the consent, of the owner.

– With the intention of permanently depriving the owner of the money or property.

3–18   For criminal fraud, the criminal act – *actus reus* – and criminal intent – *mens rea* – must exist. According to MacGregor and Hobbs[26] there are a number of key elements of fraud:

– Dishonesty, whether intentional or non-intentional (*i.e.* closing one's mind to matters which would have indicated that the conduct was dishonest).

– Deception.

– Gain, loss and risk.

Irish law relating to fraud

3–19   Irish law recognises a large number of criminal offences involving fraud. Several offences carry different penalties depending on whether the manner of commission of the offence involved any fraud. Among the offences (the list is not exhaustive) that include, or may include, an element of fraud are:

– Larceny under section 2 of the Larceny Act 1916.

– Obtaining credit by fraud under section 13 of the Debtors Act (Ireland) 1872.

---

[25] Edelhertz, H., *The Nature, Impact, and Prosecution of White Collar Crime*, U.S. Government Printing Office, 1970, as quoted in *Litigation Services Handbook. The Role of the Accountant as Expert,* (2nd ed., Weil, R.L., Wagner, M.J. and Frank, P.B. (eds), John Wiley & Sons, Inc., New York, 1995), p. 23.2.

[26] MacGregor and G., Hobbs, I., *Expert Accounting Evidence: A Guide for Litigation Support* (Accountancy Books, London, 1998), Chap. 31.

- False accounting under section 1 of the Falsification of Accounts Act 1875.
- Keeping fraudulent accounts and wilfully destroying or mutilating books of account under sections 82 and 83 of the Larceny Act 1861.
- Forgery under the Forgery Act 1913.
- Fraudulent conversion under section 20 of the Larceny Act 1916.
- Carrying on business with intent to defraud creditors of a company or creditors of any other person, or for any fraudulent purpose under section 297 of the Companies Act 1963 as substituted by section 137 of the Companies Act 1990.
- Several tax statutes, where typically penalties are doubled where fraud has been involved in the non-payment of appropriate tax.
- Fraud and misuse of electronic signatures under section 25 of the Electronic Commerce Act 2000.
- The common law offence of conspiracy to defraud.

3–20 The main legal provisions (the list is not exhaustive) relating to fraud are summarised in Table 3.3. Most of the provisions are contained in the Larceny Acts 1861 to 1990 and in the Forgery Act 1913.

Table 3.3: Main legal provisions relating to fraud

Provision	Legislation
Obtaining credit under false pretences	Section 13(1), Debtors Act (Ireland) 1872
False accounting	Section 1, Falsification of Accounts Act 1875
Keeping fraudulent accounts	Section 82, Larceny Act 1861 (as amended)
Wilfully destroying or mutilating books of account	Section 83, Larceny Act 1861 (as amended)
Forgery of documents and instruments	Forgery Act 1913
Simple larceny	Section 2, Larceny Act 1916 (as amended)
Larceny of embezzlement by an employee	Section 17, Larceny Act 1916 (as amended)
Fraudulent conversion	Section 20, Larceny Act 1916 (as amended)
Obtaining money or security by false pretences	Section 32, Larceny Act 1916 (as amended)
Fraudulent trading	Sections 297 and 297A, Companies Act 1963
Insider dealing	Part V, Companies Act 1990
Company investigations	Part II, Companies Act 1990
Keeping of proper books of account	Sections 203 and 204, Companies Act 1990
Disqualification of directors, auditors, liquidators, receivers, examiners and other officers	Part VII, Companies Act 1990

Source: Adapted from the *Report of the Government Advisory Committee on Fraud* (Government Publications, Dublin, 1992), pp. 24–28.

Tort of deceit[27]

3–21 Deceit is the name given to the civil wrong committed through the perpetration of a fraud by one party on another. A deceit generally arises from a fraudulent misrepresentation made by the offending party to the wronged party. There is an overlap between the concept of negligent misstatement, to which the principles of negligence apply, and deceit, in that deceit is, in effect, "negligence with intent". This implies that negligence is easier to prove, and that therefore a prospective plaintiff has a greater chance of success if he pursues the defendant in negligence. Nevertheless, where the constituents of the tort of deceit are present it is generally worthwhile advancing such a case as the damages recovered are likely to be greater than those for negligence.

3–22 In order to establish deceit, a plaintiff must prove that:

– the defendant made a representation of fact either knowing that the representation was false or being reckless as to whether it was true;

– the plaintiff acted on the representation and suffered damage as a result;

– the defendant intended that the representation would be relied upon by the plaintiff.

3–23 The leading case in this area has been referred to in many subsequent cases, notably *Superwood Holdings plc v. Sun Alliance and London Insurance plc*,[28] in which Denham J. said:

> "The foundation case is *Derry v. Peek* (1889) 14 App. Cas. 337. In that case an Act incorporating a tramway company provided that the carriages might be moved by animal power, and, with the consent of the Board of Trade, by steam power. The directors of the company issued a prospectus wherein it was stated that by their Act the company had the right to use steam power instead of horses. The plaintiff bought shares on the faith of that statement in the prospectus. Later the Board of Trade refused consent to the use of steam power and the company was wound up. The plaintiff brought an action of deceit against the directors founded upon the false statement, and was unsuccessful. The House of Lords held that there was no fraud, Lord Herschell stating, at p. 374: –
>
> > 'First, in order to sustain an action of deceit, there must be proof of fraud, and nothing short of that will suffice. Secondly, fraud is proved when it is shown that a false representation has been made (1) knowingly, or (2) without belief in its truth, or (3) recklessly, careless whether it be true or false. Although I have treated the second and third as distinct cases, I think the third is but an instance of the second, for one who makes a statement under

---

[27] This is dealt with in McMahon, B. and Binchy, W., *Law of Torts* (3rd ed., Butterworths, Dublin, 2000).

[28] [1995] 3 I.R. 303.

such circumstances can have no real belief in the truth of what he states. To prevent a false statement being fraudulent, there must, I think, always be an honest belief in its truth. And this probably covers the whole ground, for one who knowingly alleges that which is false, has obviously no such honest belief. Thirdly, if fraud be proved, the motive of the person guilty of it is immaterial. It matters not that there was no intention to cheat or injure the person to whom the statement was made.'

That analysis of the law remains true today, and is applicable to this case."[29]

3–24 The measure of damages arising from a successful action in deceit was dealt with by the Supreme Court in *Northern Bank Finance Corporation Ltd. v. Charlton*. Here O'Higgins C.J. said:

"The measure of damages for the tort of deceit is the actual loss flowing directly from the fraud. I adopt in this respect the views of Lord Atkin in *Clark v. Urquhart* [1930] A.C. 28 at page 68 of the report."[30]

Also commenting on the measure of damages, Henchy J. said in the same case:

"As far as the tort of fraud or deceit is concerned it is well settled that the measure of damages is based on the actual damage directly flowing from the fraudulent inducement, and that the award may, in an appropriate case (of which this may not be an example), include consequential damages representing what was reasonably and necessarily expended as a result of acting on the inducement: *Doyle v. Olby Ltd* [1969] 2 Q.B. 158."[31]

Causes and categories of fraud

Causes of fraud

3–25 Fraud can be once-off or systematic. Once-off fraud is likely to be for a large, once-off sum. However, fraud is frequently partially motivated by habit. The perpetrator may need to obtain cash regularly, for example to feed a drug habit or to deal with personal financial pressures.

Perpetrators of fraud

3–26 Moulton[32] identifies "red flags" to watch for in trying to spot fraudsters. These include large egos, substance abuse problems or gambling addiction, living beyond apparent means, self-absorption, hard working (taking few holidays),

---

[29] [1995] 3 I.R. 303 at 327–328.
[30] [1979] I.R. 149 at 187.
[31] *ibid.* at 199.
[32] Moulton, G.E., "Profile of a fraudster" (Deloitte Touche Tohmatsu, www.deloitte.ca, 1994).

under financial pressure from (say) heavy borrowings and sudden mood changes.

3–27   Edelhertz[33] classified white-collar crime by perpetrators into four categories:

(1) Ad hoc violations committed by persons for personal gain, operating in a non-business context, *e.g.* credit purchases (where there is no intention to pay), purchase by mail in another person's name, income tax offences, credit card fraud, bankruptcy fraud, social welfare fraud, insurance fraud.

(2) Criminal abuses of trust committed by persons operating inside business, government, a profession or other entity, in violation of their duty of fidelity to employer or client, *e.g.* commercial bribery and kickbacks, banking abuses by bank officials, employees and directors, embezzlement, share frauds (*i.e.* insider trading), using company funds to buy shares, petty theft and expense account frauds, computer fraud resulting in unauthorised payments.

(3) Business crimes committed incidental to and in furtherance of business operations, but which are not the central purpose of the business, *e.g.* tax fraud, infringement of competition laws, use of false financial statements to obtain credit, cheque "kiting" to obtain short-term finance, share violations (*i.e.* manipulation of the market).

(4) Fraudulent activities which are the central purpose of the business, *e.g.* medical or health frauds, share and commodities fraud, chain referral schemes, buying or pyramid schemes.

Categories of fraud

3–28   Fraud takes many forms, has an impact on the public and private sectors of our economy and affects society in many ways.[34] Fraud may be classified in a variety of ways. Table 3.4 provides some examples, some of which are discussed further in the text.

---

[33] Edelhertz, H., *The Nature, Impact, and Prosecution of White Collar Crime*, U.S. Government Printing Office, 1970, as quoted in *Litigation Services Handbook. The Role of the Accountant as Expert* (2nd ed., Weil, R.L., Wagner, M.J. and Frank, P.B. (eds), John Wiley & Sons, Inc., New York, 1995), p. 23.2.

[34] Auditing Practices Board, *Fraud and Audit: Choices for Society* (Auditing Practices Board, London, 1998).

Table 3.4: Classification of fraud

Classification	
• Definition	Fraud; Theft; Embezzlement
• By victim	Customers; Shareholders; Creditors; Competitors; Bankers; Company/Employer; Insurance companies; Government agencies
• Perpetrators of corporate fraud	Owners and Managers; Suppliers; Contractors; Customers; Employees
• Frequency	Once-off; Systematic
• Legally	Crime; Tort; Contractual
• Company	Fraud by, for or against companies (see para. **3–31**) Internal fraud; External fraud (see para. **3–32**) Transaction fraud; Statement fraud (see para. **3–33**)
• Type of fraud	Concealed fraud; Unconcealed fraud (see paras **3–36 to 3–37**)

Source: Adapted from Comer, M.J., *Corporate Fraud* (3rd ed., Gower Publishing Ltd., Aldershot, 1998), Chap. 2.

3–29   There is no standardisation on the categories or classification of fraud. Different reporting bodies use different categories for types of fraud. Examples of categorisations by three authorities in the United Kingdom are summarised in Table 3.5.

Table 3.5: Categories of fraud

Serious Fraud Office, U.K.	Metropolitan Police	Home Office
– Fraud on investors	– Computer	– Fraud by company director
– Fraud on creditors of companies	– Fraudulent trading	– False accounting
– Fraud on banks and other financial institutions	– Investment	– Other fraud
– Fraud on central and local government	– "Long firm"	– Forgery
– Fraud involving the manipulation of financial markets	– Public sector	
	– Mortgage	

Adapted from: Fraud Advisory Panel, "Study of published literature on the nature & extent of fraud in the public & private sector" (Fraud Advisory Panel, London, 1999), p. 12.

3–30   KPMG[35] in Ireland distinguished between external and internal fraud and classified internal fraud by perpetrator. The types of fraud listed by KPMG are shown in Table 3.6.

---

[35] KPMG, *Fraud Awareness Survey* (KPMG, Dublin, 1995).

Table 3.6: Internal and external fraud

Internal fraud		External fraud
Employee fraud	**Management fraud**	
Stock theft	Teeming and lading (lapping)	Cheque forgery
Misappropriation of cash	Expense account	False insurance claims
Teeming and lading	False financial statements	Credit card fraud
Cheque forgery	Misappropriation of cash	False invoices
Expense account	Unnecessary purchases	Product substitution
Petty cash	Cheque forgery	Bribe, secret commission
Kickbacks	Kickbacks	Bid rigging, price fixing
Loans/investments	Phantom vendors	False representation of funds
	Diversion of sales	

Source: KPMG, *Fraud Awareness Survey* (KPMG, Dublin, 1995), pp. 10–12.

Wells[36] establishes a classification system to explain 44 fraud schemes used by executive owners, managers and employees to defraud companies. Some fraud classifications are discussed further below.

Fraud by, for and against companies

3–31   Corporate or management fraud may be perpetrated either for the benefit of, or against companies. Fraud for the benefit of companies includes anti-competitive behaviour, corporate tax evasion, false advertising, short counts and weights and manipulation of company profits (which may in turn affect management bonuses). Frauds against the company include theft of corporate assets and embezzlement.

Internal and external frauds

3–32   Corporate or management frauds may also be categorised into internal frauds and external frauds (a category that includes frauds committed by vendors, suppliers, or contractors, who might overcharge, double charge or substitute inferior goods). Customers may try to defraud companies by feigning damage or destruction of goods, or by feigning injury from use of company products. Commercial bribery may be accompanied by manipulation of accounting records to cover up its payment and to protect the recipients from taxation on the income.

Transaction and statement fraud

3–33   Fraud in books of account can be in two major categories: transaction and statement frauds. Statement frauds involve the intentional misstatement of certain financial values to enhance (or reduce) the appearance of profitability

---

[36] Wells, J.T., *Occupational Fraud and Abuse* (Obsidian Publishing Co., Austin, Texas, 1997).

and deceive, for example, shareholders, creditors or tax authorities. Senior managers may be motivated to assist in statement fraud by reason of promotion, bonus or some other preferment. The most common ways to manipulate the profit and loss account is by changing amounts for sales or stock.

3–34 Transaction frauds are intended to facilitate the theft or conversion of company assets to individual use. Such fraud is perpetrated by employees (both at senior management level and at lower levels in the organisation). The most common forms of transaction frauds are through fictitious creditors and through the conversion of corporate assets to personal use. Mythical employees or suppliers may be added to company records to whom monies are paid for goods or services never delivered.

On-book and off-book accounting fraud

3–35 On-book frauds involve manipulation of accounting records. Off-book frauds involve misrepresentation of physical, commercial or personal realities.

Type of concealment

3–36 Comer[37] deals extensively with how fraud is concealed. Concealment may occur through falsification of realities as mentioned above for off-book fraud. Alternatively, accounting records may be falsified. Secondary concealment is also identified which includes oral and written lies, falsification of documents, destruction of documentation and falsified signatures.

3–37 There are also circumstances when fraud may not be concealed because:

– it is not necessary (*e.g.* if the victim's records do not disclose the perpetrator's identity);

– it is not possible;

– it is condoned by the victim (*e.g.* fraud carried out by senior management in a company);

– the fraudster does not know how to conceal the fraud;

– the fraud is once-off (and, say, the perpetrator absconds to another country).

---

[37]Comer, M.J., *Corporate Fraud* (3rd ed., Gower Publishing Ltd., Aldershot, 1998), Chap. 3.

Effects of fraud

3–38   Fraud has, broadly speaking, two types of consequences. First, there is the cost associated with fraud and, second, there is the effect of the fraud on victims.

Cost of fraud

3–39   The roots of fraud – greed and arrogance – are inherent in human nature. Businesses must recognise frauds as permanent risks that must be actively managed. Statistics worldwide indicate a dramatic escalation in the incidence of fraud over the past decade. This has resulted in a major demand for accountants in the field of forensic accounting as the proof of such crimes often requires forensic accounting expertise and the evidence of experts.

As there is no legal definition of fraud, attempts to quantify the incidence of fraud quickly run into difficulties.[38] Consequently, there is considerable diversity of opinion and practice among those engaged in the recording and analysis of fraud. Government departments, professional bodies, business organisations and the police have different working definitions (as already illustraed in table 3.5).

3–40   It is likely that the financial losses suffered by victims of white-collar crime such as fraud and embezzlement exceed those suffered during violent crimes such as robberies, burglaries and property theft. The cost of fraud can be quantified in a number of ways. At its simplest, it can be calculated as the financial loss suffered by the victim. This loss can also be quantified in terms of perceived cost, suspected cost, proven cost, reported cost and potential cost. The cost of fraud is often estimated using surveys of businesses. Again, the methods of quantifying this cost vary. Cost may be based on reported fraud or on extrapolations from representative samples. Such extrapolated figures may not be reliable.

3–41   The quantification of the direct cost of fraud only can ignore the consequences of fraud (*e.g.* loss of employment, business failure) to business, the wider community and the economy. Nor are the costs of regulation and policing such regulations taken into account. These additional costs arise from:

– insolvency and winding up of businesses;

– bankruptcy;

– failure of creditor/supplier businesses;

– loss of employment;

---

[38] The Fraud Advisory Panel, *First Annual Report, 1998–1999* (Institute of Chartered Accountants in England and Wales, London, 1999), p. 6.

- loss of tax revenue;

- loss of confidence in businesses;

- loss to lenders and investors;

- opportunity costs, *e.g.* diversion of management time;

- regulatory costs, such as establishing and policing regulations.

3–42 The annual cost of fraud in Ireland has been variously estimated at £26 million[39] in 1992 and £41 million[40] in 1995. A survey by KPMG in 1995 revealed that approximately 40 per cent of the top 500 Irish firms had experienced fraud in the previous two years.[41] The Small Firms Association conducted a survey of 240 member firms, all of which had an annual turnover of £3 million or less.[42] The Small Firms Association estimate that fraud had cost small firms in Ireland £225 million between 1992 and 1995. Almost 60 per cent of respondents reported having experienced a fraud. Company auditors discovered less than 10 per cent of such frauds, while one in five was reported as having been discovered by accident. In a more recent international survey conducted in October 1999, Ernst & Young found that over 50 per cent of Irish companies in its survey had experienced one or more incidents of fraud.[43] Amongst countries surveyed, Irish respondents perceived themselves to have the lowest likelihood of being hit by computer fraud.[44]

3–43 Lack of awareness of fraud at senior levels, and a tendency for company directors to ignore the problem, have both been cited in the first report of the United Kingdom's Fraud Advisory Panel as reasons for the lack of reliable information on the subject.[45] This report has warned that fraud will almost certainly increase in the future. Introducing methods for fraud prevention and detection into corporate governance rules could help to reduce fraud. Concern for the prevention and detection of fraud is also evident in Ireland. The Garda Bureau of Fraud Investigation has as one of its primary objectives "to play a pro-active role in the prevention and detection of fraud".[46] Recently, the

---

[39] *Report of the Government Advisory Committee on Fraud* (Government Publications, Dublin, 1992), p. 20.

[40] Maguire, P. Chairman of the Government Advisory Committee on Fraud, as reported in KPMG, *Fraud Awareness Survey* (KPMG, Dublin, 1995).

[41] KPMG, *Fraud Awareness Survey* (KPMG, Dublin, 1995), p. 6.

[42] Fitzgerald, K., "The £225m fraud bill", *Business & Finance*, December 14, 1995, pp. 7–8.

[43] Ernst & Young, *Fraud: The Unmanaged Risk* (Ernst & Young, 2000), p. 8.

[44] *ibid.*, p. 3.

[45] The Fraud Advisory Panel, *First Annual Report, 1998–1999* (Institute of Chartered Accountants in England and Wales, London, 1999).

[46] Garda Síochána, *Annual Report 1998* (Garda Síochána, Dublin, 1999), p. 38.

Garda Síochána and PricewaterhouseCoopers published a joint report on the issue.[47]

Victims of fraud

3–44   Victims of fraud can be divided in two groups: individuals and businesses. Individuals can suffer fraud in a variety of ways, including as consumers, employees, householders, etc. Although fraud perpetrated against individuals is, relatively speaking, more frequent than against businesses, the absolute value of the losses is comparatively smaller. However, individual victims may suffer not only financial loss, but also health and emotional problems as a result of the crime. Individual victims in the United States have been found to be younger and more highly educated.[48] Increasing computerisation makes individuals more vulnerable to fraud. Business is at risk from fraud from a variety of sources both within and outside the company. Losses are likely to be greater than for individuals, with the greatest losses arising where management are participating in the fraudulent acts.

Methods of fraud

3–45   The following discussion highlights some of the more common frauds – other sources considering fraud in more detail are cited at the beginning of this chapter. The examples cited include types of fraud adopted by employees (embezzlement is probably the most common fraud for the detection of which forensic accounting services are engaged), by managers, by those seeking to defraud Revenue and other authorities, and by those making fraudulent misrepresentations.

Bribery

3–46   Bribery represents payment or the provision of goods or services, advantage or benefit of any kind in return for actual or perceived advantage, benefit or preferential treatment. Essentially, two parties are involved: the payer and the recipient. Usually the payer, through actual or potential relationships with the recipient's principal (employer), has or wishes to obtain a benefit, advantage or preferential treatment.

---

[47] Garda Síochána and PricewaterhouseCoopers, *Fraud Alert* (Garda Síochána, Dublin, 1999).
[48] Titus, R.M., Heinzelmann, F. and Boyle, J.M. "Victimization of persons by fraud" in *Crime and Delinquency* (1995), Vol. 41, No. 1, pp. 54–72.

Cheque and credit card fraud

3–47   Cheque and credit card fraud is one of the most common types of fraud.[49] Personal or company cheques made payable to individuals may be stolen. Alternatively, blank cheques may be stolen and the signature forged. Amounts on cheques may be altered – especially the number rather than the narrative amount. Credit card fraud at its crudest arises in relation to lost or stolen cards. Fraudulent applications for cards may be made. Increasingly, frauds are being committed through mail, telephone and internet orders where credit cards are not produced to retailers. More sophisticated techniques include counterfeiting of cards.

Computer-related fraud

3–48   The use of information technology in the commission of fraud-related offences is a factor of growing importance. The Data Protection Act 1988 requires persons who keep information on computer systems to provide adequate security against unauthorised access, alteration or destruction. Inputting frauds involve changing (copying, removing, adding or altering) the data input to the computer. Processing frauds involve changing the computer program to the gain of the programmer. Changing the output of the computer (*e.g.* computer-generated cheques) can also benefit a fraudster.

3–49   The Criminal Damage Act 1991 creates offences that can involve the use of computers. These include:

– Damaging the property of another intentionally or recklessly or damaging one's own property or the property of another with intent to defraud. "Property" for these purposes is defined to include "information in a form in which it can be accessed by means of a computer and includes a program". "To damage" is defined to include: "to add to, alter, corrupt, erase or move to another medium or to a different location in the storage medium in which they are kept (whether or not property other than data is damaged thereby), or to do any act that contributes towards causing such addition, alteration, erasure or movement".

– Operating a computer within the State with intent to access any data without lawful excuse ("hacking").

---

[49] Garda Síochána and PricewaterhouseCoopers, *Fraud Alert* (Garda Síochána, Dublin, 1999), p. 28. The Garda Bureau of Fraud Investigation has a separate Cheque/Credit Card Fraud Unit to concentrate on the more serious, organised cases of cheque, credit card and counterfeit currency fraud.

Fraudulent trading[50]

3–50   Sections 297 and 297A of the Companies Act 1963 allow the court to pierce the corporate veil to impose both criminal and civil liability upon directors (including shadow directors) and officers of a company who are found guilty of fraudulent or reckless trading. Section 297 of the 1963 Act (as substituted by section 137 of the Companies Act 1990) makes it a criminal offence for any person knowingly to be a party to the carrying-on of the business of a company with intent to defraud creditors of the company, or creditors of any other person, or for any fraudulent purpose. The offence is punishable by a fine of up to £50,000 or up to seven years imprisonment or both.

In May 1996, a company director was jailed for the first time under section 297. A former insurance and investment broker whose firm collapsed with debts of more than £2 million, was sentenced to four years and three months in jail, and was also disqualified from acting as a company director, auditor or manager for 10 years. The court found that he was knowingly a party to the carrying-on of a business with the intent the defraud the creditors of the company by falsely pretending that he, as director, was engaged in the bona fide business of investing monies entrusted to him when he knew that the company was insolvent.

3–51   Section 297A of the 1963 Act, as inserted by section 138 of the Companies Act 1990, permits a court, on the application of a receiver, examiner, liquidator, creditor or contributory of a company, to declare a person responsible, with unlimited liability, for all or any part of the debts or other liabilities of the company where it appears, in the course of the winding-up or examination of the company, that that person was knowingly a party to the carrying-on of any business of the company with intent to defraud creditors of the company, or creditors of any other person, or for any fraudulent purpose, or that that person was, while an officer of the company, knowingly a party to the carrying on, of any business of the company in a reckless manner. For the purposes of this section it should be noted that the term "officer" is defined to include any auditor, liquidator, receiver or shadow director. Fraudulent trading is considered further in paras **8–55** *et seq.*

Lapping (teeming and lading)

3–52   Lapping (also called "teeming and lading") describes a scheme where the perpetrator steals cash from a business and fills the void created by its disappearance by recording cash which was intended for another use. Lapping is a type of "robbing Peter to pay Paul". Cash receipts (from, say, customer A) are taken and are replaced by subsequent cash receipts from customer B. This

---

[50]This is dealt with in Charleton, P., McDermott, P.A. and Bolger, M., *Criminal Law* (Butterworths, Dublin, 1999), pp. 914–917.

type of fraud involves careful record-keeping to remain undetected. Companies who do not contact their customers regularly (by, for example, sending out regular statements) are more prone to this type of fraud. Lapping is also facilitated by poor division of duties in organisations, particularly in the areas of debt collection and credit control.

Kiting[51]

3–53 Kiting occurs where cheques are continuously exchanged between bank accounts in two separate banks to disguise a lack of funds to back the cheques issued. Frequently, the amount "floating" between the two banks continues to grow until the scheme collapses. This involves using cheques from different banks to create the appearance of healthy cash flow. Cash is drawn from one account and lodged to a second. This gives the appearance of healthy cash receipts in the second bank account. A cheque from a third bank account can be used to prop up the account in the first bank.

Money laundering[52]

3–54 Money laundering involves the use of a legitimate financial transaction to conceal the source of cash obtained illegally (from say drug trafficking or white-collar crime) and the identities of the persons who acquired it. Money laundering is designed to enable criminals to conceal the source of illegally obtained assets and thereby avoid the effect of laws providing for the confiscation of assets derived from criminal activities (see, for instance, the Criminal Justice Act 1994).

3–55 Illegal drug sales generate more and more cash each year and, as a result, drug traffickers and other criminals must continually find new ways to launder dirty money. Laws targeting money laundering at banks and other financial institutions have encouraged traffickers to seek non-financial institutions to launder funds. As a result, many companies are vulnerable to money laundering activity. Proactive prevention programs can be designed to keep businesses free from money laundering in the future, such as establishment of customer background searches, employee training programs, compliance officers and regular ad hoc audits. With increased legislation against companies involved in money laundering, including stiff penalties and broad asset forfeiture provisions, most companies can no longer afford to assume money laundering is somebody else's problem. Cash fuels most illegal activity. The goal of money laundering is to find ways to introduce illegal gains into the legitimate money system,

---

[51] Cheque fraud generally is dealt with in Donnelly, M., "Cheque fraud: Modern treatment and future trends" in *Commercial Law Practitioner* (October 1997), pp. 216-221.
[52] See generally Ashe, M.T. and Reid, P., *Money Laundering* (Round Hall Sweet & Maxwell, Dublin, 2000).

covering tracks so that the money's original source cannot be traced. Some signs of money laundering include the following:

– activities that are not consistent with the business;

– larger than expected cash deposits, or purchases;

– withdrawals inconsistent with the cash needs of the business;

– invoices larger than normal;

– frequent deposits or purchases just under the thresholds (such as those applying to designated bodies under section 32 of the Criminal Justice Act 1994);

– unusual fund transfer activities;

– large or frequent transactions involving foreign currency amounts, offshore banks, foreign countries or shell companies;

– bank information that is insufficient or suspicious;

– accounts in false names or in the name of persons acting for a third party;

– transaction documents that appear falsified or not legally correct;

– reluctance to provide identifying information during audit;

– sudden changes in lifestyles.

3–56 Businesses most at risk of becoming unwittingly involved in money laundering are obviously those that transact business in cash. Both traditional and non-traditional financial institutions contribute to the daily flow of money. Dealers and agents of high-value items such as cars and property are also susceptible to becoming unwitting participants in such schemes. Businesses commonly used by criminals to launder cash include:

– banks;

– brokerage firms;

– insurance companies;

– gambling establishments;

– foreign currency exchanges;

– dealers in precious metals, art, blood stock, cars, boats, precious gems, etc.;

– estate agents or vendors of property;

3–57 The specific offence of money laundering was introduced to Irish law by the Criminal Justice Act 1994. Section 31 of that Act states:

   "(1) A person shall be guilty of an offence if he—

(a) conceals or disguises any property which is, or in whole or in part directly or indirectly represents, his proceeds of drug trafficking or other criminal activity, or

(b) converts or transfers that property or removes it from the State,

for the purpose of avoiding prosecution for an offence or the making or enforcement in his case of a confiscation order.

(2) A person shall be guilty of an offence if, knowing or believing that any property is, or in whole or in part directly or indirectly represents, another person's proceeds of drug trafficking or other criminal activity, he—

(a) conceals or disguises that property, or

(b) converts or transfers that property or removes it from the State,

for the purpose of assisting any person to avoid prosecution for an offence or the making or enforcement of a confiscation order.

(3) A person shall be guilty of an offence if he handles any property knowing or believing that such property is, or in whole or in part directly or indirectly represents, another person's proceeds of drug trafficking or other criminal activity."

The definitions of these offences are broad and designed to cover all possible money laundering activity. The offences carry prison terms of up to 14 years and unlimited fines. The Act goes on to impose obligations on designated bodies including banks, building societies, insurance companies, credit unions and other entities operating in the financial services industry to take measures to prevent, detect and report money laundering activities.[53] Designation is likely to be extended to accountants when the new directive on money laundering is enacted in Ireland.[54]

3–58   Section 21 of the Criminal Justice (Theft and Fraud Offences) Bill 2000 proposes to amend section 31 significantly. The proposed amendments would include within the offence of money laundering certain activities performed by someone who is reckless as to whether the property involved is, or represents, the proceeds of criminal conduct. They would also transfer to the accused in criminal proceedings the onus of establishing a reasonable doubt as to his guilt in certain circumstances.

---

[53] The Garda Bureau of Fraud Investigation has a separate Money Laundering Investigation Unit to analyse and investigate disclosures relating to suspicious financial transactions received from bodies designated under the Criminal Justice Act 1994.

[54] Council of Europe "Proposal for a Directive of the European Parliament and of the Council amending Council Directive 91/308/EEC for Prevention of the use of the Financial System for the purpose of money laundering" (Council of Europe, Brussels, 1999).

The key subsections of the proposed section 31 read as follows:

"(1) A person is guilty of money laundering if, knowing or believing that property is or represents the proceeds of criminal conduct or being reckless as to whether it is or represents such proceeds, the person, without lawful authority or excuse (the proof of which shall lie on him or her)—

    (a)   converts, transfers or handles the property, or removes it from the State, with the intention of—

        (i)   concealing or disguising its true nature, source, location, disposition, movement or ownership or any rights with respect to it, or

        (ii) assisting another person to avoid prosecution for the criminal conduct concerned, or

        (iii) avoiding the making of a confiscation order or a confiscation co-operation order (within the meaning of section 46 of this Act) or frustrating its enforcement against that person or another person,

    (b)   conceals or disguises its true nature, source, location, disposition, movement or ownership or any rights with respect to it, or

    (c)   acquires, possesses or uses the property.

. . .

(3) Where a person—

    (a)   converts, transfers, handles or removes from the State any property which is or represents the proceeds of criminal conduct,

    (b)   conceals or disguises its true nature, source, location, disposition, movement or ownership or any rights with respect to it, or

    (c)   acquires, possesses or uses it,

in such circumstances that it is reasonable to concluded that the person—

        (i)   knew or believed that the property was or represented the proceeds of criminal conduct, or

        (ii) was reckless as to whether it was or represented such proceeds,

the person shall be taken to have so known or believed or to have been so reckless, unless the court or jury, as the case may be, is satisfied having regard to all the evidence that there is a reasonable doubt as to whether the person so knew or believed or was so reckless.

(4) Where a person first referred to in subsection (1) of this section does an act referred to in paragraph (a) of that subsection in such circumstances that it is reasonable to conclude that the act was done with an intention specified in that paragraph, the person shall be taken to have done the act with that intention unless the court or jury, as the case may be, is satisfied having regard to all the evidence that there is a reasonable doubt as to whether the person did it with that intention."

Ponzi schemes

3–59   Named after Charles Ponzi, such schemes involve paying early investors with money raised from later investors.[55] These schemes are sometimes called pyramid schemes and can be found in multi-level distribution businesses such as franchises. The franchise fees are paid to the founder of the operation who may disappear with the profits.

Skimming (front-end fraud)

3–60   Skimming, also called front-end fraud, is where funds are stolen before being entered in company books. This type of fraud is commonly found in the retail trade such as bars, restaurants, shops, vending machines, etc. The cash may be taken before (or, less frequently, after) being included in the cash register.

Tax fraud

3–61   As mentioned earlier, taxation statutes generally impose higher penalties where fraud has been a part of a non-payment or underpayment of tax, and often the penalties are double those that would apply in the absence of fraud. Examples of this are contained in section 1053 and 1072 of the Taxes Consolidation Act 1997. The latter section deals with the fraudulent or negligent making of tax returns by companies. The relevant part of the section (as amended by the Finance Act 2001) states:

> "(1) Where a company fraudulently or negligently—
>> (a)   delivers an incorrect return under section 884,
>> (b)   makes any incorrect return, statement or declaration in connection with any claim for any allowance, deduction or relief in respect of corporation tax, or
>> (c)   submits to an inspector, the Revenue Commissioners or the Appeal Commissioners any incorrect accounts in connection with the ascertainment of the company's liability to corporation tax,
>
> the company shall be liable to a penalty of—
>> (i)   £500 [€630] or, in the case of fraud, £1,000 [€1,265], and
>> (ii)   the amount or, in the case of fraud, twice the amount of the difference specified in subsection (2), and
>
> the secretary of the company shall be liable to a separate penalty of £100 [€125] or, in the case of fraud, £200 [€250].
>
> (2) The difference referred to in subsection (1) shall be the difference between—
>> (a)   the amount of corporation tax payable by the company for the accounting period or accounting periods comprising the period to which the return, statement, declaration or accounts relate, and

---

[55] Parker, T.R., "White collar crime: fraud and embezzlement" in *Litigation Services Handbook. The Role of the Accountant as Expert* (2nd ed., Weil, R.L., Wagner, M.J. and Frank, P.B. (eds), John Wiley & Sons, Inc., New York, 1995), p. 23.7.

(b) the amount which would have been the amount so payable if the return, statement, declaration or accounts had been correct."

3–62 This means that, where an incorrect tax return is made negligently, the company must pay the additional tax payable on foot of the correct return, and penalties totalling £600 [€755] are also payable. By contrast, where fraud is involved the penalty is twice the additional tax and the penalties total £1,200 [€1,515].

3–63 It should be noted that the knowing or wilful delivery of incorrect returns, statements, accounts or information in connection with any tax, or the provision of assistance to do so, is an offence under section 1078 of the Taxes Consolidation Act 1997 as amended by the Finance Acts 1999 and 2001. Such offences are punishable by fines of up to £100,000 [€126,970] and imprisonment for up to five years. These issues are considered further in Chapter 11 on taxation.

Difficulties in proving fraud

3–64 Many high-profile business failures in recent years that have generally been regarded by the public as involving fraud have involved misstatement of financial information. However, it has not always been possible to obtain a successful prosecution, reflecting the difficulty of proving the elements of the crime, including deception, obtaining advantage or the causing of loss.

3–65 The Serious Fraud Office in the United Kingdom has encountered significant difficulties in proving fraud to the satisfaction of a jury in a number of high-profile cases in recent years. These "failures" are seen to reflect the inevitable problems in establishing beyond a reasonable doubt (the standard of proof necessary for criminal convictions) that the act or omission involved was intentional. There are always difficulties in proving the state of mind of a person, and the evidence needs to be very strong to overcome a denial of intent and to reach the necessary standard of proof. In addition, fraudulent activity can involve matters of a highly technical and complex nature. This can make the investigation of all the circumstances and their subsequent clear presentation to a court very difficult.

Given the difficulties in successfully prosecuting fraud, forensic accountants should exercise care not to act in place of judge or jury by pointing to the guilt or otherwise of persons subject to the investigation. Forensic accounting reports should avoid the use of terms "fraud", "fraudulent", etc., which might imply fraudulent behaviour by any person, but which could be construed as libellous.

3–66 Ireland has no direct equivalent to the Serious Fraud Office. Given the inherent difficulties in proving fraud, the formalisation of arrangements whereby all necessary skills, knowledge and expertise can be brought to bear in significant cases on behalf of the State would be very welcome.

3–67 The investigation of fraud is a service offered by the professional forensic accountant that assists in detection and quantification of fraud. Equally important to any attempt to reduce fraud is the creation of a culture and environment which is aimed at the prevention of fraud and a response policy which is designed to respond to fraud detection as effectively as possible. This is the subject-matter of the next chapter.

3–68 The Criminal Justice (Theft and Fraud Offences) Bill 2000 will, when enacted, make it easier to prosecute certain serious offences. In particular, the proposed offence of "making gain or causing loss by deception" is stated in admirably clear and brief terms. Section 6(1) of the Bill states:

> "A person who dishonestly, with the intention of making a gain for himself or herself or another, or of causing loss to another, induces another to do or refrain from doing an act is guilty of an offence."

This and other proposed provisions, if and when enacted, will help in large part to overcome some of the difficulties currently faced by the authorities in prosecuting under old statutes or common law.

Concluding comment

3–69 Accountants are notoriously paranoid about fraud. As auditors they have fought hard to limit their responsibility for the detection of fraud in companies, although they have had to accept that it is reasonable to expect an auditor to detect fraud that has a material effect on the financial statements. Even then, however, they protest that well-organised fraud involving collusion, even if material to the accounts, may well escape detection.

Although Auditing Standards support this position, and in general the courts regard auditors as watchdogs, not bloodhounds, empirical evidence suggests that public expectation is higher. Accordingly, disappointment with the audit process inevitably seems to follow the discovery of fraud.

Forensic accountants can help to bridge this "expectation gap" (as it is known among accountants). One way they can do this by offering a "fraudit" service separate and distinct from the statutory audit of the financial statements, designed to detect, and perhaps help to prevent, fraud by using their forensic and investigative skills and techniques, which are ideally suited to the task.

ACCOUNTANTS, AUDITORS AND FRAUD

CHAPTER 4

ACCOUNTANTS, AUDITORS AND FRAUD

4–01   This chapter considers the role of accountants and auditors in connection with the prevention and detection of fraud.[1]

It is the duty of a company's directors to ensure that the company has adequate controls and procedures sufficient to prevent the occurrence of fraud. This duty is normally delegated to an accounting function within a business. In addition, the company's auditors will advise and report to the board on the adequacy and operation of these controls. Auditors should design their audit so as to have a reasonable expectation of detecting material fraud. Of course, no controls or audit procedures will detect every fraud, particularly where there is collusion.

However, prevention and detection of fraud is also relevant to forensic accounting. As explained in Chapter 5, it is inappropriate for the company auditors to investigate in circumstances where fraud is suspected. This is because the quality of the audit may be in question in such circumstances. Forensic accountants would normally be asked to perform an investigation to gather evidence of the suspected fraud. Forensic accountants need to be able to arrive at a view as to whether the controls and procedures designed to prevent and detect fraud were appropriate and functioning.

Prevention of fraud

4–02   Fraud is most often detected after significant damage has been done and usually when there remains no realistic possibility of recovering any substantial proportion of the losses resulting from the fraud. Ideally, prevention is very much better than cure when it comes to fraud.

Role of company accountants

4–03   As stated in para. **4–01**, the fiduciary and other duties of company directors require them to, *inter alia*, prevent or detect fraud, which duty they

---

[1] Further discussion of these topics can be found in Bologna, G.J. and Lindquist, R.J., *Fraud Auditing and Forensic Accounting: New Tools and Techniques* (2nd ed., John Wiley & Sons Inc., New York, 1995); Comer, M.J., *Corporate Fraud* (3rd ed., Gower Publishing Ltd., Aldershot, 1998); and Davies, D., *Fraud Watch* (2nd ed., ABG Professional Information, London, 2000).

delegate to company accountants and other employees in the organisation. It is well established that directors owe a variety of duties, under statute and common law, to safeguard company assets and to ensure that companies are properly and prudently managed. These duties are owed principally to the company and, indirectly, to the shareholders. However, recent legislative developments have included the establishment of a duty on directors of companies to also take account of the interests of employees, which duty is owed to the company alone and is enforceable similarly to their other fiduciary duties.[2]

Courtney points to the risk of abuse of fiduciary duties in the case of private companies, especially those where the directors and shareholders are one and the same, whereby directors dissipate company assets to the detriment of creditors.[3]

4–04 These duties are generally regarded as implying a requirement that the directors will establish, or cause to be established, accounting systems and internal controls commensurate with the size and complexity of the company's business, and sufficient to give a reasonable expectation that fraud, irregularities and errors will be prevented or detected. Although the nature and extent of the accounting system will depend on such factors as the size of the company, the nature of its business and the specific risks to which it is exposed, all such accounting systems will have a number of common essential features. These will include:

– sufficient, appropriately qualified and trained personnel;

– systems of checks and balances, including segregation of duties;

– computerised and/or manual accounting systems to record and reconcile transactions and balances comprehensively and on a timely basis;

– a system of internal controls involving review at a senior level (possibly including review by an audit committee) of the operation of controls and accounting procedures.

The emphasis on systems of internal control has increased in recent years. An example of this in relation to quoted companies is the adoption by the Stock Exchange of the Combined Code on Corporate Governance which requires boards of directors to maintain a sound system of internal control to safeguard

---

[2] *e.g.* see s. 52 of the Companies Act 1990 which requires directors to include the interests of company employees (as well as company shareholders) in carrying out their fiduciary duties. However, this provision, standing alone, is of little practical effect.

[3] Courtney, T.B., *The Law of Private Companies* (Butterworths, Dublin, 1994), pp. 266–269.

shareholders' investments and the company's assets. The Turnbull guidance,[4] published in response to this requirement, has introduced a risk-based approach to the issue of internal control. Although only applying to listed companies, the concept of risk management in connection with internal control is gaining wider acceptance.

In most companies, the directors carry out these duties by delegating the detailed design and operation of the system and the internal controls to a number of employees.

4–05 Primary weaknesses within companies that make it easier for directors, management and employees to commit fraud include:

- lack of separation of duties;
- domination by a few managers;
- lax attitudes towards policies and rules;
- management compensation linked to short-term financial results;
- employees poorly monitored and poorly paid;
- lack of proper authorisation procedures or ability to override stated authorisation procedures.

Fraud risk assessment

4–06 Every business should be subjected to an assessment of the risk of fraud at the outset and subsequently at regular intervals. No system can be designed or implemented that provides a complete guarantee that fraud can never be perpetrated against the business. However, the risk of fraud can be very significantly reduced if the vulnerability of the business to fraud is carefully and honestly evaluated and appropriate steps are taken to address identified risks.

4–07 Management of risk is, of course, an expensive undertaking. Many owners and managers of businesses, especially smaller businesses where often the owners and the managers are the same, decide that scarce resources can better be used in growing the business and developing trading activities than in protecting against something that may never in fact occur. Indeed, the natural inclination of entrepreneurs is to allocate resources sparingly, if at all, to any activity that does not have an obviously direct and short-term impact on profitable growth.

Clearly, expenditure on management and mitigation of risk of fraud must be proportional to the degree of risk to be managed, the size of the business and available resources. However, it must always be borne in mind (and as illustrated

---

[4] Institute of Chartered Accountants in England and Wales, *Guidance for Directors on the Combined Code* (Institute of Chartered Accountants in England and Wales, London, 1999).

in Table 4.5; see para. **4–54**) that a successful fraud can be a catastrophic event from which a business may never recover.

4–08   The following extract from the report into the collapse of Barings Bank in 1995 puts this point in perspective:

> "Barings' collapse was due to the unauthorised and ultimately catastrophic activities of, it appears, one individual (Leeson) that went undetected as a consequence of a failure of management and other internal controls of the most basic kind. Management failed at various levels and in a variety of ways, described in the earlier sections of this report, to institute a proper system of internal controls, to enforce the accountability for all profits, risks and operations, and adequately to follow up on a number of warning signals over a prolonged period. Neither the external auditors nor the regulators discovered Leeson's unauthorised activities.
>
> Management and directors of all financial institutions will draw lessons for themselves. However, we would emphasise the following five significant lessons of the Barings case, which we discuss later in this section, to which particular attention needs to be paid:
>
> (a)   Management teams have a duty to understand fully the businesses they manage;
> (b)   Responsibility for each business activity has to be clearly established and communicated;
> (c)   Clear segregation of duties is fundamental to any effective control system;
> (d)   Relevant internal controls, including independent risk management, have to be established for all business activities;
> (e)   Top management and the Audit Committee have to ensure that significant weaknesses, identified to them by internal audit or otherwise, are resolved quickly".[5]

Although these conclusions arise from an investigation of a multi-billion pound fraud, it is clear that the lessons apply across the business spectrum.

Vulnerability to fraud

4–09   Vulnerability to fraud can be usefully evaluated under the following headings:

– Vulnerability inherent in the business.

– Organisational design.

– Business practices.

– External events and trading experience.

These are considered further below.

---

[5] *Report of the Board of Banking Supervision Inquiry into the Circumstances of the Collapse of Barings* (HMSO, London, 1995), p. 250.

Inherent vulnerability

4–10 Prevention of fraud begins with an assessment of the inherent vulnerability of the business to fraudulent activity. The degree of this vulnerability is dependent on several interrelated factors, including:

– size of the business;

– complexity of the business;

– number of employees;

– extent to which the activity of the business involves the handling of cash and/ or assets that are readily convertible into cash;

– degree of centralisation of the business and the extent to which the activities of employees can be supervised;

– extent to which transactions can be completed on behalf of the business in a short time or without formal approval, *e.g.* via electronic trading.

4–11 Inherent vulnerability of a business to fraud can be either increased or reduced by the business and organisational practices put in place by senior management. The attitude of senior management to the risk of fraud and the need to minimise such risk is often a key determinant of whether a business falls prey to the fraudster. This attitude is readily apparent from the manner in which the organisation is designed and the extent to which management invests in a system of checks and controls designed to make life difficult for anyone contemplating a fraud.

Organisational design

4–12 Aspects of the design of an organisation that can indicate an increased risk of fraud include:

– unnecessarily complex corporate structure;

– management dominated by one person (or a small group);

– no effective supervisory board or committee;

– absence of internal controls and procedures designed to provide a check on the appropriateness of transactions, the existence and valuation of assets, the correct recording of liabilities and the accurate and timely reporting of financial performance;

– inadequate or non-existent segregation of duties between employees responsible for handling assets of the business;

– poor or inadequate accounting records and systems;

– absence of systems for the documentation and recording of authorisation for transactions and approvals for expenditure.

Business practices

4–13 In addition to the design of the organisation, the manner in which business is conducted, and the way in which transactions are recorded and financial information is produced, can also give a good indication of the risk of fraud. The types of management practices and other events that indicate increased vulnerability to fraud include:

- internal controls being ignored or overridden by management;

- failure to correct major weaknesses in internal control previously identified;

- high turnover rate of key accounting and financial personnel;

- employees not taking holidays;

- under-staffing of the finance function;

- changes of auditors or other advisers;

- performance-based remuneration;

- inability to extract information from computer files due to lack of, or non-current, documentation of record contents or programs.

External events and trading experience

4–14 External events and trading experience can also increase vulnerability to fraud. Examples of such events include:

- inadequate working capital in the business due to difficult trading conditions, to poor profit performance or to expanding too quickly;

- increases in bad debts;

- changes in business practices or accounting policies;

- pressure to report profits at a level higher than is realistically achievable;

- significant operations or investment in an industry or product line noted for rapid change;

- unusual transactions, especially near the year end, that have a significant effect on earnings;

- unusual transactions with related parties;

- payments for services that appear excessive in relation to the services provided.

4–15 Taking all of these categories of risk assessment together and assessing the business against the general criteria listed above, and the more specific criteria relevant to the particular business and to the market in question, allows for a reasoned consideration of the vulnerability of the business to fraud.

Accounting systems and cycles

4–16   A key tool in the management of the risk of fraud is the system of internal controls in the business. *Auditing Standard 300*[6] contains a clear and useful discussion of the role and limitations of internal controls within the accounting system. While even the best system of internal controls will not guarantee that the financial statements are materially correct, the extract below makes it clear that, from the viewpoint of the external auditor, the existence of a good, working system reduces risk significantly. It states:

> "Internal controls established by the directors relating to the accounting system are concerned with achieving objectives such as:
> * transactions are executed in accordance with proper general or specific authorisation;
> * all transactions and other events are promptly recorded at the correct amount, in the appropriate accounts and in the proper accounting period so as to permit preparation of financial statements in accordance with the applicable reporting framework (eg relevant legislation and applicable accounting standards);
> * access to assets is permitted only in accordance with proper authorisation; and
> * recorded assets are compared with the existing assets at reasonable intervals and appropriate action is taken with regard to any differences.
>
> An internal control system can only provide the directors with reasonable confidence that their objectives are reached because of inherent limitations such as:
> * the usual requirement that the cost of an internal control is not disproportionate to the potential loss which may result from its absence;
> * most systematic internal controls tend to be directed at routine transactions rather than non-routine transactions;
> * the potential for human error due to carelessness, distraction, mistakes of judgment and the misunderstanding of instructions;
> * the possibility of circumvention of internal controls through collusion with parties outside or inside the entity;
> * the possibility that a person responsible for exercising an internal control could abuse that responsibility, for example by overriding an internal control; and
> * the possibility that procedures may become inadequate due to changes in conditions or that compliance with procedures may deteriorate over time.
>
> These factors indicate why auditors cannot obtain all their evidence from tests of the system of internal control."[7]

---

[6] Auditing Practices Board, *Statement of Auditing Standards 300, Accounting and Internal Control Systems and Audit Risk Assessments* (Auditing Practices Board, London, 1995).
[7] *ibid.*, paras 24 and 25.

4–17 When designing a set of controls to operate within the accounting system, it is most useful to look at the business in terms of the cycles of transaction activity that take place within it. This allows controls to be designed around the key points at which the movement of assets and the incurring of expenditures are authorised, controlled, recorded and reported. The cycles differ depending on the nature of the business. However, at a high level, controls are often built around cycles such as those outlined in Table 4.1 (see para. **4–26**).

Income cycle

4–18 The income cycle involves such activities as receiving orders for goods and services, authorisation of credit sales, recording delivery of goods or services, billing customers, credit control, collection of payments from customers, lodgment of payments received, recording all of these transactions and reporting transactions in financial statements.

Expenditure cycle

4–19 The expenditure cycle involves such activities as authorisation of purchases, ordering, tracking the receipt of goods and services, matching the details of goods and services received with those ordered, receiving invoices from suppliers and matching invoice details with goods and services received, authorisation of payments to suppliers, making of payments, recording all of these transactions and reporting transactions in financial statements.

Production cycle

4–20 In a manufacturing environment, the production cycle involves tracking the sourcing, storage and usage of raw materials, the manufacturing process including the absorption of labour and overheads in the production activity, tracking the output, storage and shipping of finished goods, the valuation of stocks and the recording and reporting of transactions.

Payroll cycle

4–21 The payroll cycle involves such activities as the input of time-based information, salary and wage levels and statutory and other deductions to the payroll system, the payment of wages and salaries, the reporting of payroll costs, the preparation of payslips and various statutory returns and the analysis of personnel costs.

Cash cycle

4–22   The cash cycle involves the recording of all cash receipts and payments, the reconciliation of bank accounts, the recording and reporting of transactions and the projection of future cash flows.

Financial reporting cycle

4–23   The financial reporting cycle involves the preparation of financial statements based on the basic transactions recorded in the basic books and records and usually involves the making of manual adjustments to the financial statements.

4–24   In most businesses, many of the activities described in the cycles above are performed by computer systems. This does not, however, obviate the need to ensure that appropriate controls are in place, within computer systems, at the points at which computer systems and manual systems interface with each other, and in relation to manual activities, to ensure that all appropriate checks and balances are in place to minimise the risk of fraud.

Evaluating internal controls

4–25   To evaluate internal controls, it is necessary first to determine, based on the nature and size of the business, the types of controls appropriate to the business. This involves obtaining a detailed understanding of the business itself and of the accounting systems and cycles (see paras **4–16** *et seq.*). It is then possible to identify specific controls relevant to the business and, conversely, to pinpoint unacceptable risks arising where controls should be in place but are not.

4–26   Types of internal controls that might be expected to exist in a business are summarised in Table 4.1. However, the stated existence of internal controls is of little use unless they are operating consistently throughout the year. It is therefore necessary not just to design, implement and document the controls; their correct operation must also be tested regularly and reported on promptly. This is normally done by internal and external auditors who will present their reports and recommendations to senior management and, where one exists, to the audit committee. These reports are valuable indicators of the effectiveness of the internal control system in a company and, by extension, of its susceptibility to fraud.

Table 4.1: Illustrative internal controls in a business

Organisational controls
- Active audit committee to which internal and external auditors report, independently of management
- Positive attitude to controls and risk management at senior management level
- Sufficient and adequately skilled resources in accounting, control, risk management and internal audit functions
- Appropriate priority given to the need to authorise and approve transactions and to review reports of financial performance and compliance with controls
- Positive attitude to the need for supervision and review of work done by employees

Income cycle controls
- Matching of orders received to goods or services supplied
- Checking that invoices to customers reflect goods or services supplied and at authorised prices
- Advancing credit to customers only with necessary approvals and only within approved credit limits
- Checking cash received from customers and ensuring the correct amount is lodged to the bank account
- Reconciliations of debtors' ledger to the debtors' balance in the nominal ledger

Expenditure cycle controls
- Written authorisations and approvals needed for ordering, accepting and paying for goods and services received
- Written reconciliations of supplier invoices to records of goods or services received and ordered
- Reconciliations of creditors' ledger to the creditors' balance in the nominal ledger

Production cycle controls
- Tracking the usage of materials, labour and overhead in the production process and reconciling volumes produced with inputs and wastage
- Physically verifying the existence and condition of stocks and reconciling physical quantities with recorded volumes

Payroll cycle controls
- Checking the calculations of wages and salaries for individual employees by reference to specified pay rates, tax and social welfare payments and other deductions, and documenting the completion of that check in writing
- Reconciling payments to Revenue authorities with amounts calculated from the payroll records

Cash cycle controls
- Ensuring segregation of duties between the receipt of cash, the recording of cash receipts and the checking of recorded receipts against bank statements
- Preparation and review of bank reconciliations, reconciling the balances advised by the bank with balances computed from the cash records
- Tracking and reconciling of petty cash receipts and payments

Financial reporting cycle controls
- Checking that basic books are reflected correctly in the financial statements
- Critically reviewing the financial statements to ensure they reflect business reality and do not reveal any cause for concern
- Ensuring that all manual adjustments to the financial statements are properly authorised

Methods of detecting fraud

Detectable symptoms of fraud

4–27   The term "red flags" of fraud is used to denote potential symptoms existing within a company's business environment that would indicate a higher risk of an intentional misstatement of the financial statements. Some are these are listed in Table 4.2.

Table 4.2: "Red flags" of fraud

Management
- Too much control vested in key employees
- Lack of ethics at senior management levels
- No organisation charts, job descriptions
- Profit is the only criterion for performance evaluation
- Lax management
- Lack of management review of proper reports
- Conflict and in-fighting among senior management
- Authoritarian management, oppression, exploitation of employees by management
- Unstable management

Employees
- Failure to pre-screen employees (*e.g.* to discover criminal record of employees)
- Low morale and motivation among employees
- Employees with unexpected wealth
- Financial pressures on employees
- Standard of living clearly beyond the financial means of employees
- Employees having outside business interests
- Marked personality changes in employees

Recording and accounting
- Lack of reporting cycles, no timetables for financial reporting
- Poor or no budgetary control
- Lack of supporting documentation to substantiate transactions
- Understaffed accounting departments
- Missing files or documentation
- Altered documentation
- Outstanding reconciling items
- Unmonitored system logs
- Inaccurate records

Commercial issues
- Large number of complaints from customers, suppliers, regulatory agencies
- Rising expenses
- Excessive bad debt write-offs
- Rising stock values
- High debt load
- Unexpected increases in volume of transactions with specific suppliers
- No transactions with certain suppliers

Sundry
- Inside tips
- Known conflict of interest not well managed

Techniques for detecting fraud

4–28   There are many ways in which the symptoms of fraud can be uncovered. Comer quotes a survey conducted in 1980 which shows that frauds were most likely to be detected by accident – survey results showed that 51 per cent of frauds were detected by accident, 19 per cent by auditors, 10 per cent by management controls and 20 per cent by "disgruntled mistresses and lovers".[8]

However, techniques do exist to detect fraud and companies should have specified procedures for detecting fraud. Comer describes a technique of "critical point auditing" which he has developed.[9] He cautions against using data mining packages and comments that these have given disappointing results and are expensive. However, he seems more supportive of specially written computer programs for use in specialist situations.[10]

4–29   Bologna and Lindquist state:

"Detecting fraud is a matter of acknowledging:
1.   That fraud exists.
2.   That any organization can become either a victim of fraud or a perpetrator of fraud.
3.   That certain weaknesses in internal controls and human character can be conducive to fraud.
4.   That certain tests of internal controls and tests of the organization's motivational environment can provide some insight on the possibility of fraud in that environment.
5.   That the key to fraud auditing is training the mind to see both the doughnut and the hole."[11]

Detecting fraud involves consideration of exceptions, rather than general rules – consideration of small exceptions may provide significant insights. Bologna and Lindquist point to the importance of identifying small differences, inconsistencies and oddities in detecting fraud, commenting that the external audit is orientated to detecting large or material differences impacting on the financial statements. Exceptions that should be looked for are:

"1. Transactions that are odd as to:
   Time (of day, week, month, year or season)
   Frequency (too many, too few)
   Places (too far, too near, and too 'far out')
   Amount (too high, too low, too consistent, too alike, too different)
   Parties or personalities (related parties, oddball personalities, strange and

---

[8] Comer, J., *Corporate Fraud* (3rd ed., Gower Publishing Ltd., Aldershot, 1998), p. 11.
[9] *ibid.*, Chap. 9.
[10] *ibid.*, p. 239.
[11] Bologna, G.J. and Lindquist, R.J., *Fraud Auditing and Forensic Accounting: New Tools and Techniques* (2nd ed., John Wiley & Sons Inc., New York, 1995), p. 133.

estranged relationships between parties, management performing clerical functions).

2. Internal controls that are unenforced or too often compromised by higher authorities.

3. Employee motivation, morale, and job satisfaction levels that are chronically low.

4. A corporate culture and reward system that supports unethical behaviour toward employees, customers, competitors, lenders, and shareholders".[12]

Benford's law[13]

4–30 Fraud leaves predictable patterns which can be detected. A statistical theory developed more than 100 years ago, combined with modern computer technology, has resulted in an effective, objective technique for detecting fraud. This theory, known as Benford's law (or as the "first digit phenomenon"), reveals inconsistencies in a wide variety of financial documents, including annual reports, tax returns, stock lists, expense accounts and in debtors and creditors. As code breakers in the Second World War discovered, there are patterns in the way single letters occur in words – E is the most common letter, followed by T, then A, and so on. Similar patterns occur in the way single digits appear in numbers. The numbers 0, 1 and 2 appear most frequently in tabulated data. The physicist Frank Benford presented evidence on the expected probabilities of various digits in their various positions. In general, the greatest percentage of numbers begin with a 1, a smaller percentage with a 2 and so on, all the way down to 9, the least frequent digit.

4–31 Benford's law can be applied to detect white-collar crime. Numbers in most financial documents conform closely to Benford's law while assigned or randomly selected numbers do not. When individuals commit fraud, they may invent numbers. The digit patterns of invented numbers cause sets of data to appear unnatural when compared to the patterns predicted by Benford's law. A simple package such as Microsoft Excel can be used, or more specialist computer programs (for larger data sets), to analyse data and reveal signs of fraud as well as errors and processing inefficiencies. Perpetrators cannot "Benfordise" their fraudulent activities by using more realistic number patterns. To do so would either create detectable inconsistencies or would reduce the benefits of the fraud. A Benford investigation can show up fraud or error that might escape traditional methods of detection.

---

[12] Bologna, G.J. and Lindquist, R.J., *Fraud Auditing and Forensic Accounting: New Tools and Techniques* (2nd ed., John Wiley & Sons Inc., New York, 1995), pp. 134–135.

[13] See Maxima Partnering Limited, "Detecting fraud and Benford's law ..." in *Inside Fraud Bulletin* (March 1999), p. 12; York, D., "Benford's law" in *Accountancy* (July 2000), p. 126; and Drake, P.D. and Nigrini, M.J., "Computer assisted analytical procedures using Benford's law" in *Journal of Accounting Education* (2000) Vol. 18, pp. 127–146.

Detecting money laundering

4–32   Money launderers create multiple layers of transactions to obscure the source of their income. However, even the most sophisticated money laundering activities can be uncovered. "Red flags" (as shown in Table 4.3) can indicate suspicious financial activity in both bank and non-bank institutions. Such activity can be traced and documented until the entire laundering process is revealed. Forensic accountants are experienced at performing intense financial investigations, sifting through layers and following electronic trails of evidence to spot unusual patterns or activity.

Table 4.3: "Red flags" of money laundering

Cash transactions
• Larger cash deposits or purchases than should be expected
• Frequent deposits or purchases just under the reporting threshold
• Withdrawals inconsistent with the cash needs of a business
• Unusual fund transfer activities
• Large or frequent transactions involving foreign currencies, offshore banks, foreign countries or apparent shell companies
• Changes in cash needs of business without corresponding increases in cash transaction reports
• Increased electronic cash transfer activity

Banking activities
• Bank information that is insufficient or suspicious
• Accounts in false names or in the names of persons acting for a third party
• Increasing use of safety deposit boxes

Commercial activities
• Activities that are not consistent with the business
• Invoices that are inordinately larger or smaller than would be expected
• Transfers by lawyers or accountants on behalf of clients
• Transactions where both parties appear to be related entities
• Transaction documentation that appears falsified or not legally correct

Behaviour of staff
• Attempts to avoid reporting requirements
• Requests to be placed on a cash transaction report exemption list
• Reluctance to provide identifying information during an audit
• Sudden changes in employees' lifestyles
• Employees who are resistant to taking vacations

Auditors and fraud

4–33   The functions of a statutory audit include the expression of opinion by auditors on: (i) the truth and fairness of the financial statements; (ii) whether they have obtained all the information and explanations they consider necessary;

(iii) whether proper books of account have been kept; and (iv) whether the accounts agree with the books of account. However, the general public expects auditors to discover fraud, often without regard to the materiality of the amounts involved.

Detection of fraud by auditors

4–34 The activities of external auditors, while not directed specifically for the purpose of detecting fraud, are designed to have a reasonable expectation of detecting fraud that is sufficiently large to give rise to a material misstatement in the financial statements. As a result, the work done and guiding principles used by auditors in this area are highly relevant to a discussion of the detection of fraud. *Auditing Standard 110: Fraud and Error* is the guidance given to auditors by the Auditing Practices Board, the body that sets auditing standards for the accountancy profession in the United Kingdom and Ireland. It introduced an explicit requirement for auditors to assess the risk of material misstatements arising from fraud:

> "When planning the audit the auditors should assess the risk that fraud or error may cause the financial statements to contain material misstatements."[14]

4–35 Under *Auditing Standard 110*, auditors are required to design audit procedures to provide reasonable assurance that published financial statements are free from material misstatements caused by the fraud:

> "When auditors become aware of information which indicates that fraud or error may exist, they should obtain an understanding of the nature of the event and the circumstances in which it has occurred, and sufficient other information to evaluate the possible effect on the financial statements. If the auditors believe that the indicated fraud or error could have a material effect on the financial statements, they should perform appropriate modified or additional procedures.
>
> . . .
>
> The auditors should consider the implications of suspected or actual error or fraudulent conduct in relation to other aspects of the audit, particularly the reliability of management representations.
>
> . . .
>
> When the auditors become aware of, or suspect that there may be, instances of error or fraudulent conduct, they should document their findings and, subject to any requirement to report them direct to a third party, discuss them with the appropriate level of management."[15]

---

[14] Auditing Practices Board, *Statement of Auditing Standards 110: Fraud and Error* (Auditing Practices Board, London, 1995), para. 24.
[15] *ibid.*, paras 29, 38, 33.

4–36 The difficulties perceived by auditors in the detection of fraud as part of the audit are evident from the detailed guidance contained in the same statement:

"Auditors plan, perform and evaluate their audit work in order to have a reasonable expectation of detecting material misstatements in the financial statements arising from error or fraud. However, an audit cannot be expected to detect all errors or instances of fraudulent or dishonest conduct. The likelihood of detecting errors is higher than that of detecting fraud, since fraud is usually accompanied by acts specifically designed to conceal its existence, such as management introducing transactions without substance, collusion between employees or falsification of records. Consequently, 'reasonable expectation' in the context of fraud must be construed having regard to the nature of the fraud and, in particular, the degree of collusion, the seniority of those involved and the level of deception concerned.

An audit is subject to the unavoidable risk that some material misstatements of the financial statements will not be detected, even though the audit is properly planned and performed in accordance with Auditing Standards. This risk is higher with regard to misstatements resulting from dishonest or fraudulent conduct. The reasons for this include the following:
 • the effectiveness of audit procedures is affected by the inherent limitations of the accounting and internal control systems and by the use of selective testing rather than the examination of all transactions
 • much of the evidence obtained by the auditors is persuasive rather than conclusive in nature
 • dishonest or fraudulent conduct may take place over a number of years but may only be discovered in a later year (for example because a fictitious asset becomes material to the financial statements), and
 • dishonest or fraudulent conduct may involve conduct designed to conceal it, such as collusion, forgery, override of controls or intentional misrepresentations being made to the auditors. [16]

4–37 *Auditing Standard 110* highlights the particular difficulties in detection where management is involved in the fraud. It points to the particular difficulty when senior management perpetrates the fraud:

"While the existence of effective accounting and internal control systems may reduce the probability of misstatement of financial statements resulting from fraud and error, there is always some risk of internal controls failing to operate as designed. Furthermore, any accounting and internal control systems may be ineffective against fraud committed by management, particularly if it involves collusion, internally or with third parties."[17]

Even the most effective accounting and internal control system may not be capable of detecting management fraud:

[16] Auditing Practices Board, *Statement of Auditing Standards 110: Fraud and Error* (Auditing Practices Board, London, 1995), paras 18–19.
[17] *ibid.*, para. 21.

"The detection of fraud committed by management poses particular difficulties for the auditor because management can be in a strong position to commit a fraud and conceal it from others within the entity and from the auditors. Actions that management may take to commit and conceal fraud include:

- introducing complexity into the corporate structure, commercial arrangements with third parties, transactions or internal systems;

- collusive acts with employees or third parties, whether related parties or otherwise;

- the override of internal controls set up to prevent or detect fraud;

- influencing accounting policies, financial statement presentation and accounting estimates affecting financial information used within the business or for external reporting;

- manipulating evidence available to, or responses to evidence requested by, the auditors, delaying the provision of evidence or making representations and responses to audit enquiries that lack integrity or are deliberately untruthful."[18]

More recently, the Auditing Practices Board has commissioned research which shows that directors and senior management were actively involved in most of the major frauds included in its survey.[19] Based on these results, the Auditing Practices Board concluded that most management frauds would not be detected without a significant increase in the scope of the audit. [20]

4–38 It is clear from paras **4–36** and **4–37** that auditors themselves, and the body charged with the responsibility for setting standards for their performance, believe that their obligation to detect fraud is limited as is their consequent legal liability. While the courts might disagree in specific cases as to where the boundary lies, the legal position in principle does not differ materially from the view of the accountancy profession.

Fraud audits

4–39 From this it can be seen that the detection of fraud can be fraught with difficulty. However, some tools are available to auditors to assist where a specific search for fraud (*i.e.* a fraud audit, or "fraudit") is warranted. A fraud audit can be performed in response to a specific concern or suspicion that a fraud has taken place, or can be used as a deterrent. Fraud audits differ from traditional statutory audits in that they focus more extensively on vulnerable areas of the

---

[18] Auditing Practices Board, *Statement of Auditing Standards 110: Fraud and Error* (Auditing Practices Board, London, 1995), para. 22.

[19] Auditing Practices Board, *Fraud and Audit: Choices for Society* (Auditing Practices Board, London, 1998), p. 9.

[20] *ibid.*, p. 11.

company. They also do not exclude items from consideration on the grounds of materiality in the context of the annual financial statements, as is the case with statutory audits. Weak and poorly monitored internal controls provide an inviting environment for fraud.

4–40 During a fraud audit, controls within the organisation can be assessed, weaknesses and vulnerabilities can be highlighted and a plan of action can be devised to reduce risk. Tools that can be used as part of a fraud audit include analytical techniques such as:

– Vertical and horizontal analysis: In vertical analysis, all figures in the profit and loss account or balance sheet are expressed as a percentage of sales or capital employed or some other base figure. This is sometimes called constructing common size statements. It highlights over several years how the sales/profitability pattern or financial structure of a company is changing.

– Ratio analysis: Ratios are mathematical expressions of relationships of one item with another. They provide a means of helping to understand what is happening in a company, providing pointers to the reasons behind performance and can give warnings of impending risk.

4–41 In addition, checklists for indications of fraud can be useful. Such a checklist could include some or all of the questions shown in Table 4.4.

Table 4.4: Anti-fraud checklist

Business policy
- Is there a published ethics policy with definitions of fraud?
- Is fraud included in the company's overall business risk assessment?
- Is there a plan in place to respond to risk and to limit damage to the business?

Staff
- Does the company take up job applicants' references and get certificates for qualifications for appointments at all levels?
- Are staff trained to notice signs of all types of fraud?
- Are whistle blowers encouraged to come forward?

Commercial activities
- Does the company follow strict credit-management practice and enforce credit limits?
- Does the company follow good practice on credit card fraud and counterfeit money?
- Are goods received and their prices checked against delivery notes and invoices?
- Is ownership checked on product-refund requests?

Security
- Have physical security arrangements been reviewed recently?
- Are visitors identified and accompanied?

Source: Adapted from Moody, M., "Fraud – enemies within" in *Director* (April 2000), p. 16.

Reporting of fraud by auditors

4–42 The responsibilities imposed on auditors in relation to reporting fraud have been increasing in recent years arising from both statutory requirements and from professional standards.

Statutory requirements

4–43 Under section 194 of the Companies Act 1990, auditors have a duty to report to the Registrar of Companies if, in their opinion, proper books of account are not being kept.[21] Section 74 of the Company Law Enforcement Act 2001 amends section 194 of the 1990 Act. It also imposes a requirement on the Registrar of Companies, where he has received notice from the auditors that the company is not keeping proper books of account, to notify the Director of Corporate Enforcement.

4–44 The Act also introduces a requirement on auditors to report suspected breaches of the Companies Acts and suspicions of illegal activity to the Director of Corporate Acts Enforcement. Of significance in relation to fraud is the extension of section 194 by inclusion of subsections (5) and (6) to require auditors to report suspicions (based on "reasonable grounds") of the commission by the company or its officer or agent of an indictable offence under the Companies Acts. Legal protection and immunity is provided to auditors complying with these requirements by section 74(6) of the Act. The new subsections are as follows:

> "(5) Where, in the course of, and by virtue of, their carrying out an audit of the accounts of the company, information comes into the possession of the auditors of a company that leads them to form the opinion that there are reasonable grounds for believing that the company or an officer or agent of it has committed an indictable offence under the Companies Act, the auditors shall, forthwith after having formed it, notify that opinion to the Director and provide the Director with details of the grounds on which they have formed that opinion.
>
> (6) No professional or legal duty to which an auditor is subject by virtue of his appointment as an auditor of a company shall be regarded as contravened by, and no liability to the company, its shareholders, creditors or other interested parties shall attach to, an auditor, by reason of his compliance with an obligation imposed on him by or under this section."

4–45 Section 57 of the Criminal Justice (Theft and Fraud Offences) Bill 2000 proposes to impose a duty to report theft and fraud offences on accountants

---

[21] Only 48 such notifications were reported to the Registrar in the five-year period 1995–1999: *The Report of the Review Group on Auditing* (Government Publications, Dublin, 2000), p. 84. Also available at www.entemp.ie/publications.htm.

(who are not employees of the firm) and on auditors as follows:

> "(2) Where the accounts of a firm, or as the case may be any information, document mentioned in subsection (1)(b), indicate that—
>
> (a) an offence under this Act ... may have been committed by the firm concerned, or
>
> (b) such an offence may have been committed in relation to its affairs by a partner in the firm or, in the case of a corporate or unincorporated body, by a director, manager, secretary or other employee thereof, or by the self-employed individual concerned,
>
> the relevant person shall, notwithstanding any professional obligations of privilege or confidentiality, report that fact to a member of the Garda Síochána."

"Relevant person" is defined in subsection (1) as the auditor or accounting adviser (other than an employee) to the firm. Non-compliance with the proposed duty to report would carry a maximum fine of £1,500 or a prison term not exceeding one year or both.

Section 1079 of the Taxes Consolidation Act 1997 imposes an additional obligation on auditors and certain other advisers to take certain actions if they become aware in the course of their work that the company is or has knowingly or wilfully delivered a false tax return or false information in connection with tax, or claims a relief to which it is not entitled or produces false documentation or otherwise fails materially to comply with certain aspects of the Tax Acts. The section requires the auditor or adviser, unless the situation is rectified, to cease work with the company and to advise an appropriate officer nominated by the Revenue authorities of such cessation.

Section 34 of the Stock Exchange Act 1995 also imposes "whistle-blowing" obligations on auditors of approved stock exchanges and authorised member firms. The section requires the auditors to report to the Central Bank of Ireland in a variety of circumstances, including the insolvency of the auditor's client, inaccuracies or omissions in returns made by the client to the Central Bank, material defects in the client's accounting or control systems and any intention of the auditor to qualify the audit opinion.

Professional standards

4–46 According to the Auditing Practices Board,[22] *Auditing Standard 110* is unique in introducing for the first time a requirement that auditors assess the need to report a fraud to the authorities. As stated earlier, since publication of *Auditing Standard 110*, legislation has introduced a similar but broader requirement to report fraud and related offences.

---

[22] Auditing Practices Board, *Fraud and Audit: Choices for Society* (Auditing Practices Board, London, 1998), p. 7.

Auditing Standard 110 states:

> "The auditors should as soon as practicable communicate their findings to the appropriate level of management, the board of directors or the audit committee if
>
> (a) they suspect or discover fraud, even if the potential effect on the financial statements is immaterial (save where SAS 110.12 applies), or
> (b) material error is actually found to exist.
>
> . . .
>
> Where the auditors become aware of a suspected or actual instance of fraud they should
>
> (a) consider whether the matter may be one that ought to be reported to a proper authority in the public interest; and where this is the case
> (b) except in circumstances covered in SAS 110.12, discuss the matter with the board of directors, including any audit committee.
>
> Where, having considered any views expressed on behalf of the entity and in the light of any legal advice obtained, the auditors conclude that the matter ought to be reported to an appropriate authority in the public interest, they should notify the directors in writing of their view and, if the entity does not voluntarily do so itself or is unable to provide evidence that the matter has been reported, they should report it themselves."[23]

The above guidance provides for exceptions SAS 110.12 deals with circumstances where directors are suspected of involvement in fraud, and it states:

> "When a suspected or actual instance of fraud casts doubt on the integrity of the directors auditors should make a report direct to a proper authority in the public interest without delay and without informing the directors in advance."[24]

4–47 In introducing a requirement for auditors to report findings of fraud to "an appropriate authority in the public interest", the Auditing Practices Board recognises the conflict between maintaining client confidentiality and public reporting. SAS 110 discusses this conflict as follows:

> "Confidentiality is an implied term of the auditors' contract. The duty of confidentiality, however, is not absolute. In certain exceptional circumstances auditors are not bound by the duty of confidentiality and have the right or duty to report matters to a proper authority in the public interest. Auditors need to weigh the public interest in maintaining confidential client relationships against the public interest in disclosure to a proper authority. Determination of where the balance of public interest lies requires careful consideration. Auditors whose suspicions have been aroused need to use their professional judgment to determine

---

[23] Auditing Practices Board, *Statement of Auditing Standards 110: Fraud and Error* (Auditing Practices Board, London, 1995), paras 41, 50, 51.
[24] *ibid.*, para. 52.

whether their misgivings justify them in carrying the matter further or are too insubstantial to deserve reporting."[25]

The statement goes on to describe situations where auditors may conclude that the directors are implicated in a fraud:

"Examples of circumstances which may cause the auditors no longer to have confidence in the integrity of the directors include situations:

- where they suspect or have evidence of the involvement or intended involvement of the directors in possible fraud which could have a material effect on the financial statements, or
- where they suspect or have evidence that the directors are aware of such fraud and, contrary to regulatory requirements or the public interest, have not reported it to a proper authority within a reasonable period."[26]

The statement then addresses the highly sensitive issue of the potential exposure of auditors where they decide to "blow the whistle":

"Auditors are protected from the risk of liability for breach of confidence or defamation provided that

- in the case of breach of confidence
  - disclosure is made in the public interest, and
  - such disclosure is made to an appropriate body or person, and
  - there is no malice motivating the disclosure, and
- in the case of defamation
  - disclosure is made in their capacity as auditors of the entity concerned, and
  - there is no malice motivating the disclosure.

In addition, auditors are protected from such risks where they are expressly permitted or required by legislation to disclose information (see paragraph below)."[27]

4–48 Another difficulty in the requirement to report fraud is defining the term "public interest". SAS 110 attempts to provide clarification of this term as follows:

"'Public interest' is a concept that is not capable of general definition. Each situation must be considered individually. Matters to be taken into account when considering whether disclosure is justified in the public interest may include

---

[25] Auditing Practices Board, *Statement of Auditing Standards 110: Fraud and Error* (Auditing Practices Board, London, 1995), para. 53.
[26] *ibid.*, para. 54.
[27] *ibid.*, para. 55.

- the extent to which the suspected or actual fraud is likely to affect members of the public
- whether the directors have rectified the matter or are taking, or are likely to take, effective corrective action
- the extent to which non-disclosure is likely to enable the suspected or actual fraud to recur with impunity
- the gravity of the matter, and
- the weight of evidence and the degree of the auditors' suspicion that there has been an instance of fraud.

When reporting to proper authorities in the public interest it is important that auditors only report to one which has a proper interest to receive the information [See *Initial Services v. Putterill* [1967] 3 All E.R. at 145 and *Lion Laboratories Ltd v. Evans* [1984] 2 All E.R. at 417]. Which body or person is the proper authority in a particular instance depends on the nature of the fraud. Proper authorities ... in the Republic of Ireland could include the Garda Fraud Squad, the Revenue Commissioners, the Irish Stock Exchange and the Department of Enterprise and Employment. In cases of doubt as to the appropriate authority auditors are advised to consult with their professional body ...".[28]

4–49 Auditors are understandably concerned about the risks of litigation that might increase as a result of the new reporting requirements:

"Auditors receive the same protection even if they only have a reasonable suspicion that fraud has occurred. Auditors who can demonstrate that they have acted reasonably and in good faith in informing an authority of an instance of fraud which they think has been committed would not be held by the court to be in breach of duty to the client even if, an investigation or prosecution having occurred, it were found that there had been no offence.

Auditors may need to take legal advice before making a decision on whether the matter should be reported to a proper authority in the public interest.

Auditors need to remember that their decision as to whether to report, and if so to whom, may be called into question at a future date, for example on the basis of
- what they knew at the time
- what they ought to have known in the course of their audit
- what they ought to have concluded, and
- what they ought to have done.

Auditors may also wish to consider the possible consequences if financial loss is occasioned as a result of fraud which they suspect (or ought to suspect) has occurred but decide not to report."[29]

---

[28] Auditing Practices Board, *Statement of Auditing Standards 110: Fraud and Error* (Auditing Practices Board, London, 1995), paras 56–57.
[29] *ibid.*, paras 58–60.

Auditor liability for undetected fraud

4–50   The liability of auditors and accountants generally is dealt with in Chapter 12. In relation specifically to the auditor's liability for the detection of fraud, it is worth noting that the courts have attempted on several occasions over many decades to establish appropriate principles in this area. A useful judgment is that of Hanna J. in the High Court in the case of *Leech v. Stokes Bros and Pim*.[30] The learned judge, whose decision to find no negligence on the part of the defendant auditors was upheld unanimously on appeal to the Supreme Court, reviewed a number of authorities on the scope of the auditor's responsibility as follows:

> "The case of *In re Kingston Cotton Mill Company (No. 2)* [1896] 2 Ch. 279 dealt with the question whether it was reasonable for auditors, without making a personal examination, to take the return of the manager as to the stock, and it was held that, it being no part of the duty of the auditors to take stock, they were justified in relying on the certificates of the manager, a person of acknowledged competence and high reputation, and they were not bound to check his certificates in the absence of anything to raise suspicion, and that they were not liable for dividends wrongly paid out on their certificate. Lindley L.J. said at p. 284:—
>
> > 'I protest however, against the notion that an auditor is bound to be suspicious as distinguished from reasonably careful.'
>
> But an important distinction between that case and the present is that the manager who made the return had no personal interest and there was no conflict between his interest and his duty. Lindley L.J. says at p. 287:—
>
> > 'His position was not similar to that of a cashier who has to account for the cash which he receives, and whose own account of his receipts and payments could not reasonably be taken by an auditor without further inquiry.'"[31]

Hanna J. then took the opportunity to refer to what may well be the most quoted judicial pronouncement on the subject of auditor liability:

> "At p. 288 Lopes L.J. said:—
>
> > 'It is the duty of an auditor to bring to bear upon the work he has to perform that skill, care and caution which a reasonably competent, careful, cautious auditor would use. What is reasonable skill, care and caution must depend upon the particular circumstances of each case. An auditor is not bound to be a detective, or, as was said, to approach his work with suspicion or with a foregone conclusion that there is something wrong. He is a watchdog, not a bloodhound. He is justified in believing tried servants of the Company in whom confidence is placed by the Company. He is entitled to assume that they are honest, and to rely upon their representations, provided he takes reasonable care. If there is anything calculated to excite suspicion he should

---

[30] [1937] I.R. 787.
[31] *ibid.* at 794.

probe it to the bottom; but, in the absence of anything of that kind, he is only bound to be reasonably cautious and careful.'

At p. 290 he says:—

> 'Auditors must not be made liable for not tracking out ingenious and carefully laid schemes of fraud when there is nothing to arouse their suspicion, and when these frauds are perpetrated by tried servants of the Company and are undetected for years by the directors.'"[32]

The learned judge went on to approve the boundaries around auditor liability set out in the dictum of Pollock M.R.:

> "In the case of *In re City Equitable Fire Insurance Co.* [1925] 1 Ch. 407, Pollock M.R. said at p. 509:—
>
> > 'What is the standard of duty which is to be applied to the auditors? That is to be found, and is sufficiently stated, I think, in *In re Kingston Cotton Mill Company (No.* 2) [1896] 2 Ch. 279. As I have already said, it is quite easy to charge a person after the event and say: 'How stupid you were not to have discovered something which, if you had discovered it, would have saved us and many others from many sorrows.' But it has been well said that an auditor is not bound to be a detective or to approach his work with suspicion or with a foregone conclusion that there is something wrong. 'He is a watchdog, but not a bloodhound.' That metaphor was used by Lopes L.J. in *In re Kingston Cotton Mill Co (No. 2).* Perhaps, casting metaphor aside, the position is more happily expressed in the phrase used by my brother Sargant L.J., who said that the duty of an auditor is verification and not detection. The *Kingston Cotton Mill Case* is important, because expansion is given to those rather epigramatic phrases. Lindley, L.J. says at p. 287: 'It is not sufficient to say that the frauds must have been detected if the entries in the books had been put together in a way which never occurred to anyone before suspicion was aroused. The question is whether, no suspicion of anything wrong being entertained, there was a want of reasonable care on the part of the auditors in relying on the returns made by a competent and trusted expert relating to matters on which information from such a person was essential.'"[33]

4–51 Although the business environment, the complexity of the commercial world and the tools, expertise and training of auditors have all changed radically since these decisions were reached, the basic principle remains essentially unaltered. An auditor is required only to plan, conduct and report on a careful audit unless a suspicion of fraud is aroused. If it is, he must continue his investigations until he is satisfied as to the true position. In the absence of such suspicion, there is no absolute obligation to detect all fraud, or even all material

---

[32] [1937] I.R. 787 at 794–795.
[33] *ibid.* at 795.

fraud. If reasonable auditing procedures have been adopted commensurate with the size and complexity of the business and its risk profile and they did not reveal the fraud, *e.g.* because of collusion involving senior employees and/or third parties, the auditor is unlikely to be held liable. He will, however, probably require the services of an expert to assist in putting together his defence to an allegation of negligence.

Continuing problems

4–52 Notwithstanding the increased contribution to preventing fraud through the introduction of *Auditing Standard 110*, the Auditing Practices Board is aware that there are continuing problems.[34] Auditors rarely have access to conclusive evidence of fraud and can rarely determine with certainty that fraud exists. Information obtained by auditors in the course of their work may give rise to suspicions but is unlikely to be definitive or to stand up to the strict rules of courts in determining whether fraud has occurred. No matter how effective the system of control, directors and senior management are likely to be able to override the controls. Fraud is frequently perpetrated by more than one individual. Collusion, especially at senior levels in organisations, can make it difficult for auditors to discover fraud. Auditors have limited powers of investigation during an audit. For example, they are not authorised to contact third parties such as customers or suppliers without authorisation from the directors. An interesting example of difficulties experienced in this regard was provided in connection with auditors obtaining third-party confirmations from banks of client account balances. This was reported as follows:

"A dispute between the Institute of Chartered Accountants and Allied Irish Banks has been resolved, with the bank agreeing to change the procedures followed when a company auditor requests information on a client's banking business.

AIB was one of the leading banks which had recently departed from a long-standing agreement with the Institute that audit certificates relating to client firms would be forwarded directly to the auditor.

Recently, AIB had been forwarding the certificates first to the client and ten days after that to the auditor. In some cases, auditors had complained that they had received the audit certificate directly from the client firm rather than the bank.

This was preventing auditors from carrying out their function effectively, accountants claimed. Obtaining an audit certificate from a company's bank is an essential part of any audit. It is often the only third party confirmation of information on a company's assets and liabilities available to an auditor.

Representations made to AIB by Institute chief executive Brian Walsh over the procedures followed in dealing with audit certificate requests have now resulted in the scrapping of the ten-day rule.

---

[34] Auditing Practices Board, *Fraud and Audit: Choices for Society* (Auditing Practices Board, London, 1998), Chap. 2.

AIB has confirmed that when the audit enquiry letter is completed, a copy will be sent to the customer and the original sent to the auditor/accountant on the same day."[35]

Materiality

4–53 Underlying the conduct of audits is the concept of materiality. The Auditing Practices Board defines materiality as follows:

> " 'Materiality' is an expression of the relative significance or importance of a particular matter in the context of financial statements as a whole. A matter is material if its omission would reasonably influence the decisions of an addressee of the auditors' report; likewise a misstatement is material if it would have a similar influence. Materiality may also be considered in the context of any individual primary statement within the financial statements or of individual items included in them. Materiality is not capable of general mathematical definition as it has both qualitative and quantitative aspects"[36]

4–54 Many frauds are not frauds against the company but frauds by company management resulting in no loss to the company, no gain to the perpetrators but which may cause losses to third parties external to the company. Thus, if there is no loss to the company, the transaction would not be material in the context of an audit. The Auditing Practices Board has considered perceptions of the significance (*i.e.* materiality) of fraud as shown in Table 4.5. A distinction is made between frauds that cause the company to collapse and other frauds. Four categories of victim are identified: the company itself, shareholders, employees and creditors. Manipulation of accounts (*e.g.* to show management in a better light), in particular, is identified as causing no loss to the company.

Concluding comment

4–55 According to industry statistics, most fraud is detected by accident or tip offs, not through financial audit.[37] Accordingly, management and shareholders should not expect the external auditors to detect and prevent fraud. However, poor audit performance appears to be commonplace.[38] Thus, there are clearly limits on the extent to which auditors can be relied on to detect fraud.

---

[35] Boyle, P., "AIB, accountants resolve row over audit certificate requests", *Irish Independent*, August 2, 2000.

[36] Auditing Practices Board, Statement of Auditing Standard 220 *Materiality and the Audit* (Auditing Practices Board, London, 1995), para. 3.

[37] Bondy, C., "Fraud's changing dynamic", *Outlook*, Winter 1998, pp. 11–16.

[38] Tomasic, R., "Auditors and the reporting of illegality and financial fraud", *Australian Business Law Review*, Vol. 20, 1992, pp. 198–229.

Table 4.5: Perceptions of the significance of fraud

Parties affected by fraud	Company continues to trade		Company collapses
	Physical loss (theft of cash or assets)	*Manipulation of accounts*	*Either physical loss or manipulation of accounts*
Company	(a) A one-off loss (profits and net assets are reduced). (b) Reduction in earnings power, growth potential.	No loss (loss of investor confidence may lead to reduction in new capital available to finance it).	Loss including writing down of assets to break-up value.
Shareholders	(a) Market value may decline; the P/E ratio may magnify the loss. (b) Loss of a dividend.	(a) Market value almost certain to decline; the P/E ratio will magnify the loss. (b) Lower future dividends.	Total market value of the company (asset value and future earnings).
Employees	No loss; but loss in company's earnings power may cause cuts in future pay rates/bonuses.	No loss; but loss in company's earnings power may cause cuts in future pay rates/bonuses.	Loss of future earnings (and, depending on nature/extent of fraud, compensation payments and pension rights).
Creditors	No loss.	No loss.	(a) Loss of amounts owing (subject to security held over individual assets). (b) Loss of future business.

Source: Auditing Practices Board, *Fraud and Audit: Choices for Society* (Auditing Practices Board, London, 1998), p. 38.

4–56 In its response to the Auditing Practices Board consultation paper, the Fraud Advisory Panel in the United Kingdom suggested that directors' duties to provide information to auditors be tightened.[39] The Panel recommends that directors of listed companies should be required to provide disclosures in financial statements on the company's fraud prevention measures. In addition, the Panel suggests that legislation should include stiff penalties for directors who knowingly give incorrect or misleading information to the auditors. Although not specifically dealing with fraud, the recommendation of the Review Group on Auditing[40] that directors of companies be required to produce an annual statement of compliance with statutory regulations,[41] and that auditors report on this statement, could make perpetration of fraud in companies more difficult in the future if this recommendation is implemented.

---

[39] Fraud Advisory Panel, Response to the Auditing Practices Board on the Consultation Paper "Fraud and Audit: Choices for Society" (Institute of Chartered Accountants in England and Wales, London, 1999).

[40] *Report of the Review Group on Auditing* (Government Publications, Dublin, 2000), p. 218. Also available at www.entemp.ie/publications.htm.

[41] It is not intended that every single statutory provision (such as, say, the legislation on dog licences) would be affected by this recommendation. Page 217 of the report states: ". . . this should be achieved in a balanced manner that would not impose significant additional costs on companies". Page 218 of the report states: "Detailed guidance on the application of this Recommendation will be required. All relevant parties should be consulted to identify regulations and administrative provisions considered to be relevant in advance of enactment of legislation."

FORENSIC ACCOUNTING INVESTIGATIONS

FORENSIC ACCOUNTING INVESTIGATIONS

Introduction to forensic accounting investigations

5–01 As explained in Chapter 1, forensic accounting involves the application of financial knowledge and expertise to legal problems. The term forensic accountant is used in this chapter but alternative terms such as "investigative accountant" and "fraud auditor" are used in other publications.[1]

The description below of the work of a forensic accountant points to the need for accountants carrying out investigative work (especially where fraud is suspected) to take a different perspective than, say, accountants or auditors operating in other areas or aspects of accountancy:

> "A forensic accountant is someone who can look behind the façade – not accept the records at their face value – someone who has a suspicious mind that the documents he or she is looking at may not be what they purport to be and someone who has the expertise to go out and conduct very detailed interviews of individuals to develop the truth, especially if some are presumed to be lying."[2]

5–02 The range and variety of forensic accounting investigations were summarised in Table 1.3. Fraud investigation work is wide-ranging. Forensic accountants can provide expertise in complex financial fraud investigations. The same investigation assignment may lead to:

– determining whether fraud has occurred;

– identifying the nature of the fraud;

– determining the scale of the fraud;

---

[1] Further discussion of forensic investigations can be found in Bologna G.J. and Lindquist, R.J., *Fraud Auditing and Forensic Accounting: New Tools and Techniques* (2nd ed., John Wiley & Sons Inc., New York, 1995); Comer, M.J., *Corporate Fraud* (3rd ed., Gower Publishing Ltd., Aldershot, 1998); and Davies, D., *Fraud Watch* (2nd ed., ABG Professional Information, London, 2000).

[2] Randall, R.F. "A suspicious mind: Profile of a forensic accountant" in *Management Accounting* (November, 1988), p. 3.

– quantifying the amount of the loss;

– identifying and tracing fraudulent transactions;

– identifying those responsible for the loss;

– tracing lost assets;

– legal action against those responsible to recover lost assets;

– criminal proceedings against those responsible.

5–03 The scope of forensic accounting/fraud investigations is a direct product of the nature and scale of the estimated loss. This type of accounting service encompasses a wide range of activities. It can be a case of a simple review of operating statistics against either historical norms or industry averages. Alternatively, it may involve detailed verification of specific transactions. In addition to carrying out investigations in advance of a trial, forensic accountants may be asked to investigate evidence adduced in the course of litigation, either for the prosecution or the defence in criminal trials, or for the plaintiff or defendant in civil trials.

5–04 Forensic accountants search for evidence of criminal conduct, or assist in the determination of, or rebuttal of, claimed damages. Depending on the circumstances, forensic accounting investigations may themselves have legal consequences and, as a result, they are conducted in a different manner and with a different perspective than ordinary accounting investigations.[3] For instance, they may involve piecing together the elements necessary to prove that a criminal act, *actus reus*, took place, and that the available evidence shows beyond reasonable doubt that the act involved the necessary criminal intent, *mens rea*.

5–05 In forensic accounting investigations, substantive evidence is examined which is used to prove facts at issue. Forensic accountants operate in an imperfect world trying to identify strategically and logically the next piece of evidence, in pursuit of the facts. Investigations must be conducted with an understanding of the legal process and the exacting standards of the courts and with regard to the nature of evidence, the manner in which it is gathered and the applicable standard of proof.

5–06 Such investigations require delving beneath the surface and beyond the obvious, applying intuition, critical analysis and a perceptive understanding of human behaviour. One area in which forensic accounting differs from regular

---

[3] Investigation of fraud from a legal rather than accounting perspective is considered in Gallagher, E., "'Collaring' the white collar criminal" *Commerical Law Practitioner* (November 1999), pp. 263-266.

accounting is that it demands an awareness of motive. Often a pattern of evidence only becomes apparent and understandable when the forensic accountant considers possible motive. Depending on the case, there may be a mass of information and documentation to examine, analyse and classify before any view can be taken. Information from internal and external sources may have to be collected, documents reviewed for authenticity and accounting and computing records analysed. In practice, information available is usually incomplete and documentation may be missing or not available. This work can be very time-consuming and may involve a process of reconstruction from incomplete records. In reviewing documentary evidence, the forensic accountant has to consider whether available documents, and related financial information, make sense in a realistic business context.

5–07 In addition to examining financial documentation, forensic accounting investigations often have to focus on the individuals involved. Witnesses and possible suspects may have to be interviewed. Forensic accountants must combine their analytical skills with a sensitivity and understanding of the human element. In gathering and analysing incomplete financial information, the forensic accountant may be assisted in the process of reconstruction through interviews to identify the reality of the business transactions issue. Many forensic accounting investigations turn out to be more complex than is initially apparent.

5–08 The outcome of fraud investigations may have serious consequences for individuals, guilty or innocent. It is accordingly vital that the appropriate experience is brought to bear. A specialist forensic accountant is usually required because general investigation procedures are not adequate to investigate fraud. Different standards of evidence and of control and collection of material apply. The outcome of the investigation may rest not only on the quality of the investigation, but on certain decisions made during the course of the work, and it is therefore vitally important that the forensic accountant's client be appropriately advised at all stages.

5–09 Table 5.1 shows examples of a sample of forensic accounting investigations. The second example shown in the table highlights the unforeseen ramifications of a fraud investigation. During that fraud investigation, a large amount of income which had not been declared for tax purposes came to light. A consequence of the forensic investigation was a prosecution by the Revenue authorities in respect of tax offences unearthed as a by-product of the investigation.

Table 5.1: Examples of forensic accounting investigations

- Forensic accounting investigation of allegedly fraudulent transactions by a former partner and business manager of a professional practice. Questionable disbursements in accounts payable, payroll and through cash transactions were identified. A written report summarising the findings was used in settlement negotiations with the former partner.
- Forensic accounting analysis for an absent partner of the books and records of a shop to verify substantial fraud and false accounting. Large amounts of unreported income by the operating partner were uncovered. The forensic accounting report was used to obtain a favorable arbitration award for the absent partner. It was also used in a successful conviction by the Revenue authorities for tax evasion by the operating partner.
- Forensic accounting investigation of family partnership. One of the partners was suspected of embezzling funds from the partnership. The forensic accounting investigation discovered that the general partner had taken partnership funds. The forensic accountant's affidavit to the court was the impetus for an out-of-court settlement between the parties.
- Forensic accounting investigation of an alleged Ponzi scheme (see para. **3–59** for a description of Ponzi schemes) by an investment broker. An analysis of the sources and uses of cash demonstrated that very little cash came from investment returns. Conversely, most of the cash invested went to service early investors and to maintain the lifestyle of the perpetrator.
- A former employee of a retailer was accused of embezzling funds. The forensic accountant reviewed the evidence compiled by the Director of Public Prosecutions to determine whether there was sufficient accounting evidence to prove that money was actually taken.
- Forensic accountant conducted due diligence to determine whether a borrower's accounting systems and procedures were in compliance with requirements set by a lender. The forensic accountant discovered serious shortcomings and procedural inadequacies and documented major embezzlement.
- Forensic accountant uncovered money laundering activities through reconstruction of four years of cash transactions.
- Forensic accountant prepared an insurance claim in connection with an embezzlement investigation and negotiated a successful settlement for the insured.
- A fire at a computer manufacturer was suspected to be arson. The forensic accountants examined accounting records and business documents abroad. Bilingual staff members were able to deal with personnel at the manufacturer's various business locations. Evidence was provided during the litigation that ensued. The expert accounting evidence became the basis for a negotiated settlement of the damages.
- Forensic accountant provided services in connected with a fire suspected to be arson. Evidence of fraud in the financial statements submitted with the perpetrator's insurance claim was discovered. The expert report was used in pre-trial motions and, based on the report, summary judgment was granted.

Starting a forensic accounting investigation

5–10   A forensic accounting investigation often starts as a result of suspicions of dishonesty. Once such suspicions have been aroused, they must be resolved in a professional and structured manner in the interests of both the organisation and the individuals suspected of fraud or dishonesty. Careers of many honest people have been damaged by unjustified suspicions and allegations of dishonesty that were not resolved. If the matter is investigated properly, this can benefit the morale of the company by drawing together the management team in solving a difficult problem.

5–11 Sources of initial suspicions of dishonesty can range from an audit finding, an anonymous tip-off, a complaint or allegation, discovery of some accounting or other discrepancy to personal behaviour of an individual or employee. Staff should not be alerted to the fact that they are under suspicion as this might jeopardise effective investigation of the problem. If staff are alerted, guilty parties may take steps to cover their tracks by deleting or destroying vital evidence. In this respect, suspicions should only be discussed with essential personnel and as few people as possible in the organisation should be informed of the suspicions. If staff realise that an investigation is underway, they may become defensive, may be pressurised by others to act in a particular way, may become unco-operative and will not be as effective or useful as witnesses. If the forensic accountants behave as if a normal audit is taking place, they can develop a better rapport with client staff and potential witnesses.

5–12 It is in a company's commercial interests that line management continue to run the business, while a separate task force carries out the investigation. For this reason, amongst others, there are considerable advantages to employing the services of an independent professional forensic accountant to carry out the investigation and to provide an impartial assessment of the situation. Professional forensic accountants are likely to have a greater than average knowledge of legal issues – the team might include lawyers to advise on any legal aspects of the investigation. The firm that carries out the company's external audit should not generally carry out the forensic investigation – it is possible that they have contributed to the problem (*e.g.* by failing to detect it earlier in the course of their audit) and they may consequently have a conflict of interest in carrying out the investigation.

5–13 The forensic accountant should establish the merit of the allegations, and attempt to corroborate the allegations where possible. Essential to the success of any fraud investigation is the speed at which information and evidence can be obtained and, of course, the accuracy of both. In many instances, and certainly in most international fraud investigations, information must be gathered in a matter of hours, rather than days or weeks.

Planning, structuring and resourcing the investigation

5–14   Planning a forensic accounting investigation depends on the nature of the investigation. For example, if persons are suspected of continuing dishonest practices, the investigation ideally should be planned so that they can be "caught in the act" with no plausible excuse or explanation. On the other hand, if the perpetrators are thought to have ceased the fraudulent activity, a different approach will be needed. The plan for this approach will concentrate on retracing the suspects' steps and reconstructing the fraud, thereby assembling evidence linking the suspects to the fraud.

If the work relates to litigation or to an investigation by regulators (such as a tax investigation), forensic accountants can assist in preparing for such litigation or investigation. When such litigation/investigation is announced or is imminent, the forensic accountants can carry out initial inquiries to assemble the available evidence and fully inform management of the facts and their potential exposure.

5–15   Forensic accountants must ensure that the investigation has enough resources to allow it to be completed quickly – delay can act in favour of the perpetrator(s) and against the victim's interests. In assembling the team, the forensic accountant must ensure as far as possible that the appropriate skills, experience and expertise are available for the assignment. In particular, where specific industry knowledge is needed, or where the assignment demands experience of a particular investigative or analytical technique, the forensic accountant should make every effort to ensure that the necessary resources are made available to meet these needs.

5–16   Forensic accountants structure the assignment by preparing a work plan and schedule for its completion. The work plan, which should be agreed in draft form with the client, should detail all the planned tasks and work steps, the individuals with responsibility for each step and a timetable for their completion.

Objectives and outcomes

5–17   The objectives of the investigation must be agreed at the outset. The client's representatives must be perfectly clear about what their ultimate objectives are and what course of action they want to pursue in mounting a recovery effort and/or a case for prosecution. Conducting a cost-benefit analysis will often help in understanding both the risks and the costs involved.

5–18   Following on from identification of the objectives, the possible/ideal outcomes of the investigation must be discussed. These can range from criminal prosecution, recovery of amounts lost, civil action, dismissal or termination of contract. If recovery of losses in the civil courts is the objective, then the standard of proof required is based on the balance of probability. In contrast with the

English courts, Irish judges have not held that the civil standard of proof is varied in cases of fraud to bring it closer to the criminal standard. Instead, they emphasise the degree of care that is required of a judge in satisfying himself that a serious civil wrong such as fraud, which has criminal implications, has been committed. For instance, in his judgment in the Supreme Court in *O'Keeffe v. Ferris*, O'Flaherty J. said:

> "It is true that fraud is an ingredient in many criminal offences but is also an ingredient in various civil wrongs, see *Northern Bank Finance v. Charlton* [1979] I.R. 149. It is true that the proof of fraud will be to the civil standard, but it is also so that the more serious an allegation that is made in civil proceedings, then the more astute must the judge be to find that the allegation in question has been proved."[4]

If criminal prosecution is the objective, it is advisable to get the Gardaí involved at an early stage. In order to be successful in a criminal prosecution, the fraud must be proven beyond reasonable doubt. The final decision as to whether to pursue a criminal prosecution in such cases will rest with the Director of Public Prosecutions.

Section 104 of the Company Law Enforcement Act 2001 amends section 240 of the Companies Act 1990 by increasing to five years the maximum term of imprisonment for conviction on indictment of an offence under the Companies Acts for which no punishment is specifically provided. The same section of the Act deems five years to be the maximum term of imprisonment for conviction on indictment of any offence under the Companies Acts that currently carries a lesser term. Because of the provisions of section 4 of the Criminal Law Act 1997 and section 4 of the Criminal Justice Act 1984, the effect of these changes is to permit the arrest without warrant and the detention for the specified period of anyone suspected of committing an indictable offence under the Companies Acts. The stated purposes of these provisions are to facilitate the investigation of suspected indictable offences and to reflect their serious nature.

As referred to earlier in para. **2–36**, management should be made fully aware that if sensitive internal company documentation is handed over to the Gardaí, it may end up being included in the book of evidence and, in due course, being made public. Management should also be aware that once the Gardaí become involved in a case, the matter is effectively out of the company's hands.

Background data

5–19 At the outset, the forensic accountant should determine the business situation, and business relationship, of the company and its owners. It is appropriate to get as much background information about the business as possible. A starting point might be the date of acquisition of an established business or commencement date of a new business venture. In addition, the ownership

[4] [1997] 3 I.R. 463 at 472.

structure and form of the organisation needs to be identified. Major suppliers and major customers should be identified together with the company's bankers, external auditors, solicitors and other advisers. The relationship between the company and its management on the one hand, and these service providers on the other, should be examined. Recent negotiations and business deals should be considered, as should any recent changes in insurance cover.

5–20 The financial position of the business, the owners (where relevant) and employees (where relevant) may need to be examined. In addition, the degree of interdependency between the business and its owners will also be relevant, as will a history of the owners' previous experience in business. A review of the annual financial statements and supporting information should disclose details of the company's financial performance and give an indication of any underlying business problems. The history and pattern of earnings should also be examined and any significant transactions or events should be considered.

5–21 Forensic accountants analyse information from several sources to construct a chronology of the financial records of the owner, business, and third parties. In this regard, the company's financial position at the time of the investigation should be compared with other earlier periods in order to identify trends in profits and in business activity.

5–22 Any review of the status of the business must be objective. It should identify not only matters favourable to management and owners of companies, but also unfavourable matters. Unfavourable matters may be obvious (steady decline in sales, worsening creditor relations, significant withdrawal of funds, etc.). On the other hand, the owner may have put substantial sums into the business.

Forensic accounting procedures

5–23 It is difficult to be prescriptive about the specific procedures to be followed in a forensic accounting investigation – these are dictated by the circumstances and nature of the investigation. The procedures outlined here are general principles rather than specific steps to be taken in any particular investigation.

Legality of procedures

5–24 Procedures followed in carrying out the investigation, particularly in relation to the gathering of evidence, should be within the law, in order that admissibility of the evidence is not compromised in later proceedings (see Chapter 22 for more information on the rules of evidence). Investigative work must be meticulously documented and procedures must be fully auditable. At every point of the investigation, actions must be verifiable.

Company policy and authorisation levels

5–25   Forensic accountants may need to identify company policy in a wide range of areas (depending on the nature of the investigation). In addition, authorisation procedures in a variety of areas may need to be established. For example, company policy for allowable business expenses, and the system for approval and payment of goods and services, may need to be ascertained.

Role of suspect in the accounting system

5–26   Investigations should uncover evidence that establishes the suspect's job description and their role in, and knowledge of, the accounting system. They should also attempt to uncover any systematic pattern used in covering up the fraud, the extent of the fraud, and the financial position of the suspect (to establish how the perpetrator benefited from the fraud). To establish the case and prove it beyond reasonable doubt, it is wise to accord the benefit of doubt to the person suspected. Where possible, when establishing facts, patterns, including the extent of the fraud, only those examples or specific occurrences of theft or fraud or embezzlement that are unassailable should be selected.

5–27   Breaches of approved procedures should be catalogued. Expense claims and records of telephone calls made from business telephones and paid for by the business may need to be reviewed. Monitoring of the suspect's internal phone, fax, computer, files and office should be considered provided it is within the law.

5–28   It is often essential in investigating crimes against a business to obtain evidence from company employees and those who had access to the assets that were (allegedly) misappropriated. It is often necessary to establish for each person who had access that that person did not take the assets in question. It is necessary to establish whether the suspect had any power to authorise transactions and what that person's power was, *e.g.* cheque-signing powers, authorisation of purchases, granting of credit. Compliance with authorisation limits should be evaluated.

Accounting records

5–29   The accounting records are extremely important in forensic investigations. Books and accounting records of the company should be examined to determine whether reporting of sales and related costs was complete and for the presence of supporting documentation such as suppliers' invoices. Expenses should be examined to identify the nature of the expense (*e.g.* promotion, travel) and whether such payments reflect the normal course of business or indicate unusual transactions. Documents such as purchase orders, purchase invoices, contract and shipping documents should be obtained that describe the goods or services being paid for. In professional service businesses, time records may need to be examined to assess the accuracy of billing professional time.

5–30 Loan agreements may need to be examined to identify the purpose of the loan, whether any interest has been charged and collected, the repayment terms and whether any repayments have been made.

5–31 The forensic accountant may need to confirm whether all revenues are properly recorded, whether recorded sales represent all sales and whether the company has unexpectedly experienced reduced sales from customers. Unrecorded sales are difficult to detect, as there will be little or no evidence in the company records of the sale. If the company has a good stock recording system, it may be possible to detect the unrecorded sale through a reconciliation of movement in stocks with records of purchases and sales. Front-end fraud in cash sales businesses (see para. **3–60**) is especially difficult to detect, particularly if the business involves the provision of services rather than the sale of goods (Front-end fraud is where the cash is taken from the customer before it gets into the accounting system, *i.e.* usually before it is recorded in the cash register.) Often the best approach available in such circumstances will be to examine the trend in gross margin and compare actual margins achieved with industry norms.

5–32 Forensic accountants may need to confirm the adequacy of the purchasing system. It may be necessary to verify that each supplier to whom payments have been made actually exists and that the supplier actually provides goods or services of the type invoiced and required by the business. It may also be necessary to verify that the goods and services were actually provided to the company. This may be done by reference to independently completed delivery dockets.

Personal records

5–33 If possible, the personal records and financial affairs of individuals may need to be examined to help establish motive. Such an analysis of records may help to establish a lifestyle inconsistent with known income and hence the need for personal gain. Any transactions between the company and the individual will need to be scrutinised carefully. The recipient's known assets should be reviewed with a view to establishing how and when they were acquired and, where relevant, what supporting documentation exists. The possibility of a payment to a bank account in a foreign jurisdiction should also be examined.

False accounting

5–34 Businesses may receive, or be subjected to, false information and internal company records may be altered such as:

– false financial statements, *e.g.* overstating income and net worth;

– overstated amounts receivable;

– false journal entries;

– fictitious customer credit information;

– false asset valuations;

– listings of fictitious creditors.

5–35 Some of the techniques used by investigating accountants to identify false accounting might include examining whether:

– information is consistent with the underlying books and accounting records;

– journal entries are properly approved;

– journal entries are appropriate and consistent with the facts;

– transactions can be confirmed with third parties.

Gathering evidence

5–36 Forensic techniques need to be applied to ensure that evidence is gathered in accordance with law and is not contaminated or destroyed. Failure to secure and examine the evidence in line with recognised procedures could rule any evidence retrieved inadmissible in court (see Chapter 22 for a discussion of the rules of evidence).

5–37 Initial sources of information for forensic accountants are normally the financial statements and accounting records of the business. Beyond this, the accountant should seek information from others directly or indirectly connected with the business. Such sources may include the company's bankers, lawyers, accountants, customers, suppliers, insurers and government agencies. Business owners, directors and employees should also be asked to provide any personal or business records they might have where relevant, although in normal circumstances they cannot be compelled to do so. In this regard, it should be noted that the Supreme Court has held that internal memos and draft reports prepared by professional advisers for their own purposes, including final draft reports and advices, are "in the area of being preparatory and, therefore, personal to the adviser and, as such, ... not discoverable."[5] This, in effect, means that only final documents, approved (in the sense of approved by the adviser) for sight by the adviser's client can be the subject of an order for discovery. This, of

---

[5] *Bula Ltd v. Tara Mines Ltd* [1994] I.L.R.M. 111 at 114, *per* O'Flaherty J.

course, does not preclude advisers from providing documents on a voluntary basis.

5–38   Specific third-party documentation should be requested and examined as necessary. This might include certificates of incorporation, partnership or trading names, deeds, mortgages or liens relating to property, auditors' working papers, tax returns, correspondence with customers and suppliers, bank statements, deposit slips, credit/debit memos, bank credit files, details of cancelled cheques, credit files from customers, payroll information and listings of property.

5–39   Records should be examined with a view to:

- ascertaining relevant facts;

- identifying questions to be put at interviews;

- detecting any potential fraud or other unlawful activity.

5–40   All evidence should be properly recovered and kept securely and a full record of how and where it was obtained and stored should be maintained. The legal implications of discovery should be kept in mind (see Chapter 22 for more information on discovery), as should the requirement to disclose documentation arising as a result of the investigation in the event of a civil or criminal trial.

Computer-based evidence[6]

5–41   Handling computer-based evidence has unique problems that have led to the development of computer forensics. These unique problems can be summarised as follows:

- Data stored in electronic format is easily modified. Incorrect handling of computer evidence by investigators can modify the data in such a way as to jeopardise its admissibility in court.[7]

- Computer systems are increasingly complex and this presents challenges for investigators in accurately recovering evidence from a wide variety of computer systems.

- The huge volume of data held on computers makes it more difficult to find the particular information relevant to the investigation.

---

[6] May, C., "Computer-based evidence. Identification and recovery of evidence in electronic format" in *Computer Law and Security Report* (2000), Vol. 16, No. 3, pp. 162–166.
[7] A useful guide on handling computer-based evidence (based on United Kingdom law) is Association of Chief Police Officers (ACPO) of England, Wales and Northern Ireland, *Good Practice Guide for Computer Based Evidence* (ACPO, Maidstone, Kent, 1999).

Forensic computing is the science of capturing, processing and investigating data from computers so that it can be presented as evidence in court. Strict procedures must be followed, and failure to do so will jeopardise a successful investigation, and may render any evidence found inadmissible. Section 25 of the Electronic Commerce Act 2000 makes it an offence to use electronic signatures without authorisation or for "a fraudulent or other unlawful purpose". Suspects may be required to decrypt incriminating data and make it available in "intelligible form".[8] However, no powers are extended to the authorities to require disclosure of passwords, codes or other encryption devices.[9]

Capturing data

5–42 In order to make best use of computer evidence, sophisticated search and investigation software tools are used to search computer files for information.[10] Procedures should ensure that the chain of evidence is maintained. Legal rules and procedures concerning the use of electronic evidence in court are discussed in paras **22–07** *et seq.*

5–43 All potential sources of computer evidence should be considered. Internet caches (storage of web material on an individual's computer or at a central Internet server) and computer logs (containing details of all Internet accesses, unsuccessful login attempts, etc.) can contain valuable information. Digital marks can unknowingly be left on documents by many operating systems and these may reveal vital evidence such as the writer's origin, creation and amendment dates, printing details and even details of amendments. Deleted, hidden, encrypted, embedded and password-protected data can also be recovered in certain circumstances.

5–44 The data capture procedure must take an exact, byte-for-byte copy of all types of digital storage media. Making a sound reliable image of computer evidence is vital for subsequent investigation work. A fundamental principle in capturing computer evidence is that no action taken by anybody performing an investigation on a computer should change data held on that computer or other media which may subsequently be used as evidence. It has become an established and documented principle that in any instance where computer-based evidence is produced, a copy should be made of the entire target device. Partial or selective file copying is not considered acceptable. The images of computer material should be taken without compromising the evidential integrity of the data.

---

[8] Electronic Commerce Act 2000, s. 27(2)(c).
[9] *ibid.*, s. 28.
[10] For example, the *Annual Report 1999*, p. 51 of An Garda Síochána reports that the Computer Crime Unit of the Garda Bureau of Fraud Investigation retrieved computer-based evidence from 117 hard drives and 1,388 ancillary computer media.

Special techniques are required to secure computer evidence in a forensically sound manner. "Imaging" is the preferred method for capturing and securing computer evidence and is quite different from the usual backup, "file-by-file" copies of disks taken for example when computers fail. Imaging involves making perfect, forensically sound, electronic duplicates of material on computers. An image copy is a complete copy of the disk from end to end. Imaging can be conducted on-site or off-site, and evidence can be captured quickly and discreetly. On-site imaging can be conducted after hours and in such a way that no trace is left of access to the computer to ensure that the suspect is not inadvertently alerted.

5–45   Evidence obtained in this way is acceptable in court provided no rule of law has been breached in obtaining the evidence. It has the advantage of being operating-system independent. The exact copy or image contains all the information that existed on the original machine without exception. The copy will contain data which may have been deleted, hidden, or overwritten. As the image is an exact replica or clone of the suspected computer, it can be investigated in place of the original computer. The investigator can view last accessed Internet sites, read saved e-mail messages and files and navigate around the computer as if it were the original computer.

5–46   The methodology should comply with guidelines for computer-based evidence. Forensic computing specialists can accompany solicitors in conducting searches to secure computer evidence and advise on the content of discovery applications (discovery is considered in Chapter 22). Such searches can be conducted on foot of *Anton Piller* orders granted by a court (see paras **21–47** *et seq.* for further discussion of *Anton Piller* orders).

5–47   There must be a full audit trail to ensure that the continuity of the evidence is maintained and to facilitate re-creation of the imaging process. An audit trail or other record of all processes applied to computer-based evidence should be created and preserved such that an independent third party could replicate the processes and achieve the same results. Forensic accountants can provide affidavits to support the methods used to extract any evidence found.

Analysing computer data

5–48   Computer forensic specialists use powerful search facilities to identify documents relevant to the investigation. Specialist software facilitates examination of data in its original format. Certain data recovered such as logs and caches requires specialist skills to interpret. Computerised intelligence analysis tools can assist in examining high volumes of data.

5–49   Examples of forensic computing assignments are shown in Table 5.2.

Table 5.2: Examples of forensic computing investigations

- The contract for sale of a consultancy business to another company contained restraint clauses, prohibitions on the removal of confidential information, and non-solicitation of staff and client clauses. The purchaser became suspicious that the vendor was acting in breach of contract. The hard disks on the vendors' desktop and laptop computers were copied and their content analysed. Within an encrypted file, a draft business plan for a new enterprise which would compete with the consultancy business was found. Deleted files were restored and details of key clients and revenue streams were recovered. It was possible to demonstrate that information had been updated within these files after the vendor had sold the consultancy business. Taken together, the evidence was sufficient to initiate proceedings.
- An employee was suspended for suspected corruption. A forensic computing analysis of the employee's computer showed that hundreds of documents had been deleted. The deleted material was recovered and was found to be crudely encrypted. Once decrypted, the files revealed transfers to offshore bank accounts. The unfair dismissal claim submitted by the discharged employee was dropped, the employee was dismissed and the forensic accountant's findings resulted in an action for recovery against the employee.
- A paedophile ring was suspected of hoarding Internet pornography on computer. Prior to the matter being investigated, the culprits were tipped off and reformatted their hard drives. The forensic computing team imaged the suspects' machines. Once the file system was rebuilt, Internet access logs were recovered and pornographic files were downloaded.

Interviewing witnesses

5–50 Interviews need to be carefully planned in advance, with details such as interview objectives, techniques, questions, interviewers and interviewees identified at the outset. These are discussed below.

Planning interviews

5–51 To ensure that interviews are effective and achieve their objective, careful planning is needed. This will assist in ensuring that the right questions are asked at interviews. Aspects that require clarity in advance include:

– purpose and end objectives of interview;

– selection of relevant persons to interview, *i.e.* those who are likely to know answers to, or assist with, interview questions;

– background briefing and documentation required before interviews, *e.g.* organisation charts, outlines of company procedures;

– an interview outline, chart of questions or a detailed script of questions may be prepared in advance.

Objective of interviews

5–52   The ultimate objective of interviews is to ascertain relevant facts. Interviews should address relevant facts pertinent to a case such as exact dates, times, persons involved, business records, pervasiveness of the fraud and, where relevant, how the witness learnt of the fraud.

Interview techniques

5–53   Using staff trained in interview techniques is the best course of action when it comes to conducting investigations and facilitating their speedy completion. Because the art of interviewing is an especially delicate process, the danger in using untrained interviewers is that they might expose both themselves and the victim to costly litigation (such as wrongful-dismissal claims, character defamation and other risks) by the investigation's intended target. Forensic accountants need to understand and learn communication techniques because there is normally little time for the gradual development of trust among parties.

5–54   Techniques used in interviews must be defendable (*e.g.* in subsequent litigation). In this respect, it is worth taking legal advice to ensure that the techniques and procedures followed will pass the scrutiny of a legal challenge. Advice taken from lawyers in connnection with actual or contemplated litigation is generally "privileged" and will not have to be disclosed or discovered in civil or criminal litigation. For important interviews on which reliance is likely to be placed in subsequent proceedings, it is generally advisable to engage a stenographer to produce an exact record of the interview. Interviewees may also seek to be accompanied by a legal adviser and, if requested, this facility should not be denied.

5–55   By conducting face-to-face interviews, experienced interviewers can extract and obtain vital information quickly because they know which questions to ask and what to make of the answers. Interviewing colleagues, co-workers, even friends of suspected fraudsters, for example, can prove extremely useful in gaining insights into their lifestyle and identifying any recent expensive purchases such as a new car. If, for example, a witness reveals that a suspect frequently travels to a foreign jurisdiction, an investigator can immediately concentrate on looking for the flow of funds into companies or bank accounts in or near that location. The alternative is possibly to spend weeks wading through thousands of documents before somebody uncovers the personal expense report or airline tickets that pinpoint the foreign connection.

5–56   Having a local presence in a foreign jurisdiction, to ensure language does not become a barrier to the investigation, is an advantage. Local investigators are more likely to have knowledge unavailable to national investigators carrying out the same task on foreign shores.

5–57 Interviewees should be treated with respect. Interviewers should act professionally, avoid aggression, be polite and use a courteous approach. This is not inconsistent with the necessity to ask difficult questions and, at times, take a tough line. The best approach is one that maximises the level of trust between interviewer and interviewee. Interviewees should be interviewed separately. If there is more than one interviewer, they need to co-ordinate their approach and questions in advance.

5–58 Leads provided by interviewees should be followed up thoroughly. Follow-up interviews may be required (i) with interviewees, or (ii) with others as suggested or prompted in previous interviews. Also, evidence to back up information disclosed during the interviews may need to be obtained.

Interview questions

5–59 Interviews can range from structured or semi-structured to unstructured. In structured interviews, interviewees are asked the same questions which have been decided in advance. The approach is restrictive and does not allow the interview to develop beyond the specific questions. Unstructured interviews are not planned in advance and develop in accordance with the interview responses. This has the disadvantage that issues may not be addressed at the interview, and may allow for introduction of greater interviewer bias to the process. Semi-structured interviews are based on an outline of the issues/questions to be addressed but allow for some development beyond the specific questions depending on the responses received.

5–60 Failure to ask the right questions is a lost opportunity. Questions should be based on accurate background information. When asking questions of a technical nature (for example, accounting questions) of a non-specialist, non-technical language with which a lay person will feel comfortable should be used.

There are broadly two types of questions that can be asked at interviews: closed questins and open questions. Closed questions often require only "yes" or "no" type answers.

Open questions – who, what, when, where type questions – allow for the interviewee to divulge information in a more unstructured way. Answers to much of the information required may be obtained by asking the following questions:

– Who is involved?

– What has happened?

– When did an event happen?

– Where did it happen?

– What documentary evidence is there?

– How was the event carried out?

Recording of interviews

5–61 Interviewers may keep handwritten notes. In addition, tape recording equipment may be used or a stenographer may be employed to record the interview accurately. In addition to recording the verbal exchanges, persons being questioned should be observed and their physical reactions to questions should be noted.

Analysing accounting data

5–62 The accounting analysis is directed primarily towards establishing any financial benefit to the suspect. Benefit may be shown in various ways, such as:

– payment to the suspect (extortion);

– assets, such as stock, shares, property, receivables transferred to the suspect;

– insurance proceeds paid to the suspect as beneficiary under a policy;

– other benefits including obtaining an interest in a business.

5–63 When analysing financial affairs, the forensic accountant may also seek to determine the following:

– business relationships and the identity of those which whom the suspect had dealings;

– whether there were sums owing to or from the victim;

– whether the motives for the suspect's behaviour were financial or could have originated for other reasons.

Tracing and recovery of assets

5–64 Tracing and recovery of assets is very relevant to many cases of fraud. Information on assets is critical in maximising recovery in settlement situations, enforcing judgments, and in making decisions to pursue personal guarantees. The potential for recovery of assets often drives many decisions in an asset diversion, fraud or liquidation context.

Essential to an effective asset search is knowing what may be available for recovery and hence, what are the strategic options. Use of on-line databases as well as people who have extensive experience in conducting funds tracing, asset diversion and other business and financial investigations can assist in such searches. Forensic accountants have skills in finding clues that indicate assets exist, and in developing procedures for uncovering and documenting these assets.

5–65   Tracing of assets may also be a feature in matrimonial disputes, where one partner has taken matrimonial assets. Sometimes at separation, the level of assets belonging to the marriage partnership are somewhat lower than expected in an effort to reduce payments to another partner.[11]

Role of forensic accountants

5–66   The role of forensic accountants in tracing assets is covered in MacGregor and Hobbs.[12] Forensic accountants can advise if there appear to be missing assets, and can assist in tracing such missing assets, using appropriate financial and legal processes. In taking account of this possibility, the accountant must delve deeper into the financial information for areas of concern in the financial statements or accounts pointing to missing assets. He must question all financial information as to whether it is a valid and correct presentation of the financial position and performance of the company. In particular, where cash has been misappropriated by diverting it to a bank account other than one of the company's accounts, the forensic accountant can assist in tracing the cash by reviewing bank records and tracking the movement of the cash balance between accounts. Table 5.3 provides examples of cases in which forensic accountants played a role in the search for and recovery of missing assets.

---

[11] Tracing of assets in the context of matrimonial dissolution is considered in Ravano, C.P. and Gursey, D.L., "Marital dissolution: Tracing and apportionment of assets" in *Litigation Services Handbook. The Role of the Accountant as Expert* (2nd ed., Weil, R.L., Wagner, M.J. and Frank, P.B. (eds), John Wiley & Sons, Inc., New York, 1995), Chap. 27.
[12] MacGregor, G. and Hobbs, I., *Expert Accounting Evidence: A Guide for Litigation Support* (Accountancy Books, London, 1998), Chap. 17.

Table 5.3: Examples of asset tracing cases in which forensic accountants have advised

- Acting in matters involving the sequestration of assets including an appointment by the court to locate and seize the assets of a man who had gone abroad. By serving orders on accountants, close family and the Revenue, properties, shares and bank accounts were located.
- Performing forensic/investigative accounting work to discover the hidden assets of a husband. Forensic accounting findings were used to convince the husband to settle the case at terms much more favourable to the wife than had been offered previously.
- Forensic/investigative accounting work used to determine the sources and uses of funds used to procure certain assets. This information was used to identify assets acquired during the marriage, assets acquired from matrimonial funds and assets acquired using sole and separate funds. Detailed matrimonial asset schedules were prepared and expert witness evidence was offered.

To facilitate detection and asset recovery, forensic accountants can offer valuable advice by compiling a financial profile of the perpetrator and identifying his or her major assets, liabilities, expenses and sources of income during the period in question. Based on that information, the victim is then in a better position to decide whether it is in the best interests of the business to undertake a fully-fledged investigation – and, if the evidence warrants it, to pursue a civil or criminal action. Usually the first step in recovering misappropriated assets is to determine whether the perpetrator is still in possession of them. The second important consideration is whether the value of those assets warrants the time and expense involved in undertaking a thorough search. All avenues for recovery, from collateral, from guarantors and from litigation with third parties should be explored.

Sources of information

5–67 Many sources of information exist to help corporate fraud victims make informed decisions about whether to try to recover misappropriated assets. International banks and government agencies may provide information. International networks share remote resources. Proprietary databases are used to access a wide variety of financial information. Through these channels, assets can be located quickly and completely.

5–68 Because international intelligence-gathering can be time-consuming and expensive, it helps to employ experts who know their way around electronic databases. Public records, such as land titles and vehicle registries, used in conjunction with observation and surveillance techniques, are often a cost-effective way to uncover hidden assets. It also helps to establish international contacts in foreign locations. This effectively expands a company's capabilities when it comes to using public databases globally. Employed properly, these investigative tools can trigger additional leads, point to the existence of assets, provide information regarding their value and identify their owners and other relevant individuals.

International law-enforcement agencies

5–69[13]   Law-enforcement agencies also provide access to information and legal processes that can facilitate evidence-gathering. The international criminal police organisation, Interpol, was established in 1914, has its general headquarters in Lyon, France and has 178 member countries. It provides assistance to the law-enforcement community. Although it has no working police force itself, it facilitates, co-ordinates and encourages police co-operation as a means of combating international crime. In the absence of legislation, police-to-police co-operation is informal.

Evidence or information sought by a foreign authority for use in criminal proceedings can be obtained by the Gardaí or various legal agencies pursuant to a power of compulsion, or under the promise of confidentiality. The evidence is only transmitted pursuant to a court order (usually under section 51 of the Criminal Justice Act 1994). The person responsible for obtaining the evidence brings it before a District Judge, explains how he came by it (which is set down in a transcript) and the evidence is then furnished by the District Judge to the Minister for onwards transmission.

5–70   A number of mechanisms for international law enforcement co-operation are available. Two systems are in place for gathering evidence in Ireland for foreign trials. Letters rogatory are requests from judges/legal authorities in one country to judges/legal authorities in another country. They facilitate international judge-to-judge assistance, and may also be used by judges on behalf of the police or prosecutors in that country. Letters rogatory are used in criminal and civil cases. The legislation governing these is the 1959 European Convention on Mutual Assistance[14] and the 1990 Convention on Search and Seizure[15] (for criminal cases) and the Foreign Tribunals Evidence Act 1856 (for civil cases).

---

[13] The authors thank Ruth Fitzgerald for her expertise and considerable assistance in drafting much of the material in paras **5–69** *et seq*. Barry Quinlan of the Department of Justice, Equality and Law Reform was also helpful in correcting and clarifying some of the text.

[14] Council of Europe, *European Convention on Mutual Assistance in Criminal Matters*, (Council of Europe, European Treaties ETS No. 030, Strasbourg, 1959).

[15] Council of Europe. *Convention on Laundering, Search, Seizure and Confiscation of the Proceeds from Crime* (Council of Europe, European Treaties ETS No. 141, Strasbourg, 1990). Available at http://ue.eu.int/ejn/data/vol_b/4b_convention_protocole_accords/ produits_du_crime/141texten.html.

Mutual assistance conventions

5–71 Mutual assistance in criminal matters is governed by Part VII of the Criminal Justice Act 1994. The Government may by order apply Part VII of the Act to the large number of countries to which the legislation applies.[16] The 1994 legislation was introduced to give effect, not only to the European Convention on Mutual Assistance, but also to the Council of Europe Convention on Money Laundering and the United Nations Drugs Convention. Under the Act, the following assistance may, subject to certain conditions, be given:

– Under section 51, the Minister may ask the President of the District Court to appoint a judge to hear evidence which is then transmitted to the foreign court or judicial authority.

– Under section 55, the Gardaí may obtain a search warrant (or a production order under section 63) where the conduct giving rise to the offence which is being investigated or prosecuted abroad would justify obtaining a search warrant in this jurisdiction.

– Under sections 4, 9 and 24, confiscation and restraint (freezing in anticipation of a confiscation order) may be obtained (for this, see also the regulations made under section 46 of the 1994 Act).

– Under section 53, the Minister may, on the consent of a prisoner, transfer him or her to another state to give evidence there (he or she may not be prosecuted – for that an extradition warrant would be required).

– Sections 49 and 50 set up systems for the service of documents.

– The State may seek similar assistance from other countries under sections 52 and 54.

5–72 Ireland is a party to a number of multilateral mutual assistance conventions such as the European Convention on Mutual Assistance in Criminal Matters. It also has a bilateral treaty with the United Kingdom which goes slightly further than the European Convention. Ireland also has an agreement with Belgium for the spontaneous exchange of information relating to suspect financial transactions (between the Money Laundering Investigation Unit of An Garda Síochána and the Cel Voor Financiële Informatieverwerking of Belgium).

5–73 In addition, there are multilateral treaties dealing with specific crimes, and which have mutual assistance provisions attached, such as the United Nations Convention Against Terrorist Financing,[17] the Council of Europe Convention

---

[16] In excess of 140 countries are designated under the legislation.
[17] United Nations. *International Convention for the Suppression of the Financing of Terrorism* (United Nations, New York, 1999).

on Money Laundering,[18] the United Nations Convention on Organised Crime,[19] etc. Ireland has adapted into Irish law the Naples II Convention (Customs Mutual Assistance)[20] and has asked to negotiate participation in the Schengen mutual legal assistance provisions[21] (which deals with judicial co-operation).

5–74 Mutual Legal Assistance Treaties also assist in international law enforcement co-operation. They oblige signatories to assist in connection with criminal investigations in the other country. They entitle the requesting country to seek assistance in: acquiring bank records and other financial information, questioning witnesses and taking statements from witnesses; obtaining copies of government records, including police reports; serving legal documents; transferring persons in custody for purposes of co-operation; conducting searches and seizures; and repatriating stolen property or the proceeds of crime.

Stages in tracing and recovery process

5–75 As soon as a company discovers that certain of its assets have disappeared and is beginning an investigation, the victim organisation should take immediate steps to stem further losses. A slow response by senior management, or an ill-thought-out strategy when confronted with evidence of misappropriated assets, can exacerbate rather than mitigate the damage already done. It is always better in cases of suspected fraud to expect the worst and ensure that every conceivable step is taken promptly to recoup the loss. The victim organisation should ensure that:

– the suspect's privileges, such as physical-access rights, corporate credit cards, computer passwords and authority to conduct business on its behalf, are revoked;

---

[18] Council of Europe. *Convention on Laundering, Search, Seizure and Confiscation of the Proceeds from Crime* (Council of Europe, European Treaties ETS No. 141, Strasbourg, 1990). Available at http://ue.eu.int/ejn/data/vol_b/4b_convention_protocole_accords/produits_du_crime/141texten.html.

[19] United Nations. *Convention against Transnational Organized Crime* (United Nations, New York, 2000). Available at www.uncjin.org/Documents/Conventions/dcatoc/final_documents_2/convention_eng.pdf.

[20] Council of Europe. *Convention on Mutual Assistance and Cooperation between Customs Administrations* (Council of Europe, Brussels, 1997). Available at http://ue.eu.int/ejn/data/vol_b/4a_convention_protocole_accords_suite/cooperation_douaniere/c-024-23011998-1-1-en.html. This Convention was legislated for in Ireland with the enactment of the Customs and Excise (Mutual Assistance) Act 2001.

[21] Council of Europe. *Mutual Legal Assistance Convention*. (Council of Europe, Brussels, 2000). Available at www.statewatch.org/news/aug00/MLAfinal.htm.

– bank signatories are changed to prevent cash-transfer instructions from being used to remove even more funds;

– an *Anton Piller* order and/or injunction (Chapter 21 deals with injunctions and *Anton Piller* orders in more detail) is, where necessary, sought immediately without the suspect's knowledge.

– The value of the misappropriated assets must be weighed against the costs of recovery. Before proceeding with a full investigation, senior management should conduct a cost-benefit analysis to determine the likelihood of recovery and the amount likely to be recovered.

5–77   Searching for assets involves:

– A preliminary search which provides a quick assessment of obvious sources of recovery and the likelihood of collecting, attaching or recovering certain assets. The search does not involve an in-depth effort to identify all assets. Rather, it provides important indicators.

– The second phase takes into account more individualised document analysis and special areas of inquiry. While public record searches can sometimes provide clear indications that further pursuit is not advisable, they can also point to areas where a more specialised inquiry is likely to yield results. If appropriate, a personal or organisational financial profile may be developed for each legal person under suspicion, as there is no more effective way to pursue an asset search than a full-blown financial profile. While sometimes expensive, if the amounts in question are large, it may be the only feasible avenue available to achieve the desired objectives.

– Finally, the search addresses issues such as proper collection techniques or avenues for legal pursuit of the assets, should the information previously obtained justify additional efforts. In this phase, the legal status of the asset(s) and whether there are other claims on the same asset(s) will be determined. Such information can be vital to maximising asset recovery efforts.

5–77   Case history 5.1 outlines the stages in tracing and recovering assets.

Case history 5.1: Tracing assets

A major client of your firm approaches you with a request that you find out all you can about the commercial worth of a foreign businessman. He tells you that he wants to sue this man for debts outstanding and he wishes to know where the man banks and whether he is worth suing. He instructs you to ascertain how much the man is worth and where his assets are located.

Work of forensic accountant in getting the evidence
- Conflict of interest check
- Consider data protection legislation and other laws: the Data Protection Act has an exclusion where the investigation or prevention of crime is concerned (section 5 of the Data Protection Act 1988). The Act does not apply to data about corporate entities but only to personal data.
- Obtain background on the debtor and transaction details from the client
- Assess possibility of recovery of any goods that were the subject of the debt
- Obtain copies of previous cheques paid by the debtor
- Search public records and databases, including trawling the Internet
- Advise the client to instruct a private investigator
- Surveillance may provide a bank address. However, surveillance is one of the most expensive investigative techniques and, if unfocused, can be a waste of money
- Inspect the debtor's house
- Instruct a solicitor when evidence has been obtained
- Seek *Anton Piller* orders (where appropriate)

Source: Adapted from Anonymous. "Asset tracing: Ignoring the experts…" *Inside Fraud Bulletin*, Maxima Partnering Ltd, March 1999.

5–78 A multidisciplinary approach combining the skills of forensic accountants, investigators and lawyers familiar with asset-recovery processes may be of benefit, including:

– close co-ordination with overseas professionals;

– full exploitation of information-technology support to rapidly assimilate and analyse large quantities of data.

Criminal process

5–79 Where criminal conduct is involved, the Gardaí should be consulted, since they will have their own search procedures. While criminal proceedings may prove useful to the fraud victim's own investigation, investigations can move slowly. The primary goal of the criminal process is not to recover assets or move with enormous speed, but, rather, to prosecute a crime. The standard of proof is higher for criminal prosecution than for civil litigation. At an early stage, it is safer to assume when handling evidence that criminal prosecution may result. The criminal process may, however, serve two other equally important purposes: (a) to punish the fraudster and (b) to gather evidence that can lead to the missing assets. It is often more expedient to seek an *Anton Piller* order (see paras **21–47** *et seq.*) to protect a fraud victim's position and prevent the possible destruction of crucial information.

Criminal Assets Bureau

5–80   The Criminal Assets Bureau (CAB) is a confiscation agency that has considerable powers in combating crime in Ireland under the Proceeds of Crime Act 1996 (see paras **21–53** *et seq.*), the Finance Acts and the Social Welfare Acts. It has a high profile in connection with the recovery of the proceeds of drug trafficking, but is also involved in recovering the proceeds of corruption and money laundering. In addition to depriving persons of the proceeds of crime, CAB acts to ensure that the proceeds of criminal activity are subjected to tax, and that social welfare claims by criminals are investigated. From its establishment on August 1, 1996 up to December 31, 1999, CAB has, under the Proceeds of Crime Act 1996, obtained interim orders to the value of £7.6 million,[22] interlocutory orders to the value of £5.4 million[23] and receivership orders to the value of £1.2 million.[24] The activities of CAB have resulted in collection of £3.4 million[25] tax and interest and discovery of overpayments of social welfare of £0.8 million.[26]

Reporting results of the investigation

5–81   Forensic accounting reports provide written details of the forensic accounting investigation. The purpose of these reports is to provide evidence in relation to the investigation. It is not for the forensic accountant to point to the guilt or otherwise of persons subject to the investigation. This is a matter for the courts. Statements in forensic accounting reports implying fraudulent behaviour by any person could be construed as defamatory. In fact, use of terms such as "fraud", "fraudulent", etc., should normally be avoided.

Complex technical material should be presented in a manner the layman can understand. Reports should be readable and concise. Complex analysis and issues should be written in simple, jargon-free language and complex concepts should be clearly explained. The emphasis in the report should be towards a practical and useful approach. The report should be written bearing in mind the level of substantiation necessary of the facts in the report and the legal rules of evidence if the report is to be used in a court case. Liaison with lawyers can assist with

---

[22] Criminal Assets Bureau, *Annual Reports 1996–1999*. Interim orders: £2,101,000 1996; £2,334,680 1997; £1,682,545 1998; £1,500,000 1999.
[23] Criminal Assets Bureau, *Annual Reports 1996–1999*. Interlocutory orders: £2,048,000 1996; £1,496,180 1997; £1,091,413 1998; £813,659 1999.
[24] Criminal Assets Bureau, *Annual Reports 1996–1999*. Receivership orders: £993,930 1996-98; £244,289 1999.
[25] Criminal Assets Bureau, *Annual Reports 1996–1999*. Tax and interest collected: £198,231, 1997; £621,749 1998; £2,361,280 1999.
[26] Criminal Assets Bureau, *Annual Reports 1996–1999*. Overpayment of social welfare: £33,235 1996; £185,769 1997; £281,073 1998; £327,755 1999.

these issues. Reports should be tailored to the facts of the case and contain:

– relevant background;

– outline of the approach of the forensic accountants;

– summary of facts;

– list of the witnesses interviewed;

– summary of the interviews;

– copies of documents;

– chronology of events;

– schedules or exhibits.

Further discussion of forensic accounting reports can be found in Chapter 23.

Concluding comment

5–82 A competent forensic investigation may result in recovery of substantial sums for the clients. If the investigation is done well, adverse publicity/ controversy can be avoided. Forensic accountants can examine insurance policies to identify whether the policy provides cover in the event of loss due to fraud. They can also advise on forms of insurance to protect against fraud, negligence and wrongful acts. They should always ensure that there is clarity regarding the evidence to be provided to support the claim.

PART III

ROLE OF FORENSIC ACCOUNTANTS

ACCOUNTING EXPERTISE IN LITIGATION AND DISPUTE RESOLUTION

CHAPTER 6

ACCOUNTING EXPERTISE IN LITIGATION AND DISPUTE RESOLUTION

6–01   Having set out in Parts I and II a description of forensic accounting, and a discussion of fraud and forensic accounting investigations this part of the book (Part III) considers the variety of legal areas in which forensic accountants have a role to play. As already stated in Chapter 2, it is important for forensic accountants to have an overall understanding of the legal context of their work. Accordingly, this part contains a discussion of the relevant legal principles and rules applying to each area relevant to forensic accounting. This discussion is not exhaustive and is intended primarily to provide forensic accountants with an introduction only to the legal context. Each chapter, and sections within chapters, direct readers to more detailed legal sources.[1] Chapter 23 considers accounting expertise, specifically focusing on expert accounting reports and expert accounting oral evidence in court.

6–02   Before each legal area is examined in detail, this chapter deals with the general characteristics of forensic accounting engagements. As such, it applies to all legal situations discussed in the remaining chapters in this part.

The chapter first considers expert evidence generally, and then deals with forensic accounting expert evidence specifically. Experts as witnesses and the nature of the evidence given by them are first discussed. This is followed by a consideration of professional standards applying to such evidence, together with the duties and responsibilities of experts. The chapter concludes with a discussion of the terms on which experts are engaged.

---

[1] Other useful discussions of this subject are available in MacGregor, G. and Hobbs, I., *Expert Accounting Evidence: A Guide for Litigation Support* (Accountancy Books, London, 1998), Chaps 2, 3, 7, and 10; Taub, M., Rapazzini, A., Bond, C., Solon, M., Brown, A., Murrie, A., Linnell, K. and Burn, S., *Tolley's Accountancy Litigation Support* (Butterworths, London, looseleaf), Part II, paras 20 and 22; Frank, P.B., Wagner, M.J. and Weil, R.L., "The role of the CPA in litigation services" in *Litigation Services Handbook. The Role of the Accountant as Expert* (2nd ed., Weil, R.L., Wagner, M.J. and Frank, P.B. (eds), John Wiley & Sons, Inc., New York, 1995), Chap. 1; Ueltzen, M.G. "Professional standards in a litigation environment" in *Litigation Services Handbook. The Role of the Accountant as Expert* (2nd ed., Weil, R.L., Wagner, M.J. and Frank, P.B. (eds), John Wiley & Sons, Inc., New York, 1995), Chap. 2; and Kelleher, D. "Expert evidence in Ireland" in *Irish Law Times* (February 1996) pp. 42-45.

The discussion in this chapter is also relevant to the outputs of forensic accounting assignments, in the form of reports presented and evidence tendered in courts of law.

Role of expert witnesses

6–03   An expert witness is one whose opinion a court or other tribunal is prepared to admit as evidence for the purpose of assisting in the resolution of a dispute or in arriving at the truth, and whose opinion is based on the application of particular expertise and knowledge to the relevant facts. Accountants are engaged as expert witnesses in litigation to gather, analyse and interpret complex financial and other data and to express an opinion thereon in terms that juries and judges can understand.

Finlay P. in *Minister for Agriculture v. Concannon* explained the basis on which the normal rule of evidence (that a witness's opinion is inadmissible) does not apply to an expert witness. He said:

> "The courts daily accept evidence given by expert witnesses of the holding of particular qualifications as the ground, and necessary ground, for the admission of their opinions in evidence according to the principles and rules of evidence applicable to expert testimony." [2]

6–04   However, the courts have made it clear that expert evidence is never a substitute for the exercise by a court of its own judgment. Expert evidence is regarded as an ingredient (often a very important one) of the case to be used by the court to assist in arriving at a decision, but a court cannot abdicate its function in favour of an expert. An example of where the judiciary draws this particular line is seen in the judgment of Murphy J. in *T.F. v. Ireland*, a case in which the constitutionality of the Judicial Separation and Family Law Reform Act 1989 was challenged. In explaining his refusal to hear expert evidence on the essential features of a Christian marriage, the learned judge said:

> "Again I declined to hear a Catholic theologian giving evidence as to the essential features of a Christian marriage. It may well be that 'marriage' as referred to in our Constitution derives from the Christian concept of marriage. However, whatever its origin, the obligations of the State and the rights of parties in relation to marriage are now contained in the Constitution and our laws and ... it falls to me as a judge of the High Court to interpret those provisions and it is not permissible for me to abdicate that function to any expert, however distinguished." [3]

---

[2] Unreported, High Court, April 14, 1980.
[3] [1995] 1 I.R. 321 at 333–334.

6–05   A classic statement of the role of expert evidence is to be found in Beven[4] which states:

> "To justify the admission of expert testimony two elements must co-exist:
>
> (1)   The subjèct matter of the inquiry must be such that ordinary people are unlikely to form a correct judgment about it, if unassisted by persons with special knowledge.
> (2)   The witness offering expert evidence must have gained his special knowledge by a course of study or previous habit which secures his habitual familiarity with the matter in hand".

6–06   Courts are increasingly codifying rules to create express duties on experts to be impartial. While an expert needs to reconcile these rules with his or her duty to act in their instructing party's best interests, the court's intention is that the duty to the client is secondary to the higher duty to the court. The function of an expert witness is to assist the court in arriving at the truth by providing a skilled expert assessment of matters requiring a specialist appreciation of the particular problem at issue.

6–07   The position has always been that the expert's duty is to the court and not to the side by which he has been instructed. This position has been reinforced in England and Wales under the new Civil Procedure Rules which came into force on April 26, 1999. Rule 35.3 states:

> "(1)   It is the duty of an expert to help the court on the matters within his expertise.
> (2)   This duty overrides any obligation to the person from whom he has received instructions or by whom he is paid."

The fact that the expert's first duty is to the court is further emphasised by the court's right under rule 35.7. When two or more parties wish to submit expert evidence on a particular issue, the court can direct that the evidence on that issue is to be given by one expert only.

Types of expert evidence

6–08   Expert evidence generally concerns matters of such a technical nature that the judge or jury could not be expected to reach a "correct" conclusion without assistance. Hodgkinson has identified five types of expert evidence. These are summarised in Table 6.1. Examples of expert evidence provided by forensic accountants are shown for each category.

---

[4] Beven, T., *Negligence in Law* (3rd ed., Stevens and Haynes, London, 1908), p. 131.

Table 6.1: Types of expert evidence

Type of expert evidence	Example of accounting expert evidence
1. Expert evidence of opinion, based on facts	• Valuation of business or of shares
2. Explanation by an expert of technical subjects or of the meaning of technical words	• Explanation of a method of accounting such as off balance sheet financing
3. Expert evidence of fact, the observation, comprehension and description of which require expertise	• Insolvency at a point in time, *i.e.* inability of a company to pay its debts as they fall due
4. Expert evidence of fact, as a necessary preliminary to the giving of evidence in the other four categories	• Maintainable profits of a business as a basis for a share valuation
5. Admissible hearsay of a specialist nature (*e.g.* explaining content or meaning of documents prepared by others)	• Interpretation of business documents deemed admissible by section 5 of the Criminal Evidence Act 1992

Source: Hodgkinson, T. *Expert Evidence: Law and Practice* (Sweet & Maxwell, London, 1990), p. 9.

6–09 In Ireland, the practice of the courts is to permit expert evidence where there is a material matter at issue between the parties, the understanding or explanation of which would fall outside the general level of knowledge and expertise normal in society. An example (in connection with actuarial evidence) can be seen from the Supreme Court judgment of Walsh J. in *Sexton v. O'Keefe*, at a time when juries still heard personal injury actions:

> "In particular I wish to emphasise the desirability of giving a jury the benefit of the evidence of an actuary in any case in which loss of future earnings forms a substantial portion of a plaintiff's claim. It is very undesirable in such cases that a jury should be left at large to form their own impressions as to expectation of life and the computing of loss dependent upon it without the expert assistance of an actuary who can inform the jury of the precise mathematical calculations involved and to be applied according to the jury's findings on the relevant facts."[5]

6–10 However, both the value of expert accounting evidence and the limits on the extent to which courts will defer to an expert accountant's opinion were explained by Pennycuick V.C. in *Odeon Associated Theatres Ltd v. Jones*:

> "In order to ascertain what are the correct principles [of the prevailing system of commercial accountancy] it has recourse to the evidence of accountants. That evidence is conclusive on the practice of accountants in the sense of principles on which accountants act in practice. That is a question of pure fact, but the court itself has to make a final decision as to whether that practice corresponds to the correct principles of commercial accountancy. No doubt in the vast

---

[5] [1966] I.R. 204 at 213.

proportion of cases the court will agree with the accountants but it will not necessarily do so. ... At the end of the day the court must determine what is the correct principle to be applied."[6]

6–11 A similar view was expressed in the case of *Murnaghan Brothers Ltd. v. O'Maoldomhnaigh*, a case stated by the Circuit Court in relation to the definition of trading stock in a claim for tax relief which the Circuit Court judge proposed to disallow. In the High Court, Murphy J. said:

> "Whilst the learned Circuit Court Judge is undoubtedly correct in saying that the court must not abdicate to experts the role of the court in determining matters of law or fact the value of expert evidence in relation to accounting matters is well recognized. Indeed in *Fraser (Inspector of Taxes) v. London Sportscar Center* (1985) 59 T.C. 63 Nourse L.J. at p. 83 commented as follows:—
>
> > '[Counsel for the crown] also made certain submissions as to the accountancy aspects of the matter. First of all he said that Nicholls J. deferred excessively to the view of the accountants as appearing from the way in which the matter was treated in the taxpayer's accounts. We disagree. We think that what the learned Judge did was to regard the accountant's view as being good evidence, perhaps the best evidence, of the commercial reality of the arrangement. He thought that the statute was more concerned with that than with the niceties of ownership. In all of this he was perfectly correct. He certainly did not allow the accountant's view to pre-empt the construction of the statute'."[7]

6–12 Only expert witnesses may provide expert opinions. In the legal environment, expert evidence is tendered by a person who is qualified to speak authoritatively by reason of special training, skill, study, experience, observation, practice or familiarity with the subject-matter under consideration.

Role of experts in North America

6–13 Rule 702 of the United States federal rules of evidence addresses the concept of testimony by experts. Rule 702 allows expert testimony whenever it will "assist" the trier of fact. The former rule was much more restrictive. It required that the expert testimony be "necessary" for the trier of fact to understand the issues in trial. This liberalisation of the rule allowing expert testimony has dramatically increased the use of experts. Rule 702 states:

> "*Testimony of experts*. If scientific, technical or other specialised knowledge will assist the trier of fact to understand the evidence or to determine a fact in issue, a witness qualified as an expert by knowledge, skill, experience, training or education may testify thereto in the form of an opinion or otherwise."

---

[6] [1971] 2 All E.R. 407 at 414.
[7] [1991] 1 I.R. 455 at 460–461.

6–14 In *R. v. Mohan*,[8] the Canadian Supreme Court elaborated on this requirement. There, Sopinka J. stated that expert evidence must be both necessary in assisting the trier of fact and relevant. Under the heading of "necessity in assisting the trier of fact" the court made it clear that expert evidence was not to be admitted if the subject of the testimony concerned an issue which was within the common knowledge of the trier of fact. In particular, Sopinka J. quoted approvingly from *R. v. Turner*[9] in which Lawton L.J. concluded:

> "An expert's opinion is admissible to furnish the court with scientific information which is likely to be outside the experience and knowledge of a judge or jury. If on the proven facts a judge or jury can form their own conclusions without help, then the opinion of an expert is unnecessary."[10]

Similarly:

> "... the evidence must be necessary to enable the trier of fact to appreciate the matters in issue due to their technical nature."[11]

Qualities of expert evidence

6–15 The courts in Ireland, and elsewhere have variously commented on the qualities required of expert evidence. The most important of these is that the evidence be unbiased and objective. In addition, relevance, reliability and cost-effectiveness of expert evidence are also important considerations. These are discussed below.

Unbiased, objective

6–16 Expert evidence should be objective and fair:

> "... the holy grail to which professional witnesses should aspire may be summarised in two words: objectivity and fairness."[12]

Some experts will be inclined to tailor their evidence to their client's requirements and pay insufficient attention to the need to be balanced and objective. This lack of objectivity, if not exposed by the opposing expert's challenge to what they are saying, will usually be perceived readily by the trial judge in any event.

6–17 In *National Justice Companion Naviera S.A. v. Prudential Assurance Co. Ltd* Cresswell J. stated:

> "An expert witness should provide independent assistance to the Court by way

---

[8] [1994] 2 S.C.R. 9 at 23.
[9] [1975] Q.B. 834 at 841.
[10] [1994] 2 S.C.R. 9 at 24.
[11] *ibid.* at 23.
[12] Barr, J. "Expert evidence – A few personal observations and the implications of recent statutory developments" (1999) *Bar Review* 185.

of objective unbiased opinion in relation to matters within his expertise. ... An expert witness in the High Court should never assume the role of an advocate."[13]

In *Whitehouse v. Jordan* Lord Wilberforce said:

> "Expert evidence presented to the court should be, and should be seen to be, the independent product of the expert uninfluenced as to form or content by the exigencies of litigation."[14]

6–18   The role of the expert is to educate and inform decision-makers so that the truth is revealed. It can be argued that the process of obtaining written reports, and examination and cross-examination of opposing experts is more likely to reveal the truth than evidence from a single "neutral" expert. In either case, it is essential that expert evidence is given with independence and impartiality.

Forensic accountants frequently use third-party endorsements for statements in their reports to point to the objectivity of the report. Such third-party data is available, for example, from the Central Statistics Office[15] or from industry associations. Other sources might include newspapers. For example, the appointments pages would provide a useful source of salary ranges for a particular job.

6–19   It can be argued that bias is self-policing, since an overtly biased expert will soon lose credibility within the professional community and not be called by other parties in future cases. But such an argument may be fragile since the reality is that parties may "shop around" for an expert who will best support their case. Furthermore, the expert's evidence may risk being coloured by a pre-existing or continuing relationship which may exist between the expert and the lawyer or the litigant.

6–20   Nevertheless, an expert is probably shortening his useful life significantly if he compromises his independence. On the subject of expert evidence and the two characteristics – objectivity and fairness – that constitute the "holy grail to which professional witnesses should aspire", Barr J. states:

> "Any competent judge will readily recognise these virtues, or the lack of them, and where they are found the testimony of such a witness is like [*sic*] to be greatly enhanced in the mind of the judge. The converse is, of course, also true."[16]

---

[13] [1993] 2 Lloyd's Rep. 68 at 81.
[14] [1981] 1 W.L.R. 246 at 256 .
[15] Central Statistics Office, Ireland *Statistical Abstract* (Government Publications, Dublin, Annual).
[16] Barr, J. "Expert evidence – A few personal observations and the implications of recent statutory developments" (1999) *Bar Review* 185.

He goes on to say:

> "Surprisingly, experts whose testimony is found to be unreliable or unhelpful are often persons of undoubted ability in their particular fields. They are rarely dishonest or deliberately unfair, but they seem to lack a true understanding of their function, i.e., to assist the court in arriving at the truth by providing a skilled expert assessment, which is objective and fair, of matters requiring a specialised appreciation of the particular problem at issue."[17]

6–21 Forensic accountants should provide independent and objective opinions to help the judge or jury to understand the evidence or to determine a fact that is in dispute. Issues to consider in assessing whether the forensic accountant is likely be compromised are:

– Has the expert been repeatedly retained by the same firm of solicitors or continuously been retained by the plaintiff/defendant?

– Is the expert working full-time on litigation matters?

– Are the expert's opinions based on sound, independent investigation or are they tilted towards the client's views?

– Did the expert obtain the information only from the client or were outside sources used?

– How soon after being engaged did the expert form opinions?

– What are the fees being charged by the expert?

– Are any fees contingent on the outcome of the case?

Relevant

6–22 The significance of relevance can be seen from the following extract from *R. v. Wilson*[18]:

> "... lack of relevance can be used to exclude evidence not because it has absolutely no bearing upon the likelihood or unlikelihood of a fact in issue but because the connection is considered to be too remote. Once it is regarded as a matter of degree, competing policy considerations can be taken into account. These include the desirability of shortening trials, avoiding emotive distractions of marginal significance, protecting the reputations of those not represented before the Courts and respecting the feelings of a deceased's family. None of these matters would be determinative if the evidence in question were of significant probative value."

---

[17]Barr, J. "Expert evidence – A few personal observations and the implications of recent statutory developments" (1999) *Bar Review* 185.
[18][1991] 2 N.Z.L.R. 707 at 711 *per* Fisher, J.

6–23   In *R. v. Mohan*[19] the court ruled that, prima facie, expert evidence was "relevant" if it was "… so related to a fact in issue that it tends to establish it." A more academic definition of relevance is provided by Stephen[20] who says that any two facts are relevant to each other if they are:

> "… so related to each other that according to the common course of events one either taken by itself or in connection with other facts proves or renders probable the past, present, or future existence or non-existence of the other."

Reliable

6–24   Expert evidence should be able to withstand close scrutiny to determine whether it is "reliable":

> "[E]xpert evidence which advances a novel scientific theory or technique is subjected to special scrutiny to determine whether it meets a basic threshold of reliability and whether it is essential in the sense that the trier of fact will be unable to come to a satisfactory conclusion without the assistance of the expert."[21]

Cost-effective

6–25   In the same case, the issue of cost-effectiveness of expert evidence was dealt with as follows:

> "Evidence that is otherwise logically relevant may be excluded … if it involves an inordinate amount of time which is not commensurate with its value or if it is misleading in the sense that its effect on the trier of fact, particularly a jury, is out of proportion to its reliability."[22]

6–26   In addition to independence and impartiality, the following further benefits to be gained from appointing an independent expert are:

– specialist technical knowledge within a given discipline;

– highly developed investigative and analytical skills;

– a broad perspective of the issues affecting disputes;

– experience in handling disputes and contentious problems;

– an understanding of the related legal processes;

– ability to present findings and opinions with clarity and authority;

– experience in presenting evidence in a court or other tribunal.

---

[19] [1994] 2 S.C.R. 9 at 20.
[20] Stephen, J.F., *A Digest of the Law of Evidence* (12th ed., Macmillan & Co. Limited, London, 1946), p. 4.
[21] *R. v. Mohan* [1994] 2 S.C.R. 9 at 25.
[22] *ibid.* at 21.

Civil liability of expert witnesses

6–27 Expert witnesses have historically had significant protection from civil liability through a litigation privilege granted to witnesses. In *M.P. v. A.P.*[23] Laffoy J. dealt with this immunity and went on to consider whether witness immunity arising from evidence given in a civil case in court extended to providing protection to the witness from professional disciplinary proceedings:

> "There is ample authority to support the proposition advanced by counsel for the applicant that a witness is protected from civil proceedings, not merely an action for defamation, in respect of his evidence in the witness box and statements made in preparing evidence (*Watson v. M'Ewan, Watson v. Jones* [1905] A.C. 480; *Marrinan v. Vibart* [1963] 1 Q.B. 528). While no authority has been cited which supports the proposition that an expert witness is immune from disciplinary proceedings or investigation by a voluntary professional organisation to which he is affiliated in respect of evidence he has given or statements he has made with a view to their contents being adduced in evidence, having regard to the public policy considerations which underlie the immunity from civil proceedings – that witnesses should give their evidence fearlessly and that a multiplicity of actions in which the value or truth of their evidence would be tried over again should be avoided – in my view, such a witness or potential witness must be immune from such disciplinary proceedings or investigation."[24]

6–28 The current trend in the United States is to exclude negligence of friendly expert witnesses from the litigation privilege. A significant recent case is *Mattco Forge Inc. v. Arthur Young & Co.*[25] In 1992, a California court of appeals decided that statutory litigation privilege that protects lawyers, judges, jurors, witnesses and other court personnel from liability arising from publications made during a judicial proceeding does not apply to claims of negligence of the expert by the party who hired the expert. The court ruled that an expert could not assert a statutory litigation privilege against his own client. The court reasoned that the litigation privilege applies to adverse witnesses, but not to friendly witnesses. Thus, as a result of the above decision, a forensic accountant who provides expert witness services in the United States may be sued by his client, and the applicable professional standards of the accounting profession may determine the appropriate standards of care. The case suggests that expert witnesses may be subject to civil liability. Careful attention to matters such as engagement letter preparation (see paras **6–64** *et seq.*) may be helpful in avoiding civil liability, controlling legal expense and reducing professional liability insurance costs.

---

[23] [1996] 1 I.R. 144.
[24] *ibid.* at 155–156.
[25] 60 Cal. Rptr. 2d 780 (1997) (CA).

Interaction between expert witnesses[26]

6–29   Experts can sometimes obtain the assistance of others whose knowledge does not duplicate, but complements, their own, in order to provide additional support for their expert opinion. However, co-ordinating the efforts of two or more experts can be problematic.

In preparing cases for litigation, lawyers will frequently rely on assistance of expert witnesses in several areas. It is important that experts work together to produce a cohesive and defensible analysis. The approach of using a team of experts, with one leading expert providing the methodological structure and performing that part of the analysis within his expertise, may be optimal. In cases where more than one expert witness is used, only one of the team of experts might testify, indicating in so doing that he is relying on the work of other experts.

It is acceptable for one expert to rely on the opinions of other experts when putting forward expert opinion. In *T. v. P.*, Lardner J. quoted from *Phipson on Evidence*[27] as follows:

> "An expert may give his opinion upon facts which are either admitted or proved by himself or other witnesses in his hearing at the trial or are matters of common knowledge as well as upon hypothesis [sic] based thereon."[28]

Examples of other experts with whom forensic accountants may work include economists, actuaries, auctioneers and valuers, vocational experts, etc. For example, in commercial litigation, the skills of economists may be essential in providing an analysis of the economic environment, performing industry analysis or providing projections based on economic models. Consistency and correctness require a dialogue between lawyers, forensic accountants and any other experts in the case.

6–30   For example, in the process of arriving at a claim for future loss of earnings several experts from a variety of disciplines may be used. These might include:

– a doctor, to advise on the plaintiff's ability, from a physical or psychological viewpoint, to resume his pre-accident employment or to engage in alternative employment;

---

[26] For further discussion of this issue, see Evans, E.A., "Interaction between accountants and economists" in *Litigation Services Handbook. The Role of the Accountant as Expert* (2nd ed., Weil, R.L., Wagner, M.J. and Frank, P.B. (eds), John Wiley & Sons, Inc., New York, 1995), Chap. 3.

[27] Buzzard, J.H., May, R. and Howard, M.N., *Phipson on Evidence* (13th ed., Sweet & Maxwell, London, 1982), p. 561.

[28] Unreported, High Court, July 30, 1989.

- a vocational rehabilitation consultant to advise on the alternative employment opportunities available to the injured plaintiff, the likelihood and timing of recovery sufficient to enable the plaintiff to take up such opportunities, and the income differential between the plaintiff's pre-accident earnings and the alternatives;
- an accountant, to assist in the calculation of lost profits and/or the quantification of the taxation implications of the change in the individual's employment status;
- an actuary, to gather together the advice of the other experts and to translate it into quantification of the present value of future lost earnings, making appropriate assumptions regarding the difference between investment returns and wage inflation, and about life expectancy.

Cases benefit from increased interaction between doctors, vocational experts, actuaries and forensic accountants. Such professional dialogue promotes more realistic and accurate assessments of matters such as (in a personal injury case) earnings expected had the accident not occurred, and expected earnings after the accident. Interdisciplinary consultation should be the trend in evaluating financial losses of plaintiffs.

Obviously, the considerations to be taken into account by each expert are closely linked and, in certain cases, interdependent. This means that the experts must not act independently but rather should take account of the assumptions underlying each other's advices in arriving at their own conclusions. In particular, all of the other experts will be influenced by the medical advice regarding the plaintiff's likely recovery and ability to work in the future, and the actuary will need to take account of the work of all other experts in arriving at the basic lost earnings before adjustment for the time value of money, for life expectancy and the time period over which losses will be incurred.

Accountants as expert witnesses

6–31	As explained in Chapter 1 (paras 1–44 *et seq.*), accountants may appear in court in one of two situations: when giving evidence of fact and when acting as expert witnesses in giving opinion evidence. This important distinction between the two situations is explained below. The remainder of the chapter is concerned with accounting evidence in the latter situation.

Specialist as witness of fact

6–32	Forensic accountants can act as witnesses of fact where they can state as a fact, from their own knowledge and examination of a particular item, that a certain event or sequence of events occurred in a particular instance. Generally speaking, an ordinary witness providing testimony in court can only give evidence of fact, *e.g.* what they saw, heard, tasted, smelt, touched – facts collected by one of the five senses. Accountants acting as witnesses of fact should provide evidence in court based on what happened, not on supposition. They are not permitted to speculate or to give an opinion as to the circumstances leading up to an event which they have witnessed.

Specialist as expert witness who gives evidence of opinion

6–33 Forensic accountants also act as expert witnesses and in that role they can, from their own knowledge and experience, give an opinion as to why a certain event or sequence of events did or did not occur. The trial judge will decide when a witness is allowed to give expert opinion. Expert witnesses may be called upon to state their opinion on a matter within their specialised knowledge and skill where the court itself cannot form an opinion from the facts. Forensic accountants often present highly technical material to courts in terminology they can understand.

6–34 Experts are retained by litigants to provide an opinion that enables judges hearing cases to understand evidence before them and to make better decisions about disputed facts. As a guide, subject to the procedure and rules of the relevant court's jurisdiction, experts are expected to:

– undertake and observe an overriding duty to assist the court on matters relevant to the expert's area of expertise;

– be objective and fair (since the expert is not an advocate for a party);

– investigate and prepare a written report on a specific issue in dispute between the litigants;

– disclose the contents of their reports, if requested;

– if requested, attend a pre-hearing meeting of experts to try to reach a consensus of opinion and to then produce a document identifying issues on which they agree or differ. If they differ, they should specify their reasons for being unable to reach agreement;

– give their opinion in evidence, including their views on opinions offered by other expert witnesses;

– be cross-examined or re-examined on their opinion;

– act in accordance with their professional body's code of professional conduct, *e.g.* the Institute of Chartered Accountants in Ireland Guide to Professional Ethics (in particular statement 4 "conflicts of interest")[29].

---

[29] Institute of Chartered Accountants in Ireland, *Handbook - Section C Ethical Guide for Members (Institute of Chartered Accountants in Ireland*, Dublin, looseleaf).

Where expert accountants can assist

Discovery assistance

6–35 Litigation often depends on documents to prove or disprove issues at trial. An important pre-trial procedure is discovery of documents, including financial records. Forensic accountants can assist and advise in finding, understanding and explaining information from such documentation. The knowledge of financial documents can assist the lawyers in formulating requests for discovery. The issue of discovery is considered in more detail in Chapter 22.

Document management

6–36 Forensic accountants can assist in organising and summarising large volumes of data. In addition, they can provide expert advice on management systems, including computer systems.

Understanding the other side's case

6–37 Forensic accountants can assist the lawyers during a trial in framing questions to be asked in cross-examination. Aspects to consider are the opposing expert's report and its strength and weaknesses, information about the opposing side's forensic accountant and assistance in interpreting the opposing expert's responses in cross-examination.

Proof of financial facts

6–38 Experts can help develop proof of financial facts. These can be used in court to explain issues or transactions. In addition, they may be the basis for facts or assumptions included in the expert accountant's opinion.

Computation of damages

6–39 Forensic accountants often advise in the computation of damages such as actual losses incurred, expected future losses, business valuations, etc. Calculation of damages is dealt with in Part IV (Chapters 15–19).

Professional standards in a litigation environment

6–40 In providing expert assistance, experts are expected to observe professional standards in the conduct of their work. Some of these standards have been discussed already – experts should be fair, unbiased and objective, and should present evidence that is relevant, reliable and cost-effective.

Codes of professional conduct

6–41   A number of expert witness organisations have codes of practice governing the conduct of their members. By way of example, the code of the British Academy of Experts, founded in 1987, is reproduced in Table 6.2.

Table 6.2: Code of practice for members of the Academy of Experts

1. Experts shall not do anything in the course of practising as an Expert, in any manner which compromises or impairs or is likely to compromise or impair any of the following:
   (a) the Expert's independence or integrity;
   (b) a person's freedom to instruct any Expert of his or her choice;
   (c) the Expert's duty to act in the best interests of the client;
   (d) the good repute of the Expert or the Experts generally;
   (e) the Expert's proper standard of work;
   (f) the Expert's duty to the Court or Tribunal.
2. An Expert who is retained or employed in any action, suit or other contentious proceeding shall not enter into any arrangement to receive a contingency fee in respect of that proceeding.
3. An Expert should not accept instructions in any matter where there is an actual or potential conflict of interest. Notwithstanding this rule if full disclosure is made in writing the Expert may in appropriate cases accept instruction when the client specifically acknowledges the disclosure.
4. An Expert shall for the protection of his client maintain with a reputable insurer proper insurances for an adequate indemnity.
5. Experts shall not publicise their practices in any manner which may reasonably be regarded as being in bad taste. Publicity must not be inaccurate or misleading in any way.
6. Fellows and Full Members may use the Academy's plaque on their stationery. Corporate Practising Members and other firms where all principals are either Fellows or Full Members may also use the Academy's plaque on their notepaper.

Source: Academy of Experts website: www.academy-experts.org

6–42   Interesting guidance on the ethical requirements applicable to experts is given by the National Association of Forensic Economics in the United States and is reproduced in Table 6.3.

Duties and responsibilities of experts

Expert evidence

6–43   As already explained in para. **6–03**, in court proceedings an expert's opinion will, in general, be admissible unless the subject-matter does not require specialist knowledge.[30] Expert evidence, however, is not conclusive. The Supreme Court held in *Aro Road and Land Vehicles Ltd v. Insurance*

---

[30]Kelleher, D., "Expert evidence in Ireland" *Irish Law Times* (February, 1996) pp. 42-45.

Table 6.3: Ethics statement of the National Association of Forensic Economics (NAFE)

Statement of ethical principles

As a practicing forensic economist and a member of the National Association of Forensic Economics, I pledge to provide fair and accurate economic analysis associated with any litigation in which I am involved, to strive to improve the science of forensic economics, and to protect the integrity of the profession through adherence to the following tenets of ethical behavior:

Employment

While it is the right of the forensic economist to accept, at his* discretion, employment relating to any case or proceeding for which his expertise qualifies him, he should decline involvement in any litigation where he is asked to take or support a predetermined position or where he has reservations about the ethical standards to which he is being asked to adhere.

Honesty, Candor and Fairness

The forensic economist shall be accurate, equitable and fair in his analysis and shall refrain from placing before either the hiring or opposing attorney or the court, any information, through commission or omission, that he knows to be false. He shall exert due diligence and, at all times, attempt to use competent judgment to avoid the entrance of false or fictitious information.

Neutrality

The forensic economist shall attempt to operate, at all times, from a position of neutrality with respect to his calculations and analysis. Whether he is engaged by the plaintiff or the defense, his approach, methodology and conclusions should, in the end, be essentially the same.

Knowledge

The forensic economist shall attempt, at all times, to maintain a current knowledge base of his discipline and shall provide his employing attorney with the full benefit of this knowledge regardless of how it may affect the outcome of the case.

Responsibility

The forensic economist shall, at all times, strive to not only present the analysis of the case within the boundaries of honesty and fairness, but also within those of his profession. To this end, he must assume the responsibility of holding his colleagues in the profession accountable to the ethical standards promulgated herein.

* The use of "his", "he", or "him" is for convenience only and is meant to be gender neutral.

NAFE encourages all of its members to be clear about sources of information and assumptions leading to all opinions they express in a litigative arena.

Source: National Association of Forensic Economics, www.nafe.net/communication/ethics.htm

---

Corporation of Ireland[31] that the judge was the "sole and final arbiter". In relation to expert evidence on behalf of the defendant insurance company, the

---

[31] [1986] I.R. 403.

court stated that in matters of "professional competence, a profession is not permitted to be the final arbiter of standards of competence ... the insurance profession is not to be permitted to dictate a binding definition of what is reasonable."[32] Nonetheless, as pointed out in paras **6–03** *et seq.*, judges pay careful heed to the opinions of professional witnesses.

There have been similar findings in relation to accounting evidence. In *Murnaghan Brothers Ltd. v. O'Maoldomhnaigh*[33] Murphy J. referred with approval to the following passage from the judgment in the case of *Odeon Associated Theatres Ltd v. Jones*:

> "In order to ascertain what are the correct principles [of the prevailing system of commercial accountancy], [the court] has recourse to the evidence of accountants. That evidence is conclusive on the practice of accountants in the sense of principles on which accountants act in practice. That is a question of pure fact, but the court itself has to make a final decision as to whether that practice corresponds to the correct principles of commercial accountancy."[34]

Denning M.R. concurred with this view (in another case) in relation to accounting evidence – see para. **11–66**.

6–44   In the case *National Justice Compania Naviera SA v. Prudential Assurance Company Ltd ("The Ikarian Reefer")*,[35] Cresswell J. identified the following duties and responsibilities of experts acting in civil cases:

(1) The expert is to disclose those facts or assumptions upon which his opinion is based, together with any material facts which could detract from the concluded opinion.[36]

(2) The expert is to make clear when an issue or question falls outside his expertise

(3) The expert should indicate that his opinion is provisional if it is considered that insufficient data was available when the facts were being researched.[37]

(4) If an expert is unable to assert that his report contained the truth, the whole truth and nothing but the truth, then that qualification should be stated on the report.[38]

---

[32] [1986] I.R. 403 at 412.

[33] [1991] 1 I.R. 455 of 461.

[34] [1971] 2 All E.R. 407 at 414.

[35] [1993] 2 Lloyd's Rep. 68.

[36] See *Flanagan v. University College Dublin* [1988] I.R. 724 where omission of a paragraph from the defence expert's report to the plaintiff was one of the grounds for a successful application by the plaintiff for an order quashing the decision by UCD's disciplinary committee to send down the plaintiff on the grounds of alleged plagerism.

[37] See *Re J.,* [1990] F.C.R. 193, *per* Cazalet J.

[38] See *Derby & Co Ltd and other v. Wheldon and others (No. 9)* [1991] 2 All E.R. 901 *per* Staughton L.J.

(5) If, following an exchange of reports (see paras **23–26** *et seq.* for a discussion of the procedures governing exchange of expert reports), the expert changes his opinion on a material matter, then this change of opinion should be communicated to the other party to the dispute without delay.

(6) All documentation that is referred to in the expert's report should be provided to the other party at the time experts exchange reports (see para. **23–32**).

Conflict of interest and expert accountants

6–45   Ethical considerations impose on experts an obligation to disclose to their instructing solicitors in advance of each assignment any personal or financial circumstances which might influence work for the client in any way not stated or implied in the instructions. Any actual or potential conflict of interest should be reported to the solicitor as soon as it is raised or becomes apparent and, if necessary, the assignment should be declined or terminated. Particularly important are:

– any directorship or controlling interest in any business in competition with the client;

– any financial or other interest in goods or services (including software) under dispute;

– any personal relationship with any individual involved in the matter;

– existence of any other client of the expert with competing interests.

Professional regulations

6–46   Although many situations are quite clear as to whether the expert has a conflict of interest, defining exactly what is and is not a conflict of interest may not always be easy. The Institute of Chartered Accountants in Ireland has some useful literature on conflicts of interest. On the threat to objectivity caused by contingency fees, the Institute states:

> "Fees should not be charged on a percentage, contingency or similar basis in respect of audit work, reporting assignments and similar non-audit roles incorporating professional opinions including expert witness assignments. Even for the other work such methods of charging may be perceived as a threat to objectivity and should therefore only be adopted after careful consideration."[39]

The general position of the Institute is that, where the interests of two or more clients conflict, it may be possible to manage the situation rather than disengage

---

[39] Institute of Chartered Accountants in Ireland, *Handbook - Section C Ethical Guide for Members* (Institute of Chartered Accountants in Ireland, Dublin, looseleaf, statement 10, para. 4.0.).

from one of the clients. However, if this is not possible, a speedy disengagement should take place. The relevant extract from the ethical guide is:

> "A self-interest threat will arise or be seen to arise where the interests of two or more clients are in conflict.
>
> There is, however, nothing improper in a firm having two clients whose interests are in conflict with each other.
>
> In such a case the activities of the firm should be so managed as to avoid the work of the firm on behalf of one client adversely affecting that on behalf of another.
>
> Where a firm believes that the situation may be managed, sufficient . . . disclosure should be made to the clients or potential clients concerned together with details of any proposed safeguards to preserve confidentiality and manage conflict.
>
> Safeguards should include:
> (a) the use of different partners and teams of staff for different engagements, each having separate internal reporting lines;
> (b) standing instructions and all other steps necessary to prevent the transfer of confidential information between different teams and sections within the firm;
> (c) regular review of the situation by a senior partner or compliance partner not personally involved with either client;
> (d) advising all the relevant clients that, in the particular circumstances, they may wish to seek alternative independent advice; and
> (e) obtaining informed consent to act from all the clients concerned.
>
> Where the acceptance or continuance of an engagement would, even with safeguards, prejudice the interests of any of the clients involved, the engagement should not be accepted or continued, or one of the assignments should be discontinued.
>
> Where adequate disclosure . . . is not possible by reason of constraints of confidentiality the firm should disengage from the relevant assignment/s.
>
> In such circumstances disengagement should take place as speedily as possible."[40]

6–47 The American Institute of Certified Public Accountants Consulting Services Special Report 93-2 includes a decision tree to assist practitioners in reviewing potential issues relevant to evaluating a conflict of interest in a litigation service engagement. As there is no equivalent guidance for forensic accountants in Ireland, this decision tree applying in the United States is shown below in Figure 6.1.

---

[40] Institute of Chartered Accountants in Ireland, *Handbook - Section C Ethical Guide for Members* (Institute of Chartered Accountants in Ireland, Dublin, looseleaf), Statement 4, paras 4.0–4.7.

6–48   Consideration of conflicts of interests in the context of engagement letters is dealt with further on in para. **6–78**.

Case law

6–49   Judicial attitude to conflicts of interest can be traced back to the mid-nineteenth century, when Cranworth L.C. said in *Aberdeen Railway Company v. Blaikie Bros*:

> "It is a rule of universal application, that no one, having such duties to discharge, shall be allowed to enter into engagements in which he has, or can have, a personal interest conflicting, or which may possibly conflict, with the interests of those whom he is bound to protect."[41]

It is important to note that there need not be an actual conflict of interest in order to present a problem – the perception, in the eyes of the "reasonable objective person" (see below, para. **6–51**), of a conflict is normally sufficient to give rise to difficulties.

6–50   The most obvious area of conflict is where a firm finds itself advising more than one of the parties to a transaction or a dispute. The courts have taken several opportunities to express their disapproval of such behaviour, even where the family solicitor finds himself, almost accidentally, advising several family members simultaneously (see, for example, *Carroll & Carroll v. Carroll*[42]). Indeed, the courts in England in recent years have placed an onus on banks to ensure that spouses obtain separate legal advice in certain circumstances (see, for example, *Barclays Bank plc v. O'Brien*[43] and *National Westminster Bank plc v. Morgan*[44]). It is clear that the law disapproves of any apparent or real conflict of interest where one professional is advising more than one party.

6–51   Conflicts of interest can also arise when an individual or firm, having advised one party to a dispute or transaction, subsequently wishes to advise another party to the same dispute or transaction in relation to the same matter or different matters. Such a situation can arise, as in the Canadian case of *Martin v. Gray*,[45] where a former employee of a firm advising one party joins the firm advising another. In that case, the Canadian Supreme Court applied a two-stage test: did the solicitor actually receive relevant confidential information as part of the solicitor-client relationship from the first party; and, if so, would a

---

[41] (1854) 1 Macq. 461.
[42] [1999] 4 I.R. 241 – see the judgment of Barron J. at p. 266.
[43] [1993] Q.B. 109; [1992] 3 W.L.R. 593; [1992] 4 All E.R. 983 (CA); [1994] 1 A.C. 180 (HL).
[44] [1985] A.C. 686; [1985] 2 W.L.R. 588; [1985] 1 All E.R. 821.
[45] [1991] 1 W.W.R. 705; *sub nom. MacDonald Estate v. Martin* [1990] 3 S.C.R. 1235.

Figure 6.1: Conflict of interest decision tree

LITIGATION CONTACT	INITIAL DECISION POINT	INVESTIGATION OF CONFLICT	PERMITTED DISCLOSURE	FURTHER DECISION ANALYSIS

LITIGATION CONTACT

The CPA is contacted by the attorney or plaintiff/defendant regarding possible litigation engagement.

INITIAL DECISION POINT

Is the plaintiff or defendant an existing or prior client? — Yes / No

Does the CPA possess confidential information pertaining to the litigation matter (whether client or nonclient)? — Yes / No

Is the attorney or law firm a client of the CPA or involved in current or prior litigation matters that could be deemed a conflict? — Yes / No

Has the CPA testified or published an opinion on similar or related matters in conflict? — Yes / No

Is there a business consideration/relationship that may create a conflict? — Yes / No

The CPA may accept the engagement provided rule 102 of Code of Professional Conduct is satisfied.

INVESTIGATION OF CONFLICT

Determine the nature of work (e.g., attest, consulting, tax). If attest services or other services are being performed, determine whether confidential information pertaining to the litigation matter is possessed by the CPA, or if the CPA performed services in an earlier period related to litigation but the plaintiff or defendant is not currently a client. (1)

Determine the nature and sensitivity of information and whether such knowledge could impeach the CPA, or may have to be discovered in violation of the client's right to confidentiality.

Determine if confidential information or special insight is possessed by the CPA as to the attorney's strategy, style, approach, and so forth.

Determine if prior testimony or published opinion would potentially impact case or credibility of the CPA.

Determine if engagement acceptance would jeopardize other aspects of the practitioner's business, client perception, and so forth (e.g., industry loyalty and concentration).

PERMITTED DISCLOSURE

Disclose nonconfidential nature of work to the attorney and discuss the potential for conflict of interest or business relationship. (2)

To the extent possible, disclose to the attorney nonconfidential relationship or information to evaluate engagement acceptance and potential conflicts.

Disclose nonconfidential information to the attorney/client to assess situation.

Disclose such testimony and published opinions to the attorney/client to assess risk to case.

Discuss the nature of business issues and perceptions with attorneys, if appropriate, for full disclosure.

FURTHER DECISION ANALYSIS

Is the CPA willing to jeopardize the client or business relationship and accept the engagement if agreeable to the attorney? (3) — Yes / No

Are the CPA and attorney/client willing to pursue engagement acceptance? — Yes / No

Are the CPA and attorney/client willing to pursue engagement acceptance? — Yes / No

Are the CPA and attorney/client willing to pursue engagement acceptance? — Yes / No

Are the CPA and attorney/client willing to pursue engagement acceptance? — Yes / No

The CPA may not or has elected not to accept the litigation engagement.

(1) The expert testimony is that of the CPA and not the member's firm. The CPA firm's prior association with a company would generally not create any attribution of the firm's knowledge to the testifying CPA, so long as the CPA has no direct or indirect knowledge. However, such prior or current association should be disclosed to the attorney provided no sensitive information is shared.

(2) Although a CPA's firm may have a current or prior business relationship with a plaintiff/defendant through providing attest or other services, such relationships would not necessarily create a conflict of interest (provided confidential information is not possessed by the testifying CPA). However, there is likely a business or client relationship that would create a business conflict requiring the CPA to decline the engagement.

(3) Should a CPA decide to pursue litigation opposite an attest client (e.g., fraudulent conveyance litigation involving a bank), the litigation probably should not be material to the financial statements of the attest client.

"reasonable objective person" perceive a risk that the information would be used to prejudice that party?

This appears a sensible approach. It allows the court to exercise its discretion in the second leg of the test in assessing whether any confidential information would be passed between the former employee and the solicitors engaged by the other party, or conversely whether effective "Chinese walls" are in place to prevent this. Recent Australian case law also follows this general approach.[46]

6–52   The recent landmark decision of the House of Lords in *Prince Jefri Bolkiah v. KPMG*[47] has, however, broken new ground in the area of conflicts of interest and Chinese walls. The facts of the case and the detail of its progress through the courts are complex. In summary, KPMG had previously been engaged by the plaintiff, a brother of the Sultan of Brunei, to undertake a very extensive financial investigation. This resulted in KPMG becoming very familiar with a large amount of confidential information relating to the plaintiff's assets and the manner of their ownership. The firm was then asked by the Brunei government to assist in an investigation of the financial affairs of an organisation that, under the plaintiff's chairmanship, managed the government's general reserve fund. KPMG recognised that the interests of this investigation might conflict with the plaintiff's interests. However, the firm concluded that the assignment could be accepted because the plaintiff was no longer a client and adequate Chinese walls could be constructed to prevent confidential information concerning the plaintiff being disclosed to the investigation team. KPMG did not seek the plaintiff's approval for their involvement in the investigation.

6–53   In unanimously allowing the appeal from the Court of Appeal's discharge of an injunction restraining KPMG from acting in the investigation, the House of Lords set a very high standard for the duty to keep information confidential. Lord Millett said:

> "Whether founded on contract or equity, the duty to preserve confidentiality is unqualified. It is a duty to keep the information confidential, not merely to take all reasonable steps to do so. Moreover, it is not merely a duty not to communicate the information to a third party. It is a duty not to misuse it, that is to say, without the consent of the former client to make any use of it or to cause any use to be made of it by others otherwise than for his benefit. The former client cannot be protected completely from accidental or inadvertent disclosure. But he is entitled to prevent his former solicitor from exposing him to any avoidable risk; and this includes the increased risk of the use of the information to his prejudice arising from the acceptance of instructions to act for another client with an adverse interest in a matter to which the information is or may be relevant."[48]

---

[46] *Carindale Country Club Estate Pty Ltd v. Astill* [1993] 115 A.L.R. 112; 42 F.C.R. 307.
[47] [1999] 2 A.C. 222.
[48] *ibid.* at 235–236.

6–54   He went on to deal with the importance of a perception of confidentiality as well as its reality. He said:

> "It is of overriding importance for the proper administration of justice that a client should be able to have complete confidence that what he tells his lawyer will remain secret. This is a matter of perception as well as substance. ... the court should intervene unless it is satisfied that there is no risk of disclosure. It goes without saying that the risk must be a real one, and not merely fanciful or theoretical. But it need not be substantial."[49]

6–55   In relation to the effectiveness of Chinese walls, Lord Millett had this to say:

> "There is no rule of law that Chinese walls or other arrangements of a similar kind are insufficient to eliminate the risk. But the starting point must be that, unless special measures are taken, information moves within a firm. . . . The Chinese walls which feature in the present case, however, were established ad hoc and were erected within a single department. ... In my opinion an effective Chinese wall needs to be an established part of the organisational structure of the firm, not created ad hoc and dependent on the acceptance of evidence sworn for the purpose by members of staff engaged on the relevant work."[50]

6–56   This decision has far-reaching implications for the management of perceived and actual conflicts of interest in all professions. Despite the fact that it obviously does not bind Irish courts, professional firms in Ireland would be ill-advised to ignore its implications. In particular, a simple solution is the adoption of a blanket policy of refusing all new work in situations where information has previously been obtained from a client, and new work would involve "the acceptance of instructions to act for another client with an adverse interest in a matter to which the information is or may be relevant".[51]

6–57   However, it is likely, in a market as relatively small as Ireland, that such a blanket policy would be unworkable or would seriously hamper the profitable growth of a practice. In such situations, it would be necessary to establish as a formal part of the organisational structure of the firm, an effective system of Chinese walls that would eliminate any real risk of disclosure.

6–58   Of course, it is possible that this decision would not be followed in Ireland, or that its impact will be watered down in England in the future. However, in the current climate in Ireland it would be unwise to plan on the basis that any compromise in this area of professional standards or ethics would be received sympathetically.

---

[49] [1999] 2 A.C. 222 at 236–237.
[50] *ibid.* at 237, 239.
[51] *ibid.* at 236.

6–59 It is safe to assume that the law will generally perceive a conflict of interest to arise where a financial interest of any kind in a party to a dispute or transaction in which the firm is engaged is held by any partner in the firm or any member of staff engaged on the assignment. This is because such an interest will give rise to at least a perception of, if not actual, impairment of independence in advising a party to the dispute or transaction. An example of the Irish judicial attitude to such a situation arising in the accountancy profession is the following extract from the High Court judgment of Barron J. in *Allied Pharmaceutical Distributors Ltd v. Walsh*:

> "What had occurred was that Mr. Walsh had placed himself in a position where his interest and his duty were in conflict. His duty was to offer advice only so long as he was being remunerated as a partner in an accountancy firm. The interests of the client were paramount. He allowed himself to depart from this role by becoming a shareholder, a director and an executive. Having built up a position of trust within the company, he abused that trust. Not surprisingly the ethical code of his profession advised against members of that profession having share holdings and directorships with client companies. It advised also against making loans to or taking loans from clients. This advice was given to protect its members from the very conflict between interest and duty which enmeshed Mr. Walsh."[52]

Selecting expert accountants

6–60 Choosing an expert has always been a critical element in litigation case management. There are a number of forensic accountants operating in Ireland. An expert witness guide for Ireland is published annually which contains a list of forensic accountants.[53] The professional accounting bodies may have lists of members specialising in forensic accounting and litigation services (see useful addresses of such bodies in Appendix 6). The *Golden Pages* and newspaper advertisements are other means. A growing source of information is forensic accounting Internet sites (especially in North America), many of which contain a list of references from prior clients who can be contacted to gauge their level of satisfaction. In practice, person-to-person referrals are probably the most common means of selecting an expert accountant.

Selection criteria

6–61 If a decision is made to appoint an independent expert then it is essential that the right person is selected. A poor appointment could have a significant impact on the outcome of the case. The process of selecting a forensic accountant requires careful consideration of several criteria. The question must be asked

---

[52] [1991] 2 I.R. 8 at 16.
[53] *Expert Witness Directory*, Supplement to the *Irish Law Times* (Round Hall Sweet & Maxwell, Dublin, 1999).

whether the expert to be appointed is in fact an expert in the required subject.

In selecting a forensic accountant, some important criteria that should be considered are summarised in Table 6.4. The broad areas to consider are the education and qualifications (especially professional) of the expert, any subsequent training, relevant post-qualification experience, availability of resources to the expert and finally, as already emphasised, the independence of the expert.

Table 6.4: Criteria to consider when selecting an expert

Education	**Area of expertise**
• College attended	• Practice concentration – which areas
• Year of graduation	• Experience of a specific industry
• Degree conferred	• Activity in the industry today
• Post-graduate education	• Involvement in industry training
• Professional qualifications	• Up-to-date in trends and developments in the industry
	• Membership of any related trade organisations and bodies
Training	
• Where trained	**Publications**
• Additional training in which areas	• Articles in professional journals
• Expert witness training	• Academic articles
	• Books
Experience	**Resources**
• Years in practice	• Size of firm
• Prior business experience	• Availability to research issues
• Prior forensic experience	• Professional support for advice
• Previous court appearances	• Library and research facilities
• Previous reports written	
	Independence of expert
	• Previous relationships with plaintiff or defendant
	• Relationships with other persons involved in the litigation

6–62   There is no perfect firm size in the accounting industry and selection based on firm size will to some extent depend on the nature of the assignment. Some assignments might be appropriate for a very specialist sole practitioner working in a narrow field of expertise. International accounting firms, with offices around the world and a large staff, may be suitable for projects that cross international borders or that require a significant time and human resource input.

6–63   Cost is a relevant consideration in selecting a forensic accountant. Fees and related costs should be discussed in advance. Forensic accountants will explain the procedures and billing of fees during the selection process. These matters are discussed more fully in paras **6–80** *et seq.* and **6–89** *et. seq.*

Engaging expert accountants

6–64 The process of engaging an expert accountant requires careful consideration so that both the client and the expert accountant have a common understanding of the terms, objectives and expectations of the engagement in advance.

Timing of engagement

6–65 If forensic accountants are hired early enough in a case, they can make a significant difference to its outcome. The expert can become more involved in the case and can contribute more extensively to the manner in which it is conducted. Lawyers often devote considerable efforts in dealing with the liability side of the case, with less attention spent on considering the damages aspects. Even when damages issues are considered, without the advice of an expert, the lawyers may fail to obtain the necessary documents to support the damages calculations.

Lawyers may be tempted not to hire an expert early in the case in order to keep costs down. In the long run, this may be counterproductive if the damages side of the case suffers as a result. The importance of bringing an expert into a case early is eloquently illustrated (in a United States context) as follows:

> "A typical disaster scenario. The damage expert gets hired two days before the deadline for expert disclosure. A pile of documents and depositions arrive at the expert's office a week later. When the expert calls the attorney to ask for key data that was not in the pile, the litigator says 'It looks like we never asked for that in the document request or at depositions. Oh, by the way, they want to take your deposition next week.' The expert must do damages analyses that makes assumptions about key facts and then alter those assumptions depending on trial testimony. This often results in poorer analysis and increases expert's costs by a factor of 2 or 3."[54]

Terms of engagement

6–66 Forensic accountants should receive clear instructions from solicitors, preferably in writing. Experts have more to lose by not agreeing terms in advance, but such agreement should also be in the interests of the instructing solicitor and the client to ensure the contractual relationship with the expert is clear.

Accepting the assignment

6–67 The agreed terms of the engagement should include the nature and extent of the services to be provided, responsibilities of the parties to the engagement,

---

[54] Plummer, J. and McGowin, G., "Ten most frequent errors in litigating business damages" *Association of Business Trial Lawyers* (1995) Vol. 5, No. 1.

and other business terms including the method of determining fees for the services, and the dates the fees are to be paid. The expert is advised to only accept an assignment where he has the:

- knowledge, experience, qualifications and professional training appropriate for the assignment;

- resources to complete the assignment within the agreed timescales and to the standard required.

Experts should not accept instructions if they are not able to prepare a report within reasonable time, having regard to the timetable of the case. A time frame for production of the report should be agreed in advance.

6–68 Forensic accountants should make clear to solicitors, in advance, what can and cannot be expected on completion of the assignment. In particular, as soon as possible after being instructed, they should identify any aspects of the engagement with which they are unfamiliar, or which they are not competent to handle, or on which they require further information or guidance.

6–69 If any part of the assignment is to be undertaken by persons other than the individual instructed, then:

- prior agreement from the instructing solicitors must be obtained; and

- the names, qualifications and experience of such persons should be provided.

When a firm has been instructed, the names of the members of the team to work on the assignment should be provided, if requested.

Engagement letters

6–70 Experts are not required to use engagement letters when providing services. However, using engagement letters provides a convenient means of outlining the engagement, of documenting the parties' understanding of the engagement, and of providing for a method of resolving future disputes should they arise. Engagement letters can help prevent misunderstandings about the services to be provided, responsibilities of the parties, and the terms of engagement. In addition, they may help to make clear that the expert's opinions, work output, and the facts known or relied upon by the expert are protected from discovery by the opposing party until the lawyer decides that he expects to call the expert to testify.

6–71 The content of engagement letters will vary depending on the court system, circumstances, professionals and clients involved.[55] Issues to be covered

---

[55] Gafford, W.W., "Engagement letters for experts in valuing damages in personal injuries and wrongful deaths" (1996) *Litigation Economics Digest*, Vol. 2, No. 1, pp. 31–53.

might include some of the considerations discussed below. A sample forensic accounting engagement letter, from the Institute of Chartered Accountants in Australia, is shown in Appendix 2. The discussion below is cross-referenced to that Appendix.

Identification of parties to the engagement

6–72   Direct engagement of the expert by the solicitor (or the solicitor and the client) may be the first step that the solicitor can take to protect expert information from discovery by the opposing party until the solicitor decides to call the expert to give evidence. This is particularly the case if the initial briefing of the expert regarding the issues at hand effectively amounts to an advisory consultation at a time when legal proceedings are yet to be initiated.

6–73   If the client hires the expert without the solicitor being a party to the engagement, expert information may not be as easy to protect from discovery by the opposing party. The reason for this is the rule on legal professional privilege (this rule is discussed at paras **22–06**, **22–30**, **22–50**, **22–52**, **23–36** and at paras **23–52** *et seq.*). This rule protects from disclosure any communications between parties and lawyers made in contemplation or furtherance of litigation, or for the purpose of obtaining legal advice. However, the inclusion of the client (along with the solicitor) as a party to the engagement may have the advantage of helping to prevent misunderstandings and disputes regarding the selection of the expert, the expert's services and the expert's fees.

Identification of the case and parties to the litigation

6–74   Identifying the case and the parties to the litigation helps document that the expert was retained in anticipation or contemplation of litigation or for preparation for trial. This is another key element in protecting expert information from discovery by the opposing party.

Effective date of engagement

6–75   The effective date of engagement should be specified in the letter.

Initial services to be completed and expected timing

6–76   The engagement letter should describe any initial services to be provided and, if possible, the expected completion times (See Appendix 2, paras 1 and 2).

Availability of information

6–77   Details of the documentation and information to be supplied to the expert by the solicitor and/or client should be identified. A standard paragraph appearing, for example, in an audit representation letter[56] might also be included in the expert's letter of engagement to the effect that to the best of the lawyers' and client's belief the information or documents provided are true, complete and correct. The effect on the engagement of the client/solicitor not supplying the information in a timely manner may also be described (*e.g.* see Appendix 2, para. 2.1). The effect of the availability of information on forensic accounting assignments is further considered in paras **23–60** *et seq.*

Conflicts of interest

6–78   Engagement letters should include an affirmative statement that the expert is not aware of any conflicts of interest. If the expert has conflicts of interest that have been waived by the appropriate parties, the statement should be changed to describe the conflicts of interest (see Appendix 2, para. 3).

The lawyers and the expert should consider the effect on the strength and credibility of the expert when conflicts of interest exist. If the lawyers restrict the engagement to an advisory role that is protected from discovery by the opposing party, and with no requirement for expert evidence to be given in court, this may not be a concern. For further discussion of conflicts of interest in the specific context of forensic accounting assignments see paras **6–45** *et seq.*

Discovery of information, opinions and work output of experts

6–79   The expert witness's work product is usually not available through discovery to the opposing side unless, in personal injury cases, it falls within the items covered by S.I. No. 391 of 1998 (see paras **23–27** *et seq.*). This is because it normally attracts the privilege associated with the contemplation or furtherance of litigation, referred to above (See also Appendix 2, para. 4).

In general, discovery is allowed for any unprivileged documents containing material relevant to the case. Discovery may even be allowed for information that is not admissible at trial if the information appears reasonably calculated to lead to the discovery of admissible evidence. Discovery is considered in more detail in Chapter 22.

Amount and timing of fee payments

6–80   The agreed terms of engagement should indicate arrangements concerning fees – whether an hourly rate, a fixed fee or amount recoverable on taxation (see paras **6–89** *et seq.*; paras **2–47** *et seq.* and paras **2–67** *et seq.*). The hourly

---

[56] Auditing Practices Board, *Statement of Auditing Standard 440:Management Representations* (Auditing Practices Board, London, 1995), p. 7 provides a sample management representation letter. This letter includes the following representation by the directors to the auditors: "We acknowledge as directors our responsibility under the Companies Act for preparing financial statements which give a true and fair view and for making accurate representations to you."

rate charge is generally the most advantageous for the expert. The terms should be agreed at the outset (see Appendix 2, para. 5) and should cover all matters including:

– expert's method of charging;

– basis of expert's charges (rate of hourly charge, amount of retainer, etc.) including any different rates for attendance at court;

– identities of staff working on the assignment;

– rates chargeable for each member of staff;

– rates for support staff;

– charging rates during travel time and waiting;

– whether cancellation fees are chargeable;

– whether disbursements are to be charged by the expert or absorbed in his fee;

– frequency of billing;

– payment arrangements.

6–81 An example of a basic fee schedule and retainer agreement is shown in Table 6.5. It provides a guideline on various aspects to be agreed concerning fees.

6–82 As already referred to in para. **2–50** responsibility for payment of the accountant's fees usually rests with the instructing solicitor, and not the client, unless the parties come to a different arrangement.

Difficulties may arise where the amount of work required turns out to exceed initial estimates. Where this is the case, the instructing solicitor should be informed as soon as practicable (see Appendix 2, para. 5.8). The solicitor then has the option of not having the extra work done.

6–83 Clear communication in the engagement letter about the expert's fees is important in preventing misunderstandings. By way of example, the model terms of engagement applying to experts generally of the Expert Witness Institute (EWI) are reproduced in Table 6.6 on page 183. These model terms deal with 10 issues, seven of which relate to the expert's fees. Expert accountants may wish to adapt this using more professional forms of expression.

Limitations that may require other experts

6–84 The development of, reliance on and ability to support certain assumptions in relation to valuations of damages in personal injuries, wrongful death and in

Table 6.5: Example fee schedule and retainer agreement*

Fee schedule
- Retainer (Non-Refundable) $1,000
- Research, Document Review and Valuation Work $175 Per Hour
- Deposition Fee $350 Per Hour
- Trial, Arbitration or Mediation Fee $350 Per Hour
- Plus any reimbursable expenses incurred throughout the course of the case.
- Retainer is due prior to work commencing on file. Billing is done on an hourly basis. Payment is due upon receipt of invoice.
- Make checks payable to: [insert expert's, or expert's company's, name]
- Travel time and expenses incurred for depositions will be billed to the retaining attorney per [insert file invoice reference number]

Retainer agreement
- [name expert] requires a minimum $1,000 non-refundable and non-transferable retainer before work commences;
- [name expert] bills for its services on an hourly basis. Rates are $175 per hour for document review, research, valuation, travel and on-call time; $350 per hour for deposition, arbitration and trial testimony;
- [name expert] is retained by the attorney; not the attorney's client;
- [name expert] will look solely to the retaining attorney for the payment of professional services rendered;
- [name expert] will bill as work is completed or on a monthly basis for work-in-progress;
- Payment is due upon receipt of invoice;
- [name expert] reserves the right to be unavailable for deposition, arbitration or trial testimony if the balance on previous billing has not been paid;
- [name expert] requires receipt of pertinent information in a timely manner in order to provide a quality product;
- Valuations are prioritized on the basis of court-imposed deadlines;

[name expert] is being retained to quantify the following economic damages (check appropriately):
[ ] Loss of Earnings/Earning Capacity, [ ] Loss of Support, [ ] Loss of Household Services, [ ] Cost of Future Medical Care, [ ] Loss of Profits, [ ] Financial Condition (i.e., Net Worth/Net Profit).

_____   _____
Print Case Name   Case Number

I agree to the above terms and wish to retain [name expert] in the above-referenced case.

_____   _____
Signature (required)   Date

_____
Print Name

_____
Print Firm

*Source: Zengler Economics, http://home.earthlink.net/~zengler (adapted).

business valuations may require additional experts, over and above those with accounting qualifications (see paras. **6–29** *et seq.*). Other experts that the case might require include engineering, actuarial experts, and experts in medical, psychiatric, psychological and vocational rehabilitation fields. Determining the appropriate evidence to present in the case is a legal matter for which the lawyers are responsible.

Update of written report prior to giving oral evidence

6–85 Considerable time may elapse between preparation of the expert report and the case coming to trial. A paragraph in the engagement letter might provide for the expert's report to be updated prior to giving evidence, or at the lawyers' request.

Limitation on responsibility

6–86 Many factors may affect the resolution or outcome of a case. The expert is hired to provide objective opinions and work product (*i.e.* without taking account of whether the plaintiff or defendant will benefit). The lawyers are not required to accept or use the opinions or work product of the expert.

An expert's responsibilities must be limited to his opinions and work product. Those responsibilities must not extend to all factors that affect the ultimate resolution or outcome of the case. Such a limitation of responsibility in an engagement letter will help clarify that the expert is not a biased "hired gun". (See Appendix 2, para. 6).

Resolving disputes

6–87 Methods of resolving disputes involving experts include out-of-court negotiations, settlement by the parties, litigation and non-litigation alternatives. Arbitration is a common alternative to litigation. The sample engagement letter might include a contractual agreement for any disputes to be decided by arbitration. It might also specify the arbitration rules to be followed. In addition, responsibility for payment of the costs of arbitration might also be set out.

Terminating engagements

6–88 Engagement letters might include provisions for terminating, *e.g.* as a result of:

- fees not being paid;

- change in lawyers and/or parties involved in the case; or

- information becoming available that makes the expert's services inappropriate. Such a situation might arise where there is disagreement between the lawyers and the expert concerning the contents of the expert opinion. The expert has a duty to provide an objective opinion.

Table 6.6: Model terms of engagement

Terms of Engagement currently in use by experts differ significantly in length, complexity and style having regard to the different fields of experts. The model terms have been prepared with the aim of covering all possible points giving the opportunity for Members to amend or omit particular paragraphs at their discretion, if not appearing relevant to their needs or their appointment. Members may wish to request instructing solicitors or, if applicable, direct clients to abide by the EWI Model Terms of Engagement and then highlight and summarise the most important of these in letters of engagement as follows.

My current terms of engagement are:
1. My current hourly fee rate is £   for all time spent on the case.
2. My daily rate for attending Court Hearings is £   , which includes time for travelling and waiting. I expect payment even if I do not give oral evidence.
3. All reasonable expenses will be charged at cost. Any necessary mileage will be charged at   per mile. Copies of receipts will be provided should they be requested.
4. My accounts are subject to VAT at current rates.
5. In legally aided cases (where my fees constitute a disbursement) I expect you to make a prompt claim to the Legal Aid Board, and to advise me of any expected delay in settlement. In all other cases I expect payment within [30]* days of invoice date from you my client irrespective of whether your client has paid you.
6. Should accounts not be settled within the agreed period, at my discretion, I have the right to charge interest on unpaid accounts at the rate of 2% per month, or part of a month, until full settlement is received.
7. I am not prepared to have my fees reduced as a result of a process of taxation and look to you, my client, to fund any shortfall against taxed costs should this arise, at any time.
8. I will use my experience, care and skill in fulfilling your instructions to the best of my ability. Please remember that I am an independent witness.
9. Please let me have your full instructions, together with any further relevant information you may have, and confirm your agreement in writing to the above terms.
10. Please keep me closely informed on the progress of the case. I can probably help in the period before trial, if indeed the matter proceeds to that stage.

*The terms of credit may be varied to reflect members' practice.

Source: Expert Witness Institute website: www.ewi.org.uk

Accountants' fees

The issue of accountants' fees has already been touched upon in para. **2–47** *et seq.*, **2–67** *et seq.* and para. **6–80** *et seq.*

Contingent fees and expert testimony

6–89   If the client's ability to pay the fee were dependent on the outcome of the case, this would amount to a situation akin to a contingency fee arrangement. This in turn might lead to accusations of lack of objectivity on the part of the expert and may undermine the credibility of the expert. As an expert should be, and should be seen to be, independent and objective,[57] the employment of an expert witness on a contingency fee basis would generally be inappropriate. The code of practice for experts shown above in Table 6.2 (item 2) prohibits the payment of fees on a contingency, *i.e.* no win/no fee basis. Under the professional ethics[58] of the professional accountancy bodies, accountants acting as expert witnesses are not allowed to accept instructions on a contingency fee basis.

6–90   If the instructing solicitor is being paid on a contingency fee basis, it is important to make it clear that such a basis for charging is neither appropriate nor allowable for someone acting as an expert witness.

Records

6–91   Daily records of time spent and expenses incurred by each member of staff should be kept. The daily record should also cover the activities and nature of the work being done on each day. Daily contemporaneous attendance notes/ time records should, if completed properly, ensure compliance with the requirements associated with the taxation of costs (see paras **6–92** *et seq.*), where necessary.

Order for costs, taxation of costs and legal aid

6–92   Orders for costs, taxation of costs and legal aid in relation to forensic accounting fees are all dealt with in Chapter 2 paras. **2–47** *et seq.* Courts give parties to litigation wide discretion in deciding whether to call expert witnesses. If costs are awarded to one party, they will normally not be able to object to the costs of an expert witness, unless they can show that it was unnecessary to call that witness – even where the expert is not actually heard by the court.[59]

Getting paid

6–93   Table 6.7 provides some useful guidelines for the forensic accountant to ensure he gets fully and promptly paid.

---

[57] See *Whitehouse v. Jordan* [1981] 1 W.L.R. 246 at 256, *per* Lord Wilberforce: "Expert evidence presented to the court should be, and should be seen to be, the independent product of the expert uninfluenced as to form or content by the exigencies of litigation".

[58] Paragraph 4.0 of statement 10 of the Institute of Chartered Accountants in Ireland *Ethical Guide for Members* states: "Fees should not be charged on a percentage, contingent or similar basis in respect of audit work, reporting assignments, due diligence and similar non-audit roles incorporating professional opinions including expert witness assignments."

[59] *Duan v. Freshford Creamery Ltd* (1942) I.L.T.R. 220; *Smyth v. Tunney*, [1993] 1 I.R. 451.

Table 6.7: Key rules to being promptly paid

1. Ensure the instructing solicitor and not the client is responsible for the fee.
2. Provide sufficient details of work to be done and cost thereof.
3. Get agreement of costs and payment terms before commencing the assignment.
4. If agreed costs will be exceeded, advise instructing solicitor as soon as possible and renegotiate agreed fees.
5. Provide invoices regularly throughout the assignment rather than one large invoice at the end.
6. Send regular reminders in respect of outstanding fees.

Source: Adapted from "Getting paid", *Forensic Group News*, May 1999, p. 5.

Future trends

6–94   The current system in Ireland where both parties to litigation call their own witnesses has been criticised as expensive. Several recommendations for reform have been made, some in relation to expert witnesses, including[60]:

– use of single, court-appointed "neutral" experts;

– courts should have the power to compel expert witnesses to meet in advance and agree issues;

– reports of expert witnesses should be taken as their evidence in chief.

Civil procedure rules in the United Kingdom

6–95   In the United Kingdom, Lord Woolf's final report on access to justice was scathing of the litigation-support industry. This led to new Civil Procedure Rules which have redefined the role of the expert witness. These new rules came into force in England and Wales on April 26, 1999. The rules, described by the Lord Chancellor as "the most fundamental change to the civil justice system in England and Wales in over 100 years," were designed better to achieve the "overriding objective of enabling the court to deal with cases justly."[61]   In this context, Part 1 of the Rules states to dealing with a case justly includes, so far as is practicable:

a.   ensuring that the parties are on an equal footing;

b.   saving expense;

c.   dealing with the case in ways which are proportionate:
     (i)   to the amount of money involved;

---

[60] See Kelleher, D., "Expert evidence in Ireland" *Irish Law Times* (February 1996) pp. 42-45.
[61] Lord Chancellor's foreword to the Civil Procedure Rules. Available at www.open.gov.uk/lcd/civil/procrules_fin/cforefr.htm.

    (ii) to the importance of the case;

    (iii) to the complexity of the issues; and

    (iv) to the financial position of each party;

d.   ensuring that it is dealt with expeditiously and fairly; and

e.   allotting to it an appropriate share of the court's resources, while taking into account the need to allot resources to other cases.

6–96   The new Civil Procedure Rules have introduced a much more active role for the court itself in the process by which expert evidence is assembled and adduced. The new rules reinforce the long-established principle that the expert is not simply engaged to appear in court and give one side of the story. His primary duty is to the court. The expert must ensure that he is suitably qualified, as his credibility is highly important. He is there to put his opinion forward – he is not an advocate. It is clear that the new rules intended to sweep away any inefficiencies or poor practices that had become part of the existing system over the decades.

6–97   Part 35 of the Rules deals with "Experts and Assessors". Among the rules contained in Part 35 is rule 35.1, which states: "Expert evidence shall be restricted to that which is reasonably required to resolve the proceedings" and rule 35.3 (cited earlier in para. **6–07**) which indicates that the duty of an expert is to the court and that this overrides any instructions from his client.

6–98   The fact that the expert's first duty is to the court is further emphasised by the court's right under rule 35.7. When two or more parties wish to submit expert evidence on a particular issue, the court can direct that the evidence on that issue is to be given by one expert only.

6–99   As well as the power referred to above to direct that a single joint expert gives expert evidence, the court also has the power under rule 35.4 to restrict expert evidence. This is done:

– by prohibiting expert evidence without the permission of the court;

– in the application for permission to call an expert or put his report in evidence, by requiring identification of the field in which expert evidence is required and, where practicable, the proposed expert to be used; and

– by limiting the amount of the expert's fees and expenses that may be recovered from the other side.

6–100   The Rules also require that expert evidence be given in a written report unless the courts direct otherwise, and rule 35.10 specifies the contents of the report as follows:

"(1) An expert's report must comply with the requirements set out in the relevant practice direction.

(2) At the end of the expert's report there must be a statement that –
   (a) the expert understands his duty to the court; and
   (b) he has complied with that duty.

(3) The expert's report must state the substance of all material instructions, whether written or oral, on the basis of which the report was written.

(4) The instructions referred to in paragraph (3) shall not be privileged against disclosure but the court will not, in relation to those instructions –
   (c) order disclosure of any specific document; or
   (d) permit any questioning in court, other than by the party who instructed the expert,
   unless it is satisfied that there are reasonable grounds to consider the statement of instructions given under paragraph (3) to be inaccurate or incomplete."

Concluding comment

6–101   Ireland will have the benefit over the next few years of observing the effects on the litigation process of the radical new rules now in force in the United Kingdom. It will be helpful to assess the successes and failures of the new rules before deciding whether, and if so what, changes should be made in Ireland.

Having said that, there is little doubt that the use of forensic accountants as experts in Ireland in general is at best inefficient. Many cases that would benefit from forensic accounting input do not get it, or get it too late. In other cases, several experts appear where fewer, or even one, would suffice in all the circumstances. New rules would help, but the onus is ultimately on parties to litigation, and on their lawyers, to make adequate and appropriate use of the skills available to them.

PERSONAL

PERSONAL

7–01   This chapter examines civil litigation affecting individuals. It has a number of separate sections each of which deals with the legal aspects of various situations affecting individuals, including personal injuries, fatal accidents, employment disputes, matrimonial disputes and bankruptcy.

Most of these sections have three subsections: legal context, role of forensic accountants and accounting calculations. The legal context is briefly introduced to give forensic accounting readers an understanding of the legal background for such cases. This discussion is not exhaustive and is intended primarily to provide forensic accountants with an introduction only to the legal context. Where appropriate, readers are referred to other texts which deal with the legal issues in more detail.

Following this discussion is a consideration of the role of forensic accountants in each legal context.

The final subsection in each section briefly summarises the accounting calculations arising. These accounting calculations in civil litigation affecting individuals are covered in greater depth in Part IV of the book. The legal principles applying generally in the calculation of damages are considered in Chapter 15, while the accounting calculations relating to damages for personal injuries and fatal accidents are discussed in detail in Chapter 16. Valuation of businesses may also be required to calculate damages (for example, where the owner of a business is injured, or in matrimonial disputes) and this is covered in Chapter 18. As personal injury damages may relate to various time periods, the time value of money is relevant to many calculations of damages and is considered in Chapter 19.

General background

7–02   A considerable number of cases entail calculating loss of earnings or other economic damages suffered by individuals and forensic accountants can assist lawyers in such cases. They must ensure that a proper basis exists for the calculations, that assumptions on which the calculations are based are reasonable and are adequately highlighted, and that the issue of mitigation of damages is considered. Forensic accountants can assist in a number of ways. They can:

- help identify key issues;

- advise in pre-trial strategies;

- provide initial assessment of the financial aspects of the claim;

- prepare an expert report for use in (i) negotiation and (ii) litigation;

- advise solicitors and barristers during and throughout the trial;

- act as expert witnesses.

Personal injury – loss of earnings cases

7–03   Most successful personal injuries cases culminate in a monetary award or settlement in compensation for the injuries suffered. Forensic accountants will be involved in cases where there are significant special damages (*i.e.* damages substantially capable of exact calculation). They would not normally advise in the assessment of general damages for pain and suffering.[1] The most significant special damages in personal injury cases often arise in connection with lost earnings. Forensic accountants are commonly brought into such cases to assist in the calculation of lost earnings which are defined broadly as the present value of the lost opportunity to earn suffered by the plaintiff as a result of the actions of the defendant.

Legal context

7–04   This section briefly outlines the legal background to civil cases involving personal injury. The classic Irish legal text in this area is White.[2]

Litigation arising out of personal injuries can originate in a wide variety of circumstances. Table 7.1 summarises the common law and statutory basis for claims for personal injuries in some of the more frequent situations that arise in practice. As can be readily appreciated from the table, which is illustrative and not comprehensive, actionable personal injuries can arise from a wide array of sources. However, the exercise of valuing the consequence of the injuries has common characteristics across all of these situations.

Negligence

7–05   In order to succeed in an action alleging negligence, a plaintiff must establish, on the balance of probabilities, that:

- the defendant owed a duty of care to the plaintiff;

---

[1] Special and general damages are discussed further in paras **7–18** *et seq.* and in Chap. 15.

[2] White, J.P.M., *Irish Law of Damages for Personal Injury and Death* (Butterworths, Dublin, 1989).

Table 7.1 Common law and statutory basis for claims for personal injuries

Source of personal injury	Common law basis for claim	Statutory basis for claim
• Road traffic accidents	Negligence Breach of duty	Road Traffic Act 1961 Road Traffic (Traffic and Parking) Regulations 1997
• Accidents at work	Negligence Employer's liability	Safety in Industry Acts Safety, Health and Welfare at Work Act 1989, and Regulations thereunder
• Trip and fall accidents, accidents on other property	Negligence Misfeasance	Occupiers Liability Act 1995
• Assault	Trespass to the person	
• Defective products	Negligence	Liability for Defective Products Act 1991 Sale of Goods Acts
• Medical treatment	Medical negligence	Occupiers Liability Act 1995
• Fire	Negligence	Accidental Fires Act 1943
• Animals	Negligence Strict liability	Animals Act 1985 Control of Dogs Act 1986

– the defendant breached that duty of care; and

– the plaintiff suffered foreseeable damage as a result of that breach.

7–06 The tort of negligence is a breach of the legal duty to take care. The duty of care is designed to protect a person from damage to his person, his property and to his economic interests. It is in this latter respect that many forensic accountants give evidence in court cases.

7–07 In medical malpractice, it is often argued that the defendant cannot be found to be negligent if he has followed the customary or common practice of his profession. However, the courts have held that following custom is not conclusive evidence that the defendant has met the necessary standard of care. Even if the defendant had followed the accepted practice of the profession, he could not escape liability if such practice did not meet the requirement of care to the patient. Customary practice may not conform to the standard of care required for a reasonably prudent professional. In such a case, it is not a good defence that the defendant acted in accordance with the customary practice. In the words of Walsh J. in the Supreme Court in *O'Donovan v. Cork County Council*, often quoted in later judgments on the issue of professional negligence:

> "If there is a common practice which has inherent defects, which ought to be obvious to any person giving the matter due consideration, the fact that it is shown to have been widely and generally adopted over a period of time does not

make the practice any the less negligent. Neglect of duty does not cease by repetition to be neglect of duty."[3]

Breach of duty

7–08   A plaintiff has a cause of action under this heading where he can establish on the balance of probabilities that the defendant had a duty and breached it, resulting in damage to the plaintiff. Establishing a duty can be difficult unless the duty in question is enshrined in a statute. For this reason, breaches of duty pleaded by plaintiffs tend to be breaches of statutory duty. For example, when a defendant breaks a red light causing a collision with, and injury to, a plaintiff, the defendant, as well as being guilty of negligence, has breached a duty under the Road Traffic (Traffic and Parking) Regulations 1997.[4]

Employer's liability

7–09   Employers owe a general duty of care to have regard to the safety, health and welfare of their employees. This general duty is supported by specific duties enshrined in legislation, including the Safety in Industry Acts and the Safety, Health and Welfare at Work Act 1989. Although the latter Act specifically provides that civil claims may not be pursued on foot of a breach of some of its provisions, this prohibition does not extend to the myriad of detailed regulations made by statutory instrument under the Act.

Trespass to the person

7–10   The tort of trespass to the person describes the civil law equivalent of criminal assault. It grounds a claim for damages arising from injury caused by personal assault.

Strict liability

7–11   Strict liability refers to wrongs that give rise to liability even where there has been no negligence, recklessness or malicious intent. Strict liability tends to arise in respect of wrongs (*e.g.* parking offences, liability for defective products) where the penalty is not too large.

Role of forensic accountants

7–12   Forensic accountants are often asked to advise on calculations in respect of loss of earnings arising from personal injuries sustained by individuals. Forensic accountants acting for plaintiffs can provide expert accounting reports avoiding unrealistic speculation, but which properly reflect the amount of the

---

[3] [1967] I.R. 173 at 193.
[4] S.I. No. 182 of 1997.

Table 7.2: Examples of personal injury cases in which forensic accountants have advised

---

ACTING FOR PLAINTIFFS

Negligence
- Calculating loss of earnings for a self-employed individual arising from a road accident
- Providing evidence for a self-employed doctor injured in a car accident concerning lost earnings resulting from closure of medical practice
- Preparing forensic accounting report calculating loss of earnings and associated tax implications where the lost income would have been receivable in a foreign location.

Injuries to employees
- Providing expert evidence on earnings and pensions, including dependency calculations, for actual and undeclared income, with comparable earnings, for a wide variety of careers, including PAYE and self-employed persons
- Preparing loss of earnings and pension loss incorporating probable career promotions, but also alternative careers
- Preparing forensic accounting reports calculating loss of income and benefits from the different career paths open to a person who might, but for the injury, have worked in both Ireland and abroad.

Other cases
- Calculating the value of a lost business opportunity where the plaintiff was denied access to a business opportunity as a result of a personal injury
- Calculating the diminution of value suffered by a business as a result of the personal injury of a key manager/owner.

Challenging expert testimony of the other side
- Calculating loss of earnings, examining the opposing expert's calculations, and providing expert witness evidence
- Reviewing the economic loss calculation of the opposing expert and providing legal team with the strengths and weaknesses of the opposing expert's calculation thereby assisting counsel to settle the case.

ACTING FOR DEFENDANTS
- Acting on behalf of the defendant insurance company, rebutting the plaintiff's expert accounting evidence demonstrating that (i) the projected earnings in the plaintiff's damages analysis were unreasonable and unreliable and (ii) that the plaintiff failed to mitigate his damages
- Giving evidence on behalf of a defendant insurance company in a personal injury matter, showing that the plaintiff's claimed damages were significantly overstated due to inappropriate assumptions regarding working life expectancy, mitigating income and potential lost earnings
- Acting on behalf of defendant insurance company in relation to an individual who claimed that his personal injuries in a car accident were so bad that the business was forced into liquidation. Testifying that the plaintiff's business had been failing for several years and demonstrating that the plaintiff's claim for damages was grossly inflated
- Preparing an alternative analysis using appropriate assumptions regarding past and future lost earnings and fringe benefits.

claim. When acting for defendants, forensic accountants can significantly reduce the quantum of claims, by focusing on an analysis of historical data or the assumptions used. Forensic accountants can assist insurance companies and the insured's lawyers in quantifying the loss of income caused by a personal injury arising from a motor vehicle accident, medical malpractice, a recreational accident or occupiers' liability. Examples of personal injury claims in which forensic accountants have acted are shown above in Table 7.2.

7–13 Loss and damage to individuals can arise as a result of professional negligence on the part of members of a variety of professions. A forensic accountant may be asked to advise:

– in relation to cases involving members of his own profession, in which he may be asked to express a view on whether the professional was negligent; and

– in relation to other professionals, where he may be asked to assist in quantifying the loss suffered by the client.

Accountants' liability for professional negligence is dealt with in Chapter 12. Examples of assignments involving professional negligence and quantification of losses as a result of professional negligence (by accountants, solicitors or other professionals), including losses of business opportunities, are shown in Table 7.3.

Table 7.3: Examples of negligence cases in which forensic accountants have advised

Accounting professional negligence
• Acting for shareholders, regulators or for a professional accounting body investigating auditing and accounting negligence, *e.g.* quality of audit work
• Considering the role of reporting accountants in relation to directors' profit forecasts in prospectuses concerning acquisitions or management buy-outs
• Providing opinion on the failure of an accountant to make appropriate tax loss claims in time and to submit correct computations, leading to claims of negligence in tax and VAT advice
• Assessing the quality of work performed by reporting accountants under the Solicitors' Accounts Rules in solicitors' indemnity fund investigations

Other professional negligence
• Calculating quantum of damages in building disputes involving architects, surveyors and other situations of professional negligence
• Preparing schedules of special damages including calculations of loss of earnings and pension
• Calculating the economic loss associated with an individual who suffered a disability as a result of alleged medical malpractice and providing expert witness testimony

Case histories

7–14　Case history 7.1 shows how forensic accountants might be involved in a personal injury case, acting either for the plaintiff or the defendant. In this case, the forensic accountant acting for the defendant insurance company advised on financial matters in such a way as to bring about a significant reduction in the amount of the damages.

Case history 7.1: Loss of earnings as a result of a traffic accident

Incident
A security consultant was involved in a car accident caused by another driver. Some months later, the injured party served notice of a lawsuit claiming £300,000 for present and future income loss for his injuries and those of his wife.

Injury
According to the plaintiff, the accident caused him psychological problems that made it impossible to continue his business or seek alternative employment. He also claimed that his wife, who had earlier left her job as a secretary to join his business, had to stay home and take care of him.

Claim
The claim was for loss of future earnings of the injured party until age 65. There was also a claim for £25,000 a year for loss of his wife's salary. This was based on the premise that she could work as a secretary if she did not have to care for her husband.

Involvement of forensic accountant
The forensic accountant was retained by the solicitor for the driver's insurance company to assess the validity of the plaintiff's financial claim (the validity of his medical injuries was a separate issue).

Methodology

Plaintiff's forensic accountant
The plaintiff was aged 50 at the time of the accident. In his claim, which was for loss of future earnings until age 65, he declared that he had been taking in approximately £290 a week or £15,000 annually from his business. However, the plaintiff's forensic accountant calculated the plaintiff's income based on the average annual income of a similar business, which was £29,000.

Defendant's forensic accountant
The increase over actual earnings was not backed up by any documentation indicating that the plaintiff's business would eventually have achieved the industry average. Study of the plaintiff's accounts showed a business in decline. His only major customer accounted for almost 70 per cent of his business revenue prior to his accident. For the four months prior to the accident, the forensic accountant for the defendant calculated that the plaintiff and his wife had a combined monthly salary of £600, before deductions for loan payments. Based on that data, it was concluded that had the accident not occurred, the business would have soon folded.

　　The forensic accountant for the insurance company calculated the plaintiff's loss assuming that, had there been no accident, he and his wife could have generated revenue similar to that actually earned for the two years preceding the accident. As it was highly questionable that the wife needed to stay at home to care for her husband (this issue would be a matter for the medical experts involved with the case), the forensic accountant argued that the wife could mitigate the loss by resuming work as a secretary at £25,000.

According to the report prepared by the plaintiff's own forensic accountant, his maximum annual loss would be £29,000. Assuming this to be reasonable (in fact, it was doubtful that the plaintiff would have achieved his profession's average), and taking into account the wife's £25,000 salary, the forensic accountant for the defence assessed that the maximum financial loss that arose from the accident was approximately £4,000 per annum.

Outcome
Prior to the release of the defendant insurance company's forensic accountant's report, the plaintiff's legal counsel was unwilling to entertain a reasonable out-of-court settlement. Once the report was presented, the lawyers agreed to settle for £30,000 including costs, approximately 10 per cent of the amount originally claimed.

Source: Adapted from Johnson, P., "Forensic accounting – a legal support" *Commercial Law Practitioner* (September 1996) pp. 206-210.

7–15 Case history 7.2 describes a typical personal injury case. A forensic accountant might assist in such a case in preparing schedules of actual medical costs incurred up to the date of the trial and schedules to support the claim in relation to future medical costs thereafter.

Case history 7.2: Past and future medical costs

Incident
A woman hired a contractor to build a house for her. She walked out on the deck during a visit to the site and the deck collapsed, injuring her.

Injury
In addition to abrasions on her face and leg, and soft-tissue injuries to her head, neck and back, she developed a haematoma in her right leg. The fall also aggravated a pre-existing back condition, requiring surgery with some resulting impairment. In addition, the woman had daily headaches that interfered with her regular activities. Her medications caused hair loss and weight gain.

Claim
The woman sued the contractor who built the deck on temporary supports and claimed, *inter alia*, £194,619, *i.e.* £48,839 in past medical expenses and £145,780 in future medical costs. Settlement efforts ended with the woman asking for £750,000 and receiving an offer of £150,000. The case went to full trial.

Outcome
The contractor was found liable and ordered to pay £790,472 as follows: £135,272 for past and future medical expenses and £655,200 for pain and suffering. The subcontractor was held not liable.

Source: Adapted from Expert Search www.expertsearch.com/index.html

7–16 Case history 7.3 describes injuries involving economic losses in the form of both loss of earnings and extra expenses comprising future medical bills. The forensic accountant would have had an important role to play in the case in estimating these losses/extra costs.

Case history 7.3: Severe permanent brain damage

Incident

Straightforward knee surgery on a 29-year-old man went badly wrong when gas made its way into the man's abdominal cavity, entered his chest and displaced his heart and lungs, causing cardiac respiratory arrest.

Injury

The patient emerged from the ordeal with severe, permanent brain damage from lack of oxygen and remained hospitalised in a vegetative coma, leaving his wife to raise their three young children on her own. The wife sued on behalf of them both.

Involvement of forensic accountant

The forensic accountant advised on loss of earnings, past and future medical costs and provided a report backing up his estimate of loss suffered.

Outcome

All but one defendant settled before the trial.

Source: Adapted from Expert Search www.expertsearch.com/index.html

Accounting calculations

7–17 Accounting calculations in relation to personal injury claims are considered in more detail in Chapter 16.

Heads of damages

7–18 Generally there are two heads of damage recognised in law. The first does not concern financial losses and concentrates on loss and damage not readily quantifiable in financial terms such as pain and suffering, both physical and psychological. This type of non-pecuniary damage is usually referred to in Ireland as general damages. General damages for pain and suffering account for a substantial portion of court awards, but it is the least well defined and most variable component of awards (nor is there a well specified definition of what pain and suffering is, or how it should be measured). A variety of subjective methods are therefore applied to compensate plaintiffs for pain and suffering.

Judges have wide discretion and little guidance, other than precedent, in their decisions. Awards for pain and suffering consequently vary widely on a case-by-case basis and are generally viewed as subjective and somewhat unpredictable. The courts have established indicative upper limits on compensation for pain and suffering, but have also recognised that such limits are dynamic and must be open to change. Based on a variety of cases that have come before the Supreme Court in recent years, awards of general damages significantly in excess of £300,000, even for the most serious injuries, may not survive on appeal (*e.g.* see *Walsh v. Family Planning Services Ltd*;[5] *Dunne v.*

---

[5] [1992] 1 I.R. 496.

National Maternity Hospital[6]; and *Reddy v. Bates*[7]; *Sinnott v. Quinnsworth Ltd*[8]; and *Coppinger v. Waterford County Council*[9]).

7–19 The second head of damage concerns material and financial loss. This type of pecuniary or economic damage is referred to in Ireland as special damages. Forensic accountants are employed to assist in calculations in relation to special damages.

Calculating special damages

7–20 Estimates of damages suffered by plaintiffs, and damages calculations following personal injury include consideration of loss of earnings, pension rights and other elements of remuneration. To determine lost earnings, the forensic accountant has to gather and analyse financial information and then provide informed opinions based on the analysis of outcomes. The accountant must be careful to provide an independent opinion that can be defended. He must also ensure that he only deals within his sphere of competence, *e.g.* an assessment of alternative employment is ordinarily performed by a vocational assessor and not by an accountant. The accountant will assist in quantifying the losses once the remuneration associated with the likely future employment of the plaintiff is compared with his actual pre-accident remuneration from employment.

7–21 Forensic accountants will usually include assessments of financial damages in a formal report with supporting calculations and schedules. To assist in calculation of an award of damages, accountants may be asked to provide evidence as to the amount of loss suffered. This work may involve an analysis of factors giving rise to the loss, an estimation of the financial consequences arising from the negligence, and an estimation of the financial consequences if the alleged negligence had not arisen.

7–22 In some personal injury cases, the damage suffered by the plaintiff is so severe that the loss continues for many years into the future. The amounts arising from calculations of such losses can be sizeable and the importance of employing experienced forensic accountants cannot be overstated. In order that the plaintiff may be compensated now a lump sum must be calculated representing the present value of all future losses attributable to the injury. A number of elements are required in this calculation. The accounting calculations are based on:

– an estimate of loss of annual earnings/annual loss. This calculation may need to take into account pre-injury income, post-injury income, cost of living

---

[6] [1989] I.R. 91.
[7] [1983] I.R. 141.
[8] [1984] I.L.R.M. 523.
[9] [1998] 4 I.R. 220.

increases, social welfare benefits, other offsetting income and taxation. The plaintiff's business ownership interests may need to be reviewed to determine the nature and extent of income from those interests. Loss of income may have to be calculated where there are incomplete records and may involve a search for previously unreported income;

- pension loss;

- estimate of the period of damage;

- multiplier to be applied to the estimate of earnings/annual loss (usually provided by an actuary);

- alternative career scenarios, including a comparison of probable career promotions with alternative (post-injury) careers (usually provided by a vocational assessor);

- dependency claims where appropriate;

- schedules of other special damages, *e.g.* medical costs, life care, costs of adapting house for injured party, etc.

7–23   A causal relationship between the wrong committed and the loss suffered must be established. Only damages caused by the wrong can be recovered. The liability for loss suffered may be reduced as a result of actions or omissions by the plaintiff. For example, awards for damages may be reduced if contributory negligence by the plaintiff is found. Forensic accountants can assist the plaintiff in proving that the defendant's actions caused the damages or, alternatively, assist the defendant in refuting that the defendant's actions caused any or all of the loss or damage.

7–24   A fundamental principle governing the calculation of damages for negligence is that the claimant must be restored to the position in which he would have found himself had the negligence not occurred. Calculations quantifying losses arising from negligence are difficult because they must inevitably make assumptions as to events that might never have occurred.

Personal injury – fatal accidents

7–25   Although not dissimilar to personal injuries litigation, there are some differences in the legal context applying to fatal accidents and, in particular, to the calculations of damages arising from fatal accidents. One obvious difference is that the plaintiff in fatal accident cases is a dependant of the deceased and not the injured party. As for personal injury cases, forensic accountants assist with the calculation of special damages. However, the total losses resulting from the death must be reduced to take account of the proportion of the amounts lost that would have been spent on the deceased himself, had he survived.

Legal context

7–26   Under the Civil Liability Act 1961, as amended, only the surviving
dependants can make a claim for loss of dependence on income. The relevant
provisions of the Act are clear and explain concisely the limits in a claim for
fatal injuries. Section 48 establishes the entitlement to make a claim for fatal
injuries and identifies the appropriate claimants:

> " (1)   Where the death of a person is caused by the wrongful act of another such
>   as would have entitled the party injured, but for his death, to maintain an
>   action and recover damages in respect thereof, the person who would have
>   been so liable shall be liable to an action for damages for the benefit of the
>   dependants of the deceased.
>   (2)   Only one action for damages may be brought against the same person in
>   respect of the death.
>   (3)   The action may be brought by the personal representative of the deceased
>   or, if at the expiration of six months from the death there is no personal
>   representative or no action has been brought by the personal representative,
>   by all or any of the dependants.
>   (4)   The action, by whomsoever brought, shall be for the benefit of all the
>   dependants.
>   (5)   The plaintiff shall furnish the defendant with particulars of the person or
>   persons for whom and on whose behalf the action is brought and of the
>   nature of the claim in respect of which damages are sought to be recovered."

Section 49 goes on to deal with the damages available on foot of a successful
fatal injury claim:

> (1) (a)   The damages under section 48 shall be—
>   (i)   the total of such amounts (if any) as the judge shall consider
>   proportionate to the injury resulting from the death to each of the
>   dependants, respectively, for whom or on whose behalf the action
>   is brought, and
>   (ii) subject to paragraph (b) of this subsection, the total of such amounts
>   (if any) as the judge shall consider reasonable compensation for
>   mental distress resulting from the death to each of such dependants.
>   (b)   The total of any amounts awarded by virtue of subparagraph (ii) of
>   paragraph (a) of this subsection shall not exceed £20,000.
>   (c)   Each amount awarded by virtue of paragraph (a) of this subsection
>   shall be indicated separately in the award.
>   (2)   In addition, damages may be awarded in respect of funeral and other expenses
>   actually incurred by the deceased, the dependants or the personal
>   representative by reason of the wrongful act.
>   (3)   It shall be sufficient for a defendant, in paying money into court in the action,
>   to pay it in one sum as damages for all the dependants without apportioning
>   it between them.
>   (4)   The amount recovered in the action shall, after deducting the costs not
>   recovered from the defendant, be divided among the persons entitled in
>   such shares as may have been determined.

Section 50 contains important provisions making it clear that the existence of life insurance policies, pension and other benefits payable on the death of the deceased does not affect the assessment of damages for fatal injuries.

> 50.—In assessing damages under this Part account shall not taken of—
>> (a) any sum payable on the death of the deceased under any contract of insurance,
>> (b) any pension, gratuity or other like benefit payable under statute or otherwise in consequence of the death of the deceased."

7–27 In *Duncan v. Baddeley*[10] the Alberta Court of Appeal ruled that, unlike in Ireland, the estate of the deceased could file a claim even if the deceased had left no dependants. If the function of tort law is to compensate the victim, it is difficult to understand why an estate should be compensated. Alternatively, if the view is that the function of the law is to encourage individuals to take those precautions for which the benefit (reduced accident costs) exceeds the cost, the full cost of each and every accident should be borne by the responsible party. The full costs of a fatal accident are not only the costs borne by the survivors. They also include the cost of the death of the victim.

Role of forensic accountants

7–28 Table 7.4 provides examples of fatal accident cases in which forensic accountants have advised.

Table 7.4: Examples of fatal accident cases in which forensic accountants have advised

• Computing lost income and other damages in connection with wrongful death action • Preparing an expert forensic accounting report for a dependency claim in respect of potential equity and pension loss, unearned income and other benefits • Calculating the lost business value for a self-employed business owner.

Accounting calculations

7–29 Damages are measured solely by reference to the financial loss suffered by a dependant as a result of a person's death. Apart from any amount payable in compensation for mental distress, the loss must relate to a pecuniary loss arising out of a personal relationship between the deceased and the plaintiff, not a loss resulting from the deceased's death disrupting or ending a business or commercial relationship.[11] The loss is calculated by reference to the actual pecuniary loss incurred, together with any reasonable expectation of benefit had the life continued. This amount is reduced by any pecuniary benefit arising

---

[10][1997] 145 D.L.R. (4th) 708; [1994] 161 A.R. 357 (Q.B.).
[11]*Hall v. Great Northern Railway Co of Ireland* (1890) 26 L.R. Ir. 289 (Ex Div).

as a result of the death except for those benefits in respect of which a statutory provision prohibits the making of any deduction. Damages will not be awarded based on guesswork.[12] The courts require explicit evidence that as accurately as possible estimates the monetary loss sustained by each dependant as a result of the death. Damages are given purely by way of compensation and are not punitive in nature. The damages may be reduced if the deceased is found to have been guilty of contributory negligence.

Employment law – unfair and wrongful dismissals

7–30   This section introduces aspects of civil litigation arising from employment disputes. Such disputes arise in two very distinct circumstances: (i) unfair and wrongful dismissals; and (ii) discriminatory employment practices. These are considered separately, as discrimination actions do not necessarily result in wrongful dismissal. Only employment laws considered to be directly relevant to the work of forensic accountants are discussed here. Given the breadth of the subject-matter, this discussion is necessarily incomplete and is intended primarily to provide forensic accountants with an introduction only to the legal context of areas in which they are likely to become involved.[13]

As for personal injury and fatal accident cases, the involvement of forensic accountants will often be directed towards the calculation of compensatory damages. These calculations will use as a basis the historical earnings of the wronged employee, or, alternatively, industry averages or other appropriate benchmarks. Forensic accountants may also need to have a knowledge of personal taxation for the purposes of these calculations. Mitigation of the loss is important in all calculations of compensatory damages. This is particularly so in employment disputes and must be considered by forensic accountants.

Legal context

7–31   Claims for unfair dismissal are statutory, *i.e.* are brought under the provisions of the Unfair Dismissals Acts 1977–1993, and proceedings will

---

[12] *Hall v. Great Northern Railway Co of Ireland* (1890) 26 L.R. Ir. 289 (Ex Div); *Applebe v. West Cork Board of Health* [1929] 1 I.R. 107 (S.C.); *Horgan v. Buckley (No. 1)* [1938] I.R. 115 (S.C.); *Gallagher v. ESB* [1933] I.R. 558 (S.C.); *Byrne v. Houlihan* [1966] I.R. 274 (S.C.).

[13] For more information on employment law see Forde, M., *Employment Law* (2nd ed., Round Hall Sweet & Maxwell, Dublin, 2000); Madden, D. and Kerr, T., *Unfair Dismissal* (2nd ed., Irish Business and Employers Confederation, Dublin, 1996); Redmond, M., *Dismissal Law in Ireland* (Butterworths, Dublin, 1999); and Von Prondzynski, F., *Von Prondzynski and McCarthy on Employment Law in Ireland* (London, Sweet & Maxwell, 1989).

usually be commenced in the Employment Appeals Tribunal. Claims for wrongful dismissal are brought under common law and such proceedings are in the courts. Claims usually relate to dismissals arising in one of three ways: breach of contract; constructive dismissal; and unfair dismissal.

7–32 The term "dismissal" is defined in section 1 of the Unfair Dismissals Act 1977 as follows:

"'[D]ismissal', in relation to an employee, means—

(a) the termination by his employer of the employee's contract of employment with the employer, whether prior notice of the termination was or was not given to the employee,

(b) the termination by the employee of his contract of employment with his employer, whether prior notice of the termination was or was not given to the employer, in circumstances in which, because of the conduct of the employer, the employee was or would have been entitled, or it was or would have been reasonable for the employee, to terminate the contract of employment without giving prior notice of the termination to the employer, or

(c) the expiration of a contract of employment for a fixed term without its being renewed under the same contract or, in the case of a contract for a specified purpose (being a purpose of such a kind that the duration of the contract was limited but was, at the time of its making, incapable of precise ascertainment), the cesser of the purpose".

Breach of contract

7–33 The Terms of Employment (Information) Act 1994 entitles all employees to be advised in writing of the terms of their employment. The Act identifies express terms which must be specified, and these include the employee's job title and duties, the expected duration and termination of fixed-term contracts, the rate of pay and the notice period. Other express terms, not specified in the Act, are often included in employment contracts, such as the duration of the probation period (which cannot exceed one year), the employer's health and safety policy, details of trade union membership arrangements, the employer's grievance, disciplinary and dismissal procedure and the company's policy in relation to sexual harassment. Wrongful dismissal can arise where employment is terminated in breach of conditions in the employment contract.

7–34 In interpreting the obligations of parties under an employment contract, certain terms can be implied into the contract if not expressly stated. Common law implies a number of terms into an employment contract where they are not expressed in it. These include: a duty to pay remuneration for work done (see *Mackey v. Jones*[14]); a duty to take reasonable care for the safety of employees (now incorporated in the Safety, Health and Welfare at Work Act 1989 and regulations made thereunder); and a duty of mutual trust between employer and employee (*e.g.* see *Flynn v. Power*[15]).

7–35 Certain terms are also implied into employment contracts by statute. Various statutes provide for minimum terms which prevail over the contract unless the contract contains express terms that are more favourable to the employee. For example, the Worker Protection (Regular Part-Time Employees) Act 1991 extends a variety of protections to part-time employees who work for an employer for at least 13 consecutive weeks and are normally expected to work for a minimum of eight hours per week.

7–36 Another important statute that implies terms into an employment contract is the Minimum Notice and Terms of Employment Act 1973. This Act sets out the minimum notice periods that an employer must give to an employee when the employer wishes to terminate the contract of employment. The requirements of the Act apply to the termination of the contract of any employee who has worked for the employer for 13 weeks or more. The minimum notice periods range from one week (where the employment has lasted less than two years) up to eight weeks (for more than 15 years service). In all cases, an employee must give a week's notice of departure to the employer. In many cases, these terms will be varied by contractual terms that are more favourable to the employee, and courts may imply longer periods into contracts where there is no period specified, especially in the cases of senior employees.

7–37 It should be noted that no notice is required where summary (*i.e.* immediate) dismissal is warranted. This can only arise in cases of serious or gross misconduct, such as theft (*e.g.* see *Leacy v. Harney*[16]).

Constructive dismissal

7–38 Constructive dismissal arises where an employee is not formally dismissed but is subjected to such intolerable working conditions that the employee has no reasonable alternative but to leave. In such cases, the employee terminates the employment contract with or without notice and is entitled to do so because of the employer's conduct.

7–39 Part (b) of the definition of "dismissal" set out above in para. **7–32** corresponds to constructive dismissal. In general, constructive dismissal is very

---

[14][1993] I.L.T.R. 177.
[15][1985] I.R. 648.
[16][1991] E.L.R. 213.

difficult to prove, as, once an employer disputes the dismissal, the onus will fall on the employee to show that he was dismissed. Only when the employee has discharged this burden does the onus revert to the employer to show that the dismissal was fair (*e.g.* see *Kennedy v. Foxford Inns Ltd*[17]).

Unfair dismissal

7–40 The statutory scheme surrounding unfair dismissal is set out in the Unfair Dismissals Act 1977. Essentially, the scheme works on the basis that all dismissals are deemed to be unfair unless the dismissal was justified on substantial grounds. This is clear from section 6 of the Act which states:

> "(1) Subject to the provisions of this section, the dismissal of an employee shall be deemed, for the purposes of this Act, to be an unfair dismissal unless, having regard to all the circumstances, there were substantial grounds justifying the dismissal."

7–41 Section 6 of the Act, as amended, goes on to list several specific cases where a dismissal is deemed to be unfair. These include situations where the dismissal results wholly or mainly from one or more of the employee's:

- trade union membership;
- religious or political opinions;
- involvement in civil or criminal proceedings being taken against the employer;
- availing of parental leave, maternity leave, adoptive leave, protective leave, natal care absence;
- race, colour, sexual orientation, age or membership of the travelling community;
- pregnancy, giving birth, breastfeeding;
- selection for redundancy contrary to agreed procedures.

7–42 The section also lists a number of grounds on foot of which a dismissal will be deemed not to be unfair. These include situations where the dismissal results wholly or mainly from:

- capability, competence or qualifications of the employee for performing work of the kind which he was employed by the employer to do;
- conduct of the employee;
- redundancy of the employee;
- employee being unable to work or continue to work in the position which he held without contravention (by him or by his employer) of a duty or restriction imposed by or under any statute or instrument made under statute.

---

[17] [1995] E.L.R. 216.

7–43 In these cases, the onus is on the employer to show that the dismissal resulted wholly or mainly from one or more of the matters specified or that there were other substantial grounds justifying the dismissal (*e.g.* see *McElroy v. Floraville Nurseries Ltd*[18]).

7–44 It should be noted that, even when an employer has valid, substantial grounds for dismissal, fair procedures must be followed. These normally include a verbal warning, a written warning, a final written warning and, especially in cases of alleged misconduct, an appropriate opportunity for the employee to be heard and for his views to be considered (*e.g.* see *Bolger v. Showerings Ltd*[19] and *Mooney v. An Post*[20]). In the latter of these cases, Barrington J., for the Supreme Court, said

> "Certainly the employee is entitled to the benefit of fair procedures but what these demand will depend upon the terms of his employment and the circumstances surrounding his proposed dismissal. Certainly the minimum he is entitled to is to be informed of the charge against him and to be given an opportunity to answer it and to make submissions."[21]

7–45 Where an employee has been unfairly dismissed, the Unfair Dismissals Act 1977 provides for three different remedies: reinstatement, re-engagement and monetary compensation. Section 7 of the Act states:

> "Where an employee is dismissed and the dismissal is an unfair dismissal, the employee shall be entitled to redress consisting of whichever of the following the rights commissioner, the Tribunal or the Circuit Court, as the case may be, considers appropriate having regard to all the circumstances:
>
>> (a) re-instatement by the employer of the employee in the position which he held immediately before his dismissal on the terms and conditions on which he was employed immediately before his dismissal together with a term that the re-instatement shall be deemed to have commenced on the day of the dismissal, or
>>
>> (b) re-engagement by the employer of the employee either in the position which he held immediately before his dismissal or in a different position which would be reasonably suitable for him on such terms and conditions as are reasonable having regard to all the circumstances, or
>>
>> (c) (i) if the employee incurred any financial loss attributable to the dismissal, payment to him by the employer of such compensation in respect of the loss (not exceeding in amount 104 weeks remuneration in respect of the

[18] [1994] E.L.R. 15.
[19] [1990] E.L.R. 184.
[20] [1998] 4 I.R. 288 at 298.
[21] *ibid.* at 298.

employment from which he was dismissed calculated in accordance with regulations under section 17 of this Act) as is just and equitable having regard to all the circumstances, or

(ii) if the employee incurred no such financial loss, payment to the employee by the employer of such compensation (if any, but not exceeding in amount 4 weeks remuneration in respect of the employment from which he was dismissed calculated as aforesaid) as is just and equitable having regard to all the circumstances,

and the references in the foregoing paragraphs to an employer shall be construed, in a case where the ownership of the business of the employer changes after the dismissal, as references to the person who, by virtue of the change, becomes entitled to such ownership. "

7–46 The Employment Appeals Tribunal or the Circuit Court will expect an employee to have attempted to mitigate his losses by seeking alternative employment following his dismissal and failure to do so will reduce the compensation awarded.

7–47 It should be noted that an aggrieved employee need not use the machinery of the Employment Appeals Tribunal to take his case. He can choose instead to take a civil action for wrongful dismissal in the courts, pleading breach of the employment contract, and possibly other civil wrongs such as misrepresentation or negligent misstatement. Recent case history shows higher paid employees choosing to take this route, probably on the assumption that damages will be higher as the Tribunal tends to hear large numbers of smaller claims. In addition, the courts can be availed of in certain circumstances to obtain an interim injunction preventing the employer from dismissing the employee (see Chapter 21 for further discussion of the use of injunctions in litigation). This helps the employee's negotiating position as he continues to receive remuneration from the employer (*e.g.* see *Boland v. Phoenix Shannon plc*;[22] *Harte v. Kelly*;[23] and *Doyle v. Grangeford Precast Concrete Ltd*[24]).

Role of forensic accountants

7–48 Plaintiffs may look for a declaration that the dismissal was in breach of contract and/or may look for damages in compensation for the wrongful dismissal. Forensic accountants may be asked to advise in calculating a quantum for the damages suffered. The circumstances leading to the dismissal may vary and will influence the calculations. Forensic accountants may be asked to advise in unfair dismissals/breach of contract employment cases in various ways:

---

[22] [1997] E.L.R. 207.
[23] [1997] E.L.R. 125.
[24] Unreported, High Court, O'Donovan J., January 19, 1998.

– calculation of loss suffered by/compensation due to employees unfairly dismissed. This may involve calculations based on of remuneration data, fringe benefits and employee share options;

– calculation of any tax-related consequences relating to the loss suffered by employees unfairly dismissed, including consideration of PAYE matters. Corrigan sets out the tax treatment of such awards.[25] Section 123 of the Taxes Consolidation Act 1997 provides that damages awards made on termination of an office or employment for unfair dismissal are taxable. However, section 201 exempts payments not exceeding £8,000 [€10,161] plus £600 [€765] per year of service from income tax. In addition, a further £4,000 [€5,080] is exempt in respect of the first such termination payment claim, if claimed within six years of the end of the tax year in which the payment is treated as income;

– calculation of any pension-related consequences relating to the loss suffered by employees unfairly dismissed. This may entail valuation of individual pension benefits under schemes such as final salary (defined benefit) company schemes, contributory and non-contributory schemes and money purchase schemes;

– calculation of effect of unfair dismissal on employment prospects of employee;

– calculation of effect of unfair dismissal on employee share options;

– giving evidence on skills required of an employee (*e.g.* in-house accountant, company secretary or company director).

Forensic accounting aspects of employment disputes are considered further in MacGregor and Hobbs.[26]

7–49 Table 7.5 provides brief examples of unfair dismissals cases in which forensic accountants might have advised.

---

[25] Corrigan, K., *Revenue Law* (Round Hall Sweet & Maxwell, Dublin, 2000), Vol. II, Chap. 28.
[26] MacGregor, G. and Hobbs, I., *Expert Accounting Evidence: A Guide for Litigation Support* (Accountancy Books, London, 1998), Chap. 25.

Table 7.5: Examples of unfair dismissals cases in which forensic accountants have advised

---

Quantification of lost earnings
- Quantifying the loss suffered by an employee with a long-term contract at a high remuneration
- Calculating economic loss arising from lost opportunity for future employment as a result of unfair dismissal

Valuations
- Valuing the loss of benefits relating to share options, property, health care and motor vehicles
- Valuing a wide range of pension schemes, *e.g.* final salary schemes, contributory and non-contributory schemes and money purchase schemes

Job market research
- Researching the availability of comparable positions in relation to wrongful dismissal
- Reviewing the job market for employment opportunities closely related to the plaintiff's lost employment to provide information to demonstrate whether the plaintiff had adequately looked for alternative employment

Sundry cases involving forensic accountants
- Assessing allegations of constructive dismissal because the employee intended to disclose purported discriminatory loan practices. Forensic accountant could prepare statistical analysis to show that there was no statistical basis for the allegations of discriminatory loan practices
- Assessing claim by employees that employee share option scheme was manipulated for the benefit of the company and its executives
- Testifying as an expert in a wrongful dismissal case on behalf of the defendant employer to show that there were no economic damages because the plaintiff's new business or employment provided more income than would have been earned had the employee stayed with the employer

---

Accounting calculations

7–50 Where an employee is successful in proving unfair dismissal or wrongful dismissal, the question of the correct measure of compensation will arise.

Wrongful dismissal – breach of contract

7–51 Where an employee with a fixed-term contract is wrongfully dismissed, he is entitled, subject to the rules of mitigation, to damages equivalent to the earnings he would have earned under the contract from the date of dismissal to the end of the contract.[27] The correct measure for damages for pension loss should be the additional pension rights which would have accrued from the date of dismissal up to the time when the employment contract would have been lawfully terminated. Any pension benefits that become payable as a result of

---

[27] Redmond, M., *Dismissal Law in Ireland* (Butterworths, Dublin, 1999), p. 160, para. 11.04.

dismissal should not reduce the amount of damages payable by way of compensation.[28]

Financial compensation under the Unfair Dismissals Act 1977

7–52 As already stated in para. **7–45**, under section 7 of the Unfair Dismissals Act 1977, a dismissed employee is entitled to one of three alternative remedies to redress the dismissal. One of these is monetary compensation. If the employee incurred any financial loss attributable to the dismissal, he should be paid compensation that is just and equitable, but not exceeding 104 weeks' remuneration. Most successful claims for unfair dismissal result in awards of compensation.

7–53 "Financial loss" is defined in section 7(3), as amended, of the Unfair Dismissals Act 1977 as: (i) any actual loss; and (ii) any estimated prospective loss of income attributable to the dismissal; and (iii) the value of any loss or diminution, attributable to the dismissal, of the rights of the employee under the Redundancy Payments Acts 1967 to 1991; or the value of any loss or diminution in relation to superannuation.

7–54 The calculation of compensation is based on the dismissed employee's remuneration. Remuneration is defined in the same subsection to include "allowances in the nature of pay and benefits in lieu of or in addition to pay." The object of compensation is to make full reparation for the loss suffered by the employee. The applicant must prove his loss but he does not have to bring precise and detailed proof of every item of loss.[29] The Unfair Dismissals (Calculation of Weekly Remuneration) Regulations 1977[30] describe how to calculate weekly remuneration, especially where the amount varies from week to week. This is done by taking average figures for a period of 26 weeks ending 13 weeks before the date of dismissal. If the employer was paying the employee less than he should have been paying under law, the calculation is based on what should have been paid (see *Kinsella v. Banagher Concrete Ltd*;[31] and *Sheridan v. Walker & Co.*[32]).

7–55 Estimation of past and future lost earnings includes wages or salary, fringe benefits, pension consequences of termination, employment alternatives and mitigation efforts. The Employment Appeals Tribunal computes an employee's net loss from dismissal to the date of the hearing, taking into account

[28] *Hopkins v. Norcross* [1993] 1 All E.R. 565.
[29] Redmond, M., *Dismissal Law in Ireland* (Butterworths, Dublin, 1999), p. 455.
[30] S.I. No. 287 of 1977.
[31] U.D. 706/1980.
[32] U.D. 470/1981.

basic pay, average bonuses and average overtime pay. In addition, prospective loss of income must be estimated. This involves estimating any reduction in future earnings and fringe benefits arising from the dismissal. The definition of financial loss requires that both past and future loss be taken into account. In practice, this can be difficult to calculate and has been described as being "full of imponderables"[33] and "highly speculative".[34] Examples of losses that could be included in the computation are illustrated by the case of *Ogden v. Harp Textiles Ltd*[35] in which the Employment Appeals Tribunal allowed compensation for the loss of rights under a pension scheme, the use of a company house and a company car, the Voluntary Health Insurance premium paid by the employer and the expense incurred in moving house (necessitated by the dismissal) together with the cost of temporary accommodation.[36]

7–56 Expenses incurred by the claimant may also be taken into account, such as costs of obtaining a new job, cost of preparing a C.V., legal costs, etc. Compensation may also include an amount for loss of rights under the Redundancy Payments Acts. These rights would only have applied had the employee been made redundant, and it is not known whether this would have happened (but for the dismissal). The Employment Appeals Tribunal has tended to calculate the compensation for lost redundancy by taking a percentage of the total redundancy lump sum, *i.e.* the percentage measuring the risk of the employee being made redundant (see, *e.g. Richardson v. H. Williams Ltd*[37]; and *Keenan v. Ferrans Stud Ltd*[38]).

7–57 Once the financial loss has been calculated, a number of deductions may be made. Section 7(2) of the Unfair Dismissals Act 1977, as amended, states that regard shall be had to:

> "(a) the extent (if any) to which the financial loss . . . was attributable to an act, omission or conduct by or on behalf of the employer,
> (b) the extent (if any) to which the said financial loss was attributable to an act, omission or conduct by or on behalf of the employee,
> (c) the measures (if any) adopted by the employee or, as the case may be, his failure to adopt measures, to mitigate the loss aforesaid, and
> (d) the extent (if any) of the compliance or failure to comply by the employer, in relation to the employee, with the procedure referred to in subsection (1) of section 14 of this Act or with the provisions of any code of practice relating to procedures regarding dismissal approved of by the Minister,

---

[33] *Kearns v. Chesterton International B.V.* U.D. 85/1979.
[34] *Groarke v. Hygiene Distributors Ltd* U.D. 93/1980.
[35] U.D. 112/1979.
[36] See also Redmond, M., *Dismissal Law in Ireland* (Butterworths, Dublin, 1999), pp. 459-466.
[37] U.D. 17/1979.
[38] U.D. 79/1979.

(e) the extent (if any) of the compliance or failure to comply by the employer, in relation to the employee, with the said section 14, and

(f) the extent (if any) to which the conduct of the employee (whether by act or omission) contributed to the dismissal."

Section 14 of the Act imposes obligations on the employer to advise employees in writing of the procedures the employer will observe before dismissing an employee and, if requested by a dismissed employee, to furnish the employee with particulars in writing of the principal grounds for dismissal.

7–58 The Employment Appeals Tribunal may make certain deductions from the compensation awarded. The two main deductions made are in respect of contributory fault and failure to mitigate the loss (*e.g.* claimant makes insufficient effort to get another job). The deduction is made on a rule-of-thumb basis, often in the form of a percentage deduction, rather than being a precise calculation.

Actual loss

7–59 The first component of any compensation is the actual loss between the date of dismissal and the date of the hearing. The calculation is based on net of tax amounts.[39] The compensation includes regular overtime, bonuses or premia if applicable. The valuation of economic loss suffered by the plaintiff must include (in addition to weekly or monthly pay) fringe benefits such as medical and life insurance, share options, profit sharing plans, contribution towards pension benefits, lost pension rights and benefits, car allowances, holiday pay, company cars, free accommodation, etc. These are taken into account in calculating the remuneration figure.[40] Payments under the Social Welfare Acts in the periods following dismissal and under the Income Tax Acts consequent on dismissal are ignored in the calculations, pursuant to section 7(2A) of the 1977 Act as inserted by section 6 of the Unfair Dismissals (Amendment) Act 1993.[41]

Estimated prospective loss

7–60 Once the employee's compensation package has been valued, both (i) the compensation package before and after dismissal from the original job and (ii) the period of unemployment following dismissal must be examined. A forensic accountant may have to quantify the plaintiff's future economic loss arising from the wrongful dismissal. The value of any pension benefit lost should be taken into account in assessing lost remuneration. In addition, the value of

---

[39] *Glover v. B.L.N. Ltd (No. 2)* [1973] I.R. 432.

[40] In *Bunyan v. United Dominions Trust (Ireland) Ltd* [1982] I.L.R.M. 404, remuneration included salary, bonus, pension contributions, use of company car, lunches, subscriptions, employee PRSI and State pension contribution. Discretionary payments by the employer were excluded from the calculation of remuneration on the grounds that they were not a payment for services.

[41] Unfair Dismissals (Amendment) Act 1993, s. 6(c).

the loss of future pension entitlement as a result of dismissal must be taken into account.

The assessment of lost pension rights is one of the major heads of claim in unfair dismissal and wrongful dismissal claims. Actuarial advice may be necessary to estimate this loss and an actuary may be required to present the evidence.

Where an employee is wrongfully discharged from an employment contract, and later finds work at lower pay, the amount of earnings of the employee in his replacement employment is subtracted from the amount he would have earned had he not been wrongfully dismissed.

Period of loss

7–61   Calculation of future loss requires the estimation of the period of loss. This will be limited and will depend on how long the plaintiff takes (i) to find alternative work and (ii) to reach the previous level of remuneration. The employee must take reasonable steps to mitigate the loss. In this respect, the reasonableness of the period of unemployment must be considered. The employee's activities during the period of unemployment and the efforts made to search for alternative employment should be examined. Employment prospects in the industry should be considered. Surveys of labour markets and wages in the local area might also be conducted.

7–62   In addition, an estimate of the period the employee would have remained with the employer may be relevant. This depends on a number of factors, including income, educational level, age, job type, industry, how long the employee was with the employer, and how often the employee had changed jobs. The appropriate period of unemployment constitutes the period of loss and this period is not necessarily the actual period of unemployment experienced by the plaintiff. A survey of work habits of 65,000 in the United States[42] showed that age, income, education and the length of time with the current employer are important factors in determining how long an employee would stay in the job.

7–63   The financial losses suffered in wrongful dismissal cases are not typically as long-lasting as in physical injury cases. For example, the dismissed employee has the same skills and experience after the event as he had before it, and is likely to be employed elsewhere. If the alternative employment is initially at lower pay, the reduction is likely to catch up with his original earning capacity after a certain period. Relatively speaking, the plaintiff's primary damage will not be long-lasting. If the labour market is working efficiently, the employee will eventually find that his inherent worth will be recognised by other employers.

---

[42]Trout, R., "Duration of employment in wrongful termination cases" in *Journal of Forensic Economics* (Summer 1995) Vol. 8, No. 2, pp. 167–177.

Mitigation

7–64 There is a duty on plaintiffs to take all reasonable steps to reduce or mitigate the loss consequent on the wrong[43] (see para. **15–74** for further discussion of mitigation). Compensation will be reduced if the employee does not take reasonable steps to find alternative work or otherwise reduce the loss suffered. Under section 7(2)(c) of the Unfair Dismissals Act 1977, "the measures (if any) adopted by the employee or, as the case may be, his failure to adopt measures to mitigate the loss aforesaid" must be taken into account.

Employment law – discrimination

7–65 As explained in para. **7–30**, forensic accountants have a role to play in employment disputes alleging discrimination. The calculation of compensatory damages arising from a successful claim for discrimination is similar to that described in the previous section dealing with wrongful and unfair dismissals. In addition, however, forensic accountants may be asked to advise and collect financial data in order to support or repudiate the claim of discriminatory practices. In providing such evidence, whereas forensic accountants will gather and analyse detailed micro-economic financial data, they may also liaise with economists who will supply broader macro-economic statistics relevant to the case.

Legal context

7–66 Fair employment laws attempt to ensure that employers base their employment practices on performance and merit rather than on non-job related characteristics. As indicated above, the Unfair Dismissals Act 1977 incorporates effective legal protection against dismissal on such grounds as trade union membership, religious or political opinions, commitments arising from parenthood, maternity, adoption and pregnancy, race, colour, sexual orientation, age or membership of the travelling community.

The law, however, also recognises that unfair practices other than dismissal can arise in the workplace. Discrimination can make the workplace unacceptably unpleasant, can adversely affect pay, promotion and career prospects and can result in constructive or actual dismissal. The Employment Equality Act 1998 addresses these areas. It renders unlawful, *inter alia*, dismissals involving victimisation.

Role of forensic accountants

7–67 Table 7.6 provides brief examples of employment discrimination cases

---

[43] Unfair Dismissals Act 1977, s. 7(2)(c).

in which forensic accountants have advised. In such cases, forensic accountants might be asked to provide statistical data from the company's records or market data from the industry to support or reject the claim of discrimination. Saad provides a useful discussion of employment discrimination litigation from a forensic accounting point of view.[44]

Table 7.6: Examples of discrimination cases in which forensic accountants have advised

---

Assessing whether there was discrimination
- Assessing a charge of discrimination by reference to promotion and compensation practices
- Assessing a charge of racial discrimination against employer by examining payroll records
- Earnings and regression analyses of payroll records regarding the disparity in wages between male and female employees to identify whether the wage disparity was job-related or discriminatory.

Calculating damages arising from discrimination
- Calculating loss of earnings due to wrongful termination on the grounds of discrimination
- Calculating unequal pay as a result of sexual discrimination, including provision of expert evidence in support of the calculations
- Reviewing the economic loss calculation of an opposing expert in an employment discrimination claim, providing lawyers with the strengths and weaknesses of the calculation.

Accounting calculations

7–68 Lost earnings might arise in a variety of employment discrimination situations such as breaches of equality legislation, failure to hire and failure to promote ("glass ceiling").

7–69 Where discriminatory practices are alleged, experts may be asked to provide evidence in relation to the variable (gender, age, racial characteristics, etc.) forming the basis for the alleged discrimination, to ascertain whether the defendant's employment practices are biased. Statistical techniques such as regression analysis might be used to determine if a particular variable is discriminatory in an equation in which employment termination is a dependent variable. Regression analysis can be used to provide statistically valid evidence of discrimination. With modern computer packages, such regression analysis is relatively straightforward, subject to the expert having access to the data necessary to input into the regression equation.

---

[44] Saad, A., "Employment discrimination litigation" in *Litigation Services Handbook. The Role of the Accountant as Expert* (2nd ed., Weil, R.L., Wagner, M.J. and Frank, P.B. (eds), John Wiley & Sons, Inc., New York, 1995), Chap. 11.

In cases of alleged employment discrimination, multiple regression techniques can be used to demonstrate the presence or absence of discrimination on the basis of gender or some other personal characteristics protected under the law. Common independent variables include gender or other characteristics the subject of discrimination litigation. Typically, the dependent variables in the analysis are salary, hire status, promotion status or termination status. The independent variables are chosen because they are believed to explain in part the variation in the dependent variable, *e.g.* measures of worker productivity such as education, training experience and level of output. Assuming gender is the discriminatory variable, the question to be answered by the regression analysis is: "for given qualifications and productivity levels, are female employees paid significantly differently than male employees?"

Matrimonial disputes[45]

7–70 A growing area of dispute is that involving marriage break-up. A civil marriage is a contractual relationship. Matrimonial disputes may result in proceedings for nullity (on the basis that there was no valid marriage), judicial separation (following which neither party has the legal right to remarry) or divorce. In modern society, matrimonial separation and divorce are increasingly commonplace.

Where the assets or income of one or both parties are substantial, it will be necessary for forensic accountants to (i) assist in ascertaining the financial position of the parties and (ii) advise on the quantum and method of payments to be made by one spouse to another.

Forensic accountants need to have some familiarity with the laws governing matrimonial cases. This is particularly so given that the legislation dealing with judicial separation and divorce contains quite explicit guidance on the financial parameters for the transfer of assets and income between the parties. The legal context for such proceedings is introduced in this section, primarily focusing on the aspects involving accounting and financial calculations.[46]

Among the biggest elements of judicial separation or divorce proceedings are the distribution of matrimonial property and the making of payments between the parties. This frequently involves valuation of non-cash assets. Particularly

[45] We are indebted to Anne Dunne SC for her assistance to us with this section of the chapter.
[46] More information on matrimonial law can be obtained in Coggans, S. and Jackson, N., *Family Law (Divorce) Act 1996* (Round Hall Sweet & Maxwell, Dublin, 1998); Duncan, W.R. and Scully, P.E., *Marriage Breakdown in Ireland: Law and Practice* (Butterworths, Dublin, 1990); Wood, K. and O'Shea, P., *Divorce in Ireland: the Options, the Issues, the Law* (The O'Brien Press Ltd, Dublin, 1997); Shatter, A.J., *Shatter's Family Law* (4th ed., Butterworths, 1997); and Shannon (ed.), *Family Law Practitioner* (Round Hall Sweet & Maxwell, 2000).

difficult, and involving considerable accounting expertise, is valuation of businesses. Valuation in matrimonial dissolution is distinct from valuation for other purposes. Recognising the unique aspects of separation and divorce is crucial to achieving an accurate, defensible valuation for companies whose owners are going their separate ways.

Legal context

7–71 The question of how the property should be distributed between the parties is affected by several statutes. The principal statute in divorce cases is the Family Law (Divorce) Act 1996, and for judicial separations, it is the Judicial Separation and Family Law Reform Act 1989, as amended by the Family Law Act 1995. Both judicial separation and divorce are also affected by the Guardianship of Infants Act 1964 and the Family Home Protection Act 1976. The two principal Acts give the court wide powers to direct how assets are to be divided and the size and frequency of payments to be made. Regardless of the statutory rules on how property is to be distributed and payments are to be made, a proper valuation of the matrimonial assets will be necessary.

7–72 In both the High Court and the Circuit Court, a spouse can, in the context of judicial separation or divorce proceedings, seek an order for discovery requiring disclosure of all documents and materials relevant to the proceedings which are in the custody, power or possession of the other spouse and which are not privileged. Privilege claimed in relation to documents may be argued before the court, which may direct that the documents be disclosed initially (to enable the court to make the decision as to whether they are privileged) without a requirement that they be made available for inspection.

Under the Circuit Court Rules,[47] wherever financial relief is being sought ancillary to the decree of judicial separation or divorce, the spouses must exchange affidavits of means. Assets to be disclosed in the affidavit include assets held on trust such as pension-scheme entitlements, including death-in-service entitlements, as well as assets jointly held with others or held beneficially by others on behalf of either of the parties.

The rules dealing with the form and content of the affidavit of means provide as follows:

> "18. Without prejudice to the right of each party to make application to the Court for an Order of Discovery pursuant to the Rules of this Honourable Court and without prejudice to the jurisdiction of the Court pursuant to section 12(25) of

---

[47]The relevant rules are rules 7, 10, 18 and 19 and Form 2 of Order 78 of the Rules of the Circuit Court 1950 as substituted by Circuit Court Rules (No. 1) 1997 (Judicial Separation and Family Law Reform Act, 1989 and Family Law Act, 1995 and Family Law (Divorce) Act, 1996) (S.I. No. 84 of 1997).

the 1995 Act and section 17(25) of the 1996 Act, in any case where financial relief under the Acts is sought, the parties shall file Affidavits of Means in accordance with Rules 7 and 10 hereof in respect of which the following Rules shall be applicable—

> (a) either party may request the other party to vouch any or all items referred to therein within 14 days of the request;
> (b) in the event of a party failing to properly comply with the provisions in relation to the filing and serving of Affidavits of Means as set down in these Rules or failing to properly vouch the matters set out therein the Court may on application grant an Order for Discovery and/or may make such Orders as the Court deems appropriate and necessary (including an Order that such party shall not be entitled to pursue or defend as appropriate such claim for any ancillary reliefs under the Acts save as permitted by the Court upon such terms as the Court may determine are appropriate and/or adjourning the proceedings for a specified period of time to enable compliance) . . .

19. The Affidavit of Means shall set out in schedule form details of the party's income, assets, debts, expenditure and other liabilities wherever situated and from whatever source and, to the best of the deponent's knowledge, information and belief the income, assets, debts, expenditure and other liabilities wherever situated and from whatever source of any dependent member of the family and shall be in accordance with the form set out in Form 2 herein or such modification thereof as may be appropriate. Where relief pursuant to section 12 of the 1995 Act is sought, the Affidavit of Means shall also state to the best of the deponent's knowledge, information and belief, the nature of the scheme, the benefits payable thereunder, the normal pensionable age and the period of reckonable service of the member spouse and where information relating to the pension scheme has been obtained from the trustees of the scheme under the Pensions Acts 1990-1996, such information should be exhibited in the Affidavit of Means and where such information has not been obtained a specific averment shall be included in the Affidavit of Means as to why such information has not been obtained."

7–73   As pension rights can represent one of a family's largest assets, they are significant considerations in judicial separation and divorce.[48] Until 1995, the courts could not divide up pensions as a specific asset on separation, although couples could privately agree on a division under maintenance clauses in a separation agreement. The Family Law Act 1995 sets out rules to deal with pension rights on judicial separation. The Family Law (Divorce) Act 1996 also gives courts power to divide pension assets in the same way as other assets.

---

[48] See Pensions Board, *The Pension Provisions of the Family Law Act, 1995 and the Family Law (Divorce) Act, 1996* (Pensions Board, Dublin, 1999).

Only pension rights which accumulated during the marriage may be taken into account on divorce or separation.

Under the Family Law Act 1995 and the Family Law (Divorce) Act 1996, spouses may seek a pension adjustment order. The court may transfer pension rights from one spouse to another or set aside benefits due to be paid at a future date by a process known as "earmarking". Pension adjustment orders may be made against employed members of a company pension scheme and against self-employed persons.

Alternatively, spouses may use the pension benefit as a bargaining tool to secure an immediate financial settlement without interfering with the pension scheme. Spouses may settle the issue of the division of pension entitlement without recourse to a pension adjustment order. This can be done by adjusting the non-pension assets, leaving pension benefits intact. Improved maintenance can be given in lieu of pension entitlements, or property could be vested by way of property adjustment orders as a substitute for the share of pension benefits. Pension adjustment orders are complex and are considered in more detail in Finucane and Buggy.[49] Where any adjustment whatever is made in relation to a pension scheme or policy, a court order is required.

7–74 Separation may be by agreement, in which case the separation agreement is a private contract drawn up voluntarily. Separation may also be by order of the court (*i.e.* a decree of judicial separation is granted). Where a decree of judicial separation is granted, the court may make a maintenance order in favour of the dependant spouse and children up to the age of 18 (or 23 if in full-time education, or if child is incapacitated). The Judicial Separation and Family Law Reform Act 1989, as amended by the 1995 Act, sets out the parameters within which the court will make orders when granting a decree of judicial separation.

Amongst the matters usually dealt with in separation agreements are future ownership of property, maintenance payments and lump sum payments, indemnity for the debts of the other spouse and taxation. Maintenance clauses make provision for one spouse (usually the husband) to pay the other spouse maintenance for her support, and for the support of any dependant children of the marriage. Details of the maintenance are a matter of negotiation between the parties. The law does not permit one party to contract out of future maintenance payments. Forensic accountants may advise either party in relation to relevant financial calculations. A useful checklist is included in Duncan and Scully[50] in relation to the income, expenses and assets of both spouses. The checklist is summarised in Table 7.7.

---

[49] Finucane, F. and Buggy, B., *Irish Pensions Law and Practice* (Oak Tree Press, Dublin, 1996).
[50] Duncan, W.R. and Scully, P.E., *Marriage Breakdown in Ireland: Law and Practice* (Butterworths, Dublin, 1990), pp. 221–226, paras 9.018–9.021.

Table 7.7: Checklist of income, expenses and assets of spouses in maintenance cases

---

Income
From employment, including "unofficial"
Benefits in kind (car, petrol, motor tax, VHI)
From trade, profession, etc.
Income from trust
Rental income
Dividends
Interest

Expenses
House – rent, mortgage, house insurance, phone, gas, electricity, fuel, television
    licence, household equipment, household repairs, etc.
Food
Clothes and shoes
Medical expenses
Insurance
Transport costs
School, university expenses, books, school outings, school lunches, etc.
Extracurricular expenses – lessons outside school, sport, hobbies, etc.
Miscellaneous – babysitting, childminding, holidays, socialising

Assets
Property in addition to family home – land, farm, holiday house
Valuables – paintings, antiques, boat, caravan, jewellery, silver
Life insurance policies close to maturity
Inheritance prospects
Cash from all sources
Shares
Business Expansion Scheme (BES) assets

Hidden assets
Hidden, undisclosed bank accounts, *e.g.* offshore
Assets held in offshore companies
Illegal earnings, earnings undeclared for tax purposes

7–75 Property clauses in a separation agreement vary according to the circumstances and wishes of the parties concerned. For example, the parties may agree to sell the family home and to divide the proceeds.

Maintenance orders by the courts

7–76 The Family Law (Maintenance of Spouses and Children) Act 1976 governs applications by spouses for maintenance orders where no other matrimonial or family law proceedings are in existence. Under section 5(1), the court may make a maintenance order if it appears "on application to it by a spouse, that the other spouse has failed to provide such maintenance for the applicant spouse as is proper in the circumstances". It is not clear what maintenance is "proper". The maintenance payments must be "adequate and reasonable, having regard to the circumstances". If no evidence is provided to the court of failure to provide proper maintenance, no maintenance order can be made under the Act. In deciding whether to make a maintenance order, and the amount to be awarded, under section 5(4) of the Family Law (Maintenance of Spouses and Children) Act 1976, the court must have regard to all the circumstances of the case and in particular to:

> "(a) the income, earning capacity (if any), property and other financial resources of
>
> (i) the spouses and any dependent children of the family, and
> (ii) any other dependent children of which either spouse is a parent, including income or benefits to which either spouse or any such children are entitled by or under statute, and
>
> (b) the financial needs and other responsibilities of:
>
> (i) the spouses towards each other and towards any dependent children of the family, and
> (ii) each spouse as a parent towards any other dependent children, and the needs of any such children including the need for care and attention."

7–77 Earnings are defined in section 3(1) of the Act as any sums payable to a person:

> "(a) by way of wages or salary (including any fees, bonus, commission, overtime pay or other emoluments payable in addition to wages or salary or payable under a contract of service);
>
> (b) by way of pension or other like benefit in respect of employment (including an annuity in respect of past services, whether or not rendered to the person paying the annuity, and including periodical payments by way of compensation for the loss, abolition or relinquishment, or diminution in the emoluments, of any office or employment)."

7–78 Section 43(e) of the Family Law Act 1995, as amended by section 52(o)(ii) of the Family Law (Divorce) Act 1996, requires spouses to provide details of their property and income such as "may reasonably be required for the purpose of the proceedings".

7–79 Case law on determining maintenance payments has produced varied and inconsistent results. However, the courts have laid out certain principles to be applied in assessing how much maintenance should be paid to spouses. A full discussion of these principles and their development is beyond the scope of this book. However, an indication of the approach of the courts can be gleaned from the judgment of McGuinness J. in the high Court in *J.D. v. D.D.*[51] The case involved a situation where the parties, in the words of the learned judge, were:

> "fortunate in that this is a family with ample financial resources, sufficient to

---

[51] [1997] 3 I.R. 64.

provide for both parties. The Court is not, therefore, faced with the all too common situation where a family has barely enough resources to provide for one household and where the breakdown of the marriage brings both parties below the poverty line."[52]

McGuinness J. went on to deal with the determination of maintenance, including the appropriate level of lump sum payment in the circumstances. She cited section 16 of the Family Law Act 1995, which lists the matters to be considered by the court in using its wide discretion to make financial orders and to determine their provisions. She then continued:

"It is clear that very many of these guidelines are relevant to the present case. Even given these guidelines however, the court still has a wide area of discretion particularly in cases where there are considerable financial assets. In these cases should the court seek simply to provide for actual day to day needs of the dependant spouse or should it endeavour to divide the family assets in a more equal way by the operation of a lump sum and/or property adjustment order? In such a division of the family assets, should the 'stay at home' wife be treated differently from the wife who works outside the home? Since the enactment of the Act of 1989 [Judicial Separation and Family Law Reform Act 1989] there has been little or no development of a body of case law in this jurisdiction in regard to such questions: where there have been written judgments, and they are few, each case has been specifically dealt with on its own facts."[53]

Bearing in mind the paucity of Irish case law, the learned judge then reviewed developments in England:

"Apart from its emphasis on the 'clean break' much of the English legislation covering ancillary relief on marriage breakdown is very similar to that in this jurisdiction and includes the same breadth of judicial discretion. There is a large body of English case law in this area and it is instructive to consider some of the approaches to calculating financial relief which have been introduced and tested in the English courts.

For many years the English courts operated what is known as 'the one third rule', whereby the wife received in or about one third of the husband's income as periodic maintenance and in addition in or about one third of the capital assets of the family. The rule had its origins in the operation of the old ecclesiastical courts and is classically expressed by Denning M.R. in the case of *Wachtel v. Wachtel* [1973] 1 All ER 829. At p. 840 of the report Lord Denning sets out the position thus: –

'In view of [a wife's] these calls on [her husband's] his future earnings, we do not think she can have both – half the capital assets, and half the earnings. ... Giving it the best consideration we can, we think that the fairest way is to start with one third of each. If she has one third of the family assets as her own – and one third of the joint earnings – her past contributions are

[52][1997] 3 I.R. 64 at 73.
[53]*ibid.* at 91.

adequately recognised, and her future living standards assured so far as may be . . . We would emphasise that this proposal is not a rule. It is only a starting point. It will serve in cases where the marriage has lasted for many years and the wife has been in the home bringing up the children. It may not be applicable when the marriage has lasted only a short time, or where there are no children and she can go out to work.'

However, the operation of this arithmetical rule has been much criticised in recent years and it is now regarded as more or less obsolete.

More recently what might be described as a dual approach has been adopted by the English courts, depending on the income of the parties in question. Where low income families are concerned what is described as the 'subsistence level approach' is used. This term is reasonably self-explanatory and is not relevant in the present case. In the case of wealthy couples the tendency is to follow the approach used in *Duxbury v. Duxbury* [1987] 1 F.L.R. 7. In that case the parties had been married for 22 years and had three adult children. The wife had brought no capital to the marriage nor had she engaged in any paid employment during the course of the marriage. The couple had had a luxurious lifestyle. The husband had considerable capital and a very large income. On the breakdown of the marriage the husband went to live with his mistress and the wife remained in the family home and began living there with a man of very modest means who was fourteen years her junior. The husband agreed to the transfer of the house to the wife but argued against the award of a lump sum lest it fall into the hands of the wife's lover. He sought the making of an order for periodical maintenance only. The Court rejected this approach and made a lump sum order of £600,000 based on actuarial calculations, which would produce a net income of £28,000 *per annum* for the wife which, the Court felt, should support her in the luxurious lifestyle to which she was accustomed for the remainder of her life.

The *Duxbury* approach, and indeed the method of calculation used in the case, has been widely followed in the English courts, although it has been frequently been stressed that it is only a guideline – see for example *B v. B (Financial Provisions)* [1990] 1 F.L.R. 20, *Gojkovic v. Gojkovic* [1990] 1 F.L.R. 140, *Hodgson v. Trapp* [1989] A.C. 807.

In *Gojkovic v. Gojkovic*, the approach was varied to take account of the fact that the wife had made a crucial and continuing contribution to the building up of the family's successful business. In that case the Court of Appeal held that in deciding whether to exercise its powers to order a very wealthy man to pay to his former wife a lump sum, the Court was not limited to calculating the wife's share according to her needs and awarding her a lump sum which would produce sufficient income to make her self-sufficient but, instead, if the wife had made an exceptional contribution to the creation of the family assets the Court should award her the share of the assets which she had earned. The facts in *Gojkovic v. Gojkovic* have no application in the present case, but the decision of the Court of Appeal illustrates the approach which may be taken where family wealth permits it.

Both *Duxbury* and *Gojkovic* were decided on 'clean break' principles and, for the reasons which I have set out above, are not directly applicable to the situation in this jurisdiction. Nevertheless, I feel that the approach of the English courts in cases involving wealthy families is both instructive and persuasive. From the English case law, I would deduce the principle that in the case where there are considerable family assets the court is not limited to providing for the dependant spouses actual immediate needs through a periodic maintenance order, but may endeavour, through the making of a lump sum order, to ensure that the applicant will continue into the future to enjoy the lifestyle to which she was accustomed."[54]

7–80 Section 42 of the Family Law Act 1995 provides for courts to make lump sum maintenance orders either instead of, or in addition to, periodical payments. Courts may secure maintenance payments on assets belonging to the respondent (paying) spouse. The Family Law (Maintenance of Spouses and Children) Act 1976 introduced attachment of earnings orders which attach the periodic maintenance payments to the earnings of the paying spouse. The court may require the paying spouse to provide a statement of earnings, expected earnings, resources and needs. In addition, the court may require the employer to supply details of earnings and expected earnings.

7–81 Section 24 of the 1976 Act requires maintenance orders to be paid without deduction of tax. Such payments are deductible from the paying spouse's gross earnings prior to them being assessed to income tax. Conversely, maintenance is taxable in the hands of the recipient spouse. However, the spouses can elect to continue to be taxed jointly and maintenance is treated as payable net in such circumstances.[55]

Sections 1025 and 1027 of the Taxes Consolidation Act 1997 provide that:

(1) Payments under maintenance arrangements for the benefit of one party to the marriage or former marriage by the other party are effectively made gross, *i.e.* the paying party is not entitled to make any deduction from the payment in respect of income tax, and the receiving party is liable to income tax on the payment. Subject to making the appropriate application, the paying party may deduct the payment in computing total income for tax purposes.

(2) Payments under maintenance arrangements for the benefit of a child of the paying party are effectively made net, *i.e.* the paying party is not entitled to make any deduction from the payment in respect of income tax, but the payment is not deemed to be the income of the child for tax purposes, and the paying party may not deduct the payment in computing his total income for tax purposes.

(3) Payments pursuant to an order under Part II of the Judicial Separation and Family Law Reform Act 1989, an order under the Family Law Act 1995 (other than section 12 of that Act) or an order under the Family Law (Divorce) Act 1996

---

[54] [1997] 3 I.R. 64 at 92–93.
[55] Taxes Consolidation Act 1997, s. 1026.

(other than section 17 of that Act) are made without deduction of income tax. Section 12 of the Family Law Act 1995 and section 17 of the Family Law (Divorce) Act 1996 deal with pension adjustment orders.

7–82 Maintenance in support of children may be ordered by the courts under section 11(2) of the Guardianship of Infants Act 1964 and under sections 5, 7 and 8 of the Family Law (Maintenance of Spouses and Children) Act 1976, as well as the Family Law Act 1995 and the Family Law (Divorce) Act 1996.

7–83 Section 20 of the Family Law (Divorce) Act 1996 deals with the legal provisions concerning financial arrangements in divorce cases. Subsection (1) states:

> "(1) In deciding whether to make an order under section 12, 13, 14, 15(1)(a), 16, 17, 18 or 22 and in determining the provisions of such an order, the court shall ensure that such provision as the court considers proper having regard to the circumstances exists or will be made for the spouses and any dependent member of the family concerned."

7–84 The orders referred to in subsection (1) include orders for maintenance pending suit, periodical payments, lump sum payments, orders conferring on one spouse the right to occupy the family home to the exclusion of the other spouse, financial compensation orders, pension adjustment orders, orders for the provision for a spouse out of the estate of the other deceased spouse and subsequent variations of certain of these orders.

7–85 Subsection (2) lists the factors to be considered by a court in assessing the appropriate financial arrangements to be made between the parties to the divorce. This is a useful and informative list as it shows that the court will take a full and well-informed view of a wide variety of relevant factors before deciding how assets and income should be split. The full list is:

> "(2) Without prejudice to the generality of subsection (1), in deciding whether to make such an order as aforesaid and in determining the provisions of such an order, the court shall, in particular, have regard to the following matters:
> (a) the income, earning capacity, property and other financial resources which each of the spouses concerned has or is likely to have in the foreseeable future,
> (b) the financial needs, obligations and responsibilities which each of the spouses has or is likely to have in the foreseeable future (whether in the case of the remarriage of the spouse or otherwise),
> (c) the standard of living enjoyed by the family concerned before the proceedings were instituted or before the spouses commenced to live apart from one another, as the case may be,
> (d) the age of each of the spouses, the duration of their marriage and the length of time during which the spouses lived with one another,
> (e) any physical or mental disability of either of the spouses,

(f) the contributions which each of the spouses has made or is likely in the foreseeable future to make to the welfare of the family, including any contribution made by each of them to the income, earning capacity, property and financial resources of the other spouse and any contribution made by either of them by looking after the home or caring for the family,

(g) the effect on the earning capacity of each of the spouses of the marital responsibilities assumed by each during the period when they lived with one another and, in particular, the degree to which the future earning capacity of a spouse is impaired by reason of that spouse having relinquished or foregone the opportunity of remunerative activity in order to look after the home or care for the family,

(h) any income or benefits to which either of the spouses is entitled by or under statute,

(i) the conduct of each of the spouses, if that conduct is such that in the opinion of the court it would in all the circumstances of the case be unjust to disregard it,

(j) the accommodation needs of either of the spouses,

(k) the value to each of the spouses of any benefit (for example, a benefit under a pension scheme) which by reason of the decree of divorce concerned, that spouse will forfeit the opportunity or possibility of acquiring,

(l) the rights of any person other than the spouses but including a person to whom either spouse is remarried."

7–86 Subsection (4) lists the factors to be taken into account by the court when deciding on the terms of any order to be made in favour of a dependant member of the family as follows:

"(4) Without prejudice to the generality of subsection (1), in deciding whether to make an order referred to in that subsection in favour of a dependent member of the family concerned and in determining the provisions of such an order, the court shall, in particular, have regard to the following matters:

(a) the financial needs of the member,

(b) the income, earning capacity (if any), property and other financial resources of the member,

(c) any physical or mental disability of the member,

(d) any income or benefits to which the member is entitled by or under statute,

(e) the manner in which the member was being and in which the spouses concerned anticipated that the member would be educated or trained,

(f) the matters specified in paragraphs (a), (b) and (c) of subsection (2) and in subsection (3),

(g) the accommodation needs of the member."

Importantly, the court is required to have an overriding regard to the interests of justice before deciding to make an order in favour of a spouse or dependant. Section 20(5) states:

"The court shall not make an order under a provision referred to in subsection (1) unless it would be in the interests of justice to do so."

7–87 Under section 13 of the Family Law (Divorce) Act 1996, financial settlements are either in the form of a lump sum or periodical payments or a combination of both. Courts are likely to prefer lump-sum settlements rather than periodic maintenance payments. This is because no party will have to return to court to change the level of maintenance, nor will problems of enforcing the maintenance order arise in the case of lump-sum settlements.

Irish courts have no power to make lump sum settlements in the context of a "clean break". Divorce laws in Ireland have been criticised on the basis that they do not provide for "clean break" settlements. At all times, maintenance remains as the one aspect of a divorce which in Ireland is not terminated by the granting of a decree. The impossibility of obtaining an absolute divorce is a distinctive and deliberate hallmark of Irish divorce – unlike the United Kingdom where clean break settlements are allowed as full and final settlement. In Ireland, even where lump-sum settlements have been paid, there is always a possibility that a spouse may return to court for maintenance whether on a periodical payment basis or on a lump-sum payment basis.

Matrimonial property

7–88 The Family Home Protection Act 1976 prohibits the sale of the family home without the consent of the non-owning spouse. An exclusive right to reside in the family home to the exclusion of the other spouse may be conferred on one spouse under the Family Law Act 1995 and under the Family Law (Divorce) Act 1996. These Acts also provide the courts with powers to grant property adjustment orders in judicial separation and divorce cases. Factors to be considered in making such orders include the conduct of the spouse concerned, the contribution by each spouse to the welfare of the family including any contribution made "to the income, earning capacity, property and financial resources of the other spouse and any contribution made by either of them by looking after the home or caring for the family."[56]

7–89 Section 36 of the Family Law Act 1995 deals with the resolution of property disputes between spouses. Section 36(1) allows for an application to be made to the Circuit Court or the High Court by "either spouse to determine any question arising between them as to the title to or possession of any property." Section 36(3) provides for spouses and children to apply to the court "where it is claimed that the other spouse has had in his or her possession or under his or her control":

(a) monies to which such spouse was beneficially entitled; or

---

[56] Family Law (Divorce) Act 1996, s. 20(2)(f) and Family Law Act 1995, s. 16(2)(f).

(b) property to which, or to an interest in which, such spouse was beneficially entitled.

Role of forensic accountants

7–90 Forensic accountants may play an important role in divorce proceedings, divorce settlements and in matrimonial disputes.[57] Matrimonial disputes can involve a variety of taxation and valuation issues. Early advice from forensic accountants can result in savings later.

7–91 Forensic accountants can act for either spouse. They can assist lawyers and mediators in the determination of net family property and other financial aspects of family law including determining the origin of, and tracing the movement of, various assets and investigating representations by spouses concerning business and personal income. Forensic accountants may also assist in evaluating the tax consequences of potential settlement scenarios.[58] They may be asked to calculate the value of the matrimonial estate for the purpose of determining child support, maintenance or any of the variety of periodical and lump-sum payments and property and pension adjustment orders envisaged in the relevant legislation.

Forensic accountants may play an important role in pre-trial negotiations. Their understanding of the numbers and the financial and taxation implications of the proposals can be helpful in settling the case. Many matrimonial cases are settled before trial and participation by the forensic accountant at that stage can greatly assist in settlement negotiations.

A forensic accountant may also be needed if either spouse is of significant individual financial worth. In this case, assets may need to be located, valued and allocated between the two parties. Where the proceedings are contested, forensic accountants may assist in reviewing records to search for matrimonial assets and in negotiating agreed valuations.

---

[57]This is considered from a U.K. perspective by Lemar, C.J. and Mainz, A.J. (eds), *Litigation Support* (4th ed., Butterworths, London, 1999), Chap. 7; MacGregor, G. and Hobbs, I., *Expert Accounting Evidence: A Guide for Litigation Support* (Accountancy Books, London, 1998), Chap. 24; Taub, M., Rapazzini, A., Bond, C., Solon, M., Brown, A., Murrie, A., Linnell, K. and Burn, S., *Tolley's Accountancy Litigation Support* (Butterworths, London, looseleaf), Part VI, para. 105; and from a U.S. perspective by Levi, V.A., "Marital dissolution: Professional goodwill and related intangibles" in *Litigation Services Handbook. The Role of the Accountant as Expert* (2nd ed., Weil, R.L., Wagner, M.J. and Frank, P.B. (eds), John Wiley & Sons, Inc., New York, 1995), Chap. 26; and Ravano, C.P. and Gursey, D.L., "Marital dissolution: Tracing and apportionment of assets" in *Litigation Services Handbook. The Role of the Accountant as Expert* (2nd ed., Weil, R.L., Wagner, M.J. and Frank, P.B. (eds.), John Wiley & Sons, Inc., New York, 1995), Chap. 27.
[58]Corrigan, K., *Revenue Law* (Round Hall Sweet & Maxwell, Dublin, 2000), Vol. I, paras 7–255 *et seq.*

7–92   Examples of matrimonial cases involving forensic accountants are shown in Table 7.8. The forensic accountant can act at different stages of separation and divorce cases:

– undertaking an initial review of financial affairs and accounts in order to provide detailed matrimonial questionnaires;

– identifying further information required resulting from the answers to questionnaires to ensure that all assets are discovered and valued correctly;

– preparing expert reports dealing with the values of assets;

– giving advice on the tax implications of transfers of assets which may be required;

– reporting on Irish assets for divorce actions outside Ireland.

Table 7.8: Examples of matrimonial cases in which forensic accountants have advised

Investigative work • Undertaking an initial review of financial affairs and accounts • Identifying further information required resulting from the initial review to ensure that all assets are discovered and valued correctly • Giving advice on the tax implications of transfers of assets • Investigating a company controlled by one party
Accounting calculations • Preparing detailed schedules of net disposable income and income tax calculations for maintenance support • Preparing and quantifying the matrimonial and non-matrimonial assets and liabilities for distribution purposes.
Valuations • Providing expert evidence on share and business valuations (see Chapter 18). • Valuing interests in property companies, professional practices, etc. (see Chapter 18).
Expert evidence • Evidence on compensation of one party • Expert evidence regarding the value of a business and the owning party's level of annual income

7–93   The various activities of forensic accountants in matrimonial proceedings are summarised in Table 7.9.

Business valuations

7–94   Forensic accounting work may include a business valuation (see Chapter 18), if a spouse is a principal in a business. If the husband and wife have joint ownership of a private company, a partnership or an unincorporated business, then the entity needs to be valued for financial breakdown.

Table 7.9: Activities of forensic accountants in matrimonial cases

Calculation of net family property
- Marshalling the assets
- Preparation of schedules of income
- Preparation of detailed budgets of expenditure
- Pension considerations
- Valuation of a closely held business or of shares in a private company
- Valuation of a professional practice
- Tax consequences of the proposed settlement

Forensic investigations
- Tracing of assets
- Asset recovery
- Discovery of unreported cash
- Fraudulent transfer of matrimonial property

Pre-trial
- Preparing the expert report
- Helping negotiate a settlement
- Mediation of financial matters

Trial
- Giving evidence
- Assisting the barrister in cross-examination of the opposing expert

7–95 When one or both of the spouses owns a business or professional practice, a judicial separation or divorce can involve two sets of lawyers, experts and many months or years of expensive wrangling. Forensic accountants can calculate a value for the business. However, there may be a big difference between the opposing forensic accountants' opinions on value. A judge then will decide which expert to believe and the future of the parties is placed in his hands.

As an alternative to court proceedings, a mediator can draft an agreement which can be turned by the lawyers into a formal property settlement and dissolution agreement. It is important to remember, however, that under the terms of the Family Law (Divorce) Act 1996, a divorce can only be granted, following compliance with various provisions designed to encourage reconciliation, by a court and the court retains very significant discretion, both at the time of the granting of the divorce and thereafter, and irrespective of the terms agreed between the parties, over the financial arrangements to be made.

Accounting calculations

7–96 In divorce and matrimonial separation cases, accounting issues can involve valuing the business owned by one or both spouses, valuing the joint assets, searching for joint cash flow and considering of cost of living issues.

Forensic accountants assist in identifying the source and disposition of profits and assets, developing asset distribution models, planning the tax aspects and related analyses. It is beyond the scope of this book to cover the complex tax issues arising in matrimonial separation and divorce.[59]

7–97 Spousal and child support awards generally depend on the court's evaluation of the estimated cash available for spending by each spouse. Therefore, the court needs data sufficient to assess an appropriate support award. Forensic accountants can assist by examining the historic income and expenditures of the parties and advising on the level of available discretionary income (*i.e.* remaining income after essential expenditure is deducted).

7–98 The American system of equitable distribution does not apply in Ireland and Irish law does not require the use of equitable distribution.

Given Ireland's increasing prosperity, economic aspects of marriages, including valuation and division of matrimonial property as well as tax considerations, are likely to grow in importance. However, jurisprudence in the High Court in relation to orders pursuant to the Judicial Separation and Family Law Reform Act 1989, as amended by the Family Law Act 1995, and the Family Law (Divorce) Act 1996 is very sparse. Consequently, it is difficult to predict what any court will do in relation to distribution of assets.

The court will provide what it considers to be "proper" provision (see para. **7–83**) by giving a dependant spouse sufficient income and assets to provide a reasonable lifestyle. "Proper" provision does not necessarily mean an equal division of the assets. Where the assets are not substantial, this might result in an equal distribution of the assets especially where children are involved. Where, however, children are not involved there may not be an equal distribution. The distribution depends on several factors, including the ages of the parties, and the length of the marriage.

7–99 Given the relatively recent advent of divorce in Ireland, practice is still evolving and there are no hard and fast rules or principles laid down governing the distribution of matrimonial property. However, developments following the introduction of judicial separation under the Judicial Separation and Family Law Reform Act of 1989 indicate that the principle that, regardless of relative income-earning history, spouses contribute equally to a marriage does appear to be gaining acceptance in Ireland. This, of course, does not necessarily result in an equal distribution of assets because the law recognises the needs of all family members and takes a special interest in the provisions necessary for children. Therefore, in cases where there are no children, the courts are likely to start

---

[59] This aspect of matrimonial disputes is dealt with by Corrigan, K., *Revenue Law* (Round Hall Sweet & Maxwell, Dublin, 2000), Vol. I, paras 7–255 *et seq.*; and Walpole, H., "Tax pitfalls of divorce" (2000) 13 *Irish Tax Review* 449.

from a position where the spouses are entitled to equal shares in assets, less related liabilities, accumulated during the marriage and to adjust that distribution based on reasonable grounds for exceptions. For example, the duration of the marriage and the relative assets positions of the parties prior to marriage will be taken into account. Where there are dependant children of the marriage, however, the courts are more likely to look at the needs of each family member and approve a distribution that is as fair as possible to all.

In many equitable distribution cases, a three-step analysis is required:

– first, property owned by the parties must be characterised as matrimonial or non-matrimonial;

– next, the property must be valued;

– finally, monetary adjustments may be made to take account of assets which will not be equitably distributed (*e.g.* pension adjustment orders in respect of pension rights– see para. **7–73**).

7–100   The need to consider the position of children, even where they were not dependant, was emphasised by Barron J. in *R.C. v. C.C.*[60] when, in comparing the constitutional provision dealing with divorce and the corresponding wording in the statute, he said:

"It is to be noted that the provisions of clause 3 of Article 41, s. 3, sub-s. 2 of the Constitution differ from the corresponding statutory provision. The former requires:

'such provisions as the Court considers proper having regard to the circumstances exists or will be made for the spouses, any children of either or both of them and any other person prescribed by law',

whereas the latter provides for:

'such provision as the Court considers proper having regard to the circumstances exists or will be made for the spouses and any dependant [*sic*] members of the family.'

Since the jurisdiction invoked is that contained in the Constitution and not that amplified by the Act, it is necessary for the court to consider the position of the children."

In the case in question, the assets were substantial and the court was entitled to take all the children into account. More often, the assets are not substantial, and the principles articulated by Barron J. in relation to the children would not necessarily apply.

---

[60][1997] 1 I.R. 334 at 339.

7–101 Other factors that may be taken into account in determining a fair distribution include:

- age;
- the physical and emotional health of the parties;
- the income or property brought to the marriage by each party;
- the standard of living established during the marriage;
- any written agreement made by the parties before or during the marriage concerning property distribution;
- the economic circumstances of each party at the time the division of property becomes effective – the income and earning capacity of each party;
- the contribution of each party to the education, training, or earning power of the other;
- the contribution of each party to the acquisition, dissipation, preservation, depreciation, or appreciation in the amount or value of the matrimonial property;
- the contribution of each party as a homemaker.

7–102 Even if an asset is subject to distribution, there may be legal questions as to how it is to be treated. If a closely held business was acquired prior to the marriage and has appreciated/declined in value, what share should the non-entitled spouse receive, if any? Should the same treatment be extended to other "passive" assets acquired prior to the marriage?

7–103 The distribution process has been characterised as having three steps. These are to:

- identify or list the property subject to distribution, *i.e.* marshalling the assets;
- determine its value for purposes of distribution. Forensic accountants can assist in valuing closely held businesses and professional practices. Other valuation experts may be required to value other assets such as residential property, commercial property, etc. Actuaries may be the best experts to value pension and related retirement benefits;
- decide on an allocation based on the principles outlined above.

Matrimonial and non-matrimonial assets

7–104 Forensic accountants determine pre- and post-matrimonial assets using bank records and related documentation. Forensic accountants can also assist in identifying separate property intermingling with matrimonial property. Intermingling occurs when separate property has been "mixed" with property earned during the marriage. Accountants can assist in distinguishing such separate property so that it is properly accounted for in the settlement.

7–105 Property acquired by either spouse prior to marriage or by third-party gift or inheritance during marriage is termed separate property and may not necessarily be subject to distribution on divorce.

7–106 The legislation allows for pension sharing on divorce. Personal pensions are treated as joint matrimonial property and should therefore be capable of being split in divorce. In the case where one spouse's personal pension is more valuable than the other's, a payment may be required from one to the other, or to a new personal pension.

Asset valuations

7–107 In family law proceedings, the court's aim is to assess the income and assets of each party and to divide these between the parties in an equitable manner. Assets and income must be distributed in a way that best enables the spouse and dependants to maintain themselves. At separation, some assets are not so easily valued, such as the family business. Other assets, such as bank accounts, are difficult to locate. Forensic accountants can assist in determining a fair value for property, and in advising on the relevant information required for a settlement. A forensic accountant can identify any gaps in information provided to determine the value of matrimonial property. When valuing matrimonial assets, the following need to be investigated:

– business ownership interests;

– intellectual property;

– potential unreported business income or assets;

– appropriateness of business write-offs;

– special issues surrounding "cash" businesses;

– personal lifestyle (to reveal possible undisclosed income or property);

– pensions;

– annuities;

– financial amount in the accounts, industry data, etc.

7–108 The importance of accurately valuing pension plans for divorce cannot be over-emphasised. Viewed as an asset, the present value of a pension will often constitute the largest portion of the matrimonial estate (see also para. 7–73). Pension valuation reports include a substantial amount of valuable information in support of the present value calculations and detailed explanations of any assumptions used. Depending on the specifics of the case, consideration of the following may be necessary:

- passive earnings adjustments;
- early retirement;
- pensions in pay-out status;
- lack of vesting;
- tax adjustments;
- cost of living adjustments;
- non-qualified deferred compensation.

Valuation of closely held businesses or shares in private companies

7–109   When either or both parties to a separation or divorce has a business or professional practice, it may be necessary for the court to establish the fair market value for purposes of the fair distribution of the matrimonial assets. The value of a business is the price a willing buyer and a willing seller would theoretically arrive at. Different models can be used, but essentially fair market value is represented by the present value of the future net cash flows to be generated by the business. Business valuation models are discussed in Chapter 18.

7–110   In cases where shares in a family company are included within the matrimonial assets, forensic accountants are often asked to form an opinion on the value of the shares. Where two spouses between them own a family business, the court is not interested in a valuation of each spouse's shares in the business and each party's rightful interest. The business will not be broken up or sold (assuming there are other assets available for settlement between the parties) and the court will merely take the value of the business into account in assessing the total assets of the couple. It will also look at other assets and income of each party to assess how best to structure the division of assets between them. The valuation is based on the business as a whole, and each shareholding is calculated on the percentage holding, with no discount for (for example) minority holdings. However, a forensic accountant might discount the value of a spouse's shareholding on the basis that it represents early receipt of the compensation for the shares, which would otherwise not have been received until the eventual sale of the business.

7–111   When analysing a company, the accountant must focus on the earnings capability of the business, as the company might not be financially stable at the time of proceedings. To accomplish this, the accountant must determine the possible borrowings and distributable cash flow to assist the court in determining proper settlement. The objective of a divorce-related business valuation is to establish a realistic value, often with limited information. The forensic accountant must appreciate that due to the acrimonious nature of the proceedings, some available financial data may not be furnished for evaluation. Any data that is presented may not fairly present the true financial picture.

Tracing assets

7–112 Sometimes at separation the level of assets belonging to the marriage partnership are somewhat lower than expected. Forensic accountants can advise if there appear to be missing assets, and can assist in tracing such missing assets, using appropriate financial and legal processes. Tracing and recovery of assets is also considered in paras **5–64** *et seq*.

Lump sums

7–113 Forensic accountants may be asked to advise on the calculation of lump-sum settlements in respect of spouse and child support. In such circumstances, the court may consider that the spouse should be able to live on a combination of capital and income arising from the lump sum in much the same way as an annuity. A simple annuity approach to the calculations may be sufficient in certain circumstances.

7–114 *Duxbury* calculations are used in the United Kingdom to calculate the quantum of large, lump-sum adjustments in "clean break" divorce cases. They are known as *Duxbury* calculations after *Duxbury v. Duxbury*,[61] the first case in which they were used. Although, as stated earlier "clean break" settlements do not apply in Ireland, these calculations may be used in Irish proceedings as guidelines.

A computer model has been developed which was used in that case. The model calculates the capital sum necessary to provide the net after-tax annual sum necessary to meet the spouse's reasonable requirements, assuming she will live for a period exactly equal to her average actuarial expectation of life.[62] The model includes various relevant factors including inflation, after-tax return on investment of the capital sum, after-tax capital growth of the capital sum and estimates of changes in tax rates.

Bankruptcy[63]

7–115 Bankruptcy is a process whereby the property of an individual, who is either unable or unwilling to pay his debts, is transferred to a trustee to be sold and distributed among his creditors.[64] Many accountants are familiar with the

---

[61] [1990] 2 All E.R. 77.
[62] Lemar, C.J. and Mainz, A.J. (eds.), *Litigation Support* (4th ed., Butterworths, London, 1999), p. 111, para. 745 *et seq*.
[63] We are indebted to Mark Sanfey, B.L. and Alacoque Condon, B.L. of the Examiner's Office for comments on and assistance with the material in this section of the chapter.
[64] Rubotham, N. "Bankruptcy: A view from the inside" *Courts Service News*, Vol. 1, No. 2, p. 12.

principles underlying company receiverships, liquidations and examinerships and the role that accountants can play in such situations. Less familiarity exists with the equivalent for individuals of corporate liquidations, *i.e.* bankruptcy. However, the involvement and advice of forensic accountants can be useful in advancing a bankruptcy situation to a fair solution.

Bankruptcy administration in Ireland is provided almost exclusively as a service of the court (through the Official Assignee, an official of the court) and, in practice, while it is possible, it is rare for a private trustee to be appointed to administer the estate of a bankrupt.

In practice, forensic accountants are rarely, if ever, involved in bankruptcy cases. This is because limited resources are available to pay for such services. This is not to say that forensic accountants do not have a valuable contribution to make in such cases. If involved, their work is likely to be limited and focused on particular aspects of the process. Where the bankrupt has a substantial business which can be sold as a going concern, it is likely the price obtained for the business would be greater if the business could continue in operation *(e.g.* under management of an accountant acting as a quasi-receiver) while a buyer is being sought for the business. A proper and professional search for a buyer, and sale of the business as a going concern by accountants, is likely to generate more funds for creditors.

Normally, creditors are paid a certain number of pence per pound owing, depending on the proceeds obtained from sale of the bankrupt's assets. Section 40 of the Bankruptcy Act 1988 also envisages the possibility of agreeing a composition with creditors by paying creditors by instalment. Skills of the forensic accountant are particularly valuable where assets need to be valued and the financial position of a bankrupt determined. Such information may be needed in order to agree a composition with the bankrupt's creditors, although to date this has rarely been done in practice.

Legal context[65]

7–116   Bankruptcy arises when a person cannot or will not pay his debts and is adjudicated a bankrupt in accordance with section 14 of the Bankruptcy Act 1988. Section 7 of the Act defines situations in terms of an "act of bankruptcy" as follows:

> "(1) An individual (in this Act called a 'debtor') commits an act of bankruptcy in each of the following cases—
> (a) if in the State or elsewhere he makes a conveyance or assignment of all or substantially all of his property to a trustee or trustees for the benefit of his creditors generally;
> (b) if in the State or elsewhere he makes a fraudulent conveyance, gift, delivery or transfer of his property or any part thereof;

---

[65] A useful legal source on bankruptcy law is Sanfey, M. and Holohan, B., *Bankruptcy Law and Practice in Ireland* (The Round Hall Press, Dublin, 1991).

(c) if in the State or elsewhere he makes any conveyance or transfer of his property or any part thereof, or creates any charge thereon, which would under this or any other Act be void as a fraudulent preference if he were adjudicated bankrupt;

(d) if with intent to defeat or delay his creditors he leaves the State or being out of the State remains out of the State or departs from his dwelling-house or otherwise absents himself or evades his creditors;

(e) if he files in the Court a declaration of insolvency;

(f) if execution against him has been levied by the seizure of his goods under an order of any court or if a return of no goods has been made by the sheriff or county registrar whether by endorsement on the order or otherwise;

(g) if the creditor presenting a petition has served upon the debtor in the prescribed manner a bankruptcy summons, and he does not within fourteen days after service of the summons pay the sum referred to in the summons or secure or compound for it to the satisfaction of the creditor.

(2) A debtor also commits an act of bankruptcy if he fails to comply with a debtor's summons served pursuant to section 21(6) of the Bankruptcy (Ireland) Amendment Act, 1872, within the appropriate time thereunder, and section 8(6) of this Act shall apply to such debtor's summons."

7–117   Section 84 of the Company Law Enforcement Act 2001, which section is scheduled to come into operation on March 1, 2002, extends the definition of undischarged bankrupt in section 2 of the Companies Act 1963 to include those adjudged bankrupt in any foreign jurisdiction, as follows:

"'[U]ndischarged bankrupt' means a person who is declared bankrupt by a court of competent jurisdiction, within the State or elsewhere, and who has not obtained a certificate of discharge or its equivalent in the relevant jurisdiction."

At present the definition is limited to undischarged bankrupts in Ireland and the United Kingdom.

Under section 183 of the Companies Act 1963, undischarged bankrupts are disqualified to act as director or officers of companies (see para. **10–28**). Section 40 of the Company Law Enforcement Act 2001 provides to provide a mechanism to allow the Director of Corporate Enforcement to intervene where he suspects that an undischarged bankrupt is acting as a company director and to permit the court to make a disqualification order against such a director. No date has yet been fixed for this section to come into effect.

7–118   An individual becomes adjudicated bankrupt on foot of an order of the court following the hearing by the court of a petition presented either by a creditor, or by the bankrupt himself. A debtor can petition the court for his own bankruptcy, provided the estate will produce at least £1,500, and this option may be availed of where the bankrupt is being vigorously pursued by individual creditors. The legal process provides some protection to the bankrupt. An adjudication in bankruptcy prevents the exercise by unsecured creditors of the usual remedies available. Following bankruptcy, creditors must take the benefit of the bankruptcy and cannot proceed to execute their judgments separately against the bankrupt.

The petition must be founded on an act of bankruptcy, as defined, which took place within three months before the presentation of the petition. In addition, a petition can only be presented against a debtor who is domiciled in the State or has been ordinarily resident in, or has carried on business in, the State within a year before the petition is presented. The amount of the debt must be a liquidated sum of £1,500 or more. An act of bankruptcy (principally those specified in section 7 of the Act) can consist of a voluntary or involuntary action or a default, *e.g.* failure to comply with a bankruptcy summons requesting payment.

7–119   Once adjudicated bankrupt, the debtor is obliged under section 19 of the Act to:

> "(a) unless the Court otherwise directs, forthwith deliver up to the Official Assignee such books of account or other papers relating to his estate in his possession or control as the Official Assignee may from time to time request and disclose to him such of them as are in the possession or control of any other person;
>
> (b) deliver up possession of any part of his property which is divisible among his creditors under this Act, and which is for the time being in his possession or control, to the Official Assignee or any person authorised by the Court or otherwise under the provisions of this Act to take possession of it;
>
> (c) unless the Court otherwise directs, within the prescribed time file in the Central Office a statement of affairs in the prescribed form and deliver a copy thereof to the Official Assignee;
>
> (d) give every reasonable assistance to the Official Assignee in the administration of the estate;
>
> (e) disclose to the Official Assignee any after-acquired property."

In addition, the petitioning creditor shall, after adjudication, and at the request of the Official Assignee, provide all information he may have relating to the trade, dealings, affairs, or property of the bankrupt, and produce to the Official Assignee any relevant books of account and documents in his possession.

7–120   The legal process of bankruptcy is mainly for the benefit and relief of the people to whom the bankrupt owes money, *i.e.* the creditors. The object is to enable the creditors to recover amounts due to them or as much of those amounts as possible. If there are insufficient funds in the bankrupt's estate to pay all creditors, monies raised through disposal of the bankrupt's assets during bankruptcy are divided rateably among the unsecured creditors, after discharge of the costs, expenses and fees of the Official Assignee and the petitioning creditor, and after any preferential creditors.

7–121   When a person is made bankrupt (referred to by the courts as "adjudicated bankrupt"), under section 44 of the Act, that person's property vests by law in the Official Assignee, a court-appointed official whose role and duties are defined by statute. The bankrupt's property will be sold and the proceeds distributed to his creditors.

The Official Assignee's function is to realise the bankrupt's property and to distribute the proceeds among his creditors. He does not have the power to carry on the bankrupt's business after bankruptcy. Under the Bankruptcy Act 1988, the Official Assignee may agree costs not exceeding £1,000. This is to avoid the delay of taxing the costs. The Minister for Justice may increase or reduce this limit. The Official Assignee may also agree the charges of accountants, auctioneers, brokers or other persons without referring the matter to the Taxing Master.

7–122 An alternative to bankruptcy is arrangement. If a debtor in financial difficulties feels he is unable to meet his debts he can apply to the court to make an arrangement with his creditors. Arrangement procedures are similar to examinerships for companies. The principle is the same in that the arranging debtor gets a breathing space in which he is "protected until further order from action or other process" to enable him to put together a proposal for his creditors.

This process has the advantage of providing some protection to the debtor, who can also avoid the disabilities and disqualifications resulting from being bankrupt, and afford him some measure of privacy to protect his name, standing and credit.

There are two kinds of arrangement. Voluntary arrangements are outside the control of the court and can avoid the disabilities and disqualifications resulting from being adjudged a bankrupt. In involuntary arrangements, the debtor first seeks the protection of the court with a view to reaching a compromise with creditors, 60 per cent (in number and value) of whom must accept the proposal, which must then be approved by the court.

Role of forensic accountants

7–123 Accountants may be involved in bankruptcy in the following circumstances:

- as trustees in voluntary arrangements;
- as trustees acting with a committee of inspection appointed by the court;
- as members of a committee of inspection (*e.g.* on behalf of a financial institution);
- as receiver/manager of property of the bankrupt or arranging debtor;
- as a creditor's assignee;
- as an expert witness;
- as advisers to unsecured creditors (*e.g.* financial institutions), or to debtors/ bankrupts contemplating a composition with creditors;
- as provider of professional services to the Official Assignee.

Although the bankrupt is required to make full disclosure of his assets, the Official Assignee will carry out his own investigation of the bankrupt's asset position. In practice, forensic accountants are most likely to be involved in bankruptcy proceedings primarily for the purpose of identifying assets which may have been secreted away, or in establishing what proportion of joint assets (such as a family home) may be attributed to the bankrupt. Such a function could be carried out on behalf of the Official Assignee, although the Official Assignee is largely restricted to funding investigative activities from the assets of the bankruptcy, which are usually meagre. Such a role could also be performed by or on behalf of an accountant acting as a trustee in bankruptcy under section 110 of the 1988 Act or by a receiver or manager appointed by the court pursuant to section 73 of the 1988 Act. The assets of the bankrupt would have to be substantial to fund the forensic accounting work.

7–124 Accountants may be appointed by the court under section 73 of the Act as receiver or manager to take possession of the bankrupt's property or part of it.

Receivers/managers are normally appointed by the court on application by a mortgagee. The assignment may involve the sale of a business of the bankrupt as a going concern. The court has the power under section 73 to appoint "a receiver or manager of the whole or part of the property of the bankrupt or arranging debtor". This may be done at any time after the adjudication or after the granting of an order for protection. The receiver/manager must submit accounts to the Official Assignee.

In practice, however, appointments as receiver/manager are rare. This may not be the case in the future as Ireland grows more prosperous. Such an appointment is justified where the bankruptcy is substantial and there are sufficient assets to fund the appointment.

7–125 In the case of *Re Dolan, a bankrupt*,[66] the bankrupt was given liberty by the court to continue proceedings arising out of his interest in certain property, and these proceedings resulted in the payment of £10,000 in compensation for the benefit of the bankrupt. An accounting firm with a statutory mortgage on the property pursued a claim in the bankruptcy and, despite the existence of a letter undertaking to lodge any compensation received with a specified bank, the accounting firm's claim succeeded. In addition, legal and accounting costs and expenses arising subsequent to the date of the court order giving the bankrupt liberty to continue the proceedings were also allowed.

Accountants may also wind up the bankrupt's estate under a court order to do so under section 110 of the Act as a trustee in bankruptcy if the requisite three-fifths in number and value of the creditors voting at the statutory sitting vote in favour of such a course. Again, to date such appointments have been rare.

---

[66] [1981] I.L.R.M. 155.

Concluding comment

7–126 The value to litigation of the knowledge, expertise, experience and training of an accountant should never be underestimated. This value can be seen readily in many aspects of the legal process. On a day-to-day basis, however, the involvement of accountants in the quantification of damages for personal injuries can often go unnoticed. In many cases, lost income or earnings, when converted to a present value, can represent a multiple of the likely compensation for pain and suffering. The work of the accountant in calculating such losses, and in making appropriate adjustments for taxation, often goes largely unchallenged. Expert accountants need to be aware of the significance of their calculations to the total damages to be recovered by an injured plaintiff and should be careful to ensure that the accounting principles, tax rules and working assumptions they use are appropriate to the situation. They can also assist in performing sensitivity analysis to show how the value of a claim can vary when assumptions change. The ability to do this, particularly using a computer model that incorporates tax effects and other consequences of changed assumptions (*e.g.* by distinguishing fixed and variable costs in profit calculations) can be enormously valuable and can also have the effect of highlighting the importance of the expert accountant to the process.

CRIMINAL

CHAPTER 8

CRIMINAL

General background

8–01   This chapter provides an introduction to criminal law and to criminal offences related to which forensic accountants might advise.[1] Civil and criminal cases have been introduced and compared in Chapter 2 (paras **2–25** *et seq.*). Criminal prosecutions require a higher standard of proof than civil cases. For a criminal prosecution to succeed, the guilt of the accused must be proven "beyond reasonable doubt".[2] In civil cases, the standard of proof required is the "balance of probability", which is generally understood to mean that the plaintiff has established to the satisfaction of the court that it is more likely than not that the defendant committed the wrong of which the plaintiff complains. Procedure in criminal trials is considered in more detail in Chapter 20.

Role of forensic accountants

8–02   Most litigation involving forensic accountants arises from allegations of civil wrongs. However, with the growth of white-collar crime in general and fraud in particular, forensic accountants are increasingly becoming involved in criminal actions. Forensic accountants may act for either the State (usually represented by the Director of Public Prosecutions for serious cases) or for the defendant.

---

[1] Recommended for a more detailed consideration of criminal law, particularly Chap. 10 on Property Offences and Chap. 11 on Corporate Crime, is Charleton, P., McDermott, P. A. and Bolger, M. *Criminal Law* (Butterworths, Dublin, 1999). Forensic accounting aspects of criminal litigation in a U.K. context, including issues of fraud and false accounting, are considered by Taub, M., Rapazzini, A., Bond, C., Solon, M., Brown, A., Murrie, A., Linnell, K. and Burn, S., *Tolley's Accountancy Litigation Support* (Butterworths, London, looseleaf), Part VIII, para. 171.

[2] In *People v. Byrne* [1974] I.R. 1 at 9 (CCA) Kenny J. stated: "The correct charge to a jury is that they must be satisfied beyond reasonable doubt of the guilt of the accused, and it is helpful if that degree of proof is contrasted with that in a civil case. It is also essential, however, that the jury should be told that the accused is entitled to the benefit of the doubt and that when two views on any part of the case are possible on the evidence, they should adopt that which is favourable to the accused unless the State has established the other beyond reasonable doubt".

8–03 Various aspects of fraud and false accounting have been discussed in Part II (Chapters 3, 4 and 5). Fraud is notoriously difficult to prove in the courts notwithstanding that many laws on the statute books exist to punish crimes involving fraud. This is partly due to the fact that fraud involves an intent to deceive, and such intent, being a state of mind, is by definition difficult to establish beyond a reasonable doubt. The difficulties associated with attempting to prove criminal fraud are exacerbated by a lack of resources available to, and dedicated to, the investigation of corporate fraud.

Forensic accountants may be asked to advise in a variety of criminal actions involving fraud, including:

- acting on behalf of prosecuting authorities such as the Director of Public Prosecutions;

- advising on defalcation of funds, *e.g.* misappropriation of monies in solicitors' client accounts;

- investigating allegations concerning directors' and employees' responsibilities, *e.g.* provision of key accounting information in criminal actions against directors;

- dealing with VAT and PAYE and other taxation fraud (taxation is dealt with in Chapter 11);

- tracing and recovery of assets (see also paras **5–64** *et seq.*);

- investigations under the Companies Acts (Chapter 13 covers such investigations);

- criminal injuries compensation claims.

The role of forensic accountants is further referred to in this chapter in cases of larceny, embezzlement and theft and in the context of fraudulent conversion. Forensic accountants have a role in many other criminal situations but it is difficult to be prescriptive, as the cases are so many and varied. Many crimes can involve an element of fraud and where this is the case, the forensic accountant can provide valuable input. The nature and size of the fraud will, to a certain extent, determine the involvement of the forensic accountant.

8–04 Criminal law is highly technical and procedural. In many cases, the constituent elements of the crime and the procedures necessary to convict the criminal are set out in detailed legislation. Failure to comply with any aspect of the relevant legislation or to satisfy any detailed requirement for a proof can be fatal to the case. For these reasons, it is essential that the forensic accountant becomes familiar with the law in the area relevant to the case in question. It is beyond the scope of this book to deal comprehensively with the criminal law. However, an outline of the relevant legal provisions is given in each of the areas in which forensic accountants are most likely to become involved.

The specific areas considered relevant to forensic accounting and covered in this chapter are: offences involving fraud or interfering with accounting records, offences under company law, and criminal offences under competition law.

In addition to the material on criminal law in this chapter, an overview of the procedural aspects of criminal cases is set out in Chapter 20.

Criminal offences under Irish law generally

8–05   There are a relatively small number of criminal offences under Irish law dealing with fraud. The primary criminal offences include[3] :

– simple larceny;

– larceny by clerk or servant;

– embezzlement;

– fraudulent conversion;

– obtaining by false pretences;

– conspiracy to defraud;

– falsification of accounts;

– blackmail, extortion, demanding money with menaces;

– handling stolen property;

– forgery/counterfeiting.

8–06   The Criminal Justice (Theft and Fraud Offences) Bill 2000, if and when enacted, would repeal, *inter alia*, the Forgery Act 1861, the Falsification of Accounts Act 1875, the Forgery Act 1913, the Larceny Act 1916, the Larceny Act 1990 and most of the Larceny Act 1861. This would have the effect of abolishing the various offences involving larceny (including simple larceny and embezzlement) and the offences of fraudulent conversion, obtaining by false pretences and handling stolen property, created by the 1916 Act (as amended by the 1990 Act). It would also result in the abolition of the existing offences of forgery (created by the Forgery Act 1913, as amended by the Criminal Law Act 1997 and the Finance Act 1989) and false accounting (created by the Falsification of Accounts Act 1875). The offences of blackmail, extortion and demanding money with menaces (created by the Criminal Justice (Public Order) Act 1994) and of conspiracy to defraud (a common law offence) would remain unaffected.

---

[3] Gallagher, E., "'Collaring' the white collar criminal" *Commercial Law Practitioner* (November 1999), pp. 263-266.

The abolished offences would be replaced by new offences including theft, deception, false accounting, handling stolen property, forgery, using or copying a false instrument and counterfeiting. The new offences are discussed more fully at paras **8–15** *et seq.,* **8–30** *et seq.,* **8–40** *et seq.,* and **8–47** *et seq.*

8–07   Other more recent statutes creating offences of a "white-collar" nature include:

– the Criminal Damage Act 1991, which introduced provisions to deal with computer crime (see paras **8–45** *et seq.*);

– the Criminal Justice Act 1994, which deals with the proceeds of drug trafficking and with money laundering generally (see paras **8–96** *et seq.*);

– the Investment Limited Partnerships Act 1994, which introduced criminal offences to deal with persons (or companies) falsely holding themselves out as investment limited partnerships;

– the Investment Intermediaries Act 1995, which introduced criminal offences to deal with persons (or companies) falsely holding themselves out as investment business firms (beyond the scope of this book);

– the Stock Exchange Act 1995, which introduced criminal offences to deal with persons (or companies) falsely holding themselves out as stock exchanges (beyond the scope of this book);

– the Taxes Consolidation Act 1997, which gathered together and consolidated several existing offences arising from non-compliance with Revenue law (taxation is covered in paras **8–49** *et seq.* and in Chapter 11);

– the Companies Act 1990, which introduced several new or expanded offences, including fraudulent trading (by inserting a new section 297 into the Companies Act 1963 – see paras **8–55** *et seq.*), insider dealing (section 108 of the 1990 Act – see paras **8–91** *et seq.*), failing to disclose directors' interests in a company (section 196), making a false or misleading statement to an auditor (section 197), failing to keep proper books of account (section 202 – see paras **8–63** *et seq.*), furnishing false information (section 242 – see paras **8–72** *et seq.*) and falsifying company documents (section 243 – see paras **8–76** *et seq.*);

– the Competition (Amendment) Act 1996, which prohibits agreements, decisions and concerted practices whose object or effect is the prevention, restriction or distortion of competition in trade (section 4) and which creates as an offence the abuse of a dominant position in trade (section 2) (competition law is covered in paras **8–103** *et seq.* and **9–123** *et seq.*).

Many of these statutes, in addition to creating criminal offences, provide for the personal liability of individuals for losses caused by their unlawful behaviour.

8–08   Criminal offences related to which forensic accountants are likely to be retained, and which are discussed below, include:

– larceny, embezzlement, theft;

– fraudulent conversion;

– obtaining money/credit by false pretences;

– conspiracy to defraud;

– falsification of accounts.

8–09   Other criminal offences that involve financial matters which might involve the services of forensic accountants, but which are not discussed in this chapter are:

– bankruptcy offences under the Debtors (Ireland) Act 1872, including frauds by bankrupts, fraudulent transfers, concealment of property and false claims by creditors;

– customs offences under the Customs Consolidation Act 1876, including fraudulent entries and claiming drawback;

– offences by banking and financial institutions under the Central Bank Act 1971, the Credit Union Act 1997 and the Industrial and Provident Societies (Amendment) Act 1978, including fraud and misappropriation of property, failure to keep records, failure to keep proper accounts, failure to present annual accounts and fraud by officers.

Larceny, embezzlement and theft

8–10   The crimes of larceny and embezzlement have been on the statute books for some time. The Criminal Justice (Theft and Fraud Offences) Bill 2000 proposes to replace these offences with a single offence of theft.

Simple larceny/larceny by clerk or servant

8–11   The current law relating to theft can be found in the Larceny Acts 1861 (the principal Act), 1916 and 1990.[4] Given the age of the principal Act, some of the language used is somewhat old fashioned. As already discussed in the context of definitions of fraud in para. **3–08**, section 1 of the Larceny Act 1916 defines stealing in the following terms:

> "... a person steals who, without the consent of the owner, fraudulently and without a claim of right made in good faith, takes and carries away anything capable of being stolen with intent at the time of such taking permanently to deprive the owner thereof ..."

---

[4] For further discussion of this legislation, see McCutcheon, J.P., *The Larceny Act 1916* (Round Hall Press, Dublin, 1988).

Section 2 of the Larceny Act 1916 provides that "[s]tealing...shall be simple larceny and a felony...".

Embezzlement

8–12   Embezzlement occurs when property is stolen before it comes into the possession of the thief's employer. The difference between larceny and embezzlement (by a servant) revolves around whether the property is, or is not, in the master's possession. At common law, a servant who misappropriated his master's property was guilty of larceny only if the property was in actual or constructive possession of the master. Embezzlement, on the other hand, takes place when the servant misappropriates property entrusted to him by a third party on behalf of the master. Section 17 of the 1916 Act deals with larceny and embezzlement by clerks or servants as follows:

> "Every person who—
> (1) being a clerk or servant or person employed in the capacity of a clerk or servant—
>   (a) steals any chattel, money or valuable security belonging to or in the possession or power of his master or employer; or
>   (b) fraudulently embezzles the whole or any part of any chattel, money or valuable security delivered to or received or taken into possession by him for or in the name or on the account of his master or employer..."

8–13   The distinction between larceny and embezzlement has, in practice, little practical consequence.[5] Section 17 of the Larceny Act 1916 only applies to clerks or servants (*i.e.* generally employees), which are different from officers, agents or contractors.

8–14   Definitions of fraud are considered in Chapter 3 (paras **3–04** *et seq.*). The term "fraudulently" (as used in sections 1 and 17 of the 1916 Act, quoted above in paras 8–11 and 8–12) was considered in *The People (Attorney General) v. Grey*[6] and is accepted as referring to something dishonest or morally wrong. McCutcheon cites Stephen who points out that "[i]t is essential to fraud that the fraudulent person's conduct should not merely be wrongful, but should be intentionally and knowingly wrongful...".[7] In *Superwood Holdings plc v. Sun Alliance and London Insurance plc*, Denham J. referred back to the judgment of Lord Herschell in the seminal case of *Derry v. Peek* as follows:

> "The foundation case is *Derry v. Peek* (1889) 14 App. Cas. 337. In that case an Act incorporating a tramway company provided that the carriages might be moved by animal power, and, with the consent of the Board of Trade, by steam power. The directors of the company issued a prospectus wherein it was stated that by

---

[5] McCutcheon, J.P., *The Larceny Act 1916* (Round Hall Press, Dublin, 1988), p. 54.
[6] [1944] I.R. 326 at 332.
[7] McCutcheon, J.P,. *The Larceny Act 1916* (Round Hall Press, Dublin, 1988), p. 17.

their Act the company had the right to use steam power instead of horses. The plaintiff bought shares on the faith of that statement in the prospectus. Later the Board of Trade refused consent to the use of steam power and the company was wound up. The plaintiff brought an action of deceit against the directors founded upon the false statement, and was unsuccessful. The House of Lords held that there was no fraud, Lord Herschell stating, at p. 374:—

> 'First, in order to sustain an action of deceit, there must be proof of fraud, and nothing short of that will suffice. Secondly, fraud is proved when it is shown that a false representation has been made (1) knowingly, or (2) without belief in its truth, or (3) recklessly, careless whether it be true or false. Although I have treated the second and third as distinct cases, I think the third is but an instance of the second, for one who makes a statement under such circumstances can have no real belief in the truth of what he states. To prevent a false statement being fraudulent, there must, I think, always be an honest belief in its truth. And this probably covers the whole ground, for one who knowingly alleges that which is false, has obviously no such honest belief. Thirdly, if fraud be proved, the motive of the person guilty of it is immaterial. It matters not that there was no intention to cheat or injure the person to whom the statement was made.'

That analysis of the law remains true today, and is applicable to this case."[8]

This judgment would indicate that fraud must be proved and to do so involves showing that the fraud was carried out "knowingly", or "without belief in its truth" or "recklessly" as to its truth or falseness.

Theft under the Criminal Justice (Theft and Fraud Offences) Bill 2000

8–15   The whole of the Larceny Act 1861 (except sections 12–16, 24 and 25) and the whole of the Larceny Acts 1916 and 1990 are proposed for repeal by the Criminal Justice (Theft and Fraud Offences) Bill 2000. The Bill envisages replacement of many of these offences by new offences, including:

— theft under section 4, defined as the dishonest appropriation of property without the consent of its owner and with the intention of depriving its owner of it (see below, para. 8–16);

— making gain or causing loss by deception under section 6, the definition of which involves dishonestly inducing a person to do or refrain from doing an act;

— obtaining services by deception under section 7;

— making off with the intention of avoiding payment on the spot under section 8;

---

[8] [1995] 3 I.R. 303 at 327–328.

– dishonestly operating a computer with the intention of making gain or causing loss to another person under section 9 (see para. **8–44** *et. seq.*);

– false accounting under section 10;

– dishonestly suppressing documents and executing valuable security by deception under section 11;

– forgery under Part 4;

8–16   Under section 4 of the Bill, theft would be defined as:

"(1) Subject to section 5, a person is guilty of theft if he or she dishonestly appropriates property without the consent of its owner and with the intention of depriving its owner of it.

(2) For the purposes of this section a person does not appropriate property without the consent of its owner if—

    (a)   the person believes that he or she has the owner's consent, or would have the owner's consent if the owner knew of the appropriation of the property and the circumstances in which it was appropriated, or

    (b)   (except where the property came to the person as trustee or personal representative) he or she appropriates the property in the belief that the owner cannot be discovered by taking reasonable steps,

but consent obtained by deception or intimidation is not consent for those purposes.

. . .

(4) If at the trial of a person for theft the court or jury, as the case may be, has to consider whether the person believed—

    (a)   that he or she had not acted dishonestly, or

    (b)   that the owner of the property concerned had consented or would have consented to its appropriation, or

    (c)   that the owner could not be discovered by taking reasonable steps,

the presence or absence of reasonable grounds for such a belief is a matter to which the court or jury shall have regard, in conjunction with any other relevant matters, in considering whether the person so believed."

8–17   Section 5 proposes to provide exceptions to the offence of theft, including property or rights transferred with defective title and theft of land, wild vegetation and wild animals.

Role of forensic accountants in larceny, embezzlement and theft cases

8–18   As in other areas of criminal law, accountants can appear as witnesses of fact in prosecutions for larceny, embezzlement and theft. Such appearances will arise most often where a fraud has been perpetrated on a company or business, either by an employee or officer or by a third party. Company accountants may be required to give evidence of fact as to the discovery of the fraud, the audit trail of paper and/or computer records that helps to describe the nature of the fraud and to identify its perpetrator and the scale of the fraud in financial terms.

Section 54(1) of the Criminal Justice (Fraud and Theft Offences) Bill 2000 proposes that accountants may be required by the trial judge to explain accounting transactions to juries, as follows:

> "In a trial on indictment of an offence under this Act, the trial judge may order that copies of any or all of the following documents shall be given to the jury in a form that the judge considers appropriate:
>
> . . .
>
> (f) any other document that in the opinion of the trial judge would be of assistance to the jury in its deliberations including, where appropriate, an affidavit by an accountant summarising, in a form which is likely to be comprehended by the jury, any transactions by the accused or other persons which are relevant to the offence."

8–19 There is also scope, however, for forensic accountants to act as experts in such cases. Evidence relevant to whether an accused person is guilty of an offence tends to be of a factual nature and it is only when relevant facts need to be assessed or interpreted by an expert (*e.g.* by examination of accounting or computer records) that an expert will be necessary. Forensic accountants can, nevertheless, have a role in quantifying the scale of a fraud and this in turn has implications for the seriousness of the crime and, potentially, for the severity of the sentence.

Fraudulent conversion

8–20 As already mentioned in para. 8–12, section 17 of the Larceny Act 1916 only applies to clerks or servants (*i.e.* to employees). Actions of officers, agents and independent contractors are considered under section 20 which deals with wrongful conversion of property by fiduciary agents. The essence of fraudulent conversion is that the accused obtained the property in a fiduciary capacity and subsequently converted it with intent to defraud (*i.e.* to dishonestly devote the property to some other purpose). Section 20 states:

> "20.—(1) Every person who —
>
> (i)   being entrusted either solely or jointly with any other person with any power of attorney for the sale or transfer of any property, fraudulently sells, transfers, or otherwise converts the property or any part thereof to his own use or benefit, or the use or benefit of any person other than the person by whom he was so entrusted; or
>
> (ii) being a director, member or officer of any body corporate or public company, fraudulently takes or applies for his own use or benefit, or for any use or purposes other than the use or purposes of such body

> corporate or public company, any of the property of such body corporate or public company; or
>
> . . .
>
> (iv) (a) being entrusted either solely or jointly with any other person with any property in order that he may retain in safe custody or apply, pay, or deliver, for any purpose or to any person, the property or any part thereof or any proceeds thereof; or
>
>   (b) having either solely or jointly with any other person received any property for or on account of any other person;
>
> fraudulently converts to his own use or benefit, or the use or benefit of any other person, the property or any part thereof or any proceeds thereof;
>
> shall be guilty of a misdemeanour …".

8–21   The essence of this offence is that the accused acquired the property in a fiduciary capacity and subsequently converted it wrongfully to his own use. In other words, the property was entrusted to the individual for a purpose other than his own benefit and he subsequently appropriated it for himself. This offence is distinguished from the offence of obtaining by false pretences in that the latter offence involves the transfer to the individual taking place on foot of a false pretence (see para. **8–26** *et. seq.*) by him, meaning that there has been no genuine entrustment by the transferor. This distinction is seen clearly in the judgment of the Court of Criminal Appeal, delivered by Maguire C.J. in *People (Attorney General) v. Heald*:

> "In the opinion of this Court it must be shown that the applicant had authority to receive the money on behalf of the nuns before she can be convicted of the offence of fraudulent conversion. … In argument, Mr. D'Arcy admitted that if a complete stranger to the nuns had imposed on these two old ladies in precisely the same way as the applicant that the correct charge would be that of obtaining money by false pretences and not fraudulent conversion."[9]

According to Ó Dálaigh J. sitting in the Court of Criminal Appeal:

> "In the case of fraudulent conversion the fiduciary element in [*sic*] the essential basis of the offence, and the entrustment is a genuine entrustment in which the fiduciary ownership has been lawfully obtained but which, so to speak, subsequently goes wrong. The term "conversion" of itself indicates this."[10]

8–22   As for the offences of larceny and embezzlement, the legislation dealing with fraudulent conversion would be repealed and replaced by the offence of theft under section 4 of the Criminal Justice (Theft and Fraud Offences) Bill 2000.

---

[9] [1954] I.R. 58 at 62.

[10] *People (A.G.) v. Singer* [1960] 1 Frewen 214 at 227.

8–23 Fraud and misappropriation of property belonging to credit unions is an offence under section 173 of the Credit Union Act 1997.

Role of forensic accountants in fraudulent conversion cases

8–24 Again, accountants are more likely to appear as witnesses of fact than as expert witnesses in cases involving allegations of fraudulent conversion. Accounting personnel in commercial organisations may well have important evidence to give relating to the basis on which property was given to an employee and the manner in which it was expected to be used.

8–25 Forensic accounting activity in such cases is likely to be limited to involvement in the valuation of losses, and such input can be especially useful where the value of the property in question is difficult to calculate, where the calculation involves the application of accounting rules and standards or where there are consequential effects (*e.g.* lost profits) arising from the fraudulent conversion.

Obtaining by false pretences

8–26 An example of larceny by false pretences is where goods are paid for by cheque when the issuer of the cheque knows there are no funds to meet the cheque. Section 32 of the Larceny Act 1916 is concerned with obtaining by false pretences as follows:

"Every person who by any false pretence—

(1) with intent to defraud, obtains from any other person any chattel, money or valuable security, or causes or procures any money to be paid, or any chattel or valuable security to be delivered to himself or to any other person for the use or benefit or on account of himself or any other person, or
(2) with intent to defraud or injure any other person, fraudulently causes or induces any other person—
  (a) to execute, make, accept, endorse, or destroy the whole or any part of any valuable security; or
  (b) to write, impress, or affix his name or the name of any other person, or the seal of any body corporate or society, upon any paper or parchment in order that the same may be afterwards made or converted into, or used or dealt with as, a valuable security;

shall be guilty of a misdemeanour and on conviction thereof liability to a term of imprisonment not exceeding ten years or a fine or both."

8–27 Ó Dálaigh C.J. has set out the elements of the offence of obtaining by false pretences[11]:

---

[11] *People (A.G.) v. Bristow (No. 2)*, unreported, Court of Criminal Appeal, March 27, 1962.

- accused must have obtained money;

- money must have been obtained by false pretence;

- false pretence related to an existing fact;

- victim was induced to part with his money by the pretence;

- perpetrator knew that the pretence was false;

- false pretence was made with intent to defraud.

8–28 Examples of obtaining by false pretences include counterfeiting (*i.e.* holding out the money to be genuine, when it is known to be counterfeit), bouncing cheques (where the issuer of the cheque knew there was no money in the account to meet the cheque), using a stolen credit card number, etc.

Obtaining credit by false pretences

8–29 Section 13(1) of the Debtors Act (Ireland) 1872 is concerned with obtaining credit by false pretences or fraud as follows:

> "Any person shall in each of the cases following be deemed guilty of a misdemeanour, and on conviction thereof shall be liable to be imprisoned for any time not exceeding one year, with or without hard labour; that is to say,
> (1) if in incurring any debt or liability he has obtained credit under false pretences, or by means of any fraud ...".

Section 11(3) of the Criminal Law Act 1997 provides that no person shall be sentenced by a court to imprisonment with hard labour.

Deception under the Criminal Justice (Theft and Fraud Offences) Bill 2000

8–30 The Criminal Justice (Theft and Fraud Offences) Bill 2000 introduces new offences to replace the variety of offences involving deception. Section 6 introduces an offence of making gain or causing loss by deception as follows:

> "(1) A person who dishonestly, with the intention of making a gain for himself or herself or another, or of causing loss to another, induces another to do or refrain from doing an act is guilty of an offence."

8–31 Obtaining services by deception is set out in section 7 as follows:

> "(1) A person who dishonestly, with the intention of making a gain for himself or herself or another, or of causing loss to another, by any deception obtains services from another is guilty of an offence."

8–32 Section 8 of the Bill deals with dishonesty making off in the knowledge that payment on the spot is expected or required, with the intention of avoiding payment.

8–33   Section 9 proposes to extend section 6 to persons who dishonestly operate computers with the intention of making a gain or causing a loss (see para. **8–47**).

Conspiracy to defraud

8–34   A conspiracy is an agreement, arising from a conscious understanding of a common design, to perform an unlawful act. Conspiracy to defraud is an offence at common law and involves two or more parties agreeing to act in a manner that enriches themselves (or another party) at the expense of the third party. It is likely that where there is evidence of substantive offences having been committed, these will be charged and pursued in court by reference to the relevant statute in preference to common law charges.

This offence was dealt with by Geoghegan J. in the High Court in the recent extradition case of *Myles v. Sreenan*. The learned judge defined the offence as follows:

> "The best definition of the common law offence of conspiracy to defraud is probably to be found in the English case of *Scott v. Metropolitan Police Commissioner* [1975] A.C. 819. That definition reads as follows at p. 840:
>> '... an agreement by two or more by dishonesty to deprive a person of something which is his or to which he is or would be or might be entitled and an agreement by two or more by dishonesty to injure some proprietary right of his, suffices to constitute the offence of conspiracy to defraud.'
>
> In *O'Sullivan v. Conroy* (unreported, High Court, Barr J., July 31, 1997) stated the following:
>> 'It is not in dispute that the offence of conspiracy to defraud is part of the common law in Ireland, as in England ...'."[12]

Geoghegan J. went on to conclude that the common law offence had been carried over into Irish law under the Constitution.

False accounting/falsification of accounts

8–35   There are a number of general criminal offences dealing with books of account and accounting information variously termed false accounting, keeping fraudulent accounts and wilfully destroying or mutilating books of account. In addition, there are two further offences under company law – falsification of accounts and furnishing of false information – which are considered in paras **8–71** *et seq.*

False accounting

8–36   False accounting is dealt with under section 1 of the Falsification of Accounts Act 1875 (as amended by section 11 of the Criminal Law Act 1997)

---

[12] [1999] 4 I.R. 294 at 298.

which provides:

> "That if any clerk, officer, or servant, or any person employed or acting in the capacity of a clerk, officer, or servant shall wilfully and with intent to defraud, destroy, alter, mutilate, or falsify any book, paper, writing, valuable security, or account which belongs to or is in the possession of his employer or has been received by him for or on behalf of his employer, or shall wilfully and with intent to defraud make or concur in making any false entry in, or omit or alter, or concur in omitting or altering, any material particular from or in any such book, or any document, or account, then in every such case the person so offending shall be guilty of a misdemeanour, and be liable to be kept in penal servitude for a term not exceeding seven years, or to be imprisoned for any term not exceeding two years."

Section 11(1) of the Criminal Law Act 1997 provides that "no person shall be sentenced by a court to penal servitude."

8–37   Section 1 makes it clear that the falsification must (i) be deliberate and (ii) be carried out with intent to defraud. The terms "clerk, officer, or servant" are interpreted as applying to employees only.[13] Thus, accountants providing bookkeeping services to clients cannot be charged under this legislation.

Fraudulent accounts

8–38   Keeping fraudulent accounts and wilfully destroying or mutilating books of account are offences under sections 82 and 83 of the Larceny Act 1861. Section 82 states:

> "Whosoever, being a director, public officer, or manager of any body corporate or public company, shall as such receive or possess himself of any of the property of such body corporate or public company, otherwise than in payment of a just debt or demand, and shall with intent to defraud, omit to make or cause or direct to be made a full and true entry thereof in the books and accounts of such body, shall be guilty of a misdemeanour."

Wilfully destroying or mutilating books

8–39   Section 83 of the Larceny Act 1861 deals with wilfully destroying or mutilating books of account:

> "Whosoever, being a director, manager, public officer, or member of any body corporate or public company, shall, with intent to defraud, destroy, alter, mutilate, or falsify any book, paper, writing or valuable security belonging to the body corporate or public company, or make or concur in the making of any false entry, or omit or concur in omitting any material particular, in any book of account or other document shall be guilty of a misdemeanour."

---

[13] *R. v. Solomons* [1909] 2 K.B. 980.

False accounting under the Criminal Justice (Theft and Fraud Offences) Bill 2000

8–40   The Criminal Justice (Theft and Fraud Offences) Bill 2000 envisages the replacement of some of these offences by new offences. As set out above, when enacted, the new legislation will effect the repeal of, *inter alia*, the Falsification of Accounts Act 1875 and most of the Larceny Act 1861.

8–41   If the Criminal Justice (Theft and Fraud Offences) Bill 2000 is enacted as drafted, section 1 of the 1875 Act (see above, para. **8–36**) will be repealed and replaced by section 10 of the Bill in the following terms:

> "(1) A person is guilty of an offence if he or she dishonestly, with the intention of making a gain for himself or herself or another, or of causing loss to another—
> - (a) destroys, defaces, conceals or falsifies any account or any document made or required for any accounting purpose,
> - (b) fails to make or complete any account or any such document, or
> - (c) in furnishing information for any purpose produces or makes use of any account, or any such document, which to his or her knowledge is or may be misleading, false or deceptive in a material particular.
>
> (2) For the purposes of this section a person shall be treated as falsifying an account or other document if he or she—
> - (a) makes or concurs in making therein an entry which is or may be misleading, false or deceptive in a material particular, or
> - (b) omits or concurs in omitting a material particular therefrom."

8–42   The draft new provisions are significantly wider in that they appear to apply not only to officers and employees but also to anyone involved in the preparation of accounts or documents for accounting purposes. This wider group would appear to include accountants engaged in the provision of accounting or bookkeeping services to clients, and auditors engaged in the audit of accounts. The provisions appear wide enough to apply to anyone, including for example IT staff who make false entries in a computerised accounting system. Auditors may also be alarmed to discover that the effect of subsection (1)(c) may well be to expose them to significant criminal sanction where they issue a clean audit report based on accounts or documents that they know are or may be misleading, false or deceptive in a "material particular".

If proceedings were taken on this latter point, a forensic accountant is likely to play a key role in assessing the state of knowledge of the auditor at the time he made his report.

8–43   Dishonestly suppressing documents and executing valuable security by deception is covered under section 11 of the Bill:

> "(1) A person is guilty of an offence if he or she dishonestly, with the intention of making a gain for himself or herself or another, or of causing loss to another,

destroys, defaces or conceals any valuable security, any will or other testamentary document or any original documents of or belonging to, or filed or deposited in, any court or any government department or office.

(2) (a) A person who dishonestly, with the intention of making a gain for himself or herself or another, or of causing loss to another, by any deception procures the execution of a valuable security is guilty of an offence.

   (b) Paragraph (a) shall apply in relation to—

      (i) the making, acceptance, endorsement, alteration, cancellation or destruction in whole or in part of a valuable security, and

      (ii) the signing or sealing of any paper or other material in order that it may be made or converted into, or used or dealt with as, a valuable security,

as if that were the execution of a valuable security."

Computer crime

8–44 Computer crime can encompass any one of the following categories of crime:

– computer fraud (see paras **3–48** *et seq.* and paras **5–41** *et seq.*

– damage to data or programs (often referred to as computer abuse and misuse);

– theft of information.

Computer abuse and misuse

8–45 The Criminal Damage Act 1991 includes sections designed to make computer abuse, particularly by computer hackers, a criminal offence. Three aspects of computer abuse are dealt with by the legislation:

– entering computers to steal or damage data;

– damaging computer operating systems;

– perpetrating financial fraud.

The 1991 Act creates offences in respect of causing damage to property, threatening to damage property, unauthorised access to a computer and possession of anything with intent to cause damage to data. So far, no prosecutions have taken place in the Irish courts in respect of computer misuse.

Where a person has been convicted of criminal damage, the court may order that the injured party be compensated. The injured party is defined under section 2 as any person who has suffered loss other than consequential loss as a result of the actions of the accused. The compensation cannot exceed the amount that the injured party would have received in a civil action against the accused person.

8–46 Section 22 of the Data Protection Act 1992 creates an offence of gaining unauthorised access to personal data. The provision does not apply to employees or agents and appears to be aimed at hackers and others who gain access to such data without authorisation.

8–47　As already mentioned in para. **8–33**, section 9 of the Criminal Justice (Theft and Fraud Offences) Bill 2000 proposes to extend offences dealing with unlawful use of computers to include fraudulent intent as well as actual damage. The proposed section states:

> "(1) A person who dishonestly, whether within or outside the State, operates or causes to be operated a computer within the State with the intention of making a gain for himself or herself or another, or of causing loss to another, is guilty of an offence."

Theft of information

8–48　Two difficulties face any attempt to invoke the law of theft in an informational context:

– unless the information is held on some storage device which is also removed, it is difficult to see how the requirements of section 1 of the Larceny Act 1916 (*i.e.* the requirement of taking and carrying away – see para. **8–11**) or of the proposed Criminal Justice (Theft and Fraud Offences) Bill 2000 (*i.e.* the requirement to dishonestly appropriate – as the owner is still in possession of the information, though not exclusive possession – see para. **8–16**) can be applied;

– section 5 of the Criminal Justice (Theft and Fraud Offences) Bill 2000 defines theft as the appropriation of "property". It is not clear whether information can be regarded as property for the purposes of the laws of theft.

Other offences involving fraud

Tax fraud

8–49　There are several tax statutes where, typically, penalties are increased (usually doubled) where fraud has been involved in the non-payment of appropriate tax. These are considered in Chapter 11.

8–50　The Taxes Consolidation Act 1997 gathers together in section 1078 a variety of tax offences which had previously appeared in the Finance Acts of 1983, 1986, 1989, 1992 and 1996. The effect of this consolidation exercise is that most of the Revenue offences relating to income tax, corporation tax, capital gains tax, capital acquisitions tax, value added tax, stamp duty and excise duties and residential property tax are dealt with in one place in the tax code.

8–51　Section 1078 is a wide-ranging section designed to encompass all types of offences that can arise in relation to the various taxes referred to above. Section 1078(2) states:

"A person shall, without prejudice to any other penalty to which the person may be liable, be guilty of an offence under this section if the person—

    (a) knowingly or wilfully delivers any incorrect return, statement or accounts or knowingly or wilfully furnishes any incorrect information in connection with any tax,

    (b) knowingly aids, abets, assists, incites or induces another person to make or deliver knowingly or wilfully any incorrect return, statement or accounts in connection with any tax,

    (c) claims or obtains relief or exemption from, or repayment of, any tax, being a relief, exemption or repayment to which, to the person's knowledge, the person is not entitled,

    (d) knowingly or wilfully issues or produces any incorrect invoice, receipt, instrument or other document in connection with any tax,

 (dd) (i) fails to make any deduction of dividend withholding tax . . .

    (e) (i)   fails to make any deduction required to be made by the person under section 257(1),

    (f) (i)   fails to make any deduction required to be made by the person under section 734(5) . . .

    (g) knowingly or wilfully fails to comply with any provision of the Acts requiring—

        (i)   the furnishing of a return of income, profits or gains, or of sources of income, profits or gains, for the purposes of any tax,

        (ii) the furnishing of any other return, certificate, notification, particulars, or any statement or evidence, for the purposes of any tax,

        (iii) the keeping or retention of books, records, accounts or other documents for the purposes of any tax, or

        (iv) the production of books, records, accounts or other documents, when so requested, for the purposes of any tax,

    (h) knowingly or wilfully, and within the time limits specified for their retention, destroys, defaces or conceals from an authorised officer—

        (i)   any documents, or

        (ii) any other written or printed material in any form, including any information stored, maintained or preserved by means of any mechanical or electronic device, whether or not stored, maintained or preserved in a legible form, which a person is obliged by any provision of the Acts to keep, to issue or to produce for inspection,

 (hh) knowingly or wilfully falsifies, conceals, destroys or otherwise disposes of, or causes or permits the falsification, concealment, destruction or disposal of any [certain] books, records or other document[s] . . .

    (i) fails to remit any income tax payable pursuant to Chapter 4 of Part 42, and the regulations under that Chapter, or value-added tax within the time specified in that behalf in relation to income tax or value-added tax, as the case may be, by the Acts, or

    (j) obstructs or interferes with any officer of the Revenue Commissioners, or any other person, in the exercise or performance of powers or duties under the Acts for the purposes of any tax."

8–52 Liability of directors is addressed at subsections(5) and (6):

"(5) Where an offence under this section is committed by a body corporate and the offence is shown to have been committed with the consent or connivance of any person who, when the offence was committed, was a director, manager, secretary or other officer of the body corporate, or a member of the committee of management or other controlling authority of the body corporate, that person shall also be deemed to be guilty of the offence and may be proceeded against and punished accordingly.

(6) In any proceedings under this section, a return or statement delivered to an inspector or other officer of the Revenue Commissioners under any provision of the Acts and purporting to be signed by any person shall be deemed until the contrary is proved to have been so delivered and to have been signed by that person."

8–53 Section 1079 imposes an additional obligation on company auditors and on company advisers who provide assistance or advice in the preparation or delivery of information that is used or is likely to be used for any taxation purpose. The obligation arises when the auditor or adviser, while acting in that capacity, obtains information indicating that the company has committed, or is in the course of committing, a relevant offence. In such circumstances, the auditor or adviser must advise the company of the position without undue delay, request that the matter be rectified and, unless the matter is rectified, resign as auditor or adviser. A resigning auditor in these circumstances must give written notice of the resignation to the company and to an appointed officer of the Revenue Commissioners. Failure to comply with these obligations is a criminal offence.

The relevant portions of section 1079 are reproduced below and read as follows:

"(1) . . . In this section—
'relevant person', in relation to a company and subject to subsection (2), means a person who—
(a) (i) is an auditor to the company appointed in accordance with section 160 of the Companies Act, 1963 (as amended by the Companies Act, 1990), or
(ii) in the case of an industrial and provident society or a friendly society, is a public auditor to the society for the purposes of the Industrial and Provident Societies Acts, 1893 to 1978, and the Friendly Societies Acts, 1896 to 1977,
or
(b) with a view to reward, assists or advises the company in the preparation or delivery of any information, declaration, return, records, accounts or other document which he or she knows will be or is likely to be used for any purpose of tax;

'relevant offence' means an offence committed by a company which consists of the company—

(a) knowingly or wilfully delivering any incorrect return, statement or accounts or knowingly or wilfully furnishing or causing to be furnished any incorrect information in connection with any tax,

(b) knowingly or wilfully claiming or obtaining relief or exemption from, or repayment of, any tax, being a relief, exemption or repayment to which there is no entitlement,

(c) knowingly or wilfully issuing or producing any incorrect invoice, receipt, instrument or other document in connection with any tax, or

(d) knowingly or wilfully failing to comply with any provision of the Acts requiring the furnishing of a return of income, profits or gains, or of sources of income, profits or gains, for the purposes of any tax, but an offence under this paragraph committed by a company shall not be a relevant offence if the company has made a return of income, profits or gains to the Revenue Commissioners in respect of an accounting period falling wholly or partly in the period of 3 years preceding the accounting period in respect of which the offence was committed;

...

(2) For the purposes of paragraph (b) of the definition of 'relevant person', a person who but for this subsection would be treated as a relevant person in relation to a company shall not be so treated if the person assists or advises the company solely in the person's capacity as an employee of the company, and a person shall be treated as assisting or advising the company in that capacity where the person's income from assisting or advising the company consists solely of emoluments to which Chapter 4 of Part 42 applies.

(3) If, having regard solely to information obtained in the course of examining the accounts of a company, or in the course of assisting or advising a company in the preparation or delivery of any information, declaration, return, records, accounts or other document for the purposes of tax, as the case may be, a person who is a relevant person in relation to the company becomes aware that the company has committed, or is in the course of committing, one or more relevant offences, the person shall, if the offence or offences are material—

(a) communicate particulars of the offence or offences in writing to the company without undue delay and request the company to—

(i) take such action as is necessary for the purposes of rectifying the matter, or

(ii) notify an appropriate officer of the offence or offences,

not later than 6 months after the time of communication, and

(b) (i) unless it is established to the person's satisfaction that the necessary action has been taken or notification made, as the case may be, under paragraph (a), cease to act as the auditor to the company or to assist or advise the company in such preparation or delivery as is specified in paragraph (b) of the definition of 'relevant person', and

(ii) shall not so act, assist or advise before a time which is the earlier of—

    (I) 3 years after the time at which the particulars were communicated under paragraph (a), and

    (II) the time at which it is established to the person's satisfaction that the necessary action has been taken or notification made, as the case may be, under paragraph (a).

(4) Nothing in paragraph (b) of subsection (3) shall prevent a person from assisting or advising a company in preparing for, or conducting, legal proceedings, either civil or criminal, which are extant or pending at a time which is 6 months after the time of communication under paragraph (a) of that subsection.

(5) Where a person, being in relation to a company a relevant person within the meaning of paragraph (a) of the definition of 'relevant person', ceases under this section to act as auditor to the company, then, the person shall deliver—

    (a) a notice in writing to the company stating that he or she is so resigning, and

    (b) a copy of the notice to an appropriate officer not later than 14 days after he or she has delivered the notice to the company."

Criminal offences under company law

8–54 The Companies Acts contain over 280[14] separate criminal offences from minor summary offences to serious indictable offences carrying maximum sentences of ten years' imprisonment and of fines of up to £200,000. Three categories of offence of particular relevance to forensic accountants are considered in this section, which concludes by examining sundry other criminal offences under company legislation. These offences are:

– fraudulent trading;

– failure to keep proper books of account; and

– false accounting.

Fraudulent trading

8–55 The offence of fraudulent trading is dealt with in section 297 of the Companies Act 1963. This is to be distinguished from the more recently enacted civil offence of reckless trading which is considered in paras **10–59** *et seq.* Fraudulent trading is defined in section 297(1) as where:

---

[14] *Report on the Working Group on Company Law Compliance and Enforcement* (McDowell Report) (Government Publications, Dublin, November 1998), p. 9. – this figure only includes offences in the Companies Acts 1963–1990. The two 1999 Companies Acts and the Company Law Enforcement Act 2001 add further offences to the list.

> ". . . any person is knowingly a party to the carrying on of the business of a company with intent to defraud creditors of the company or creditors of any other person or for any fraudulent purpose...".

The original section 297 in the 1963 Act dealt with both criminal and civil liability for fraudulent trading. Section 297 in its present form, which deals only with criminal liability, was inserted by section 137 of the Companies Act 1990. A new section, section 297A, dealing with civil liability for reckless or fraudulent trading where a company is being wound up or is in examinership, was inserted by section 138 of the Companies Act 1990. Unlike reckless trading, as can been seen from section 297 quoted above, liability for fraudulent trading applies to "any person" and is not restricted to officers of the company.

8–56 Accordingly, for criminal liability for fraudulent trading to arise, it must be proved beyond a reasonable doubt that the person so accused was "knowingly" a party to the wrongful trading, and that the business was carried on "with intent" to defraud creditors of the company or of another person or "for any fraudulent purpose". These provisions raise questions as to the state of knowledge and the state of mind of the accused person and proof of such subjective matters beyond reasonable doubt is likely to be difficult. Courtney discusses the difficulties inherent in this.[15]

8–57 Section 297 has been interpreted by the courts in the leading case on the equivalent provisions in English law as follows:

> "[I]f a company continues to carry on business and to incur debts at a time when there is, to the knowledge of the directors, no reasonable prospect of the creditors ever receiving payment of those debts, it is, in general, a proper inference that the company is carrying on business with intent to defraud."[16]

It should be noted in relation to the above (and as discussed in para. **3–04**) there is currently no legal definition of fraud.

8–58 The original section 297, which provided for both criminal and civil sanctions for fraudulent trading, has been tested on a number of occasions in the Irish courts. Only civil claims have been taken,[17] presumably due to the difficulties in proving fraud to the criminal standard of proof.

8–59 The case of *Re Hunting Lodges Ltd*[18] concerned the sale of a pub, where the purchaser paid a sum to the company and, in addition, paid the principal

---

[15] Courtney, T.B., *The Law of Private Companies* (Butterworths, Dublin, 1994), pp. 325–330.
[16] *Re William C. Leitch Bros Ltd* [1932] 2 Ch. 71.
[17] Charleton, P., McDermott, P.A. and Bolger, M., *Criminal Law* (Butterworths, Dublin, 1999), p. 915.
[18] [1985] I.L.R.M. 75.

shareholder a side payment. The parties (*i.e.* the vendor, his wife and the purchaser) were found to be "knowingly parties" to the transaction and that the transaction was conducted with the necessary intent to defraud creditors (*i.e.* the Revenue authorities) or for fraudulent purposes. Thus, all the parties were found to be personally responsible for the debts of the company. The judge then had to decide on the amount of liability for each party to the fraud. Even though no money was lost through the behaviour of the vendor's wife, she was found personally liable because of the moral blame that could attach to her from her actions.

8–60 Other cases resulting in findings of fraudulent trading include *Re Kelly's Carpetdrome Ltd*[19]; *Re Aluminium Fabricators Ltd*[20]; and *Re Contract Packaging Ltd.*[21] In all three cases, the company failed to keep proper books of account, intent to defraud was found and personal liability for company debts was imposed on various parties associated with the companies. Liability can extend to anyone who knew of the fraudulent intent or purpose. In the case of *Re Contract Packaging Ltd*, two directors of the company were forced to sell private assets to repay company debts. In the case of *Re Kelly's Carpetdrome Ltd*, the order under section 297 was made against a respondent who was neither a director nor a member of the company and who in fact occupied no overt position in relation to the company. In both *Re Kelly's Carpetdrome Ltd* and *Re Aluminium Fabricators Ltd*, personal liability for all the debts was imposed on the respondents.

8–61 The first person to be given a prison term for fraudulent trading is the investment broker Mark Synnott. He operated an investment company Mark A. Synnott (Life and Pensions) Brokers Ltd. He took money from investors and, instead of investing the money as he had undertaken to, he lodged the proceeds which he used to pay a return to the more demanding of this clients (which he called "bonding in arrears").

8–62 An example of issues that may arise in a case of fraudulent trading is shown in Case History 8.1.

Failure to keep proper books of account

8–63 The importance of keeping proper book cannot be over-emphasised. The failure of many businesses to keep proper books of account has, in many cases, led to their downfall.

---

[19] Unreported, High Court, Costello J., July 1, 1983.
[20] [1984] I.L.R.M. 399.
[21] *The Irish Times* January 16, 17 and 18, 1992.

Case History 8.1: Fraudulent trading

A Limited has gone into liquidation leaving no cash in the bank and assets with a £nil realisable value. Consequently, creditors will get nothing.

Scenario 1
Shortly before the company went into liquidation, the business of A Limited was transferred to New A Limited which has the same directors as A Limited.

Scenario 2
The owner of A Limited had lent £2 million to the business, which amount had not been repaid at the time of the liquidation. This asset was transferred to New A Limited which subsequently traded profitably and repaid the loan to the owner.

Issues
• Was the establishment of New A Limited a ruse for the owner to recover his loan of £2 million?

• Was the establishment of New A Limited a legitimate method of developing fresh business opportunities?

Source: Adapted from Burns, S. "Jumping the queue" in *Accountancy* (June 1999), p. 42.

Requirement to keep proper books of account

8–64   Companies are required to keep proper books of account, on a continuous and consistent basis, under section 202 of the Companies Act 1990 as follows:

> "(1) Every company shall cause to be kept proper books of account, whether in the form of documents or otherwise, that —
>> (a)   correctly record and explain the transactions of the company,
>> (b)   will at any time enable the financial position of the company to be determined with reasonable accuracy,
>> (c)   will enable the directors to ensure that any balance sheet, profit and loss account or income and expenditure account of the company complies with the requirements of the Companies Acts, and
>> (d)   will enable the accounts of the company to be readily and properly audited."

Subsections 1(6) and (2) makes it clear that the requirement is continuous and accordingly that the records must be maintained continuously, *i.e.* not, say, prepared just once a year when accounts are being drawn up:

> "(2) The books of account of a company shall be kept on a continuous and consistent basis, that is to say, the entries therein shall be made in a timely manner and be consistent from one year to the next."

Subsection 3 is quite precise as to the level of detail required to comply with the requirement to keep proper books:

"(3) Without prejudice to the generality of subsections (1) and (2), books of account kept pursuant to those subsections shall contain —
  (a) entries from day to day of all sums of money received and expended by the company and the matters in respect of which the receipt and expenditure takes place,
  (b) a record of the assets and liabilities of the company,
  (c) if the company's business involves dealing in goods —
    (i) a record of all goods purchased, and of all goods sold (except for those sold for cash by way of ordinary retail trade), showing the goods and the sellers and buyers in sufficient detail to enable the goods and the sellers and buyers to be identified and a record of all the invoices relating to such purchases and sales,
    (ii) statements of stock held by the company at the end of each financial year and all records of stocktakings from which any such statement of stock has been, or is to be, prepared, and
  (d) if the company's business involves the provision of services, a record of the services provided and of all the invoices relating thereto."

8–65 Section 149 of the 1963 Act requires the profit and loss account and balance sheet to give a true and fair view respectively of the company's profit or loss for the financial year and its state of affairs at the end of the financial year. This requirement is repeated in section 3 of the Companies (Amendment) Act 1986. It is also referred to in section 202(4) of the 1990 Act which indicates that if the books of accounts give a true and fair view, this, together with compliance with the requirements of subsections (1), (2) and (3), will result in compliance with the requirements to keep proper books of account:

"(4) For the purposes of subsections (1), (2) and (3), proper books of account shall be deemed to be kept if they comply with those subsections and give a true and fair view of the state of affairs of the company and explain its transactions."

Criminal offences for failure to keep proper books of account

8–66 Company law sets out the following criminal offences in connection with failure to keep proper books:

– wilful failure to ensure proper books of account are maintained[22];

– a company's insolvency contributed to by a failure to have kept proper books of account[23];

– failure of auditor to serve notice of his opinion that the company is not maintaining proper books.[24]

---

[22] Companies Act 1990, s. 202.
[23] *ibid.*, s. 203.
[24] *ibid.*, s. 194.

8–67   Subsection 202(10) makes it a criminal offence to fail to keep proper books of account, in the following terms:

> "A company that contravenes this section and a person who, being a director of a company, fails to take all reasonable steps to secure compliance by the company with the requirements of this section, or has by his own wilful act been the cause of any default by the company thereunder, shall be guilty of an offence".

However, subsection 202(10) also provides for a defence, and a mitigation of penalty, in the following terms:

> "(a) in any proceedings against a person in respect of an offence under this section consisting of a failure to take reasonable steps to secure compliance by a company with the requirements of this section, it shall be a defence to prove that he had reasonable grounds for believing and did believe that a competent and reliable person was charged with the duty of ensuring that those requirements were complied with and was in a position to discharge that duty, and
>
> (b) a person shall not be sentenced to imprisonment for such an offence unless, in the opinion of the court, the offence was committed wilfully."

Also an officer may be ordered by the court to be personally liable for the debts of the company where proper books of accounts have not been kept.

Section 42 of the Company Law Enforcement Act 2001 extends the grounds for disqualification of directors to persons found guilty of two or more offences under section 202(10). No date has yet been fixed for the coming into operation of this provision.

On November 1, 2000, *The Irish Times* reported convictions for failure to keep proper books as follows:

> "Successful convictions were also obtained for the first time last week against companies and directors for failing to keep proper books and records.
>
> The prosecutions were brought on the basis of notifications to the Companies Office by the companies' auditors who could not determine if proper books and accounts had been kept.
>
> Auditors are obliged to make such notification under company law."

This newspaper account is not accurate. The first conviction was obtained against two directors of the Mean Fiddler Ltd in June 1999. In total, there were nine successful summary prosecutions in 1999 and 2000.[25]

8–68   For companies in liquidation, where failure to keep proper books of account has contributed to the company's inability to pay its debts then, under section 203 of the Companies Act 1990, officers of the company may be liable to a fine or a term of imprisonment:

---

[25] The authors are grateful to Peter Durnin of the Department of Enterprise, Trade and Employment for this information.

"(1) If—

    (a) a company that is being wound up and that is unable to pay all of its debts, has contravened section 202, and

    (b) the court considers that such contravention has contributed to the company's inability to pay all of its debts or has resulted in substantial uncertainty as to the assets and liabilities of the company or has substantially impeded the orderly winding up thereof

every officer of the company who is in default shall be guilty of an offence and liable—

      (i) on summary conviction to a fine not exceeding £1,000 or to imprisonment for a term not exceeding 6 months or to both, or

      (ii) on conviction on indictment, to a fine not exceeding £10,000 or to imprisonment for a term not exceeding 5 years or to both.

(2) In a prosecution for an offence under this section, it shall be a defence for the person charged with the offence to show that—

    (a) he took all reasonable steps to secure compliance by the company with section 202, or

    (b) he had reasonable grounds for believing and did believe that a competent and reliable person, acting under the supervision or control of a director of the company who has been formally allocated such responsibility, was charged with the duty of ensuring that the section was complied with and was in a position to discharge that duty."

8–69   Auditors have certain duties under section 202. Civil consequences of failure to keep proper books imposed on officers of companies are considered in paras **10–32** *et seq*.

Investment business firms

8–70   Section 19 of the Investment Intermediaries Act 1995 deals with provisions for keeping proper books of account by investment business firms. Section 19 only relates to books and records specified by the regulatory authority (*i.e.* the Central Bank) but subsection (3) states that the requirements of section 19 are in addition to requirements to keep proper books in other Acts. Section 19 provides:

"(1) (a) An investment business firm shall keep at an office or offices within the State such books and records (including books of accounts) or other documents as may be specified from time to time by a supervisory authority and shall notify the supervisory authority of the address of every office at which any such books or records are kept."

The penalties arising from a breach of this provision can be severe. Section 54 of the Act empowers the court to impose on any officer or former officer unlimited personal liability for part or all of the debts and liabilities of an authorised investment business firm where:

"(a) … an authorised investment business firm is being wound up and is unable to pay all of its debts and has contravened section 19 ... of this Act, and

(b) the Court considers that such contravention has contributed to the inability of an authorised investment business firm to pay all of its debts or has resulted in substantial uncertainty as to the amount, location, ownership or otherwise of the assets and liabilities of an authorised investment business firm or of the money or investment instruments of clients of the said authorised investment business firm or has substantially impeded its orderly winding-up ...".

In addition, failure to comply with section 19(1)(a) above and failure by a director of an authorised investment business firm to "take all reasonable steps to secure compliance by an authorised investment business firm with the requirements of section 19 ... of this Act, or has by his own wilful act been the cause of any default by an authorised investment business firm thereunder"[26] are both criminal offences under section 79 of the Act. These offences carry penalties of fines up to £1,000,000 and prison terms of up to 10 years.

Falsification of accounts

8–71   The Companies Acts provide for other offences (*i.e.* in addition to failure to keep proper books of account) in relation to the books of account of companies. Two types of offence are identified:

– furnishing of false information;

– destroying, mutilating or falsifying books or documents.

Furnishing of false information

8–72   Section 242 of the Companies Act 1990 deals with the provision of false information.

"(1) A person who, in purported compliance with any provision of the Companies Acts, answers a question, provides an explanation, makes a statement or produces, lodges or delivers any return, report, certificate, balance sheet or other document false in a material particular, knowing it to be false, or recklessly answers a question, provides an explanation, makes a statement or produces, lodges or delivers any such document false in a material particular shall be guilty of an offence.

(2) Where a person is guilty of an offence under subsection (1) and the court is of opinion that any act, omission or conduct which constituted that offence has—
   (a) substantially contributed to a company being unable to pay its debts;
   (b) prevented or seriously impeded the orderly winding-up of the company; or
   (c) substantially facilitated the defrauding of the creditors of the company or creditors of any other person,

---

[26] Investment Intermediaries Act 1995, s. 54(6).

that person shall be liable on conviction on indictment to imprisonment for a term not exceeding 7 years or to a fine not exceeding £10,000 or to both."

8–73 The inclusion of false statements in prospectuses[27] and in statements in lieu of prospectuses[28] are offences, as is making false statements in connection with returns, reports, certificates, balances sheets or other documents required under the Companies (Amendment) Act 1986.[29] The wilful making of false statements in connection with the provisions exempting very small companies from the audit requirement is an offence.[30]

8–74 Providing misleading, false or deceptive material in directors' statements concerning the allotment of shares[31] is also an offence, as is providing misleading, false or deceptive statements to an expert carrying out a valuation or making a report in connection with non-cash allotment of shares.[32]

8–75 In ministerial investigations of the ownership of shares and debentures of companies (considered in Chapter 13), failure to give information or giving false information is an offence.[33]

Destroying, mutilating or falsifying books or documents

8–76 Section 243 of the Companies Act 1990 provides for offences in relation to destroying, mutilating or falsifying books or documents (or being privy thereto) and fraudulently parting with, altering or making an omission in any book (or being privy thereto):

"(1) A person, being an officer of any such body as is mentioned in paragraphs (a) to (e) of section 19(1) who destroys, mutilates, or falsifies or is privy to the destruction, mutilation or falsification of any book or document affecting or relating to the property or affairs of the body, or makes or is privy to the making of a false entry therein, shall, unless he proves that he had no intention to defeat the law, be guilty of an offence.

(2) Any such person who fraudulently either parts with, alters or makes an omission in any such book or document, or who is privy to fraudulent parting with, fraudulent altering or fraudulent making of an omission in, any such book or document, shall be guilty of an offence."

The reference to paragraphs (a) to (e) of section 19(1) serves to include within the scope of section 243 the officers of companies formed and registered under

---

[27] Companies Act 1963, s. 50.
[28] *ibid.*, ss. 35(7) and 54(5).
[29] Companies (Amendment) Act 1986, s. 22(3).
[30] Companies (Amendment) (No. 2) Act 1999, s. 37.
[31] Companies (Amendment) Act 1983, s. 24(6).
[32] *ibid.*, s. 31(3).
[33] Companies Act 1990, s. 15(3).

the Companies Acts, existing companies within the meaning of those Acts and companies not formed under the Acts but registered or eligible for registration under the Acts.

8–77   It is a defence to show that the accused had no intention to defeat the law. Subsection (2) introduces a fraudulent element into the offence which would require the accused knowingly to perpetrate some deceit or falsehood.

8–78   Similar provisions concerning books of account of companies in liquidation are contained in section 293 of the Companies Act 1963 (as amended), as follows:

> "... if any person, being a past or present officer of a company which at the time of the commission of the alleged offence is being wound up, whether by the court or voluntarily, or is subsequently ordered to be wound up by the court or subsequently passes a resolution for voluntary winding up—
>
>   . . .
>
> (c)   does not deliver up to the liquidator, or as he directs, all books and papers in his custody or under his control belonging to the company and which he is required by law to deliver up; or
>
>   . . .
>
> (f)   makes any material omission in any statement relating to the affairs of the company; or
>
>   . . .
>
> (h)   after the commencement of the winding up prevents the production of any book or paper affecting or relating to the property or affairs of the company; or
>
> (i)   within 12 months next before the commencement of the winding up or at any time thereafter conceals, destroys, mutilates or falsifies or is privy to the concealment, destruction, mutilation or falsification of any book or paper affecting or relating to the property or affairs of the company; or
>
> (j)   within 12 months next before the commencement of the winding up or at any time thereafter makes or is privy to the making of any false entry in any book or paper affecting or relating to the property or affairs of the company; or
>
> (k)   within 12 months next before the commencement of the winding up or at any time thereafter fraudulently parts with, alters or makes any omission in, or is privy to the fraudulent parting with, altering or making any omission in, any document affecting or relating to the property or affairs of the company;
>
>   . . .
>
> he shall ... be liable, on conviction on indictment, to imprisonment for a term not exceeding 2 years or to a fine not exceeding £2,500 or to both, or, ... on summary conviction, to imprisonment for a term not exceeding 6 months or to a fine not exceeding £500 or to both."

8–79 Falsification of accounts of credit unions is an offence under section 174 of the Credit Union Act 1997 and furnishing false information relating to credit unions is an offence under section 175.

Other criminal offences applying to directors and officers

8–80 A large number of criminal offences apply to directors and officers of companies. These can be categorised as offences relating to:

– disqualification of directors;

– prohibited transactions with directors;

– failure to provide information concerning transactions with directors;

– failure to provide information generally;

– accounts preparation;

– winding up of companies;

– company investigations and inspections;

– requirements relating to shares.

Disqualification of directors

8–81 Legislation dealing with qualifications of directors is considered in paras **10–28** *et seq*. There are a number of criminal sanctions where these requirements are not observed, as follows:

– disqualified director acting in contravention of disqualification order[34];

– director, officer or member knowingly acting with the instructions of a disqualified director[35];

– failure of director charged with an offence, or subject to civil proceedings, involving alleged fraud or dishonesty, to advise the court of directorships.[36] This information is of interest to the court as a conviction on indictment gives rise to an automatic disqualification order.

Prohibited transactions with directors

8–82 Directors have fiduciary responsibilities, first to companies and thereafter to shareholders, creditors and employees. Directors are also in a privileged position in dealings with their companies. In their transactions with companies, company law seeks to limit the scope of directors to put their own financial interests above those of companies Additional statutory duties are imposed on

---

[34] Companies Act 1990, s. 161.
[35] *ibid.*, s. 164.
[36] *ibid.*, s. 166.

directors in relation to their transactions with the company, including their share dealings, borrowing by directors from the company and contracts between the company and its directors. Failure to observe these additional duties may result in criminal penalties. The additional statutory requirements relating to directors, which if contravened carry criminal penalties, are:

- prohibition on dealing by directors in options to buy or sell securities of the company (the buying of a right to subscribe for securities that themselves confer a right to subscribe for further securities is not covered by this prohibition)[37];

- prohibition on certain loans, guarantees and similar transactions with directors and connected persons.[38]

Failure to provide information concerning transactions with directors

8–83   In addition to certain transactions with directors being prohibited, company law also imposes additional duties on directors to disclose information concerning their dealings with their companies. Again, this reflects the privileged position of directors in the management of company affairs. It is a criminal offence for directors or officers of companies not to comply with any of these disclosure requirements. The disclosures relate to directors' interests in company shares and debentures and directors' contracts with the company. The offences are:

- failure by director to notify interests in shares or debentures of company[39];

- failure by director to notify grant of right to spouse/children in shares or debentures of company[40];

- failure by director to ensure notification of acquisitions and disposals of shares or debentures of company[41];

- failure to keep a company register to record directors' interests in shares and debentures of the company as required under section 53 of the Companies Act 1990[42];

- failure by director to notify his interest in a contract or proposed contract with the company[43];

- failure by licenced bank to maintain or permit inspection of register of certain substantial contracts with directors excluded from publication.[44]

---

[37] Companies Act 1990, s. 30.
[38] *ibid.*, s. 40.
[39] *ibid.*, s. 53.
[40] *ibid.*, s. 64.
[41] *ibid.*, s. 58.
[42] *ibid.*, ss. 60, 61 and 62.
[43] Companies Act 1963, s. 194.
[44] Companies Act 1990, s. 44.

Failure to provide information generally

8–84   Directors also have duties to disclose certain dealings in the shares of public limited companies. It is an offence for a director of a public limited company to fail to notify the company of the acquisition of a shareholding of 5 per cent or more of the company by him and his family or by parties acting in concert with him.[45]

It is also an offence for a quoted company to fail to notify the stock exchange of interests in its shares or debentures notified to it by one of its directors.[46]

8–85   Section 34 of the Investment Intermediaries Act 1995 makes it an offence for officers or employees of investment intermediary businesses to supply misleading, false or deceptive information to the auditors. It is also an offence to fail to supply information requested by the auditors within a specified period of time,[47] although there is a defence to this.

Accounts preparation

8–86   Directors also have duties to account to shareholders for their management and stewardship of the company and its assets. Criminal penalties are imposed in the event that these duties are not observed by directors and officers of companies.

– failure to present accounts at annual general meetings[48];

– failure to comply with required form and content of accounts[49];

– failure of directors to ensure accounts comply with companies legislation[50];

– failure to present group accounts at annual general meeting of holding company[51];

– failure to prepare and attach to the accounts a directors' report[52];

– circulating prospectus of foreign companies in contravention to sections 361 to 364 of the Companies Act 1963[53];

– failure to call extraordinary general meeting where assets are less than half the share capital.[54]

---

[45] Companies Act 1990, s. 79.
[46] *ibid.*, s. 65.
[47] Within two working days.
[48] Companies Act 1963, s.148.
[49] *ibid.*, s. 149.
[50] Companies (Amendment) Act 1986, s. 22.
[51] Companies Act 1963, s. 150.
[52] *ibid.*, s. 158.
[53] *ibid.*, s. 365.
[54] Companies (Amendment) Act 1983, s. 40.

Winding up offences

8–87 Twenty six criminal offences are identified under section 293 of the Companies Act 1963 which apply to directors and officers of companies in liquidation. In addition, section 295 provides for offences in respect of frauds committed by officers of companies which have gone into liquidation, as follows:

> "If any person, being at the time of the commission of the alleged offence an officer of a company which is subsequently ordered to be wound up by the court or subsequently passes a resolution for voluntary winding up—
>
> (a) has by false pretences or by means of any other fraud induced any person to give credit to the company;
>
> (b) with intent to defraud creditors of the company, has made or caused to be made any gift or transfer of or charge on, or has caused or connived at the levying of any execution against, the property of the company;
>
> (c) with intent to defraud creditors of the company, has concealed or removed any part of the property of the company since or within 2 months before the date of any unsatisfied judgment or order for payment of money obtained against the company;
>
> he shall be liable, on conviction on indictment, to imprisonment for a term not exceeding 2 years or to a fine not exceeding £2,500 or to both or, on summary conviction, to imprisonment for a term not exceeding 6 months or to a fine not exceeding £500 or to both."

Investigations and inspections

8–88 Criminal offences are also provided for in respect of officers of companies who fail to co-operate in company investigations and inspections as follows:

– failure to keep and make available for inspection a report and register of the results of an investigation under section 83 of the Companies Act 1990[55];

– exercising or purporting to exercise rights over shares restricted by ministerial order[56];

– issuing shares in contravention of restrictions[57];

– failure to provide books, documents, explanations or statements required by ministerial direction[58];

– Obstruction of exercise of right of entry or search under warrant[59];

---

[55]Companies Act 1990, s. 88.
[56]*ibid.*, s. 16.
[57]*ibid.*, s. 16.
[58]*ibid.*, s. 19.
[59]*ibid.*, s. 20.

– Unauthorised publication of any information, book or document.[60]

Investigations and company inspections are considered in more detail in Chapter 13.

Requirements relating to shares

8–89   Offences identified in company legislation are committed by directors where the company:

– gives financial assistance for the purchase of its own shares without observing the requirements of section 60 of the Companies Act 1963;

– acquires its own shares other than on a permitted basis[61];

– fails to maintain and make available for public inspection a register of interests in its shares[62];

– fails to re-enter as soon as practicable an entry in its register of interests in shares that was improperly removed[63];

– fails to retain and permit inspection of contracts for purchase of own shares[64];

– fails to deliver return to registrar concerning purchase of own shares[65];

– fails to comply with ministerial regulation concerning purchase of own shares[66];

– contravenes various procedures concerning restrictions regarding purchase of shares.[67]

Failure by a quoted company to notify a recognised stock exchange of the purchase of its own shares[68] and failure to comply with a notice issued by a company requiring information of a person believed to have an interest in the company's shares[69] are also offences.

Extension of offences beyond directors and officers

8–90   Section 56 of the Criminal Justice (Theft and Fraud Offences) Bill 2000 proposes to extend liability for offences under its provisions committed by

---

[60] Companies Act 1990, s. 21.
[61] Companies (Amendment) Act 1983, s. 41.
[62] Companies Act 1990, s. 80.
[63] *ibid.*, s. 87.
[64] *ibid.*, s. 222.
[65] *ibid.*, s. 226.
[66] *ibid.*, s. 228.
[67] *ibid.*, s. 234.
[68] *ibid.*, s. 229.
[69] *ibid.*, s. 85.

businesses beyond officers of companies to any person who purported to act as an officer of the company and consented to or who connived in committing the offence, as follows:

"(1) Where—
- (a) an offence under this Act has been committed by a body corporate, and
- (b) the offence is proved to have been committed with the consent or connivance of, or to have been attributable to any neglect on the part of, a person who was either—
  - (i) a director, manager, secretary or other officer of the body corporate, or
  - (ii) a person purporting to act in any such capacity,

that person, as well as the body corporate, is guilty of an offence and liable to be proceeded against and punished as if he or she were guilty of the first-mentioned offence.

(2) Where the affairs of a body corporate are managed by its members, subsection (1) shall apply in relation to the acts and defaults of a member in connection with the member's functions of management as if he or she were a director or manager of the body corporate.

(3) The foregoing provisions shall apply, with the necessary modifications, in relation to offences under this Act committed by an unincorporated body."

Insider dealing

8–91 In publicly quoted companies, parties privy to inside knowledge have the opportunity to use this knowledge to trade in the company's shares at a personal gain. For example, if the financial controller of a business knows that the company is going to release exceptionally good results, he could buy shares before the information is released to the market and sell them at a profit after the announcement of the good results has caused the share price to rise.

Insider dealing is dealt with in Part V of the Companies Act 1990 (see sections 107 to 118). Insider dealing is both a criminal offence and a civil wrong. Four offences are identified in the Act:

1. Insider dealing – unlawfully dealing in securities – as defined in section 108 of the Companies Act 1990 is deemed an offence under section 111.

2. It is an offence under section 112 for a person to deal in securities within 12 months of a prior conviction under section 111 or section 112.

3. Section 113 extends to agents – it is an offence for a person to deal with another person with reasonable cause to believe it is insider dealing.

4. Finally, failure by stock exchange personnel to observe professional secrecy is an offence.[70]

---

[70]Companies Act 1990, s. 118.

Section 114 sets out the penalties for insider dealing. The maximum penalties for conviction on indictment are a 10-year term of imprisonment and/or a fine of £200,000.

Sectin 109 deals with civil liability for insider dealing. Charleton, McDermott and Bolger[71] suggest that the imposition of criminal liability for insider dealing in the terms set out in the 1990 Act may be unconstitutional on the grounds that liability appears to be determined based on the civil standard of negligence. This point has not been tested in the Irish courts to date. The topic of insider dealing is covered comprehensively in Ashe and Murphy.[72]

Criminal offences relating to auditors

8–92 Although a number of criminal offences are laid down in statute, civil actions against auditors are more common and to date there have been no criminal prosecutions of auditors in the Irish courts. Company law provides for a large number of criminal offences that relate to the audit function and these are summarised in Table 8.1.

8–93 Section 74 of the Company Law Enforcement Act 2001 imposes additional reporting requirements on auditors. In particular, the existing obligation under section 194 of the Companies Act 1990 to notify the company and the Registrar of Companies that the auditors have formed the opinion that the company is not keeping proper books has been extended to require notice also to be given to the Director of Corporate Enforcement. Section 74 also requires the auditors to notify the Director where they have reasonable grounds to believe that the company or its officer or agent has committed an indictable offence under the Companies Acts. No date has yet been fixed for the coming into operation of section 74. Section 57 of the Criminal Justice (Theft and Fraud Offences) Bill 2000 proposes to add, an additional requirement for auditors to report suspicions of offences. This has already been discussed in paras **4–42** *et seq.*

Criminal offences applying to receivers and liquidators

8–94 Company legislation also identifies a number of criminal offences applying to receivers and liquidators, as follows:

– undischarged bankrupt acting as officer, liquidator or examiner[73];

– failure to submit statement of affairs to receiver within two months of appointment[74];

---

[71] Charleton, P., McDermott, P.A. and Bolger, M., *Criminal Law* (Butterworths, Dublin, 1999), p. 918.
[72] Ashe, M.T. and Murphy, Y., *Insider Dealing* (Round Hall Press, Dublin, 1992).
[73] Companies Act 1963, s. 183.
[74] *ibid.*, s. 320.

Table 8.1: Criminal offences relating to the audit function under company legislation

Failure to give the Minister notice of ministerial power to appoint auditor if no auditors have been appointed at the annual general meeting	Section 160 (5A) of the Companies Act 1963 as inserted by section 183 of the Companies Act 1990
Failure to notify registrar of companies within 14 days of passing of resolution removing an auditor	*ibid.*
Failure of auditor to notify registrar of companies of his resignation as auditor	Section 185, Companies Act 1990
Failure of auditor to include required material in notice of resignation	*ibid.*
Failure to send copies of auditor's notice of intention to resign and circumstances of the resignation	*ibid.*
Failure to convene general meeting on requisition by auditor	Section 186, Companies Act 1990
Failure to send to persons entitled and to registrar of companies auditor's further statement at his request	*ibid.*
Failure to send former auditor notices of meeting and related documents	*ibid.*
Failure of auditor to serve notice of his opinion that the company is not maintaining proper books	Section 194, Companies Act 1990
Person acting as auditor when disqualified to do so	Section 187, Companies Act 1990
Person with disqualification order serving as partner in firm of auditors	Section 195, Companies Act 1990
Failure of subsidiary company or its auditors to give holding company auditors information	Section 196, Companies Act 1990
Failure of holding company to obtain information needed for audit from subsidiary	*ibid.*
Making misleading, false or deceptive statement to auditor	Section 197, Companies Act 1990
Failure to provide explanations to auditor within two days of requisition	*ibid.*
Failure of recognised professional body to provide list of registered auditors to registrar of companies	Section 199, Companies Act 1990
Failure of recognised professional body to provide, within one month of qualification, list of newly registered auditors to registrar	Section 200, Companies Act 1990

- failure of company-nominated liquidator in a creditors' voluntary winding up to refrain from exercising certain powers, to attend the creditors' meeting or to apply to court for directions in certain circumstances[75];

- failure of receiver/liquidator to incorporate certain information in a periodic account[76];

- failure of receiver/liquidator to file periodic account[77];

- failure of liquidator to inform the court of person acting as director of the company who was restricted from acting as a director.[78]

Sundry other criminal offences

8–95 A number of other company law offences attract criminal penalties. These include:

- failure of persons acting together in concert to keep each other informed[79];

- failure of purchaser to ensure that his agent notifies him of acquisitions and disposals of interests in shares of a public company[80];

- failure to repay surplus business expenses[81];

- contravention of various sections of the Act dealing with investment companies[82];

- failure by stock exchange personnel to comply with obligation of professional secrecy regarding information obtained in the course of exercising functions relating to the disclosure of interests in shares.[83]

Financial services and money laundering

8–96 Money laundering is any system of turning the proceeds of crime or any money from suspect sources into legitimate funds, with a view to concealing the proceeds of criminal activity. The legislation dealing with money laundering is contained in the Criminal Justice Act 1994. Section 31 of the Act defines the offence of money laundering in the following terms:

---

[75] Companies Act 1990, s. 131.
[76] Companies Act 1990, s. 144.
[77] *ibid.*, s. 145.
[78] *ibid.*, s. 151.
[79] *ibid.*, s. 79.
[80] *ibid.*
[81] *ibid.*, s. 36.
[82] *ibid.*, s. 262.
[83] *ibid.*, s. 94.

"(1) A person shall be guilty of an offence if he—
  (a) conceals or disguises any property which is, or in whole or in part directly or indirectly represents, his proceeds of drug trafficking or other criminal activity, or
  (b) converts or transfers that property or removes it from the State, for the purpose of avoiding prosecution for an offence or the making or enforcement in his case of a confiscation order.

(2) A person shall be guilty of an offence if, knowing or believing that any property is, or in whole or in part directly or indirectly represents, another person's proceeds of drug trafficking or other criminal activity, he—
  (a) conceals or disguises that property, or
  (b) converts or transfers that property or removes it from the State, for the purpose of assisting any person to avoid prosecution for an offence or the making or enforcement of a confiscation order.

(3) A person shall be guilty of an offence if he handles any property knowing or believing that such property is, or in whole or in part directly or indirectly represents, another person's proceeds of drug trafficking or other criminal activity."

8–97   Thus, two elements may be present: (1) disguising or concealing the proceeds of crime and (2) intending to avoid prosecution or a confiscation order. Irish banks and other financial institutions are now required to carry out detailed customer identity checks, to maintain customer and transaction records, to report suspicions of money laundering to the Gardaí and to educate and train staff in their statutory obligations to prevent money laundering and in how to recognise suspicious transactions.[84]

8–98   In money laundering cases, especially where the fraudster has disappeared or has no identifiable assets, defrauded plaintiffs have sought to seek redress from those who have assisted in the fraud (*e.g.* by assisting in disposing of the proceeds). In order to succeed in such cases, the plaintiff must show that the party assisting in the fraud was knowingly assisting. Five states of knowing assistance have been identified[85] :

1. Actual knowledge.

2. Wilfully shutting one's eyes to the obvious.

3. Wilfully and recklessly failing to make the inquiries which an honest and reasonable person would make.

4. Knowledge of the circumstances which would indicate the facts to an honest and reasonable person.

5. Knowledge of the circumstances which would put an honest and reasonable person on inquiry.

---

[84] Ashe, M. and Reid, P., "Equity and the pursuit of hot money – warning to banks" *Commerical Law Practitioner* (September 1997) pp. 188-194.
[85] *Baden v. Sociéte Générale* [1992] 4 All E.R. 161.

8–99   One such case, *Agip (Africa) v. Jackson,*[86] involved a firm of accountants. Agip's chief accountant altered names of payees on payment orders and diverted payments to English companies which were incorporated by the firm of accountants, two of whose partners acted as directors. Funds from Agip were first paid to the English companies which were then put into liquidation. Thereafter the monies were paid to another English company and then on to a French company – a partner in the accounting firm was a director of both these companies. The partners of the accounting firm were held personally liable to pay Agip even though they had not benefited personally from the Agip monies. They were held liable because they knowingly assisted in a fraudulent and dishonest design – and assisted in furtherance of the fraud.

8–100   Under sections 3 and 4 of the Proceeds of Crime Act 1996, an officer authorised by the Revenue Commissioners or a member of the Garda Síochána can apply to the court for an order the effect of which is to freeze assets known or suspected to be, or to be related to, the proceeds of crime. Such an order can be made on an interim basis (under section 3) on foot of an *ex parte* application, and also following an interlocutory hearing (under section 4). In addition, assets frozen by an interlocutory order for more than seven years can be the subject of a disposal order under which the assets are transferred to the Minister or such other person as the court may determine.

Under section 4 of the Criminal Justice Act 1994, the Director of Public Prosecutions can seek a confiscation order in respect of the proceeds of drug trafficking. In addition, under section 30 of the Misuse of Drugs Act 1977 a court may make a forfeiture order in respect of anything related to an offence committed under the Act.

Further information on money laundering issues in a United Kingdom context is contained in Taub *et al.*[87]

Criminal offences under competition law

8–101   Competition law is considered in somewhat more detail in Chapter 9 (paras **9–123** *et seq.*). Of relevance to this chapter are the five criminal offences created by the Competition (Amendment) Act 1996. The 1996 Act introduced criminal penalties into competition law in respect of the offences originally defined as civil wrongs in sections 4 and 5 of the 1991 Competition Act.

Section 4 prohibits anti-competitive agreements, decisions and concerted practices in the following terms:

---

[86] [1990] 1 Ch. 265; [1991] Ch. 547 (C.A.).
[87] Taub, M., Rapazzini, A., Bond, C., Solon, M., Brown, A., Murrie, A., Linnell, K. and Burn, S., *Tolley's Accountancy Litigation Support* (Butterworths, London, looseleaf), Part VIII, para. 174.

"(1) Subject to the provisions of this section, all agreements between undertakings, decisions by associations of undertakings and concerted practices which have as their object or effect the prevention, restriction or distortion of competition in trade in any goods or services in the State or in any part of the State are prohibited and void, including in particular, without prejudice to the generality of this subsection, those which—

  (a) directly or indirectly fix purchase or selling prices or any other trading conditions;

  (b) limit or control production, markets, technical development or investment;

  (c) share markets or sources of supply;

  (d) apply dissimilar conditions to equivalent transactions with other trading parties thereby placing them at a competitive disadvantage;

  (e) make the conclusion of contracts subject to acceptance by the other parties of supplementary obligations which by their nature or according to commercial usage have no connection with the subject of such contracts."

Section 5 prohibits the abuse of a dominant position in the following terms:

"(1) Any abuse by one or more undertakings of a dominant position in trade for any goods or services in the State or in a substantial part of the State is prohibited.

(2) Without prejudice to the generality of subsection (1), such abuse may, in particular, consist in—

  (a) directly or indirectly imposing unfair purchase or selling prices or other unfair trading conditions;

  (b) limiting production, markets or technical development to the prejudice of consumers;

  (c) applying dissimilar conditions to equivalent transactions with other trading parties, thereby placing them at a competitive disadvantage;

  (d) making the conclusion of contracts subject to the acceptance by other parties of supplementary obligations which by their nature or according to commercial usage have no connection with the subject of such contracts."

Sections 4 and 5 closely mirror the equivalent provisions of the Treaty on European Union.[88]

8–102 Four criminal offences committed by undertakings are identified in the 1996 Act. Under section 2(2):

"(a) An undertaking shall not—

  (i) enter into, or implement an agreement, or

  (ii) make or implement a decision, or

  (iii) engage in a concerted practice.

(b) an undertaking which contravenes this section shall be guilty of an offence."

---

[88] Articles 81 and 82 of the Treaty, formerly Articles 85 and 86 of the E.C. Treaty.

The terms "agreement", "decision" and "concerted practice" are defined as those agreements between undertakings, decisions by associations of undertakings and concerted practices which have as their object or effect the prevention, restriction or distortion of competition in trade in any goods or services in the State or in any part of the State.

Substantial fines are provided for, up to a maximum of the greater of £3 million or 10 per cent of turnover. Section 2(2)(c) provides for a number of defences to section 2(2)(a).

Section 2(5)(b) of the 1996 Act creates the offence of not complying with the conditions of a licence granted by the Authority.

8–103 Two offences are created in respect of unilateral behaviour by dominant firms. One extends a criminal sanction to section 5 of the 1991 Act. Acting in a manner prohibited by section 5 of the 1991 Act is an offence under section 2(7) of the 1996 Act. The other creates a criminal sanction for non-compliance with an order (in respect of divestment concerning dominant position) made by the Minister under section 14 of the 1991 Act.

8–104 Section 3(4)(a) of the 1996 Act provides that where an undertaking has committed any one of the four offences described above, then any director, shadow director, manager, secretary or other similar officer "… or any person purporting to act in such capacity" who authorised, consented to, or connived at, the acts that constitute the offence is also guilty of an offence.

The Competition Authority was reported as having successfully taken its first criminal prosecution under competition law in connection with price fixing.[89]

Concluding comment

8–105 It is ironic that in this age of automation, when all but the tiniest businesses have computer systems to track transactions and keep accounts, it has been necessary to increase the scope of, and penalties for, offences relating to the keeping of "books of account" by companies. Even the term "books of account" sounds as though it is from a different time. However, the problems caused by failure to keep proper financial records are very real in today's business world. The consequences of such failure can range from the frustration of late, incomplete or inaccurate information to the insolvent winding up of the company.

An assessment of the quality of record-keeping has therefore become an important part of the assessment of whether proceedings should be initiated in many situations. The training and experience of forensic accountants is usually

---

[89]McManus, J., "Competition watchdog seeking to extend its winning streak", *The Irish Times*, October 20, 2000, p. 7.

very valuable in this process, although for that value to be maximised, the accountant should be engaged at an early stage. In making the assessment, the accountant will have regard to prevailing record-keeping practices in the real world and may conclude in certain situations that the literal requirements of the Companies Acts (*e.g.* the requirement that the books of account must "at any time enable the financial position of the company to be determined with reasonable accuracy"[90]) may be unduly idealistic.

---

[90] Companies Act 1990, s. 202(1)(b).

CHAPTER 9 — CONTENTS

COMMERCIAL

COMMERCIAL

9–01 This chapter examines civil litigation arising from the conduct of commerce. Most such litigation involves companies, as either plaintiff or defendant or both. Chapter 10 deals with litigation of companies also, but only in the context of the governance of such companies.

Commercial disputes involving economic damage may arise in a variety of business situations. The chapter has a number of separate sections, each of which deals with the legal aspects of various commercial disputes. Topics considered include breach of contract, breach of warranty (including mergers and acquisitions litigation), product liability, insurance losses and claims, construction, intellectual property rights, competition law, computers, piracy and e-commerce and, finally, expropriation/compulsory acquisition.

A brief overview of the legal context, forensic accounting involvement and accounting calculations in each of these situations is given. Accordingly, most of the sections referred to above have three subsections: legal context, role of forensic accountants and accounting calculations. The legal context is briefly introduced to give forensic accounting readers an understanding of the legal background for such cases. This discussion is not exhaustive and is intended primarily as an introduction only to the legal context. Readers are referred to other texts for a more detailed consideration of the legal issues introduced in the chapter.[1] Following this discussion is a consideration of the role of forensic accountants in each legal context. The final subsection in each section briefly summarises the accounting calculations arising. These accounting calculations are covered in greater depth in Part IV of the book.

9–02 In commercial loss claims, forensic accountants can assist in analysis of liability and damage issues, evaluation of damages, quantification of damages, performance of economic impact assessments, reconstruction of records, dispute resolution and provision of expert testimony. The legal principles applying to the calculation of damages are discussed in Chapter 15. The accounting calculations dealing with business interruption and consequential loss of profits, involving loss of goodwill, losses arising from loss of opportunity, losses arising from price erosion, valuing businesses, etc., are briefly considered. Such

---

[1] A legal overview is given in Forde, M., *Commercial Legislation* (Round Hall Sweet & Maxwell, Dublin, 1996).

calculations are examined in more detail in Chapters 17 and 18. As damages may relate to various time periods, the time value of money is considered in Chapter 19.

9–03 Commercial litigation cases usually fall into one or more of four categories:

1. Breach of contract: Contracts are voluntary agreements of rights and duties to be assumed between two or more persons or entities. One party is liable to the other for failure to perform his obligations under the contract.

2. Tort: A tort is a private or civil wrong or injury other than a breach of contract. It is based on the duties of one person to another imposed by law. Examples of torts that might affect companies are trespass, nuisance, slander, libel, conspiracy and many aspects of negligence.[2]

3. Anti-competitive behaviour: competition law prohibits anti-competitive behaviour by businesses (see paras **9–123** *et seq.*).

4. Fraud: Fraud is a deception practiced in order to secure unfair or unlawful gain. In a business context, fraud may involve falsification of business records, embezzlement, attempts to deceive regulatory authorities and deliberate misrepresentation of facts. Criminal law, including criminal offences involving fraud, is covered in Chapter 8.

Breach of contract

9–04 This section introduces breach of contract cases. The law of contract is not discussed in full. The types of contract terms arising in commercial agreements are discussed. Legal issues are then considered, with emphasis on situations where damages arise. The involvement of forensic accountants in such cases, and the types of accounting calculations arising, are then considered.[3]

---

[2] See paras **9–04** *et seq.* for further discussion of breach of contract and tort actions, and the considerations to be taken into account in deciding whether to take a breach of contract or tort action or both.

[3] Legal issues are more comprehensively covered in Chitty, J., *Chitty on Contracts* (28th ed., Sweet & Maxwell, London, 1999); Clark, R. and Clarke, B., *Contract Cases and Materials* (2nd ed., Gill & Macmillan, Dublin, 2000); Clark, R., *Contract Law in Ireland* (4th ed., Round Hall Sweet & Maxwell, Dublin, 1998); Friel, R., *The Law of Contract* (2nd ed., Round Hall Sweet & Maxwell, Dublin, 2000); and, in a forensic accounting context, MacGregor, G. and Hobbs, I., *Expert Accounting Evidence: A Guide for Litigation Support* (Accountancy Books, London, 1998), Chap. 16.

Types of breach of contract disputes

9–05 Commercial disputes involving breach of contract can arise from a variety of aggreements, including:

– agreements with suppliers or customers;

– royalty agreements;

– franchise agreements;

– management agreements;

– employment agency agreements;

– employee agreements;

– exclusive distributorship agreements;

– representation agreements;

– warranty agreements;

– oral agreements.

Express and implied terms

9–06 Contracts contain express terms and, in addition, some terms may be implied into a contract by law. Express terms are clearest if provided in writing, but oral express terms are also possible. Implied terms are not expressly included in the contract. They may be implied in five different situations as follows:

1. "officious bystander" test;

2. a custom in the business;

3. terms implied by common law;

4. terms implied by statute;

5. fundamental rights of individuals.

Each of these is discussed below.

Implied terms in contracts

"Officious bystander" test

9–07 Where it is apparent from the relevant circumstances and facts that the parties to the contract had, or reasonably must have, intended to agree the term (for example, where in the absence of the term the contract would not be workable), the term will be implied into the contract. This is sometimes known as the "officious bystander test", *i.e.* terms that are so obviously needed that they go without saying, and in respect of which, in the words of MacKinnon

L.J. (quoting from an essay he had written years previously) in *Shirlaw v. Southern Foundries (1926) Ltd*:

> "If, while the parties were making their bargain, an officious bystander were to suggest some express provision for it in their agreement they would testily suppress him with a common 'oh, of course!' "[4]

This test was referred to and approved by the Supreme Court as recently as 1997 in the judgment of Murphy J. in *Sullivan v. Southern Health Board*.[5]

A custom in the business

9–08 A term may be implied to give effect to a custom in the business. However, the conditions necessary for a custom to be established are demanding. Maguire P. expressed the test as follows in *O'Reilly v. Irish Press* when he said that for a practice to be a custom on usage it must be:

> " ... so notorious, well known and acquiesced in that in the absence of agreement in writing it is to be taken as one of the terms of the contract between the parties."[6]

Although somewhat tautologous when used to describe how a custom might be implied into a contract, this explanation gives a flavour of the difficulty in establishing a custom generally.

Terms implied by common law

9–09 Terms may be implied by common law where a court forms the view that it is necessary to do so. This situation arises most often in employment contracts (*e.g.* see *Carvill v. Irish Industrial Bank Ltd*[7]), in landlord and tenant cases (*e.g.* see *Howard v. Dublin Corporation*[8]) and agency contracts. For example, in the first of these categories, a company's managing director who had been dismissed summarily took proceedings alleging unfair dismissal. Although there was no express contractual term setting out the minimum period of notice for his dismissal, O'Keeffe J., giving the judgment of the Supreme Court, implied such a term into the employment contract as follows:

> "I think that the plaintiff must be regarded as employed under a contract from year to year as managing director, and that it must be implied also that such contract could not be determined without such notice as is appropriate to an engagement of the kind mentioned. The trial judge considered that a year's notice

---

[4] [1939] 2 K.B. 206 at 227.
[5] [1997] 3 I.R. 123.
[6] [1937] I.L.T.R. 194 at 195.
[7] [1968] I.R. 325.
[8] [1996] 2 I.R. 235.

(or salary in lieu of notice) was appropriate, and the defendants have not submitted that such length of notice was excessive, although they have contended that no notice at all was required. In the circumstances I see no reason for disturbing the finding of the trial judge that the appropriate period of notice was a year, although I might not myself have fixed so long a period."[9]

Terms implied by statute

9–10 Terms may be implied by statute – examples of such implied terms can be found in the Sale of Goods Acts 1893 and 1980, the Organisation of Working Time Act 1997 and the Minimum Notice and Terms of Employment Act 1973. For example, under the Sale of Goods and Supply of Services Acts 1893–1980 there is an implied condition that goods sold are of merchantable quality.

Fundamental rights of individuals

9–11 The fundamental rights of individuals embodied in and developed from the Constitution give rise to implied terms in contracts, particularly in the employment area. Examples include the right to bodily integrity first recognised by the Supreme Court in *Ryan v. Attorney General*.[10]

Types of express terms

9–12 Contracts are generally regarded as containing two types of express terms: conditions and warranties (see paras **9–34** *et seq.* for a discussion of breach of warranty).

Conditions

9–13 The term "condition" is not defined in statute, but is generally regarded as including all terms with which compliance is necessary for the contract to achieve its intended purpose. A condition of a contract is therefore so fundamental to the contract that, where a party fails to comply with a condition, the innocent party can consider himself discharged from the contract and can sue for damages for any loss suffered.

Warranties

9–14 The term "warranty" is defined in section 62 of the Sale of Goods Act 1893 as a term that is "collateral to the main purpose" of a contract. It is therefore not fundamental to the achievement of the intended purpose of the contract, and it is this that distinguishes it from a condition.

---

[9] [1968] I.R. 325 at 344.
[10] [1965] I.R. 294.

Remedy depends on term

9–15 Businesses can experience breaches of contract and courts will compensate them for any damages arising. Remedies available to an aggrieved party for breach of the contract by the other party can vary depending on the nature of the breach. For instance, if the breached term is a condition, then the aggrieved party may either rescind or affirm the contract and may seek damages. If the breached term is a warranty, the aggrieved party remains bound by the contract but may seek damages for the breach.

Legal context

9–16 A valid contract typically involves enforceable promises by one party in consideration for which another party makes a payment or a reciprocal promise. When one party does not perform its promise, a breach of contract may have occurred and a lawsuit may follow.

When a case is taken alleging breach of contract, the first step the court must take is to determine whether, in fact, a breach of contract did occur. If it is determined that no breach occurred, then the case is concluded. Only if a court determines that a breach of contract occurred will it consider the evidence from the plaintiff concerning the extent of damages incurred.

Breaches of contract by sellers – buyers' damages

9–17 Contracts involving the sale of goods are governed by the provisions of the Sale of Goods Act 1893 as amended by the Sale of Goods and Supply of Services Act 1980. Section 51 of the Sale of Goods Act 1893 measures damages as follows:

> "(2) The measure of damages is the estimated loss directly and naturally resulting, in the ordinary course of events, from the seller's breach of contract.
>
> (3) Where there is an available market for the goods in question, the measure of damages is prima facie to be ascertained by the difference between the contract price and the market or current price of the goods at the time or times when they ought to have been delivered, or, if no time was fixed, then at the time of the refusal to deliver."

Subsection 3 of section 51 gives a statutory basis for protecting the buyer in a market where prices are rising. Although this measure of damages includes no compensation for lost profits on resale of the goods by the buyer, it is based on the not unreasonable premise that the buyer can restore his ability to earn that profit by simply purchasing replacement goods at the market price. Where the goods are not freely available at the date of breach, this simple measure of damages might not be sufficient, as envisaged by subsection (3) above. The courts have interpreted the term "available market" as referring to a market for identical goods, *e.g.* in *Lazenby Garages v. Wright*,[11] the general second-hand car market was not regarded as specific enough to be an available market. In any event, this measure is of a prima facie nature, and can therefore be varied for good reason.

9–18   Breaches of contracts by sellers may arise from any one of the following events:

– failure to deliver the goods;

– failure to deliver the goods anticipated by the seller and notified to the buyer in advance of the agreed date for delivery;

– delayed delivery of goods;

– delivery of wrong (*i.e.* not conforming to the specifications in the contract) or damaged goods.

Buyers may reject the goods and repudiate the contract where the seller has committed a serious breach of one of the contract terms. In addition, the buyer may be entitled to damages. The amount of the damages will vary depending on the nature of the breach of contract.

9–19   Where goods are not delivered in compliance with the contract of sale, buyers are entitled to claim for damages. The buyer is entitled to be put into the same situation as if the contract had been performed. This would include the difference between the contracted agreed sale price and the price at which the buyer was able to acquire replacement goods, together with any loss of profit arising from the breach. In these cases, the agreed contract price and the price for replacement goods are central to the calculation of damages.

Litigation can arise out of claims of decline in sales leading to loss of profits due to late shipment of stock by a vendor. Such claims can be rebutted or reduced on several grounds, such as failure to use an alternative supplier, inaccurate sales projections, and replacement sales of different products.

9–20   When the seller breaches, the buyer's damages are lost profits and any additional costs incurred. Where a supplier breaches a contract and the buyer is injured, difficulty can arise in determining the buyer's lost value. One option open to the buyer is to withhold payment to the supplier. However, this will not fully compensate the buyer for the profits lost by not having access to the goods contracted for. The amount of the loss depends on the nature of the intended use of the goods. If the buyer obtains the goods elsewhere, the loss of value may be mitigated. In buyer cases, damages may extend to the entire business. Where breach of the contract by the seller caused the buyer's business to collapse.

---

[11] [1976] 1 W.L.R. 459.

Breaches of contract by buyers – sellers' damages

9–21 In specific contracts, when a buyer breaches, the seller's damages are the differential between contracted sales price, net of costs that were not incurred due to the breach, and net realisable value obtained. Where a buyer wrongfully refuses to accept delivery of goods, he may be required to pay damages in respect of the expenditure incurred in attempting to deliver the goods and in storing the goods. In addition, the seller will be entitled to obtain the loss of the bargain and be compensated so as to put him into the same situation as if the contract had been performed. Thus, the seller will be entitled to recover the profit he would have made from the sale.

Where a buyer breaches a contract that a seller/supplier has fully performed, calculating the supplier's damages is relatively straightforward. The supplier is awarded the full value of the performance due from the buyer plus interest to compensate for the delay in payment. Where, however, the buyer's breach precedes complete performance by the supplier, damages are more difficult to calculate. Such cases commonly arise in construction contracts, employment contracts and sale of goods. In both buyer and seller cases, however, damages may extend to the entire business.

For example, damages involving the entire business could arise where a seller had an exclusive contract to supply a service to a manufacturer and the manufacturer decided to supply the service itself. If the loss of the contract was so catastrophic, it might put the seller out of business. If the entire business of the seller was affected this would have to be reflected in the damages claim. The seller must be compensated for the profits lost arising from termination of the contract. The calculation of profits lost is based on past actual profit. The damages are the sales of the product at historical profitability of the seller (*i.e.* sales less cost of sales, expenses and overhead).

In another example, a buyer did not purchase goods as agreed under his contract with a supplier and warned the seller to mitigate (*i.e.* take action to reduce) his damages. The seller sued for 100 per cent of the contract. A differential analysis showed that the seller had sold the goods to an alternative buyer, incurring some additional costs in obtaining the alternative buyer. The net profit earned on the alternative sales was the mitigation, and the buyer was entitled to use that profit to reduce the standard contract price for the purposes of the seller's claim for breach of contract.

Non-compete covenants

9–22 A common form of contract case involves covenants not to compete, possibly for a specified period of time. This is common in sale-of-business agreements or in employment contracts in service businesses concerning employees leaving, for example, to set up on their own. The damage calculations involve isolating specific damages that result exclusively from the illegal competition. In a service business, where the breach involves stealing of clients, the calculations may be more straightforward and the specific damages easier to isolate.

Role of forensic accountants

9–23   Most claims for damages arising from breaches of commercial contracts will involve calculation of profits that the plaintiff lost due to the defendant's breach. Certain contracts contain provisions that provide for a type of forensic examination of underlying records in order to substantiate claims made by one of the parties. Contract damages claims revolve around compensation for reasonable expenditures, provided there was prudent action to mitigate (*i.e.* reduce) damages.

9–24   Examples of a variety of breach of contract cases involving forensic accountants are shown in Table 9.1.

Table 9.1: Examples of breach of contract cases in which forensic accountants have advised

Breaches of contract generally
• Calculating the value of a lost business opportunity resulting from a breach of, and interference with a contract, preparing exhibits and providing expert witness testimony
• Calculating the economic loss on the breach of a covenant not to compete by an employee who founded a competing company, analysing the monthly revenue that the defendant had received from the plaintiff's customers, choosing the proper method to use in calculating the amount of damage, *i.e.* the amount of gain to the ex-employee or the amount of lost profit to the former employer
• A financial services company forced a computer sales company out of business by an allegedly wrongful repossession of stock. A calculation of profits lost to the time of trial and projected future losses became the basis of a settlement
• A claim that the failure of the plaintiff's business was due to lack of promotional and other support promised by the defendant. Defendant counter-claimed that the plaintiff's failure denied the defendant promised royalty payments and promotion fees
• Defendant, an investment bank, orally guaranteed that it would perform an initial public offering (IPO) which would allow the plaintiff to expand. The defendant subsequently reneged on its guarantee, leaving the plaintiff in a precarious financial position after expending significant funds and efforts preparing for the IPO. Damages were calculated as the profit the plaintiff would have earned if the IPO had gone forward less actual profits earned
• Alleged breach of contract for failure by the owner of a shopping centre to operate its business continuously in relation to the anchor tenant. Forensic accountant's work included performing a financial analysis of the shopping centre and giving evidence regarding anticipated rates of return for the centre at the date the anchor tenant's lease was signed

- Analysing the financial records of a film distribution company whose breach of contract was alleged to have caused the film to fail because the distribution company did not use its best efforts to market and distribute the film
- Analysing damages in connection with a franchise termination dispute leading to damages associated with shutdown costs, lost contribution and a claim for loss of the initial investment. Preparing an alternative analysis of damages considering the plaintiff's actual operating results and industry trends.

Breaches of contract by buyers – sellers' damages
- Determining compensation for termination of supply contract without agreed notice
- Calculating the economic loss associated with the breach of a supply contract which resulted in bankruptcy of the plaintiff's business. Assisting in establishing a causal link between the loss of the contract and the loss of profits and destruction of the business. Performing a business valuation to demonstrate the lost business value and providing expert witness testimony
- Following cancellation of a long-term supply contract, analysing the validity of the lost profits claim and preparing an alternate calculation for presentation at trial, based on documentation obtained through discovery.

Case histories

9–25 Three more detailed examples of breach of contract cases, describing the involvement of forensic accountants are shown below. Case History 9.1 involves a breach of contract by a seller.

Case History 9.1: Breach of contract by seller/supplier

Incident
A manufacturing company entered into a contract with a supply company, for the supply of equipment to improve its efficiency. The supplier was chosen as it had recently developed a new system which included numerous features not available on any other systems. The supplier assured the manufacturer that the system was fully tested and that it was capable of meeting the manufacturer's requirements. A contract was duly entered into by both parties. The system was supplied at a discount of approximately 70% of retail price.

Claim
The system did not live up to expectations and, despite two years of modifications and improvements by the supplier, was eventually replaced by the manufacturer. The manufacturer took an action against the supplier for recovery of costs suffered in replacing the system and for damages.

Involvement of the forensic accountant
The forensic accountant prepared a report based on actual costs incurred in replacing the system and fully supported these costs by third-party invoices. The legal team then considered the issue of damages including loss of business reputation, deterioration in staff morale and profits lost due to communication difficulties. Due to the subjective nature of these issues, it was deemed appropriate that the forensic accountant would not attempt to quantify these matters. Therefore the report produced by the forensic accountant related solely to actual matters of fact.

Source: Adapted from Donohoe, D., "Forensic accounting" in *Accountancy Ireland* (October 1997), pp. 6 and 8.

9–26   Case History 9.2 involves a breach of contract by a buyer.

Case History 9.2: Breach of contract by buyer

Incident

A foreign subsidiary of a major multinational corporation entered into a written contract with a local service provider. The contract was for a fixed period of two years. At the end of two years, no new contract was entered into but the service provider continued to provide the same type of services.

Claim

A year later the multinational obtained a substantial new client. The local serivce provider claimed that it was entitled to a commission payment for arranging the meetings with the new client, arising from a clause in the new "oral" contract entered into on the termination of the fixed term contract. When the request was rebuffed litigation ensued. At this point it was realised that no due diligence had been done on the service provider and absolutely nothing was known about it.

Involvement of forensic accountant

Forensic accountants were instructed by the multinational corporation to establish the background of the service provider and to assist in identifying weaknesses in the service provider's case. Enquiries revealed that the service provider had a history of manipulating commercial relationships to bring fictitious claims. Its corporate structure spread over many jurisdictions in each of which it, or a related company, had broken local laws. The forensic accountants also established that in three cases company officers fabricated evidence to support litigation.

Outcome

The evidence of, and information gathered by, the forensic accountants assisted the client in winning its case.

Source: Adapted from the Risk Advisory Group Ltd, www.riskadvisory.net/ci/ciex/html

9–27   Case History 9.3 involves a breach of contract by a landlord.

Case History 9.3: Breach of contract by landlord

Incident

A handwritten contract was entered into by the owner of a shopping centre, and by the company operating the centre, stipulating the number of separate units which could be provided within the centre. Difficulties arose when the shopping centre was not ready at the agreed time, and subsequently shops were only able to open as units became available.

Claim

The shopping centre operator took an action against the owner for damages for loss of profit as a result of breach of contract. As the operator's income depended on the numbers of customers at each shop, losses suffered could not be determined with certainty.

Involvement of forensic accountant

The forensic accountant prepared a calculation of estimated losses which formed the basis for negotiations to reach a settlement. In situations of this nature where the calculation deals with an event that did not actually occur (because of the breach of contract), it is not possible to be definitive. As the calculations were based on estimation, the report included detailed notes highlighting the assumptions used and the basis of preparation of the estimates.

Source: Adapted from Donohoe, D., "Forensic accounting" in *Accountancy Ireland* (October 1997), pp. 6 and 8.

Accounting calculations

9–28   Parties to a contract can incur loss in a number of ways. A party may lose profits due to the breach. In addition, incidental or consequential losses may also be incurred. Incidental losses may arise because extra costs were incurred as a result of the breach. Consequential losses are those that the plaintiff incurred as an indirect result of the defendant's wrongful actions.

9–29   In seeking a remedy for breach of contract, the plaintiff generally has three possible avenues of recovery: damages, restitution and specific performance:

1.   Damages refer to compensation in the form of money to compensate the injured party for the effects of the breach.

2.   Restitution involves requiring the breaching party to account for the benefit that the injured party has conferred on him. Restitution is commonly used to avoid the unjust enrichment of the defendant by requiring the party in breach to pay the fair value of the performance that the plaintiff has rendered.

3.   When a court awards specific performance, the defendant is required to render the promised performance "as nearly as is practicable".

However, the plaintiff does not have complete discretion in choosing among these remedies.

Damages arising from breach of contract

9–30   The measurement of damages for a specific breach of contract depends on the terms of the contract and related documents. Thus, a thorough review of the contract and related documentation is necessary to establish a framework for the damages analysis.

The basic rule in claims for damages for breach of contract is that the plaintiff is entitled to be placed, as far as money can do it, in the same position as he would have been if the contract had been performed in accordance with its terms. Accordingly, damages may arise from two sources:

- actual losses from the breach;

- losses consequent on the breach, which are called consequential losses.

9–31   The loss to the injured party is the market value of the benefit he has been deprived of as a result of the breach. To calculate damages (sometimes referred to as "compensation for loss of bargain", the plaintiff's financial position as a result of the breach has to be compared with what if would have been "but for" the breach of contract by the defendant. A plaintiff cannot, in general, make a profit out of the contractual claim. Although exemplary (or punitive) damages are available in certain circumstances in tort claims (a tort is a private or civil wrong or injury, other than a breach of contract), the general rule is that no such damages can be awarded in a claim for breach of contract. This is because the parties to the contract had the opportunity to deal in advance with the consequences of a breach when agreeing the terms of the contract. Limited exceptions to this general rule have arisen in cases of breaches of employment contracts and in breaches of contract that involve bad faith or serious disregard for personal safety.

As a result of these considerations, where a claim can be grounded both in contract and in tort, plaintiffs are slow to abandon a claim in tort, and usually pursue both initially, where there is any prospect of exemplary damages.

9–32   In addition, the courts have historically been very reluctant to enforce a term in a contract that has the effect of penalising a party to an extent that is clearly disproportionate to the damage caused by the breach, even if the term (known as a penalty clause) has been freely agreed to by both parties. The test was stated by Costello J. in *Irish Telephone Rentals Ltd v. Irish Civil Service Building Society.*[12] He dealt with a clause that, it was argued, imposed a disproportionate penalty on the defendant and reviewed relevant case law as follows:

> "The defendant has submitted that the sum calculated in accordance with the condition does not represent a genuine pre-estimate of the actual loss which the plaintiff sustained as a result of the wrongful repudiation of the hiring agreement but is a penalty clause which the court should not enforce. The courts have evolved various rules for considering whether a stipulated sum is a penalty or a genuine pre-estimate. That which is relevant to the present case is that stated by Lord Dunedin in *Dunlop Pneumatic Tyre Co. Ltd. v. New Garage and Motor Co. Ltd.* [1915] A.C. 79 at 87:
>
> > 'It will be held to be a penalty if the sum stipulated for is extravagant and unconscionable in amount in comparison with the greatest loss that could conceivably be proved to have followed from the breach.'

---

[12][1991] I.L.R.M. 880.

The application of this principle is to be seen in the majority decision of the Court of Appeal in England in *Robophone Facilities Ltd. v. Blank* [1966] 1 W.L.R. 1428 in which the court considered a contract for the hiring of a telephone-answering machine for a seven year period which was repudiated before the hiring began. The hiring agreement contained a clause which made provision in the event of premature termination for the payment of agreed liquidated damages equal to 50% of the total of the rentals due. In deciding that the sum of 50% was a genuine pre-estimate of loss and not a penalty Lord Diplock examined what would be recoverable by way of damages assessed on common law principles and concluded that because 50% of the gross rent would not produce a figure which was 'extravagantly greater' than those damages the clause was enforceable."[13]

Costello J. then applied these principles to the case at hand:

"Before considering in greater detail the operation in this case of clause 11, I should give some more detail of how the plaintiff's claim is made up.

The plaintiff has calculated that there were nine full years of the agreement to run from the date of termination. The annual rent at that time (which had been increased over the years pursuant to the rent revision clause) was then £1,438.16. This annual rent was discounted over a nine year period by 5% giving a discounted figure of £10,222.15. There was added to this one quarter's rent unpaid in 1988 (that is, £359.51 [*sic*]) giving a total of £10,581.66. A figure of 25% of this sum was then calculated, that is a sum of £2,645.42. This was deducted from the sum of £10,581.69 [*sic*] giving a figure of £7,936.27. It is to be noted that the gross rent for the unexpired nine year period of the hiring was £13,043.62 according to these calculations.

I have come to the conclusion that the formula contained in clause 11 does not produce a liquidated sum that can properly be regarded as a genuine pre-estimate made at the date of the contract of the loss which the plaintiff would suffer should the contract be prematurely determined and that it is in reality a penalty and therefore unenforceable."[14]

It is clear from this analysis that, where a clause in a contract provides for a payment, on a breach, that significantly exceeds any genuine pre-estimate of the loss caused by the breach, the courts will regard it as a penalty clause and will not enforce it.

Consequential loss

9–33 A head of damages commonly included in breach of contract claims is "consequential loss". Consequential loss is such loss as the claimant could prove over and above that which arose as a direct result of such breaches of contract that the claimant could prove.[15] The topic of consequential loss has occupied the attention of the Supreme Court on a number of occasions, notably in

---

[13] [1991] I.L.R.M. 880 at 889.
[14] *ibid.* at 889–890.
[15] *British Sugar plc v. NEI Power Projects* [1997] 87 B.L.R. 42 (CA).

Superwood Holdings plc v. Sun Alliance and London Insurance plc[16] and in *Mogul of Ireland Ltd v. Tipperary North Riding County Council.*[17] In the former case, the term "consequential loss" was defined in the contract under which the dispute arose. In the latter case, the matter at issue was whether consequential losses were recoverable in an action for malicious damage under the then prevailing legislation.

None of the judgments in these cases contains a definition of the term consequential loss, with the learned judges preferring to deal with the concept using its ordinary, natural meaning. The fact that these and other cases deal extensively with consequential losses without the necessity of a definition implies that the ordinary meaning of the term is well understood judicially. In other words, consequential losses can be taken to be those losses resulting from the event in question, other than such losses as flow directly from the event.

In some circumstances, it may be too difficult to calculate the loss suffered as a result of the breach. In such cases, an alternative measure of damages might be used, such as out-of-pocket expenses incurred.

Breach of warranty

9–34 Warranties are a form of assurance given by vendors to purchasers and which form part of a contract of sale. Many warranty clauses common in purchase/sale contracts relate to accounting, financial reporting and purchase price issues. From a buyer's perspective, warranties generally serve three purposes:

– they assist the buyer in understanding the purchase;

– they enable the buyer to recover damages if the seller makes inaccurate representations;

– they allow the buyer to abort the transaction if the seller makes false representations.

Warranties are common in connection with merger and acquisition agreements which normally include extensive financial warranty clauses. Warranties are included in contracts to limit the general contractual principle of *caveat emptor* – let the buyer beware. The role of forensic accountants, and the calculations necessary, in such disputes, are briefly discussed here.[18]

---

[16] [1995] 3 I.R. 303.
[17] [1976] I.R. 260.
[18] Further information on forensic accounting aspects of breach of warranty can be found in Lemar, C. J. and Mainz, A. J. (eds), *Litigation Support* (4th ed., Butterworths, London, 1999), Chap. 3; and Taub, M., Rapazzini, A., Bond, C., Solon, M., Brown, A., Murrie, A., Linnell K. and Burn, S., *Tolley's Accountancy Litigation Support* (Butterworths, London, looseleaf), Part VI, para. 80.

Legal context

9–35 A warranty is a term of a contract the breach of which gives rise to an action for damages, but which does not allow the innocent party to treat himself as discharged from the contract. Thus, a breach of warranty does not constitute a breach of the contract itself.

Mergers and acquisitions

9–36 This section briefly considers disputes arising from breach of warranty in mergers and acquisitions, focusing in particular on disputes that might require expert accounting input. Mergers and acquisitions also give rise to actions in tort for misrepresentation which are considered in paras **10–73** *et seq*. The law dealing with mergers and acquisitions is comprehensively covered in Clarke.[19]

9–37 Mergers and acquisitions often result in disputes. Accountants are usually involved in due diligence[20] and in the negotiation stages of merger and acquisition activity. However, they also have significant opportunities to provide forensic accounting services in connection with any disputes arising. Merger and acquisition agreements commonly include clauses dealing with accounting and financial reporting matters. These clauses often affect the purchase price and are, therefore, commonly the subject of disputes. Examples of such clauses are:

- financial statements show a true and fair view;
- accounting policies are consistent with prior years;
- full title is held on the assets of the company and the assets are adequately insured;
- financial statements are presented in accordance with generally accepted accounting principles;
- no undisclosed liabilities exist;
- full provision for taxes due has been made;
- no material adverse change has occurred in the company's business since the date of the most recent audited balance sheet.

In addition, such clauses may also indicate how changes in financial position in the period between pre-closing and closing are to be dealt with and how the

---

[19] Clarke, B., *Takeovers and Mergers Law in Ireland* (Round Hall Sweet & Maxwell, Dublin, 1999).

[20] Due diligence is described by Clarke, *ibid.*, as an "exercise to confirm the details given to [the purchaser] by the vendor and to satisfy itself as to the state of affairs of the company", p. 495.

Case History 9.4: Breach of warranty

Incident

A property development company purchased the premises and business of a prominent hotel. One million pounds of the selling price of the hotel was placed in an escrow fund (*i.e.* money held by a third party until conditions of an agreement are fulfilled) to indemnify the property development company against any breach of warranties or representations made by the sellers in the sale agreement. Subsequently, the property development company claimed that the financial statements of the hotel had not been prepared in accordance with generally accepted accounting principles, in that they did not disclose potential redundancy costs of £1.25 million in connection with terminating employees.

Claim

As a result of this alleged breach of warranty, the property development company demanded and received payment of £350,000 from the escrow agents. The vendors of the hotel filed suit for return of the funds.

Involvement of the forensic accountant

The hotel vendors retained a forensic accountant to provide an opinion on the accounting and financial statement disclosures which the property development company claimed were omitted contrary to generally accepted accounting principles.

Methodology

- The sale agreement was reviewed and it was determined that amongst the accounting records, audited financial statements had been included and seen by the property development company prior to sale. These financial statements showed a business that, whilst having a large turnover, was barely breaking even. The largest expense related to payroll costs. It seemed clear that the property development company was attempting to fund the redundancies via the escrow account.
- During the course of the sale and immediately following, the property development company made a number of public statements to the effect that no redundancies would take place. Subsequently, a large number of staff were made redundant.
- It was necessary to establish the appropriate accounting treatment for the redundancy costs. Accounting standards were considered first. Following this, common practice was considered which required a detailed review of disclosure in available comparable financial statements. In addition, specific examples of redundancy disclosure were considered.
- The key issue relating to the case revolved around the definition of "liability" and "contingent liability" in the accounting literature. Based upon the facts available, it was clear that the potential redundancy costs did not meet the criteria to be accounted for as either a liability or a contingent liability. Accordingly, the hotel vendors were correct in (i) not recognising and (ii) not disclosing the amount in their financial statements.

Outcome

As a result of the forensic accountant's report, the property development company did not contest the financial statements disclosure aspects of the claim at the hearing.

Source: Adapted from Johnson, P., "Forensic accounting–a legal support" *Commercial Law Practitioner* (September 1996) pp. 206-210.

seller will operate the business prior to closing and handover to the purchaser. Earn out clauses may also be included. Such clauses attempt to mitigate the acquiror's risk by making the consideration payable to the vendor contingent on the future performance of the acquired company. These clauses usually stipulate that the acquired company must achieve certain predetermined performance levels, often expressed in terms of sales revenue or pre-tax profits.[21]

Role of forensic accountants[22]

9–38 Forensic accountants may be asked to advise in relation to liability and to assist in proving (or otherwise) a breach of financial warranty. In addition, they may calculate the quantum of damages flowing from the breach. Calculation of damages depends on the nature of the warranty and will be based on the difference between the position the person relying on the warranty would have been in had the representations been true and the actual position he is in as a result of the breach of warranty (*e.g.* see *Bank of Ireland v. Smith*[23]).

9–39 An example of a breach of warranty case in which a forensic accountant advised is shown in Case History 9.4.

9–40 Forensic accountants can assist parties in merger and acquisition disputes in a variety of ways. They can advise on formulating the dispute by identifying areas which do not conform to the purchase/sale agreement and by listing sections of the agreement that have been violated. Forensic accountants can calculate adjustments to the accounts necessary to comply with the agreement, can identify breaches in observing generally accepted accounting principles, and can quantify the effect of such breaches.

Forensic accountants can also assist in advising on the financial information that should be requested of the other side during the discovery process. They can then analyse the facts and documentary evidence obtained during the discovery, and advise the client on liability issues and on calculation of damages.

9–41 Forensic accountants can also identify the strengths and weaknesses of the client's position, can advise on the likely response from the other side and can advise on a counter-response from the client. When the case comes to trial forensic accountants can advise on questions for cross-examination. Table 9.2 describes cases in which forensic accountants have acted as advisers in disputes concerning mergers and acquisitions.

---

[21] Sudarsanam, P.S., *The Essence of Mergers and Acquisitions* (Prentice Hall, London, 1995), pp. 190–193.
[22] This is considered in Perks, B.W., Haller, M.W. and Kreb, K.D., "Mergers, acquisitions and divestitures: the nature of disputes and the role of the CPA" in *Litigation Services Handbook. The Role of the Accountant as Expert* (2nd ed., Weil, R.L., Wagner, M.J. and Frank, P.B. (eds), John Wiley & Sons, Inc., New York, 1995), Chap. 14.
[23] [1966] I.R. 646.

Table 9.2: Examples of mergers and acquisitions cases in which forensic accountants have advised

- Providing expert evidence on the breach of a covenant not to compete, testifying about the difficulty in establishing a causal link between the breach and any economic loss, including a description of possible intervening causes of any economic loss
- Investigating sales and profit figures provided, where the purchasers were unable to achieve the level of turnover and profit quoted by the vendor. Inspection of the accounting records of both parties to assess the accuracy of the statements made on the sale and why the purchasers had achieved such poor results
- Verifying valuations of assets which were the subject of warranties in company acquisitions
- Comparing the tax position of an entity post-acquisition with the position as warranted on sale and calculating damages based on this comparision

Accounting calculations

9–42 A breach of warranty is a contract-related claim. There are two types of warranties in a contract for sale of goods: express or implied. In express warranties, the seller clearly identifies the particular characteristics of the goods that he guarantees. In an implied warranty, the promise is less clearly stated and a more general guarantee is given, such as general merchantability.

The normal standard of warranty-related damages is the difference between the value of the goods as warranted and the value of the goods that were sold. Consequential loss as a result of breach of warranty is the difference between the value of an asset or the business if the situation had been as warranted and its actual value. The terms of the warranty may define how the loss is to be calculated. Calculation of damages will be based on the difference between the position the person/company would have been in had the warranty representations been true and the actual position he/it is in as a result of the warranty being untrue.[24]

Mergers and acquisitions

9–43 In a merger or acquisition, the effect of this is that the damages recoverable on foot of a breach of warranty in the sale and purchase agreement amount to the difference between the market value of the company had the warranties been true compared with the actual market value. The market value of the company had the warranties been true is normally taken to be the actual purchase price paid for the company.

---

[24] *Firbank's Executors v. Humphreys* (1886) 18 Q.B.D. 54 at 60 (CA).

9–44   If the price was based on a multiple of earnings, and the breach of warranty affects future profits, damages may be based on a multiple of the overstatement of net profit.[25] This may apply even where the original price was not based on an earnings multiple.[26] Where there is a deficiency of assets warranted by the vendor, the amount of damages is the amount of the deficiency.

Product liability

9–45   Manufacturers of defective products are exposed to liability in tort, contract or under statute in respect of defects. Claims under statute may only be brought where the liability exceeds £350 (see para. **9–52**). Many claims far exceed this limit, and forensic accountants are often involved in such cases because of the size of claims and the complexity of the necessary calculations.

Legal context

9–46   Liability for such claims can arise in three ways: through claims of negligence by the producer (tort), under contract and under statute. Each of these is discussed below.

Liability in tort

9–47   Liability in tort depends on the injured party establishing a number of matters including that the manufacturer of the product owed the injured party a duty of care and that the manufacturer has failed to discharge this duty and that the loss or damage suffered by the injured party was caused by the defect of which he complains.

Liability under contract

9–48   Under contract law, the injured party may only have a contractual relationship with the retailer of the product as opposed to the manufacturer of the product. The absence of a contractual relationship with the manufacturer of the product may cause difficulties if the retailer of the product does not have sufficient means (*i.e.* insurance) to meet the injured party's claim. It is also possible that the injured party has no contractual relationship with either the retailer or the manufacturer.

9–49   It is not uncommon for suppliers to insert exclusion clauses in contracts

---

[25] *Senate Electrical Wholesalers Ltd v. Alcatel Submarine Networks Ltd, The Times*, June 26, 1998.
[26] *ibid.*

in respect of their products. An exclusion clause is a contractual term which purports to limit or exclude liability for breach of contractual terms. However, the other party may rely on the doctrine of fundamental breach which will not allow one party to evade liability for breach of one of the fundamental elements of the contract. This issue arose in *Clayton Love & Sons (Dublin) v. British and Irish Steam Packet Co Ltd*[27] where the Supreme Court held that the failure to keep the product being transported (scampi) frozen was a breach of a fundamental term of the contract notwithstanding two exclusion terms in the contract. In addition, under the sale of goods legislation, the exclusion clauses must be fair and reasonable.

9–50 By providing that the liability of a producer for damage caused by a defect in his product arises in tort, section 2(1) of the Liability for Defective Products Act 1991 (see para. **9–52**) has the effect that the injured party does not have to establish a contractual relationship with the manufacturer of the product as a precondition to establishing liability.

Statutory liability

9–51 The sale of goods legislation implies a condition into every contract of sale that the goods supplied are of merchantable quality and reasonably fit for any purpose for which they are supplied.[28] The Liability for Defective Products Act 1991 provides victims/injured parties of defective products with an additional remedy against the producer. Producers (which term is broadly defined) are required to ensure that products placed on the market are safe. Under the 1991 Act, the injured party is not required to establish the existence of a duty of care. However, the onus remains on the injured party to prove the damage, the defect and the causal relationship between the two.[29]

9–52 Section 2 of the Act imposes liability on producers of defective products. "Producers" are defined for this purpose, as follows:

"(1) The producer shall be liable in damages in tort for damage caused wholly or partly by a defect in his product.

(2) In this Act, 'producer' means—

(a) the manufacturer or producer of a finished product, or

(b) the manufacturer or producer of any raw material or the manufacturer or producer of a component part of a product, or

---

[27] (1970) 104 I.L.T.R. 157.
[28] Sale of Goods Act 1893, s. 14, as amended by s. 10 of the Sale of Goods and Supply of Services Act 1980.
[29] Liability for Defective Products Act 1991, s. 4.

(c) in the case of the products of the soil, of stock-farming and of fisheries and game, which have undergone initial processing, the person who carried out such processing, or

(d) any person who, by putting his name, trade mark or other distinguishing feature on the product or using his name or any such mark or feature in relation to the product, has held himself out to be the producer of the product, or

(e) any person who has imported the product into a Member State from a place outside the European Communities in order, in the course of any business of his, to supply it to another, or

(f) any person who is liable as producer of the product pursuant to subsection (3) of this section.

The Act imposes liability on the supplier of goods in certain circumstances where the producer cannot be identified. The first £350[30] of damage that would otherwise arise under the Act is excluded from liability.

9–53   Section 5 of the Act defines when a product is defective for the purposes of the Act:

> "(1) For the purposes of this Act a product is defective if it fails to provide the safety which a person is entitled to expect, taking all circumstances into account, including—
>
> (a) the presentation of the product,
>
> (b) the use to which it could reasonably be expected that the product would be put, and
>
> (c) the time when the product was put into circulation.
>
> (2) A product shall not be considered defective for the sole reason that a better product is subsequently put into circulation."

9–54   The Act provides a number of possible defences for producers, including the situation where the state of scientific and technical knowledge at the time when the producer put the product into circulation was not such as to enable the existence of the defect to be discovered.

Role of forensic accountants

9–55   Damages will be awarded to place the person who suffered damage into the position which he was before the actions of the defendant. Forensic accountants can assist in assessing the quantum of the damages. Table 9.3 describes product liability cases in which forensic accountants have advised.

---

[30]Liability for Defective Products Act 1991, s. 3.

Table 9.3: Examples of product liability cases in which forensic accountants have advised

---

Preparing claims/analysis of damages
- Preparing a claim for lost profits on behalf of a manufacturer that was sold defective equipment. Calculating the company's lost profits by determining what the company's profits would have been but for the defective equipment, including components of damages such as increased costs, inefficiencies, lost productivity and additional capital expenditures
- Preparing an alternative analysis for damages associated with the failure of a machine, analysing the claim presented and determining that damages were appropriate, documented and accurate
- Analysing out-of-pocket costs and lost profit resulting from the downtime arising from claims against a transport company for losses caused by delivery of a contaminated product
- Calculating loss associated with the failure of a generator, including fluctuating product prices and raw material prices in the calculations
- Calculating loss associated with faulty equipment after considering machine downtime for scheduled maintenance.

Auditing product liability claims
- Auditing, on a sample basis, out-of-pocket costs claimed by farmers associated with crop damage to fields treated with herbicide
- Auditing product recall claims resulting from defective ingredients and packaging, requiring verification of the out-of-pocket costs of the recalls and the analysis of claims for lost sales including claimed long-term effects, as well as marketing costs incurred to regain market share
- Auditing costs incurred in product recalls. Evaluating profits lost as a result of the recalls, and negative publicity by analysing market share data.

Accounting calculations

9–56   The producer is liable for damage caused wholly or partially by a defect in his product. Not all damage is covered by the Liability for Defective Products Act 1991. Damage is defined in the Act as damage, personal injury or loss, or damage to, or destruction of any item of property other than the defective product itself. However, in the case of damage affecting property, the damaged property is required to be of a type normally intended for private use or consumption, and was used by the injured person mainly for his own private use or consumption. The 1991 Act appears to exclude recovery for damage to property used commercially in the course of a trade, business or profession.

9–57   Occasionally, losses may arise as a result of a product recall by a supplier of defective products or due to an impairment of operations caused by the failure of a sub-component or part purchased from a supplier. Often in such circumstances the product has be recalled, repairs made and in some cases rebates or other accommodations paid to customers. Claims arising from defective products and product tampering typically involve a considerable volume of

318   *Forensic Accounting*

detailed records supporting the costs incurred in the recall and can include complex claims for lost sales based on market share reports or other data. Forensic accountants use this data to arrive at an estimate of damage comprising costs incurred and revenues foregone.

9–58   There may be limited availability of exemplary or punitive damages in product liability cases where a court determines that a producer should be publicly punished for putting defective products in circulation. This is likely to arise where the defect exposed consumers to significant risk of injury and the producer was either grossly negligent or put the defective product into circulation knowing of the defect. In such circumstances a court might use exemplary or punitive damages both to punish the wrongdoer and to discourage similar behaviour in the future. In such a case the individual plaintiff would enjoy a windfall gain that is likely to exceed significantly the value of the damage done to him.

Insurance losses and claims

9–59   It is beyond the scope of this book to consider the complex legal issues concerning the law of insurance.[31] However, there is a clear role for forensic accountants in the calculation of lost profits and in the valuation of lost or damaged assets arising from an insured risk.

9–60   Forensic accountants are generally only involved in insurance cases in relation to claims for losses. Insurance policies normally lay down the procedures governing claims. The insured person must demonstrate that insurance existed to cover the loss claimed. Even where the loss is covered by an insurance policy, and the insurers are prima facie liable to pay the insured, there are circumstances where the insurers are entitled to reject the claim and to repudiate liability. These include:

– breach of conditions in the insurance policy by the insured;

– non-disclosure: All facts material to the assessment of risk by the insurer must be disclosed. If it can be shown that non-disclosure induced the insurer to enter the contract, the insurer can avoid the liability and repudiate the contract;

– fraud: Insurers can avoid liability where a claim is fraudulent because: (i) the insured deliberately caused the loss; or (ii) where the loss was not in fact caused by one of the perils insured against; or (iii) the loss suffered was inflated or overstated.

---

[31] Further information on legal aspects of insurance are available in Buckley, A.J., *Insurance Law in Ireland* (Oak Tree Press, Dublin, 1997); O'Regan Cazabon, A., *Irish Insurance Law in Ireland* (Round Hall Sweet & Maxwell, Dublin, 1999); Corrigan, M. and Campbell, J.A. (eds), *A Casebook of Irish Insurance Law* (Oak Tree Press, Dublin, 1993).

The sum payable under an insurance contract depends on the terms of the policy. Insurance policies fall into one of the following categories:

— valued policies, *i.e.* the full value of the policy is paid where the loss is a total loss, regardless of the value of the loss;

— unvalued policies, *i.e.* the actual value of the loss is paid at the time the loss is incurred. Such policies may refer to an amount for which the risk is insured. This amount represents the maximum that can be claimed in respect of the loss.

Legal context

9–61 A contract of insurance is a contract whereby one party, the insurer, agrees in return for a payment (the premium) to pay a sum of money to the insured on the happening of a certain event, or to indemnify the insured against the loss caused by the occurrence of a specified event. Contracts of insurance cover areas such as life insurance, personal accident, public liability, damage to property, professional indemnity and general liability. Many insurance contracts provide for alternative dispute resolution mechanisms such as arbitration and, hence, many insurance cases do not come before the courts (see Chapter 14).

9–62 Economic losses suffered by businesses may be covered by insurance and may be claimable, depending on the clauses in the insurance policy. Examples of items covered by insurance policies and examples of insurance claims are shown in Table 9.4.

Table 9.4: Civil liability and insurance claims

Business	**Personal injury**
• Contents	• Motor vehicle accidents
• Stock losses	• Slips and falls
• Product liability	• Recreational accidents
• Professional negligence	• Medical malpractice
• Property damage	• Occupiers' liability
• Rental loss	• Fatality
• Third party liability	
• Employee compensation claims	
Fraud	
• Arson	
• Other insurance fraud	
• Employee dishonesty	

Types of insurance claims

9–63 As Table 9.4 illustrates, there are many different types of insurance claims.

Business insurance loss evaluations may arise from all types of disasters such as fires, floods, and machinery accidents. Claims for increased costs arising directly from the disaster may also be made. These include temporary hire of replacement machinery, temporary relocation of the business following damage to the original premises, additional transport costs, etc. The insurance claim may include amounts for increased working costs. It may not be practical to look at individual invoices to extract the additional costs. An alternative approach might be to compare actual costs and budgeted costs in the absence of any damage (adjusting the budgeted figures for any variation between historic actual and budgeted activity). Conversely, any savings that the business experiences as a result of the incident must also be taken into account. Management accounts are often the best place to look for potential cost savings.

Fire and property insurance

9–64 Insurance claims can arise as a result of natural disasters such as fires, floods and earthquakes. Fire and property insurance policies are generally limited to material damage such as damage to property. Separate insurance contracts are issued to cover consequential losses such as reduction in business.

9–65 One of the most common insurance risks where forensic accountants can become involved is loss of stock. Forensic accountants may advise in relation to stock losses arising from natural events such as fires, floods, etc., from robbery and theft, and from stock losses during transportation. Claims for fire or flood damaged stock require consideration of three main issues:

1. Existence of stock.

2. Stock quantities.

3. Stock values.

The existence of stock and the estimation of quantities of stock depend on the adequacy of the system for recording stock. In more sophisticated businesses, there may be "real time" stock recording systems that update recorded stock levels on an item-by-item basis, supplemented by regular verification through stock counts. Such a system can provide information on stock on hand at any particular date. However, in many businesses continuous stock records are not maintained and stock must be physically counted at regular intervals to ascertain stock levels. Commonly, businesses that conduct periodic (often annual only) stock counts maintain no records of stock levels in the intervening periods. In the case of a catastrophe such as a fire or a flood, calculating stock quantities may involve a "roll forward" from the previous physical stock count. A roll forward involves adjusting for purchases and sales of stock during the period, and for any wastage that might have occurred. For example, in a roll forward, amounts in the previous stock count are adjusted for sales, purchases and wastage in the period since the stock count up to the date of the fire/flood.

9–66   In an insurance claim, the wording of the policy may influence stock valuations. Stock valuation can be a subjective matter and, consequently, susceptible to manipulation. When a manufacturer sustains a loss of stock, the cost to replace such stock is a key question. On the one hand, to mitigate loss of business income, the manufacturer may need to expedite replacement of stock by authorising overtime. Other types of stock may not warrant such emphasis if demand for the product by the firm's customers is not a factor. Retail, wholesale and manufacturer losses may need to be analysed for these issues. In addition, a regular issue affecting the quantum of claim is provisions for slow-moving or obsolete stock.

9–67   Care must also be taken not to double count losses. For example, any stock claim would need to be examined against the associated loss of profits claim, to ensure that there is no double counting.

Consequential loss/business interruption insurance[32]

9–68   An ordinary property damage policy does not cover loss of profits or loss of market arising from damage to property. A separate insurance contract is required to cover loss of trade in the form of reduced turnover and/or increased operating costs arising from (say) a fire. Such policies are variously referred to as business interruption, consequential loss or loss of profits policies. As with all policies of indemnity, recovery depends on the terms and conditions of the particular policy. Policies usually specify a method of measuring the loss of earnings.

Normal interruption policies provide that, where the business of the insured is interrupted, the insurer pays the insured the amount of the loss resulting from the interruption subject to a material damage proviso and a maximum liability limit. The cost of replacing goods or material will be met by the material damage insurance.

The purpose of such insurance is to put the insured in the position they would have been in had there been no interruption of the business. The extent of the

---

[32] An authoritative work on this subject is Cloughton, D., *Riley on Business Interruption and Consequential Loss Insurance* (8th ed., Sweet & Maxwell, London, 1999). Other useful books on this topic include Gamlen, E. and Philips, J., *Business Interruption Insurance* (Buckley Press, London, 1992); Hickmott, G.J.R., *Interruption Insurance: Proximate Loss Issues* (Witherby & Company Limited, London, 1990); and Hickmott, G.J.R., *Interruption Insurance: Practical Issues* (Witherby & Company Limited, London, 1999).

loss is generally calculated in accordance with the terms of the policy by reference to the performance of the business in previous accounting periods, adjusting for any variations or trends in the business. Generally, policies require the insured to take all reasonable steps to restore the business to normal trading levels as quickly as possible. Policies will reimburse the insured for expenditure in avoiding or reducing the loss during the indemnity period in consequence of the damage, but not exceeding the sum produced by applying the rate of gross profit to the amount of the reduction thereby avoided.[33]

In order to obtain payment under consequential loss policies, a material damage section must be included in the policy. Thus, any property in which there is an insurable interest, but which is not insured against material damage, is excluded from the consequential loss cover.

Role of forensic accountants

9–69 Forensic accountants assist those insured, their representatives and insurance companies in their evaluation of insurance claims. They prove, evaluate and assist in a variety of claims including fraud investigations, business valuation, and business interruption. As insurance claims get larger, the need to involve experts in the process increases. Forensic accountants, as a result, often specialise in loss evaluation. The decision to involve a forensic accountant usually involves a cost/benefit analysis.

9–70 In some insurance cases, the need for a forensic accountant is unavoidable – for example, in a professional indemnity claim against an accountant, where an expert accountant is required to express an opinion on the reasonableness of another accountant's work. In other insurance claim cases, such as fire insurance claims, the need for a forensic accountant is not so obvious. Forensic accountants often assist injured parties in preparing insurance claims to maximise loss recovery for plaintiffs by strengthening their clients' positions in their negotiations with insurers. Alternatively, forensic accountants may act for defendant insurance companies to minimise excessive claims. A clear understanding of the claim requires a full appreciation of the underlying business. The wording of the policy must also be considered. Table 9.5 describes insurance cases in which forensic accountants acted as advisers.[34]

---

[33] Buckley, A.J., *Insurance Law in Ireland* (Oak Tree Press, Dublin, 1997), p. 354.
[34] Forensic accounting aspects of insurance are dealt with in Taub, M., Rapazzini, A., Bond, C., Solon, M., Brown, A., Murrie, A., Linnell, K. and Burn, S., *Tolley's Accountancy Litigation Support* (Butterworths, London, looseleaf), Part VI, para. 90; and reinsurance contract disputes are considered in Lemar, C.J. and Mainz, A.J. (eds), *Litigation Support* (4th ed., Butterworths, London, 1999), Chap. 11.

Table 9.5: Examples of insurance cases in which forensic accountants have advised

Acting for the plaintiff
- Testifying that defendant insurance company, in bad faith, delayed payment for insured losses arising from a fire in plaintiff's office and that the defendant's actions cut off plaintiff's cash flow, forcing plaintiff to lay off personnel and suspend marketing activities, resulting in lost profits
- Valuing lost profits and incentives associated with an explosion at a factory, factoring other intervening causes of loss into the calculations
- Reconstructing three years of incomplete accounting records to document the claim settlement amount in an insurance claim dispute over valuation of stocks
- Reviewing the finances of an entity spanning several years, proving the misdirection of funds by seeking recovery from the insurer, and assisting in civil and criminal remedies
- Investigating and documenting incident of embezzlement, preparing insurance claim and negotiating successful settlement.

Acting for the defendant insurance company
- Analysing multiple business interruption claims brought in connection with flooding caused by the failure of a sprinkler system, with a view to demonstrating that the claims did not compare with the actual operating results of the business and were overstated
- Monitoring and auditing the cost of decontaminating and repairing a facility, following a nuclear power plant incident
- Auditing claims for property losses sustained as a result of natural disasters
- Monitoring and auditing the clean-up and repair costs claimed as a result of an explosion and fire, providing financial expertise to lawyers throughout the resulting arbitration process and giving evidence before to the arbitrators
- Auditing the business interruption and extra expense losses as well as the property damage loss as a result of explosion
- Testifying concerning the net worth and annual profits during the punitive damages phase of an insurance bad faith matter, based on review of financial statements.

Insurance fraud
- Examining accounting records and business documents at various business locations relating to a fire suspected to be arson. Supporting lawyers in discovery and during the trial
- Providing consulting services related to arson, discovering evidence of fraud in the financial statements submitted with the perpetrator's insurance claim.

Accounting calculations

9–71 Forensic accountants are experienced in dealing with business interruption, stock loss and surety claims,[35] as well as asset recovery. Whether acting for the plaintiff or the defendant, forensic accountants can:

– interpret the financial aspects of the terms of the contract;

---

[35] Surety bonds are agreements by insurance companies to be responsible for the debts or obligations of an insured party.

- ascertain compliance with contract terms;

- reconcile such terms with the business realities;

- present findings in a manner acceptable to the insurance industry and the courts.

Forensic accountants can assist in the following types of accounting calculations:

- business interruption losses;

- business loss of profits;

- extra expenses;

- stock counts, reconstruction and valuation;

- personal earnings losses.

9–72   Forde[36] discusses various methods of valuing insurance losses. In fire and other property insurance, the value of the loss is the difference between the values before and after the damage occurred. Alternatively, the cost of repairs may be deducted from the value of the property after repair, which value is compared with the original value of the property. Four different calculations were considered in *St Albans Investment Co v. Sun Alliance*,[37] in respect of a premises completely destroyed by fire: market value, replacement cost, reinstatement cost of new building and replacement cost of building similar to the one destroyed.

Loss of profits claims

9–73   Loss of profits can be measured relatively accurately by reference to turnover, by comparing turnover in the months following damage with that in the corresponding period in the 12 months preceding the event, subject to appropriate adjustment for special circumstances and trends in the business. Thus, the shortage of turnover throughout the period of interruption is ascertainable and provides an accurate basis for measuring the insured's loss. Focusing on turnover provides a measure which can take account of seasonality. In addition, the effect of trends on turnover can be estimated.

Reduction of turnover is a reliable index for measuring the proportionate effect an insured event on earnings. Loss of turnover is not the same as loss of profits. When turnover falls, variable production costs will also fall. The loss to be compensated therefore should only take into account indirect, fixed overheads (*e.g.* factory rent, factory manager's salary, depreciation on production

---

[36] Forde, M., *Commercial Law* (2nd ed., Butterworths, Dublin, 1997), pp. 294–297.
[37] [1983] I.R. 363.

machinery) and the related loss of net profit. Thus, the proportionate loss is measured by reference to the normal ratio of overheads and net profit to turnover (called the net profit plus standing charges approach) as follows:

$$\text{Loss of profits} = \text{Fall in turnover} \times \frac{\text{Fixed overheads} + \text{net profit}}{\text{Turnover}}$$

An alternative (and more logical) way of approaching this calculation is the turnover less variable costs approach as follows:

$$\text{Loss of profits} = \text{Fall in turnover} - \text{variable costs}$$

Forensic accountants can assist in the calculation of the profits the business would have made had the insured event not occurred. The first step is to calculate the lost sales and then to calculate the lost gross profit on those sales. Any consideration of lost sales will involve looking at historic sales patterns, but also at future prospects. Businesses often find themselves poised for expansion at the time of a particular incident. In these circumstances, it becomes necessary to consider budgets and forecasts, investment valuations and market surveys. It is also important to consider the market conditions in which the business operates. Another issue is the need to distinguish between variable and fixed costs (*i.e.* those costs that vary directly according to production/sales and those that do not). In practice, the distinction is not an easy one to draw and some costs may be partially variable.

Interruption of trading may also involve additional expenditure, such as to minimise the loss of turnover or to resume normal trading as quickly as possible. This additional expenditure will also be compensated under the policy.

Thus, in summary, compensation under loss of profits policies comprise:

— loss of net profit due to reduction in turnover;

— loss due to increased ratio of fixed costs to a reduced turnover;

— loss due to additional expenditure.

Construction[38]

9–74 Building contracts, whereby one person (the contractor) agrees to carry out construction or engineering works for another (the employer), are governed

---

[38]Useful sources for building and civil engineering contract claims are Duncan Wallace, I.N., *Hudson's Building and Engineering Contracts* (11th ed., Sweet & Maxwell, London, 1994); Powell-Smith, V. and Sims, J., *Building Contract Claims* (3rd ed., Blackwells, London, 1997); Powell-Smith, V., Stephenson, D. and Redmond, J., *Civil Engineering*

by the general law of contract. All of the elements of a simple contract are required to be present, and the general rules of performance, discharge, breach and so on apply. However, building contracts have developed into a rather peculiar and complex area of law. A number of the matters covered in building contracts are summarised below.

Building contracts differ from many other types of contracts in the level of detail specified in relation to the quantification of damages where the contract is breached. Contracts normally prescribe exact calculations, based on financial and accounting terms which are usually defined explicitly. Attempts to interpret and then apply these terms to individual cases can be assisted by expert accountants. Thereafter, the calculation of damages will also normally involve expert accountants. Construction contracts also often invoke arbitration when breached. Expert accountants may be required to assist, or even act as arbitrators.

The contract will provide for the contractor to carry out and complete the works in accordance with detailed drawings and specifications. The contract will identify the various parties engaged to carry out professional responsibilities in relation to the works and will define those responsibilities. The architect or engineer is given the power to issue instructions to the contractor on behalf of the employer, and the contractor is required to comply with those instructions. To the extent that there are cost implications to the contractor in complying with the instructions, then the contract will provide for how such costs should be dealt with.

Most building agreements in Ireland are based on the use of standard form contracts. The terms in these standard form contracts lay down the principles by which the conflicting interests of the parties are to be resolved throughout the progress of the contract. There are four standard contracts used in Ireland:

1. Basic, original form – primarily used for substantial contracts.

2. Government departments and local authorities (GDLA) form – used where the work is to be paid wholly or partly from public exchequer funds.

3. Shorter form (SF88) – used for small or simple contracts.

4. Plain language contract – this is intended to have the same legal effect as the standard form, but is written in a simple style and clauses in the contract are more logically set out.

Claims (3rd ed., Blackwells, London, 1999); Trickey, G. and Hackett, M., *The Presentation and Settlement of Contractors' Claims* (2nd ed., Spon Press, London, 2001). Such claims are discussed from a forensic accounting perspective in Regan, D.P. and Johns, C.A., "Litigation consulting: Construction claims" in *Litigation Services Handbook. The Role of the Accountant as Expert* (2nd ed., Weil, R.L., Wagner, M.J. and Frank, P.B. (eds), John Wiley & Sons, Inc., New York, 1995), Chap. 16, and in Lemar, C.J. and Mainz, A.J. (eds), *Litigation Support* (4th ed., Butterworths, London, 1999), Chap. 5.

9–75 A contractor for the construction of a large project commits to complete the construction to specifications, within an agreed time period and for an agreed price/pricing method. Building contracts have three basic elements:

1. Offer – the contractor offers by way of tender to perform the works.

2. Acceptance – the employer accepts the offer.

3. Consideration – the contractor's offer is for a certain sum of money, *i.e.* the consideration.

Such a contract is notable for bringing together a large number of parties to the contract, including the owner (employer), architects, engineers, contractors and subcontractors. Changes during construction can alter the ability to meet contractual obligations and the ability to earn profit on the contract. The combination of interdependency among the parties to the project, and the cost of the impact of a disruption, make construction litigation and arbitration common. Construction litigation may include claims for extra work, delays, escalation, acceleration, disruption, contractor termination, unabsorbed overhead and cost of capital.

Construction cases often involve allegations of failure to complete construction on time, or according to the specifications of the contract. Other construction cases concern who pays certain costs and whether cost overruns can be passed on to the builder. Generally speaking, the employer is only liable for such delay or disruption to the building project if the problems were within his power to control or are otherwise stated to be his risk. Contractors take all the remaining risks unless the terms of the contract state otherwise.

Delay claims

9–76 Extension-of-time provisions may empower the architect or engineer to extend the date for completion of the works, upon the occurrence of certain events specified in the contract. The contractor may have the right to obtain reimbursement for loss and/or expense incurred in execution of the works from the employer, to the extent that the loss has occurred based on events set out in the contract.

A contractor is normally entitled to compensation if he suffers loss as a result of delay caused by another party to the contract. The contractor may obtain a time extension and reimbursement for damages. Excusable delay arises when unforeseeable events beyond control, fault or negligence, such as unusually bad weather, occur. When excusable delays occur, the contractor may only receive a time extension.

Where a contractor did not receive an appropriate time extension for an excusable delay, the contractor may have incurred extra costs through acceleration attempts to meet timetables. This in turn may lead to a claim for damages. Critical path analysis may be used in such claims. It helps to calculate the minimum length of time in which a complex project can be completed, and which activities should be prioritised in order to complete by that date.

Entitlement to damages in the event of delay can take one of two forms. General damages are left to be determined by the courts. Liquidated damages can be resolved in advance (*i.e.* specified in the contract) by estimating the damage the employer would suffer due to delay (referred to as "liquidated or ascertained damages" in the standard form contracts). Such liquidated or ascertained damages will not normally be overturned by the courts provided they are a genuine pre-estimate of damage, not amounting to a penalty. The amount should comprise the loss suffered by the employer in the event of delay, and may include interest payable during the delay period, loss of profit, loss of rent, rent costs of alternative premises, extra costs and inflation.

9–77 Some contracts contain no damage-for-delay clauses and these have generally been upheld by the courts. In fact, as a matter of general principle, where a contract does not provide an express right to repudiate if a time-limit is not met, the law treats time as not being of the essence of the contract and, consequently, a delay of itself will not confer such a right. Instead, the court will look to the presumed intention of the parties in making the contract, and only when it is reasonable to presume that they intended time to be of the essence will this be held to be the case. Keane J. (as he then was) referred to this principle in relation to a contract for the sale of land in a Supreme Court judgment in *Kramer v. Arnold*:

> "It is well known that the courts of equity adopted a more liberal attitude to stipulations as to time in contracts than was the case in the common law courts. Thus, in contracts for the sale of land, equity would not treat the contract as voidable by reason only of the failure of either party to complete on the date fixed for completion. In general, time was not of the essence of the contract in respect of completion unless the parties had expressly so stipulated and, following the enactment of the Judicature (Ireland) Act, 1877, the common law courts applied the same rule."[39]

9–78 Because time is not of the essence unless so specified explicitly in the contract, a common feature of building contracts is the express provision for the payment of damages to the employer if the contractor fails to complete the works within the stipulated time. Many building contracts provide for liquidated damages (*i.e.* pre-determined amounts) in the event of late completion of the contract, payable by the building contractor to the owner of the property or employer of the contractor. The contract will provide for a set sum to be payable for each day or week beyond the agreed completion date (or any approved

---

[39] [1997] 3 I.R. 43 at 60.

extension of time for completion), based on a genuine pre-estimate of the loss likely to be suffered by the contractor's failure to perform. Agreed damages clauses are valid and enforceable provided the amount is a reasonable estimate (or lower) of the loss that is likely to be caused by late completion. In many cases, the liquidated damages are nominal compared with the actual loss incurred by the owner/employer as a result of the delay. Such a clause has the effect of limiting the contractor's liability and defines the risk to which the contractor is exposed when the contract is undertaken. Liquidated damages clauses also obviate the need to calculate and prove the actual loss, which could be difficult in practice.

Where contracts include penalty clauses rather than liquidated damages clauses, the owner or employer may sue the contractor for the actual loss incurred which is recoverable by way of unliquidated damages.

Changes in specifications/variations

9–79 Some contracts will be for a fixed price, but with allowances for fluctuations or escalations in the cost of construction. Contracts which do not provide for fluctuations or escalations are usually short-term contracts where the works can be completed speedily, and the contractor is willing to take the risk that he can perform within the stipulated time at the set contract price and make a profit. In contrast, and more frequently, the contract will provide for the contract sum to be adjusted based on specified cost factors, such as the prices of materials and wages payable in the industry. If the cost of these specified factors fluctuates, then the contract sum may be adjusted accordingly. The engineer or architect is responsible for certifying what adjustments (if any) should be made to the contract sum by reason of any of these events.

Claims for extra work arise from changes in the specifications and in the scope of the contract requested by the employer. These must show the scope of the extra work, that the extra work is not within the scope of the contract, and the detailed calculations of the extra materials, labour, equipment, other costs, and profit arising.

Contractors' direct loss/expense

9–80 Contractors may be entitled to payment where the contract has been prolonged or disrupted. Direct costs are expenses incurred in performing the contract which the contractor properly and directly incurs as a result of disruption or prolongation. Direct losses and expenses are to be distinguished from indirect or consequential losses or damages. The damages will be the loss reasonably foreseeable by the parties at the time the contract was entered into.

Legal context for calculation of losses

9–81 A United States court summarised the precision required by plaintiffs when computing and presenting claims[40]:

> "Courts have modified the 'certainty' rule into a more flexible one of 'reasonable certainty'. In such instances, recovery may often be based on opinion evidence, in the legal sense of that term, from which liberal inferences may be drawn. Generally, proof of actual or even estimated costs is all that is required with certainty.
>
> Some of the modifications which have been aimed at avoiding the harsh requirements of that 'certainty' rule include: (a) if the fact of damage is proven with certainty, the extent or the amount thereof may be left to reasonable inference; (b) where a defendant's wrong has caused the difficulty of proving damages, he cannot complain of the resulting uncertainty; (c) mere difficulty in ascertaining the amount of damage is not fatal; (d) mathematical precision in fixing the exact amount of damage is not required; (e) it is sufficient if best evidence of the damage which is available is produced; and (f) the plaintiff is entitled to recover the value of his contract as measured by the value of his profits."

9–82 The courts in the United States have also addressed the level of imprecision that may prove fatal to the plaintiff. They concluded that the damages presented must not be based on "mere speculation, guess or conjecture".[41] They have also recognised that "especially in sizeable construction claims when mathematical precision is impossible", damage computations must reasonably approximate the amounts that the plaintiff may recover from the defendant.[42]

Whilst the Irish courts have not dealt with this issue to the same extent, it is reasonable to assume that a similar approach would be taken. In particular, a lack of absolute precision in the calculation of damages would not be fatal to a claim, provided the damages has been established and a reasonable basis for a calculation of a range of values for the damages has been advanced.

Role of forensic accountants

9–83 Forensic accountants can be very useful both in defining the parameters of such a range of values for damages and in calculating its upper and lower ends. Forensic accountants can assist quantity surveyors in assessing direct costs, overheads and profits. This service is invaluable in agreeing the settlement of contractors' claims whether or not they proceed to court or arbitration. Forensic accountants may need to work with engineers and other financial analysts with experience in construction-related issues, industry practices, risk evaluation, dispute prevention and resolution techniques to help owners, developers, contractors, engineers, and lawyers devise cost-effective solutions to construction disputes.

---

[40] *M & R Contractors & Builders v. Michael*, 215 Md. 340 at 348–349; 138 A. 2d 350 at 355 (1958).
[41] *Zirin Laboratories Int'l v. Mead-Johnson & Co*, 208 F. Supp. 633 (E.D. Mich.) (1962).
[42] *Joseph Pickard's Sons Co, v. United States*, 532 F. 2d 739 (Ct Cl.) (1976).

9–84   Table 9.6 describes cases in the construction industry in which forensic accountants acted as advisers.

Table 9.6: Examples of construction claim cases in which forensic accountants have advised

Acting for contractor
- Assisting contractor in preparing a claim against the property owner (employer) for damages associated with delays in the completion of the project
- Assisting contractor in assembling a claim for damages associated with the rehabilitation of a bridge structure
- Performing detailed investigative accounting analyses and preparing a claim in regard to the construction of a nuclear power plant, including assisting legal team with case strategy and with settlement negotiations.

Acting for property owner
- Auditing contractors' job cost records to audit the subcontractors' claims
- Calculating the economic loss on a construction delay case, demonstrating that average daily costs increased as a result of a delay caused by the contractor
- Reducing a substantial consequential loss of profit claim arising from delays in the installation of new plant by, *inter alia*, assessing the market share and the margin at which the plaintiff's product would have been sold
- Reviewing and evaluating claims of the general contractor and four prime contractors associated with the construction of a convention centre, including development of alternative claim methodology
- Investigating a relocation cost claim and providing counter arguments for a subcontractor in a construction defect case
- Providing guidance on the reasonableness of executive compensation of a contractor.

9–85   Case History 9.5 provides a more detailed example of the involvement of a forensic accountant in a construction claim.

Accounting calculations

9–86   In the case of a construction contract, if the buyer repudiates the contract before the contractor has begun the construction work, the damages award will equal the amount the builder would have received for complete performance, less the expenditure saved that would otherwise have been incurred in completing the contract. If the buyer's repudiation comes after the builder has commenced work, the amount expended on the contract, less any materials which the contractor can use on other contracts will have to be calculated and will form part of the damages calculation. Damages for lost profits will be the contract price less the expenditure that would have been incurred had the contract been completed. Total damages will be the profit that would have been earned had the contract been completed, plus any irrecoverable expenditure to date on the contract.

Case History 9.5: Construction claim – Digging under the road

Incident
A construction company was contracted to lay a sewer under a major road. Due to unexpected soil conditions, the contractor had to complete the work using manual labour instead of a mechanical digger.

Claim
The contractor claimed that this unanticipated development resulted in considerable costs for design revisions and additional manual labour and filed a £1.5 million claim.

Involvement of the forensic accountant
The services of a forensic accountant were obtained to respond to the claim. The contractor's claim had been prepared by its own accountants. The forensic accountant was provided with a summary that divided the contractor's costs into three categories:
1. Budgeted costs.
2. Costs that would have been incurred if no problems had been encountered.
3. Actual costs.

In addition to analysing the financial components of the claim in detail, the bid and estimation process was considered to assess the accuracy of the contractor's initial quote. The amount of its claim had been determined by taking the difference between the actual final cost of the contract and the estimated original cost. From the examination, which was conducted with the help of an expert from the construction industry, it appeared that the contractor had underbid in order to win the contract. This led to the hypothesis that the contractor might be attempting to recover low margins and/or losses through the claim.

The claim itself was examined in detail. It was concluded that the contractor knew all along that the work would have to be done manually. The discovery of problems was a fortuitous accident from which it decided to benefit. Further examination of the claim revealed costs had no relation to the stoppage caused by the soil conditions. For example, the claim included charges for cranes that were engaged at other work sites.

Outcome
As a result of the investigation, damages were £225,000 rather than £1.5 million.

Source: Adapted from Johnson, P., "Forensic accounting–a legal support" *Commercial Law Practitioner* (September 1996) pp. 206-210.

9–87 When a contractor is entitled to compensation under the terms of the contract in respect of delay, forensic accountants must estimate the related costs. Many contractor costs are time sensitive and form the basis for a claim for compensation. Costs due to delay generally arise from extended contract performance, escalation and acceleration. Escalation claims require proof that costs incurred in later periods had higher unit prices than the prices that would have existed had no delay occurred. Acceleration results when a contractor revises the contract schedule to complete the remaining activities in less time than planned. This is done by adding manpower and shifts, increasing overtime and revising work sequences. The contractor may receive compensation for any additional costs incurred. The contractor's acceleration claim must prove that the employer or employer-representative decided to accelerate.

9–88 Disruption of the contractor's workforce by the employer resulting in reduced productivity can also contribute to a claim for compensation by the contractor. Forensic accountants ascertain the affected activities and then calculate the affected and unaffected productivity rates for these activities. The incremental costs associated with the lower productivity experienced in the affected period becomes the core of the contractor's disruption claim. An alternative to the affected versus unaffected approach uses the contractor's experience from other projects or uses industry productivity standards.

9–89 A contractor's interest cost claim usually depends on the terms of the contract, and on whether there is any linkage between the costs incurred on the project and money borrowed by the contractor to finance these costs in whole or in part.

Intellectual property rights

Infringement of intellectual property rights

9–90 Breaches of intellectual property rights usually result in loss of business and/or loss of profit margin (through competition from the infringer) for the holders of those rights. Accordingly, damages claimed for such breaches are usually based on financial and accounting data, and the amounts involved can be significant. The accepted methods for calculating damages are based on measures of lost profits. The need for expertise in the selection and use of these measures often leads to the involvement of forensic accountants in such claims.

There are four main forms of intellectual property rights – patents, copyrights, trade marks and trade secrets.[43] Remedies for interference with rights relating to unregistered trade marks and trade secrets are determined under common law. Remedies available in connection with infringement of patents, copyrights and registered trade marks are determined by statute.

---

[43] Intellectual property law is considered comprehensively in Clark, R. and Smyth, S., *Intellectual Property Law in Ireland* (Butterworths, Dublin, 1997).

Patent infringement

9–91   Patents give inventors exclusive rights to use and sell their inventions for a limited time. Section 9 of the Patents Act 1992 states that an invention "shall be patentable under this Part if it is susceptible of industrial application, is new and involves an inventive step." The Act goes on specifically to exclude certain items from patentability, including:

(a) a discovery, a scientific theory or a mathematical method;

(b) an aesthetic creation;

(c) a scheme, rule or method for performing a mental act, playing a game or doing business, or a program for a computer;

(d) the presentation of information;

(e) a method (but not a product, and in particular a substance or composition, for use in any such method) for treatment of the human or animal body by surgery or therapy and a diagnostic method practised on the human or animal body;

(f) an invention the publication or exploitation of which would be contrary to public order or morality, provided that the exploitation shall not be deemed to be so contrary only because it is prohibited by law;

(g) a plant or animal variety or an essentially biological process for the production of plants or animals other than a microbiological process or the products thereof.[44]

9–92   Patents (other than short-term patents) have a life of 20 years from the date of publication of their grant in the Patents Office Journal. A short-term patent, which can be granted where the relevant invention is new and susceptible of industrial application provided it is not clearly lacking an inventive step, lasts for 10 years. In exchange for publicly disclosing an invention, a patent holder receives what amounts to a legal monopoly, *i.e.* the exclusive right to exploit the invention (through product sale or licencing). The exclusiveness of the patent means the "winner takes all".

After patent protection expires, the invention becomes public property and anyone may make, use or sell it.

9–93   The rights of a patent holder to pursue a civil remedy where a patent is infringed are set out in section 47 of the Patents Act 1992. This section allows a plaintiff to claim damages in respect of the alleged infringement of his patent, or to claim for an account of the profits derived by the defendant from the alleged

---

[44] Patent Act 1992, ss. 9 and 10.

infringement. However, the court is permitted to award only one of these reliefs to a successful plaintiff. The full text of section 47 is:

> "(1) Civil proceedings for infringement of a patent may be brought in the Court by the proprietor of the patent in respect of any act of infringement which he alleges he is entitled under sections 40 to 43 and section 45 to prevent and (without prejudice to any other jurisdiction of the Court) in those proceedings a claim may be made—
> (a) for an injunction restraining the defendant from any apprehended act of such infringement;
> (b) for an order requiring the defendant to deliver up or destroy any product covered by the patent in relation to which the patent is alleged to have been infringed or any article in which the product is inextricably comprised;
> (c) for damages in respect of the alleged infringement;
> (d) for an account of the profits derived by the defendant from the alleged infringement;
> (e) for a declaration that the patent is valid and has been infringed by the defendant.
> (2) The Court shall not, in respect of the same infringement, both award the proprietor of a patent damages and order that he shall be given an account of the profits."

9–94 Section 49 of the Act provides an important relief against proceedings for patent infringement in favour of a party who was unaware of the existence of the patent. The relevant subsection states:

> "In proceedings for the infringement of a patent damages shall not be awarded, and no order shall be made for an account of profits, against a defendant who proves that at the date of the infringement he was not aware, and had no reasonable grounds for supposing, that that patent existed, and a person shall not be deemed to have been so aware or to have had reasonable grounds for so supposing by reason only of the application to a product of the word 'patent' or 'patented' or any word or words expressing or implying that a patent has been obtained for the product, unless the number of the relevant patent accompanied the word or words in question."

Patent infringement may be direct or contributory. Direct infringement refers to the unauthorised use of the patented product. Contributory infringement results when one party facilitates infringement by others. The plaintiff may bring an action against both the direct infringer and the party facilitating the infringement. Defences to allegations of patent infringement include claims of non-infringement and that the patent is not valid.

Copyright infringement

9–95 Section 17 of the Copyright and Related Rights Act 2000 (the "2000 Act"), most of the provisions of which came into force on January 1, 2001, recognises that copyright is a property right:

"...whereby, subject to this Act, the owner of the copyright in any work may
undertake or authorise other persons in relation to that work to undertake certain
acts in the State, being acts which are designated by this Act as acts restricted by
copyright in a work of that description."

Under the 2000 Act and subject to its detailed terms, copyright will subsist in
"original literary, dramatic, musical or artistic works".[45] Copyright also attaches
to databases in certain circumstances. Copyright does not subsist in a literary,
dramatic or musical work or an original database "until that work is recorded in
writing or otherwise by or with the consent of the author".[46]

9–96   Copyright infringement can therefore take many forms. Section 37 of
the 2000 Act defines, subject to certain exceptions, the acts restricted by copyright
in terms of the copyright owner's exclusive right to undertake or authorise others
to undertake all or any of the specified acts in relation to the work in question.
The specified acts are:

"(a) to copy the work;
 (b) to make available to the public the work;
 (c) to make an adaptation of the work or to undertake either of the acts referred
     to in paragraph (a) or (b) in relation to an adaptation".

9–97   The exceptions to the exclusive right include the right to play a sound
recording in public (provided the appropriate payments are made to the relevant
licensing body). They also include exemptions for:

– fair dealing for the purposes of research or private study, or for criticism or
  review accompanied by sufficient acknowledgment;

– incidental inclusion in another work;

– copying in preparation for instruction, in the course of instruction or for
  examination;

– inclusion of a short passage in an anthology for educational purposes, with
  sufficient acknowledgment;

– certain other educational purposes, including lending;

– anything done for purposes of parliamentary or judicial proceedings or
  statutory inquiries or under statutory authority;

– back-up copies of computer programs;

– anonymous works where it is reasonable to assume that the copyright has
  expired;

---

[45] Copyright and Related Rights Act 2000, s. 17(2)(a).
[46] *ibid.*, s. 18(1).

– abstracts of scientific or technical articles;

– advertisements of artistic works.

Section 37 of the 2000 Act goes on to state that the copyright in a work is infringed by a person who, without the licence of the copyright owner, undertakes, or authorises another to undertake, any of the acts restricted by copyright.

As well as direct infringement through an unlawful breach of the exclusive right referred to above, copyright can be infringed by adaptation of a work and by secondary infringement through the making and use of an infringing copy.

9–98 An infringement of a copyright in a work is actionable by the copyright owner.

Section 127 of the 2000 Act expressly states that all relief by way of damages, injunction, account of profits or otherwise as is available in respect of the infringement of any other property right is available for infringement of copyright. Section 128 of the 2000 Act deals with the award of damages in an action for infringement of copyright. It states:

> "(1) The court may, in an action for infringement of copyright award such damages as, having regard to all the circumstances of the case, it considers just.
>
> (2) Without prejudice to any other remedy, where, in an action for infringement of the copyright in a work, it is shown that at the time of the infringement the defendant did not know and had no reason to believe that copyright subsisted in the work to which the action relates, the plaintiff is not entitled to damages against the defendant.
>
> (3) In exercising its powers under subsection (1) in addition to or as an alternative to compensating the plaintiff for financial loss, the court may award aggravated or exemplary damages or both aggravated and exemplary damages."

9–99 Section 140 of the 2000 Act creates offences for infringement of copyright and these offences carry penalties of up to £100,000 in fines and up to five years imprisonment for conviction on indictment.

Trade mark infringement

9–100 A trade mark is any word, name or symbol, or device or any combination thereof used by a business to distinguish its goods and services from those of others. Trade marks identify products so that consumers may choose those they know and like, while the manufacturer can benefit from building a strong consumer following. Trade mark law protects any designs, distinctive features of clothing and buildings, sounds and even fragrances and packaging, as well as business names.

9–101 While patent and copyright law aim to encourage innovation, trade mark law aims to avoid deceiving and confusing customers and to protect a firm's investment in reputation and goodwill. Section 6 of the Trade Marks Act 1996 defines the term "trade mark" in simple terms as follows:

"In this Act a 'trade mark' means any sign capable of being represented graphically which is capable of distinguishing goods or services of one undertaking from those of other undertakings."

This definition implies that trade marks must be distinctive. However, one may not trademark a product feature actually determined by the product's purpose. This is clear from section 8(1)(c) of the Act, which prohibits from registration "trade marks which consist exclusively of signs or indications which may serve, in trade, to designate the kind, quality, quantity, intended purpose, value, geographical origin, the time of production of goods or of rendering of services, or other characteristics of goods or services." Section 8 contains several other absolute grounds for refusal of registration.

9–102 Trade mark ownership derives from the registration process set out in the 1996 Act. The property in a trade mark is defined by section 7 of the Act as follows:

"A registered trade mark is a property right obtained by the registration of the trade mark under this Act and the proprietor of a registered trade mark shall have the rights and remedies provided by this Act."

Trade marks are registered initially for a period of 10 years and can be renewed indefinitely, subject to various provisions regarding revocation of the trade mark, for further periods of 10 years. Non-use of the trade mark for five years can give rise to revocation.

9–103 Section 13 of the Trade Marks Act 1996 bestows on the proprietor of a registered trade mark exclusive rights in the trade mark. Section 14 sets out the circumstances in which a trade mark will be deemed to be infringed. These include use of the trade mark by someone other than its proprietor and use of a similar or identical mark for identical or similar goods or services in a manner likely to cause confusion among the public.

Infringement of a trade mark is actionable in the same way as any other property right. Section 18 of the Act states:

"(1) Where a registered trade mark is infringed, the infringement shall be actionable by the proprietor of the trade mark.

(2) In an action for infringement of a registered trade mark all such relief by way of damages, injunctions, accounts or otherwise shall be available to the proprietor as is available in respect of the infringement of any other property right."

In trade mark infringement cases, the courts examine factors such as the similarity of marks, the similarity of products or services, the geographic area involved, the manner of concurrent use, the strength of the defendant's allegedly infringing mark, the likelihood of confusion in the market place and the defendant's intention.

9–104 Fraudulent use of a trade mark is also a criminal offence, carrying fines of up to £100,000 and imprisonment for up to five years for conviction on indictment. Falsely representing a trade mark as registered is also a criminal offence.

Passing off

9–105 It should be noted that the tort of "passing off" gives protection under the common law where someone attempts to deceive the public into believing that his products or services are those of another whose products or services have acquired a reputation or goodwill.[47] Thus, where what is in effect a trade mark has not been registered, it is open to the offended party to institute proceedings in passing off. A judgment that considers this cause of action is that of Kinlen J. in the High Court case of *An Post v. Irish Permanent plc*[48] in which the plaintiffs sought and obtained an injunction preventing the defendant from using the name "Savings Certificates" for a new product.

9–106 Successful passing off actions almost invariably result in the award of an injunction (see chapter 21) in favour of the plaintiff restraining the defendant from continuing the behaviour that led to the confusion between the products or services of the parties. It is well established that an injunction will not normally be granted by a court unless damages would be an inadequate remedy in the circumstances, and the courts have accepted that damages are extremely unlikely to be adequate to compensate a plaintiff in a passing off action. This is mainly because the extent of the damage caused, which normally comprises loss of customers and appropriation of the reputation and goodwill of the injured party, is virtually impossible to measure.[49] For this reason, damages are rarely awarded in passing off actions.

Accounting calculations

9–107 Broadly speaking, there are three forms of remedy for infringement of intellectual property rights: injunction, damages and account of profits. In addition to these remedies, the successful party will normally be awarded costs against the other party.

Like many other types of dispute, breaches of intellectual property rights are often initially dealt with by the plaintiff applying for an injunction to stop the breach. If an intellectual property case proceeds to hearing in England, the proceedings are usually divided into two phases:

---

[47] It should be noted that an intention to deceive is not a necessary ingredient of the tort of passing off, although the courts have recognised that proof of such an intention is a clear indication of passing off.

[48] [1995] 1 I.R. 140.

[49] *e.g.* see *Polycell Products Ltd v. O'Carroll* [1959] Ir. Jur. Rep. 34.

– establishment of liability; and

– calculation of quantum of damages.

Intellectual property disputes typically involve accountants where damages have to be quantified, and forensic accountants will therefore mainly participate in the second phase.[50]

9–108   If the purpose of litigation is to obtain damages for infringement, the plaintiff must prove its loss. Damages are normally intended to be compensatory, not punitive. There are three approaches to compensating plaintiffs. The most common remedy sought is damages for lost profits, but alternative methods of calculating damages include "an account of profits" and "reasonable royalty".

These remedies can be claimed at the option of the holder of the intellectual property rights and, in the two-phase English system, the election does not have to be made until the question of liability is determined. Forensic accountants can advise plaintiffs on whether to elect for an inquiry for damages or for an account of profits. In addition, courts have discretion in deciding the appropriate basis for the calculation of damages to be awarded.

Damages

9–109   The amount of damages is essentially a question of fact and damages cannot be completely speculative,[51] but need not be proven with absolute precision.[52] Proper quantification of infringement damages requires detailed quantitative analysis supported by sound finance, investment and valuation theory, including qualitative analysis.

Damages are awarded on the basis of compensation for the loss suffered as a result of infringement. Proof of lost profits must include two elements:

---

[50] Damages issues relating to intellectual property infringements in a U.S. context are considered in Evans, E.A., Samuelson, M.S. and Sherwin, R.A., "Economic analysis of intellectual property rights" in *Litigation Services Handbook. The Role of the Accountant as Expert* (2nd ed., Weil, R.L., Wagner, M.J. and Frank, P.B. (eds), John Wiley & Sons, Inc., New York, 1995), Chap. 17; Strong, G.G., "Damages issues of copyright, trademark, trade secret, and false advertising cases" in *Litigation Services Handbook. The Role of the Accountant as Expert* (2nd ed., Weil, R.L., Wagner, M.J. and Frank, P.B. (eds), John Wiley & Sons, Inc., New York, 1995), Chap. 33; Frank, P.B. and Wagner, M.J., "Patent infringement damages" in *Litigation Services Handbook. The Role of the Accountant as Expert* (2nd ed., Weil, R.L., Wagner, M.J. and Frank, P.B. (eds), John Wiley & Sons, Inc., New York, 1995), Chap. 34. Intellectual property disputes in a U.K. context are covered in Taub, M., Rapazzini, A., Bond, C., Solon, M., Brown, A., Murrie, A., Linnell, K. and Burn, S., *Tolley's Accountancy Litigation Support* (Butterworths, London, looseleaf), Part VI, para. 100; and in Lemar, C.J. and Mainz, A.J. (eds), *Litigation Support* (4th ed., Butterworths, London, 1999), Chap. 10.

[51] See, for instance, the judgment of Lord Wilberforce in *General Tyre & Rubber Co. v. Firestone Tyre & Rubber Co. Ltd* [1976] R.P.C. 197.

[52] See, for instance, *Gerber Garment Technology Inc v. Lectra Systems Ltd* [1995] R.P.C. 383.

1. Only damages that can be shown as having been caused by the infringement can be recovered, *e.g.* loss of profit on sales, loss of licence income and losses arising from product reputational damage.

2. Evidence supporting the computation of the loss of profits must be provided.

9–110 In most commercial cases, damages are the difference between the profits the property owner would have earned but for the actions of the defendant, and the profits/losses he actually earned. The principle underlying damages for patent infringement is that the patent holder or holder of some other intellectual property right is entitled to be placed, as far as money can do it, in the position which he would have been in if his patent had not been infringed. Damages for breach of intellectual property rights are intended to compensate the owner for the fair value of the loss resulting from the infringement.

Damages are usually assessed as a percentage of sales of the infringing goods, on the basis of the usual commercial practice of voluntarily licencing the intellectual property rights in exchange for royalty on sales. Damages calculations can take account of:

– decline in the overall market value of the work;

– reduced sales revenue arising from price depression – the patent holder may have reduced prices due to the increased competition arising from the infringement;

– lost profits from operations;

– effects on cost structure such as loss of economies of scale;

– increase in costs such as advertising due to the presence in the market of the infringer;

– lost royalties where the intellectual property is licenced to others.

9–111 The courts have examined the issue of how much damage should be compensated when awarding damages for patent infringement, *i.e.* whether to include indirect loss of profits on goods or services other than those resulting from direct infringement. Courts may also allow damages based not only on profit from the patented product but also on non-patented parts of the business. This is referred to as the "Entire Market Value Rule". Following this principle, several supplemental damages theories exist which are designed to compensate the plaintiff for the total harm done as a result of the infringement (subject to the claim not being speculative). In order to compensate for losses arising from infringement, supplemental damages may include price erosion, convoyed sales and accelerated market entry damages.[53] In addition to core damages in respect

---

[53] Walsh, J.E. and Hoffman, M.E., "Injunctive and damages remedies available in a patent infringement case" in *St Louis Bar Journal* (Fall 2000). Available at www.bamsl.org/barjour/fall20/walsh_.htm.

of loss of profits arising from lost sales, in the United Kingdom infringement case *Gerber Garment Technology Inc v. Lectra Systems Ltd*[54] the judge in the patent court awarded four additional heads of damages[55]:

1. Parasitic damages – damages in respect of lost profits on sales of products other than the infringed products (accessory products – sometimes called convoyed sales) which would have been made but for the infringement.

2. Springboard damages – beneficial effect of infringement on start-up or launch of new product by the infringer (called "springboard" or "accelerated market entry" effect) adversely impacting on the victim company's business, resulting in further depressed sales for the wronged company.

3. Reasonable royalty – royalties which would have been paid to the victim company but for the depressed sales arising from the infringement.

4. Price depression – price cuts in response to the increased competition from the infringer.

Damages and calculation of lost profits

9–112   Lost profits can be calculated in a number of different ways. The most basic computation is incremental lost profits. One method of calculating loss of incremental profits is shown in Table 9.7. Incremental lost profits comprise lost sales less direct costs of those lost sales, less any other variable costs relating to those lost sales. Alternatively, lost profits can be calculated as units sold by the infringer multiplied by the patentee's incremental profit margin. The norm in such calculations is to assume that the infringer's sales would have been the patentee's. In both calculations, the ability to distinguish between fixed costs (those that do not vary with production levels) and variable costs (those that vary with production) is essential – as only variable costs are deductible in calculating incremental lost profit. In practice, this distinction can be difficult and the subject of dispute between forensic accountants as costs may not be perfectly fixed or variable but instead may display both fixed and variable behavioural properties. See Chapter 17 and Table 17.1 in this regard.

---

[54] [1995] R.P.C. 383.
[55] Floyd, C., "Damages in intellectual property disputes" *The Forensic Accountant* (1996), Issue 14, pp. 6–7.

Table 9.7: Loss of incremental profits

	€	€
Lost sales		XXX
Direct cost of lost sales		
Raw materials	XXX	
Direct labour	XXX	
Manufacturing overhead	XXX	
Other manufacturing costs	<u>XXX</u>	(XXX)
Gross profit		XXX
Variable costs in relation to lost sales		(XXX)
Lost contribution (= lost profits)		XXX

In addition to being deprived of profits on sales made by the infringer, the profits of the patentee from its remaining business may also be adversely affected by the infringer's actions. When the infringer enters the market, the price may be affected by the increased competition generated by the new market entrant. This can lead to lower prices received by the patent owner. It can be difficult to measure the price effect in these situations. The increased competition and patent infringement will lead to lower volumes of output and sales for the injured company, which in turn may also have adverse affects on the cost structure of the business and, in particular, on the ability of the company to benefit from economies of scale. Again, measuring these damages may be difficult.

Alternative – "Account of profits" approach

9–113 The measurement of the infringer's profits may play an important role when it is difficult to measure the patentee's lost profits. As an alternative to damages based on lost profits which the plaintiff would have earned but for the infringement, the plaintiff can elect to require the infringer to account for the profits made on the infringing activities. As a result of this option, discovery has particular importance in infringement cases. Plaintiffs are normally awarded discovery of the infringer's documents related to the quantum of profits, sufficient to assist in making the election between lost profits and an account of profits. In *Celanese International Corporation v. BP Chemicals Ltd*[56] (see below para. **9–115**) these documents were held to include the management accounts of the relevant division of the defendant.

In an account of profits, the infringer cannot be required to pay more than the profits it actually made. The rationale behind the "account of profits" approach is to ensure that the infringer does not profit from his wrongful act. Accordingly, where an account of profits is likely to yield a higher amount than a damages calculation (in other words where the ill-gotten gains of the infringer exceed the losses to the property-holder flowing directly from the infringer's

[56][1999] R.P.C. 203.

wrong) then an account of profits should be claimed. Such a situation can arise where the infringer makes sales to customers who are not customers of the property owner and/or at higher prices.

9–114 Assessment of the profits made as a result of the infringement, as distinct from ordinary business profits, is often a difficult and complex matter. Forensic accountants can assist in the calculation of the profits for which the infringer may be required to account. The input of forensic accountants in calculating profits can involve the complete construction of a profit and loss account for the infringer's unlawful activities for the relevant period, or can be limited to certain elements of the profit and loss account where undisputed information is available. The tasks of the forensic accountant may include:

– estimation of volume of sales for the relevant period based on available records of the infringer (usually available by way of discovery) and, where appropriate, information available within the industry and elsewhere from third parties;

– calculation of sales revenues based on actual or assumed selling prices;

– estimation of direct costs associated with the sales (note: indirect, or fixed, costs would ordinarily be excluded from the calculation of profits on the basis that they would be incurred in any event by the infringer even if he had not infringed);

– estimation of other costs (*e.g.* interest, taxation) and revenues (*e.g.* income ancillary to the sale of the product such as service or repair revenues, or interest income) attributable to the sales;

– provision of any other relevant advice in relation to the profits earned by the infringer and the damage suffered by the plaintiff.

9–115 The records of the infringing entity, even if obtained by way of discovery, may well be incomplete. As a result, forensic accountants may need to reconstruct records based on available information such as cash receipts and payments, machine usage, etc.

Until recently, there has been little guidance from the courts on how an account of profits should be prepared, and on the detailed accounting principles to be applied in preparing such an account.[57] The judgment in *Celanese International Corporation v. BP Chemicals Ltd*[58] clarified issues surrounding the calculation of profits by a patent infringer, arising from the election by the plaintiff for an account of profits rather than a claim for damages:

---

[57] For further details of this case, see Mainz, A., Price, R. and Tarcyzycki, T., "Called to account" in *Forensic Accounting Ltd* (2001). Available at www.forensicaccounts. demon.co.uk/Resources/Articles/Hoechst_Article/hoechst_article.html.
[58] [1999] R.P.C. 203.

– Profits were to be based on a fair apportionment of the total actual profit made by the infringer, based on what proportion of the total profit was attributable to the infringing activities.

– The onus is on the defendant to show that apportionment is appropriate, but neither the plaintiff nor the defendant bears the onus of establishing the appropriate apportionment of costs.

– The fair allocation of profit should start with "base allocated profit" calculated as an even spread of profit across the different activities (infringing and otherwise) in the production process. A weighting (increase or decrease) may then be applied to "base allocated profit" to take into account the relative merit of the infringing process. This was called "differential" profit. Thus, the total account of profit comprised the base allocated profit and the differential profit.

– Infringing revenues were based on arm's length prices, rather than actual prices between connected group companies.

– Costs unrelated to the infringing process were ignored.

– Costs relating directly to production and sale of the infringing product were allowed fully.

– Costs common to the infringing and non-infringing activities were allocated between the products on an appropriate basis – usually by reference to ordinary accounting principles or the practices normally adopted by the defendant.

– Finance charges incurred in relation to plant were included in the account.

– The profit paid over by the infringer should be net of tax, including any tax refund subsequently recovered by the infringer arising from the payment of profits to the plaintiff.

Reasonable royalty approach[59]

9–116   When actual damages cannot be proved, or are not sought for reasons of difficulty of proof, trial strategy or otherwise, damages in the form of reasonable royalty may be sought.

Intellectual property may be licenced to others in exchange for a royalty. Usually, a reasonable royalty is defined as that which a willing licensor and a willing licensee would have negotiated at the beginning of the infringement period. There are two types of royalty: running royalties and lump sum royalties. Running royalties are variable and are expressed either as a percentage of

---

[59]There were 15 factors considered in attempting to estimate the reasonable royalty in the U.S. case *Georgia-Pacific Corp v. United States Plywood Corp* 243 F. Supp. 500 at 521; 146 U.S.P.Q. (BNA) 228 at 246 (S.D.N.Y.) (1965).

revenue, gross profits, net profits or as a per-unit cost. Lump sum royalties are a fixed sum in return for rights to use the intellectual property in a manner that is not related to usage volume.

9–117 A patent holder is entitled to lost profits but these should never be less than a reasonable royalty. The purpose of the royalty alternative is not to direct the form of compensation, but to set a floor below which an award of damages might otherwise run the risk of falling unjustly short of the wrong committed by the infringer.[60] The objective is to compute a reasonable royalty high enough to compensate the plaintiff for the loss suffered as a result of the infringer's actions. Thus, in calculating damages, the royalty rate and the sales to which the royalty rate is to be applied must be identified.

In practice, this often means that courts award a reasonable royalty as a consolation prize for intellectual property owners who cannot prove their lost profits. For products that are produced in competitive industries with constant returns to scale and no significant sunk costs, there should be little or no difference between the two standards (*i.e.* between the calculation of damages and the calculation of a reasonable royalty) when appropriately measured. In such conditions, owners will realise the full incremental benefit of their intellectual property regardless of whether they produce the product themselves or whether they licence the intellectual property for others to produce the product. Although the courts in the United States have stated that reasonable royalties should be a floor for damage measurements, they may compromise in cases where reasonable royalty damages exceed lost profits and where evidence shows that the owner would not have licenced the infringer at normal third party rates. In such cases, the courts may award an amount equal to lost profits (even if less than reasonable third party royalties), but no less than what a reasonable royalty payment from the infringer alone would have been. This exception prevents the infringer from profiting from the infringement.

9–118 Royalty fees can be used as a basis for damages, even where the patent is not actually used to generate revenue in that way. In such cases a hypothetical royalty may be used, based for example on royalty rates for similar products in the market.

There are a variety of methods for calculating reasonable royalties including[61]:

1. Established royalty.

---

[60] See, for instance, the judgment of Lord Shaw in *Watson, Laidlaw & Co Ltd v. Pott, Cassels and Williamson* [1914] 31 R.P.C. 104.

[61] Wise, R.M., "Quantification of infringement damages" (Paper presented at the Federated Press Protecting & Managing Intellectual Property Assets Conference, Toronto, Ontario, September 23/24, 1997). Available at www.wbbusval.com/articles1.htm.

2. Hypothetical or notional royalty.

3. Analytical approach – excess of anticipated profits on infringing sales over "normal" profit, which excess is taken to represent the royalty rate on infringing sales.

4. Rule of thumb – such rules of thumb are used on occasion in the United States, *e.g.*:
   - 25 per cent Rule: 25 per cent of pre-tax gross profit of the business owning the intellectual property;
   - 5 per cent of sales method.

Other factors to be considered in establishing a reasonable royalty include:

- projected profitability to the infringer of the patented product at the beginning of the infringement period;

- actual royalties received by the patent holder for licensing the patent in question;

- royalties paid by licensees for "comparable" patents;

- patent holder's established licensing policies;

- relationship between licensor and licensee (*e.g.* are they competitors?);

- duration of patent and term of license;

- value of the licensed item in generating sales of non-patent items.

9–119 Patent holders are also entitled to recover a reasonable royalty on the sales made by the infringer which the patent holder would not have made. This is on the principle that even in respect of those sales the patent holder is entitled to compensation for the use of his property by payment of a reasonable hire charge or royalty. A reasonable royalty in this context is one which would have been agreed between a willing licensor and a willing licensee.

9–120 In summary, the lost profits approach is generally preferred – it generally exceeds reasonable royalty damages. However, it is advisable to consider both calculations in preparation for the case. Reasonable royalty is generally used when lost profits cannot be established with sufficient accuracy and provides a floor for damages.

Role of forensic accountants

9–121 Forensic accountants can advise on amounts due in respect of royalties from patent and copyright infringements. Trade marks, copyright, and patents may need to be valued in connection with litigation suits. Forensic accountants can also assess damages due to infringement of any rights associated with intellectual property, and in the calculation of profits earned on foot of the infringement, where an account of profits is claimed. Forensic accountants assist in resolving intellectual property-related disputes and help trial lawyers assess both infringement liability and damage assessments. Examples of the kind of litigation in relation to intellectual property rights involving the services of forensic accountants are given in Table 9.8.

Table 9.8: Examples of intellectual property rights infringement cases in which forensic accountants have advised

- Testifying on behalf of the plaintiff in wrongful manufacture and marketing of products featuring the plaintiff's concept; dealing with sales of the products and the calculation of a royalty on those sales
- Calculating lost profits in connection with copyright violations, assisting the plaintiff by developing a financial model to calculate the profits it would have earned but for the violations and analysing the profit made by the defendant on the products in question
- Calculating lost profits associated with a license agreement for the use of certain proprietary formulas
- Preparing a claim against the contractor for lost profits for an architect whose construction plans were utilised without compensation to him, including a gross profit analysis of all homes constructed using the intellectual property (the plans) of the architect
- Calculating the quantum of losses in intellectual property "passing off" action, including assisting and representing the plaintiff at mediation
- Calculating damages in patent infringement cases by evaluating the demand for the patented product, the availability of substitute products and capacity to meet demand
- Calculating damages in a patent infringement case arising from a competitor's reverse engineering of the plaintiff's product, including understanding demand for the product, the existence of non-infringing substitutes, ability of the company to manufacture and market the product, and the profit the plaintiff would have realised but for the infringement
- Calculating the reasonable royalty associated with the use of certain patented technology, providing expert witness evidence regarding the reasonable royalty as well as rebuttal evidence regarding the reasonable royalty calculation prepared by an opposing expert

9–122 Courts may require qualified expert testimony as an aid to calculating damages or reasonable royalty in a variety of circumstances. Forensic accountants can assess damages due to infringement of rights associated with intellectual property, and in the calculation of profits earned on foot of the infringement, where an account of profits is claimed. Forensic accountants can advise on amounts due in respect of royalties from patent and copyright infringements. In addition, in some circumstances, trade marks, copyright and patents may themselves need to be valued in connection with litigation and forensic accountants with appropriate valuation expertise can provide valuable assistance in such cases.

Competition law

9–123 The issues involved in competition cases are often complex and advisers in such cases commonly include economists, statisticians, accountants, financial analysts, industry experts, transactional database managers, and valuation and market research consultants.

One of the factors influencing the profitability of businesses is the conduct of other participants in the market, including suppliers, customers and competitors. Where it can be shown that the conduct is wrongful, the injured firm may seek compensation in the form of lost profit damages. Such calculations usually involve forensic accountants.

This section considers competition law generally.[62] Criminal offences specifically arising under competition law are referred to in paras **8–103** *et seq.*

9–124 The primary reason why mergers, acquisitions and joint ventures are challenged by competition or anti-trust authorities is fear of collusion – that is, where the number of competing firms is reduced by such transactions, the remaining competitors could act in concert. An expert may, however, show that, even though the concentration levels within the relevant market would normally be considered high, collusion is unlikely.

Competitive practices, and unfair methods of competition, are not necessarily in themselves wrong, and losses arising from such practices cannot be recovered in the form of damages. However, Forde[63] identifies various forms of competition which may give rise to actions for damages or applications for injunctions. These include:

- activities specifically prohibited by law, *e.g.* under the Competition Act 1991, anti-competitive agreements, and prohibited abuse of dominant position;

- persuasion of a third party by a competitor to breach a contract or a competitor inducing employees to give up their jobs are actionable wrongs under tort law;

- unlawful interference with contracts by competitors, *e.g.* interfering with performance of a contract or disrupting the performance of a contract;

- injurious falsehood, *e.g.* making disparaging criticisms of a competitor's goods or business;

---

[62] Additional sources for information on competition law are Cook, C.J. and Kerse, C.S., *EC Merger Control* (3rd ed., Sweet & Maxwell, London, 1999); Cregan, B.J. *Competition Law in Ireland: Digest and Commentary* (Gill & Macmillan, Dublin, 1997); Massey, P. and O'Hare, P., *Competition Law and Policy in Ireland* (Oak Tree Press, Dublin, 1996); and Maher, I., *Competition Law Alignment and Reform* (Round Hall Sweet & Maxwell, Dublin, 1999).

[63] Forde, M., *Commercial Law* (2nd ed., Butterworths, Dublin, 1997), pp. 431–440.

- passing off, *i.e.* presenting goods as if they were those of a competitor;
- obtaining access to confidential information about a competitor;
- conspiracy (with say a group of traders) to cause damage to a competitor.

The above list shows that there are quite a variety of actions that originate from anti-competitive practices of one sort or another. This section deals with only one of these – those actions contrary to the statutory provisions under competition laws.

Regulation and enforcement of competition law

9–125 Competition laws derive from two sources: the European Community competition rules and Irish laws. European Community competition rules are enforced by DG IV, the Commission Directorate, which can investigate infringement of competition rules, and prosecute such infringements. The European courts also have a role in enforcement of European Community competition rules. DG IV only has power to impose fines for infringement of the rules, whereas private litigation in national courts enables claims for damages to be made – an option not available at European Community level.

Irish competition rules are enforced by the Competition Authority, the courts and, in some cases, by the Minister for Enterprise, Trade and Employment.

Role of the Minister

9–126 The Mergers, Take-overs and Monopolies (Control) Act 1978 (as amended by the Mergers, Take-overs and Monopolies (Control) Act 1978 (section 2) Order 1993 enables the Minister to prohibit, or to permit subject to conditions, certain take-overs and mergers which would impede competition. The Act generally only applies to mergers where the turnover and gross assets of the two enterprises respectively exceed £20 million and £10 million. If the Minister considers that the public interest warrants it, he may declare that the Act is to apply to a particular business combination notwithstanding that it does not meet the statutory limits. As similar roles are conferred on the Competition Authority by the Competition Act 1991, there is some confusion between these two pieces of legislation.[64]

Importance of EU case law

9–127 The Irish courts have considered alleged breaches of the Competition Acts, and by extension of Articles 81 and 82[65] of the EC Treaty, on several occasions since the passing of the Acts. A recent and very instructive case is *Chanelle Veterinary Ltd v. Pfizer (Ireland) Ltd*[66] where the High Court judgment

---

[64] Ellis, H., *Irish Company Law for Business* (Jordans, Bristol, 1998), pp. 406–407.
[65] Formerly Articles 85 and 86 of the Treaty of Rome.
[66] [1999] 1 I.R. 365 at 391.

of O'Sullivan J. contains a very useful discussion of several important European cases on various aspects of competition law. The force of European case law dealing with Article 85 as precedent for the Irish courts is accepted by O'Sullivan J. when he quotes the judgment of Costello P. in *Donovan v. Electricity Supply Board*[67] as follows:

> "Section 4 is in identical terms to Article 85 of the Treaty, around which has grown up in the past thirty years a very considerable volume of case law from decisions of the Commission and the Court of Justice. These decisions are not binding on our courts but in view of (a) the provisions of the Act's preamble which declares that its object is to prohibit by analogy with Article 85 the prevention, restriction and distortion of competition, and (b) the fact that Article 85 of the Treaty is part of Irish domestic law and the Irish courts are required to follow decisions of the Court of Justice in relation to it on inter-state trade, it seems to me that the decisions of both the Commission and the Court of Justice on the construction of Article 85 should have very strong persuasive force."

The judgment of O'Sullivan J. is lengthy and repays careful study for anyone involved in a similar dispute. In the specific case, the plaintiff failed in its action and the decision of O'Sullivan J. was upheld on appeal to the Supreme Court.

Role of the Competition Authority

9–128   The Competition Authority was established under the Competition Act 1991. Its functions are defined in the Competition Acts 1991 and 1996. The Competition (Amendment) Act 1996 gives the Competition Authority power to investigate breaches of competition law and, where necessary, to bring civil and criminal court actions in order to stop anti-competitive arrangements or abuses of dominant positions.

The main objective of the Authority is to promote greater competition in the Irish economy by tackling anti-competitive practices, and so contributing to an improvement in economic welfare. It aims to do this primarily by effectively enforcing the Competition Acts. Agreements which have as their objective or which effect prevention, restriction or distortion of competition are null and void under section 4 of the 1991 Act. In this context, the Competition Authority issues certificates and grants licences for agreements notified to it under section 7 of the 1991 Act.

Role of the Director of Corporate Enforcement

9–129   Section 31 of the Company Law Enforcement Act 2001 amends section 21 of the Companies Act 1990 (as already amended by the Companies (Amendment) (No.2) Act 1999) to allow the Director of Corporate Enforcement to disclose otherwise confidential information for the purpose of the performance by the Competition Authority of any of its functions. Section 18 of the 2001 Act

---

[67] [1994] 2 I.R. 305 at 322.

permits the Competition Authority to disclose to the Director any information that may relate to the commission of an offence under the Companies Acts. No date has yet been fixed for the coming into operation of sections 18 or 31 of the 2001 Act.

Legal context

9–130 The objective of the Competition Act 1991 is to prohibit the prevention, restriction or distortion of competition and the abuse of dominant position in trade in the State in the interests of the common good.

Under the 1991 Act, the primary means of enforcement was private actions in the courts by aggrieved parties, either seeking injunctions to restrain the illegal acts or for damages. The 1996 Act created criminal offences, prosecutable either summarily or on indictment by the Director of Public Prosecutions.

The offences referred to are those arising under sections 4 and 5 of the Competition Act 1991, which are dealt with below.

Anti-competitive agreements, decisions and concerted practices

9–131 Article 81 of the EC Treaty of Rome prohibits certain anti-competitive agreements, decisions and concerted practices. This prohibition is reflected in section 4 of the Competition Act 1991, which makes such practices automatically void and unenforceable, as follows:

> "(1) Subject to the provisions of this section, all agreements between undertakings, decisions by associations of undertakings and concerted practices which have as their object or effect the prevention, restriction or distortion of competition in trade in any goods or services in the State or in any part of the State are prohibited and void, including in particular, without prejudice to the generality of this subsection, those which—
> (a) directly or indirectly fix purchase or selling prices or any other trading conditions;
> (b) limit or control production, markets, technical development or investment;
> (c) share markets or sources of supply;
> (d) apply dissimilar conditions to equivalent transactions with other trading parties thereby placing them at a competitive disadvantage;
> (e) make the conclusion of contracts subject to acceptance by the other parties of supplementary obligations which by their nature or according to commercial usage have no connection with the subject of such contracts."

9–132 The term "concerted practice" was defined in *Imperial Chemical Industries Ltd v. Commission*[68] as a form of co-operation between undertakings which, without having reached the stage where an agreement properly so-called has been concluded, knowingly substitutes practical co-operation between them for the risks of competition.

---

[68] [1972] E.C.R. 619.

9–133 In *Société Technique Minière v. Maschinenbau Ulm GmbH*,[69] the European Court of Justice listed a number of factors to be considered in order to determine whether an agreement is capable of preventing, restricting or distorting competition. These included:

1. Nature and quantity of the products concerned (*i.e.* market share of the product market).

2. Position and size of the parties concerned, relative to the market.

3. Whether the agreement is an isolated one or is part of a series of similar agreements.

4. Severity of the clauses in the agreement.

5. Possibility of other commercial currents acting on the same products (*i.e.* parallel imports or exports).

9–134 In *R.G.D.A.T.A. Ltd v. Tara Publishing Company Ltd*,[70] Murphy J. in the High Court held that the existence of a non-competition clause in an agreement for the sale of an undertaking did not necessarily mean that such an agreement was in breach of the provisions of Article 85 (now Article 81 of the EC Treaty). In order to determine whether such restrictive clauses offended the competition provisions of the Treaty, it was necessary to determine whether they were required for the legitimate protection of the undertaking which was being transferred and the development of competition within the particular market in question.

9–135 The Competition Authority took its first criminal prosecution under the legislation and criminal convictions were obtained in October 2000 when an oil company was convicted on two charges of price fixing. The oil company was accused of entering into an agreement with a garage which was designed to restrict or distort competition in trade in goods contrary to section 2 of the Competition (Amendment) Act 1996 and the Competition Act 1991. It was a condition of the agreement that the garage not reduce its prices below specified levels unless the oil company reduced its own scheduled prices. An economist working for the Competition Authority provided expert evidence in the case. The judge found that the agreement distorted competition.[71]

Damages

9–136 Section 6 of the Competition Act 1991 provides for remedies for persons aggrieved under the legislation as follows:

---

[69] [1966] E.C.R. 235.
[70] [1995] 1 I.R. 89.
[71] As reported in McLaughlin, B. and Reid, L., "Oil company fined after 'unique' price-fixing case", *Irish Independent*, October 5, 2000, p. 3.

"(1) Any person who is aggrieved in consequence of any agreement, decision, concerted practice or abuse which is prohibited under section 4 or 5 shall have a right of action for relief under this section.

. . .

(3) The following reliefs, or any of them, may be granted to the plaintiff in an action under this section:
(a)   relief by way of injunction or declaration,
(b)   subject to subsection (6), damages, including exemplary damages."

Thus, the legislation provides for damages and, in addition, exemplary damages. Subsection 6 provides that damages cannot be awarded where the Competition Authority has granted a certificate (in respect of an agreement notified to it). Maher[72] points out that damages are rarely awarded as cases in the Irish courts have rarely proceeded to full hearing. She states that damages have never been awarded in the Irish courts in respect of restrictive practices agreements contrary to European Community law.

In *Donovan v. Electricity Supply Board*,[73] the Supreme Court held that the function of an award of damages under section 6 is to compensate parties who have suffered as a result of the abuse. The intentions of the abusing party are irrelevant except in relation to exemplary damages.

Abuse of dominant position

9–137   The principle concern of mergers regulators is to prevent acquisitions or mergers that create or enhance market power to an excessive extent. Market power is demonstrated by the ability of firms to raise prices above the competitive level for a significant time period. To measure market power, it is first necessary to define the relevant market. European law deals with the relevant product and geographical market by reference to the principles set out in Article 82 of the EC Treaty of Rome. Article 82 states:

"Any abuse by one or more undertakings of a dominant position within the common market or in a substantial part of it shall be prohibited as incompatible with the common market in so far as it may affect trade between member states."

9–138   This principle is reflected in section 5 of the Competition Act 1991, as follows:

"(1) Any abuse by one or more undertakings of a dominant position in trade for any goods or services in the State or in a substantial part of the State is prohibited.
(2) Without prejudice to the generality of subsection (1), such abuse may, in particular, consist in—

---

[72]Maher, I., *Competition Law Alignment and Reform* (Round Hall Sweet & Maxwell, Dublin, 1999), p. 143.
[73][1997] 3 I.R. 573.

(a) directly or indirectly imposing unfair purchase or selling prices or other unfair trading conditions;
(b) limiting production, markets or technical development to the prejudice of consumers;
(c) applying dissimilar conditions to equivalent transactions with other trading parties, thereby placing them at a competitive disadvantage;
(d) making the conclusion of contracts subject to the acceptance by other parties of supplementary obligations which by their nature or according to commercial usage have no connection with the subject of such contracts."

Abuse of dominant position in a market for goods or services in any substantial part of the State is prohibited. The Act creates a tort-like right of action for any person aggrieved by such anti-competitive behaviour.

9–139 The relevant product market was defined in the European case of *Instituto Chemicoterapico Italiano SpA and Commercial Solvents Corporation v. Commission*[74] as being a market in which products are substantially interchangeable. The relevant geographical market was defined in *United Brands Co v. Commission*[75] as being the market in which "objective conditions of competition applying to the product in question must be the same for all traders."

9–140 The Department of Justice in the United States defines the relevant market as all firms that, should they act in concert, would be able to profitably impose a "small but significant and nontransitory" price increase. It has stated that a price increase of five per cent for one year in most contexts will constitute a "small but significant nontransitory" increase in price.[76] In the *United Brands* case, the court defined an excessive price as one which bears no reasonable relation to the economic value of the product. This, of course, raises the question as to how the economic value of a product is to be determined. In litigation, the consideration of this issue tends to involve expert economists.

9–141 In the European Union, concentrations are policed under Regulation 4064/89,[77] which applies to mergers, acquisitions and concentrative joint ventures between firms whose combined worldwide turnover exceeds a specified amount, where the combined turnover in the European Union of two or more of the firms exceeds a specified level and where those European Union activities are not overly concentrated in a single Member State. A concentration to which the Regulation applies will be permitted if it does not "create or strengthen a dominant position as a result of which effective competition would be impeded in the common market or a substantial part of it."[78]

---

[74] [1974] E.C.R. 223.
[75] Case 27/76 [1978] E.C.R. 207 at 274; [1978] 1 C.M.L.R. 429 at 485.
[76] U.S. Department of Justice, *Merger Guidelines*, 49 Fed. Reg. 28, 823 (1984).
[77] [1990] O.J. L257/13.
[78] Regulation 4064/89, Art. 2(2).

9–142	*Donovan v. Electricity Supply Board*[79] involved a challenge to the proposed introduction by the defendant of a scheme under which it would supply electricity to installations carried out by electrical contractors only on production of a completion certificate signed in a prescribed manner. Costello P. in the High Court held that the defendant was in a dominant position and had been unintentionally abusing that dominant position. The Supreme Court held on appeal, *inter alia*, that:

1.	Whilst Article 85 (now Article 81 of the EC Treaty (section 4(1) of the Act of 1991) and Article 86 (now Article 82 of the EC Treaty (section 5 of the Act of 1991) of the Treaty of Rome were complementary in their joint aim to eliminate the distortion of competition, they were independent as they addressed two different problems.

2.	An undertaking which was in a dominant position in one market and used this dominance so that it affected competition in a sub-market where it was not dominant could be guilty of an abuse contrary to section 5 of the Act of 1991 even where the undertaking gained no competitive advantage by its actions.

3.	The effect of the defendant's trading conditions was, by virtue of its dominant position in the market for the supply of electricity, that it imposed, directly or indirectly, unfair trading conditions in the sub-market for low voltage installations in which the plaintiffs operated.

4.	An award of damages was justified pursuant to section 6(3) of the Act of 1991, as the defendant had been guilty of abusing its dominant position regardless of the fact that such abuse was unintentional.

9–143	*H.B. Ice Cream Ltd v. Masterfoods Ltd*[80] involved a challenge to the plaintiff's prohibition on the storage by retailers of other manufacturers' products in freezer cabinets provided to the retailers by the plaintiff. The dispute in the case arose over the de-listing by the defendant of the plaintiff as an authorised distributor of the defendant's products. The plaintiff alleged that this de-listing was anti-competitive and in breach of Article 85 of the Treaty of Rome and of section 4 of the Competition Act 1991. The plaintiff sought damages, various declarations, an injunction restraining the defendant from de-listing the plaintiff and an order requiring the defendant to supply product to the plaintiff. Lynch J. in the High Court held that the defendant had raised a fair question to be tried as to whether the plaintiff enjoyed a dominant position in the market in ice-cream products in Ireland, but not as to whether the plaintiff's cabinet agreements might affect trade between the Member States or might prevent, restrict or distort

---

[79] [1997] 3 I.R. 573.
[80] [1990] 2 I.R. 463.

competition within the market or amount to an abuse of its dominant position contrary to Articles 85 and 86 of the Treaty of Rome.

Predatory pricing

9–144 Predatory pricing is pricing a firm's products below cost with the intent of driving one's competitors from the market and thereafter raising the firm's prices to supra-competitive levels. In the first decision of the European Court of Justice on predatory pricing, *AKZO Chemie v. Commission*,[81] the court distinguished between lowering prices to win new customers and doing so to eliminate a competitor. The court said it may be necessary to determine the motivation of the party in question, and in the specific case held that the entity's "avowed intention" had been to eliminate one of its competitors.

9–145 Although many courts agree with the stated definition, there is no general agreement on the cost measures to be used to calculate below-cost pricing. The most widely used cost standard is that a price above reasonably anticipated short-run marginal cost is non-predatory.[82] As analysts rarely have access to marginal cost data, reasonably anticipated average variable cost might be used as an alternative.[83] Courts have accepted other cost measures – the details of the particular case may determine the relevant cost analysis. Although an average variable cost analysis may be appropriate for a mature firm, it may not be for a start-up business. Having decided on the appropriate cost measure, the expert may need to consider joint costs. The time frame over which the firm's costs are analysed between fixed and variable is also important. The shorter the time period, the fewer the variable costs. Another issue is the level of output considered in categorising costs between fixed and variable.

9–146 In addition to cost estimation in predatory pricing analysis, market analysis is also significant. For a campaign of predatory pricing to be successful and for its anti-competitive effects to occur, the firm engaging in this behaviour must be able to recoup its losses. It needs to be demonstrated that it will obtain and retain market power as a result of the predatory pricing.

Role of experts

9–147 Competition law relies heavily on economic analysis which plays an important role in liability and damage issues. It is not enough to perform financial calculations – an understanding of the underlying economic theories and concepts

---

[81] [1991] E.C.R. I–3359; [1993] 5 C.M.L.R. 215.
[82] Areeda, P. and Turner, D.F., "Predatory pricing and related practices under section 2 of the Sherinan Act" in *Harvard Business Law Review* (1975) Vol. 88, p. 697.
[83] Areeda, P. and Turner, D.F., *Antitrust Law* (Little, Brown & Company, New York, 1978), p.148.

and how they fit into the framework of competition law is vital. The need for economic input to many disputes involving alleged anti-competitive behaviour is apparent from the fact that a rare legislative reference to expert evidence appears in section 4 of the Competition (Amendment) Act 1996:

> "(1) In proceedings for an offence under section 2 of this Act, the opinion of any witness who appears to the court to possess the appropriate qualifications or experience as respects the matter to which his or her evidence relates shall, subject to subsection (2) of this section, be admissible in evidence as regards any matter calling for expertise or special knowledge that is relevant to the proceedings and, in particular and without prejudice to the generality of the foregoing, the following matters, namely—
>
> (a) the effects that types of agreements, decisions or concerted practices may have, or that specific agreements, decisions or concerted practices have had, on competition in trade,
>
> (b) an explanation to the court of any relevant economic principles or the application of such principles in practice, where such an explanation would be of assistance to the judge or, as the case may be, jury.
>
> (2) Notwithstanding anything contained in subsection (1) of this section, a court may, where in its opinion the interests of justice require it to so direct in the proceedings concerned, direct that evidence of a general or specific kind referred to in the said subsection shall not be admissible in proceedings for an offence under section 2 of this Act or shall be admissible in such proceedings for specified purposes only."

9–148 Table 9.9 provides examples of cases in the area of competition involving expert advice from either accountants or economists.

Table 9.9: Examples of competition cases in which experts have advised

- Examining calculations involving alleged actions by the defendant claimed to have been designed to depress a majority-owned subsidiary's earnings, thus enabling the defendant to complete the acquisition of the subsidiary at artificially depressed prices based on an earnings formula, contrary to competition laws

- Calculating plaintiff's damages in a case where independent service organisations contended that the defendant's refusal to sell them parts allowed the defendant to monopolise the servicing of its equipment and restrained competition in refurbishing and selling used equipment

- Identifying key accounting data necessary to quantify the economic loss sustained by a private hospital as a result of the unfair business practices of a public sector health care body and preparing a preliminary economic loss calculation

- Quantifying the economic loss sustained by an airport refueling operation as a result of the unfair business practices of a national supplier and distributor of aircraft fuel, including analysing an economic loss report prepared by the opposing expert

9–149 It is worth noting that several pages of O'Sullivan J.'s *Chanelle Veterinary Ltd v. Pfizer (Ireland) Ltd*[84] judgment are given over to an analysis of the expert evidence given by a noted Irish economist, Mr Moore McDowell, and by an eminent London economist, Dr William Bishop. Significant reliance is placed on this evidence.

Accounting and economic calculations

9–150 Forensic accountants are commonly asked to provide analyses of both liability and damages issues relating to competition, pricing and benchmarks.

Assessment of dominant position

9–151 In assessing whether, as a matter of fact, an entity (before or after a proposed merger, acquisition or joint venture) is dominant within the relevant market, several factors can usefully be considered by the expert. These include:

1. Market share – where this exceeds 50 per cent there is a strong argument favouring dominance; however, depending on the structure of the market, shares much lower than this can be dominant (*e.g.* in *United Brands Co v. Commission*[85] a share of 40–45 per cent was regarded as dominant where the nearest competitors in the market had shares of 16 per cent and 10 per cent).

2. Resources – the more physical and technological resources an entity has and the stronger its balance sheet, the greater its ability to take short-term and long-term steps to dominate a market.

3. Vertical integration – the power to act independently of the market is greatly enhanced by control over supply of raw materials and over the distribution and marketing of products.

4. Barriers to entry – the more difficult it is for a new competitor to enter the market, for whatever reason, the easier it is for the entity already there to dominate.

5. Past behaviour – in *Eurofix Ltd and Bauco v. Hilti AG*,[86] the Commission's decision said that Hilti's discriminatory treatment of its customers was "witness to its ability to act independently of, and without due regard to, either competitors or customers in the relevant markets in question."

9–152 Economic and financial analysis of a proposed merger must first identify the relevant product and geographic markets. The analysis should include not

---

[84] [1999] 1 I.R. 365.
[85] Case 27/76 [1978] E.C.R. 207; [1978] 1 C.M.L.R. 429.
[86] [1989] 4 C.M.L.R. 677 at 704–705.

only firms directly competing with the parties involved in the proposed merger but also firms producing substitute products and firms that would enter the market or expand their current output should the merged firm impose a supra-competitive price.

9–153   Having defined the relevant product and geographic markets, the expert should then measure the concentration within the markets. The correct measure of concentration depends on the economic facts of each case but two common measures are the concentration ratio and the Herfindahl-Hirschman Index.

9–154   The expert might also consider whether reasons exist for the merger other than the purchase of a competitor's exit. The expert should also investigate whether the merger will increase output. In cases alleging violation of competition laws, assessment of damages must be causally linked to the anti-competitive acts cited in the complaint. Thus, an expert on damage issues should show that the damages relate to those acts that injure competition, not merely to acts that injure a competitor.

Damages

9–155   In tort actions, damages are calculated to put the injured party back in the position it would have been had the injury not been inflicted. Massey and O'Hare[87] question whether this would deter the anti-competitive behaviour which is likely to be highly profitable. They point to the award of triple damages in the United States as more likely to deter offending businesses.

Computers, piracy and e-commerce

9–156   Forensic accountants will not often be involved in litigation arising from increased use of technology in commerce. Exceptions to this include the use of e-commerce for fraudulent financial gain and for the infringement of property rights in electronic goods. In addition, there have been some notable cases involving alleged anti-competitive behaviour in the information technology industry. Such cases may involve expert accountants.

   This section briefly considers civil laws relating to information technology. Criminal offences are covered in Chapter 8 (paras **8–44** *et seq.*).[88]

---

[87] Massey, P. and O'Hare, P., *Competition Law and Policy in Ireland* (Oak Tree Press, Dublin, 1996), p. 222.

[88] Consideration of Irish law applying to information technology generally is to be found in Kelleher, D. and Murray, K., *Information Technology Law in Ireland* (Butterworths, Dublin, 1997). Forensic accounting aspects of computer disputes are considered in Lemar, C.J. and Mainz, A.J. (eds), *Litigation Support* (4th ed., Butterworths, London, 1999), Chap. 12.

Legal context

9–157   The main problems relating to computers which may give rise to civil litigation are:

- infringement of copyright;

- counterfeit and piracy;

- competition law.

These are considered below.

Computer copyright infringement

9–158   Computer copyright problems most often concern pirating or direct copying of software. The major concern of computer program copyright owners is the reproduction, publication or adaptation of their work. Regulation 8(1) of the European Communities (Legal Protection of Computer Programs) Regulations 1993[89] details several rights which are particular to computer programs. Three infringements are identified:

> "(a) any act of putting into circulation a copy of a computer program knowing, or having reason to believe, that it is an infringing copy, or
> (b) the possession for commercial purposes, of a copy of a computer program knowing, or having reason to believe, that it is an infringing copy, or
> (c) any act of putting into circulation, or the possession for commercial purposes of, any means the sole intended purpose of which is to facilitate the unauthorised removal or circumvention of any technical device which may have been applied to protect a computer program."

9–159   Before the owner of copyright in a computer program or a database can pursue a claim for breach of that copyright, he must first be in a position to prove he is its owner. Prior to the enactment of the Copyright and Related Rights Act 2000, there were no provisions for the registration of copyright in a computer program or database. However, section 2 of the Act specifically includes "a computer program" in the definition of a "literary work" for the purposes of copyright, and defines a computer program as "a program which is original in that it is the author's own intellectual creation and includes any design materials used for the preparation of the program." Thus, the author of any computer program satisfying this definition can avail of the protections provided by the Act. The Act also provides for copyright protection in respect of an original database, which is defined at section 17(2)(d) as "a database in any form which by reason of the selection or arrangement of its contents constitutes the original intellectual creation of its author."

---

[89] S.I. No. 26 of 1993.

9–160 In deciding whether copying of a work has occurred, the court must first decide whether there is substantial similarity between the original works and the copy. In such cases, the courts must then decide whether there is also a causal connection – the copyright work must be the source from which the infringing work is derived. Evidence of substantial similarity provides prima facie evidence of causal connection.

9–161 The Irish courts have considered computer copyright infringement in *News Datacom Ltd v. Lyons (t/a Satellite Decoding Systems).*[90] In that case, the plaintiff complained that the defendant was producing decoding cards to unscramble television signals previously scrambled by the plaintiff and that to do so the defendant must have been copying the plaintiff's coding algorithms. Flood J. refused to grant an injunction restraining infringement of copyright, finding that there was no positive evidence giving rise to an implication of copying and that behaviour involving questionable ethics or morality was not of itself sufficient to justify the granting of an injunction.

Counterfeit and piracy

9–162 The European Communities (Counterfeit and Pirated Goods) Regulations 1996[91] lays down measures to prohibit the free circulation, export, re-export or entry of counterfeit or pirated goods which may include computer programs. The copyright owner may apply to the Revenue Commissioners requesting them to suspend the release of any counterfeit or pirated goods or to detain them. The suspension will remain in force for three months or such further period as the Revenue Commissioners may decide.

Computers and competition law

9–163 The computer industry has always been prone to control by a small number of large corporations. The European Commission has taken proceedings against IBM for anti-competitive practices under Article 85 of the Treaty of Rome.[92] IBM was also the subject of complaint by Phoenix Computers Ltd.[93] Novell also complained to the Commission that Microsoft was in breach of Article 86 of the Treaty of Rome.[94] Providers of on-line services, such as America Online and Europe Online, and computerised reservation systems have also been the subject of complaint.[95]

---

[90] [1994] 1 I.L.R.M. 450.
[91] S.I. No. 48 of 1996.
[92] Fourteenth and Twenty Fourth Commission Reports on Competition Policy (1985 and 1994).
[93] Twenty Second Commission Report on Competition Policy (1992).
[94] Twenty Fourth Commission Report on Competition Policy (1994).
[95] Kelleher, D. and Murray, K., *Information Technology Law in Ireland* (Butterworths, Dublin, 1997), p. 153.

Role of forensic accountants

Computer copyright infringement

9–164 The remedies available for breach of copyright under the Copyright and Related Rights Act 2000 are discussed at paras **9–95** *et seq.* These remedies are available, subject to the detailed provisions of the Act, to the owner of a copyright in a computer program or database where that copyright is breached.

Accounting calculations

Computer copyright infringement

9–165 Damages for copyright infringement are intended to compensate the plaintiff for actual loss incurred as a result of the infringement. This might be calculated on the basis of royalties that would have been payable to the plaintiff had the defendant instead of infringing copyright obtained a licence for the acts in question.

Expropriation/compulsory acquisition

9–166 There may be circumstances in which forensic accountants might be asked to advise in cases involving compulsory purchase of assets.[96]

9–167 Expropriation or nationalisation of business and private assets is where states nationalise private property for a public purpose. Such rights are accepted for reasons of public utility and similar aims. Compulsory acquisition is concerned with the taking of immovable property, or of limited rights therein, by a community agency or public utility against the wishes of the owner of the property. In Ireland, expropriation of property must be accompanied by payment of compensation. Compensation is limited to the enrichment realised by the nationalising state, with no compensation for lost profit. Fair compensation will only consist of the just price of what was expropriated, *i.e.* the value to the undertaking at the moment of dispossession.

Compulsory purchase

9–168 In claims for compensation for compulsory purchase of business premises, the concept of extinguishment valuation can arise. Most businesses facing a compulsory purchase order will seek to relocate. Generally, if the cost of relocation exceeds the present value of the business, the court may limit the compensation to the lower value (known as extinguishment value). However, following a 1995 English decision,[97] the fact that the cost of relocation exceeds the present value of the business is not an absolute bar to assessing compensation

---

[96] This issue is comprehensively covered in McDermott, S. and Woulfe, R., *Compulsory Purchase and Compensation: Law and Practice in Ireland* (Butterworths (Ireland) Ltd., Dublin, 1992).
[97] *Buildings and Lands Director v. Shun Fung Ironworks Ltd* [1995] 4 All E.R. 907 (C.A.).

by reference to the cost of relocating. It depends how a reasonable businessman using his own money would behave in the circumstances.

9–169 Businesses are entitled to compensation in respect of assets compulsorily acquired. There are 16 rules in assessing compensation deriving from the Acquisition of Land (Assessment of Compensation) Act 1919, the Local Government (Planning and Development) Act 1963 and the Housing Act 1966.[98] Five of the rules deal with matters to be disregarded in determining market value. Four rules require that certain matters be taken into account when valuing land under compulsory acquisition, *i.e.* that the value of land is its open market value, subject to the four regard rules. The rules are summarised in Table 9.10.

Role of forensic accountants

9–170 Forensic accountants are most likely to advise in relation to damages relating to relocation. Forensic accountants can assist businesses and State authorities where the business is either:

– able to relocate and is able to claim compensation for losses arising from temporary disruption of business operations (loss of sales and profits), out-of-pocket expenses (moving expenses) and future costs that may be incurred at the new location; or

– unable to relocate and may be entitled to compensation in the form of termination allowance which is generally calculated with reference to the value of goodwill.

Business losses will result from disruption of business due to relocation and/or the new location not being as favourable a location as the property which was expropriated. In order to determine the amount of business lost, a projection of what the income would have been had the expropriation not taken place is required. Historical data and industry and government statistics are gathered to determine trends using simple or statistical models. The loss of income for the period can then be estimated.

The business loss calculation does not include moving expenses. Such expenses include the direct costs attributable to relocation which include costs of operations which could have been avoided had the expropriation not taken place. They are temporary costs required to effect the move. There may be costs incurred in moving stock to the new premises. These costs will include employee time and transport costs. Equipment may need to be rented.

There may also be costs associated with the wind-down of the old location and the start-up of the new location. There may also be additional costs associated with doing business in the new location.

---

[98] McDermott, S. and Woulfe, R., *Compulsory Purchase and Compensation: Law and Practice in Ireland* (Butterworths (Ireland) Ltd., Dublin, 1992), p. 211.

Commercial 365

Table 9.10: Rules in assessing compensation in respect of compulsory acquisitions

• No allowance for acquisition being compulsory • Open market valuation **Disregard rules** • Special suitability or adaptability to inflate price above market value • Increase in value by virtue of use for illegal purposes • Depreciation/appreciation by virtue of land being included in development or amenity plan • Value attributable to any unauthorised structure or unauthorised use • Proposals of local authority to develop the land. **Regard rules** • Any restrictive covenants entered into by the acquirer when the land is compulsorily purchased • Restriction on development of land for which any compensation has already been paid • Restriction on development of land imposed by legislation • Contribution required of any planning authority as a condition precedent to development of the land. **"Equivalent restatement" rules** • Compensation should be based on reasonable cost of equivalent reinstatement • Cost of an equivalent reinstatement building should not exceed the estimate cost of buildings, taking into account the depreciation on the building compulsorily acquired. **Disturbance rule** • The provisions of rule 2 (open market valuation) should not affect the assessment of compensation for disturbance or any other matter not directly based on the value of land. **Definition and purchase notice rules** • Definition of terms • Exclusion of allowance for disturbance or severance from compensation in certain circumstances. *Source*: Adapted from McDermott, S. and Woulfe, R., *Compulsory Purchase and Compensation: Law and Practice in Ireland* (Butterworths (Ireland) Ltd., Dublin, 1992), Chap. 10.

Accounting calculations

9–171 Disturbance may be defined as the loss or expense suffered by an owner as a result of the compulsory acquisition of his land, apart from the value of the land, arising from loss of the lands or from injury to any lands retained.

The courts interpret the value of land as including the personal loss suffered by the owner over and above the market value of the land compulsorily acquired. There are four principal tests for a valid disturbance claim[99]:

[99] McDermott, S. and Woulfe, R., *Compulsory Purchase and Compensation: Law and Practice in Ireland* (Butterworths (Ireland) Ltd., Dublin, 1992), p. 240.

– loss must have been sustained, or must reasonably be expected to be sustained in the future;

– loss must flow from compulsory acquisition;

– loss must not be too remote;

– loss must be the reasonable consequence of the dispossession of the owner.

Generally speaking, losses or expenses incurred prior to date of service of notice are not recoverable in a disturbance claim. Compensation should not exceed total loss. A claimant must take all reasonable steps to mitigate the loss consequent on compulsory acquisition. Claimants are also entitled to compensation for parts of land injured by the compulsory acquisition. Professional fees incurred in dealing with the notice received from the appropriate authority indicating its intention to acquire the property compulsorily and inviting submissions as to the nature of the interest in the property and the compensation sought (known as the notice to treat) are also recoverable. There is no specific valuation date for disturbance compensation. Where new assets replace old assets, regard must be had for any benefit or cost saving which will accrue to the owner.[100] Table 9.11 lists the losses that are compensatable for disturbance arising from compulsory acquisitions.

9–172   The question of the extent to which a party whose property is subject to compulsory purchase is entitled to compensation for all the losses flowing from the purchase came before the High Court, and on appeal before the Supreme Court, in *Dublin Corporation v. Underwood*.[101] The issue was referred as a case stated by the property arbitrator. In the High Court, Budd J. reviewed the relevant legislation (Acquisition of Land (Assessment of Compensation) Act 1919) and case law. He held that where lands were taken under compulsory powers, the owner or occupier was entitled not just to the market price, but also to compensation for loss which he suffered in consequence of the acquisition, *i.e.* compensation for disturbance. He also held that the costs of acquiring alternative premises were not allowable unless they had been incurred or might reasonably be expected to be incurred.

9–173   In the Supreme Court, Keane J. (as he then was) dismissed the plaintiff's appeal. He noted, having reviewed several English authorities, that there was no Irish authority directly in point and stated:

> "The matter, accordingly, must be decided by this Court, as it was in the High Court, as a matter of principle. In the High Court, Budd J., was of the view that the defendant was entitled to be compensated on the basis of equivalence and

[100] *Tamplins Brewery v. Brighton Corporation* (1971) 22 P. & C.R. 746; *Anderson v. Glasgow Corporation* [1974] 14 R.V.R. 398.
[101] [1997] 1 I.R. 69.

Table 9.11: Compensable losses for disturbance

- Cost of seeking and acquiring alternative premises, *e.g.* acquisition costs, survey costs, bridging loan interest
- Cost of adapting new premises, not increasing value of new premises and not exceeding compensation payable for closing the business
- Removal expenses, *e.g.* disconnecting and refitting equipment, value *in situ* of fittings left behind, losses on forced sale of stock
- Double overheads in period running two premises between vacating old premises and moving into new premises
- Increased overheads
- Claimant's time and trouble, including travelling and out-of-pocket expenses
- Loss of goodwill
- Inherent goodwill

Source: Adapted from McDermott, S. and Woulfe, R., *Compulsory Purchase and Compensation: Law and Practice in Ireland* (Butterworths (Ireland) Ltd, Dublin, 1992), Chap. 11.

that he should recover neither more nor less than his total loss. That was also the view taken by Carroll J. and it is fully in accord with the statement of the law by Scott, L.J. in *Horn v. Sunderland Corporation* [1941] 2 K.B. 26. I am satisfied that Budd J. was correct in applying that principle in the present case. It would be patently unjust, in my view, for the dispossessed owner to receive less than the total loss which he has sustained as a result of the compulsory acquisition: such a construction of the relevant legislation would be almost impossible to reconcile with the constitutional prohibition of unjust attacks on the property rights of the citizens.

In the present case, it is accepted that the claimant held these properties as an investment and would have continued to hold them as such if they had not been compulsorily acquired. He wishes to replace them with a corresponding investment. The payment to him of the market value of the properties will enable him, so far as money can do it, to replace the acquired properties, but he will sustain additional expenses in the form of stamp duty, legal and agent's fees. If he is not paid these latter sums, he will not have been compensated in full for the loss of his existing investment property. "[102]

Concluding comment

9–174   It appears clear that e-commerce is with us to stay – but to what extent, in what form, and for what specific business purposes, remains a mystery. The development of the law in this area is in its infancy in most parts of the world, but lawmakers (and lawbreakers) have begun to realise that the location of

---

[102] [1997] 1 I.R. 69 at 129.

business in an intangible, regulation-free location – cyberspace – presents a new and difficult set of problems. Multinational businesses are familiar to us – but not those that have no physical presence anywhere. The difficulties consequent on an inability to specify the residences of a business include problems in imposing taxes and duties on such businesses. Legislators would be well advised to consult lawyers and accountants, who together have vast experience of cross-border business and of drafting and analysing tax codes, to assist in overcoming these difficulties.

COMPANIES AND PARTNERSHIPS

COMPANIES AND PARTNERSHIPS

10–01   Commercial litigation, which primarily affects companies, has been covered in Chapter 9. This chapter considers litigation affecting companies also, but only in the context of the governance of such companies. In addition, disputes affecting partnerships are also dealt with in this chapter.

Aspects of disputes and litigation arising from the governance of companies include shareholder disputes, disputes concerning directors, examinerships and insolvency, reckless trading and misrepresentation.

10–02   Forensic accountants are likely to be involved in these issues in a number of circumstances:

- where the dispute or litigation relates to accounting issues (such as disputes over the calculation of business profits, valuation of shares, etc.);

- directors' duties and responsibilities, particularly where these involve accounting issues;

- whether company business plans justify making use of examinership with a view to rescuing rather than winding up the company;

- considering accounting issues consequent on winding up of companies;

- helping to decide whether companies continued to trade in circumstances where the directors knew, or ought to have known, that the company was unable to pay its debts as they fell due;

- disputes arising from false or misleading accounting or financial information included in company documents;

- advising in partnership disputes concerning accounting aspects of the business and the allocation of profits and assets between the partners;

- in the calculation of financial sums for the purpose of negotiating towards settlement of any of the above matters.

Shareholder disputes

10–03 Shareholder disputes might involve any one of the following[1]:

- disputes in relation to the memorandum and articles of association, where members have rights to have rules of the company enforced;

- disputes arising out of shareholder agreements;

- oppression of minority shareholders.

Legal context

Statutory contract – memorandum and articles of association

10–04 The memorandum of association sets out the basic provisions concerning a company's existence, objectives and powers. The articles of association are the internal rules which govern relations between the company and its members and between the members themselves (*inter se*). These two documents form the corporate constitution of the company.

By virtue of section 25 of the Companies Act 1963, these documents comprise a contract. This statutory contract binds the members and the company, and the members to the members. It is enforceable by the members against the company, by the company against the members and by the members *inter se*. Thus, a member can take legal proceedings against another member who fails to observe the provisions of the memorandum and articles of association. The statutory contract (*i.e.* the memorandum and articles of association) is only enforceable by members against members in their capacity as members.

Many cases in this context relate to clauses concerning pre-emption rights attaching to shares, whereby existing shareholders have rights to acquire shares from other members before these can be transferred to non-members.

Shareholder agreements

10–05 Shareholder agreements are common and are used to supplement the memorandum and articles of association. They have the advantage over the memorandum and articles of association (copies of which are placed on a file in the Companies Office and are available to the public) in that they are confidential to the parties. In addition, shareholder agreements can give certain rights and impose certain obligations that cannot legally be included in the memorandum and articles of association. They may change the rights and powers of groups of shareholders.

Shareholder agreements are contracts that bind the parties and are therefore enforceable under contract law.

---

[1] These issues are fully considered in Courtney, T.B., *The Law of Private Companies* (Butterworths, Dublin, 1994), especially Chaps 5 and 11.

Shareholders' rights

10–06   Shareholders have a number of rights (subject to whether the type of share held by them confers the right) as follows:

- right to dividends;

- right to attend and vote at meetings;

- right to vote in the election or removal of directors;

- right to receive copies of the annual accounts, directors' report and auditor's report before the annual general meeting;

- right to vote on changes to the memorandum and articles of association;

- right to requisition extraordinary general meeting (subject to there being a minimum number and/or value of shareholders making the request);

- right to participate in bonus and rights issues of shares;

- right to transfer shares, subject to restrictions for private companies.

10–07   Following the rule in *Foss v. Harbottle*,[2] the rights of individual shareholders to initiate proceedings is restricted to wrongs done to the shareholder personally, rather than to the company. There are three types of personal shareholder rights:

- rights arising from the memorandum and articles of association (and any shareholders' agreement) which are fundamental to the individual;

- rights arising from directors' fiduciary duties to individual shareholders personally;

- statutory rights, *e.g.* to receive copies of the accounts before the annual general meeting.

Oppression of minority shareholders[3]

10–08   The Companies Acts permit the majority of members to control most constitutional aspects of companies. As a result of this democratic approach to conducting the affairs of companies, individual shareholders, if out-voted on an issue, have limited grounds for redress. However, where corporate majority decisions wrongfully affect shareholders' individual rights, these individual or minority shareholders are given some protection by:

- judicial exception to the rule in *Foss v. Harbottle*[4];

---

[2] (1843) 2 Hare 461; (1843) 67 E.R. 189.
[3] See Hollington, R., *Minority Shareholders' Rights* (Sweet & Maxwell, London, 1990).
[4] (1843) 2 Hare 461; (1843) 67 E.R. 189.

- protection against the oppression of minorities under section 205 of the Companies Act 1963;

- right of minority shareholders to petition the court to wind up the company under section 213 of the Companies Act 1963.

10–09 Prior to the enactment of section 205 of the Companies Act 1963, the rights of minority shareholders were constrained by the rule in *Foss v. Harbottle*.[5] The rule embraces several principles, but in its most fundamental form it establishes that, in general, where a company suffers a wrong only the company itself, and not the shareholders individually, can seek that the wrong be righted and/or compensated for. The rationale for the rule is that the majority of shareholders should be able to determine the actions and strategies of the company. However, the inevitable outcome of the rule is that a majority can impose its will and thereby oppress a minority. For this reason, section 205 was introduced in order to provide a mechanism for the courts to intervene in favour of minorities in cases of oppression.

10–10 The basic principle articulated in *Foss v. Harbottle*[6] that individual shareholders cannot sue the company is subject to four exceptions at common law:

- if the act is illegal or *ultra vires* the company;

- if the act has not been properly sanctioned by a special resolution of the company;

- if there is a fraud on the minority committed by the majority shareholders;

- if the act infringes the individual rights of the shareholders.

10–11 In such cases the minority shareholders' remedy is either:

- personal, *i.e.* when it arises from an act infringing his individual membership rights;

- derivative, *i.e.* when it derives from an injury to a company rather than to individual shareholders; or

- representative, *i.e.* when it is brought on behalf of a number of shareholders.

10–12 Section 205 is widely used to protect the rights and interests of minority shareholders in private companies. It should be noted that relief is often sought under section 213 of the Companies Act 1963 at the same time as under section

---

[5] (1843) 2 Hare 461; (1843) 67 E.R. 189.
[6] *ibid*.

205. Section 213 permits the court to wind up a company in any of a number of circumstances, including where the court is of the opinion that it is just and equitable that the company shall be wound up, and where the court is satisfied that:

> " ... the company's affairs are being conducted, or the powers of the directors are being exercised, in a manner oppressive to any member or in disregard of his interests as a member and that, despite the existence of an alternative remedy, winding up would be justified in the general circumstances of the case so, however, that the court may dismiss a petition to wind up under this paragraph if it is of opinion that proceedings under section 205 would, in all the circumstances, be more appropriate."[7]

10–13   Section 205 provides the mechanism for individual shareholders to apply to the court for an order in circumstances where a member believes that the affairs of the company are being conducted, or that the powers of the directors are being exercised, in a manner oppressive to the member or any shareholders or in disregard of their interests as shareholders.

10–14   Examples of oppression include:

- where directors, being the majority shareholders, exercise their power in relation to restriction of transfer of shares to outsiders (as set out in the articles of association) such that the shares could only be sold to the directors at an undervaluation;

- where directors' remuneration absorbs such a high proportion of the profits of the company that none is available for distribution to the shareholders in the form of dividends.

10–15   Section 205(3) gives the court very wide powers as follows:

> "If, on any application ... the court is of opinion that the company's affairs are being conducted or the directors' powers are being exercised as aforesaid, the court may, with a view to bringing to an end the matters complained of, make such order as it thinks fit, whether directing or prohibiting any act or cancelling or varying any transaction or for regulating the conduct of the company's affairs in future, or for the purchase of the shares of any members of the company by other members of the company or by the company and in the case of a purchase by the company, for the reduction accordingly of the company's capital, or otherwise."

10–16   Where there is a complaint of oppression, the shareholder can avail of section 205 even if he suffered the alleged oppression in a capacity other than as

---

[7] Companies Act 1963, s. 213(g).

shareholder (*e.g.* as director or creditor) – see the judgment of Gannon J. in *Re Murph's Restaurants Ltd.*[8]

10–17 The most common remedy granted by the courts under section 205 is to require the oppressing majority, or the company itself, to acquire the shares of the petitioning shareholder at the value they would have in the absence of the oppressive conduct, *e.g.* see *Re Greenore Trading Co Ltd.*[9] However, as noted above, the court's discretion is wide and various other remedies have been granted, including restraining a company from implementing the oppressive decision that is the subject of the complaint, *e.g.* see *Re Williams Group Tullamore Ltd.*[10] In that case, a single act of oppression was deemed sufficient to attract relief under section 205.

10–18 In a recent case involving the dismissal of a director who was also a shareholder, *McGilligan v. O'Grady*,[11] Keane J. (as he then was) in the Supreme Court summarised the general objective of section 205 in the following terms:

> "It is important to bear in mind the object of s. 205 of the Companies Act, 1963. Until its enactment, a majority of the shareholders in the company could, perfectly lawfully, use their powers in a manner which was harsh and unfair to the minority and had no regard to their interests. Unless the aggrieved shareholders could point to some illegality, whether flowing from a breach of the company's constitution or the general statutory or common law applicable to companies, the law could afford them no relief.
>
> Section 205 was enacted primarily in order to remedy that defect in company law. Consequently, the fact that, in a case such as the present, the shareholders are perfectly entitled as a matter of law - s. 205 apart - to remove a director even when that is in breach of a contract between him and them is not a material factor in considering whether that action, either taken in isolation or as part of a general course of conduct intended to exclude a particular body of shareholders from participation in the company, is a ground for relief under that section. Neither is it a relevant consideration in determining whether, in an appropriate case, that conduct should lead to the winding up of a company on the just and equitable ground: that is the effect of the decisions in *In re Westbourne Galleries Ltd.* [1973] A.C. 360 and *In re Murph's Restaurants Ltd.* [1979] I.L.R.M. 141."[12]

10–19 In *Horgan v. Murray*, Murphy J. in the Supreme Court expanded on the role of the court in section 205 proceedings as follows:

> "It seems to me that there is an issue to be tried first as to whether there was oppression and, if there was, the appropriate remedy or solution for the court to

---

[8] [1979] I.L.R.M. 141.
[9] [1980] I.L.R.M. 94.
[10] [1985] I.R. 613.
[11] [1999] 1 I.R. 346.
[12] *ibid.* at 361–362.

provide. Whilst the petitioner has indicated in some detail the remedy which he believes is the one appropriate 'with a view to bringing to an end the matters complained of' it is by no means certain that the judge hearing the application would accept that this is so. The function of the court is to resolve an existing problem. It goes without saying that that function must be exercised without creating injustice to either party." [13]

10–20   In *Irish Press plc v. Ingersoll Irish Publications Ltd*[14] the Supreme Court held that damages cannot be awarded in section 205 proceedings.

10–21   Minority shareholders can complain about majority decisions on a variety of grounds, many of which can be categorised as either that:

– the majority did not act bona fide for the benefit of the company; or

– the decision gave the majority an advantage that was denied to the minority.

Role of forensic accountants

10–22   Forensic accountants can advise in shareholder disputes, whether or not a shareholders' agreement is in place. These disputes usually come down to the value of a stake in the business. Share valuations are often required and there are well-established valuation principles and methods in such cases (see Chapter 18).

10–23   An example of an oppression of minorities case in which a forensic accountant might be involved is shown in Case History 10.1.

Accounting calculations

10–24   When oppression of minority cases, or disputes concerning rights of shareholders concern financial or accounting issues, accountants may be required to advise and give expert evidence. As already explained, many of these cases will involve share valuations, which are considered in Chapter 18. But other accounting calculations may be relevant. For example, minority shareholders might claim the majority shareholder mismanaged the company by taking excess compensation. A forensic accountant could examine whether in fact this claim was appropriate and whether the compensation was reasonable. Alternatively, shareholders may be accused of disrupting the operations of the business, resulting in excess expenses and lost profits. Forensic accountants could testify regarding damages incurred as a result of the disruptive behaviour of such shareholders.

---

[13] [1997] 3 I.R. 23 at 41.
[14] [1995] 2 I.R. 175.

Case History 10.1: Oppression of minorities

A minority shareholder in a business believes that profits are being understated and that the majority owner is siphoning off revenue for his own use. As a result, artificially small dividends are being paid to shareholders. The minority shareholder believes that the majority owner is putting lucrative contracts through an unincorporated business – sole tradership – that he also owns.

Problem

The minority shareholder cannot prove his suspicions. Minority shareholders have very few rights. For example, they have no access to the books and records of the company.

Possible solution

The minority shareholder could persuade another director that all is not as it should be. Directors are entitled to examine the books and records of a company. In that way the minority shareholder might obtain evidence and/or redress.

Source: Derived from Burns, S., "Minority rights" *Accountancy* (February 1999), p. 46.

Directors

10–25 Directors have fiduciary duties which are owed to companies and not to their shareholders. Thus, actions against directors are normally taken by companies rather than by shareholders. Examiners, receivers and liquidators on behalf of companies often initiate such litigation. However, increasingly in private companies, directors are found to owe fiduciary duties to shareholders. In addition, the courts and legislation have extended directors' duties to creditors of insolvent companies and to employees (under section 52 of the Companies Act 1990).[15]

Forensic accountants may be asked to advise where breaches of fiduciary or other duties relate to accounting aspects of companies. Increasingly, breaches concerning the legal requirement to keep proper books of account are coming to court (see paras **8–67** and **10–34** *et seq.*). Such cases will frequently involve expert accountants.

Legal context

Directors' responsibilities

10–26 As already stated, directors owe a number of fiduciary duties to companies, shareholders, creditors and employees:

---

[15]These issues are examined in Courtney, T.B., *The Law of Private Companies* (Butterworths, Dublin, 1994), Chap. 8.

- directors must act bona fide, *i.e.* in good faith in the interests of the company as a whole;

- directors must avoid situations where their personal interests are in conflict with those of the company;

- directors must not make an undisclosed profit from their positions, and must account for any profits which they secretly derive from their position, *i.e.* any profit earned by a director from his position is regarded as having been earned for the company and must be paid over to the company.[16] In this context, under section 194 of the Companies Act 1963, transactions between directors and the company must be disclosed to the board of directors. In addition, acquisitions by directors of non-cash assets of the company (and acquisitions by companies of non-cash assets from directors) must first be approved at a general meeting of the company[17];

- directors are required to carry out their duties with due care, skill and diligence.

10–27 On top of these general duties, directors also have specific statutory duties as set out in the Companies Acts.

Restriction and disqualification of directors

10–28 Provisions for restriction and disqualification of persons from acting as directors are contained in Part VII of the Companies Act 1990. In addition to bodies corporate and the company's auditors, the following are prohibited from being directors of companies:

1. Under section 183 of the Companies Act 1963, as substituted by section 169 of the Companies Act 1990, an undischarged bankrupt cannot be a director. Section 40 of the Company Law Enforcement Act 2001 inserts a new section 183A in the 1963 Act permitting the Director of Corporate Enforcement to enquire into the solvency status of any company director and to make a disqualification order against a director on the grounds that he is an undischarged bankrupt. No date has yet been fixed for the coming in to operation of section 40.

2. Section 150 of the Companies Act 1990 requires the High Court to declare that, where a company is wound up and is found to be unable to pay its debts, any person who was a director or shadow director of the company at the date of, or within 12 months before, the commencement of the winding up shall not be appointed as, or act in any way as, a director or secretary of any company or participate in the formation or promotion of any company

---

[16] See, *e.g. Regal (Hastings) Ltd v. Gulliver* [1942] 1 All E.R. 378; *Industrial Development Consultants Ltd v. Cooley* [1972] 2 All E.R. 162.
[17] Companies Act 1990, s. 29.

below a specified size unless the court is satisfied that the person acted honestly and responsibly and it would not be just and equitable to impose such restrictions on him. Section 150(4A) of the 1990 Act, newly inserted by section 41 of the Company Law Enforcement Act 2001, provides that an application for a declaration under section 150 may be made to the court by a liquidator or receiver or by the Director of Corporate Enforcement. No date has yet been fixed for the coming into affect of section 41 of the 2001 Act.

10–29   Under section 160(1) of the Companies Act 1990, a person convicted of an indictable offence in relation to a company or involving fraud or dishonesty may, on the application of the prosecutor, be prevented by the court from acting as a company director. Section 160(1A) of the 1990 Act, inserted by section 42 of the Company Law Enforcement Act 2001, deems disqualified a director who fails to make the necessary notification, required by section 3A(1) of the Companies (Amendment) Act 1982 or by section 195(8) of the Companies Act 1963, of his disqualification under the laws of another state to act as a director. These sections (3A(1) and 195(8)) are newly inserted respectively by sections 101 and 91(a) of the 2001 Act. No date has yet been fixed for the coming into operation of the said sections 42, 101 or 91(a). In addition, under section 160(2) of the Companies Act 1990, the High Court can make a disqualification order against directors for such periods as the court sees fit, in the following circumstances:

– on its own motion or on an application by the Director of Public Prosecutions, or in certain cases by the registrar of companies or any member, contributory, officer, employee, receiver, liquidator, examiner or creditor of a company in relation to which the person in question was or is being proposed as a director, or in any proceedings, if the court is satisfied that:

(a) the person has been guilty of fraud in relation to the company, its members or creditors;

(b) the person has been guilty of any breach of his duty;

(c) a declaration has been granted under section 297A of the Companies Act 1963 that the person is responsible for all or any part of the debts or other liabilities of the company having been knowingly a party to reckless or fraudulent trading;

(d) the person's conduct makes him unfit to be concerned in the management of a company;

(e) the person has been persistently in default in the delivery of notices, returns, accounts or other documents to the registrar of companies;

(f) the person has been guilty of two or more offences in relation to the requirement to keep proper books of account;

(g) the person was a director of a company struck off the register for failing to file returns following the sending of a letter to the company by the Registrar of Companies except where the person can show that the company had no actual or contingent liabilities when it was struck off;

(h) the person is disqualified under the law of another state for conduct that would, in the view of the court, give rise to a disqualification order if it had occurred in the State.

Categories (f), (g) and (h) above were added to section 160 by section 42 of the 2001 Act, in respect of the coming into operation of which no date has yet been fixed.

10–30 The courts have considered both section 150 and section 160 since the enactment of the Companies Act 1990. In *Robinson v. Forrest*,[18] Laffoy J. compared the two sections, and referred to the judgment of Murphy J. in *Business Communications Ltd v. Baxter*,[19] as follows:

"The seminal authority on s. 150 is the decision of Murphy J. in *Business Communications Ltd. v. Baxter* (Unreported, High Court, Murphy J., 21st July, 1995). In his judgment Murphy J. pointed to two significant features of s. 150(1); first, it is mandatory and the court has no discretion unless the person against whom an order is sought establishes that the case falls within one or other of the three exceptions set out in s. 150(2); and, secondly, the period of the restriction is a fixed period of five years and, in the first instance at any rate, the court has no discretion to impose a lesser restriction. Murphy J. expressed some concern about the duration of the period of restraint and in general the lack of flexibility in section 150. Nonetheless, he highlighted a distinction between a disqualification order under s. 160 of the Act of 1990 and a restriction order under section 150. The former is comprehensive in its effect in that the person against whom it is made may not be appointed or act as an auditor, director or other officer, receiver, liquidator or examiner or be in any way concerned or take part in the promotion, formation or management of any company, however much the paid up capital thereof, whereas the latter order does not extend to participation in a company which meets the requirements set out in section 150(3). In relation to this distinction, Murphy J. commented as follows at p. 14:

'Financially and commercially this is clearly a well founded distinction. It is hardly unreasonable to require a person who was a director of a failed company in respect of which he had committed no misconduct but for which he neglected to exercise an appropriate degree of responsibility from resuming such an office in another company, again with the privilege of limited liability except on condition that a stipulated and not excessive sum was provided for the paid-up capital thereof. The figure of £20,000 must

---
[18] [1999] 1 I.R. 426.
[19] Unreported, High Court, July 21, 1995.

represent a very modest sum as the capital for any commercial enterprise and a very limited obstacle to anyone wishing to engage in trade through the medium of a limited liability company. Indeed, it might not be unreasonable to suggest that every limited liability company should be required to have paid-up capital of at least that amount. It would seem that the more serious penalty which the restraining order imposes is the stigma which attaches as a result of the making of the order and its filing in the Companies Office.' "[20]

10–31   As mentioned above, Part 4 of the Company Law Enforcement Act 2001:

– extends the scope of the current legal provisions concerning the restriction and disqualification of directors; and

– gives the Director of Corporate Enforcement power to apply to the court for restriction and disqualification of directors.

It should be noted that when section 41 of the 2001 Act becomes operational it will increase the figure of £20,000 referred to by Murphy J., being the minimum nominal value of the paid-up share capital of a company (other than a plc) necessary to permit a restricted director to be involved with its formation or promotion to £50,000. The same section increases the equivalent figure for a plc from £100,000 to £250,000. Also the new provisions will provide the new Director of Corporate Enforcement, liquidators and receivers with the right to apply to the court for restriction orders to be imposed on directors.

Failure to keep proper books of account

10–32   The requirements to keep proper books of account under section 202 of the Companies Act 1990 have been set out in paras **8–64** *et seq*. Failure to keep proper books may lead to criminal prosecutions under section 203 of the Companies Act 1990 and these are also considered in Chapter 8 in para. **8–68**. Auditors' responsibilities for proper books of account under section 194 of the Companies Act 1990 are considered in paras **4–43** *et seq*. In addition, legislation provides for civil penalties for failure to keep proper books of account under section 204, which mirrors section 203 (which imposes criminal penalties).

10–33   Civil consequences arise in respect of companies being wound up which are unable to pay all of their debts and have failed to keep proper books of account. Officers, and former officers, can be held personally liable, without limitation of liability, for the debts and other liabilities of such companies. The court must find that failure to keep proper books of account has contributed to the company's inability to pay its debts or has resulted in substantial uncertainty

[20][1999] 1 I.R. 426 at 432–433.

as to the company's assets and liabilities or has impeded the company's orderly winding up. Section 204 states:

"(1) Subject to subsection (2), if—
>   (a) a company that is being wound up and that is unable to pay all of its debts has contravened section 202, and
>   (b) the court considers that such contravention has contributed to the company's inability to pay all of its debts or has resulted in substantial uncertainty as to the assets and liabilities of the company or has substantially impeded the orderly winding up thereof,

the court, on the application of the liquidator or any creditor or contributory of the company, may, if it thinks it proper to do so, declare that any one or more of the officers and former officers of the company who is or are in default shall be personally liable, without any limitation of liability, for all, or such part as may be specified by the court, of the debts and other liabilities of the company.

(2) On the hearing of an application under this subsection, the person bringing the application may himself give evidence or call witnesses."

Subsection 2 is a rare instance in which legislation refers to the use of expert witnesses, who almost certainly will be accountants, to assist in securing a conviction.

10–34 The first case in which a company director was made personally liable under section 204 of the Companies Act 1990 for part of the company's debts, arising from his failure to keep proper books of account, is *Re Mantruck Services Ltd: Mehigan v. Duignan*.[21] The official liquidator of Mantruck Services Ltd found "significant and extensive" omissions in the company's records and that these resulted in substantial uncertainty as to the assets and liabilities of the company. By reason of the absence of records, the liquidator was unable to determine the financial position of the company with reasonable accuracy. This led to the liquidator expressing the view that the failure to keep books of account had resulted in substantial uncertainty as to the assets and liabilities of the company and had substantially impeded its orderly winding up.

10–35 Shanley J. held that before a director can be held personally liable under section 204 of the Companies Act 1990, the court must be satisfied that there has been a failure to keep proper books under section 202. According to Shanley J.: "In other words, the court must be satisfied that a criminal offence has been committed by the company."[22] The learned judge went on to hold that section 204 itself does not create a criminal offence and that Irish law applies the same standard of proof in respect of all civil wrongs.

On this construction, personal liability under section 204 will be imposed if

---

[21] [1997] 1 I.R. 340.
[22] *ibid.* at 356.

it is proven to the criminal standard (beyond reasonable doubt) that proper books of account have not been kept by the company *and* it is proven to the civil standard (on the balance of probabilities) that the other conditions necessary for section 204 liability have been satisfied *and* if the court thinks it proper to do so.

He pointed out that the obligation to keep proper books is not an obligation to act as a mere passive custodian but rather the positive obligation to create proper books and records in a particular form with specified contents and that section 202 entails a continuing obligation.

10–36   Shanley J. held that before liability can be imposed under section 204 it must be established that:

- the company is being wound up;

- the company is unable to pay its debts;

- the company has failed to keep proper books;

- the failure to keep proper books has: (i) contributed to the company's inability to pay all its debts; or (ii) has resulted in substantial uncertainty as to the assets and liabilities of the company; or (iii) has substantially impeded the orderly winding up of the company;

- the definition of officer or former officer knowingly and wilfully authorised or permitted the contravention by the company of section 202 or the officer is a person convicted under sections 194, 197 or 242;

- the definition of officer or former officer is not restricted to executives of the company and may include auditors and any person convicted of providing false information.

10–37   The court held that the principal director was personally liable for the debts of the company, and in addition he was disqualified from acting as a director under section 150 of the Companies Act 1990 for a period of five years.

It is interesting to note that expert accounting evidence was relied upon in this case to establish a central component of liability under section 204. Shanley J. referred to this evidence in his judgment as follows:

> "... a fellow of the Institute of Chartered Accountants, gave evidence. He is a former member of the Council of the Institute and of the Auditing Practices Review Committee. In addition, he is a member of the Consultative Committee of Accountancy Bodies. He gave evidence of having received all the records that were before the applicant (including the books obtained on the 20th June, 1996). In his opinion these books and records did not contain a record of the assets and liabilities of the company. He drew attention to the failure to record stocks for February, 1992, and thereafter; the failure to list creditors after March, 1992, and the failure to record fixed assets after March, 1991. Because of such

deficiencies, he was of the opinion that one could not properly prepare a balance sheet, or indeed, a set of accounts for the company. He said that he would have expected to see copies of all credit notes and copies of any leases so as to properly explain the transactions of the company."[23]

10–38 Failure to keep proper books of account may also be deemed to be reckless trading (see paras **10–59** *et seq.*) which may also result in directors being held personally liable for the debts of the company.[24]

Role of forensic accountants

Directors' responsibilities

10–39 Table 10.1 shows examples of breach of fiduciary duty cases in which forensic accountants have been involved.

Table 10.1: Examples of breach of fiduciary duty cases in which forensic accountants have advised

- Advising in litigation alleging breach of fiduciary responsibility by a director of a company, where the company was sold to another company of which the director was a major shareholder
- Investigating the beneficial ownership of a competitor company which established that the managing director of a group subsidiary was, in fact, the beneficial owner of the competitor and had been so while he was employed by the group when he made a number of questionable decisions that adversely affected the trading performance of the company. Providing sufficient evidence to allow the company to take legal action against the subsidiary's managing director and other former employees

Restriction and disqualification of directors

10–40 A forensic accountant may be asked to give expert advice and evidence in relation to the possible disqualification or restriction of directors.[25] In particular, he may be asked to give an opinion, based on his experience, as to whether, in the context of a proposal that a court would make a declaration under section 150(1) of the Companies Act 1990, the director in question qualifies under the exemptions set out at section 150(2), *i.e.* that the director "has acted honestly and responsibly in relation to the conduct of the affairs of the company

[23] [1997] 1 I.R. 340 at 347.
[24] Courtney, T.B., *The Law of Private Companies* (Butterworths, Dublin, 1994), p. 137. See *Re Produce Marketing Consortium Ltd (No. 2)* [1989] B.C.L.C 520.
[25] The role of forensic accountants in disqualification of directors in the U.K. is considered in MacGregor, G. and Hobbs, I., *Expert Accounting Evidence: A Guide for Litigation Support* (Accountancy Books, London, 1998), Chap. 29; and in Taub, M., Rapazzini, A., Bond, C., Solon, M., Brown, A., Murrie, A., Linnell, K. and Burn, S., *Tolley's Accountancy Litigation Support* (Butterworths, London, looseleaf), Part VIII, para. 173.

and that there is no other reason why it would be just and equitable that he should be subject to the restrictions imposed by this section". This would involve an assessment of the performance of the director in relation to the affairs of the company and would require the forensic accountant to review all available evidence of that performance, including board minutes and other records of decisions made.

10–41 Also, where an application is made under section 160(2) for a disqualification order against a director (or other promoter, officer, auditor, receiver, liquidator or examiner) of a company, a forensic accountant may be engaged to advise, and give evidence, in relation to the factors to be considered by the court in deciding whether to grant the application. Although several of these matters are factual in nature, the forensic accountant should be in a position to assist in assessing whether the individual in question has been in breach of duty, and whether his conduct makes him unfit to be concerned in the management of a company. Again, the forensic accountant should be provided with all available information to allow him to advise comprehensively.

Examinerships[26]

10–42 The concept of examinerships was introduced in Ireland on the enactment of the Companies (Amendment) Act 1990, which has since been amended by the Companies (Amendment) (No. 2) Act 1999.

The legislation provides for a moratorium from their creditors for companies in financial difficulties. Under the Act, an examiner is appointed by the High Court to investigate the company's affairs to see if there is any prospect of rescuing the business. The provisions provide such companies with the opportunity of obtaining from the High Court protection from creditors for a limited period of time (generally three months under the 1990 Act, reduced to 70 days under the 1999 Act) to allow a survival package to be put together by an independent, court-appointed examiner. Among the effects of appointment of an examiner is to freeze all new litigation involving the company and to prevent both secured and unsecured creditors from levying execution against the company's assets. If there is a prospect (a "reasonable prospect" under the 1999 Act) of the company's survival, the examiner reports back to the court and then seeks to negotiate a compromise with creditors, with a view to putting forward a scheme of arrangement for approval by the courts.

---

[26] The topic of examinerships is considered more comprehensively from a legal point of view in O'Donnell, J.L., *Examinerships The Companies (Amendment) Act, 1990* (Oak Tree Press, Dublin, 1994); and in Forde, M., *The Law of Company Insolvency* (The Round Hall Press, Dublin, 1993), Part II.

Legal context

10–43 Applications for appointment of examiners are made initially by applying *ex parte* (*i.e.* the other side – in this context the company's creditors – is not present at the hearing) to the court on the day the petition seeking the appointment is presented. The court may treat this application as the hearing of the petition or it may fix a later date for the hearing. On the initial *ex parte* application, the utmost good faith is required and the petition to the court should be factually correct and provide an accurate account of the company's position. Where it is subsequently found that there were inaccuracies in the initial petition, the courts may refuse to sanction the proposed scheme of arrangement.[27]

10–44 Under section 3(4)(a) of the Companies (Amendment) Act 1990, the affidavit accompanying the petition presented to the High Court should be accompanied by the signed consent of the person nominated to act as examiner. The rules provide for the appointment of an interim examiner pending the hearing of the petition. Where an interim appointment is sought, the reasons for this should also be set out in an affidavit.

The primary function of examiners is to examine the situation, affairs and prospects of the company. Examiners investigate the viability of companies and formulate survival proposals for presentation to meetings of shareholders and creditors and, ultimately, the court. Examiners do not have any role in relation to management of the company, unless expressly authorised to do so by the court. Appointment of an examiner has no direct effect on the management or running of the company. Examiners are not officers of the company – they are officers of the court. They must report to the court within 21 days of their appointment or such longer period as the court may allow, and formulate proposals, put them before meetings and report back to the court again within 35 days of their appointment or such longer period as the court may allow. Examiners must, as officers of the court, act honestly and with impartiality. No professional qualifications are required. However, a person cannot act as an examiner if he is not qualified to act as a liquidator.

In investigating companies, examiners are given power to obtain information and explanations from company officers and agents. Section 244A of the 1963 Act (inserted by section 125 of the 1990 Act) prevents any person from withholding from the examiner documents, etc. belonging to the company or relating to the company's affairs. Examiners may also obtain documents and other information from persons other than agents and officers of the company such as employees, shareholders, etc. Examiners may require directors to produce documents relating to bank accounts which may have been used for undisclosed company transactions and improprieties.

---

[27] *Re Wogans (Drogheda) Ltd (No. 2)*, unreported, High Court, Costello J., February 9, 1993.

Role of independent accountants

10–45　Section 3A of the Companies (Amendment) Act 1990, which was inserted by section 7 of the Companies (Amendment) (No. 2) Act 1999, requires petitions to the court for appointment of examiners to be accompanied by a report from an independent person (the company's auditors, or another independent accountant qualified for appointment as examiner) supporting the request for appointment of an examiner.

The legislation specifies the matters to be covered in the independent accountant's report under section 3B, also inserted by the 1999 Act. These include:

- names and permanent addresses of the company officers and others in accordance with whose instructions directors are accustomed to act;

- names of other bodies corporate of which the directors are also directors;

- statement of affairs, including details of assets and liabilities (including contingent and prospective liabilities) and names and addresses of creditors;

- whether there is evidence of disappearance of property;

- whether the company has a reasonable prospect of survival as a going concern, together with conditions for survival;

- whether the proposals would offer a reasonable prospect for survival;

- whether an attempt to continue the business would be more advantageous for members and creditors than winding up;

- recommendations for the company;

- whether there are indications concerning reckless or fraudulent trading;

- details of funding required;

- recommendations as to which liabilities should be paid;

- whether the work of the examiner would be assisted by a creditors' committee;

- any other relevant matters.

The independent accountant's report will deal with the state of the company's affairs and will be made by someone other than a director, secretary, manager, shareholder or employee of the company. The opinion will specify the objectives to be achieved by appointing an examiner. Provision of a neutral assessment of the company's position will assist the court in deciding whether to make the order. The report should give as clear a picture as possible of assets, liabilities, cash flow and forecasts of profit and loss, together with the availability of any finance required during the administration and any other relevant data. Such reports should be as brief and concise as possible and should not involve undue expense and delay. An order will only be made where the court is satisfied that there is a reasonable prospect of the survival of the company as a going concern. Unless the court has this evidence, the court will not appoint an examiner.

Insolvency

10–46 Insolvency law is considered in this section only to the extent[28] where it is directly relevant to insolvency cases that might involve forensic accountants. This is likely to arise where directors have made a false declaration of solvency (in a voluntary winding up), or where the company continued to trade when it was unable to pay its debts as they fell due, where failure to keep proper books of account contributed to the company's inability to pay its debts or resulted in uncertainty as to the assets and liabilities of the company.

Legal context

10–47 Under Irish insolvency law, legal provisions can give rise to both criminal proceedings and civil litigation. Some of these have been mentioned already in Chapter 8 in connection with criminal litigation.

Criminal offences under insolvency law

10–48 The principal legislative provisions that can give rise to criminal proceedings that might involve expert accounting evidence are as follows:

1. Requirement to make a statutory declaration of solvency, including a statement of affairs, in a voluntary winding up under section 256 of the Companies Act 1963, as substituted by section 128 of the Companies Act 1990. This statutory declaration and statement of affairs must be supported by a report and statement of an "independent person" who must be qualified to act as auditor, but who is not necessarily the company's auditor.

2. Destruction, mutilation, or falsification of books or other records of a company being wound up, or making of a false or fraudulent entry in a company document with intent to defraud, by an officer or contributory of the company under section 243 of the Companies Act 1990 (see para. **8–76**).

3. Frauds by officers of companies prior to their liquidation under section 295 of the Companies Act 1963, including inducement by false pretences of persons to give credit to the company, and transfer or concealment of company property with intent to defraud creditors (see para. **8–87** where this section is reproduced).

---

[28] More detailed discussion of legal aspects of insolvency law can be found in Lynch, I., Marshall, J. and O'Ferrall, R., *Corporate Insolvency and Rescue Law and Practice* (Butterworths, Dublin, 1996); and Forde, M., *The Law of Company Insolvency* (The Round Hall Press, Dublin, 1993).

4. Being knowingly a party to the carrying on of the business of a company with intent to defraud creditors of the company or creditors of any other person or for any fraudulent purpose under section 297 of the Companies Act 1963 – fraudulent trading is considered in more detail in paras **8–55** *et seq.*

5. Where a company that is being wound up and is unable to pay its debts has contravened its obligation to keep proper books of account pursuant to section 202 of the Companies Act 1990 and the court considers that such contravention has contributed to the company's inability to pay its debts or has resulted in substantial uncertainty as to the assets and liabilities of the company or has substantially impeded the company's orderly winding up under section 203 of the Companies Act 1990.

Civil actions under insolvency law

10–49 Circumstances that can give rise to civil actions that might involve forensic accountants include:

1. Under section 256 of the Companies Act 1963, the court can declare a director personally responsible without limitation of liability for all or any of a company's debts or other liabilities where the company was proven to be unable to pay its debts, and the director was a party to a statutory declaration of solvency for a voluntary winding up of the company without having reasonable grounds for the opinion that the company would be able to pay its debts.

2. Fraudulent preferences made by a company within six months (or two years in respect of transactions in favour of persons connected with the company) before the commencement of its insolvent winding up are invalid under section 286 of the Companies Act 1963.

3. The court can declare personally responsible, without limitation of liability for all or any of a company's debts or other liabilities, any person who was, while an officer of the company, knowingly a party to the carrying on of any business of the company in a reckless manner, or any person who was knowingly a party to the carrying on of any business of the company with intent to defraud creditors of the company or creditors of any other person or for any fraudulent purpose under section 297A of the Companies Act 1963 (reckless trading is considered in more detail in paras **10–59** *et seq.*).

4. The court can assess damages in favour of a company being wound up against any promoter, past or present officer, liquidator, receiver or examiner of the company or any director of the company's holding company who has misapplied, retained or become liable or accountable for any money or property of the company or has been guilty of any misfeasance (improper performance of an otherwise lawful act) or breach of duty or trust in relation to the company under section 298 of the Companies Act 1963, as amended by section 142 of the Companies Act 1990 (see also para. **10–55**).

5. Breach of the duty of a receiver selling property to get the best possible price reasonably obtainable under section 316A of the Companies Act 1963 can give rise to liability for the receiver (see also para. **10–54**).

6. The court can declare a director of a company or of its holding company or a person connected to such a director personally responsible without limitation of liability for all or any of the company's debts or other liabilities where the company is being wound up and is unable to pay its debts and the court considers that the company's inability to pay its debts has been materially contributed to, or the orderly winding up of the company has been substantially impeded, by the making of a loan or quasi-loan by the company to the person in question, or the entry by the company into a credit transaction or guarantee or other security in favour of the person, under section 39 of the Companies Act 1990.

7. The court can declare officers of a company personally liable without any limitation of liability for all or any part of the liabilities of the company where the company is being wound up, is unable to pay its debts and has contravened its obligation to keep proper books of account pursuant to section 202 of the Act and the court considers that such contravention has contributed to the company's inability to pay its debts or has resulted in substantial uncertainty as to the assets and liabilities of the company, or has substantially impeded the company's orderly winding up under section 204 of the Companies Act 1990.

10–50 These examples are not exhaustive, but are indicative of the large range of situations where an insolvency can lead to legal proceedings. In most cases, services of forensic accountants can be very valuable in identifying and evaluating the relevant issues and considerations, in assessing the risks in the proceedings, in pursuing a settlement of civil claims and in advising the court by way of expert evidence. In particular, the court has very wide discretion in most of the situations described and the evidence of an expert would be given considerable weight by the court when deciding the manner and extent to which that discretion should be exercised.

10–51 Insolvency frequently leads to cases alleging reckless or fraudulent trading. Many such cases involve expert testimony by forensic accountants. Reckless trading is considered separately in the next section (paras **10–59** *et seq.*), while fraudulent trading is covered in Chapter 8 (paras **8–55** *et seq.*).

Statutory declaration of solvency and statement of affairs

10–52 "Independent" accountants may be required to report on directors' declarations of solvency, which are accompanied by a statement of affairs, in voluntary liquidations.

Proof of debts

10–53 Creditors wishing to be treated for the purpose of voting at creditors' meetings are required to submit a formal claim known as proof of debt to the liquidator. Repayments to creditors by the liquidator are made only to those creditors whose proofs have been lodged and admitted. Accountants may be asked to assist in this process. The provisions of the Companies Acts regarding proof of debts must be read in conjunction with the provisions of the Bankruptcy Act 1988 and with the Rules of the Superior Courts 1986, in particular Order 74, rules 102–111. Section 283 of the Companies Act 1963 states that in addition to quantified debts, debts payable on a contingency, future claims (whether certain or contingent) and claims for damages can be proven against companies being wound up. In the case of contingent debts or damages, the section states that a "just estimate" should be made.

Duties of care and good faith

10–54 Receivers and liquidators have duties in connection with the sale of company assets. Receivers (but not liquidators) are required under section 316A of the Companies Act 1963 (as inserted by section 172 of the 1990 Act) to exercise all reasonable care to get the best price reasonably obtainable for the assets. Although there is no equivalent statutory requirement of liquidators, common law would impose on them a similar duty.[29] Being fiduciaries, liquidators must exercise their powera bona fide and for the benefits of the liquidation.

Actions by liquidators against wrongdoing

10–55 Provisions are available under company law to enable liquidators to obtain redress against persons involved in running insolvent companies, in particular, holding such persons personally liable for all or part of the company's unpaid debts. Such actions may involve expert accounting evidence, depending on the nature of the wrongdoing. Persons being rendered accountable must have been involved in some wrongdoing against the company or its creditors. Section 298 of the Companies Act 1963, as amended by section 142 of the Companies Act 1990, provides a swift and simple procedure for obtaining redress against certain categories of wrongdoing against companies in liquidation. Section 298(1) applies where any officer (which has been found to include company auditors) has:

> ". . . misapplied or retained or become liable or accountable for any money or property of the company, or has been guilty of any misfeasance or other breach of duty or trust in relation to the company."

---

[29] See, for example, *Re Brook Cottages Ltd* [1976] N.I. 78; *Van Hool McArdle Ltd v. Rohan Industrial Estates Ltd* [1980] I.R. 237.

10–56 The section has provided a remedy for misappropriation of company property or funds, retention of undeclared profits, preference of certain creditors and several other abuses of directors' powers. Dishonesty is not required for a finding of wrongdoing – improper actions or gross negligence may also give rise to an adverse finding by the courts. Costello J. has said:

> "It is not every error of judgment that amounts to misfeasance in law and it is not every act of negligence that amounts to misfeasance in law…[S]omething more than mere carelessness is required, some act that, perhaps, may amount to gross negligence in failing to carry out a duty owed by the director to his company."[30]

Role of forensic accountants

10–57 Forensic accountants can assist in a variety of cases involving insolvency matters such as:

– identifying potential preferential payment to creditors;

– identifying reversible insider transactions;

– determining the existence and location of misappropriated assets;

– determining whether any director's or officer's actions amounted to a breach of fiduciary duty;

– determining whether third party professional malpractice caused any of the damages.

10–58 Table 10.2 sets out various scenarios involving forensic accounting expertise in insolvency cases.[31]

Reckless trading

10–59 The Companies Act 1990 introduced the concept of "reckless trading" into Irish law, which attempted to deal with many of the criticisms made of the narrow scope of the laws on fraudulent trading (considered in paras **8–55** *et seq.*).[32]

---

[30] *Re Mont Clare Hotels Ltd: Jackson v. Mortell*, unreported, High Court, Costello J., December 2, 1986.

[31] Forensic accounting aspects of insolvency are also covered in MacGregor, G. and Hobbs, I., *Expert Accounting Evidence: A Guide for Litigation Support* (Accountancy Books, London, 1998), Chap. 30; and in Taub, M., Rapazzini, A., Bond, C., Solon, M., Brown, A., Murrie, A., Linnell, K. and Burn, S., *Tolley's Accountancy Litigation Support* (Butterworths, London, looseleaf), Part VIII, para. 173.

[32] The subject of reckless trading is considered more comprehensively in Courtney, T.B., *The Law of Private Companies* (Butterworths, Dublin, 1994, pp. 314-325); Forde, M., *The Law of Company Insolvency* (The Round Hall Press, Dublin, 1993), pp. 261–267; and Lynch, I., Marshall, J. and O'Ferrall, R., *Corporate Insolvency and Rescue Law and Practice* (Butterworths, Dublin, 1996), Chap. 8.

Table 10.2: Examples of insolvency cases in which forensic accountants have advised

- Reviewing records of an insolvent company for a bank, reporting trends and providing evidence of illegalities which substantiated the bank's position in settlement negotiations
- Providing research and expert report for a dissident group of shareholders objecting to a company reorganisation in respect of a company in receivership
- Advising in respect of funds claimed by the receivership, regarding the circumstances of payments and amounts due to the receivership
- Acting for creditors of an insolvent firm in an action against the auditor of the company
- Investigating payments by an insolvent company to uncover evidence of fraudulent preference payments
- Performing an insolvency analysis in certain fraudulent conveyance actions and preparing an affidavit to the court reporting the results and support for the insolvency analysis
- Acting for major creditors to defend a fraudulent conveyance action filed by a liquidator of an insolvent company. Reviewing and critiquing an insolvency analysis prepared by the liquidator's accountants and preparing an alternative solvency analysis

Forensic accountants apply a degree of judgment in assisting in the assessment as to whether directors have, in fact, acted with a degree of recklessness. This is because such an assessment involves comparing the actions of directors with those reasonably expected of a person of similar knowledge, skill and experience. Accountants, especially those in public practice, have the opportunity to observe from the inside the operations of many businesses in a variety of industries in the course of their work. They also tend to advise at senior management levels in organisations and this allows them to observe the business practices of directors at close quarters. Furthermore, the training and continuing professional education in accountancy practices keeps them abreast of best practices in the area of corporate governance. Thus, expert accountants can make use of broad business experience in assisting in the assessment of possible recklessness.

Legal context

10–60   Under section 297A of the Companies Act 1963 (as inserted by section 138 of the Companies Act 1990) the court may, on the application of the receiver, examiner or liquidator or of a creditor or contributory of a company that is in the course of being wound up or is in examinership, declare personally responsible without limitation of liability for all or any part of the debts or other liabilities of the company any person (being an officer of the company) who was knowingly a party to the carrying on of the company's business in a reckless manner. Section 297A(1) states:

> "If in the course of the winding up of a company … it appears that—
>   (a)   any person was, while an officer of the company, knowingly a party to

the carrying on of any business of the company in a reckless manner; or

(b) any person was knowingly a party to the carrying on of any business of the company with intent to defraud creditors of the company, or creditors of any other person or for any fraudulent purpose;

the court, on the application of the receiver, examiner, liquidator or any creditor or contributory of the company, may, if it thinks it proper to do so, declare that such person shall be personally responsible, without any limitation of liability, for all or any part of the debts or other liabilities of the company as the court may direct."

10–61 Provisions relating to reckless trading differ in three respects from fraudulent trading. The section only applies to officers of companies, which includes auditors, liquidators, receivers and shadow directors. Mere employees, agents and third parties cannot be held responsible for reckless trading. Section 297A on reckless trading does not provide for criminal sanctions. Finally, liability for reckless trading is related to the loss caused by the activity in question.

10–62 The Companies Acts do not define reckless trading. However, certain situations are specifically deemed to constitute reckless trading, although the specified examples are expressly stated not to be exhaustive. This means that the court has discretion in determining whether a given set of circumstances constitutes reckless trading.

The specified situations are set out as follows in subsection (2) of section 297A of the Companies Act 1963:

"… an officer of a company shall be deemed to have been knowingly a party to the carrying on of any business of the company in a reckless manner if—

(a) he was a party to the carrying on of such business and, having regard to the general knowledge, skill and experience that may reasonably be expected of a person in his position, he ought to have known that his actions or those of the company would cause loss to the creditors of the company, or any of them, or

(b) he was a party to the contracting of a debt by the company and did not honestly believe on reasonable grounds that the company would be able to pay the debt when it fell due for payment as well as all its other debts (taking into account the contingent and prospective liabilities)."

10–63 A declaration under section 297A that an individual is personally responsible for the debts or other liabilities of a company as a result of reckless trading can only be made if the company is deemed unable to pay its debts and the applicant (if creditor or contributory) or any person on whose behalf the application is made has suffered a loss as a result of the reckless trading. Where the declaration is being considered under (b) above (*i.e.* where a debt was contracted when the individual did not honestly believe on reasonable grounds that the company would be able to pay the debt when it fell due for payment as well as all its other debts) the court is also required to take account of whether the creditor was aware of the company's financial position and nevertheless assented to the incurring of the debt.

10–64 Because of the very serious consequences flowing from a finding of reckless trading (unlimited liability, disqualification from acting as company officer), liability must be clearly and unequivocally established. Section 297A(6) gives the court discretion to relieve the individual from some or all of the relevant personal liability in certain circumstances, as follows:

> "Where it appears to the court that any person in respect of whom a declaration has been sought ... has acted honestly and responsibly in relation to the conduct of the affairs of the company or any matter or matters on the ground of which such declaration is sought to be made, the court may, having regard to all the circumstances of the case, relieve him either wholly or in part, from personal liability on such terms as it may think fit."

10–65 It has been argued that section 297A proceedings (for civil liability) were in fact of a criminal nature, and imposed criminal sanctions that bore all the hallmarks of criminal charges. Consequently, the constitutionality of the section was challenged in *O'Keeffe v. Ferris, Ireland and the Attorney General*.[33] In rejecting the plaintiff's claim, O'Flaherty J., speaking for the Supreme Court, said:

> "While much stress has been laid by counsel for the plaintiff on the need to protect the citizen from injustice in the course of proceedings, the entitlement of victims of wrongdoing to be safeguarded is something to which the Court must also have regard and the Court, therefore, upholds the paramount objective of this legislative provision, which is to protect those who may have been wronged."[34]

10–66 The leading Irish case on reckless trading in the context of these legislative provisions is *Re Hefferon Kearns Ltd (No. 2)*.[35] Although this case dealt with the provisions of section 33 of the Companies (Amendment) Act 1990, this section was repealed and replaced by section 297A and the relevant provisions in the two sections are identical. The case involved an application to make directors of a company in examinership personally liable for the debts of the company on the grounds of their knowing involvement in reckless trading. In his judgment, Lynch J. interpreted certain aspects of the section and these

---

[33] [1993] 3 I.R. 165 (High Ct – Murphy J.); [1997] 3 I.R. 463 (Sup. Ct).
[34] [1997] 3 I.R. 463 at 472.
[35] [1993] 3 I.R. 191.

interpretations are of significant assistance to legal and forensic accounting practitioners in advising on the scope and applicability of the section. He said:

> "At the outset I should say that I am satisfied that s. 33 of the Act of 1990 does not impose a collective responsibility on a board of directors as such in respect of the manner in which a company has been run. Section 33 operates individually and personally against the officers (which includes the directors) of a company and the onus rests on the plaintiff to prove in relation to each of the defendants in this case that his conduct falls within the ambit of conduct prohibited or liable to be penalised by section 33."[36]

10–67 He went on to deal with the significance of the word "knowingly" in establishing whether a finding of liability is justified:

> "The inclusion of the word 'knowingly' in s. 33, sub-s. 1 (a) must have been intended by the Oireachtas to have some effect on the nature of the reckless conduct required to come within the sub-section. I think that its inclusion requires that the director is party to carrying on the business in a manner which the director knows very well involves an obvious and serious risk of loss or damage to others, and yet ignores that risk, because he does not really care whether such others suffer loss or damage or because his selfish desire to keep his own company alive overrides any concern which he ought to have for others."[37]

10–68 He then dealt with the concept of "ought to have known" as it appeared in the section:

> "What sub-s. 2 (a) requires is knowledge, or imputed knowledge, that the first defendant's actions or those of the company *would* cause loss to creditors: it is not sufficient that there might be some worry or uncertainty as to the ability to pay all creditors."[38]

10–69 In relation to the question of liability arising as a result of the company incurring a debt when it was unlikely to be able to pay that and all its other debts, Lynch J. said:

> "Paragraph (b) of sub-s. 2 appears to be a very wide ranging and indeed draconian measure, and could apply in the case of virtually every company which becomes insolvent and has to cease trading for that reason. If, for example, a company became insolvent because of the domino effect of the insolvency of a large debtor, it would be reasonable for the directors to continue trading for a time thereafter, to assess the situation and almost inevitably they would incur some debts which would fall within para. (b) before finally closing down. It would not be in the interests of the community that whenever there might appear to be any significant

---

[36] *ibid.* at 219.
[37] [1993] 3 I.R. 191 at 222.
[38] *ibid.* at 223.

danger that a company was going to become insolvent, the directors should immediately cease trading and close down the business. Many businesses which might well have survived by continuing to trade, coupled with remedial measures, could be lost to the community.

I think that it is because sub-s. 2 and especially para. (b) is so wide-ranging, that sub-s. 6 was included in s. 33 of the Act."[39]

Subsection 6 of section 297A was the provision, quoted at para. **10–64** above, that gave the court power to relieve persons from liability in certain circumstances.

10–70   It should be noted that Carroll J. held in *Re Hunting Lodges Ltd (in liquidation)*[40] that a single isolated transaction can constitute "carrying on of any business of the company". In the same case, various participants in the fraudulent activities of the company in question were declared personally responsible for different portions of the company's debts, emphasising the discretion of the courts in determining such responsibilities (see also para. **8–59**).

10–71   Failure to keep proper books of account may be construed as reckless trading.[41]

Role of forensic accountants

10–72   The most likely involvement of the expert accountant in the context of an application under section 297A is to assist in the assessment of whether the person(s) involved was knowingly a party to reckless trading in the terms of the section and whether any of the other considerations that might serve to reduce or eliminate exposure to personal liability applied to their involvement.

As can be seen from the above summary of the legislative provisions and the manner in which they have been interpreted by the courts, the determination of whether a declaration of responsibility should be made is based on criteria that are largely subjective. Forensic accountants can assist in such judgment calls by arriving at an opinion based on experience in the commercial world as to matters such as:

- What is the level of general knowledge, skill and experience that may reasonably be expected of someone in the person's position?

- Were there reasonable grounds for an honest belief that a debt contracted by the company would be paid when it fell due, along with all other debts?

- Did the applicant creditor suffer a loss as a consequence of the reckless trading complained of?

---

[39] *ibid.* at 224–225.
[40] [1985] I.L.R.M. 75.
[41] *Re Produce Marketing Consortium Ltd. (No. 2)* [1989] B.C.L.C. 520.

- Was the creditor aware of the company's financial position when the debt was incurred?

- Did the person act honestly and responsibly?

In order to render these opinions, a forensic accountant needs to draw on relevant experience and also needs to be provided with all available information that touches on any of these questions.

Forensic accounting aspects of these issues in the United Kingdom are considered in MacGregor and Hobbs.[42]

Misrepresentation

10–73   Misrepresentation cases requiring expert accountants are likely to do so for two purposes: either to establish the misrepresentation, which will usually relate to financial and/or accounting data if a forensic accountant is involved; or to quantify the financial effect of the misrepresentation.

Legal context

10–74   Misrepresentation involves a misstatement of an existing fact or a false statement of past or existing fact that is intended to, and which actually does, induce another to enter into a contract. This is not to be confused with a statement of opinion or belief. However, it is a misrepresentation of fact for someone to state an opinion which he does not believe, which might in turn misrepresent a fact. As stated by Bowen L.J. in *Smith v. Land and House Property Corporation*:

> "It is often fallaciously assumed that a statement of opinion cannot involve the statement of a fact. In a case where the facts are equally well known to both parties, what one of them says to the other is frequently nothing but an expression of opinion. But if the facts are not equally well known to both sides, then a statement of opinion by the one who knows the facts best involves very often a statement of a material fact, for he impliedly states that he knows facts which justify his opinion."[43]

10–75   In order for there to be misrepresentation, there must be an asymmetry of information between parties to a transaction. Litigation for misrepresentation by businesses is common, for example in mergers and acquisitions where the purchaser alleges that information provided by the vendor misrepresented the facts.

---

[42] MacGregor, G. and Hobbs, I., *Expert Accounting Evidence: A Guide for Litigation Support* (Accountancy Books, London, 1998), Chap. 33.
[43] (1884) 28 Ch. D. 7 at 15.

Misrepresentation in prospectuses

10–76   Cahill[44] identifies four common law investor remedies in connection
with information in prospectuses: omission constituting misrepresentation,
deceitful misrepresentation, negligent misstatement, and actions for rescission.
In order to base an action on misrepresentation, the plaintiff must also be able
to prove that the misrepresentation was unambiguous. The representation must
also be material, *i.e.* one which could affect the judgment of a reasonable person
in deciding whether or on what terms to enter a contract. In order to prove
misrepresentation, the plaintiff must prove the representation induced the contract.

Omission of information

10–77   Damages against persons responsible may be granted for misrepresentation, but the misrepresentation must be shown to have been deceitful,
which will require showing that the deceit was in the form of "active
misrepresentation" and that it affected the judgment of the prospective investor.
Loss must be shown to have resulted from reliance on the misrepresentation.
The term "misrepresentation" implies the positive act of a statement made.
However, omission of information may be classified as "active misrepresentation" in certain circumstances.

   Mere omission of material facts in itself does not provide a basis for an
action of damages for misrepresentation, except where the omission has the
effect of making what had been disclosed absolutely false.[45] Courts will consider
the substantive effect of the omission to see if the omission materially affects
the truth of statements in the prospectus.[46]

   In order to establish deceitful misrepresentation, an element of fraud must
be shown.[47]

Negligent misrepresentation

10–78   In a purely tortious context, a person relying on misrepresentation may
have a remedy under the *Hedley Byrne*[48] principle, *i.e.* that a person who made
a negligent statement could owe a duty of care to a person who suffered economic
loss through reliance on the statement. A person may be entitled to rely on the
care and skill of the person making the statement. Thus, for example, in the
context of prospectuses, directors who are negligent in respect of misstatements
or omissions in prospectuses may have a potential liability in negligence to
investors. Directors may be found to owe a duty of care to investors in such
situations. For such an action to be successful, the plaintiff must show that:

---

[44] Cahill, D., *Corporate Finance Law* (Round Hall Sweet & Maxwell, Dublin, 1999),
   p. 129.
[45] *Peek v. Gurney* (1873) L.R. 6 H.L. 377.
[46] *Components Tube Co v. Naylor* [1900] 2 I.R. 1; *Peek v. Gurney* (1873) L.R. 6 H.L. 377.
[47] *Derry v. Peek* (1889) 14 A.C. 337.
[48] *Hedley Byrne & Co Ltd v. Heller & Partners Ltd.* [1964] A.C. 465.

- the maker of the statement owed a duty of care to the plaintiff;
- the statement constituted a breach of that duty of care;
- the plaintiff suffered loss as a consequence of the breach.

Fraudulent misrepresentation

10–79 A person may have a remedy under the tort of deceit where the misrepresentations are fraudulent. The significance of a plaintiff being able to prove fraud no longer lies in the fact that he may be able to bring an action for deceit. It will be easier and generally just as effective to bring an action in negligence. Damages for deceit will compensate for "all the actual damages directly flowing from the fraudulent inducement"[49] whereas those for negligence are limited to damage which is reasonably foreseeable, but this is rarely likely to be of great significance. The real significance of proving fraud lies rather in its effect on any disclaimers or exclusions which the representor attaches to his statement. In general, proof of fraud has the effect that disclaimers cannot be invoked and no finding of contributory negligence is made against the plaintiff if he succeeds.

Comparison of negligent and fraudulent misrepresentation

10–80 The normal measure of damages in negligent misrepresentation is to restore the plaintiff to the position he would have been in had the misrepresentation never occurred, subject to remoteness of damages. Where fraud is involved, all damages flowing from the fraudulent inducement can be recovered, regardless of whether or not it was reasonably foreseeable. Costello J. referred to the principle of restoring the plaintiff to the pre-wronged position when describing the manner in which damages are calculated in a case of fraudulent misrepresentation in *McAnarney v. Hanrahan*:

> "Where damages are claimed for fraudulent misrepresentation then they are assessed so as to put the plaintiff in the position he would have been in if the representation had not been made to him. This is different to the case where damages are being assessed in the case of a claim based on breach of warranty - then damages are assessed on the basis that the warranty was true."[50]

10–81 There is no contributory negligence in an action for fraud. Thus, for example, any due diligence work carried out by the plaintiff will not affect the amount of damages in a fraudulent misrepresentation case.

10–82 In actions for negligent misrepresentation, it is necessary to show a duty of care, which exists where there is a special relationship. In an action for

---

[49] *Doyle v. Olby (Ironmongers) Ltd* [1969] 2 Q.B. 158 at 167; [1969] 2 All E.R. 119 at 122 (CA), *per* Lord Denning M.R.
[50] [1993] 3 I.R. 492 at 498.

deceit there is no need to show the existence of a special relationship. Therefore, where a misstatement is alleged, it may only be possible to pursue the action where there is an allegation of fraudulent misrepresentation.

10–83 Section 71 of the Statute of Limitations 1957 states:

> "(1) Where, in the case of an action for which a period of limitation is fixed by this Act, either—
>> (a) the action is based on the fraud of the defendant or his agent or of any person through whom he claims or his agent, or
>> (b) the right of action is concealed by the fraud of any such person,
>
> the period of limitation shall not begin to run until the plaintiff has discovered the fraud or could with reasonable diligence have discovered it.
>
> (2) Nothing in subsection (1) of this section shall enable an action to be brought to recover, or enforce any charge against, or set aside any transaction affecting, any property which has been purchased for valuable consideration by a person who was not a party to the fraud and did not at the time of the purchase know or have reason to believe that any fraud had been committed."

Because of this limitation, some actions for misrepresentation may only be possible if fraud is alleged.

10–84 Directors may be insured for civil liability, but the policy is very unlikely to extend to cover allegations of fraud.

10–85 Negligent and fraudulent misrepresentation are compared in Table 10.3.

Table 10.3: Comparison of negligent and fraudulent misrepresentation

	Negligent misrepresentation	Fraudulent misrepresentation
Damages	Restore person to position pre-wrongful action	Reparation for all damages flowing from fraudulent inducement
Contributory negligence	✔	✗
Duty of care	✔	✗
Insurance cover	✔	✗
Statute of limitations	Generally 6 years from date of misrepresentation	Generally 6 years from time fraud is discovered

Action for rescission

10–86   Shareholders may be able to rescind their contract acquiring the shares where there is omission of information, negligent misrepresentation or fraudulent misrepresentation. Cahill[51] identifies the pre-conditions that must be present for rescission to be granted:

- the party making the representation must have been aware that the prospective shareholder would subscribe for shares on foot of the misrepresentation;

- the misrepresentation must have been responsible for inducing the investor to invest;

- the investor must have acted promptly in seeking the remedy of recission once the misrepresentation came to light;

- *restitutio in integrum* (plaintiff restored to the position he would have been in if the misrepresentation had not been made) must still be possible.

Role of forensic accountants

10–87   Broadly speaking, forensic accountants will have two distinct roles in cases involving misrepresentation. Where the misrepresentation relates to accounting data, expert accountants may be asked to give expert evidence to the court on the nature and extent of the misrepresentation. For instance, most share sale agreements will warrant that the financial statements of the entity being sold have been prepared in accordance with generally accepted accounting principles. An expert accountant will assist the court in determining whether this warranty amounts to a misrepresentation.

Forensic accountants may have a role to play in assisting to ensure in advance that there is no misrepresentation. For example, section 31 of the Companies Act 1990 prohibits loans, guarantees, etc. to/for directors. There is an exception to this under section 32 where the value of the arrangement/total amount outstanding is less than 10 per cent of the relevant assets of the company. Forensic accounting is likely to be required in evidence where the section 32 exception is relied upon. This is important in practice and many deals proceed on the basis of auditors' certificates that section 32 applies.

Most often the forensic accountant will be involved in the calculation of the excess consideration paid by a party on foot of a misrepresentation. Depending on the nature of the misrepresentation, this calculation could involve a full share valuation exercise, or a valuation of specific assets or cash flows.

---

[51] Cahill, D., *Corporate Finance Law* (Round Hall Sweet & Maxwell, Dublin, 1999), pp. 148–149.

Accounting calculations

10–88   Where misrepresentation is established, the remedy is the recovery of damages by investors. The loss is the reduction in value of the shares up to a maximum loss of the amount the investor paid for the shares.[52] However, this approach has been questioned.[53] The issue of whether additional consequential damages should be recoverable has also been raised.[54]

10–89   Statutory remedies may also be available under the Companies Acts. Under section 49 of the Companies Act 1963, investors in public companies (the provision does not apply to private companies) may claim compensation for misstatements in prospectuses. The compensation to be paid is for the "loss or damage they may have sustained by reason of any untrue statement" in a prospectus. Section 50 also imposes criminal sanctions for misstatements in prospectuses.

Partnership disputes

10–90   Partnerships have particular characteristics that make them more prone to disputes than companies. Companies are obliged to have a written constitution (*i.e.* the memorandum and articles of association) setting out the initial ownership structure, and the manner in which formal business is to be conducted. By contrast, many partnerships come into being from ad hoc arrangements between individuals and no formal written partnership agreement is put in place at the outset. Thus, when any dispute arises in such situations, there is no pre-defined mechanism or set of rules (other than the Partnership Act 1890) by which the dispute can be resolved.

Because of this, and because many businesses are conducted through partnerships, this is fertile territory for disputes. Many of these disputes involve forensic accountants as they frequently relate to financial matters such as share of profits, allocation of expenses between the partnership and individual partners, conduct of business for the benefit of individual partners rather than for the partnership, etc. Departures of partners (arising from death, resignation, retirement or dismissal, or for other reasons) frequently involve goodwill valuations. Such valuations usually require expert accounting input.

As discussed in Twomey,[55] partnerships themselves may be involved in litigation in a number of different ways, *e.g.* they may be sued or may themselves

---

[52]Cahill, D., *Corporate Finance Law* (Round Hall Sweet & Maxwell, Dublin, 1999), p. 138.
[53]*Clark v. Urquhart, Stacey v. Urquhart* [1930] A.C. 28 at 67.
[54]*Potts v. Miller* (1940) 64 C.L.R. 282 at 298–299.
[55]Twomey, M.J, *Partnership Law* (Butterworths, Dublin, 2000), Chap. 12.

initiate litigation against others. The material here is more concerned with disputes between partners *inter se*.

Legal context

10–91 Twomey considers partnership disputes in section C of his book and identifies the following matters which may give rise to disputes between partners:

- management rights of partners;
- financial rights of partners;
- fiduciary duties of partners;
- partnership property;
- partnership capital;
- goodwill of partnerships;
- shares in partnerships.

10–92 In relation to the financial rights of partners, Twomey identifies the following matters:

- sharing of profits and losses;
- outlays and advances by partners;
- payments by firms for the services of partners;
- payment of interest;
- partnership books of account.

Most disputes arising out of these issues will relate to legal considerations. Issues involving forensic accountants are set out below.

Partnership accounts

10–93 Partners under section 28 of the Partnership Act 1890 are required to:

> "... render true accounts and full information of all things affecting the partnership to any partner or his legal representative."

Partnerships are generally not required to file accounts as, given the unlimited liability of partners, there is less need to regulate to protect creditors. Regulation 6 of the European Communities (Accounts) Regulations 1993[56] require partnerships to file accounts where the partners are themselves limited liability companies. The liability of such partnerships is in effect limited to the share capital of the underlying partner companies.

---

[56] S.I. No. 396 of 1993.

Partnerships are required to keep accounts for the purpose of providing an account of the firm's financial dealings to the individual partners. This issue was recognised by the Supreme Court in *Baxter v. Horgan*.[57]

As discussed by Twomey,[58] where items are recognised in accounts they may imply that this was agreed by the partners:

> "If there had been a settlement of account, containing this item, in the first year of the partnership, that would be fair ground for saying that there was an agreement between the partners to that effect…".[59]

Fiduciary duties

10–94 As set out by Twomey,[60] partners have a number of fiduciary duties to each other, including:

– partners must act in the firm's interest (rather than in the partner's own personal interest);

– partners must act in good faith in their dealings with each other;

– partners must not abuse their powers;

– partners must treat each other as equals (unless otherwise specified in the partnership agreement);

– partners owe each other a duty of honesty;

– partners must render true accounts and full information to each other;

– partners must account for private profits;

– partners must account for profits of a competing business;

– partners must share post-dissolution profits.

Role of forensic accountants

10–95 Forensic accountants can assist in partnership disputes relating to financial matters. Such financial disputes are most likely to relate to partners' share of income and share of net assets from the business. This may involve computation of share of profits/losses, including allocation of expenses to the partnership, calculation of partners' partnership remuneration, and valuation of tangible assets and of goodwill of the partnership.[61] Where there is a written

---

[57] Unreported, High Court, Murphy J., May 28, 1990, unreported, Supreme Court, June 7, 1991.

[58] Twomey, M.J., *Partnership Law* (Butterworths, Dublin, 2000), pp. 114–115.

[59] *Hutcheson v. Smith* (1842) 5 I. Eq. R. 117 at 123.

[60] Twomey, M.J., *Partnership Law* (Butterworths, Dublin, 2000), Chap. 15.

[61] A useful guide to valuing partnerships and goodwill in partnerships is Peelo, D., *Valuations, Mergers and Sales of Professional Practices* (Peelo & Partners, Dublin, 1998).

partnership agreement, the forensic accountant will be required to apply its terms and may be required to interpret terms that are unclear. The forensic accountant also needs to be aware that the provisions of the Partnership Act 1890 apply to certain aspects of the conduct of the partnership in the absence of a written agreement dealing with those aspects.

The law on damages (as discussed in Chapter 15) would also apply to partnership disputes. An individual partner might be entitled to damages from his partners where there has been a breach of fiduciary duty or where the rules applying to the allocation of income and assets have been breached to his detriment.

Accounting calculations

Computation of partnership profits/losses

10–96 The Partnership Act 1890 does not define what constitutes profits. Twomey points out that the definition of profits has not been much considered by the courts.[62] In older cases, profit has been taken to mean the change in value of assets from one date to another. Twomey suggests that the meaning of profit would involve consideration of generally accepted accounting principles. He points out that in a United States case, *McDonald v. Fenzel*,[63] the cash basis of accounting was rejected by the court – profits should be accounted for using the accruals method of accounting. Twomey comments that:

> "It is particularly helpful if at the time of the creation of the partnership, the partners enlist the services of their accountant to determine, for example, whether extraordinary expenses are to be paid out of ordinary income or out of borrowings or capital, whether work in progress is to be taken into account in determining the profit share of each partner, the value to be attributed to doubtful debts, the amount of depreciation of fixed assets, etc."[64]

Reimbursement of expenses incurred

10–97 Partners are entitled to be reimbursed for payments made by them individually on behalf of the partnership. This extends to client entertainment expenses. Conversely, payments made by the partnership in respect of the private business of one of its partners should be reimbursed by the individual partner to the partnership.

---

[62] Twomey, M.J., *Partnership Law* (Butterworths, Dublin, 2000), pp. 320–321.
[63] 638 N.Y.S. 2d 15 (1996).
[64] Twomey, M.J., *Partnership Law* (Butterworths, Dublin, 2000), p. 321.

Remuneration of partners

10–98 Unless expressly provided for in the partnership agreement, partners are not entitled to remuneration for services, including management services, provided to the partnership. There is an exception to this principle where the partnership business is carried on after its dissolution (for example, because one of the partners died). In such cases, the remaining partners working in the business are entitled to be remunerated in calculating the post-dissolution profits due to the deceased partner.

Valuation of partnership property and goodwill

10–99 Goodwill may be valued according to the terms of the partnership agreement, or otherwise. Valuation of goodwill is considered generally in Chapter 18 (para. **18–45**, para. **18–58** *et seq*. and para. **18–94** *et seq*.), Case law indicates that goodwill should be valued at its market value rather than book value.[65]

Damages for breach of fiduciary duties

10–100 The usual remedy for losses caused by breach of fiduciary duty by a partner is damages or an account for profits. Account of profits is the statutory remedy under the Partnership Act 1890 in the case of breaches of fiduciary duties arising from private profits, profits of a competing business and post-dissolution profits. Breach of fiduciary duties may also lead to dissolution of the partnership. In some cases, the breach may amount to repudiation of the partnership agreement. Costs may be awarded against the partner in breach of his fiduciary duty.[66] In addition, courts may order that the initial capital contributed by a partner be returned to him in cases of breach of duty.

Concluding comment

10–101 Recent enactments in the area of company law in Ireland have had the effect of exposing company directors to a wide range of possible penalties, including unlimited personal liability for debts of the company in various circumstances. Whilst, as a matter of principle, making those who enjoy the power and privileges associated with managing a business accountable to those who can be affected by their decisions (including creditors and shareholders), a good case can be made to suggest that the legislation has not struck the right balance between risk and reward. This is particularly the case for the non-

---

[65] See, for example (in the context of partnership property), *Barr v. Barr*, unreported, High Court, Murphy, J., July 29, 1992.

[66] *Baxter v. Horgan*, unreported, High Court, Murphy, J., May 28, 1990; unreported, Supreme Court, June 7, 1991.

executive director who, by definition, will not be as familiar with the day-to-day activities of the company as his executive colleagues on the board. Although several of the provisions imposing possible liability on directors recognise that some may be in a better position of knowledge and influence than others, individuals considering an offer to join a board are justified in thinking very carefully and weighing up risks and rewards before accepting. It would be a pity if legislation were to have the effect of depriving companies of valuable expertise, or of making the acquisition of that expertise prohibitively expensive.

TAXATION

CHAPTER 11

TAXATION

11–01 This chapter considers the issue of taxation in a limited way. In particular, only aspects relevant to the practice of forensic accounting are dealt with.[1,2]

Forensic accountants are likely to act in:

— interpretation of accounting principles relevant to the determination of tax liabilities;

— disputes arising from tax avoidance schemes;

— tax evasion, amounting to tax fraud.

In the first two situations, the forensic accountant may be employed at various stages in the case and will tend to act as an expert witness. In the third situation, the earlier legal and forensic accounting advice (rather than tax advice) is obtained the better. A recent paper advocates caution where a criminal prosecution in relation to tax is envisaged:

> "A taxpayer under criminal investigation will not be content to leave his/her defence in the hands of a tax practitioner. I don't imagine a tax practitioner wants to have that role in any event. This requires legal expertise and legal representation. Consequently when a case is signalled as a criminal investigation one, the practitioner should advise the client that legal representation is required."[3]

The chapter deals with the process by which taxation disputes are determined. In all cases other than judicial review cases such disputes are first heard by the Revenue Appeal Commissioners. Thereafter, their decisions may be appealed to the courts. Also leave to take judicial review proceedings may be granted provided all appeal processes have been exhausted. Judicial reviews are where

---

[1] The authors are grateful to Kieran Corrigan, Patrick Donnelly and James Skehan for their advices in relation to this chapter.

[2] Tax investigations are also considered from a forensic point of view (in a U.K. context) in Taub, M., Rapazzini, A., Bond, C., Solon, M., Brown, A., Murrie, A., Linnell, K. and Burn, S., *Tolley's Accountancy Litigation Support* (Butterworths, London, looseleaf), Part IX, para. 180. A more comprehensive consideration of all aspects of Irish taxation is to be found in Corrigan, K., *Revenue Law* (Round Hall Sweet & Maxwell, Dublin, 2000).

[3] Donnelly, P., "The future role of prosecutions" (Paper delivered at the Joint Institute of Taxation/Revenue Tax Audit Conference, Kilkenny, November 3/4, 2000).

the appeal is against the process, *e.g.* where a decision-making body has exceeded its authority or acted in bad faith.[4] The taxation appeals procedure is described and an overview of the prosecution of tax offences is given. Relevant tax case law, including cases dealing with accounting issues, is then considered.[5] The chapter concludes by examining the role of forensic accountants in tax disputes.

Areas falling outside the scope of this chapter include those where taxation specialists act in an advisory capacity in relation to tax matters generally, and where tax accountants act as agents for their clients in the preparation and submission of tax returns and the negotiation and determination of interpretations of tax legislation.

Forensic accountants may be approached to advise either the Revenue authorities or the taxpayer in tax investigations and in litigation involving tax issues. Forensic accountants should consider the time commitment and the requirement for specialised knowledge before accepting any such engagement.

Tax appeals procedure[6, 7]

11–02   In a general sense, an appeal is a formal expression of dissatisfaction by a taxpayer against an assessment made, an action taken, or a decision made, by a Revenue official. There are three types of appeal – those involving interval reviews in Revenue, those where the Ombudsman is asked to intervene and those that involve a formal appeal to the Appeal Commissioners. Forensic accountants will most often be asked to advise in appeals to the Appeal Commissioners, acting for either the Revenue or for the taxpayer.

Appeals to the Appeal Commissioners

11–03   The role of the Appeal Commissioners is to decide all questions of fact and law other than constitutional issues which are confined to the superior courts. A taxpayer has the right to enter a formal appeal to the Appeal Commissioners against any determination of the Revenue in relation to:

– an estimated assessment of income or profit raised as a consequence of a

---

[4] *State (Calcul International Ltd and Solatrex International Ltd.) v. Appeal Commissioners* 3 I.T.R. 254 is such a case where Barron J. discusses, *inter alia*, the powers of Revenue Appeal Commissioners compared with those of the courts.

[5] The Institute of Taxation in Ireland has an extensive publication list of books, cases, CD-ROM material, articles, etc. on Irish taxation – these can be viewed at www.taxireland.ie/info/index.htm.

[6] A practical description of bringing a case to the Appeal Commissioners and thereafter through the courts is provided in Somers, J. and Lockhart, G., "Taking a VAT case through the courts, Erin a case study" (1998) 11 *Irish Tax Review* 149.

[7] For a consideration of appeal procedures in respect of customs and excise duties see Herbert, L. and Somers, J., "The new appeals procedures for customs and excise duties" (1996) 9 *Irish Tax Review* 106.

person's failure to submit a return or because the inspector is of the opinion that the return received is either insufficient or incorrect, or any other determination by the Revenue;

— a Revenue decision in relation to excise duties or customs tariffs, or certain administrative acts such as classifications or valuations under the European Union Customs Code;

— an assessment to Capital Acquisitions Tax[8] or to Stamp Duty;[9]

— decisions of the Revenue Commissioners as to the market value of any real property for the purposes of Capital Acquisitions Tax;[10]

— a determination, assessment or certain other decisions made in relation to Value Added Tax;[11]

— claims to allowances, deductions and reliefs;

— all claims to exemption; and

— all claims for repayment of taxes or duties.

11–04 An appeal, in the context of taxation, means a formal hearing before an independent arbiter, an Appeal Commissioner, who is appointed by the Minister for Finance for this purpose. An appeal must generally be lodged by giving notice in writing to the inspector or other officer appointed by the Revenue Commissioners who made the relevant assessment within 30 days of the date of the notice of assessment. Notices of assessment inform taxpayers of the right of appeal. As a general rule, no appeal may be lodged against an estimated assessment of income or profit until a completed return is submitted and the tax due by reference to the return, including interest and costs, is paid.

Grounds of appeal

11–05 The right to appeal an assessment to income tax, corporation tax or capital gains tax to the Appeal Commissioners is afforded to any person who is "aggrieved" by the assessment.[12] The inspector or other appointed Revenue officer who made the assessment can refuse the application to appeal. However, such refusal, which must be notified, with reasons, to the applicant, can itself be appealed to the Appeal Commissioners.

---

[8] Capital Acquisitions Tax Act 1976, s. 52.
[9] Stamp Act 1891, s. 13 as inserted by s. 109 of the Finance Act 1994.
[10] Capital Acquisitions Tax Act 1976, s. 51.
[11] See sections 8, 23A, 25 and 37 of the Value Added Tax Act, 1972 as amended by the Finance Acts 1973, 1983, 1991, 1992, 1995, 1997, 1998, 2000 and 2001.
[12] Taxes Consolidation Act 1997, ss. 933 and 945.

11–06 In addition, under the provisions of section 811 of the Taxes Consolidation Act 1997, the Revenue Commissioners may:

− form an opinion that a transaction is a tax avoidance transaction;

− calculate the resulting tax advantage;

− determine the relevant tax consequences; and

− calculate relief from double taxation.

Any person aggrieved by such opinion, calculation or determination may appeal to the Appeal Commissioners. Such appeals may only be made on the following grounds:

− the transaction specified in the notice of opinion is not a tax avoidance transaction; or

− the amount of the tax advantage calculated by the Revenue is incorrect; or

− all or part of the tax consequences determined by the Revenue are not just and reasonable; or

− the amount of relief from double taxation which it is proposed to give the person is insufficient or incorrect.

Appeal procedure

11–07 The procedure applicable to most appeals made to the Appeal Commissioners is dealt with in section 934 of the Taxes Consolidation Act 1997.

The appeal process is initiated by the taxpayer making a formal, written appeal to the inspector of taxes, who acknowledges its receipt. In making the appeal, the taxpayer is usually expressing dissatisfaction with the income or profit figures on which he has been assessed for tax purposes and not the resulting tax liability based on the assessed income or profit figures.

11–08 In advance of the hearing of the appeal, the inspector of taxes issues a Form AH1 setting out the points at issue and relevant legislation. The taxpayer and his adviser are invited to comment and agree the terms of the Form AH1. Form AH1 should contain a statement of matters in dispute rather than agreed facts.

In many cases, appeals may be settled, without recourse to the Appeal Commissioners, by the inspector and the taxpayer (and/or his agent) coming to an agreement in writing that the assessment is to stand or be amended in a particular way. An appeal may be settled by agreement also where it has been partly heard or when it has been adjourned to allow the Appeal Commissioner to make a determination. Tax practitioners and taxpayers must weigh up the costs of the appeal, and the probability of losing, against the amount of tax involved. In many cases, tax practitioners may settle with the Revenue even though they do not agree with its interpretation.

11–09   Appeal Commissioners are appointed by the Minister for Finance under section 850 of the Taxes Consolidation Act 1997. There are normally three Appeal Commissioner posts. Since 1993, there have been two Commissioners. Appeal Commissioners carry out a largely administrative function although they have certain judicial-like discretionary powers (subject to some restrictions), such as the power:

– to administer an oath and examine persons under oath;

– to issue precepts (*i.e.* orders) to obtain information and documentation of assistance in determining the appeal;

– to determine liability;

– to adjourn a case;

– to state a case for the opinion of the High Court; and

– to dismiss an appeal.

As pointed out in para. **11–26**, the role of the Appeal Commissioners can be critical in relation to findings of fact.

11–10   The Appeal Commissioners hear appeals not withdrawn or agreed. They are responsible for appointing the time and place for the hearing of an appeal. The clerk to the Appeal Commissioners advises the tax inspector of the time and place of the hearing. The tax inspector, in turn, notifies the taxpayer and his agent at least 21 days in advance. Many appeals are settled in the 21-day interval between the notice and the date of the appeal hearing.

11–11   The Appeal Commissioners hear appeals by taxpayers against assessments and decisions of the Revenue Commissioners relating to taxes and duties. Appeal procedures, dealt with under section 934 of the Taxes Consolidation Act 1997, are quite legalistic and are similar to court proceedings. Cases involve preparing agreed statements of facts, providing written submissions and often engaging counsel.

11–12   Despite the intention that the appeal process would be a tribunal where taxpayers could plead on their own behalf, the vast majority of appellants are professionally represented by accountants and, in some cases, by solicitors and barristers. Section 934(2) of the Taxes Consolidation Act 1997 deals with representation before the Appeal Commissioners and states:

"(a) On any appeal, the Appeal Commissioners shall permit any barrister or solicitor to plead before them on behalf of the appellant or the inspector or other officer either orally or in writing and shall hear—

    (i)   any accountant, being any person who has been admitted a member of an incorporated society of accountants, or

    (ii) any person who has been admitted a member of the body incorporated under the Companies Act, 1963, on the 31st day of December, 1975, as 'The Institute of Taxation in Ireland'.

  (b) Notwithstanding paragraph (a), the Appeal Commissioners may permit any other person representing the appellant to plead before them where they are satisfied that such permission should be given."

11–13   Cases coming before the Appeal Commissioners are increasingly complex, frequently involving legal counsel on both sides and consideration of extensive oral and documentary evidence. The Appeal Commissioners hear a number of appeals arising from assessments raised by inspectors in the Criminal Assets Bureau.[13] They also have authority to determine whether the Revenue can re-open earlier years, where the taxpayer has availed of the tax amnesty under the 1993 tax amnesty legislation (Waiver of Certain Tax, Interest and Penalties Act 1993), and they determine whether certain powers can be exercised by a Revenue officer.

11–14   Technically speaking, witnesses (other than the taxpayer and the inspector) should wait outside until called. In practice, they may attend throughout the hearing if the parties agree. At an appeal hearing, the Appeal Commissioner hears both sides and makes a decision/determination based on the evidence presented and the relevant legislation, including precedents. Submissions may be both oral and written.

11–15   The two Appeal Commissioners do not normally sit together but rather hear appeals individually. The Appeal Commissioners are not a court of record and all hearings are heard *in camera*. Members of the public are not admitted to hearings and the Appeal Commissioners' and Revenue Commissioners' staff are bound by oath to preserve the confidentiality of the taxpayer's affairs.

11–16   Hearings are relatively informal within the parameters of fair procedure. Either side may call witnesses. It is also common in complex cases and, provided both sides agree, to employ a stenographer to record the proceedings.[14]

    The format of an appeal hearing may include some or all of the following stages:[15]

---

[13] Unlike most other situations, tax inspectors in the Criminal Assets Bureau work anonymously. Thus, in practice, these assessments are raised in the name of the CAB, unlike other tax assessments which are raised in a tax inspector's own name. This is permitted by s.859 of the 1997 Act.

[14] Somers, J. and Lockhart, G., "Taking a VAT case through the courts, Erin a case study" (1998) 11 *Irish Tax Review* 149 at 151.

[15] This is discussed in more detail in Dolan, E., "Income tax appeal hearings" (1999) 12 *Irish Tax Review* 584.

- the hearing usually begins with an opening submission by the taxpayer (possibly including documentary evidence). This is because, in a case of appeal against an assessment, the onus of proof is clearly put upon the taxpayer to show why the assessment is unreasonable. The taxpayer must open the case;[16, 17]

- the taxpayer and taxpayer's witnesses may then be called;

- the inspector may then cross-examine the taxpayer and his witnesses;

- the taxpayer and taxpayer's witnesses may then be re-examined;

- the Revenue makes opening submissions;

- the Revenue calls Revenue witnesses;

- the taxpayer may cross-examine Revenue witnesses;

- the Revenue may re-examine Revenue witnesses;

- the taxpayer makes final submissions;

- the Revenue makes final submissions;

- the taxpayer can then make a final submission, *i.e.* the taxpayer always has the last word.

11–17   In relation to an assessment, an Appeal Commissioner, on the basis of the lawful evidence submitted at a hearing, can decide to:

- increase the assessment;

- reduce the assessment; or

- order that the assessment stand.

11–18   Sections 935 to 938 of the Taxes Consolidation Act 1997 set out the procedures in relation to additional information to be supplied to the Appeal Commissioners. Section 935 gives the Commissioners power to demand schedules containing particulars for their information, as follows:

> "(1) Where notice of appeal has been given against an assessment, the Appeal Commissioners may, whenever it appears to them to be necessary for the purposes of the Tax Acts, issue a precept to the appellant ordering the appellant to deliver to them, within the time limited by the precept, a schedule containing such

---

[16]*Norman v. Golder* (1944) 24 T.C. 293.

[17]However, in the case of a tax avoidance opinion issued by the Revenue under section 811 of the Taxes Consolidation Act 1997, the onus of proof would appear to be clearly on the Revenue. In such cases the Revenue rather than the appellant might open the case.

particulars for their information as they may demand under the authority of the Tax Acts in relation to—

(a) the property of the appellant,
(b) the trade, profession or employment carried on or exercised by the appellant,
(c) the amount of the appellant's profits or gains, distinguishing the particular amounts derived from each separate source, or
(d) any deductions made in determining the appellant's profits or gains.

(2) The Appeal Commissioners may issue further precepts whenever they consider it necessary for the purposes of the Tax Acts, until complete particulars have been furnished to their satisfaction.
(3) A precept may be issued by one Appeal Commissioner.
(4) A person to whom a precept is issued shall deliver the schedule required within the time limited by the precept."

The inspector of taxes may, in turn, object to any information included in any schedule furnished under this provision, stating reasons for the objection.[18] The Appeal Commissioners may question the additional information supplied and may ask for further information.[19] They may summon any person (*e.g.* an employee) to give evidence on oath concerning the taxpayer's assessments.[20]

11–19 The Appeal Commissioner determines the income or profit figures on which the taxpayer is liable to tax and/or the allowances, reliefs, etc. to which the taxpayer is entitled. The Appeal Commissioner does not determine the tax liability. The tax inspector computes this based on the Appeal Commissioner's determination. The Appeal Commissioner records his determination on a prescribed form at the time it is made, and transmits that form to the relevant tax inspector within 10 days. The determination may be given at the hearing or reserved and given subsequently by post.

11–20 The Appeal Commissioner's decisions are final and conclusive, subject to the taxpayer's right to bring the matter before the courts. Application to do so must be made in writing within 10 days after the determination by the Appeal Commissioners. Neither the determination nor the assessment made to give effect to that determination can be altered, unless the taxpayer requires the appeal to be reheard *de novo* by a Circuit Court judge.[21] Unlike the taxpayer, the tax inspector does not have the option of a Circuit Court rehearing except in relation to capital acquisitions tax matters.[22] Either the taxpayer or the tax inspector, however, may require a case to be stated for the opinion of the High Court where there are questions concerning points of law.[23]

[18] Taxes Consolidation Act 1997, s. 936.
[19] *ibid.*, s. 938.
[20] *ibid.*, s. 939.
[21] *ibid.*, s. 942.
[22] Capital Acquisitions Tax Act 1976, s. 52(5)(b).
[23] Taxes Consolidation Act 1997, s.941.

11–21 In relation to customs and excise appeals, there is no right of appeal to the Circuit Court for either party. However, an appeal to the High Court can be made on a point of law. Under the European Union treaties, a customs case, pending decision before the Appeal Commissioners or a court, in which a question is raised and for which there is no judicial remedy under national law, may be referred to the European Court of Justice.

11–22 Appeals are classified as either "quantum", involving a question of fact, or "technical", involving a question of law, although in some cases the appeal will be based on a mixed question of fact and law. Quantum appeals usually require a short hearing. A quantum appeal normally entails the Appeal Commissioner adjudicating between the tax inspector and the taxpayer, based on arguments and assertions made at the appeal hearing. The subject-matter is very often the disputed level of the income or profit figure on which the taxpayer should be assessed for tax following a Revenue audit.

11–23 Technical appeals are more complex involving the application or interpretation of legislation and case law precedents. The subject-matter is usually the correct tax treatment to be applied to particular income or expenditure figures and may result in significant decisions involving points of tax law. A technical appeal may also be a test case brought by the Revenue to seek clarification on a particular point of law. In such cases, the Revenue lists just one test case, which may be representative of a significant number of similar appeals. The Appeal Commissioner's decision is then applied to all such similar cases. Technical appeals may be time-consuming and generally require, in the first instance, a briefing note from the tax inspector setting out the technical and tax issues involved. Either party may engage legal counsel and expert witnesses may be summoned. On average, the Revenue engages counsel in about 40 appeal cases each year.[24] The Appeal Commissioners will also require both parties to make submissions setting out their arguments prior to the commencement of the hearing. They are also expected to cite the authorities they intend to rely upon.

Circuit Court appeals

11–24 Under section 942 of the Taxes Consolidation Act 1997 any person aggrieved by a determination of the Appeal Commissioners in any appeal against an assessment made on that person may, on giving notice in writing to the inspector or such other officer as the Revenue Commissioners shall authorise within 10 days after such determination, require that the appeal shall be reheard

---

[24] *Department of Finance, Report of the Steering Group on the Review of the Office of the Revenue Commissioners* (Government Publications, Dublin, 2000), para. 7.26.

by a judge of the Circuit Court. A small number of appeals, about 10 to 15 a year,[25] proceed from the Appeal Commissioner to the Circuit Court.

The formal appeal process is largely self-contained. Its purpose is mainly to determine either the income or profit figure that should be taxed or the tax treatment of an agreed income or profit figure. However, the appellant, the inspector or the Revenue officer may, if dissatisfied with the determination of the appeal by the judge as being erroneous in point of law, declare such dissatisfaction immediately after the determination and may subsequently, within 21 days, require the judge to state a case for the opinion of the High Court.[26] Any decision of the High Court on the case stated can be appealed to the Supreme Court. This procedure is analogous to the procedure for the statement of a case for the opinion of the High Court following the determination of the Appeal Commissioners.

Even though the statement of a case to the High Court is more expensive, it may in the long run provide a quicker resolution of the dispute and reduce overall costs. Consequently, appeals to the Circuit Court can end up costing substantially more than estimated at the outset. Whether or not the issue is a question of fact or a question of law is very important in this respect, as the High Court can only determine issues of law. There is a better chance that the Circuit Court will give a decision of fact which will not be overturned by the High Court.

High Court hearings

11–25   The statement of a case for the opinion of the High Court following a determination of the Appeal Commissioners is formally instituted by the appellant or the inspector giving notice in writing addressed to the Clerk to the Appeal Commissioners. This notice requires the Appeal Commissioners to state and sign the case to be referred to the High Court. In practice, the case stated is drafted by the losing side and is agreed by the other side for submission to the Appeal Commissioners. In complicated cases, a case stated can take years to agree. The Appeal Commissioners, with the aid of this agreed submission, will then formulate questions to the High Court based on the points of law disputed, and must ask the High Court whether the Appeal Commissioners were correct in law in reaching their decision. This document forms the basis for the High Court appeal hearing.

11–26   Ordinarily, only points of law may be argued before the High Court on a case stated. The distinction between law and fact is a critical distinction, and a determination of fact will only be reviewed by the court if it is clear from the objective facts that no reasonable Commissioner could have made the inferences

---

[25] *Department of Finance, Report of the Steering Group on the Review of the Office of the Revenue Commissioners* (Government Publications, Dublin, 2000), para. 7.27.
[26] Taxes Consolidation Act 1997, s. 943.

that they did from the evidence before them. In this respect, all questions of fact to be determined on a case stated are better described as mixed questions of fact and law.

Thus, the Appeal Commissioners' role is critical in that the High Court will not entertain the re-hearing of questions of fact. The High Court will only overturn questions of fact where the decision is perverse or could not have been reached by any reasonable Commissioner. Provided there are reasonable grounds on which the Commissioner could have reached the decision, it cannot be overturned in the High Court simply because a High Court judge might have arrived at a different decision on the same facts.[27] Given that many critical aspects of Revenue law are matters of fact, this means that decisions of the Appeal Commissioners can often be the most important decisions, especially as far as the Revenue is concerned as they do not have the option, which is open to the taxpayer, to appeal a decision of the Appeal Commissioners to the Circuit Court for a full rehearing.

Supreme Court

11–27   In order to initiate an appeal to the Supreme Court, it is necessary to lodge a notice of appeal with the Registrar of the Supreme Court, requesting an appeal of the High Court decision and establishing the particular questions of law to be considered in the appeal. Care must be taken when drafting the notice of appeal that the matters in issue arise from the facts established before the lower courts as no new facts may ordinarily be presented to the Supreme Court.

11–28   The document grounding the appeal to the Supreme Court must include: (i) the notice of appeal; (ii) the High Court order; (iii) the High Court judgment; and (iv) the case stated to the High Court. After lodging the appeal, submissions setting out the arguments to be made to the Supreme Court must also normally be lodged.

Judicial reviews[28]

11–29   Judicial review is concerned with the fairness of the decision-making process (see also para. **13–03**). Taxpayers may bring an action by way of judicial review to the High Court to challenge the fairness or propriety of administrative acts having a public character. This process is quite different and distinct from the appeals system. Subjecting the Revenue to judicial review has been successfully employed in a number of cases. The grounds for judicial review against a public body such as the Revenue include:

–   lack or excess of jurisdiction;

---

[27] *Mara v. Hummingbird* [1982] I.L.R.M. 421.

[28] For a fuller discussion of this see Hunt, P., "Judicial review in Revenue matters – a brief outline" (1996) 9 *Irish Tax Review* 21.

–   error of law on the face of the record;

–   abuse of jurisdiction;

–   disqualification due to bias or special interest.

11–30   In addition, judicial review may be available where Revenue actions interfere with taxpayers' legitimate expectations. Four different types of relief are relevant in judicial review proceedings against the Revenue:

1.   An order of certiorari from the High Court can quash a determination of, for example, the Appeal Commissioners.

2.   An order of mandamus is a command from the High Court to a public body to perform a public duty of a legal nature.

3.   A declaration determines the rights or legal position of parties to an action by means of a clear statement or declaration of the relevant law by the High Court.

4.   An order of prohibition is directed to an inferior tribunal to prevent it from usurping a jurisdiction.

It is important to note that a judicial review action cannot be taken prior to exhaustion of all other appeal procedures. It is also important to note that judicial review is concerned with the decision-making process and not the decision itself. It is not the function of the court to substitute its opinion on the actual matter in question for that of the authority making the decision such as the Revenue Commissioners.

Tax offences

11–31   Broadly speaking, there are two categories of tax offences. They are (i) the non-submission of returns and (ii) tax evasion under both tax and customs and excise legislation. Forensic accountants are unlikely to be involved in cases concerning failure to submit returns.

Non-submission of returns

11–32   These are relatively routine prosecutions, of which some 1,200 are taken each year.[29] There are no reported problems in relation to these prosecutions. In the case of non-submission of returns, sanctions vary in severity from the charging of interest, surcharges and penalties, together with the publication of the defaulter's name where a penalty is incurred, to the prosecution

---

[29] The Report of the Steering group on the Review of the Office of the Revenue Commissioners (Department of Finance, Government Publications, 2000) states that 1,224 convictions for the non-submission of returns were obtained in 1999.

of the offender and the imposition by the court of a fine or prison sentence, followed again by publication of the offender's name and other relevant details. Cases where taxpayers have not submitted returns are identified by inspectors of taxes and the details of a number of them are notified to the Revenue solicitor who issues formal warning letters. If the warning is not heeded and the return remains outstanding the Revenue solicitor, or outside the Dublin area the appropriate State solicitor, institutes proceedings in the District Court.

11–33 A recent change in the law was an amendment[30] to allow the prosecuting solicitor to apply to the District Court for an order requiring the convicted taxpayer to submit the tax returns outstanding. Previously, conviction did not always result in the submission of tax returns.

Tax evasion

11–34 Most criminal tax investigations requiring accounting work usually involve suspicions of one or more of the following:

– false statements on returns;

– aiding/abetting.

Tax evasion has been described as:

> "...the illegal act of not paying the correct amount of tax which is due. This may involve, for instance, non-disclosure, fraud or forgery and it is invariably a criminal offence when engaged in."[31]

11–35 In a tax fraud case, the taxpayer should normally employ a forensic tax accountant at the earliest possible stage. The objective might be to reach a settlement in advance of trial, as the publicity associated with a court case, even where the taxpayer is successful, can have adverse consequences for his business and personal reputation.

11–36 Tax fraud involves actions knowingly taken by taxpayers with the intention of defrauding the State. The Revenue authorities respond to serious tax evasion by:

– negotiating monetary settlements of tax due, interest thereon and civil penalties;

– the direct prosecution of serious offenders; and

– providing experienced assistance to the Criminal Assets Bureau (CAB) for the purpose of assessing and collecting tax on illegal gains.

---

[30] Taxes Consolidation Act 1997, s. 1078(3A) as inserted by s. 211(c) Finance Act 1999.
[31] Corrigan, K., *Revenue Law* (Round Hall Sweet & Maxwell, Dublin, 2000), para. 24–02.

Serious tax fraud is more often resolved by monetary settlements (which include interest and penalties) than by prosecution. The position has recently been described as follows:

> "...there are very substantial differences between investigations carried out with a view to a monetary settlement and those carried out with a view to prosecution. A criminal investigation is focused on gathering evidence and must be conducted within the demanding rules which apply in the Criminal Justice System whereas an investigation into a tax liability can be conducted within the less demanding rules of the tax code. A suspect in a criminal investigation is not normally obliged to co-operate with the investigation, but a taxpayer whose liability is under enquiry does not have the same constitutional backing for a refusal to co-operate."[32]

Where it appears that the Revenue is not pursuing a financial settlement route, the taxpayer and tax adviser should seek legal advice.

Section 58 of the Taxes Consolidation Act 1997 empowers the Revenue to tax illegal profits (under the general heading "Miscellaneous income"). This is a practical, and sometimes advantageous, alternative to freezing assets from criminal activities. If the taxpayer can show that the income has come from legal sources, the freezing provisions will not be successful.[33] However, there is no need to prove the source is illegal for the income to be taxable.

11–37 According to the *Report of the Steering Group on the Review of the Office of the Revenue Commissioners*,[34] 17 cases have come before the courts since 1996. Proceedings have been completed in 12 of these resulting in 13 convictions (in two of the cases, a conviction was secured against both the company and the director involved) and one acquittal. The tax at risk in these cases was about £3.3 million. Prison sentences were imposed in two cases but were suspended. Fines were imposed in the other cases.

11–38 Following audits and investigations, the Revenue deals with defaulting taxpayers mainly by negotiating monetary settlements (including interest and penalties). In addition to penalties, defaulters also frequently suffer publication of the details in the national newspapers.

Only a small percentage of cases alleging tax evasion are brought before the courts.[35] In the year 2000 there were 32 serious tax fraud cases in the pipeline

---

[32] Donnelly, P., "The future role of prosecutions" (Paper delivered at the Joint Institute of Taxation/Revenue Tax Audit Conference, Kilkenny, November 3/4, 2000).

[33] Statutory freezing orders are covered in paras **21–52** *et seq*.

[34] Department of Finance, (Government Publications, Dublin, 2000), para. 3.48.

[35] This is primarily due to the difficulties associated with successfully prosecuting tax fraud, but the Revenue Commissioners have been using their powers to greater effect. They "conducted two searches under District Court Warrants (Section 905(2)(A) TCA 1997). In the cases in question there was strong suspicions of breaches of the tax code. The searches were conducted in such a manner as to ensure that the material gathered

for prosecution. The tax at risk in these cases is approximately £7 million. Five of these are at present before the courts and 27 are at various stages of investigation or reporting to the Director of Public Prosecutions. These statistics exclude the operations of the CAB.[36]

11–39   There were only eight reported prosecutions for serious tax fraud in the Irish courts in the period between 1997 and June 2000.[37] The major obstacle to mounting successful prosecutions was the burden of evidence required for a conviction.[38] Experience shows that the major obstacle to obtaining a conviction for serious tax evasion is securing the very detailed evidence and onerous proofs required. The issues here go beyond Revenue prosecutions and are common features of the prosecution of "white-collar" crimes. Essentially, evidence, once obtained, must be proved in order to be introduced into a criminal trial.

11–40   The process of a criminal investigation is not directly concerned with the assessment or collection of tax. Separate monetary settlement investigations take place to secure the tax, usually following the prosecution. The amount of tax ultimately collected in a case may exceed the amount involved in the offences prosecuted. Consequently, the figures quoted above for tax at risk are approximations.

Securing a successful conviction in a prosecution case is both time-consuming and resource intensive and requires the involvement of specialist staff. A particular difficulty associated with securing a criminal conviction is the standard of proof that must be met by the prosecution before the courts.

11–41   Chapter 4 of Part 38 of the Taxes Consolidation Act 1997 affords to the Revenue Commissioners very significant powers, including powers of inspection, in relation to tax. These powers include:

---

can be used as evidence if the cases come before the Courts. This type of action is not necessary in every potential prosecution case but it serves to illustrate the different approach which may be necessary in some instances. We have also been making applications to the Courts for access to financial records for the purposes of obtaining evidence for prosecutions (Section 908A TCA 1997). This mirrors the approach the Gardai (sic) use under the Bankers Books of Evidence Act 1879 and is distinguished from the powers contained in Section 906A, 907 and 908 TCA 1997, where certain information in financial institutions can be accessed for inquiry purposes." Quoted from Donnelly, P., "The future role of prosecutions" (Paper delivered at the Joint Institute of Taxation/Revenue Tax Audit Conference, Kilkenny, November 3/4, 2000).
[36] *ibid.*
[37] Dowling, B. and O'Keeffe, A., "Tax cheats face jail in Revenue shake up", *Irish Independent*, September 6, 2000, p. 1.
[38] Department of Finance, *Report of the Steering Group on the Review of the Office of the Revenue Commissioners* (Government Publications, Dublin 2000, para. 7.39).

– a general power to make all necessary inquiries to establish the accuracy of information submitted in relation to the tax affairs of a party;

– power to require the production of accounts, books and documents where the inspector is dissatisfied with the information, if any, provided by the taxpayer;

– power to apply to court for an order requiring a person who has custody or possession of any books or papers relating to income tax or corporation tax to deliver such papers;

– power to obtain from certain persons details of transactions and documents relating to the tax liability of a taxpayer;

– various powers to enter premises and to inspect, remove and take copies of records and documents;

– power to apply to court for an order requiring a financial institution to furnish information in relation to a taxpayer.

Civil and criminal penalties

11–42 The Tax Acts contain a number of sections which set out fines for breaches of the tax code. In addition, there are penalties for criminal offences under tax legislation. The Revenue can proceed to impose fines or, alternatively, bring a case through the courts, in which case the court will apply the appropriate penalties.

11–43 Part 47 of the Taxes Consolidation Act 1997 sets out the various penalties for acts or omissions that have the object or effect of the evasion of income tax, corporation tax or capital gains tax. Sections 1052 to 1058 set out penalties for certain income tax and capital gains tax breaches of the tax code as follows:

– failure to make certain returns – fines of up to £1,200 [€1,520];

– fraudulently or negligently making incorrect returns – penalties of up to £250 [€315] together with the difference (or, in a case of fraud, twice the difference) between the actual tax payable and the tax that would have been payable if the incorrect return had been correct;

– assisting in making incorrect returns – fine of £500 [€630];

– making a false statement to obtain an allowance – depending on the scale of the amount of tax that would have been evaded and on the seriousness of the offence, a fine of up to twice the tax that would have been evaded and/or a prison term of up to eight years;

– obstructing a tax officer in the execution of his duties – fine of £100 [€125].

11–44 Sections 1071 to 1075 impose equivalent penalties for certain corporation tax offences as follows:

- failure to make certain returns – fines of up to £1,000 [€1,265] for the company and up to £200 [€250] for the company secretary;

- fraudulently or negligently making incorrect returns – penalties of up to £1,000 [€1,265] together with the difference (or, in a case of fraud, twice the difference) between the actual tax payable and the tax that would have been payable if the incorrect return had been correct;

- failure of new company to supply certain information – penalty of £500 [€630] for the company and £100 [€125] for the company secretary;

- failure to give notice of liability to corporation tax – penalty of £500 [€630]for the company and £100 [€125] for the company secretary;

- failure to furnish certain information – penalty of £500 [€630] for the company and £100 [€125] for the company secretary;

- fraudulently or negligently furnishing certain incorrect information – penalties of up to £1,000 [€1,265] for the company and up to £200 [€250]for the company secretary.

11–45 In addition to these penalties, Chapter 4 of Part 47 of the 1997 Act as amended by the Finance Act 1999 is concerned with penalties for specified Revenue offences which are imposed by the criminal courts. Section 1078(2) specifying the relevant offences states:

> "A person shall, without prejudice to any other penalty to which the person may be liable, be guilty of an offence under this section if the person—
>
> > (a) knowingly or wilfully delivers any incorrect return, statement or accounts or knowingly or wilfully furnishes any incorrect information in connection with any tax,
> >
> > (b) knowingly aids, abets, assists, incites or induces another person to make or deliver knowingly or wilfully any incorrect return, statement or accounts in connection with any tax,
> >
> > (c) claims or obtains relief or exemption from, or repayment of, any tax, being a relief, exemption or repayment to which, to the person's knowledge, the person is not entitled,
> >
> > (d) knowingly or wilfully issues or produces any incorrect invoice, receipt, instrument or other document in connection with any tax,
> >
> > (dd) (i) fails to make any deduction of dividend with holding tax . . .
> >
> > (e) (i) fails to make any deduction required to be made by the person under section 257(1),
> >
> > (f) (i) fails to make any deduction required to be made by the person under section 734(5), . . .

    (g) knowingly or wilfully fails to comply with any provision of the Acts requiring—
        (i) the furnishing of a return of income, profits or gains, or of sources of income, profits or gains, for the purposes of any tax,
       (ii) the furnishing of any other return, certificate, notification, particulars, or any statement or evidence, for the purposes of any tax,
      (iii) the keeping or retention of books, records, accounts or other documents for the purposes of any tax, or
      (iv) the production of books, records, accounts or other documents, when so requested, for the purposes of any tax,
    (h) knowingly or wilfully, and within the time limits specified for their retention, destroys, defaces or conceals from an authorised officer—
        (i) any documents, or
       (ii) any other written or printed material in any form, including any information stored, maintained or preserved by means of any mechanical or electronic device, whether or not stored, maintained or preserved in a legible form, which a person is obliged by any provision of the Acts to keep, to issue or to produce for inspection,
   (hh) knowingly or wilfully falsifies, conceals, destroys or otherwise disposes of, or causes or permits the falsification, concealment, destruction or disposal of any [certain] books, records or other document[s] . . .
    (i) fails to remit any income tax payable pursuant to Chapter 4 of Part 42, and the regulations under that Chapter, or value-added tax within the time specified in that behalf in relation to income tax or value-added tax, as the case may be, by the Acts, or
    (j) obstructs or interferes with any officer of the Revenue Commissioners, or any other person, in the exercise or performance of powers or duties under the Acts for the purposes of any tax."

The penalties for these offences, which, as noted above, are additional to any other penalties, are specified in subsection (3):

"A person convicted of an offence under this section shall be liable—
    (a) on summary conviction to a fine of £1,500 [€1,900] which may be mitigated to not less than one fourth part of such fine or, at the discretion of the court, to imprisonment for a term not exceeding 12 months or to both the fine and the imprisonment, or
    (b) on conviction on indictment, to a fine not exceeding £100,000 [€126,970] or, at the discretion of the court, to imprisonment for a term not exceeding 5 years or to both the fine and the imprisonment."[39]

The section also provides for the situation where the offence is committed by a body corporate and imposes penalties on certain individuals who consented or connived in the commission of the offence as follows:

---

[39] Taxes Consolidation Act 1997, s. 1078(3) as amended by the Finance Acts 1999 and 2001.

"Where an offence under this section is committed by a body corporate and the offence is shown to have been committed with the consent or connivance of any person who, when the offence was committed, was a director, manager, secretary or other officer of the body corporate, or a member of the committee of management or other controlling authority of the body corporate, that person shall also be deemed to be guilty of the offence and may be proceeded against and punished accordingly."[40]

11–46 Part 47 of the 1997 Act also provides for interest on overdue tax, surcharges and other sanctions for the making of late returns. Section 1086 of the Act provides for the publication of the names of tax defaulters.

11–47 Section 512 of the Income Tax Act 1967 gave extensive powers to the Revenue Commissioners and to the Minister for Finance to mitigate any fine or penalty arising in relation to tax. The section also empowered the Revenue Commissioners to order the discharge of any person imprisoned for any offence before the term of imprisonment had expired. However, these powers of mitigation were restricted significantly by the Waiver of Certain Tax, Interest and Penalties Act 1993 (which enacted what is often referred to as the 1993 Tax Amnesty).

The relevant sections of the 1967 and 1993 Acts were repealed by the Taxes Consolidation Act 1997 and replaced by section 1065 of that Act. Section 1065 provides that no mitigation shall be allowed to a person who could have availed of the 1993 Tax Amnesty and failed, either by making a false declaration or by making no declaration at all, to declare all taxable income and chargeable gains in respect of which tax due and payable had not been paid.

It is noteworthy that section 11 of the 1993 Act, now repealed and re-enacted as section 1056 of the Taxes Consolidation Act 1997, imposed severe penalties where a false statement is made in any return, statement or declaration as to tax or to obtain an allowance, reduction, rebate or repayment of tax. These penalties include a mandatory prison sentence of up to eight years in cases where the effect of the false statement would be to reduce the person's tax liability by £100,000 or more.

11–48 An interesting consideration of taxation penalties can be found in *DPP v. Redmond*[41] in relation to the tax affairs of George Redmond, a former Dublin county manager. The judgment of Hardiman J. examines, *inter alia*, the interaction between civil and criminal tax penalties. He concludes that, in considering imposition of criminal penalties, courts should have regard to any civil penalties paid.

---

[40] Taxes Consolidation Act 1997, s. 1078(5).
[41] unreported, Supreme Court, December 21, 2000.

Effect of voluntary disclosure[42]

11–49 Taxpayers subject to Revenue audit can elect to make voluntary disclosures to the Revenue. Such voluntary disclosures occur during Revenue audits, but voluntary disclosures can occur in other circumstances (*e.g.* taxpayers "walk in off the street"). It is normal procedure at the commencement of a Revenue audit for the Revenue auditor to invite the taxpayer to make a voluntary disclosure. Such disclosures can give the taxpayer substantial benefits and allow the taxpayer a second chance to regularise his affairs without facing the full rigours of the law. Such disclosures can influence the Revenue positively to settle the taxpayer's affairs in a financial manner. Civil penalties arising from monetary settlement will be influenced by the taxpayer's behaviour during audit. In addition, the taxpayer is less likely to find his name in the Revenue's quarterly list of defaulters. The benefits of voluntary disclosure are:

– Possible avoidance of publication of details of the case;

– mitigation of penalties;[43]

– reduced likelihood of prosecution by the Revenue.

11–50 It is important from a legal point of view that clients are made aware of the importance of this process and of the consequences of making erroneous voluntary disclosure. On receipt of a Revenue audit notification, it is essential that there be a consultation between the client and the tax adviser to ascertain whether the case is likely to be a normal revenue audit or whether the case could fall within the prosecution criteria. If the practitioner is misled by his client into believing that none of the criteria exist for prosecution, the practitioner may inadvertently advise the client to make a voluntary disclosure which could have very serious adverse consequences for the client.

11–51 Appendix 3 of the Code of Practice for Revenue Auditors[44] sets out nine offences which are likely to be prosecuted, including:

– use of forged and falsified documents;

– systematic scheme to evade tax;

– false claims for repayments;

---

[42] This topic is discussed more fully in Corcoran, N., "Voluntary disclosure and prosecutions" (1999) 12 *Irish Tax Review* 149.

[43] Maximum mitigation of penalties under the Taxes Acts is 95% (*i.e.* there is an automatic penalty of 5%). Mitigation available is as follows. For full disclosure: unprompted 60%, prompted 40%; full co-operation during Revenue audit 30%; scale and gravity of the offences 15% or less.

[44] Revenue Commissioners (November, 1998). Available at www.revenue.ie/pdf/audcop.pdf.

- failure (as distinct from minor delays) in remitting fiduciary taxes;

- deliberate and serious omissions from tax returns;

- use of offshore bank accounts to evade tax;

- insidious schemes of tax evasion;

- aiding and abetting the commission of a tax offence;

- offences under the Waiver of Certain Tax, Interest and Penalties Act 1993.

11–52 The voluntary disclosure must be made before an examination of books and records begins as part of the Revenue audit process. Under the code of practice, any voluntary disclosure made will be written down by the Revenue auditor. The statement will be read back to the taxpayer to ensure it reflects what has been said. The taxpayer will be asked to confirm his agreement with the written note of the voluntary disclosure and will then initial the page and note the time and date.

Tax case law dealing with accounting principles and practice

11–53 Profit is a key theme common to both accounting and taxation. Accountants seek to record and report it; the Revenue authorities seek to tax it. Where necessary, the courts will decide on the appropriate accounting treatment in computing taxable profits. Normally expert accountants are asked to provide expert opinion in such cases.[45] Cuddigan and Burke[46] point out: "The question of what is correct accounting practice is complicated even with the benefit of expert evidence from accountants." Freedman[47] states:

> "So, it is for the court, in the light of the evidence of accountants, to decide what are the correct principles of commercial accountancy to apply in calculating taxable profits, subject, of course, to any specific statutory provisions. Although this sounds simple, it leaves open some fundamental issues, the central question being whether there are principles of tax law, established by judicial decision or in some way inherent in income tax law, which can override the correct principles of commercial accountancy for tax purposes."

It is therefore appropriate to consider the case law dealing with the interface between accounting and taxation.

---

[45] See para. **6–10** for Pennycuick V.–C.'s famous dictum on this issue.
[46] Cuddigan, J. and Burke, C., "Accounting principles and the computation of tax" (1997) 10 *Irish Tax Review* 434.
[47] Freedman, J., "Defining taxable profit in a changing accounting environment" (1995) No. 5 *British Tax Review* 434-444.

11–54 Case law on this issue has evolved over a period of decades. As there were no accounting standards until the 1970s, courts developed rules of thumb on how to treat certain transactions for tax purposes. However, as accounting standards have become more numerous, the courts are increasingly relying on them. This trend started in *Symons v. Weeks*[48] and continued with *Gallagher v. Jones*.[49]

11–55 Except for a decision of Carroll J. in *Carroll Industries plc v. Ó Cúlacháin*[50] the Irish courts have always endorsed the importance of accounting principles in determining profits for tax purposes. Recent case law in the United Kingdom also positively embraces accounting principles for the purpose of calculating taxable profit. This is probably, at least in part, because accounting standards are recognised explicitly in United Kingdom company legislation but are not referred to specifically in the equivalent statutes in Ireland. In the United Kingdom, the Companies Act 1985, as amended, in England and Wales and the Companies (Northern Ireland) Order 1986, as amended, require annual accounts to state whether they have been prepared in accordance with applicable accounting standards and to give particulars of any material departure from those standards and the reasons for it. Company law in Ireland contains no equivalent provision and while this does not reduce the authority of the standards from the point of view of the preparation of accounts, it undoubtedly gives less prominence to both the use of, and departures from, accounting standards in the preparation of accounts. Tax legislation in the United Kingdom also requires profits to be calculated based on accounting principles, and embraces the fundamental requirement that accounts should show a true and fair view.[51] Nevertheless, it is submitted that it would be very unwise for any party to attempt to argue that they need not pay any heed to the accounting standards adopted by the accountancy bodies in Ireland.

Principles in tax law relevant to accounting

11–56 For tax purposes, financial statements must be prepared in accordance with generally accepted accounting principles. However, a number of legal principles have generally been held by the courts to override any conflicting accounting principles.

---

[48] [1983] S.T.C. 195.
[49] [1993] S.T.C. 537.
[50] [1988] I.R. 705.
[51] s. 42(1) of the United Kingdom Finance Act 1998 provides that income taxable under Schedule D, Case I or Case II, must be "computed on an accounting basis which gives a true and fair view".

Accounting principles – Decisions of United Kingdom courts[52]

11-57 A number of decisions in the United Kingdom indicate that the courts are increasingly taking cognisance of accounting principles, particularly in relation to determining allowable tax deductions. The importance of accounting principles in calculating taxable profits was recognised in *Sun Insurance Office v. Clark* as follows:

> "It is plain that the question of what is or is not profit or gain must primarily be one of fact, and of fact to be ascertained by the tests applied in ordinary business. Questions of law can only arise when ... some express statutory direction applies and excludes ordinary commercial practice, or where, by reason of its being impracticable to ascertain the facts sufficiently, some presumption has to be invoked to fill the gap."[53]

11–58 In *Whimster & Co v. IRC,* it was held by the Court of Session in Scotland that accounting treatment must conform with both ordinary accounting principles and the rules of the Income Tax Act:

> "... the account of profit and loss to be made up for the purposes of ascertaining that difference must be framed consistently with the ordinary principles of commercial accounting so far as applicable and in conformity with the rules of the Income Tax Act."[54]

11–59 In *Odeon Associated Theatres Ltd v. Jones*, the view was also put forward that accounts should be prepared to conform with generally accepted accounting principles, and should then be adjusted for an express prohibition in the relevant statute:

> "... first one must ascertain the profits of the trade in accordance with ordinary principles of commercial accountancy.... Secondly, one must adjust the account by reference to the express prohibitions contains in the relevant statute...."[55]

Both the *Whimster* and *Odeon* cases have been considered in the Irish courts and are discussed in this context in paras **11–64** *et seq.*

11–60 In the joint cases *Gallagher v. Jones* and *Threlfall v. Jones*,[56] the taxpayer claimed a deduction when it was paid. The Revenue argued that the payment would be recorded in the accounts over a number of years and should

---

[52] See generally Freedman, J. "Defining taxable profit in a changing accounting environment" (1993) No. 6 *British Tax Review* pp. 434-444; and Freedman, J. "Ordinary principles of commercial accounting – clear guidance or a mystery tour?" *British Tax Review* (1995) Vol. X, No. 5 pp. 468-478.
[53] (1912) 6 T.C. 59 at 78, *per* Lord Haldane.
[54] (1925) 12 T.C. 813 at 823, *per* the Lord President.
[55] [1971] 2 All E.R. 407 at 413, *per* Pennycuick V.C.
[56] [1993] S.T.C. 537.

therefore be allowed for tax purposes in a similar way. The Court of Appeal
accepted the Revenue's argument. In so doing, the courts were accepting the
overriding importance of the commercial substance of the transaction over its
strict legal form (see paras **11–73** *set seq.*). The arguments set out in the judgment
are discussed by Cuddigan and Burke.[57] They state that Harman J. supported
the appeal by the taxpayer, basing his decision on the two cases: *Vallambrosa
Rubber Company Ltd v. Farmer*[58] and *Duple Motor Bodies Ltd v. Ostime*[59]
Harman J. in the Chancery Division said:

> "In the result, it seems to me that because of the principle I see established by
> the House unanimously and in clear words in Duple Motor actual expenditure
> properly incurred and referable to the trade is properly chargeable in the accounts
> for the year in which it falls due notwithstanding that prudent and proper principles
> of commercial accounting would draw the commercial accounts of the trading
> enterprise on a different basis and would spread forward the actual expenditure
> incurred over future years so as to give a more balanced view of the nature of the
> success or failure of the trade."[60]

11–61 The Crown successfully appealed this decision. Bingham, M.R.
disagreed with Harman J.'s conclusions stating that it was doubtful whether it
was intended to lay down general overriding rules in the earlier decisions cited
by Harman J. He stated:

> "… in the ordinary way the computation of a taxpayer's trading profits and losses
> for tax purposes must be made according to the ordinary principles of commercial
> accountancy. But they also agreed that the application of such principles is subject
> to any rule of tax law, statutory or otherwise which precludes or limits such
> application."[61]

In discussing the role of accounting principles in computing taxable profits,
Bingham M.R. had this to say:

> "… Subject to any express or implied statutory rule, of which there is none here,
> the ordinary way to ascertain the profits or losses of a business is to apply accepted
> principles of commercial accountancy. That is the very purpose for which such
> principles are formulated. As has often been pointed out, such principles are not
> static: they may be modified, refined and elaborated over time as circumstances
> change and accounting insights sharpen."[62]

Bingham M.R. found that judges could only overrule a generally accepted
accounting treatment in limited circumstances, as follows:

---

[57] Cuddigan, J. and Burke, C., "Accounting principles and the computation of tax" (1997)
10 *Irish Tax Review* 434.
[58] (1910) 5 T.C. 529.
[59] (1961) 39 T.C. 537.
[60] [1993] S.T.C. 199 at 216.
[61] [1993] S.T.C. 537 at 544.
[62] *ibid.* at 555.

"... I find it hard to understand how any judge-made rule could over-ride the application of a generally accepted rule of commercial accountancy which (a) applied to the situation in question, (b) was not one of two or more rules applicable to the situation in question and (c) was not shown to be inconsistent with the true facts or otherwise inapt to determine the true profits or losses of the business."[63]

11–62 In *Johnston v. Britannia Airways Ltd*,[64] the taxpayer was obliged under air navigation rules to have a major overhaul of its engines every 17,000 miles. The companies applied the accruals basis of accounting[65] and charged overhaul costs based on an estimate calculated by reference to the number of airmiles flown. The Revenue argued that the deduction should be based on actual expenditure incurred, rather than on an allocation against income based on an estimate of the actual future overhaul costs to be paid for. The court found in favour of the taxpayer, supporting the application of generally accepted accounting principles in the calculation of taxable profits. This judgment confirmed the decision in *Owen v. Southern Railways of Peru Ltd*[66] when it was held that a tax deduction based on a provision (rather than actual expenditure) was acceptable provided (i) exclusion of the provision would render the company accounts inaccurate and (ii) the provision is accurately calculated. Knox J. said:

"the Court is slow to accept that accounts prepared in accordance with the accepted principles of commercial accountancy are not adequate for tax purposes as a true statement of the taxpayer's profits for the relevant period."[67]

11–63 Two more recent cases[68] in the United Kingdom provide further confirmation of the importance of generally accepted accounting principles as conclusive for tax purposes, in the absence of a specific statutory rule.[69] The authorities held that provisions were allowable tax deductions, contrary to the Inland Revenue's argument that they anticipate future expenditure and, as such, should not be deductible in arriving at taxable profit. Of particular interest, is the Inland Revenue's acceptance of these decisions by (i) not appealing the decisions and (ii) its statement that "there is no longer a rule of law which denies provisions for "anticipated" losses or expenses."[70]

---

[63] [1993] S.T.C. 537 at 555–556.
[64] [1994] S.T.C. 763.
[65] Whereby costs are charged against revenue as incurred rather than when paid in cash.
[66] (1953–1956) 36 T.C. 602.
[67] [1994] S.T.C. 763 at 782.
[68] *Herbert Smith (a firm) v. Honour* [1999] S.T.C. 173; and *Jenners Princes Edinburgh Ltd v. IRC* [1998] S.T.C. (SCD) 196.
[69] Macleod, J.S., "Tax law and accountancy practice" (2000) 13 *Irish Tax Review* 171.
[70] "Tax provisions move closer to accounting practice" Inland Revenue Press Release 137/ 99, July 20, 1999.

Accounting principles – Decisions of Irish courts

11–64   Two United Kingdom cases (*Whimster* and *Odeon*) (see paras **11–58** *et seq.*) have been considered by the Irish courts. More recent United Kingdom cases have not yet been addressed in Irish cases. The larger cases clearly give great weight to the importance of accounting principles in arriving at taxable profit. Thus, the United Kingdom courts have recognised the fundamental importance of accountancy principles in arriving at taxable profits. It is likely that the Irish courts will also place considerable emphasis on accounting principles, especially given the growth in accounting standards and pronouncements which provide guidance on what constitutes generally accepted accounting principles which would not have been available in older cases.

11–65   At least three significant Irish tax cases deal with the interaction of accounting principles and tax law. These decisions lend general support to the view that accounting treatment should also be followed for tax purposes unless there are specific tax provisions which outlaw the accounting treatment. There is a fundamental acceptance of the *Odeon* principle by the Supreme Court in two of the three Irish cases. The judgment of Carroll J. in the third case is not so supportive of *Odeon*.

In *Cronin v. Cork & County Property Ltd,*[71] the Revenue's case was that on ordinary principles of commercial accountancy the profit or loss should be based on the accounts, adjusted where necessary in accordance with statutory provisions. Both the High Court and the Supreme Court found for the Revenue, affirming the *Whimster* and *Odeon* decisions that the use of ordinary principles of accountancy in ascertaining the correct mode of dealing with the profits of a trade.

In *Carroll Industries plc v. Ó Cúlacháin,*[72] the plaintiff attempted to persuade the courts that taxable profits should be calculated by reference to current cost accounting principles (*i.e.* accounting principles that would take into account the effects of inflation – at that time Ireland suffered from high rates of inflation). The case was vigorously argued and no less than nine accountants gave evidence.

This case also discussed whether the prevailing (*i.e.* current) system of accounting is the correct test (in the context of the case, whether historic cost accounting principles (the prevailing system) or current cost accounting principles should be applied). Carroll J. stated:

> "I do not think that the 'prevailing' system is the correct test. Time and again the courts have held that no one system should be applied. If there is a system of commercial accounting which is appropriate to the company involved and which correctly ascertains the full profits for tax purposes being the receipts during the year and the expenditure laid out to earn those receipts, then it is possible that the system may be accepted. But conversely, if there is a system of commercial accounting which is appropriate to the company involved but which does not

[71] [1986] 1 I.R. 559; (1984) 4 I.T.R. 300.
[72] [1988] 1 I.R. 705; [1988] 4 I.T.R. 135.

correctly ascertain the full profits for tax purposes then that system cannot be used for the computation of tax."[73]

Carroll J. discussed the judgments in *Whimster* and *Odeon* and favoured *Whimster*. However, the judgment appears to suggest that ordinary principles of commercial accountancy should be followed unless they fall foul of a statutory provision or otherwise fail to achieve the objective of measuring income and expenditure appropriately.

In *Murnaghan Bros Ltd v. O'Maoldomhnaigh*,[74] it was held that the accounting treatment was strong evidence of the commercial reality of the transaction and the judgment in *Odeon* was cited to support this view.

Accounting principles and revenue versus capital expenditure

11–66   In dealing with the question of what is revenue and what is capital expenditure, the courts have consistently held that the principles of commercial accountancy must be observed. In the *Odeon* case, Pennycuick V.-C. granted the taxpayer's appeal in the Chancery Division and the Crown's appeal of this decision was dismissed. On appeal, Salmon L.J. stated in the Court of Appeal:

> "In my judgment the principle is well established, namely, that, in determining what is capital expenditure and what is revenue expenditure in order to arrive at the profit for tax purposes in any particular year, the Courts will follow the established principles of sound commercial accounting unless they conflict with the law as laid down in any statute."[75]

Denning M.R., however, expressed reservations about following generally accepted principles in all cases, as follows:

> "The Courts have always been assisted greatly by the evidence of accountants. Their practice should be given due weight; but the Courts have never regarded themselves as being bound by it. It would be wrong to do so. The question of what is capital and what is revenue is a question of law for the Courts."[76]

This view (treatment of expenditure in accordance with the ordinary principles of commercial accountancy) was confirmed in two Irish cases: *S Ltd v. O'Sullivan*[77] and *Dolan v. AB Co Ltd*.[78]

11–67   Whether the distinction between capital and revenue expenditure is a question of fact or law has been considered in a number of cases. This is important

---

[73][1988] 1 I.R. 705 at 716.
[74][1991] 1 I.R. 455.
[75][1973] Ch. 288 at 294.
[76]*Heather v. P-E Consulting Group Ltd* (1972) 48 T.C. 293.
[77][1972] 2 I.T.R. 602.
[78][1968] 2 I.T.R. 515.

in relation to whether an appeal is heard by the Circuit Court or the High Court (the High Court can only hear cases stated on questions of law – see discussion at paras **11–25** *et seq.*). After a lengthy discussion of the issue, Corrigan concludes that what is capital and what is revenue appears to be a question of fact and law, informed by the correct principles of commercial accountancy.[79] That this is so is endorsed by the decision of the Supreme Court in *Brosnan v. Mutual Enterprises Ltd*[80] where it was held that a foreign exchange loss was correctly treated as being revenue in nature.

Valuation of stocks and work-in-progress

11–68   Although some issues concerning stock have come before the Irish courts, the issue of stock valuation *per se* has not been so considered. In the case *Duple Motor Bodies Ltd v. Ostime*,[81] the taxpayer valued stock on the basis of direct costs only, excluding indirect costs. The court accepted that either method of accounting for stock was in accordance with accepted accounted principles and was not in contravention of any income tax rules. This case has been superseded by considerable developments in commercial accountancy principles. In particular, is it now widely accepted (and, for example, required by SSAP 9 *Stocks and Long-Term Contracts*) that stock valuation should include indirect production overheads and, in some cases, indirect overheads not specifically of a production nature. In *Pearce (Inspector of Taxes) v. Woodall Duckham Ltd*,[82] in the context of valuation of contract work-in-progress, attributable overheads and a proportion of profit were included in the valuation, consistent with the recommendations of SSAP 9.

Accounting for provisions and contingencies

11–69   Provisions have been accepted by the courts as valid deductions for tax purposes provided they can be calculated with reasonable accuracy. In the case of *Owen v. Southern Railway of Peru Ltd*, a charge in respect of contingent payments was also accepted as a tax deduction, provided it could be calculated with reasonable reliability:

> "... whatever the legal analysis, I think that, for liabilities as for debts, their proper treatment in annual statements of profit depends not upon the legal form but on the trader's answer to two separate questions. The first is: have I adequately stated my profits for the year if I do not include some figure in respect of these

---

[79]Corrigan, K. *Revenue Law* (Round Hall Sweet & Maxwell, Dublin, 2000), para. **11–429** *et seq.*
[80][1995] 1 I.L.R.M. 45.
[81](1961) 39 T.C. 537.
[82][1978] 1 W.L.R. 832; [1978] 2 All E.R. 793.

obligations? The second is: do the circumstances of the case, which include the techniques of established accounting practice, make it possible to supply a figure reliable enough for the purpose?"[83]

11–70 This case was approved and upheld in *Johnston v. Britannia Airways Ltd* [84] and in *Herbert Smith (a firm) v. Honour*.[85] It is important to point out that the Irish Revenue authorities have issued a tax briefing confirming that provisions computed in accordance with FRS 12 *Provisions, Contingent Liabilities and Contingent Assets* will be deductible.[86]

Prior year adjustments

11–71 The court found in *Pearce (Inspector of Taxes) v. Woodall Duckham Ltd*[87] that prior year adjustments should be taxed in the year of adjustment rather than in prior years.[88]

In the 1929 case, *Commissioner of Income Tax (Bombay) v. Ahmedabad New Cotton Mills Company Ltd*,[89] opening stocks were undervalued. The Court of Appeal held that they should be valued correctly even though this breached the consistency principle that opening stock should be the same as the closing stock of the previous period. This would under modern day accounting principles also be treated as a prior year adjustment arising from a fundamental error rather than a change in accounting policy. However, Orr L.J. distinguished this case from the *Pearce* case on the grounds that the *Bombay* case was a correction of an undervaluation, rather than a change in the basis of valuation.

11–72 The Irish Revenue has referred to the treatment of prior year adjustments for tax purposes arising from a change in accounting policy on the implementation of FRS 12. They state:

> "The treatment, for tax purposes, of such an accounting adjustment [i.e. a prior year adjustment] will depend on whether the provision was allowed for tax purposes for the period in which it was made.
>
> • If the provision was allowed for tax purposes for the period in which it was made, the accounting adjustment should be included in the profits for tax purposes of the period in which the change in accounting policy took place."[90]

---

[83] (1953–1956) 36 T.C. 602 at 644, *per* Lord Radcliffe.

[84] [1994] S.T.C. 763.

[85] [1999] S.T.C. 173.

[86] "Accounting rules and taxation" *Tax Briefing* (September 2000) 41 pp. 14-15. Available at www.revenue.ie/publications/txbrefng/tb41.pdf.

[87] [1978] 1 W.L.R. 832; [1978] 2 All E.R. 793.

[88] See Ramsay, C., "Pearce (Inspector of Taxes) v Woodall-Duckham Ltd." (2000) 13 *Irish Tax Review* 389.

[89] [1929] 46 T.L.R. 68.

[90] "Accounting rules and taxation" *Tax Briefing* (September 2000) 41 p. 15. Available at www.revenue.ie/publications/txbrefng/tb41.pdf.

Commercial substance over strict legal form

11–73   As discussed in paras **11–57** *et seq.*, a number of recent cases in the
United Kingdom have considered the application of generally accepted
accounting principles for tax purposes. Under generally accepted accounting
principles, transactions should be accounted for in accordance with the
commercial substance of the transaction rather than its strict legal form. This
raises the question whether the substance over form approach should also apply
in calculating taxable profits. The issue of substance over form has been
considered in a number of United Kingdom cases. In *Commissioners of Inland
Revenue v. Duke of Westminster*[91] the House of Lords stated:

> "If, on the other hand, the doctrine [of substance over form] means that you may
> brush aside deeds, disregard the legal rights and liabilities arising under a contract
> between parties, and decide the question of taxability or non taxability upon the
> footing of the rights and liabilities of the parties being different from what in law
> they are, then I entirely dissent from such a doctrine."

11–74   The decisions in *McGrath v. McDermott*[92] and in *O'Sullivan v. P.
Ltd*[93] also confirmed the doctrine of the *Irc v. Duke of Westminster*[94] case
(which did not consider accounting issues *per se*) – it is the legal relationships
created between the parties rather than the commercial substance of a transaction
that should determine how the transaction should be taxed.

11–75   Thus, following this judgment, for tax purposes the strict legal form of
a transaction overrode its commercial substance. However, this decision has
more recently been considered by the courts with a different outcome. Cases,
such as *Furniss v. Dawson*,[95] have found in favour of the "substance over form"
principle and have found that the commercial substance of a transaction can be
more important than its strict legal form in determining its treatment for tax
purposes. The statutory provisions dealing with tax avoidance transactions,
introduced by following the *McGrath v. McDermott* case by section 86 of the
Finance Act 1989 and now enshrined in section 811 of the Taxes Consolidation
Act 1997, show the intention of the legislature to impose taxation where the
legal form of a transaction might cause tax to be avoided in circumstances where
the commercial substance represents a transaction that would ordinarily be
taxable.

---

[91] [1936] A.C. 1.
[92] [1988] I.R. 258.
[93] [1962] 2 I.T.R. 464; (1962) 3 I.T.C. 355.
[94] [1936] A.C. 1 at 25 *per* Lord Russell of Kilburn.
[95] [1984] A.C. 474.

Role of forensic accountants in taxation cases

11–76   As stated at the beginning of this chapter, forensic accountants are likely to act in disputes arising from tax avoidance schemes, in cases involving interpretation of accountancy principles and in cases of tax evasion, amounting to tax fraud.

Whereas tax accountants will almost always be involved in an advisory capacity, and sometimes as witnesses of fact, forensic accountants can provide independent expert evidence (frequently in tax avoidance cases) of the taxpayer's financial circumstances.

Where Revenue offences have allegedly been committed, forensic accountants have more limited roles and will be involved less often in such cases. However, an important ingredient in the more serious offences, and by definition those offences that are likely to attract the stiffest penalties, is the extent to which the taxpayer knowingly, willingly, intentionally or fraudulently committed the offence. Where such issues arise, forensic accountants may well be engaged on one or both sides to examine the available evidence demonstrating or casting doubt on the intent behind the actions of the taxpayer and to express an expert opinion on the existence and degree of such intent.

11–77   Forensic accountants should make sure to:

– give advice appropriate to the circumstances. It is important that the forensic accountant understand the perspective of the regulatory authorities being dealt with;

– obtain legal advice himself if in doubt.

11–78   There are significant difficulties and disincentives in attempting to prosecute serious tax fraud in Ireland. The nature of the criminal process can make it all too easy to escape prosecution (while not necessarily avoiding liability).

Concluding comment

11–79   The discussion above demonstrates that an issue central to almost all significant tax disputes is the determination of the appropriate accounting treatment for specified transactions. Indeed, if current trends continue, the relevant accounting standards and rules will be the single most important element of this determination. Forensic accountants can have a major role to play here. They can:

– examine the nature and size of the transactions in question;

– identify the acceptable accounting treatments applicable to the transactions;

- quantify the effect of the use of various possible accounting treatments;
- advise on the most appropriate treatment and the arguments for and against each one;
- assess the position taken by the other side.

This analysis can be vitally important in preparing for and delivering a case arising from a tax dispute.

ACCOUNTANTS' LIABLITY

CHAPTER 12

ACCOUNTANTS' LIABLITY

12–01   One area for which the experience and expertise of expert accountants is ideally suited (but in which accountants are often reluctant to become involved) is the liability, usually arising from negligence, of accountants themselves. The common reluctance of accountants to participate in such cases as an expert is normally based on a feeling of "there but for the grace of God go I". However, the involvement of expert accountants on all sides of such cases is essential to their proper conduct. In practice, accountants do act as experts for either side in cases involving liability of members of their profession, and provide a very valuable service in doing so.

12–02   In what circumstances can an auditor or a reporting accountant be found legally liable on the strength of a report signed by him? This is a question that has exercised the minds of accountants in professional practice for decades. In recent years, as the size and frequency of claims against auditors has increased, the question has also affected the economics of the practice of accountancy, as the providers of professional indemnity insurance cover have demanded increasingly higher premium levels to reflect the increasing risk.

12–03   In fact, many claims against auditors are compromised before the litigation has been seen through to its conclusion, as insurers take over the decision-making process and determine that the risk of an enormous award is too great to run. Many audit firms that have settled claims will admit privately that they would have preferred to have taken the case to a conclusion, both on its merits and in an attempt to deter future potential litigants from taking cases against auditors.

12–04   The difference in views between insurers and their clients does not, however, merely reflect a different attitude to risk; it also arises because the law differs between jurisdictions and cannot be regarded as settled.

12–05   Issues that must be addressed by the court in deciding whether an accountant is liable for his negligence are as follows:

– a duty of care must be shown to have been owed by the accountant to the plaintiff;

– the accountant must be shown to have been negligent;

447

– the plaintiff must be shown to have suffered loss or damage;

– the negligent action(s) must be shown to have caused the plaintiff's loss or damage.

12–06 Before addressing aspects of the law of negligence as it applies to the liability of accountants in particular, it is worth noting certain principles that apply in the context of professional negligence generally. This chapter examines liability of accountants from three different perspectives. First, the duty of care is considered. Secondly, standards of care in determining whether there was professional negligence are examined. The chapter concludes with a discussion of the role of expert accountants in such cases.[1]

Duty of care

12–07 Liability for a loss suffered due to negligence on the part of an accountant or other professional is based on a duty of care owed to the complaining party by the professional. Such a duty of care can be established relatively easily where there is either a contract between the professional and the other party (in which case an action probably lies in breach of contract also) or where the other party is an addressee of the report from the accountant. A duty of care may also exist between the accountant and another party who, although not an addressee of the report, relies on it with the knowledge and agreement of the accountant. Whether an accountant owes a duty of care to a party who relies on his report without the accountant's express knowledge or agreement is a much more difficult area.

Duty of care of auditors to third parties

12–08 For many years, accountants and other professionals believed, with justification, that, whilst they clearly owed a duty of care to the parties to whom their reports were addressed (usually the shareholders of a company), no duty of care to any other party arose other than in very specific and restricted circumstances, such as fraud or through the existence of some other clearly defined contractual or fiduciary duty. However, this comfortable position became a thing of the past with the landmark decision in *Hedley Byrne & Co Ltd v. Heller and Partners Ltd*,[2] which effectively became Irish law through the

---

[1] Further information on accountants and professional negligence is to be found in Lemar, C.J. and Mainz, A.J. (eds), *Litigation Support* (4th ed., Butterworths, London, 1999), Chapter 8; MacGregor, G. and Hobbs, I., *Expert Accounting Evidence: A Guide for Litigation Support* (Accountancy Books, London, 1998), Chap. 26; and Taub, M., Rapazzini, A., Bond, C., Solon, M., Brown, A., Murrie, A., Linnell, K. and Burn, S., *Tolley's Accountancy Litigation Support* (Butterworths, London, looseleaf), Part VI, para. 95.
[2] [1964] A.C. 465.

judgment of Davitt P. in *Securities Trust Ltd v. Hugh Moore and Alexander Ltd.*[3] Those decisions had the effect of extending the duty of care beyond actual contractual relationships to where there was a "special relationship" equivalent to a contract between the parties. The learned judge in the latter case summarised the extended duty of care as follows:

> "The proposition that circumstances may create a relationship between two parties in which, if one seeks information from the other and is given it, that other is under a duty to take reasonable care to ensure that the information give is correct, has been accepted and applied in the case of *Hedley Byrne & Co. Ltd. v. Heller and Partners Ltd.*, recently decided by the House of Lords."[4]

In the words of Lord Morris in *Hedley Byrne*:

> "… if in a sphere in which a person is so placed, that others could reasonably rely upon his judgment or his skill or upon his ability to make careful inquiry, a person takes it upon himself to give information or advice to, or allows his information or advice to be passed on to, another person who, as he knows, or should know, will place reliance upon it, then a duty of care will arise".[5]

Duty of care of professionals to third parties

12–09 The courts have grappled with the issue of duty of care of professionals to third parties on many occasions since the seminal case of *Hedley Byrne & Co Ltd v. Heller & Partners Ltd*[6] An example of an Irish court recently addressing the matter at length is *Doran v. Delaney*[7] in which the central issue was whether the solicitor of the vendor of a property owed a duty of care to a third party (the purchaser of the property) with whom he had no contractual relationship. In his judgment, Keane J. (as he then was) relied on the judgment of Devlin L.J. in *Hedley Byrne* in describing the potential breadth of liability of professionals:

> "In the course of his speech in *Hedley Byrne & Co. Ltd. v. Heller & Partners Ltd.* [1964] A.C. 465, the case which, as applied in a number of decisions in this jurisdiction, is authority for the proposition that liability for negligent mis-statements can arise in our law, even in the absence of a contractual relationship, Devlin L.J. said, at pp. 528 and 529:
>
> > 'I think, therefore, that there is ample authority to justify your Lordships in saying now that the categories of special relationship, which may give rise to a duty to take care in word as well as in deed are not limited to contractual

---

[3] [1964] I.R. 417.
[4] *ibid.* at 421.
[5] [1964] A.C. 465 at 503.
[6] [1964] A.C. 465.
[7] [1998] 2 I.R. 61.

relationships or to relationships of fiduciary duty, but include also relationships which in the words of Lord Shaw in *Nocton v. Lord Ashburton* [1914] A.C. 932 at p. 972 are "equivalent to contract" that is, where there is an assumption of responsibility in circumstances in which, but for the absence of consideration, there would be a contract. Where there is an express undertaking, an express warranty as distinct from mere representation, there can be little difficulty. The difficulty arises in discerning those cases in which the undertaking is to be implied. In this respect the absence of consideration is not relevant. Paying for information or advice is very good evidence that it is being relied on and that the informer or adviser knows that it is. Where there is no consideration, it will be necessary to exercise greater care in distinguishing social and professional relationships and between those which are of a contractual character and those which are not. It may often be material to consider whether the adviser is acting purely out of good nature or whether he is getting his reward in some indirect form.' "[8]

Keane J. went on to apply this reasoning to the case at hand:

"... while the primary duty of the solicitor acting for the vendor in circumstances such as arose here, is, under common law and by virtue of contract, to protect his own client, that obligation is perfectly consistent with the existence of a duty of care in certain circumstances to the purchaser."[9]

He then placed boundaries around the liability to third parties, by relying on a different English case:

"It is also clear that the transmission by a solicitor to a third party of information which turns out to be inaccurate and upon which the third party relied to his detriment does not, of itself, afford a cause of action in negligence to the injured third party. The factors necessary to give rise to liability were set out by Jauncey L.J. in the passage so frequently referred to in the present case in *Midland Bank v. Cameron, Thom Peterkin and Duncans* [1988] S.L.T. 611 as follows at p. 616:

'In my opinion four factors are relevant to a determination of the question whether in a particular case a solicitor, while acting for a client, also owed a duty of care to a third party:-
   (1) the solicitor must assume responsibility for the advice or information furnished to the third party.
   (2) the solicitor must let it be known to the third party expressly or impliedly that he claims, by reason of his calling, to have the requisite skill or knowledge to give the advice or furnish the information;
   (3) the third party must have relied upon that advice or information as a matter for which the solicitor has assumed personal responsibility; and

[8] [1998] 2 I.R. 61 at 73.
[9] *ibid.* at 73–74.

(4) the solicitor must have been aware that the third party was likely so to rely.'

It is clear that, at least in cases where those four factors are present, a solicitor may be held liable in negligence to a third party under the more general principle laid down in *Hedley Byrne & Co. Ltd. v. Heller & Partners Ltd.* [1964] A.C. 465."[10]

12–10 It is clear that the courts are quite prepared, in appropriate circumstances, to find that a negligent professional is liable to a third party for losses suffered by that party as a result of the negligence, even where the professional owes no direct contractual or other duty to the third party.

Circumstances in which a duty of care is owed

12–11 In the years since the *Hedley Byrne* decision the limits on the liability of auditors to third parties have changed frequently, first resulting in an expansion of the range of situations in which auditors could be found to owe a duty of care, and later reducing that range. The House of Lords took the opportunity to clarify the position somewhat in the celebrated case *Caparo Industries plc v. Dickman.*[11] This decision was widely interpreted as being favourable to accountants in that it appeared to set restrictive boundaries around the circumstances in which a duty of care to third parties could arise. However, it can be seen from the judgments themselves, and from subsequent case law, that the issue cannot be resolved by a comprehensive set of rigid rules –judgment must still be exercised in each set of specific circumstances. This is clear from the conditions necessary for a duty of care to arise, as set out in the *Caparo* decision, which can be summarised as follows:

(i) the damage to the third party was reasonably foreseeable by the accountant;

(ii) there was sufficient "proximity" between the third party and the accountant – this usually means that the accountant knew of the existence of the third party and knew that the third party would probably rely on the accountant's work for a particular transaction; and

(iii) it would be fair, just and reasonable to impose a duty of care in all the circumstances of the case.

12–12 Clearly all three of these conditions, but especially the third, require the application of significant judgement. In addition, the words of Lord Bridge emphasise the lack of precision in the second condition:

"The concepts of proximity and fairness…are not susceptible of any such precise definition as would be necessary to give them utility as practical tests, but amount

---

[10] [1998] 2 I.R. 61 at 74.
[11] [1990] 2 A.C. 605

in effect to little more than convenient labels to attach to the features of different specific situations which, on a detailed examination of all the circumstances, the law recognises pragmatically as giving rise to a duty of care of a given scope."[12]

The decision in *Caparo* is therefore regarded as having had less than the hoped-for effects on the appetite for litigation of putative plaintiffs, and on the related potential exposure of professional accountants to large awards of damages and prohibitive professional indemnity insurance costs.

12–13   It is apparent that the courts have been unwilling or unable to define a clear set of principles to allow determination of when a duty of care exists and instead look to the specific circumstances of each particular case before deciding the criteria to apply. As a consequence, the law continues to develop in this area.

A number of broad principles can probably be stated, however, to help guide an analysis based on the current state of the law. These are:

1.   An auditor owes a duty of care to those to whom his report is addressed – usually the shareholders.

2.   Where an auditor or accountant is a party to a contractual relationship and provides information within the terms of that contract, he owes a duty of care to any other party to the contract who relies on that information.

3.   Where an auditor or accountant is guilty of fraud, he will be liable to the full extent of all losses flowing from the fraud, without any deduction for contributory negligence.

4.   Although an auditor or accountant owes no general duty of care to third parties, a duty of care does arise in certain circumstances. Generally, if all of the following conditions are fulfilled, a duty of care arises:
     (a)   the damage to the third party was reasonably foreseeable by the accountant;
     (b)   there was sufficient "proximity" between the third party and the accountant – this usually means that the accountant knew of the existence of the third party and knew that the third party would probably rely on the accountant's work for a particular transaction; and
     (c)   it would be fair, just and reasonable to impose a duty of care in all the circumstances of the case.

12–14   The position in England has been thrown into further uncertainty by a number of recent cases where the decisions of lower courts on applications to strike-out actions in negligence against accountants were appealed. It should be noted that, because strike-out applications are preliminary in nature and do not

---

[12][1990] 2 A.C. at 618.

consider all the evidence that would be adduced at a full trial, general conclusions cannot be safely deduced from court decisions in such cases. One of these cases, *Electra Private Equity Partners v. KPMG Peat Marwick*[13] had an Irish dimension. Here the plaintiff had invested in Cambridge Group plc, an Irish company, which subsequently went into receivership. Having lost its full £10 million investment, the plaintiff instituted proceedings against KPMG, whom Electra had engaged to perform due diligence procedures in advance of the investment, and against KPMG Stokes Kennedy Crowley, Cambridge's auditors.

In this case, the Court of Appeal decided that it is not necessary to establish a conscious assumption of responsibility on the part of the auditor in order to prove negligence. The court also held that the involvement of due diligence advisers did not *per se* remove the possibility that the auditors had assumed responsibility to the investors. However, the overriding message from the Court of Appeal was unhelpful in attempting to arrive at a clear set of guidelines against which to measure particular circumstances for the purposes of advising on potential exposures in negligence.

The court in effect cautioned against granting applications by defendant accountants to strike out claims at a preliminary stage before all facts are known to the court because such cases are notably facts-sensitive.

Irish law on duty of care

12–15 There is relatively little recent case law in Ireland on the subject of the liability of auditors and accountants. In the cases of *Primor plc v. Stokes Kennedy Crowley* and *Primor plc v. Oliver Freaney and Co*,[14] the Supreme Court heard appeals against High Court decisions in both cases together. Although the principal matter at issue in the appeals was whether the plaintiff should be allowed to proceed with the cases given the delay of the plaintiff in progressing the proceedings, the Supreme Court took the opportunity to address in general terms the issue of negligence of auditors. In his judgment, O'Flaherty J. summarised the position as follows:

> "Many years ago, in the Court of Appeals of New York, Cardozo C.J., in a passage often quoted since, warned against extending the liability of accountants too far when he said:—
>
>> 'If liability for negligence exists, a thoughtless slip or blunder, the failure to detect a theft or forgery beneath the cover of deceptive entries, may expose accountants to a liability in an indeterminate amount for an indeterminate time to an indeterminate class. The hazards of a business conducted on these lines are so extreme as to enkindle doubts whether a flaw may not exist in the implication of a duty that exposes to these consequences': *Ultramares Corporation v. Touche* [1931] 255 N.Y. 170, at page 179.

---

[13] unreported, Court of Appeal (Civil Division), April 23, 1999.
[14] [1996] 2 I.R. 459.

As already pointed out, the accountants' obligations to the plaintiff are discharged if they exercise reasonable care. They must bring reasonable skill and competence to their task. But they are not required to act as super-humans; nor are they to be faulted simply because an expert witness is produced who says that, if he had been in charge of things, affairs might have been ordered better . . . Nor, it is hardly necessary to add, is the defendants' conduct to be viewed with the wisdom of hindsight.

Further, I believe that any liability in negligence of accountants would have to be established having regard to the legislative framework in which they carry out their duties. In England — and I do not understand our relevant company legislation differs in any material respect in this regard — the position was summarised as follows by Lord Jauncey of Tullichettle in the course of his speech in *Caparo Industries plc v. Dickman* [1990] 2 A.C. 605 at p. 660:—

> 'Three matters emerge from the statutory provisions, namely: (1) that the responsibility for the preparation of accounts giving a true and fair view of the company's financial state is placed fairly and squarely on the shoulders of the directors; (2) that the role of the auditors is to provide an independent report to the members on the proper preparation of the balance sheet and profit and loss account, and as to whether those documents give a true and fair view respectively of the state of the company's affairs at the end of the financial year and of the company's profit and loss for that year. Their role is thus purely investigative rather than creative; (3) that the company's accounts, including the auditors' report, will be furnished to all members of the company as well as to debenture holders and any other persons entitled to receive notice of general meeting. The accounts will, of course, also be available to any member of the public who chooses to examine the company file in the office of the Registrar of Companies.'"[15]

12–16 Although arguably not part of the *ratio decidendi* of the case and therefore being *obiter dicta*, nevertheless these remarks and quotations are probably a good indication of the attitude of the Supreme Court to the general issue of the liability of auditors. They indicate a high degree of approval for the approach to the topic taken by the House of Lords in the *Caparo* case.

Standards of care

12–17 Of course, even if a duty of care does exist between an accountant and a third party, no liability arises unless the accountant is held to have been negligent in the performance of his duties and the third party has suffered loss as a result of that negligence. The question of whether the accountant has been negligent is determined by a comparison of his actual performance with the standard of care

---

[15][1996] 2 I.R. 459 at 502–503.

required of him in the particular circumstances. It is in the making of this comparison that the expert accountant plays an important role.

12–18   For example, an auditor may give an unqualified (*i.e.* clean) opinion on financial statements that are subsequently found to have been materially misstated by failing to include the effects of a significant fraud. A shareholder who has suffered a loss through the fraudulent dissipation of the company's assets may proceed against the auditor on the grounds that, had the auditor detected the fraud, it could have been stopped and the loss of assets could have been reduced. In such a situation, it is not sufficient to show that the auditor owed a duty of care to the shareholder and that the shareholder suffered a loss as a result of the fraud. It is necessary also to show that the audit performed by the auditor fell short of the appropriate standard and that, had it not done so, the fraud would have been detected and the loss reduced.

12–19   It is clear, therefore, that a crucial element of the case will be the determination by the court as to what constitutes the appropriate standard and whether the auditor met that standard. The court will need to be assisted in making this assessment and usually both sides to the dispute will engage experts in this capacity.

Customary practice

12–20   When assessing whether a professional person has been guilty of negligence in the performance of his profession, courts pay great regard to what is described as "customary practice". In preference to making an assessment against a notional standard of care that may be too high (if derived from ideal standards) or too low (*i.e.* the lowest common denominator), the courts attempt to arrive at a standard that reflects the reality of how things are done in practice. However, the courts reserve the right to decide whether current practice is acceptable.

12–21   This concept was well enunciated by Walsh J. in *O'Donovan v. Cork County Council* in the context of a claim for medical negligence. He said:

> "Challenge, unsupported by evidence, is not sufficient to put the matter in issue. A medical practitioner cannot be held negligent if he follows general and approved practice in the situation with which he is faced: see *Daniels v. Heskin* and the cases referred to therein.
>
> That proposition is not, however, without qualification. If there is a common practice which has inherent defects, which ought to be obvious to any person giving the matter due consideration, the fact that it is shown to have been widely and generally adopted over a period of time does not make the practice any the less negligent. Neglect of duty does not cease by repetition to be neglect of duty."[16]

---

[16][1967] I.R. 173 at 193.

12–22   This statement of principle is not restricted to the medical profession. In *Roche v. Peilow*[17] the Supreme Court made it clear that the same principle applied to the solicitors' profession and, by extension, to other professions. In his judgment, in which he quoted with approval and explained further the passage of Walsh J. set out above, Henchy J. said:

> "The general duty owed by a solicitor to his client is to show him the degree of care to be expected in the circumstances from a reasonably careful and skilful solicitor. Usually the solicitor will be held to have discharged that duty if he follows a practice common among the members of his profession: see *Daniels v. Heskin* [1954] I.R. 73 and the cases therein referred to. Conformity with the widely accepted practice of his colleagues will normally rebut an allegation of negligence against a professional man, for the degree of care which the law expects of him is no higher than that to be expected from an ordinary reasonable member of the profession or of the speciality in question. But there is an important exception to that rule of conduct. It was concisely put as follows by Walsh J. in *O'Donovan v. Cork County Council* [1967] I.R. 173, at p. 193:
>
>> 'If there is a common practice which has inherent defects, which ought to be obvious to any person giving the matter due consideration, the fact that it is shown to have been widely and generally adopted over a period of time does not make the practice any the less negligent. Neglect of duty does not cease by repetition to be neglect of duty.'
>
> The reason for that exception or qualification is that the duty imposed by the law rests on the standard to be expected from a reasonably careful member of the profession, and a person cannot be said to be acting reasonably if he automatically and mindlessly follows the practice of others when by taking thought he would have realised that the practice in question was fraught with peril for his client and was readily avoidable or remediable. The professional man is, of course, not to be judged with the benefit of hindsight, but if it can be said that if at the time, on giving the matter due consideration, he would have realised that the impugned practice was in the circumstances incompatible with his client's interests, and if an alternative and safe course of conduct was reasonably open to him, he will be held to have been negligent."[18]

More recent cases have confirmed these statements of principle, *e.g.* see *Dunne v. National Maternity Hospital*.[19]

Standards of care applying to auditors

12–23   Auditors are expected to exercise reasonable skill and care in carrying out their responsibilities. These are not clearly defined in law. In the oft-quoted case of *Re Kingston Cotton Mill Company (No. 2)*, Lopes J. said:

---

[17] [1985] I.R. 232.
[18] [1985] I.R. 232 at 254–255.
[19] [1989] I.R. 91.

"It is the duty of an auditor to bring to bear on the work he has to perform that skill, care, and caution which a reasonably competent, careful and cautious auditor would use. What is reasonable skill, care and caution must depend on the particular circumstances of each case. An auditor is not bound to be a detective or, as was said, to approach his work with suspicion or with a foregone conclusion that there is something wrong. He is a watchdog, but not a bloodhound. He is justified in believing tried servants of the company in whom confidence is placed by the company. He is entitled to assume that they are honest, and to rely upon their representations, provided he takes reasonable care. If there is anything calculated to excite suspicion he should probe it to the bottom; but in the absence of anything of that kind he is only bound to be reasonably cautious and careful."[20]

12–24   In the case of *Re City Equitable Fire Insurance Co Ltd*, Pollock M.R. referred to this passage and added some additional explanation to it:

"What is the standard of duty which is to be applied to the auditors? That is to be found, and is sufficiently stated, I think, in *In re Kingston Cotton Mill Company (No. 2)*. As I have already said, it is quite easy to charge a person after the event and say: 'How stupid you were not to have discovered something which, if you had discovered it, would have saved us and many others from many sorrows.' But it has been well said that an auditor is not bound to be a detective or to approach his work with suspicion or with a foregone conclusion that there is something wrong. 'He is a watchdog, but not a bloodhound.' That metaphor was used by Lopes L.J. in *In re Kingston Cotton Mill Co (No. 2)*. Perhaps, casting metaphor aside, the position is more happily expressed in the phrase used by my brother Sargant L.J., who said that the duty of an auditor is verification and not detection. The *Kingston Cotton Mill Case* is important, because expansion is given to those rather epigramatic phrases. Lindley, L.J. says (at p. 287): 'It is not sufficient to say that the frauds must have been detected if the entries in the books had been put together in a way which never occurred to any one before suspicion was aroused. The question is whether, no suspicion of anything wrong being entertained, there was a want of reasonable care on the part of the auditors in relying on the returns made by a competent and trusted expert relating to matters on which information from such a person was essential.'"[21]

12–25   In the Irish case of *Leech v. Stokes Bros and Pim*, Hanna J. in the High Court explained the point succinctly:

" ... the duty upon an auditor is, under the circumstances of the particular case and of his employment, to exercise such care and skill as a diligent, skilled and cautious auditor would exercise according to the practice of the profession."[22]

Interestingly, on appeal to the Supreme Court, Meredith J. sounded a warning bell by suggesting that an auditor should keep a distance from his client. He said:

---

[20] [1896] 2 Ch. 279 at 288–289.
[21] [1925] 1 Ch. 407 at 509–510.
[22] [1937] I.R. 787 at 798.

"The business of an accountant and auditor is innately unsympathetic, and it is liable to suffer in efficiency when undertaken in a more or less obliging and friendly spirit."[23]

12–26 The judgment in *Bank of Credit and Commerce International (Overseas) Ltd v. Price Waterhouse* provides a more recent view of the duties of auditors:

"The auditor is employed by the company to exercise his professional skill and judgment for the purpose of giving the shareholders an independent report on the reliability of the company's accounts. In the course of professional life of an average auditor he will carry out audits for numerous clients involved in widely differing businesses. The skill he offers and for which he is paid is the skill in looking at a company's accounts and the underlying information on which they are or should be based and telling the shareholders whether the accounts give a true and fair view of the company's financial position. He is not in possession of facts or qualified to express a view as to how the business should be run, in the sense of what investments to make, what business to undertake, what prices to charge, what lines of credit to extend and so on. Not only does he not normally have the necessary expertise but those are areas in respect of which his advice is not sought. When the company engaged an auditor, it is not seeking his help in steering the management into making better management decisions. There are others who hold themselves out as able to give that sort of assistance."[24]

12–27 As might be expected, and can be readily seen even from the limited number of judgments quoted above, there is no simple formula or set of rules establishing the standard of care required of an auditor or accountant. However, certain materials are regarded as authoritative and most courts would attach significant weight to them. These materials include:

1. Statutory duties (imposed by legislation).

2. Professional standards developed and published by the accountancy profession, including Auditing Standards, Accounting Standards,[25] Ethical Standards and Rules of Professional Conduct.

3. Textbooks by reputable experts in the relevant field.

---

[23] *ibid.* at 832.

[24] [1999] B.C.C. 351 at 369, *per* Laddie J.

[25] In the case of *Lloyd Cheyham & Co Ltd v. Littlejohn & Co* [1987] B.C.L.C. 303 at 313, Woolf J. stated:

"While they are not conclusive, so that a departure from their terms necessarily involves a breach of duty of care, and they are not as the explanatory foreword makes clear, rigid rules, they are very strong evidence as to what is the proper standard which should be adopted and unless there is some justification, a departure from this will be regarded as constituting a breach of duty."

4. Manuals, particularly those adopted by the accountant or auditor or his firm.

5. Best practice as described in journals, other publications and exposure drafts of proposed future professional standards.

12–28 The court will expect an expert to interpret these authorities in a manner that can be readily understood and to apply them to the specific circumstances of the case in a clear and careful way.

Other considerations

12–29 In addition to showing that an accountant owed a duty of care to the plaintiff and was negligent, the plaintiff must be shown to have suffered loss or damage and the negligent action(s) must be shown to have caused the plaintiff's loss or damage.

Foreseeability

12–30 Even where the defendant's negligence caused the loss, no award for damages will be made unless the loss was foreseeable. This point is dealt with, *inter alia*, in Chapter 15 (paras **15–62** *et seq.*).

Remoteness and causation

12–31 The chain of causation between the negligent act and the loss suffered by the plaintiff must be established if an award of damages is to be made. Only the loss caused by a breach of duty by the accountant can be recovered. The chain of causation may be broken by an act or omission of the plaintiff or by some other person. This in turn may result in a reduction in damages awarded against the accountants. In particular, the negligence of directors and management of companies is relevant in actions against auditors. Decisions of the courts on this issue have varied. Some have supported the application of negligence to directors and management,[26] others have not.[27]

12–32 In this regard, the provisions of Part III of the Civil Liability Act 1961 should be noted. Section 12 of the Act deals with situations where there is more than one negligent party (known as concurrent wrongdoers) and renders each

---

[26] *Morgan Crucible plc v. Hill Samuel Bank* [1991] 1 All E.R. 148; *Nelson Guarantee Corporation Ltd v. Hodgson* [1958] N.Z.L.R. 609; *Daniels v. Anderson* [1995] 16 A.S.C.R. 607; *Dairy Containers Ltd v. Auditor General* [1995] 2 N.Z.L.R. 30.
[27] *Henderson v. Merrett Syndicates Ltd* [1994] 3 All E.R. 506; *Simonius Vischer & Co v. Holt and Thompson* [1979] 2 N.S.W.L.R. 322.

such negligent party liable for the whole of the damage for which that party is a concurrent wrongdoer (see also para. **12–07**). The effect of these provisions is that an injured plaintiff is free to collect his full damages against any one of the concurrent wrongdoers, and it is then up to the party who has paid up to pursue the other concurrent wrongdoers for their share of the damages. This means that, even if the directors are held to be partially responsible for losses suffered by a plaintiff, in the absence of appropriate insurance cover or sufficiently deep pockets on the part of the directors, the auditor may end up footing the entire bill in any event.

12–33   In *Galoo Ltd v. Bright Grahame Murray*,[28] the issue of causation in respect of an action against the company's auditors was considered. The court set out two aspects that should be considered in determining causation: whether the negligent act allowed an "occasion for damage" to occur and whether the act was the "effective or dominant cause" of such damages. An act that merely provides the occasion for loss cannot necessarily be said to have caused the damage.

Role of expert accountants

12–34   As in all cases where an expert witness is engaged to give evidence to a court in a dispute, the first duty of that expert is to the court (see Chapter 6). Nevertheless, experts will usually be engaged, in the first instance, by one or other party to the dispute, and the expert will have to view the case from the perspective of the party that engages him as well as from the perspective of the court.

12–35   Before accepting appointment, the expert should have satisfied himself that he has the appropriate level of expertise necessary for the assignment. As business life has become increasingly complex and specialised, so also are the requirements of expert witnesses. For this reason, it is probably no longer advisable, for instance, for an auditor to undertake an expert witness assignment in a case alleging negligent auditing unless he can bring to bear extensive experience and expertise, not just in auditing generally but in auditing in the particular industry or type of business involved in the case as well as in forensic accounting.

12–36   In carrying out the assignment, the expert will have a role in advising on both liability and quantum. Professional indemnity policies are invalidated where there is fraud. As such policies do not cover fraud, forensic accountants should be careful to avoid using the term (this has already been referred to in paras **3–03**, **3–65** and **5–81**) as this might invalidate the claim.

---

[28][1995] 1 All E.R. 16.

Liability

12–37   To advise on liability, the expert accountant will need to examine closely all evidence of the work performed by the accountant. In most cases, this will involve a careful examination of the accountant's working papers. These will be available to the accountant's own expert and access to them will be sought (and, if necessary, obtained by a court order for discovery – see paras **22–18** *et seq.*) on behalf of the plaintiff.

12–38   In reviewing working papers, the expert needs to take account of several factors:

1.   Whether there is any defined format or content for the working papers, and if so whether they comply with the defined requirements.

2.   Whether the working papers demonstrate compliance with the necessary standard of work as determined by professional standards, audit manuals, etc.

3.   Whether significant or material areas have received a level of careful attention commensurate with their importance.

4.   Whether the number and qualifications of the staff used on the engagement were appropriate and adequate.

5.   Whether the appropriate level of supervision and review of the audit process by someone of significant experience was applied to the engagement.

6.   Whether the significant areas of judgment were properly identified, referred to senior personnel for consideration and appropriately considered and resolved.

7.   Whether the appropriate level of independence and expertise was brought to bear on the engagement.

Experts must be careful to ensure that they do not apply hindsight in evaluating the work of the accountant – they must attempt, as far as possible, to put themselves in the position in which the accountant found himself at the relevant time.

Sources of difficulties giving rise to a claim in negligence are often in areas of judgment that may not have been subjected to, and may not have been susceptible to, detailed work by the accountant. In these circumstances, it will be important for the expert to review all available papers, not just those evidencing detailed work, to establish the extent to which the relevant issues were discussed and carefully considered.

12–39   The process by which the expert gathers together and presents the result of his work, both by way of written report and in evidence, is discussed in Chapter 23.

Quantification of damages

12–40   Expert accountants may also be asked to assist in quantifying the losses suffered by the plaintiff, arising from the accountants' negligence. This requires an assessment of the factors causing the loss and an evaluation of the financial consequences of the negligent acts. It is difficult to be more prescriptive concerning the accounting calculations involved in quantifying such damages. Every case is unique, and turns on its own facts.

12–41   Table 12.1 provides some examples of circumstances in which accountants acted as experts in cases involving negligence by accountants and auditors.

Table 12.1: Examples of accountants' liability cases in which forensic accountants have advised

---

Quality of accountants' work
- Reporting on the quality of work carried out by an accountancy firm
- Acting on a negligence claim against an accountancy firm for its role as reporting accountants in relation to a directors' profit forecast
- Assessing auditors' work on:
  - accounts which it is alleged contained substantial fictitious debtors as a result of a fraud
  - accounts in the retail sector, which were relied on by third party investors
  - internal and external audit assignments for an organisation where a senior employee had misappropriated funds
- Reviewing and opining on the quality of work performed by reporting accountants under the solicitors' accounts rules after client moneys had been stolen and where irregularities in the records ought to have been reported to the Law Society

Quantification of losses arising from negligence of accountants
- Quantifying the loss suffered as a result of accountants' failure to make the appropriate tax loss claims in time and to submit correct computations

---

Disciplinary proceedings

12–42   In relation to accountants' liability specifically, expert accountants have a role to play not only where the accountant is the subject of a legal action, but also where his conduct becomes the subject of a complaint which may subsequently be investigated by his professional body. The professional accountancy bodies in Ireland have varied approaches to disciplining their members.[29] Where disciplinary proceedings are taken against accountants by their professional bodies, expert accountants may be required to assist in the

---

[29] See Review Group on Auditing *Report of the Review Group on Auditing* (Government Publications, Dublin, 2000), pp. 85–91. Also available at www.entemp.ie/ publications.htm. See also comment in para. **13–02**.

determination of the issues. Although complaints against accountants can arise in a variety of circumstances, the situations most likely to involve expert accountants will be those where there have been an alleged breach of auditing standards, or an alleged breach of a code of professional conduct.

Concluding comment

12–43   Forensic accountants are uniquely well placed to add real value where an auditor or accountant is accused of negligence. In attempting to do so with zeal they need to avoid some possible pitfalls, such as:

– the use of hindsight – "surely it was obvious …";

– the application of today's standards to yesterday's world: "but best practice would suggest …";

– applying an ideal, rather than a practical, approach: "but why didn't you examine all the transactions …";

– forgetting that the primary responsibility for the accounts rests with the directors: "but the accounts the auditors prepared were wrong …".

A practical approach is needed, and knowledge of what does happen, as well as what should happen, is of immense value to the court.

It is also worth noting that there may be a trend emerging towards limiting the liability of auditors where their negligence is not the sole cause of a loss.

The recently published Final Report of the Company Law Review Steering Group in the United Kingdom contains some important recommendations that may at last provide some relief to auditors.[30] The report recognises that "… auditors' so-called 'deep pockets' have ensured that, of the possible targets of professional negligence claims for financial loss caused by misstatement in accounts, they are the favourite."[31] It then rejects the 'proportionality solution' (*i.e.* modifying the principle of joint and several liability referred to at para **12-32** above by fixing auditors only with the amount of damages proportionate to their share of the blame for the loss) as contrary to principle, stating that:

> "The effect of the proportionality approach would be to impose on a plaintiff who is wholly innocent the risk that a party in the wrong may be unable to satisfy a claim, rather than imposing that burden on another party (the auditor) whose fault caused the loss."[32]

---

[30] The full text of the report, *Modern Company Law for a Competitive Economy*, is available at www.dti.gov.uk/cld/final_report.
[31] Paragraph 8.136 of the report.
[32] Paragraph 8.138 of the report.

However, the report goes on to make an important recommendation relating to the prohibition on the contractual limitation of his liability by an auditor contained in section 200 of the Companies Act 1963. The report states:

> "In addition, we recommend that auditors should be able to limit their liability contractually with the company in tort (or delict) with third parties. Contractual limitation should be achieved by the repeal of the prohibition on auditors' and companies' so limiting the liability. Such limitation should be publicised in the auditors' report and such notice should bind those who rely on the report (i.e. thus achieving limitation of liability in tort). In both cases the limitation would not be effective without prior approval by shareholders."[33]

This proposal has been welcomed by accountants in the United Kingdom. Its implementation is, of course, by no means certain, although the membership of the Steering Group, the fact that it was established by the DTI and the extent of consultation undertaken before final recommendations were made all suggest that the proposals will be given serious consideration.

---

[33] Paragraph 8.143 of the report.

COMPANY INVESTIGATIONS AND TRIBUNALS OF INQUIRY

CHAPTER 13

COMPANY INVESTIGATIONS AND TRIBUNALS
OF INQUIRY

13–01   A defining characteristic of a court is that it is engaged in the resolution
of disputes and the apportionment of liability between two or more parties. This
is usually done using an adversarial system involving the presentation of the
opposing cases, the cross-examination of witnesses and the determination of
the matter by the court. This process means that not only are findings of fact
made, but those findings result in the imposition of penalties or an award of
damages or other relief.

By contrast, tribunals of inquiry and other non-court investigations have as
their object the finding of facts and the gathering of information. Although the
facts and information may be highly relevant to separate court proceedings, the
tribunals/investigations themselves will not result in any sanction (except possibly
for costs of the proceedings) for any party.

In most personal (Chapter 7), commercial (Chapter 9) and company and
partnership (Chapter 10) litigation, forensic accountants are involved, *inter alia*,
in the computation of damages. Because awards of damages do not arise in
tribunals/investigations, the role of forensic accountants in such matters is more
limited. Nevertheless, forensic accountants can play an important role in
gathering, assimilating and analysing financial and accounting data to assist in
these proceedings. Investigative and auditing skills are particularly useful in
carrying out such activities. Some of the techniques described in Chapters 4 and
5 in relation to detecting and investigating fraud may be relevant to activities
described in this chapter.

The McDowell report recognised the contribution accounting expertise can
make in company investigations as follows:

> "...it is clearly desirable that dedicated accountancy resources are made available
> to [company investigations] ... Persons of considerable skill in auditing and
> forensic accounting are required for this work."[1]

Brady[2] sets out the multitude of investigative agencies referred to in legislation

---

[1] *Report of the Working Group on Company Law Compliance and Enforcement* (McDowell
Report) (Government Publications, Dublin, November, 1998), p. 58.
[2] Brady, R., "Tribunals and politics: A fundamental review" in *Contemporary Issues in
Irish Law and Politics* (2000) No. 3, p. 159.

in Ireland, the most important of which, from a forensic accounting point of view, are:

- the Garda Síochána (referred to in para. **3–43**, especially the Garda Bureau of Fraud Investigation);
- the Criminal Assets Bureau (considered in Chapter 5 at para. **5–80** and in Chapter 11 at paras **11–13, 11–36**);
- office of the Director of Corporate Enforcement;
- the Appeal Commissioners (considered in Chapter 11 at paras **11–02** *et seq.*);
- Oireachtas Committees (especially the Committee of Public Accounts, which is not considered here as it is outside the scope of this book);
- inspectors appointed under the Companies Acts;
- authorised officers appointed under the Companies Acts; and
- tribunals of inquiry.

This chapter considers the latter three types of investigations in two sections – (i) company investigations and (ii) tribunals of inquiry. Company investigations were briefly touched upon in Chapter 8 in the context of criminal offences in relation to such investigations (see para. **8–88**).

In addition, the Insurance Act 1989 provides for appointment of inspectors to entities covered by that legislation.

13–02   Hogan and Morgan[3] also refer to "domestic" tribunals established by groups such as professions to apply rules of the body to members, possibly to determine the culpability or otherwise of members and any consequent sanction that may be appropriate. Although such tribunals are generally free to establish and follow their own rules of procedure, they are subject to the overriding requirements of natural justice.

The two most important and fundamental rules of natural justice are: *audi alteram partem* (*i.e.* a party under investigation or against whom allegations are made must be afforded adequate opportunity to present his own case) and *nemo judex in causa sua* (*i.e.* nobody should be a judge in his own cause, meaning that the tribunal must be, and must be seen to be, independent and objective in the consideration of the matters before it). These basic principles have given rise to the development of detailed guidance, based on case law, for the constitution and conduct of non-judicial tribunals and investigations.

13–03   Where a party believes that the rules of natural justice are not being followed or a tribunal is otherwise exceeding its authority, that party may apply to court for leave to institute judicial review proceedings for the purpose of

---

[3] Hogan, G. and Morgan, D.G., *Administrative Law in Ireland* (3rd ed., Round Hall Sweet & Maxwell, Dublin, 1998), p. 255.

having a court decide the issue (see also paras **11–29** *et seq.*). It is important to recognise that judicial review proceedings are not concerned with the merits of decisions made by tribunals, but rather with the manner in which decisions were made. Such proceedings are therefore very different from appeals of decisions. The difference was illustrated clearly in the famous words of Lord Brightman in *Chief Constable of North Wales Police v. Evans*, when he said:

> "Judicial review is concerned, not with the decision, but with the decision-making process. ... Judicial review, as the words imply, is not an appeal from a decision, but a review of the manner in which the decision was made." [4]

This extract was quoted with approval by Griffin J. and referred to by Finlay C.J. in the Supreme Court in *State (Keegan & Lysaght) v. Stardust Victims Compensation Tribunal* [5] and in several other subsequent reported Irish cases.

Company investigations[6]

13–04   The importance of accounting to company investigations is evidenced by the frequent appointment of accountants to act as either authorised officers or as company inspectors. In addition, accountants are frequently engaged to work behind the scenes with inspectors or authorised officers.

As stated in Chapter 3, forensic accountants are often involved in investigating fraud. Many company investigations are instigated arising from suspicions of fraud of one type of another. As the first report of the Company Law Review Group commented:

> "The ability to conduct investigations into the affairs or ownership of companies is an important component of the company law framework. It provides a mechanism whereby evidence of wrongdoing, fraud and breaches of law can be obtained with a view to further proceedings. It can provide reassurance to interested parties in dispelling unfounded suggestions of misconduct and, by holding out the possibility of close scrutiny, can discourage such activities by those transacting business through the company vehicle." [7]

13–05   Part II of the Companies Act 1990 introduced extensive new provisions in Ireland in relation to investigation of companies. Until then, only a limited scheme for appointment of inspectors by the Minister for Industry and Commerce existed under sections 165 and 166 of the Companies Act 1963. Very little use was made of these powers with only five appointments – one each in 1965,

---

[4] [1982] 1 W.L.R. 1155 at 1173.
[5] [1986] I.R. 642.
[6] The authors thank Paul Appleby, Gerard Hogan and George Moloney for assistance with this section of the chapter.
[7] Company Law Review Group, First Report (Government Publications, Dublin, 1994), p. 18, para. 3.2.

1974 and 1978 and two in 1979.[8] McCormack[9] suggests that these investigations were less than effective, mainly due to legal difficulties encountered. Further applications were made for the appointment of inspectors during that time but, according to Courtney,[10] the outcome of those applications is not known. This is because the annual *Companies Reports* published by the Department recorded the applications made under sections 165 and 166 of the Companies Act 1963 but say nothing of the outcome of those applications.[11]

13–06   Under section 166(a) of the Companies Act 1963, the Minister could initiate an inspection where the court ordered that one be carried out, or where the company itself by special resolution declared there should be one. The Minister also had discretion, under section 165(1), to appoint inspectors where a minority of members of a company called for an investigation and could show good reason for seeking one.

13–07   The Companies Act 1990 considerably extended the scope for appointment of inspectors. This was in response to problems associated with the old procedures including limitations as to the circumstances in which an investigation could be initiated and constitutional doubts as to the power of the Minister to appoint inspectors.[12] The most important changes were neatly summarised as follows by Murphy J. in the High Court in a judgment delivered on February 7, 1992:

> "Part II of the Act of 1990 differs from its predecessors in that it confers the power to appoint inspectors to investigate 'the affairs of the company' on the High Court instead of the Minister and it confers the new and distinct power on the Minister in certain circumstances to appoint an inspector or inspectors to investigate and report on 'the membership of any company and otherwise with respect to the company for the purpose of determining the true persons who are or have been financially interested in the success or failure (real or apparent) of the company or able to control or materially to influence the policy of the company'. In addition, the powers conferred upon any inspector appointed under the Act of 1990 are more extensive in certain respects than those conferred on inspectors by earlier legislation. The statutory effect of the inspector's report has

---

[8] McCormack, G., *The New Companies Legislation* (The Round Hall Press, Dublin, 1991), p. 37.
[9] *ibid.*, pp. 37–38.
[10] Courtney, T.B., *The Law of Private Companies* (Butterworths, Dublin, 1994), p. 807.
[11] We are grateful to Brian Hutchinson of the Law Faculty, University College Dublin and author of "Investigation of Private Companies", *i.e.* Chap. 20 in Courtney, *ibid.*, for this information.
[12] McGrath, D., "Investigations under the Companies Act 1990" (1993) 11 *Irish Law Times*, p. 264.

been extended by the Act of 1990. The report is now admissible in civil proceedings (by virtue of s. 22 of the Act of 1990) not merely as evidence of the opinion of the inspector but also of the facts set out in the report."[13]

13–08　Thus, two types of investigation are possible under the 1990 Act – those ordered by the High Court and those ordered by the Minister. The scope of court-ordered investigations differs from that of those ordered by the Minister.[14] Applications to the court for court-ordered inspections by members and creditors are now possible. Under section 7(3) of the Companies Act 1990 applicants may be required by the court to give security for costs for the investigation not exceeding £100,000. This figure will increase to £250,000 on the date (yet to be fixed) that section 20 of the Company Law Enforcement Act 2001 comes into operation.

Company inspectors/authorised officers

13–09　As stated above, inspectors/authorised officers may be appointed in one of two ways: by the Minister or by the court. The Minister's power to appoint inspectors under section 14 of the Companies Act 1990 will be transferred to the Director of Corporate Enforcement at a date yet to be specified, when section 14 of the Company Law Enforcement Act 2001 comes into operation.

Appointment of inspectors by the Minister (section 14)

13–10　Under section 14 of the Companies Act 1990, the Minister may appoint one or more competent inspectors to investigate and report on the membership of a company for the purpose of determining the identity of the true persons who have or have had a financial interest in the company. Section 14 provides

> "(1) The Minister may, subject to subsection (2), appoint one or more competent inspectors to investigate and report on the membership of any company and otherwise with respect to the company for the purpose of determining the true persons who are or have been financially interested in the success or failure (real or apparent) of the company or able to control or materially to influence the policy of the company.

---

[13] *Chestvale Properties Ltd v. Glackin* [1993] 3 I.R. 35 at 43–44.

[14] Section 14 of the Company Law Enforcement Act 2001 (implementing the recommendations of the McDowell Report *Report of the Working Group on Company Law Compliance and Enforcement* (Government Publications, Dublin, November 1998) transfers to the Director of Corporate Enforcement the Minister's powers under sections 14, 15 and 16 of the Companies Act 1990 to appoint inspectors, to require information as to persons with interests in the company's shares and debentures, and to impose restrictions on such shares and debentures. No date has been fixed for the coming into effect of these tasks.

(2) An appointment may be made by the Minister if he is of the opinion that there are circumstances suggesting that it is necessary —
   (a) for the effective administration of the law relating to companies;
   (b) for the effective discharge by the Minister of his functions under any enactment; or
   (c) in the public interest.

(3) The appointment of an inspector under this section may define the scope of his investigation, whether as respects the matters or the period to which it is to extend or otherwise, and in particular may limit the investigation to matters connected with particular shares or debentures."

New provisions inserted into section 14 by section 26 of the Company Law Enforcement Act 2001 will, when in operation, permit the court, on the application of the Director of Corporate Enforcement, to direct repayment to the Director by a company under investigation of the cost of the investigation.

13–11 In connection with investigating the ownership of shares/debentures of a company, the Minister is also empowered under section 15 to obtain any information on the present and past interests in the shares without appointing an inspector.

Appointment of authorised officers by the Minister

13–12 Section 19 of the Companies Act 1990 gives the Minister power to require information to be provided by a company, body corporate or insurance undertaking to the Minister or to any officer authorised by the Minister. Under section 19, the Minister or an authorised officer may require the production of books or documents, if the Minister is of the opinion that there are circumstances suggesting that:

(a) examination of the books and documents is necessary with a view to determining whether an inspector should be appointed to conduct an investigation under the Companies Acts;

(b) the affairs of the company or body in question are being, or have been, conducted with intent to defraud its members or creditors or the creditors of any other person;

(c) the affairs of the company or body are being, or have been, conducted for a fraudulent purpose or in a manner unfairly prejudicial to some part of its members;

(d) any act or proposed act or omission of or on behalf of the company or body is, or would be, unfairly prejudicial to some part of its members or is likely to be unlawful; or

(e) the body was formed for a fraudulent or unlawful purpose.

13–13   Section 19 also confers on the Minister or the authorised officer the power:

(a)   to require the production of the books and documents from anyone who appears to be in possession of them, subject to any lien that person may have over the documents;

(b)   to take copies of the books and documents produced; and

(c)   to require the person producing the books and documents, or any other person who is a present or past officer of, or is or was at any time employed by, the body in question, to provide an explanation of any of the books and documents.

Failure to comply with obligations under section 19 is an offence.

13–14   Section 19 has been used on several occasions in recent years, principally to allow the Minister to make an informed judgment as to whether an application to court for the appointment of an inspector under section 8 of the Companies Act 1990 is justified (see paras **13–17** *et seq.*). On a number of occasions, the Minister has acted on foot of a report prepared by an authorised officer following a section 19 investigation by applying to court for the appointment of an inspector under section 8. Evidence obtained under section 19 has also been used in legal proceedings against companies and directors for failure to comply with obligations under the Companies Acts.

Section 29 of the Company Law Enforcement Act 2001 repeals section 19 of the 1990 Act and replaces it with an entirely new section 19. The new section re-enacts the provisions summarised above at paras **13-12** and **13-13**, replacing the Minister with the Director of Corporate Enforcement, and grants the following additional powers to the Director:

–   The power to require the production of specified books and documents by a body if the Director is of the opinion that there are circumstances suggesting that the body may be in possession of such books or documents containing information relating to the books or documents of a body which comes within the terms of one or more of (a) to (e) in paragraph **13-12** above.

–   The power to require the production of copies of books or documents of a body.

–   The power to require production of books or documents which may relate to any books or documents of a specified body, subject to a requirement that, unless there is a reasonable risk of concealment, falsification, destruction or disposal of the documents, the party in possession of the documents be notified in advance of the Director's intention to require production of the documents and be given an opportunity to respect.

These are significant new provisions, in that they empower the Director to require production of documents by parties other than the body under investigation (*e.g.* the body's bankers or advisers). No date has yet been fixed for the coming into operation of these provisions.

13–15   Section 59 of the Insurance Act 1989 gives the Minister power to appoint authorised officers to entities governed by the Insurance Acts for the purposes of obtaining any information which the Minister may require. Such an authorised officer may obtain any books, documents or records relating to the issue of, or acceptance of, any premium relating to any policy, bond, certificate or other instrument of insurance. Section 60 of the Act also gives the authorised officer power to enter premises in furtherance of his investigations.

Appointment of inspectors by the court on application of members and creditors

13–16   Section 7 of the Companies Act 1990 deals with circumstances in which members (at least 100, or the holders of at least 10 per cent of the company's paid up share capital), a director, a creditor or the company may apply to the High Court requesting appointment of an inspector. Under section 7, the court may appoint one or more competent inspectors to investigate the affairs of a company in order to enquire into matters specified by the court and to report thereon as directed by the court. No investigation has been undertaken under this section to date.[15]

Appointment of inspectors by the court on application of the Minister

13–17   The High Court may also appoint one or more competent inspectors to investigate and report on the affairs of a company on application by the Minister[16] under section 8 of the Companies Act 1990. The application will only be granted if the court is satisfied that there are, in relation to the company in question, circumstances suggesting:

> "(a) that its affairs are being or have been conducted with intent to defraud its
>   creditors or the creditors of any other person or otherwise for a fraudulent or
>   unlawful purpose or in an unlawful manner or in a manner which is unfairly
>   prejudicial to some part of its members, or that any actual or proposed act
>   or omission of the company (including an act or omission on its behalf) is
>   or would be so prejudicial, or that it was formed for any fraudulent or
>   unlawful purpose; or

---

[15] Company Law Enforcement Bill 2000, Explanatory and Financial Memorandum (Government Publications, Dublin), p. 7.
[16] The Director of Corporate Enforcement will take over this power from the Minister on a date, yet to be fixed, when section 21 of the Company Law Enforcement Act 2001 comes into operation.

(b) that persons connected with its formation or the management of its affairs have in connection therewith been guilty of fraud, misfeasance or other misconduct towards it or towards its members; or

(c) that its members have not been given all the information relating to its affairs which they might reasonably expect."[17]

13–18 Section 21 of the Company Law Enforcement Act 2001, when in operation, will empower the Director of Corporate Enforcement to appoint one or more of his officers as inspectors – this acknowledges that such staff may already have acquired knowledge of a company's affairs through preliminary investigations.

13–19 Section 9 of the Companies Act 1990 gives inspectors appointed under section 7 or section 8 of the Act power to extend their investigations to related bodies corporate (which term is defined in section 140(5) of the Act), provided they have the approval of the court so to do. Section 22 of the Company Law Enforcement Act 2001 broadens the definition of "related body corporate" in the 1990 Act to include "a body corporate with which the company has a commercial relationship, and the commercial relationship exists where goods or services are sold or given by one party to another". A date has yet to be fixed for the coming into operation of section 22.

13–20 Table 13.1 summarises the activities under the above mentioned sections of the Companies Act 1990 and the Insurance Act 1989 from their commencement to December 2000. The investigation provisions in Part II of the Companies Act 1990 have been used on 21 occasions, five involving appointment of inspectors under section 8, three involving appointments under section 14 and a further 13 involving the appointment of authorised officers under section 19.

Table 13.1: Use of investigation provisions under Part II of the Companies Act 1990 and under the Insurance Act 1989

Section	Completed No.	Ongoing No.	Total No.
Section 8, Companies Act 1990	2	3	5
Section 14, Companies Act 1990	3	–	3
Section 19, Companies Act 1990	6	7	13
Section 59, Insurance Act 1989	–	1	1
	11	11	22

Source: Department of Enterprise, Trade and Employment as reported in the *Companies Reports* (Government Publications, Dublin, annual).

13–21 Table 13.2 lists the 22 investigations. In eight cases, inspectors were appointed, while in 14 cases authorised officers were appointed. Accountants

---

[17] Companies Act 1990, s. 8(1).

Table 13.2: Appointment of inspectors/authorised officers under the Companies Act 1990 and under the Insurance Act (IA) 1989

	Year	Issue	Company	Inspector[1]/ Authorised officer[2]	Qualification	Section of Act
1.	1991*	"Greencore affair" – purchase of shares in Irish Sugar and sale to Greencore at a profit	Sugar Distributor (Holdings) Ltd	Maurice Curran[1]	Solicitor	Section 14
2.	1991*	As above	Siúcre Éireann cpt	{Ciaran Foley[1] / Aidan Barry[1]}	Barrister / Chartered accountant	Section 8
3.	1991*	"Telecom affair" – sale of site in Ballsbridge to Telecom Éireann at twice the previous year's valuation	Chestvale Properties and Hoddle Investments	John Glackin[1]	Solicitor	Section 14
4.	1993*	Purchase of a controlling interest in Countyglen plc which was suspected of purchasing its own shares	Countyglen plc	Peter Fisher[2]	Management accountant	Section 19
5.	1994*	As above	Countyglen plc	Frank Clarke[1]	Barrister	Section 8
6.	1994*	Financial irregularities	Clonmannon Retirement Village group of companies	Martin Cosgrove[2]	Chartered accountant	Section 19
7.	1997*	Involvement of Mr Jim Stanley and Mir Oil Development Ltd in beneficial ownership of shares	Bula Resources (Holdings) plc	Lyndon MacCann[1]	Barrister	Section 14
8.	1997	Following report of the McCracken Tribunal on payments by Dunnes Stores	Celtic Helicopters Ltd	Gerard Ryan[2]	Chartered accountant	Section 19
9.	1997*	As above	Garuda Ltd (t/a Streamline Enterprises)	Peter Fisher[2]	Management accountant	Section 19
10.	1998*	Following interim report of Celtic Helicopters Ltd investigation	Ansbacher (Cayman) Ltd	Gerard Ryan[2]	Chartered accountant	Section 19
11.	1998	As above	Guinness & Mahon (Ireland) Ltd	Gerard Ryan[2]	Chartered accountant	Section 19
12.	1998	As above	Hamilton Ross Co. Ltd	Gerard Ryan[2]	Chartered accountant	Section 19
13.	1998*	As above	Irish Intercontinental Bank Ltd	Gerard Ryan[2]	Chartered accountant	Section 19
14.	1998	Following allegations by RTÉ that insurance policies had been used to facilitate tax evasion	National Irish Bank Financial Services Ltd	Martin Cosgrove[2]	Chartered accountant	Section 59, IA 1989
15.	1998	Following allegations by RTÉ of fee loading and interest surcharging	National Irish Bank Ltd	{John Blayney[1] / Tom Grace[1]}	Retired judge / Chartered accountant	Section 8
16.	1998	Following interim reports on investigations into Irish Intercontinental Bank Ltd and Guinness & Mahon (Ireland) Ltd	Kentford Securities Ltd	Gerard Ryan[2]	Chartered accountant	Section 19
17.	1998	Following report of authorised officer into allegations by RTÉ that insurance policies had been used to facilitate tax evasion	National Irish Bank Financial Services Ltd	{John Blayney[1] / Tom Grace[1]}	Retired judge / Chartered accountant	Section 8
18.	1998**	Following interim reports on investigations into Irish Intercontinental Bank Ltd and Guinness & Mahon (Ireland) Ltd	Dunnes Stores (ILAC Centre) Ltd	{George Maloney[2#] / Gerard Ryan[2]}	Certified accountant / Chartered accountant	Section 19
19.	1998**	As above	Dunnes Stores Ireland Company	{George Maloney[2#] / Gerard Ryan[2]}	Certified accountant / Chartered accountant	Section 19
20.	1998*	To examine books and documents recording transactions relating to Dunnes Stores companies	Faxhill Homes Ltd	George Maloney[2]	Certified accountant	Section 19
21.	1999	Arising from Ansbacher (Cayman) operations	College Trustees Ltd	Gerard Ryan[2]	Chartered accountant	Section 19
22.	1999	Following receipt of the authorised officer's report	Ansbacher (Cayman) Ltd	{Declan Costello[1#] / Paul Rowan[1] / Noreen Mackey[1] / Seán O'Leary[1] / Michael Cush[1]}	Retired judge / Chartered accountant / Barrister / Serving judge / Barrister	Section 8

* Investigation completed   ** Under judicial review

#Mr Maloney resigned as authorised officer shortly after appointment and was replaced by Mr Gerard Ryan. Mr Justice Costello resigned as inspector and was replaced by His Honour Judge Seán O'Leary and Mr Michael Cush SC in 2000.

Source: Department of Enterprise, Trade and Employment, including the *Companies Reports 1988–1991*, *Companies Reports 1992–93, 1993–94, 1995, 1996, 1997, 1998 and 1999* (Government Publications, Dublin).

have played a substantial role in the conduct of company investigations. All the authorised officers were professionally qualified accountants (also all but one were civil servants). Of the 15 inspectors appointed, four were accountants, two were solicitors, five were barristers and four were serving/retired judges.

The appointment as inspectors of individuals from a variety of professional backgrounds reflects the fact that the relevant expertise is valuable in the conduct of the investigations and that the role of the inspector is investigative rather than judicial. This is borne out by a judgment of Murphy J. in the High Court when it was submitted to him that directions sought from the court by an inspector amounted to the administration of justice. He said:

> "It seems to me that most of the matters in respect of which the court would make an order under s. 7, sub-s. 4 are matters which the inspector might do within his own discretion but which he might prefer for his own protection or some reason to have sanctioned by an order of the court confirming the propriety of his action. When it is recognised that the investigation by the inspector is not itself the administration of justice — though from time to time it may involve the requirement to act judicially — it is difficult to see how or why guidance or directions as to how those functions should be carried out could themselves constitute the administration of justice."[18]

The Company Law Review Group rejected suggestions that civil servants and other government officers should not be eligible for appointment as inspectors on the grounds of lack of competence, exposure to ministerial interference and inability to retain confidentiality.[19] It is worth noting that with the recent appointment of the first Director of Corporate Enforcement from the ranks of the civil service, appointment of civil servants as company inspectors may also be a feature in the future.

Powers of inspectors

13–22   Inspectors appointed by the High Court under section 7 or section 8 of the 1990 Act are empowered to investigate the affairs of the company and report thereon as directed by the court. The term "affairs" is not defined by the legislation. The term has been interpreted broadly in the English courts.[20]

The scope of investigations ordered by the Minister under section 14 of the 1990 Act is more restricted, *i.e.* into the membership of the company for the purpose of determining the true owners of the company. Section 14(4) of the Act states:

> "Subject to the terms of an inspector's appointment his powers shall extend to the investigation of any circumstances suggesting the existence of an arrangement

---

[18] *Re Countyglen plc* [1995] 1 I.R. 220 at 225.
[19] Company Law Review Group, First Report (Government Publications, Dublin, 1994), p. 19, para. 3.13.
[20] *R. v. Board of Trade ex parte St Martins Preserving Co Ltd* [1965] 1 Q.B. 603.

or understanding which, though not legally binding, is or was observed or likely to be observed in practice and which is relevant to the purposes of his investigation."

13–23   Section 10 imposes duties on all officers and agents of the company whose affairs are under investigation by inspectors appointed by the court under section 7 or section 8 of the 1990 Act, and confers corresponding powers on the inspectors. The effect of these duties and powers is that inspectors can require officers and agents to produce all books and documents of, or relating to, the company, to attend before the inspectors when required so to do and otherwise to give to the inspectors all assistance in connection with the investigation which they are reasonably able to give. Section 10(4) gives an inspector power to examine on oath the officers and agents of the company. Failure on the part of an individual to comply with the obligations imposed by section 10 can result in a court punishing the offender. When amendments to this section pursuant to section 23 of the Company Law Enforcement Act 2001 comes into operation the court will have wide discretion as to the order to be made consequent on non-compliance.

13–24   In addition, section 10(3) extends the power to permit an inspector, in certain circumstances, to require a present or past director or shadow director to produce all documents relating to bank accounts maintained by that person. The relevant circumstances include where money paid into or out of the account has resulted from or been used in the financing of certain transactions, arrangements or agreements that should have been disclosed in the company's accounts or a register of such transactions and was not, or where the money was used in connection with misconduct by the director towards the company or its members. This additional power applies to court-appointed inspectors only – thus inspectors appointed under section 14 cannot access directors' personal bank accounts notwithstanding the contrary judgment in *Glackin v. Trustee Savings Bank*.[21]

Section 18 of the Act provides that answers given by a person to questions put to him in exercise of powers under section 10 may be used in evidence against him. The constitutionality and proportionality of this provision have been upheld by the Supreme Court,[22] although the admissibility of the evidence was held by Barrington J. not to extend in general to confessions for the purposes of criminal proceedings unless in a particular case the trial judge was satisfied that the confession was voluntary. When amendments to this section pursuant to section 28 of the 2001 Act come into operation, the power to use answers given in evidence against the individual giving them will not extend to their use in criminal proceedings other than proceedings for perjury.

---

[21][1993] 3 I.R. 55. See McGrath, D., "Investigations under the Companies Act 1990" (1993) 11 *Irish Law Times* 264.

[22]*Re National Irish Bank (No. 1)* [1999] 3 I.R. 145.

Conduct of an investigation

13–25 Inspectors are not bound by strict rules of natural justice until such time as a determination on an issue which is contentious is made.[23] Thereafter, basic procedural fairness must be observed.

Production of books and records

13–26 Sections 10 and 19 of the Companies Act 1990 deal with information to be disclosed by officers and agents of companies (and related companies under section 9) to inspectors (section 10) and authorised officers of the Minister (section 19).

13–27 As already stated (see para. **13–23** *et seq.*), under section 10(1) of the Companies Act 1990 inspectors can require the production of books and documents relating to companies under investigation and related companies and can examine persons on oath. Where an officer or agent of the company or a related company, or any other person considered by the inspectors to be in possession of any information concerning the company's affairs, refuses to produce the books and documents requested, to attend before the inspectors or to answer any question concerning the affairs of the company, the inspectors may certify such refusal to the court. It is this certification that triggers the court's power to punish the offender following an inquiry into the matter.

13–28 The material supplied to the inspector must be that which in the honest opinion of the officers and agents of the company may be of assistance to the inspector.[24] The Company Law Review Group recognised that there may be difficulties arising from the element of subjective judgment as to what information should be provided. However, the Group was of the opinion that section 10 strikes the correct balance between powers of inspectors and presumed co-operation of respondents.[25] The information does not have to be the property of the company.[26]

13–29 Amendments to these requirements will come into effect when a date is fixed for the coming into operation of section 23 of the Company Law Enforcement Act 2001 with three consequent effects:

---

[23] See Courtney, T.B., *The Law of Private Companies* (Butterworths, Dublin, 1994), pp. 817–820, paras 20.019 to 20.023 for a more detailed discussion of the issues.

[24] McGrath, D., "Investigations under the Companies Act 1990" (1993) 11 *Irish Law Times* 264.

[25] Company Law Review Group, First Report (Government Publications, Dublin 1994), p. 20, para. 3.15.

[26] *Chestvale Properties Ltd v. Glackin* [1993] 3 I.R. 35 at 53.

- A lien on company books or documents will not be prejudiced by the legislation – this amendment limits the scope for legal objection to producing the material to inspectors thus facilitating progress of the inspection.

- Recalcitrant companies or company officers will be open to punishment at the discretion of the court.

- Under section 10 of the Companies Act 1990, books and records must be produced by "officers and agents" of the company. Section 23 of the 2001 Act extends the definition of agents to include accountants, bookkeepers and taxation advisers, as well as auditors as previously.

13–30   In circumstances described in para. **13–12**, section 19 of the Companies Act 1990 requires companies to produce books and documents as specified by the Minister or his authorised officer. The books and documents can be requested of any person believed to be in possession of them. Persons required to produce the books and documents must state their whereabouts. Such a statement can be used in evidence against the person.

13–31   Section 23(1) of the Companies Act 1990 exempts from the requirements to disclose information to inspectors or authorised officers any information that the person involved would, in the opinion of the court, be entitled to refuse to produce on the grounds of legal professional privilege. Others such as banks[27] or journalists[28] are not protected by privilege. Section 23(2) provides that, in a section 19 investigation, bank records relating to the affairs of customers must only be required to be produced where it appears to the Minister that such production is necessary for the purposes of the investigation or where the customer is a person on whom a requirement has been imposed under section 19.

13–32   Section 29 of the Company Law Enforcement Act 2001 replaces section 19 of the Companies Act 1990. The power of examination of books and documents is transferred from the Minister to the Director of Corporate Enforcement. In addition, the books and documents examinable are extended to include books and documents of other companies but which contain information about the company being investigated. Powers of inspection of the books and documents are extended under subsection (5) and would allow for:

- copies to be taken;

- provision of explanations to the Director of Corporate Enforcement by present and past officers and employees of the company being investigated, including those employed in a professional, consultancy or similar capacity;

---

[27] *Glackin v. Trustee Savings Bank* [1993] 3 I.R. 55.
[28] *Re an inquiry under the Company Securities (Insider Dealing) Act 1985* [1988] A.C. 660.

- statements of where the books and documents are located in the event that they are not produced to the Director of Corporate Enforcement;

- provision of all assistance to the Director of Corporate Enforcement.

13–33   Section 19(8) of the 1990 Act as inserted by section 29 of the 2001 Act will, when operative, make it an offence, notwithstanding, to destroy, mutilate, falsify or conceal any book or document the subject of a direction for its production.

13–34   To ensure that the examination of books and records under section 19 is as comprehensive as possible, section 32 of the Act widens the terms of section 23(2) of the Companies Act 1990. This change enables bank documents to be accessed even where the company under examination is not a customer of the bank. No date has yet been fixed for the coming into operation of section 32.

Access to company minutes

13–35   Section 19 of the 2001 Act amends section 145 of the Companies Act 1963 to allow the Director of Corporate Enforcement access to records of decisions of companies. It requires minutes of company meetings and of meetings of directors and board committees to be produced to the Director of Corporate Enforcement on request. No date has yet been fixed for the coming into operation of section 19.

Tribunals of inquiry[29]

13–36   Where accountants appear publicly in tribunals, it is almost always as witnesses of fact rather than as forensic accounting experts. When asked to give evidence as a witness of fact, an accountant should not respond without taking legal advice and considering it carefully. In particular, he should be aware that his evidence may give rise to an investigation of the accountant himself under the rules of his professional body.

This is not to say that forensic accountants do not have a role to play in tribunals. However, this role is mostly played behind the scenes in providing expert support and assistance to the tribunal or, alternatively, to those witnesses of fact appearing before it. Tribunals involving forensic accountants are those concerning allegations of financial irregularities. The investigative skills of forensic accountants are invaluable in this work in analysing transactions through large volumes of company records and multiple bank accounts, and in tracing

---

[29] The authors are indebted to Christopher Doyle, Gerard Hogan and Michael Moriarty who provided very helpful advice on tribunals.

the movements of cash from account to account and through large numbers of jurisdictions.

13–37 Hogan and Morgan[30] list examples of the many and various types of tribunals in Ireland. They define a tribunal as "...a body, independent of the Government or any other entity but at the same time not a court, which takes decisions affecting individual rights, according to some fairly precise (and usually legal) guidelines and by following a regular and fairly formal procedure".[31] A category of inquiry, statutory inquiries, is identified, which has two sub-categories: what Hogan and Morgan describe as "decision inquiries" (which are required for determining outcomes in a wide spectrum of areas such as planning and disciplinary matters) and "post-mortem" inquiries.[32]

Post-mortem inquiries investigate accidents, natural disasters and other matters of public interest. Normally such inquiries take the form of public hearings where witnesses give detailed evidence under oath in response to questions from tribunal lawyers and may be subject to cross-examination on behalf of other interested or affected persons. The principal Act, the Tribunals of Inquiry (Evidence) Act 1921, established the procedures and powers of tribunals of inquiry and provided for such tribunals to take evidence. This Act has been amended four times: in 1979, 1997 and twice in 1998. Section 2 of the Tribunals of Inquiry (Evidence) (Amendment) Act 1979 provides for a tribunal of one or more persons "sitting with or without an assessor or assessors appointed by the instrument appointing the tribunal or any instrument supplemental thereto". Much of the new legislation stemmed from the decision in *Re Haughey*.[33] In that case, key sections of the Committee of Public Accounts of Dáil Éireann (Privilege and Procedure) Act 1970 was found to be unconstitutional because (in effect) it purported to permit a tribunal to determine that a witness was in contempt and send that person forward for sentence only to the High Court, so that the tribunal was given a form of jurisdiction in criminal cases. The invalidation of that Act cast a shadow over the constitutionality of section 1 of the 1921 Act and this was only partly cured by the 1979 Act which provided that such conduct (contempt) would henceforth be an offence, triable in the ordinary way.

The events disclosed in the Report of the Tribunal of Inquiry (Dunnes Payments) (the "McCracken Report") showed that, short of a potentially long and complex criminal prosecution, the absence of a contempt power on the part of the tribunal meant that there was no effective means of enforcing its orders. Accordingly, it was necessary of the Oireachtas to give the High Court (via section 4 of the 1997 Act) the power to enforce orders of the tribunal.

---

[30] Hogan, G. and Morgan, D.G., *Administrative Law in Ireland* (3rd ed., Round Hall Sweet & Maxwell, Dublin, 1998), Chap. 6.
[31] *ibid.*, pp. 256–257.
[32] *ibid.*, pp. 293 *et seq.*
[33] [1971] I.R. 217.

13–38 The Report of the Tribunal of Inquiry (Dunnes Payments) (the "McCracken Report") illustrated an apparent weakness in the legislation such that, despite the tribunal's finding that much of the evidence given by Mr Charles Haughey to the tribunal could not be accepted, the tribunal did not have the power to order Mr Haughey to pay any of the tribunal's own costs. The Tribunals of Inquiry (Evidence) (Amendment) Act 1997 addressed this issue by providing to the tribunal or its chairperson the power to order the payment by any other person, of part or all of, not only the costs of any person appearing before the tribunal represented by counsel or solicitor but also the costs incurred by the tribunal itself.

13–39 This Act also confers certain immunities and privileges on persons who produce or send documents to a tribunal pursuant to an order of that tribunal. It also establishes a mechanism whereby orders of tribunals can be enforced by the High Court. The Tribunals of Inquiry (Evidence) (Amendment) Act 1998, and the Tribunals of Inquiry (Evidence) (Amendment) (No. 2) Act 1998 provide for the amendment of a tribunal's terms of reference in restricted circumstances when such amendment is sought by the tribunal or is consented to by the tribunal following consultation with the Attorney General.

13–40 The function of a tribunal is as a finder of fact. It has no power to impose a criminal sanction or to adjust legal rights.[34]

"The Tribunal has no jurisdiction or authority of any description to impose a penalty or punishment on any person . . . It is a simle fact-finding operation, reporting to the legislative."[35]

Establishment of tribunals

13–41 Section 1 of the 1921 Act provides for the appointment of a tribunal where both Houses of the Oireachtas consider that one is required to inquire into a definite matter of urgent public importance. Table 13.3 overleaf lists the tribunals convened over the years since 1922. Most of the early tribunals dealt with issues not of concern to accountants. Exceptions include:

– the Great Southern Railway Stock Tribunal in 1943 which concerned allegations of improper dealings in shares; and

– the Sale of Locke's Distillery Tribunal in 1947 which concerned allegations of political interference in the sale of the distillery.

13–42 Commencing with the Beef Tribunal in 1992, appearances by accountants (in various capacities) at tribunals have now become regular occurrences.

---

[34] Brady, R., "Reflections on tribunals of inquiry" (1997) 3 *Bar Review* 121.
[35] *Goodman International v. Hamilton* [1992] 2 I.R. 542 at 588, *per* Finlay, J.

Table 13.3: Appointment of tribunals by Houses of the Oireachtas

Year	Tribunal	Chairman
1928	Shooting of Timothy Coughlan	Cussen J.
1937	Fire at Pearse St, Dublin	Maguire J.
1943	Fire at St Joseph's Orphanage, Cavan	McCarthy J.
1943	Great Southern Railway Stock – improper dealings in shares	Overend J.
1946	Monaghan Curing Company	O'Byrne J.*
1947	Sale of Locke's Distillery	O'Byrne J.*
1967	Death in Custody of Liam O'Mahony	Fitzgerald, W.O'B., SC
1970	RTÉ "Seven Days" programme on money lending	De Buitléir J.
1975	Allegations by two TDs against Minister for Local Government	Henchy J.
1980	Whiddy Island oil disaster	Costello J.
1982	Stardust nightclub fire	Keane J.
1985	Kerry babies	Lynch J.
1992	Beef processing industry (Goodman Tribunal)	Hamilton P.
1997	Blood Transfusion Service Board – Hepatitis C	Finlay J.
1997	Dunnes payments to politicians	McCracken J.
1997	Financial affairs of Charles Haughey and Michael Lowry	Moriarty J.
1997	Planning and other payments	Flood J.
1999	Blood Transfusion Service Board – HIV	Lindsay J.
2000	Post-mortem inquiry	Dunne, A., S.C.

Source: Adapted from O'Doherty, S. [1988] I.C.L.S.A. 60–42.

*These were unusual tribunals in that three judges (rather than the customary one) formed the tribunal: O'Byrne J. (Sup. Ct.), O'Hanrahan J. (High Ct.), and Shannon J. (Circ. Ct.).

Powers of tribunals

13–43 Where the instrument by which a tribunal is appointed or any instrument supplemental thereto provides that the 1921 Act (as amended) applies, the tribunal has all the powers, rights and privileges as are vested in the High Court on the occasion of an action in respect of:

– enforcing attendance of witnesses and examination of them on oath or affirmation;

– compelling the production of documents; and

– subject to rules of court, issuing a commission or request to examine witnesses abroad.

Offences

13–44 Section 1 of the 1921 Act, as amended, lists several offences, including: disobeying a summons to appear as a witness before the tribunal; refusing to take an oath or affirmation; refusing to produce a document legally required by the tribunal to be produced; refusing to answer a question; giving evidence, material to the inquiry, to the tribunal knowing it to be false or not believing it to be true; obstructing or hindering the tribunal in the performance of its functions; failing, neglecting or refusing to comply with an order of the tribunal; and otherwise doing or omitting something where such act or omission would be contempt of the High Court if the tribunal had been that court. These offences are punishable by a fine of up to £10,000 or up to two years imprisonment or both.

Costs

13–45   Powers to order that the legal costs of any person appearing before the tribunal be paid by another person are provided to tribunals under section 6(1) of the Tribunals of Inquiry (Evidence) (Amendment) Act 1979:

> "Where a tribunal, ... is of the opinion that, having regard to the findings of the tribunal and all other relevant matters, there are sufficient reasons rendering it equitable to do so, the tribunal ... may by order direct that the whole or part of the costs of any person appearing before the tribunal by counsel or solicitor, as taxed by a Taxing Master of the High Court, shall be paid to the person by any other person named in the order."

13–46   As pointed out above in para. **13–38**, this power was extended in the 1997 Act to allow the tribunal to order another person to pay all or part of the costs of the tribunal itself. In order to exercise this power the tribunal or its chairperson must be:

> "... of opinion that, having regard to the findings of the tribunal and all other relevant matters (including the terms of the resolution passed by each House of the Oireachtas relating to the establishment of the tribunal or failing to co-operate with or provide assistance to, or knowingly giving false or misleading information to, the tribunal), there are sufficient reasons rendering it equitable to do so".[36]

13–47   In the case of the Beef Tribunal, almost all costs were awarded to parties represented at the tribunal. However, it should not be assumed that this would happen in all tribunals. For example, all except one application for costs in the Whiddy Tribunal were rejected.[37] Carroll J. interpreted the Act of 1979 to mean that only witness expenses relating to witnesses who actually give oral evidence before a tribunal are recoverable.[38] However, it should be re-iterated that the ground rules for costs have been greatly changed and pre-1997 practice and case law will be to that extent modified by the 1997 Act.[39]

---

[36] Tribunals of Inquiry (Evidence) (Amendment) Act 1997, s. 3(1).
[37] See Hogan, G. and Morgan, D.G., *Administrative Law in Ireland* (3rd ed., Round Hall Sweet & Maxwell, Dublin, 1998), pp. 303–306 for a discussion on this point.
[38] *Minister for Finance v. Flynn*, unreported, High Court, February 9, 1996.
[39] See generally judgment of Laffoy J. in *Minister for Finance v. Goodman* [1999] 3 I.R. 333.

Examining tribunal witnesses

13–48 Section 5 of the 1979 Act provides that any statement or admission made to a tribunal is not admissible as evidence against the person making the statement or admission in criminal proceedings other than in proceedings in relation to the giving of evidence which the witness knows to be false or does not believe to be true. The section appears to be designed to encourage candid disclosure on the part of persons dealing with tribunals without fear of self-incrimination in general terms, but excepting situations where persons seek to mislead tribunals themselves by false or untruthful testimony.

13–49 A consequence of public tribunals is the sacrifice of the constitutional right of citizens to privacy and confidentiality in favour of the public's right to know where matters of urgent public concern are involved. The courts have upheld such public interest primacy.[40]

Role of accountants in investigations and tribunals

13–50 Accountants may become involved in company investigations either as witnesses of fact (*e.g.* as officers or employees of the company being investigated) or in a forensic accounting capacity in any one of the following ways:

– as inspectors;

– as agents of inspectors;

– as persons authorised by the Minister under section 19 of the Companies Act 1990;

– acting on behalf of clients.

Accountants may provide forensic accounting services in the context of tribunals in more limited circumstances:

– as agents of the tribunal; or

– acting on behalf of clients.

Indeed, whilst it has been almost invariable practice to have tribunals chaired by serving or retired judges, there is no reason in principle why an accountant with appropriate expertise should not chair a tribunal.

---

[40] *Goodman International v. Hamilton* [1992] 2 I.R. 542; *Haughey v. Moriarty* [1999] 3 I.R. 1; *Redmond v. Flood* [1999] 3 I.R. 79; *J. Murphy v. Flood* [2000] 2 I.R. 298.

13–51 The normal considerations regarding skills, expertise, experience and resources apply when a forensic accountant is given the opportunity to act in such a case. A discussion of the necessary skills and expertise is contained in Chapters 4 and 5.

Concluding comment

13–52 The explosion of company investigations and tribunals in Ireland in recent years shows no sign of slowing down. As the various investigations and tribunals develop, it is becoming apparent that the skills of investigative accountants and auditors can be highly relevant and very useful to inspectors, authorised officers and tribunals. In fact, the careful following of a paper trail and the verification of explanations of transactions, so essential to the success of some of the ongoing investigations, constitute the daily work diet of many accountants in practice. There is clearly an opportunity here both for accountants to become more involved and for hard-worked inspectors, authorised officers and tribunals to benefit from relevant skills. Should such involvement expedite the conclusion of certain matters, so much the better.

Recent trends suggest that accountants will play an increasing role in investigations (at a minimum) and possibly in tribunals of inquiry. Establishment of the new Office of Corporate Enforcement points to increased activity of this nature, with the consequent increasing involvement of accountants in such activities.

CHAPTER 14 — CONTENTS

ALTERNATIVE DISPUTE RESOLUTION

ALTERNATIVE DISPUTE RESOLUTION

CHAPTER 14

ALTERNATIVE DISPUTE RESOLUTION

14–01   Alternative dispute resolution (ADR) is defined in the glossary to the Civil Procedure Rules in the United Kingdom as:

> "A collective description of methods of resolving disputes otherwise than through the normal trial process".[1]

Increasingly, individuals and companies are trying to find ways of settling disputes without going to trial. Spurred by cost considerations, the number of claims settled by the use of alternative methods of dispute resolution is growing.[2] A key trend, borne out by statistics, is a growing shift away from courtroom confrontations. Litigation suffers from drawbacks which make other forms of dispute resolution more attractive. The judicial system can be slow and expensive. The large number of cases filed relative to the supply of judicial resources can lead to delay. Faced with increasing litigation, the Irish courts system is under strain resulting in inevitable delays, especially in non-urgent work. The costs involved and the delay in the court system encourage the parties to accept other methods of dispute resolution.

The role of forensic accountants in the courts has been described in Chapters 7 to 12. Their role in ADR proceedings is similar. Disputes that tend to go to arbitration are distinguished by being more technical and often involving cross-border aspects than cases that go to court, *e.g.* disputes arising out of large construction projects. Irrespective of the technical nature of the dispute, and of the number of jurisdictions involved, there will almost always be financial calculations to be performed. These calculations are no different to the ones described in earlier chapters, except that the arbitration agreement may prescribe a formula for damages. Forensic accountants appearing in disputes subject to ADR should appreciate the different procedures operating in such circumstances.

This chapter provides a summary of types of ADR. It also examines procedure

---

[1]   The Civil Procedure Rules (S.I. 1998 No. 3132) (L.17) (HMSO, London, 1998). Available at www.hmso.gov.uk/si/si1998/98313202.htm.

[2]   For example, "an increasing number of couples are avoiding courtroom separation battles by seeking help from a State-run mediation service. Last year, more than 1,000 couples went to the Family Mediation Service (FMS) – 20 per cent of the total over the past 13 years", "Couples turn to mediation" in *Sunday Independent*, September 3, 2000.

concerning arbitration, concluding with a consideration of the role of forensic accountants in these processes.[3]

14–02 If parties to a dispute cannot reach a settlement, they may be required (usually by a contract) to submit to ADR. Even if ADR is not required, the parties may consider arbitration or mediation as a potentially faster and less expensive alternative to litigation in court. Within business organisations, disputes often arise that can only be resolved when an independent review has been made of accounting records. ADR, including arbitration, mediation and mini-trial, has become a viable alternative to traditional litigation. It is particularly suitable for parties who wish to retain a working relationship after the dispute is over.

14–03 Besides arbitration and mediation, ADR can involve a neutral party's early evaluation of the strengths of the opposing cases or a mini-trial of the issues.

14–04 Although there is no specific policy in the Irish legal system that ADR is to be preferred in any particular circumstances, judges have made it clear in several cases that the process of arbitration has their support and that the courts should be slow to interfere with the determinations of validly appointed arbitrators. Barron J. in *Vogelaar v. Callaghan*[4] put it as follows:

> "Arbitration is an alternative to litigation through the courts. Its merit is that it is cheaper and speedier. At the same time it is an acknowledgement by the parties that they are placing their problem before an arbitrator for his final decision. It must, therefore, be only in rare circumstances where justice can obviously be seen not to have been done that the courts should entertain applications to set aside such awards or to remit them to the arbitrator for further consideration. Such steps on the part of the court should be taken only where there is some form of misconduct either by the arbitrator or in the course of the proceedings in some other way. This is indicated by ss. 31 and 38 the Arbitration Act, 1954. Much of the complaint made by the plaintiffs in the present case is in reality an effort to appeal the decision of the arbitrator and as such is a misunderstanding of the function of the arbitrator and the system of arbitration itself."

---

[3] The laws applying to arbitration are considered by Forde, M., *Arbitration Law & Procedure* (The Round Hall Press, Dublin, 1994); Walton, A. and Vitoria, M. *Russell on the Law of Arbitration* (20th ed., Stevens & Sons London, 1982); and in a forensic accounting context in MacGregor, G. and Hobbs, I., *Expert Accounting Evidence: A Guide for Litigation Support* (Accountancy Books, London, 1998), Chap. 14; Lemar, C.J. and Mainz, A.J. (eds), *Litigation Support* (4th ed., Butterworths, London, 1999), Chap. 20; Taub, M., Rapazzini, A., Bond, C., Solon, M., Brown, A., Murrie, A., Linnell, K. and Burn, S., *Tolley's Accountancy Litigation Support* (Butterworths, London, looseleaf), Part VII, para. 160.

[4] [1996] 1 I.R. 88 at 93.

Alternative forms of dispute resolution

14–05 Disputes can be resolved by a variety of means other than litigation. Alternative dispute resolution includes techniques such as negotiation, mediation, conciliation and arbitration. The former three methods are non-binding on the parties to the dispute. Arbitration has the advantage of being binding on the parties.

Non-binding procedures

14–06 Negotiation, mediation and conciliation differ from litigation and arbitration in that the parties are not bound to accept the final result. This means that there is no binding verdict, although such agreements can in practice be very durable. The function of the negotiator/mediator/conciliator is to bring the parties together to facilitate reaching a settlement agreement.

Negotiation

14–07 Negotiations are direct communications between parties or their representatives for the purpose of reaching a settlement or agreement.[5] Negotiation usually involves representatives of each party communicating directly with each other without the presence of an independent person. This process is used most often when there is some agreement on, or at least appreciation of, the boundaries surrounding the range of possible solutions to the dispute (*e.g.* in financial settlement negotiations, the maximum and minimum reasonable or realistic amounts). This gives a context and focus for the discussions and the parties generally proceed to state the important elements and arguments supporting their point of view with a view to moving towards their preferred boundary. When all parties have stated their cases, there is generally a better understanding all round of the relative strengths and weaknesses of the position of each party.

14–08 Each party will also give some advance thought to their planned negotiation strategy. They will be influenced in this regard by the relative strength of the positions of the parties and their knowledge of the strategy likely to be adopted by the other parties. Attempts will be made to identify possible concessions that have more value to one party than to another, *i.e.* opportunities to give a little and get a lot because the little given is valued highly by the recipient. Thought will also be given to whether the opening position should be an extreme one, allowing significant room for apparent movement and concession,

---

[5] Chernick, R., Strong, G.G. and Shea, J.S., "Roles and techniques of an accountant in alternative dispute resolution" in *Litigation Services Handbook: The Role of the Accountant as Expert* (2nd ed., Weil, R.L., Wagner, M.J. and Frank, P.B. (eds), John Wiley & Sons, Inc., New York, 1995), p. 9.2.

or whether this would serve only to annoy a well-informed opponent who wishes to negotiate from the outset on a realistic basis.

14–09   Often, there will be an implied (but not necessarily explicitly stated) threat of legal proceedings in the event of failure of negotiations. When this is the case, each party will factor into their thinking the likely costs, delays and uncertainties of litigation. These factors tend to introduce some room for manoeuvre on all sides.

14–10   Negotiation is regarded as the most direct way of reaching a solution but differences in negotiation strength may mean that the solution is unfair or short-lived. A more structured form of negotiation is the mini-trial, presided over by a neutral third party (see para. **14–15**) where each side's case is presented before a panel of persons with authority to propose settlement terms.

Mediation

14–11   The key characteristic of mediation is that the mediator does not decide the issue in dispute. The essential feature of mediation is the presence of a third party co-operating with the disputing sides to find a solution, rather than imposing one (as a judge would). The mediator facilitates a process by which the parties attempt to agree a resolution between them. A mediator interposes between two or more parties in dispute for the purpose of reconciling their differences. A mediator will assist the parties to recognise the strengths and weaknesses of their relative positions, and the positions of opposing parties. The mediator may suggest compromises and strategies to resolve the dispute. In theory, this provides greater flexibility and allows the parties to exercise greater control over the procedures and results. Once the resolution is agreed it is reproduced in writing. Experts will often provide assistance in the mediation process by bringing objectivity to bear on matters of liability and quantum.

14–12   Mediation is most used in matrimonial cases.[6] Legislation governing divorce and judicial separation in Ireland requires that the parties involved be given an opportunity to consider mediation before deciding to proceed with a break-up. In particular, the Family Law (Divorce) Act 1996 states that the solicitor acting for an applicant for divorce must, before instituting divorce proceedings:

> ". . . discuss with the applicant the possibility of engaging in mediation to help to effect a separation (if the spouses are not separated) or a divorce on a basis agreed between the applicant and the other spouse and give to the applicant the names and addresses of persons qualified to provide a mediation service for spouses who have become estranged".[7]

---

[6] "Couples turn to mediation", *Sunday Independent*, September 3, 2000.
[7] Family Law (Divorce) Act 1996, s. 6(2)(b).

14–13 The other party's solicitor is required to do the same as soon as possible after being instructed in relation to the proceedings. The Judicial Separation and Family Law Reform Act 1989 contains similar provisions in relation to judicial separation.

14–14 Mediation can take different forms, such as mini-trials or "shuttle diplomacy", where the mediator presents different versions of a proposal to the parties in turn until agreement is reached.[8]

14–15 A mini-trial[9] is an early short trial, usually no longer than a day, where both sides present their case to individuals who have authority to propose settlement terms for the matter (*e.g.* the chief executive in an employment dispute in a company). The process does not bind the parties, nor can they use information learned in the proceedings in a subsequent trial of the dispute. The mini-trial has no formal rules of procedure or evidence. Decision makers discuss the case and attempt to resolve the dispute. The mini-trial is most often used in commercial disputes in the United States, but is not common in Ireland.

14–16 The mediation process is voluntary and informal. The outcome of mediation is non-binding and must be agreed to by all the parties. The process is private, and the arguments, evidence and outcome are not subject to disclosure unless both parties agree.

14–17 The London Court of International Arbitration provides sample procedures or rules for mediation of disputes.[10]

Conciliation

14–18 In conciliation, a third party helps the parties to reach their own agreement, rather than actively suggesting solutions. It can be seen as a form of mediation. Conciliation is most useful when the parties involved will need to continue a working or close commercial relationship after the dispute has been resolved. It is designed to find a solution that both sides ultimately find agreeable, or at least acceptable. It is used where the parties have a good appreciation of the merits of the positions taken by the other, but for tactical, public relations or other reasons they cannot be seen to "give in without a fight". Conciliation procedures are often followed in labour disputes over pay increments, productivity changes and redundancy.

---

[8] Doherty, B., "Should arbitration be like litigation?" (1995) 2 C.L.P. 204.

[9] Frank, P.B., Wagner, M.J. and Weil, R.L., "The role of the CPA in litigation services", in *Litigation Services Handbook: The Role of the Accountant as Expert* (2nd ed., Weil, R.L., Wagner, M.J. and Frank, P.B. (eds), John Wiley & Sons, Inc., New York, 1995), p.1.7.

[10] London Court of International Arbitration, www.lcia-arbitration.com/rulecost/mediation.htm.

Arbitration

14–19 By contrast with a mediator, an arbitrator will hear the parties to an arbitration and will make a determination of the issue, which will be binding on the parties. Arbitration is therefore much closer to litigation than is mediation. Both statute law and the common law govern arbitration.

14–20 Arbitration is a contractual process by which a dispute is resolved by an independent person, selected on the basis of expertise, reputation, training and experience as an arbitrator.[11] For centuries, arbitration has been the procedure of choice of parties in shipping and commodity disputes. One of the earliest arbitrations held by the merchants of Dublin involved a dispute about ownership of the cargo of the *Ouzel Galley*, which returned to Ireland following a dramatic voyage, at the beginning of the eighteenth century.[12]

14–21 Arbitration as a means of dispute resolution, alternative to the courts, is growing and developing in Ireland. This alternative to litigation is supported both by the legislature and by the courts in Ireland. Arbitration has developed as a favoured alternative to litigation because it combines procedural flexibility with binding decisions which can be supervised by the courts.

What is arbitration?

14–22 There is no statutory or judicial definition of arbitration. Arbitration can be defined as a process for resolving disputes based on an enforceable agreement to arbitrate.[13] It is a private dispute resolution mechanism. The arbitrator is required to act judicially (not merely as expert or valuer) in relation to a dispute that relates only to formulated differences of some kind. This means that the parties to the agreement are bound by the terms of their agreement and can only refer to arbitration disputes that fall to be resolved by arbitration under the terms of the agreement. As a result, there can be serious wrongs (usually of a tortious nature) not dealt with in the contract and therefore not covered by the arbitration clause. Consequently, the arbitrator, once appointed, can clearly define the limits of his powers and his scope to make findings in favour of one party or the other. This leads to an attractive degree of certainty as to the range of possible outcomes of the arbitral process.

14–23 The process usually involves appointment of an arbitrator selected by

---

[11] MacGregor, G. and Hobbs, I., *Expert Accounting Evidence: A Guide for Litigation Support* (Accountancy Books, London, 1998), p. 201.
[12] Chartered Institute of Arbitrators, Irish Branch, www.arbitration.ie.
[13] Mustill, M.J.M. and Boyd, S.C., *The Law and Practice of Commercial Arbitration in England* (2nd ed., Butterworths, London, 1989), p. 31.

the parties or, in default of agreement, by a nominated third party (often the President of a relevant professional body or of an Institute of Arbitrators), and results in a binding decision known as an award. The fact that an arbitrator's award is enforceable summarily in the courts makes arbitration a unique alternative to litigation when compared with other means of dispute resolution.

14–24 Although arbitration may be imposed by statute (*e.g.* see section 8 of the Prompt Payment of Accounts Act 1997), more commonly it tends to be consensual and is binding on the parties by virtue of an arbitration clause in an agreement between them. The arbitration clause will normally indicate the events triggering its operation. It will contain a mechanism for the selection of an arbitrator, and will indicate the rules to be applied by the arbitrator. Such an agreement may be contained in a contract predating the dispute, or the parties to a dispute may make the agreement after the dispute has arisen.

14–25 Almost any dispute which can be resolved by litigation in the courts can be settled by arbitration. Areas where arbitration has proved especially effective include: purchase price disputes; potentially misleading or false financial statements; valuation matters; building and civil engineering contracts; shipping; rent review clauses in commercial leases; partnership disputes; insurance; manufacturing generally; computer applications; imports and exports; processing industry; general trading; commodities and the engineering industry.

14–26 Insurance policies commonly include arbitration provisions to apply when disputes arise over whether an event and/or party is validly insured under the policy. In recent years, most travel contracts provide that disputes will be referred to arbitration. Commercial parties have increasingly adopted arbitration clauses as the dispute resolution method of choice in contracts for financial services, insurance, reinsurance, technology transfer, distributorship agreements, entertainment agreements, service agreements and sales contracts including consumer sales and services.

14–27 An advantage of arbitration over litigation in court is that the parties have the opportunity to have their dispute heard and resolved by an individual or individuals with expertise in their field of activity and full familiarity with business and commercial practices in their industry. Typically, parties to a specialist contract (*e.g.* in construction) will agree that the arbitrator will be appointed by agreement or, where agreement cannot be reached, by someone in their industry (*e.g.* the President of the Institute of Engineers). This should ensure a knowledgeable arbitrator rather than a well-intentioned, but less than fully informed member of the judiciary whose brief is far too wide to allow him to become expert in all industries or fields of activity that feature in cases before him.

14–28 Arbitration can also be especially useful in settling international disputes where it might be unclear which country's courts have jurisdiction.

Statutory provision for arbitration

14–29 Although the arbitration agreement is a private one between the parties, it is supported by public law, notably by supervision of the courts. Legal privileges under arbitration derive from the Arbitration Acts 1954 to 1998 which provide a structural legal framework for both domestic and international arbitrations. In addition, case law has bestowed on arbitration a status not enjoyed by other procedures.

14–30 There are three pieces of legislation in Ireland dealing with arbitration. They are the Arbitration Act 1954, the Arbitration Act 1988 and the Arbitration (International Commercial) Act 1998. This body of legislation deals with:

– the irrevocable authority of arbitrators, subject only to the court;

– penalties for false evidence given to an arbitrator;

– the power of the parties and of the court in certain circumstances to appoint arbitrators or to fill a vacancy arising in an arbitration;

– the manner in which an arbitration is conducted, including the time it is deemed to commence, the power of the arbitrator and of the court to summon and examine witnesses in arbitration proceedings, the power of the court in relation to an arbitration to order security for costs, to order discovery and inspection of documents, to order the securing of property and to order injunctions;

– the power of the court to stay court proceedings in favour of arbitration, subject to the rights of the parties to avail of the alternative procedure set out in the rules of court for small claims;

– the power of the arbitrator to make interim and final awards, the binding nature of the awards and the powers of enforcement of awards available to the parties;

– the arbitrator's power to deal with costs and interest on the award;

– the statement of a case by an arbitrator for decision by the court;

– the power of the court to remit an award back to the arbitrator for reconsideration;

– the power of the court to remove an arbitrator on the grounds of delay or misconduct or to revoke his authority on the grounds of bias on the part of the arbitrator or fraud on the part of one of the parties to the arbitration;

– the power of the court to set aside the award of an arbitrator on the grounds of an arbitrator's misconduct or the improper procurement of the arbitration or the award;

– the application of the statutes of limitations to arbitrations;

– the enforcement in the State of awards under foreign arbitrations;

– the incorporation in Irish law of the Geneva Protocol, the New York Convention and the Washington Convention.

14–31 The Acts specifically exclude arbitrations arising from employment or industrial relations disputes from the effect of their provisions.

Who can use arbitration?

14–32 Any company or other legal person, capable of entering into a binding legal contract, can agree to refer present and/or future disputes to arbitration. The process is based on the written contractual agreement of the parties.

Disputes which are not suitable for arbitration

14–33 Matters not suitable for arbitration include wrongs that attract a criminal sanction such as a fine or prison sentence and matrimonial matters such as divorce, custody and so on. Furthermore, an arbitrator's award is a private matter and cannot, therefore, be effective against anyone who is not party to the dispute. This means that arbitration cannot be used in a dispute which necessarily involves parties outside the arbitration agreement.

14–34 Where any of the parties to an agreement are not willing to commit to refer present or future disputes to arbitration then arbitration cannot be invoked to resolve the dispute unless it is mandated by statute. The jurisdiction of the arbitration tribunal is generally based entirely on the written contract of the parties.

Comparison of different forms of dispute resolution

Advantages of arbitration

14–35 Arbitration offers a number of advantages over litigation. Some of the advantages of arbitration are outlined on the website of the Irish Branch of the Chartered Institute of Arbitrators.[14]

Privacy and confidentiality

14–36 Arbitration is conducted outside of court and in private. In many cases, the whole arbitration process will be considered private and confidential. Arbitral

---

[14] www.arbitration.ie.

awards are private and do not become binding precedents. This can avoid embarrassment for the parties to the dispute and damage to existing commercial relationships. Litigation, on the other hand, must be held in public (unless the rare and exceptional powers of the court or under statute are availed of to permit *in camera* hearings). The risk of publicity can inhibit potential litigants.

Choice of arbitrator

14–37   As already discussed in para. **14–27**, the parties or a nominating body will normally appoint an arbitrator who is an expert in the matter under dispute. The arbitrator is typically chosen by the parties or, where the parties cannot agree, is nominated by a trusted third party. Some arbitrations involve more than one arbitrator – often three, with one appointed by each party and a third agreed by the parties or appointed by an independent body. In litigation, parties have no control over the choice of judge, who may not have the special knowledge or skills that could assist greatly in dealing with the dispute.

Procedural flexibility

14–38   The parties may control, at least to some extent, the manner of the proceedings having regard to the nature of the dispute and to their precise needs. The parties may indicate the degree of formality or informality of the procedure, unless there are pre-ordained rules or the parties are uncertain as to the procedure to adopt, in which case the arbitrator will direct an appropriate procedure. The parties may, for instance, choose documents-only and expedited hearing procedures. Subject only to the provisions of the Arbitration Acts 1954 to 1998, which do not constrain the parties significantly in the manner in which they choose to conduct the arbitration, the parties are free to agree on the procedure to follow.

In practice, to avoid either a very lengthy arbitration clause in the agreement or protracted discussions when it is invoked, parties often agree in advance to adopt one of several internationally recognised sets of rules for the conduct of arbitrations (*e.g.* the rules of the Chartered Institute of Arbitrators – Irish Branch) and this set of rules is incorporated into the arbitration clause in the agreement.

In this regard, it is worth noting that some international arbitral organisations have several sets of rules, depending on the nature and significance of the dispute. Also, it is open to the parties to agree on a set of rules but to specify in their agreement certain amendments to those rules in order to adapt them to their specific circumstances.

14–39   Litigation is confrontational and can be lengthy. Parties cannot control procedures as these are established by statute or by the rules of the court. The parties are subject to rigid precedents. Different judges may hear different stages of a case. All of these factors make litigation less flexible and less easy to adapt to the specific circumstances of the dispute between the parties.

Efficiency

14–40 The parties can decide on the location, language and, to a great extent, the timing of the hearing to facilitate the parties and their witnesses. In litigation, parties have little or no choice over the venue and timing, and this may result in undue travel time for both sides and inconvenience to witnesses and others. Greater speed can result in cost savings.

Informality

14–41 The process is less formal than court. The rules of evidence are not applied to the same extent and matters such as the physical surroundings, the attire of legal representatives and the arbitrator and the absence of formal language reduce the degree of formality. It is also open to the parties in conjunction with the arbitrator to decide on the extent of legal representation in the arbitration. In court litigation, the process and the surroundings tend to be formal and can, in some circumstances, be unnecessarily intimidating.

Certainty, finality and enforceability of the award

14–42 Section 41 of the Arbitration Act 1954 renders an arbitral award enforceable, with the leave of the court, in the same way as a court order or judgment and permits judgment to be entered in terms of the award. Subject to the provisions of the Arbitration Acts 1954 to 1998, the award of the arbitrator is final, binding and enforceable upon the parties. The arbitral award may only be challenged in the High Court on specified limited grounds and there is no other right of appeal of an arbitrator's award. These grounds are:

1. Under section 39 of the 1954 Act, a party can apply to court to have the arbitrator's award set aside on the grounds of misconduct by the arbitrator or improper procurement of the award or of the arbitration.

2. Under section 36 of the 1954 Act, a party can apply to court to have the award remitted to the arbitrator for reconsideration.

14–43 Order 56 of the Rules of the Superior Courts provides that these challenges to the award must be made by special summons within six weeks of the making and disclosure of the award by the arbitrator.

Costs

14–44 Arbitration may be less costly than litigation as the use of the expert as arbitrator can save time on explanations of a technical nature. In addition, an arbitrator will normally be able to attend the hearing at a location to suit the convenience of the parties. The costs of arbitration are primarily time-related and will depend upon the matters in dispute, the procedure chosen by the parties and their choice of representative.

Disadvantages of arbitration

14–45 Arbitration does have some potential or actual disadvantages when compared with litigation. These include:

– the arbitrator may be inexperienced in the process and procedure of dispute resolution, whereas judges gain considerable experience in practice before being eligible for appointment as judges;

– there is no defined procedure to get a judgment in default of appearance or a defence;

– there are no powers available to an arbitrator that correspond with the power of the court to compel the attendance of witnesses (other than the parties to the arbitration and all persons claiming through them), the production of evidence in the possession of third parties and the discovery of documents in the custody, power or possession of third parties;

– the arbitrator and venue are not publicly funded, whereas the State pays for the courtroom and the judge;

– there are generally no binding precedents in arbitration and this can cause uncertainty;

– it may prove necessary to resort to the courts during or after an arbitration, because of delay, bias, problems with the conduct or outcome of the arbitration, issues arising requiring court interpretation or difficulties in obtaining payment on foot of the award. Where a need arises to apply to court for some of these reliefs this would seem to negate, at least in part, the advantages of arbitration.

Thus, to summarise, the theoretical flexibility of procedure can be limited in practice.

14–46 However, it should be noted that it is possible to obtain qualifications in arbitration and that many arbitrators are experienced in industry-specific arbitration and in the law as it applies to arbitration. The qualifications held by an arbitrator can be indicative of both a level of academic attainment and a degree of practical experience as an arbitrator and this can help to overcome some of the perceived drawbacks of arbitration. The Chartered Institute of Arbitrators, through its Irish branch, administers training and examinations for various levels of membership among Irish arbitrators and maintains lists of those individuals who have attained the various levels of experience and proficiency in arbitration.

Arbitration agreements

14–47 An arbitration agreement must be in writing and may address either present or future disputes or both. An agreement to refer an existing dispute to arbitration is often referred to as an "ad hoc reference". The arbitration agreement may incorporate specific requirements of the parties. For example, it may stipulate the place and language of the arbitration. Subject to public policy, it may have provisions relating to the law governing the arbitration. The parties are free to specify the number of arbitrators and their qualifications.

14–48 The Chartered Institute of Arbitrators offers advice on the correct form for an arbitration clause in a contract. The Institute recommends the following standard wording:

> "Any dispute or difference arising out of or in connection with this contract shall be determined by the arbitration of a single arbitrator to be agreed between the parties, or failing agreement within fourteen days after either party has given to the other a written request to concur in the appointment of an arbitrator, by an arbitrator to be appointed by the President or Vice President of the Chartered Institute of Arbitrators."[15]

14–49 The Irish branch of the Institute uses a slightly different form of wording. Parties to a contract who wish to have any dispute referred to arbitration under the rules are recommended to insert in their contract an arbitration clause in the following form:

> "Any dispute or difference of any kind whatsoever which arises or occurs between the parties in relation to any thing or matter arising under, out of, or in connection with this agreement shall be referred to arbitration under the arbitration rules of the Chartered Institute of Arbitrators – Irish Branch."[16]

Some of the differences in the wording arise as a result of relevant Irish case law.

14–50 The London Court of International Arbitration provides sample arbitration rules, recommended clauses and costs.[17] The Chartered Institute of Arbitrators also provides sample arbitration rules on its website to help parties and arbitrators take maximum advantage of the flexible procedures available in arbitration for the resolution of disputes quickly and economically.[18] The rules

---

[15] www.arbitrators.org/materials/arb/arbclause.htm.
[16] Chartered Institute of Arbitrators – Irish Branch, www.arbitration.ie/agreement.htm.
[17] London Court of International Arbitration, www.lcia-arbitration.com/rulecost/english.htm.
[18] www.arbitrators.org/materials/arb/rules.htm.

incorporate relevant provisions of the Arbitration Act 1996 in the United Kingdom and have also taken cognisance of the new Civil Procedure Rules effective there from April 26, 1999. The rules provide that the wishes of parties regarding procedure will be respected so far as possible, but they also seek to ensure that the arbitrator will have sufficient powers to direct the proceedings if the parties cannot agree on procedure or will not co-operate. The Rules may be used without reference to the Institute unless the Institute is required to act as appointing authority in accordance with Article 3.

14–51   Table 14.1 summarises the sections in the two sets of rules – the London Court of International Arbitration rules appear more comprehensive, but the simpler Chartered Institute of Arbitrators rules may be appropriate for most disputes.

Enforcement of arbitration agreements

14–52   The Irish courts have consistently decided cases in favour of upholding the validity of arbitration agreements. In doing so, they have both followed the lead given by the English courts and also made it clear that, as a matter of policy, they would be very slow to deem an arbitration agreement invalid other than in the most exceptional circumstances.

14–53   In the recent case of *Doyle v. Irish National Insurance Co plc*,[19] Kelly J. took the opportunity to look at the views of the judiciary in England as well as Irish precedent in this area. The case itself involved a motorist whose insurance company, when investigating a claim by the motorist, discovered that he had failed to disclose to them a previous conviction under the Road Traffic Act 1961 when renewing his insurance policy. As this was a breach of the terms of his insurance, the insurance company indicated that they would not indemnify him in respect of his claim. The motorist instituted legal proceedings for specific performance of the contract of insurance. The insurance contract contained an arbitration clause and the insurance company applied to have the specific performance proceedings stayed under section 5 of the Arbitration Act 1980 pending arbitration in relation to the dispute. In response to the application for a stay, the motorist argued that if, as the insurance company asserted, the insurance agreement was no longer valid because of the breach, then the arbitration clause, as part of the agreement, could not survive.

14–54   Kelly J. held that the arbitration clause could survive independently of the agreement. He started his analysis by quoting from a leading English case:

---

[19][1998] 1 I.R. 89.

Table 14.1: Comparison of the arbitration rules of the London Court of International Arbitration and the Chartered Institute of Arbitrators

London Court of International Arbitration	Chartered Institute of Arbitrators
1. The request for arbitration	1. Introductory
2. The response	2. Commencement of the arbitration
3. The LCIA court and registrar	3. Appointing authority
4. Notices and periods of time	4. Appointment of the arbitrator
5. Formation of the arbitral tribunal	5. Communications between parties and arbitrator
6. Nationality of arbitrators	
7. Party and other nominations	6. Arbitration procedure
8. Three or more parties	7. Powers of the arbitrator
9. Expedited formation	8. Form of procedure
10. Revocation of arbitrator's appointment	9. Awards
11. Nomination and replacement of arbitrators	10. Costs
12. Majority power to continue proceedings	11. General
13. Communications	12. Definitions
14. Conduct of the proceedings	
15. Submission of written statements and documents	
16. Seat of arbitration and place of hearings	
17. Language of arbitration	
18. Party representation	
19. Hearings	
20. Witnesses	
21. Experts to the arbitral tribunal	
22. Additional powers of the arbitral tribunal	
23. Jurisdiction of the arbitral tribunal	
24. Deposits	
25. Interim and conservatory measures	
26. The award	
27. Correction of awards and additional awards	
28. Arbitration and legal costs	
29. Decisions by the LCIA court	
30. Confidentiality	
31. Exclusion of liability	
32. General rules Recommended arbitration clauses Schedule of costs	
Source: www.lcia-arbitration.com/rulecost/english.htm	Source: www.arbitrators.org/rules2.htm

"The starting point for my consideration of this issue is the decision of the House of Lords in *Heyman v. Darwins Ltd.* [1942] A.C. 356, which drew a distinction between an arbitration clause and the remaining provisions of a contract. In the course of his judgment Macmillan L.J. said at pp. 373 and 374.

'. . . an arbitration clause in a contract . . . is quite distinct from the other clauses. The other clauses set out the obligations which the parties undertake towards each other . . . but the arbitration clause does not impose on one of the parties an obligation in favour of the other. It embodies the agreement of both parties that, if any dispute arises with regard to the obligations which the one party has undertaken to the other, such dispute shall be settled by a tribunal of their own constitution . . . what is commonly called repudiation or total breach of a contract . . . does not abrogate the contract, though it may relieve the injured party of the duty of further fulfilling the obligations which he has by the contract undertaken to the repudiating party. The contract is not put out of existence, though all further performance of the obligations undertaken by each party in favour of the other may cease. It survives for the purpose of measuring the claims arising out of the breach, and the arbitration clause survives for determining the mode of their settlement. The purposes of the contract have failed, but the arbitration clause is not one of the purposes of the contract.'"[20]

Kelly J. went on to apply this logic to the facts of the case at hand:

"Whilst that decision speaks of repudiation or total breach of contract the principle decided by it is equally applicable in circumstances where one party seeks to void or rescind a contract on the ground of misrepresentation or non-disclosure. That is so whether the misrepresentation or non-disclosure is fraudulent, negligent or innocent. Provided that the words of the clause are sufficiently wide, these are matters which can be referred to arbitration. (*vide* Mustill and Boyd: The Law and Practice of Commercial Arbitration in England: 2nd ed. at p. 112)."[21]

Kelly J. then cited subsequent cases when the same principles had been followed:

"*Heyman* has been consistently applied by the courts in England since it was decided in 1942. In *Bremer Vulkan v. South India Shipping* [1981] 1 A.C. 909 at p. 980 Diplock L.J. was able to say without further explanation:

'The arbitration clause constitutes a self-contained contract collateral or ancillary to the shipbuilding agreement itself: *Heyman v. Darwins Ltd.*'

Similarly in *Mackender v. Feldia A.G.* [1967] 2 Q.B. 590, the Court of Appeal, following the *dicta* in *Heyman*, found that non-disclosure relating to the practice of smuggling did not abrogate a foreign jurisdiction clause contained in an insurance policy. The non-disclosure only made that contract voidable and the dispute as to non-disclosure was one arising under the policy and remained within the arbitration clause.

More recently in *Harbour Assurance Ltd. v. Kanza Ltd.* [1993] Q.B. 701, the Court of Appeal concluded that an insurance agreement which one of the parties sought to declare void *ab initio* on the basis of non-disclosure of material facts and misrepresentation did not render the arbitration clause invalid. In so doing the court reviewed the case law and found that the *Heyman* doctrine was a common thread running through all the cases. The court went so far as to say that an issue as to the initial illegality of the contract was also capable of being referred to arbitration, provided that any initial illegality did not directly impeach

[20] [1998] 1 I.R. 89 at 92–93.
[21] *ibid.* at 93.

the arbitration clause. The issue is whether the illegality goes to the validity of the arbitration clause and not whether the illegality goes to the validity of the contract.

In *Hurst v. Bryk* [1997] 2 All E.R. 283, which concerned repudiation of a partnership agreement, Simon Brown L.J. relied on the established principle in *Heyman* in order to find that a repudiatory breach did not extinguish the contract altogether and the contract's clause pertaining to the apportionment of profits and losses of the firm remained intact." [22]

Kelly J. then cited an Irish authority before reaching his conclusion:

"In Ireland, Morris J. (as he then was) declared *Heyman* to be a correct statement of the law when he held that the issue of fundamental breach in a building contract should be sent to arbitration; vide *Parkarran Ltd. v. M. & P. Construction Ltd.* [1996] 1 I.R. 83.

In these circumstances I am therefore satisfied that the plaintiff's contention that the arbitration clause in the instant case is no longer valid is not well founded as a matter of law." [23]

14–55 The finality of an award made by the property arbitrator was tested in the case of *Dublin Corporation v. Building and Allied Trade Union*.[24] The plaintiff had paid compensation to the defendant some years previously on foot of an award determined by the property arbitrator who had clearly based his award on the defendant's submission that the property involved was a unique building that would need to be rebuilt. The award was for reinstatement cost, which was significantly in excess of open market value. When the defendant failed to rebuild the property, the plaintiff sued for the difference between the amount paid and the open market value, arguing that the defendant had been unjustly enriched in the circumstances. The plaintiff's claim succeeded in the High Court but this decision was overturned on appeal to the Supreme Court. On the subject of the finality of an arbitral award, Keane J. (as he then was) had this to say:

"It is accepted by the Corporation that the award in this case was final and binding on both it and the union. The doctrine of *res judicata* applicable to this, as to every final judgment or award of any competent court or tribunal, has the consequence that the parties are estopped between themselves from litigating the issues determined by the award again. The justification of the doctrine is normally found in the maxim *interest rei publicae ut sit finis litium* and it is important to bear in mind that the public interest referred to reflects, in part at least, the interest of all citizens who resort to litigation in obtaining a final and conclusive determination of their disputes. However severe the stresses of

---

[22] [1998] 1 I.R. 89 at 93–94.
[23] *ibid.* at 94.
[24] [1996] 1 I.R. 468.

litigation may be for the parties involved – the anxiety, the delays, the costs, the public and painful nature of the process – there is at least the comfort that at some stage finality is reached. Save in those exceptional cases where his opponent can prove that the judgment was procured by fraud, the successful litigant can sleep easily in the knowledge that he need never return to court again.

That finality is, of course, secured at a cost. The defendant who discovers as soon as the case is over that the award of damages against him is grossly excessive because of facts of which he was wholly unaware and was unable to bring before the court cannot, in the absence of fraud, resist the enforcement of the judgment against him. The plaintiff who similarly finds out that his damages are far less than those which would have been awarded had the court been in possession of evidence not available at the hearing is equally precluded from disputing the finality of the judgment. The interest of the public in that finality is given precedence by the law over the injustices which inevitably sometimes result. "[25]

14–56   In *Doyle v. Kildare County Council,*[26] Hamilton C.J., in reversing the decision of Flood J. in the High Court to set aside an award, emphasised the reluctance which courts should have to interfere with arbitral awards. He first summarised the basis for the High Court decision:

> "The ground upon which the learned trial judge ultimately set aside the award made by the second defendant, was that he was of the opinion that there was *prima facie* evidence of an inconsistent basis of calculation of the market value of certain parts of the land subject to acquisition or effective sterilization.
>
> He stated, at p. 430, that:—
>
> > 'In my opinion this inconsistency is sufficient to invalidate the mathematical calculation of the appropriate amount of the award and the award is accordingly invalid.'
>
> On that basis, he made an order setting aside the award."[27]

Hamilton C.J. then explained his reason for allowing the appeal:

> "Under the provisions of the Arbitration Act, 1954, the learned trial judge had no jurisdiction to set aside the award in the absence of any finding that the second defendant had misconducted himself or the proceedings.
>
> At common law, a court has jurisdiction to set aside an award where an error of law appears on the face of the award.
>
> This is a jurisdiction which should only be exercised sparingly and where an award shows on its face an error of law so fundamental that the courts cannot stand aside and allow it to remain unchallenged." [28]

---

[25] [1996] 1 I.R. 468 at 481.
[26] [1995] 2 I.R. 424.
[27] *ibid.* at 445.
[28] *ibid.* at 445.

14–57 However, the courts will interfere in exceptional cases. In *Administratia Asigurarilor de Stat v. I.C.I.*, O'Hanlon J. refused to stay court proceedings pending arbitration. Granting leave to revoke an arbitrator's powers, he held that in large and complex cases where there was an allegation of fraud and where it was unlikely that, when agreeing to refer disputes to arbitration, the parties envisaged the circumstances that transpired subsequently, the courts might be a more appropriate forum. He said:

> "For a claim of the magnitude and complexity of the present claim, proceedings by way of arbitration can present many problems, which would not arise if the matter were being processed by way of ordinary litigation before the court. Resort must be had to the court in any event for orders of discovery, interrogatories, and for many other forms of relief incidental to the proceedings. Questions of law may be referred by case stated from an arbitrator or umpire to the court, and must be if so directed by the court. The control which can be exercised by the arbitrators or umpire over the course of the proceedings is not as satisfactory as that which can be exercised by the court, using the comprehensive code of procedure provided by the Rules of the Superior Courts." [29]

14–58 The final word on the finality of arbitral awards should go to the late McCarthy J., whose dictum when giving the judgment of the Supreme Court in *Keenan v. Shield Insurance Company Ltd* forms the basis of many of the later decisions on the point. He said:

> "Arbitration is a significant feature of modern commercial life; there is an International Institute of Arbitration and the field of international arbitration is an ever expanding one. It ill becomes the courts to show any readiness to interfere in such a process; if policy considerations are appropriate as I believe they are in a matter of this kind, then every such consideration points to the desirability of making an arbitration award final in every sense of the term. *Church and General Insurance Company v. Connolly and McLoughlin* (Unreported, High Court, Costello J., 7th May, 1981) itself is an example of the type of fine-combing exercise which courts should not perform when it is sought to review an arbitration award." [30]

Arbitrators

14–59 As already discussed in paras **14–27** and **14–37**, arbitrators are independent, impartial and selected by the parties (or on their behalf by an appointing authority, *e.g.* the Chartered Institute of Arbitrators). Arbitrators

---

[29] [1990] 2 I.R. 246 at 257.
[30] [1988] I.R. 89 at 96.

are appointed on the basis of their arbitral/technical expertise, reputation and experience in the field of activity in which the dispute arises.

14–60   Any person can be an arbitrator – the law does not set any minimum qualifications. In appointing an arbitrator, it is advisable to ensure that the person appointed is properly trained and knowledgeable in the arbitral process and in the technical field of commerce or law in, or likely to be in, issue. Parties are advised to ensure that the appointed arbitrator has demonstrated a competence as an arbitrator in the particular field.

14–61   Generally, cases are heard by one arbitrator, but a panel of three or more can be requested. There is no appeal mechanism as such against decisions or awards of the arbitrator. However, the "case stated" procedure provided for in section 35 of the Arbitration Act 1954 allows the arbitrator to refer a point of law or an award or any part thereof to the court. In addition, the same section provides that the court can order a case to be stated by the arbitrator on a point of law or an award or part thereof. The court invokes this latter power to require a case stated on application of a party to the arbitration. As pointed out previously, the Arbitration Act empowers the court to remit an award back to the arbitrator for reconsideration and, in exceptional cases, to set aside the award.

14–62   An arbitral tribunal can consist of a sole arbitrator. The trend in international arbitration is for a tribunal of three to be appointed – one by each side (with the consent of the other side) and a chairperson. Section 14 of the Arbitration Act 1954 presumes, in the absence of agreement to the contrary, that there will be a single arbitrator. Under the Arbitration (International Commercial) Act 1998, there is a presumption of a three-person tribunal in the absence of agreement to the contrary.

14–63   Legislation contains procedures for the appointment and replacement of arbitrators by the High Court where the parties fail to agree a candidate, or where the appointed arbitrator refuses to act, dies or becomes incapable of acting. Under section 18 of the 1954 Act, the court is empowered, where the parties fail to agree on the appointment of a replacement within a specified time, to make the appointment.

Arbitrators are advised to get the parties to agree to exclusion of liability clauses in the agreements appointing them, as it is not clear whether they are immune from suits of negligence. Section 12 of the Arbitration (International Commercial) Act 1998 extends immunity from personal suit to arbitrators in international arbitrations provided they have not acted in bad faith. Sections 24 and 37 of the Arbitration Act 1954 provide for removal of an arbitrator for misconduct or for failure to use reasonable dispatch.

Powers of arbitrators

14–64 The arbitrator derives his authority and powers from the consent of the parties as articulated in the arbitration agreement. In the case of disputes arbitrated under statute, arbitrators derive their power from statute rather than from agreement of the parties. The arbitrator's power to conduct the arbitration and to give direction to parties derives principally from the contract under which he was appointed and also from the law contained in the Arbitration Acts 1954 to 1998.

Arbitrators' fees

14–65 Arbitrators should agree fees in advance before accepting an appointment. The agreement can either be a fixed fee or a time-based arrangement. In more complex or lengthy cases, the arbitrator will normally agree on a schedule of payments of his fees and expenses. Whether or not interim payments are made, normal practice is for the arbitrator not to release his award until his final bill has been paid. The process of "taking up the award" (*i.e.* obtaining the decision of the arbitrator, often after payment of his outstanding fees) therefore involves one or more parties to the arbitration, on being advised of the availability of the award, paying the outstanding fees and expenses of the arbitrator and obtaining his decision in return.

Arbitral procedure

14–66 Parties must ensure that the procedures employed are fair and just; not to do so might render any award unenforceable. Stages and issues to consider in the conduct of an arbitration are summarised in Table 14.2.

14–67 Arbitral procedures can be set by law or by agreement of the parties. In practice, they are a combination of the two. Most arbitration agreements make reference either to a standard set of rules of procedure published by a recognised body (*e.g.* the Chartered Institute of Arbitrators or the International Chamber of Commerce) or to the Arbitration Acts. In either case, the arbitrator will be free, subject to the rules of natural justice and fair procedure, to fill in any gaps in the rules referred to by making procedural decisions of his own.

14–68 Procedures can range from the straightforward to more complex procedures mirroring High Court procedure. The form of procedure is usually initially agreed by the parties, and is implemented by the arbitral tribunal as the arbitration proceeds. The types of detailed matters that, if not covered in rules incorporated in the arbitration agreement, will need to be addressed by the parties and determined by the arbitrator include[31]:

---

[31] Adapted from Hutchinson, B., "Arbitration: When and why?" in *Irish Business Law* (February 1999), p.2.

Table 14.2: Stages in and issues to consider in the conduct of an arbitration

- Arbitration agreement
- Choice of arbitrator
- Identification of issues
- Preparation and the hearing
  - Representation of the parties by lawyers
  - Timetable
  - Time-limit on oral presentations
  - Form of submissions – oral, in writing or both
  - Presentation of cases separately, or in the absence of the other party (*ex parte*)
  - Response to other party's case
  - Cross-examination
  - Use of expert witnesses
  - Arrangements for witnesses
  - Conduct of hearing
  - Venue for hearing
  - Language for proceedings
  - Recording of hearings
- Award
- Enforcement of the award
- Costs
- Security for costs

Adapted from: Lemar, C.J. and Mainz, A.J., *Litigation Support* (4th ed., Butterworths, London, 1999), pp. 254 and 259; and MacGregor, G. and Hobbs, I., *Expert Accounting Evidence: A Guide for Litigation Support* (Accountancy Books, London, 1998), p. 203.

– *Pleadings*: How are they to be made? What are the time-limits? To whom should they be sent? By what means should they be sent? Should a secretary or registrar be appointed to deal with day-to-day administration of the case?

– *Hearing*: Will a hearing be necessary? Where and when will it be held? Will stenographers be required? Will *ex parte* hearings be permitted on any aspects or issues in the case?

– *Evidence*: How is the evidence to be presented? Will the presentation of evidence be adversarial or inquisitorial? Will expert witnesses be required or permitted? Will hearsay evidence be admissible or will strict standards apply? Will evidence be given on oath?

– *Discovery, interrogatories, inspection of premises or materials*: How will these be effected?

– *Award*: How is it to be disclosed? Who will take it up? Who will pay the arbitrator's fees? Will the parties require reasons to be given in the award?

14–69 A competent arbitrator should be able to deal with these matters at a preliminary meeting with the parties. Sample rules of procedure are available from the arbitral professional bodies such as the International Chamber of Commerce, the London Court of International Arbitration or the Chartered Institute of Arbitrators. Rules may also be available through industry associations (such as the Irish Travel Agents' Association).

14–70 Parties may prefer to have their disputes settled in accordance with "principles of equity and fairness" or in accordance with "general principles of international business". In Ireland, Articles 28(2) of UNCITRAL Model Law,[32] which applies to international arbitration, permits the application of non-legal standards.

Involvement of the courts

14–71 Involvement of the courts in the arbitration process is derived from the Arbitration Acts 1954 to 1998, common law and the Constitution. The Arbitration Acts provide procedures to assist arbitrations. These generally allow the courts to intervene in arbitrations to prevent injustice. Interventions such as the following are possible[33]:

- staying proceedings (section 12 of the 1980 Act);

- appointing an arbitrator (sections 18 and 40 of the 1954 Act);

- compelling the attendance of a prisoner as a witness in an arbitration (section 21 of the 1954 Act);

- ordering security for costs, discovery, inspection, interrogatories, affidavit evidence, preservation or sale of goods or property, security of the amount in dispute, an interim injunction and the appointment of a receiver (section 22 of the 1954 Act);

- extending time for making an award (section 23 of the 1954 Act);

- removing the arbitrator on the grounds of delay (section 24 of the 1954 Act) or misconduct (section 37 of the 1954 Act);

- determining a point of law or an issue relating to an award in response to a case stated by the arbitrator (section 35 of the 1954 Act);

- remitting an award back to the arbitrator for reconsideration (section 36 of the 1954 Act);

- setting aside an award on the grounds of misconduct by the arbitrator or the

---

[32] United Nations Commission on International Trade Law (UNCITRAL) Model Law on International Commercial Arbitration (United Nations Commission on International Trade Law, Vienna, 1985). Available at www.uncitral.org/en-index.htm.

[33] Doherty, B., "Should arbitration be like litigation?" *Commercial Law Practitioner* (September 1995), pp. 204-206.

improper procurement of the award or of the arbitration (section 38 of the 1954 Act);

– revoking the power of the arbitrator on the grounds of bias by the arbitrator or alleged fraud by a party to the arbitration (section 39 of the 1954 Act);

– enforcing an award (section 41 of the 1954 Act).

Awards

14–72 For arbitration to have value, the awards must be final, binding and enforceable. The parties to the dispute have a choice between a reasoned and unreasoned award. In a reasoned award, the arbitrator describes how he arrived at his decision. This reassures the parties that the arbitrator reached a decision after proper consideration. In addition, an appeal to the courts is more difficult with an unreasoned award.

Damages first

14–73 The traditional approach to dispute resolution is to decide liability issues first, and damages issues secondly.[34] The damages first approach is advantageous in commercial cases because it may increase the chance of settlement before significant expense is incurred in resolving liability. The damages first approach:

– reduces overall uncertainty regarding award outcomes, by narrowing the range of possible damage outcomes;

– reduces one area of disagreement between the parties, making it easier for them to negotiate from a common information set, thus increasing the probability of settlement;

– reduces errors in damage estimates due to incomplete information. When the damage estimate is more accurate, the parties will be less willing to spend resources pursuing liability theories not justified by the size of the potential award.

14–74 In *Manning v. Shackleton*,[35] Keane J. (as he then was) in a Supreme Court judgment held that the property arbitrator, although he was exercising a quasi-judicial function, was not required to give a reasoned judgment, since:

---

[34] Chernick, R., Strong, G.G. and Shea, J.S., "Roles and techniques of an accountant in alternative dispute resolution" in *Litigation Services Handbook: The Role of the Accountant as Expert* (2nd ed., Weil, R.L., Wagner, M.J. and Frank, P.B. (eds), John Wiley & Sons, Inc., New York, 1995), pp. 9.9–9.10.
[35] [1996] 3 I.R. 85.

- either party could ask him to specify the amount awarded in respect of any particular matter;

- the Acquisition of Land (Assessment of Compensation) Act of 1919 allowed a special case to be stated to the High Court on a point of law;

- the Act of 1919 and the Act of 1954 provided the High Court with a supervisory jurisdiction;

- the High Court also had discretion to judicially review the decision of a property arbitrator in an appropriate case;

- to require a reasoned judgment in every case would encourage attempts to appeal awards by way of judicial review, contrary to the policy of the legislation to afford a procedure which avoided the necessity for litigation and was final and binding.

Interest

14–75 Section 34 of the Arbitration Act 1954, as substituted by section 17 of the Arbitration (International Commercial) Act 1998, provides for the award of interest (simple or compound) on the arbitrator's award. Unless otherwise agreed between the parties, the arbitrator has significant discretion in the amounts on which interest is payable, the periods in respect of which interest is calculated and the applicable rate of interest. The relevant provisions state:

> "(1) The parties to an arbitration agreement may agree on the powers of the arbitrator or umpire as regards the award of interest.
>
> (2) Unless otherwise agreed by the parties, the arbitrator or umpire may award simple or compound interest from the dates, at the rates and with the rests that he or she considers meet the justice of the case—
>> (a)   on all or part of any amount awarded by the arbitrator or umpire, in respect of any period up to the date of the award;
>> (b)   on all or part of any amount claimed in the arbitration and outstanding at the commencement of the arbitration but paid before the award was made, in respect of any period up to the date of payment.
>
> (3) Unless otherwise agreed by the parties, the arbitrator or umpire may award simple or compound interest from the date of the award (or any later date) until payment, at the rates and with the rests that he or she considers meet the justice of the case, on the outstanding amount of any award (including an award of interest under subsection (2) and an award of costs)."[36]

---

[36] Arbitration (International Commercial) Act 1998, s. 17.

Costs of arbitration

14–76 Section 29 of the Arbitration Act 1954 deals with the arbitrator's power to award costs and the manner in which costs disputes can be resolved. The section states:

> "(1) Unless a contrary intention is expressed therein, every arbitration agreement shall be deemed to include a provision that the costs of the reference and award shall be in the discretion of the arbitrator or umpire who may direct to and by whom and in what manner those costs or any part thereof shall be paid, and may, with the consent of the parties, tax or settle the amount of costs to be so paid or any part thereof, and may award costs to be paid as between solicitor and client.

> (2) Where an award directs any costs to be paid, then, unless the arbitrator or umpire, with the consent of the parties, taxes or settles the amount thereof—
> - (a) the costs shall be taxed and ascertained by a Taxing Master,
> - (b) the procedure to obtain taxation and the rules, regulations and scales of costs of the Court relative to taxation and to the review thereof shall apply to the costs to be so taxed and ascertained as if the award were a judgment or order of the Court."

Role of forensic accountants in arbitration

14–77 With an increasing number of disputes being resolved outside the courtroom, lawyers should consider the role accountants can play in alternative dispute resolution (ADR). An increasing number of lawyers are including accountants on the panel of arbitrators in commercial cases and in cases involving personal damages. These cases often involve complex damage calculations, as well as interest and tax issues. Bringing an accountant into the process early can often save time and professional fees and may reduce the client's financial burden. Clients in the preliminary stages of business dissolution or divorce, for example, may want to discuss property valuation issues and the tax consequences of various settlement options with an accountant to gain a realistic understanding of the situation.

14–78 Forensic accountants can participate in ADR in many ways. They can assist settlement negotiations by assessing damages early. They can be mediators, arbitrators, expert witnesses or settlement consultants.

Forensic accountants can play a role as mediator, either alone or as co-mediator with someone who has formal legal training. Alternatively, forensic accountants could be engaged to provide reports or expert evidence to the mediator.

Forensic accountants can play the role of the arbitrator, either as the sole arbitrator or as a panel member. The accountant could alternatively be engaged to provide a report or expert evidence to the arbitrator. Matters involving financial, economic and accounting issues often require the specialist knowledge of a forensic accountant.

14–79 In summary, an accountant can play one of two roles in ADR:

– as an expert witness engaged to provide an independent evaluation of economic damage. This role is similar to the expert's role in civil litigation except the arbitrator may have more specialist knowledge than a judge or jury. As in civil litigation, the forensic accountant might critique the opposing side's report and expert evidence and may also provide the barrister with questions for cross-examination of the opposing expert;

– as a neutral alone or in conjunction with a neutral who has legal training (*e.g.* a lawyer or former judge).

Benefits from appointing independent experts

14–80 The accountant as arbitrator offers a number of advantages. The accountant's special expertise allows the lawyers to spend less time explaining the issues. Accountants can educate other panel members by explaining complex financial issues and helping the panel reach a sensible decision.

14–81 A dispute destined for arbitration is likely to be technically complex. The successful resolution of such a dispute can be dependent upon how well the parties to the dispute convey these technically complex matters to the arbitrator. In some instances, a consideration of the technical matters may be prepared in-house by the parties to the dispute. It is often the case that the party or parties to the dispute have the expertise within their own organisations, and that their members of staff are more than capable of giving a valid opinion on the matters in dispute. However, it is vital that such an opinion is given with independence and impartiality. An opinion or report that can be shown to be biased will be given little weight by the arbitrator. In other instances, an independent forensic accountant may be appointed by a party to the dispute to prepare an expert's report and give expert evidence on one or more of the issues in dispute.

14–82 In addition to this independence and impartiality, the British Academy of Experts cite the following further benefits to be gained from appointing an independent expert[37]:

– specialist technical knowledge within a given discipline;

---

[37] Kenyon, M., "Appointing an expert" (1992), http://trett.com/digest/i9a2.htm.

– highly developed investigative and analytical skills;

– a broad perspective of the issues affecting disputes;

– experience in handling disputes and contentious problems;

– an understanding of the related legal processes;

– ability to present findings and opinions with clarity and authority;

– experience in presenting evidence in a court or other tribunal.

Concluding comment

14–83 The courts continue to encourage arbitration, and arbitration continues to flourish. Although arbitration and litigation each have their advantages and disadvantages, one issue stands out as setting them apart – that is the technical knowledge, experience and expertise of the skilled arbitrator in the area in which he is appointed. It is no accident that the international construction industry, which involves engineering issues of great complexity, provides significant work for arbitrators. However, another conclusion arises from this: there is now a greater need than ever before for judicial specialisation and training so that litigants can benefit from specific expertise and experience in the same way as parties to arbitration. There is no doubt that Irish judges are of a very high calibre – specialist training in selected technical areas would result in a judicial system that, as well as being of the highest competence, would enjoy the confidence of potential litigants regardless of the nature and complexity of the subject-matter of the dispute. If this were to happen, forensic accountants need not feel threatened; judges are less likely to dispense with experts than to test them more closely, based on a better understanding of what they say.

Part IV

FORENSIC ACCOUNTING CALCULATIONS

THE LAW ON DAMAGES

THE LAW ON DAMAGES

15–01 As already explained in Chapters 7 and 9, forensic accountants are often involved in calculating damages in personal injury and commercial litigation. Various aspects of such personal injury and commercial damages, including the ways in which they are calculated, are considered in Chapters 16 to 19 to follow. This chapter deals with the law generally concerning damages.[1]

15–02 Much of forensic accounting work involves computation of damages arising from various different aspects of civil litigation. Well-founded damage analysis combines *inter alia* accounting and actuarial science, business insight, and an understanding of the law.

The foundation of every case is facts. Relevant documents must be examined and pertinent information extracted to address both damage and liability issues. Provision of information is essential to provide the factual basis for a sound case strategy and to identify the facts to which legal, scientific and business principles must be applied.

When damages arise

15–03 Damages constitute pecuniary compensation for an injury or wrong sustained from a breach of contract or tortious act (a tort is a "civil wrong, independent of contract"[2]) or from a breach of duty. Liability to pay damages, therefore, arises as a remedy for a civil wrong committed by one party against another.

---

[1] More detailed consideration on the topic can be found in Kemp, D., *Damages for Personal Injury and Death* (7th ed., Sweet & Maxwell, London, 1998); McGregor, H., *McGregor on Damages* (16th ed., Sweet & Maxwell, London, 1997); Munkman, J., *Damages for Personal Injuries and Death* (10th ed., Butterworths, London, 1996); and White, J.P.M., *Irish Law of Damages for Personal Injuries and Death* (Butterworths (Ireland) Ltd, Dublin, 1989).

[2] Murdoch, H., *Murdoch's Dictionary of Irish Law* (3rd ed., Topaz Publications, Dublin, 2000), p. 795.

Breach of contract

15–04 Breaches of contract have already been considered in paras **2–29** and **9–04** *et seq.* A contract is an agreement between two or more persons entered into voluntarily and is concerned with the mutual rendering of benefits. A binding contract must include an offer, the acceptance of the offer, consideration of some kind and an intention to create legal relations (*i.e.* to be legally bound by the commitments made).

15–05 An action in contract will most often arise from a breach of an express or implied term in a contract. A person in breach of contract is in breach of an obligation he has agreed to assume. However, disputes over contracts can also arise due to mistake on the part of one or both parties entering into the contract, misrepresentation by one party to another or duress exerted by one party over another. Contracts can also fall foul of other rules rendering them illegal (*e.g.* contracts to commit a crime or otherwise contrary to public policy) or void (*e.g.* contracts in restraint of trade). The law of equity (*i.e.* fairness) can also intervene in a contract (*e.g.* where there is undue influence by one party over another). It is clear that contracts represent fertile ground for those who specialise in the resolution of disputes.

15–06 Remedies available to an aggrieved party for breach of the contract by the other party can vary depending on the nature of the breach. For instance, if the breached term is a condition of the contract, then the aggrieved party may either rescind or affirm the contract and may seek damages. If the breached term is a warranty, the aggrieved party remains bound by the contract but may seek damages for the breach (see also paras **9–34** *et seq.*).

Remedies under contract law are primarily concerned with ensuring that the party in breach does what he contracted to do. If one party defaults on performing his side of the agreement, then the loss to the other party is the market value of the benefit of which he has been deprived. The plaintiff is entitled to compensation for the loss of his bargain. The purpose of an award of contractual damages is referred to in *Robinson v. Harman* as being a situation:

> ". . . where a party suffers loss by reason of a breach of contract, he or she is, so far as money can do it, to be placed in the same situation, with respect to damages, as if the contract had been performed."[3]

This objective is usually achieved by awarding damages for the lost performance of the contract.

15–07 As already explained in para. **9–13**, the term "condition" is not defined in statute, but is generally regarded as including all terms compliance with which

---

[3] (1848) 1 Ex. 850.

is necessary for the contract to achieve its intended purpose. Section 11(2) of the Sale of Goods Act 1893, as substituted by section 10 of the Sale of Goods and Supply of Services Act 1980, states:

> "Whether a stipulation in a contract of sale is a condition, the breach of which may give rise to a right to treat the contract as repudiated, or a warranty, the breach of which may give rise to a claim for damages but not to a right to reject the goods and treat the contract as repudiated, depends in each case on the construction of the contract. A stipulation may be a condition, though called a warranty in the contract."

15–08 The award in contract is prospective – its objective is to put the plaintiff in the position that would have existed had the contractual promise been fulfilled.

Breach of statutory duty

15–09 There is no absolute rule governing the imposition of civil liability on persons who breach a statute. Some statutes specifically impose a duty of care on one party towards another (*e.g.* Occupiers Liability Act 1995). Others create duties, but expressly preclude a right of action in civil proceedings on foot of breaches of those duties (*e.g.* section 60 of the Safety, Health and Welfare at Work Act 1989). Most create duties and leave it to the courts to determine whether breaches of duty can ground civil proceedings. Ordinarily, courts will allow breaches of statutory duty to be pleaded unless this is specifically precluded by legislation or precedent, and in many cases courts will look less favourably on a defendant where a breach of statutory duty has been established than where the only wrong is a tort.

Torts

15–10 Torts have already been introduced in paras **2–28** and **9–03**. A tort is a breach of general duty imposed by the civil law, where a person, his property or his rights have been damaged in some way. Torts occur because the law has imposed a duty on persons generally. Examples of torts include negligence, defamation, deceit, trespass, as well as breaches of duties such as the duty of an employer to provide a safe place for employees to work. Liability in tort may also arise through the intentional infliction of bodily harm (known as "trespass to the person"), and from strict liability associated with certain wrongs such as defective products. Although there is a wide range of torts, many (but not all) are examples in one form or another of the effects of negligence.

15–11 The primary remedy in tort is an award of damages compensating a person for his loss. The purpose of an award of damages in tort for economic loss is to seek to restore the plaintiff to the financial position that existed prior to the commission of the tort. The task of the court is essentially retrospective. It looks at the plaintiff's economic state before he relied on the defendant's conduct and compares that with the actual financial position following that reliance. This differs from the award for contractual damages which is (as stated above) prospective. However, in compensation for the affects of a tort the court will have regard to the plaintiff's reasonable expectations regarding the future and, if the wrong has adversely affected his ability to achieve those expectations (*e.g.* through diminished earning power caused by an injury), then he will be compensated to the extent of the present value of his estimated future losses.

15–12   The function of tort law is to compensate "worthy" victims, creating a presumption that the wrongful party will be found responsible. This is one view of the function of tort law – it compensates victims for harms that have already occurred.

15–13   Notwithstanding that this is the objective stated by the courts, some court decisions can be more easily understood if it is assumed that they are trying to influence future behaviour than if it is assumed they are attempting to "right past wrongs". Courts will often consider the impact that current rulings can be expected to have on individuals' future behaviour. In this view, the function of damages for torts is not merely to compensate particular plaintiffs for past wrongs; it is also to protect potential plaintiffs from future harmful behaviour. The courts recognise that any decision made in the current case may influence the behaviour of parties in similar, future cases. Hence, it becomes important to set a precedent which will direct future parties to behave in a socially desirable manner. In particular, economic analysis predicts that the courts will prefer those rules that encourage parties to select cost-minimising behaviours.[4]

15–14   A defendant should only be found liable if he failed to take those actions that would have been taken by a "reasonable" person. If the function of the law is to encourage behaviour that maximises social benefits minus social costs, a "reasonable" action will be one for which the benefits exceed costs.

Other remedies

15–15   It should be noted that, whilst the resolution of most civil wrongs will result in the payment of damages (or a pecuniary settlement if the case is resolved before it is heard), damages are not the only remedy available. In deciding how to resolve a case, the court will usually attempt as far as possible to place the injured party back in the position he was before he was "wronged".

---

[4] Bruce, C., "Applying economic analysis to tort law" in *Expert Witness Newsletter* (Summer 1998), Vol. 3, No. 2, www.economica.ca/ew32p2.htm.

Specific performance

15–16 In cases of breach of contract, therefore, a court may order specific performance of the contract, requiring the wrongdoer to abide by the terms of the contract he breached. This is a particularly effective remedy where the matter at issue is a contract for the sale of land.

Injunctions

15–17 Another remedy available in certain cases is an injunction, which is usually used to prevent the carrying out or continuation of an action that is or would be a civil wrong. For instance, a court order preventing the unlawful picketing of a business premises is likely to be of far greater benefit to the owner of the business than an order for damages, following weeks of lost business, against a group of individuals or a trade union. An injunction is normally granted only where damages would be an inadequate remedy in the circumstances of the case. Injunctions are discussed in more detail in Chapter 21.

Types of damages

15–18 Damages divide into two categories: compensatory and other. Other damages include aggravated damages, exemplary (*i.e.* punitive) damages and nominal damages. These are discussed below.

Damages involving forensic accounting calculations

15–19 Forensic accountants would normally only be involved in calculation of compensatory damages. Other damages are therefore only briefly described in this chapter.[5]

Compensatory damages

15–20 Compensation awarded by a court is unconditional and is usually in the form of a lump sum payable at one time. The object of an award of damages is to compensate a plaintiff for the damage, loss or injury he has suffered. The compensatory damages to be recovered by a plaintiff are, in money terms, the court's best measurement of the plaintiff's actual loss. The measure of damages has been defined as:

"... that sum of money which will put the party who has been injured, or who

---

[5] Further discussion of damages from a forensic accounting point of view is to be found in MacGregor, G. and Hobbs, I., *Expert Accounting Evidence: A Guide for Litigation Support* (Accountancy Books, London, 1998), Chap. 18.

has suffered, in the same position as he would have been in if he had not sustained the wrong for which he is now getting his compensation ... ".[6]

15–21   As with even the most straightforward principles of law, there are exceptions to the general rule and courts will interpret principles in a way that lends itself to the justice of the case (limitations of damages are considered in paras **15–52** *et seq.*). The relevant principles underlying the law on damages are:

– *Restitutio in integrum.*

– Principles of mitigation.

– Remoteness of damages.

These principles are considered later in the chapter.

15–22   In a recent High Court case, *Doran v. Delaney (No. 2)*, Geoghegan J. dealt at some length with the principles associated with measuring compensatory damages. He said:

> "At the hearing of the action there was a good deal of discussion about distinctions between the measure of damages for breach of contract and the measure of damages in tort. There is of course a theoretical distinction but for the reasons which I will be demonstrating I do not think that it makes any practical difference in this case. If a party to a contract breaks that contract the other party is entitled to be compensated on the basis of what he has lost by reason of the contract not being performed. On the other hand the measure of damages appropriate for the tort of negligence is the loss sustained by reason of the breach of duty or in other words in the case of say negligent misrepresentation the plaintiff must be restored to the position he would have been in if the misrepresentation had not been made. The hallowed phrase used is *restitutio in integrum*. These rules, whether it be the contractual measure or the tortious measure are always subject to the special principles of mitigation of damages and remoteness of damage."[7]

15–23   In summary, the court will award compensatory damages in an amount that restores the injured party to the position in which he would have found himself had he not suffered the wrong of which he complains, subject to two principal *caveats*:

– the court will draw a line beyond which damage or injury, although flowing from the wrong, is too remote and not therefore eligible for compensation (but losses reasonably within the contemplation of the parties at the inception of the contract or the commission of the tort will not fall beyond the line); and

---

[6] *Livingstone v. Rawyards Coal Company* (1880) 5 App. Cas. 25 at 39, *per* Lord Blackburn.
[7] [1999] 1 I.R. 303 at 308.

— the court will expect that the plaintiff will have made all reasonable attempts to mitigate the damage and will adjust the damages downwards where it finds that this was not the case.

Damages not normally involving forensic accounting calculations

Aggravated damages

15–24　Aggravated damages are awarded to provide additional compensation to the injured plaintiff where his sense of injury resulting from the tort is justifiably heightened by the manner in which, or the motive for which, the defendant behaved.[8] Most often, aggravated damages are awarded in situations where the defendant continued to injure the plaintiff or to behave maliciously or wrongfully towards him after the complaint was made and sometimes up to and during the hearing. The most frequent example of such behaviour is when a defendant in defamation proceedings pleads justification in his defence. Essentially he is responding to the claim of defamation by claiming that, although he made the statements complained of, he was justified in doing so. This is a high-risk strategy for a defendant because, by raising this defence he is essentially repeating the defamation and doing so up to the hearing of the case. If his defence fails, he falls squarely within the parameters of an award of aggravated damages.

15–25　The courts have recognised this position on numerous occasions. A recent example is in the judgment of O'Flaherty J. in *Burke v. Central Independent Television plc.*[9] The matter at issue in the case was whether documents could be withheld from the process of discovery on the grounds that to disclose them would imperil life. The documents in question contained potentially defamatory statements and the issue arose as to whether a plea of justification would be raised in response to a claim of defamation. In this regard, O'Flaherty J. commented:

> "If, of course, the plea of justification fails, then the case becomes one which may call for the award of aggravated damages. The defeat of such a plea, after persistence in it at a trial, would call for aggravated damages in the ordinary way. The weakness or otherwise of the sources of information on which allegations were based would not add any additional dimension to this head of damages in my view."[10]

---

[8] White, J.P.M., *Irish Law of Damages for Personal Injury and Death* (Butterworths, Dublin, 1989), p. 7, para. 1.2.02.
[9] [1994] 2 I.R. 61.
[10] *ibid.* at 89.

Exemplary or punitive damages

15–26 Punitive damages have been defined as those damages beyond compensatory damages that have the purpose of "punishing the defendant or of setting an example for similar wrongdoers" and as "private fines levied by civil juries to punish wrongful conduct and deter its future occurrence".[11] Exemplary or punitive damages are additional damages awarded to plaintiffs for the purpose of making an example of, and punishing the defendant for exceptionally reprehensible conduct. They are distinguished from aggravated damages by virtue of the fact that they are not designed to compensate the plaintiff and are not therefore measured with compensation in mind, but rather are intended to teach the defendant, and others of like mind to the defendant, a lesson. It therefore follows that exemplary damages can result in a windfall for the fortunate plaintiff who happens to be the one whose case is used to punish the defendant. As explained in para. **15–13** and paras **15–89** *et seq.*, such damages are only available in tort actions and do not arise in breach of contract cases.

15–27 The development of exemplary or punitive damages has been somewhat controversial, but they have survived as a weapon in the armoury of the courts. In *Rookes v. Barnard*,[12] the House of Lords attempted to limit to three categories the cases in which exemplary damages could be awarded. This categorisation has been subject to criticism, but is still used as a touchstone where exemplary or punitive damages are being considered. These categories are:

1. Oppressive, arbitrary or unconstitutional action by servants of government.

2. Where the defendant's conduct has been calculated by him to make a profit for himself which may well exceed the compensation payable to the plaintiff.

3. Where exemplary damages are expressly authorised by statute.

15–28 In *Garvey v. Ireland*,[13] McWilliam J. in the High Court held that the plaintiff, a former Garda Commissioner removed from office by the Government, was entitled to exemplary damages because of the oppressive conduct of the Government in dismissing him. The learned judge cited the first *Rookes v. Barnard* category in support of his decision.

15–29 Punitive damages are provided for under the Civil Liability Act 1961. Subsections (4) and (5) of section 14 state:

"(4) Where the court would be prepared to award punitive damages against one

---

[11] *Gertz v. Robert Welsh, Inc.*, U.S. 323, 350 (1973).
[12] [1964] A.C. 1129.
[13] [1981] I.L.R.M. 266.

of concurrent tortfeasors, punitive damages shall not be awarded against another of such tortfeasors merely because he is a concurrent tortfeasor, but a judgment for an additional sum by way of punitive damages may be given against the first-mentioned tortfeasor.

(5) The judgment mentioned in subsection (4) of this section may specify that such additional sum is awarded by way of punitive damages, and no contribution shall be payable in respect thereof by a tortfeasor against whom such judgment could not properly have been given."

15–30   Exemplary damages are also mentioned in the same Act in the context of the survival of causes of action vested in a deceased person. Section 7(2) of the Civil Liability Act 1961 states:

"Where, by virtue of subsection (1) of this section, a cause of action survives for the benefit of the estate of a deceased person, the damages recoverable for the benefit of the estate of that person shall not include exemplary damages, or damages for any pain or suffering or personal injury or for loss or diminution of expectation of life or happiness."

15–31   These provisions would suggest at first glance that a distinction is being drawn between exemplary damages and punitive damages by the legislature. Hamilton P. (as he then was) attempted to draw a distinction between the two in *Kennedy v. Ireland*,[14] based on the use of the terms in different places within the Civil Liability Act 1961. However, the Supreme Court subsequently held that there was no real difference between the two. The Supreme Court's discussion of this issue arises within the judgment of Finlay C.J. in *Conway v. Irish National Teachers Organisation*.[15] The relevant excerpt neatly summarises the various categories of damages as follows:

"Having considered these submissions and also the authorities to which we were referred, I have come to the following conclusions as to the principles of law which are applicable. In respect of damages in tort or for breach of a constitutional right, three headings of damages in Irish law are, in my view, potentially relevant to any particular case. They are: —
1.   Ordinary compensatory damages being sums calculated to recompense a wronged plaintiff for physical injury, mental distress, anxiety, deprivation of convenience, or other harmful effects of a wrongful act and/or for monies lost or to be lost and/or expenses incurred or to be incurred by reason of the commission of the wrongful act.
2.   Aggravated damages, being compensatory damages increased by reason of
     (a)   the manner in which the wrong was committed, involving such elements as oppressiveness, arrogance or outrage, or

[14][1988] I.L.R.M. 472.
[15][1991] 2 I.R. 305.

    (b) the conduct of the wrongdoer after the commission of the wrong, such as a refusal to apologise or to ameliorate the harm done or the making of threats to repeat the wrong, or

    (c) conduct of the wrongdoer and/or his representatives in the defence of the claim of the wronged plaintiff, up to and including the trial of the action.

        Such a list of the circumstances which may aggravate compensatory damages until they can properly be classified as aggravated damages is not intended to be in any way finite or complete. Furthermore, the circumstances which may properly form an aggravating feature in the measurement of compensatory damages must, in many instances, be in part a recognition of the added hurt or insult to a plaintiff who has been wronged, and in part also a recognition of the cavalier or outrageous conduct of the defendant.

3.   Punitive or exemplary damages arising from the nature of the wrong which has been committed and/or the manner of its commission which are intended to mark the court's particular disapproval of the defendant's conduct in all the circumstances of the case and its decision that it should publicly be seen to have punished the defendant for such conduct by awarding such damages, quite apart from its obligation, where it may exist in the same case, to compensate the plaintiff for the damage which he or she has suffered. I have purposely used the above phrase 'punitive *or* exemplary damages' because I am forced to the conclusion that, notwithstanding relatively cogent reasons to the contrary, in our law punitive and exemplary damages must be recognised as constituting the same element."[16]

15–32   Irish courts have awarded exemplary or punitive damages on several occasions. There is now clear recognition that they form part of the reliefs available to aggrieved plaintiffs in appropriate cases. One example of the approval of such an award arose in *McIntyre v. Lewis*[17] when a jury's decision to award exemplary damages against the State in a case of malicious prosecution was appealed to the Supreme Court. In his judgment upholding the award of exemplary damages (but reducing the amount), Hederman J. said:

"I believe that in the circumstances of this case the jury were entitled to award exemplary damages both for the assault and false imprisonment on the one hand and for the malicious prosecution on the other. Equally they were entitled to award exemplary damages in respect of one or other or both. They chose to award what were obviously exemplary damages in relation to the malicious prosecution. In cases like this, where there is an abuse of power by employees of the State the jury are entitled to award exemplary damages. One of the ways in which the rights of the citizen are vindicated, when subjected to oppressive conduct by the employees of the State, is by an award of exemplary damages."[18]

---

[16] [1991] 2 I.R. 305 at 316–317.
[17] [1991] 1 I.R. 121.
[18] *ibid.* at 134.

15–33 While there is no statutory guidance or cap on the amount of exemplary or punitive damages in Ireland, the courts will have regard to the circumstances of the individual case in arriving at a reasonable award. On this point, in the same case, Hederman J. said:

> "...the amount awarded for exemplary damages should bear some relation to the amount that would be proper for general damages."[19]

15–34 This implies a link between the compensation properly payable to the plaintiff and the appropriate amount of exemplary damages. However, in his judgment in the same case, McCarthy J. said:

> "Exemplary or punitive damages are intended to reflect disapproval - they are peculiarly appropriate for assessment by a jury. The damages reflect the standing of both the abused and the abuser but one should look, in particular, to the standing of those responsible for the malicious prosecution ... In my opinion, the damages appropriate to a case of this kind must reflect the proper indignation of the public at this conduct, whatever windfall it may prove for the plaintiff in the result."[20]

15–35 The judgments of the Supreme Court in *Conway v. Irish National Teachers Organisation*[21] were delivered subsequent to the judgments in *McIntyre v. Lewis*[22] and must be regarded as a clearer and more authoritative statement of the law. Accordingly, the categorisation of the types of damage set out in the *Conway* case (see above, para. **15–31**) can be regarded as the appropriate guide.

15–36 Courts in many jurisdictions, none more so than in the United States, have awarded punitive damages with increasing frequency and in progressively larger amounts. This creates a growing demand for financial experts to analyse and explain the consequences of the defendant's actions and its financial status.

15–37 Where relevant, and given the choice, most plaintiffs' lawyers elect for tort rather than breach of contract actions, so that the plaintiff has a better opportunity to claim exemplary damages. Exemplary damages are not a feature of actions for breach of contract because the contract is a creation of the parties to it, and they therefore are regarded as having the power to provide between them for the consequences of any breaches of their agreement. In torts, on the other hand, the injured party must by definition be complaining of an act or omission (*e.g.* negligence) that offends principles and practices of relevance to the community as a whole. This is not necessarily the case in a private agreement.

---

[19] [1991] 1 I.R. 121 at 135.
[20] *ibid.* at 138.
[21] [1991] 2 I.R. 305.
[22] [1991] 1 I.R. 121.

It is therefore more likely that a court will wish to "make an example" of a defendant in an action in tort so as to attempt to protect the community from future similar acts or omissions inimical to its interests.

Nominal damages

15–38   The term nominal damages is used to describe awards made when a court finds that, although the plaintiff's legal rights have been infringed, he has suffered no damage or injury requiring compensation, and exemplary damages are not justified. Nominal damages arise in situations, such as trespass and libel, where the tort itself is actionable without proof of damage.

15–39   In a dissenting judgment in *Walsh v. Family Planning Services Ltd,*[23] McCarthy J. recognised the concept of nominal damages for a technical assault. He criticised the practice of attempting to elevate such claims to the status of actions for breach of constitutional rights in order to increase the possibility of obtaining substantial damages:

> "A breach of a constitutional right is a very grave matter, but assault actions should not be dressed up in a constitutional guise. Defamation and trespass to property may theoretically offend against some of the guarantees in respect of personal rights contained in Article 40 of the Constitution. It is, however, the State which is enjoined by its laws to protect as best it may from unjust attack and in the case of injustice done to vindicate the life, person, good name and property rights of every citizen. Claims to attack such rights unjustly may well be resisted calling in aid the constitutional guarantee; the guarantee, however, is not to be used to elevate the status of a trifling cause of action. There being a technical assault, in my judgment nominal damages was the true measure and I would assess them at one penny."[24]

15–40   It should be noted that the award of nominal damages by a judge or jury does not imply any criticism of the plaintiff, who will usually have taken the proceedings in order to vindicate his rights rather than to obtain damages. This absence of criticism is evident from the fact that the successful plaintiff who is awarded nominal damages will normally be awarded his costs.

15–41   In situations where a plaintiff has a technical right to succeed but the court disapproves of his behaviour, or of his taking the case in the circumstances, very small damages will be awarded, but costs (which will far exceed the damages) may be awarded against the plaintiff. Not to be confused with nominal damages, these are sometimes known as "contemptuous damages".

---

[23] [1992] 1 I.R. 496.
[24] *ibid.* at 522.

Liquidated damages

15–42   Parties to a contract may elect to make an explicit agreement as to what each party's remedy is in the event of a breach. Such an agreement is referred to as a "liquidated damages" clause. Liquidated damages clauses are usually written in contracts at the time of contracting and stipulate the approximate monetary value of losses which would be sustained in the event of a breach of contract. They may become an issue of contention in cases where actual damages suffered by the plaintiff are less than those stipulated in the contract. When actual damages are the lesser amount, the reasonableness of the liquidated damages clause may be challenged on the grounds that such clauses may not be enforceable under contract law (see para. **9–32**).

Such a clause is particularly suitable for contracts to complete works, such as building activities, within a period of time. In the old case of *Toomey v. Murphy*,[25] the defendant agreed to complete building work by a specified date, in default of which he would pay £5 per week to the plaintiff. This was held to be a liquidated damages clause. Liquidated damages also arise in the sale and purchase of property, where courts have held that a deposit can be retained as liquidated damages when the purchaser fails to complete the purchase.[26]

15–43   The purpose of specifying in an agreement an amount payable on foot of a breach is to attempt to avoid the lengthy and expensive processes of having a court or other tribunal measure the appropriate compensation, or battling acrimoniously towards a settlement, when the parties themselves are best positioned at the outset to measure the damage should it arise.

15–44   The courts recognise that actions to recover liquidated amounts are, or should be, more straightforward than other cases and provide an accelerated means of pursuing such claims (*e.g.* by summary summons in the High Court – see Appendix 3 (Glossary) for brief explanation of term.

15–45   For a liquidated damages clause to be enforceable, the amount of damages resulting from a breach of contract must be a reasonable forecast of the plaintiff's damages at the time the contract is made. A court will not enforce a liquidated damages clause which the court believes to be a penalty or to be punitive in nature. This is because the goal of the law is generally not to compel a party to perform, but instead to redress breach through compensation. Thus, a disproportionately high liquidated damages clause will be invalidated.[27]

---

[25] [1897] 2 I.R. 601.

[26] See *e.g. Stud Managers Ltd v. Marshall* [1985] I.R. 83.

[27] A leading case setting out this principle is *Dunlop Pneumatic Tyre Co Ltd v. New Garage & Motor Co Ltd* [1915] A.C. 79. The judgment of Dunedin L.J. was cited with approval by Barron J. in the Supreme Court in *Pat O'Donnell & Co Ltd v. Truck and Machinery Sales Ltd* [1998] 4 I.R. 191 at 214–215.

Valuation of damages

15–46   Irish law recognises several methods for defining economic damages.
Damage awards under breach of contract can be classified under one of three
contract damages principles: reliance, restitution and expectation of loss. These
are discussed below

Actual losses incurred

15–47   One type of damage recovery is the actual loss incurred. This form of
restitution applies in fraud cases. A common method used to calculate actual
losses is the out-of-pocket measure of damages computed as the difference
between what the plaintiff paid for something and the actual value received.

Expectations remedy/benefit of the bargain

15–48   Another common valuation method, especially in breach of contract
cases, is the expected profits from a proposed contract or deal. Using this method,
the breaching party pays an amount that makes the plaintiff's firm as well off as
it expected to be if the contract has been properly fulfilled. This is often called
the benefit-of-the-bargain approach to computing damages in contract disputes.

A similar valuation method to the expectations remedy is the "but for"
method. This applies where plaintiffs claim lost profits in business litigation.
The loss can be measured as the amount the plaintiff's actual earnings fall short
of the earnings that would have been earned "but for" the illegal actions of the
defendant. This can be described as the differences between "but for" profits
and actual profits.

Reliance loss

15–49   Another type of recoverable damage is called the "reliance loss". This
takes into account costs incurred by the plaintiff in the reasonable expectation
that the contract would go ahead. This measure of loss is based on arriving at a
figure that compensates the plaintiff for losses arising because he acted on the
assumption that the contract would be fulfilled. From a compensation point of
view, this means that a plaintiff in a breach of contract action is entitled to any
monies paid to third parties in expectation of the contract (and possibly the
opportunity cost or foregone interest on the loss).

Restitution loss

15–50   In addition to out-of-pocket expenses, the plaintiff is also entitled to
claim any monies paid directly to the defendant. Restitution loss involves
restoring to the buyer any payment made to the seller for goods not delivered.
Although similar to reliance loss, restitution loss can only involve the parties to
the breached contract, whereas reliance loss can include compensation for

payments made to third parties in reliance on the contract where the breach of the contract caused inadequate (or no) value to be received from the third party.

Other losses

15–51   Other losses such as consequential losses can also arise. These tend to be specific to individual cases and must be justified on their individual merits in order to be recoverable.

Limits on recovery of damages

15–52   Certain rules apply that may operate to reduce the award of damages. In tort, the tests of causation, remoteness and foreseeability apply.

15–53   Courts will limit damages awards to losses incurred by the plaintiff that were reasonably foreseeable by the defendant. In addition, where the plaintiff can limit or mitigate damages by taking reasonable steps following a breach, courts will expect him to do so. Finally, the courts will not award damages where the plaintiff's damages claims are too uncertain or too speculative. See *Gommell v. Wilson*[28] judgment quoted in para. **16–63**).

Causation

15–54   To succeed in claiming compensatory damages for a wrong, it is essential that the plaintiff prove to the satisfaction of the court that the damage for which he seeks to be compensated resulted from the wrong of which he complains and that the wrong was committed or caused by the defendant.

Causation and tort

15–55   One of the most complex issues in tort law concerns the determination of causation. To succeed in a claim for damages in tort, a plaintiff must establish that:

– the defendant caused the damage complained of;

– the damage is not too remote from the action of the defendant;

– a consequent legal liability arises, on foot of which the defendant is required to compensate the plaintiff.

It is only when these elements have been established that the question of the measure of damages arises.

15–56   In order to establish the first element, causation, it is necessary to show that the defendant caused the damage as a matter of both fact and law. An investigation of the circumstances will normally reveal, at least as a matter of

---

[28][1982] A.C. 27.

probability, whether the defendant did as a matter of fact cause the damage. For instance, an engineer inspects a machine that caused an injury to an individual working in a factory, and the engineer determines that the machine had not been properly maintained and failed to have standard and appropriate safety features. It is likely that the plaintiff's employer will be found to have caused the accident as a result of negligence.

15–57   The usual way that the courts assess factual causation is by using what is known as the "but for" test, *i.e.* if the damage would not have occurred but for the act or omission of the defendant then the defendant caused it. This simple and rather attractive maxim must, however, be tempered by the realisation that it could give unacceptable results where a plaintiff's injuries were caused by two independent but culpable defendants, *e.g.* in a multiple collision where the plaintiff's vehicle is impacted by two others. Clearly, the "but for" rule has the potential to exempt each defendant from liability on the grounds that the plaintiff would have suffered damage anyway as a result of the acts of the other. Happily, the law modifies the rule in such circumstances to ensure that justice is done by allowing the plaintiff to proceed and recover against both parties in the same proceedings.

15–58   Having established the factual cause or causes of damage, the courts will then determine whether this cause, or any of them, amounts to a legal cause of damage. Here the court will look for a voluntary act or omission or an unusual set of circumstances giving rise to the damage. In other words, normal events, even if they cause damage (*e.g.* fog, causing reduced visibility on a road), will not normally be held to be legal causes of an accident.

Causation and breach of contract

15–59   Any breach of contract entitles the plaintiff, at a minimum, to nominal damages. For an injured party to recover more, he will have to demonstrate that the conduct of the defendant caused his loss and he will have to provide a reasonable estimate of the extent of his injury, measured in money.

15–60   Generally, the plaintiff will be able to prove with relative certainty his expenditures arising due to the defendant's breach. Actual expenditures will be easily proven, once the plaintiff has maintained a record of such expenses. Similarly, where an established market exists, the plaintiff may be able to demonstrate his loss based on market values. Determining damages becomes more difficult where the plaintiff claims damages based on profits he might have made in subsequent transactions but for the defendant's breach. In such cases, the plaintiff is denied recovery if his claim for lost profits is considered too uncertain or too speculative. Courts generally require that lost profits be shown with "reasonable certainty".

15–61 From the perspective of causation, the court will seek to satisfy itself that whatever damage is cited by the plaintiff flowed from the breach. Again, this is generally a matter of investigation and proof of the relevant facts. In *Gunning v. Dublin Corporation*, Carroll J. said:

> "In breach of contract the test for quantum of damage is not *de facto* loss. The aggrieved party is only entitled to recover such part of the loss actually resulting as was at the time of the contract reasonably foreseeable as liable to result from the breach either in the ordinary course of things or due to special circumstances known to the offending party. In tort the tortfeasor takes his victim as he finds him. The test for quantum of damage is whether the damage is of a type to be foreseeable, in which case damages can be recovered even if the degree of damage is unforeseeable." [29]

Remoteness/foreseeability

15–62 A head of damages which is not foreseeable is said to be too remote in fact. A doctrine also applies called "remoteness in law". Plaintiffs are not entitled to compensation from defendants for damage which is held to be too remote in law, though it may undoubtedly be a consequence of the defendant's wrong.

15–63 Damages are recoverable only for those injuries that the defendant had reason to foresee were a probable result of his acts or omissions or of his breach of contract. The basis for this limitation when applied to a breach of contract is grounded in the realisation that the liability for unforeseen loss might impose on the defendant a burden disproportionate to the risk he originally thought he was assuming under the contract, and the corresponding benefit that he stood to gain. The rationale for this principle in tort cases is that the law should not give rise to behaviour that is excessively risk averse, *i.e.* it should not discourage otherwise valuable activity that may be an indirect and remote cause of damage.

15–64 In the High Court case *Doran v. Delaney (No. 2)*, referred to earlier, Geoghegan J. said on the subject of remoteness of damage:

> "In considering the proper measure of damages in this case therefore I must at all times bear that principle in mind and be careful not to assess damages which should be disallowed on the grounds of remoteness. But reasonably foreseeable loss flowing either from a breach of contract or from a negligent misrepresentation relied upon cannot be considered too remote." [30]

After citing various English authorities, he concluded:

> "It can be seen from these passages, therefore, that loss is not too remote if it

---

[29] [1983] I.L.R.M. 56 at 63.
[30] [1999] 1 I.R. 303 at 310.

could have been reasonably within the contemplation of the parties at the time of
entering into the contract (in the case of breach of contract) or at the time of
making the misrepresentation or committing the breach of duty (in the case of
tort)."[31]

These remarks help to establish boundaries around the legal liability of parties
where, although their acts, omissions or breaches of contract had the ultimate
effect of causing damage, they could not have foreseen such damage.

15–65   The legal concept of *novus actus interveniens* is relevant here. This
term describes a situation where the causal link between the act or omission of
the defendant is broken by an intervening event which, because of its occurrence
and nature, is regarded as the primary cause of the damage. Where the intervening
event could not reasonably have been foreseen, the resulting damage is regarded
as too remote from the defendant's act or omission for the purposes of establishing
legal liability.

15–66   The question of foreseeability tends to be decided on the facts of each
individual case and it is difficult, if not impossible, to arrive at a clear and
exhaustive set of guidelines in this area. It is useful, however, to look at one
judgment as an example of the manner in which the courts approach the issue.
The case of *Crowley v. AIB, Defendant, and O'Flynn, Green, Buchan &
Partners, Third Party*[32] involved a fall from the roof of a bank premises by the
plaintiff, a schoolboy, who was awarded damages for negligence. The third party,
a firm of architects, successfully appealed to the Supreme Court an apportionment
of 30 per cent liability against them. The High Court had made the apportionment
on the grounds that their design had rendered the roof of the defendant's premises
easily accessible to children.

In allowing the appeal by the third party against the 30 per cent finding,
Finlay C.J. held that because AIB knew that boys played on the roof, and did
nothing to prevent them doing so, this was the primary cause of the accident and
the architects should not share the blame. He said:

> "I am satisfied that having regard to the express finding made by the jury that
> the defendant, its servants or agents, was aware of the fact that boys, including
> the plaintiff, were liable to play on this unguarded roof and to the absence of
> evidence (which was not tendered at any part of the hearing) that they had
> attempted to prevent or prohibit the plaintiff and the other boys from playing on
> this roof, it was not open to the learned trial judge to hold that a sufficient nexus
> or connection existed between any negligence or default on the part of the third
> party and the happening of this accident so as to constitute the third party a

[31] [1999] 1 I.R. 303 at 315.
[32] [1987] I.R. 282.

concurrent wrongdoer with the defendant and therefore liable to make contribution or indemnity."[33]

He went on to hold that the architects could not have foreseen the bank's willingness to allow boys to play on the roof when the danger of a fall was so obvious:

"It was not suggested that any part of the design required by the defendant in the reconstruction of these bank premises involved an intended use of this lower roof otherwise than such use as might occasionally be required for the purpose of maintenance or repair. Accepting as this Court must, on appeal, the finding of the learned trial judge that it had been established that access to this lower, unguarded roof was easy, certainly for a fit boy of sixteen years of age, either by stepping over the wall adjoining the stone steps or by dropping down 4 or 5 feet from the parapet wall of the upper roof, there does not appear to me to have been any evidence which would indicate that the third party should reasonably have foreseen that boys would be permitted by the servants or agents of the defendant to play energetic games upon this unguarded roof which so obviously carried the ever-present danger of a fall from it. "[34]

Finlay C.J. then cited earlier authority for his reasoning:

"The legal position with regard to the potential liability of a third party in circumstances such as these is, in my view, correctly stated in the decision of this Court in *Conole* v. *Redbank Oyster Co.* [1976] I.R. 191 in the judgment of Henchy J. where, dealing with the alleged liability to contribute of a firm named Fairway, who had, on the evidence constructed an unseaworthy boat, he said at p. 196 as follows: —

'Assuming that Fairway were negligent in sending forth an unseaworthy boat, reliance on this negligence must, on the authorities, be confined to those whom Fairway ought reasonably to have foreseen as likely to be injured by it. Furthermore, the negligence must be such as to have caused a defect which was unknown to such persons. If the defect becomes patent to the person ultimately injured and he chooses to ignore it, or to an intermediate handler who ignores it and subjects the person ultimately injured to that known risk, the person who originally put forth the article is not liable to the person injured. In such circumstances the nexus of cause and effect, in terms of the law of tort, has been sundered as far as the injured person is concerned.' "[35]

He summarised the position in the *Crowley* case as follows:

"There can be no doubt on all the evidence in this case that the servants or

---

[33] [1987] I.R. 282 at 287.
[34] *ibid.* at 287.
[35] *ibid.* at 287

agents of the defendant, prior to the happening of this accident were completely and fully aware of the danger of permitting boys to play upon this unguarded roof and that, in the words of the extract which I have just read from the judgment of Henchy J., they ignored that danger and, by permitting the continuation of the playing by the boys upon the unguarded roof, subjected them to the risk which caused this accident. In these circumstances, I am satisfied that the third party is entitled to succeed on the first ground argued on its behalf in this appeal."[36]

15–67 Damages are foreseeable when they arise naturally. The defendant is not required to have actual foresight of the extent of damages which occur but merely to have reason to foresee generally that damages could occur. It is not necessary for the plaintiff to show that the defendant should have contemplated the specific resulting injury or should have implied or expressly promised to compensate the plaintiff for such injury in case of breach. Nor is it required that the defendant would have foresight that the breach would cause the plaintiff the loss of a specific sum of money. However, if only one party to a contract is aware of, or could reasonably foresee a risk of loss, the other party generally is not liable if such a loss occurs. Thus, if the defendant can prove that he did not know or have reason to know of any special circumstances which would create unusual risk of loss to the plaintiff, then the defendant will not be liable for such extraordinary loss.

Remoteness and tort

15–68 The concept of remoteness of damage is concerned with the extent of the defendant's liability for losses caused by his negligence. Once negligence has been established and found to have caused the injury or damage complained of, the court asks a further question: should the defendant be required to compensate the plaintiff or is the injury or damage too remote a consequence of the defendant's negligence?

15–69 If the injury or damage is found to be too remote, the defendant is not required to compensate the plaintiff even though the injury or damage was caused by the defendant's negligence. The concept of remoteness is used to limit the damages recoverable by the plaintiff to those losses that are not too far removed from the defendant's breach.

15–70 Case law shows that the modern test of remoteness of damage is that of reasonable foreseeability of damage. The remoteness of damage question does not arise until it has been established that the defendant has failed to take reasonable precautions against a reasonably foreseeable risk of injury or damage, and that the negligence caused the injury or damage.

---

[36] [1987] I.R. 282 at 288.

Remoteness and breach of contract

15–71 The test of remoteness used in cases of breach of contract is that of "common knowledge and reasonable contemplation". This is regarded as a narrower test than the "reasonable foreseeability" test used in tort.[37] However, where the plaintiff has a cause of action in both contract and tort, the test used in tort is applied.

15–72 The requirement of remoteness protects the defendant from being exposed to a liability that is out of proportion to the risk contemplated at the signing of the contract. Remoteness is governed by the rule in *Hadley v. Baxendale*.[38] Alderson B. stated the rule in that case as follows:

> "... where two parties have made a contract which one of them has broken, the damages which the other party ought to receive in respect of such breach of contract should be such as may fairly and reasonably be considered either arising naturally, i.e. according to the usual course of things, from such breach of contract, or such as may reasonably be supposed to have been in the contemplation of both parties, at the time they made the contract, as the probable result of the breach of it."

15–73 This formulation has been approved on several occasions in the Irish courts, recently by the Supreme Court in the judgment of O'Flaherty J. in *Primor plc v. Stokes Kennedy Crowley*[39] (this case is considered in paras **12–15** *et seq.*) A plaintiff who claims in respect of damage which does not arise in the "usual course of things" must bring the claim within the second limb of the rule in *Hadley v. Baxendale*. Under the first part, it is implied that the defendant is a reasonable person with knowledge of the ordinary course of things. In contrast, liability under the second part arises from actual knowledge of the defendant. The basis of the rule is said to be that the defendant with actual knowledge is undertaking to bear a greater loss.

The development of the rule in *Hadley v. Baxendale* was discussed by Henchy J. in *McGrath v. Kiely*.[40] He explained the rule as it had evolved in some detail, citing the position as set out in a 1949 judgment of the English Court of Appeal, as follows:

> "The rule in *Hadley v. Baxendale* [(1854) 9 Exch. 341] has been re-stated and refined by the English Court of Appeal in *Victoria Laundry (Windsor) Ltd v. Newman Industries Ltd* [[1949] 2 K. B. 528] (at p. 539) as follows:

---

[37] See the House of Lords' decision in *The Heron II; Koufos v. Czarnikow* [1967] 3 All E.R. 686.

[38] (1854) 9 Ex. 341 at 354–355.

[39] [1996] 2 I.R. 459.

[40] [1965] I.R. 497.

'(1.) It is well settled that the governing purpose of damages is to put the party whose rights have been violated in the same position, so far as money can do so, as if his rights had been observed: (*Sally Wertheim v. Chicoutimi (Pulp) Company* [[1911] A.C. 301]. This purpose, if relentlessly pursued, would provide him with a complete indemnity for all loss *de facto* resulting from a particular breach, however improbable, however unpredictable. This, in contract at least, is recognised as too harsh a rule. Hence,

(2.) In cases of breach of contract the aggrieved party is only entitled to recover such part of the loss actually resulting as was at the time of the contract reasonably foreseeable as liable to result from the breach.

(3.) What was at that time reasonably so foreseeable depends on the knowledge then possessed by the parties or, at all events, by the party who later commits the breach.

(4.) For this purpose, knowledge "possessed" is of two kinds; one imputed, the other actual. Everyone, as a reasonable person, is taken to know the "ordinary course of things" and consequently what loss is liable to result from a breach of contract in that ordinary course. This is the subject matter of the "first rule" in *Hadley v. Baxendale* [(1854) 9 Exch. 341]. But to this knowledge, which a contract-breaker is assumed to possess whether he actually possesses it or not, there may have to be added in a particular case knowledge which he actually possesses, of special circumstances outside the "ordinary course of things", of such a kind that a breach in those special circumstances would be liable to cause more loss. Such a case attracts the operation of the "second rule" so as to make additional loss also recoverable.

(5.) In order to make the contract-breaker liable under either rule it is not necessary that he should actually have asked himself what loss is liable to result from a breach. As has often been pointed out, parties at the time of contracting contemplate not the breach of the contract, but its performance. It suffices that, if he had considered the question, he would as a reasonable man have concluded that the loss in question was liable to result (see certain observations of Lord du Parcq in the recent case of *A/B Karlshamns Oljefabriker v. Monarch Steamship Company Limited* [[1949] AC 196].

(6.) Nor, finally, to make a particular loss recoverable, need it be proved that upon a given state of knowledge the defendant could, as a reasonable man, foresee that a breach must necessarily result in that loss. It is enough if he could foresee it was likely so to result. It is indeed enough, to borrow from the language of Lord du Parcq in the same case, at p. 158, if the loss (or some factor without which it would not have occurred) is a "serious possibility" or a "real danger." For short, we have used the word "liable" to result. Possibly the colloquialism "on the cards" indicates the shade of meaning with some approach to accuracy.' "[41]

---

[41] [1965] I.R. 497 at 512–513.

Mitigation/avoidability

15–74 Many forensic accountants fail to take account of mitigating factors in calculating losses. Forensic accounting reports should contain a section dealing with mitigation. Reference to mitigation will add credibility to such reports.

Once a party to a contract knows that the other party has breached or will breach the contract, the non-breaching party has an obligation to make reasonable efforts to mitigate his damages. An injured party is never awarded damages for losses he could have avoided by reasonable efforts and without substantial risk of further loss. Under the mitigation principle, the injured firm's actual position, which incorporates the effects of the wrongful act, is adjusted to take account of avoidable but unavoided effects. There is a duty on the plaintiff to take all reasonable steps to mitigate (*i.e.* reduce) the loss consequent on the wrong.

15–75 The meaning of the term mitigation in the context of an assessment of damages concerns the avoiding of the consequences of a wrong, whether in tort or in contract. McGregor[42] states that the term mitigation contains three interrelated rules. Plaintiffs:

– cannot recover for avoidable loss;

– can recover for loss incurred in reasonable attempts to avoid loss;

– cannot recover for avoided loss.

15–76 The principle of mitigation of damage is referred to frequently in the courts. In a judgment quoted above in para. **15–22**, Geoghegan J. made reference to the principle. In *Kelly v. Hennessy*, Hamilton C.J. gave a helpful summary of the principle when he said:

> "In addition the defendant has appealed against the finding by the learned trial judge that the plaintiff, by not having treatment for her depressive condition which would prove beneficial and aid her recovery, had not failed to mitigate her damages.
> There is a duty on all plaintiffs to take all reasonable steps to mitigate the damages or loss which they claim against another party.
> The duty is to take all reasonable steps having regard to the nature of their injuries or illness and the circumstances of the case and the onus is on the defendant to establish such failure on the balance of probabilities."[43]

---

[42] McGregor, H., *McGregor on Damages* (16th ed., Sweet & Maxwell, London, 1997), p. 185, n.1.
[43] [1995] 3 I.R. 253 at 264–265.

15–77 It is important to note that the plaintiff is only required to take steps that are considered to be reasonable, not ones that are extravagant or that have a low chance of success. In attempting to mitigate his damage, the plaintiff is not required to incur considerable expense or inconvenience, disorganise his business or break other contracts. The injured party is, however, required to make reasonable attempts to limit his damages.

Effect of mitigation

15–78 If the plaintiff makes reasonable attempts to mitigate his damage, but fails to do so, he is not penalised. So long as the plaintiff's attempt is reasonable, regardless of whether it proves successful, he can recover for the expense or for the loss caused by the lack of success. The economic justification for this rule is to encourage an injured party to do what he can to minimise the injury caused by a breach. In practice, pre-trial loss generally allows for good faith errors – taking into account that the plaintiff took what he thought was the best course of action (even if this did not lead to the maximum mitigation, *i.e.* the minimal loss). Thus, the pre-trial loss calculation is based on the actual post-accident income – not on what should have been generated (given the benefit of hindsight). This principle is well illustrated by the judgment of Keane J. (as he then was) in *Lennon v. Talbot Ireland Ltd*:

> "It is often easy after an emergency has passed to criticise the steps which have been taken to meet it, but such criticism does not come well from those who have themselves created the emergency. The law is satisfied if the party placed in a difficult situation by reason of the breach of a duty owed to him has acted reasonably in the adoption of remedial measures, and he will not be held disentitled to recover the cost of such measures merely because the party in breach can suggest that other measures less burdensome to him might have been taken."[44]

Limits on mitigation

15–79 There are three important limits on the duty to mitigate in respect of contracts:

1. Mitigation cannot arise until a breach has taken place. See *White and Carter (Councils) Ltd v. McGregor*.[45]

2. Where repudiation precedes the time for performance, it is not part of the mitigation rules to decide whether the plaintiff acted reasonably in trying to terminate or to continue with performance.

---

[44]Unreported, High Court, December 20, 1985.
[45][1962] A.C. 413.

3. The principles do not apply unless damages have actually been claimed. Therefore, if a plaintiff is unable to frame a claim for the recovery of a sum, no question of mitigation will arise.

Duty of care

15–80 For damages to be recoverable on foot of a claim in tort, in addition to showing that the damage was caused to the plaintiff by the defendant, and that causation is not defeated by remoteness, it is also necessary to show that the defendant owed a duty of care to the plaintiff, that the duty of care was breached and that the plaintiff suffered damage as a result of the breach. In other words, the non-remote cause of damage to the plaintiff must constitute a breach of a duty of care owed by the defendant to the plaintiff. The issue of duty of care has already been discussed in paras **12–07** *et seq.* in relation to accountants' liability.

15–81 Many lengthy, learned and comprehensive works have been written on the subject of the law of torts and the duty of care. The leading Irish text in this area is McMahon and Binchy.[46] It is beyond the scope of this work to deal in any significant detail with this area of the law, and readers are encouraged to consult McMahon and Binchy's work and other relevant material for a full discussion of the issues.

15–82 Since the famous "snail in a bottle" *Donoghue v. Stevenson* case, the general duty of care owed by one party to another has been extended and further defined. The part of Lord Atkin's judgment in that case that has been cited with approval most often in Irish cases is:

> "You must take reasonable care to avoid acts or omissions which you can reasonably foresee would be likely to injure your neighbour. Who, then, in law, is my neighbour? The answer seems to be—persons who are so closely and directly affected by my act that I ought reasonably to have them in contemplation as being so affected when I am directing my mind to the acts or omissions which are called in question".[47]

15–83 O'Flaherty J. quoted this passage as recently as 1997 in the case of *Madden v. Irish Turf Club*.[48]

In *W. v. Ireland (No. 2)*,[49] Costello P. reviewed the law relating to duty of

---

[46] McMahon, B.M.E. and Binchy, W., *Law of Torts* (3rd ed., Butterworths, Dublin, 2000).
[47] *M'Alister (or Donoghue) v. Stevenson* [1932] A.C. 562 at 580.
[48] [1997] 2 I.R. 184.
[49] [1997] 2 I.R. 141.

care as it exists in Ireland. He made reference to the judgment of McCarthy J. in *Ward v. McMaster*[50] in the following terms:

> "In his judgment (with which the Chief Justice, Walsh J., and Griffin J. agreed) McCarthy J. referred in detail to the loan scheme and then reviewed the authorities in Northern Ireland and in England and Australia to which he had been referred. In particular he referred to *Anns v. Merton London Borough* [1978] A.C. 728 and to a well-known passage in the judgment of Wilberforce L.J. (at pp. 751 and 752) (which he stated he did not 'seek to dilute') as follows (at p. 347): —
>
> > 'the position has now been reached that in order to establish that a duty of care arises in a particular situation, it is not necessary to bring the facts of that situation within those of previous situations where a duty of care has been held to exist. Rather the question has to be approached in two stages. First one has to ask whether, as between the alleged wrongdoer and the person who has suffered damage there is a sufficient relationship of proximity or neighbourhood such that, in the reasonable contemplation of the former, carelessness on his part may be likely to cause damage to the latter—in which case a prima facie duty of care arises. Secondly, if the first question is answered affirmatively, it is necessary to consider whether there are any considerations which ought to negative, or to reduce or limit the scope of the duty or the class of persons to whom it is owed or the damage to which a breach of it may give rise.'
>
> The judgment of McCarthy J. then went on to review the views expressed in later cases in England which analysed the test propounded by Wilberforce L.J. and heavily qualified it as well as the court's decision in the case. He rejected these criticisms...".[51]

15–84 Costello P. went on to say:

> "The view of the Irish courts has been that *Anns* was a 'confirmation' of the long established principles of the law of tort contained in *Donoghue v. Stevenson* [1932] A.C. 562 and was not (as some commentators in England seem to consider) a major innovation in the law of tort."[52]

15–85 Thus, the essential ingredient in the duty of care now appears to be sufficient proximity between the plaintiff and the defendant. Although this term is not defined, it imparts the essence of the required relationship between the parties.

15–86 Once sufficient proximity has been established, a duty of care can arise in a wide array of circumstances, *e.g.*:

---

[50] [1988] I.R. 337.
[51] [1997] 2 I.R. 141 at 151–152.
[52] *ibid.* at 153.

- employer to employee;
- occupier of property to visitor;
- driver to other road users;
- professional person to his clients;
- manufacturer or seller of products to buyers and customers;
- builder to customer;
- neighbour to neighbour;
- owner of animals to others;
- company to owner of a corporate brand or identity;
- individuals to others in the context of, *e.g.* the right to one's good name, the right to enjoy one's property, the right to privacy and the right to bodily integrity.

15–87   An act of negligence under any of these, and a variety of other headings, that causes damage to another is likely to constitute a breach of a duty of care.

Misfeasance/nonfeasance

15–88   Even if the defendant has foreseen the harmful event, he will often not be found to owe a duty of care if his failure to act is one of nonfeasance (*i.e.* failing to perform an act that would have prevented the damage) rather than misfeasance (*i.e.* performing a lawful act in a way that caused or failed to prevent the damage). If it is the actions of the defendant which create the circumstances in which a third party may be harmed, failure to take precautions to avert that harm is called misfeasance. In that circumstance, the defendant will be held to owe a duty of care. If, however, the defendant has merely observed that a third party may be harmed if a certain precaution is not taken, but has not taken that precaution, that failure to act is termed nonfeasance. In that circumstance, the defendant may be found to owe no duty of care. The individuals whose actions initiate a harmful situation owe a duty of care to those who are (potentially) harmed.

Availability of damages

15–89   Given the choice, most plaintiffs' lawyers elect for tort rather than or in addition to breach of contract actions. This is because it can often be easier to bring a set of circumstances within the general boundaries of a duty of care than within the strict limits imposed by the terms of a specific contract. In addition, a claim in tort can include a claim for exemplary (*i.e.* punitive) damages (see paras **15–26** *et seq.*) whereas a claim in contract cannot. The availability of the choice is effectively confirmed by the judgment of Hamilton C.J. in *Kennedy v. Allied Irish Banks plc*,[53] where he stated:

---

[53] [1998] 2 I.R. 48.

"I accept this to be the correct statement of the law *viz.* that where a duty of care exists, whether such duty is tortious or created by contract, the claimant is entitled to take advantage of the remedy which is most advantageous to him subject only to ascertaining whether the tortious duty is so inconsistent with the applicable contract that, in accordance with ordinary principle the parties must be taken to have agreed that the tortious remedy is to be limited or excluded."[54]

Standards in measuring damages

15–90   Although both breach of contract and tort actions seek compensatory damages, they do not share an identical standard for such damages:

"The primary aim in measuring damages is compensation, and this contemplates that the damages for a tort should place the injured person as nearly as possible in the condition he would have occupied if the wrong has not occurred, and that the damages for breach of contract would place the plaintiff in the position he would be in if the contract had been fulfilled."[55]

15–91   In tort, no question of loss of bargain can arise. The plaintiff is not complaining of a failure to implement a promise but a failure to leave him alone. The measure of damages in tort is therefore to be assessed on the basis of restoring as far as possible the *status quo ante*.

15–92   Table 15.1 summarises the differences in terms of effect on damages between breach of contract and tort actions.

Table 15.1: Comparison of assessment of damages in contract and in tort

	Tort	Contract
Claim for damages		
Standard for damages	• Restore to pre-injury position – *status quo ante*	• Restore to post-completion of the contract position
Valuation of damages		
Perspective	• Retrospective	• Prospective
Claim for exemplary damages	• Allowed	• Not possible
Limitations on recovery		
Causation	• Probable cause	• Direct result of breach
Remoteness	• Reasonably foreseeable	• Reasonable contemplation
Mitigation	• Plaintiff must try	• Plaintiff must try

---

[54] [1998] 2 I.R. 48 at 56.
[55] McCormack, C.T., *Handbook on the Law of Damages* (West Publishing Company, St. Paul, Minnesota, 1935), p. 560.

Measuring the amount of damages

15–93 Forensic accountants are frequently involved in assisting in establishing the quantum of a claim. Quantum (derived from Latin, meaning amount) is the amount of money that is due, or the amount of money that is lost, arising from the tort or breach of contract. There is no specific rule to decide the quantum of damages.

15–94 In personal injury cases, where the person has suffered bodily injuries, some guidance is available on quantum of general damage (see, for example, Pierse[56]). Experts in the medical and para-medical fields advise in relation to such personal injuries. Forensic accountants are concerned with estimating loss arising from lost earning power of individuals suffering personal injury and other special damages. Calculation of such damages depends on the individual circumstances of the case, and it is not possible to provide even broad guidelines on quantum. However, Chapter 16 attempts to provide guidelines on methods of calculation.

Types of damages

Restitution of damages in tort actions

15–95 The fundamental principle on which tort damages are calculated in common law courts is *restitutio in integrum* – the victim's damages are to equal his loss such that they restore him to his position before the wrong was committed. This doctrine is usually justified on the grounds that the function of tort law is to compensate the victim for the wrong perpetrated on him.

15–96 In the case of non-pecuniary losses, such as pain and suffering occasioned by the plaintiff's injuries, *restitutio in integrum* cannot be achieved. The compensatory principle in its application to the assessment of damages for such losses requires that the plaintiff be awarded such sum as, in the view of the court, represents a reasonable satisfaction for such losses.

15–97 A simple rationale for *restitutio* is that it is intended to ensure that the negligent party is required to bear a level of cost which equals the value of the costs created by his negligent activity. This level of cost is necessary to ensure that potential defendants will weigh the full benefits of all possible precautions (as measured by savings in accident costs) against the costs of those precautions.

---

[56] Pierse, R., *Quantum of Damages for Personal Injuries* (2nd ed., Round Hall Sweet & Maxwell, Dublin, 1999).

Restitution in breach of contract cases

15–98   Restitution damages are available in breach of contract cases only where the plaintiff has not fully or substantially completed his performance of the contract. If the plaintiff has substantially or completely performed his contractual obligations, then his damages will be limited to his expectation damages under the contract. Accordingly, restitution will be denied in those cases where the injured party has fully performed and all that remains is for the defendant to pay a contractually specified sum of money. The policy for denying restitution under such circumstances is to avoid placing the courts in a position of valuing a performance for which the parties have already established a value by their contract. However, if the plaintiff contracts merely to pay a specified amount, and pays this amount, and the defendant fails to perform his contractual obligations, restitution may be ordered through the return to the plaintiff of the amount paid.

Restitution damages generally

15–99   In contrast to cases in which a court grants expectation damages or reliance damages, restitution is awarded to prevent the unjust enrichment of the party in breach. The goal of the court in awarding restitution damages is not to protect either the expectation interest or the reliance interest of the injured party. Rather, the objective is to return the breaching party to the position he would have occupied had the contract not been made. Consequently, the award of restitution damages is measured by the value rendered to the defendant, regardless of the plaintiff's reliance or expectation damages. Thus, unlike reliance damages, restitution damages are not limited by the amount of the contract.

15–100   A simple example of restitution is where the plaintiff pays the defendant a sum in advance after which the defendant refuses to perform. In such a case, the plaintiff can bring an action for restitution to obtain return of his money. The money will be returned even where the performance, if rendered, would have been less valuable to him than the amount he paid. This can be seen from the judgment of Griffin J. for the Supreme Court in *United Dominions Trust (Ireland) Ltd v. Shannon Caravans Ltd*:

> "As to the second question, where a plaintiff has paid money in pursuance of his obligations under a contract and the consideration for which he entered into the contract totally fails, he may bring an action for the return of the money so paid . . . or he may sue for damages for breach of contract."[57]

15–101   One rationale for this approach is that the courts are reluctant to permit a defendant to use his breach as a method of limiting recovery by the plaintiff, thereby rewarding him for his breach. In *Hickey & Co Ltd v. Roches Stores*

---

[57] [1976] I.R. 225 at 233.

(Dublin) Ltd,[58] Finlay P. said that if a wrongdoer calculates that he will profit by breach of contract, such *mala fide* conduct should lead the courts to look both at the injury suffered by the victim and the profit or gain unjustly obtained by the wrongdoer, and damages should be increased to deprive the wrongdoer of any profit still obtained after quantifying the victim's loss.

Restitution may also be awarded to avoid unjust enrichment in circumstances where no binding contract existed.

Reliance damages

15–102   With reliance damages, the goal of the court will be to place the injured party in as good a position as he occupied prior to the making of the contract. If the plaintiff has acted in reliance on the contract, he can usually prove the extent of his expenditures in reliance on the contract even if he cannot prove lost profits. In such cases, the plaintiff is entitled to recover damages based on his reliance less any benefit he has received through salvage or otherwise.

Expectation damages

15–103   The general principle governing the measurement of damages for breach of contract is that the objective of the award of damages is to put the injured party in as good a position as he would have occupied had the contract been performed. Such damages are referred to as expectation damages because they seek to preserve the plaintiff's expectation interest in the contract. In calculating expectation damages, the injured party is entitled to recover:

> "... the loss in the value to him of the other party's performance caused by its failure or deficiency, plus ... any other loss, including incidental or consequential loss, caused by the breach, less ... any cost or other loss that he has avoided by not having to perform."[59]

15–104   When a court awards reliance damages, there is a possibility that the plaintiff could be put in a better pecuniary position than he would have been in had the contract been fully performed. This possibility exists where the plaintiff, rather than making a profit, would have suffered a net loss from full performance. If the defendant can demonstrate that the plaintiff would have lost money on the contract, the plaintiff's recovery may be limited to his expectation damages. It is noteworthy that under this scenario the burden of proof shifts to the defendant.

15–105   When measuring expectation damages, courts employ a subjective standard. Courts measure a plaintiff's expectation damages based on what

[58]Unreported, High Court, July 14, 1976.
[59]See Manley, D.H. and Reed, M.D., "Legal Framework for the Calculation of Damages in Commercial Litigation" *Journal of Forensic Economics,* Vol. 6, No. 3, 1993, pp. 219 at 220.

specific worth the contract would have had to the plaintiff, not to some hypothetical reasonable person.

15–106 Additionally, if the breach caused the plaintiff other incidental or consequential losses, he may be entitled to recover for these, provided that such additional losses were foreseeable at the time the contract was formed. Incidental damages include costs which arise from the plaintiff's reasonable efforts to avoid loss after a breach has occurred. Consequential damages include losses sustained by the injured party which the breaching party knew or had reason to know would result from his breach.

15–107 From the plaintiff's damages calculations are subtracted any amounts saved by the plaintiff by not having to complete his performance. When calculating the savings, there is some question as to whether expenses such as overheads should be included in the plaintiff's savings. At least one authority has suggested that the proper treatment of overhead expense depends on whether the costs involved are fixed or variable. Generally, variable costs can be treated as costs which the plaintiff has saved. Fixed costs which cannot be avoided by the plaintiff irrespective of his contractual responsibilities will generally not be deducted from an award of damages.

15–108 There are certain circumstances in which courts will not award plaintiffs their full expectation damages (*i.e.* including all incidental and consequential losses). For example, in some instances the cost of curing a breach will be clearly disproportionate to the diminution in value suffered by the plaintiff. In such circumstances, the court will limit recovery to the difference in value between the performance required by the contract and the defective performance.

Collateral benefits

15–109 It is possible for a plaintiff to be compensated for his injuries from more than one source (see also paras **16–45** *et seq.*). The most common such occurrence is where, as a result of personal injuries caused by actionable negligence, a plaintiff has valid social welfare claims and also seeks full compensation for his pain, suffering, expenses and lost earnings from the defendant via legal proceedings.

Some such possibilities have been eroded by statute. For instance, section 75 of the Social Welfare (Consolidation) Act 1993 (as amended by section 20 of the Social Welfare Act 1994) reduces damages for personal injuries by reference to disability benefit and disablement benefit in the following terms:

> "Notwithstanding section 2 of the Civil Liability (Amendment) Act, 1964, and section 236 of this Act, in an action for damages for personal injuries (including any such action arising out of a contract) there shall in assessing those damages be taken into account, against any loss of earnings or profits which has accrued

or probably will accrue to the injured person from the injuries, the value of any rights which have accrued or will probably accrue to him therefrom in respect of disability benefit payable by virtue of section 53 (disregarding any right in respect of the said disability benefit payable by virtue of section 210, after the death of the injured person) or disablement benefit (disregarding any increase thereof under section 57 in respect of constant attendance) for the 5 years beginning with the time when the cause of action accrued."

15–110   Such deductions have been the subject of some criticism from commentators and the courts on the grounds that they have the effect of penalising plaintiffs to the benefit of insurance companies.

On the other hand, legal commentators find the concept of collateral benefits to be one of the great puzzles in tort law. Why should plaintiffs be double compensated – once from his insurer or employer and once from the defendant? The economic analysis of *restitutio* suggests one possible explanation for this rule: that the function of torts is not only to compensate the victim but also to deter the injurer. In this light the concept makes sense. If the defendant did not have to pay damages because the plaintiff was insured or worked for a benevolent employer, then a finding of liability would have no (or a reduced) deterrent effect. Using this rationale, the source of payments to the plaintiff is less irrelevant to the determination of the damages payable by the defendant. Whether the plaintiff receives benefits from an insurance company, a benevolent employer, a charity, family, friends, the State, etc., the principle still applies that the tortfeasor will only take the full impact of his actions into account if he is required to play full value of the damages to the plaintiff.

Concluding comment

15–111   Irish courts have been slow to award aggravated damages and punitive damages over the years. This reluctance is understandable, as most successful civil cases are founded on a wrong committed by a defendant on a plaintiff, the rectification of which has the dual effect of depriving the defendant of the benefit of his wrongful act and restoring the corresponding cost to the plaintiff.

Nevertheless, situations do arise where these two elements – the benefit of the wrong to the wrongdoer and its cost to the wronged – are not equal. Where the wrongdoer's ill-gotten gains exceed the cost to the plaintiff, courts are still often reluctant to grant the windfall to the plaintiff, but they will, if to do so is the only effective way to punish the wrong adequately, and if they are persuaded of the justice of this approach. For this reason, forensic accountants, when quantifying a plaintiff's case, should always have regard to the benefits derived from the wrong by the defendant as well as to the plaintiff' losses – a careful and clear analysis of these benefits could significantly increase the damages ultimately payable to the plaintiff.

ACCOUNTING CALCULATIONS – PERSONAL INJURY DAMAGES

CHAPTER 16

ACCOUNTING CALCULATIONS – PERSONAL INJURY DAMAGES

16–01   Chapter 7 has considered the legal context applying to personal injury cases. This chapter considers the accounting calculations arising in personal injury litigation.[1]

16–02   The chapter commences by considering personal injury cases generally. This is followed by a discussion of computations involved in calculating personal injury damages. A consideration of fatal accident cases follows. Calculation of damages in fatal accident cases is similar to personal accident cases – any differences are highlighted in the chapter. The chapter then looks at the payment of awards and taxation of awards. The chapter concludes by considering sundry accounting issues relevant to calculation of personal injury and fatal accident damages.

16–03   Damages in personal injury and fatal accident cases use a more or less standard methodology which does not differ significantly between cases. The methodology usually includes projecting lost earnings and related fringe benefits over the work life of the plaintiff. Victims may suffer a reduction in life expectancy, which may in turn reduce the person's expected working life. The

---

[1] Other useful sources on this topic include Berenblut, M.L. and Rosen, H.N., *Litigation Accounting: The Quantification of Economic Damages* (Carswell Thomson Professional Publishing, Ontario, 1995); Brookshire, M.L., deSeve, C.W. and Slesnick, F.L., "Estimating damages in personal injury and wrongful death cases" in *Litigation Economics* (Gaughan, P.A. and Thornton, R.J. (eds) JAI Press, Greenwich, Connecticut, 1993); Lemar, C.J. and Mainz, A.J. (eds), *Litigation Support* (4th ed., Butterworths, London, 1999), Chap. 6; MacGregor, G. and Hobbs, I., *Expert Accounting Evidence: A Guide for Litigation Support* (Accountancy Books, London, 1998), Chap. 21; Martin, G.D. and Vavoulis, T., *Determining Economic Damages* (James Publishing Inc, California, 1999); Taub, M., Rapazzini, A., Bond, C., Solon, M., Brown, A., Murrie, A., Linnell, K. and Burn, S., *Tolley's Accountancy Litigation Support* (Butterworths, London, looseleaf), Part VI, para. 70; and Ugone, K.R., Taylor, C.R. and Miller, G., "Calculation of lost earnings" in *Litigation Services Handbook. The Role of the Accountant as Expert* (2nd ed., Weil, R.L., Wagner, M.J. and Frank, P.B. (eds), John Wiley & Sons, Inc., New York, 1995), Chap. 32.

value of those lost working years must also be calculated. Information on life expectancy and working life expectancy can be obtained from statistical data, usually available from an actuarial expert.

The calculation of lost earnings is based initially on historical data. Those earnings are projected using assumed growth rates. The projected earnings (lost because of the accident) are then discounted to present value using an appropriate discount rate.

Personal injuries cases

16–04 Personal injury cases usually involve a temporary or permanent disruption to the personal income or benefits of individuals or to their ability to earn an income.

Stages in personal injuries cases

16–05 Table 16.1 shows the stages involved in a personal injury case. Some of the terms in the table are discussed in Chapter 20 and are explained in the glossary in Appendix 3.

Initially, the main concern is to show that the defendant was negligent and is liable for the damage caused. Once liability is regarded as likely to be established in the plaintiff's favour quantum will become an issue. As with other claims arising from tortious damage, the underlying objective is to place the injured party back in the position in which he would have found himself had the defendant's negligence not occurred.

Damages in personal injuries cases

16–06 Damage is an injury, loss or reduced condition of the property or person of another. If it has resulted from a legal wrong, its value may be recovered through litigation. As previously discussed in paras **7–18** *et seq.*, the elements comprising heads of damages in personal injury awards are usually classified under the two headings "special damages" and "general damages". Special damages include pre-trial pecuniary losses, such as out-of-pocket expenses directly resulting from the injury sustained (*e.g.* medical expenses), measurable future expenses, past loss of earnings and the present value of estimated future loss of earnings. General damages comprise pre-trial and future non-pecuniary losses, *i.e.* pain and suffering and loss of amenities of life for the past, present and future to the extent that such losses are a result of the injuries sustained.

Table 16.1: Steps in personal injury damage award cases

Investigate facts and circumstances of accident
↓
Conclude that there is a reasonable cause of action
↓
Identify all possible defendants (taking account of issues of causation and remoteness)
↓
Issue letters seeking admission of liability and compensation and threatening proceedings
↓
Estimate value of claim*
↓
Choose correct jurisdiction and identify all relevant causes of action
↓
Issue proceedings *
↓
Respond to Notice for Particulars *
↓
Reply to Defence, where necessary *
↓
Issue Notice for Particulars and seek and make Discovery and Interrogatories where necessary *
↓
Enter into settlement discussions and/or consider defendant's lodgment where appropriate *
↓
Update details of damage (past and future) *
↓
Set matter down for trial
↓
Furnish reports of expert witnesses pursuant to S.I. No. 391 of 1998 (High Court only)
↓
Hearing *
↓
Judgment

* The forensic accountant can have significant input at all of these stages.

16–07   Table 16.2 identifies general and special damages arising from personal injuries.

Table 16.2: Damages in personal injury cases

Pecuniary (special) damages
- Lost earnings (including other compensation, fringe benefits, etc.) (see paras **16–23** *et seq.*)
  - During injury period (past and future)
  - Consequent on potential for higher periods of unemployment
  - Due to reduced life expectancy
- Pension rights lost (see paras **16–40** *et seq.*)
- Additional health care and living expenses (see paras **16–78** *et seq.*)
- Other actual costs (past and future) arising from the injury

Mitigating (reduction in) damages (see paras **16–44** *et seq.*)
- Earnings post-injury (past and future)
- Income tax
- Social welfare

Non-pecuniary (general) damages
- Reduced life expectancy (see paras **16–58** *et seq.*)
- Increased pain and suffering
- Reduced quality of life
- Reduced likelihood of marrying or of remaining happily married

---

16–08   Table 16.3 list items frequently omitted in claims for damages.

Table 16.3: Top 10 list of losses plaintiffs often overlook

---

1. Loss of household services such as cooking, cleaning and transporting children
2. Loss of future social security or pension benefits
3. Loss of holiday pay
4. Loss of future health insurance and life insurance benefits
5. Loss of deferred compensation from a lost job
6. Loss of long-term or short-term disability insurance
7. Loss of benefits from promotions that were expected or likely
8. Loss of personal possessions damaged in an accident
9. Loss of estate accumulation, including contributions to retirement plans
10. Cost of mileage to and from medical treatment

Source: Adapted from Long, S., "Top ten things plaintiffs forget in personal injury cases" in *Frankenfeld Report Newsletter* (November 1998), Vol. 1, No. 1, www.frankenfeld.com.

16–09   In *Reddy v. Bates*[2], McCarthy J. had this to say about the nature of the injuries compensable by general damages:

"In contrast with the approach to a review of an award under the headings of past and future actual loss, the Court's approach in reviewing an award of general damages may, essentially, be one of first impression. Such damages are frequently

---
[2] [1983] I.R. 141 at 151.

stated to be for pain and suffering; they would be better described as compensation in money terms for the damage, past and future, sustained to the plaintiff's amenity of life in all its aspects, including actual pain and suffering, both physical and mental, both private to the plaintiff and in the plaintiff's relationships with family, with friends, in working and social life and in lost opportunity."

16–10   This chapter does not deal further with general damages because, as can be appreciated from the above quotation, there is little or no role for forensic accountants in advising the courts in this area. However, it is worth noting that, despite occasionally asserting that this should not be done (*e.g.* see the judgment of McCarthy J. referred to above), courts will often look at the accumulated total of all damages. The figure for general damages will be adjusted to make the total of both the special and the general damages appear to more appropriately reflect the injuries (*e.g.* see the judgment of O'Hanlon J. in *Connolly v. Dundalk Urban District Council*[3] and the decision of the Supreme Court in *Sinnott v. Quinnsworth Ltd*[4]).

There is a possible role for forensic accountants in applying inflationary factors to general damages awarded in past cases in order to arrive at reasonable amounts in a case. However, such an exercise is fraught with the difficulties associated with attempting to measure "pain and suffering" or "loss of amenity" and the inevitable argument that "no two cases are the same".

Pecuniary damages

16–11   As shown in Table 16.2, pecuniary damages typically consist of lost earnings (both past and future), additional health care, rehabilitation and medical expenses (both past and future), special education or retraining costs and household services lost and other out-of-pocket expenses. Non-pecuniary damages typically include allowances for past and future pain and suffering and reduced quality of life (*e.g.* loss of job satisfaction).

16–12   In assessing loss of future earnings, loss of earning capacity (rather than loss of earnings *per se*) is the object of the calculations. The loss of earnings capacity assessed in the Irish courts is based on what the plaintiff *would* have earned rather than what he *could* have earned. This is clear from a large number of decisions of the courts over the years. Barron J. put it simply and clearly in *Doran v. Dublin Plant Hire Ltd*[5] when he said:

"Although it may be difficult to determine the facts which give rise to future loss of earnings, it still must be done. The fundamental matter is to determine the

---

[3] [1990] 2 I.R. 1.
[4] [1984] I.L.R.M. 523.
[5] [1990] 1 I.R. 488 at 497–498.

natural and probable financial loss to the plaintiff. There are two parts to the equation:

  (1) What would the plaintiff have earned throughout his working life, if he had not met with the accident; and

  (2) What will he now earn over the same period."

16–13   Table 16.4 shows the various elements comprising the estimate of pecuniary loss.

Table 16.4: Estimate of pecuniary loss

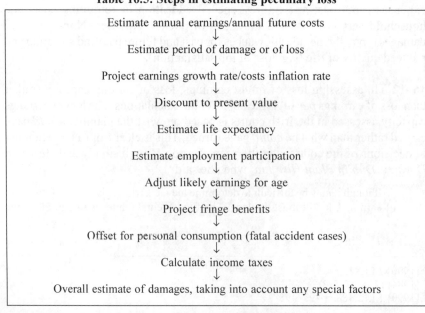

Total estimated pecuniary loss includes present value of:	

• Lost net earnings:
    + Reduction in gross earnings
    + Reduction in fringe benefits
    - Unemployment probability
    - Income taxes
    - Work-related expenses
 • Lost household services
 • Costs of lifetime health care and living expenses
 • Other recurring future costs (*e.g.* equipment)
 • Funeral and burial costs (fatal accident cases)
 • Other out-of-pocket costs
	Multiplier reflecting duration of losses and time effects of payments in the future applied to the sum of these amounts

16–14   The steps involved in estimating loss of earnings are summarised in Table 16.5.

Table 16.5: Steps in estimating pecuniary loss

Estimate annual earnings/annual future costs
↓
Estimate period of damage or of loss
↓
Project earnings growth rate/costs inflation rate
↓
Discount to present value
↓
Estimate life expectancy
↓
Estimate employment participation
↓
Adjust likely earnings for age
↓
Project fringe benefits
↓
Offset for personal consumption (fatal accident cases)
↓
Calculate income taxes
↓
Overall estimate of damages, taking into account any special factors

This exercise is normally undertaken by an actuary who uses appropriate mortality tables and assumptions regarding investment returns and wage inflation together with the available relevant information concerning the plaintiff (*e.g.* age, pre-accident earnings after taxation, likely post-accident earnings after taxation and likely duration of the losses).

Calculating damages in personal injuries cases

16–15   The Irish courts hear a large number of personal injuries cases every year. Although no two cases are identical, the high volume of cases, many of which have similar characteristics, has led to a degree of standardisation in the approach used to calculate damages. However, despite this, the calculation of damages is not an exact science and can be highly complex. For this reason, the assistance of experts, including accountants, actuaries and other professionals, is often sought by the legal teams of the parties involved.

Difficulty in quantifying awards

16–16   The difficulty in assessing damages is not a basis for a refusal to make an award in the plaintiff's favour. In fact, the courts have stated that it is not appropriate to substitute an increase in general damages for an item of special damage on the grounds that the latter is difficult to quantify. On this point, Barron J. in the High Court in *Doran v. Dublin Plant Hire Ltd* said:

> "This submission was made as part of a general submission as to the admissibility of actuarial evidence and to contest the use of an actuarial multiplier to a presumed weekly loss of earnings. It was submitted that there was no evidence to support such a calculation and that such evidence as there was as to future loss of earnings should lead to an additional award of general damages for loss of job opportunity. I appreciate his wish to prevent an automatic use of actuarial figures. Yet it seems to me that to award general damages for what is in fact special damage merely because of difficulty in assessing the amount to be awarded must be wrong in principle. ... Although it may be difficult to determine the facts which give rise to future loss of earnings, it still must be done. The fundamental matter is to determine the natural and probable financial loss to the plaintiff."[6]

16–17   Difficulties in estimation are common in cases concerning the loss of an opportunity for the plaintiff arising from the wrong of the defendant. In the nature of things, these damages are speculative and much depends on the evidence in a particular case. An obvious and usual example is damages for lost profits. If absolute certainty were required as to the precise amount of the loss that the

---

[6] [1990] 1 I.R. 488 at 497–498.

plaintiff had suffered, no damages would be recovered at all in a majority of cases. In awarding damages, courts are required to take account of uncertainties such as lost earnings capacity, loss of profits and future costs.

Assumptions

16–18 Many questions concerning personal injuries calculations cannot be answered with precision, even with the benefit of expert evidence, because they relate to the future. Accordingly, the experts, and ultimately the court, must make certain assumptions about the future in order to arrive at an estimate of the present value of future lost earnings. In making such assumptions, the court must consider the probability of occurrence of possible future events (*e.g.* promotion, change of job, redundancy, death, further disabling accident, etc.) and the relative probabilities of these events must be factored into the award for future loss of earnings.

16–19 It is accepted in the courts that these calculations of damages will be based on assumption and estimation.[7] Table 16.6 lists some assumptions that might be necessary in a personal injury damages calculation.

Table 16.6: Assumptions necessary in calculation of personal injury damages

Assumptions
Discount rate
Fringe benefits
Life expectancy
Labour force participation
Unemployment rate
Rate of growth of earnings
Plaintiff's retirement age

Probability versus possibility

16–20 Henchy J., when addressing a High Court jury on this subject (at a time when juries heard personal injury actions), commented on the distinction between probability and possibility. His charge to the jury was quoted by O'Dalaigh C.J. in the Supreme Court appeal of the jury's decision in *Kennedy v. East Cork Foods*[8]:

> "In dealing with future loss of earnings, the judge told the jury that unless there was a very heavy recession in the food-processing business the plaintiff was unlikely to be laid off as he was seventh in seniority in a group of 14 or 15 fitters,

---

[7] *Mallett v. McMonagle* [1970] A.C. 166.
[8] [1973] I.R. 244 at 252–253.

and that the probability was that they might say that the plaintiff would hold his job permanently. The judge continued as follows:—

> 'The one risk is if he gets sacked he would find it difficult to get another job. He would drop to being an unskilled man and earning £14 per week as an unskilled man. He has got a group certificate in the technical school and he is a satisfactory maintenance fitter. It is for you to say whether in fact in the future he would ever lose any wages because of this accident. If you think, on the other hand, that the probability is that he will lose wages, you must be satisfied of it as a matter of probability, not as a possibility. Damages are awarded not because something may possibly happen, but because something will probably happen, because if damages were awarded for possibilities some enormous damages would be awarded, because many things are possible in this life, but in terms of law we look only to probabilities. If you think that the probability is that at some future time he will have a loss of earnings because of this accident, then award him a sum under this heading. I don't know, but those of you who are in business, as most of you are, will be able to come to a reasonable and sensible sum.'"

16–21   The later case of *Reddy v. Bates*[9] is regularly referred to in personal injuries cases to this day as it is regarded as having established as a matter of law that the present value of future loss of earnings, as calculated using actuarial techniques and the best estimate of probable actual losses in the future, should be reduced to take account of a degree of uncertainty as to whether a plaintiff would be employed continuously for the period assumed by the calculations. In fact, as can be seen from the judgment of Griffin J. in the Supreme Court, although reference was made to the fact that actuarial calculations of future loss of earnings do not typically take account of "the marriage prospects of the plaintiff" or "any risk of unemployment, redundancy, illness, accident or the like", the court found only that the possibility of unemployment or redundancy should be considered in mitigation of the award, and even then, "the matter should be canvassed in evidence and in argument". Griffin J. said:

> "When actuarial evidence first came into regular use in our courts in cases such as this, employment was reasonably stable and so continued for many years thereafter. During that period of comparative stability, actuarial figures could be applied by juries with reasonable confidence, even though they have always been directed by trial judges that such figures are intended only as a guideline for the assistance of juries and that they are not bound to accept the figures. Whilst the mathematical calculations made by an actuary may be constant and correct, they should be applied in the particular circumstances of every case with due regard to reality and common sense. There is now a high rate of unemployment not only in this country but in Great Britain and in most of the member States of the European Economic Community. The great increase in recent years in the number of employees becoming redundant and in the number of firms being

---

[9] [1983] I.R. 141.

closed – firms which would have been regarded hitherto as of unshakeable financial soundness – must inevitably lead to the conclusion that there is no longer any safe, much less guaranteed, employment. In my view, this is a factor which juries should be required to take into account in assessing future loss of earnings in any given case, but the matter should be canvassed in evidence and in argument."[10]

16–22   It is clear that the reduction envisaged by Griffin J. in that case related specifically to the possibility of redundancy and was linked to the very difficult economic circumstances of the day. It is at least arguable that this decision should have considerably less effect, in terms of reductions in awards, in the current economic climate in Ireland given the availability of jobs and the dramatically reduced unemployment figures. It is interesting also to note that in *Reddy v. Bates*, having raised the possibility of such a reduction in the award for future loss of earnings, Griffin J. failed to make one.

Loss of earnings

16–23   Lost earnings comprise the monetary loss, expressed in present values, arising from the individual's inability or reduced ability to provide certain services. The calculation of past and future earnings capacity has a substantial impact on the amount of compensatory damages recoverable in personal injury litigation. Lost earnings damages due to the plaintiff comprises the present value at the date of injury of the difference between the plaintiff's projected "but for" earnings and the actual earnings. The calculations include both actual or estimated lost past earnings and projected lost future earnings.

This can be summarised in the following equation:

Lost earnings =
("But for" – actual past earnings) + Present value ("But for" – projected future earnings)

16–24   The legal principles for calculating damages were set out in the United Kingdom in *Cookson v. Knowles*[11] as follows:

– past lost earnings can include expected increases in income (*e.g.* wage increases that have been granted to employees performing similar tasks as the plaintiff);

– future loss is based on earnings at the date of the trial, *i.e.* no allowance for inflation. However, account may be taken for expected increases in earnings (*e.g.* arising from promotion);

---

[10][1983] I.R. 141 at 146–147.
[11][1979] A.C. 556.

- future loss is usually calculated by applying a multiplier (derived from annuity tables) to the multiplicand (*i.e.* the estimate of the annual loss).

- An uncertainty arising in *Cookson v. Knowles* as to the date from which the multiplier should be calculated in a fatal case was resolved by the House of Lords in *Graham v. Dodds.*[12] It was held that, while the pre-trial loss and the future loss may be treated separately for the purpose of capital assessment, the overall multiplier must be calculated from the date of death (see paras **16–69** *et seq.* for discussion of timing of calculation of damages). To calculate the multiplier from the date of the trial would be to ignore the uncertainty which affects everything that might have happened to the deceased after the date of his death.

Calculation of past earnings loss

16–25   Past losses of earnings incurred between the date of injury and the date of trial must be pleaded as special (*i.e.* pecuniary) damages. Past losses may be calculated by applying to a periodic (*i.e.* weekly, monthly, annual) amount (called the multiplicand) a multiple for the period of loss. Adverse contingencies must be taken into account (such as ill-health, strikes, unemployment) which would have reduced the plaintiff's earnings in the pre-trial period had he not been injured. This adjustment is similar to that in calculating future losses (see below, para. **16–49**), except that a deduction for life expectancy is not appropriate.

Estimate of annual earnings

16–26   Earnings will include basic earnings, additional revenues, shift premiums, bonuses, commissions, fringe benefits and deferred benefits. Finding appropriate base earnings requires the accountant to identify the amount of earnings of the injured party prior to the accident. The plaintiff's earnings history prior to the incident is a good source for understanding the base-year earnings. Earnings should be reduced by taxation (see paras **16–123** *et seq.*) and certain social welfare payments[13] (see paras **16–112** *et seq.*) and by any costs incurred by the plaintiff in making those earnings such as travel costs and clothing costs.[14] In the case of foreign currency earnings lost, the court will award damages in the foreign currency[15] or convert the foreign currency amount at an appropriate rate (*e.g.* see *Conley v. Strain*[16]).

---

[12][1983] N.I. 22.
[13]*Cooke v. Walsh* [1984] I.L.R.M. 208 at 217.
[14]*Lim Poh Choo v. Camden and Islington Area Health Authority* [1980] A.C. 174.
[15]*Hoffman v. Sofaer* [1982] 1 W.L.R. 1350.
[16][1988] 1 I.R. 628.

Fringe benefits

16–27 Lost earnings may include lost fringe benefits. Fringe benefits are part of a person's earnings. If the earnings are lost, the benefits that accompany them are generally also lost and should therefore be included in lost earnings calculations. Fringe benefits are compensatable damages[17] because their absence is an economic loss to the plaintiff (or to dependants in fatal accident cases) which must be replaced and they are part of the payment for the injured person's services. Details of the benefits the plaintiff was receiving before the accident, and was likely to receive in the future, should be obtained. Lost fringe benefits then need to be estimated. The courts have compensated plaintiffs for loss of board and lodging,[18] loss of the opportunity to buy duty free goods,[19] etc. In cases where the employer and employee share the cost of the fringe benefit, the calculation should only include the employer's contribution towards the fringe benefit.

16–28 In Ireland, the inclusion of fringe benefits and the deduction of expenses directly attributable to employment are generally accepted practices and these adjustments to the basic earnings figures tend to be made in the actuary's report and to form part of the actuary's calculations. The general principle that the amount recoverable by a plaintiff is limited to the difference between losses resulting from the damage and any gains arising as a consequence of the accident was well stated by Walsh J. in the Supreme Court in *O'Looney v. Minister for the Public Service*[20]:

> "In assessing the compensation the judge must make an award which includes the medical or surgical expenses incurred or likely to be incurred by the applicant and he must give damages for the pain and suffering occasioned by the injuries and for any disease or tendency to disease caused by the injuries. In addition he is required to examine the effects, if any, on the future earning power of the applicant and, in so doing, he is dealing in effect with a special heading of damages namely, economic loss. As in any other case the term 'economic loss' must take into account any sums gained as a result of the injuries and the award for economic loss should be the sum appropriate to compensate for the amount by which the actual prospective loss exceeds the actual or prospective gain."

Projection of future earnings

16–29 In an award where a plaintiff is compensated for the loss of earnings capacity, the court compares the plaintiff's pre-accident earning capacity with

---

[17] *Glover v. B.L.N. Ltd (No. 2)* [1973] I.R. 432.
[18] *Liffen v. Watson* [1940] 1 K.B. 556.
[19] *Ashley v. Esso Transportation Co Ltd* [1956] 1 Lloyd's Rep. 240; *The Times*, February 8, 1956.
[20] [1986] 1 I.R. 543 at 547.

his post-accident earnings capacity, and awards damages to represent the difference. In theory, compensation under this head of damages is for the loss of a capital asset (*i.e.* the ability to earn) rather than for loss of income in the form of earnings. (*e.g.* see the judgment of Barr J. in the High Court in *Phelan v. Coillte Teoranta*[21]).

16–30   In order to calculate a lump sum to compensate for loss of future earnings, a projection of future earnings will be required. A growth rate must be determined to project future earnings over the expected working life of the injured person (see discussion of life expectancy in para. **16–52**). This is the percentage rate that earnings would be expected to increase during the damage period. The growth rate must accurately reflect the expected increases in the plaintiff's earnings. A variety of sources are used to estimate this rate including industry standards, historical data and government statistics. The plaintiff's historical earnings are frequently used as a predictor of future earnings growth rates. If a solid historical record is available, it may be used to calculate a growth rate directly. Alternatively, it may be necessary to resort to average earnings statistics for the relevant occupation. The accountant may project "but for" earnings based on the past trend in the plaintiff's earnings, provided these follow a consistent pattern and are a reliable indicator of the future. Earnings may also increase because of the plaintiff's prospects of promotion,[22] even where the prospects of promotion are not certain[23] (see also *State (Thornhill) v. Minister for Defence*[24]).

16–31   When arriving at an appropriate multiplier to apply to calculated loss of earnings, the actuary will often make an assumption as to the extent to which investment returns will exceed wage inflation over the period of the losses. In doing so, the actuary is building into his calculation of the present value of future lost earnings an assumption in relation to increases in income and simultaneously applying a discount to arrive at the capital value today of the future income stream that the plaintiff has lost. If it is accepted that, over the long term, wage inflation and investment returns move approximately in tandem with a relatively constant differential between them, this approach has the effect of making it unnecessary to project specific pay rises into the future. However, such a calculation ignores any pay adjustments arising from factors other than inflation (*e.g.* by virtue of promotion, productivity changes, etc.) that the plaintiff might enjoy, and these therefore need to be factored into the calculation separately.

16–32   Projecting income streams for self-employed persons is likely to be

---

[21] [1993] 1 I.R. 18.

[22] *Mitchell v. Mulholland (No. 2)* [1972] 1 Q.B. 65 at 83–84 (C.A.).

[23] *Ratnasingam v. Kow Ah Dek* [1983] 1 W.L.R. 1235.

[24] [1986] 1 I.R. 1.

more difficult than for employees. For self-employed persons, a distinction must be made between their income from equity in the business (which should not be affected by the injury) and income in compensation for their work in the business. One approach is to calculate what it would cost to pay a manager to do the work of the owner.

16–33   As stated earlier, the measure of damage is not loss of earnings *per se* but rather loss of earning capacity. The effect of loss of earning capacity is that the plaintiff is disadvantaged in competing with others for work in the labour market. Thus, damages will also be awarded in respect of "disadvantage in the labour market" where the plaintiff's employment prospects are adversely affected by the injury.[25] The quantum of damages depends on the present value of the risk that the plaintiff will, at some future time, suffer financial damage because of his disadvantage in the labour market.

Projection of future earnings of children

16–34   Calculating the lost earnings of children involves greater estimation and subjective judgment than for adults. Two approaches have been used, the latter being less likely in practice:

1.   The use of government statistics of average earnings (possibly subject to adjustment for the particular circumstances of the individual child).[26]

2.   A calculation based on the earnings and employment history of the child's father.[27]

16–35   In *McNamara v. Electricity Supply Board*,[28] the plaintiff was 11 years old at the time of the accident and 17 when the case came to trial. The Supreme Court held that is was not unreasonable to base compensation on the plaintiff becoming a chef, as this was the occupation he stated in evidence that he would have pursued and one of his brothers was a trainee chef at the time of the trial. In *Cooke v. Walsh*,[29] the plaintiff came from a working-class background and the court found that his earnings should be assessed by reference to the average earnings of a semi-skilled worker. The award in this case was subsequently set aside on unrelated grounds (that no deduction had been made for income tax

---

[25] In the U.K., see *Smith v. Manchester Corporation* [1974] 17 K.I.R. 1 (C.A.); in Ireland, see *Kennedy v. East Cork Foods Ltd* [1973] I.R. 244.

[26] A wealth of interesting statistics can be found in an annual publication, Central Statistics Office Ireland, *Statistical Abstract* (Stationery Office, Dublin, Annual).

[27] *Cassel v. Hammersmith and Fulham Health Authority* [1992] P.I.Q.R. Q168.

[28] [1975] I.R. 1.

[29] [1983] I.L.R.M. 429; [1984] I.L.R.M. 208.

and social welfare payments that would have been made by the employee, and that the deduction for adverse contingencies was inadequate[30]).

16–36   On the other hand, in *Lindsay v. Mid-Western Health Board*,[31] Morris J. (as he then was) in the High Court did not consider that there was "anything like sufficient evidence to base a claim for past or future loss of earnings". The case involved a child who, at the age of eight, had suffered irreversible brain damage and who, at the time of trial, had been in a deep coma for 18 years. Although the Supreme Court allowed an appeal against the High Court finding of negligence against the defendant, the finding that there was no evidence to ground a claim for lost earnings was not disturbed.

16–37   An obvious difference between this case and *McNamara v. Electricity Supply Board*[32] was the inability of the plaintiff in *Lindsay v. Mid-Western Health Board*[33] to give evidence herself as to what her career hopes and expectations would have been had she not suffered injury. If this was the sole or principal reason for denying an award of future loss of earnings, it could be argued that it was an inappropriate basis for such a decision. Instead, a clear statement from the courts would be welcome as to the extent, if at all, to which either general (*i.e.* non-pecuniary) damages or special (*i.e.* pecuniary) damages (or both) should differ where the plaintiff is not in a position to appreciate the extent of her injuries. Finlay C.J. referred to this issue in *Dunne v. National Maternity Hospital*[34] when he said:

> "No submission was apparently made at the trial and no argument was certainly presented on this appeal to the effect that as a matter of principle a person who, as a result of injuries tortiously inflicted, has no awareness of his condition should be entitled under the heading of general damages to nil or nominal damages only. I, therefore, express no view on any such proposition."

A view on this issue would be very helpful to litigants and their advisers in cases that are, by definition, among the most tragic.

16–38   In some cases the injury to a child, while not so severe as to interfere completely with the injured person's ability to earn, adversely affects his education or training such that he can only earn a living in a less well paid job. Such a plaintiff is entitled to compensation for the consequential loss of earnings.[35]

---

[30] [1984] I.L.R.M. 208 at 216–217.
[31] [1993] 2 I.R. 147 at 177.
[32] [1975] I.R. 1.
[33] [1993] 2 I.R. 147.
[34] [1989] I.R. 91 at 119.
[35] *Jones v. Lawrence* [1969] 3 All E.R. 267; *Joyce v. Yeomans* [1981] 2 All E.R. 21 (C.A.); *Clancy v. Commissioners of Public Works in Ireland* [1992] 2 I.R. 449.

Other lost benefits

16–39 In some cases, the plaintiff's earning capacity is so reduced that he will not be able to make social welfare contributions resulting in lower social welfare entitlements than before the accident. The claim for damages should include the lost social welfare benefits.

Account is taken of each plaintiff's special circumstances (*e.g.* variations by geographical region are taken into account) and additional information (*e.g.* implications of different retirement ages) is provided to help evaluate non-earnings losses such as lost social welfare benefits or pension rights. Factors such as levels of economic activity and employment are also considered.

Valuation of pension benefits lost

16–40 In some personal injury cases, the lost compensation includes lost pension rights or benefits which would have been earned after the working life and retirement of the plaintiff. The projected lost pension benefits must be added to lost earnings in calculating damages. Generally speaking, there are two types of pension plans – defined contribution and defined benefit plans. Calculating pension benefits under defined benefit plans is easier than under defined contribution plans, but both calculations are likely to require the assistance of an actuary. The formula for defined benefit after retirement generally includes parameters for years of service, salary levels and the date of retirement.

16–41 There are two ways of calculating the present value of the loss. The open market approach involves obtaining quotations on the insurance market for the amount of lost pension for the plaintiff. Alternatively, an actuary can be asked to assess the present value of payment for life of the amount of the loss of pension commencing at the date of retirement of the plaintiff.

16–42 The method used in *Auty v. National Coal Board*[36] for calculating pension loss in personal injury claims has been accepted in England as the primary way for computing losses of pension in lump sum calculations. The open market approach was followed, together with the application of a five per cent discount rate. In the calculations, various "imponderables" were relevant in discounting the pension benefit loss including voluntary redundancy, dismissal, ill health, disablement and death. A further discount relating to early receipt of lump sum payments should also be taken into account. Credit is usually given in one of two ways:

– deducting the actual lump sum from the projected lump sum as if lost at retirement date and discounted to trial date;

– discounting the projected lump sum to date of receipt of actual lump sum and deducting one from the other.

---

[36] [1985] 1 All E.R. 930.

16–43 In *Longden v. British Coal Corp*,[37] it was held that the early receipt of a pension benefit before retirement age should not be deducted from the loss of pension benefit. Given that lump sums are merely a payment of a future pension income stream, this approach raises an inconsistency of treatment between two parts of the same element of damages and is difficult to justify from a theoretical viewpoint. For this reason, it may not survive a review in the future.

In *Sexton v. O'Keeffe*,[38] a case well known for its endorsement by the Supreme Court of the value of actuarial evidence, damages awarded to the plaintiff included lost pension benefits which were calculated by Kingsmill Moore J. by applying to the plaintiff's annual loss a multiplier taken by him from the "5 per cent tables to be found at page 74 of Innwood's Tables".[39]

Mitigating lost earnings

16–44 As explained in Chapter 7 (para. **7–64**) and Chapter 15 (paras **15–74** *et seq.*), plaintiffs have a duty to take reasonable steps to minimise the damages they incur, for example, by finding alternative employment after an accident. Actual earnings after the injury may not be the best measure of damage mitigation – the plaintiff may not have made a sufficient effort to mitigate damages.

16–45 The basic rule is that damages are based on the net consequential loss. Receipts arising from the accident must therefore be deducted from the plaintiff's losses. However, the general rule in Irish law is that compensating benefits are not taken into account in reducing the plaintiff's damages for loss of earnings in a personal injury action. The Irish courts have long held that receipt of insurance proceeds should be ignored in assessing plaintiff damages.[40] Section 2 of the Civil Liability (Amendment) Act 1964 states:

> "In assessing damages in an action to recover damages in respect of a wrongful act (including a crime) resulting in personal injury not causing death, account shall not be taken of–
>
> (a) any sum payable in respect of the injury under any contract of insurance,
>
> (b) any pension, gratuity or other like benefit payable under statute or otherwise in consequence of the injury."

This section sets out the rules for non-deduction of monetary receipts in calculating damages. These provisions have been qualified to some extent by later provisions in the Social Welfare Acts. In particular, in actions for damages for personal injuries, account is taken, against any loss of earnings or profits

---

[37] [1998] A.C. 653.
[38] [1966] I.R. 204.
[39] *ibid.* at 211.
[40] *Woodman Matheson & Co. Ltd v. Brennan* (1941) 75 I.L.T.R. 34.

arising from the injuries sustained, of the value of any related rights to disability benefit or disablement benefit for the five years following the accident (see also paras **15–109** *et seq.*).[41] For actions for personal injuries arising from road traffic accidents, account is taken of the value of any related rights to sickness benefit or invalidity pension for the same period.[42]

16–46 The amended provisions are:

> "75.—(1) Notwithstanding section 2 of the Civil Liability Act, 1964, and section 236 of this Act, in an action for damages for personal injuries (including any such action arising out of a contract) there shall in assessing those damages be taken into account, against any loss of earnings or profits which has accrued or probably will accrue to the injured person from the injuries, the value of any rights which have accrued or will probably accrue to him therefrom in respect of disability benefit payable by virtue of section 53 (disregarding any right in respect of the said disability benefit payable by virtue of section 210, after the death of the injured person) or disablement benefit (disregarding any increase thereof under section 57 in respect of constant attendance) for the 5 years beginning with the time when the cause of action accrued."

> "237.—(1) Notwithstanding section 2 of the Civil Liability Act, 1964, and section 236, in assessing damages in any action in respect of liability for personal injuries not causing death relating to the use of a mechanically propelled vehicle (within the meaning of section 3 of the Road Traffic Act, 1961), there shall be taken into account the value of any rights arising from such injuries which have accrued, or are likely to accrue, to the injured person in respect of sickness benefit (including any amount payable therewith by way of pay-related benefit) or invalidity pension under Part II for the period of 5 years beginning with the time when the cause of action accrued."

16–47 Other items to be considered include:

– Statutory sick pay which should be deducted.[43]

– Redundancy payments which should not be taken into account in assessment of damages.[44]

– Savings on living expenses (*e.g.* travel costs to/from work) which should be deducted as an expense to earn lost earnings.[45]

---

[41] Social Welfare (Consolidation) Act 1993, s. 75, as amended by s. 20 of the Social Welfare Act 1994.

[42] Social Welfare (Consolidation) Act 1993, s. 237, as amended by s. 17 of the Social Welfare Act 1997.

[43] *Palfrey v. GLC* [1985] I.C.R. 437.

[44] *Mills v. Hassal* [1983] I.L.R. 330; see also *O'Loughlin v. Teeling* [1988] I.L.R.M. 617.

[45] Discussed in *Dews v. National Coal Board* [1988] 1 A.C. 1.

– Tax rebate which must be deducted from lost earnings.[46]

16–48   Although defendants have attempted to have entitlements to pension rights or accelerated payment of pensions taken into account in assessing compensation for loss of earnings by plaintiffs, this has been resisted by the courts. For such benefits to be taken into account in assessing loss-of-earnings claims would be to allow the wrongdoer to benefit from his wrong.

Multipliers

16–49   Given that damages are usually awarded in the form of a lump sum rather than in the form of an income stream, the assessment of damages requires the conversion of an annual figure into a capital sum. Actuaries generally advise, and the courts generally apply, a multiplier approach. A multiplier based on the expected duration of the loss is applied to an amount representing the annual losses and expenses (called the multiplicand) producing a capital figure. In personal injury actions, the multiplier is determined at the date of trial. Invariably an actuary advises on the appropriate multiplier.[47]

16–50   Actuarial evidence has long been a feature of personal injury actions in the Irish courts, as evidenced by the following dictum of Walsh J. in *O'Leary v. O'Connell*:

> "It has been decided by this Court in many cases that, where there is a substantial element of future loss of earnings involved in any claim, the evidence of an actuary is not merely desirable but necessary. It is immaterial whether the prospective loss is in respect of a long period or in respect of a short period, and whether the period has already commenced or whether it will arise at some stage in the future. The appropriate actuarial evidence is necessary in all these cases to enable the jury to arrive at a reasonably accurate mathematical computation of the present value of the actual loss which they find will be incurred."[48]

In *Cooke v. Walsh*,[49] the court found that:

> "... the function of an actuary is to ascertain what is the capital sum, payable at the time of the hearing of the action, which is equivalent to a loss of each £1 per week for a specified period, taking into account that the capital sum can be invested and earn interest, the probabilities of the plaintiff surviving that period, and inflation."

---

[46] *Hartley v. Sandholme Iron C. Ltd* [1975] Q.B. 600.
[47] This is in contrast to the practice in the U.K. where multipliers are based on actuarial tables called Ogden Tables.
[48] [1968] I.R. 149 at 156.
[49] [1984] I.L.R.M. 208 at 216.

16–51   A number of factors considered below and in Chapter 19 influence the amount of the multiplier including:

– life expectancy (paras **16–52** *et seq.*);

– time value of money (para. **16–55** and Chapter 19);

– discount rate (para. **16–55** and Chapter 19);

– period of loss (paras **16–69** *et seq.*).

Life expectancy

16–52   In the United Kingdom and Ireland, life expectancies are obtained from actuarial tables, and actuaries use these tables as an important input to the determination of the appropriate multiplier. Life expectancy can be affected by a plaintiff's general medical and social history, but is normally taken to be the average for a person of the gender and age of the plaintiff, as disclosed by the actuarial tables.

16–53   Irish courts are very accustomed to hearing the evidence of actuaries and using their calculations of multipliers to take account of life expectancies, whether normal or reduced. An example is *Conley v. Strain* where Lynch J., in the High Court, found:

> "Regarding future loss of earnings, the plaintiff's actuary, on the basis of a life expectancy of 25 years, indicated that the capital value of each pound per week of lost earnings would be £932. This figure does not however take into account the contingencies of redundancy, unemployment, sickness, accident and matters of an economic nature which might interrupt the continuity of the plaintiff's employment. Taking these matters into account, the defendants' actuary indicated a multiplier of £870 for each pound per week. Each of these figures is on the basis of applying the multiplier to the net take home pay."[50]

16–54   The multiplier is the number of weeks or years of loss of earnings, discounted to account for the early receipt of a lump sum. The multiplier is designed to reflect many factors, in particular, the plaintiff's life expectancy and the time value of money (see para. **16–55**. and Chapter 19 for further discussion of this topic). In personal injury cases, courts have traditionally relied on doctors for opinions on plaintiffs' remaining life expectancy where it has been shortened by the effects of the injuries. However, even eminent physicians are unable to answer such questions with any degree of precision. The analogy with life insurance is helpful. When applying for a life insurance policy, the doctor first examines the patient to assess various risk factors. The results are transferred to the insurance company's actuaries, who use a risk profile to assess life expectancy. Thus, both medical and statistical/actuarial skills are needed.

---

[50] [1988] 1 I.R. 628 at 645.

Only a physician is qualified to appraise the individual, and only a statistician or actuary is qualified to turn the appraisal into a life expectancy.

Time value of money

16–55   As the money intended to compensate for the future loss is being received at the time the calculation is made (*i.e.* at the time of the judgment or settlement of the action), rather than when the loss or expense is actually incurred, the multiplier is adjusted downwards to take into account the time value of money. If the loss is not expected to begin until some time in the future, there must be an additional adjustment of the discount for accelerated receipt (this issue is considered in more detail in Chapter 19). A further and separate downward adjustment will be made to the multiplier to reflect the contingencies of life. The multiplier should also take into account the rate of return on investment of the lump sum in the future. These principles apply to both future expense and loss of future earnings. In order to effect the discount of accelerated receipt, it is necessary to apply a notional rate of interest which the plaintiff is assumed to obtain by investing the "accelerated" lump sum.

Calculating damages using multipliers

16–56   The multiplier is often provided to the court when the facts concerning rate of growth of earnings, discount rate, and age of retirement are not in dispute but there is some disagreement concerning the plaintiff's starting salary. The determination and agreement of multipliers is usually less difficult than might be expected for two reasons. First, experts rarely differ significantly with respect to the discount rate or the plaintiff's retirement age. Thus, multipliers would have to be provided only for a selection of growth rates of earnings. Second, growth rates of earnings tend to be associated very closely with educational level. Simply by calculating a multiplier for each of four levels of education can provide a comprehensive range of multipliers: primary school, secondary school, university, and post-graduate.

16–57   Kemp[51] sets out two approaches to calculating damages using multipliers. The single multiplier method is based on average net annual earnings and one multiplier.[52] The split multiplier approach caters for the changing earning capacity of the injured party and applies an increasing amount of earnings (multiplicand) to the multiplier.[53] These two approaches are illustrated in Table 16.7.

---

[51] Kemp, D., *Damages for Personal Injury and Death* (7th ed., Sweet & Maxwell, London, 1988), pp. 177–179.
[52] Examples of where this method has been applied include *Brightman v. Johnston, The Times*, December 17, 1985; and *Housecroft v. Burnett* [1986] 1 All E.R. 332 (C.A.).

Table 16.7: Use of multipliers in calculating lump sums

Single multiplier method
Multiplicand, i.e. average net annual earnings €20,000
Multiplier: 15 times
Present value of plaintiff's future earnings stream is: €300,000

Split multiplier method

	Multiplicand	Multiplier	Lump sum
	€		€
Initially	15,000	4	60,000
Then	20,000	6	120,000
Finally	25,000	5	125,000
Present value of plaintiff's future earnings stream is:			€305,000

Lost years deduction

16–58   Irish law allows a plaintiff whose life expectancy has been shortened to recover loss of earnings and other pecuniary benefits in respect of his "lost years", *i.e.* years in which the plaintiff would have been alive and earning but for the accident.[54] In *Doherty v. Bowaters Irish Wallboard Mills Ltd*,[55] a Supreme Court appeal, Walsh J. said:

> "The evidence of the actuary called on behalf of the plaintiff was that the capitalised value at the date of the trial of the plaintiff's loss of earnings for the future would be £9,335. That was on the assumption of an actual life expectancy of 28 years. This figure was taken and acted upon on the assumption that the plaintiff was not entitled to recover, as part of his damages, any sum in respect of the loss of wages for the number of years by which his expectation of life had been reduced, which in this case was approximately ten years. On this matter the learned trial judge expressed the view that that was the correct legal position. In my opinion the period or the length of time by which the expectation of life has been reduced must also be taken into account, though of course for that particular period the sum to be considered would not be the gross loss of wages for the period but the surplus, if any, after providing for what it would have cost him to live during those years if he had not had the accident."

---

[53] Examples of where this method has been applied include *Brittain v. Gardner, The Times*, February 18, 1988; and *Burke v. Tower Hamlets Health Authority, The Times*, August 10, 1989.

[54] The leading case on this in the U.K. is *Pickett v. British Rail Engineering* [1980] A.C. 136. However, the matter was addressed in an earlier Irish case in *Doherty v. Bowaters Irish Wallboard Mills Ltd* [1968] I.R. 277.

[55] [1968] I.R. 277 at 285.

16–59   A more recent example of the application of this principle occurred in the High Court case of *Coppinger (Dermot) v. Waterford County Council*. In his judgment Geoghegan J. said:

> "I accept the principle put forward by the actuary, Mr. Lynch and approved by Walsh J. in *Doherty v. Bowaters Irish Wallboard Mills Ltd.* [1968] I.R. 277, that the future loss of earnings should not be discounted by reference to loss of life expectancy except to the extent of monies which would have gone to the support of the plaintiff or would not have been used for the benefit of his family."[56]

16–60   Lost years are calculated by reference to the likely life expectancy of the plaintiff were it not for the accident compared with his life expectancy after the accident. A plaintiff's injuries often result in a reduced life expectancy such that he is expected to die before the "normal" retirement age. In such cases, the court will determine compensation for the income which the individual would have earned between the (expected) age of death and the (previously expected) age of retirement. In principle, the pleasure which consumption of this residual would have provided during the years which have been lost can be replaced by consumption during the plaintiff's now-shortened lifetime.

Calculation of "lost years" damages

16–61   A plaintiff whose life expectancy has been shortened will not need to be compensated for the full value of the income lost during the years which he/she will not now live. Three alternative approaches to this calculation are set out in Table 16.8:

- alternative 1 proposes no compensation for lost years;

- alternative 2 proposes full compensation for lost years;

- alternative 3 proposes compensation for lost years comprising the full loss reduced for the saving of living expenses on the death of the injured party.

Alternative 3 is the one normally followed and is the approach approved by the dicta of Walsh J. and Geoghegan J. quoted above at paras **16–58** and **16–59** respectively.

16–62   Numerous theories have been put forward for the determination of the amount of compensation to be made for lost years. These range from:

- reducing full income for those components of income absolutely necessary to the maintenance of life; to

- reducing full income for the entire value of the plaintiff's projected expenditure on consumption (*i.e.* deduction of the entire value of income except savings).

---

[56][1998] 4 I.R. 220 at 239.

Table 16.8: Alternative approaches in calculating lost years deduction

Injury suffered by 45-year-old woman
Life expectancy reduced to age 52
Absent injury, she would have worked to age 62, earning €30,000 per year.

Restitutio would require that the plaintiff be compensated during those lost years (*i.e.* between ages 52 to 62) (in addition to her loss of future earnings from age 45 to 52 years).

Amount of compensation:

Alternative 1
No compensation required as defendant will not be alive during the period after age 52 – this approach ignores the fact that the plaintiff has lost the right to enjoy the income she would have earned between the ages 52 to 62.

Alternative 2
Entire value of her foregone income, *i.e.* a lump sum present value of approximately €180,000 (€30,000 x 10 years x discount factor of 0.60) – this ignores the fact that the plaintiff would not have enjoyed as excess income the full value of her income as some would have been used for living expenses.

Alternative 3
Value of forgone income [(€30,000 x 10 years), net of living expenses for each year (say 50%: €15,000 x 10 years)] x discount factor of 0.60, *i.e.* a lump sum present value of approximately €90,000.

Adapted from: Beesely, S., "Shortened life expectancy: The 'lost years' calculation" in *Expert Witness* (Spring 1996),Vol. 1, No. 1, http://economica.ca.

A calculation based on reasonable assumptions as to likely future patterns of spending on essential living expenses will usually be sufficient.

16–63   Pecuniary benefits which form the subject of a "lost years" claim are not confined to, but mainly relate to, lost earnings. The size of the claim depends on the age of the plaintiff and his life expectancy at the date of trial. The House of Lords in England[57] rejected the suggestion that only a modest award of damages, akin to compensation for loss of expectation of life, should be made where future lost earnings were involved. Their Lordships held that, except for situations (*e.g.* cases involving young children) where a reasonable estimate of lost future earnings is impossible, an estimate should be made and damages should be awarded based on that estimate. They stated:

> "The correct approach in law to the assessment of damages in these cases presents, my Lords, no difficulty, though the assessment itself often will. The principle must be that the damages should be fair compensation for the loss suffered by the deceased in his lifetime. The appellant in Gammell's case was disposed to argue by analogy with damages for loss of expectation of life, that, in the absence of cogent evidence of loss, the award should be a modest conventional sum.

[57] *Gammell v. Wilson* [1982] A.C. 27.

There is no room for a 'conventional' award in a case of alleged loss of earnings of the lost years. The loss is pecuniary. As such, it must be shown, on the facts found, to be at least capable of being estimated. If sufficient facts are established to enable the court to avoid the fancies of speculation, even though not enabling it to reach mathematical certainty, the court must make the best estimate it can. In civil litigation it is the balance of probabilities which matters. In the case of a young child, the lost years of earning capacity will ordinarily be so distant that assessment is mere speculation. No estimate being possible, no award – not even a 'conventional' award – should ordinarily be made. Even so, there will be exceptions: a child television star, cut short in her prime at the age of five, might have a claim: it would depend on the evidence. A teenage boy or girl, however, as in Gammell's case may well be able to show either actual employment or real prospects, in either of which situations there will be an assessable claim. In the case of a young man, already in employment (as was young Mr. Furness), one would expect to find evidence upon which a fair estimate of loss can be made. A man, well established in life, Mr. Pickett, will have no difficulty. But in all cases it is a matter of evidence and a reasonable estimate based upon it."[58]

Calculation of living expenses

16–64 The primary difficulty arising in applying this approach concerns the measurement of the value of living expenses. Where the experts often disagree is with respect to the measurement of personal living expenses. One method is to approximate this figure using the average family's expenditures on such categories as food, clothing, shelter and transportation. If the plaintiff were a member of a family, not all of the income would have been spent on that family member. Indeed, it is known from fatal accident litigation in the United States that the total amount which most individuals spend on goods and services which benefit them alone is approximately 30 per cent of after-tax income. As only some portion of that percentage is spent on necessities, the deduction for personal necessities may be as little as 10–15 per cent. However, most of the reported cases assume that all expenditures on food, shelter, clothing, transportation, and health care are necessary.

16–65 A number of approaches to calculating the deduction have been applied in the United Kingdom:

– the deduction has been calculated similarly to the value of dependants' dependency in fatal accident cases (see paras **16–103** *et seq.* below)[59];

[58] *Gammell v. Wilson* [1982] A.C. 27 at 78, *per* Lord Scarman.
[59] *Benson v. Biggs Wall & Co Ltd* [1983] 1 W.L.R. 72; *Harris v. Empress Motors Ltd* [1983] 3 All E. R. 561; [1984] 1 W.L.R. 212.

- damages have been limited to the sums which the victim would have invested as savings during the lost years[60];

- damages have been calculated by reference to the available surplus remaining, after deducting from the net earnings the cost of maintaining the victim in his station of life.[61]

16–66　Given these different approaches to the calculation of the deduction of living expenses, the Court of Appeal in the combined appeals, *Harris v. Empress Motors Ltd* and *Cole v. Crown Poultry Packers Ltd*[62] provided some general guidance as to the principles to be applied. In both cases, the judge had adopted the United Kingdom Fatal Accidents Act 1976 dependency approach and had deducted 25 per cent from the net earnings in assessing damages for the lost earnings during the lost years. Three principles were set out:

- the elements comprising living expenses should be the same regardless of the age of the injured party;

- the sum to be deducted as living expenses should be the proportion of the victim's net earnings spent on maintaining himself at the standard of living appropriate to his case;

- sums expended to maintain others should not form part of the victim's living expenses and should not be deducted from net earnings.

16–67　In relation to the last two items, clarification was provided in respect of shared living expenses such as rent, mortgage interest, rates, heating, electricity, gas, cost of household car, telephone, television licence. Such shared expenses are to be allocated on a pro rata basis over the number of persons in the household. Only the victim's share of the joint living expenses should be deducted. No further more precise guidelines were provided in relation to the proportion of net earnings that should be deducted as an estimate of living expenses.

16–68　Pecuniary loss is not confined to lost earnings and has included loss of other reasonable expectations such as the prospect of marriage and the prospect

---

[60] *Sullivan v. West Yorkshire Passenger Transport Executive*, unreported, Mustill, J., December 17, 1980, as cited in *Harris v. Empress Motors Ltd* [1983] 3 All E. R. 561; [1984] 1 W.L.R. 212.

[61] *White v. London Transport Executive* [1982] 1 Q.B. 489; *Clark v. Sugrue Brothers Ltd*, unreported, January 28, 1983.

[62] [1983] 3 All E. R. 561; [1984] 1 W.L.R. 212.

of an inheritance.[63] Loss of pension benefit in the lost years may also be claimed.[64]

Date of assessment and period of damage

Date of assessment of damages

16–69 The general rule is that damages are assessed on a once-and-for-all basis as of the date that the cause of action arose – usually the date of injury. There are, however, exceptions to this rule. The court will look at the state of affairs prevailing at the date of hearing of the action and, if necessary in order to give appropriate compensation, it may update the claim to that date. In practice, most claims are asserted in terms that envisage the recovery of all losses attributable to the wrong, whenever they arise.

16–70 The plaintiff's cause of action in damages must be complete by the time the action is brought. The plaintiff cannot, for example, recover as damages in a breach of contract case money which would have been payable at a later date, as that term of the contract has not yet been breached. In tort, a plaintiff is entitled to have the damages assessed from the moment that the cause of action is complete. In a personal injury action based on negligence, this would be when the injury was first sustained. Such assessment should take into account all future losses.

In certain instances, damages may be difficult to assess. However, difficulty in assessing the claim is not a bar to recovery.

Period of damage

16–71 The damage period to be used for the calculation of losses attributable to an accident is the full period of time during which the injured party is expected to experience those losses. In general in personal injury cases the period will run from the date of the accident until there is no longer any financial effect directly attributable to it.

The period for which losses are calculated will depend on the circumstances of each case. The damage period may be for: (i) the whole of the plaintiff's expected life; (ii) the plaintiff's full working life expectancy; and/or (iii) until early retirement. In the case of medical expenses for severely injured plaintiffs, the expense will be incurred over the whole of the plaintiff's life. Statistics on life expectancies will be relevant here. In the case of lost earnings, there would be a shorter period of loss, *i.e.* to the date of retirement, although the multiplier

---

[63] See *Adsett v. West* [1983] Q.B. 826. See also *Marley v. Ministry of Defence*, unreported, Queen's Bench Division, Machin J., July 30, 1984.

[64] *Marley v. Ministry of Defence*, unreported, Queen's Bench Division, Machin J., July 30, 1984.

will still take account of the probability of death before retirement age. Thus, it may be appropriate to apply different multipliers to different heads of damages. Even within the same head of damages, it may be appropriate to use different multipliers each, say, involving different levels of expenses. Again, actuaries are used extensively in Irish litigation to consider these issues and advise on the appropriate multipliers.

Judicial discount

16–72 In loss of earnings cases, one of the consequences of the focus on loss of earnings capacity (see para. **16–12**), rather than loss of earnings, is that a reduction in the award under this head is sometimes made on account of what is know as the "vicissitudes of life", *e.g.* illness, unemployment, redundancy. In Ireland, this is usually referred to as the "*Reddy v. Bates* adjustment", following the dictum of Griffin J. in *Reddy v. Bates*.[65] In fact, as pointed out earlier (see above, para. **16–21**), Griffin J. advocated an adjustment in respect of reduced periods of employment. In essence the court does not assume that the plaintiff would be able to exercise his earning capacity for the whole of the rest of his working life. However, the wider "vicissitudes" have been recognised in several subsequent decisions (*e.g. Clancy v. Commissioner of Public Works in Ireland*[66]).

16–73 In the past (before the *Wells v. Wells*[67] decision), judges in the United Kingdom routinely reduced multipliers by anything up to 20 per cent on the grounds of "unspecified contingencies" or the "vicissitudes of life". The House of Lords' *Wells v. Wells* decision pointed out that some of such manifold contingencies are already taken account of in the medical assessment of life expectancy and in the actuarial tables and multiplier used.[68] In the future multipliers in England may not be reduced unless there are specific reasons to do so.

16–74 In Ireland in recent times, there has been an effort on the part of the Supreme Court to curb the inflation of damages awards. This has manifested itself in increasing discounts for "adverse contingencies" such as ill health and unemployment of the plaintiff in assessment of damages for lost earnings capacity. White[69] argues:

> ". . . recent judicial interventions aimed at minimising damages awards for personal injuries are misconceived and productive of injustice to plaintiffs without reciprocal benefits to society as a whole".

---

[65][1983] I.R. 141.
[66][1992] 2 I.R. 449.
[67][1998] 3 All E.R. 481.
[68]*ibid.* at 498 *per* Lord Lloyd.
[69]White, J.P.M., *Irish Law of Damages for Personal Injury and Death* (Butterworths, Dublin, 1989), p. 119.

16–75   There is undoubtedly merit in this argument. In addition, there is a strong argument that the placing by the courts of arbitrary limits on general (*i.e.* non-pecuniary) damages is also misconceived as a policy. This practice has its roots in a decision of the Supreme Court in *Sinnott v. Quinnsworth Ltd.*[70] In that case, the Supreme Court reduced an award of general damages made by a jury to the plaintiff who had been rendered quadriplegic in a car accident. The jury's award of £400,000 was reduced to £150,000. The court indicated the basis that should be used to arrive at a figure for general damages, saying that it should represent fair and reasonable compensation for the loss and injury sustained by the plaintiff, taking account of the total sum awarded in respect of past and future loss or expense, ordinary living standards prevailing in the country, the general level of incomes and the things on which the plaintiff might reasonably be expected to spend money. O'Higgins C.J. went on to say that general damages should not exceed this figure "in a case of this nature".

The effect of this decision has been to constrain awards for general damages since then, although the amount has been "updated" to take account of inflation, as for instance evidenced by the judgment of Geoghegan J. in the High Court in *Coppinger (Dermot) v. Waterford County Council*:

> "In *Connolly v. Bus Éireann* (Unreported, High Court, Barr J., 29th January, 1996), the judge considered among other matters what kind of upward adjustment should be made to the figure of £150,000 suggested by the Supreme Court in *Sinnott v. Quinnsworth* [1984] I.L.R.M. 523, as a maximum figure for general damages. Barr J. came to the conclusion that a fair equivalent of that figure would now be £200,000. I think it reasonable to follow that view and I do so in the context that I consider this is clearly a case where the maximum figure for general damages should be awarded."[71]

In *Kealy v. Minister for Health,*[72] Morris P. awarded general damages of £250,000 to the plaintiff who had developed hepatitis as a result of being injected with contaminated anti-D blood products. The judge distinguished the case from the *Sinnott case* on the grounds that this case did not involve the award of very large sums for special damages which, following *Sinnott*, would require the court to take into account the total award when measuring damages for pain and suffering.

16–76   It is clear that the view of the Supreme Court in *Sinnott* was that awards were in danger of becoming unrealistically high. To solve this by placing an absolute cap on general damages, however, is to use a very blunt instrument that is bound to lead to injustice. There is no doubt that all cases are different and should be looked at on their own merits. To select one set of facts, however horrific, and say in effect that "nothing could be worse than this" is to deny the infinite variation in human experience.

---

[70] [1984] I.L.R.M. 523.
[71] [1998] 4 I.R. 220 at 241.
[72] [1999] 2 I.R. 456

Further, inflation is hardly the only factor that should give rise to the need to change even an arbitrary maximum. There is certainly little doubt that the expectation of quality of life enjoyed by most Irish citizens at the start of the twenty-first century is markedly higher than it was in the early 1980s. In fact, the ingredients of the decision that resulted in the cap of £150,000 as quoted above, being "ordinary living standards prevailing in the country, the general level of incomes and the things on which the plaintiff might reasonably be expected to spend money", have undoubtedly encountered a steep change since then.

Finally, the concept of arriving at general damages by "taking account of the total sum awarded in respect of past and future loss or expense" appears fundamentally flawed if one accepts that general damages are designed to compensate for effects not measurable in financial terms.

16–77   For these reasons, it is submitted that the Supreme Court should take an appropriate opportunity to review the ongoing relevance of the policy espoused in *Sinnott v. Quinnsworth Ltd*.[73]

Expenses

16–78   For expenses to be recovered, it must be demonstrated that the expenses are necessary because of the defendant's wrong.[74] Only reasonable expenses may be recovered.[75] In cases of severe injury, additional expenses may have to be considered such as additional health care, rehabilitation and medical expenses (both present and future), and special education or retraining costs (*e.g.* see *Conley v. Strain*[76]). In the case of severe injuries, calculation of the annual loss should be based on loss of earnings and on any annual nursing/medical costs to be incurred by the plaintiff. Where health care costs include a stay in a medical or paramedical institution, the element of that cost relating to the value of board and lodgings must be deducted, as the plaintiff would have had to maintain himself had he not been injured.[77] The courts have also allowed expenses of special accommodation and adaptations to existing accommodation in the case of severe injuries.[78]

16–79   Three criteria are generally relevant in evaluating future medical costs. They must be directly related to the wrong of which the plaintiff complains,

---

[73] [1984] I.L.R.M. 523.

[74] White, J.P.M., *Irish Law of Damages for Personal Injury and Death* (Butterworths, Dublin, 1989), p. 230.

[75] *Cunningham v. Harrison* [1973] Q.B. 942; *Cassel v. Riverside Health Authority* [1995] P.I.Q.R. Q168.

[76] [1988] 1 I.R. 628.

[77] *Shearman v. Folland* [1950] 2 K.B. 43; *Lim Poh Choo v. Camden and Islington Area Health Authority* [1980] A.C. 174.

[78] *Doherty v. Bowaters Irish Wallboard Mills Ltd* [1968] I.R. 277; *Fitzgerald v. Lane* [1987] 2 All E.R. 455.

generally acceptable by the medical profession and reasonable in amount.[79] The process of estimating medical expenses in a court case involves the following:

- the medical expert determines the medical goods and services required by the plaintiff, and the time period over which these will be necessary;

- the cost of these goods and services are then projected into the future according to an index. As Walsh[80] has pointed out, a general price index may not be suitable as medical cost inflation may differ from general levels of inflation;

- the projected medical costs are discounted to present value.

16–80 Multipliers in relation to future expenses should not be set so as to allow recovery for lost years (relating to reduced expectation of life), in contrast to the case with future earnings (see paras **16–58** *et seq.*). As pointed out by Smith,[81] compensation for the cost of future care of an individual whose life expectancy is demonstrably impaired need obviously be less than that required for someone whose anticipation of a future lifetime is normal.

Personal/household services

16–81 Since individuals make valid contributions through their efforts at both paid and unpaid work, the courts have concluded that they should be compensated when they are unable to pursue either type of employment. In the field of personal injury litigation, this has implied that calculation of a plaintiff's damages should include the loss (or impairment) of the individual's ability to perform household services. Controversy remains, however, concerning the method which should be used to establish the economic value of that loss. There are two components of the loss of household services: direct labour, including most general house-keeping duties; and management or indirect labour.[82]

16–82 *Daly v. General Steam Navigation Co*[83] provided a precedent-setting judgment involving a claim for household services. Two main principles set out in *Daly* deal with the pre-trial and future loss of household services.

First, a future loss of household services was allowed, regardless of the intent, or lack of it, on the part of the plaintiff to hire replacement household labour to compensate for the lost capacity to undertake household work:

---

[79] Slesnick, F.L., "Forecasting medical costs in tort cases" in *Litigation Economics* (Gaughan, P.A. and Thornton, R.J. (eds), JAI Press, Greenwich, Connecticut, 1993).

[80] Walsh, B., *Medical Care Inflation* (University College Dublin, Working paper, 1999).

[81] Smith, H.G., "lost years maybe, lost care–never" in *Expert Witness* (Spring 1997), Vol. 2, No. 1. Available at www.economica.ca/ew21p4.htm.

[82] *Brouwer v. Grewal* [1995] 168 A.R. 342 at 353–354.

[83] [1980] 3 All E.R. 696.

"It is really quite immaterial, in my judgment, whether having received those damages the plaintiff chooses to alleviate her own housekeeping burden ... or whether she chooses to continue to struggle with the housekeeping on her own and to spend the damages which have been awarded to her on other luxuries ..."[84]

16–83   The second aspect relates to additional costs incurred in the pre-trial period as a result of the accident. The cost of those replacement services was not considered an appropriate measure of the loss of housekeeping ability. The loss, rather, should have been assessed as a part of the plaintiff's general damages, and the additional pain, suffering and loss of amenity experienced by the plaintiff should be the measure of that loss. This approach to the impairment of housekeeping ability which awards the plaintiff for loss of ability rather than relying on the prior "antiquated if not sexist" approach (that sought to calculate the value of the services lost by measuring the loss from the point of view of a third party who had previously benefited from the services provided by the victim) has been supported in the Canadian courts.[85] In addition, in some instances, the household services which were performed by a plaintiff or the deceased cannot be replicated by replacement labour.[86]

Extent of loss

16–84   While there seems to be consensus that the loss of household services is compensable, there is less agreement concerning the evidence that should be brought forward to substantiate the extent of the loss:

"Precise proof is manifestly impossible, but if a basis for reasonable ascertainment of the amount of damages has been established, the court will make the assessment as best it can with what it has."[87]

16–85   Courts in Canada have expressed concern at the lack of appropriate data on this issue.[88] There are instances in which the court relies on the plaintiff and/or the plaintiff's family as the primary source of information in the estimation of the loss of household services.[89] In many cases, however, additional evidence, as well as documentation, has been required such as statistical data, specific information regarding the plaintiff and time spent by paid help or family members in replacement of the plaintiff's duties.[90] Use of statistical evidence has been

---

[84] [1980] 3 All E.R. 696 at 701.
[85] *Fobel v. Dean* [1991] 6 W.W.R. 408 (Saskatchewan Court of Appeal).
[86] *Taguchi v. Stuparyk* [1994] 16 Alta. L.R. 3d 72.
[87] *Mason v. Peters* [1982] 139 D.L.R. 3d 104 at 110.
[88] *Acheson v. Dory* [1993] 8 Alta. L.R. 3d 145.
[89] *Gilchrist v. Oatway* [1995] 168 A.R. 56.
[90] *Simmie v. Parker and Unger* [1994] 164 A.R. 178.

found to enhance the validity of the claim.[91] Loss of household services may be adjusted in light of other factors in the plaintiff's life such as the employment circumstances of the plaintiff, as well as an active social and family life.[92]

16–86 Quantification of an individual's, or an estate's, loss of household services in such a way as to return the plaintiff to pre-injury status involves the estimation of hours contributed prior to the accident, currently, and in the future. Determination of this loss would appear to be a clear-cut matter of identifying the individual's contribution prior to the accident, and reducing this pre-accident contribution, in the case of an injured party, to the extent that the injured party is still able to perform those duties. In reality, however, the process of estimating, after the fact, the extent to which an individual has contributed to the myriad duties required to keep a household functioning, from meal preparation to maintenance of the physical structure itself, is a matter that is neither straightforward nor obvious.

16–87 In *Reddy v. Bates*,[93] Griffin J. in the Supreme Court dealt with an appeal against a jury's finding under the heading "household assistance". His judgment gave a valuable insight into judicial attitudes in Ireland to the extent to which a plaintiff should be compensated for loss of household services. In dealing with the defendant's appeal against the amount awarded by a jury under this heading, he first summarised the relevant expert evidence proffered by the plaintiff and the counter-arguments advanced by the defendant:

> "In relation to the household assistance which the plaintiff would require in the future, a witness was called from the National Manpower Service. The effect of this evidence being that the employment of a housekeeper for five days would cost approximately £130 per week, and that the cost of a relief housekeeper for the remaining two days would be approximately £40 per week—making a total of £170 per week. The defendant's case on this issue was that the reality is that it was extremely likely that the plaintiff's family, being a very close-knit family, would continue to look after her and that, at best, only assistance on a part-time basis would be necessary …".[94]

Griffin J. then explained that, although the plaintiff's evidence purported to justify compensation of £170 per week under this heading, and although the jury awarded only £123 per week, or just over 70 per cent of the amount claimed, nevertheless both he and the trial judge felt the amount awarded was excessive. However, because the amount awarded was within an acceptable range, Griffin J. made no alteration to the amount on appeal:

[91] *Brouwer v. Grewal* [1995] 168 A.R. 342; *O'Hara v. Belanger* [1989] 98 A.R. 86.
[92] *Mackie v. Wolfe* [1994] 153 A.R. 81.
[93] [1983] I.R. 141.
[94] *ibid.* at 145.

"Under this heading the jury awarded a sum of £115,000. At the actuarial calculation of £1,812, this works out at a sum of £123 per week, constantly increasing annually throughout life. The plaintiff was contending for £170 per week, but the jury clearly did not accept that figure. The learned trial judge invited the jury 'to keep their feet on the ground' in considering the damages under this heading and he invited the jury to be reasonable about this particular heading of damage. It is unlikely that the plaintiff will require any more assistance than would an elderly feeble person. Although the sum awarded was higher than the figure I would award in the particular circumstances, and was clearly higher than the sum the learned trial judge would have awarded had he been assessing the damages, it is nevertheless within the range of damages which, on the evidence, could be found by the jury and I would not interfere with it." [95]

16–88   When a claim is made for loss of household services capacity, the claimant's pre-accident household service contribution must be determined and compared to the post-accident capacity for household services. The difference between the pre-accident contribution and the current contribution represents the claimant's loss of household service capacity. One simple way of measuring this loss is to calculate the number of additional hours that it would take a replacement worker to perform all of the tasks which the claimant can no longer do. However, the number of additional hours that a claimant would require to complete the chores which can no longer be performed may overstate the amount of time required by replacement workers. Therefore, using this estimate based on the claimant's rate of work without adjustment could overstate the claimant's true loss. Accordingly, an adjustment may need to be made to estimate accurately the claimant's loss. Replacement workers will typically be more productive than the claimant, so the loss of household service hours may need to be adjusted downwards to reflect this productivity. Three wage-based household services valuation methods are:

1.   opportunity cost method;

2.   generalist market replacement method; and

3.   specialist market replacement method.

Opportunity cost method

16–89   Valuation of household services utilising the opportunity cost method is based on the assumption that when an individual chooses to undertake unpaid work, such as household activities, the possibility of spending that time at paid work is precluded. Thus, the salary associated with that employment is foregone. Wages sacrificed to allow the individual to spend time at unpaid work are thus

---

[95] [1983] I.R. 141 at 147.

said to be representative of the economic value that the individual places on the unpaid activity. For example, if the individual has chosen to give up 20 hours a week of employment paying €10 per hour, in order to engage in 20 hours of housework, the opportunity cost approach concludes that the value of that housework must have been at least €10 per hour.

16–90   There are various problems associated with adopting the opportunity cost method to evaluate household services, not least of which is the determination of the wage that has been sacrificed to allow the individual to participate in unpaid work. More problematic is the assumption, underlying the opportunity cost method, that the amount which must be spent to restore the plaintiff to the pre-accident position is the value which the plaintiff had placed on the household services which have been lost.

Generalist and specialist market replacement methods

16–91   The approach taken in both these replacement cost methods is to value household services according to what it would cost to hire an individual who offers those services on the market. The difference between the two market substitute methods is that the generalist method assumes that an individual who does general domestic work could replicate these services. The specialist method, on the other hand, assumes that to replace household services it would be necessary to hire individuals with expertise in specific areas that comprise the various components of household duties.

16–92   The use of replacement cost methods in the valuation of household services is recommended in personal injury claims, as they best meet the following criteria:

–   relative ease of computation;

–   distributional equity; and

–   probability of restoring plaintiffs (as much as is possible) to their pre-accident position.

16–93   Of the two replacement cost methods, the specialist approach necessitates more subjectivity than the generalist approach. Arguably, the generalist variant of the replacement method best calculates the loss of household services in personal injury cases. It is only when the generalist approach is clearly inappropriate, such as when the plaintiff provided services to the household which could only be replaced by a skilled tradesperson, that use of the specialist method would be recommended. The *caveat* still holds, however, that an estimate derived using the replacement cost method is only as reliable as the factors used in its calculation, specifically the determination of the number of hours requiring replacement and the hourly cost of the replacement services.

Calculating damages in fatal accident cases

16–94   Relatives of, and survivors of, the victims of a fatal accident can seek compensation for the victim's wrongful death if it was caused by negligence or another culpable act. For such cases, the economic loss of the plaintiff is not simply the lost earnings of the deceased. It consists of the portion of the deceased's earnings that would have benefited the plaintiff.

16–95   Claims for fatal accidents are brought under Part IV of the Civil Liability Act 1961. Where the deceased had initiated proceedings before his death, the case normally survives for the benefit of his estate under the provisions of Part II of the same Act.

16–96   The amount of lost earnings payable as a result of fatal injuries is calculated as a multiple of the proportion of the deceased's earnings lost to his dependants by virtue of his death. The amount of earnings of the deceased must be calculated at the date of his death and must also be estimated or projected as at the date of trial (as the multiplier is applied at the date of trial). In addition, the value of dependency (usually expressed as a percentage of the deceased's earnings) must be calculated. Finally, the multiplier is applied to the value of dependency.

16–97   The stages in calculating a lump sum in fatal accident cases are summarised in Table 16.9.

Table 16.9: Calculating lump sums in fatal accident cases

Estimate deceased's earnings at date of death
↓
Calculate the dependency rate at date of death
↓
Calculate value of dependency at date of trial
(Projected earnings at date of trial X Dependency rate)
↓
Select multiplier
↓
Calculate lump sum (Multiplicand X Multiplier)

16–98   An example case history concerning loss of earnings and the role played by the forensic accountant in a fatal accident case is shown below.

Multiplier in fatal accident cases

16–99   The calculation of the amount of damages involves estimating the deceased's earnings, deducting from that sum his personal and living expenses

Case history 16.1: Loss of earnings in fatal injury action

Incident and injury

John Smith was a self-employed driver who operated his own haulage company. He was killed when his friend's rifle accidentally discharged. He was 35 at the time of his death and was survived by his wife and three children.

As a result of the accident, John Smith's wife assumed the administrative tasks (obtaining contracts, invoicing, etc.) of the business and hired a full-time driver at €12 per hour. This enabled the wife to generate gross revenues similar to what would previously have been achieved. Had Mr. Smith not passed away, however, he would have performed the administrative duties and the truck driving.

Involvement of forensic accountant

The forensic accountant was retained by the family's solicitor to assess past (*i.e.* from the time of the accident until the time of the assessment) and future losses. The assessment of income loss for a self-employed person is difficult because of the unpredictable flow of earnings. Therefore, it was essential to prepare an approach that accurately reflected the reality of how the haulage business operated.

The forensic accountant estimated that John Smith would have spent 2,000 hours a year on administrative duties and the truck driving. Using the €12 per hour rate for both the truck driver and the wife, the total lost income was calculated (to an estimated retirement age of 65) as €292,000.

Outcome

The matter proceeded to trial, during which the court accepted the calculations.

Source: Adapted from Johnson, P., "Forensic accounting – a legal support" (1996) 3 C.L.P. 206.

and applying a multiplier to that amount to obtain the lump sum of damages.[96] The multiplier is calculated from the date of the deceased's death,[97] not from the date of the trial (unlike personal injury cases where the multiplier is calculated from the date of trial). In a fatal accident case, where a large number of years have elapsed between the date of death and the date of trial, only part of the lump sum will represent compensation for future losses or expenses. Therefore, to take account of the receipt of the lump sum the actuary will normally apply a smaller discount.[98]

16–100 A number of factors influence the actuarial calculation of the loss, including the age and expected working life of the deceased and the life expectancy of the dependants. The future prospects of the deceased had he not been killed can also affect the calculation, which may be higher where there were prospects of advancement and promotion. However, in *McDonagh v.*

---

[96] *Davies v. Powell Duffryn Associated Collieries Ltd* [1942] A.C. 601 at 617.
[97] *Cookson v. Knowles* [1979] A.C. 556 at 575–576. See also *McDonagh v. McDonagh* [1992] 1 I.R. 119.
[98] *Corbett v. Barking, Havering and Brentwood Health Authority* [1991] 2 Q.B. 408.

McDonagh,[99] Costello J. cast some doubt on this when, in rejecting an actuarial calculation that took account of changes in family income following the death, he said:

> ". . . the loss should be based on the actual contribution which the deceased made out of her wages for the maintenance of her children".

16–101 In England, a widow/widower's remarriage and any consequent benefit to children from step-parents should not be taken into account in calculating damages.[100] However, the prospect of divorce resulting in a reduced period of dependency should be taken into account.[101]

16–102 In Ireland, the possibility of remarriage by the deceased's widower has been held to be a valid factor giving rise to a reduction in the amount payable in respect of services gratuitously rendered by the deceased prior to her death (see *McDonagh v. McDonagh*[102]).

Personal consumption expenses/payments for the benefit of dependants

16–103 Broadly speaking, the deceased's income will have been spent either on himself or on the family. Damages are based on the proportion of the deceased's income devoted to his dependants. This amount can be calculated from two different perspectives:

– calculate the deceased's personal consumption and assume the remaining income is for his dependants;

– calculate the expenditure on the family and assume any remaining income is for the personal consumption of the deceased.

16–104 Ideally, these two calculations should give the same answer, and often the accountant or actuary will take both approaches thereby checking the accuracy of one against the other.

Personal consumption expenses

16–105 All or a portion of the deceased's personal consumption should be deducted from lost earnings in death cases. As the survivors would no longer have to spend a portion of the family income on the deceased, an award that included that amount would overcompensate the relatives leaving an extra amount

---

[99] [1992] 1 I.R. 119 at 125.
[100] *Stanley v. Saddique* [1992] Q.B. 1; *Topp v. London Country Bus (South West) Ltd* [1993] 3 All E.R. 448.
[101] *Owen v. Martin* [1992] P.I.Q.R. Q151.
[102] [1992] 1 I.R. 119.

for them to consume. Although the personal consumption of the deceased should be deducted, any expenditure on family items should not be deducted.

16–106   The best source of information is the actual spending by the deceased person. A specific personal consumption history for the deceased is likely to be preferred by the court because specific information is more convincing than data based on averages. However, actual data may not be available. In practice, percentages may be used as estimates in the absence of actual data on the deceased's personal consumption.

16–107   A number of researchers in the United States have produced data on personal consumption expenditures which might be useable (possibly with some modification for different lifestyles) in the Irish courts.[103]

Payments for the benefit of dependants

16–108   The expenditure on family including housekeeping money, mortgage repayments, payments for utilities, holidays, clothes, school fees, insurance and gifts can be calculated. In Ireland it is normal for an expert actuary or accountant to gather and analyse the available information, sourced from records, from documentation and directly from the individual dependants, and to calculate from this information and from first principles the amounts spent on the deceased and on the dependants.

16–109   In England, instead of attempting a detailed calculation of the costs and expenses incurred by the deceased for his own personal benefit, a simpler method was applied in *Harris v. Empress Motors Ltd*[104] using a rule of thumb percentage. Once the deceased's net income is calculated, a percentage (one third where there were no children) is applied to deduct the deceased's personal expense. Two-thirds net earnings is taken as the value of the dependency. This percentage would depend on family circumstances such as the number and ages of the children. The one-third/two-thirds rule of thumb is only applied in "normal" cases and there have been circumstances where the court has not applied the rule of thumb, arguing that the value of dependency must depend on the facts.[105]

---

[103] Cheit, E., "Measuring economic loss due to death and disability" in *Injury and Recovery in the Course of Employment* (Wiley, New York, 1961), pp. 76–82; Harju, M.W. and Adams, C.H., "Estimating personal expenditure deductions in multi-income families in cases of wrongful death" in *Journal of Forensic Economics* (1990) Vol. 4, No. 1, pp. 65–81; and Patton, R.T. and Nelson, D.M., "Estimating personal consumption costs in wrongful death cases" in *Journal of Forensic Economics* (1991) Vol. 4, No. 2, pp. 233–240.

[104] [1983] 3 All E. R. 561; [1984] 1 W.L.R. 212.

[105] *Owen v. Martin* [1992] P.I.Q.R. Q151.

16–110 It is commonly accepted that the surviving spouse would have benefited from approximately 70 per cent of the (after-tax) incomes of each of the deceased and the survivor – with the remaining 30 per cent of the combined after-tax incomes of both spouses having benefited the deceased alone.[106] What is not agreed, however, is whether the 30 per cent of the survivor's income which would previously have benefited the deceased should now be deducted from the survivor's dependency damages. (When this deduction is made, it is said that a "cross dependency" approach has been used; whereas when the deduction is not made, it is said that a "sole dependency" approach has been used.)

16–111 Private means of the dependants also influence the rule of thumb, reducing the dependency percentage where there are substantial means.[107] However, where a dependant resumes work as a result of the fatality, damages are not reduced by the dependant's earning capacity.[108]

Social welfare benefits

16–112 Part V of the Civil Liability Act 1961 deals with claims for damages arising from fatal injuries caused by a wrongful act, neglect or default. Section 50 of the Act states:

> "In assessing damages under this Part account shall not be taken of—
>
> (a) any sum payable on the death of the deceased under any contract of insurance, or
>
> (b) any pension, gratuity or other like benefit payable under statute or otherwise in consequence of the death of the deceased."

16–113 The effect of this provision is that, *inter alia*, social welfare benefits payable as a result of the death are not deducted from any damages payable in respect of a claim arising from the death. An exception to this, under section 75(3) of the Social Welfare (Consolidation) Acts 1993, is that any death benefit by way of grant for funeral expenses payable under the occupational injuries benefits provisions of that Act may be taken into account in the assessment of damages in respect of total injuries.

Payment of awards

16–114 Damages are assessed once and for all, and such damages are awarded in the form of a lump sum, rather than as an income stream. In settling claims in

---

[106] *Coward v. Comex Houlder Diving Ltd* [1984] 1 W.L.R. 212; *Crabtree v. Wilson* [1993] P.I.Q.R. Q24.

[107] *Davies v. Hawes*, unreported, High Court, Ogden J., May 9, 1990.

[108] *Howitt v. Heads* [1973] 1 Q.B. 64.

the United Kingdom, the parties may, as an alternative, agree that some or all of the damages form part of a structured settlement, under which an annuity paid for by the defendant will provide the plaintiff with an income. However, the recipient of the settlement will need to take care to be satisfied that the future payments are properly and adequately secured. Structured settlements are not a feature of the resolution of personal injury claims in Ireland.

Structured settlements

16–115   A structured settlement is a contract between the plaintiff and defendant in which the plaintiff agrees to accept damages in the form of periodic payments over a period of time rather than a lump sum payment. Structured settlements may comprise elements of both systems, with some damages being paid as a lump sum and others being paid over a period. The periodic payment may or may not be uniform in amount, consisting of a lump sum element, monthly payments, etc. Structured settlements, agreed by both parties, are an alternative to lump sum payments. The major reason why structured settlements are attractive to plaintiffs is that they prevent the recipient from spending the money soon after receipt. A structured settlement can be administratively easier from the claimant's point of view and can avoid the worry of administering a large lump sum. In addition, the annual income can be protected against inflation and can be guaranteed for life. Annuities have features that qualify them as the ideal tool to deliver a specified sum to a specified party at specified times.

Annuities

16–116   An annuity is an investment vehicle that makes periodic payments consisting of interest and principal, until such time as the fund becomes extinguished. In this manner it resembles a mortgage in reverse, where the annuitant assumes the role of the bank and the insurance company that of the borrower. The annuitant may elect to have the term of the payments set out as a specific period of time (*i.e.* a specified number of years) or set to some undetermined eventuality (*e.g.* the death of the annuitant), or a combination thereof. The term of a life annuity is the life of the annuitant (or in the case of structured settlement annuities, the life of the individual nominated as the measuring life). A life annuity provides payments that continue for life, regardless of how long the claimant remains alive. By taking advantage of the annuity issuer's capacity to spread the risk of "living too long" amongst many annuitants, an individual claimant does not need to provide for such a contingency.

16–117   Annuities suitable for structured settlements should ideally:

– be index-linked;

– be guaranteed for a minimum number of years or for the duration of the plaintiff's life;

– allow for streamed lump sum payments in the future in addition to regular sums, in anticipation of the changing needs of the plaintiff.

The first structured settlement in the United Kingdom took place in July 1989.

Case suitability

16–118   Preferences for structured settlements will depend on risk perceptions, income tax rates, and the spot annuity rate of return relative to other rates of return.

16–119   When a structured settlement is constructed, the present value of an award is used to buy an annuity. However, the actual return on the annuity will be determined by the internal rate of return prevailing on annuities on the date of purchase. Thus, the present value of an earnings stream at one rate of discount is used to purchase an annuity whose payout is determined by a different rate of return. The annuity rate of return prevailing on the date the annuity is purchased will affect the amount that the recipient of an award settlement actually receives. If the rate of return on an annuity is greater than the original rate of discount used to calculate the present value of the award the recipient will receive more – and vice versa.

16–120   It has been said that "only the very large cases" merit consideration for a structured settlement. Some suggest that the list should be expanded to include actions that involve minors and/or those otherwise incapable of managing their own resources. Typically, those cases most suitable for structuring include:

– infants;

– those claimants not mentally capable of managing their own resources;

– claimants whose future life expectancy may be in doubt;

– claimants who are in high income tax brackets;

– cases involving a cost of future care claim;

– the elderly who wish to control the distribution of their estates.

Methodology

16–121   The methodology for converting lump sums into equivalent streams of periodic payments has become an issue in the English courts. Forensic accountants are often required to convert a present value award into a stream of periodic payments. Courts must approve the proposed structured settlement. It is usual for the proposals to be accompanied by an accountant's report dealing with the financial advantages of the settlement to the claimant, with particular emphasis on life expectancy and the likely future medical and nursing costs.

Forensic accountants in such cases will be required to prepare comprehensive damage evaluations which provide a thorough review of the accounting issues as well as the amounts at issue. Careful analysis and verification of the facts and timely reporting pave the way for prompt and equitable resolution of each case.

16–122 In arriving at the details of a structured settlement, consideration must be given to medical, rehabilitation, custodial and health care costs, adjusted for anticipated inflation. Future education costs (for both the claimant and/or the claimant's family) and loss of future income estimates should also be discussed during the settlement negotiation process. Ideally, a structured settlement specialist should attend that meeting and work with the plaintiff and his other advisers.

Taxation of personal injury damages

16–123 The present and future tax implications of any awards or settlements in respect of personal injury or fatal accidents must always be considered. This section touches on this topic, which is dealt with in more detail by Corrigan in an Irish context and others in a United Kingdom context.[109] He summarises the position as follows:

1. Lump sum personal injury awards are not taxable. Individuals pay tax under Schedule E (if employed) or Schedule D (if self-employed). Personal injury damages are not taxed upon receipt because they either (i) do not arise from employment or (ii) are not profits from a trade.

2. The interest element of a damages award is subject to tax under certain Schedule D Case III provisions, similar to the tax treatment of other types of interest.

3. However, under section 189 of the Taxes Consolidation Act 1997, income earned on a damages award in respect of someone permanently and totally incapacitated, where the income is the person's sole or main source of income, is exempt from taxation. Thus there is a difference in the taxation of income earned on lump sum awards between permanently and non-permanently incapacitated individuals.

---

[109] Corrigan, K., *Revenue Law* (Round Hall Sweet & Maxwell, Dublin, 2000), Vol. II, Chap. 28. Taxation of damages (in a U.K. context) is also covered in Lemar, C.J. and Mainz, A.J. (eds), *Litigation Support* (4th ed., Butterworths, London, 1999), Chap. 15; and in MacGregor and G., Hobbs, I., *Expert Accounting Evidence: A Guide for Litigation Support* (Accountancy Books, London, 1998), Chap. 19.

4. Capital gains on investments (except for government securities) are not exempt from capital gains tax.

16–124 Income tax can have two effects on damages calculations for lost earnings. First, it reduces earnings lost by the plaintiff which, in turn, decreases the present value of the award which must replace the loss. However, income tax also reduces the interest to be earned in the future on the lump sum award (called the "reverse tax effect") which increases the present value of the award. In some cases, the two effects are offset. In other cases, the award may be increased/decreased as a result of income tax.

Taxation on lost earnings

16–125 The benchmark case *British Transport Commission v. Gourley*[110] set a precedent (*Gourley* principle) whereby the recipient of damages could not be under or over compensated for the incidence of taxation. Prior to the *Gourley* case, the tax aspects of plaintiff compensation were not usually considered relevant to the quantification of the amount payable. By a six-to-one majority, the House of Lords laid down the principle that tax should be taken into account. The general principle on which damages are to be assessed is:

> "A successful plaintiff is entitled to have awarded to him such a sum as will, so far as possible, make good to him the financial loss which he has suffered and will probably suffer as a result of the wrong done to him for which the defendant is responsible."[111]

16–126 In relation to taxes on damages:

> "[To] ignore the tax element at the present day would be to act in a manner which is out of touch with reality. Nor can I regard the tax element as so remote that it should be disregarded in assessing damages. The obligation to pay tax … is almost universal in its application. That obligation is ever present in the minds of those who are called upon to pay taxes, and no sensible person any longer regards the net earnings from his trade or profession as the equivalent of his available income. Indeed, save for the fact that in many cases … the tax only becomes payable after the money has been received, there is, I think, no element of remoteness or uncertainty about its incidence."[112]

Where damages are not subject to tax when received by the individual, but represent compensation for the loss of monies which would have been received net of tax, then the damages should be calculated net of tax. Alternatively, if the damages fall to be charged to tax upon receipt, then the compensation should be awarded gross of tax.

[110] [1956] A.C. 185.
[111] *ibid.* at 212, *per* Lord Reid.
[112] *ibid.* at 203, *per* Earl Jowitt.

16–127 This issue was not considered in the Irish courts until 1973. The principle in *Gourley's* case was considered and approved by Kenny J. in the Irish High Court in *Glover v. B.L.N. Ltd (No. 2)*.[113] The court ruled that taxation should be taken into account even where it is difficult to estimate the effect of taxation as follows:

> "An award of damages by a court is intended to compensate the plaintiff for the loss which he has suffered: in some cases the damages may be punitive but compensation or restoration (so far as money can do it) to the position before the accident is the main element. Therefore, it is irrelevant that the defendant will profit by an allowance being made for tax against the loss. If the damages ... are not chargeable to tax while the lost remuneration would have been, the plaintiff would be getting an award which would exceed the loss which he had suffered by being deprived of the remuneration. Income tax enters into the economic lives of so many of our citizens that the law cannot ignore it when assessing damages. ...
>
> In my opinion, the rule adopted by the majority in *Gourley's Case* accords with reason and principle and should be applied to ... the damages for loss of salary, fees and commission in this case."[114]

The approach was confirmed in *Cooke v. Walsh*.[115]

16–128 Accordingly, income taxes and employee social welfare contributions[116] should be deducted from the calculation of lost earnings for the purpose of determining compensation. Damages in these types of cases are tax free, while the lost earnings of the plaintiff would have been taxed as regular income. Not to take into account this tax effect would be to overcompensate the plaintiff. Although the calculation of lost earnings should be net of tax, the damage calculations should take into account the tax on any interest to be earned in the future on investing the lump sum award (sometimes called the reverse tax effect). These two taxes will not necessarily be offsetting given differences in timing and possibly in the tax treatment applying to the two different types of earnings.

16–129 There are conflicting views in the courts about whether the tax deduction is calculated based on current rates of taxes at the time of trial[117] (as an estimate of future rates of taxes) or whether the liability for taxes might be assumed to reduce.[118]

---

[113] [1973] I.R. 432.

[114] *ibid.* at 441–442.

[115] [1984] I.L.R.M. 208 at 217.

[116] *Cooper v. Firth Brown* [1963] 1 W.L.R. 418.

[117] *British Transport Commission v. Gourley* [1956] A.C. 185; and *Glover v. B.L.N. Ltd* [1973] I.R. 432.

[118] *Daniels v. Jones* [1961] 1 W.L.R. 1103; and *Griffits v. Van Raaj* [1985] I.L.R.M. 582.

Effect of taxation on calculations

16–130   Consider a simple example in Table 16.10. Were there no income tax, a payment of €10,000 at an assumed interest rate of 10 per cent would be sufficient to pay the medical costs of €11,000 in one year's time. However, a tax gross-up is required of €232.56 to cover income tax payable at 25 per cent on the interest. This extra amount is known as the tax gross-up. Usually, the gross-up is reported as a percentage of the un-grossed up award. The gross-up is determined by calculating the plaintiff's tax liability prior to considering the award for damages. This is compared to the liability including income generated from the award. The gross-up is the additional capital required to fund the resulting tax liability.

Table 16.10: Effect of taxation on personal injury compensation

Plaintiff requires €11,000 to pay health care expenses for one year from now. Assume an interest rate of 10% Assume at an income tax rate of 25% Lump sum required now to pay for cost of care of €11,000 in one year's time	
	€
Lump sum	10,232.56
Interest 10%	1,023.26
Income tax 25% on interest earned	(255.82)
After tax amount	11,000

16–131   The tax gross-up is affected by a variety of factors. To estimate the gross-up, details about the future cost-of-care requirements (and the associated tax credits) are required as well as information about all of the plaintiff's expected income, including future employment income and any additional interest income that he will earn (especially from loss of income awards). The higher the plaintiff's expected income, the greater the percentage gross-up resulting from income being taxed at a higher marginal tax rate. To summarise, some of the factors which influence the value of the gross-up include:

1. Plaintiff's marginal rate of income tax.

2. Damages award: a larger award will generate more interest and more tax. Thus it will lead to a higher gross-up.

3. Post accident employment income: greater post accident employment earnings will lead to a larger gross-up.

4. Tax-deductible expenses: the greater the portion of tax-creditable expenses, the less tax will be paid. Thus, the tax gross-up will be lower.

5. Timing of consumption: if a large portion of the award will be consumed early in the plaintiff's life, then this will lead to a lower gross-up.

6. Age: young plaintiffs will generally require larger gross-ups than will old plaintiffs, both because they will have more interest income and, therefore, be in higher tax brackets, and because their awards will continue much further into the future.

Accounting data

16–132   Accounting numbers are essential in computing and supporting the financial calculations. The foundation of the calculation must be built securely on all available data. Forensic accountants can assist in the early stages of a case in the acquisition of information by formulating interrogatories, requests to produce documents and requests to admit facts. Forensic accountants may also assist in evaluating the quality, integrity and sufficiency of the data available in respect of his client's case. All accounting information must be evaluated for its relevance, reliability, comprehensiveness and accuracy. Inadequate information will lead to flawed calculations.

Forensic accountants need to double check the foundations and assumptions on which their calculations are based. Instructing solicitors should:

– double-check the accountant's calculations to make sure all relevant information is included therein;

– make sure the forensic accountant has been provided with all available financial information.

The use of third-party endorsements for statements in forensic accounting reports will add to the credibility of the report. For example, Central Statistics Office data[119] or data from industry associations can assist in confirming the accounting data (*e.g.* average industrial wage, wages in a specific industry) used in the report. Newspaper appointments pages can also provide a useful source of salary ranges for a particular job. A telephone survey of businesses might also be a way of obtaining salary data.

16–133   Forensic accountants are limited by the information provided to them. The failure to use all available data or to have knowledge of what is available can be very damaging for a case.

16–134   There are occasions, particularly in relation to self-employed persons, where the accounts and the returns to the Revenue do not reveal the true financial performance of the business. In the United Kingdom, the courts have found that a plaintiff may be compensated for lost earnings even where these were not disclosed to the Inland Revenue.[120]

---

[119] Central Statistics Office Ireland, *Statistical Abstract* (Government Publications, Dublin, Annual).
[120] *Duller v. South East Lincs Engineers* [1981] C.L.Y. 585.

Opportunity cost versus replacement cost

16–135   Many calculations carried out by forensic accountants in personal injury cases use either an opportunity or a replacement cost approach. An opportunity cost approach is based on what an individual sacrificed to obtain something (see also **16–88** *et seq.*). A replacement cost approach is based on what one would have to pay to replace something. The availability of reliable data creates advantages and disadvantages for each approach depending on circumstances. Deciding which method to use depends on the fit of each approach to the valuation task at hand. In some circumstances, the replacement cost approach is appropriate. In others, only the opportunity cost approach will work. For example, an opportunity cost approach is the only one appropriate in the case of valuing lost future earnings of a seriously injured minor. In contrast, any valuation of a life-care plan must be performed with a replacement cost approach.

Concluding comment

16–136   There are several aspects of the way in which the courts compensate the victims of personal injuries arising from legal wrongs that merit review. These include:

- The arbitrary limit placed on general damages payable for pain and suffering in the most tragic and extreme cases.

- The somewhat unclear and imprecise deduction made by courts from calculated special damages to take account of future uncertainties – the so-called "*Reddy v. Bates* deduction".

- The effective subsidisation of the insurance industry by the State that results from the calculation of damages on a "net of tax" basis.

- The assumptions made routinely in actuarial calculations regarding the long-term differential between wage inflation and investment returns – a small change in this assumption can have a very significant effect on the calculation of damages (see also Chapter 19).

A clear indication of current judicial and/or legislative thinking in these areas would assist legal practitioners, and forensic accountants, in achieving greater precision in the calculation of damages for personal injuries.

CHAPTER 17

ACCOUNTING CALCULATIONS –
COMMERCIAL DAMAGES

ACCOUNTING CALCULATIONS – COMMERCIAL DAMAGES

17–01   Commercial damage is a business loss of profits or loss of asset value resulting from the actions of another party.[1] Commercial litigation has been considered from a legal perspective in Chapters 9 and 10.

The majority of business litigation actions arise from contractual disputes. Commercial litigation can also involve disputes ranging from civil actions concerning competition issues or claims of patent infringement to allegations of tortious interference with business relationships.

17–02   These actions may involve a temporary or permanent interruption of business, breach of contract or losses due to fraud. The economic damage to be calculated in a commercial suit will follow from either a lost profit or lost asset value model. The former is frequently associated with business interruption cases and the latter with business valuation and share fraud cases. Either model might be appropriate in breach of contract, commercial tort, or competition cases depending on the situation. In such commercial loss claims, forensic accountants can assist in evaluation and quantification of damages, reconstruction of records, dispute resolution and provision of expert testimony.

17–03   This chapter examines the accounting aspects of calculations of damages arising in commercial litigation. Related to commercial damages is valuation of business and of shares in businesses and this is discussed in Chapter 18.[2]

---

[1] Foster, C.B., Trout, R.R. and Gaughan, P.A., "Losses in commercial litigation" in *Journal of Forensic Economics* (1989), Vol. 6, No. 3, pp. 179–196.

[2] Consideration of commercial damages in greater depth can be found in Anastasi, J.T., "Business interruption claims" in *Litigation Services Handbook. The Role of the Accountant as Expert* (2nd ed., Weil, R.L., Wagner, M.J. and Frank, P.B. (eds), John Wiley & Sons, Inc., New York, 1995), Chap. 15; Berenblut, M.L. and Rosen, H.N., *Litigation Accounting* (Carswell Thomson Professional Publishing, Ontario, 1995); Dunn, R.L., *Recovery of Damages for Lost Profits* (4th ed., Lawpress Corporation, Westport, CT, 1992); Freeman, N.W. and Spielmann, J.A., "Lost profits" in *Litigation Services Handbook. The Role of the Accountant as Expert* (2nd ed., Weil, R.L., Wagner, M.J. and Frank, P.B. (eds), John Wiley & Sons, Inc., New York, 1995), Chap. 30; Gaughan, P.A., *Measuring Commercial Damages* (John Wiley & Sons, Inc, New York, 2000); Knapp, C.L., *Commercial Damages, A Guide to Remedies in Business Litigation* (Matthew Bender, New York, NY, 1993); Lemar, C.J. and Mainz, A.J. (eds), *Litigation*

The chapter first considers loss of profits issues generally. Methods of calculating lost profits are then introduced followed by discussions of the detailed loss of profits calculations. The taxation implications of commercial damages awards are then outlined. The chapter concludes by considering sundry forensic accounting issues.

Loss of profits

17–04 Whereas there is a fairly standard approach to calculating damages in personal injury and fatal accident cases (see Chapter 16), commercial damages calculations tend to vary considerably as the circumstances vary widely from case to case. In addition, the industries involved may be very different and may present unique issues. As a result of this variability, commercial damages cases present a greater degree of complexity for the damages expert.

Tort and breaches of contract

17–05 Legal aspects of commercial disputes have already been considered in Chapters 9 and 10. They are briefly summarised again here, with an emphasis on computing commercial damages.

17–06 While a claim for profits lost as a result of relying on an incorrect statement is normally pursued only in a contract action, in suitable circumstances a plaintiff may recover lost profits in a tort action. The plaintiff, in seeking to recover for the loss of a commercial opportunity, is entitled to have the damages assessed by reference to the chance that the opportunity would otherwise have been successfully exploited had the wrong not been committed. Theoretically, this differs from the objective in contract actions in which a plaintiff may recover "expectation losses" so as to put him in the position in which he would have found himself had the contract been performed.

Damages

17–07 Businesses can incur economic damage as a result of actions by other parties. If the damage can be shown to have been caused by the wrongful conduct of another party, such damages may be recoverable by the injured party. Damages comprise the compensation in money for the detriment suffered from the unlawful act or omission of another.[3] Recoverable economic damages usually consist of the profits lost to the damaged business. Damages are the discounted sum of projected profits but for the alleged action, minus projected profits including the

---

Support (4th ed., Butterworths, London, 1999), Chap. 2; Martin, G.D. and Vavoulis, T., *Determining Economic Damages* (James Publishing Inc, California, 1999).

[3] Foster, C.B. and Trout, R.R., "Computing losses in business interruption cases" in *Journal of Forensic Economics* (1989), Vol. 3, No. 1, pp. 9–22.

effects of the action. The legal principles concerning damages generally have already been considered in Chapter 15.

17–08 In seeking remedies for injury, the law provides the injured party and the courts with the flexibility to address a myriad of factual settings from which such cases arise. The alternative remedies of damages, restitution and specific performance are adaptable to precise situations while sharing the general goal of returning the parties to the position which they either held or reasonably expected to hold before the breach occurred.

Length of damage period

17–09 Determining the damage period can be relatively straightforward or may be difficult. The choice of length of a damage period depends on the length of time necessary for the damaged firm to complete its adjustment to the loss caused by the wrongful act so that the remaining effects of the wrong suffered are negligible. In a business interruption case, losses may be measured until such time as the sales or profits of the plaintiff's business have recovered. The length of time must also take account of the fact that other causal influences on the firm's profits may overwhelm the influence of the wrongful act. If the incremental profit margin shrinks with each successive period and/or if the discount rates fully incorporate risk factors, then usually the present value of each future year's lost profit will fall off quickly. As the present value in each period decreases towards zero, it will normally be clear where the damage period can be cut-off without materially affecting the present value of future losses.

17–10 In breach of contract cases the damage period is defined by the life of the contract. The period remaining on the contract from the date of the wrongful act defines the duration of the plaintiff's losses and courts will apply their own interpretation where the time period under the contract is unclear. The actual length of the contract period may also be an issue in dispute – for example in cases of early termination or where there are option clauses. Where the period of the contract is very long courts in the United States have ruled that the projected losses are too speculative or uncertain.[4] Courts have ruled that losses must be shown with reasonable certainty.

The further into the future one forecasts, the greater is the uncertainty surrounding the forecast. Accordingly, courts may not award damages for the full period of the contract. As a result, losses will only be recoverable within the time period within which they can be shown with reasonable certainty. In a United States case,[5] the court ruled that "as a general principle" lost future

---

[4] *Hawkinson v. Johnston*, 122 F 2nd 724 (8th Cir. 1941). In this case the court decided that losses should not run beyond 10 years even though the contract had 60 years to run.
[5] *Cargill v. Taylor Towing Services, Inc*, 642 F 2d 239 at 241 (8th Cir. 1981).

profits are deemed too speculative to allow a recovery for their loss unless the plaintiff presents sufficient proof to bring the issue outside the realm of conjecture, speculation or opinion unfounded on definite facts. In the United States, the legal basis for establishing damages to the satisfaction of the courts requires that[6] :

- damages must be proven with a reasonable degree of economic certainty;

- damages may be estimated and do not have to be exactly measured;

- damages cannot be speculative.

17–11   Under some contracts, the loss period is uncertain. The loss period and the magnitude of the losses may depend on the investment required to complete performance of the contracts. This is open to interpretation by the courts. In one extreme example in the United States, the court awarded damages for the time period of the sole trader's life expectancy even though the contract between the parties was terminable with 10 day's notice.[7] Another uncertainty is whether option clauses in contracts would have been exercised. The courts in the United States have determined that making an assumption regarding the exercise of options is too speculative.[8]

17–12   In the case of litigation arising from, say, anti-competitive behaviour the period for recovery of damages is less obvious. If the wronged business is in a start-up situation, the period of damages may only be a few years to avoid excessively speculative calculations. An alternative period of damages might be the average product life cycle in the industry.

17–13   Where the wrongful act has caused the plaintiff to go out of business, the loss period is infinite. Although the loss period may have no definite termination date, this does not imply that the losses themselves are infinite. The practice of discounting projected lost profits to present value means that losses in the future are discounted to increasingly lower values, reducing to negligible amounts.

The Irish courts will tend to look at the specific circumstances of each individual case and to rely, where appropriate, on the evidence of experts when deciding on the appropriate period to use for the calculation of damages for business interruption. An example of this arose in *Herlihy v. Texaco (Ireland) Ltd*[9] where Pringle J. arrived at a loss period of two years, in a case involving

---

[6] Gaughan, P.A., "Economic and financial issues in lost profits litigation" in *Litigation Economics* (Gaughan, P.A. and Thornton, R.J. (eds), JAI Press, Greenwich, Connecticut, 1993), p. 182 quoting Cerillo, W., *Proving Business Damages* (Wiley, New York, NY, 1991), pp. 1–20.

[7] *Charles R. Combs Trucking Inc v. International Harvester Co*, 12 Ohio St 3rd, 241; 466 NE 2nd 883 (1984).

[8] *Birge v. Toppers Mensware, Inc*, 473 SW 2d 79 (Tex. Civ. App. 1971).

[9] [1971] I.R. 311.

the termination of a tenancy, partly on the basis of evidence given by a chartered surveyor.

Standards of proof

17–14   Proving the existence of lost profits is subject to a standard that has been described as "reasonable certainty". The key issue is to satisfy the court on the balance of probabilities that lost profits have resulted from the alleged wrong. To so satisfy the court requires that uncertainty as to the occurrence of lost profits be reimbursed. Once that is demonstrated, proving the level of lost profits is subject to the more liberal standards of "best available evidence" and a "reasonable estimate". These standards allow plaintiffs and defendants wide latitude in the use of facts, expert witnesses and methodologies.

Computation of damages

17–15   The computation of damages can be expressed as follows:

$$\text{Lost profits} = \text{Loss of sales revenue} - \text{Savings in variable costs due to reduced output} + \text{extra costs incurred due to the injury}$$

These equations may need to be modified depending on particular circumstances. For example, in some cases there may be no loss of revenues, only additional costs incurred. In other situations, there may be a loss in sales revenue without a corresponding saving in variable costs.

Computation of lost profits

17–16   The law does not clearly define lost profit damages – rather they vary by type of action and jurisdiction. There are various reasons for awarding lost profit damages, including:

– to compensate the victim for damage caused;

– to put the plaintiff in the same position in which he would have been had the wrongful act not occurred;

– to punish the wrongdoer;

– to restore to the plaintiff that which has been taken from him.

The general principles guiding the calculation of lost profits are, on the face of it, simple. Net profits (defined as revenues less costs) that the plaintiff would have received but for the defendant's actions, must be computed. The computation can be broken down into a number of steps as follows:

- define the damage period;
- estimate lost revenues from sales;
- subtract costs associated with lost revenues;
- subtract revenues (less variable costs) associated with mitigating efforts;
- express net lost revenues in present value terms;
- estimate any residual loss of worth.

17–17   The estimation of loss of profits in a business resulting from a fire, flood or similar incident does not involve as much guesswork as might initially appear. Forensic accountants use their experience of similar businesses to calculate losses in a logical manner. In assessing business interruption losses forensic accountants must have the skills and experience to:

- survey the physical damage to assess the extent of business interruption during restoration;
- estimate the period of interruption;
- analyse sales and production records to determine pre-loss and projected activity;
- determine the business interruption value through a review of the profit and loss accounts;
- determine the actual loss sustained, allowing for sales made-up, fulfilment of demand with quantities on hand, potential purchase and resale of products, etc.

17–18   To assist in these activities, the forensic accountant will require all relevant available information, including:

- production experience if the loss involves manufacturing operations;
- sales experience and history, if there is evidence of loss of sales;
- cost of sales and expense history;
- continuing normal operating expenses;
- extra expenses.

17–19   The first step is to calculate lost sales and then to calculate the lost gross profit on those sales. Sales are a function of volume sold and unit price. This will involve looking at historic sales patterns and at future prospects. In a typical commercial damages case, the projection of revenues that the plaintiff firm has lost as a result of the alleged wrongdoing is based on the plaintiff firm's historical rate of revenue growth, as well as other relevant factors. An expanding business will have to support claims made by reference to budgets, forecasts, investment appraisals and market surveys. Market conditions in the industry generally also need to be considered. Losses are measured by projecting revenues and then converting these amounts into profits through the application of a relevant profit margin. These profits may then be further adjusted for the impact of other relevant factors such as the time value of money (see Chapter 19).

17–20   Lost profits are defined as the revenues or sales not received or consummated as a result of the actions of another party, less the costs associated with producing those sales. The lost profit model requires a comparison of the plaintiff's profits after the injury with the profit the plaintiff might have expected if no injury had occurred. Economic loss with this model requires that profits be measured before and after the injury. For breach of contract, this means the contract price less cost of performance, or cost of completion, or, as it is sometimes put, "expenses saved" as a result of the plaintiff being excused from performance by the other party's breach.

17–21   However, the basis of calculation for compensation for loss of profits is often set out in the relevant insurance policy and, if so, this will determine the components of the compensable loss and the manner in which it is calculated (*e.g.* see *Superwood Holdings plc v. Sun Alliance Insurance London plc*[10]). In particular, if only losses in excess of a predetermined amount are recoverable, this will be factored into the calculation. Also, any conditions or limitations imposed on margins recoverable under the policy must also be considered.

17–22   In general, defendants are only required to compensate plaintiffs for net profits, not gross profits or gross selling price.[11] In the United Kingdom, the Court of Appeal held that damages for loss of gross profit or gross contribution can only be claimed if the overheads could not reasonably be avoided and/or where there was no substitute business available.[12]

17–23   To summarise, the computation of lost profits is a four-step exercise[13]:

(1) Estimate "but for" revenues (paras **17–32** *et seq.* and para. **17–61**).

(2) Estimate associated costs (paras **17–78** *et seq.*).

(3) Examine fixed cost patterns (paras **17–58** *et seq.*).

(4) Compute lost profits.

---

[10] [1995] 3 I.R. 303.

[11] *West Coast Winery, Inc v. Golden West Wineries*, 69 CA 2d 166 (1945).

[12] *Western Web Offset Printers Ltd v. Independent Media Ltd* (1995) 139 Sol. J. 212 LB.

[13] Foster, C.B. and Trout, R.R., "Computing losses in business interruption cases" in *Journal of Forensic Economics* (1989), Vol. 3, No. 1, pp. 9–22.

Concepts of profit

17–24   The profit calculation in the financial accounts consists of sales revenues for the period less all expenses incurred in that period. The concept of profit in calculating damages or lost profits in civil litigation is quite different. Lost profit is incremental revenue lost less incremental (variable) expenses saved in not earning those revenues.

17–25   It is usually not possible or advisable to measure these net profit streams directly. Rather the before and after gross revenue streams are measured or estimated, and the related costs are then deducted in arriving at profit. Sales are easier to forecast than profit, even where profit is properly defined. Firms usually account separately for sales and keep accurate and detailed sales data. Trends and seasonal patterns are usually easy to observe. Profits, however, are a residual. Cost/expense accounting errors, whether costs are recorded on a cash or accruals basis, result in profit patterns that can be difficult to forecast. Easily available historical measures of profit such as the gross profit margin or the net profit margin are unlikely to be suitable to measure the change in net profits that resulted from the wrongful acts.

17–26   An understanding of why the gross or net profit margin is not suitable for measuring the change in profits is a most important concept in lost profits analysis. A better measure is the change in the incremental profit margin. The incremental profit margin measures the change in net profits as a result of change in revenue. The incremental profit margin lies somewhere between the gross profit margin and the net profit margin. The gross margin (in percentage terms) is sales less cost of sales, divided by sales. The net margin is sales less total costs, divided by sales. The incremental profit margin is the incremental (additional) sales less incremental costs associated with the lost incremental (additional) sales, divided by the lost incremental (additional) revenue.

17–27   A common technique to calculate the incremental profit margin is to identify each expense category (using profit and loss accounts or more detailed underlying financial data such as adjusted trial balance amounts) as being fixed or variable. The distinction lies in the importance of distinguishing between which categories of cost are fixed (do not vary with the level of revenue) and which are variable (do vary with the level of revenue). Another way of expressing this is that variable costs are those costs that can be cut back or avoided after the revenue loss occurs. Fixed costs are those that would be incurred with or without the revenue loss. This issue is considered again in paras **17–78** *et seq.*

Avoid double counting

17–28   Double counting can occur in making loss of profit claims especially where expenses and loss of profits are both claimed. Plaintiffs cannot claim both additional expenditure and loss of profits. They must decide whether to seek to be put back into the position they would have been if the contract had not been made (*i.e.* recover expenditure outlay) or claim the profits that could have been made but for the breach of contract (*i.e.* lost profit).[14]

Damages where revenues and profits have increased

17–29   Damages may exist even where revenues and profits have increased. There may be circumstances where damages are recovered even where growth after interruption exceeds pre-interruption growth. It is possible that a plaintiff is damaged by not being able to achieve an even higher growth rate than the actual rate as a result of the wrong, even where the actual growth rate is higher than historical rates. However, the analytical and evidentiary burdens of proving such damages may be greater.

Disaggregation of revenue

17–30   Analysing total revenues may not capture the relevant trends if only a certain segment of the business is affected by the defendant's actions. One method of proving loss in such circumstances might be to disaggregate revenue figures for different product lines or business segments to isolate falls in revenues from individual products or business segments.

Spillover costs

17–31   The defendant's actions may also cause spillover costs. This is where the injured part of the business has spillover effects on other parts of the business. Spillover effects must be proved – possibly by a product-by-product revenue analysis, showing trends not only in total revenues but also in its disaggregated components.

Methods of calculating lost profits

17–32   When a company has been damaged or forced out of business, the most reasonable measure of damages is generally lost profits. Lost profits claims typically rest on a comparison between the injured firm's "but for" situation and its actual situation. The "but for" situation is a hypothetical construction of the facts as they would exist but for the wrongful conduct, a scenario based on

---

[14] *Cullinane v. British "Rema" Manufacturing Co. Ltd* [1954] 1 Q.B. 292 at 308.

the premise that the wrongful conduct never occurred. The difference between the "but for" and actual is a measure of the firm's loss – the extent to which the firm is worse off because the wrongful conduct occurred.

17–33   The nature of the "but for" versus actual comparison to be made depends on the ramifications of the wrongful act. Given the complexity of business enterprises, wrongful conduct frequently has fundamental and long-lasting consequences for the injured firm. Wrongful conduct may disrupt the stream of transactions by upsetting the firm's market relationships or internal workings. Many lost profits cases involve continued transactional losses from continuing wrongful conduct. When a firm's operations are disrupted, the changes forced on the firm can be expected to impair profitability for some time, or may be so drastic that the firm is unable to recover and must liquidate. To assess the extent of the loss caused by such disruption entails a longer view of the divergence between "but for" and actual. The focus is on the firm's capacity to make profits, not solely on the profit lost on a particular transaction.

17–34   Determining the revenue that would have been received had the damage not occurred can be difficult. There are a number of methods the plaintiff can employ to prove lost profits. Three distinct economic loss models can be used in varying types of commercial litigation cases. Lost profits are generally calculated using one or more of the following methods:

(1) "Before and after" approach – business profits before, during and after the defendant's alleged acts are examined to show specific losses suffered by the plaintiff.

(2) "Yardstick" approach – financial information about companies similar to the plaintiff is obtained and used as a yardstick to estimate the profits the plaintiff would have earned but for the wrong perpetrated by the defendant.

(3) "Market model" approach – a model to project lost profits is developed using assumptions arising from a study of the industry and the plaintiff's operating results in the context of the industry.

17–35   Other methods of proving business damages can be developed through the use of expert assistance. Using a variety of approaches, an expert witness may testify as to the likely range of that amount of profits the injured party has lost as a result of the defendant's actions. In recent years, courts have shown a greater receptivity to proof by expert opinion and to the use of sophisticated economic and financial data.

"Before and after" approach

17–36   In calculating damages, a method of accounting called the "before and after" method is often used. This method is also called the "with and without" method or "differential analysis". The "before and after" method compares the plaintiff's profits prior to the alleged violation with profits after the violation using historical data such as the injured plaintiff's past volume of production and sales. Applying this method generally involves estimating lost revenue and then multiplying it by the incremental profit margin. The concept is to isolate factors that changed as a result of the wrongful acts or events. The "before and after" method computes the differences between actual results and assumed results that would have been achieved, based on historic records in the company itself, in the absence of the wrongful acts or events.

The logic of the assumed results rests on a series of hypothetical assumptions that can be subject to dispute. Basing those assumptions on verifiable third party data such as industry, professional or economic trends is always preferable. It is essential to compare the economic, industry and business conditions in the pre-interruption and post-interruption periods to make sure that the assumption that both periods are comparable is valid, or to adjust the calculations accordingly where such assumption is not appropriate. It is unwise to ignore differences in the before and after time periods, even if this complicates the calculations. Study and comparison must be made of factors such as changes in the economic environment, changed industry conditions, the customer base, business facilities (where the interruption entailed a move of premises), etc. The defendant may try to undermine the damages calculation by proving that the external environment in the "after period" is different to the "before period", and that this difference and not the injury led to some or all of the reduction in profits. For example, the defendant may allege that the plaintiff's own mismanagement was responsible for poorer performance in the after period.

Yardstick approach

17–37 Another means of proving lost profits, called the "yardstick" approach, involves the plaintiff introducing evidence of the profits made by a business operating in similar market conditions that was not subject to the defendant's breach. In situations where it is difficult to forecast the lost revenues of the plaintiff firm, an acceptable alternative approach is to compare the sales growth, or level of sales, of the injured firm with another firm (unaffected by the injury) in the same line of business. This method, for example, is useful where there is an insufficient track record to apply the before and after method where the injured business is relatively new. Alternatively, the method can be used to buttress the findings of the "before and after" method.

17–38 This approach is obviously less persuasive in that it is based not on the actual performance of the business in question but on a notional performance determined by comparison. This means that inaccuracies arise in the resulting calculation, as a result not only of approximations inherent in assumptions generally, but also because of the inevitable differences between the business in question and the business with which it is being compared. In other words, the defendant will argue that the so-called comparable business is not really comparable. Lack of comparability can derive from many sources. The defendant's experts will attempt to put forward reasons (other than the defendant's actions) justifying the difference in performance between the plaintiff and the comparable company.

17–39 The yardstick approach has been used in start-up situations (see para. **17–44** *et seq.*), where businesses with no past history of profits have been permitted to introduce evidence of the profits of similar businesses. Its use has the obvious problem of locating a proper proxy firm. Acceptable proxy firm candidates should be similar in size, product line, markets and other relevant factors. Caution should be used before applying the yardstick approach, given the difficulty in locating appropriate proxy firms.

Market model/market share approach

17–40 In the market model/market share approach, revenues in the pre- or post-loss period are used to establish the firm's relationship to the total market. The total market data are then used to determine the lost revenues. The following information is required to use the market approach:

– definition of the relevant product market;

– historic sales for the relevant market;

– past sales of the plaintiff firm for the same historic period;

– demonstration that the plaintiff could have continued to compete in the market.

17–41 The first step in developing a market model is to study and evaluate the plaintiff company's business plan, marketing strategy, and forecasts to identify relevant information and assumptions. The use of information prepared prior to the alleged injury helps to overcome the assertion that damages are too speculative. Then some research of the industry should be conducted to determine typical growth rates, expenses/cost ratios, cash flow ratios, capital expenditures, etc., for similar businesses (if they exist).

17–42 Once the research is complete, a model is developed to forecast the plaintiff's lost profits over the time period during which the damages are likely to continue. By using knowledge of total market sales during the injury period, sales for the injured firm can be estimated by applying the firm's market share to total market sales. Variable or direct costs can then be subtracted to arrive at lost profits. When few sales data are available from periods not affected by commercial injury, it may be necessary to assume the enterprise would have maintained a constant share of some relevant product market if the injury had not occurred. Estimated lost profits are then discounted to arrive at present value. An advantage of this approach is that highs and lows in local, regional or national economic cycles are automatically accounted for.

Variations in lost profits calculations

17–43 The three standard methods for calculating lost profits have been described. Deciding which method to use depends on the particular circumstances giving rise to the lost profits calculation and on the nature of the business. Three circumstances are briefly considered here:

– calculating losses in start-up businesses;

– business interruptions of various types;

– losses so substantial as to cause the business to fail.

Start-up business[15]

17–44 For businesses not well established (or entirely unestablished), the concept of business interruption is difficult to prove and may be speculative unless the economics or past experience, or both, indicate a successful venture. In the United States, courts generally do not award lost profits damages to new companies because such damages are speculative:

"... loss of profits is a definite element of damages in an action for breach of contract or in an action for harming an established business which has been operating for a sufficient length of time to afford a basis for estimation with some degree of certainty as to the probable loss of profits, but that, on the other hand, loss of profits from a business which has not gone into operation may not be recovered because they are merely speculative and incapable of being ascertained with the requisite degree of certainty."[16]

17–45 The court's position in the United States has evolved over time. Cerillo[17] writes:

"Courts adopting this 'new business' rule include *Main Realty Co. v. Blackstone Valley Gas & Electric Co.*, 59 R.I. 29, 193 A. 879 (1937) (in dicta); *Keener v.*

[15] This is considered in Barchas, I.D. and Weil, R.L. "Loss profits damages to new businesses" in *Litigation Services Handbook. The Role of the Accountant as Expert* (2nd ed., Weil, R.L., Wagner, M.J. and Frank, P.B. (eds), John Wiley & Sons, Inc., New York, 1995), Chap. 31.

[16] *Evergreen Amusement Corp v. Milstead* 206 Md. at 618 (1955), 112 A 2d at 904–905.

[17] Gaughan, P.A., "Economic and financial issues in lost profits litigation" in *Litigation Economics* (Gaughan, P.A. and Thornton, R.J. (eds), JAI Press, Greenwich, Connecticut, 1993), p. 194 quoting Cerillo, W., *Proving Business Damages* (Wiley, New York, NY, 1991), pp. 1-20.

Sizzler Family Steak Houses, 597 F. 2d 453 (5th Cir. 1979) (Under Texas law, prospective profits are not recovered for a newly established business or businesses operated at a loss); *Sambo's of Ohio v. City Council*, 466 F. Supp. 177, 181 (N.D. Ohio 1979) ('The law is well settled that loss of profits from a new business enterprise is too speculative to be allowed as an element of damages. Only where the evidence establishes a history of profitable operations, followed by the actionable wrong and a diminution of profits, can there be any recovery'); *St. Paul at Chase Corp. v. The Manufacturer Life Insurance Company*, 262 Md. 192, 278 A. 2d 12 (1971); *Dieffenback v. McIntyre*, 208 Okla. 163, 254 P. 2d 346 (1952)."

Nonetheless, it is possible in exceptional circumstances for a new business to recover lost prospective profits.[18]

17–46   Computing lost profits in a start-up business presents unique challenges for a damages expert due to the complete absence of historical data (unestablished business) or to the availability of only limited data (newly established business). In computing lost profits in a start-up business, the expert is generally limited to using the market model approach (see para. **17–40** *et seq.*). Alternatively, proxy firms may be used, *i.e.* those which are similar in every respect (size, product line, capitalisation) to the plaintiff. In the latter case it will be necessary to satisfy the court that the plaintiff firm is truly like the proxy firm. This may be possible in certain types of businesses such as franchises. The existence of, and applicability of data for, proxy firms would need considerable research. The "before and after" approach is typically ruled out because the company has little or no historical operating results to show a pattern of growth or profitability.

To establish a claim for lost profits for a start-up business, the plaintiff must overcome the likely assertion that forecasted profits are too speculative. However, many courts are willing to award lost profits to a start-up business, provided they can be established with "reasonably certainty". The expert must consider the amount of time it would have taken the start-up business to conquer the "learning curve" inherent in any start-up. The defendant will attempt to undermine the reliability of the projections to create the impression that the calculations are purely speculative.

If lost profits for a start-up cannot be projected with reasonable certainty, an alternative measure of damages would be the plaintiff's out-of-pocket costs in starting the business. With adequate record keeping, this claim should be relatively simple to prove.

---

[18] *Hunters Int. Mfg. Co v. Christiana Metals Corp*, 561 F. Supp. 614 (ED Mich. 1982); aff'd, 725 F. 2d 683 (7th Cir. 1983). In *Fera v. Village Plaza, Inc* 396 Mich. 639; 242 NW 2d 372 (1976) the plaintiffs leased space in a new shopping centre but the landlord gave their space to another tenant. The plaintiffs successfully sued for loss of profits. The judgment held that courts should not interpret the new business rule to exclude all claims for lost profits.

17–47 When a new venture or start-up business fails, the uncertainty surrounding lost profits and value lost can be even more controversial. Three principal views of what is lost have been identified.[19] The measure of damages varies depending on the view taken of what is lost. The three views of what has been lost are:

(1) Investment – the amount invested in the start-up business. This is the least uncertain of the three methods and can be estimated based on actual records of expenditure. However, this method ignores the value arising from the prospect of the start-up business being successful (or vice versa in the case of the start-up business failing).

(2) Opportunity – the expected value of the lost profits. This approach attempts to take into account the lost opportunity to earn profits in the future. This measure of loss is based on expectations at time of injury. No consideration is given to actual experience or new information after the wrongful act and this is the main deficiency with this method.

(3) Outcome – the actual value of the profits lost. This method seeks to overcome the deficiency of the opportunity method by taking into account all information available after the injury about what would have happened but for the wrongful act. It seeks to restore the plaintiff to the position it would have been in "but for" the wrongful event. The outcome is calculated based on experience to date. However, this method has practical difficulties in that a large amount of evidence and information about post-wrongful act events is required. Where the time between the wrongful act and the trial is substantial the amount of evidence required is even greater.

Defendants will attempt to show that the business was subject to very high levels of risk which caused the failure. The burden of proof is placed on the plaintiff and it can be very difficult to provide acceptable evidence, especially where the defendant provides data on the other risk factors that might have caused the business to collapse.

Types of business interruption claims

17–48 Today's complex business interrelationships in manufacturing, distribution, services and outsourcing create significant problems in properly establishing business interruption values and evaluating maximum business interruption loss exposure. Accounting data needs to be properly interpreted to accurately report business interruption values. Exposures at various business locations need to be evaluated, given the potential interdependency of various production and distribution facilities. Business interruption and consequential

---

[19]Bodington, J.C. "Appraising the profits lost by a failed new venture" in *Journal of Forensic Economics* (1990), Vol. 4, No. 1, pp. 7–14.

loss of profits give rise to a variety of types of claim, such as:

- business interruption insurance claims;
- third party liability claims;
- uninsured tort claims.

Business interruptions can impair the sales and profits of an enterprise for many years, damage business reputation, and undermine relations with customers, suppliers and lending institutions. They may also involve extra expense, rental losses and soft cost claims (*e.g.* relating to intellectual capital and intangibles).

17–49   Business interruptions can be classified as closed, open, or infinite[20]:

- With a closed interruption, the loss period has ended before the loss computations are performed. The forecaster has normal (*i.e.* un-interrupted) sales data before and after the loss.

- With an open interruption, sales have not returned to normal at the time of the loss computations, and the company is still in business. The forecaster has only pre-loss period normal sales data to work with, and may have to forecast the end of the loss period as well as the magnitude of the losses themselves. The issue of how far into the future to measure lost profits is as much a legal issue as an economic issue.

- An interruption is infinite if the company went through a period of operating losses, then went bankrupt or was sold at a reduced value. There is only pre-loss normal sales data, and the forecast is used to compute losses up to the date of the bankruptcy and the market value of the company at that date. If the firm is forced out of business, the comparison of "but for" and actual profits may extend to the period for which the firm would probably have continued but for the wrongful conduct. The calculation of lost profits in such a situation would compare the "but for" profits with the actual profits (€nil if the company goes out of business), discounted to present value less liquidation value for the business.

Losses causing business failure

17–50   In severe cases, losses suffered by a business consequent on injury are so great that they cause the business to fail.[21] The dilemma for the lost profits expert is to quantify and separate out the influence of the wrongful act from other causal forces that may have also contributed to failure. One technique is break-even point analysis of price and sales volume. This is a method of

---

[20] Foster, C.B. and Trout, R.R., "Computing losses in business interruption cases" in *Journal of Forensic Economics* (1989), Vol. 3, No. 1, pp. 9–22.
[21] *Bader v. Cerri*, 96 Nev. 352; 609 P. 2d 314 (1980).

examining the relationship between changes in volume, sales, expenses and net profit based on a knowledge of how costs behave, *i.e.* whether costs are fixed or variable with sales. The objective is to establish the impact on financial results if a specified level of activity/volume fluctuates. The contribution (*i.e* sales revenue less variable costs) of each product must be known.

17–51   The law clearly distinguishes between the failure of a young, unestablished business and that of an established business. If a business is young, small and undercapitalised, then it is considered to be vulnerable to a myriad of different causes of failure and, consequently, it may be difficult to prove that the wrongful act was the fatal blow. Experts for the defendant will frequently point to the high failure rate of small businesses in their first years of operation. Plaintiff experts will point out that the risk of failure goes down dramatically if the firm survives a certain period.

17–52   For larger firms that are clearly established businesses it is possible to measure the impact of a particular loss of revenue on the financial ratios of the firm. Then, it is possible to draw inferences from the change in those key financial ratios to the risk of failure of the firm. There is considerable literature on predicting the failure rate of larger firms based on the changes in key financial ratios.

Where the wrongful act clearly caused the failure, damages must be stated in terms of loss of the business *per se*. Such loss may be assessed from three different perspectives:

– book value of the assets;

– replacement value of the assets;

– fair market value.

Fair market value is generally accepted as the most appropriate method to use. Fair market value is the price the business would be exchanged at, given a willing buyer and willing seller, and assuming neither are under compulsion to buy/sell and both are reasonably informed as to the relevant facts. Two methods of computing fair market value are capitalised net profits/earnings and loss of future net profits/earnings. These methods are discussed in Chapter 18. The position of the firm being valued and the economics of the industry as a whole must be factored into the calculations.

17–53   When a business fails as a result of a wrongful act, and the owners have gone on to alternative employment, the earnings or profits from the alternative employment during the damage period are off-set in mitigation against lost profits.

Measuring lost profits resulting from loss of customers

17–54   A common type of lost profits involves the loss of customers, *e.g.* as a result of business interruption customers may be lost because the ability of the plaintiff to supply products or services was interrupted. Alternatively, particular customers may have been poached through illegal actions of the defendant such as the defendant priating clients (*e.g.* former employees of the plaintiff firm). Litigation involving claims of damages for lost customers is not uncommon.

   In order to calculate damages, a breakdown of sales by customer is required over an historical period. One way of measuring loss due to customer loss is to base projections of lost sales on historical sales to lost customers. However, this method assumes that all the lost customers would have remained with the plaintiff firm during the loss period at pre-existing levels of business. In practice, most businesses suffer some customer attrition due to competition and for other business reasons. On the other hand, volumes of business with customers can also increase over time. The simple calculation is appropriate only if the firm can justify the assumption of 100 per cent retention. Where relevant, the historical attrition rate should be factored into the model. Such analysis of historical attrition rates may be difficult where there is limited data.[22]

17–55   A more accurate calculation would include statistical methodology that specifically measures the historical customer attrition rate. This methodology can be applied to the projected revenues for lost customers to arrive at the adjusted revenue projection. In addition, customer growth rates might also be considered – this is desirable if customer growth rates vary and/or display considerable cross-sectional variation, *e.g.* if the age profile of customers is very varied. Once the appropriate growth rates have been selected, and the annual revenues per lost customer have been projected, an adjustment is required for the probability that each specific customer could have terminated its business relationship with the plaintiff over the loss projection period (for reasons other than the alleged wrongdoing). This is called survival probability analysis and is gaining popularity with social scientists to calculate duration of business cycles, marriages, lifetimes of firms, etc. Using this technique will correct one of the drawbacks commonly associated with simplistic lost profits analysis in cases where the plaintiff claims lost customers as a result of an alleged transgression. The technique can be used by plaintiffs to make damages projections more realistic. It can also be used by defendants to correct the overestimation of damages often present in many plaintiff's claims where it is assumed that, were it not for the action of the defendant, all customers would have remained with the plaintiff.

---

[22] For more information on this issue, see Bonanomi, L., Gaughan, P.A. and Taylor, L.W., "A statistical methodology for measuring lost profit resulting from a loss of customers" in *Journal of Forensic Economics* (1998), Vol. 11, No. 2, pp. 103–113.

Patent infringement and intellectual property damages

17–56   The accounting calculations in patent and intellectual property infringement have already been considered in Chapter 9 (paras **9–90** *et seq.*). Two approaches were outlined – (1) the account of profits approach and (2) the reasonable royalty approach.

Account of profits approach

17–57   The formula for computing lost profits in a patent infringement case is simple in theory but complex in practice. Lost profits generally equal the revenues from lost sales less the additional costs of producing those sales. The cost component of the formula is similar to that in other lost profits cases. However, calculation of the sales component is unique because of the presence of the infringer.

It may not be an accurate assumption that the patent holder's lost sales are equal to the sales of the infringer. For example, the infringer may have superior marketing capabilities, a larger advertising budget, more efficient distribution channels or may operate in better geographical locations. These and other factors must be taken into account in determining the patent holder's lost sales.

Once potential lost sales are taken into account, the patent holder's ability and capacity to manufacture the additional product must be considered. Both the patent holder's physical production facilities and its level of utilisation of those facilities during the infringement period must be analysed. In some cases the patent holder may claim that it would have expanded its production capacity to meet the additional demand. This is a very difficult assertion to prove and, if proven, requires that the cost of increasing the capacity be included in the calculations.

17–58   Typically, damages are based on prices actually charged by the patent holder for its own sales. However, the patent holder might argue that the price charged would have been higher but for the infringement because competition with the infringer depressed prices for both parties. If this argument were successful, the lost profits calculation would also have to take into account the lost sales revenue (because of lower prices) on the patent holder's own sales. Conversely, it could be argued that had the price been higher this would have depressed demand resulting in lower sales volumes.

Reasonable royalty approach

17–59   Damages in a patent/intellectual property infringement case should never be less than the national royalties lost through the infringement. The issues in such a calculation are discussed in paras **9–116** *et seq.*

Establishing lost profits in a patent infringement case may impose a heavier burden on the plaintiff than in other types of cases. The availability of reasonable royalty damages in the event that lost profits are deemed too speculative may cause courts to demand a greater precision in proving lost profits in such cases.

Estimation of lost revenues

17–60   Lost profits can be measured by projecting lost incremental revenue and applying a relevant profit margin to the projected lost revenues. Thus, the first step in calculating lost profits is to determine the level of sales or revenues that would have been received but for the actions of the other party. The estimate of lost revenues depends on a wide range of data and estimates.

"Before and after" approach

17–61   How the business performed before and after the business interruption sheds considerable light on how it could have performed but for the interruption. If the impact of the wrongful act is a loss of revenue to a firm, past revenues can be projected forward in time from historical data, assuming past rates of growth will remain constant. This works best for firms that have steady rates of growth, are in industries with steady rates of growth, and do not exhibit seasonality or business cycle patterns.

Market model/market share approach

17–62   Otherwise, it is necessary to examine how the whole industry (or, more accurately, the relevant market) has behaved before and after the date of the wrongful act. It may be necessary to examine how market shares have changed and how those market shares were impacted by the actions of the defendant.

Hybrid approach

17–63   When the wrongful act involves the diversion of plaintiff revenue to the defendant, one approach is to use the revenue gained by the defendant as the best available measure of the level of revenue lost by the plaintiff. This can lead to the hybrid approach of estimating lost profits by multiplying the revenue gained by the defendant by the profit margin of the plaintiff.

Forecasting techniques and choosing a forecast model

17–64   The terms forecast and projection are used interchangeably, although in practice they relate to quite different types of financial statements. The distinction between these two terms is not always clear. The auditing guideline exposure draft *Prospective Financial Information*[23] defined a forecast as:

> ". . . management's best expectation of the most likely future results, financial position or changes in financial position of an enterprise for one or more future dates or periods based on assumptions representing management's judgement

---

[23] Institute of Chartered Accountants in England and Wales, *Auditing Guideline Exposure Draft 'Prospective Financial Information'* (Institute of Chartered Accountants in England and Wales, London, 1990), para. 8.

of both the conditions likely to prevail and the course of action it is most likely to take. Due to the need for reliability a forecast should only exceptionally extend beyond the current accounting period."

17–65 A projection, on the other hand, is defined as either:

"(a) management's best expectation of the future results, financial position or changes in financial position which is subject to more uncertainty than a forecast because of the quality of the corroborative evidence available to support the amounts. This could be due to such factors as:
 • how far ahead the future period is;
 • lack of sufficient trading record;
 • volatility of the business;
 • especially uncertain business environment; and
 • highly subjective assumptions; or
(b) management's illustration of the future results, financial position or changes in financial position based on hypothetical assumptions which may or may not prevail over the period but which are nevertheless within a reasonable range."[24]

Thus, a forecast is the best judgment of what is going to happen, whereas a projection can be based on hypothetical, what-if assumptions. Several possible scenarios can be considered in projections.

17–66 More recently, the Institute of Chartered Accountants in England and Wales has issued a discussion paper which suggests a change to these definitions as follows:

"We propose departing from international practice by offering a new distinction between forecasts and projections based upon the directors' degree of belief and confidence. In the case of a forecast, directors need to be prepared to say that 'this is highly likely to happen'. In the case of a projection, directors need to be prepared to say that 'this is reasonably likely to happen'."[25]

The discussion paper provides further proposed guidance in relation to the distinction between projection and forecast.

17–67 Economic forecasting models may be used for estimation of lost revenues. A number of forecasting techniques are available. Various projection techniques from basic to more sophisticated can be used to create a "but for" revenue stream over the relevant loss period. Forecasting revenues can vary

---

[24] Institute of Chartered Accountants in England and Wales, *Auditing Guideline Exposure Draft 'Prospective Financial Information'* (Institute of Chartered Accountants in England and Wales, London, 1990), para. 8.
[25] Institute of Chartered Accountants in England and Wales, *Prospective Financial Information: Challenging the Assumptions. A Discussion Paper* (Institute of Chartered Accountants in England and Wales, London, 2000), para. 4.22.

from basic historical growth rate extrapolation methods to more sophisticated curve-fitting techniques. There is a multitude of forecasting models available to choose from. Forecasting methods can be divided into two broad categories: time series models and econometric models. The forecast model should be simple and easily understood by a court.

The nature of the sales data available to the forecaster will also influence the choice of forecast method. Both time series and econometric methods require that a considerable amount of sales revenue data be available for time periods not affected by the injury that gave rise to the loss. The number of years data available, the frequency of the data (daily, weekly, monthly, etc.) and whether the sales pattern is regular (*e.g.* shop) or irregular (*e.g.* contract business) are considerations.

Trends and horizontal analysis

17–68 Basic growth rate extrapolation is a common revenue forecasting method. The appropriate revenue base is identified and a growth rate is selected and applied to the chosen revenue base to project the "but for" revenues. This very simple form of estimation is based on an analysis of percentage change of revenues and expenses from year to year based on several years' historical data or other information. The rates of change are calculated (possibly producing an average rate of change) and are applied to predict what the profit would have been had prior relationships and circumstances continued. The resulting projected profit is then compared with actual results and the loss computed. This method may not produce defensible results if prior profits have been erratic or if the particular industry has been affected by recent economic events.

Trend lines and curve fitting models

17–69 These are simple forecasting techniques. The idea is to estimate the equation of a line or curve that fits (*i.e.* lies close to) the observed actual sales figures outside the interruption period. Trend or curve fitting can be used in any situation where the pre-loss pattern is established.

Regression analysis

17–70 Curve fitting methods define a line or polynomial curve which "best fits" the historical data. The statistical technique (*i.e.* linear regression analysis) analyses historical data such that the line/curve of best fit is placed in the middle of the historical data points. The data is plotted on a graph for the given period of time and a straight line/curve of "best fit" is determined. This then enables estimation of each relevant variable. From the line/curve of best fit, each variable such as sales and expenses can be forecast. Projected net profit is then computed and compared with actual profits to arrive at the business loss due to the injury. This approach is similar to the previous one except that the use of statistical methods may result in more accurate calculations. The choice depends on a consideration of the extra cost in using the more accurate linear (or other) regression methodology compared with the additional benefits derived from more accurate calculations. In addition, limited availability of data may preclude the use of this method of estimation of revenues.

Time series models

17–71   Times series analysis is a form of regression analysis that uses time as the independent variable. Most forecasting techniques involve identifying and measuring patterns in time series data. The pattern is then projected into the future as a forecast. There are two important components to a pattern – trend and seasonal variation. The trend may be up or down and linear or nonlinear. Abrupt changes in sales patterns (such as the post-introduction phase of a new product) and random outliers (abnormally large once-off transactions) are also of concern to a forecaster.

The simplest time series models are curve fitting or deterministic. The pattern of revenues in periods when no injury occurred is approximated by a mathematical curve. The equation of this curve can be used to forecast the "but for" revenues for a period where there was a loss arising from the commercial injury. The equation can be linear, quadratic, logarithmic or S-shaped, depending on the pattern observed. Many of the curve fitting models can be expanded to allow for seasonal variation in monthly or quarterly revenues. A common application of deterministic models is in business interruption cases.

Time series models require knowledge of the firm's sales revenue only, while econometric models require knowledge of a number of other explanatory variables as well. The choice of a particular forecasting model will depend on the nature of the commercial injury, the pattern observed in pre-injury revenues, the accuracy required, the cost and complexity of the model, and the amount of data available.

Classical decomposition

17–72   Classical decomposition is an extension of trend and curve fitting to cases where sales show seasonal variation. Seasonality may not be important where annual revenues are projected. However, forecasts within a year may need to be adjusted to take into account the fact that many businesses experience seasonal variations. Seasonal adjustment facilitates comparison of values at different times in the seasonal cycle and leads to more accurate short-term forecasting. With seasonal decomposition, historical sales patterns are smoothed or averaged out to eliminate the seasonal variation. The normal sales data are smoothed out, then compared with the original figures to estimate seasonal factors. A trend curve is fitted to the smoothed sales series and projected over the loss period. These projected sales trend figures are then adjusted by the appropriate seasonal factors to obtain the desired forecasts. The seasonally adjusted revenues are then used to construct a smoothed forecast. Classical decomposition can be used in any situation where seasonal factors are important.

Smoothing methods

17–73 Smoothing involves averaging out the highs and lows in a series of sales figures. The resulting smoothed series may more clearly reveal the underlying patterns than the original series, thereby facilitating the choice of a forecast model. Used this way, smoothing can be an antecedent of any forecast method. In certain circumstances, smoothing can generate the forecasts themselves. The models adapt themselves gradually to pre-interruption patterns. When the loss period begins, the updated pattern is projected as a forecast. Smoothing method forecast models should not be used in closed interruption cases (see para. **17–49** for explanation) or where sales data are recorded at irregular intervals (as projected levels may not correspond closely to actual values, especially in the post-loss period).

Models incorporating other external factors

17–74 Econometric models may attempt to incorporate the effects that the marketplace and the economy have on the profitability of the business. Thus, a relationship between the profitability of the company and both commercial and economic events is established as an indicator independent of the wrongful event.

17–75 Curve fitting models (described in para. **17–69** *et seq.*) do not work well when the sales data do not exhibit a clear pattern. In such instances, an econometric model may be needed to estimate the revenues during a loss period. An econometric model uses regression analysis (see **17–70**) to measure the dependence of one variable on a set of explanatory variables. The appropriate variables to select depends on four characteristics: type of interruption, database, normal sales patterns and simplicity of technique.

17–76 The accuracy of the econometric model used to forecast is difficult to demonstrate in business interruption cases. Actual figures against which to compare the forecast are never available in such cases – the uninterrupted, lost sales can never be observed. The forecaster must be able to demonstrate the credibility and goodness of fit of the forecast model. The forecast model should be widely known, and with a proven track record. The forecast level of sales should track closely with actual sales during the normal pre- or post-loss periods.

Reasonableness of forecast

17–77 Notwithstanding which forecasting method is used, the overall reasonableness of the resulting forecast needs to be examined critically. A common-sense perspective has to be taken. Where the forecast results do not fit the known facts, or where they produce extreme results, they are likely to be rejected by the court.

A common mistake is to project revenues beyond the capacity constraints of the business (even where it can be shown there is a demand for such a high level of sales). The presence of capacity constraints may not automatically preclude a forecast beyond the plaintiff's capacity level but the plaintiff will have to demonstrate in a convincing way how the capacity constraints would have been overcome.

Industry data (such as productivity data) may be used to test the forecast for reasonableness. In addition, an examination of the firm's market share implied by the forecast compared with the pre-injury market share may be revealing.

Effect of costs

17–78   The definition of profit used in lost profit calculations should include all variable or direct costs, such as sales commission, and certain variable labour costs (regardless of where these items are included or charged in the accounts either in arriving at gross profit or later on in the profit and loss account).

There are two aspects to costs in calculating lost profits:

(1) Avoidable variable costs – this, in turn, requires consideration of the differences between fixed and variable costs.

(2) Extra costs incurred due to the injury.

Avoidable variable costs

17–79   Avoidable costs are those costs which are avoided where sales are reduced. It will be important to determine how different costs vary with levels of service provision or production. Costs that vary with production should be included in the lost profit calculation, while those that are fixed should be excluded. The cost of producing the sales includes sales commissions, materials, direct labour and distribution costs. These costs will not be incurred in relation to the sales revenue lost. Lost revenues should be reduced by these avoidable costs in the lost profits calculation. The greatest problem in estimating costs is identification of how they behave against output or sales revenue, *i.e.* the fixed and variable elements of costs.

Fixed and variable costs

17–80   The important revenues and costs in a claim for loss of profits are the marginal or variable revenues and costs. Products generally involve more than one type of cost and product costs can be analysed in different ways. One way is by reference to their behaviour against output. Costs may be analysed between direct (which are variable) costs incurred solely or specifically to produce a product or deliver a service, and indirect (which comprise variable and fixed elements) costs, such as factory overheads, which are not directly related to a particular product or service. Most lost profits calculations require costs to be classified between fixed and variable.

17–81 Variable costs are those that vary with the level of production or with sales levels. Variable costs in other accounting periods are the best evidence of the avoided marginal cost to the firm of not earning lost revenue in the loss period. Examples of variable costs include direct materials, direct labour, production overheads, etc. Most variable costs are included in cost of sales. However, other costs such as sales commission, delivery expenses and some administration costs may also vary with output. In lost profits calculations, it is necessary to determine the extent to which variable costs fall when revenues fall.

17–82 Fixed costs, such as rent, remain the same at a variety of production/ sales levels. In most models fixed costs are assumed to remain constant except for possible temporary overhead expenditures directly related to the interruption. Where long run interruption occurs this assumption may not remain valid. The historic cost-output relationship may change. Costs that are fixed over the short term may increase or decrease in the long run in a step, ramp or steady/gradual manner.

17–83 In estimating costs, variable and fixed costs need to be identified and separated. Some costs can be classified as all fixed or all variable for a specified period of time. It cannot be assumed, however, that costs are perfectly fixed or variable. In between behaviour is also found. As illustrated in Table 17.1 and Figure 17.1, some costs may contain both fixed and variable components – sometimes called semi-fixed (step) or semi-variable (mixed) costs. Step costs increase or decrease abruptly at intervals of activity because their acquisition comes in indivisible chunks. Mixed costs contain both mixed and variable elements, *e.g.* a telephone bill which contains fixed line rental charge and variable call charges.

Table 17.1: Examples of cost behaviour patterns

Variable costs	Fixed costs
Direct labour	Depreciation on machinery
Oil for machines in factory	Factory rental
Royalty payments	Advertising
	Factory manager's salary
Mixed costs	**Step costs**
Electricity (flat basic, variable usage charge)	Supervisor (one per X number employees)
Telephone charges (fixed line rental, variable call charges)	Call centre operator (one per X number of calls)

17–84   Figure 17.1 presents the four cost behaviour patterns (variable, fixed, step and mixed) in diagrammatic format.

Figure 17.1: Cost behaviour patterns

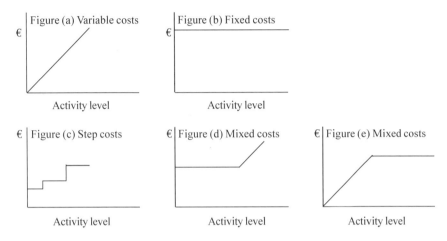

The fixed and variable behaviour pattern of historical costs may also change after the injury. Additionally, the lost incremental profit as a result of the injury may alter as the period from the date of the wrongful act gets longer. This shrinkage of incremental profit margin over time is related to the obligation of the plaintiff to mitigate damages.

17–85   The example in Table 17.2 serves to illustrate the importance of variable or marginal costs in loss of profits analysis. The important measure of profit in such cases is the difference between incremental revenue and associated costs. This is called contribution.

Statistical methods for estimating variable and fixed costs

17–86   Statistical techniques can be used to measure the correlation coefficient between revenue and various cost categories. The correlation coefficients can be ranked from most variable to least variable depending on the size of the correlation coefficient. Perfectly variable costs will have a correlation coefficient of one whereas fixed costs will have a correlation coefficient of zero.

17–87   A more precise statistical technique for measuring the degree of variability of cost to revenue is linear regression analysis (see para. **17–70**). Simple regression analysis can be used when it is not straightforward whether costs are variable or fixed. Regression analysis studies a series of historic cost relationships and reduces them to an algebraic line formula. Individual observations (which may be monthly, quarterly or annual) of cost and revenue

Table 17.2: Example of loss of profits consequent on breach of contract

Assume a printing company has 10 contracts each with an annual sales value (excluding VAT) of €100,000 p.a. The variable cost for each contract (comprising raw materials) is €20,000. Because the business requires sophisticated, technologically-advanced, expensive machinery, computer equipment and software, it has high fixed costs of €700,000 p.a.

The annual profit and loss account for such a business would be as follows:

	€000
Sales (€100,000 x 10 contracts)	1,000
Variable costs (€20,000 x 10 contracts)	(200)
Contribution	800
Fixed costs	700
Net profit	100

Assuming the business loses one of its 10 contracts, the following would be the profit and loss account for the year:

	€000
Sales (€100,000 x 9 contracts)	900
Variable costs (€20,000 x 9 contracts)	(180)
Contribution	720
Fixed costs	700
Net profit	20

Annual profits of the company have reduced from €100,000 to €20,000 – a reduction of €80,000. This is due to the loss of the contract which has cost the company €80,000. The following shows the make-up of this loss:

	Original	*After loss of contract*	*Change*
	€000	€000	€000
Sales (€100,000 x 10/9 contracts)	1,000	900	(100)
Variable costs (€20,000 x 10/9 contracts)	(200)	(180)	20
Contribution	800	720	(80)
Fixed costs	700	700	
Net profit	100	20	

Thus, the annual loss of profits of €80,000 is entirely due to the loss in contribution from the lost contract (*i.e.* variable revenue (€100,000) less variable cost (€20,000)). The contribution is high (at 80%) because of the nature of the business – one that has high fixed costs.

are plotted and a line of best fit is obtained. After the observed costs have been plotted, a line can be mathematically determined that represents estimated costs at various levels of production. Regression analysis can be used to separate costs that vary with sales from those that do not.

This technique is more precise than the other methods used by accountants to separate out variable and fixed cost elements. It has, however, limitations from a statistical point of view which could be attacked by the other side. For example, if the amount of variation explained by the regression is low, it could be argued that other factors explain more of the variation in revenue. By examining this information, an accountant can estimate the foregone overhead costs associated with the lost sales.

17–88   To obtain greater confidence in any cost estimation, the analyst can evaluate whether an estimate is reasonable by comparing the results under more than one methodology. The results can be compared with historical data, with independent estimates or with industry statistics.

Cost estimation

17–89   Like lost revenues, costs may not be susceptible to precise calculation, in which case they must be estimated. Unfortunately, most financial statements do not distinguish between fixed and variable costs. Given this difficulty in using aggregate amounts as disclosed in financial statements, individual cost categories must be examined to decide which vary with the level of revenue.

17–90   The appropriate estimation technique depends on the purposes of the analysis and, in some cases, the information available. The proper sorting of accounting costs into variable and fixed overhead categories requires considerable experience and judgment. The method of estimation itself can become an issue during litigation. Costs can be estimated by analysing historical information and applying professional judgment and/or analytical techniques. In some cases, reports already available within the company may contain cost information; in other cases, data accumulated by the company's accounting systems may be analysed to estimate costs. If this data is unavailable, the analyst may be required to rely on outside information from government or industry sources. In the absence of adequate information on variable costs, gross profit percentages from a similar industry can be substituted.

The use of the methods described above may be further complicated by factors such as inflation, volume discounts, technological change and accounting principles.

Owners' compensation from profits

17–91   Generally speaking, management salaries are fixed annual amounts and should not be deducted in calculating lost profits. An exception to this might be where it can be shown that management time was diverted from more profitable activity with the result that the business suffered. Plaintiffs may need to record details of such management time, as the court will not speculate on quantum by awarding some percentage of expenditure.[26] Where management or other compensation varies with revenue (*e.g.* sales commission) it should be deducted.

---

[26] *Tate and Lyle Food and Distribution Ltd v. Greater London Council* [1981] 3 All E.R. 716.

Where compensation is payable to the owners of the business, a similar distinction should be made between fixed and variable costs, fixed salaries to owners should not be deducted in lost profits calculations. It should be noted, however, that there have been numerous legal decisions in the United States requiring that owners' compensation be deducted in arriving at the amount of lost profits in contrast to generally not deducting management compensation.[27]

Extra costs incurred due to the injury

17–92   Generally, in computing lost profit, fixed costs are ignored. This is because fixed costs generally would have been incurred with or without business interference. However, there are occasions where some fixed costs would be included in lost profits computations. Extra costs incurred by the plaintiff as a result of the injury or interruption must be added to the other losses. For example, the injured party may have to incur fixed costs in an attempt to mitigate the damages caused by the other party.

Additional costs (sometimes called incidental costs) incurred as a result of the commercial injury are generally not difficult to calculate. Fixed costs before and after the business interruption may need to be examined to see if any have risen as a result of the interruption. An analysis of fixed costs trends will help to identify any additional fixed costs so incurred. The interruption may cause extraordinary expenses that should be added to the claim. Examples include penalties incurred for any contracts cancelled as a result of the injury, out-of-pocket expenses, costs of mitigation and plant closure costs. Plaintiffs typically itemise such costs explicitly in their statement of claim and may also provide supporting documentation. Care should be taken not to double count costs already included in the loss of profits calculation.

Methods of cost estimation

17–93   Methods of estimating costs include:

– direct costs assignment;

– account analysis;

– cost accounting analysis.

Direct costs assignment

17–94   Direct costs assignment is generally simple and reliable in the appropriate circumstances (*e.g.* a dispute over the cost of a particular product). The analysis uses information concerning costs related directly to a product

---

[27]Gaughan, P.A. "Economic and financial issues in lost profits ligitation" in *Litigation Economics* (Gaughan, P.A. and Thornton, R.J. (eds) (JAI Press, Grenwich, Connecticut), pp. 180–181.

(such as raw materials, direct labour) often obtained from invoices or financial statements. Because these costs can be volatile (particularly material prices), fluctuation in price must be considered. Also, use of certain accounting principles may require adjustment to the financial data.

Account analysis

17–95   In account analysis, various expense categories are reviewed to judge those costs that are fixed and those that are variable. These costs can be divided by the appropriate number of units sold or manufactured to obtain the cost per unit. One drawback to this approach is the difficulty in classifying semi-variable and semi-fixed costs. This introduces an element of subjectivity into the calculation.

Cost accounting analysis

17–96   Cost accounting analysis often involves two methodologies: ratio analysis and regression analysis. Ratio analysis involves establishing relationships between certain costs and some measure of production such as units produced, units sold, sales revenue or direct labour hours. For example, total overhead cost might be divided by total direct labour hours. This approach might not be appropriate under all circumstances, however, such as cases in which the marginal or incremental cost is at issue and is likely to differ significantly from variable costs. In addition, it may be necessary to perform an analysis over several previous years to evaluate the relevance and accuracy of current financial information.

Ex ante *and* ex post *approaches to damage calculations*

17–97   Controversy surrounds whether projections of losses should be based on expectations at the time of the injury or at the time of compensation. There are two choices for measuring lost profits, based on fundamentally different temporal perspectives, which can significantly affect the amount of damages calculated:

(1) The *ex ante* approach (also called the lost going concern value) treats a harm to profitability as a loss in the firm's value suffered at the time of impact, which by definition ignores the effect of post-impact events on the firm's expected "but for" and actual experience. The extent of loss may be measured *ex ante, i.e.* at the point of impact when the injured firm's "but for" and actual prospects begin to diverge. Such an assessment compares the expectations, at the time of impact, of the firm's subsequent experience "but for" the wrongful conduct and expectations, at the time of impact, of the firm's subsequent experience taking into account the wrongful conduct's effects. Because time may elapse between wrongful conduct and its impact on the injured firm, a different *ex ante* approach could be adopted that is

based on expectations at the time of the wrongful act. A time of impact perspective, however, is more attuned to judging the propriety of the conduct at issue or matters of causation (both of which can be judged at time of impact), rather than to estimating the extent of lost profits (which may be best judged in the light of events occurring after the time of impact consequent on the wrongful act).

– The *ex post* approach (also called the lost future profits approach) treats the harm as a stream of profit losses suffered after impact, which allows post-impact events to influence the measurement of the losses. The extent of loss may be measured *ex post*, *i.e.* at the time the damages are being litigated. The critical difference is that a time of trial assessment permits reliance on post-impact events in constructing the firm's "but for" and actual experience.

17–98 The two methodologies can yield radically different estimates of the plaintiff's losses as is illustrated in Table 17.3. Two sets of calculations are shown in this table – one based on the *ex ante* time of impact approach and the other based on the *ex post* time of trial approach.

The date of the wrongful act is assumed to be January 2000. In the *ex ante* time of trial case, the "but for" profits are based on the company's projections at the time of the wrongful act. The "actual" results are based on revised company projections – revised immediately after the wrongful act, based on expectations at the time of the injury and taking its effect into account. Assuming the projections are reliable, the projected future losses amount to €510,000. These losses would need to be discounted to present value to take account of the time value of money and any risk factors inherent in the business. These figures are taken at the time the injury occurred and rest entirely on expectations at the time of the injury.

The date of trial is assumes to be 20X2. By that time, it is apparent that events have not turned out as expected at the time of the wrongful act. By the time of trial, the reduction in actual profits (projected at time of impact/wrongful act) has not materialised and actual profits have recovered well after the injury. In this *ex post* time of trial approach the lost profits comprise actual profits lost up to the date of trial and projected lost profits thereafter (discounted to present value to take the time value of money into account). The "but for" profits are the projected profits before the wrongful act but these projections have been adjusted to take account of changes in assumptions in the light of post-injury actual events. The total lost under this approach is considerably less at €180,000.

To summarise, there is a variation in the calculation of lost profits based on these two approaches of €330,000 (€510,000$_{Ex\ ante}$ − €180,000$_{Ex\ post}$). In this example, under the *ex ante* approach, projected future losses are €330,000 higher than under the *ex post* method.Clearly, the *ex post* method is the preferable approach in that it takes into account all known facts available at the time the case is being heard.

Table 17.3: Comparison of the *ex ante* and *ex post* approaches to measuring lost profits

Year	Ex ante Time of impact "But for" – Actual profits €000	Difference €000	Ex post Time of trial "But for" – Actual profits €000	Difference €000	Time of impact v. Time of trial €000
20X0[1]	240–210	(30)	240–210	(30)	0
20X1	270–195	(75)	270–210	(60)	15
20X2[2]	300–210	(90)	285–240	(45)	45
20X3	330–225	(105)	300–270	(30)	75
20X4	360–255	(105)	315–300	(15)	90
20X5	390–285	(105)	330–330	(0)	105
		(510)		(180)	330

[1] Time of injury
[2] Time of trial

Source: Adapted from Taurman, J.D. and Bodington, J.C., "Measuring damage to a firm's profitability: ex ante or ex post?" in *The Antitrust Bulletin* (Spring 1992), pp. 57–106.

Lost profits or lost cash flow

17–99   The choice of time at which calculations are performed can have a substantial impact on the amount of damages, as shown in the *ex ante* and *ex post* approaches just discussed. As can be seen from Chapter 16 on damages, the law does not provided detailed guidance for forensic accountants on how to calculate damages. No exclusive or prescriptive ways of performing the calculations are laid out in statute for example. A further complication in relation to the calculations is whether the forensic accountant bases calculations on lost profits or lost cash flow.[28] A number of factors influence the choice, as follows:

(1) Type of damages – damages may be in the form of out-of-pocket losses or lost profits. Out-of-pocket losses are generally calculated on a cash basis. Damages are the total amount of cash paid out less any cash received. Less guidance is available concerning which approach to use in calculating lost profits – either the profit or cash approach is valid and may be acceptable to the courts.

(2) Amount of capital expenditure on fixed assets – profits are calculated after deducting a charge for depreciation representing the proportion of the fixed asset cost utilised in the period. Under the cash approach, the cost of the fixed asset is deducted at the time of its acquisition when it is paid for. Over the total life of the fixed asset there will be no difference between the two methods, but there may be differences during the useful life of the asset and

---

[28] Wagner, M.J., "How to measure damages? Lost income or lost cash flow" in *Journal of Accountancy* (February 1990), pp. 28–31 and 33.

present values also differ where costs are recognised in different time periods. Such differences can be substantial where the value of fixed assets is substantial, *e.g.* in Table 17.4 shown below, profits amount to €800,000 per annum for the five years, whereas under the cash method, there is a nil cash flow in 20X0, and a net cash inflow of €1 million in the four years thereafter. Over the five-year period, as shown by the total column, there is no overall differences between the two methods of calculating the performance of the business.

Table 17.4: Comparison of lost profits and lost cash flow approaches

Year	20X0	20X1	20X2	20X3	20X4	Total
	€000	€000	€000	€000	€000	€000
Income	1,000	1,000	1,000	1,000	1,000	5,000
Depreciation	(200)	(200)	(200)	(200)	(200)	(1,000)
Profit	800	800	800	800	800	4,000
Cash inflow	1,000	1,000	1,000	1,000	1,000	5,000
Cash outflow	(1,000)	—	—	—	—	(1,000)
Net cash flow	nil	1,000	1,000	1,000	1,000	4,000

(3) Timing – as shown in the calculations above, the timing of the calculation of the expense write off will, under the two methods, result in differing amounts of damages (except at the end of the asset's useful life).

Under the two methods there is a difference in the timing of recognising expenses. This difference in timing of recognition may then have knock-on effects on the net present value calculations and calculations of pre-judgment interest (see Chapter 19 for further consideration of these two topics). Because the capital expenditures on fixed assets are paid for in the first year, lower damages are projected in the early years under the cash basis, which results in lower cumulative discounted damages (and vice versa for the profit-based approach). Thus, normally there is a higher net present value of future damages under the profit approach rather than cash flow approach – but this is not always the case and both calculations should be considered at the outset. The differences between the two methods will be greater the higher the discount rate, the longer the loss period and the greater the differences in the quantum costs of assets.

Opportunity cost

17–100   In addition, opportunity cost must be taken into account. The concept of loss of profits and loss of opportunity must be distinguished. The concept of lost opportunity caused by a wrongful act is the loss of the chance to earn profits in the future, rather than the loss of profits themselves. The courts normally regard loss of profits as a form of pure economic loss. Future economic loss is less likely to be recoverable on the grounds of uncertainty. A number of cases have argued that damages for loss of opportunity should be recoverable but to date there have been no conclusive authorities on the point. However, in *Dunne v. Fox*,[29] where the matter at issue was the basis on which recoverable costs should be calculated on behalf of a firm of accountants engaged in providing non-party discovery, Laffoy J. recognised the concept of opportunity costs and held that they were an appropriate basis for the calculation of costs incurred by the firm (see para. **22–35** for further discussion of this case).

If the plaintiff is to recover damages in respect of opportunity costs, he must satisfy the courts that he had a reasonable expectation of obtaining the benefits of the opportunity he claims to have lost. A person who is wrongfully deprived of an opportunity to obtain a benefit may recover damages for the loss of an opportunity even though it cannot be proved with certainty that the opportunity would have been taken or any benefit obtained.[30] Courts may discount the opportunity costs for some element of uncertainty therein.[31]

17–101   One of the most common opportunity costs considered is the return on capital, were the capital invested elsewhere. Just as future losses are discounted to present value, past losses should be adjusted to present value. This requires the firm's opportunity cost to be measured. If the injured firm had access to lost profits, it could have invested these in the firm's operations. These reinvested profits would have earned a return at the firm's cost of capital.[32] Opportunity costs are ignored in accounting records as they do not represent out-of-pocket expenses. This can very easily lead to double counting with actual costs. Extreme care must be taken in including opportunity costs in any calculation of damages suffered.

Other damage calculation considerations

17–102   There are a number of additional issues to be considered by forensic accountants in damages calculations. The role played by assumptions in such calculations and the presentation of lost profits calculations are discussed below.

Role of assumptions

17–103   Assumptions play a crucial role in damages calculations. Expert evidence is often based on the use of such assumptions. Reference has been made throughout this chapter to the use of assumptions, for example, in projecting revenues. Chapter 23 also refers throughout to the use of assumptions in drafting expert reports. Assumptions may be made by the expert accountants or may

---

[29] [1999] 1 I.R. 283.
[30] *Allied Maples Group Ltd v. Simmons and Simmons* [1995] 4 All E.R. 907.
[31] *First Interstate Bank of California v. Cohen Arnold & Co* [1996] P.N.L.R. 17.
[32] The cost of capital of a firm is the rate of return the firm must earn which is just sufficient to maintain the value of the business.

derive from instructions to the expert from the solicitor and client. The expert may have to make assumptions to compensate for missing information. Assumptions are often outside the expert's own area of expertise and he will have to rely on the input of another expert (*e.g.* an actuary or an economist). The assumptions relied upon should be clearly stated in the expert's report.

The assumptions used in making the projections are matters for vigorous cross-examination, and demand a firm basis and foundation. Some assumptions cannot be made in the realm of accounting principles on their own. However, the accountant can quantify the effect of the assumptions of other experts on financial results.

Types of assumptions

17–104 Experts may rely on three types of assumption[33]:

(1) Factual assumptions: Experts may be asked to assume various facts. To the extent possible and practical the expert should try to verify the facts given to him as part of his brief. Where assumptions of fact are based on evidence to be given in the proceedings, the forensic accountant should discuss with his instructing lawyers the relative strength and persuasiveness of the evidence.

(2) Assumptions of other experts: As already stated in para. **17–103**, it is common to use multiple experts. Each expert may have to rely on the assumptions of other experts. Forensic accountants, in particular, will commonly rely on economists, whereas actuaries tend to rely on accountants.

(3) Economic and financial assumptions: These are the assumptions provided by the expert in the damage calculations. Examples include the rate of inflation, discount rate, rate of growth, etc.

Defence tactics concerning assumptions

17–105 Significant reductions in the amount of damages awarded can be achieved where assumptions used by plaintiffs' experts are attacked and undermined by the defence. It is therefore essential that the defence identifies and understands all assumptions used by the plaintiff. The effect of each assumption on calculations should be established and sensitivity analysis should be performed to assist in identifying those assumptions that are most important to the damages calculation.

Presentation of lost profits calculations

17–106 The previous paragraphs have discussed the calculation of lost profits

---

[33] Gaughan, P.A., *Measuring Commercial Damages* (John Wiley & Sons, Inc, New York, 2000), pp. 38–39.

consisting of lost revenues, less associated variable costs, plus any additional overhead and other costs incurred by the damaged party as a result of the interruption. Lost profit calculations are often presented as pro forma statements (see example in Table 17.5). The actual performance and the performance "but for" the injury can be shown side-by-side in the familiar profit and loss account format. Common size ratios can be used in such pro-forma statements, such that each cost is presented as a percentage of sales. The pro-forma "but for" figures can be compared with the actual results, the difference being the lost profits. The pro-forma statement can be expanded to include calculations based on different assumptions, resulting in a range of forecasts.

Table 17.5: Example pro-forma profit and loss account

	Actual results		"But for" results		Difference (Lost profits)
	€000	%	€000	%	€000
Sales	2,000	100.0	3,000	100.0	(1,000)
Cost of sales – variable costs	(700)	(35.0)	(1,050)	(35.0)	350
Cost of sales – fixed costs	(400)	(20.0)	(400)	(13.3)	—
Gross profit	900	45.0	1,550	51.7	(650)
Distribution costs	(250)	(12.5)	(375)	(12.5)	125
Administration expenses	(150)	(7.5)	(150)	(5.0)	—
Net operating profit	500	25.0	1,025	34.2	(525)
Interest paid	(80)	(4.0)	(80)	(2.7)	—
Profit after interest before tax	420	21.0	945	31.5	(525)
Taxation @ 20%	(84)	(4.2)	(189)	(6.3)	105
Profit after interest after tax	336	16.8	756	25.2	(420)

Loss of asset values

17–107   As well as advising on loss of profits, forensic accountants may be asked to value individual assets of the business for the purpose of quantifying loss of value of those assets. The particular type of assets to be valued must be researched. Market value has to be determined through research, trial marketing, and experience in selling such assets. Examples of such assets include:

– intellectual property such as brands, copyrights, mastheads;

– stocks;

– debtors.

Lost asset model

17–108   The value of an asset is the discounted present value of expected future net cash flows which derive from the asset. Any asset that has value and is marketable may command a market price, since a knowledgeable buyer may be willing to pay for the right to receive the asset's future cash flows. The price such buyers would be willing to pay is called the fair market value of the asset.

17–109 If a wrongful act reduces or eliminates the expected cash flows of an asset, increases the variability or riskiness of those cash flows, or reduces the marketability (liquidity) of the asset, then the market price of the asset may be reduced and the current owner of the asset may have suffered a loss. The lost asset model is as follows:

Loss = Value of asset before wrongful act – Value of asset after wrongful act

17–110 Both the before and after valuations must be calculated at the same point in time. The value at each point of time is the capitalised value of the net cash flows, defined as the present value of future cash revenues less future cash costs, associated with the asset.

Property damage cases

17–111 These cases are often ones where accounting records are least relevant. Damages in such cases usually consist of a decline in the fair market value of the damaged property. Accounting records do not purport to show fair value, although they may be useful in evaluating the condition, age and utility of the asset. Depreciated replacement value of an asset is easily calculated, but economic value is even more important because of the utility of the asset.

Goodwill damages

17–112 Goodwill is defined as the excess of the fair value of the business as a whole over the fair value of the total of the individual net tangible and other intangible assets of the business. Goodwill is a synergistic residual of all of the net tangible assets of a business along with intangible assets and other assets not measured, such as the value of the clientele, location, reputation, and competitive advantage of the business.

17–113 Goodwill damages are difficult to assess. Normally, goodwill is only recognised in financial statements when it has been paid for. Internally generated goodwill is not recognised, mainly because it is so difficult to measure objectively. Determining goodwill may be based on any one of a number of available formulas, such as capitalising excess profits at a risk rate of interest. Goodwill damages require the establishment of the existence of goodwill before some event, and a decline in this value directly caused by the event, and not by economic or other conditions.

Loss of working capital

17–114   If the wrongful act involves loss of working capital (current assets less current liabilities) to the plaintiff, financial analysis can be used to estimate the amount of lost profit that would have been generated by the lost work capital (this would be in addition to compensation for the lost working capital itself). The following statement of financial relationships can be useful:

$$\text{Profit} = \frac{\text{Profit}}{\text{Revenue}} \quad \times \quad \frac{\text{Revenue}}{\text{Working Capital}} \quad \times \text{Working Capital}$$

The ratio of profit to revenue is the lost profit margin. The ratio of revenue to working capital is a standard financial ratio – for which industry standards may be available. If the wrongful act results in a loss of working capital to the plaintiff then its impact on profit can be estimated by multiplying the loss of working capital by the two standard ratios.

If the wrongful act involves damage to stock (*e.g.* fire, flood, theft), then the expert can similarly use the stock turnover ratio (the revenue to stock ratio) to arrive at a lost profits estimate:

$$\text{Profit} = \frac{\text{Profit}}{\text{Revenue}} \quad \times \quad \frac{\text{Revenue}}{\text{Stock}} \quad \times \text{Stock}$$

Effect of taxation on commercial damages

17–115   The effect of taxation on personal injury damages has been considered in paras **16–123** *et seq*. Similar principles apply to the calculation of commercial damages. However, the effect is quite different – mainly because personal injury lump sum awards are not subject to income tax whereas commercial damages are generally taxable. Compensation payments are taxable according to the nature of what they are compensating.[34]

---

[34] This section touches on this topic, which is dealt with in more detail by Corrigan: Corrigan, K., *Revenue Law* (Round Hall Sweet & Maxwell, Dublin, 2000), Vols I and II, Chaps 11 (paras 11–366 *et seq.*) and 28. Taxation of damages is considered in Lemar, C.J. and Mainz, A.J. (eds), *Litigation Support* (4th ed., Butterworths, London, 1999), Chap. 15. MacGregor, G. and Hobbs, I. *Expert Accounting Evidence: A Guide for Litigation Support* (Accountancy Books, London, 1998), Chap. 19. Taub, M., Rapazzini, A., Bond, C., Solon, M. Brown, A., Murrie A., Linnell, K. and Burn, S., *Tolley's Accountancy Litigation Support* (Butterworths, London, looseleaf), Part VI, para. 115.

Taxation of commercial damages

17–116 From a taxation point of view, business can be divided into two groups: sole traders or partnerships whose profits are subject to income (and other) tax – the tax payer being the owner(s), and incorporated businesses, whose profits are subject to corporation tax.

Damages awarded to sole traders/partnerships

17–117 Damages paid to a sole trader in compensation for loss of profits are fully taxable under Schedule D Case I. Compensation for loss of profits is taxed as income.[35]

17–118 Compensation for damages to business capital assets are not subject to income tax but may be subject to capital gains tax under section 535(2)(a) of the Taxes Consolidation Act 1997.

Damages awarded to companies

17–119 It is generally agreed that the appropriate measure of a firm's loss is the after-tax net cash flow. The award of pre-tax lost income only yields the correct compensation if: (i) the time between loss and compensation spans no change in tax rates or relevant tax law; (ii) discounting is performed with after-tax rates; and (iii) the injury causes no changes in the timing of after-tax income, extra tax costs or the loss of tax benefits. The proponents of after-tax estimates of damages also propose that an allowance for tax on an award be added to the damage request.

Taxable commercial damages

17–120 In non-personal injury cases, payment received in compensation (for example for breach of contract) is generally treated as a trading receipt in the accounts of the business and is taxable on receipt. In *London and Thames Haven Oil Wharves Ltd v. Attwooll*, it was explained that such compensation should be calculated gross:

> "Where, pursuant to a legal right, a trader receives ... compensation for the trader's failure to receive a sum of money which ... would have been credited to ... profits ... the compensation is to be treated for income tax purposes in the same way as that sum of money would have been treated if it had been received instead of the compensation."[36]

17–121 The general principle is that a lump sum paid in compensation, even if described as a capital sum, is treated for tax purposes as trading income rather than as a capital receipt if it is made in lieu of revenue receipts forgone or

---

[35] *Hickey & Co Ltd v. Roches Stores* [1980] I.L.R.M. 107.
[36] [1967] Ch. 772 at 815 *per* Lord Diplock.

revenue expenditure incurred. In *Corr v. Larkin*,[37] a sum received under a loss of profits insurance policy, although described as a capital sum, was held to be a revenue receipt. Similarly, compensation for loss of profits arising from the bombing of a business premises in Belfast, even though business was never recommenced, was held to be a trading receipt by the Northern Ireland Court of Appeal in *Lang v. Rice*.[38]

Commercial damages not taxable

17–122   However, there are exceptions. Where the compensation is awarded to replace a particular asset, or where the trader can establish that the non-performance of a contact resulted in the loss of the whole, or substantially whole, structure of his profit-making apparatus, then the compensation may be treated as a capital receipt, *e.g.* see *Van den Berghs Ltd v. Clark*.[39] For example, a business reliant on one contract may treat the compensation for loss of this contract as a capital receipt, not to be treated as part of taxable profits. However, capital receipts give rise to capital gains tax liabilities and, hence, are also to be awarded gross.

Compensation for loss of profits

17–123   The receipt of compensation may not always be taxed in the way that the lost profits for which the payment compensates would have been taxed. The principal difference is the timing of the imposition of tax on the amount in question. Typically, the compensation is calculated, using appropriate discounting techniques, as the lump sum that is required to replace the lost profits over the period of the loss. However, although the lost profits, had they been earned, would have been taxed by reference to the period in which they were earned, the tax on the compensation will be payable in respect of the period in which the compensation is received. Accordingly, the tax is normally paid sooner than it would have been had the wrong that caused the lost profits not occurred, and an appropriate adjustment to the compensation would be necessary to allow for this difference in timing.

17–124   The taxation characteristics attaching to compensation in respect of loss of profits, and the taxation treatment of the compensation, were considered in *Corr v. Larkin*.[40] This judgment is the definitive Irish judgment on the tax treatment of insurance proceeds of loss of profits policies.

This case involved a claim for loss of profits following a fire in the insured's bakery. At the time, insurance coverage against lost profits was uncommon and

[37][1949] I.R. 399.
[38](1983) 57 T.C. 80.
[39](1935) 19 T.C. 390.
[40][1949] I.R. 399.

the circumstances of the case were regarded as quite special. However, the principles established by Maguire J. in the High Court, in considering a case stated by the Circuit Judge, are of general application. The court decided that the compensation was a revenue rather than a capital receipt, representing a trading receipt to be taxed as income. The judge also considered the timing for accounting for and taxing the compensation. Following his decision, the compensation is taken into account for tax purposes in the accounting period immediately following that in which the compensation can first be ascertained and not the period covered by the loss nor when the compensation is paid. Where stage payments are made the same criteria apply.

Gourley *principle*

17–125   The *Gourley* principle has already been considered in paras **16–125** *et seq.* in the context of personal injury damages. A distinction can be drawn between personal injury cases and commercial cases – personal injury damages awards are generally not taxable in the hands of recipients whereas, as set out above, commercial damages are taxable.

   In applying the *Gourley* principle, gross damages are reduced to take into account the plaintiff's tax liability (*i.e.* personal plaintiffs are not liable to tax and so the damages award is reduced for the consequent tax saving) – but this is only done where the damages or compensation are tax free. In order to apply this rule, the forensic accountant needs to know the tax treatment of the original loss and the tax treatment of the damages or compensation. The plaintiff's tax position needs to be known to calculate the exact amount of damages. The calculation can take into account tax planning opportunities.

17–126   Application of the well-known *Gourley* principle to loss of profits cases was tested in the United Kingdom in *Amstrad plc v. Seagate Technology Inc.*[41] In a product liability case, Amstrad was awarded damages of £56 million in respect of loss of profits arising from hard disk drives supplied by Seagate that were defective. The corporation tax rate at the time of the loss was 34 per cent whereas it had reduced to 31 per cent at the time of the judgment for damages. The argument put forward by Seagate's legal team was that the award would overcompensate Amstrad since Amstrad would be taxed at a lower rate on the award (31 per cent) compared with the tax the company would have paid (34 per cent) had the lost profits actually been earned.

   Amstrad, on the other hand relying, *inter alia*, on the court of appeal judgment in *Parsons v. BNM Laboratories Ltd,*[42] was of the view that no account should be taken of taxation on lost income if the damages would be subject to taxation,

---

[41] (1997) 86 B.L.R. 34. See also Ellison, J. and Chandler, B., "Damages and interest in loss of profits claims" in *The Forensic Accountant* (1998), Issue 17, pp. 2–3.
[42] [1964] 1 Q.B. 95.

even if the basis of taxation were different. The justification for this view was that the calculation of damages could become unnecessarily complicated and difficult. In line with this, Amstrad also argued that the effect of taxation should be ignored.

The judge did not uphold this argument on the grounds that it would result in damages greater than the actual loss. He stated:

> "It is therefore clear that unless account is taken in the assessment of damages of the incidence of taxation, the award will be more than the loss which Amstrad is taken to have suffered. Am I compelled to ignore the incidence of taxation and to give judgement for more than Amstrad's supposed actual loss? I think not."[43]

Compensation for premises, plant and machinery

17–127   Subject to certain exceptions, compensation by way of capital sum for damage or injury to an asset, for destruction or dissipation of an asset or for any depreciation or risk of depreciation of an asset gives rise to a disposal for the purposes of the capital gains tax, even though no asset is acquired by the person paying the compensation (see section 535 of the Taxes Consolidation Act 1997). This point was confirmed in the case of *Golding v. Kaufmann*.[44]

Roll-over relief

17–128   Section 536 of the Taxes Consolidation Act 1997 provides for a limited form of roll-over relief when the compensation monies received are reinvested. In practice, three such scenarios can occur where the compensation monies are reinvested in whole or in part and no disposal is deemed to arise. These are:

– the asset is not fully destroyed and the compensation is fully reinvested;

– the asset is destroyed totally and the compensation is fully reinvested;

– part only of the compensation is reinvested.

The tax treatment varies depending on which of these three scenarios arise. There is no full roll-over relief as would apply where an asset is sold and the proceeds reinvested in a similar business asset.

17–129   Under section 980 of the Taxes Consolidation Act 1997, where compensation constitutes a disposal of certain specified assets (including land, minerals, certain shares and goodwill of a trade) and exceeds £100,000, the insurance company or court must deduct 15 per cent of the compensation and pay this amount directly to the Revenue, unless the plaintiff can produce the necessary tax certificate.

---

[43] *Amstrad plc v. Seagate Technology Inc* (1997) 86 B.L.R. 34 at 52, *per* Lloyd J.
[44] [1985] S.T.C. 152.

Role of forensic accountants

17–130 Proceedings involving a claim for lost profits or damage to asset values offer significant opportunities for forensic accountants to become involved. Some of the areas of potential involvement have been identified in this chapter. In such cases, the forensic accountant will need to consider carefully his approach to the task and to consider possible pitfalls. Some of these are summarised below.

Consideration of financial statements

17–131 The profit and loss account is typically the focus in calculating damages in terms of lost profits to a business. However, the profit and loss account is only one of three key financial statements to be considered in calculating an accurate damage analysis. Without examining the information in the balance sheet and cash flow statement the forensic accountant may not have all the financial information needed to make an accurate calculation. For example, a growing business needs to finance increased working capital requirements – the additional cash needs (and related interest costs) of this extra requirement should be taken into account. Other increasing business needs that should be considered include investment in fixed assets such as plant and equipment. The forensic accountant needs to analyse the cash flow implications of such requirements otherwise the forecasted operational needs of the business may be misstated. These types of problem often arise when businesses project significant increases in sales, but fail to factor in the additional cash and debt financing needs.

17–132 Accounting records are prepared on an accruals basis of accounting, whereby revenues and costs are recognised and included in the financial statements when they are earned or incurred, not when they are received or paid in cash. The cash basis of accounting may be more appropriate in certain circumstances.

Reliability

17–133 Quality of the data is an important consideration. Forensic accountants should not assume that the financial statements can be relied upon when using financial statement data for calculating lost profits. There are a number of reasons why financial statements may not be reliable:

– transactions included in the financial statements may not have occurred in that period (*e.g.* booking revenue early, before the revenue has been properly realised);

– unreported transactions;

– inaccurate measurement of revenues and expenses;

– inaccurate description of revenues and expenses.

17–134 Financial statements of companies will generally have been subject to audit, whereas the financial statements of a sole trader or partnership may have been prepared but not audited by a firm of accountants. The latter financial statements may be less reliable than audited financial statements.

17–135 Consistency in accounting methods from one period to another is important. Income can be raised or lowered by judicious selection of accounting policies. Comparison of the policies with those of similar companies in the same industry may highlight such selections. Disclosures may be incomplete or misleading. Disappearing accounting records may also be a problem. Records may have been mislaid or discarded.

17–136 Forensic accountants are limited by the information provided to them. Accounting numbers are essential in computing and supporting the financial calculations. The foundation of the calculation must be built securely on all available data. The failure to use all available data, or to have knowledge of what is available, can be very damaging to a case. Forensic accountants can assist in the early stages of a case in the acquisition of information by formulating interrogatories, requests for voluntary discovery and requests to admit facts. Forensic accountants may also assist in evaluating the quality, integrity and sufficiency of the data available in respect of their client's case.

Reconstruction of accounting records

17–137 Accounting records may need to be re-created in various circumstances. The initial objective is to create or re-create the books. Relational databases (*i.e.* that links data together) may be used in the reconstruction of accounting records. Table 17.6 shows the various circumstances in which forensic accountants might be involved in reconstructing accounting records.

Recasting profits

17–138 In private companies certain expenses charged to the company may not strictly relate to the company (*e.g.* personal and household expenditure of the principal shareholders). Private companies often control taxable income through the use of expenses that are in reality distributions to shareholders. Shareholders in, say, a family company may choose to take some of their return in the form of directors' emoluments rather than dividends. In addition, compensation paid to the owner and family members may be more or less than the market rate that would be paid to a third party performing the same tasks. Thus, the net profit history of the company may show only limited profits. The true profitability of the business may need to be reconstructed. A series of add-backs will need to be identified in such cases, together with related tax effects, in order to calculate the true profitability of the business.

Table 17.6: Examples of incomplete records cases in which forensic accountants have advised

---

Civil litigation
- Reconstructing accounting records claimed to have been lost or stolen
- Reconstructing profit and loss statements that were destroyed, *e.g.* as a result of a fire or flood
- Reconstructing accounts from the limited accounting information available in the case of a sole trader where no accounts have been prepared.

Criminal litigation
- Reconstructing incomplete tax records
- Reconstructing cash transactions in support of proof of money laundering activities
- Reconstructing accounting records from incomplete supporting documentation for defence against Revenue criminal charges
- Reconstructing accounting records misstated as a result of manipulation by accounting and management personnel.

Approach by expert accountant for the defendant

17–139 A view often expressed is that defendants should not provide expert evidence in relation to the amount of damages as this might add credibility to the concept that there are measurable damages. It is widely considered that defence experts should only be used to attack the plaintiff's detailed damages calculations, but should not prepare alternative figures. Even where a defence expert provides evidence that the plaintiff's claim for damages is overstated, his lower estimate may only be used to provide an average of the higher plaintiff's estimate and the lower defence estimate. Conversely, if a defence damages calculation is not available, the plaintiff's calculations may be accepted in the absence of any alternative.

Conduct a causation investigation

17–140 It may be preferable to begin with a causation investigation. The expert reviews the injury and attempts to identify other potential causes of the alleged damages. For example, the expert might conduct market research to determine whether changes in the marketplace caused the plaintiff's business to lose profits. The expert's researches might indicate that the damages were self-inflicted or that a new competitor entered the market thereby causing the plaintiff to lose sales. This information is available from a variety of sources including annual reports, the Internet or interviews with other companies in the industry.

A causation investigation is valuable for a number of reasons. First, it allows the expert to begin work before obtaining the opposing expert's analysis. In addition, if the expert can provide defence counsel with strong evidence of alternative causes, the importance of evidence on damages may be reduced.

Test the plaintiff's expert's model

17–141 The first step in this process is to challenge the fundamental assumptions in the opposing expert's damages model. Differences between experts can arise based on technical lost profit assumptions such as rates of revenue growth, incremental lost profit margin for calculating lost profits, appropriate discount rate for arriving at present value of future lost profits and how far out the damages period should extend. Experts should consider whether the assumptions used are valid and supportable.

The sensitivity of the plaintiff's damages model to these assumptions needs to be considered. If the expert can show that the amount of damages calculated by the plaintiff's model changes dramatically with small changes in assumptions, the opposing expert's credibility may be impaired. Other relevant questions to be addressed include: Does the opposing expert use the appropriate methodology to calculate lost profits? Is there a reasonable basis for the discount used in calculating present value? Have mitigation issues been considered? The opposing expert should also test the mechanical accuracy of the plaintiff's expert's model. Simple mistakes can cause damages to be significantly misstated.

Create an alternative damages model

17–142 As pointed out above, many defence lawyers are reluctant to offer an alternative damages model in case it will establish a "floor" (*i.e.* the minimum amount of damages to be awarded). However, providing an alternative damages model may lend credibility to the defence and provide an alternative to the plaintiff's high damages number. An alternative damages model is most important when the plaintiff's case has merit – it the best way to contain the damages. Alternatively, if the plaintiff's case is frivolous, an alternative damages model is probably not necessary.

There are other difficulties involved when the duration of the loss period (in open interruption cases) or the future fair market value of the company (in infinite interruptions) are in question.

Concluding comment

17–143 The calculation of commercial damages is an area that gives the forensic accountant an opportunity to move centre stage. He is likely to be familiar not only with the legal principles surrounding the exercise but also with the business issues and accounting rules underlying the calculation. This leads to a chance to play a significant role in quantifying the claim and moving the matter to a resolution.

However, in these circumstances it is easy for the forensic accountant to fall prey to the temptation to demonstrate through his report, and possibly through his evidence, the breadth and depth of his knowledge. In doing so he can easily find himself emphasising areas that turn out to be of little or no relevance or significance to the issues at hand or the calculation itself.

The forensic accountant should always remember that, irrespective of the extent of his knowledge, the real value he adds is in remaining focused on the significant issues and in providing clear, understandable input on those issues that make a real difference to the outcome of the case.

CHAPTER 18

ACCOUNTING CALCULATIONS – VALUING BUSINESSES

CHAPTER 18

ACCOUNTING CALCULATIONS – VALUING BUSINESSES

18–01   There are many cases in litigation where knowledge of business valuation techniques and methods is necessary. Valuations may be required in a variety of legal situations such as divorce, oppression of minority shareholders cases, other shareholder disputes, partnership dissolution, etc. Valuations may involve quoted, or more usually unquoted, businesses and shares. Valuation of publicly quoted companies is the easier of the two as the shares are traded and valued daily (provided trading in the shares is active). However, in Ireland there are only approximately 100 publicly quoted companies so forensic accountants are much more likely to have to value private, closely held companies.

The subject of business valuations is complex and worthy of an entire book. This chapter is only intended to be an introduction and readers are referred to other sources for more detailed discussion.[1]

18–02   Business valuation is the process of assigning value to financial assets (*e.g.* shares) for which there is usually no financial trading market available. Accountants are often asked to give their opinion on the value of shares in a limited company. Chapters 7, 9 and 10 have indicated situations in which business valuations are required in litigation. This chapter provides some guidance on the valuation principles, techniques and methods involved in valuing private, closely held companies.

18–03   Establishing the real or market value of a business is rarely a simple process. Each business has unique circumstances requiring different (but acceptable) approaches to each valuation. A valuation substantiates a company's worth by setting values for all tangible and intangible assets. This requires a multidimensional analysis of the business, including a thorough review, analysis and interpretation of pertinent financial, economic, tax and industry data.

---

[1] More detailed discourses on share valuations can be found in Eastaway, N., Booth, H. and Eamer, K. *Practical Share Valuation* (4th ed., Butterworths, London, 1998); Giblin, B.H., *Valuation of Shares in Private Companies* (3rd ed., Institute of Taxation in Ireland, Dublin, 1999); Lokey, O.K. and Cefali, S.L., "Business valuations" in *Litigation Services Handbook. The Role of the Accountant as Expert* (2nd ed., Weil, R.L., Wagner, M.J. and Frank, P.B. (eds), John Wiley & Sons, Inc., New York, 1995), Chap. 29; Lemar, C.J. and Mainz, A.J. (eds), *Litigation Support* (4th ed., Butterworths, London, 1999), Chap. 4; Taub, M., Rapazzini, A., Bond, C., Solon, M., Brown, A., Murrie, A., Linnell, K. and

Business valuation is an area requiring expertise and is often unforgiving of attempts by non-specialists to produce values based on instinct or generic formulae.

Methodologies

18–04 Many different approaches and methods of valuation analysis should be reviewed and considered for use in relation to a specific business or asset being valued. A well-grounded estimate of fair market value, book value or investment value can be vastly different from true fair market value. It is essential to select the most appropriate methodologies and the relevant types of analysis, such as sophisticated mathematical calculations, ratio analysis, industry comparisons, economic and market analysis and relative business risk assessment, to achieve a competent valuation.

The date of valuation may also influence the choice of valuation methods. Methods of valuation used in practice have changed over the years. Valuers may have to use valuation techniques applicable at a date of valuation in the past, as well as earnings multiples applicable at that time. For example, in the 1970s and 1980s net assets values were considered more important in valuations (for example, purchase prices had to be underpinned to a great extent by net assets). Old text books can provide useful guidance on valuation practices at particular periods of time.

18–05 The courts have recognised that valuation is not an exact science, and that expert valuers can, with perfect legitimacy, hold widely differing opinions as to the value of the same business or asset. In a recent case, it was held that a valuer was not negligent in valuing an asset for more than it subsequently realised where the result was "within a proper bracket of valuation".[2] In another case,[3] a margin of 15 per cent was considered a reasonable margin of error where the property was unusual and it was difficult to achieve a level of precision as a result.

18–06 The human qualities inherent in the process underscore the subjective nature of business valuation and the resulting fact that no single approach can be applied to every situation. Valuations should be based on a reasonable methodology – as has been stated by one judge "valuation is an art and not a science but is not astrology …".[4]

Information

18–07 In order to ensure that the full economic valuation is arrived at it is important that all relevant information and facts are considered. The most current

---

Burn, S., *Tolley's Accountancy Litigation Support* (Butterworths, London, looseleaf), Part VI, para. 85.

[2] *Axa Equity & Law Home Loans Ltd v. Goldstack & Freeman* [1994] 1 E.G.L.R. 175.

[3] *Private Bank & Trust Co Ltd v. S (UK) Ltd* [1993] 67 P. & C.R. 166.

[4] *Platform Home Loans Ltd v. Oyston Shipways Ltd* [1996] 49 E.G. 112.

information possible relative to the valuation date should be used.[5] However, the use of knowledge gathered at a later date[6] or concerning subsequent events[7] may not be permissible.

Establishing an accurate assessment of value for any business, enterprise or intangible asset requires an in-depth specialised knowledge. Valuation includes an analysis of the financial statements, projections and other relevant data.

Knowledge of the industry

18–08 Numbers, facts, figures, balance sheets and financial statements on their own are simply not adequate to measure accurately the true fair market value of an asset. It is very important to gain at least a basic knowledge of the business and its industry. The microeconomic aspects of the overall industry, the marketplace and the environment of the business to be valued need to be understood to appreciate the different economic forces that will impact on the business. The forensic accountant should ensure that he understands the underlying factors in the business – products sold, manufacturing processes, customers, pressing concerns of the industry, importance of business location to its ongoing success, government and regulatory requirements, major competitive threats, threats from technological obsolescence, etc. This information can be obtained through discussion with the business owner, inquiries of industry sources, industry publications, etc. Business valuations need to reflect each company's unique character and valuation principles should be tailored to that purpose.

Role of forensic accountants

18–09 In the absence of willing buyers and sellers,[8] establishing a company's fair market value requires the assistance of experts who understand the valuation methods to apply to given situations. The importance of experts in this area is well illustrated by the judgment of Kenny J. in *Attorney General v. Jameson*. The case involved a dispute over the value to be applied for taxation purposes to shares in the company, owned by the Jameson family, which operated the well-known distillery of the same name. The learned judge said:

> "It seems to me that this Court is not competent to give an opinion as to the value of these shares. The matter is one for the Commissioners of Inland Revenue themselves, with or without the aid of an expert whose business it is to make such valuations and to calculate the chances in any given state of circumstances."[9]

---

[5] *Central Trust Co v. United States*, 305 F. 2d 393 (Ct Cl. 1962).

[6] *Trustees of Johan Thomas Salvesen v. IRC* [1930] S.L.T. 387.

[7] *IRC v. Marr's Trustees* [1906] 14 S.L.T. 585; *Holt v. IRC* [1953] 2 All E.R. 1499.

[8] For a consideration of the term "willing seller" in the context of share valuation see *Short v. Treasury Commissioners* [1948] A.C. 534. See also *Attorney General v. Jameson* [1904] 2 I.R. 644.

[9] [1904] 2 I.R. 644 at 663.

However, this statement of principle did not deter Kenny J. from setting out a helpful list of factors to support his view that the price at which the shares would "in the opinion of the Commissioners, fetch if sold in the open market" was neither necessarily the par value of the shares (£100) nor the price that would be paid in an unrestricted market. The list of factors included:

> "The possibility of a sale by private agreement at a higher price to a member of the limited class of permissible transferees; the payment of a large dividend; the position, stability and character of the Company; the special pre-emption rights attaching to the ownership of the shares, would all be, in my opinion, elements in the estimation of a price …".[10]

Boyd J. in the same case addressed the nature of the industry and the use of dividend history as a basis for valuation in the following terms:

> "We know, from our experience of what has befallen several well-known distilleries in this city, which for long years produced large profits for their proprietors, how uncertain and fluctuating are the profits of this business; and I do not think much stress can be laid on the fact of the dividends which have for some years been paid by the company in this case as being any test of the value of the shares."[11]

Qualifications of the forensic accountant and the expertise required to value shares may depend on each particular circumstance. In *Whiteoak v. Walker*,[12] in the United Kingdom it has been found that the auditors who performed occasional valuations had the appropriate expertise. This decision was made on the grounds that the articles of association did not require a specialist valuation expert.

18–10 The expert should consider how various factors may affect a company's value, and he can apply common sense, informed judgment and a reasonable approach to the valuation process in doing so. In order to be of greatest benefit, objective, independent experts capable of defending the valuation in case of litigation or dispute should conduct valuations.

18–11 It is essential that valuations be carried out in accordance with established procedures if they are to constitute credible evidence in court. Valuations should be thorough and comply with accepted standards of professional practice. A complete and thorough valuation reduces questions and ambiguities which, in turn, will reduce exposure to legal repercussions. The use of a forensic accountant for such a valuation exercise provides third party objectivity, independence and credibility. Evidence in the report that the forensic

---

[10] [1904] 2 I.R. 644 at 675.
[11] *ibid.* at 680.
[12] [1988] 4 B.C.C. 122.

accountant has some understanding of the industry and the background to the business, beyond the financial figures, will enhance the credibility and weight of the valuation.

18–12   The valuation report should fully explain how the valuation was carried out and should include details of the principles and methods of valuation, information on which the valuation is based and steps followed in preparing the valuation. The forensic accountant should point out where information necessary for the valuation has not been made available and should indicate any assumptions, restrictions and other limitations in his valuation as a result.

18–13   Where valuations are based on assumptions, the forensic accountant should be able to justify the assumptions used.[13] A small change in an assumption can have a large impact on the amount at which the business is valued. Courts are likely to subject valuation techniques and assumptions to careful scrutiny.

18–14   Some examples of actual situations involving forensic accountants and business valuations are shown in Table 18.1.

Business and share valuations

18–15   A useful outline of the steps involved in preparing a business valuation provided by Trout[14] is reproduced at Figure 18.1. The initial steps involve obtaining background information such as historical financial data and information on underlying relationships (financial and otherwise) in the business. The data necessary for the particular valuation method to be used is then assembled. For example, where discounted cash flow is to be used the market discount rate needs to be selected. The method of valuation selected is then applied to the relevant data to produce a value for the business. Trout's approach involves considering several valuation models, the accounting book value and any recent prior sales of shares.[15] This value may then be discounted for lack of control (in the case of a minority holding) or is increased to take account of the premium payable for a controlling interest in a company (in the case of a majority holding).

---

[13] *Anangel Atlas Compania Naviera SA v. Ishikawajima-Harima Heavy Industries Co Ltd (No. 2)* [1990] 2 Lloyd's Rep. 526.
[14] Trout, R., "Business valuations" in *Measuring Commercial Damages* (Gaughan, P.A. (ed.), John Wiley & Sons, Inc., New York, 2000), Chap. 8.
[15] In *McNamee v. Revenue Commissioners* [1954] I.R. 214 arm's length sales prior to the date of valuation were held to be of assistance in valuing shares.

**Table 18.1: Examples of business valuations where forensic accountants
have advised**

Matrimonial disputes
- Valuing interests in two property companies in connection with a divorce, including appearance as expert witness
- Valuing interests in two separate (and unrelated) solicitor's practices in connection with divorce, with appearance as expert witness
- Valuing a medical practice in connection with a divorce including expert witness testimony
- Valuing a dental practice in connection with a divorce which assisted in settlement.

Shareholder disputes
- Preparing an expert valuation of a business "owned" by two brothers who had fallen out before the promised transfer of shares from one brother to the other had taken place
- Assisting in dispute over share values after falling out between two directors with 50/50 shareholdings
- Valuing a manufacturing business to determine the "fair value" of a dissenting minority interest
- Valuing a medical products company using a "fair value" and a "fair market value" standard to resolve a dispute with a group of dissident minority shareholders
- Testifying that the plaintiff expert's valuation of the business was significantly overstated, that the value of goodwill was much lower and that the claims for unfinished and future business were overstated, which led to settlement for a much lower amount than claimed.

Mergers and acquisitions
- Valuing shares in a travel company on the basis of the exclusion, and then the inclusion, of a material third party liability not addressed in a share sale agreement.

Assisting counsel
- Providing analysis on business valuations submitted by opposing counsel, as well as questions for cross-examination of the other expert or consultant
- Providing assistance to counsel regarding the difference between "fair market value" and "fair value" in a dissident shareholder case. Providing information regarding minority discounts, marketability discounts and key person discounts
- Performing a valuation on developmental computer software including expert testimony regarding the fair market value of the software.

Purpose of the valuation

18–16 Company worth is influenced by the motivation behind the valuation. Business owners seek business valuations for a variety of reasons, and each reason may carry a distinct set of influencing factors and valuation methods and standards. Different valuation methods are used depending on the purpose of, or the reasons for, the valuation, and they result in different values for the business.

Forensic accountants may be asked to value businesses for a variety of purposes, including inheritance tax, death duties, matrimonial disputes (dealt with in Chapter 7), business break-ups and in connection with agreements for the purchase or sale of businesses.

Figure 18.1: Pathway to valuation

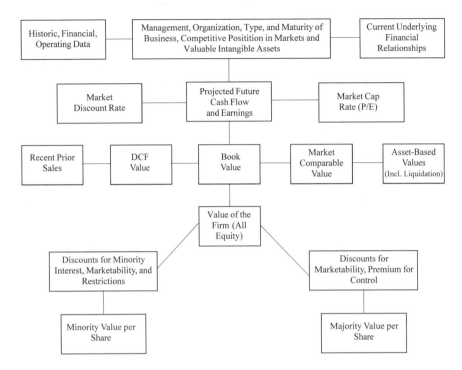

(*Source*: Trout, R., "Business valuations" in *Measuring Commercial Damages* (Gaughan, P.A. (ed.), John Wiley & Sons, Inc., New York, 2000), p. 237.

18–17   Forensic accountants are often involved in business valuation in connection with legal disputes such as those shown in Table 18.2:

Table 18.2: Circumstances in which business valuations may be required

Personal litigation	Commercial litigation	Corporate litigation
• Employment disputes involving employee share ownership plans • Divorce and matrimonial disputes	• Lost profit analysis • Business interruption leading to company liquidation • Mergers and acquisitions	• Shareholder disputes • Minority shareholder litigation • Partnership disputes

Financial statements

18–18   Financial statements can provide a wealth of information, and may highlight items previously undisclosed. They provide a good opportunity to gain an understanding of the financial aspects of the business. A historical consideration of the company's operations is vital in appreciating the patterns and trends in the business, as well as in providing an understanding of any anomalies therein. Multi-year analysis will assist in an understanding of the major expense categories, and any unusual, out-of-line changes that have occurred in any particular year. A review of the most recent five years' profit and loss figures may highlight any changes in gross profit percentages in that period. A preliminary analysis can help flag specific revenues, expenses, margins or years that merit further investigation.

18–19   It is important to undertake an initial review and analysis of the company's profit and loss account, cash flow statement and balance sheet. Interim financial statements or internal management accounts may highlight interesting and significant differences between the year end and other accounts. Forensic accountants should also be especially sensitive to the existence of additional companies, related entities and related party transactions, etc.

18–20   The financial statements or tax returns of a business cannot necessarily be accepted at face value. They almost always require investigation and some degree of restatement for the purpose of their use in a valuation exercise. Therefore, it is useful at an early stage to have a forensic accountant review the profit and loss account and balance sheet numbers and report on their reliability for determining value and income.

18–21   A starting point for assembling the valuation is to put several years' (usually five) profit and loss and balance sheet data on a spreadsheet. The spreadsheet may be accompanied by supporting documentation and schedules. Any adjustments to the figures should also be documented.

Levels of business ownership

18–22   A key element in determining value is the level of ownership that a given interest represents. There are three primary levels, listed in order of declining value:

– controlling interest, which carries with it the power to influence strategy, structure and policy;

– marketable minority interest, which is highly liquid but carries little or no control; and

– non-marketable minority interest, which is typical of minority interests in closely held businesses.

Basis of valuation

18–23   There are a number of methods for valuing firms and there is never a single "right" answer. Every private company is unique but the available valuation techniques are the same for every business. The valuation will also vary depending on the type of shareholding being valued and on the identity of the purchaser – whether there is a "willing" buyer or seller or there is a special purchaser, whether there is a minority holding or a 50/50 holding of shares, etc. Not everyone is a willing buyer/seller and this can create anomalies in share valuations.

18–24   Forensic accountants use a number of valuation methodologies to build up a robust core valuation range. The best method should be identified and justified as such in the specific circumstances on the basis of economic reasoning. However, other methods should also be used to support the best method and to indicate the size of the range of possible values. Viewing an approach from an economic perspective provides insights concerning the necessary assumptions associated with each approach. Economic reasoning should be applied when explaining to a court the logic of a particular assumption within a given method. With an understanding of the assumptions necessary for each valuation approach, the expert can aid the court by choosing the approach which minimises the speculation involved in valuing the firm.

18–25   The method of valuation should specify:

– the standard of value to be used (see paras **18–26** *et seq.*);

– the premise of value (see paras **18–33** *et seq.*); and

– the discounts to be applied for lack of control and lack of marketability and any premia to be applied (see paras **18–108** *et seq.*).

While parties to a dispute may agree on the valuation approach, there may be disagreement over the appropriate *standard* of value and the appropriate *premise* of value.

Valuation standards

18–26   Various valuation standards are shown in Table 18.3, together with a brief explanation of each. Valuation standards include fair market value, book value, historical cost, etc. A variety of methods that can be employed to determine the value of an asset, and each has its special advantages and disadvantages.

Table 18.3: Valuation terminology and standards of value

Term	Definition
Valuation standards	
• Book value	Value of net assets (*i.e.* assets – liabilities) as shown in the financial accounts or books of the company
• Historic cost	Original price paid for the asset
• Depreciated historic cost	Book value (see above) on the historic cost basis
• Replacement cost/price	Price it would cost to replace assets in the business
• Depreciated replacement cost	Price or cost to replace by purchasing a similar asset equivalently worn out
• Fair value	Value in an arm's length transaction between informed and willing parties
• Fair market value/open market value	Value assuming all willing market participants are informed adequately of the proposed sale and of the details of the asset
• Intrinsic value	What an asset ought to sell for, considering its potential future cash flow to an investor/owner
• Net present value	Value of future stream of earnings/payments based on today's monetary values
• Net realisable value	Value that could be obtained if the asset had to be sold, less all marketing, selling and distribution costs
• Value in use	Value of asset to the business based on its continued use in the business
Premise of value	
• Going concern value	Price assuming the business will continue in operation and will not significantly curtail its operations
• Forced sale value	Price that could be obtained if seller was forced to sell it now
• Liquidation value	Cash received by owners were business to be wound up

Fair value

18–27 Fair value is a concept often used in valuing a minority shareholder's holding. It may be required under the articles of association or by agreement between the parties. Fair value is not the same as open market value – fair value may take into account the special circumstances of a special buyer. It is a special purpose valuation where the value of the asset is considered from the perspective of a particular buyer. This method of valuation takes into account market value and at the same time factors reflecting the relative position of the vendor and purchaser in the specific transaction. For various reasons (see below), a purchaser may be willing to pay an above market price for a controlling interest in a company.

Fair market value

18–28 The concept of fair market value is commonly used to determine the value of assets and businesses that are subject to acquisition, estate planning, estate taxation, buy-sell agreements, ownership dissolution and other situations. Fair market value is usually defined as the price a willing buyer would pay a willing seller, where the market has reasonable knowledge of the relevant facts. It assumes that the buyer is not under any compulsion to buy and the seller is not under any compulsion to sell. As has already been stated, this is often not the case and this can affect the valuation, either:

– by increasing the value (adding a premium on the valuation) in the case of a special purchaser (say, if acquisition of the shares creates a majority holding); or

– by decreasing it where a minority holding is being sold.

In practice, there is a move away from the concept of willing buyer/seller as this is not appropriate to real life situations.

Open market value

18–29 Businesses may be valued at open market value – by which is meant the fair price which might be paid in an even-handed transaction for the item in question.

Open market value is the price a willing buyer would pay and a willing seller would accept for the purchase of an entire business or the entire share capital of a business. Open market value is largely synonymous with "fair market value".[16]

18–30 Open market value was defined by Swinfen Eady L.J. in *IRC v. Clay*[17] as:

> "A value ascertained by reference to the amount obtainable in an open market shows an intention to include every possible purchaser. The market is to be the open market as distinguished from an offer to a limited class only, such as the members of the family. The market is not necessarily an auction sale. The Section means such amount as the land might be expected to realise if offered under conditions enabling every person desirous of purchasing to come in and make an offer and if the proper steps were taken to advertise the property and let all likely purchasers know that the land is in the market for sale."

This definition was further expanded on by Lord Morris of Borth-Y-Gest in the

---

[16]For a consideration of the term "willing seller" in the context of share valuation see *Short v. Treasury Commissioners* [1948] A.C. 534. See also *Attorney General v. Jameson* [1904] 2 I.R. 644.
[17][1914] 3 K.B. 466 at 475.

House of Lords in *Lynall v. IRC*[18] as follows:

"... 'open' market in which the property is offered for sale to the world at large so that all potential purchasers have an equal opportunity to make an offer as a result of its being openly known what it is that is being offered for sale. Mere private deals on a confidential basis are not the equivalent of open market transactions".

The intention of the courts in arriving at a valuation of shares at open market value is to include every possible purchaser, including special purchasers. However, the courts have found that if the existence of a special purchaser is not known, such a special purchaser may not affect prices.[19] This is not always realistic and it might be wrong to base the valuation on anything other than those special factors.

18–31 In the Irish taxation statutes, several definitions of market value are used. One typical such definition is contained in section 15 of the Capital Acquisitions Tax Act 1976 in the following terms:

"Subject to the provisions of this Act, the market value of any property for the purposes of this Act shall be estimated to be the price which ... such property would fetch if sold in the open market on the date on which the property is to be valued in such manner and subject to such conditions as might reasonably be calculated to obtain for the vendor the best price for the property."

The market value approach generally values a business as a going concern (see para. **18–34**). This involves determining the representative earnings and/or cash flow levels of the company and applying multiples based on the value of publicly traded stock (or of private transactions, if available) of comparable companies.

Agreed value

18–32 Agreed value, established in a buy-sell agreement, is another standard of value, but it is not necessarily binding. Courts have been known to ignore an agreed value if the intrinsic value of a company's shares may be greater than the buy-sell value.

Premise of value

18–33 The premise of value depends on the future of the subject business: will it continue to operate as a going concern or will it be liquidated? And if the latter, will it be an orderly liquidation or a forced liquidation? The answers to these questions can have a dramatic impact on value. Before embarking on a detailed valuation exercise, it is essential to decide which of the two fundamental

---

[18] [1971] 3 All E.R. 914 at 922.
[19] *IRC v. Crossman* [1936] 1 All E.R. 762.

bases is to be used. These are the liquidation (break-up) basis, which arrives at the value of what remains after all assets are sold and all debts are paid, and the going concern basis, which considers goodwill and the company's ability to generate cash flow and income in the future.

Going concern valuation

18–34 Going concern is not a method of valuation but indicates that the business is being valued on the basis that it will continue in operation for the foreseeable future.

Forced sale/liquidation valuation

18–35 Assets sold on a forced sale or liquidation basis will realise significantly less than would be the case if they were sold in the normal course of trading on a going concern basis. Assets such as specialised machinery, stock, work-in-progress and debtors would have significantly lower values were the business to cease trading.

18–36 Whether shares should be valued on a going concern or break-up basis will be determined by an assessment of the circumstances prevailing at the time. In general, a business will be presumed to be a going concern unless there is clear evidence to the contrary. An example of such a case arose in *Re William Courthope*.[20] In the context of the specific circumstances of the case, the judge stated:

> "… that it is a better proposition to look at it from the point of view of what it would be worth wound up rather than from the point of view of what it would make carrying on. If you tried to find a purchaser for these shares, in my view, he would probably say to himself 'well this is a thing to buy to wind up'."

Methods of valuing businesses

18–37 There are three general perspectives from which to choose, any two or all three of which may be used to establish value: the assets approach, the income approach and the market approach. These approaches and methods of valuation are summarised in Table 18.4. The methods of valuation discussed in the following paragraphs follow this table. The assets approach is first described, followed by three income-based methods: discounted cash flow, capitalisation of earnings and excess earnings. The market earnings multiple approach is then considered.

Assets approach to valuing businesses

18–38 The net assets value approach can be used to value a business either as a going concern or on a liquidation basis. It focuses on the company's balance

---

[20] [1928] 7 A.T.C. 538.

Table 18.4: Methods of valuing businesses

Assets perspective (see paras **18–38** *et seq.*)   • Market value   • Book value   • Adjusted book value   • Liquidation value
Income perspective   • Discounted cash flow (see paras **18–46** *et seq.*)   • Capitalisation of earnings (see paras **18–56** *et seq.*)   • Excess earnings/super profits method (see paras **18–58** *et seq.*)
Market approach   • Earnings multiple/price earnings approach (see paras **18–68** *et seq.*)   • Recent purchase offers, and sales of comparable businesses
Other   • Dividend yield basis (see paras **18–82** *et seq.*)   • Buy-sell agreement formulae to determine value   • Heterogenous, hybrid or mixed approach   • Key man approach   • Revenue multiples based on prior/forecast sales   (Possibly applying different multiples to different revenue streams)   • Capitalisation of cash flow   • Book value multiples

sheet rather than its income or cash flow. Net assets valuation, incorporating the valuations of the underlying assets or divisions of the business, may be appropriate in some circumstances, *e.g.* when the value of the business is highly related to its assets rather than to its performance and earnings. The assets approach is useful for a business that has substantial tangible and intangible assets and whose recent earnings may not reflect its intrinsic value (*e.g.* property companies, banks and start-up businesses).

18–39 The net asset value approach values the firm as the net value of the tangible assets (*i.e.* physical assets excluding *e.g.* goodwill) of the firm. The advantage of this approach is that the assumptions required by the expert are limited. The net assets approach is illustrated in Table 18.11.

18–40 Applying the net assets approach requires choosing a standard of value (see para. **18–26** *et seq.*) with which to value the individual assets of the business. A number of these are briefly discussed here including market value, book value, adjusted book value and liquidation value. The circumstances in which the valuation is being carried out will suggest which standard of value is most appropriate.

Book value and liquidation values may be useful as indicators of the minimum or floor value of the business but otherwise the assets approach will rarely be used on its own as a method of valuation. This approach would only be valid when it yields a value greater than the present value of a stream of earnings realised when the firm retains the assets and uses them on an on-going basis. If the net asset value approach yields a lesser value, its use would undervalue the firm. Thus, the value of the firm as an on-going business must be calculated as a comparison.

Market value of assets

18–41   Market value is the price someone would pay for the business. Fair value and open market value (and the differences between the two) have been discussed earlier in paras **18–28** *et seq.* in the context of standards of value. Open market value and fair market value are closely related.

The approach consists of determining the fair market value of the company's individual assets and subtracting the fair market value of the company's liabilities. To place a market value on the tangible assets, the expert may need to get an independent valuation. Such a valuation should be conducted by an objective, third-party firm that employs full-time expertise and is capable of defending the valuation in case of litigation or dispute.

Book value of assets

18–42   Book value is equal to the net worth of the company as shown in its current balance sheet. While it is often the simplest method of valuation, it is very rarely an accurate indicator of a business's true value.[21] Book values of property, plant, equipment (which will generally be shown at depreciated historic cost) and stock may differ significantly from their market values. Book value does not take into account many subjective factors that are key to arriving at a defensible fair market value.

Adjusted book value

18–43   For companies whose primary value derives from specific assets, an adjusted net asset approach may be appropriate. The starting point for such a valuation is the book value of the business. Book values are then adjusted to market value. The measure of market value can vary depending on the availability of information. This will depend on whether there is a ready market for the asset or, alternatively, whether the asset is very specialised and therefore difficult to value.

Methods of valuation (to determine the adjustment to market value) can range from net realisable value, to value-in-use, to replacement cost, depreciated replacement cost, etc. The adjusted book value method involves consideration

---

[21] Twomey, M., *Partnership Law* (Butterworths, Dublin, 2000), p. 400, para. 16.81. In *Barr v. Barr*, unreported, High Court, November 3, 1983, Barron J. held that balance sheet values for partnership property should only be used where the partnership agreement expressly provides for this method of valuation. See also *Cruickshand v. Sutherland* [1923] 128 L.T. 449.

of market value for some or all of the assets, together with the worth of goodwill and other intangible assets. A drawback of adjusted book value (and asset valuation generally) is that it may value the business at a higher/lower level than earnings and sales forecasts would support.

Liquidation value

18–44 Another valuation concept is liquidation value which is the net cash inflow that would be received if the business were wound up. This is a last resort and is a method of valuation to be used in the most exceptional and pessimistic situations. It assumes there is no value in the business continuing and that the best value would be obtained by closing the business and selling off the net assets. Liquidation value, in turn, depends on whether the liquidation is an orderly liquidation or on a forced sale basis. Much lower valuations are likely to be obtained by valuing assets on a break-up or forced sale basis. For example, debtors are unlikely to realise book value if the debtors are not to do business with the company in the future. Equally, stock will probably be sold at much lower values. The break-up value of fixed assets will be much lower than the value generated by continuing to use the assets in the business. To make matters worse, the liabilities are likely to have to be settled at book value.

Although all of these factors apply to both an orderly liquidation and a forced sale, these two scenarios can result in very different valuations. This is because, in an orderly liquidation time can be taken to identify all possible buyers, to pursue debtors and generally to obtain the best prices reasonably available. In a forced sale, often the first offer must be accepted due to the urgency of the circumstances.

Goodwill

18–45 The treatment of goodwill by the courts may depend on the purpose of the valuation. Goodwill is generally defined as the excess of the value of the business over the value of its net tangible assets (and other intangible assets capable of valuation. A business may have two types of goodwill, business (or practice) goodwill and personal (or professional) goodwill. Business goodwill is associated with the firm or practice as an entity, and may be attributable to established relationships with customers, clients, employees and suppliers. Business goodwill is quantifiable and can be bought or sold. Personal goodwill is attributable to the individual's/practitioner's skill, training and reputation. Such goodwill is not saleable as it attaches to an individual. A distinction must be made in identifying goodwill as either personal or business goodwill.

Different methods can be used to value goodwill.[22] These include:

---

[22] Mason, M.E. and Cohen, M.S., "From a matrimonial lawyer's perspective – the ten (and a few more) most frequent errors made by business appraisers" (American Academy of Matrimonial Lawyers website www.aaml.org/Articles/2000-1/10mistakes.htm), pp. 10–15.

- capitalisation of excess earnings/super profits approach (see para. **18–58**) – although some courts in the United States consider this method of valuation to be too speculative and formulistic;

- comparable sales, *i.e.* goodwill valuations in sales of/offers to buy comparable businesses;

- fair market value of business minus tangible assets.

Whatever the method of valuation chosen, the calculations must be tailored to meet the particular needs and circumstances of each case.

Discounted cash flow

18–46 Discounted cash flow is a method of valuation based on an income perspective (rather than assets or market perspective). Discounting future cash flows is generally the most comprehensive, and thus most widely favoured approach (from a theoretical perspective) to determining the fair market value of a business. However, many methods of valuation can be interpreted as methods of calculating the present value of a stream of future earnings.

18–47 Discounted cash flow is based on the generally accepted theory that the value of the business depends on its future cash flows measured at present day values. The time value of money and present values are discussed more fully in Chapter 19.

This approach values the business as a going concern, estimating the present value of an investment by discounting all future economic income by a rate of return known as a discount rate. It involves sophisticated analyses and restrictive assumptions that require professional judgment. Future cash flows arising from the business are calculated at present value, based on a discount factor which will take risk into account. The value of a firm is the present value of the stream of future cash flow generated by the firm, where:

$$V = \sum \frac{E_i}{(1 + r)^i}$$

V = Value of the company
E_i = Earnings in the ith year
r = Rate of return or capitalisation rate or discount rate required

The discounted cash flow approach is a step by step procedure of calculating the present value of the future stream of earnings of the firm as an on-going concern. While being the most theoretically correct method, discounting future cash flows is rather subjective and can be sensitive to minor changes in assumptions. To compensate for that sensitivity, secondary valuation methods may be worked into the calculation.

Taken at face value, this approach makes little direct use of market-generated information. Thus, the details of the assumptions that the experts must make may be regarded as highly speculative. So, although few experts would object to the discounted cash flow approach on a theoretical basis, its implementation may in practice detract from its validity.

18–48   For an individual shareholder, the value of the shares is the discounted value of the future cash flowing from (i) dividends and (ii) the future sale price of the shares. Investors discount their expectation of future cash flow and thus determine the future current market price. Ultimately, all future cash flows are represented by a stream of dividend payments. This is illustrated in Table 18.5.

Table 18.5: Example dividend approach to valuing a business

Nominal value of share €1.00
Assume current dividend is 10 cent per share
Dividends are expected to grow by 10% per annum over the next 8 years and by 4% thereafter
The discount rate is 8%

Value of dividend

Year	Dividend [€0.10 x (1.10)^t]	Discount factor	Present value
1	0.110	0.926	0.102
2	0.121	0.857	0.104
3	0.133	0.794	0.106
4	0.146	0.735	0.107
5	0.161	0.681	0.110
6	0.177	0.630	0.112
7	0.195	0.583	0.114
8	0.214	0.540	0.116
Total present value of dividend for years 1–8			0.871

Value of share
Dividend from year 9 onwards is expected to grow by 4%. Therefore, the dividend in year 9 will be year 8 dividend of €0.214 by 1.04 = 0.2226. The capital value at the end of year 8 necessary to give a return in year 9 onwards of €0.2226 is 0.2226/0.04 = €5.56

Net present value at a discount rate of 8% of €5.56 = 5.56/(1.08)^8 = €3.004

Value of share today = Present value of dividends for years 1–8 + present value of capital sum required to produce dividend in the future: €0.871 + €3.004 = €3.875

18–49   Buying a business is equivalent, in financial terms, to buying the future cash flows which it will generate. Valuing that future cash means taking a view on:

– how much money will be generated by the business, *i.e.* the expected future profit (proxy for cash flows);

– when will the cash be generated, or how much cash will be generated in the distant future. Cash flows in the more distant future are worth less than those in the short term;

– the likelihood of expectations being met or the risk of expectations not being met;

– the alternative uses for the price being paid or the cost of financing the purchase.

18–50   A fully detailed approach to the valuation will look at each of these factors separately, consider the appropriate value (or range of values) and combine them to arrive at a result. The result can be considered as a whole, along with its sensitivity to changing different assumptions, and, ultimately, a view can be taken.

18–51   Assumptions are required for three variables in this approach:

– forecast of the stream of future expected cash flow (projection of future income);

– duration of the cash flows;

– appropriate risk-adjusted discount rate used to calculate present value, *i.e.* the required rate of return for a hypothetical prospective buyer.

There are different strategies for making these three assumptions which are discussed below.

Forecasting cash flow

18–52   Relevant cash flows appropriate to the valuation must be defined. This may be problematic as there is no agreement as to which cash flow definition to use. Future values of cash flow (however defined) must then be forecast. Even if the expert developed an acceptable econometric model for cash flow, there would be explanatory variables which would also need to be forecasted, which might invite controversy.

Value of the business is determined based on discounting the business's future cash flows (or earnings in lieu). As already stated, the use of projected future income represents the perspective of future buyers who are interested in the business's future (not past) performance. In projecting future income, a modest (or no) growth rate might be assumed. A major problem with using future income is preparation of income projections. Projections of income can be materially inaccurate, especially in respect of relatively small companies with negligible market share control. Nevertheless, the approach is a valid one.

Projection period

18–53   The length of time over which future cash flows can be reliably estimated is often an issue. The important factor in selecting a projection period is the ability to forecast future cash flows reliably for the full period. This in turn will be influenced by the nature of the business, the financial history of the company and the future prospects for the company and its industry. Company valuers frequently calculate present values based on five-year cash flows which, together with the present value of the firm in its fifth year, gives the current value. Current value is the sum of the present values of the cash flows for the next five years added to the discounted value of the firm at the end of the fifth year. The value at the end of the fifth year must be estimated and discounted back to present value.

Discount rate

18–54   The discount rate is used to determine the current value of the future cash flows. The discount rate or required return is a function of risk and investment alternatives. It reflects the amount of money investors would pay to receive some estimated level of cash in the future, taking account of the risk of not receiving those future cash flows. This in turn is influenced by the relative riskiness of the company's own business and the industry in which it operates.

The rate of return required for an investor to invest in the business needs to be estimated. The estimated future amount of cash to be received is not guaranteed and is not known with any certainty. For this reason the discount rate must be risk-adjusted. The higher the risk, the higher the (risk-adjusted) discount rate, with lower current values as a result. Risk and economic value are inversely related.

Non-operating assets

18–55   If the business has assets that are not considered necessary operating components in order for it to generate its revenue, then those assets should be treated separately and their market value added to the value thus determined. Equally, the earnings must be based on operating income exclusive of income from non-operating assets.

Discounted cash flow is somewhat sophisticated and other methods discussed below are more commonly found in practice. An example of this method of valuation is shown in Table 18.10.

Capitalisation of earnings

18–56   An alternative method of valuation based on an income perspective is the capitalisation of earnings approach. This is encapsulated in the following formula:

$$V = \frac{I \times (1 + G)}{R - G}$$

V = Value of the company
I = Most recent maintainable profit
G = Expected sustainable growth rate of the net profit of the company
R = Rate of return that a prospective buyer would require

The capitalisation of earnings method is often applicable to mature businesses (*i.e.* those likely to achieve relatively modest growth in earnings and net cash flows). This method is unacceptable for high growth companies because it only considers history and not future performance. Although the capitalised earnings approach appears to relieve the expert of the need to forecast earnings, this is not the case – the forecast is implicit rather than explicit.

The capitalisation of earnings approach consists of defining earnings, forecasting earnings growth and calculating the present value. The difference between this method (and the discounted cash flow approach) is that all of the future earnings values are assumed to be equal and to continue indefinitely. The assumption that future earnings remain constant allows the present value to be readily calculated.

The definition of earnings and the value of the discount rate must be determined with the capitalised earnings approach. In practice, there is often little agreement in the definition of earnings but there is some agreement on the discount rate, which must incorporate risk. It should be noted that a slight change in anticipated growth rate can have a dramatic impact on value. If growth is slowing, and the business is mature and cyclical, a growth rate may be chosen that is in line with the consumer price index or some other standard measure of inflation. If the industry and business are performing strongly, it may be appropriate to choose a higher growth rate. An example of the capitalised earnings method of valuation is shown in Table 18.10 (see para. **18–80**).

The capitalisation approach is regularly used in business valuations. It is also appropriate in cases where the plaintiff alleges a permanent destruction of business.[23]

Risk rate

18–57 The development of the risk rate to use begins with an analysis of the risk-free rate at the time of the valuation. Investors would expect a higher return than the risk-free rate when they invest in a company. Historically, for public companies the actual return tends to be several percentage points higher than the risk-free rate. In addition, a greater return would be expected of private companies with less predictability as to future income, profitability and marketability of shares.

The specific company risk premium is intended to measure the additional risk assumed by the buyer of a private company, and takes into account the strength of management, quality of the labour force and other strategic issues. If at the time of valuation the company is performing poorly in comparison to its peers, a risk premium at the higher end of the range may be chosen (and vice versa).

---

[23] *Taylor v. B. Heller & Co*, 364 F. 2d 608 (6th Cir. 1966).

Excess earnings/super profits method

18–58　This approach to valuing a company divides the value of a firm into two parts: the value of its tangible assets (and any intangible assets capable of valuation separate from the business) and the value of its other intangible elements (*i.e.* goodwill, customer lists, etc.). The tangible assets (and separable intangible assets) are valued and are added to the value of other intangible assets determined using the excess earnings method. Having identified the tangible assets, a reasonable or "normal" level of earnings or a reasonable return on those assets must be determined.

This method is particularly apposite where there are large goodwill values such as in professional practices or services businesses. However, the method can be somewhat formulistic and should only be used where there are no better methods (*e.g.* market comparables) available for valuing the intangible assets of the business.

The excess earnings approach may not be suitable for businesses that have negative or low earnings.

18–59　The excess earnings method of calculating goodwill has been used in several important cases in the United States, especially in family law cases.[24] The courts there have ruled that the excess earnings method of measuring loss of business goodwill reasonably quantifies the loss even though other acceptable methods exist to value goodwill.[25] This method was also used in the English case of *Findlay's Trustees v. IRC*[26] where the business was valued at eight times the net profit after interest and after tax. There was some disagreement between the expert valuers on whether the multiple of eight should be applied to the average profits or to the most recent profit figure. However, in *Buckingham v. Francis*[27] the court rejected the use of the super profits method of valuation in favour of a valuation based on future maintainable earnings.

18–60　The basic excess earnings formula is as follows:

Normal earnings = Fair value of tangible assets x Rate of return

Excess earnings = Maintainable earnings − Normal earnings

Intangible asset value = Excess earnings x Multiplier

Value of business = Fair value of tangible and intangible assets

---

[24] *Re marriage of Watts*, 171 Cal. App. 3d 366; 217 Cal. Rptr. 301 (1985); *Re marriage of Garrity and Bishton*, 181 Cal. App. 3d 675; 266 Cal. Rptr. 485 (1986); and *Re marriage of Slivka*, 183 Cal. App. 3d 159; 228 Cal. Rptr. 76 (1986).
[25] *Department of Transportation v. Muller*, 36 Cal. 3d 263; 681 P. 2d 1340; 203 Cal. Rptr. 225 (1985).
[26] [1938] 22 A.T.C. 437.
[27] [1986] 2 All E.R. 738.

Rate of return

18–61   This return should provide reasonable compensation for the owner and is usually a rate that is typical for the industry. Reliable information on this may not, however, be readily available. What is available typically may show major fluctuations from year to year which would suggest a certain level of unreliability. The margin of error in any publicly available information can be several percentage points in either direction. In the absence of information on the return on investment in a particular industry, a suitable substitute rate to use is one that reflects what would be expected as a reasonable rate of interest on the funds invested in the subject company.

18–62   The normal income must then be calculated. In the case of a professional practice, this might be the earnings of the practitioner were he to be employed by a large firm without the benefit of his goodwill. This would be similar to the amount that one would have to pay a qualified professional to work in place of the subject practitioner. In other words, statistics setting forth average earnings for self-employed practitioners, be they partners or sole practitioners, would serve as a reference point for determining excess earnings.

Maintainable profit/earnings

18–63   Maintainable earnings are the reasonable and probable earnings of the business based upon a continuation of the current level of business activity. In private companies, in particular, certain expenses charged to the company may not strictly relate to the company (*e.g.* personal and household expenditure of the principal shareholders). In addition, compensation paid to the owner and family members may be more or less than the market rate that would be paid to a third party performing the same tasks. Another issue to take account of is the possibility of the business owning assets which are not used to generate profits of the business. The profits of the business should be adjusted for the use of these redundant assets.

The profit and loss accounts of the business would be used as a starting point to determine maintainable earnings. The adjusted, maintainable profit must be calculated. Adjustments should ensure that the earnings and the related expenses reflect market conditions. Such adjustments might include the following:

– Rent: adjust to market rate of rent (for example, where business premises are owned).

– Loss/gain of product lines.

– Loss of key customer.

– Discontinued operations.

– Interest on capital: risk-free return on capital in the business.

- Non-recurring or exceptional items.

- Changes in accounting policies.

- Compensation levels/owner's remuneration: the business should only be charged with the compensation for its employees, including the owners, based on market rates on an arm's length basis.[28] Determining a fair compensation level can be a difficult task. Job responsibilities, skill, experience, capability, number of hours worked, roles filled, particular expertise of the owners, the fair rate of compensation in the general marketplace for that type of person, the fair compensation in that particular marketplace would all have to be considered.

- Inflation.

- Non-operating assets: (such as shares in other companies) which do not contribute to the ongoing trading operations of the business. The practice is to exclude the income from such assets from maintainable earnings and to value the non-operating assets separately. Thus, the value of the business is a multiple of its maintainable earnings, excluding income from non-operating assets, plus the value of its non-operating assets.

18–64   The courts in the United States have held that a company's past earnings trend, with adjustments made for any exceptional or non-recurring items, should be analysed in arriving at a historical earnings level to use in assessing the fair market value of a company's shares. The courts there also found that greater weight should be given to the most recent periods.[29] An example of the calculation of maintainable earnings with greater weighting for more recent periods is shown in Table 18.6.

18–65   An example of the excess earnings/super profits method of valuation, including adjustment to maintainable earnings, is shown in Table 18.7. Maintainable earnings in the example are taken to be an average of the most recent three years' profits. Where there is an obvious trend in profits, the most recent year's profits might be weighted more heavily than the more out of date profits, *e.g.*:

$$\text{Profits}_{\text{Year 3}} \times 3 + \text{Profits}_{\text{Year 2}} \times 2 + \text{Profits}_{\text{Year 1}} \times 1 = \text{Total} \div 6_{(3+2+1)} = \text{Average profit}$$

The example is based on valuing goodwill based on a multiple of four. Alternatively, different multiples might be applied to different segments of profit.

Multiple/capitalisation rate

18–66   The adjusted maintainable profit, less a reasonable return on the tangible assets, represents the before tax excess income/super profit. A multiplier or

---

[28] *Woodward v. Quigley*, 257 Iowa 1077; 133 NW 2d 38 (1965).
[29] *Central Trust Co v. United States*, 305 F. 2d 393 (Ct Cl. 1962).

capitalisation rate is applied to the excess and the resulting figure is goodwill. This is added to the value of the company. The resulting amount is the value of the tangible assets of the company as a whole.

The appropriate capitalisation rate (this should be the before tax capitalisation rate) should be applied to the excess earnings to give the capitalised value of the intangible assets of the business. The capitalisation rate is the inverse of the multiplier. If the capitalisation rate is 20 per cent, this means divide by 20 per cent or multiply by 5. The multiplier is in effect saying: "How many years am I willing to pay for the intangible value of the business?"

18–67 Evidence of goodwill valuation in the courts is sparse.[30] There is a long established practice that goodwill should be valued within the range of a multiple of one to five (20 per cent to 100 per cent).[31] The choice between these ranges depends on a variety of factors including trading record, profitability, trend of profits, nature of the business, etc. If there are comparable companies with significant multipliers, and the company has solid expectations of continued growth and profitability, the market might reward such a company with a large multiplier.

The above approach leaves significant discretion to the court. The court must decide reasonable values for normal earnings and the excess earnings multiplier. In many respects the above formula allows just enough discretion, while at the same time it provides an opportunity to create an important degree of uniformity in valuations.

Earnings multiple/price earnings approach

18–68 The most commonly used method of valuing a business is using price earnings (p/e) ratios. The earnings multiple/price earnings approach is a method of valuation based on the market perspective and is heavily reliant on capital markets data, particularly the earnings multiple as shown by the price earnings ratio. The p/e ratio is the market price per share divided by the earnings per share.[32] It assumes that earnings (*i.e.* profit after tax) are similar to cash flows, and that the p/e ratio provides an approximation of the present value of future cash flows. Where available, the p/e ratio of a comparable publicly quoted company is used as a basis for valuation. Taking into consideration the inefficiencies in the market, it is clear that quoted p/e ratios can only give a rough approximation of value.

---

[30] *Reed v. Lowestoft Borough Council* [1973] 227 E.G. 835.
[31] McDermott, S. and Woulfe, R., *Compulsory Purchase and Compensation: Law and Practice in Ireland* (Butterworths (Ireland) Ltd, Dublin, 1992), p. 257.
[32] An accounting standard, FRS 14 *Earnings per Share*, provides guidance on how earnings per share should be calculated. Earnings for the purpose of earnings per share are those attributable to ordinary shareholders and comprise consolidated profit after tax, minority interests and preference dividends.

Table 18.6: Example calculation of maintainable earnings

	20X3 €000	20X2 €000	20X1 €000
Land and buildings	3,000		
Plant and machinery (cost €2.8 million)	1,120		
Investments at cost	600		
Net current assets	1,120		
12.5% Secured loan	(520)		
	5,320		
Ordinary shares	3,200		
10% Preference shares	960		
Profit and loss account	1,160		
	5,320		
Profit for year	628	512	612
Investment income included in profit	50	40	36
Market value of land and buildings	3,600		
Market value of investments	440		
Market yield on preference shares	15%		
p/e multiple of comparable company	5		

The secured loan would be repaid out of the proceeds of the investments
The plant and machinery has a replacement cost of €3.4 million
The company has a policy of providing depreciation at a rate of 20% per annum on cost

	20X3 €000	20X2 €000	20X1 €000
Maintainable earnings			
Profit for year	628	512	612
Investment income	(50)	(40)	(36)
Depreciation at replacement cost rates ([3,400 – 2,800] @ 20%)	(120)	(120)	(120)
Loan interest not payable in the future (12.5% @ 520)	65	65	65
Adjusted profit	523	417	521
Preference dividend	(96)	(96)	(96)
	427	321	425
Weighting	x3	x2	x1
	1,281	642	425

Valuation based on earnings multiple
Maintainable earnings ([1,281+ 642 + 425] ÷ 6)	391
Capitalisation rate/multiple	x 5
Value of the company	1,955

Net asset value
Book value (5,320 – 960)	4,360
Increase in value of property (3,600 – 3,000)	600
Decrease in value of investments (600 – 440)	(160)
	4,800

Conclusion: Valuation on a net assets basis yields a much higher result and may be more appropriate than an earnings-multiple valuation

Table 18.7: Example excess earnings/super profits approach to valuing a business

Summarised balance sheet of a company at December 31, 20X3 is as follows:

		€000
Fixed assets		
Freehold property		600
Plant, machinery and equipment		150
Goodwill		200
		950
Quoted investments		350
Current assets		
Stock	120	
Debtors	500	
Bank	17	
	637	
Creditors: Amounts due within one year	(237)	
Net current assets		400
Creditors: Amounts due after more than one year		(200)
Total net assets		1,500
Share capital		
Ordinary shares of €1 each	500	
6% Preference shares of €1 each	250	750
Profit and loss account		750
Total		1,500

Profits for the three years 20X1, 20X2 and 20X3 were €220,000, €300,000 and €160,000 respectively.

It was agreed that the company would be valued on the basis of a normal return of 12.5% on net tangible assets, together with goodwill which was to be valued at four times the excess earnings or super profits.
The value was agreed subject to the following information:
• Long term creditors would be redeemed at a discount of 20%
• The current rental value of the property is €80,000 per annum. It is agreed that the market value of commercial property is approximately 10 times annual rentals .
• The yield on quoted investments is 5% on the market value which is €500,000. As these investments are surplus to the main requirements of the business it was agreed they would be included in the valuation at their market value.
• The accounts of the company in 20X2 show an exceptional profit of €30,000 on disposal of a building of the company

Valuation of ordinary shares	€000
Value per the balance sheet	1,500
Adjustments	
Preference shares redeemed at par	(250)
Goodwill (to be valued separately)	(200)
Uplift on value of property	200
Quoted investments (to be valued separately)	(350)
Discount on redemption of long term creditors €200,000 x 20%	40
Net tangible value of the assets of the business	940

	20X1	20X2	20X3	Total
Maintainable earnings	€000	€000	€000	€000
Profit per accounts	220	300	160	680
Income from quoted investments	(25)	(25)	(25)	(75)
Exceptional item		(30)		(30)
Preference dividend	(15)	(15)	(15)	(45)
	180	230	120	530
Average maintainable profit for one year (530 ÷ 3 years)				177
Less: Normal return €940,000 (net tangible assets) x 12.5% (normal rate of return)				(117)
Excess earnings/super profits				60
Value of goodwill = 4 times				240

Value of company	€000
Net tangible assets	940
Quoted investments	500
Goodwill	240
	1,680

A layering approach to valuations using multiples may also be appropriate. Different multiples may be applied to different layers of earnings reflecting different vulnerability to competition, different barriers to entry, etc., applying to different parts of the business.

18–69   Other relevant ratios are the market to book value[33] and the price/revenue ratio.[34] For certain industries which have a large proportion of their assets in the form of fixed assets, use of market to book ratios in valuing the business may be appropriate. Where fixed assets are proportionately large, market to book ratios of the subject business may be compared with market to book ratios of a group of comparable publicly quoted companies. A price/revenue model may also be used – small businesses and professional practices are often sold on the basis of a multiple of revenue rather than a multiple of net earnings. In many businesses, the revenue figures may be considered to be more reliable than earnings (*e.g.* due to drawings by owners, possible expense manipulation, etc.) and better indicators of the size and potential profitability of the business. The price/revenue method of valuation may be useful for such businesses and where an alternative method of valuation is not available.

18–70   Comparing the company to be valued with industry peers is helpful in doing a business valuation. Comparable quoted companies are those engaged in the same or a similar line of business that are listed on an exchange. A common measure of relative value for a company is the price earnings ratio. If reasonably comparable publicly traded companies can be found, the value of a privately held company can be predicated based on the price earnings ratios of those comparable companies. The earnings multiple/price earnings approach is where the "maintainable" level of earnings is capitalised by the application of a multiple based on the price earnings ratio of a similar publicly quoted company (see also examples in Tables 18.6, 18.11 and 18.12). This methodology is convenient and simple due to the accessibility of public company data. An example of the price earnings ratio (p/e ratio) is shown in Table 18.8.

Table 18.8: Example price earnings ratio

p/e ratio = <u>Market price per share in cent</u>   Earnings per share in cent
Example Publicly quoted price of the ordinary shares of A plc is €1.20 The earnings per share of A plc (from the latest financial statements) is 10 cent p/e ratio = € <u>1.20</u> = 12   0.10 cent A plc is valued at 12 times earnings

---

[33] Market to book value is the market value per share divided by the book value (*i.e.* the value as recorded in the books of account) per share.

[34] Price/revenue ratio is the price per share divided by the sales per share.

18–71   The price earnings ratio is a multiple and represents the number of times' earnings investors are willing to pay for the firm. Earnings per share is disclosed in the annual accounts of publicly quoted companies and the market price is available from the relevant stock exchange and in the business press.

18–72   The discounted cash flow (or earnings) approach requires a projection of future cash flow (income), which is then discounted in order to determine value. Theoretically, discounting earnings is a better approach to the earnings multiple method – businesses are purchased for earnings they are expected to generate in the future, not for their past earnings. However, the use of past earnings has some merit as a guide to what might be generated in the future. The use of price earnings ratios also provides a more objective basis of valuation. In addition, the market tends to factor into the p/e ratio its evaluation of the maintainability and quality of historical earnings.

18–73   When the earnings multiple approach is used the expert can to a large extent rely on market-generated information to value a firm. The expert can calculate the value of the firm as the product of the market-generated price earnings ratio of publicly traded companies in the same industry (or the average for the industry) and the most recent earnings of the firm. Earnings multiple has the advantage of taking direct market-generated information, and as such may reduce speculation and be more appropriate for use by the expert in assisting the court.

18–74   The price earnings approach is an all-inclusive value. The value arrived at with price earnings ratios is a value for the entire company including goodwill (if any). Price earnings ratios are quoted after tax and should therefore be applied to after tax profits.

Selecting the multiple/price earnings ratio

18–75   To use the price earnings (earnings multiple) approach there must be publicly traded companies with which to compare the company to be valued. In practice this can be difficult. It requires at least one company, but preferably a few companies, that are publicly traded and that are sufficiently comparable with the subject company to make meaningful comparisons. The first step is to identify companies in similar or related industries, and then refine that initial identification to those that are comparable. Sources of information include analysts and/or brokers' reports on the industry, databases, trade organisations, the owners of the business, clients and suppliers of the business and publicly available information. Factors to be considered as indicators of similarity include industry, size, historical growth, and by comparing various financial ratios across firms.

18–76   It is usual to find a wide diversity in price earnings ratios of publicly quoted companies in the same industry. An analysis of the reasons for these differences might provide additional insights. One reason that must be investigated is the possibility that the companies follow different accounting treatments and have different accounting methods and policies.

Comparison of market capitalisation and book value is important. A high price earnings ratio might indicate a company with a high book value, or might indicate a company with a strong growth track record with expectations of continued growth, and therefore a willingness of the market to pay a greater multiple for that company's shares. Taking all these factors into account, the subject company and comparable public companies need to be compared to determine a price earnings ratio. One approach might be to compute median price earnings ratios from a group of five to 10 comparable companies and apply this to the subject business to be valued.

Problem of non-comparability

18–77   Comparable price earnings ratios purport to compare the value of private companies with the market values of public company shares. When the earnings multiple approach is used with the market-generated price earnings ratio, the only necessary assumption is that the firm in question is not significantly different from the average firm in the industry in terms of expected earnings growth rate and risk (or that the differences offset each other). Market forces which are common to all firms in the industry will, to some extent, control the growth rate and earnings. Assuming average performance is *a priori* a reasonable assumption.

18–78   However, valuation of private interests by comparison with public company shares is often an apples-and-oranges situation. Even when companies in the same industry have been identified, true comparability may remain difficult. Size and extent of diversification may be problems. Even if a few companies were comparable in terms of product this might help. If only one company is comparable it is questionable whether any basis for comparison has been established.

Typically publicly traded companies are larger than most private companies. Private companies usually have a narrower product focus and are less diverse than public companies, making comparisons more difficult. There are other factors such as geographical dispersion and depth of management that weigh negatively in comparing private and public companies. The comparison can become even more difficult for smaller, more specialised closely held companies.

18–79   If comparison companies have been identified, these comparison companies need to be examined from as many angles as possible to determine how they compare to the company being valued and to further understand how their strengths and weaknesses relate to their price earnings ratios. Additional detailed comparison is required in relation to quality and depth of management, market share, geographical diversity, product diversity, sales growth rates, net profit growth rates, gross and net profit relationships, return on capital, adequacy of capital structure and risk profile. A simple example of the earnings multiple approach is shown in Table 18.9 (see also Tables 18.6, 18.11 and 18.12).

Table 18.9: Example earnings multiple approach to valuing a business

	A Ltd €000	B Ltd €000
Maintainable profits after taxation	8,000	2,000
Share capital – ordinary €1 shares	20,000	
– ordinary 25 cent shares		10,000
Price earnings ratio of comparable quoted company	10	12
Value of company	80,000	24,000

18–80 Table 18.10 shows the discounted cash flow, capitalisation of earnings and super profits approaches to valuation applied to a simple case.

Table 18.10: Example discounted cash flow, capitalisation of earnings and super profits approach to valuing a business

Company has net tangible assets of €45 million
Maintainable earnings before tax are currently and are forecast at €13.5 million per annum
The normal return on investments is 20%, as is the discount rate
The price/earnings ratio is 5
Goodwill is to be valued at three years' excess earnings or super profits

Capitalisation of forecast earnings
€13.5 million x p/e 5 = €67.5 million

Super profits	€m
Actual maintainable earnings	13.5
Normal return €45 million x 20%	(9.0)
Excess earnings/super profits	4.5
Goodwill €4.5 million x 3	13.5
Net tangible assets	45.0
	58.5

Discounting	€m	
Present value of €9 million for 10 years at 20%	37.728	(€9m x 4.192$_{\text{Note 1}}$)
Present value of €4.5 million for three years at 20%	9.477	(€4.5m x 2.106$_{\text{Note 2}}$)
	47.214	

Note 1: The factor of 4.192 is obtainable from annuity tables and is the present value of an annuity at an interest rate of 20% after 10 years.

Note 2: The factor of 2.106 is obtainable from annuity tables and is the present value of an annuity at an interest rate of 20% after 3 years.

18–81   The net assets approach and capitalisation of earnings approaches are applied to a simple example in Table 18.11.

Dividend yield basis

18–82   The dividend yield basis is usually used to value a minority shareholding. As illustrated in Table 18.5 (see para. **18–48**), dividend valuations do not differ fundamentally from other cash flow valuations. The past or future assumed level of dividend is valued based on the investment return, taking into account an appropriate weighting for risk.

Valuation of minority parcels of shares in private companies is often based on the capitalisation of dividends rather than maintainable earnings. This recognises that minority shareholders are not in a position to direct the company or influence the distribution of dividends or the investment of retained profits. As a result, the value of such shareholdings is generally restricted to the right to receive dividends. The dividend yield method involves computing a capital value for the shares such that, when the dividends paid are expressed as percentage of this capital value, it produces a reasonable yield when compared with the yield that could be obtained from a comparable publicly quoted company. Some discount would normally be applied to reflect any restrictions on transferability of the shares and the absence of a ready market in the shares. An example of the earnings multiple and dividend yield approaches shown in Table 18.12.

18–83   As the examples above have shown, different approaches to valuation give different results. In the United States, the courts have rejected valuations that did not give appropriate weightings to a variety of factors such as net asset values, earnings and dividend-paying capacity.[35] They have accepted that price earnings multiples of public companies can help to assess the fair market value of a closely held company – but should not be the only method used. A valuation should not rely solely on one method or approach to value, but rather on a combination of approaches.[36]

Factors affecting the valuation

18–84   Many business owners have an idea of what their business is worth, based on such factors as the value of its assets minus liabilities, recent sales of competing companies, industry traditions and their own entrepreneurial instincts. Forensic accountants must determine the fair value of the business taking into account both qualitative and quantitative factors associated with the specific business. The complexity of carrying out a full valuation cannot be under-estimated – it requires research into the business, its industrial and commercial context, the market and the economy together with a substantial degree of judgment.

---

[35] *Estate of Andrews v. Commissioner*, 79 T.C. U.S. 938 (1982).
[36] *Ronald v. 4-Cs Electronic Packaging, Inc*, 168 Cal. App. 3d 290; 214 Cal. Rptr. 225 (1985).

Table 18.11: Example net assets and capitalisation of earnings approaches to valuing a business

Example

The summarised balance sheets of C Ltd for the three years ending December 31, 20X1, 20X2 and 20X3 are as follows:

	20X1	20X2	20X3
	€000	€000	€000
Freehold property	3,700	3,700	3,700
Plant, machinery and equipment	1,800	1,600	1,400
Stock	1,860	2,160	2,320
Debtors	840	810	980
Creditors	(1,020)	(1,000)	(1,040)
Bank overdraft	(200)	(90)	(80)
	6,980	7,180	7,280
Share capital	4,000	4,000	4,000
Retained earnings	2,980	3,180	3,280
	6,980	7,180	7,280

- The freehold property has a market value of €5 million
- Plant, machinery and equipment is shown in the books at depreciated cost. It has a realisable value of €100,000, but it would have to be replaced in the near future at a cost of €3 million. The replacement equipment would have a 10-year useful life and would be valueless thereafter
- The value of stock, taking into account obsolescence factors not recognised in the accounts at the end of 20X1, 20X2 and 20X3, was €1.86 million, €2.09 million and €2.2 million respectively
- If stock were sold on a forced sale basis it would have a realisable value 20% lower than book value (net of obsolescence factors)
- Included in the debtors at December 31, 20X3 are debts of €80,000 expected to be irrecoverable
- The owners of the business, Mr and Mrs Bloggs, are elderly and do not work in the business. They are paid directors' fees of €600,000. The management is paid €700,000 per annum
- Annual dividends amount to €200,000
- If Mr and Mrs Bloggs sold their shares, they could invest the proceeds at a yield of 12.5% per annum
- Earnings are to be based on maintainable earnings, averaged over the last two years.

Net assets valuation	Going concern value	Break-up valuation
	€000	€000
Freehold property	5,000	5,000
Plant, machinery and equipment	100	100
Stock	2,200	1,760
Debtors	900	900
Creditors	(1,040)	(1,040)
Bank overdraft	(80)	(80)
Valuation	7,080	6,640

Multiple of earnings		20X2		20X3
		€000		€000
Profit for the year retained	(3,180–2,980)	200	(3,280–3,180)	100
Add: Dividends paid		200		200
Profit attributable to ordinary shares		400		300
Adjustments				
Directors' fees		600		600
Stock written down to net realisable value:				
Opening stock		—		70
Closing stock		(70)		(120)
Write off bad debt		—		(80)
Adjusted profit		930		770
Average			850	

Capitalising earnings of €850,000 ÷ 12.5% = €6.8 million

Conclusion

The range of valuations is therefore €7.08 to €6.8 to €6.64 million.

Once the purpose of the valuation is identified, the forensic accountant will examine those factors that are relevant to that purpose. The principal factors to take into account in arriving at such a valuation are summarised in Table 18.13. Six categories of factors are identified:

(1) Economic factors: macroeconomic factors relating to the general economy should be taken into account in valuing businesses, as should microeconomic factors affecting, say, the particular industry in which the business operates. Knowledge of the industry may be essential to do a proper valuation. In smaller businesses the regional and local business environment may be more important.

(2) Firm-specific factors: these are factors relating to the business itself, such as its earning capacity, dividend paying capacity, etc.

(3) Management: the management of the business needs to be considered, including, in smaller family owned businesses, the role of the owner.

(4) Shareholdings in the business: distribution of the shares of the company, the different rights attaching to the shares and other share-related considerations will have an important influence on value.

(5) Financial information: financial data, both internal and external to the firm, is of course essential in a proper valuation of any business, and includes the book value per share, market prices of comparable companies, etc.

(6) Assets: individual assets may also be significant in the valuation, especially intangibles such as goodwill.

18–85 Special factors may have an important bearing on the valuation. Industry and local effects will normally be included in the valuation through a risk-adjusted discount rate or choice of multiplier. Eastaway, Booth and Eamer[37] discuss case law on the treatment by the courts of various factors in business and share valuations.

Impact of unreported income on valuation of a business

18–86 A problem frequently encountered in the valuation of private companies is the failure to record all its income in its financial statements – possibly for tax reasons. Unreported cash is often an issue in matrimonial cases where one of the spouses claims that the business makes more money than the financial statements indicate (and therefore that the business is worth more than it appears).

This situation raises two difficulties:

– What is the amount of the unreported income?

---

[37] Eastaway, N., Booth, H. and Eamer, K., *Practical Share Valuation* (4th ed., Butterworths, London, 1998), Chap. 5.

Table 18.12: Example earnings multiple and dividend yield approaches to valuing a business

The following are the summarised accounts of Family A Ltd for the past five years

	20X5 €000	20X4 €000	20X3 €000	20X2 €000	20X1 €000
Balance sheet					
Fixed assets	3,520	3,320	3,100	2,790	2,660
Net current assets	870	600	440	310	170
	4,390	3,920	3,540	3,100	2,830
Share capital (25 cent shares)	640	640	640	640	640
Profit and loss account	3,750	3,280	2,900	2,460	2,190
	4,390	3,920	3,540	3,100	2,830
Contingent liabilities	1,040	810	550	220	190
Profit and loss account					
Profit before tax	760	620	670	650	570
Tax	(118)	(68)	(80)	(250)	(220)
Profit after tax	642	552	590	400	350
Dividends	(172)	(172)	(150)	(130)	(110)
Profit retained	470	380	440	270	240

Share price

Comparable plcs	High	Low	Current	Dividend	Dividend Cover	Dividend Yield	p/e
A plc (50 cent shares)	277	201	202	6.23	3.5	4.7	9.3
B plc (25 cent shares)	168	132	132	3.27	5.6	3.8	7.2

Q: How should A Family Ltd be valued?

Multiple of earnings valuation

	Latest profit €000	Average profit €000	Weighted average profit €000
	642		
Profit after tax $(590_{20X3} + 552_{20X4} + 642_{20X5}) \div 3$		595	
Profit $(590_{20X3} \times 1 + 552_{20X4} \times 2 + 642_{20X5} \times 3) \div 6$			603
Number of shares	2,560	2,560	2,560
Earnings per share	25.1 cent	23.2 cent	23.6 cent
Using A plc multiple	9.3	9.3	9.3
Value per share	€2.33	€2.16	€2.19
Using B plc multiple	7.2	7.2	7.2
Value per share	€1.81	€1.67	€1.70

Conclusion: Value of shares are in the price range €1.67 to €2.33

Dividend yield valuation

Range 6.72 cent/$0.038_{B\,plc}$ to 6.72 cent/$0.047_{A\,plc}$ = Share value €1.77 cent to €1.43 cent
Given the dividend cover, the higher valuation based on the yield on B plc's shares might be favoured

Net assets valuation	€000	
Book value of assets:	4,390	
Contingent liabilities	(1,040)	
Valuation based on available information	3,350	2,560 shares = €1.31 per share

It is likely that current net assets are worth more than their book value. The book valuation is likely to be the lowest acceptable value for the shares.

Note: Taxation on dividends has been ignored.

– What are the implications of disclosing the unreported income?

Typically, unreported cash will not appear in the books and accounts of the business, or in its bank statements. One way to estimate the unreported cash is to examine the owner's personal sources and uses of cash. If uses exceed sources over a period of time, this provides an indication that under-reporting is occurring and the forensic accountant can estimate the amount, for the purposes of valuing the business. Another indicator of the existence and scale of unreported cash can be found by applying an expected or industry standard margin to the costs of the business and comparing expected revenues, as reported in the accounts.

Adjustments to accounting records

18–87 Valuations should be based on underlying data and should be justifiable on the basis of underlying facts. Valuation of businesses may involve an add-back to reported earnings for "above-market" owner compensation. The above-market compensation may be paid not only to owners but also to family of owners. In valuing the company, the possibility that these "employees" could be replaced at lower cost must be considered. Conversely, an owner may accept below-market compensation if, for example, the company is in financial difficulties. To calculate the adjustment, the actual compensation paid by the company to be valued must be compared with that paid by other companies to employees with similar duties and skills. Such benchmark compensation may need to be adjusted to take into account the years of service, knowledge of the market, management skills and other factors relating to the employee. In comparing compensation, it is important to consider all sources of compensation including salary, share options, pension plans, bonus plans, fringe benefits, etc.

18–88 A basic principle of business valuations is that events subsequent to the valuation date should not be considered in determining fair market value – except to the extent they were reasonably foreseeable at the valuation date. The courts have drawn a distinction between subsequent events that could not have been foreseen that have an impact on value (*e.g.* discovery of oil) – which should not affect the valuation and subsequent events which provide evidence of value at the valuation date (*e.g.* actual sale of property of the business shortly after the valuation date which throws light on the value of the property at the valuation date).

Valuation of businesses for divorce

18–89 Of all types of cases in which a business value is a primary issue, divorce cases tend to be the most acrimonious. A primary reason why many divorce valuation cases go to court is that the relevant valuation guidelines tend to be ambiguous and to offer a variety of options to the parties.

Table 18.13: Factors to consider in a valuation assignment

Economy/industry
- Outlook for the economy in general
- Outlook for the industry affecting the business
- Industry forecasts
- Maturity of the industry
- Competitiveness of the industry
- Information on the local economy and local competitive position
- Industry events of relevance at or around the valuation date, *e.g.* changes in regulation
- Investor risk that is inherent to the industry
- Information on similar companies in the industry
- Details of recent sales of similar companies in the industry

Business
- Nature of the business
- History of the business
- Maturity of the business
- Memorandum and articles of association
- Shareholder or other relevant agreements
- Board and management minutes
- Organisation charts
- Quality of management
- Quality of employees
- Major customers
- Major competitors

Management
- Management depth
- Executive compensation
- Importance of involvement of current owner
- Viability and value of the business without the current owner

Shares
- Ownership of shares
- Share option and share incentive schemes
- Recent sales and other transactions in shares
- Percentage of the company being valued
- Rights attaching to class of shares in question, including transferability of shares
- Market price of similar listed or quoted company shares
- Investor risk of the business

Financial
- Financial accounts
- Management accounts
- Recent financial history
- Budgets and forecasts
- Financial projections
- Amount and trend of net profits
- Business's earning capacity
- Dividend history
- Dividend paying capacity

Assets
- Clarification of ownership of assets
- Valuation of individual assets, *e.g.* property, plant, etc.
- Valuation of specialist assets, *e.g.* intellectual property rights
- Book value and financial condition
- Value of goodwill

18–90   Establishing business value for the purposes of matrimonial dissolution is one of the more common reasons for using a business valuation specialist. Perhaps more than in any other scenario divorce-related valuation requires that the forensic accountant bring to bear all of his analytical and investigative skills. There are at least three reasons for this:

- First, the spouse claiming a share of the business operated by the other spouse will often contend that the business has hidden assets.

- Secondly, to refute or substantiate that contention, a forensic accountant will have to review the company's financial statements thoroughly. If these are not recent, or if they incorporate personal, non-business transactions, he will be unable to produce a reliable valuation without reviewing the underlying records and transactions.

– Thirdly, the peculiar nature of divorce often makes it difficult to establish and maintain an effective valuation date. As a result, the analyst may need to be more active than normal in producing financial statements that accurately reflect the company's assets, operations and financial health. He also will need to understand how judicial attributes and combativeness between the parties make business valuation in matrimonial cases different from its application to other contexts.

Method of valuation

18–91   The most common method used in divorce is the multiple of earnings method. While fair market value is appropriate for most valuations, it is not always applicable in divorce. For example, valuation of non-marketable professional goodwill cannot be based on fair market value because such assets cannot be sold in any marketplace. In such cases, the intrinsic value standard, *i.e.* what an asset is deemed to be worth, notwithstanding its value on the market – may be more appropriate.

Unrecorded assets, liabilities, earnings and expenses

18–92   In relation to the balance sheet, forensic accountants must take account of the possibility that there are unrecorded assets and liabilities. Examples include: fully depreciated assets shown in the balance sheet at nil valuation (but which may be of significant value), unrecorded leases, misstated stock, ownership of patents, franchises or royalty rights, under-funded pension liabilities, pension schemes with surplus assets and the cash surrender value of insurance policies.

In addition, amounts shown in the balance sheet must be carefully examined. For example, property and investments may be included at cost, whereas market value could be significantly greater. Assets may be reduced in value due to high levels of depreciation and amortisation, or due to substantial provisions (against, say, stock and debtors).

18–93   Profit and loss accounts also need to be carefully analysed. Earnings may be understated and expenses overstated. Amounts for turnover may exclude unrecorded cash sales. On the expenses side, personal expenses such as travel and entertainment may be included when they do not strictly relate to the business or they may be inflated. Adjustments to management salaries and transactions with related parties should be particularly scrutinised.

Goodwill

18–94 As explained in paras **7–70** *et seq.*, jurisprudence in judicial separation and divorce cases is very limited and the Irish courts have not considered the valuation of goodwill in matrimonial disputes. Theoretically speaking, there are three choices in the treatment of goodwill by the courts. The choice depends on whether the goodwill is considered to be personal goodwill relating to the individual or to be practice or enterprise goodwill relating to the business:

(1) The courts may refuse to place a value on any type of goodwill.

(2) Personal goodwill may be considered to be the separate property of an individual and not a divisible matrimonial asset.

(3) However, in some cases, practice goodwill may be considered to be a distributable matrimonial asset.

Goodwill may be a distributable asset if the practice has a value independent of the presence or reputation of a particular individual. In such cases, valuers will have to isolate enterprise goodwill from personal goodwill for asset allocation purposes.

Peelo[38] suggests, in an Irish context, that "goodwill does not have a monetary value to the individual partner in a large professional practice" and that "goodwill does not exist to an extent attributable to an individual partner". As there are few legal cases in Ireland or the United Kingdom on this issue, judgments in other jurisdictions may be looked at for guidance.

18–95 Divorce courts in the United States have difficulty dealing with non-transferable goodwill after a marriage is dissolved. First, if the goodwill was produced by the combined efforts of several partners, it is not merely a matrimonial asset, but that which may be jointly held by others. Secondly, if the business was discontinued after dissolution of the marriage, then there would be a loss of goodwill. For these reasons, divorce courts in the United States have differed over whether goodwill, particularly for professionals, should be considered an asset and what value, if any, to place on it.

In the United States, professional goodwill was not regarded as a divisible matrimonial asset until the case of *Golden v. Golden*[39] decided that matrimonial property valuations for matrimonial dissolution involving professional practices had to include an estimate of professional goodwill.

---

[38] Peelo, D., *Valuations, Mergers and Sales of Professional Practices* (Peelo & Partners, Dublin, 1998), p. 10.
[39] 270 CA 2d 401 (1969).

Most American states consider goodwill to be an asset to be included in valuing a business, provided it is independent of the owner's professional reputation.[40] For example, the Indiana Supreme Court overturned a 10-year court decision and held that personal goodwill in a professional practice is not a divisible marital asset.[41] The basis for the decision was that personal goodwill is "nothing more than the future earning capacity of the individual" and, therefore, is not a divisible asset. The court stated that goodwill that "depends on the continued presence of a particular individual is a personal asset."[42] According to the same judgment, enterprise or practice goodwill, on the other hand, is a divisible asset. The court stated, in the context of a medical practice with contracts to provide services to two local hospitals, that enterprise goodwill was not based "on the identity of the physicians but on the exclusive service contracts that were attributes of the business". It should be noted that there were two dissenting judges who considered that some element of personal goodwill should be treated as a distributable matrimonial asset.

Thus, consistent with the views of the two dissenting judges referred to above, Californian courts have held that personal goodwill is a "community" (*i.e.* matrimonial) asset. In *Re: Marriage of Nichols* it was stated:

> "It is a community asset because husband's experience, reputation and skill, which enable him to command this high income were developed while he was marriage [*sic*] to wife".[43]

In the earlier case of *Re: Marriage of Fenton* the court held:

> "The practice of the sole practitioner husband will continue, with the same intangible value as it had during marriage. Under the principles of community property law, the wife, by virtue of her position of wife, made to that value the same contribution as does a wife to any of the husband's earnings and accumulations during the marriage. The wife is as much entitled to be recompensed for that contribution as if it were represented by the increase in value of stock in a family business."[44]

---

[40] Mason, M.E. and Cohen. M.S., "From a matrimonial lawyer's perspective – the ten (and a few more) most frequent errors made by business appraisers" (American Academy of Matrimonial Lawyers website www.aaml.org/Articles/2000-1/10mistakes.htm), pp. 10–15.

[41] *Yoon v. Yoon*, 711 NE 2d 1265 (Ind. 1999).

[42] Baker, C., "From the bench: Case notes: Court excludes personal goodwill from marital estate" in *The Expert Litigation Services Journal*, www.gmgcpa.com/DOCS/The %20Expert%20Litigation%20Services20%Journal.htm.

[43] 33 Cal. Rptr. 2d 13 (CA App. 1994), as cited in Mason, M.E. and Cohen, M.S., "From a matrimonial lawyer's perspective – the ten (and a few more) most frequent errors made by business appraisers" (American Academy of Matrimonial Lawyers website www.aaml.org/Articles/2000-1/10mistakes.htm.), p. 15.

[44] 184 Cal. Rptr. 597 (CA App. 1982), as cited in Mason, M.E. and Cohen, M.S., *ibid.*

18–96   Professional goodwill may be seen as the present value of the professional spouse's future earning capacity and therefore the separate property of the spouse. Alternatively, professional goodwill may be seen as part of the value to which the non-professional spouse has contributed. For purposes of a matrimonial dissolution, the parties are primarily concerned with the existence, value, and consequences of the "goodwill" of a professional business in an economic sense, as distinguished from legal or accounting concepts.[45] Although intangible, goodwill is no less certain or real than other assets. In fact, the calculated value of goodwill can be more certain and less speculative than the calculated value of other more tangible assets. Including professional goodwill in the concept of matrimonial property requires a correct understanding of the relation between present asset values and future earnings. In other words, it is important to realise that the value of an asset reflects the future earnings or cash flows to be derived from it. Once the existence of the non-professional spouse's ownership of a matrimonial interest in future excess earnings has been established, the method of goodwill valuation outlined in case law follows logically.

18–97   Goodwill is calculated in divorce proceedings by discounting future matrimonial excess earnings and represents an asset to be divided. The earnings on which the calculation of goodwill is based should not therefore form part of the basis for calculating maintenance payments. Suppose future excess earnings were included in the income basis used to calculate maintenance, the spouse receiving such payments would receive a proportion of future excess earnings as part of maintenance payments, in addition to a share of the matrimonial goodwill. This would, in effect, be a double count.

These principles apply whenever property or monetary assets are transferred. If the spouse is awarded a wholly-owned house, then the future income of the paying spouse is reduced by the fair market value of the housing services forgone. If the paying spouse transfers cash to the other spouse as the latter's matrimonial interest in a rental property, retaining ownership of the property after dissolution, then the property's future rental income should be excluded from the income basis used to calculate maintenance. An economic asset is always interchangeable with, and a mirror image of, future income from the asset.

18–98   To deny the existence of goodwill as a matrimonial asset would be to neglect heated discussions of goodwill occurring in sales of professional practices, in the admission of new partners to a partnership, and in various negotiations of covenants not to compete. In these examples, goodwill is considered a property right which can be bought and sold separate from the personage of the original professional.

---

[45] *Marriage of Lopez*, 38 CA 3d 93 at 108 (1974).

Although the legal and verbal definitions of goodwill may be considered somewhat elusive and changeable over time, the economic and tax definitions have remained relatively constant. Economists have avoided verbal confusion by defining goodwill according to its method of calculation. The presence of goodwill and its value, therefore, rests upon excess earnings over and above a fair return on tangible net assets. In a professional practice, the concept of "tangible net assets" should be expanded to include labour services of the professional and his assistants. Goodwill value is derived from the discounted future excess earnings of the professional practice. Excess earnings for a professional practice may relate to business location, personality of the professional, unusual talent, etc.

Withdrawing partner

18–99   The value of an interest in a business is typically based on a price that would be paid by a hypothetical willing buyer. The value of an interest in a practice, in which a buyer intends to practice as a professional, could be defined as the ability to generate earnings above what the buyer could earn as an employee. Arguably, practice goodwill creates such value. A hypothetical buyer would derive little value from the remaining practitioners' professional goodwill, which would generally not be included in the valuation.

The value of a business depends on its ability to generate cash flows for its owners. Data on sales of comparable companies can also provide meaningful insight into the value of a business.

Although net profit or cash flow are generally most important, the turnover may provide a good indicator of value if there is some certainty concerning the costs associated with such level of turnover. In such cases, the net profit can be reasonably estimated.

Compulsory acquisition

18–100   As explained in Chapter 9, businesses are entitled to be compensated for disturbance, *i.e.* loss or expense suffered as a result of the compulsory acquisition of property. Loss of goodwill is one of the items for which compensation can be claimed. Where business premises are acquired, the owner will be entitled to compensation where, as a result of the acquisition, the goodwill of the business is either lost or diminished. Goodwill in this situation has been described as the ability to derive a future profit out of the premises from which the plaintiff has been dispossessed.[46]

The goodwill to be compensated is to be determined on the basis of its value to the owner, which cannot be less than market value.[47] As was stated in *Afzal v. Rochdale Metropolitan Borough Council*[48]:

---

[46] *Reed Employment Ltd v. London Transport Executive* [1978] 246 E.G. 233.
[47] *R.C. Handley Ltd v. Greenwich London Borough Council* [1970] 214 E.G. 213.
[48] [1980] R.V.R. 165.

"The market value of the claimant's goodwill is not the measure of what the council are required to pay. In respect of a business extinguished on compulsory acquisition the measure is always that of value to the claimant not that of value in the market".

Start-up businesses

18–101   Any valuation approach is difficult to use when dealing with a company with the potential for explosive growth. If the company being valued is on the cutting edge of some technological, scientific discovery or some other advance, traditional valuation approaches may not be relevant.

Valuation of closely held businesses

18–102   Information may be readily available about how to determine the worth of a publicly traded company, but finding trained professionals capable of determining the value of a closely held private business is a more difficult task. In cases of closely held companies, data may be more difficult to obtain than from public companies. Without access to reliable earnings data, the valuer lacks information on which to postulate earnings growth rates required to compute present values of future earnings. As a result, the valuer must rely on alternative information as a proxy for earnings. If a record of dividends is available, then dividends can be used as a substitute for earnings data, acknowledging that past dividends could have a weak relationship with the company's dividend paying capacity. The valuation of a closely held business will take account of:

– future cash inflow from owning the business;

– comparison with the sale of any similar companies;

– value of the physical assets.

18–103   Closely held businesses requiring valuation, such as sole proprietorships, partnerships and private companies, may be found in the manufacturing, distribution, retail and other sectors. Professional practices also frequently need to be valued as a result of disputes such as partnership disputes or in the context of divorce proceedings. The valuation process is complex and requires not only an understanding of the line of business in which the company operates but also an understanding of relevant economic principles together with the analytical skills necessary to interpret financial statements.

18–104   The determination of fair market value of shares in the case of a closely held company is more complex than the determination for a widely held public company. The traditionally accepted definition of fair value is determined by the price negotiated between a willing buyer and a willing seller when the former is not under any compulsion to buy and the latter is not under any compulsion to sell, both parties having reasonable knowledge of relevant facts. For the shares in a closely held company, there is no directly analogous representative transaction in an established market. Thus, fair market value depends on the circumstances and relevant facts as determined by a valuer who exercises informed judgment and reasonableness.

18–105 Frequently, valuers of shares in closely held companies use the prices of publicly quoted shares of companies in the same industry as a guide. Valuation of shares on this basis is in fact a prediction of the future based on facts available at the date of valuation. This is because the prevailing share prices of public companies reflect the market consensus as to the future for the company and its industry as well as market sentiment generally. When shares are closely held, they are traded infrequently in an erratic market. As a result, some other measure of value may be appropriate. Nevertheless, when valuing shares which are not publicly traded, it is acceptable for the valuer to make comparisons with the prices of listed shares of comparable companies in a similar line of business, providing he also takes into account factors reflecting the essential differences between the company being valued and the public entity being used for comparison.

18–106 Important factors to consider in valuing closely held shares are: the company's earnings and dividend payout capacity; the history of the company from incorporation; the general economic outlook and the outlook for the specific industry; the book value of the shares; the financial condition of the business, previous sales of the shares[49]; and the size of the block of shares to be valued.

18–107 When access to records is not restricted certain ratios can also be calculated and used to assist valuation. The price to earnings ratio, the price to operating profit ratio and the price to sales ratio should yield similar results. The price to book value ratio will not because it depends on past rather than current expenditure values. Ratios based on current earnings are more useful predictors of future values.

Premiums and discounts of private company valuations

18–108 Regardless of the valuation method used, there may be a need for a premium or (more likely) a discount on the calculated value. The issue of discounts and premiums presupposes a valuation approach based on a continuing business. In a net asset or liquidation valuation, one assumes the shareholders would get their pro rata share of the proceeds of sale. The courts have found that shareholdings of an individual in different capacities should be aggregated.[50]

---

[49] In *McNamee v. Revenue Commissioners* [1954] I.R. 214 the sales price in a previous sale was taken into account by the judge in deciding a value for the shares.
[50] *Barclays Bank v. IRC* [1961] A.C. 509.

Once the overall value of the business has been determined, a valuation adjustment or discount can be applied to specific ownership interests. Such discounts can be used to recognise minority interests that lack control over business policies and procedures and non-marketability issues related to the owners' freedom to sell their shares. These discounts can range from 5 per cent to over 50 per cent, depending on the ownership interests being evaluated.

Discounts for minority holdings and premia for majority holdings are not applied in the valuation of quasi-partnership private companies. Instead, such shares are valued on a pro-rata basis.[51]

Premium for controlling interest

18–109 A controlling interest in a business is sometimes worth a premium over its pro rata value. A controlling interest can direct the company, determine compensation, and enforce the implementation of most key decisions.

There is no premium for control in valuing a 100 per cent holding. The premium for control cannot raise the value of shares to exceed the value of a company in its entirety. A premium might be paid for a controlling interest to reflect potential economies of scale, to achieve a reduction in competition, or to secure a source of supply or outlet for the company's products. Such a premium attaches to particular purchasers willing to pay over and above what the general purchaser would pay. Courts in the United States have held that there should be no premium for a minority shareholding.[52]

Discount for lack of marketability of the shares

18–110 In *McNamee v. Revenue Commissioners*[53] Maguire J. held that in estimating the price which shares would fetch if sold in the open market, the court should have regard to the number of prospective purchasers the shares would attract, the earning capacity of the company, the dividend policy of the directors, the resources of the company, its capital and replacement requirements, its business difficulties and competitors, the nature of the trade and the inability to dispose of the shares freely, once bought.

18–111 There are at least two broad general types of discount common in the valuation of private companies that decrease value:

– discount for minority interest reflecting lack of control; and

– discount for lack of marketability.

[51] Courtney, T.B., *The Law of Private Companies* (Butterworths, Dublin, 1994), pp. 417–419.
[52] *Estate of Bright v. United States*, 658 F. 2d 393 (Ct Cl.1962).
[53] [1954] I.R. 214.

These discounts reduce the value of an ownership interest below its pro rata share of the business's overall value. Thus, how a company's ownership is divided can have a major impact on its cumulative market value and the value of any ownership interest.

As explained earlier, valuations based on public companies (*e.g.* using price earnings ratios) are discounted in the case of private company shares. The discount for lack of marketability can have a significant impact on the valuation of closely held businesses. Courts in the United States have upheld discounts for minority interests and lack of marketability.[54] In the United Kingdom the courts have applied a substantial discount because of restriction of transfer of shares.[55] In *Re William Courthope deceased*[56] a discount of one-third was applied to a 49 per cent shareholding, whereas in a more recent case[57] a 12.5 per cent discount was applied to the same percentage shareholding. In the case of *Re Castleburn Ltd*[58] the court upheld discounting of the value of a minority shareholding.

18–112 The rationale for marketability discounts is that if there is a thin market for the shares, it would require time and effort and expense to sell the shares. It could be argued that such an approach is double counting the discount, if the discount has already been taken into consideration in the valuation method used. Most approaches to valuing private companies factor in and provide for typical marketability discounts in the development of the capitalisation rate or multiple used.

Discount for minority interests

18–113 If one does not control a company, especially a private company, it is likely that the value of the minority interest is less than the pro rata share of the whole value of the company. A minority interest or an interest with lack of control is at a disadvantage in that it cannot influence the direction of the company, level of salaries, hiring of management, etc. As a consequence of this lesser power it is not unusual to expect the minority value to be somewhat less than the pro rata value of a controlling interest. Minority interest or lack of control discounts can range between 10 per cent and 40 per cent. Ignoring the discounted values of minority ownership can create a large (and avoidable) tax burden.

Conversely, price earnings ratios tend to be based on small minority blocks of shares. If an entire company is being valued a premium for control might be applied to a price earnings ratio based on minority interests. Table 18.14 summarises the discount rates applied in a variety of situations to valuing shares in private companies.

---

[54] *Hardwood v. Commissioner*, 82 T.C. (U.S.) 239 (1984).
[55] *Trustees of Johan Thomas Salvesen v. IRC* [1930] S.L.T. 387.
[56] [1928] 7 A.T.C. 538.
[57] *Battle v. IRC* [1980] S.T.C. 86.
[58] [1991] B.C.L.C. 89.

Table 18.14: Table of discounts for valuing shares in private companies

Source	Discount	
Case law		
Holt v. IRC [1953] 2 All E.R. 1499 at 1502	33.33%	
Lynall v. IRC [1971] 3 All E.R. 914 at 928	25–50%	
Giblin[1]		
50% shareholding (where the rest of the shares are held by one other individual)	20–30% of value of company	
25–49% shareholdings	30–40% of value of company	
	20–40% of p/e ratio	
1–24% shareholdings	50% of value of company	
	50% of value on dividend yield basis	
Revenue Commissioners[2]	Capital gains tax	Capital acquisitions tax
75–100% shareholdings	Nil%	Nil–5%
51–74% shareholdings	10%	10–15%
50% shareholdings	30%	20–30%
Over 25% shareholdings	40%	35–40%
Up to 25%		Value by reference to dividends; or discounted earnings, range 50–70%
15–24% shareholdings	60%	
10–14% shareholdings	70%	
1–9% shareholdings	80%	

[1] Giblin, B.H., *Valuation of Shares in Private Companies* (3rd ed., Institute of Taxation in Ireland, Dublin, 1999), p. 56.
[2] Revenue Practice Manuals on Share Valuations, e.g. Part 7, "CAT share valuation" in *Capital Acquisitions Tax Work Manual and Staff Guidelines* (Revenue Commissioners, Dublin).

Traditional approach

18–114   The traditional approach relies on studies that identify discounts on the sale of restricted shares in publicly traded companies or compare discounts on the sale of shares in closely held companies before and after an initial public offering. This data is used to determine the median discount and the resulting quantitative adjustments to reflect differences between the subject business and those involved in the empirical studies. This approach is not very precise as the studies typically show a wide range of discounts.

Quantitative Marketability Discount Model (QMDM)

18–115   A new mathematical model for estimating the discount is gaining acceptance in the United States. Developed by Mercer,[59] the quantitative

---

[59] Mercer, Z.C., *Quantifying Marketability Discounts* (Peabody Publishing, Memphis, Tennessee, 1997).

marketability discount model (QMDM) has a number of advantages over traditional methods. QMDM focuses on the subject company rather than comparisons with other businesses. QMDM attempts to replicate the quantitative aspects of the investment decision-making process. The model relies on five key assumptions an investor would consider in evaluating the purchase of a minority interest in a privately held company. These are:

– expected growth rate for the underlying value of the equity interest;

– expected dividend yield;

– expected dividend growth rate;

– expected holding period;

– required rate of return over the holding period.

These five assumptions are intuitively appealing as they reflect real-life factors that influence the price an investor will pay for the shares.

Portfolio discount

18–116   The underlying assets of a business may have less value when grouped together than they would if considered separately. Normally, as already stated, minority interests in private companies are discounted for lack of marketability and lack of control. However, there may be circumstances where discounts for lack of marketability are appropriate even where a 100 per cent acquisition is being valued. This would occur where there is a lack of a ready market for the shares which could be caused by:

– in the case of an asset holding company, difficulty in finding a buyer interested in the company's portfolio of assets;

– costs associated with sale of 100 per cent interest;

– an uncertain time horizon for finding a buyer;

– uncertainty about the form of proceeds.

The amount of the discount is influenced by factors such as whether liquidation of the company is contemplated (little discount for marketability) and whether there is an active acquisitions market for the type of business being valued (reduced discount for marketability).

18–117   Forced sale of a block of shares in a closely held company may result in a price that is higher or lower than fair market value. The price may be higher when, for example, the buyer needs the holding to gain control of the company. The price may be lower when minority shareholders are required to liquidate their holding in a thin market.

    Such a valuation may be required in personal injury cases. For example, if an employee with shares in a company is required to leave the company because of personal injury, that employee may, under the terms of the employee share scheme, need to sell the shares on leaving. Generally speaking, holdings of shares in companies are considered to be investments which are not subject to recovery as economic loss. However, shares held by employees can form part of the compensation (*i.e.* work incentive) package designed by senior management to align employee and firm interests. It may be a condition of employment that employees hold shares in the employer company. By being forced through personal injury to leave the employment, the shares may have to be relinquished, depriving the injured employee of significant employment compensation in the form of dividends from the shares and the capital gain attaching to the shares.

Legal framework for valuing companies and shares in companies

18–118   Valuations for the purpose of litigation must in general be carried out following principles developed through the courts. Often the valuer will have to be familiar with the relevant statutory requirements, case law or other peculiarity of the event relating to the valuation. Many valuations require the advice of lawyers. However, the courts have laid down few overriding principles in this area and the reported decisions of Irish courts have usually been very specific to the circumstances of the case in question. In addition, the basis of valuation of shares where a dispute arises, and the manner in which the valuation is performed, is often specified in a contract between the parties and the agreed terms will normally prevail (*e.g.* see *Horgan v. Murray*[60]).

18–119   The forensic accountant's opinions on business valuations are based on assumptions about certain legal rights. These assumptions may involve the application of statutes, case law, articles of association, byelaws, partnership agreements, shareholder agreements, etc. When forensic accountants examine legal rights and restrictions, they do so to determine how hypothetical willing buyers and sellers would view these rights and restrictions.

Valuation of businesses

18–120   Many of the share valuation cases coming before Irish courts arise as a result of section 205 of the Companies Act 1963 which deals with oppression of minorities (see Chapter 10 for details). Subsection (3) confers on the court wide discretion to have regard to all the circumstances in arriving at a fair valuation:

> "(3) If on any application under subsection (1) or subsection (2) the court is of opinion that the company's affairs are being conducted or the directors' powers

---

[60][1997] 3 I.R. 23.

are being exercised as aforesaid, the court may, with a view to bringing to an end the matters complained of, make such order as it thinks fit, whether directing or prohibiting any act or cancelling or varying any transaction or for regulating the conduct of the company's affairs in future, or for the purchase of the shares of any members of the company by other members of the company or by the company and in the case of a purchase by the company, for the reduction accordingly of the company's capital or otherwise."

In some cases the court will determine the value of shareholdings.[61]

Going concern valuation – non-assets basis of valuation

18–121 According to Courtney,[62] the issue of valuation was considered in *Irish Press plc v. Ingersoll Irish Publications Ltd*[63] where conflicting valuations were provided by opposing expert valuers. The valuations are shown in Table 18.15. The Irish Press valuer approached the valuation from the perspective of

Table 18.15: Valuations in *Irish Press plc v. Ingersoll Irish Publications Ltd*

Valuation date	Nov. 14, 1991	Dec. 21, 1993
Irish Press valuation	£m	£m
Value of masthead:		
(25% of 1991 turnover of £29 million)	7.25	
(20% of 1993 turnover of £27 million)		5.40
Deficit on shareholders' funds	(3.00)	(7.50)
Funding requirement to restore profitability		(13.00)
Value/(Deficit)	4.25	(15.10)
Irish Press valuer	4.25	nil
Ingersoll valuation		
Projected turnover of £30.5 in 3 years time x 1.75 turnover multiple of comparable U.K. quoted newspaper companies = £53 million		
Net present value in 1993 of £53m, assuming a required rate of return of 30%	24.00	24.00
Required capital injection	(14.00)	(14.00)
Uplift for special purchaser's cost savings	2.00	2.00
Deterioration between 1991 and 1993	2.00	
Ingersoll valuer	14.00	12.00
Barron J.'s valuation	10.00	4.5

Source: Adapted from Giblin, B.H., *Valuation of Shares in Private Companies* (3rd ed., Institute of Taxation in Ireland, Dublin, 1999), pp. 177–181.

---

[61] *Colgan v. Colgan*, unreported, High Court, July 22, 1993, *per* Costello J.; *Re Clubman Shirts Ltd* [1991] I.L.R.M. 43, *per* O'Hanlon J.; *Irish Press plc v. Ingersoll Irish Publications Ltd*, unreported, High Court, May 13, 1994, *per* Barron J.

[62] Courtney, T.B., *The Law of Private Companies* (Butterworths, Dublin, 1994), p. 416, para. 10.087.

[63] Unreported, High Court, Barron J., May 13, 1994; [1995] 2 I.R. 175.

valuing the newspaper titles or mastheads. Ingersoll's valuer used a multiple of turnover methodology, basing the multiple on comparable publicly quoted newspaper companies in the United Kingdom.

The principal difficulty for the judge in this case was that the two opposing experts used conventional methods of valuations, both of which were non-assets based. Barron J. considered both methods unsuitable to the company's business and financial condition. He valued the shares at November 14, 1991 on the basis of a previous transaction in the shares, *i.e.* on the basis that Ingersoll had paid £5 million for a 50 per cent interest in Irish Press in 1989 and the judge did not believe the value had dropped since then. On appeal to the Supreme Court Barron J.'s determination that the value of the shares was £10 million was not disturbed as it was held to be a finding of primary fact supported by credible evidence. However, Barron J.'s award of damages in the case (which was based on the £10 million valuation less the likely remaining cost of "turning around" the Irish Press Group) was overturned by the Supreme Court on the grounds that section 205 of the Companies Act 1963 does not permit the award of compensation or damages, but rather allows the court only to make orders "with a view to bringing to an end the matters complained of".

Going concern valuation – net assets basis of valuation

18–122   A court will address the specific circumstances of the case in deciding on the appropriate valuation basis for use in proceedings. The going concern basis of valuation was considered in *Buckingham v. Francis.*[64] On the other hand, in the case of *Re Clubman Shirts Ltd*[65] O'Hanlon J. said:

> "... I take the view that the petitioner's shareholding as of 31 July 1980, was unsaleable in the open market; had no value if assessed on a dividend yield or earnings yield basis, and the petitioner must fall back on a net asset valuation basis to support a claim for payment when the shares are to be acquired by the parties resisting his claim."

O'Hanlon J. added that the net assets valuation basis he was recommending should be based on a "break-up" basis and not in relation to their value to a company which could continue in business as a going concern.[66]

18–123   In the case of *Colgan v. Colgan,*[67] a valuation report valuing the company's properties at £7.37 million was available. Courtney attributes to the trial judge a deduction of £300,000 from this sum in respect of "current liabilities over current creditors".

---

[64] [1986] 2 All E.R. 738.
[65] [1991] I.L.R.M. 43 at 54.
[66] *ibid.* at 55.
[67] Unreported, High Court, Costello J., July 22, 1993 See Courtney, T.B., *The Law of Companies* (Butterworths, Dublin, 1994), p. 417.

Fair value under articles of association or by agreement between the parties

18–124   Where a shareholders' agreement or the company's articles of association provide for an extra-judicial mechanism for valuing shares the courts generally decline jurisdiction and insist that the parties exhaust the ordained procedure.[68]

The leading case on fair value is *Dean v. Prince*.[69] In this case, the court considered the valuation because the auditor had, in an attempt to achieve agreement, given reasons for his determination of the fair value of the shares. The auditor, in certifying a fair value for the shares, explained that he had not valued the company as a going concern as this would be inappropriate given the company's persistent losses. The judge held the valuation invalid and not binding because the auditor had not attributed a premium to the shareholdings when they were a majority and represented a controlling interest in the company. This finding was rejected by the Court of Appeal which supported the auditor's view that the shares should be valued pro rata to the company's worth, which should not be based on a going concern valuation given the losses.

Valuation of shares

18–125   Most share valuations commence with the valuation of the company as a whole and then proceed to assess the value of the shareholding in question. There is no universal rule followed by the courts in valuing shareholdings.

The main difficulty in valuing a shareholding is deciding whether the shares should be valued on a pro rata basis, or whether the shareholding should be subject to a premium (for majority holdings) or discount (for minority holdings). It is generally accepted by the courts that premiums or discounts should not be applied to minority or majority shareholdings in family owned quasi-partnership private companies[70] – all such shares should be valued on a pro rata basis.

Discount for minority interest

18–126   As already referred to in para. **18–108**, not discounting shares of quasi-partnerships[71] has been accepted in law in Ireland in *Colgan v. Colgan*, where Costello J. said:

---

[68]See *re XYZ Ltd* [1986] 2 B.C.C. 520.
[69][1954] 1 Ch. 409.
[70]See Courtney, T.B., *The Law of Private Companies* (Butterworths, Dublin, 1994), pp. 417–419.
[71]A quasi-partnership is "a company which although formed and registered under the Companies Acts 1963 to 1990, is in substance a partnership vehicle for its members". See Courtney, T.B., *ibid.*, p. 27, para. 1.080.

"… all the authorities indicate that there should not be a discount when dealing with a quasi partnership".[72]

18–127 It is also accepted that share values should not be discounted when sold pursuant to a court order under the oppression of minorities provisions (section 205) of the Companies Act 1963. Nourse J. set out the rationale for this ("section 75" refers to the English equivalent of section 205 of the Companies Act 1963):

> "I would expect that in a majority of cases where purchase orders are made under section 75 in relation to quasi-partnerships the vendor is unwilling in the sense that the sale has been forced upon him. Usually he will be a minority shareholder whose interests have been unfairly prejudiced by the manner in which the affairs of the company have been conducted by the majority. On the assumption that the unfair prejudice has made it no longer tolerable for him to retain his interest in the company, a sale of his shares will invariably be his only practical way out short of a winding up. In that kind of case it seems to me that it would not merely not be fair, but most unfair, that he should be bought out on the fictional basis applicable to a free election to sell his shares in accordance with the company's articles of association, or indeed on any other basis which involved a discounted price. In my judgment the correct course would be to fix the price pro rata according to the value of the shares as a whole and without any discount, as being the only fair method of compensating an unwilling vendor of the equivalent of a partnership share. Equally, if the order provided, as it did in *In re Jermyn Street Turkish Baths Ltd* [1970] 1 W.L.R. 1194, for the purchase of the shares of the delinquent majority, it would not merely not be fair, but most unfair, that they should receive a price which involved an element of premium."[73]

18–128 This approach was implicitly approved by Barron J. in *Horgan v. Murray*.[74]

Valuations in partnerships

Valuation of property

18–129 Dissolution of partnerships may require partnership property to be valued. The courts will value partnership property at current value rather than book value.[75] Where the partnership does not specify the method of valuation for a departing partner's share, the court is likely to order that the departing partner's share be acquired at valuation.[76]

---

[72] Unreported, High Court, July 22, 1993 at p. 7.
[73] *Re Bird Precision Bellows Ltd* [1984] Ch. 419 at 430.
[74] [1997] 3 I.R. 23.
[75] Twomey, M.J., *Partnership Law* (Butterworths, Dublin, 2000), p. 400, para 16.81. In *Barr v. Barr*, unreported, High Court, November 3, 1983, Barron J. held that balance sheet values for partnership property should only be used where the partnership agreement expressly provides for this method of valuation.
[76] *Sobell v. Boston* [1975] 2 All E.R. 282.

Valuation of partnership goodwill[77]

18–130 The Partnership Act 1890 does not mention goodwill. The question of whether a departing partner should be entitled to his share of goodwill in a partnership should be expressly stated in the partnership agreement. It is common (and can be advantageous for tax reasons[78]) for partnership agreements to expressly state that goodwill is to have no value for the purposes of admitting new partners and for calculating outgoing partner's share of the partnership. This also has practical advantages to the partnership as a whole. However, in some cases, goodwill has to be valued. The accounts or book value of goodwill is not an acceptable means of valuation.[79] Partnership goodwill represents the present value of a future income stream. As the circumstances of a partnership are completely different from a company, the basis of valuing partnership goodwill will be different to that of companies. No definitive formula exists for valuing partnership goodwill. Possible approaches include:

– multiple of profits (or proportion of profits), based on average profits for a specified previous period;

– multiple of annual fee income.

Peelo[80] suggests that goodwill in professional practices should not exceed a multiple of two times future profits. He also points out that in some practices, no goodwill is attributable to individual partners, as it is only vested in the continuing partners of the practice.

Interest

18–131 O'Hanlon J. refused to award interest in *Re Clubman Shirts Ltd*[81] even though 10 years had passed since the original findings giving rise to a need to value the shares.

Date of valuation

18–132 Where shares in private companies are valued under the terms of a shareholder agreement or the articles of association of the company, the valuation date is governed by the terms of the agreement or articles – typically the date of death of a deceased member, date of service of a transfer notice or the occurrence of an event giving rise to compulsory sale of the shares.[82]

---

[77] A useful guide to valuing goodwill in partnerships is Peelo, D., *Valuations, Mergers and Sales of Professional Practices* (Peelo & Partners, Dublin, 1998).
[78] Carroll, B.A. and O'Reilly, M., *Carroll's Tax Planning in Ireland* (Sweet & Maxwell, London, 1986), paras 13.2.1 *et seq.*
[79] *Davidson v. Wayman* [1984] 2 N.Z.L.R. 115.
[80] Peelo, D., *Valuations, Mergers and Sales of Professional Practices* (Peelo & Partners, Dublin, 1998), p. 10.
[81] [1991] I.L.R.M. 43.
[82] Courtney, T.B., *The Law of Private Companies* (Butterworths, Dublin, 1994), p. 420, para. 10.098.

18–133   Where shares are sold arising from an oppression of minorities action under section 205 of the Companies Act 1963 generally speaking, as set out by Nourse J., the date is taken as the date of the court order ordering the shares to be sold:

> "If there were to be such a thing as a general rule, I myself would think that the date of the order or the actual valuation would be more appropriate than the date of the presentation of the petition of the unfair prejudice. Prima facie an interest in a going concern ought to be valued at the date on which it is ordered to be purchased. But whatever the general rule might be it seems very probable that the overriding requirement that the valuation should be fair on the facts of the particular case would, by exceptions, reduce it to no rule at all."[83]

18–134   This general rule has been departed from in many cases. The date has been variously set as the date of oppression,[84] the date of the petition in the absence of oppression,[85] the date of a previous valuation (where the petitioner had previously unreasonably rejected fair value offers to purchase the shares)[86] and a date a few weeks before the court's order to purchase the shares.[87]

18–135   In *Irish Press plc v. Ingersoll Irish Publications Ltd*[88] Barron J. set the valuation date at five days before making his judgment, explaining the position as follows:

> "It has been submitted on behalf of the respondent that the date of presentation of the petition should be the date at which the shares should be valued. This may be the correct approach when the wrongdoer is being compelled to buy the shares but not if their value has already fallen by that date by reason of the oppression. A totally different situation arises when it is the wrongdoer who is being compelled to sell his shares. His actions have caused loss and the value of the shares has gone down. This factor must be reflected in the price which the petitioner will be required to pay for the respondent's shares. Here this fall has taken place, not only in the value of the respondent's shares but also in the value of the petitioner's shares. Clearly the appropriate date for valuing the respondent's shares must be the date of valuation. In addition, additional compensation must be provided for any drop in value of the petitioner's shares."

18–136   As indicated earlier, events that occur subsequent to the valuation date should be ignored.[89] Only to the extent that a knowledgeable investor could reasonably anticipate, as of the valuation date, that a subsequent event would occur, should the valuation reflect such an event. Conversely, contingent assets

---

[83] *Re London School of Electronics Ltd* [1985] 3 W.L.R. 474 at 484.
[84] *Re Clubman Shirts Ltd* [1983] I.L.R.M. 323; *Re OC (Transport) Services Ltd* [1984] B.C.L.C. 251.
[85] *Scottish Co-operative Wholesale Society Ltd v. Meyer* [1959] A.C. 324.
[86] *Re A Company* [1983] 1 W.L.R. 927.
[87] *Colgan v. Colgan*, unreported, High Court, July 22, 1993, *per* Costello J.
[88] Unreported, High Court, May 13, 1994 at p. 85.
[89] See *Bader v. United States*, 172 F. Supp. 833 (SD Ill. 1959).

and liabilities (*i.e.* assets and liabilities which depend on the occurrence or non-occurrence of a future event) at the valuation date should be taken into account even though they are difficult to quantify because of the uncertainty surrounding the magnitude and likelihood of the contingent event.

Date for valuation of matrimonial assets

18–137 One critical issue in valuations for the purpose of judicial separation/divorce is the valuation date. There is no consensus on the issue and, in the absence of jurisprudence, there is confusion about the date that should be chosen to value different assets. The valuation date may be anytime from the date of the commencement of the action to the date of the trial. The date may depend on the type of asset or on the nature of ownership of the asset, and also on the time the court is asked to make the valuation (especially where there has been a long delay between issuing proceedings and the hearing date). The following valuation dates may be pertinent to a divorce proceeding:

- the date the divorce complaint is filed;
- the date closest to trial or settlement;
- the date of separation;
- the date of marriage.

Courts may set the date the parties should use for valuation of each asset.

18–138 The date closest to trial or settlement generally applies to more complex companies whose value depends on a variety of factors such as workforce, location, underlying asset values, etc. The date of separation is more likely to apply to small or simple businesses whose revenues are directly attributable to the involved spouse. Examples include professional practices, skilled trades, and service businesses that are inseparable from the owner. (Using this valuation date assumes that the parties can agree on the date that they separated.)

A date of marriage valuation is applicable where one of the parties owned the business before the marriage began and the other spouse may be entitled to only half of the net growth that occurred while they were married. In such cases, the increase in value from the date of marriage to either the date of separation or the date of trial will need to be calculated by valuing the business as of the starting and ending dates. Various allocation formulae can then be applied to determine the matrimonial portion of the business to be divided.

In practice, the valuation date is almost always the complaint date. However, there are a number of variations on this. The valuation date may be the trial date. It is unusual for the date of valuation to tie in nicely with the financial year end of the business or professional practice to be valued. In such circumstances, the previous year's accounts might be a starting point from which to work.

Valuation by auditors

18–139   Auditors are often required under shareholders' agreements or under company articles of association to carry out the share valuation. Auditor valuations are rarely questioned by the courts, except where there is clearly an error, mistake or proof of some improper motive[90] or where auditors give reasons for their valuations.[91] In *Burgess v. Purchase and Sons (Farms) Ltd*[92] the company's articles provided that the shares should be valued at fair value which was to be determined by the company's auditors whose determination was to be final, binding and conclusive. The judge held that a "speaking valuation" could be impugned notwithstanding that the articles provided that it was final, binding and conclusive.

Concluding comment

18–140   To summarise, an overview of a valuation assignment is shown in Table 18.16.

Table 18.16: Overview of a valuation assignment

Purpose of valuation
Scope of valuation
Valuation date
Precise business, shares, assets to be valued
Time-frame for preparing the valuation
Format of valuation report
Information to support valuation
Third parties to contact
Limitations surrounding valuation
Restrictions on using valuer's report
Methods of valuation
Build up method to determine capitalisation rates
Data required
Economic factors
Industry factors
Risk-free rate
Equity risk premium
Small company risk premium
Company-specific factors
Specific company risk premium
Business growth rate

---

[90] *Colliwer v. Mason* (1858) 25 Beav. 200, *per* Sir John Romilly M.R.; and *Johnston v. Chestergate Hat Manufacturing Co Ltd* [1915] 2 Ch. 338, *per* Sargant J.
[91] [1983] 1 Ch. 217.
[92] *ibid.*

18–141 It is clear from the discussion in this chapter that the valuation of businesses is anything but an exact science and is fraught with difficulty and complexity. Accountants engaged in valuations to be used in litigation should remember that the purpose of the exercise is not to reveal the exact value of the business – because in fact no such exact value exists – but rather to assist the court in an assessment of the likely value or range of values applicable in the particular circumstances. Thus, an expert valuation that is supported by a list of key assumptions and by sensitivity analysis showing how the value changes when assumptions are altered is of significantly greater value to the court than a single figure. The courts will readily recognise that precision is not possible and will greatly value the opportunity to test the range of values proposed by reference to a variety of likely scenarios. While this poses a challenge to the expert, as he needs to be extremely well prepared to give the necessary evidence, by the same token it allows him to demonstrate the real value of expert knowledge.

CHAPTER 19

INTEREST, DISCOUNT AND THE TIME VALUE OF MONEY

INTEREST, DISCOUNT AND THE TIME VALUE OF MONEY

19–01   This chapter deals with the effects of the time value of money on awards for damages. Two distinct time periods are at issue relating to the period of loss. These are:

(1) Pre-judgment period – the period between the date of injury and the date of judgment. The award of damages may take account of the opportunity costs of past losses. If the plaintiff is awarded the exact sum of the loss he may be under-compensated – had he not suffered losses those monies would have been available to the plaintiff for investment and the plaintiff would have earned a return in the form of interest. In such cases interest may be added to compensate for the lost purchasing power during the period the plaintiff did not have constructive use of the money. This is illustrated in Table 19.1 below.

Table 19.1: Example opportunity cost of lost interest

A Ltd has cash now of €10,000
Rate of interest 7.5%
Flow of future income €750 per annum
A Ltd loses the cash of €10,000 due to the wrongful actions of B Ltd
Assume an interest rate of 7.5%
The wrongful actions of B Ltd will result in (i) loss of cash of €10,000 and (ii) a reduction in income of A Ltd of €750 per annum
(either reduced interest earned on cash or increase in interest paid on borrowings)
Decline in future earnings = "Opportunity cost"

(2) Post-judgment period – between the date of judgment and the date future losses end (*i.e.* subsequent to the date of judgment). If the plaintiff is compensated in full at the date of judgment for future losses he will be over-compensated – the plaintiff is gaining access to monies earlier than in the normal course of business. He could invest those monies and earn interest therefrom.

Two aspects are considered in this chapter:

– application of discount rates in the calculation of present values; and

– awards of interest in calculating damages.

In relation to these two aspects of the damage calculations, two stages are involved in the computations:

– selection of the discount rate and the pre-judgment interest rate;

– calculation of the present value of damages at the date of judgment.

19–02 The chapter has four sections. The first deals with discount rates generally. Discount rates in personal injury damage calculations and in commercial damages are then discussed. The chapter ends by considering interest on damages.[1]

19–03 Economists will provide expert evidence on most of the topics in this chapter. However, accountants have a central role to play in providing the raw data to which an interest rate or discount rate is applied. They may also carry out calculations using the rates and time periods determined by other experts. Accountants and lawyers should fully understand the assumptions used by economists, both for their own client and the other party to the litigation, in order to fully understand the methodology applied in calculating damages.

Any expert evidence provided may need to be amended or adjusted for delays in the trial date.[2] This is because:

(1) The two periods of time will change – the pre-judgment period from date of accident to date of judgment will increase and the post-judgment period from date of judgment to the date future losses are incurred will shorten. This will usually result in a higher quantum of damages because the pre-judgment amounts are not discounted but are claimed at their full value plus interest, while future losses will be discounted over a shorter period as a result of the delay. However, in theory the difference should be sufficient merely to compensate the plaintiff for the additional delay in receiving the present value of the damages, i.e. the new present value should be the present

---

[1] These issues are also considered in Berenblut, M.L. and Rosen, H.N., *Litigation Accounting* (Carswell Thomson Professional Publishing, Ontario, 1995), Chaps 3 and 11; Dilbeck, H.R., "The time value of money" in *Litigation Services Handbook. The Role of the Accountant as Expert* (2nd ed., Weil, R.L., Wagner, M.J. and Frank, P.B. (eds), John Wiley & Sons, Inc., New York, 1995), Chap. 38; Gaughan, P.A., *Measuring Commercial Damages* (John Wiley & Sons, Inc, New York, 2000), Chap. 7; Lemar, C.J. and Mainz, A.J. (eds), *Litigation Support* (4th ed., Butterworths, London, 1999), Chap. 14. MacGregor, G. and Hobbs, *Expert Accounting Evidence: A Guide for Litigation Support* (Accountancy Books, London, 1998), Chap. 20; Martin, G.D. and Vavoulis, T., *Determining Economic Damages* (James Publishing Inc, California, 1999), Chap. 11; Phillips, J.R. and Freeman, N.W., "Interest as damages" in *Litigation Services Handbook. The Role of the Accountant as Expert* (2nd ed., Weil, R.L., Wagner, M.J. and Frank, P.B. (eds), John Wiley & Sons, Inc., New York, 1995), Chap. 40; Weil, R.L., "Compensation for the passage of time" in *Litigation Services Handbook. The Role of the Accountant as Expert* (2nd ed., Weil, R.L., Wagner, M.J. and Frank, P.B. (eds), John Wiley & Sons, Inc., New York, 1995), Chap. 37.

[2] See, generally, Martin, G.D. and Vavoulis, T., *Determining Economic Damages* (James Publishing Inc, California, 1999), para. 1141.

value at the earlier date plus interest to the later date.

(2) The discount rate may change between different trial dates – this is less likely, but possible due to changes in prevailing interest rates or in assumptions made by economists. This would have the effect of changing the present values at both the earlier and later dates.

Discount rates

19–04 The calculation of pecuniary damages is an important aspect of lawsuits relating to personal injury and fatal accident cases, and in relation to compensation for commercial losses.

Litigation damages that are related to future losses are always calculated based on the present value of those losses. This requires that future projected losses must be converted to present value. If an award for damages is made at the date of judgment, but future losses would not be incurred until some time in the future, then the early receipt of the same amount would constitute over-compensation of the plaintiff because he could invest that amount and end up with more at the date of the loss than he was deprived of by the injury.

Compensation for economic loss usually comprises a lump sum representing the present value of a future stream of payments. The compensation might represent compensation for lost profits, earnings, fringe benefits or medical expenses to be incurred in the future. Successful plaintiffs have the right to recover damages reflecting the likely future timing of the expected losses and expenses resulting from the injury sustained.

In order to compute the present value of a future amount, a discount rate must be selected. The discount factor chosen is applied to the future losses to discount them to present value. The rate may include a premium over a risk-free rate to account for the riskiness of a projected income stream. The convention in personal injury loss analysis is to select a risk-free rate as risk adjustments will already have been made by economists and actuaries against the estimate of future earnings. For example, future earnings are adjusted for the risk that the plaintiff might have experienced periods of unemployment in the future, and for expectations concerning worklife (taking into account risks thereto). By contrast, in commercial damages the risk adjustment process is often incorporated in the discount rate.

19–05 This section starts by introducing the basic concepts. Methods of selecting the discount rate are then discussed, followed by a consideration of the effect of risk and of other factors on the discount rate.

Introduction to the basic concepts

19–06 An understanding of some basic concepts is necessary before the discount rates can be considered. Basic concepts dealing with compounding, discounting, derivation of present value, interest rates and rates of inflation, and real interest rates are introduced.

Compounding

19–07   It is first useful to consider compounding, which is the opposite of discounting and which is more familiar to most. Compounding is the addition of interest each period to a sum of money in order to determine its value at some time in the future. In arithmetical terms it is a geometric progression. The future value of a sum of money after n periods, where interest is compounded at an interest rate of r each period, is expressed as follows:

$$\text{Future value} = \text{Present value} \times (1 + r)^n$$

(In this calculation r is expressed as the decimal equivalent of the interest rate, *e.g.* 5% is expressed as 0.05).

Once the interest rate has been chosen, annuity tables of factors relating to each interest rate are available which make the calculations relatively straightforward. Table 19.2 shows a simple application of this calculation.

Table 19.2: Compounding

Assume
Plaintiff requires compensation now (December 31, 20X5) for losses of €100,000 incurred in each of the past five years.
No inflation
Plaintiff could have invested his profits over the past five years at a deposit interest rate of 5%
Assume that the losses occurred at the end of each year

Compound value

Year	Calculation	Compound value
20X5	100,000 x 1	100,000
20X4	100,000 x 1.05^1	105,000
20X3	100,000 x 1.05^2	110,250
20X2	100,000 x 1.05^3	115,762
20X1	100,000 x 1.05^4	121,551
		552,563

Alternatively, using tables:
€100,000 x 5.52563 (terminal value of an annuity at 5% rate of interest) = €552,563
Thus, plaintiff would need to be paid €552,563 on December 31, 20X5 to compensate him for:
(1) his lost profits in each of the previous five years; and
(2) the loss of the use of those monies which could have been invested at a 5% return

Discounting

19–08   Discounting seeks to convert a future sum to present value, and is therefore the inverse of compounding. The present value will depend on the rate of interest in each period, and the number of such periods over which the sum is expected to arise. The present value of a future sum received after n periods, discounted at an interest rate of r, is expressed as follows:

$$\text{Present value} = \text{Future value} \times \frac{1}{(1+r)^n}$$

Discounting, as with compounding, reflects the time value of money. One euro today is worth more than €1 at some future time because of its potential to earn interest.

Once the discount rate has been chosen, tables of factors relating to each discount rate are available which make the calculations relatively straightforward. Table 19.3 shows a simple application of this calculation.

Table 19.3: Discounting

Assume
Plaintiff is compensated now (January 1, 20X1 for losses of €100,000 to be incurred in each of the next five years, starting on December 31, 20X1.
Discount rate of 5%
No inflation
The compensation to be awarded is the present value of €100,000 payable over the next five years

Present value calculation as at January 1, 20X1

Year	Calculation	Present value
20X1	$100,000 \div 1.05^1$	95,238
20X2	$100,000 \div 1.05^2$	90,703
20X3	$100,000 \div 1.05^3$	86,384
20X4	$100,000 \div 1.05^4$	82,270
20X5	$100,000 \div 1.05^5$	78,353
		432,948

Alternatively, using tables: €100,000 x 4.32948 (present value of an annuity at 5% rate of interest) = €432,948

19–09 Expert actuarial and financial testimony is frequently provided to assist judges and juries in establishing the present value of a future stream of payments or losses such as lost earnings. Several aspects of discounting losses have been debated in the economics literature. Whether economists and actuaries can make reliable present value estimates of pecuniary damages in personal injury and fatal accident cases has been a source of ongoing debate.

In all cases a discount rate must be employed. Although the subject of much controversy, the selection of a rate of discount to use in calculating present value of economic loss for forensic purposes is a well-defined problem. In general, five variables should be considered in determining the present value of a future payment stream such as earnings:

(1) Expected working life or time period over which the payment stream will extend or would have extended.

(2) Amount of beginning payment or earnings.

(3) Year-by-year anticipated rate of growth/inflation in the payment stream.

(4) Year-by-year interest rate.

(5) Discount rate at which the expected stream of earnings is discounted to present value.

The level of the discount rate used to measure present value is inversely proportional to the net result, *i.e.* the higher the discount rate, the lower the present value and vice versa. It is therefore essential to include all relevant factors in arriving at the discount rate.

Derivation of present value

19–10 It is well established in both law and economics that a lump sum payment today is equivalent to, and interchangeable with, a flow of future income. It is this equivalence which justifies a present lump sum payment as a substitute for future economic damages. This occurs regularly in personal injury and fatal accident cases, and in damages for commercial losses. These principles also apply in cases of divorce and judicial separation, although provision is often made in such cases for regular ongoing payments into the future, and this can obviate the need to determine the present value of such payments.

19–11 A further example of a present value calculation in a personal injury context is shown in Table 19.4.

Table 19.4: Example of present value calculation

Assume
- Plaintiff incurred severe personal injuries requiring full-time medical care over the next five years
- Medical costs of €200,000 would be incurred at the beginning of each of the next five years, commencing immediately
- Discount rate 15%

Present value calculation

Year	Calculation	Present value
20X1	$200,000 \div 1$	200,000
20X2	$200,000 \div 1.15^1$	173,913
20X3	$200,000 \div 1.15^2$	151,229
20X4	$200,000 \div 1.15^3$	131,503
20X5	$200,000 \div 1.15^4$	114,351
		770,996

- This means that €200,000 paid now, together with €570,996 invested at 15% interest per annum, will be sufficient to meet the five annual medical bills of €200,000.
- This can be seen from the following table:

Year	Opening balance	Amount spent	Amount reinvested	Interest at 15%	Closing Balance
20X1	770,996	200,000	570,996	85,649	656,645
20X2	656,645	200,000	456,645	68,497	525,142
20X3	525,142	200,000	325,142	48,771	373,913
20X4	373,913	200,000	173,913	26,087	200,000
20X5	200,000	200,000	—	—	—

Interest rates and rates of inflation

19–12   In making awards, courts must take into consideration two main factors: inflation and the ability of the money to earn interest. In practice, these two factors may, in effect, cancel each other out. If the interest rate received over, say, the next 30 years on a lump sum payment is equal to the inflation rate, the money will grow in size by interest and at the same time its buying power will diminish correspondingly because of the effects of inflation.

Real ("true") rate of interest

19–13   The question that faces the legal system is: "How much does the plaintiff have to be compensated today, in order to ensure that the plaintiff will have enough money to pay for future losses incurred as a result of the injury?" The answer to the question depends on two variables:

– the effect of the rate of inflation on future costs; and

– the rate of interest at which the plaintiff can invest the award.

19–14   The key distinction is between nominal and real interest rates. The nominal rate is the rate of interest quoted to depositors by financial institutions. Nominal rates of interest take no account of inflation and the real purchasing power of money. The purchasing power of a sum of money today is likely to be quite different to the purchasing power of the same sum of money in, say, 10 years' time. This is especially so in periods of high inflation. The rate of inflation is crucial to evaluating the real (net of inflation) return on the money. The real rate of return is the rate in excess of inflation. The nominal rate of interest is equal to the real rate of return plus the expected rate of inflation. To obtain the real return, the effect of the rate of inflation has to be removed from the nominal interest rate. The equation is as follows:

Real interest rate = [(1+nominal interest rate)/(1+rate of inflation)] – 1

The difficulty with this equation is that the rate of inflation in the future is not known.

19–15   The discount rate used in damages calculations is usually the real interest rate at which it is assumed plaintiffs will invest their awards in order to replace their future streams of losses, *i.e.* the expected observed rate of interest adjusted for the expected rate of inflation. When awarding lump sums, courts must factor the "real interest" rate into any award. This can be done either by applying the real rate (*i.e.* the nominal rate less the inflation rate) to the likely future losses expressed in terms of today's prices, or by adding projected inflation to the amounts of future losses and then applying the nominal interest rate. Both calculations should yield the same present value.

Economic theory suggests that interest rates are at least in part a function of inflation – as inflation rises or falls interest rates will tend to follow. Accordingly, the differential between interest rates and inflation representing the real interest rate can be estimated to be a broadly constant or predictable rate over the long term. Actuaries tend to assume a constant real rate which is often fixed at circa 4 per cent.

19–16   There is considerable debate over the interest rate at which plaintiffs are assumed to invest their awards in order to replace their future streams of losses. For example, should it be assumed that investors will invest in completely safe investments that provide a low risk-free rate of return or should the rate be based on, say, the higher but riskier return that can be earned on equities. Many complex factors impinge on real interest rates. Walsh[3] discusses these and concludes that real interest rates have been in the region of 1 per cent over the past century. He refers to a survey of forensic economists in the United States[4] in which most economists surveyed favoured a real rate of interest (discount rate) in the region of 2 per cent. Finally, Walsh cautions against using a discount rate greater than 4 per cent and opines that an appropriate rate to apply in an Irish context is 2 per cent or lower.

19–17   In reality, actuaries often use real rates of 4 per cent when giving expert opinions in Irish courts and this is probably too high over the long term.[5] The effect of an overestimate of real rates is to discount the future losses by too much, thereby under-compensating the plaintiff and causing a likely future shortfall between funds available and the losses as they are incurred.

19–18   Financial experts have used the real rate of interest to discount future losses because it has been less volatile than the nominal or market rate of interest. (The nominal rate increases and decreases with the rate of inflation while the underlying real rate remains stable.) Recently, however, the real rate has been almost as variable as the nominal rate. Nevertheless, because the courts have become accustomed to the use of the real rate, forensic accountants and actuaries follow that convention.

19–19   The example in Table 19.5 illustrates the point.[6] The amount needed now to permit a plaintiff to pay an inflation-adjusted cost in the future can be

---

[3] Walsh, B., "The real interest rate" (Working paper, University College Dublin, 1999).

[4] Brookshire, M. and Slesnick, F., "A 1996 survey of 'prevailing practice' in forensic economics" *Journal of Forensic Economics* (1997), Vol. 10, No. 1, pp. 1–28.

[5] *Business & Finance* (2-8 August 2001) reported the lowering of the interest rate assumption to 2 per cent in a case awarding personal injury damages of £2.3 million. The article predicts that this lower rate of interest will be followed in other courts leading to increased awards for damages.

[6] Adapted from Bruce, C., "What is a 'discount rate'?" in *Expert Witness* (Spring 1996), http://economica.ca.

calculated by multiplying the current cost of the expense to be compensated by (1 + rate of inflation) divided by (1 + nominal rate of interest). The inverse of the figure, less 1, is the figure which expert witnesses use to determine the present, or lump sum value of a future cost. It is called the real rate of interest because it has the effect of "netting out" or extracting the impact of inflation from the observed, or nominal, interest rate, leaving only that element of interest payments which is independent of inflation – the "real" rate of interest.

Table 19.5: Example discount rates based on the real rate of interest

Arising from the injury, medical costs will be incurred one year in the future, costing in today's prices €1,040
Assume inflation of 2.5% applies to medical expenses ➡ The medical expenses in one year's time will amount to €1,040 x 1.025 = €1,066
Assume risk-free rate of interest on secure investment is 6.6% ➡ €1,000 invested now will yield €1,066 in one year's time; €1,000 is the present value (sometimes called the commuted value) of €1,066.
Deriving the discount rate The real interest rate is the difference between the rate of inflation (2.5%) and the rate of return (6.6%). The real interest rate is (1.066/1.025) – 1 = 1.04 – 1 = 4%
In other words, a 4% real return will be sufficient to convert €1,000 into enough cash, €1,040 in today's terms, to pay the health care bill in a year's time.

19–20   It is interesting to note that, as of the time of writing, real interest rates in Ireland are probably negative given recent increases in local inflation and low interest rates determined by the European Central Bank. It may be time for analysts and actuaries to adjust their models to take account of the new scenario whereby movements in interest rates and exchange rates are outside the control of Irish regulators.

19–21   Five variables were identified in para. **19–09** as relevant to calculation of net present value. Two of these variables (expected working life or the time period over which the payment stream will extend, and the amount of the beginning payment or earnings) are readily subject to estimation with a reasonable degree of economic certainty in most cases. However, three variables (year-by-year earnings growth rate, the inflation rate and the resulting discount rate) cannot be predicted with reasonable certainty. Nonetheless, because the valuation process revolves around a somewhat predictable average differential between the anticipated rate of growth/rate of inflation and the discount rate, the resulting present value estimates can be calculated with a degree of precision.

19–22   General measures of inflation may not adequately reflect inflation in relation to a particular set of goods or services. For example, Walsh[7] finds that the cost of medical services is rising faster than the cost of living index in Ireland.

19–23 A present value figure should be calculated for each damage item. Thus, damages based on the loss of 52 weekly wage payments require 52 present value calculations. While 30 years' worth of such damages results in 1,560 line items, such calculations are no longer excessively burdensome given the availability of computers. The short cut of an annual payments convention (or mid-year convention) in place of accurate calculations could place plaintiffs at a disadvantage.

Selecting the discount rate for lost profits

19–24 Since the lump sum present value of a future stream of payments will differ according to the discount rate used, arriving at the appropriate rate is of major importance in such calculations. Damages are the discounted sum of projected experience but for the alleged action minus projected experience including the effects of the action. This can be expressed as follows:

After tax present value of damages =

$\sum$[(Earnings/Profit (were there no injury) – Earnings/Profit (including the effects of the injury)]

x After tax risk-adjusted discount rate

Two assumptions are implicit in the above expression. First, the discount rate is assumed to be the same in each time period. This is a common convenience in practice. The incremental effort in adjusting the discount rate over time is generally considered to exceed the incremental precision in the results. Secondly, the discount rate is either the same under the no injury and injury scenarios, or an appropriate rate can be derived for the difference between the two. An illegal action may alter the uncertainty surrounding the two projections, whereas a single risk-adjusted rate implies uniform uncertainty.

The appropriate discount rate may be a composite of several rates determined by the line items affected by an injury.

19–25 Experts must provide evidence concerning the forecasted value of the real interest/discount rate. There are a number of techniques for obtaining such a forecast and for providing an estimate of the real rate of interest. Three methods have been used to forecast real discount rates,[8] each of which has its strengths and weaknesses. Of the three techniques for forecasting real interest rates, the least satisfactory is the one based on historical rates. As those rates have varied so widely since the early 1970s, they convey little reliable information concerning the future.

---

[7] Walsh, B., "Medical care inflation" (Working paper, University College Dublin, 1999).
[8] Bruce, C., "Selecting the discount rate" in *Expert Witness* (Autumn 1996), http://economica.ca.

Historical approach

19–26 This approach assumes that the average rate which has been observed in the past will continue into the future. Analysis of historical rates indicates that real rates were fairly stable over the period 1950–1970, at approximately 3 per cent. During the oil crisis of the early 1970s, real interest rates fell, sometimes becoming negative. Towards the end of that decade, however, they began to rise again to more than 3 per cent. Since 1983 real interest rates have consistently remained above that level. Indeed, until recently real interest rates had remained above 4 per cent for a long period.

Forecasting agencies

19–27 Some consulting firms provide forecasts of various economic variables including the real rate of interest. Caution must be used when employing these firms' long-term forecasts. Long-term forecasts cannot be made without imposing assumptions about many factors which are outside the mathematical models developed by these agencies. Private forecasters have little incentive to produce accurate long-term forecasts. The forecasts on which agencies' accuracy is evaluated are those which have been made into the near future, not the distant future. The real rate of interest, on the other hand, must commonly be forecast 20 or 30 years into the future.

Market/nominal rates

19–28 Information concerning future real rates of interest is available on the money market. Market interest rates take three factors into account:

– pure productivity of, or return on, capital;

– a premium to pay the lender for inflation during the period of the loan;

– a premium to pay the lender for the risk that the borrower will not repay or will default on the loan.

A purchase of 20-year government securities paying 6 per cent, believing that inflation will average 2 per cent per year, suggests an expected real rate of interest averaging approximately 4 per cent over those 20 years (*i.e.* 6 per cent nominal or true rate of interest, net of the 2 per cent inflation). Forecasts of the rate of inflation can be used to deflate nominal market rates of interest to obtain the implicit, underlying real rates. Such forecasts can be obtained with some accuracy.

The emergence of index-linked government securities in the United Kingdom, which guarantee a fixed risk-free return in excess of the rate of inflation, has provided a market-based measure of real interest rates for the first time. The use of these investment products as indicators of appropriate discount rates for the calculation of damages has been approved by the House of Lords in *Wells v. Wells.*[9]

---

[9] [1998] 3 All E.R. 481.

19–29   Most economists prefer the market-based technique. Index linked government securities are not available in the Irish Market. When selecting a discount rate for calculating the present value of an earnings loss, where there is a choice, most experts in Ireland opt for the average of appropriate-term government interest rates.

Risk

19–30   Generally speaking, the higher the level of risk of an investment, the higher its rate of return. If an award is invested at a rate of return higher than the risk-free rate, the higher return represents a compensatory return to risk incurred in the post-award situation and should have no bearing on the pre-award calculation of economic loss or in selection of the discount rate.

Risk-free rate

19–31   In personal injury cases, awards of lost earnings are typically based on conservative estimates of future wages and relevant actuarial data. The calculation of expected future earnings often takes into account the various risk factors such as death and unemployment in personal injury cases. Given the degree of certainty with which the future income stream can be predicted, it is appropriate to apply a risk-free return. Subjecting the expected amount, which has already been adjusted for risk factors, to a future risk adjustment by discounting with non risk-free rates could result in under-compensation for the plaintiff.

The discount rate to be applied is the rate of return for safe investment of capital to an ordinary person unschooled in making investments and the rate at which an ordinary and prudent person – an unskilled investor – would invest funds for such a term. Available interest and bank rates should provide a guide to the rate of discount. As far back as 1966, Kingsmill Moore J. in the Supreme Court was satisfied with the use of a discount rate of 5 per cent per annum in *Murphy v. Cronin*.[10]

The issue has not, however, been determined on a definitive basis in the Irish courts to date. In England the House of Lords addressed the question in *Wells v. Wells*.[11] Their Lordships focused their attention on whether investment returns assumed in such calculations of lost earnings should be the returns on equities (which involve significant investment risk) or on Indexed Linked Government Securities (which are a much safer form of investment the effect of which is to protect the capital sum from the effects of inflation and provide a return to the investor). All five law lords held that the latter approach was the appropriate one. Lord Lloyd of Berwick said:

[10] [1966] I.R. 699.
[11] [1998] 3 All E.R. 481.

"Investment in ILGS is the most accurate was of calculating the present value of the loss which the plaintiffs will actually suffer in real terms.

Although this will result in a heavier burden on these defendants, and, if the principle is applied across the board, on the insurance industry in general, I can see nothing unjust. It is true that insurance premiums may have been fixed on the basis of the 4 to 5% discount rate indicated in *Cookson v Knowles* [1978] 2 All E.R. 604, [1979] A.C. 556 and the earlier authorities. But this was only because there was then no better way of allowing for future inflation. The objective was always the same."[12]

Lord Steyn said:

"...the Court of Appeal have assumed that the same investment policy would be suitable for all investors, regardless of special needs. The premise that the plaintiffs, who have perhaps been very seriously injured, are in the same position as ordinary investors is not one that I can accept. Such plaintiffs have not chosen to invest: the tort and its consequences compel them to do so. ... Typically, by investing in equities an ordinary investor takes a calculated risk which he can bear in order to improve his financial position. On the other hand, the typical plaintiff requires the return from an award of damages to provide the necessities of life. For such a plaintiff it is not possible to cut back on medical and nursing care as well as other essential services. His objective must be to ensure that the damages awarded do not run out. It is money that he cannot afford to lose."[13]

Although these judgments would appear to rely heavily on the availability of ILGS, of which there is no equivalent in the Irish financial markets, it is noteworthy that the court did not stop at approving the use of such investments to calculate the appropriate differential. The lords went on to extract from the evidence presented to them the appropriate percentage, and all agreed that, instead of the figures of 4% to 5% commonly used, the correct differential for the cases before them was 3%, reflecting the altered investment environment and the availability of a suitable benchmark. It is noteworthy that with effect from June 2001 a rate of 2.5% has received legislative recognition in the United Kingdom (see para. **19-49**). It is submitted that 3% is likely to be much closer to an appropriate differential in Ireland today than figures of 4% and higher that are commonly used.

19–32   A risk-free rate in Ireland is the rate of return currently available on a government security whose maturity date corresponds to the end of the period over which the relevant losses are projected.

   Although it is generally correct to adopt a risk-free rate, this position assumes

---

[12] *Ibid.* at 493.
[13] *Ibid.* at 504.

all markets for labour and capital are perfect and complete. The award of a lump sum in advance confers the ability to enter capital markets to an extent not previously available to the recipient. This may result in award over-payments as current methodologies for calculations of economic loss implicitly assume severe risk aversion in capital markets.

Risk adjusted discount rates

19–33   The effect of risk on the discount rate may also have to be calculated. A risk-free rate of interest is an appropriate discount rate only when applied to projected losses which are themselves risk-free. Conversely, as elements of uncertainty or speculation enter into the projection of future losses, either those elements must be removed from the analysis or the discount rate must be increased commensurately to maintain parity in risk. To do otherwise would yield an award which over-compensates the plaintiff.

19–34   A risk-adjusted discount rate should be applied when calculating the present value of future losses for a company. An appropriate rate is the after-tax, risk-adjusted opportunity cost of capital.

The cost of capital is the weighted-average cost of various forms of capital such as equity (ordinary shares) and debt (borrowings). Each type of capital has a different claim on the firm's assets and distributions. The cost of capital relating to ordinary shares is normally expressed as a nominal risk-free rate plus a risk premium. Analytic efforts focus on estimating the appropriate risk premium. The Capital Assets Pricing Model developed in the 1960s links the premium to the relationship between changes in the return on an asset and changes in the return on a diversified market portfolio. The relationship is captured in a regression coefficient known as beta. More recently, Arbitrage Pricing Theory links the premium to a series of betas, being a series of more firm-specific factors.

Other factors to consider in determining discount rate

19–35   As has already been stated, the correct choice of interest rate is subject to debate and is determined by:

– the timing of the harmful incident giving rise to damage;

– the timing of the effects of the damage arising from the harmful incident;

– the timing of payment of compensation for damage to the plaintiff.

A small difference in the rate can have a substantial impact on the amount of damages.

19–36   A number of other factors need to be taken account of in determining the discount rate.

Time period

19–37 Regardless of the choice of interest rate, the time span over which the rate applies (*i.e.* the term to maturity) is also a relevant factor. Long-term interest rates are usually, although not always, higher than short-term interest rates. The duration of the investment on which the discount rate is based should match the time period to which the damages compensated for by the investment relate. Accordingly, attributes of appropriate investments must include maturity dates falling within or around the damage period.

Tax-free rate

19–38 The difference between the sum of all future values and the present value of an award is the interest which is assumed to be earned on the award. The interest is taxable income to the recipient. If taxed, the full value of after-tax earnings is not replaced. This implies the use of a risk-free rate minus some effective tax rate.

Average over some reasonable time span

19–39 The time span should be long enough to smooth out short-term fluctuations in nominal and real rates of interest. But it should not be so long as to include historical periods with radically different economic structures. The discount rate should be averaged over the same period as an earnings growth rate is measured.

An approximate discount rate choice is a fairly short-term government rate, with perhaps a tax adjustment, averaged over several business cycles.

Range of rates

19–40 Generally, no single rate is perfectly appropriate. A range of acceptable rates should be determined, from which a selection can be made. The average might be used, or the high end may be used to produce a conservative result. Both a high and a low may be used to produce a range of damage amounts, leaving the choice to the judge or jury. Such a range adds credibility as well as reality.

Discount rate in personal injuries damages

19–41 Somewhat different considerations apply in the choice of discount rates in personal injury damages compared with commercial damages.

Discount rate to be applied to the multiplier

19–42 The approach to discount rates in litigation differs considerably between Ireland and the United Kingdom where multipliers from actuarial tables (called

Ogden Tables) have been used. A multiplier reflects the number of years by which the agreed annual loss is multiplied to compensate the plaintiff. By contrast, Irish courts allow expert actuaries to take the lead role in advising on this issue.

A number of recent judgments in the United Kingdom are important, even in the Irish legal context.

Pre- Wells v. Wells – *the "ordinary prudent investor"*

19–43 In the past, the courts in the United Kingdom held that plaintiffs would invest their money on a long-term basis in the same way as "an ordinary prudent investor", *i.e.* that they would invest in a mix of equities and government stock. Thus, prior to the *Wells v. Wells*[13] judgment, it was assumed that personal injury victims could invest lump sums in a mixture of equities and government stocks (also known in the United Kingdom as gilts).

19–44 In 1979, the House of Lords in *Cookson v. Knowles*[14] set guidelines for assessing future loss. One of these was that the multiplier used to calculate the present value of future losses would be based on a rate of return between 4 and 5 per cent. As a result, the practice developed of calculating multipliers on the basis of an assumed return on investment of 4.5 per cent.

Wells v. Wells *decision – minimum risk basis*

19–45 On July 16, 1998 the House of Lords delivered its long-awaited judgment in the so-called "multiplier" cases of *Wells v. Wells, Thomas v. Brighton Health Authority* and *Page v. Sheerness Steel Co plc.*[15] The effect of this decision is to substantially increase compensation payable where claims are made for future losses following personal injury.

The cases centred on the correct method of calculating damages in respect of claims for future years' loss of earnings, cost of nursing care and other future losses generally. Fundamental to this process is the choice of correct multiplier, *i.e.* the number of years by which the agreed annual loss is multiplied to take account of the "accelerated receipt" by plaintiffs of their compensation. The principal factors relevant in arriving at the correct multiple is the likely rate of return on money invested by plaintiffs (*i.e.* the discount rate). The lower the rate of return/discount rate the higher the multiplier required.

The choice of rate of interest/discount rate was at the heart of the cases. The issue to be decided was whether the approach used following *Cookson v. Knowles*[16] of using a discount rate in the region 4 to 5 per cent remained appropriate in today's economic environment.

---

[13] [1998] 3 All E.R. 481.
[14] [1979] A.C. 556.
[15] [1998] 3 All E.R. 481.
[16] [1979] A.C. 556.

19–46 The Lords decided that a plaintiff was entitled to invest the lump sum compensation award on a minimum risk basis (not as previously on the basis of the "ordinary prudent investor"). Index linked government securities (ILGS) offers an annual return, together with the "guarantee" of the return of the index linked capital sum. The cost for obtaining the guarantee of the value of the capital sum is a lower rate of interest. The plaintiffs had argued that the multipliers should be based on the lower rates of return, while the defendants had argued that the higher returns available on the stock market suggested that the 4.5 per cent rate was appropriate.

It was decided that the discount rate should be determined by reference to ILGS and that the appropriate rate was 3 per cent. It was additionally decided that the guideline figures of 4–5 per cent set out in the *Cookson v. Knowles*[17] case should now be replaced by a figure of 3 per cent for general use pending a figure being set under the Damages Act 1996. Under this Act, the Lord Chancellor is permitted to fix an assumed rate of return on investments to be used in all calculations of future pecuniary loss. The Lord Chancellor also has the power to prescribe different rates of return for different types of cases. To date, he has not exercised any of these powers. Section 1 reads:

> "(1) In determining the return to be expected from the investment of a sum awarded as damages for future pecuniary loss in an action for personal injury the court shall, subject to and in accordance with rules of court made for the purposes of this section, take into account such rate of return (if any) as may from time to time be prescribed by an order made by the Lord Chancellor.

> (2) Subsection (1) above shall not however prevent the court taking a different rate of return into account if any party to the proceedings shows that it is more appropriate in the case in question."

19–47 There are three key aspects to the decision in *Wells v. Wells*[18]:

(1) As discussed above, multipliers will be based on a discount rate of 3 per cent instead of 4.5 per cent.

(2) Judicial discount has been discouraged. In the past courts have routinely reduced multipliers by anything up to 20 per cent.

(3) The minor anomaly that the rate of return used for calculating the cost of special accommodation was fixed at 2 per cent when the interest rate assumed for multipliers was 4.5 per cent has been removed and both have been adjusted to 3 per cent in line with the risk-free returns now assumed elsewhere.

The combined potential effect of these changes is to increase damages substantially.

---

[17] [1979] A.C. 556.
[18] [1998] 3 All E.R. 481.

19–48 The difference in tax rates in different countries was the issue in *Van Oudenhoven v. Griffin Inns Ltd.*[19] Where there was no evidence that the effect of higher taxes abroad would erode an award for damages for future loss of earnings to a substantially greater extent than in the United Kingdom, the trial judge had erred in finding the claim exceptional and uplifting the multiplier.

19–49 Two conflicting decisions regarding the rate of return to be used for future losses have been recently reached. In *Barry v. Ablerex Construction (Midlands) Ltd,*[20] on the basis of material which showed that a rate of 3 per cent was no longer appropriate in calculating damages for future costs of care, the rate of discount to be applied to the multiplier was 2 per cent. But in *Warren v. Northern General Hospital Trust*[21] the Court of Appeal said that it was for the Lord Chancellor, using his power under the Damages Act 1996, to revise the rate of return from the current 3 per cent and not the court. The Court of Appeal noted that the Lord Chancellor had issued a consultation paper and that a new rate should be promulgated in the near future. In fact, the Lord Chancellor has recently set a rate of 2.5 per cent.[22]

Discount rates in Irish courts

19–50 Walsh[23] has considered the *Wells v. Wells* decision as it would apply in Ireland. He points out that there are no investments in Ireland like the index linked government securities (ILGS) referred to in this decision and that it would be unreasonable for Irish investors to be exposed to exchange rate fluctuations arising from investing in sterling. He finds the *Wells v. Wells* judgment applicable to Irish plaintiffs, and that the appropriate discount rate to use in Ireland is that obtained from a low-risk investment such as government stocks (historically in the region of 2 per cent after inflation). However, there is no indication yet that the Irish courts, or indeed the actuaries advising them, intend making any significant or fundamental change to the rates used in Ireland or the assumptions underlying their use.

19–51 Peelo[24] challenges current practice in the Irish courts of assuming that lump sums are capable of being invested at a real (*i.e.* higher than inflation) rate of return of 4 per cent per annum. He suggests that the practice of using this real rate of 4 per cent derived from the semi-state Housing Finance Agency having

---

[19] [2000] 1 W.R.L. 1413
[20] Times Law Reports, March 30, 2000.
[21] [2000] 1 W.L.R. 1404.
[22] This takes effect from June 28, 2001 and was set in the Damages (Personal Injury) Order 2001 (S.I. No. 230 of 2001).
[23] Walsh, B., "The implications of *Wells v. Wells* for calculating capital values" (Working paper, University College Dublin, 1999).
[24] Peelo, D., "The calculation of a lump sum award to an incapacitated plaintiff" (Working Paper, Peelo & Partners, Dublin, 2000).

issued index-linked 30-year stock in 1985 that guaranteed a return of 4 per cent above inflation. This stock is no longer available to investors.

Assuming an average inflation rate of 2.3 per cent (based on historical rates for the period 1998 to 1999) and investment management advisory fees of 1 per cent, Peelo argues that the real rate of return available on risk-free investments such as deposits or gilts is nil or, at best, 1 per cent. Only by investing in equities, which involves some risk, can investors obtain a real rate of return higher than this. He cites the Trustee (Authorised Investments) Order 1998[25] as justification for growing acceptance of the appropriateness of investing in equities. This statutory instrument now allows the Wards of Court Office to invest in equities (subject to certain conditions), whereas previously the Office was only permitted by legislation to invest in government securities, bank and building society deposits and Bank of Ireland and AIB shares. Assuming a 70/30 investment split between equity and government securities, Peelo argues that a real rate of return of 2.5 per cent (not the current 4 per cent applying in Irish courts) is more realistic.

Discount rate and business damages

19–52   Whenever damages for lost profits are awarded in compensation, it is necessary to calculate the present value of the expected future income stream being compensated.

Discounting lost profits

19–53   Courts have long recognised the need to discount projections of lost profits to present value equivalent. Courts recognise that discounting is necessary to reflect the plaintiff's opportunity to invest and earn a return on the award. Furthermore, courts recognise that discounting is a means of adjusting for uncertainty surrounding projections of losses. In spite of court recognition of the importance of discounting, it is not always insisted upon and courts have, in the past, awarded un-discounted losses. This would be unusual, however, and could have arisen, for example, if the defendant did not object to the plaintiff's methodology.

19–54   There is considerable controversy surrounding choice of discount rates employed when calculating the present value of lost profits. Estimating discount rates is an inexact science. An error that is sometimes made in plaintiff lost profits calculations is to use a riskless interest rate (discount rate) to convert future lost profits to present value. Although the use of a riskless interest rate may be common in personal injury actions, it is rarely appropriate in lost profits analysis. The earning of business profits involves substantial risks and a lot of illiquidity for equity investors. These risks and illiquidities are particularly high for smaller closely-held businesses, and extremely high for younger firms. In

[25] S.I. No. 28 of 1998.

estimating lost profits, which are inherently subject to unknown or uncontrolled future events, a risk premium may therefore be necessary for discounting purposes depending on the applicable law.

19–55   Estimating appropriate discount rates for firms' losses in the context of litigation is complex. When a firm's injury is characterised as lost profits, discounting at the injured firm's cost of capital appears appropriate. Finance theory suggests that the value of a firm is the present value of the projected profits discounted at its cost of capital. The injury causes projected profits to fall, and this in turn reduces the value of the firm by the present value of the change in projections. However, this assumes that the cost-of-capital effect of the injury is similar to that of the firm. A single estimate of cost of capital as the discount rate provides accurate compensation only if three conditions hold:

(1) The illegal action did not change the uncertainty associated with a projection of any element (*i.e.* of any underlying revenue or cost) making up the loss of profits – this assumption, although not necessarily appropriate, is often used for convenience due to the difficulty in measuring any change in discount rate.

(2) All underlying revenues and costs must be injured proportionately – this is rarely true, and when fixed costs are considered, it is almost certainly not true.

(3) The above two conditions must hold in every period.

19–56   The calculation of damages should not assume that the cost-of-capital effect of the injury is a copy of the uninjured firm. The appropriate after-tax, risk-adjusted discount rate may be a combination of rates corresponding to the combination of revenues and expense items making up the lost profit. Although this discussion indicates that a single cost of capital is appropriate in only certain limited cases, finding the correct rate is more complex and difficult than estimating the uninjured firm's cost of capital.

19–57   Estimating the appropriate discount rate for losses can be approached from two perspectives. First, appropriate discount rates can be estimated for the revenues and costs underlying the profit calculation. Alternatively, the firm's uninjured and injured costs of capital can be estimated. The discount rate chosen is for the firm as a whole.

Discounting in valuing a business

19–58   The role of discount rates in valuing businesses is complex. An injury may have an effect on the appropriate discount rates, not captured by standard methods of valuation. Application of standard valuation methods may lead to under- or over-compensation. Courts, perhaps because no party to litigation has forced the issue, have tended to apply standard business valuation models. They have not recognised that litigation places unique demands on these methods.

19–59   When business valuations are done for established small to medium sized companies that are closely held, the price earnings ratios can be as low as 4 to 7. This implies a discount rate (reciprocal of the price earnings ratio) in the range of at least 14 to 25 per cent to fully incorporate the risk and illiquidity present. If these kinds of discount rates are used in lost profits analysis, then measuring present value of future lost profits is very similar to measuring the diminution in the value of the firm as a result of the wrongful act. The only way of valuing damages for a firm that ceased to exist because of the wrongful acts of the defendant may be to value the firm prior to the date of the wrongful acts.

19–60   Using the above logic, it would be unusual for the present value of future lost profits to substantially exceed the value of the firm. This is a logically consistent position, and a good cross-check against inflated damages analyses. One exception is when a small business is owned and operated by persons whose alternative income will be much less if the firm is put out of business as a result of the wrongful act. In this case, the lost profits analysis is effectively converted into a lost earnings analysis for the promoters.

Interest on damages

19–61   Interest is designed to compensate plaintiffs for the delay in payment of damages. Damages now often include an amount representing the loss of use of money. Interest is not an award of damages, but represents a payment to plaintiffs for being out of pocket. In other words, interest is not a component of general damages, but rather is a head of special damage.

19–62   Interest is a recurring issue in damages claims (and can be more of a legal issue than an accounting one). Interest calculations are required to compensate for the passage of time, during which the plaintiff was out of pocket. In theory, the delay in resolving a case is the principal factor giving rise to interest damages. Therefore, in theory the party that causes the delay should bear the interest cost. This, however, may be impractical particularly because the process of litigation itself necessarily takes more time. When interest is clearly a cost incurred it is clearly justified and should be added to the computation of damages.

19–63　Interest is not automatically awarded and must be claimed by the plaintiff. Claims for interest are usually included in the closing paragraphs (known as the "prayer for relief") of the statement of claim.

19–64　The Courts Act 1981 empowers the court to award interest in addition to any award of money, including damages, subject to certain exceptions. The award of interest can be in respect of all or any part of the award and in respect of the whole or any part of the period between the date the cause of action accrued and the date of the judgment. The exceptions include prohibitions on:

– the award of interest on interest;

– the award of interest by the court when interest is already payable on the debt concerned;

– the award of interest on damages for personal injuries or in respect of a death, in so far as the damages are in respect of (a) any loss occurring after the date of the judgment for the damages or (b) any non-pecuniary loss occurring between the date when the cause of action accrued and the date of judgment.

The effect of this latter provision is that a court cannot award interest on an award of general damages (*i.e.* damages for pain and suffering) in a personal injury case, even if the court's judgment is given several years after the injury was sustained. This exception does not extend, however, to awards of special damages, such as out-of-pocket expenses incurred or loss of earnings suffered as a result of the injury, and interest can be awarded on such losses.

19–65　The rate at which interest can be awarded by the court under section 22 of the Courts Act 1981 is specified as the rate per annum standing specified for the time being for the purposes of section 26 of the Debtors Act (Ireland) 1840. This rate was fixed at 11 per cent per annum by section 19 of the Courts Act 1981 and changed by statutory instrument in 1989[26] to 8 per cent per annum.

19–66　Forensic accountants should be familiar with the law of interest damages. Many cases requiring expert accounting evidence span several years and interest can form a large part of the plaintiff's damages. Where legal interest rates exceed market borrowing rates, forensic accountants can point out the advantages of speedy settlements to defendant clients.

19–67　Statutory provisions and the rules established by case law can be confusing and need to be fully understood by forensic accountants to ensure no mistakes are made in the calculations. In particular, careful note should be taken of the fact that the prohibition in section 22 of the Courts Act 1981 on "interest

---

[26] Courts Act 1981 (Interest on Judgment Debts) Order, 1989 (S.I. No. 12 of 1989).

on interest" has the effect of precluding the compounding of interest, even if the period involved is one of several years.

19–68 There have been considerable developments in the law concerning the ability of the plaintiff to receive interest on a "primary" loss for the period between the sustaining of the loss and the date of judgment. In particular, many of the statutes in the area of employment law confer specific power on the court or other body that determines a claim to award interest at the rate specified under the Courts Act 1981 on all or any part of the award and for the period relevant to the claim.

19–69 There is an issue as to whether interest could be awarded in circumstances where, although claimed in the pleadings, the matter was not addressed in court until after the court's final award (which did not include interest) was perfected. This was addressed by McCracken J. in *Concorde Engineering Co Ltd v. Bus Atha Cliath.*[27] In his judgment the learned judge said:

> "The award of interest under the Courts Act, 1981, is a discretionary award. There is authority that in what I might call a purely commercial case interest should as a general rule be awarded, but this is not quite such a case. This is in fact an action for damages for negligence arising out of a traffic accident. I certainly cannot say that at the time of the hearing I had actually decided or intended to make such an award, nor can I say that, if I had been asked to award interest at the time, I would have done so. In fact, had such a request been made, I would have sought the views of the defendant's counsel, and I would have made a determination based on the arguments before me. I know of no authority which says that a court can re-open an issue, after a final order has been made, in the sense of hearing arguments which were not addressed to the court in the course of the action, and making a finding based on such arguments.
> In those circumstances, I must refuse this application."

Pre-judgment and post-judgment interest

19–70 In personal injury, fatal accidents and business loss the calculation of damages is performed subsequent to the loss period. Because damages are calculated at a time subsequent to the source of the loss, the plaintiff will have been out of pocket for an amount of money equal to the damages for the period between the date of the wrongful act and the date of judgment. An allowance for interest as a compensable head of damage provides a mechanism to allow the plaintiff to recover the interest lost over this period.

The date on which judgment is made is deemed to be the dividing point when considering awards of interest. Before this date, interest awarded is referred to as pre-judgment interest and is allowable on a variety of different heads of

---

[27] [1995] 3 I.R. 212 at 215–216.

damage. After this date, interest is referred to as post-judgment interest and is calculated by reference to the entire damage award.

Pre-judgment interest

19–71   There are several reasons why a pre-judgment rate of return may need to be applied to pre-trial losses. The first is to place the parties in the same position they would have been in had the wrongful acts not occurred. Providing the plaintiff with a damage award in respect of monies it would have had access to in earlier years (but for the injury) under-compensates the plaintiff. This is because the plaintiff does not have the use of the monies in the period between the date of injury and the date of the award. Some return needs to be applied to the compensation for this period of loss up to the date of judgment.

Adding pre-judgment interest ensures the plaintiff is fully compensated. In addition, the liability for pre-judgment interest may provide the defendant with an incentive not to prolong the litigation.

Common law generally allows pre-judgment interest on liquidated damages from the date on which the damages become liquidated, but not on unliquidated damages.[28] Liquidated damages are damages for which one can determine an amount without a judicial finding (e.g. specified under the terms of a contract – see paras **15–42** *et seq.*). Unliquidated damages are not known until the court renders judgment – they generally arise at least in part from non-pecuniary losses.

19–72   There are differing views as to the appropriate rate to apply to historical damages to bring them to trial date terms.[29] Three possible rates (in order of size) have been identified:

(1) At a minimum, the risk-free rate should be applied.

(2) Another possibility is to use the defendant's rate on borrowings (debt rate), based on the debt the defendant owed the plaintiff during the period as a result of the defendant's wrongful actions.

(3) Lastly, it can be argued that the plaintiff lost investment opportunities by being deprived of the profits during the period. On this view, it can be argued that the best measure of this loss is the plaintiff's cost of capital (expected rate of return on the investment/type of business the plaintiff would have invested in).

---

[28]Phillips, J.R. and Freeman, N.W.,, "Interest as damages" in *Litigation Services Handbook: The Role of the Accountant as Expert* (2nd ed., Weil, R.L., Wagner, M.J. and Frank, P.B. (eds), John Wiley & Sons, Inc., New York, 1995), p. 40.7.

[29]Gaughan, P.A., *Measuring Commercial Damages* (John Wiley & Sons, Inc., New York, 2000), p. 216.

Plaintiffs are likely to prefer the cost of capital rate as it is likely to be the highest and will therefore lead to larger awards for damages. Conversely, defendants will prefer the lowest risk-free rate.

The interest should not be calculated for the entire period, as this would assume the losses and extra expenses arose at the start of the period, whereas in practice the losses are likely to have been incurred throughout the period.

Post-judgment interest

19–73   Post-judgment interest is incurred in the time between judgment and payment of any damages awarded. Under sections 26 and 27 of the Debtors Act (Ireland) 1840, post-judgment interest applies to all pecuniary awards, including awards of costs, whether compensatory or punitive, and acts to compel the defendant to make payment of the award. A full discussion of the right to interest on costs can be found in the judgment of Murphy J. in *Best v. Wellcome Foundation (No. 2)*.[30] Although the judgment should be read in full to appreciate the manner in which Murphy J. reconciles some apparently contradictory Supreme Court authorities on the subject, his main conclusion relates to the right of a plaintiff to recover interest on costs from the date of a High Court judgment against him where that judgment is subsequently overturned on appeal. He reaches this conclusion based on the decision of the Supreme Court in *Cooke v. Walsh*,[31] and states it in the following terms:

> "On the face of it that judgment would seem to establish with the full authority of the Supreme Court the propositions, first, that an award of costs *simpliciter* by the High Court or the Supreme Court carries with it interest at the rates fixed pursuant to the provisions of s. 26 of the Debtors (Ireland) Act, 1840, and, second, that interest runs from the date of the High Court order in respect of the costs of the High Court proceedings which should have been awarded but were not until corrected by the subsequent order of the Supreme Court."[32]

Contracts

19–74   The terms and conditions of many contracts provide for interest in respect of amounts due. If a contract provides for interest, discretionary interest is not awarded by the court as this would amount to double counting (see section 22(2)(b) of the Courts Act 1981). Where the contract does not provide for interest, the court awards interest as damages in limited circumstances.

Under contract law, plaintiffs have the right to pre-judgment interest on liquidated damages, calculated using any lawful interest rate stipulated by the contract. If the contract does not stipulate a rate, then the courts use the legal or statutory rate.

---

[30] [1995] 2 I.R. 393.
[31] [1989] I.L.R.M. 322.
[32] [1995] 2 I.R. 393 at 399.

746   *Forensic Accounting*

Interest in personal injury cases

19–75   Interest is usually awarded in personal injury cases. Guidelines on the calculation of interest were set out in *Jefford v. Gee*[33] and, subsequently, in *Cookson v. Knowles.*[34] The purpose of awarding interest is to compensate the claimant for the late receipt of the income, which is received after the trial, rather than at the time it would have been earned.

19–76   The principles for calculating interest on loss of earnings are:

– calculation based on past loss from date of accident to date of judgment;
– no interest on future loss of earnings;
– simple interest;
– interest is added to the loss of earnings after tax (no tax is deducted from the interest).

19–77   Tort law allows pre-judgment interest at the discretion of the court for the purpose of compensating plaintiffs' losses. The law concerning interest damages in tort actions distinguishes between economic losses, where the law allows interest, and non-pecuniary losses, where it does not.

19–78   Damages for future loss bear no interest. As explained above, such damages are discounted to present value to take into account the early receipt of the monies.[35]

Interest on commercial damages

19–79   In general, interest will be awarded pursuant to the provisions of the Courts Act 1981 in commercial cases where the terms of the matter in dispute (usually a contract) do not themselves provide for interest. Where a contract or other arrangement provides for interest in the circumstances giving rise to the dispute, the Courts Act 1981 precludes the court from making an award of interest (see also paras **19–74**).

19–80   In addition to damages for lost profits, interest is awarded to compensate plaintiffs for the loss of the use of those profits. In *Amstrad plc v. Seagate Technology Inc,*[36] it was successfully argued that interest should be based on the after tax loss of profits. The judge accepted that there is no point in awarding interest on that part of the lost profits which would have been paid in corporation tax.

---

[33] [1970] 2 Q.B. 130.
[34] [1979] A.C. 556.
[35] Kemp, D., *Damages for Personal Injury and Death* (7th ed., Sweet & Maxwell, London, 1998), Vol. 1, para. 16–015.
[36] (1997) 86 B.L.R. 34.

Calculation of interest

19–81 The calculation of interest requires two estimates:

– the time period between past loss and payment of damages; and

– the rate of interest to be applied in the calculation to the past loss.

19–82 A number of principles are applied in the calculation of interest. The rate of interest paid is that prescribed in the Courts Act 1981 for cases of death and personal injury. In other cases, it is decided at the court's discretion. It usually accrues from the date of the tort or of the breach of contract.

Compound interest

19–83 When damages are awarded, if interest is granted by the court it is on a simple rather than on a compound basis. Section 22 of the Courts Act 1981 allows simple interest only. Plaintiffs may plead for restitution damages, instead of pleading for compensatory damages plus interest. Restitution requires a defendant to forfeit all ill-gotten profits, including interest, as well as principal.

Income tax on plaintiffs' interest awards

19–84 When the plaintiff is a taxable entity, three possible income tax rates must be considered[37]:

– the income tax rate the plaintiff would have paid on amounts it would have collected but for the defendant's wrongdoing;

– the income tax rate the plaintiff would have paid on amounts it would have earned on the after tax amounts retained from above;

– the rate the plaintiff will pay on the damage settlement awarded.

19–85 The rate of income tax will be the actual (or effective) rate of tax suffered by the taxpayer, rather than the marginal rate of tax. The actual rate of tax is often lower than the marginal rate of tax as many companies and wealthy individuals reduce their tax rate by availing of tax avoidance measures and other tax planning strategies. The existence of tax bands for income tax also has the effect of reducing the overall tax rate below the marginal rate.

19–86 In *Polaroid Corp v. Eastman Kodak Co*[38] in the United States, Kodak was found to have infringed Polaroid's patents. Polaroid successfully argued that, had Kodak not infringed, Polaroid would have located additional

---

[37] Weil, R.L., "Compensation for the passage of time" in *Litigation Services Handbook: The Role of the Accountant as Expert* (2nd ed., Frank, P.B., Wagner, M.J. and Weil, R.L. (eds), John Wiley & Sons, Inc., New York, 1995), p. 37.6.

[38] 16 U.S.P.Q. 2d 1481 (D. Mass., 1990, as corr. 1991).

manufacturing capacity in Ireland, where taxes were reduced for such manufacturing facilities to encourage entities to locate manufacturing plants there.[39]

Concluding comment

19–87   The courts, and therefore those advising parties in the settlement of the many cases that never get as far as a court, pay scant attention to the assumptions underlying calculations of the effects of the passing of time on the value of monetary awards. As a result, it is quite possible that the bulk of awards and settlements fail to provide the level of compensation for which they are designed. Such a conclusion can, however, be nothing more than speculation until such time as a definitive study is undertaken of how successful plaintiffs cope with their damages and, in particular, whether they are able to meet all projected expenses out of the award/settlement plus interest thereon. Until then, however, the suspicion will remain that, due to a combination of judicial caution in relation to gross amounts and neglect of the need to address the impact of falling interest rates on the real return available on investments, plaintiffs do not, in general, recover sufficient capital sums to compensate them properly for the effects of the wrongs from which they suffer.

[39]Weil, R.L., "Compensation for the passage of time" in *Litigation Services Handbook: The Role of the Accountant as Expert* (2nd ed., Frank, P.B., Wagner, M.J. and Weil, R.L. (eds), John Wiley & Sons, Inc., New York, 1995), p. 37.6.

PART V

PROCEDURAL ASPECTS OF FORENSIC ACCOUNTING

PROCEDURE IN LITIGATION AND LEGAL TERMINOLOGY

CHAPTER 20

PROCEDURE IN LITIGATION AND LEGAL TERMINOLOGY

20–01 This chapter summarises the manner in which a case is initiated and progressed through the courts system in Ireland (readers are referred to Chapter 2 for a general overview of the legal system in Ireland and for references to other works dealing with the Irish legal system[1]).The purpose of this chapter is to provide the forensic accounting expert with a general understanding of the stages in the litigation process and the way in which court proceedings find their way through the legal system to a conclusion. It is not intended to be an exhaustive description of all possible eventualities, but rather an overview of the typical progression of a case from initiation to conclusion.

Procedure is described under the headings of the two main branches of the law – civil and criminal. The procedure described and the terms explained are not intended to be comprehensive, but rather to give the reader a point of reference for the situations most likely to be encountered by a forensic accountant in litigation. Note that Appendix 3 contains a glossary of accounting and legal terms.

20–02 The chapter starts with civil proceedings taken in the High Court, as this is the jurisdiction by far the most likely to be encountered by expert accountants. However, certain procedural steps not encountered in the High Court are also explained as they arise. It should be noted that much of the procedure used in the High Court are applicable directly, or by analogy, to other courts and, indeed, to other dispute resolution environments (alternative dispute resolution is dealt with in Chapter 14).

Many disputes are resolved before going to full plenary hearing(*i.e.* full hearing with witnesses giving oral evidence). This is especially the case in the event that an injunction is obtained. As injunctions play such a vital role, particularly in commercial disputes, they are considered separately in Chapter 21.

A similar approach is followed in describing criminal procedure. Criminal proceedings, especially if they involve allegations of fraud, may involve the services of forensic accountants.

---

[1] Other useful legal texts are Charleton, P., McDermott, P.A. and Bolger, M., *Criminal Law* (Butterworths, Dublin, 1999); Collins, A.M. and O'Reilly, J., *Civil Proceedings and the State in Ireland: A Practitioner's Guide* (The Round Hall Press, Dublin, 1990); and Ó'Floinn, B. *Practice and Procedure in the Superior Courts* (Butterworths, Dublin, 1996).

Overview of civil procedure

20–03 Most civil cases involving forensic accountants take place in the High Court.[2] Thus, this overview is based on a High Court action. Civil cases in the Circuit and District Courts are briefly considered in paras **20–43** *et seq.*

A typical civil case in the High Court can best be understood as a series of sequential steps leading to the eventual outcome of the proceedings. It is important to note that the parties can settle a civil dispute themselves at almost any stage and on almost any terms. The various stages are:

– communications before action (see para. **20–04**);

– parties and pleadings (see paras **20–05** *et seq.*);

– interlocutory hearings (see paras **20–22** *et seq.*);

– preparation for trial (see paras **20–25** *et seq.*);

– the full hearing (see paras **20–31** *et seq.*);

– judgment (see paras **20–37** *et seq.*);

– appeal (see paras **20–40** *et seq.*);

– execution of judgments and orders (see paras **20–41** *et seq.*).

Communications before action

20–04 Although not strictly part of the legal proceedings, the existence of a dispute and the essential cause for complaint and disagreement are normally communicated between the parties before formal legal proceedings are issued. In many cases (*e.g.* family disputes, alleged unfair dismissals, etc.) the circumstances of the dispute will be well known, and probably well rehearsed, between the parties before proceedings are commenced. In other cases, the first intimation that a proposed defendant will have of a possible suit will be a letter, sometimes called a "letter before action", from or on behalf of the proposed plaintiff. This letter will set out the principal causes for complaint, suggesting that the defendant acknowledge liability and agree compensation in order to avoid legal proceedings.

---

[2] As explained in paras **2–19** *et seq.*, a civil case involving a claim for damages of an amount less than £5,000 is generally heard in the District Court and a civil case involving a claim for damages of between £5,000 and £30,000 is heard in the Circuit Court. These limits are due to be increased with effect from January 1, 2002. Forensic accountants are more likely to be engaged in higher value cases heard in the High Court, where there is no limit on the damages that can be claimed.

The advantages of communications before action are that they provide an opportunity to resolve matters quickly and to avoid legal costs in doing so. They also provide a defence to any allegation made in court at a later stage that proceedings were unnecessary to resolve the dispute. However, in cases of any complexity or where there are material disagreements relating to the matters at issue, the case tends to progress quickly to the next stage.

Parties and pleadings[3]

Identification of defendants by plaintiffs

20–05 Before preparing a summons and presenting it to the Central Office of the High Court for subsequent issue, the prospective plaintiff must decide on who the appropriate defendants to the proceedings will be. Although parties can be added to proceedings at a later date (see paras **20–18** *et seq.* for further explanation), it is preferable that all defendants, where possible, are identified in the originating summons. The court has discretion to refuse leave to add parties to the proceedings.

20–06 In deciding on the appropriate defendants, the plaintiff needs to consider all of the damage he is alleging and the related reliefs he is seeking, all of the wrongs alleged which gave rise to the damage and all possible perpetrators of those wrongs. In particular, the plaintiff needs to take account of the fact that legal liability can extend beyond parties immediately involved in the cause of action. For instance:

- where an employee commits a fraud on a customer of a business while exercising his duties at work, his employer may also be liable;

- where a driver causes damage in a motor vehicle, the owner of the vehicle may also be liable;

- where damage is occasioned in a premises or on land, the occupier of the premises or land may be liable in addition to other parties involved;

- where breach of contract and negligence are both pleaded[4] in relation to the same damage, there may be a negligent party who was not a party to the contract but owed a duty of care to the plaintiff in the circumstances;

- where defamation is alleged, the medium through which the defamatory statement was made (*e.g.* newspaper, television station, etc.) may be liable as well as the statement's author;

- where the plaintiff wishes to proceed against an organ of the State he will need to be advised carefully as to who the defendants should be.

---

[3] See App. 3 (Glossary) for brief explanation of term.
[4] See paras **15–90** *et seq.* for an explanation of why pleadings alleging both breach of contract and tort might be taken.

20–07   For these and other reasons, the plaintiff needs to take care before issuing proceedings to ensure that he has identified the correct defendants. However, he can take comfort from section 12(1) of the Civil Liability Act 1961, which states:

> "Subject to the provisions of sections 14, 38 and 46, concurrent wrongdoers are each liable for the whole of the damage in respect of which they are concurrent wrongdoers."

The effect of this provision is that, where more than one party is responsible for the damage caused to the plaintiff then, subject to specific exceptions, judgment in respect of the whole of the damage is recoverable from each of the wrongdoers. As a result, the plaintiff can transfer to the wrongdoers the problem of dividing the liability between them in the appropriate proportions by pursuing just one of them, provided that one is found to be liable in some way and to some extent for the damage. The specific exceptions relate to situations: (i) where the plaintiff agrees to an apportionment of damages between defendants; (ii) where one defendant is entitled to mitigation of damages in a defamation action; (iii) where the plaintiff is found guilty of contributory negligence; and (iv) in certain maritime cases. This rule means, of course, that defendants must also ensure that they initiate proceedings against any other party that may be liable and that has not been included in the proceedings by the plaintiff.

Statute of Limitations

20–08   The legislation that sets out time-limits governing the issue of legal proceedings is the Statute of Limitations 1957, as amended by several subsequent Acts, including the Civil Liability Act 1961, the Succession Act 1965, the Sale of Goods and Supply of Services Act 1980 and, most notably, the Statute of Limitations (Amendment) Act 1991.

20–09   In general, actions arising under contract cannot be commenced more than six years after the cause of action arises. The six-year limitation period also applies to actions in tort, with one exception. Where a claim for damages for negligence, nuisance or breach of duty includes a claim for damages for personal injury, the time limit is three years from the date of the occurrence of the cause of action or, if later, from the date of knowledge. The date of knowledge is the date the injured person (or, if that person is deceased, his or her personal representative) first became aware of the significance of the injury, its cause, the person who caused it and, if the defendant is to be a different person, the identity of and reason for proceeding against the defendant. The time-limit for actions taken on an instrument executed under seal and for actions (other than by the State) to recover land is 12 years.

20–10   The issue of a summons has the effect of commencing the proceedings and "stopping the clock" for the purpose of compliance with the Statute of

Limitations. Accordingly, the various limitation periods are measured against the period of time between the date the cause of action accrued or, if applicable, the date of knowledge, and the date on which the summons instituting the proceedings was issued by the Central Office of the High Court.

Issue of summons by plaintiffs

20–11   The issue of a summons (see Appendix 3 for explanation of term) marks the institution of most formal legal proceedings in the High Court. (Note that certain family law matters and some company law matters are initiated by a document called a "petition": and many company law proceedings are initiated by a document called an "originating notice of motion"). The term "statute-barred" is used to describe the phenomenon whereby an otherwise valid claim cannot be pursued because proceedings have not been issued within the statutory time-limits (see paras **20–08** *et seq.* for further explanation).

20–12   Once issued by the Central Office of the High Court, a summons remains valid for a year (unless renewed by the court for further periods of six months), and the summons can be served on the defendant or defendants at any time within the period of validity. Service on individual defendants in the State is generally required to be effected in person, although the court may grant permission for service to be effected in another manner if reasonable efforts to serve the defendant in person have been made and have failed. Section 379 of the Companies Act 1963 states that service on a company can be effected at its registered office or, where no registered office has been notified to the Registrar of Companies, at the Companies Registration Office. Service on defendants resident outside the State is governed by detailed procedures set down in the Rules of the Superior Courts and the Brussels,[5] Hague[6] and Lugano[7] Conventions. These Conventions are agreements between the Contracting States (including all European Union states) as to the rules for establishing the country whose court has jurisdiction over specific legal proceedings that involve parties domiciled in different countries and also for the service of documents and the enforcement of judgments in other countries.

Entering an appearance by defendants

20–13   When a defendant receives a plenary or summary summons, he is required by the Rules of the Superior Courts to "enter an appearance" (see Appendix 3 for explanation of term) to the summons within eight days of service

---

[5] Hague Convention on the Service Abroad of Judicial and Extra Judicial Documents in Civil and Commercial Mattters, Signed at Brussels on September 27, 1968; [1975] O.J. L204/28; [1978] O.J. L304/77.
[6] Signed at The Hague on November 15, 1965.
[7] Signed at Lugano on September 16, 1988; [1988] O.J. L319/9-48.

of the summons. An appearance may be entered to a special summons at any time.[8] Lodging in the Central Office of the High Court (in most cases) a document identifying the defendant's solicitor, or stating that the defendant intends to defend the action in person, effects the entry of an appearance. A copy of this document, stamped by the Central Office, must be served on the plaintiff or the plaintiff's solicitor. If a defendant fails to enter an appearance in time the plaintiff can seek judgment in default of appearance, but a defendant will almost invariably be given additional time by the court to enter an appearance if he so requests.

Statements of claim by plaintiffs

20–14   Once served, a plenary summons (see Appendix 3 for explanation of term) should be followed within 21 days by a statement of claim (see Appnedix 3 for further explanation of term), setting out in some detail the basic facts underlying the plaintiff's claim, details of the allegations that give rise to the basis for a legal claim arising from the facts, and a description of the damage suffered for which the plaintiff believes he should be compensated. For example, where a plaintiff alleges that a defendant has breached a commercial contract with him, causing loss of business and profits, the statement of claim will:

- identify the parties to the case;

- give details of the contract, citing the parties to it, its date and its principal terms;

- identify the particular terms allegedly breached by the defendant, giving details of the timing and manner of the alleged breaches;

- give details of the losses allegedly suffered by the plaintiff and the basis for attributing those losses to the alleged breach of contract by the defendant;

- state the grounds for legal liability on the part of the defendant;

- claim damages, interest and costs (and possibly specific performance which is a request to the court to order the defendant to refrain from the breach and comply with the terms of the contract).

Requests for further particulars by defendants

20–15   Having received a statement of claim, a defendant will usually seek from the plaintiff further details of the claim being made against him before preparing his formal defence. A request for such further details is made in the form of a notice for particulars (see Appendix 3 for explanation of term) and the replies thereto are described as replies to particulars (see Appendix 3 for explanation of term). An additional request is usually called a notice for further and better particulars. Although not pleadings in the formal sense in High Court

---

[8] For a brief definition of "special summons" see App. 3 (Glossary).

cases, notices and replies to particulars form an important part of the exchange of information between the parties.

Defence and counterclaim

20–16   The defendant's response to the statement of claim is the defence (see Appendix 3 for explanation of term) or defence and counterclaim (see Appendix 3 for explanation of term). Typically, all allegations other than matters that are self-evidently true or are uncontroversial are either denied or explicitly not admitted in the defence, as a result of which the plaintiff must prove his allegations on the balance of probability (see para. **2–30** and para. **8–01** for further discussion of standards of proof). It should be noted, however, that a judge may choose to penalise a defendant (*e.g.* by way of costs) if he finds that a fact denied by the defendant should have been admitted.[9]

Where the defence contains a counterclaim or other allegation against the plaintiff by the defendant, the plaintiff may prepare and serve a reply. Allegations in the reply may also merit a response, and so on. When all such documents have been served between the parties the pleadings close.

Lodgment

20–17   The term "lodgment" when used in relation to court proceedings most often refers to the payment into court of a sum of money by a defendant for the purpose of satisfying all or a specified element of the plaintiff's claim against that defendant (see also paras. **20–52** *et seq.*). It should be noted that the State as a defendant is now permitted to avail of the lodgment system by making settlement offers without the requirement to lodge the funds in court.

The lodgment process is governed by Order 22 of the Rules of the Superior Courts and the policy behind it is to encourage the settlement of claims before the costs of preparing for and appearing in court are incurred. The Rules permit a defendant to lodge amounts in court within certain specific periods during the course of the proceedings. The permissible payments and specified periods vary depending on the nature of the proceedings. General rules for all proceedings are varied in the case of proceedings for damages for personal injuries caused by negligence, nuisance or breach of duty or for fatal injuries, and for certain other types of proceedings. In all cases the plaintiff is given a specified period within which he can accept the lodgment in settlement of his claim against the defendant or of the specified element of the claim. If he does so the proceedings are stayed (*i.e.* suspended). If the plaintiff declines the lodgment the matter proceeds and the court is not told the amount of the lodgment (or, in certain cases, that there is a lodgment) until all questions of liability and amount of debt or damages have been decided. If the amount awarded to the plaintiff does not exceed the amount paid into court then, subject to the judge's discretion to

---

[9] See Order 21, rule 8 of the Rules of the Superior Courts 1986.

direct otherwise for special reasons, the plaintiff becomes liable for the costs of the action from the time the payment into court was made. This potential costs penalty can be very substantial and serves to focus the mind of a plaintiff on the amount he feels he is likely to recover in comparison with the amount of the lodgment.

Addition of third parties to proceedings by plaintiffs and defendants

20–18 At any stage in the case it may become apparent to either the plaintiff or the defendant that an additional defendant should be part of the proceedings. This can arise in a variety of ways and usually results from the further investigation of the circumstances of the cause of action by both parties through the process of exchange of particulars, discovery and the engagement of experts to advise on the facts. For example, investigation by a consultant engineer of the facts surrounding an industrial accident, on foot of which an injured party has issued proceedings against his employer, may reveal that an independent contractor was responsible in some way for the accident.

20–19 The courts generally facilitate the addition of parties to proceedings in the interests of efficiency and justice, provided no party is excessively prejudiced by the addition. The relevant rule states:

> "No cause or matter shall be defeated by reason of the misjoinder or non-joinder of parties, and the Court may in every cause or matter deal with the matter in controversy so far as regards the rights and interests of the parties actually before it. The Court may at any stage of the proceedings, either upon or without the application of either party, and on such terms as may appear to the Court to be just, order that the names of any parties improperly joined, whether as plaintiffs or as defendants, be struck out and that the names of any parties, whether plaintiffs or defendants, who ought to have been joined, or whose presence before the Court may be necessary in order to enable the Court effectually and completely to adjudicate upon and settle all the questions involved in the cause or matter, be added."[10]

20–20 Where a plaintiff wishes to join an additional defendant after proceedings have been issued he applies to the court for leave to do so. Existing defendants rarely object to the addition of a new defendant. Having obtained the leave of the court, an amended summons and statement of claim are served on the new defendant.

20–21 Where a defendant feels that another person who is not a party to the proceedings initiated by the plaintiff may be liable on foot of the circumstances of the case, he applies under Order 16 of the Rules of the Superior Courts to join the new party as a "third party" to the proceedings (see Appendix 3 for

---

[10] Rules of the Superior Courts 1986, Ord.15, r.13.

explanation of term). The plaintiff receives notice of the defendant's intention and may apply to add the proposed third party as a defendant. If so, the procedure described in para. **20–20** is invoked. If not, and if the court grants leave to the defendant to do so, a third party notice is served on the new party. This explains the basis for the defendant's belief that the third party is liable and, in effect, commences a parallel set of proceedings between the defendant and the third party.

The hearing of proceedings against third parties usually takes place immediately after the hearing of the original action, provided the plaintiff's claim has succeeded against the defendant. If the plaintiff fails against the defendant and has not joined the third party as a defendant he has no subsequent recourse against the third party in the proceedings. For this reason it is usually prudent for the plaintiff to join a proposed third party as a defendant, unless there is no basis for a claim against that party by the plaintiff. Where the plaintiff succeeds against the defendant, the court will then be asked to determine the issue between the defendant and the third party so that the defendant may be able to recover (partly or fully) from the third party the amount of the plaintiff's award.

Interlocutory hearings

20–22   In certain circumstances the assistance of the court may be required by one or more parties to proceedings to resolve an issue in advance of the full hearing. Examples include situations where without immediate relief irreparable damage may be done, in which case an injunction may be sought asking for a court order to prevent such damage (see Chapter 21). Where the court is satisfied that the urgency of the matter is such as to justify the provision of relief (normally of a temporary nature) before the case can be heard in full, an interlocutory hearing will be held at which the parties will argue their sides of the urgent matter in question, and usually based on evidence contained in affidavits rather than given by witnesses in person. If the court grants relief following an interlocutory hearing the relief will normally be of a temporary or interim nature pending the outcome of the full hearing.

Notice of motion

20–23   A notice of motion is a document used to initiate certain court applications. Except for motions which are expressly permitted to be made without notice to the other party or parties in a case (known as *ex parte* applications), applications by motion are made on notice. The notice of motion will contain details of the time and place at which the court application will be made and the nature of the relief sought. It will also indicate the basis on which the relief is sought and will refer to any supporting documents (*e.g.* affidavits) on which the moving party intends to rely. An example of an application made by notice of motion by a plaintiff is an application for judgment in default of defence, *i.e.* the plaintiff is seeking judgment in his favour because the defendant has failed to deliver a defence to the proceedings. An example in respect of a defendant is a motion to join a third party to the proceedings.

Affidavit

20–24 An affidavit is a document containing the sworn evidence of its signatory, who is known as the "deponent". It is the equivalent of sworn oral testimony given at a court hearing, except that the truthfulness of the content of the affidavit cannot itself be tested on cross-examination at the time that it is sworn. There is therefore a high degree of formality involved in the preparation and swearing of an affidavit for use in court proceedings. The formalities include requirements that the affidavit be written in the first person, contain the name, description and address of the deponent and be sworn before a solicitor or commissioner for oaths (other than the swearing party's own solicitor), who must indicate where and when it was sworn and that he knows the deponent. Affidavits are used to set out facts in support of court applications, but not to plead the relevant law. In most cases, such as for proceedings commenced by summary summons, a party receiving an affidavit filed on behalf of the opposing party can serve a notice to cross-examine the deponent, and unless the deponent submits to cross-examination his evidence cannot be used without special leave of the court.

Preparation for trial

20–25 The period between the exchange and close of pleadings and the hearing of the action can be anything between a few days and several years. Typically, the period will last at least a number of months. This period of time is used by all parties to gather and analyse all relevant evidence, to identify and arrange for the attendance of all necessary witnesses, and to prepare all appropriate legal and other submissions.

Engagement of experts

20–26 As pointed out in paras **1–18, 1–39, 1–40** and **6–65**, it is important to engage experts at as early a stage as possible so that they can assist in the gathering and organisation of documents and other evidence. The number of experts necessary and their areas of expertise will, of course, depend on the matters at issue in the proceedings. Accountants, engineers, doctors, actuaries, architects and others will often find that the courts need to avail of their services in order to throw light on areas of technical complexity. If the experts are engaged prior to the discovery process they can contribute significantly to the identification of the central issues, the strengths and weaknesses in the relative cases of the parties and the organisation of the case generally. In particular, the organisation of documents in large and complex cases is a major challenge and experts can assist greatly in this process.

Discovery

20–27 In the majority of complex cases both sides seek discovery (see Appendix 3 for further explanation of term). Although specific known documents may be requested of one party by the other in the process of discovery, the overriding obligation on all parties is to provide copies of all documents relevant to any of the matters at issue in the proceedings specified in the order for discovery that are in the custody, possession or power of each party – in other words, those relevant documents that the party has or can obtain. In addition, discovery of relevant documents can be sought from a party not involved in the proceedings, and an order for such discovery is usually forthcoming provided the relevance of the requested material has been established and the requesting party covers the reasonable costs incurred by the third party.[11]

20–28 Discovery will be sought on a voluntary basis initially, and the request for voluntary discovery must comply with the detailed provisions of the Rules of the Superior Courts.[12] If not provided voluntarily the requesting party will normally apply to court seeking an order compelling discovery. In response to a discovery order, the party providing the discovery will do so by swearing an affidavit (see para. **20–24** and Appendix 3 for explanation of term) listing separately: (i) the documents being provided; (ii) the documents in the party's custody, power or possession over which a privilege (see paras **22–03** *et seq.* para. **22–30** and para. **22–35**) exempting their disclosure is claimed; and (iii) the documents previously but no longer in the party's custody, power or possession together with an indication of what has become of them. The affidavit will confirm that the total of the three lists is a complete list of all relevant documents that are or have been in the party's custody, possession or power.

Interrogatories

20–29 Interrogatories (see Appendix 3 for further information) are used to seek answers to specific questions relevant to the matters at issue, typically where those answers are not expected to appear in, or arise from the content of, documents. Because of the importance of discovery and interrogatories to the nature and extent of the involvement of expert accountants in litigation they are dealt with more fully in Chapter 22.

20–30 Once the process of discovery and interrogatories is complete, each party will set about organising the evidence for trial. This will involve asking the expert witnesses to prepare and complete their expert reports, obtaining statements of fact from witnesses and researching the relevant legal principles. Documents obtained on discovery will be examined carefully for evidence

---

[11] See Order 31, rule 29 of the Rules of the Superior Courts 1986.
[12] See Rules of the Superior Courts (No. 2) (Discovery) 1999 (S.I. No. 233 of 1999).

relevant to the matters in dispute. In the meantime, the hearing will be scheduled by the court on application by the parties, who will have attempted to identify dates suitable for the attendance of all witnesses.

The hearing

Presentation of plaintiff's case

20–31   With a small number of exceptions a judge sitting alone hears civil cases in the High Court. When the case first comes before a court for hearing it is opened by counsel for the plaintiff, who will usually summarise the nature and key features of the case before calling his first witness. The plaintiff's case is presented first. The order in which witnesses are called is determined by the plaintiff's legal team, who will balance the (sometimes conflicting) considerations of tactics, availability of witnesses and a desire to present the case in a clear, logical and easy-to-follow fashion.

Direct, cross- and re-examination

20–32   When being questioned by the plaintiff's counsel, the plaintiff's witnesses are undergoing "direct examination". Counsel may not ask leading questions (*i.e.* questions that anticipate a specific answer) in direct examination or cross-examine a witness called by him except on rare occasions.

20–33   When direct examination of a plaintiff's witness is complete, defence counsel's cross-examination of the witness begins. Leading questions are permissible in cross-examination and, as a result, cross-examination tends to be more robust than direct examination. In general, questions concentrate on matters raised in direct examination and matters to be raised on direct examination of the defence's own witnesses, but can stray outside these boundaries. It is important that significant evidence to be given by defence witnesses is put to the relevant plaintiff witnesses to give them an opportunity to respond to it. If this is not done, plaintiff's counsel may object successfully to the introduction of the evidence at a later stage. It is worth noting that, if the court rises during cross-examination of a witness (*e.g.* for lunch or overnight) counsel for the party who called the witness is not permitted to communicate with the witness during the break or at any subsequent stage until cross-examination is complete.

20–34   Following cross-examination of the plaintiff's witness, plaintiff's counsel has an opportunity to ask the witness further questions ("re-examination"), but such questions are restricted to clarification of matters raised in cross-examination. New evidence cannot be given at this stage.

Defence

20–35   When all the plaintiff's witnesses have given evidence the defence then begins direct examination of its own witnesses. The same rules govern the conduct of direct examination by defence counsel, cross-examination by plaintiff's counsel and re-examination by defence counsel as for the presentation of the plaintiff's evidence. The judge can (and frequently does) join in the questioning of witnesses at any stage for the purpose of clarifying the evidence given.

20–36   It should be noted that, in general, documents, even those produced on foot of a court order for discovery, do not constitute evidence in the case until "proven" by oral evidence. In other words, most documents must be identified by a witness who must describe their origin, nature, content and significance.

Judgment

20–37   When all the evidence has been presented and counsel have summed up their cases, the judge will either render a verdict immediately or will reserve judgment. Decisions that are given immediately on the conclusion of a case (known as *ex tempore* judgments) are usually confined to simple cases, or occasionally matters of urgency. Reserved judgments are often given in more complex cases. The parties may have to wait some weeks or months for a reserved judgment. When it is given the judge will usually read the judgment in full, and written copies will then be distributed to the parties.

20–38   Depending on the result, one side will usually seek their costs against the other, as costs usually, but not always, follow the event.

20–39   If the losing party plans to consider an appeal, their counsel will normally apply for a stay on any order, including the order for costs, made on foot of the judgment. Whether or not to grant a stay is within the judge's discretion and he will consider the specific circumstances of the case before deciding. The effect of a stay is to postpone the effect of the judgment until either an appeal has been heard and determined or the time for lodging an appeal has expired and no appeal has been lodged.

Appeal

20–40   Appeals from High Court civil cases are to the Supreme Court. Depending on the nature of the case, the appeal will be heard by a court of either three or five judges. Appeals are based on points of law, or on mixed points of fact and law, as determined by the High Court. The Supreme Court will overturn a pure finding of fact only in the most exceptional circumstances. Witnesses do not give evidence in a Supreme Court hearing, and the court will be very slow to second-guess the determination of a High Court judge as to the credibility of witness evidence, where the High Court judge has had the opportunity to observe the witness giving his evidence and being cross-examined on it.

Although in certain cases it is possible to appeal a Supreme Court decision by way of reference to the European Court of Justice, in general the Supreme Court is the last port of call.

Execution of judgments and orders

20–41   Once judgment has been entered in favour of a party to proceedings that party is entitled to recover the amount of the decree (which specifies the amount payable in damages) of the court, subject only to any stay on the order made by the court or the fulfilment of any condition on which the judgment is dependent.

Enforcement of judgment

20–42   If the amount of the judgment is not paid, the party seeking to enforce the judgment proceeds to the process of execution. Depending on the nature of the judgment and on the likelihood of assets being available to meet it, one or more of the following procedures may be considered and undertaken:

- taking out an order for sequestration, under which assets of the losing party can be seized and retained until the judgment is met;
- taking out an order for *fieri facias*, directing the sheriff to seize goods or assets up to the amount of the judgment, and following which an order of *venditioni exponas* can be entered authorising the sale of the goods and assets to meet the judgment;
- taking out an order for attachment which authorises the successful litigant to obtain payment directly from another party who is indebted to the defaulting party;
- seeking to put the losing party into bankruptcy (if an individual) or liquidation (if a company);
- seeking an order for the committal of a party under section 6 of the Debtors Act (Ireland) 1872.

Details of the procedure involved in these and other methods of recovery are beyond the scope of this book.

Circuit Court civil procedure

20–43   Civil procedure in the Circuit Court is similar in most respects to the equivalent High Court procedure. Circuit Court procedure is governed by the Rules of the Circuit Court 1950 as amended (new Circuit Court rules are expected in the near future). The last rule in the 1950 rules illustrates the close link between the procedure of the Circuit Court and that of the High Court:

> "Where there is no Rule provided by these Rules to govern practice or procedure, the practice and procedure in the High Court may be followed."[13]

Differences between High Court and Circuit Court civil procedure

20–44 The principal differences between civil procedure in the two jurisdictions are:

(1) The originating document for proceedings in the Circuit Court is a civil bill. A civil bill combines the functions of both the summons and the statement of claim in the High Court. Depending on the nature of the proceedings the type of civil bill will differ. Most cases begin with an ordinary civil bill, but, for example, actions for ejectment commence with one of a number of ejectment civil bills. Cases in which equitable relief (such as an injunction or specific performance (see Appendix 3 for an explanation of this term) of a contract) is sought are commenced with an equity civil bill. Notwithstanding differences in title, each civil bill must contain the facts and assertions necessary to ground the claim.

(2) Because the jurisdiction of the Circuit Court is limited (by reference to the nature of the case, the size of the claim, the rateable valuation of land in certain circumstances, or the geographical area involved) the civil bill generally needs to contain sufficient information to confirm that the Circuit Court in the particular circuit in which the proceedings are being issued has jurisdiction to hear the case.

(3) Ten days are allowed from the date of service of the civil bill to the entry of an appearance, and a further 10 days are allowed from then for the delivery of the defence by the defendant.

(4) Requests for particulars and replies to particulars are also a feature of cases in the Circuit Court and, unlike in the High Court, they are regarded as pleadings in their own right.

District Court civil procedure

20–45 Civil proceedings in the District Court are commenced with a civil summons, which is required to set out concisely the nature and basis of the claim. The procedure does not provide for a formal defence, but rather for a "notice of intention to defend". Because the District Court deals with a high volume of relatively small claims, procedure is less formal than in the Circuit Court and the High Court.

---

[13] Order 59, Rule 14, Rules of the Circuit Court 1950.

Security for costs

20–46   A fundamental principle of litigation is that the loser is usually liable for all or a significant proportion of the winner's costs. However, if the losing party has insufficient funds the successful litigant may have difficulty in enforcing the order for costs.

Where a defendant loses and is unable to pay the plaintiff's costs, this is usually a foreseeable outcome and the risk that it will happen should have been assessed by the plaintiff before he initiated proceedings. The position of the successful defendant who is unable to recover his costs is, however, different. This is because he did not institute the proceedings and therefore had no choice but to incur costs in his defence.

From the defendant's point of view, one approach to this problem is to apply to the court for an order for security for costs. The purpose of an application for security for costs is to safeguard a successful defendant from failing to recover his costs from the claimant. Such an order requires the plaintiff to lodge into court a sum to be used in discharge of the defendant's costs should the plaintiff's action fail. If the plaintiff cannot meet the order for security for costs the case will be delayed until such time as the order is met. A successful application for an order for security for costs may have the effect of deterring the plaintiff from pursuing the case.

Security for costs may be awarded against a defendant where the defendant is making a counterclaim (see para. **20–16**). In such circumstances, the defendant can be ordered to give security for costs of the counterclaim.[14]

Legal context

Companies

20–47   Security for costs provides protection for successful defendants, where the plaintiff either cannot pay the costs and damages awarded, or is resident outside the jurisdiction where an order for costs made by an Irish court might be difficult or impossible to enforce. The issue of security for costs in respect of companies is legislated for in the Companies Act 1963.

Section 390 of the Companies Act 1963 makes provisions for security for costs by companies as follows:

"Where a limited company is plaintiff in any action or other legal proceedings,

---

[14]The issue of security for costs from a forensic accounting perspective is considered further in Lemar, C.J. and Mainz, A.J. (eds), *Litigation Support* (4th ed., Butterworths, London, 1999), Chap. 13; MacGregor, G. and Hobbs, I., *Expert Accounting Evidence: A Guide for Litigation Support* (Accountancy Books, London, 1998), Chap. 27; Taub, M., Rapazzini, A., Bond, C., Solon, M., Brown, A., Murrie, A., Linnell, K. and Burn, S., *Tolley's Accountancy Litigation Support* (Butterworths, London, looseleaf), Part IV, para. 45.

any judge having jurisdiction in the matter, may, if it appears by credible testimony that there is reason to believe that the company will be unable to pay the costs of the defendant if successful in his defence, require sufficient security to be given for those costs and may stay all proceedings until the security is given."

From a forensic accounting point of view, the importance of this section is in the credible testimony that must be provided to show that the plaintiff company will be unable to meet the (successful) defendant's costs. The defendant has to prove (by credible testimony) that the plaintiff will be unable to pay any costs that may ultimately be awarded in the defendant's favour.

20–48   Security for costs cannot be ordered against plaintiff companies except where, at the discretion of the court, having regard to all the circumstances of the case, it is equitable to do so. It is not enough to show the plaintiff has financial difficulties. This point was made in the judgment of Kingsmill Moore J. in *Peppard & Co Ltd v. Bogoff,* as follows:

> "... the section does not make it mandatory to order security for costs in every case where the plaintiff company appears to be unable to pay the costs of a successful defendant, but that there still remains a discretion in the court which may be exercised in special circumstances."[15]

The court may exercise its discretion "in special circumstances". It is up to the plaintiff company to show there are special circumstances. In *Jack O'Toole Ltd v. MacEoin Kelly Associates,* Finlay J. stated:

> "... if the plaintiff company seeks to avoid an order for security for costs ... it must, as a matter of onus of proof, establish to the satisfaction of the judge the special circumstances which would justify the refusal of an order."[16]

The court has complete discretion in deciding whether to award security for costs.[17] A number of principles have been articulated by the courts, as follows[18]:

– impecunity of the plaintiff is, in itself, insufficient justification for an order for security for costs;

– the court must weigh the potential injustice to the plaintiff if he is not permitted to pursue his claim against that to the defendant if security is not ordered;

– the court will consider the plaintiff's prospects of success in making its decision;

---

[15] [1962] I.R. 180 at 188.
[16] [1986] I.R. 277 at 283.
[17] See *Sir Lindsay Parkinson & Co v. Triplan Ltd* [1973] 2 All E.R. 293; *Proetta v. Neil* [1996] 1 I.R. 100; and *Fares v. Wiley* [1994] 2 I.R. 379.
[18] *e.g.* see *Keary Developments Ltd v. Tarmac Construction Ltd* [1995] 3 All E.R. 534. See also *Lismore Homes Ltd (in liquidation) v. Bank of Ireland Finance Ltd* [1999] 1 I.R. 501; *Lancefort Ltd v. An Bord Pleanála* [1998] 2 I.R. 511; *Pitt v. Bolger* [1996] 1 I.R. 108; and *Maher v. Phelan* [1996] 1 I.R. 95.

- any amount can be ordered as security for costs up to the full amount applied for;

- the court will take into account the plaintiff's resources and any other sources of funding available.

20–49 A number of grounds on which security for costs have been ordered in High Court actions against corporate plaintiffs have been identified as follows:

(1) The bona fides of the defendant – courts will not grant an order for security for costs where there is evidence that the defendant is not acting bona fide.

(2) The strength of the plaintiff's case – this will influence whether an order is made.

(3) Insolvency of the plaintiff caused by the defendant's actions – an order for security for costs is less likely in such circumstances.

(4) Existence of individual co-plaintiffs – this can have various effects.

(5) Plaintiff company in liquidation – defendants' costs will rank in order of priority of repayment following normal rules and procedures.

Individuals and partnerships

20–50 Because an order can be enforced by the Irish courts against an Irish resident, security for costs is not granted against individual plaintiffs resident in Ireland.[19]

An individual who is a national of and ordinarily resident in another Member State of the European Union cannot be required to provide security for costs solely on the grounds that he resides out of the jurisdiction of the Irish courts.[20]

The rules relating to partnerships follow those applicable to individuals.

Role of forensic accountants

20–51 Defendants must be able to provide courts with good grounds justifying the order for security for costs. Assistance from forensic accountants is frequently sought in connection with application for security for costs. Financial evidence in the form of a sworn statement (affidavit) can assist the court in its decision. The forensic accountant may be required to prepare a report or affidavit expressing his opinion on whether or not the plaintiff is likely to be able to meet an order for costs from existing resources. The purpose of the statement is to show that the plaintiff does/does not have adequate collateral to discharge the bill of costs if he loses the case.

---

[19] *Maher v. Phelan* [1996] 1 I.R. 95.
[20] *Proetta v. Neil* [1996] 1 I.R. 100.

All information publicly available concerning the plaintiff's financial position will have to be obtained. More information will be available concerning companies (rather than individuals) such as from the following sources:

- audited accounts from the Companies Registration Office (these may be quite out of date depending on how efficient the plaintiff is with filing its accounts);

- reports on the credit standing of the plaintiff from credit rating agencies;

- financial information concerning the plaintiff as included in case documents.

The issues to be included in the forensic accounting report will depend on the specific circumstances of the case. Security for costs may not be awarded if the financial difficulties of the plaintiff are found to be due to the defendant's wrongful actions. The defendant, supported by his expert evidence, will have to show that the plaintiff's financial difficulties arose independently of the defendant's actions.

Forensic accountants should be conscious that the evidence they provide in connection with applications for security for costs may be referred to again at the full hearing of the case. If the expert evidence is not accepted, or if doubt is cast on its quality, this may disadvantage the expert evidence at the full hearing.[21,22]

Payments into court

Legal context

20–52 A defendant may provide some protection for itself when assessing the risk of losing the case. Defendants in civil cases have the option to pay a sum into court (called a lodgment) as an offer to settle (see also para. **20–17**). The sum of money should cover the expected award of damages, together with interest, in the event that the judge finds against the defendant. If the sum awarded to the plaintiff is less than the lodgment, the plaintiff will be held liable for both parties' costs to the extent that they arose after the date the lodgment was made. Thus, even though the plaintiff may be the successful litigant, costs arising after the lodgment may be payable by him.

The settlement offer must be made in writing and the defendant must identify whether the offer relates to all or only part of the claim.

In claims other than debt or damages, it is possible to make "without prejudice except as to costs" written offers to settle – these are called Calderbank letters.

---

[21] MacGregor, G. and Hobbs, I., *Expert Accounting Evidence: A Guide for Litigation Support* (Accountancy Books, London, 1998), p. 182.

[22] Useful examples of a model affidavit that might be used by forensic accountants in such applications can be found in Lemar, C.J. and Mainz, A.J. (eds), *Litigation Support* (4th ed., Butterworths, London, 1999), App. G; Taub, M., Rapazzini, A., Bond, C., Solon, M., Brown, A., Murrie, A., Linnell, K. and Burn, S., *Tolley's Accountancy Litigation Support* (Butterworths, London, looseleaf), App. 9.

Calderbank letters are often used in arbitration, offering to settle a dispute on specified terms and stating that it may be used in connection with costs if the offer to settle is refused. If the offer is not accepted and the other party is awarded a lesser sum by the court, the offeror gets costs from the period after the Calderbank letter.

Role of forensic accountants

20–53   Forensic accountants have an important role to play in assisting defendants estimate the quantum of damages which, in turn, will influence the amount to be lodged in court.

Overview of criminal procedure

20–54   As explained in para. **2–26**, criminal cases are prosecuted on behalf of the people, usually by the Director of Public Prosecutions (the "DPP"). The objective of such cases is to establish the guilt of a person or persons alleged to have committed a breach of a specific law with a view to having them convicted of the crime and punished accordingly. The party taking the case is described as the prosecution and the accused person is called the defendant or the accused.

20–55   Procedure in criminal trials can be quite different from civil cases – proper observance of the rules of procedure and evidence in criminal trials is very important. Where proper procedure is not followed, a criminal trial may collapse. Criminal procedure in the Irish courts can be complex and technical, and an overview only is given here.

Types of prosecution

20–56   There are two distinct types of prosecution, and they give rise to different procedure for the disposal of the case. Serious crimes are prosecuted on indictment while less serious crimes are subject to summary prosecution. Many statutes prescribe different penalties depending on whether a conviction follows a summary prosecution or a prosecution on indictment. For example, under section 2(4) of the Non-Fatal Offences against the Person Act 1997, the less serious crime of assault envisages only summary prosecution by setting out its penalty as follows:

> "A person guilty of an offence under this section shall be liable on summary conviction to a fine not exceeding £1,500 or to imprisonment for a term not exceeding 6 months or to both."

Under section 3(2) the more serious crime of assault causing harm attracts the following penalties:

"A person guilty of an offence under this section shall be liable—
- (a) on summary conviction to imprisonment for a term not exceeding 12 months or to a fine not exceeding £1,500 or to both, or
- (b) on conviction on indictment to a fine or to imprisonment for a term not exceeding 5 years or to both."

The even more serious crime of causing serious harm envisages only trial on indictment under section 4:

"(1) A person who intentionally or recklessly causes serious harm to another shall be guilty of an offence.

(2) A person guilty of an offence under this section shall be liable on conviction on indictment to a fine or to imprisonment for life or to both."

Summary prosecution

20–57 Summary prosecution normally involves the issuance of a summons by a clerk of the District Court (or some other person authorised by statute), usually on application of a member of the Garda Síochána. The summons contains details of the alleged offence and directs the accused person to appear at a hearing of the District Court to answer the charge. Ordinarily there is no further paperwork involved in the case, although documentary evidence (*e.g.* results of a test of blood or urine for alcohol content in a drunk driving case) may be necessary.

Prosecution on indictment

20–58 Prosecution on indictment is far more complex, involving as it does all of the most serious crimes. Several agencies can initiate a prosecution, but most are commenced by the Garda Síochána, who assemble evidence and send a file to the Director of Public Prosecutions (DPP) for consideration. The DPP will decide whether to proceed, based on his assessment of the likelihood of a conviction based on the assembled evidence and on public policy grounds.

20–59 Following a decision by the DPP to proceed, the accused is brought before the District Court to be charged. If the offence involved is an indictable one (*i.e.* it can be prosecuted and attract a penalty on indictment) it falls into one of two categories – it is either one of a number of indictable offences specified by statute as triable summarily or it is not one of those offences.

Summary trials

20–60 The Constitution restricts the summary trial of offences in the District Court to minor offences only. The District Court can deal summarily with indictable offences in any of the following situations:

(1) Where an offence is specified by statute to give rise to the possibility of

either summary conviction or conviction on indictment. There are many such offences and in these cases the prosecuting authority decides, based on the seriousness of the specific offence allegedly committed, whether to proceed summarily (limiting the severity of the sentence that can be imposed) or on indictment. Where the prosecution decides to proceed summarily and the District Judge agrees that the offence in question is minor, the trial can proceed.

(2) Offences scheduled in section 2 of the Criminal Justice Act 1951, as amended, provided that the District Judge is of the opinion that the offence is minor and the accused waives his right to trial by jury. These scheduled offences include certain offences under the Larceny Acts (the consent of the DPP to a summary trial is required for some of these) and under the Forgery Act 1913, the Falsification of Accounts Act 1875 and the Debtors Act (Ireland) 1872.

(3) Offences, other than a list of very serious offences (including murder, rape, aggravated sexual assault, treason, piracy and genocide), dealt with on a plea of guilty provided the DPP consents.

(4) Minor offences under certain Acts with the consent of both the accused and the DPP, including offences under section 3 of the Tribunals of Inquiry (Evidence) (Amendment) Act 1979 and section 57 of the Companies (Amendment) Act 1983.

(5) Offences (other than homicide) allegedly committed by children.

(6) Criminal prosecution for publishing a libel.

A summary trial proceeds before a District Judge, who hears the evidence for the prosecution and the defence and decides on guilt or innocence and on sentence.

Trial on indictment

20–61 If the case cannot be dealt with summarily but the accused pleads guilty in the District Court, the judge will send the case to a higher court for sentencing only.

If the case is to proceed to trial on indictment, either because it cannot be tried summarily or not all the necessary conditions listed above are fulfilled, a District Judge conducts a preliminary examination. In advance of this the book of evidence, containing details of the charges against the accused, the names and statements of all witnesses to be called by the prosecution and a list of all exhibits and other relevant material to be used as evidence, is served on the accused. Based on the book of evidence, and on sworn deposition of prosecution witnesses if taken by the defence, the District Judge decides whether there is a sufficient case to send forward for trial.

20–62 Depending on the offence involved, the case will be sent forward to either the Circuit Criminal Court or the Central Criminal Court (the name used by the High Court when hearing criminal cases). When the accused comes before the trial court the formal indictment listing the charges against him is read – this process is called the arraignment. The accused is asked to plead not guilty or guilty at this stage. If the plea is not guilty, a jury is empanelled to hear the case. A guilty plea will lead directly to sentencing.

20–63 It should be noted that trials of virtually all serious criminal offences can be transferred to the Special Criminal Court by virtue of their being offences specifically scheduled for this purpose or on foot of a certificate of the DPP in a prescribed form. The Special Criminal Court is presided over by three judges (usually one each from the High Court, the Circuit Court and the District Court) without a jury. It is designed for trials of offences in respect of which the ordinary courts are deemed inadequate to secure the effective administration of justice and the preservation of public peace and order.

Initiation of criminal proceedings

20–64 The investigation of a crime centers around the gathering of admissible evidence that an offence has been committed by a suspected individual. The evidence is normally gathered by members of the Garda Síochána (although sometimes by other agencies under specified powers) using their authority granted by statute and common law. The authority of the Gardaí can include powers to demand information, to require the production of documents, to enter onto premises[23] or to search without a warrant.[24] The Gardaí also have power in certain circumstances to seek and obtain a search warrant and to seize and retain as evidence items seized in a lawful search.[25] However, where evidence is obtained as a result of a deliberate and conscious violation of citizen's constitutional rights it is inadmissible at trial in the absence of extraordinary excusing circumstances.[26]

Where evidence is obtained illegally but not by a conscious and deliberate violation of a constitutional right the court may decide at its own discretion whether to admit the evidence at trial.[27]

---

[23] *e.g.* Licensing (Ireland) Act 1874, s. 23; Health Act 1947, s. 94; and Finance Act 1926, s. 26.

[24] *e.g.* Misuse of Drugs Act 1977, s. 23; Criminal Law Act 1976, s. 8.

[25] *e.g.* Criminal Law Act 1976, s. 9; Criminal Justice Act 1994, s. 55; Criminal Assets Bureau Act 1996, s. 14; Central Bank Act 1997, s. 76; Non-Fatal Offences Against the Person Act 1997, s. 7; Criminal Justice (Miscellaneous Provisions) Act 1997, s. 10; and Child Trafficking and Pornography Act 1998, s. 7.

[26] *People (DPP) v. Kenny* [1990] 2 I.R. 110 at 134, *per* Finlay C.J.

[27] *DPP v. McMahon* [1986] I.R. 393 at 399, *per* Finlay C.J.

Where there is no arrest initially, criminal proceedings commence with the issue of a summons on foot of a complaint, usually made by a Garda, and stated on the summons. The complaint comprises details of the offence alleged to have been committed and the summons directs the defendant to appear in court to answer the complaint. In general, for minor offences the complaint must be made within six months of the date the offence was allegedly committed. There is no general statutory time-limit for the institution of proceedings for serious offences, although significant delay may be held to have prejudiced the accused's right to a fair trial and can lead to the case being struck out.

Arrest and questioning of suspects

20–65 A suspect may be arrested either with a warrant or without a warrant depending on the circumstances. An arrest warrant can be issued:

– in respect of an indictable offence, in lieu of a summons;

– where a person fails to appear in answer to a summons;

– where a defendant on bail breaches the terms of his recognizance (a recognizance is a written and signed acknowledgment by a bailed person and by his sureties of a debt due in the event that the bailed person fails to fulfil the conditions of his bail, such as to appear in court at a specified time and date; a surety is a person who guarantees a payment on behalf of the bailed person in the event that the bailed person fails to fulfil the conditions of his bail).

In addition, many statutes give members of the Garda Síochána power to arrest without a warrant. For instance, section 49(6) of the Road Traffic Act 1961 as amended gives such a power where a Garda suspects a person of driving while intoxicated. Generally, such powers are restricted to circumstances where the suspect is caught "red handed". However, where a Garda suspects with reasonable cause that someone is about to commit a felony he can make an arrest without a warrant.

A suspect has, in general, a right to remain silent without any adverse inference being drawn from such silence. However, this is not an absolute right and, for example, section 52 of the Offences Against the State Act 1939 empowers a Garda to demand an account of his movements from a person detained under section 30 of that Act. A further example of an exception to the right to silence arises in sections 18 and 19 of the Criminal Justice Act 1984 which provides that inferences as to the guilt of an accused may be drawn from his silence in certain circumstances.

20–66 Once arrested, except in very limited circumstances, a suspect must be charged or released, *i.e.* he cannot be detained to "assist the Gardaí with their enquiries", except under specific statutory provisions set out in section 30 of the Offences Against the State Act 1939 and section 4 of the Criminal Justice

Act 1984. These sections allow such detention for specified periods on suspicion of commission of a serious offence and subject to strict rules surrounding the manner in which the detention is conducted. These rules include the right to consult a solicitor and the right to inform another person of the detention.

Subject to the above exceptions, an arrested person must be brought before a District Judge as soon as is practicable. Particulars of the charges with which the suspect is faced are entered on a charge sheet in most cases.

Book of evidence

20–67 Most criminal proceedings in which forensic accountants become involved are in respect of offences that are serious enough to warrant trial by jury, *i.e.* indictable offences. Where an indictable offence is not dealt with summarily (*i.e.* by a District Judge sitting alone – see above, para. **20–60**) it is progressed by serving on the accused a "book of evidence",[28] containing a number of specified items. These include:

– a statement of the charges;

– copies of any sworn information in writing on which the proceedings were initiated – such sworn statements are usually obtained by the Gardaí;

– a list of witnesses to be called at the trial;

– statements of evidence to be given by each of the witnesses; and

– copies of certain documents;

– a list of exhibits (such as documents; exhibits are usually numbered for convenience) to be produced at the trial.

A copy of the book of evidence must also be furnished to the court. Where further evidence becomes available after the book of evidence has been prepared, an additional book of evidence may be served on the accused and provided to the court.

Where an accused pleads guilty the offence may, with the consent of the Director of Public Prosecutions, be dealt with summarily by the District Court, or the accused may be sent forward for sentence to the court where the offence would have been tried.

20–68 Prior to the coming into effect of Part III of the Criminal Justice Act 1999 a preliminary examination was conducted in the District Court before an accused was sent forward for trial on indictment, tried summarily or discharged. This procedure was abolished with effect from October 1, 2001.

---

[28] The term "book of evidence" does not appear in the relevant legislation but is understood to mean the documents specified in s. 6 of the Criminal Procedure Act 1967 as amended – see the judgment of Walsh J. in *People (Attorney General) v. Cummins* [1972] I.R. 312 at 321–322 for judicial recognition of the term.

Under section 4A of the Criminal Procedure Act 1967 as inserted by section 9 of the Criminal Justice Act 1999, an accused charged with an indictable offence is now sent forward by the District Court to the Court before which he is to stand trial unless the case is being tried summarily, the accused pleads guilty or the accused is unfit to plead. The court of trial will be the Circuit Criminal Court in the appropriate circuit, unless:

(a) the offence involved is one of those reserved to the Central Criminal Court;

(b) the offence is an indictable offence scheduled under the Offences Against the State Act 1939, in which case the accused is sent forward to the Special Criminal Court; or

(c) the DPP issues the necessary certificate to transfer the trial of a non-scheduled offence to the Special Criminal Court.

Before sending the accused forward the District Judge gives an alibi warning, advising the accused that he must give the prosecution notice of any intention to present alibi evidence at his trial.[29] Bail is also dealt with at this stage. If the accused has already been refused bail in the District Court he will ordinarily remain in custody until arraignment and trial. If already on bail the accused's bail expires when he is sent forward for trial, but will normally be renewed.

20–69 After the accused is sent forward an indictment is prepared on behalf of the DPP. The indictment is the formal charge preferred against the accused and it is drafted based on the book of evidence in a format set out in the Criminal Justice (Administration) Act 1924. It identifies the court, the prosecutor and the accused and contains a statement of the offence alleged and particulars of the offence. Each offence charged on an indictment is referred to as a "count".

20–70 The arraignment of the accused then takes place. This involves the indictment being read to the accused in court. The accused is required to plead guilty or not guilty to each count. When he pleads guilty to a count, he stands convicted and the prosecution need not prove the case, no jury hears evidence on that count and the court hears only evidence of the accused's previous criminal record, if any, in order to assist in sentencing. Where the accused will not or is unable to plead, a plea of not guilty is entered on his behalf.

20–71 Where the State wishes to discontinue proceedings it can do this at any time after the indictment is read and before a verdict is delivered. This is done by entering a *nolle prosequi*. This is not necessarily a bar to a fresh prosecution in respect of the same offence at a later date, although in practice a further prosecution of the same offence rarely follows.

---

[29] See s. 20 of the Criminal Justice Act 1984.

20–72 Where an accused has been convicted or acquitted of an offence, however, fresh proceedings cannot be brought in respect of the same offence. If an accused wishes to avoid such "double jeopardy" he can do so at his arraignment or at any later stage before a verdict is given by a "plea in bar" – known as *autrefois acquit* or *autrefois convict.*

Overview of the progress of a criminal case in the courts

The trial

20–73 If a trial is to proceed following arraignment a jury is empanelled (unless the trial is before judges sitting without a jury in the Special Criminal Court).

Procedure at hearing in the criminal courts is similar to the civil courts, with certain specific differences:

(1) The rules of evidence are applied more strictly in criminal cases, probably because personal liberty is often at stake.

(2) In a criminal trial the accused need not present any evidence and, in particular, need not give evidence himself – guilt may not be inferred from this.

(3) At the end of the prosecution's case the accused may apply to the judge for a direction, *i.e.* he asks the judge to direct the jury to find him not guilty of one or more offences on the grounds that the prosecution's case, taken at its height, does not disclose a prima facie case based on evidence that a jury might reasonably accept as establishing the guilt of the accused.

(4) The standard of proof differs: the prosecution must prove the accused's guilt beyond a reasonable doubt; the standard in civil cases is proof "on the balance of probabilities" (see paras **2–30, 8–01** and **20–16** for further discussion).

20–74 Prosecution counsel opens the case and points out the matters he intends to prove, the facts on which his proof will be based and an outline of the evidence to be called. Witnesses are then called for direct examination by the prosecution, followed by cross-examination by the accused's counsel and, if necessary and permitted, re-examination by the prosecution.

Any argument concerning the admissibility of evidence takes place in a *voire dire*, or trial within a trial, in the absence of the jury and the trial judge adjudicates on the issue.

20–75 When the prosecution's case closes the defence can apply to the judge for a direction that there is "no case to answer", again in the jury's absence. If such a direction is given the accused is acquitted.

If no direction is applied for or given, the defence opens its case. The accused is not compelled to give evidence in his defence. Witnesses are called and direct examination, cross-examination by the prosecution and re-examination follow. Closing speeches are then made, first by the prosecution and then by the defence. The trial judge sums up for the jury, dealing with the burden of proof, the standard of proof (beyond reasonable doubt) required to convict the accused, other relevant issues of law, a summary of the important issues of fact and the relevant evidence, the necessary ingredients of the offence and any necessary warnings.

20–76 A jury's verdict need not necessarily be unanimous, provided sufficient time has been given to the jury to reach a unanimous verdict, but at least 10 jurors must agree on the verdict. If the verdict is to convict, sentencing follows and may be deferred to allow the defence to prepare submissions in mitigation or for certain reports to be obtained.

20–77 Sentencing is determined by several factors, including the judge's assessment of the seriousness of the offence or offences of which the accused has been convicted, the accused's past record, any mitigating circumstances, including those disclosed in psychological or other reports and the discretion available to the judge as set out in the relevant statute. In this regard, while most statutes imposing criminal liability provide for fines and/or terms of imprisonment as sentences, the Criminal Justice (Theft and Fraud Offences) Bill 2000[30] proposes to permit the court, in addition to imposing such a sentence, to order restitution of stolen property, or money in lieu thereof, to anyone entitled to recover the stolen property.

Criminal legal aid

20–78 The Criminal Justice (Legal Aid) Act 1962 governs the right of an accused to legal aid (see also paras. **2–52** *et seq.*). Where an accused is faced with a charge of a serious offence and he is unable to pay for the necessary legal assistance, the Supreme Court has held that the accused should be given the opportunity of obtaining such assistance at the State's expense.[31]

The criminal legal aid scheme excludes certain types of proceedings from entitlement to legal aid, including extradition proceedings, but certain of these are covered by an alternative non-statutory scheme known as the "Attorney General's scheme".[32]

The 1962 Act provides that the District Court may make a final, non-appealable, decision, based on the means of the accused, the gravity of the charge and any exceptional circumstances, as to whether the interests of justice require that legal aid be granted. If so, a legal aid certificate appropriate to the stage of the proceedings is granted. The types of certificate that can be granted include a

---

[30] See s. 53 of the Bill.
[31] *State (Healy) v. Donoghue* [1976] I.R. 325.
[32] Information is available on the Attorney General's scheme from the Office of the Attorney General or through the website at www.irlgov.ie/ag/agscheme.htm.

Legal Aid (Trial on Indictment) Certificate, a Legal Aid (Appeal) Certificate and a Legal Aid (Case Stated) Certificate.

Appeal of criminal cases

20–79   The methods by which a decision in a criminal case can be appealed are many and varied. Conviction by summary trial in the District Court can be appealed by way of a new, *de novo* hearing in the Circuit Court before a judge alone. In addition, either side can sometimes appeal on a point of law:

- by way of "consultative case stated" while the District Court hearing is still in progress; or

- by "case stated" at the conclusion of the case to the High Court from the District Court.

The decision of the High Court can be appealed further to the Supreme Court (the appeal of a decision on a consultative case stated requires leave of the High Court judge; the High Court decision on the case stated at the end of the District Court hearing can be appealed without leave). In certain specific and rare cases, the prosecution can appeal an acquittal in the District Court to the Circuit Court. The decision by the Circuit Court following the *de novo* hearing is final and cannot be appealed.

Article 117 of the Treaty of Rome permits any court to seek a preliminary ruling from the European Court of Justice on, *inter alia*, the interpretation of the Treaty and the validity of acts of the European Union institutions.

In addition, the manner in which any judicial decision is made can be referred to a higher court by way of judicial review proceedings (see also paras **11–29** *et seq.* and para. **13–03**).

20–80   The Court of Criminal Appeal, comprising three judges (one of the Supreme Court and two of the High Court), hears appeals against convictions, and against sentence (by either side), by the Circuit Criminal Court, the Central Criminal Court and the Special Criminal Court. It is the final appeal court for serious criminal cases, except where the Court of Criminal Appeal, the DPP or the Attorney General certifies that a point of exceptional public importance has arisen, in which case a further appeal can lie to the Supreme Court. Because (except for decisions of the Special Criminal Court) the conviction in the lower court is based on findings of fact made by a jury, appeals against conviction taken to the Court of Criminal Appeal must be based essentially on points of law or procedure. It is intended that the Court of Criminal Appeal will be abolished and its functions taken over by the Supreme Court.[33]

---

[33] See s. 4 of the Courts and Court Officers Act 1995.

Standards of proof

20–81   As explained in paras **2–30, 20–16** and **20–73**, in criminal cases, the prosecution is required to prove its case "beyond a reasonable doubt". This is a high standard reflecting the presumption of innocence. The general view is that, within reason, it is better that people who are probably guilty of a crime should be let go than that people whose innocence is reasonably possible should be deprived of their liberty. The courts have on several occasions attempted to explain what "beyond a reasonable doubt" actually means. One such attempt that is frequently referred to was made by Denning J.:

> "If the evidence is so strong against a man as to leave only a remote possibility in his favour, which can be dismissed with the sentence 'of course it is possible but not in the least probable' the case is proved beyond reasonable doubt, but nothing short of that will suffice."[34]

Concluding comment

20–82   An understanding of civil and criminal procedure is extremely helpful to the forensic accountant in preparing to provide input to proceedings. It also serves to convince most experts that the disadvantages of being absent from important parts of a trial far outweigh the costs saved by such absence. An expert accountant should take on the sometimes difficult task of convincing his instructing client and solicitor that their case will benefit significantly if he is present for all the important evidence – and if he succeeds, he should be sure to deliver on his promise and attend the hearing for that evidence.

---

[34] *Miller v. Minister for Pensions* [1947] 2 All E.R. 372 at 373–374.

CHAPTER 21

INJUNCTIONS

CHAPTER 21

INJUNCTIONS

21–01 This chapter introduces the topic of injunctions, which are a powerful legal weapon in disputes.[1] Injunctions are very important especially in commercial cases. Put simply, an injunction is an order of the court requiring a party either to perform an act or to refrain from performing an act.

21–02 Only a small number of cases proceed to trial where a plaintiff is successful in an application for an injunction. This is because injunctive relief is only available where damages would not be an adequate remedy to "right the wrong" that has been committed. As a result, when an injunction is granted it is usually the best and most desirable outcome from the point of view of the plaintiff. Thus, the injunction may be the beginning and end of a commercial case. Even where a case goes to full trial, the outcome of injunction proceedings will often have a significant bearing on the final outcome of the case.[2]

21–03 In legal terms an injunction is an equitable remedy. This means that it derives not from the historically rigid common law or from statute but rather from attempts over a lengthy period by courts to provide an overlay of justice and flexibility for the otherwise harsh strictures of the law. Equity is the ingredient that softens the law and allows it to bend a little in the interests of justice where it would otherwise break on the application of the rules laid down by courts and legislators.

Because an injunction is an equitable remedy, a court will have wide discretion in evaluating the merits of the case and deciding whether to grant the application for an injunction. In performing this evaluation and making the decision, the court will have regard to several principles, or "maxims", of equity (*i.e.* fairness). These include:

– the plaintiff must come to the case with "clean hands", *i.e.* equitable relief is

---

[1] Legal issues dealing with injunctions are dealt with more comprehensively in Delany, H., *Equity and Law of Trusts in Ireland* (2nd ed., Round Hall Sweet & Maxwell, Dublin, 1999); Keane, R., *Equity and the Law of Trusts in the Republic of Ireland* (Butterworths, Dublin, 1988); and Courtney, T.B., *Mareva Injunctions and Related Interlocutory Orders* (Butterworths, Dublin, 1998).

[2] In fact, this argument (that granting an injunction would affect the final outcome of the case) was unsuccessfully used by the defendant and an injunction was granted in *Symonds Cider and English Wine Co Ltd v. Showerings (Ireland) Ltd* [1997] 1 I.L.R.M. 481.

generally not granted to a party that has itself also committed a wrong related to the same matter;

– the plaintiff must be prepared to act fairly towards the defendant in the course of the proceedings and thereafter – "he who seeks equity must do equity";

– the plaintiff must act without undue delay in order to succeed – "delay defeats equity";

– the equity imputes an intention to fulfil an obligation.

Equitable remedies are discretionary in nature. Legal rules developed by judges can be divided into rules of common law and rules of equity. Rules of equity are based on the justice or equity of cases. Section 28(11) of the Judicature (Ireland) Act 1877 provides that where there is a conflict between the common law rules and rules of equity, the latter prevails. Thus, judges take fairness into consideration in coming to a decision. This is especially so in the case of injunctions.

21–04 Injunctions developed initially as a means of doing justice in cases where the traditional common law remedy of damages could not achieve such an aim. An injunction is an equitable remedy available to a party to prevent another from acting in such a way as to interfere with his rights.

Use and role of injunctions

21–05 Injunctions are often classified into three types:

(1) Mandatory injunctions, which are used by a court to order a defendant to perform a particular act, including an act necessary to bring to an end the wrong complained of (see paras **21–08** *et seq.*).

(2) Prohibitory injunctions, which are used by a court to restrain a defendant from continuing or repeating a wrongful act.

(3) *Quia timet* injunctions, which are used by a court to order a defendant to refrain from committing a wrong where the plaintiff has a "well-founded apprehension of injury – proof of actual and real danger – a strong probability, almost amounting to moral certainty" – see the judgment of Henchy J. in *C.& A. Modes v. C. & A. (Waterford) Ltd*,[3] quoting Fitzgibbon L.J. in *Attorney General v. Rathmines & Pembroke Joint Hospital Board*.[4]

21–06 Injunctions are therefore typically used where the urgent performance or cessation of activity by a defendant is more valuable to a plaintiff than damages might be at some future date following the commission, repetition or continuation

[3] [1976] 1 I.R. 198 at 213.
[4] [1904] I.R. 161 at 171.

of the wrong. Such situations arise in a variety of circumstances, such as in relation to land and buildings (*e.g.* where an injunction restraining demolition of a building is preferable to obtaining damages to fund its reconstruction), employment (where an injunction restraining the dismissal of an employee is preferable to damages combined with loss of reputation following an unfair dismissal), industrial relations (where an injunction restraining an unlawful picket is preferable to an attempt to recover lost profits, lost business and lost goodwill following a cessation of work) and defamation (where an injunction restraining the publication of libelous material is preferable to an award of damages combined with an unjustly damaged reputation).

21–07 In proceedings for claims for damages the full claim may take some time to come before the courts. Either party may seek an interim remedy to protect any interests which the delay might affect. Injunctions are used to attempt to maintain the position of the parties pending the full hearing of an action (or to maintain the status quo between the parties).

Mandatory injunctions

21–08 Mandatory injunctions can be classified as restorative or enforcing. Restorative injunctions require the defendant to put right the consequences of his actions. Enforcing injunctions require the performance of some positive obligation, often of a continuing nature.

21–09 The courts have traditionally been reluctant to grant mandatory injunctions at the interlocutory stage (see paras **21–28** *et seq.*). Such a remedy has been characterised by Denham J. as "an exceptional form of relief".[5] Plaintiffs must establish a "strong and clear case so that the court can feel a degree of assurance that at a trial of the action a similar injunction would be granted".[6] Despite its exceptional nature, courts will not hesitate to grant a mandatory injunction in an appropriate case, *e.g.* see *Boyle v. An Post*,[7] where Lardner J. granted a mandatory injunction ordering the payment of wages and salaries to the plaintiffs by the defendant where he perceived an undisputed breach of contract leaving no serious issue to be tried at the hearing of the action.

21–10 Plaintiffs must be able to specify with sufficient precision the action required of the defendant to comply with the terms of the injunction. The terms must be certain enough to enable it to be ascertained whether the defendant is complying with the injunction granted. Courts are more cautious in granting mandatory injunctions because their enforcement implies a degree of supervision that courts are reluctant to undertake.

---

[5] *Boyhan v. Beef Tribunal* [1992] I.L.R.M. 545 at 556.
[6] *ibid.*
[7] [1992] 2 I.R. 437.

Conditions for granting an injunction

21–11 The High Court has jurisdiction to grant an interlocutory injunction[8] (see paras **21–28** *et seq.*). Order 50, rule 6(1) of the Rules of the Superior Courts 1986 which regulates the practice and procedure in the High Court and Supreme Court provides:

> " The court may grant ... an injunction ... by an interlocutory order in all cases in which it appears to the court to be just or convenient to do so."

21–12 Certain important principles are applicable in all cases where a court is asked to grant an injunction. Case law has developed three specific conditions that must be fulfilled in order for an injunction to be granted. An injunction will not be granted unless:

– there is a serious question to be tried;

– the balance of convenience lies with the granting of the injunction; and

– damages would not be an adequate remedy for the wrong of which the plaintiff complains.

These conditions are discussed below.

Serious question to be tried

21–13 The last 30 years have seen significant development in the law of injunctions. Prior to this, the test generally applied by a court in deciding whether an interlocutory injunction was justified on the facts presented was whether those facts established a prima facie case on the part of the plaintiff, *i.e.* a probability that the plaintiff would succeed at the eventual hearing.[9]

A modified, and less onerous, test of "a serious question to be tried" was first approved by the British House of Lords in the celebrated *American Cyanamid* case.[10] Plaintiffs seeking interlocutory injunctions now must establish that there is a "serious" or "fair" question to be tried which is not frivolous or vexatious. The Irish courts adopted the *Cyanamid* principle in *Campus Oil Ltd v. Minister for Industry and Energy (No. 2)*[11] and *Irish Shell Ltd v. Elm Motors Ltd*,[12] using the term "fair question to be tried" rather than the British "serious question to be tried". The *Campus Oil* case, in which the judgment of Keane J. (as he then was) in the High Court was upheld on appeal to the Supreme Court,

---

[8] This jurisdiction derives from s. 28(8) of the Judicature (Ireland) Act 1877.
[9] See *Educational Co of Ireland Ltd v. Fitzpatrick* [1961] I.R. 323; *Esso Petroleum Co Ltd v. Fogarty* [1965] I. R. 531.
[10] *American Cyanamid Co v. Ethicon* [1975] A.C. 396.
[11] [1983] I.R. 88.
[12] [1984] I.R. 200.

is the leading Irish case on the conditions necessary for the grant of an injunction. Its principles have been followed in a number of more recent cases (*e.g.* see the judgment of O'Flaherty J. in *Hinde Livestock Exports Ltd v. Pandoro Ltd*[13]).

Balance of convenience

21–14 Once a plaintiff establishes that there is a serious case to be tried the courts will then determine the matter on the basis of the balance of convenience. Applicants must establish that the balance of convenience lies on the side of granting the application for the injunction, and this usually involves the preservation of the status quo until the trial of the action. Balance of convenience is seen as weighing financial and material loss of the plaintiff against that of the defendant if the injunction is granted. As stated by Lord Diplock in the *Cyanamid* case:

> "... it would be unwise to attempt to list all the various matters which may need to be taken into consideration in deciding where the balance lies, let alone to suggest the relative weight to be attached to them."[14]

21–15 In assessing where the balance of convenience lies, the court attempts to measure the likely damage to the plaintiff if the injunction were to be refused and the plaintiff were to subsequently succeed at trial, against the likely damage to the defendant if the injunction were to be granted and the plaintiff were subsequently to fail at trial.

Damages not an adequate remedy

21–16 If the plaintiff would be sufficiently compensated by an award of damages should he succeed in his action, an injunction should not be granted.[15] Thus, where an alternative remedy, such as damages, would provide an adequate and fair outcome in the event that the plaintiff were successful, an injunction will not be granted.

21–17 The court must be satisfied that there is a real possibility of injurious and unlawful action being committed and that the plaintiff would thus be denied justice if he were denied the right of application for immediate relief. In certain types of actions, *e.g.* infringement of copyright or unfair dismissal, damages will rarely provide an adequate form of remedy. While some of the plaintiff's loss will be pecuniary in nature, he may also suffer loss of goodwill and injury to reputation which cannot be compensated for by monetary payments. Courts must consider:

---

[13] [1998] 2 I.R. 203.
[14] *American Cyanamid Co v. Ethicon* [1975] A.C. 396 at 408.
[15] See *e.g.* the judgment of Blayney J. in the Supreme Court in *Ferris v. Ward* [1998] 2 I.R. 194.

(a) whether the plaintiff can be adequately compensated by awards for damages;

(b) whether the defendant can meet the liability; and

(c) whether the plaintiff's losses are exclusively pecuniary in nature.

Where there is a high probability that a defendant will be unable to comply with the terms of an order, then an application for an injunction may be refused.

21–18 Conversely, the court will consider the consequences if an interlocutory injunction is granted and the defendant subsequently succeeds at trial:

(a) whether the defendant would be adequately compensated by payment of damages by the plaintiff;

(b) whether the plaintiff would be able to pay the damages in such circumstances.

In applying for injunctive relief, the plaintiff must normally give an undertaking as to damages confirming that he will compensate the defendant in respect of damages suffered and costs incurred should the injunction turn out to have been wrongly sought and granted.

21–19 Where compliance with an injunction would result in the committal of an unlawful act, then such an order will not be granted.[16] Where it can be shown that the plaintiff is guilty of an illegal act or other misconduct in relation to the issue at hand, relief will be denied.[17]

Discretionary factors considered by the court

21–20 Courts may take into account other factors in deciding whether to grant interlocutory relief. Such considerations to be taken into account by courts relate not only to the nature of the right sought to be enforced and to the potential consequences of the decision to grant or refuse relief but may also include factors relating to the conduct of the person invoking the court's jurisdiction. If the plaintiff has been guilty of some impropriety or disreputable conduct the injunction may be refused following the maxim "he who comes to equity must come with clean hands".[18] The court has discretion in applying this maxim and the principle is applied flexibly. For it to succeed as a defence to an application for an injunction, the defendant would have to show that the plaintiff acted very improperly indeed. The principle was applied by the Supreme Court in *Curust Financial Services Ltd v. Loewe-Lack-Werk*.[19] Finlay C.J. referred to the

---

[16] See *e.g. Pride of Derby and Derbyshire Angling Association Ltd v. British Celanese Ltd* [1953] Ch. 149 at 181.

[17] This is an example of one of the maxims of equity – "he who comes to equity must come with clean hands."

[18] *Dering v. Earl of Winchelsea* (1787) 1 Cox 318 at 319–320.

[19] [1994] 1 I.R. 450.

principle in the following terms:

> "I accept that, the granting of an injunction being an equitable remedy, the court has a discretion, where it is satisfied that a person has come to the court, as it is so frequently expressed, otherwise than 'with clean hands', by that fact alone to refuse the equitable relief of an injunction. It seems to me, however, that this phrase must of necessity involve an element of turpitude and cannot necessarily be equated with a mere breach of contract."[20]

Types of injunctions

21–21 Depending on the circumstances surrounding the application for an injunction and the urgency of the need for relief, different types of injunction may be sought and granted. The principal different types are:

– interim injunctions;

– interlocutory injunctions;

– perpetual injunctions

– *Mareva* injunctions; and

– proprietary injunctions.

These different types of injunctions are discussed below.

21–22 Injunctions can impose obligations that are negative (restraining the performance or continuance of a wrongful act) or positive (requiring the performance of an act). Interim and interlocutory injunctions are granted before the full plenary hearing of an action, whereas perpetual injunctions are granted as an outcome of the hearing. Interim injunctions are obtained for a limited period only, in contrast with interlocutory injunctions which last until the final hearing of the action.

Interim (*ex parte*) injunctions

21–23 Interim injunctions are usually granted on foot of an application made *ex parte, i.e.* in the absence of the opposite party. Such applications are normally made in respect of matters of extreme urgency, where there is a real risk that in the absence of an immediate injunction an act will take place that would be difficult and costly to reverse once done. Interim injunctions are obtained for a limited period only (usually a matter of a few days) and will have effect only until a further order is sought in the immediate aftermath of the granting of the interim relief.

---

[20] [1994] 1 I.R. 450 at 467.

Procedure in obtaining an interim injunction

21–24   The applicant for an injunction may apply to court, without notice to the other party to the proceedings, to seek an interim injunction from the court restraining the activities complained of until a named date. An interim injunction of a particularly urgent nature may be obtained from a High Court judge outside normal court hours. Generally, only the plaintiff's legal representatives attend the application for interim relief. The application to the court is brought on an issued plenary summons, provided there is time to issue such a summons. Alternatively, oral evidence may be given. A reasonable explanation must be provided for the non-issue and non-service of the summons. Usually counsel for the plaintiff will give an undertaking that a summons will be issued at the earliest opportunity. The defendant is unlikely to be aware of the application at this stage.

21–25   Only the plaintiff's affidavits are read before the judge. The court decides whether to grant an injunction after reading the affidavits and hearing counsel for the plaintiff. The affidavit will usually contain details of the background to the dispute, details of conduct which is alleged to be unlawful and an estimate of damage suffered by the plaintiff.

21–26   The decision to grant or refuse the injunction lies in the discretion of the court since the injunction is a remedy developed by the courts of equity. Plaintiffs must give an undertaking to pay damages if the injunction is later found to be unwarranted. It is also expected that, as is the case for all *ex parte* applications, the applicant will, in addition to stating his own case, point out any weaknesses in his case and the thrust of the other side's anticipated case so that the court can take a balanced view.

21–27   The terms of the order will grant an interim injunction for a limited period, and usually with liberty to issue a notice of motion seeking an interlocutory injunction. The order will also usually permit shorter notice of the hearing of such an application than would normally be required and permitting service of the notice on the opposing party in a manner that will expedite the hearing, even if this manner of service does not comply with normal rules for service. This latter order is known as an order for substituted service. The notice of motion is usually returnable for the day the interim order expires – this means that the application for an interlocutory injunction will be scheduled to be heard on that day. The party affected by an interim injunction is normally free to apply to court have the injunction discharged.

Interlocutory injunctions

21–28   The main difference between the effects of interim and interlocutory injunctions is that the former is of relatively short duration, while the latter remains in force until the full plenary hearing of the case, which can take some time to come to court. The purpose of an interlocutory injunction is normally to preserve the status quo between the parties to the action until the trial of the issues in dispute can take place when the courts can finally determine the rights of the parties. The rationale behind granting interlocutory injunctions is to prevent plaintiffs suffering irreparable prejudice by reason of the delay which must necessarily occur between the institution of proceedings and trial of the action dealing with the substantive issues.

Applicable circumstances

21–29   Interlocutory injunctive relief is needed because of the inevitable delays involved between the time the plaintiff is wronged and the time when the plaintiff is eventually granted relief by the courts. Interlocutory injunctions are heard on notice to the defendants and both sides are entitled to be present and legally represented in court.

Procedure

21–30   If an interim injunction is granted, notice of the order is served on the other party, and a date is fixed for hearing the application for an interlocutory injunction, at which both sides will be heard.

21–31   If the court declines to grant an interim injunction, it may grant leave to the applicant to serve notice on the other party of his intention to apply for an interlocutory injunction, and the court may in these circumstances allow shorter notice of that application than usual. Alternatively, the court may grant the interim injunction and allow service of a shorter notice.

21–32   Applications for interlocutory orders are normally heard on affidavit (voluntary sworn written statement of facts). However this is not always the case and the court may use its discretion to allow oral evidence. If the defendant provides the court with a replying affidavit it may be difficult for the court to resolve conflicting evidence without oral evidence and cross-examination.

21–33   Interlocutory orders are binding against whom they are granted. Once granted, the injunction continues until full trial. However, defendants may apply by issuing a notice of motion to have the injunction order discharged before its expiry. Plaintiffs are required to serve a statement of claim on defendants within two weeks of the date of the order. Defendants then have a further two weeks to file a defence after which plaintiffs have a further two weeks to reply. A date is then fixed for a full trial of the action.

Perpetual injunctions

21–34   A perpetual injunction will only be granted after a full hearing of the action. The plaintiff must establish a right and demonstrate the actual or threatened infringement of that right by the defendant. If issued, the injunction lasts forever and an award for damages and costs will simultaneously be made. Appeals against decisions to grant or deny, or against the terms of the injunction, may be directed from the High Court to the Supreme Court.

***Mareva* injunctions**

21–35   A *Mareva* injunction is an order of the court granted before or after judgment restraining the party to whom it is directed from disposing of or dealing with his own assets. The novelty of *Mareva* injunctions is that defendants can be restrained in the use of their own assets, notwithstanding that plaintiffs have no proprietary right or claim in those assets.

21–36   A *Mareva* injunction was first granted by Lord Denning who based his power to do so on the wide discretion left to the courts in the Supreme Court of Judicature Act 1873 under which the court was empowered to grant an injunction in all cases in which it shall appear to the court to be just and convenient. (The Irish equivalent of that Act is the Judicature (Ireland) Act 1877.) Lord Denning interpreted this as giving him unlimited power to grant an injunction subject only to the "just and convenient" requirement. He proceeded to create the tests to be satisfied for the grant of a *Mareva* injunction, and in summary form these are:

– a debt is due and owing by the defendant to the plaintiff;

– there is no defence to the debt;

– there is a danger that the debtor may dispose of his assets to defeat any future judgment.

21–37   These conditions have been amended and refined in subsequent cases. The current state of the law in Ireland in relation to the conditions necessary for the grant of a *Mareva* injunction is summarised below.

21–38   A *Mareva* injunction is enforced by the successful plaintiff, immediately on being granted the injunction, notifying the defendant and his bankers or other persons who hold his assets. Any breach of the order by a bank already notified of it is a contempt of court by the bank.

Applicable circumstances

21–39   *Mareva* injunctions are generally used to prevent the dissipation, destruction or anticipated removal of property from one legal jurisdiction to another, pending a trial of the matters at issue between the parties. *Mareva* injunctions do not determine any proprietary rights in the property. They do not give the plaintiff any form of security or priority over other creditors. Legal entitlement must still be proved in a civil lawsuit. Depending on the factual circumstances and the relief sought, this injunction may be granted at the same time as an *Anton Piller* order (see paras **21–47** *et seq.*).

Discharge of business, legal and living expenses

21–40   *Mareva* injunctions can be modified in a number of ways, but are normally granted *ab initio* for the maximum sums claimable.[21] They do not apply to interfere with a defendant's obligation to discharge his lawful debts. Three types of expenses have been identified as being exempt from the provisions of *Mareva* injunctions: ordinary living expenses; legal costs; and ordinary business expenses. This reduces the adverse impact of the injunction on defendants who can carry on their life and business with less disruption.

Requirements

21–41   The rules for obtaining a *Mareva* injunction are strictly applied by the courts. To arrive at a just result, the court weighs up the interests of plaintiffs and defendants before granting a *Mareva* injunction. The interest of the plaintiff is that the defendant has sufficient assets to meet the claim. However, *Mareva* injunctions may not be granted if it is clear to the court that the dominant purpose is to apply pressure on the defendant to provide some security for the plaintiff. Defendants cannot be unduly oppressed by the making of *Mareva* injunctions, especially as they are normally sought *ex parte (i.e.* in the absence of the other party). In such applications, plaintiffs are required to identify the important points for and against their applications.

21–42   The following are the requirements to obtain a *Mareva* injunction[22]:

– only granted in support of existing substantive causes of action;

– good arguable case – this is a higher standard than is required in the case of other injunctions;

– proof that the defendant has assets inside/outside the jurisdiction;

– real risk of the defendant disposing of or dissipating his assets with the objective of ensuring that a judgment will not be met.

---

[21] See below, para. **21–58** for a discussion of maximum sum orders.
[22] Adapted from Clohessy, G.M., "Mareva injunctions" *Commercial Law Practitioner* (June 1994) pp. 151-155; and from Courtney, T.B., "Mareva injunctions: proving an intention to frustrate judgment" *Commercial Law Practitioner* (January 1996) pp. 3-11.

Procedure

21–43   The relevant procedural requirements to be followed and observed in applying for *Mareva* injunctions were summarised by Murphy J. and quoted with approval by Hamilton C.J. in *O'Mahony v. Horgan* as follows:

> "1.   The plaintiff should make full and frank disclosure of all matters in his knowledge which are material for the judge to know.
> 2.   The plaintiff should give particulars of his claims against the defendant, stating the grounds of his claims and the amount thereof and fairly stating the points made against it by the defendant.
> 3.   The plaintiff should give some grounds for believing that the defendant had assets within the jurisdiction. The existence of a Bank Account is normally sufficient.
> 4.   The plaintiff should give some grounds for believing that there is a risk of the assets being removed or dissipated.
> 5.   The plaintiff must give an undertaking in damages, in case he fails."[23]

21–44   In the same case, Hamilton C.J. said:

> "... a *Mareva* injunction will only be granted if there is a combination of two circumstances established by the plaintiff i.e. (i) that he has an arguable case that he will succeed in the action, and (ii) the anticipated disposal of a defendant's assets is for the purpose of preventing a plaintiff from recovering damages and not merely for the purpose of carrying on a business or discharging lawful debts."[24]

This case is the leading authority on *Mareva* injunctions under Irish law and the judgments of Hamilton C.J. and O'Flaherty J. (in the same case) summarise clearly the development of the law in this area and its application in Ireland.

Proprietary injunctions

21–45   Proprietary injunctions arise where plaintiffs have, or claim to have, proprietary interests in assets which are in possession of defendants. In such cases, plaintiffs may obtain an interlocutory injunction to restrain defendants from dealing in such assets. These injunctions are to be distinguished from *Mareva* injunctions on the basis that in a *Mareva* injunction the plaintiff seeks to freeze the defendant's assets, whereas a proprietary injunction seeks to restrain the defendant from dealing with assets in which the plaintiff claims a legal or beneficial interest, *i.e.* to freeze assets that may be the plaintiff's.

---

[23] [1995] 2 I.R. 411 at 416.
[24] *ibid.* at 418.

Requirements

21–46 Courtney[25] summarises the conditions for obtaining proprietary injunctions to freeze assets in which the plaintiff asserts a proprietary claim. The plaintiff must show that:

- there are reasonable grounds for claiming a proprietary interest in the assets in the defendant's possession;
- there is a fair or serious question to be tried;
- the "balance of convenience" favours making the injunction.

Courtney points out that the proofs for proprietary injunctions are not as onerous as those for *Mareva* injunctions and are therefore preferable where plaintiffs can reasonably assert proprietary claims in the assets in question. In particular, a plaintiff in such an application is not required to establish a nefarious intention on the part of the defendant.

Anton Piller orders

21–47 Asset and document searches can be conducted on foot of *Anton Piller*[26] orders granted by a court. *Anton Piller* orders are in essence a private civil search warrant. These orders are granted *ex parte* (*i.e.* where only the requesting party is present when the application is made to court). Their effect is to order the defendant (or the suspect in criminal matters) to permit the applicant to enter onto the defendant's premises to inspect and/or remove documents or other items belonging to the applicant from the premises. *Anton Piller* orders may also require the defendant to disclose to the applicant the whereabouts of specified documents or other items.

It should be noted that the Irish courts grant *Anton Piller* orders very rarely.

Requirements

21–48 Because they are granted in the defendant's absence and effectively authorise a breach of normal property rights, *Anton Piller* orders are very difficult to obtain. They do not give the plaintiff any proprietary rights to the documents or property found. They simply allow the materials to be seized and placed in safekeeping. The plaintiff's rights to the property must still be proved in court. Because these orders are an exceptional and powerful remedy, their use should be considered with a great deal of caution. Carried out improperly, they may prejudice the plaintiff's legal position and cost the plaintiff more money.

---

[25] Courtney, T.B., *Mareva Injunctions and Related Interlocutory Orders* (Butterworths, Dublin, 1998), pp. 18–19.
[26] *Anton Piller K.G. v. Manufacturing Processes Ltd* [1976] 1 All E.R. 779.

To obtain an *Anton Piller* order, the plaintiff must prove, usually by affidavit, that:

– he has a strong case;

– the potential, or actual, damage is serious;

– clear evidence exists that the suspect or another person possesses incriminating documents or other material and could well destroy them if given notice.

21–49   When acting on an order, it is extremely important not to stray from carrying out only those acts specified in it. The order must specifically:

– identify which of the plaintiff's agents—forensic accountants, investigators, or individuals knowledgeable about the documents or property to be searched for and seized—can enter the suspect's premises;

– require the attendance of a police officer to maintain the peace;

– require the plaintiff's lawyer to attend the premises to advise the suspect of his or her right to obtain independent legal advice before permitting entry.

21–50   *Anton Piller* orders were originally limited to seizing property and records in copyright infringement and cases dealing with the improper use of trade secrets. They have now been expanded to cover many other situations, among them:

– retrieving confidential information, customer lists and other documents wrongfully taken from an employer by a departing employee;

– locating funds misappropriated by employees;

– obtaining documents and assets in tax prosecution and matrimonial cases

– locating missing documents and information that help to answer how a fraud was perpetrated. (e.g. see paras **5–46, 5–75** and **5–79**).

Civil cases

21–51   *Anton Piller* orders have been granted most often in cases where intellectual property rights are allegedly being infringed (*e.g.* through unlawful copying of compact discs) and among the stringent conditions required to be fulfilled in order to obtain such an order is that the court must be convinced that there is a real danger of destruction of the documents or items if the order is not made.

Anton Piller orders have been granted in the English courts on a number of occasions (*e.g.* see the House of Lords' decision in *Rank Film Distributors Ltd v. Video Information Centre*[27]) but have rarely been considered in the Irish

---

[27] [1982] A.C. 380.

courts and could be susceptible to constitutional challenge (see, however, the judgments of Costello J. in the High Court, and Griffin J. on appeal in the Supreme Court, in *House of Spring Gardens Ltd v. Point Blank Ltd*,[28] both of which refer to an *Anton Piller* order made by Costello J. in earlier proceedings involving the same parties).

Statutory asset freezing orders

21–52   In addition to common law remedies developed by the courts in order to protect a variety of property rights, several statutes provide for the freezing and/or seizure of assets in certain circumstances.

Proceeds of Crime Act 1996

21–53   Asset forfeiture legislation in the form of the Proceeds of Crime Act 1996 (see also para. **5–80**) introduced powers under which the High Court can make orders for the preservation and disposal of property that represents the proceeds of crime. The Act provides for the making of both interim orders (which have a maximum 21-day life unless an application for an interlocutory order is made) and interlocutory orders preventing the respondent from dealing with all or a part of the specified property or diminishing its value.

Interim orders

21–54   For an interim order the court to be made must be satisfied, in an *ex parte* application by a Garda not below the rank of Chief Superintendent or by an authorised officer of the Revenue Commissioners, that the respondent is in possession or control of specified property that is, or is connected with, the proceeds of crime. The property in question must have a value in excess of £10,000. While interim orders expire within 21 days of granting, they may be replaced with interlocutory orders on the same terms.

Interlocutory orders

21–55   Interlocutory orders are similar in nature to interim orders but may remain in force for up to seven years. For an interlocutory order to be made, it must appear to the court, on evidence given by the applicant, that the respondent is in control or possession of property which is, or is connected with, the proceeds of crime. An interlocutory order will be discharged where, on the balance of probabilities, the court is satisfied on evidence given by the respondent or another person that the property is not the proceeds of crime or connected therewith or that its value is less than £10,000. The court has discretion to refuse the order if injustice would result.

---

[28] [1984] I.R. 611.

21–56   The basis for obtaining an order is unusual in that it appears to reverse (at least partly) the normal burden of proof, *i.e.* it is necessary for the respondent to satisfy the court once an apparent case is made by the applicant. A civil standard of proof is invoked and the opinion of a State official may be given as evidence that property is in some way tainted by criminality. Under this legislation, a criminal conviction is no longer necessary to confiscate assets. These provisions have survived a legal challenge on these and other grounds in *Gilligan v. Criminal Assets Bureau*[29] when McGuinness J. ruled in the High Court that the Act was not unconstitutional.

Disposal orders

21–57   The legislation also provides for disposal orders. A disposal order may be granted where an interlocutory order has been in force for not less than seven years. Such an order allows for the transfer of all rights in the property to the Minister for Finance.

Maximum sum orders in civil trials

21–58   General freezing orders obtainable under *Mareva* injunctions have been for the most part displaced in the United Kingdom by the use of "maximum sum" orders which restrict the defendants from dealing in assets not exceeding a specific sum. The "maximum sum" referred to in an order should be the maximum sum of money which a plaintiff would hope to recover at trial of the substantive issue in question. It might appear that it would be in the best interests of the plaintiff to over-estimate the claim. However, this runs the risk that the plaintiff would be subsequently held liable to compensate the defendant based on the plaintiff's undertakings. As was stated in *Jet West Ltd v. Haddican*:

> "... while it is permissible and indeed sensible, in deciding what sum he wished to put forward as being the limit below which assets cannot be reduced in accordance with the injunction, to take account of claim, interest and costs, and perhaps even take a slightly optimistic view as to what may be at stake, there comes a point at which, if you open your mouth too wide, you run a substantial risk that there may be a claim against your client under the counter indemnity."[30]

Criminal Justice Act 1994

21–59   This Act was introduced to provide for the recovery of proceeds of drug trafficking and other serious crimes and to create the offence of money laundering. The Act provides that the proceeds of drug trafficking of a person convicted on indictment of a drug trafficking offence may be confiscated on a successful application to court by the DPP. This power to confiscate is extended

---

[29] [1998] 3 I.R. 185.
[30] [1992] 2 All E.R. 545 at 549.

to situations where a person convicted on indictment of a non-drug trafficking offence is found to have benefited from the offence. The Act also empowers the High Court to prohibit a person from dealing with any realisable property where proceedings have been instituted for drug trafficking or another indictable offence and a confiscation order has been made or there are reasonable grounds to make one.

Family Law Act 1995 and Family Law (Divorce) Act 1996

21–60   These two Acts give the court wide powers to restrain or set aside any dispositions or other dealings with property done with the intention of defeating a pending or intended claim for any of a number of reliefs available under certain provisions of the Acts. In summary, the relevant provisions allow the court to protect claims, made in the context of judicial separation or divorce proceedings, for:

– maintenance;

– periodical payments;

– lump sum orders;

– property adjustment orders;

– a right to occupy the family home or to sell it and dispose of the proceeds;

– certain other dealings with property;

– financial compensation orders;

– pension adjustment orders and preservation of pension entitlements.

Involvement of forensic accountants

21–61   There is clear scope for the involvement of forensic accountants where parties are applying for or resisting injunctions. Because the issue of the adequacy of damages is so central to the determination of whether an injunction will be granted, and because the measurement of the balance of convenience inevitably involves a comparison of financial implications of various possible scenarios, the value of accountancy and financial expertise is clear.

21–62   Despite this, expert accountants are not engaged to assist in injunction proceedings nearly as often as might be expected. This is undoubtedly partly because there is no established practice of doing so, and also because by their nature injunction proceedings tend to be brought on an urgent basis in circumstances where there is little or no time available to brief experts and await their considered views.

21–63 Nevertheless, the success or failure of an application is likely to be significantly affected by the cogency and relevance of available financial evidence. In this regard, accountants can contribute in several ways. These include:

- assisting in the calculation of the maximum damages likely to flow from successful plenary proceedings, thereby facilitating an evaluation of the adequacy of damages;

- estimating the financial implications for both parties of the granting of the injunction and of a decision to refuse the injunction, thereby informing the debate on the balance of convenience;

- assessing the ability of the applicant to honour an undertaking as to damages in the event that the application is successful but the respondent prevails in the substantive proceedings;

- anticipating the financial arguments to be made by the other side and helping to prepare to respond to such arguments.

Lawyers would be well advised to consider seriously obtaining expert accountancy assistance from the earliest stage in contentious financial injunction applications.

Concluding comment

21–64 Recent case law and legislative developments have served to weaken the force of the principle of inviolability of personal and private property. Whether the mark has been overstepped will only be determined when the Supreme Court is asked to pronounce on one or more of the developments referred to above in the context of the rights granted to citizens by Article 43 of the Constitution. Although these rights are, of course, not absolute, it is worth noting that they have in the past had no express equivalent in the United Kingdom, the jurisdiction that invented the *Mareva* injunction and the *Anton Piller* order. This raises the question whether the existence of these rights renders the Irish environment sufficiently different to the United Kingdom to justify a less aggressive approach to interference with personal property than that pursued in the United Kingdom in recent years. Developments in this area will be watched with interest by observers with various interests. In the meantime, there is fertile ground for lawyers to argue and for accountants to advise.

LAWS OF EVIDENCE, DISCOVERY AND INTERROGATORIES

CHAPTER 22

LAWS OF EVIDENCE, DISCOVERY AND INTERROGATORIES

22–01 This chapter examines the rules and procedures followed by the courts in relation to evidence, discovery and interrogatories in a case. A basic introduction to these topics is provided and the chapter is written for accountants rather than for lawyers.[1]

A number of legal terms are used in the chapter (such as statement of claim, notice for particulars, affidavit, etc.) which are explained more fully in the glossary in Appendix 3.

Laws of evidence

22–02 The Irish courts work according to a straightforward principle – all information relevant to the matters at issue in legal proceedings is admissible in evidence unless it falls within one of a number of narrowly defined exceptions. The policy behind this principle is the obvious one – no party should be at a disadvantage, either in pursuing an action or in defending it, by virtue of the non-disclosure of relevant information.

There are, of course, several exceptions to the general rule. However, the courts are slow to approve new exceptions, and tend to interpret the limits of those that already exist as narrowly as can be done within the bounds of justice. In addition, the legislature has also enacted laws to define as narrowly as possible certain existing exceptions.

Admissibility

22–03 Evidence must be admissible in accordance with the rules of evidence. A full discussion of the laws of evidence in Ireland is beyond the scope of this book. However, it is useful to be aware of the principal exceptions to the general rule that all relevant evidence is admissible. These can be summarised as follows:

---

[1] Readers are referred to Fennell, C. *Law of Evidence in Ireland* (Butterworths, Dublin, 1992); and Cahill, E. *Discovery in Ireland* (Round Hall Sweet & Maxwell, Dublin, 1996) for more detailed legal discussion of the laws of evidence, discovery and interrogatories.

(1) Evidence obtained illegally is not admissible.

(2) With the notable exception of individuals giving evidence in their capacity as experts, witnesses are generally not permitted to give opinion evidence (*i.e.* to draw inferences from facts) – see paras **1–44** *et seq.*

(3) The privilege against self-incrimination allows witnesses to refuse to answer questions or to produce documents or other evidence where to do so might expose them to criminal charges, penalties or forfeitures.[2]

(4) Communications between spouses during their marriage are privileged and are therefore not admissible in evidence.

(5) Communications between lawyers in relation to a dispute that are marked "without prejudice", cannot be produced in evidence in the dispute without the consent of both the sender and the receiver of such communications.

(6) Confidential communications between a solicitor and his client made for the purpose of obtaining legal advice are privileged unless the privilege is waived by the client, provided the communications are not made in furtherance of a criminal offence. Communications made to a lawyer in order to obtain his legal assistance, as opposed to legal advice, are not privileged.

(7) Communications between a lawyer and a third party, or between the lawyer's client and a third party, the dominant purpose of which is pending or contemplated litigation, are privileged.

(8) Subject to certain exceptions, hearsay evidence is inadmissible. The rule against hearsay states that "… a statement other than one made by a person while giving oral evidence in the proceedings is inadmissible as evidence of any fact stated."[3] The main purpose of the hearsay rule is to exclude evidence of a statement made by a person who is not available to be cross-examined in relation to that statement. Hearsay is discussed more fully in paras **22–12** *et seq.*

(9) Subject to certain exceptions, evidence of previous similar facts (*e.g.* previous criminal behaviour of a defendant in a criminal trial) is inadmissible.

---

[2] However, this privilege does not always apply. For example, under s. 245(6) of the Companies Act 1963, a person cannot refuse to answer questions in a liquidation on the grounds of self-incrimination, but the answers given cannot be used in subsequent civil or criminal proceedings, except in the case of criminal proceedings for perjury in connection with any of the answers given. However, answers obtained in a s. 245 examination in *Re Aluminium Fabricators Ltd* [1984] I.L.R.M. 399 were used against a witness in fraudulent trading proceedings because these proceedings were deemed to relate to the same liquidation.

[3] Cross, Sir R. and Tapper C., *Cross on Evidence* (7th ed., Butterworths, London, 1990), p. 454.

(10) A diplomat cannot be required to give evidence and all papers and correspondence of a diplomatic mission are inviolable.

As can be readily appreciated, this list is merely a summary of some of the more important exceptions to the general rule requiring disclosure of all relevant evidence and is itself subject to a variety of exceptions. In short, the law is less than clear and less than settled on the issue of what must be produced and what may be withheld.

22–04   However, what can be stated clearly is that the Irish courts lean strongly towards the disclosure of information where possible. This general policy was clearly stated in the landmark *Murphy v. Dublin Corporation* judgment which recognised that only the courts are constitutionally mandated to decide whether a document should be discovered. Walsh J. said:

> "Under the Constitution the administration of justice is committed solely to the judiciary in the exercise of their powers in the courts set up under the Constitution. Power to compel the attendance of witnesses and the production of evidence is an inherent part of the judicial power of government of the State and is the ultimate safeguard of justice in the State. . . . If … conflict arises during the exercise of the judicial power then, in my view, it is the judicial power which will decide which public interest shall prevail."[4]

22–05   A recent example of the Supreme Court's view that restrictions on disclosure of information should be interpreted narrowly arose in the case of *Gallagher v. Stanley*.[5] The case involved a child whose birth was complicated and who suffered severe injury and disablement. Discovery was sought of all relevant hospital records, and the hospital claimed privilege over certain documents, including the statements of three nurses taken following the injury to the child. The hospital based its claim of privilege on the fact that the statements were: "not made in the ordinary course of treatment"[6] but that they:

> ". . . were made at the request of the matron of the hospital for the very reason that it was immediately apparent that the infant plaintiff had undergone an extremely difficult birth and that there was a substantial risk that he would suffer very serious injuries as a result thereof".[7]

Hence, the hospital claimed that the documents "were made for the purpose of or in contemplation of litigation."[8]

---

[4] [1972] I.R. 215 at 233.
[5] [1998] 2 I.R. 267.
[6] *ibid.* at 270.
[7] *ibid.* at 270.
[8] *ibid.* at 269.

22–06   The High Court, and the Supreme Court on appeal, rejected the claim of privilege. O'Flaherty J. adopted the "dominant purpose test", *i.e.* that in order to attract the privilege as claimed it would be necessary to show that the dominant purpose of the documents was for actual or contemplated litigation. He then held that this had not been the dominant purpose in the circumstances of the case, saying:

> "I think that the Matron would have had in the forefront of her considerations, as well as the possibility of litigation, that she should be in a position to account for how the hospital was run, as far as her domain was concerned, and how the staff under her control had conducted themselves in regard to what must have been quite a traumatic occurrence on the night in question."[9]

He pointed to the importance of the cause of justice and to assisting the course of the trial:

> "Both principles, full disclosure on the one hand and legal professional privilege on the other, are there to advance the cause of justice. Sometimes they may be on a collision course, but not, I think, here…. I believe it is likely to help the course of the trial if these documents are made available to the plaintiff's advisers now and I do not see that the principle of legal professional privilege suffers in any way."[10]

This judgment is a good example of the continuing reluctance of the courts to accede to the exclusion of evidence where there is doubt as to its admissibility.

Electronic/digital evidence[11]

22–07   The following legislation may have relevance during investigations involving computer-based evidence:

– Freedom of Information Act 1997;

– Finance Act 1997 (section 81);

– Taxes Consolidation Act 1997 (*e.g.* section 912);

– Finance Act 1995 (section 87);

– Investment Intermediaries Act 1995;

– Criminal Justice Act 1994 (section 63);

– Criminal Evidence Act 1992;

– Criminal Damage Act 1991 (section 5);

---

[9] [1998] 2 I.R. 267 at 272–273.
[10] *ibid.* at 273.
[11] A useful guide on handling computer based evidence (based on U.K. law) is Association of Chief Police Officers of England, Wales and Northern Ireland, *Good Practice Guide for Computer Based Evidence* (ACPO, Maidstone, Kent, 1999).

- Data Protection Act 1988;

- Safety, Health and Welfare at Work Act 1989.

The importance of computer evidence in criminal investigations has been discussed in paras **5–41** *et seq*. To secure all the information necessary for trial it is essential to preserve evidence carefully, whether in hard copy or in electronic form. Originals must be secured and copies taken for working purposes. Because strict procedures must be followed to ensure that evidence obtained electronically is admissible, extreme care should be taken when dealing with any such data.

22–08   There are two types of evidence generated by computers[12]:

- real evidence such as calculations and analyses; and

- documents and records held on computer which are treated as hearsay (see paras **22–09** *et seq.*).

Real evidence generated by computers will be admissible in court – in the case quoted below the evidence concerned telephone printouts of a hotel's computer:

> "Where information is recorded by mechanical means without the intervention of the human mind, the record made by the machine is admissible in evidence, provided of course, it is accepted that the machine is reliable."[13]

The House of Lords addressed this issue and clarified this statement in *R v. Shepherd*.[14] Lord Griffiths held that, irrespective of whether the human mind was involved, a document produced by a computer can only be relied upon by the prosecution if evidence is produced to satisfy section 69 of the Police and Criminal Evidence Act 1984. This section requires that, in order for a computer generated document to be admissible in criminal proceedings, there must be no grounds to believe improper use of the computer rendered the document inaccurate, and it must be shown that at all material times the computer was operating properly (or if not, that its failure to operate properly did not affect the production or accuracy of the document).

The problem with computer records is that it is often difficult to identify the author, and it is possible that a document may have had multiple authors.

Admissibility of electronic/digital evidence in criminal trials

22–09   The problem of admissibility of evidence is one of the most common reasons for collapse of criminal trails. The Criminal Evidence Act 1992 was

---

[12] Kelleher, D. and Murray, K., *Information Technology Law in Ireland* (Butterworths, Dublin, 1997), Chap. 24.
[13] Smith, J.C., "The admissibility of statements by computer" *Criminal Law Reports* (1981) 387 at 389-390, quoted with approval by the Court of Appeal in *R v. Spiby* [1990] 91 Cr. App. Rep. 186.
[14] [1993] 1 All E.R. 225.

enacted to allow business records to be admissible in court. This is a statutory exception to the hearsay rule and is of some relevance to expert accountants. Section 2 of the Act defines a document as including:

"... reproduction in a permanent legible form, by a computer ... of information in non-legible form."

Information in non-legible form is defined as including information in microfilm, microfiche, magnetic tape or disk. Section 5(1) of the 1992 Act states:

"... information contained in a document shall be admissible in any criminal proceedings as evidence of any fact therein of which direct oral evidence would be admissible if the information –

(a) was compiled in the ordinary course of a business,
(b) was supplied by a person (whether or not he so compiled it and is identifiable) who had, or may reasonably be supposed to have had, personal knowledge of the matters dealt with, and
(c) in the case of information in non-legible form that has been reproduced in permanent legible form, was reproduced in the course of the normal operation of the reproduction system concerned."

Where the document contains information which the average person would not understand without explanation, section 5(6) states that an explanation will be admissible if it is given in court by a competent person, either orally or contained in a document signed by such a competent person. The evidence must be accompanied by a certificate signed by a member of management of the business which compiled the information or by a competent person.

Admissibility of electronic/digital evidence in civil trials

22–10   Until recently, there was no legislation in Ireland dealing with evidence in civil trials. As a result, in civil cases computer records were treated as hearsay and were only admissible where they fell within one of the exceptions to the hearsay rule. The exceptions to the hearsay rule are such that it was unlikely that computer records would be admissible in civil trials.

22–11   Section 22 of the Electronic Commerce Act 2000 has made electronic evidence admissible in cases as follows:

"In any legal proceedings, nothing in the application of the rules of evidence shall apply so as to deny the admissibility in evidence of–

(a) an electronic communication, an electronic form of a document, an electronic contract, or writing in electronic form–
    (i) on the sole ground that it is an electronic communication, an electronic form of a document, an electronic contract, or writing in electronic form, or

> (ii) if it is the best evidence that the person or public body adducing it could reasonably be expected to obtain, on the grounds that it is not in its original form,

or

> (b) an electronic signature–
>> (i) on the sole ground that the signature is in electronic form, or is not an advanced electronic signature, or is not based on a qualified certificate, or is not based on a qualified certificate issued by an accredited certification service provider, or is not created by a secure signature creation device, or
>> (ii) if it is the best evidence that the person or public body adducing it could reasonably be expected to obtain, on the grounds that it is not in its original form."

Hearsay and expert accounting evidence

What is hearsay?

22–12   In the ordinary sense of the word, hearsay is a fact which has not been perceived by a person, but has been told to him by another person. The rule against hearsay, to which there are several exceptions, renders inadmissible, as evidence of the truth of an assertion, testimony that the assertion was made. Kingsmill Moore J. explained the rule in his Supreme Court judgment in *Cullen v. Clarke*:

> "In view of some of the arguments addressed to the Court, it is necessary to emphasise that there is *no* general rule of evidence to the effect that a witness may not testify as to the words spoken by a person who is not produced as a witness. There *is* a general rule, subject to many exceptions, that evidence of the speaking of such words is inadmissible to prove the truth of the facts which they assert; the reasons being that the truth of the words cannot be tested by cross-examination and has not the sanctity of an oath. This is the rule known as the rule against hearsay." [15]

Rule against hearsay

22–13   The rule against hearsay is still a feature of the rules of evidence in both civil and criminal cases in Ireland, and it tends to be applied strictly in criminal proceedings. In the context of the laws of evidence, the rule against hearsay deems inadmissible, subject to certain exceptions, evidence proffered by a witness of a statement made by another person when the objective of the evidence is to establish the truth of what is contained in the statement. Evidence of a statement does not offend the rule against hearsay, and is therefore admissible, when it is proposed to establish, by the evidence, not the truth of the

---

[15] [1963] I.R. 368 at 378.

statement but the fact that it was made. By way of example to illustrate the point, if a witness overhears, but does not see, someone admitting at the scene of a crime that he committed the crime, the evidence of what he heard is admissible as evidence of the presence of the person at the scene but not as confession evidence of his guilt.

Expert witness exceptions to the rule against hearsay

22–14   However, expert witnesses are not subject to the full rigours of the rule against hearsay. It is recognised that, for the purposes of their opinion, experts will generally have to rely on specialist facts and background knowledge, the veracity of which will not be open to challenge and cross-examination in the proceedings. The facts or data in the particular case upon which an expert bases an opinion or inference may be those perceived by or made known to him at or before the hearing. The only requirement is that the information is the type that experts in the field normally rely upon. If of a type reasonably relied upon by experts in the particular field in forming opinions or inferences upon the subject, the facts or data need not be admissible as evidence.

22–15   Opinion evidence expressed by an expert is therefore a recognised exception to the rule against hearsay, to the extent that the expert's opinion relies on assertions the truth of which, although the expert is satisfied thereof, is not tested before the court. An example of the acceptability of such evidence in an Irish court was in *Carroll Industries plc v. Ó Cúlacháin,*[16] when Carroll J. cited with approval a passage from the judgment of Pennycuick V.C. in *Odeon Associated Theatres Ltd v. Jones.*[17] The relevant extract from the letter judgment is quoted at para. **6–10**.

22–16   This "relaxation" of the rule against hearsay has been acknowledged implicitly by the Irish courts, *e.g.* in the judgment of Shanley J. in *Vogel v. Cheeverstown House Ltd* when he said:

> "Apart from the plaintiff and the complainant, there is no witness who is in a position to give first-hand evidence in relation to the allegation of sexual abuse. All the evidence proposed, and the witnesses tendered, will give hearsay evidence if permitted to do so, although it must be said of some of the witnesses that they will give evidence as experts."[18]

The effect of this "relaxation" is that, for instance, an accountant giving evidence as to the quality of audit work in a negligence case can place reliance on academic and other works describing best practice in auditing, without the necessity for the authors of those works to give their own evidence and to be available for cross-examination. In effect, because of his expertise, the expert can defend and

---

[16][1988] I.R. 705 at 714–715.
[17][1971] 2 All E.R. 407.
[18][1998] 2 I.R. 496 at 498.

be challenged on the assertions on which he relies, and cross-examination of him is deemed sufficient to test the veracity of those assertions.

22–17   Experts may testify in terms of opinion or inference and give reasons therefor without prior disclosure of the underlying facts or data, unless the court rules otherwise. Nevertheless, forensic accountants may be compelled to disclose facts or data underlying their expert opinion and should always be in a position to do so. The expert may, in any event, be required to disclose the underlying facts or data on cross-examination.

Discovery

22–18   The issue of discovery has already been touched upon in paras **20–27** *et seq.* Discovery is the formal process that allows parties to litigation to demand the disclosure and production to them of relevant documents in the custody, possession or power of other parties to the dispute or, in certain cases, of third parties. In recent years discovery has become a standard feature of all but the most straightforward and non-contentious of cases. Discovery is primarily used in civil litigation but is occasionally relevant in criminal trials.

Discovery in civil cases

22–19   The process of discovery usually commences after the plaintiff's claim in a civil case had been set out in a statement of claim (or equivalent document) (see Appendix 3 (Glossary) for explanation of the term). This is elaborated on by replies to notices for particulars (see para. **20–15** for explanation of the term) raised by one or more defendants to the claim and responded to by the defences of the defendants. At this point in the litigation, the legal basis for the plaintiff's claim should have been articulated clearly. The full extent of the case being made in response to the claim may not yet be clear, as the defence will tend to deny all but the most innocuous of the plaintiff's claims. This tactic on behalf of the defendant, is designed to force the plaintiff to prove all aspects of his claim.

22–20   The principal "missing link" for the plaintiff at this stage will usually be that, although he knows the nature of his claim and its legal basis, he does not have all the evidence necessary to support the claim. For example, a plaintiff may develop a serious respiratory disorder while working in a factory environment containing high levels of noxious fumes and dust particles. He bases his claim on the advice of his doctors who tell him that his condition has probably been caused by certain poisons carried through the air by fumes and dust. Inspection facilities will be sought on his behalf and attempts will be made to sample the air and isolate the poisons. However, the factory environment may be very different from when he worked there or the tests may be otherwise inconclusive. In any event, he will not have full details of tests carried out on an ongoing basis by his employer, the state of their knowledge of the danger at the relevant time or the safety procedures adopted by them. In order to obtain this information, the plaintiff's solicitors will request discovery of all documents in the custody, power or possession of the employers that are relevant to the plaintiff's claim. They will also specifically request documents relating to safety procedures, tests of the air and working environment, evaluations of compliance with safety standards, installation and maintenance of ventilation systems and various other relevant documents.

Request for voluntary discovery

22–21   The discovery process commences with a request from a party's solicitors that another party or parties provide the relevant documents on a voluntary basis. The Rules of the Superior Courts[19] require that, unless the court deems that urgency, the nature of the case or other circumstances warrant a departure from the rule, no order for discovery shall be made unless a written request for voluntary discovery has already been made specifying the precise categories of documents requested, explaining why they should be discovered and allowing a reasonable time for a response. The Rules also deal with the time-limits for an application for discovery and the remedies open to a party where agreed voluntary discovery is not made in the agreed time or at all. These remedies include the making by the court of an order for discovery, an order directing the trial of a preliminary issue or an order for the attachment of the party in default and an order dismissing the action (for a plaintiff in default) or striking out the defence (for a defendant in default). Sometimes the response will be a positive one, but more often there will be disagreement as to the breadth of the discovery requested. For this or other reasons, the matter may have to be resolved by an application to court.

Application for discovery to the courts

22–22   The procedure for making an application to the High Court for discovery of documents is set out in the Rules of the Superior Courts.[20] There are similar Rules for Circuit Court applications.[21] The general rules relating to discovery contained in Order 31 of the Rules of the Superior Court are:

> "12. (1) Any party may apply to the Court by way of notice of motion for an order directing any other party to any cause or matter to make discovery on oath of the documents which are or have been in his or her possession or power, relating to any matter in question therein. Every such notice of motion shall

---

[19] Rules of the Superior Courts (No. 2) (Discovery) 1999 (S.I. No. 233 of 1999).
[20] Rules of the Superior Courts 1986, Ord. 31.
[21] Rules of the Circuit Court 1950, Ord. 29 deals with discovery of documents in the Circuit Court.

specify the precise categories of documents in respect of which discovery is sought and shall be grounded upon the affidavit of the party seeking such an order of discovery which shall:

> (a)   verify that the discovery of documents sought is necessary for disposing fairly of the cause or matter or for saving costs;
>
> (b)   furnish the reasons why each category of documents is required to be discovered."

The options open to the court when an application for discovery is made are then set out:

> "(2) On the hearing of such application the Court may either refuse or adjourn the same, if satisfied that such discovery is not necessary, or not necessary at that stage of the cause or matter, or by virtue of non-compliance with the provisions of subrule 4(1), or make such order on such terms as to security for the costs of discovery or otherwise and either generally or limited to certain classes of documents as may be thought fit.
>
> (3) An order shall not be made under this rule if and so far as the Court shall be of opinion that it is not necessary either for disposing fairly of the cause or matter or for saving costs."

22–23   Rule 12 continues by dealing in sub-rule (4) with the necessity of a request for voluntary discovery described above, and with the discretion of the court in dealing with the costs of an application for an order for discovery where a prior written application was not made in time or at all.

22–24   These rules indicate that discovery must be necessary for disposing fairly of the case or for saving costs. The courts have refused applications that they deemed unnecessary.[22] Discovery must not be used for improper purposes.[23] It is a contempt of court to use documents other than for the purpose of the action.[24]

22–25   The effect of these rules is that any party to a dispute may, on notice to the other parties and having complied with the rules as to requests for voluntary discovery, ask the court to adjudicate on that party's entitlement to discovery of documents and to make an order requiring discovery to be made. The application will be supported by an affidavit (see Appendix 3 (Glossary) for explanation of term) explaining the reasons why the applicant believes the documents in question to be relevant and discoverable. This affidavit will give a brief history and status of the litigation to date. It will also set out details of the applicant's attempts

---

[22] *Murphy v. Minister for Defence* [1991] 2 I.R. 161.

[23] *Megaleasing UK Ltd v. Barrett* [1993] I.L.R.M. 497.

[24] *Allied Irish Banks plc v. Ernst & Whinney* [1993] 1 I.R. 375; *Gormley v. Ireland* [1993] 2 I.R. 75; *Wang v. Minister for Justice (No. 2)*, unreported, High Court, Denham J., March 16, 1993.

to obtain discovery of the documents on a voluntary basis, and copies of previous correspondence making these requests will be attached as exhibits to the affidavit. A representative of the party against whom discovery is being sought may swear a replying affidavit explaining why he believes the application should not be successful or why the discovery should be limited in some way.

22–26   The application is normally made to the Master of the High Court, or to a judge if the case is before the Circuit Court. Although not a judge of the High Court, the Master fulfils an important role in administering and adjudicating on a variety of applications in relation to High Court cases. In contested discovery applications the Master will read the affidavits and hear counsel for all interested parties. He will then make an order in such terms as he feels are appropriate. He may refuse to make an order.

More often than not the matter of who must pay the costs of the application for discovery will be reserved by the Master to be decided by the trial judge in the case itself, as the trial judge will be best equipped, having heard all the evidence, to decide whether the discovery application was justified. However, where the discovery applied for is granted without significant amendment or limitation by the Master and where there have been previous unsuccessful attempts to obtain the discovery on a voluntary basis, the Master may well penalise the party whom he orders to make the discovery by awarding the costs against that party.

Order for discovery and affidavit listing documents

22–27   Where an order for discovery is made by the Master it will specify that an affidavit of discovery must be sworn by an individual, nominated to do so on behalf of the party making discovery, within a specified period of time. The affidavit must be in the form specified in Appendix C to the Rules of the Superior Courts and in particular must include the following statements by the individual swearing the affidavit (known as the deponent):

"1. I have in my possession or power the documents relating to the matters in question in this suit set forth in the first and second parts of the first schedule hereto.

2. I object to produce the said documents set forth in the second part of the said first schedule hereto.

3. That [here state upon what grounds the objection is made, and verify the facts as far as may be].

4. I have had, but have not now, in my possession or power the documents relating to the matters in question in this suit set forth in the second schedule hereto.

5. The last mentioned documents were last in my possession or power on [state when].

6. That [here state what has become of the last-mentioned documents, and in whose possession they now are].

7. According to the best of my knowledge, information, and belief, I have not now, and never had in my possession, custody or power, or in the possession, custody or power of my solicitors or agents, solicitor or agent, or in the possession, custody or power of any other persons, or person on my behalf, any deed, account, book of account, voucher, receipt, letter, memorandum, paper, or writing, or any copy of or extract from any such document, or any other document whatsoever, relating to the matters in question in this suit, or any of them, or wherein any entry has been made relative to such matters, or any of them, other than and except the documents set forth in the said first and second schedules hereto."

22–28 This prescribed format requires the deponent to list all relevant documents (or groups of similar documents) which are or have ever been in the possession, custody or power of the party making discovery and to identify separately from among them:

(a) those documents which were at one time, but no longer are, in that party's possession, custody or power, stating what has become of those documents and who now has possession of them; and

(b) those documents which that party is refusing to produce, stating the basis for such refusal (usually a claim of privilege).

Failure to produce documents

22–29 Under the Rules of the Superior Courts,[25] failure to make discovery, having agreed to do so voluntarily, or to comply with an order for discovery, runs the risk for plaintiffs that their action may be dismissed for want of prosecution. Defendants run the risk that their defence may be struck out, the effect of which is to place them in the same position as if they had not defended the proceedings.[26] Both parties run the risk of attachment, a process by which an order is addressed to the Gardaí "commanding" them to attach the individual so as to have him appear before the High Court to answer for his contempt. However, it should be noted that these powers are used in only the most extreme cases, as the courts view the purpose of the relevant rules to be to ensure discovery rather than to punish those in breach. This is evident from the Supreme Court judgment of Barrington J. in *Murphy v. J. Donohoe Ltd*[27] in which he allowed an appeal from the decision of Johnson J. in the High Court, striking out the defendant's defence for non-compliance with an order for discovery:

"Order 31, r. 21, exists to ensure that parties to litigation comply with orders for discovery. It does not exist to punish a defaulter but to facilitate the administration of justice by ensuring compliance with the orders of the court.

[25] Rules of the Superior Courts, Ord. 31, r. 21.
[26] Cahill, E., *Discovery in Ireland* (Round Hall Sweet & Maxwell, Dublin, 1996), p. 12.
[27] [1996] 1 I.R. 123.

Undoubtedly cases may exist where one party may not be able to get a fair trial because of the other party's wilful refusal to comply with an order for discovery. In such cases it may be necessary to dismiss the plaintiff's claim or to strike out the defendant's defence. But such cases will be extreme cases. As Hamilton C.J. put it in *Mercantile Credit Co. v. Heelan* (Unreported, Supreme Court, 14th February, 1995):–

> 'The powers of the Court to secure compliance with the rules and orders of the Court relating to discovery should not be exercised so as to punish a party for failure to comply with an order for discovery within the time limited by the order.'" [28]

22–30 There are a number of circumstances in which parties can object to discovery and can claim privilege. However, these objections are usually made in the affidavit of discovery, allowing the party to comply with the agreement or order for discovery while declining to produce certain documents on stated grounds. Such grounds can include:

– executive privilege, claimed by the public sector;

– legal professional privilege;

– statutory right to privilege;

– privilege against self-incrimination;

– diplomatic privilege.

Discovery by third parties

22–31 The sources of relevant information obtainable by a party on discovery are not limited to the other parties to the litigation. Third parties who are not involved in the dispute but in whose possession, custody or power some relevant documents reside can be required to make discovery of those documents in the same way as parties to the dispute. The only significant difference is that, not unreasonably, the party seeking discovery from a "non-party" must indemnify the latter as to the reasonable costs of providing the information. This is because, not being a party to the dispute, the third party neither has the opportunity to profit from the litigation nor has a case to answer.

22–32 The rule relating to discovery by non-parties is Order 31, rule 29 of the Rules of the Superior Courts, which states:

> "Any person not a party to the cause or matter before the Court who appears to the Court to be likely to have or to have had in his possession custody or power any documents which are relevant to an issue arising or likely to arise out of the cause or matter or is or is likely to be in a position to give evidence relevant to any such issue may by leave of the Court upon the application of any party to the

---

[28] [1996] 1 I.R. 123 at 142.

said cause or matter be directed by order of the Court to answer such interrogatories or to make discovery of such documents or to permit inspection of such documents. The provisions of this Order shall apply *mutatis mutandis* as if the said order of the Court had been directed to a party to the said cause or matter provided always that the party seeking such order shall indemnify such person in respect of all costs thereby reasonably incurred by such person . . ."

22–33   The rules already referred to, requiring a prior application for voluntary discovery before a court order is sought, apply also to situations where non-party discovery is sought. However, courts will be somewhat slower to grant orders for discovery against individuals or entities who are not party to the proceedings on the grounds that a discovery process can be costly and can cause significant inconvenience which may be inappropriate or disproportionate when it involves a stranger to the proceedings.

22–34   These issues were canvassed in a case involving a firm of accountants in *Allied Irish Banks plc v. Ernst & Whinney*.[29] The substantive action involved allegations of negligence by the defendant firm as auditors of the failed Insurance Corporation of Ireland plc ("ICI"), which had been acquired before its collapse by the plaintiff. AIB plc sought third party discovery against the Minister for Industry and Commerce, who exercised a regulatory function in relation to ICI. The Master of the High Court granted discovery and his decision so to do was appealed successfully to the High Court. Costello J.'s decision in the High Court to overturn the Master's order was itself overturned on appeal to the Supreme Court. In ordering discovery by the Minister, Finlay C.J. recognised the different standards to be applied in cases of third party discovery. He concluded that, while the court has discretion to refuse to make an order for non-party discovery where such an order would cause undue oppression or prejudice not compensatable by the payment of costs, nevertheless the rule does not oblige the party seeking the order to be able to identify the specific documents sought. He said:

> "The provisions of r. 29, on the other hand, create a situation in which after it has been established to the satisfaction of the court that a person not a party has, or is likely to have, in his possession documents which are relevant to an issue arising, the court still has a further discretion. This arises from the fact that the rule provides that, upon that being established, the leave of the court to make the order for discovery still is required.
>
>   I take the view that the further discretion thus arising must relate, even where documents may be in the custody or procurement of a stranger to the action, and where they may have some relevance to the issues arising in the action, to a consideration of particular oppression or prejudice which will be caused to the person called upon to discover such documents, not capable of being adequately compensated by the payment by the party seeking it of the costs of making such discovery.

---

[29] [1993] 1 I.R. 375.

> I do not, however, consider that r. 29 can be construed as imposing upon a party seeking an order for discovery pursuant to it an obligation, not only to establish that the person against whom the order is sought has or is likely to have in his possession or procurement documents which are relevant to an issue arising in the cause or matter, but also to establish specific documents as distinct from categories of documents which *prima facie* are relevant."[30]

His decision was influenced by the fact that the third party was an organ of government:

> "In reaching this conclusion, I am rejecting the contention made on behalf of the Minister that having regard to the time and standard of official which would be involved in the making of this discovery, it is unduly oppressive on the Minister. I conclude that it is not, and, having regard to the fact that it is a contribution towards the administration of justice, it is particularly appropriate that a State authority should be asked, even at the cost of some inconvenience, to provide it."[31]

The late McCarthy J. held a similar view:

> "One can well envisage the serious damage that might be done to a small firm of auditors and accountants or the like if they had to take one or two members of staff to devote to an exercise of little direct importance to that firm. Such an objection taken by a Department of State, charged with monitoring the insurance industry, should not be sustained."[32]

It is clear from these judgments that third party discovery will be allowed in appropriate cases, but that the courts will keep a watchful eye on the possibility of such discovery being disproportionate to the potential benefit and will disallow third party discovery applications where they are not justified.

22–35 In relation to the costs of non-party discovery, Laffoy J. made a number of important findings in *Dunne v. Fox.*[33] She dealt, *inter alia*, with the quantum of fees charged by the defendant firm of accountants in making discovery as non-party to proceedings. She considered the appropriateness of such charges including the cost of legal advice and whether such charges should include a profit element or merely reflect the actual cost of making discovery. She dealt first with whether it was appropriate for the non-party to take legal advice regarding privilege and for the plaintiff seeking the discovery to bear the cost of such advice:

> "… it was submitted on behalf of the plaintiff that costs incurred in connection with the claim of the non-party's clients to privilege were unreasonably incurred. While acknowledging that it was not unreasonable that a firm of accountants

---

[30] [1993] 1 I.R. 375 at 389.
[31] *ibid.* at 392.
[32] *ibid.* at 395–396.
[33] [1999] 1 I.R. 283.

making discovery would be astute to ensure that its client's entitlement to privilege was preserved, it was submitted that it was unreasonable to expect the client's opponent to bear the cost of the firm consulting with the client and obtaining legal advice from a solicitor and counsel on the issue of the client's privilege. It is quite clear that the issue of the defendants' privilege was of paramount importance at all material times and it was expressly provided in the order of the 3rd October, 1994, that the order was without prejudice, *inter alia:-*

> '... to the right of the defendants to assert a claim for privilege over any documents so discovered . . . '

Apart from the non-party's responsibility to the court in making the discovery, the non-party also owed a duty of care to its clients for whom it was carrying out the investigation. In my view, the costs incurred by the non-party in consulting with its clients and their solicitors and in obtaining advice from its own solicitors and from counsel instructed by its own solicitors as outlined in Mr. Lacy's evidence were reasonably incurred and it is reasonable that they should be ultimately borne by the plaintiff, because they would not have been incurred at all but for the existence of the order of the 3rd October, 1994, which was obtained at the behest of the plaintiff for the advancement of his litigation."[34]

The learned judge then went on to deal with the fees charged by the non-party in respect of their own time spent complying with the order for discovery:

> "The principal area of controversy between the plaintiff and the non-party related to the *quantum* of the non-party's own fees. A number of points arise on this aspect of the taxation. First, in my view, the Taxing Master was correct in rejecting the submission made before him on behalf of the plaintiff that the costs to be allowed to the non-party should not include a profit element. That submission was not repeated on the review in this Court and, indeed, it was conceded, properly in my view, that the non-party was entitled to opportunity costs where it was established that fees were forgone. The argument advanced in this Court was that the non-party could only equate "costs" with fees if it could establish that those were fees forgone, that is it say [sic], that not only would the personnel deployed in the discovery process have been involved on equally remunerative work, but also that that work would have been lost to the firm. It is clear from Mr. Lacy's evidence that, had the staff engaged in the discovery process not been so engaged, they would have been engaged in other available work which would have generated profit for the firm. Whether or not that work was lost to the firm, in my view, the non-party is entitled to recoupment of the profit element, because, even if it was retained in the firm it had to be performed by other staff or it had to be postponed, with a "knock-on" effect on other work."[35]

It is suggested that this decision shows a very clear appreciation of the way in which accounting firms carry on their business and is to be welcomed by accountants who may become involved in proceedings to which their clients are a party.

---

[34] [1999] 1 I.R. 283 at 300–301.
[35] [1999] 1 I.R. 283 at 301.

Summary of discovery procedure in civil cases

22–36   Table 22.1 summarises the stages involved in the discovery process.

Table 22.1: Checklist of procedures in seeking discovery in civil cases

* Seek voluntary discovery by writing to the other party and specifying categories of documents sought and the reasons why they are relevant

If voluntary discovery unsuccessful

* Draft notice of motion and affidavit seeking order for discovery and stating that discovery is required to fairly dispose of the cause or matter or to save costs

If order for discovery is granted by the court

* Affidavit of deponent (listing documents) must be delivered within specified time period
* Seek an order for production of any document specified in affidavit or in list of documents
* Obtain a notice to inspect – inspection to take place within a specified time-limit and at a specified venue for inspection
* Documents can be inspected and copied

Documents not produced

* If deponent defaults, bring motion to seek relief (Order 31, rule 21)
* Party required to produce documents may object
* Party required to produce documents may claim privilege
* Court decides whether document is privileged

Source: Adapted from Cahill, E., *Discovery in Ireland* (Round Hall Sweet & Maxwell, Dublin, 1996), pp. 6–7.

Discoverable documents

22–37   The rules on discovery are not precise on what constitutes a document but the courts have defined the term broadly, as follows:

> "... any thing which, if adduced in evidence at the hearing of the proceedings, would be put in, or become annexed to, the court file of the proceedings".[36]

In the same case Kenny J. described a document as "... something which gives information".[37]

---

[36] *McCarthy v. O'Flynn* [1979] I.R. 127 at 129, *per* Henchy J.
[37] [1979] I.R. 127 at 131, *per* Kenny J.; cited by Murphy J. in his High Court judgment in *Keane v. An Bord Pleanála* [1997] 1 I.R. 184 at 196, and by Denham J. in the Supreme Court in the same case at 230.

22–38   The term has extended to x-rays,[38] photographs of tombstones[39] and tape recordings.[40] More recent English cases have accepted computer information on disk or digital tape.[41] Henchy J. dealt with the general definition of the word "document" in the context of the discovery rules in *McCarthy v. O'Flynn* as follows:

> "The dictionary meaning of 'document' connotes any thing that furnishes evidence but the word, as used in the Rules of the Superior Courts, varies in the scope of its meaning with the context: see, for example, the special definition of the word given by order 107, r. 1, for the purpose of that order, and see the distinction drawn in other rules between 'document' and 'exhibit'. However, I think that where the word occurs in the discovery rules it should be construed in terms of the scheme and purpose of those rules. Thus read, I consider that the word includes any thing which, if adduced in evidence at the hearing of the proceedings, would be put in, or become annexed to, the court file of the proceedings. All such things are part of the documentation of the case and qualify for preservation as part of the court archives."[42]

Kenny J. said:

> "I think that an X-ray plate and photograph are documents and that the defendant is entitled to an order for the discovery of those of the plaintiff taken between the 1st January, 1973 and the 31st December, 1973. ... Etymologically the word 'document' is derived from the Latin word 'documentum' which in turn comes from the verb 'docere'. Therefore, it is something which teaches or gives information or a lesson or an example for instruction. The main characteristic of a document is that it is something which gives information. An X-ray plate or photograph gives information and so it is a document and the defendant is entitled to discovery of it. All the better authorities support this view."[43]

Inspection of bank records and books of accounts

22–39   The Bankers' Books Evidence Acts 1879 to 1989 empower courts to make an order for the inspection and copying of entries in bankers' books by a party in any legal proceedings. Section 7 of the 1879 Act provides:

> "On the application of any party to a legal proceeding a court or judge may order that such party be at liberty to inspect and take copies of any entries in a bankers' book for any of the purposes of such proceedings. An order under this section may be made either with or without summoning the bank or any other party, and shall be served on the bank three clear days before the same is to be obeyed, unless the court or judge otherwise directs."

---

[38] *McCarthy v. O'Flynn* [1979] I.R. 127.
[39] *Lyell v. Kennedy (No. 3)* (1884) Ch. D. 1.
[40] *Grant v. South Western and County Properties Ltd* [1975] Ch. 185.
[41] *Derby & Co Ltd v. Weldon (No. 9)* [1991] 2 All E.R. 901.
[42] [1979] I.R. 127 at 129.
[43] *ibid.* at 130–131.

Bankers' books are defined in section 9(2) of the 1879 Act (as substituted by section 2 of the Bankers' Books Evidence (Amendment) Act 1959 and subsequently amended by section 131 of the Central Bank Act 1989 to:

> "(a) include any records used in the ordinary business of a bank, or used in the transfer department of a bank acting as registrar of securities, whether –
>
>   (i) comprised in bound volume, loose-leaf binders or other loose-leaf filing systems, loose-leaf ledger sheets, pages, folios or cards, or
>
>   (ii) kept on microfilm, magnetic tape or in any non-legible form (by the use of electronics or otherwise) which is capable of being reproduced in a permanent legible form, and
>
> (b) cover documents in manuscript, documents which are typed, printed, stencilled or created by any other mechanical process or partly mechanical process in use from time to time and documents which are produced by any photographic or photostatic process."

Procedure

22–40   Applications for such orders should be grounded on affidavit. Generally, the bank is a notice party to the application. However, such applications can be made *ex parte* and the bank will only become aware of the order after it has been made. Generally speaking, courts will only grant an order in respect of a party to the proceedings[44] but there have been exceptions in relation to some third party accounts.[45]

Applicable circumstances

22–41   The purpose of these provisions in the Bankers' Books Evidence Acts 1879–1989 has been explained in the following terms by Barrington J. in *Larkins v. National Union of Mineworkers*[46] in a passage in which he refers to the judgment of Murphy J. in *O'C. v. P.C.D.*[47]:

> "... the purpose of the Bankers' Books Evidence Acts ... is merely to facilitate banks by allowing them, in certain circumstances, to prove the contents of some of their books by secondary evidence. They in no way limit the powers of the court, in an appropriate case, to order discovery or inspection.
>
> Mr. Justice Murphy makes this clear in a passage which appears at p. 274 of the report. He says:–
>
> > 'Again it must be recognised that the purpose of the Bankers' Books Evidence Act was to facilitate the proof of evidence contained in books used by bankers in the day to day conduct of their profession. Presumably the removal of such crucial documentation for the purposes of litigation

---

[44] *Staunton v. Counihan* [1957] 92 I.L.T.R. 32.
[45] *M'Gorman v. Kierans* [1901] 35 I.L.T.R. 84.
[46] [1985] I.R. 671.
[47] [1985] I.R. 265.

might create considerable inconvenience. I would assume that it was for that reason that the legislature permitted, subject to important safeguards, the substitution of secondary evidence.'

Under these circumstances it appears to me that there is nothing in the Bankers' Books Evidence Acts or in Mr. Justice Murphy's decision to circumscribe the power of the High Court, in an appropriate case, to order the production or inspection of any of a bank's books, documents or computer printouts."[48]

22–42   Once an order for production of specified documents has been obtained, and the notice of inspection has issued from the other side, documents may be inspected and copied within a specified time-limit and at the venue specified. Order 31 of the Rules of the Superior Courts set-out the regulations governing inspection of bank records and of books of account:

> "17. The party to whom such notice is given, shall, within two days from the receipt of such notice, if all the documents therein referred to have been set forth by him in such affidavit or list as is mentioned in rule 13, or if any of the documents referred to in such notice have been set forth by him in such affidavit or list, then within four days from the receipt of such notice, deliver to the party giving the same a notice stating a time within three days from the delivery thereof, at which the documents, or such of them as he does not object to produce, may be inspected at the office of his solicitor, or in the case of banker' books or other books of account, or books in constant use for the purposes of any trade or business, at their usual place of custody, and stating which (if any) of the documents he objects to produce, and on what grounds.
>
> . . .
>
> 20. (1) Where inspection of any business books is applied for, the Court may, instead of ordering inspection of original books, order a copy of any entries therein to be furnished and verified by the affidavit of some person who has examined the copy with the original entries, and such affidavit shall state whether or not there are in the original book any and what erasures, interlineations, or alterations. Provided that, notwithstanding that such copy has been supplied, the Court may order inspection of the book from which the copy was made."

Statutory right to demand production of books or documents

22–43   Sections 10(2) and 19 of the Companies Act 1990 empower company inspectors and Ministers/authorised officers to request production of company books and records. Under section 10(2), company inspectors may also require persons to "attend before them and otherwise to give them all assistance". This provision extends to persons other than company officials.[49] The provisions of section 10(2) have been tested in the courts.

---

[48] [1985] I.R. 671 at 695–696.
[49] *Chestvale Properties Ltd v. Glackin* [1993] 3 I.R. 35.

In *Glackin v. Trustee Savings Bank,*[50] Costello J. held that the obligation to assist an inspector by producing documents and appearing before him must be complied with, irrespective of the existence of a confidentiality agreement between the party whose assistance is requested (in that case a bank) and the party to whom the requested documents and information relate (in that case the bank's customer).

Company investigations are dealt with in more detail in Chapter 13. The Company Law Enforcement Act 2001 has extended rights to access to books and documents. This is discussed in paras **13–29** *et seq.*

Discovery in criminal cases

22–44 In criminal cases tried before a judge and jury, the prosecution is required by law[51] to serve a book of evidence (see paras **20–61** *et seq.* on the accused, containing as follows:

- statement of charges;

- copy of sworn information in writing on which the proceedings were initiated;

- list of witnesses to be called during the trial;

- statement of the evidence to be given by each of the witnesses;

- list of exhibits;

- right to inspect the exhibits.

22–45 Because of these requirements, discovery is not as important in criminal cases as in civil actions. Discovery allows parties in civil actions to obtain documents in the absence of a statutory requirement on one party to serve documents or exhibits on another.

The Rules of the Superior Court dealing with discovery also apply in criminal cases.[52] The principles established in the *Murphy v. Dublin Corporation* judgment, set out in para. **22–04**, have been applied by the courts to criminal cases.[53] In normal circumstances privilege cannot be claimed by the Gardaí in the absence of special circumstances. The courts have applied such special circumstances to protect the identity of police informers.[54]

---

[50] [1993] 3 I.R. 55.
[51] Criminal Procedure Act 1967, s. 6(1).
[52] Rules of the Superior Courts, Ord. 125.
[53] *DPP (Hanley) v. Holly* [1984] I.L.R.M. 149; *Breathnach v. Ireland (No. 3)* [1993] 2 I.R. 458.
[54] *DPP v. Special Criminal Court* [1999] 1 I.R. 90.

Discovery of accountants' working papers relating to clients

22–46   Accountants' working papers enjoy no special exemption or immunity from discovery and the normal rules applying to documents generally apply also to such papers. In particular, where relevant to a matter in issue, working papers must be discovered except where prepared in contemplation or furtherance of litigation.

22–47   As a result of these rules, where an accountant is a party to proceedings (*e.g.* in a suit for negligent auditing or other professional work) his working papers will be directly relevant and discoverable. Indeed, in such cases the working papers can be so central to the cause of action that discovery may be ordered before the plaintiff completes the statement of claim, so that the claim can be properly particularised. This situation arose in *Law Society of Ireland v. Rawlinson and Hunter*.[55] In that case the plaintiff issued a summons against the defendants claiming that they had been negligent in the preparation of four accountants' reports concerning the practice of a solicitor whose practising certificate had been later withheld. The solicitor had subsequently died and numerous claims were made against the plaintiff in respect of alleged losses suffered by the solicitor's clients. The plaintiff had not yet delivered a statement of claim but sought and obtained an order from the Master of the High Court against the defendants for discovery of:

> "... all documents in their possession, power, control or procurement relating to the matter in question in the above entitled proceedings and in particular (but strictly without prejudice to the generality of the foregoing) all working papers, audit programmes, memoranda and other documents (howsoever described) relating to the carrying out by the defendants of their functions and duties as accountants and auditors of the firm . . .".[56]

The discovery was sought, and granted, on the grounds that it was necessary for the preparation of a properly particularised and comprehensive statement of claim. The defendants appealed on the grounds that discovery was normally made after the delivery of a statement of claim and was never ordered for the purpose of assisting the plaintiff in establishing a basis for a claim.

While acknowledging, based on legal authorities, that an order for discovery prior to the delivery of a statement of claim should only be made in exceptional cases, Morris J. (as he then was) dismissed the appeal, saying:

> "Given the complexity of the case, the nature of the plaintiff's statutory obligations to make good the solicitor's default from the compensation fund, the fact that there clearly exists a statable case capable of being pleaded in general terms and, finally, the desirability of having a concise and clear statement of claim which will enable the defendants to know the case which they have to meet, I am

---

[55] [1997] 3 I.R. 592.
[56] *ibid.* at 593–594.

satisfied that this case falls into the category of exceptional cases referred to in the authorities and I affirm the order made by the Master on the 3rd March, 1995."[57]

22–48   Where an accountant prepares records, such as a nominal ledger, on behalf of his client they remain documents within the custody, power or possession of the client and are discoverable, where relevant, by the client even if they remain in the possession of the accountant. The Supreme Court so held in *Quigley v. Burke* where Hamilton C.J. said:

> "In circumstances, where the accounts which the tax-payer himself keeps are not adequate to explain his tax affairs and where his employee, an accountant, completes those accounts by writing up a nominal ledger, I am satisfied that the accountant, acting on behalf of the tax-payer as agent, is not entitled to claim that the books should not be produced on the grounds that they are working papers. A tax-payer has to produce accounts in an intelligible form so that the basis of the computation is clear. The accountant is appearing for his client as his tax agent."[58]

It should be noted that, although referred to in the above extract as an employee, the accountant was a partner in a firm of accountants engaged by the taxpayer for a particular purpose.

22–49 Where an accountant holds relevant papers of his own, rather than as agent for another, and is not a party to the proceedings, discovery of those papers can be ordered under Order 31, rule 29 governing non-party discovery. This issue, and the costs of such an exercise, arose in *Dunne v. Fox*.[59] In 1993, the plaintiff had started proceedings under section 205 of the Companies Act 1963, alleging oppression of him by various directors of a group's holding company. Later, in connection with the proceedings, the holding company and some of its subsidiaries and related companies retained a firm of accountants to investigate a number of transactions. In 1994, the plaintiff sought by notice of motion an order for discovery pursuant to the Rules of the Superior Courts[60] of the accountants, as a non-party, of documents and working papers prepared by the firm in connection with the investigations.

An order for discovery was made allowing three weeks for the discovery and ordering that the plaintiff should pay to the firm of accountants costs of appearing on the motion and reasonable costs of complying with the order. The discovery sought was very extensive. To complete the task in three weeks the firm deployed a large number of people including partners and senior staff to ensure the work would be done without the need for rechecking, and also to

---

[57][1997] 3 I.R. 592 at 596.
[58][1995] 3 I.R. 278 at 284.
[59][1999] 1 I.R. 283.
[60]Rules of the Superior Courts, Ord. 31, r. 29.

provide the level of skill needed to complete the task in accordance with the order. At the same time, the firm was keen to protect the legitimate interests of its clients, three directors of the holding company, in the discovery process. The affidavit of discovery was duly delivered and in it a claim of privilege was made in respect of the firm's clients. On hearing a motion challenging the claim of privilege the court disallowed the claim of privilege and ordered the documents to be disclosed.

Discovery of experts' reports

22–50 A report prepared by an expert as part of the preparation of a claim or defence to a claim is clearly a document prepared in contemplation or furtherance of legal proceedings (see para. **20–03**). As such, provided it is prepared for and communicated only to the client and/or his lawyer and its sole or dominant purpose relates to the proceedings, it attracts legal professional privilege. (See Court of Appeal decision in *Derby & Co v. Weldon (No. 9)*[61]). Accordingly, if the document has been prepared in advance of the time of the preparation of an affidavit of discovery, it should be listed in the affidavit and included in the schedule of documents being withheld from disclosure on the grounds of a claim of privilege.

22–51 However, the parties may agree to exchange expert reports for the purposes of narrowing the issues and facilitating settlement negotiations. Once exchanged, the report ceases to be privileged. This process of exchanging expert reports is now a requirement in personal injuries litigation.

Discovery of experts' working papers

22–52 Again, the normal rules applying to discovery (see paras **22–18** *et seq.* generally) apply to working papers prepared by an expert in the course of his engagement as such. On the basis that it is very likely that such working papers have been prepared for the sole purpose of assisting in the furtherance of legal proceedings, they are likely to be privileged. If the working papers have a dual purpose or multiple purposes, however, they must pass the "dominant purpose" test (see para. **22–06**) in order to qualify for legal professional privilege.

Interrogatories

22–53 Interrogatories are a very close relative of discovery. The essential difference is that, while discovery only permits a party to obtain information from another party if it is contained in a document, interrogatories can be used

---

[61] [1991] 2 All E.R. 901.

to obtain other information in the knowledge of a party even if it is not in a document.

22–54   The manner in which this is done is by posing a series of written questions to the other party to which they must respond. However, the nature of the questions that may be posed is limited, principally by the requirement that the questions must relate clearly to issues relevant to the matters in dispute between the parties. They must only relate to matters of fact.[62] Interrogatories must relate to issues raised in pleadings and not to the evidence in the case. The applicable test was formulated in *Marriott v. Chamberlain*[63] and applied by Costello J. as follows:

> "The law with regard to interrogatories is now very sweeping. It is not permissible to ask the names of persons merely as being witnesses whom the other party is going to call, and their names not forming any substantial part of the material facts; and I think we may go so far as to say that it is not permissible to ask what is mere evidence of the facts in dispute, but forms no part of the facts themselves. But with these exceptions it seems to me that pretty nearly anything that is material may now be asked. The right to interrogate is not confined to the facts directly in issue, but extends to any facts the existence or non-existence of which is relevant to the existence or non-existence of the facts directly in issue."[64]

22–55   Generally, interrogatories must be capable of being answered specifically, usually by the words "Yes" or "No". These limitations generally ensure that interrogatories are not used to cast a wide net in the hope that useful information may be obtained.

22–56   Order 31 of the Rules of the Superior Courts applies to interrogatories as well as to discovery. The relevant general provisions are:

> "1.   In any cause or matter where relief by way of damages or otherwise is sought on the ground of fraud or breach of trust, the plaintiff may at any time after delivering his statement of claim, and a defendant may at or after the time of delivering his defence, without any order for that purpose, and in every other cause or matter any party may by leave of the Court, upon such terms as to security for costs or otherwise as the Court may direct, deliver interrogatories in writing for the examination of the opposite parties, or any one or more of such parties, and such interrogatories when delivered shall have a note at the foot thereof, stating which of such interrogatories each of such persons is required to answer: provided that no party shall deliver more than one set of interrogatories to the same party without an order for that purpose; provided also that interrogatories which do not relate to any

---

[62] *Bula Ltd v. Tara Mines Ltd* [1995] 1 I.L.R.M. 401.
[63] (1886) 17 Q.B.D. 154 at 163.
[64] *Mercantile Credit Co of Ireland Ltd v. Heelan* [1994] 2 I.R. 105 at 111–112.

matters in question in the cause or matter shall be deemed irrelevant, notwithstanding that they might be admissible on the oral cross-examination of a witness.

2. A copy of the interrogatories proposed to be delivered shall be delivered with the notice of application for leave to deliver them, unless the Court shall otherwise order, and the particular interrogatories sought to be delivered shall be submitted to and considered by the Court. In deciding upon such application, the Court shall take into account any offer which may be made by the party sought to be interrogated, to deliver particulars, or to make admissions, or to produce documents, relating to any matter in question. Leave shall be given as to such only of the interrogatories as shall be considered necessary either for disposing fairly of the cause or matter or for saving costs."

22–57   Interrogatories are not as widely used as many lawyers believe they should be. They are particularly useful when very specific matters are in dispute between the parties relating to events the occurrence of which has not been documented.

Role of expert accountants in discovery and interrogatories

22–58   Unfortunately, it is not uncommon for an expert to be engaged to assist in a case at a stage when the formalities of pleading the case and obtaining evidence are at a very advanced stage. This can arise for a variety of reasons, including:

(1) The lawyers and the parties to the litigation have been fully occupied in formulating the case, establishing the facts and gathering evidence and have not found the time to address their minds to the need for expert assistance.

(2) It is believed that the expert's role is, or should be limited to analysing the available evidence and rendering an opinion, and that therefore there is no need to engage the expert until the evidence has all been gathered.

(3) Counsel has not been asked until late in the proceedings to advise on the proofs necessary to present the case in the best light and little or no thought has been given until then to the role an expert might play.

(4) It is believed that costs can be minimised by engaging the expert as late in the process as possible and limiting the expert's brief as much as possible.

22–59   In fact, the prospects of success in a case, and the quantum of damages that may ultimately arise, can be influenced significantly by the early engagement of an expert. The right expert with the right mix of skills and relevant experience will be able to advise on arguments that can legitimately be pursued and on the evidence necessary to test and advance those arguments. He will also be able to advise on the various ways in which the quantum of damages can be calculated and the documents and other information that will assist in this regard.

22–60   For these and other reasons, the engagement of an expert at an early stage can be very beneficial. In particular, if the expert is engaged and briefed fully before discovery is requested or interrogatories submitted, he has an opportunity to assist in defining the information to be requested of the other parties to the litigation. The expert accountant engaged at an early stage should therefore be asked to assist:

– in isolating from the claim, as pleaded, the matters relevant to the question of liability that have an aspect related to his field of expertise, *e.g.* in an claim for negligent auditing the manner in which the audit was performed will be within the accountant's field;

– in isolating from the claim as pleaded the matters relevant to the amount of the claim that fall within his expertise, *e.g.* in a claim for lost profits the calculation of those profits based on financial statements will be relevant;

– in isolating from the defences raised to the claim any aspects which fall within his field;

– in identifying any additional aspects of the claim or defence, not already pleaded, that are relevant to the claim;

– in identifying, based on his experience and expertise, the types of evidence relevant to the various aspects that are likely to be in the possession, custody or power of other parties or non-parties and the form that that evidence is likely to take.

These steps, when carried out carefully and comprehensively, will assist greatly in the formulation of a focused request for discovery and/or list of interrogatories that is likely to elicit the maximum amount of relevant evidence.

22–61   The expert accountant has a further role after discovery has been made, and can fulfil this role even if his engagement has taken place at a time too late to allow him to advise on the application for discovery. This role is the critical review of the list of discoverable documents provided on foot of an application for discovery. The same experience and expertise that allows the expert to advise on the types of documents that should be sought can be used to identify documents or categories of documents that a party ought to be in a position to discover but which are not listed. This can be extremely useful advice in that it may lead to the disclosure of important information that otherwise, through inadvertence or deliberate concealment, might not have come to light.

22–62   Order 31 of the Rules of the Superior Courts makes provision for an application to court to disclose such information in the following terms:

"20. (3) The Court may, on the application of any party to a cause or matter at any time, and whether an affidavit or list of documents shall or shall not have already been ordered or made, make an order requiring any other party to state by affidavit whether any one or more specific documents, to be specified in the application, is or are, or has or have at any time been in his possession or power; and, if not then in his possession, when he parted with the same, and what has become thereof. Such application shall be made on an affidavit stating that in the belief of the deponent the party against whom the application is made has, or has at some time had, in his possession or power the document or documents specified in the application, and that they relate to the matters in question in the cause or matter, or to some of them."

22–63 Finally, it is worth noting that, despite its obvious advantages and its importance to the fair conduct of litigation, the process of discovery has its problems. These principally centre around the fact that, except in the most straightforward of cases, discovery can involve very significant cost and a lot of time in assembling and providing enormous amounts of material, much of which turns out to be of very marginal, if any, relevance to the case. This tendency to overload the discovery process has brought it into disrepute, but it survives in its present form in Ireland. In the words of O'Flaherty J. in *Allied Irish Banks plc v. Ernst & Whinney*:

"There has been the experience in other jurisdictions where discovery is used to swamp the opposing party with masses of material: 'one abuse referred to is the tactic of producing volumes of documents in studied chaos, either to burden the opposition or to increase the possibility that a significant document will be overlooked' (see Simpson, Bailey and Evans, *Discovery and Interrogatories* 2nd ed., at page 2).

To engage in such a tactic is as much an abuse as to withhold relevant information."[65]

O'Flaherty J. went on to close his judgment by saying:

"I conclude by expressing the hope that parties to litigation will feel able to avail of what has been set out about discovery recently in *Ambiorix Ltd v. Minister for the Environment* [1992] 1 I.R. 277, and in *Murphy v. Minister for Defence* [1991] 2 I.R. 161 and now in this case as an aid to defining the relevant issues and resolving disputes and will remember that these interlocutory matters, such as discovery and interrogatories, are a means to an end and should never be allowed to take on a life of their own."[66]

---

[65] [1993] 1 I.R. 375 at 396–397.
[66] *ibid.* at 397–398.

Concluding comment

22–64　　In England and Wales, the new Civil Procedure Rules, implemented following the proposals of Lord Woolf, have brought about significant changes to the discovery process in that jurisdiction. One of the more significant changes is that, for what is known as "fast-track" cases, discovery, now called "disclosure", is limited to documents which the party making disclosure intends to rely on in the case and documents which materially undermine that party's case or support another party's case. This change has the merit of reducing the quantity of discoverable material very significantly, but has the drawback of placing an onus on the party making discovery to judge whether documents are disadvantageous to that party's case and, if so, to disclose them. It is likely that sufficient time will be allowed to elapse to permit an evaluation of the success or failure of these changes before any similar steps are contemplated in Ireland.

CHAPTER 23 – CONTENTS

FROM THE REPORT TO THE COURT

FROM THE REPORT TO THE COURT

23–01   Chapter 6 has considered the work of accountants in a litigation environment in term of their role, professional standards applying and engagement of forensic accountants. This chapter examines the role of forensic accountants in the courtroom, focusing on the preparation of the forensic accounting report and on the provision of expert testimony.[1]

23–02   Forensic accountants provide independent and objective opinions which should be robust and capable of withstanding challenges in court. Instructing solicitors are provided with reports for use in litigation or negotiations, highlighting any errors or omissions in the claim and its strengths and/or weaknesses. Sworn evidence can be given to the court in the form of sworn affidavits and as a witness under direct examination and cross-examination at the court hearing. In addition, forensic accountants can assist during trials to help counsel formulate questions based on evidence given by the opposing accounting experts. They can assist in providing financial research for cross-examination by the lawyer. Experts may be used in defence cases. They can be asked to conduct a causation investigation. They can test the plaintiff's expert's model for theoretical soundness and they can assist the defence by creating an alternative damage model.

23–03   In order for the forensic accountant to be credible, high ethical standards and an independent approach must be followed (see discussion of independence and objectivity of expert witnesses in paras **6–15** *et seq.*). In particular, forensic accountants should understand what really happened. Unfortunately, there are

---

[1] Other useful material on these issues are to be found in Lemar, C.J. and Mainz, A.J. (eds), *Litigation Support* (4th ed., Butterworths, London, 1999), Chaps 19 and 21; MacGregor, G. and Hobbs, I., *Expert Accounting Evidence: A Guide for Litigation Support* (Accountancy Books, London, 1998), Chaps 4 and 5; Taub, M., Rapazzini, A., Bond, C., Solon, M., Brown, A., Murrie, A., Linnell, K. and Burn, S., *Tolley's Accountancy Litigation Support* (Butterworths, London, looseleaf), Part III, para. 32; Brinig, B.P., "The art of testifying" in *Litigation Services Handbook. The Role of the Accountant as Expert* (2nd ed., Weil, R.L., Wagner, M.J. and Frank, P.B. (eds), John Wiley & Sons, Inc., New York, 1995), Chap. 8; Frank, P.B., Wagner, M.J. and Weil, R.L., "The role of the CPA in litigation services" in *Litigation Services Handbook. The Role of the Accountant as Expert* (2nd ed., Weil, R.L., Wagner, M.J. and Frank, P.B. (eds), John Wiley & Sons, Inc., New York, 1995), p. 1.15–1.16.

clients who do not want to have their expert spend the necessary time to get at the basic truths. Forensic accountants must be allowed the time and resources to do the proper research for the case.

23–04 Well-prepared, carefully reasoned, clear and objective presentation of evidence carries significant weight with a judge and/or jury. Complex analyses need to be translated into simple, effective and clear testimony. Forensic accountants can act as effective communicators by translating complex financial information into simple, concise language that a judge and jury can readily understand.

Expert report writing

23–05 Regardless of who the client is, an expert's objective is to help the court to understand the evidence and to determine a fact that is in dispute. Forensic accountants should prepare reports that are easily understood by key people such as judges, juries, clients and lawyers. The audience for forensic accounting reports is composed primarily of non-accountants and others not familiar with financial information. A narrative setting out in plain language the numbers on which it is based is helpful for the layman's to understanding and is more persuasive. A narrative report backed up by tables is preferable to one which requires the reader to analyse and understand those tables in order to understand the findings.

23–06 The issues examined should be viewed from the standpoint of both parties to the dispute. The opinion should be impartial. The expert should consider his client's case from a critical perspective. The client needs to be advised of the weaknesses of the case, as well as its strengths. It is not in the client's interest for the court to reject the expert's report on the grounds that is it excessively one-sided. The expert report should be well-written, authoritative, fair and unbiased.

23–07 Expert reports should contain simple narratives describing the assignment and the instructions, outlining any assumptions (both those of the expert and those provided in the instructions from the solicitor and client), the materials assembled in preparing the report, the data extracted from those materials, the expert's opinions, and how the data and tables in the report support the opinions provided. The report should include sufficient narrative and observations to demonstrate an understanding of the business and its background. The report should contain sound financial and statistical background and a clear summary of conclusions. The degree of subjectivity and interpretation needs to be kept to a minimum. Hence, the report should not include excessive subjective interpretations or vague conclusions. Where possible and appropriate, the report should cite independent, third party authoritative sources to strengthen the work of the expert and his conclusions.

23–08 The report needs to be logical and professional. The report should follow an orderly and logical progression that leads to conclusions. Calculations in the report should be shown in a step-by-step progression. Each significant calculation should be capable of being re-checked at a later date. In writing the report, every conclusion and each supporting statement should be considered by the expert from the standpoint of being cross-examined about its basis and meaning. Narratives in expert reports must be very precise.

23–09 It is advisable to have someone (preferably familiar with litigation work) to review carefully and critically the report in draft form.[2]

Credibility of the expert report

23–10 An honest, credible, persuasive report is important. The report, for example, should make it clear where persons other than the expert did the work. The experience and qualifications of such persons should be noted, together with an indication of how they were supervised and of how their work was checked. The proportion of the work carried out by the expert personally should be identified.

23–11 The methodology employed should be that which is generally accepted. Any available alternative methods should be considered. The nature of the data relied on and sources of the data should be noted. Any work or procedures to validate the results should be discussed.

23–12 When dealing with quantum, it is more credible for the expert to provide a range of damages, rather than a single amount. Judges and arbitrators realise that arriving at a damages figure is not a simple process. In addition, key damages assumptions are often outside the expert's area of expertise. Providing a range of damages that varies according to changes in assumptions outside the expert's speciality adds to the credibility and usefulness of the report.

23–13 The expert should be prepared to discuss drafts of his report. The expert should keep a record, and make it available if required, of any changes between earlier and final drafts, together with reasons for the changes.

Preliminary reports

23–14 The report should initially be prepared as a draft for submission to the clients and their legal advisers. This will enable them to consider the material in

---

[2] Some useful additional guidance for forensic accountants on preparing expert reports can be found in MacGregor, G. and Hobbs, I., *Expert Accounting Evidence: A Guide for Litigation Support* (Accountancy Books, London, 1998), Chap. 4.

the expert's report, to provide feedback and to eliminate any technical inaccuracies, false assumptions and factual errors. Experts may have to prepare preliminary estimates, but might not be asked to finalise their report until several months later.

It is important for legal advisers to read a preliminary version of the report to see whether the expert may have misinterpreted any of the information they have provided. Sometimes important facts are given informally and may be recorded incorrectly by the expert. Sometimes documents can create misleading impressions. Lawyers can be adept at picking up errors of fact in reports. That is a very important part of the process of checking the validity of the analysis.

Sources for reports

23–15 It is advisable to provide a detailed and complete audit trail in expert reports showing every authority and source used and each step in the calculations. Often expert reports do not contain adequate citations and sources relied upon in the report. The detailed intermediate steps and calculations may also be omitted. Such omissions can convey the impression that the expert does not want the other side to understand how the calculations were arrived at, or that the expert is not confident in the calculations. The absence of such citations, sources or calculations reduces the credibility of the report, and may deprive the court of useful assistance.

Further, by obscuring sources, authorities and calculations, the expert makes his task more difficult when it comes to giving evidence. Court proceedings may take place long after the report is written and the expert may not fully recall all the sources, authorities and calculations relied on. Not only does this put pressure on the expert's memory but it may enable opposing counsel to undermine the expert's poise, the quality of the work performed and the validity of the conclusions reached.

Structure of expert reports

23–16 A number of authors have provided guidance on the structure of expert reports.[3] Sections and headings normally included in expert accounting reports are discussed below.

Overview

23–17 Reports should begin with an overview, summarising the background of the plaintiff's case/business, the nature of the plaintiff's dealings with the

---

[3] Peisley, T., "Accountants as experts" (2000) *Charter*, Vol. 71, No. 2, pp. 66–68. See also nn.1 and 2.

defendant, the allegations contained in the complaint, and a general description of the nature of the damages sought.

Expert reports should include a statement that the expert understands that his duty is to the court and that he has complied with that duty.

Description of engagement or assignment

23–18   Reports should indicate that the expert was engaged by the plaintiff or the plaintiff's lawyer and should provide a brief description of what the expert was asked to do. All instructions (written or oral) which define the scope of the report should be summarised and attached to the report. It may also include a statement that the plaintiff's legal advisers asked the expert to assume that the plaintiff will prevail on liability, and that the expert's role is limited to the calculation of damages resulting from the facts alleged in the complaint.

Expert's opinion

23–19   The expert's opinion should be stated early in the report. The opinion should, if possible, be stated in terms of the allegations and the resulting monetary impact. If there is more than one component of damages, such as lost past profits and lost future profits, the report should provide a summary in the opinion section. Reasons for each opinion should be given and the opinions should be summarised where several opinions are provided.

Nature of work performed

23–20   Work that was performed by the expert and his staff should be described in sufficient detail to provide at least a general understanding of how the expert formed his opinion. This section might state, for example, that the expert has read the complaint, reviewed various specified documents and financial records of the plaintiff, conducted independent research in the industry (including market trends), met with key employees of the plaintiff, toured facilities and developed a damages model. The report should refer to each key document that was considered by the expert in forming his opinion.

The report should highlight any limitations such as lack of information in certain areas. However, insertion of excessive qualifying concerns may weaken the report. Additionally, any limitations of expertise should be highlighted.

Basis of opinion

23–21   The basis of opinion section provides a narrative description of the various financial and non-financial data, and calculations contained in other exhibits, relied upon in arriving at the opinion. The facts, matters and assumptions upon which the report proceeds should be summarised and included in the report, as should the content of any significant documents and other materials which the expert has been instructed to consider.

Any literature or other material used, and all assumptions made, should be listed. The report might describe, for example, the number of years used to calculate lost damages, how estimated lost revenues and related costs were determined, the approach used (*e.g.* "yardstick", "before and after", etc.), and the impact of outside influences unrelated to the defendant's alleged acts (such as industry trends, government regulations, etc.).

Typically, causation issues and evidence are not part of the damage expert's testimony. If the expert has accumulated such evidence and formed an opinion, however, the basis of opinion should be set out in this section. If at any stage the expert's opinion is changed, any party who has been issued with a report should, without delay, be advised of the change.

Experts should declare that they have made all desirable and appropriate inquiries and have not withheld any matters of significance.

Qualifications

23–22 The report should identify and provide details of the expert's qualifications and those of any person who carried out any work on which the expert relies. The expert's qualifications are generally detailed in a separate section of the report, or are separately admitted (in the form of a *curriculum vitae*), or both. Some experts may include a statement that the expert's compensation is not contingent on the outcome of the litigation.

Limitations

23–23 The report should provide a qualification where it is incomplete or inaccurate. The expert should make it clear when a particular question or issue falls outside his field of expertise if it might otherwise be assumed that he considered and/or formed a view on that issue.

Things to avoid in wording reports

23–24 Table 23.1 provides some examples of things to avoid in preparing an expert report. Reports should not in general contain colloquialisms and slang.

Pre-trial procedure

23–25 Forensic accountants will be involved in certain steps that take place between the preparation of expert reports and the hearing of the case.

Exchange of reports

23–26 Exchange of expert reports has been briefly discussed in para. **6–44** and discovery of expert reports has been discussed in paras **22–50** *et seq.*

Table 23.1: Things to avoid in wording a report

(1) "This report is prepared for the purpose of assisting the defence of ..." – suggests bias

(2) "I am experienced in this field" – a commercial dispute, but attached CV only mentions personal injury work

(3) "I interviewed ..." – when it was obvious on cross-examination that it was his staff that interviewed

(4) "I believe ..." – an expert is there to give opinion, which should be based on professional opinion, experience and the facts of the case

(5) "The plaintiff holds a ... licence" – when he held but no longer holds. Tense matters in law

(6) Make sure to specify the correct piece of legislation, *e.g.* Companies Act 1990 or Companies (Amendment) Act 1990

(7) Avoid accounting jargon

(8) Define abbreviations the first time they are used

(9) Adapt the report so that it is suitable for the engagement, *i.e.* a court case or arbitration/mediation

(10) Double-check spelling of names – do not assume names are spelt correctly in any documents given to you

(11) Inclusion of material not relevant to the assessment of plaintiff's post-accident problems

Source: Adapted from *Forensic Group News* (Institute of Chartered Accountants in England and Wales, May 1999), p. 8.

Exchange of reports in personal injury cases

23–27 Until they were amended in certain respects in 1997 and 1998, the Rules of the Superior Courts 1986, which govern practice and procedure in the High Court and the Supreme Court, made no explicit reference to experts, expert witnesses or expert evidence. However, expert evidence has been very much a part of practice in these courts virtually since their establishment. The amendments to the Rules in 1997 and 1998 were made in order to require the exchange of certain reports between the parties to proceedings that involve a claim for damages in respect of any personal injuries. These provisions are designed to ensure that all parties to personal injury proceedings are aware of the case against them and are not "ambushed" at trial. This, in turn, tends to encourage settlement of such proceedings before the case is heard in court.

23–28 The relevant statutory provisions applying only to personal injuries cases, were introduced by section 45 of the Courts and Court Officers Act 1995 and supplemented by Rules of Court in October 1998.[4] These new rules apply in personal injuries litigation only. This does not include personal injuries tried by juries under section 1(3) of the Courts Act 1988 (*e.g.* in cases of alleged assault or false imprisonment by the defendant on the plaintiff).

23–29 The new rules, which apply to reports of experts, make compulsory the exchange of reports by the parties. In cases where there is no significant disagreement between the experts on both sides, there may be no need for the expert to appear in court if the parties so agree. It will be sufficient to supply the reports of the experts for consideration by the court. Even where there is divergence of opinion, pre-trial exchange of reports is likely to narrow the areas of disagreement.

23–30 The Rules of the Superior Courts as amended impose a requirement on each party to litigation involving any personal injuries to disclose any report of any expert witness on whose evidence that party plans to rely for the purposes of the litigation. The rules apply to all proceedings which were instituted on or after September 1, 1997. A party to such proceedings may only rely on a statement or report during the course of the trial of an action where that statement or report has been disclosed in accordance with these rules. The disclosure obligation is imposed in the following terms:

> "The plaintiff in an action shall furnish to the other party or parties or their respective solicitors (as the case may be) a schedule listing all reports from expert witnesses intended to be called within one month of the service of the notice of trial in respect of the action or within such further time as may be agreed by the parties or permitted by the Court.

> Within seven days of receipt of the plaintiff's schedule, the defendant or any other party or parties shall furnish to the plaintiff or any other party or parties a schedule listing all reports from expert witnesses intended to be called. Within seven days of the receipt of the schedule of the defendant or other party or parties, the parties shall exchange copies of the reports listed in the relevant schedule."[5]

23–31 Section 45 of the Courts and Court Officers Act 1995 states:

> "(1) Notwithstanding any enactment or rule of law by virtue of which documents prepared for the purpose of pending or contemplated civil proceedings (or in connection with the obtaining or giving of legal advice) are in certain circumstances privileged from disclosure, the Superior Court Rules Committee, or the Circuit Court Rules Committee as the case may be, may, with the concurrence of the Minister, make rules
>   (a) requiring any party to a High Court or Circuit Court personal injuries action, to disclose to the other party or parties, without the necessity of any application to court by either party to allow such disclosure, by such time or date as may be specified in the rules, the following information, namely—

---

[4] Rules of the Superior Courts (No. 6) (Disclosure of Reports and Statements) 1998 (S.I. No. 391 of 1998). The rules introduced by S.I.s Nos 348 and 471 of 1997 were replaced in their entirety by S.I. No. 391 of 1998.
[5] Rules of the Superior Courts 1986, Ord. 39, r.46(1).

> (i) any report or statement from any expert intended to be called to give evidence of medical or para-medical opinion in relation to an issue in the case;
>
> (ii) any report or statement from any other expert of the evidence intended to be given by that expert in relation to an issue in the case";

23–32   The term "report" for these purposes is defined widely as follows:

> "... 'report' means a report or reports or statement from accountants, actuaries, architects, dentists, doctors, engineers, occupational therapists, psychologists, psychiatrists, scientists, or any other expert whatsoever intended to be called to give evidence in relation to an issue in an action and containing the substance of the evidence to be adduced and shall also include any maps, drawings, photographs, graphs, charts, calculations or other like matter referred to in any such report."[6]

23–33   In the event of non-compliance with these provisions, the court has wide discretion, including the power to:

> "... make such order as it deems fit including an order prohibiting the adducing of evidence in relation to which such non-compliance relates."[7]

23–34   Parties that have previously disclosed their expert reports can withdraw their intention to rely on them, and when they do so any privilege that the document would have attracted prior to its disclosure is restored.

It should be noted that expert reports prepared by experts whom it is not intended to call as witnesses can be communicated in total confidence and cannot be required to be disclosed. This enables parties to engage experts to advise on various aspects of the case and to assist in assessment of the likelihood of success without fear of having to "show their hand" to the other side.

23–35   These rules will therefore affect accountants advising on the liability aspects of personal injuries cases, or relating to the assessment of damages. Time-limits are laid down for furnishing of (i) schedules of and (ii) copies of expert reports by one side to the other. Notwithstanding these new rules, some expert reports can remain privileged (*i.e.* protected from discovery). In particular, the court retains discretion to exempt a particular report or statement or part thereof from the disclosure requirement, on the application of a party, in the interests of justice.

To conclude, expert witnesses should know that their reports will become evidence in personal injuries cases and will be subject to detailed scrutiny by the trial judge and counsel on both sides of the case. Expert reports should

---

[6] Rules of the Superior Courts 1986, Ord. 39, r.45(1).
[7] *ibid.*, r.48.

therefore be factually correct and contain all relevant information necessary for a fair and objective assessment (even if prejudicial). Carefully reasoned arguments should be articulated.

Privilege

23–36　The rule on legal professional privilege (already briefly referred to in paras **6–73, 22–06, 22–30, 22–50** and **22–52**; and see also paras **23–52** *et seq.*) provides an exception to the general rule that all relevant information should be available to all parties to the dispute. The position regarding information passing to and from the solicitor, and also between the client and the third party expert, was summarised in general terms by Keane J. (as he then was) in the High Court in *Breathnach v. Ireland (No. 3)*:

> "There then arises the separate question as to whether any or all of the documents are protected from discovery because of legal professional privilege. That privilege enables a client to maintain the confidentiality of two types of communication:
> (1)　communications between him and his lawyer made for the purpose of obtaining and giving legal advice; and
> (2)　communications between him or his lawyer and third parties (such as potential witnesses and experts) the dominant purpose of which was preparation for contemplated or pending litigation." [8]

Meetings of experts before trial

23–37　It may be valuable for the instructing solicitor to brief the forensic accountant to attend preliminary meetings with the other party's expert(s) on a "without prejudice basis" (see further discussion at paras **22–03** *et seq.*) to resolve specific areas of disagreement or confusion. A "without prejudice" meeting of experts can explore resolution of issues and potential settlement without either party being bound in any way by the content of the discussions unless (*e.g.* on reaching a settlement) both parties agree to be so bound.

Meetings in personal injury cases

23–38　The usual practice is for meetings to take place in personal injury cases after exchange of reports but a meeting before this can offer advantages. Areas of agreement can be identified and undisputed facts and access to information can be agreed. It can be more difficult to reach agreement in post-report meetings – experts will be more resistant to retracting opinions set out previously in writing. However, a post-report meeting can identify weaknesses in an expert's report, and this is preferable to such weaknesses being identified in court.

23–39　Overall, these meetings can be useful in clarifying issues and reducing the costs of litigation. A meeting of experts can identify common ground and, if

---

[8] [1993] 2 I.R. 458 at 470.

possible, resolve any difference of opinion between the experts. Many inconsistencies between forensic accountants arise from differences in the facts which have been presented to them. Pre-trial meetings can help determine whether differences between the accountants' calculations are based on inconsistent understandings of the facts. If so, the inconsistency can be ironed out either between the parties or, if it is a material issue of fact that goes to central issues in the proceedings, a trial of a preliminary issue can be sought. Such meetings can greatly reduce the time spent considering a claim, thus reducing overall cost. This may act as a catalyst for the settlement of the action which could save court time and, consequently, considerable expense.

23–40 Under the new Civil Procedure Rules in England and Wales, experts can be required to hold a meeting to discuss the issues in respect of which they have been engaged. In Ireland, there are no equivalent rules of practice or procedure. However, in practice, where there are complex issues involving experts it is not uncommon for an interchange to take place between the experts, with a view to narrowing the issues or at least understanding the reasons for any significant differences between the parties on key issues.

23–41 Normally lawyers will attend meetings of experts and specify the terms of experts' meetings. Any resulting agreements between experts should be confined to matters of expert opinion, rather than to matters of fact. Experts must recognise that the instructing solicitor will set the limits to these discussions. A meeting of minds will only occur if the experts recognise that their purpose is to try and resolve differences and not engage in point scoring.[9] The tone and demeanour of the participants will determine whether the meeting is adversarial which would make the narrowing of differences between experts more difficult.

Criteria and standards for evaluating experts' qualifications

23–42 The first criterion used to determine whether a court will accept expert opinion evidence is relevance. Case law has established that, unless the court is of the view that a matter at issue is such as to require specialist knowledge and that the proposed expert has sufficient relevant knowledge and expertise, the expert will not be permitted to give opinion evidence.

23–43 The expert accountant must have the appropriate education and training in his field of expertise. Whether a witness is sufficiently qualified as an expert is a matter to be decided by the court. As this issue tends to be addressed and ruled on at the outset of a trial involving expert evidence, there is relatively

---

[9] Carter, D., "Making the most of meetings of experts" in *The Forensic Accountant* (Spring 1994), pp. 4–5.

little reported Irish case law on the issue. However, this should not be taken to indicate that the credentials of experts are rarely challenged. On the contrary, it is common, particularly in large and complex cases, for both sides to cross-examine the other's expert closely on his experience and expertise with a view to undermining the credibility of his evidence.

23–44 The court defines the criteria by which the judge determines who is and who is not an expert. An expert may be qualified as an expert by reason of knowledge, skill, training or experience. The party calling the expert must prove that the expert has scientific, technical or other specialist knowledge. Courts generally favour the admission of expert evidence unless it is clearly unnecessary and, apart from the daily procession of medical and dental practitioners and actuaries giving evidence in connection with claims for damages for pain and suffering and lost earnings arising from personal injuries, Irish courts see a wide variety of other experts from time to time, such as accountants (*e.g.* see *Murnaghan Brothers Ltd v. O'Maoldomhnaigh*[10]), construction experts (*e.g.* see *Groome v. Fodhla*[11]) and even handwriting experts (*e.g.* see *Smyth v. Tunney*[12]).

23–45 In criminal cases, the general rule is that all evidence should be heard in the presence of the jury. However, the judge may conduct a *voire dire*, or trial within a trial, in certain circumstances where there is a possibility that the jury might be prejudiced if they were to hear argument. This arises most frequently where there is some doubt as to whether certain evidence is admissible in the trial. To avoid the jury hearing evidence which may turn out to be inadmissible, the judge will exclude the jury from the hearing relating to admissibility and they will return after he has ruled on the matter.

23–46 This situation can arise when an expert is tendered by one side. As previously pointed out, the expert's opinion evidence will only be admissible if it is relevant, the issue in question is such as to require expert evidence and the proposed expert is suitably qualified. If the judge is asked to rule on the admissibility of expert evidence and if he feels that the argument on the issue could prejudice the jury he will conduct a *voire dire* in the matter.

23–47 In order to assist in establishing his suitability before the court, the accountant should retain an up-to-date *curriculum vitae*. This should be similar in many ways to one which an employee would present to a potential employer, but adapted to establish that the forensic accountant has specialised knowledge on matters for which he has been retained.

---

[10] [1991] 1 I.R. 455.
[11] [1943] I.R. 380.
[12] [1993] 1 I.R. 451.

Potential challenges to qualifications of experts

23–48 As pointed out earlier, in complex contentious cases each side will usually attempt to challenge the expertise and experience of experts tendered by the other side, with a view to influencing the court towards preferring the evidence of their own experts. The types of issues likely to be raised in this process include:

– Does the expert appear to be a theorist lacking in practical experience?

– Is the expert's knowledge broad rather than specific to the relevant issues? For example, the expert may be well-versed in valuing businesses, but may not have adequate experience of the particular type of business involved in the case.

– Is the expert a specialist in an area different from that concerning the case?

– Is the expert's professional record mediocre or flawed?

– Has the expert given any prior testimony or published works inconsistent with expert opinions offered in this case?

– Has any prior testimony or publication by the expert been rebutted or severely criticised?

Going beyond area of expertise

23–49 Expert accountants should be aware that their evidence, or parts of their evidence, may be inadmissible if they express an opinion that goes beyond their field of expertise and about which they do not hold specialised knowledge.

Laws governing expert witness testimony

Procedural rules applying to experts

23–50 Solicitors are only too well aware of the rigours of the procedural requirements of courts and tribunals. However, these requirements also apply to anyone giving expert evidence. Each jurisdiction has procedures particular to it, and expert accountants should refer to the relevant legislation, court rules, practice notes and/or guidelines for the particular jurisdiction in which they are appearing.

Rules regarding admissibility of expert testimony

23–51 As already stated in paras **6–09** *et seq.*, expert opinion testimony is admissible at trial if:

– it is relevant to the determination of the facts at issue;

– it is presented by a witness qualified as an expert;

– it will assist the judge or jury in understanding the evidence or facts at issue.

Although expert evidence often includes a significant amount of opinion and conclusions based on research and facts known to the expert but not presented as evidence in court, nevertheless courts will accept expert evidence that satisfies the criteria listed above. Where an expert uses or quotes from knowledge of research or other facts not presented in court by way of oral evidence given by the source of such information, the expert's evidence of such research or facts is hearsay. The acceptance of such evidence by a court therefore constitutes a judicially-approved exception to the rule against hearsay. For a discussion of the rule against hearsay see paras **22–12** *et seq.*

Client legal privilege

23–52   Privilege as applying to expert reports has already been discussed in paras **6–73, 22–06, 22–30, 22–50, 22–52,** and in para. **23–36**. Legal professional privilege exists to serve the public confidence in the administration of justice by encouraging full and frank disclosure by clients to their lawyers. The expert should, in conjunction with his instructing solicitor, identify the sorts of verbal or written communications and types of documents involving the expert in respect of which the client can and may need to claim privilege in order to prevent their future disclosure to the other side. If the proper procedure is not followed, a party can lose this privilege and this may have undesired consequences for the client.

23–53   All information necessary for a full assessment of the issue should be included in the expert's report, even if it could be embarrassing for the party to the litigation. However, great care should be taken in including such sensitive information.

23–54   In general, legal professional privilege has the effect of exempting from the general requirement to disclose all information relevant to the proceedings details of:

– confidential communications (but not communications made in furtherance of a criminal offence) between a party and his lawyer made for the purpose of obtaining legal advice (but not legal assistance); and

– communications between the party or his lawyer and a third party made in contemplation or furtherance of legal proceedings.

23–55   In the latter category, where there is more than one purpose involved in the communication, the courts apply the "dominant purpose" test. In *Smurfit*

Paribas Bank Ltd v. AAB Export Finance Ltd, Finlay C.J. explained the policy behind the privilege as follows:

> "The existence of a privilege or exemption from disclosure for communications made between a person and his lawyer clearly constitutes a potential restriction and diminution of the full disclosure both prior to and during the course of legal proceedings which in the interests of the common good is desirable for the purpose of ascertaining the truth and rendering justice. Such privilege should, therefore, in my view, only be granted by the courts in instances which have been identified as securing an objective which in the public interest in the proper conduct of the administration of justice can be said to outweigh the disadvantage arising from the restriction of disclosure of all the facts." [13]

23–56 In *Gallagher v. Stanley* O'Flaherty J., before adopting the dominant purpose test, gave the following helpful summary of the purpose and extent of legal professional privilege. He said:

> "The recognition of legal professional privilege goes back many centuries. The privilege attaches to confidential communications passing between lawyer and client for the purpose of obtaining legal advice or assistance and also where litigation is contemplated or pending. Litigation was obviously not in the contemplation of anyone on behalf of the plaintiff at the time that these statements came into existence and, therefore, the question is whether it can be taken as being in contemplation as far as the hospital authorities were concerned. The privilege does not attach to members of the legal profession. It is a privilege of the client, who can always waive it. Its purpose is to aid the administration of justice, not to impede it. In general, justice will be best served where there is the greatest candour and where all relevant documentary evidence is available." [14]

23–57 In the same case Lynch J. adopted the dominant purpose test in the following terms:

> "People as often as not act from mixed motives or for a number of reasons, rather than one single motive or reason. Therefore to require that the sole reason for obtaining the statements the subject matter of this appeal should have been the anticipation or contemplation of litigation is to set too high a test before privilege can arise. The true test is that the anticipation and/or contemplation of litigation should have been the dominant motive or reason. In this regard I would adopt the reasoning in the case of *Waugh v. British Railways Board* [1980] A.C. 521." [15]

23–58 It should be noted that the privilege can be waived at any time by the party in whose favour it operates (but not by the lawyer or the third party).

---

[13] [1990] I.L.R.M. 588 at 594.
[14] [1998] 2 I.R. 267 at 271.
[15] *ibid.* at 273–274.

23–59   So what does this all mean for an accountant who will act as an expert? Irish case law suggests that in most cases (except for reports prepared in personal injury cases where it is intended that the accountant will give evidence) an expert's report(s), drafts of an expert's written opinion, working papers and other documents on the expert's file will be subject to client legal privilege.

Information on which to base testimony

23–60   The responsibility for collecting information required for the expert's report is divided between the expert and the solicitor. Whereas solicitors are expected to provide information specific to a case, such as accounting and financial data, the expert is expected to collect information drawn from his area of specialisation such as knowledge about behaviour of costs (whether fixed or variable with production), methods of valuation, etc.

23–61   A forensic accountant can only base his conclusions on the materials presented. He must clearly indicate, as soon as practical, the materials required to evaluate the case properly. The instructing solicitor may provide the material. The client may also provide information. Forensic accountants rarely have the ideal full complement of information available to them. They have to proceed and do the best job with the information available. Instructing solicitors may not provide all the materials either available or requested. Often the forensic accountant is given important information at a very late stage in a case.

23–62   If the forensic accountant does not have all the materials considered necessary, any assumptions made to compensate for missing information need to be clearly stated, together with the basis for making the assumption.

Sufficient data to enable an opinion to be given

23–63   Normally the division of responsibilities is clear. But grey areas remain as was highlighted in the United States case *Re Brand Name Prescription Drugs Antitrust Litigation*.[16] Less than five days before the trial, an expert economist was asked to prepare a report on the involvement of one of the parties in this competition case. The expert relied on counsel to provide the documents necessary to formulate an opinion. At trial it was shown that counsel failed to provide a number of documents which proved crucial to the case. Not only did the court reject the expert's opinion, it criticised him for failing to obtain the relevant documents. In the court's view, an independent expert was "… obligated to request all of the information necessary to form a well-reasoned opinion and to admit when he lacked sufficient information to adequately render such an

---

[16] W.L. 351178 (ND, Ill) (1996).

opinion". It was incumbent on the expert "… to go beyond what was sent to him by his employing counsel in deciding whether he was in possession of all relevant information".[17]

23–64   In relation to expert opinion, three types of information can be identified as relevant:

Personal

23–65   This would comprise information specific to the client, be it an individual or a company. Forensic accountants need to inform the lawyer of the information needs of the case. If the information cannot be provided, the expert might consider alternative sources (*e.g.* evidence by another expert). Solicitors have been known to withhold from the expert accountant information they consider might be damaging to the client. This practice runs the risk of such information emerging during the trial, and this could be very damaging to the case. The evidence considered by the solicitor to be harmful may only be of minor significance in the view of the expert – however, its significance might be enhanced if it were sprung on the expert during the trial.

Statistical, industry or market background information

23–66   Statistical, industry or market background information applicable to the case should be obtained subject to two constraints – cost and time. It is only the parties to the case who can decide whether the missing information is sufficiently important to justify the additional cost or a delay in proceedings. If the necessary information is not made available, the expert may refuse to become involved in the case or may prepare his report based on the information that is available. In the latter case, the report should note the inadequacy of the information available.

Legal

23–67   Legal information includes information on statutes, common law and regulatory rules. It is not the role of the expert witness to claim expertise in the law. Nevertheless, the expert needs to be aware of the legal principles relevant to the case and he should have knowledge of rules concerning legal issues relevant to his calculations such as choice of discount rate, principle of *restitutio*, etc.

23–68   No expert can be held responsible for information which lies outside his expertise unless he falsely claims to be an expert in the relevant area.

---

[17] See Bruce, C., "The Role of Experts" in *Lawyers Weekly* (September 20, 1996). Also available at www.economica.ca/artic01.htm.

Tendering evidence

23–69 If a claim goes to court, the forensic accountant must be able to clearly and succinctly explain evidence included in his report under: (i) direct, examination-in-chief; (ii) cross-examination; and possibly (iii) re-examination. MacGregor and Hobbs[18] contains an excellent chapter, with copious examples, to assist forensic accountants who have to give evidence in court.

23–70 The expert witness needs to be truthful, and walk the line between advocacy, professionalism and credibility. Underlying all court testimony is the duty to give the court independent, objective and impartial evidence. There are a number of ways in which credibility of the expert can be enhanced.

23–71 The success of the expert's testimony is directly proportional to the amount of pre-trial preparation he has done. Experts and lawyers should work together in advance to discuss the major areas of direct testimony and possible cross-examination questions. A good expert should attempt to provide evidence in an interesting and lively way to keep the judge, jury or arbitration panel engaged. However, it is more important to be clear, comprehensive and credible than to entertain.

23–72 Accountants giving oral evidence may be asked to opine on a number of financial areas in which they lack industry expertise. To enhance credibility, multiple experts might be considered. For example, in a lost profits case three experts might be used – one for market penetration, one for financial considerations and a third for operational considerations. If an expert has to testify outside his main area of expertise, he should ensure that he has evidence to support his assumptions. Where he does not have the necessary information or expertise he should decline to give his opinion. To venture an unsupported or ill-informed opinion is to risk undermining all evidence given, even that which is properly supported and is within the expert's field of knowledge and expertise.

Appearing in court

23–73 When the hearing of the action in which the expert is due to give evidence approaches, counsel will consider the nature of the necessary evidence and the order in which the evidence is to be presented. Ordinarily, witnesses of fact will be heard before the expert's evidence is presented. This is because it is generally easier for the court to understand the context of the expert's evidence when all the relevant facts have already been presented. In addition, the plaintiff's full case (including the evidence of all witnesses) will be presented before the

---

[18] MacGregor, G. and Hobbs, I., *Expert Accounting Evidence: A Guide for Litigation Support* (Accountancy Books, London, 1998), Chap. 5.

defendant's evidence begins (see paras **20–31** *et seq.* for a discussion of the sequence of events at the hearing). This raises the question as to whether the experts should attend the full hearing in order to ensure that they take account in their evidence of all facts and inferences presented to the court. In general, it is advisable that each expert should attend at least all court sessions up to the time of his evidence and also the evidence of his opposite number (the opposing side's expert) if any, or, if this is not possible, that he obtains and reviews a transcript of all such evidence. In lengthy and complex cases this means that the expert may have to commit very significant amounts of time to this attendance and, if this is likely, the basis for the related costs should be specifically agreed in advance and dealt with in the engagement letter (see paras **6–70** *et seq.* for discussion of engagement letters).

Direct examination

23–74   The typical sequence of events in testifying begins by first going through a direct examination conducted by the barrister acting for the expert's party in the litigation. This may have been discussed beforehand and is generally carried out in a friendly manner. There is a risk that direct examination may lull the expert into a false sense of complacency.

23–75   Direct testimony of an expert usually commences by presenting the expert's qualifications, including education and experience. Education and experience should be stated in a manner relevant to issues in the case. For example, the expert's experience of the industry in question in the case might be brought out. Qualifications should be meaningfully explained. After stating the expert's qualifications, the direct examination usually presents the opinions of the expert, and the reasons and data supporting these opinions. Questions will also focus on the scope of the work done by the expert, the methods used and the opinion and conclusions of the expert.

23–76   As already discussed in para. **20–32**, counsel is not permitted to "lead the witness" (*i.e.* ask leading questions) in direct examination. The expert should be familiar with the detail in the report and should be able to withstand cross-examination on the report. The expert must be well prepared so that he can respond comprehensively and appropriately to the open questions asked by his counsel.

Cross-examination

23–77   Cross-examination generally follows direct examination and is conducted by the other side's barrister. Cross-examination by opposing counsel will focus on matters raised in direct testimony but must also deal with matters to be raised in direct evidence by opposing counsel's own witnesses. This latter requirement is to give the opportunity to the plaintiff's expert to respond to points that will be made by his opposite number after his own evidence has concluded. Because of the importance of this opportunity to the fair hearing of the issues, where in direct evidence the defendant attempts to raise an issue or argument not previously put in cross-examination to the plaintiff's witnesses, the judge will usually disallow the evidence, or, at a minimum, permit the plaintiff to recall his expert to rebut the evidence if he so wishes.

23–78 Cross-examination of an expert will usually involve a challenge to his qualifications, objectivity, methodology, data, validity of conclusions, and consistency with prior testimony, publications and generally accepted standards. In order to be able to deal with this, the forensic accountant should be very familiar with his report, files and other paperwork, and with the work of his associates and staff. The expert should be familiar with the detail in the report so that he can withstand cross-examination on the report. The most credible and persuasive experts are those who stand up to the pressures of cross-examination and demonstrate a complete knowledge while doing so. Forensic accountants must be extremely well-prepared and have the facts at their fingertips. There should be no loose ends.

23–79 The questions should be anticipated (if possible) so that they can be answered honestly and fully. It is not improper for forensic accountants to go through expected questions beforehand and to rehearse the responses. Considering the case from the opposing side's perspective, and imagining their probable viewpoint or line of thought, will help. In this way, possible weaknesses of the client case may be revealed.

23–80 It is not unusual for the barrister to discuss his cross-examination of the other side with his own side's expert. This is important especially where the barrister is not comfortable with financial matters or in complex financial cases. The barrister may need help in understanding the other side's expert report.

Procedural rules governing cross-examination

23–81 The scope of cross-examination can be very broad. However, the cross-examining counsel cannot try to discredit the expert's testimony by questioning the content of any technical or professional journals or writings unless those sources have been considered by the expert in reaching his opinion, or have been admitted into evidence (see, *e.g. Bobb v. Modern Products, Inc*[19]).

Re-examination

23–82 The adversarial system is designed to give each side an opportunity to present its case in turn before the judge or jury decides the matter. This process

---

[19] 648 F.2d 1051 at 1057 (5th Cir. 1981).

becomes, in relation to each witness, a single opportunity in turn for each side to examine that witness. As a result, in general there is no "second bite at the cherry" – when counsel concludes his examination of a witness he is assumed to have elicited all relevant evidence from the witness.

23–83   The exception to this rule is when a witness in cross-examination gives evidence on matters not dealt with in direct examination. In such circumstances counsel who called the witness is permitted to re-examine him, but the re-examination must be limited to matters raised in cross-examination. The prohibition on leading questions applies to re-examination in the same way as it applies to direct examination.

23–84   When being re-examined the expert should attempt as far as possible to remain consistent to his direct evidence in order to avoid damage to his credibility. The following extract from the judgment of Sullivan C.J. in *Re Hafner: Olhausen v. Powderley* is instructive in this regard:

> "The expert evidence on that matter was given by three chartered accountants:— Mr. Brock, who was examined on behalf of the plaintiff, and Mr. Purtill and Mr. Shortall, who were witnesses for the defendants. The evidence of Mr. Purtill and of Mr. Shortall would support the contention of the defendants' counsel, as would the evidence of Mr. Brock on his examination-in-chief, with which his evidence on re-examination does not seem to be quite consistent.
>
> We think that the weight of evidence on this point is in favour of the view expressed by Mr. Purtill and Mr. Shortall, and Black J., who had the advantage of seeing and hearing these witnesses, says that he was disposed to agree with that view."[20]

Questions from the bench

23–85   The trial judge is at liberty to ask questions of any witness at any time, and will often do so in order to confirm or clarify statements made in evidence. Some judges will wait until cross-examination (and, if necessary, re-examination) is complete before asking questions. Others will intervene in the course of evidence.

In all cases the duty of the expert remains the same, *i.e.* to answer truthfully and clearly in order to assist the court in the resolution of the matter at hand.

Responses to questions and cross-examination

23–86   Courtroom poise and presence is important. Some suggestions concerning the demeanour of experts is provided in Table 23.2.

---

[20][1943] I.R. 426 at 475.

Table 23.2: Demeanour of the expert

- Be frank and direct
- Be authentic
- Do not exaggerate qualifications
- Do not surrender objectivity
- Do not become defensive
- Do not be impatient or impolite
- Do not be arrogant or pompous
- Do not be evasive

23–87   Table 23.3 summarises the "Ten Commandments" of expert testimony, which are recommended subject to reservations concerning item 5. Some documents may be essential given the evidence being tendered.

Table 23.3: "Ten Commandments" of expert testimony

1. Always tell the truth but answer only the question asked
2. Think before answering
3. Never answer a question you do not understand
4. Do not guess or speculate
5. Do not bring notes, diagrams, books or other written material to the court unless required by a subpoena or the lawyer
6. Listen carefully to each objection made by the lawyer
7. Do not argue or become angry or hostile with the examining lawyer
8. Even if a question calls for a yes or no answer, ask to explain your response if you feel a qualification or explanation is required to complete your answer
9. Be wary of questions that involve absolutes
10. Do not memorise the answers before the trial

Source: adapted from Frank, P.B., Wagner, M.J. and Weil, R.L., "The role of the CPA in litigation services" in *Litigation Services Handbook. The Role of the Accountant as Expert* (2nd ed., Weil, R.L., Wagner, M.J. and Frank, P.B. (eds), John Wiley & Sons, Inc., New York, 1995), pp. 8.2–8.3.

23–88   Some dos and don'ts in giving evidence are summarised in Table 23.4 which advice might be adapted for Irish courts. Lemar and Mainz also provide a useful list of dos and don'ts in cross-examination.[21]

Things to do in giving evidence

Clarity and simplification

23–89   If a claim goes to court, the practitioner should be able clearly and succinctly to explain evidence included in the accounting expert's report under examination-in-chief and under cross-examination. A concise clear explanation

---

[21] Lemar, C.J. and Mainz, A.J. (eds), *Litigation Support* (4th ed., Butterworths, London, 1999), App. H.

Table 23.4: Strategies and tactics that the expert may employ

DO	DON'T
√ Listen carefully to each question, and be sure you understand it	✗ Don't volunteer – just answer the question asked
√ Ask that compound questions be broken down into their individual component parts. If the questioner does not do so, the expert should proceed to do this task	✗ Don't guess – if unsure, say so ✗ Don't bring any documents with you ✗ Don't let yourself be speeded up or rattled – some opposing counsel will subtly increase the tempo of the questioning in order to induce the expert to answer hastily
√ Request that the questioner define any technical terms used in questions	
√ Take time to think before answering	✗ Don't try to stretch your qualifications or your opinions
√ Ask to refer to documents if needed, especially if a question refers to one or more specific documents	✗ Don't accept implicit assumptions in questions – ask that assumptions be made explicit
√ Make each answer stand alone – it may be read back out of context	✗ Don't accept as true assumptions made by the questioner – a document may not state exactly what a lawyer says it states
√ Be polite, even if the questioner provokes or insults you	
√ Beware of hypotheticals – often they are traps. Make sure that the questioner clearly states all assumptions in the hypothetical, and then carefully repeat all of the assumptions in your answer. It is also worth stating in your answer that these assumptions do not correspond with the facts of the case at hand if this is so	✗ Don't be reluctant to admit that you have discussed things with client counsel – that is not objectionable ✗ Don't simply agree if you are asked "do you agree with the following . . . ?" –you may wish to qualify your answer to allow for exceptions or special cases
√ Beware of questions dealing in extremes with terms such as "always", "never", "certain" or "possible". The question may be designed to paint you into a corner	✗ Don't display inappropriate or distracting mannerisms.
√ Hold firm to your genuine opinions, but be open to new data. Make it clear that you keep an open mind.	

Source: Adapted from Livingstone, J.L., "Expert testimony in the United States: Some do's and don'ts" in *The Expert* (March 1997), p. 10.

of complex accounting issues can win the case. The person who is easiest to understand is often the most believable. Expert witnesses should be able to make complex financial and accounting issues understandable to a judge and jury and explain the issues in basics that are readily understandable to all.

John Previts, an actuary of considerable courtroom experience in the United Kingdom, provides very personal insights into the performance of expert witnesses "on the stand":

> "I have probably given evidence as often as any other UK actuary over a period of 30 years or so, and the over-riding lesson is that you must make a supreme effort not to get rattled while in the box.
>
> Counsel for the opposition is likely to adopt one of two techniques in cross-examination. The first is to ignore you. In the classic Perry Mason phrase, counsel will say to the judge 'I have no questions for this witness' in the hope that the judge will also ignore your evidence. The other technique, which I have certainly experienced more often, is to get you so confused and irritated that the judge will also be confused by your evidence, placing little weight on your contribution when it comes to formulate the judgment."[22]

Confidence

23–90   The only reason experts are asked to testify is to give an opinion. Opinion evidence should be given in a confident way. Expert witnesses should be accurate, firm and definite. They should state an opinion, defend their opinion and stick to the opinion because prior research has justified arriving at that opinion, and resulting documentation supports that opinion. Unconvincing phrases such as "I believe", "it seems", "it is possible" and "I would say" can quickly undermine expert opinion and are an invitation for additional cross-examination. Counsel may be able to have the entire testimony discredited because "expert guessing" is not allowed under the rules of evidence.

Open-ended questions/conciseness

23–91   If possible, questions should be answered with a yes or no response. If counsel attempts to insist on a yes or no answer to questions that cannot be answered in that fashion, the expert can state, "I cannot answer that question with a yes or no reply". It will then be up to counsel to either let the expert explain his answer or counsel may have to rephrase his question.

Open-ended questions invite long, rambling answers. Counsel may be trying to get information which will be used during cross-examination. Open-ended questions should be answered as concisely as possible, with care being taken not to provide information that was not asked for. Experts are better served by brief, succinct replies to open-ended questions. It is for counsel to ask follow-up questions.

---

[22] Previts, J., "The actuary as an expert witness" in *The Actuary* (December 1999), p. 23.

Honesty

23–92   Experts should answer questions honestly. If an expert does not know the answer to a question this should be admitted. The more the expert hesitates or tries to avoid saying "I don't know" the more emphasis may be given to this lack of knowledge by the judge or jury. If experts allow themselves to get flustered, their lack of knowledge will be emphasised to the jury.

23–93   When asked about a fact, situation, or occurrence that the expert honestly does not remember, the best answer is to admit not remembering. The simple, direct and best response is, "I don't know". There is nothing wrong with this response if the expert genuinely does not know the answer to the question. However, an endless string of "I don't knows" (or even one that may seem hard to believe) may tend to damage credibility. If the expert's response is that he does not recall counsel may then attempt to refresh his memory.

The throwaway statements that come after the "but" or "I don't know" reply help counsel by providing him with additional information. This type of reply frequently results in new lines of inquiry and detailed questioning by counsel.

Mistakes

23–94   Expert witnesses are not expected to be perfect. During a long and arduous examination, experts may make a mistake or error. If errors have been made, they should be corrected as soon as possible. Counsel may quickly challenge experts on mistakes before there is an opportunity to correct them. In that case, experts should admit errors graciously. What should be avoided after making a mistake is making the matter even worse by an inability or unwillingness to admit the mistake. This could give the appearance of bias.

Unclear and compound questions

23–95   Questions that cannot be understood should not be answered. If the question is confusing, the preferred answer is, "I don't understand the question". However, answers must be truthful and the answer, "I don't understand" is only appropriate when that is the actual case. Caution should be exercised in giving such a response – it might undermine the expert's credibility.

23–96   Frequently, barristers attempt to confuse the expert by asking compound questions; that is, two or more questions combined. Sometimes the question is asked in a stream of consciousness manner that is difficult to comprehend, let alone answer accurately. When faced with such questions, rephrasing and clarification of the question, and a breakdown into simpler questions, should be requested.

Errors to avoid in giving evidence

23–97   An expert should be thoroughly prepared and should not enter into new areas of testimony during the case which he does not fully understand and for which he is not fully prepared.

Advocacy

23–98   One mistake often made by experts is behaving as an advocate. While it is accepted that each expert represents one side, and that within reason each expert will take the position that favours his client, experts should provide testimony that is fair, even-handed, and as unbiased as possible. The expert should demonstrate that he is following the facts, not his client's emotions.

Incomplete information

23–99   Believing it to be in the best interests of their clients, experts sometimes have a tendency not to present the whole picture, thus creating an unbalanced assessment of the situation. Some people believe it is wise to filter information provided to the expert, and to hold back certain facts about the client or case from the expert. Usually this is a bad idea. It is best to assume that the opposing side knows the whole story. If that is the case, if the expert takes the stand without all the facts, the expert's testimony may be weakened. The reliability and credibility of the expert may be undermined on cross-examination if such a biased approach is taken.

23–100   Sometimes the client filters information provided to the lawyers. To guard against this, the expert should do an independent investigation of the client to reveal any inconsistencies in the client's version of the facts. The expert might examine annual reports, read newspaper articles, conduct research on the Internet, or interview other people in the same industry.

Avoid absolute words

23–101   Absolute words such as "always", "never", etc., should be avoided where possible. These are frequently an invitation to, and fertile ground for, cross-examination by counsel. Counsel will attempt to damage the expert's credibility by extracting absolute statements. Counter examples may then be used in an effort to show the falsity or inappropriateness of the statements made.

Do not elaborate or volunteer

23–102   Generally, an expert should only answer the questions asked and should not volunteer information. Volunteering information will almost always result in new lines of cross-examination. It may also disclose information to which counsel would otherwise never have become privy. Volunteering information can be one of the biggest mistakes an expert makes. Keeping answers short can help greatly in avoiding this pitfall.

Unfounded assumptions

23–103 Unfounded or unsupported assumptions should not be made in an attempt to answer questions. If the question cannot be answered, or the expert does not have an answer to the question, this should be stated. Assuming is akin to guessing and should be avoided. A better answer might be, "I don't know".

Concessions

23–104 A very common error made by experts is their failure to concede an obvious and irrefutable point out of misguided loyalty to the client's case. In answering questions honestly, occasional concessions may have to be made. Making concessions graciously may enhance the expert's confidence, integrity, and flexibility. Otherwise, in sticking rigidly to a position, the expert may appear inflexible and partisan.

Avoid slang

23–105 Slang expressions should be avoided when replying to questions. When they are transcribed and read back to a jury, these expressions diminish the value of expert responses. Most slang expressions slip from experts unintentionally. Avoidance of such slips requires concentration and focus.

Counsel's "bumble and fumble" gambit

23–106 Experts are frequently tricked into volunteering key information by counsel apparently bumbling or fumbling with some type of technical question. Counsel sometimes use this bumble and fumble technique deliberately. Experts should not assist counsel in framing questions but should wait for the question and then answer it correctly.

Speculation and hoping

23–107 Expert witnesses are under oath to tell the truth. Expert testimony will help resolve the rights and liabilities of parties who are involved in a legal dispute. Accordingly, there is no place for guesswork. Guesses are not admissible in evidence and can only damage the expert's credibility. It should be avoided.

23–108 At trial, many experts do not practice this principle and, in fact, speculate freely. One of the most common forms of speculation by experts at trial is the "I do not know, but…" reply. It is usually a mistake to use this response. First of all, if experts do not know, then any information provided after the "but" is mere speculation. Secondly, damaging information may be volunteered after the "but".

23–109   Experts should take care not to be tricked, cajoled, or forced into speculating when answering questions under oath. There is nothing wrong with the response, "I'm sorry, but I'm not going to speculate on that".

23–110   Sophisticated counsel may attempt to trap the expert witness by the use of the word "hope". If the expert inadvertently agrees with such an assertion, this may allow the lawyer to successfully call into question the reliability of the expert opinion. When confronted with an "and you are hoping ..." question, it may be best to actively refute the question. Experts should remember that passive agreement to a barrister's characterisation or mischaracterisation is in effect letting the barrister put words in the expert's mouth.

23–111   The view of the courts on speculation by experts is evident from the judgment of Morris J. (as he then was) in *Lindsay v. Mid-Western Health Board*.[23] Several expert medical witnesses gave evidence as to the likely or possible causes of a loss of consciousness and subsequent brain damage suffered by an eight-year-old girl in the aftermath of an appendix operation. Some of the defendant's expert witnesses had sought to explain the cause of the plaintiff's condition as a viral infection. Morris J. dealt with some of the expert evidence as follows:

> "Accordingly, as I see this aspect of the case the defendant is asking me to accept a viral explanation for the cause of [the plaintiff's] brain damage but, at the same time, every one of the defendant's witnesses has been at pains to stress that what they are proposing is no more than a theory and that they do not know and probably never will know what happened. Professor O'Donoghue refers to the theory as 'pure speculation'. It emerges in the course of the defendant's evidence that none of them has ever considered that it was necessary to document this theory in any of the medical journals nor lecture on it notwithstanding the fact that they are the authors of numerous publications and are actively concerned in the teaching of students. It is my opinion that I should accept the defendant's proposal as no more than what Professor O'Donoghue describes, as 'pure speculation'. I believe that if there was any weight in this theory carrying the support of such eminent medical practitioners, the risks associated with the administration of an anaesthetic where it is thought that the patient had a viral infection would have received substantial exposure. ... I think it would be quite wrong for the court to adopt a theory based on pure speculation as being a reasonable explanation for what occurred."[24]

23–112   Morris J.'s decision in favour of the plaintiff was reversed on appeal to the Supreme Court and in his judgment O'Flaherty J. modified somewhat the view expressed in the High Court judgment on the issue of speculation by the experts. He said:

---

[23] [1993] 2 I.R. 147.
[24] [1993] 2 I.R. 147 at 174–175.

"The furthest the defendant got was to suggest as possibilities other means by which the plaintiff sustained her injuries. I believe this evidence is not, however, to be regarded as totally inadmissible. It was legitimate, I believe, for the defendant to adduce evidence of possibilities, remote though they might be, as an explanation; in contradistinction to saying that it could not offer *any* explanation of any description whatsoever. It went to provide some corroboration, as well, that there was no negligence on its part in the administration of the anaesthetic."[25]

23–113   It is clear that the courts will, with reluctance, accept speculation from an expert as to the cause of an occurrence if no stronger basis for an explanation exists. Otherwise such speculation would not be allowed.

Possibility

23–114   The use of the word "possible" can be open to misinterpretation. Testifying that something is merely "possible" is most likely legally insufficient. If an opinion is only a mere possibility, the judge may well not allow it to be presented to the jury as evidence.

Concluding comment

23–115   Whilst it is tempting to believe that the greatest benefit that an expert brings to litigation is his knowledge, experience and expertise in his chosen profession, the reality to be observed in courtrooms on a regular basis is somewhat different. In practice, experts, whose relative levels of expertise are similar, will be retained in significant cases on both sides and will find that they agree on many aspects of the case and disagree on some. The task of the court is to prefer the evidence of one side (including the expert) over the other in order to resolve the issue.

In fact, the question of which expert's evidence is preferred often turns on the clarity with which the expert presents his evidence and the confidence and competence apparent from his words and body language. An ability to make complex or technical points clear and intelligible is founded on a thorough understanding of the subject-matter in addition to training in presentation and communication skills and plenty of practice. To achieve such ability requires hard work and discipline – but the enormous difference that results makes the effort worthwhile.

---

[25] *ibid.* at 184–185.

APPENDICES

APPENDICES – CONTENTS

APPENDIX 1

OUTLINE COMPLETION CHECKLIST FOR A
FORENSIC ACCOUNTING ASSIGNMENT

This appendix contains a suggested completion checklist that can be used to ensure that the forensic accountant addresses all significant issues in the acceptance, performance and reporting results of his work, and in delivering expert testimony. It does not purport to be comprehensive and clearly does not encompass all of the detailed steps carried out in any specific engagement. In addition, it does not take account of matters and issues specific to particular industries or particular types of court proceedings.

The list of questions should be used as an aide memoire to ensure that certain important steps have been considered and can be tailored for specific circumstances.

DETAILED CHECKLIST

1. Engagement acceptance

1.1 Have all the details necessary to decide whether the engagement should be accepted been obtained? These should include:
- identity of all parties to the dispute;
- identity of key individuals from each of the parties;
- identity of the key advisers (including solicitors, auditors, tax advisers, other experts and others) to each party;
- summary of the nature of the dispute and the matters in issue;
- indication of the stage that the dispute has reached;
- proposed timetable for the involvement of the expert accountant;
- projected timing for the bringing of the proceedings to a conclusion;
- any proposed restrictions on the scope of the work of the expert accountant;
- any proposed fee arrangements.

1.2 Would there be any actual or potential conflict of interest if the expert were to accept the engagement? Factors to consider in this assessment include:
- personal or family relationships with any of the parties or individuals identified as involved in the dispute;

- financial interests held by the accountant, his partners, professional colleagues or immediate family, directly or indirectly, in any of the parties;
- professional relationships, including services carried out in the past or currently being provided, involving the proposed expert or his professional colleagues and any of the parties or individuals identified as involved in the dispute;
- previous or current involvement in any material issue involved in the case, even if none of the parties was involved;
- any proposed contingent fee arrangements.

1.3 Would there be any perceived conflict of interest if the expert were to accept the engagement? Similar considerations apply here but the matter must be viewed from the perspective of the reasonable outsider.

1.4 Has it been clearly agreed, understood and acknowledged that the expert's first duty will be to the court, even if this has a potentially adverse effect on the prospects of success of the party on whose behalf he is to be engaged?

1.5 Does the expert himself have, or have within his team, the necessary competence to perform the assignment?

1.6 Does the expert himself have, or have within his team, the necessary experience in the provision of forensic accounting services, including the preparation of reports for use in such assignments and the giving of evidence in court?

1.7 Does the expert himself have, or have within his team, the necessary relevant knowledge for the assignment, including industry knowledge, general legal knowledge and knowledge of factors affecting the principal matters in dispute?

1.8 Do the proposed timetables give adequate time to complete the assignment comprehensively, including the completion of all quality control procedures?

1.9 Are any limitations placed on the scope of the expert's work reasonable and of no likely adverse effect on the quality, comprehensiveness, timeliness or objectivity of the expert's work and conclusions?

1.10 Is the basis of fees clearly understood and acceptable?

1.11 Has an overall risk assessment, performed in relation to the proposed assignment, including consultation with another senior professional if deemed necessary, concluded that the risks associated with the engagement are acceptable?

1.12 Should the engagement be accepted?

2. Engagement letter

2.1 Has an engagement letter been drafted that deals, at a minimum, with the following matters in a clear and acceptable manner:
- the provision by the instructing solicitor of full and detailed instructions and access to all relevant documentation, correspondence, legal pleadings, etc.;
- the services to be provided, including the detailed scope of the work, the timetable for its completion and the provision of reports and expert testimony;
- confidentiality of materials passing between the expert and his instructing solicitor (and their client);
- intellectual property rights of any original work of the expert;
- the extent to which the expert will attend the hearing of the action, including the oral evidence of his opposite number;
- the basis for fees and expenses and billing arrangements;
- the assumption of liability by various parties in the event that a dispute arises out of or in connection with the services provided by the expert accountant;
- resolution of disputes between the parties;
- the fact that the expert's first duty is to the court.

2.2 Has the engagement letter been signed, in advance of the commencement of substantive work by the expert or on his behalf and on behalf of the instructing solicitor?

3. Performance of work

3.1 Has the agreed work been performed competently by appropriately qualified and experienced individuals and subjected to an appropriate level of review?

3.2 Have any matters arising from review been properly and appropriately resolved?

3.3 Have any issues arising in relation to the scope of work, availability of information or other matters of dispute involving the performance by the expert of his work been satisfactorily resolved?

3.4 Have all necessary meetings and consultations (including meetings with the client, the instructing solicitors, counsel and representatives of the other side, as appropriate) been attended by the expert and issues raised resolved appropriately?

3.5 Has the expert complied with all relevant codes of professional conduct and ethical rules in the acceptance and performance of the engagement?

3.6 Have all duties of confidentiality been observed in relation to the assignment?

4. Reporting

4.1 Has a draft report dealing with all material issues been prepared in accordance with agreed arrangements? Has it been appropriately reviewed and subjected to all necessary quality review procedures?

4.2 Is the draft report clear, concise and user-friendly?

4.3 Are the expert's conclusions summarised in one section of the draft report and cross-referenced to the relevant detailed content where the basis for each conclusion is explained?

4.4 Does the draft report distinguish between matters of fact and matters of opinion? Does it distinguish between facts assumed by the expert based on his instructions, facts known to the expert or ascertained first-hand by him, facts obtained from other sources (citing the source in each case), and opinions provided by others (again citing sources)?

4.5 Does the draft report describe the background to the dispute, the presence or absence of any conflict of interest, the scope of the expert's work and a description of the work performed?

4.6 Are all relevant exhibits, listings, schedules and other similar items appended to the draft report and referred to clearly in the main body of the draft report?

4.7 Has the draft report been subjected to appropriate quality control procedures in time for issues arising from such procedures to be properly disposed of?

4.8 Have all issues raised in connection with the draft report been disposed of appropriately and have all necessary consequential amendments been made to the report?

4.9 Has the final report been signed (confirming that all opinions stated in it are those of the expert), dated and delivered in accordance with agreed arrangements?

5. Evidence

5.1 Have all necessary and appropriate preparations been made for the delivery of expert testimony?

5.2 Has all necessary and appropriate input been given by the expert to his instructing lawyers in relation to his evidence and that of his opposite number?

5.3 Has the expert given full and comprehensive evidence that is objective and fair, in accordance with the terms of engagement?

6. Completion

6.1 Has the engagement been concluded and all fees and expenses billed and collected?

6.2 Have all necessary and appropriate working papers been filed and retained and the balance of papers destroyed in accordance with policy?

6.3 Has the client been asked for feedback on the quality of service delivered by the expert and associated matters and has the feedback been received and acted upon where appropriate?

SAMPLE FORENSIC ACCOUNTING ENGAGEMENT LETTER[1]

Dear Client/Solicitor,

Litigation proceedings

We understand that *you/your client* wish/es to retain our firm in relation to *your/their* .... proceedings.

Prior to undertaking any substantial work on *your/your client's* behalf, we wish to clarify for *you/your client* the basis upon which this firm is prepared to act for *you/your client*, the way in which we would, if retained, charge for work done on your behalf and your obligations in relation to the payment of our costs.

1. Purpose and scope

1.1 We have been advised that *you/your client* would like us to:
   [insert full description of professional assignment]

1.2 To the extent *you/your client* ask us to reach conclusions or form opinions, we are obliged to do so without regard to the impact that our conclusions may have on the litigation.

1.3 We have also found that we are often required to perform additional work to that originally agreed resulting from either the findings of our initial engagement or our discussions with counsel.

1.4 We note that it is impractical to obtain instructions on every aspect of our involvement in this litigation matter and there will often be instances where we will have to use our discretion in determining the work to be performed.

---

[1] *Source:* Adapted from the Institute of Chartered Accountants in Australia Forensic Accounting Special Interest Group's submission to the Australian Law Reform Commission, June 1999.

2. Timing

2.1 *You/your client* have/has indicated to us that *you/your client* requires this engagement to be completed by *[Date of Completion]*. We anticipate that we will be able to meet this timetable, provided we receive the necessary information in a timely manner.

3. Conflict of interest

3.1 We have performed an internal search for potential client conflicts based upon the names of the parties that *you/your client* have/has provided. We are not aware of any circumstances that, in our view, would constitute a conflict of interest or would impair our ability to provide objective assistance in this matter. Should any unforeseen conflicts arise that would impair our ability to perform objectively, we would advise *you/your client* immediately and determine our continued involvement in the engagement.

4. Legal professional privilege and confidentiality

4.1 We understand that all communications between ourselves and you *[only applicable to solicitors]* as legal advisers, as well as any materials or information developed or received by us, whether oral or written, may be protected by legal professional privilege and they will as such be treated by us as confidential.

4.2 Any written reports or other documents which we prepare are to be used only for the purpose of this litigation and may not be published or used for any other purpose without our written consent.

5. Staffing and billings

5.1 The professional staff assigned to your litigation matter will perform work under the ultimate supervision of a partner or principal.

5.2 Each litigation report is unique in its preparation and presentation. It is therefore not possible for us to furnish a precise estimate of our final costs as they will be subject to many factors.

5.3 Our fees are based upon the time necessarily spent on the assignment by our staff with the appropriate level of skill and experience. Costs relating to the work performed by the people assigned to the engagement are charged on the basis of time units of *[insert method of charging]*. This method of time costing applies to all attendances, such as conferences, telephone calls, attendances at court and travelling and waiting time.

5.4 The current average hourly rate *(or detailed breakdown per level of staff)* for all professional and support staff is €......... Our charge out rates are reviewed on *[insert review dates]* each year.

5.5 Disbursements such as photocopying, courier, facsimile, telephone, search fees and travelling expenses will be itemised separately and charged as incurred.

5.6 Based on our understanding of the work that we have been asked to undertake at this time, we estimate that our fees may be in the vicinity of €....... to €......... *[Optional]* – A retainer of €........ will be payable prior to the commencement of our work and is included in our estimate of fees. This estimate of our fees excludes the cost of disbursements and any additional work undertaken by us at your request (or your counsel's request) in the future.

5.7 As we have stated above, this is an estimate only and could vary for any number of reasons. This estimate does not amend or replace our basis of charging as set out above but is indicative only and subject to additional work being undertaken during the course of our investigation, as deemed necessary by ourselves, yourself, or your client.

5.8 We will notify *you/your client* in the event that our costs will exceed the above preliminary estimate prior to additional costs being incurred. At that time we will provide *you/your client* with a further estimate of the overall fee.

5.9 As *you/your client* have/has engaged our services in this matter, our billings will be directed to *you/your client*. We understand that *you/your client* accept/s responsibility for their payment. Our fees will be billed on a *[weekly, monthly, periodic]* basis, detailing the work undertaken on your behalf during that period. Our terms require payment within *[insert days]* from the date of invoice. Any unpaid amounts will attract interest at our overdraft rate (presently ....%).

5.10 Our fee is not contingent upon the final results and we do not warrant or predict results or final developments in this matter.

5.11 If *you/your client* wish/es to retain our services, please complete the confirmation and return a signed copy of this letter to our office. Please note that we will not be able to commence any substantial work on your behalf until we have received the signed agreement *[optional – and a cheque for the retainer of €........]*. We will send you an invoice to acknowledge the payment of the retainer once it has been received by us.

5.12 In addition to our fees, *you/your client* agree/s to pay any tax or other charge imposed on us (now or in the future) in relation to any transactions arising in connection with, or as an outcome of, this agreement including (but not limited to) a goods and services tax.

6. Limitation of liability

6.1 We shall use reasonable skill and care in the provision of the services set out in this letter.

6.2 We shall accept liability to pay damages for losses arising as a direct result of breach of contract or negligence on our part in respect of services provided in connection with, or arising out of, the engagement set out in this letter (or any variation or addition thereto). However, such liability of *[insert firm name]*, its partners and staff (whether in contract, negligence or otherwise) shall in no circumstances exceed *[insert number]* times the fees paid in the aggregate in respect of all such services.

6.3 *You/your client* agree/s to hold our firm, its partners, and employees harmless from any liabilities, costs and expenses relating to, or arising from this engagement (including, without limitation, legal fees and the time of our personnel involved) incurred by reason of any action we take in good faith (unless we are negligent).

6.4 *You/your client* agree/s that if *you/your client* make/s any claim against us for loss as a result of a breach of our contract, and that loss is contributed to by *your/your client's* own actions, then liability for *your/ your client's* loss will be apportioned as is appropriate having regard to the respective responsibility for the loss, and the amount *you/your client* may recover from us will be reduced by the extent of *your/your client's* contribution to that loss.

If *you/your client* have/has any questions regarding the scope of our engagement, or if any of the terms of this agreement are otherwise unclear, please contact .... of this office and we will discuss the matter at no cost to *you/ your client*.

Please sign hereunder if you are in agreement with the terms of this engagement letter.

We look forward to hearing from *you/your client*.

Yours faithfully,

APPENDIX 3

GLOSSARY

This glossary is intended to provide helpful explanation for common accounting and legal terms. The explanations provided are not definitive – some terms may be defined more explicitly in legislation.

a fortiori: all the more so.

a priori: from pre-existing knowledge.

account: a formal record of a particular type of transaction (as indicated by the title of the account) expressed in money or other unit of measurement and kept in a ledger. These are often referred to as "T" accounts because they are written in a T format as shown by the following example:

Bank Account

Bal. b/d	100	150	Cash purchases
Cash sales	200	150	Bal. c/d
	300	300	

accounting assumptions: see accounting principles.

accounting entities: accounting entities are business units for which accounting information is prepared. Accounts are prepared for a business entity – not for the owners of that entity.

accounting period: the period of time at the end of which financial statements are prepared – usually a 12-month period.

accounting policies: the methods of accounting selected by businesses as being most appropriate to their circumstances. Examples of items for which companies generally have an accounting policy include consolidation, depreciation, stock, bad debts, research and development, etc. The accounting policies are usually shown in the financial statements at the start of the notes to the accounts.

accounting principles: the broad basic assumptions underlying the preparation of the financial statements. Five accounting principles are mentioned in the Companies (Amendment) Act 1986 – (i) accruals (also called the matching principle), (ii) consistency, (iii) going concern, (iv) prudence and (v) the prohibition on netting assets and liabilities (*i.e.* gross amounts should be shown in the financial statements, not net amounts of assets less liabilities). Accounting standards identify two of these – going concern and accruals – as fundamental accounting concepts.

881

accounting records: documents in which the accounting transactions of a business are recorded.

accounting standards: pronouncements of the accounting profession outlining accounting and disclosure rules applying to a variety of accounting transactions and items. Observance of the accounting standards provides prima facie evidence that the accounts give a true and fair view (as required by law). Older standards applicable in Ireland and the United Kingdom are called Statements of Standard Accounting Practice (SSAPs); more recent standards are referred to as Financial Reporting Standards (FRSs).

accrual accounting: also called the matching principle. The recognition of transactions, assets and liabilities when they occur, and not just when cash is received and paid. Revenues and expenses are matched in so far as their relationship can be determined and are accounted for in the same accounting period. Nearly all accounts are prepared on this basis. The alternative is the cash basis of accounting.

accruals: income earned not yet received (shown as an asset, as the income is receivable) and expenses incurred not yet paid (shown as a liability, as the payment is due in respect of the product or service already consumed by the accounting entity).

actus reus: a guilty act, usually a criminal offence, performed by someone.

ad idem: in agreement, or of the same mind.

adjudication: process by which an independent third party resolves disputes as they arise without the formality of court, arbitration or other proceedings.

affidavit: sworn written voluntary statement of facts.

allegation: unproven assertion, usually that a wrong has been committed or of an element of the wrong.

alternative dispute resolution (ADR): collective term to describe various forms of dispute resolution other than court proceedings, including arbitration, mediation and conciliation.

amortisation: the periodic allocation of the cost of fixed assets in the balance sheet to the profit and loss account. The terms amortisation and depreciation are similar – amortisation is often used in respect of intangible fixed assets.

Anton Piller order: a court order, granted *ex parte* in very unusual circumstances, on foot of which a party can seize documents and other items in the possession of another party without advance warning on the grounds that the items in question are in imminent danger of destruction and are relevant to proceedings between the parties.

appearance: the document used by a defendant on whom a summons is served to indicate to the Central Office of the High Court and to the plaintiff's solicitor the identity of the defendant's solicitor (if any) and the defendant's intention to defend the proceedings.

appellant: person who appeals.

arbitration: resolution of a dispute by an appointed arbitrator or panel of arbitrators.

arm's length prices: prices between informed and willing parties that are not related parties, other than in a forced sale.

arraignment: beginning of a criminal trial when the indictment is read to the accused and he is asked whether he pleads guilty or not.

arranging debtor: individual who is unable to meet his debts and who voluntarily submits to the jurisdiction of the court for the purpose of arriving at a compromise with his creditors.

assets: items arising from past transactions which will generate future benefit (often in the form of revenue or income).

associated companies: companies, not being subsidiaries, in which an interest is held that permits the holder of the interest to exercise significant influence – such influence is generally presumed if the investor holds more than 20 per cent of the voting shares of the associated company.

audi alteram partem: requirement of natural justice for courts or other adjudications to "hear the other side" or to hear both sides of the matter.

audit: process by which an auditor forms an independent and objective opinion as to whether the accounts fairly reflect the financial performance and financial position of a company. The financial statements of all except very small companies must be audited, generally on an annual basis.

auditor: a member of a recognised professional accounting body who holds a certificate from that body which entitles the person to carry out an audit. Thus, not all professionally qualified accountants are entitled to carry out audits.

autrefois acquit: previously acquitted.

autre fois convict: previously convicted.

aver: to allege or assert – statements of fact in an affidavit are often referred to as averments.

balance sheet: statement of assets, liabilities and capital at a specified date. The balance sheet follows the balance sheet equation (Assets – Liabilities = Capital) and therefore should balance.

before and after method: a method of computing lost profits by comparing expected performance had the injury not occurred with projected performance after the injury or wrongful action.

beyond reasonable doubt: burden of proof in criminal cases. If there is reasonable doubt regarding the evidence against the accused, that person is entitled to the benefit of the doubt and must be acquitted.

bona fide: in good faith, honestly.

book of evidence: a book of documents containing the charges, sworn statements, statements of evidence to be given, lists of witnesses and lists of exhibits which must be served on the accused in criminal trials and on which the prosecution intends to rely in a jury trial.

book value: the value at which assets and liabilities are recorded in the books, accounts and financial statements of an accounting entity. The book value may bear no resemblance to the market value of the assets had liabilities – it is merely the amount at which it is recorded for accounting purposes.

bookkeeping: methodical and systematic recording of financial data relating to business transactions. It provides the raw material for the preparation and presentation of financial statements.

brief: instructions sent by a solicitor to counsel in connection with proposed or actual legal proceedings.

burden (and standard) of proof: the party who must prove his case in order to alter the status quo bears the burden of proof. In most criminal cases the burden initially falls on the prosecution, but can transfer to the accused in the course of the trial. In civil cases the burden falls on the plaintiff, according to the maxim "he who asserts must prove".

Calderbank letter: letter written "without prejudice", often used in arbitration, offering to settle a dispute on specified terms and stating that it may be used in connection with costs if the offer to settle is refused.

capital: capital is the amount owed by the business to the providers of finance to the business. Depending on the context, the term capital may refer to all providers of finance – owners/shareholders and long-term lenders such as the banks. Alternatively, the term may only refer to monies attributable to owners of businesses, *i.e.* the sole trader, partner or shareholders depending on the type of business organisation.

Capital comprises the amounts contributed to the business by the owners, plus any profits earned by the business returnable to the owners, less any profits already withdrawn by the owners or shareholders (usually in the form of dividends if it is a company).

capital expenditure: expenditure to acquire assets for continuing use in the business (*i.e.* fixed assets). Such expenditure is initially recorded in the balance sheet and thereafter it is transferred/allocated (by means of amortisation or depreciation) to profit and loss accounts for periods to which it relates.

capital gains and losses: the gain or loss on disposal of a fixed asset. The difference between the proceeds on sale of a fixed asset and the amount at which it is recorded in the books of the accounting entity.

capital reserve: a reserve not distributable to owners/shareholders of the accounting entity. Surplus on revaluation of assets is an example.

case stated: referring a point of law to a higher court.

causation: whether the damage suffered by the complaining party can be attributed to the alleged wrong committed by another party.

certiorari: order sought in judicial review proceedings quashing the decision of another court, tribunal or administrative body.

champerty: the unlawful provision of assistance in litigation by someone with no interest in the proceedings in consideration of making a gain arising from some part of the matter in dispute.

chancery division: division of the High Court that deals with matters involving companies and other aspects of commercial law.

charge: in criminal proceedings an instruction to a jury by the trial judge summarising the evidence and outlining the applicable law.

civil bill: legal document commencing civil proceedings.

civil law: body of law providing persons with civil remedies (such as damages).

civil process: initiation of a civil claim in the District Court in a document setting out the facts and the nature of the relief sought by the plaintiff.

common law: system of laws derived from judicial decisions rather than from a written code.

company: a legal entity separate from its owners (members) incorporated under companies legislation.

competition law: area of law principally administered by competition or antitrust authorities which governs monopolies, mergers, price fixing, etc. – known as antitrust law in the United States.

conciliation: meeting for the purpose of resolving a dispute through the facilitation of settlement discussions.

consistency: a basic accounting assumption/principle that like transactions are accounted for in the same ways within the same accounting period, and from one period to the next.

consolidated accounts: financial statements for a group of companies, comprising the holding or parent company and its subsidiaries. Consolidated accounts are similar to, but not exactly the same as, group accounts (see group accounts).

consultation: meeting, usually involving counsel.

contingent liabilities: liabilities dependent on the occurrence or non-occurrence of a future event. Examples include the outcome of a court case, the guarantee of the borrowings of another company, or the repayment of government grants if the conditions of the grant agreement are not observed.

contract: an agreement between two or more parties that is enforceable at law.

contribution: variable revenue less variable costs.

contributory negligence: where the court finds the plaintiff to be partly responsible for the damage of which he complains.

counsel: barrister.

counterclaim: a claim by the defendant against the plaintiff arising out of the same circumstances that gave rise to the plaintiff's claim.

creative accounting: accounting that complies with the letter of the law and with accounting standards but not with the spirit of these regulations. By means of rule-bending and loophole-seeking, the accounts are not prepared as intended by regulations. The resulting accounts report financial results that may not accurately portray the substance of the transactions of the business.

creditors: persons or businesses to whom money is owed.

criminal law: imposition of penal sanctions (such as imprisonment) on persons who have committed offences contrary to public law.

cross-examination: questions posed by counsel for one party to witnesses called by another party. It follows direct examination and may include leading questions.

current assets: assets whose future benefit will be realised within one year. Examples include stock, debtors, and cash at bank and petty cash.

current liabilities: liabilities due within one year.

damages: money payable by order of the court to compensate the injured party for injuries suffered (and, in exceptional cases, to punish or make an example of the wrongdoer).

de bene esse: for what it's worth – usually evidence allowed by a judge even though it would not ordinarily be admissible.

de facto: as a matter of fact.

de jure: as a result of a legal right.

de nova: a new, hearing case from the beginning.

decree: a court order, embodying its judgment.

defence: formal reply by a defendant to a document (*e.g.* statement of claim) setting out details of the plaintiff's claim against him.

defendant: party against whom civil or criminal proceedings are taken.

deponent: person who swears an affidavit.

depositions: sworn testimony given other than in court and recorded for use in proceedings.

depreciation: method of allocating the cost of fixed assets to accounting periods expected to benefit from their use.

differential analysis: analysis between alternatives of incremental, extra costs and revenues, and costs saved and revenues not earned.

direct costs: costs that can be identified with or related to specific units of output or of production.

direct examination: See examination-in-chief.

discontinuance: voluntary abandonment of proceedings by a plaintiff.

discounted cash flow: a method of valuation whereby future cash flows are discounted to their present value by a discount rate which takes into account both time values and risk.

discovery: the process by which a party to proceedings gains access to all relevant documents in the possession, power or custody of another party and which relate to any matter in question in the proceedings.

double entry: a system of accounting that recognises that business assets are owed back to owners as a result of the business being accounted for as an entity separate from the owner. Every transaction has a dual effect. The double entry effect of a few simple transactions are shown by way of illustration:

Purchase of fixed asset	Dr. Fixed asset	Cr. Bank
Contribution of capital by owner	Dr. Bank	Cr. Capital
Cash sale	Dr. Bank	Cr. Sales

embezzlement: a criminal offence committed by a person who fraudulently converts, for his own use, property received by him on account of his employer.

equity, owners': see owners' equity.

escrow: money or documents held by a third party until the conditions of an agreement are met.

estoppel: principle by which a party otherwise entitled to take a particular course in law or to seek a particular relief is precluded from doing so because of something he has done.

ex parte: application to a court without notice to the other party and where the other party has no right to address the court.

ex post facto: after the event; retrospectively.

examination-in-chief: direct examination – questions posed by counsel for one party to witnesses called by that party; precedes cross-examination and may not include leading questions.

examinership: provides for a moratorium from their creditors for companies in financial difficulties. An examiner is appointed by the High Court to investigate the company's affairs to see if there is any prospect of rescuing the business.

execution of judgment: enforcing a judgment of the court against the unsuccessful party.

exemplary damages: punitive damages – damages awarded by a court for the primary purpose of punishing the wrongdoer or making an example of him. They need not bear any relation to a measure of the damage suffered by the wronged party.

expenses: costs incurred in generating the revenue recognised in that accounting period. They arise from using up assets and/or from incurring liabilities in generating revenue/income.

fair value: amount by which assets or liabilities could be exchanged in arm's length transactions.

false accounting: destroying, defacing or concealing accounting records or documents or otherwise rendering them deceptive or misleading.

fictitious assets: assets shown in the books which will generate no future benefit. Asset balances not yet written off or expensed to the profit and loss account which will generate no future revenue, against which the asset cost can be matched.

fieri facias: cause to be made – order of execution directing the sheriff to seize assets in satisfaction of a debt.

financial position: financial position or state of affairs of a business at any date is its book value as shown by assets less liabilities.

financial statements: the financial statements under company legislation comprise the profit and loss account and balance sheet. Accounting standards have added two further "primary" statements – the cash flow statement and the statement of total recognised gains and losses. The financial statements should be read together with the accounting policies and the notes to the accounts which are an integral part of the financial statements.

fixed assets: assets acquired for continuing use in a business and whose future benefit will normally be realised over a period exceeding one year. Examples include tangible, intangible and financial fixed assets such as land and buildings, plant and machinery, fixtures and fittings, goodwill, patents, trademarks, investments/shares in other companies.

fixed costs: costs that do not vary with level of activity such as sales (expressed in units or at selling price), production in units, etc.

foreseeability: extent to which a party could reasonably have been expected to anticipate the actual consequence of his actions – used to establish liability in tort claims.

form and substance: see substance over form.

fraudulent trading: a criminal offence in which a person carries on a company's business with the intent to defraud creditors. The offence may give rise to the person being found personally liable for the company's debts, and to being disqualified from acting as a company director.

further and better particulars: additional details of a claim or defence necessary for a party to have an understanding of the case being made by the opposing party.

general damages: damages for pain and suffering (in a personal injury context).

general ledger: see nominal ledger.

generally accepted accounting principles (GAAP): ways of producing financial statements that over time have gained the general support of the accounting profession. Well-established accounting conventions, rules and procedures as articulated in the pronouncements of professional accounting bodies. These generally accepted accounting principles may vary from country to country.

going concern: the fundamental assumption underlying the preparation of most financial statements that the business will continue in operational existence for the foreseeable future. This assumption has a material influence on the amount at which assets are shown in the financial statements – going concern values are usually higher than break-up valuations.

goodwill: goodwill is the measure of the future benefit from unidentified assets reflecting a company's good name, reputation, etc. There are two types of goodwill – internally-generated goodwill which is never recorded in financial statements and purchased goodwill which may be recognised in the balance sheet. Purchased goodwill is the difference between what is paid for a business and the fair value of the assets identifiable tangible and intangible assets acquired.

gross-up: calculate an item without deductions, *e.g.* calculate revenues without deduction for any expenses.

group accounts: group accounts consist of the financial statements of a group of companies comprising the parent or holding company, subsidiaries (consolidated and non-consolidated) and associated or related companies.

habeus corpus: an order of the High Court requiring the detention of a person to be justified and the grounds for detention to be certified in writing.

hearing: trial of an action, or its equivalent in arbitration.

hearsay: evidence of the words or actions of another.

historical cost accounting: a method of accounting whereby all transactions, assets and liabilities are recorded at their original cost. Because it is based on factual evidence, this is the most common method of accounting. Modified historical cost accounting is also a common alternative.

holding gains and losses: gains and losses arising from holding assets in periods of changing prices.

in camera: hearing a case in private.

income: see revenue. Accountants ascribe a meaning to the term "income" which is different to the economists' interpretation of the term.

income and expenditure account: also called "profit and loss account". However, the term "income and expenditure account" is often used in non-profit making organisations in place of "profit and loss account".

incremental costs: costs directly incurred in order to produce an additional unit of revenue.

indictable offence: a serious offence for which the accused has the right to be tried by a jury.

indictment: numbered list of charges against an accused person for which he is to be tried.

indirect costs: costs that cannot be identified with or traced to units of production, *e.g.* factory rent, cost of factory supervisor, depreciation of manufacturing plant and equipment, etc.

injunction: an order of the court requiring a party either to perform an act or to refrain from performing an act.

inspection of documents: examination, and the taking of copies, of original documents disclosed during the process of discovery.

intangibles: assets that have no physical substance, *e.g.* goodwill, patents, trademarks, newspaper titles, brands.

inter alia: among other things.

inter alios: among other persons.

inter partes: between parties.

interlocutory hearing: a hearing prior to the trial of the action involving two or more parties to the proceedings, and usually dealing with preliminary or procedural matters.

interrogatories: written questions posed by one party to be answered in sworn form by another party.

inventory: see stock – the term "inventory" is more commonly used in the
United States.
ipso facto: by that fact.

judgment: decision of the court, usually giving detailed reasons.
judicial review: application to the High Court challenging the finding of an
inferior court, tribunal or other person exercising a quasi-judicial function,
on the grounds that it acted beyond its jurisdiction or failed to apply fair
procedures.

larceny: criminal offence of theft.
ledger: collective term for all the accounts, *e.g.* nominal ledger (all the accounts
of the business), debtors ledger (all the debtor accounts), creditors ledger
(all the creditor accounts).
legitimate expectation: legal recognition of a right to expect that the law will
respect a specific entitlement.
liabilities: amounts due by persons or companies to third parties. Liabilities
included trade creditors, bank loans, lease obligations, taxes due, dividends
proposed and sundry other amounts due.
liquidated damages: a predetermined level of compensation payable in the
event that a cause of action arises, usually a breach of contract.
liquidator: person appointed to wind up a company by selling its assets, paying
creditors and distributing any remaining monies and assets to members of
the company.
lodgment: amount paid into court by a defendant in settlement of an action. If
the plaintiff refuses to accept the lodgment in settlement of the proceedings
and subsequently is awarded less than the amount of the lodgment by the
court the plaintiff must pay ordinarily the defendant's costs from the date
of the lodgment.
long-term liabilities: liabilities due after more than one year.

mala fide: bad faith.
mandamus: order of mandamus (Latin: "we command") is a command of the
High Court arising from judicial review proceedings to an inferior court,
tribunal or other person exercising a quasi-judicial function, to perform a
public duty of a legal nature.
Mareva injunction: interlocutory relief granted to a party ordering another
party to the proceedings not to dispose of any assets or a proportion of
assets where such disposal would render a judgment unenforceable.
matching principle: see accrual accounting.
materiality: an item is considered material (*i.e.* significant) if its non-disclosure
would distort the view given by the financial statements. In practice, the
interpretation of what is/is not material is very subjective.
mediation: method of alternative dispute resolution where an independent party

assists in discussions towards resolution of a dispute but does not give judgment or indicate his own view of how the matter should be resolved.

mens rea: intention to commit an offence or a wrong.

minority interest: the interest or shares in a subsidiary not owned by the parent or holding company. Minority interests only occur where a subsidiary is not wholly owned by the parent company.

misfeasance: improper performance of an otherwise lawful act.

mitigation: efforts made by a plaintiff to minimise the effect of the wrong suffered by him.

mixed costs: costs that contain both fixed and variable elements.

modified historical cost accounting: historical cost accounting modified by the revaluation of some assets of the company – usually the more valuable assets such as land and buildings.

motion: initiation of certain court applications usually by a document called a notice of motion. Except for motions which are expressly allowed without notice to the other party or parties in a case (known as *ex parte* applications), applications by motion are made on notice.

mutatis mutandis: with all necessary changes having been made.

negligence: breach of a duty of care giving rise to actionable damage caused to another party.

nemo judex in causa sua: no one can be a judge in his own cause.

net present value: the value of estimated or expected future cash flows discounted at a discount rate to its present worth.

net realisable value: the amount at which an asset can be sold, less costs of selling the asset and less the costs of putting the asset into a saleable condition.

nolle prosequi: discontinue the proceedings.

nominal ledger: a collective term to describe all the accounts in an accounting entity – also sometimes called the general ledger.

non sequitur: a statement that does not follow logically from the statement that preceded it.

notice for particulars: a list of specific questions seeking further details of matters referred to in a pleading.

notice to admit: request by a party to proceedings that another party admit certain documents or facts, failing which admission there may be a cost penalty on the party refusing to do so.

novus actus interveniens: an event, not involving the defendant, in the chain linking the acts of the defendant to the damage caused to the plaintiff, the effect of which is to negate causation.

obiter dictum: statement by a judge in the course of a judgment that is not necessary for the decision involved in the judgment and therefore not a binding precedent.

operating gains: see operating income (profit).

operating income (profit): income (or profit) earned from the activities of the business in providing its main products or services to customers. Non-operating income is that generated from activities incidental to the business (*e.g.*, income from investments outside the business, holding gains).

opportunity costs: cost or value of a benefit sacrificed as a result of taking an alternative course of action.

overheads: costs not directly related to the goods produced (indirect costs) attributable to running the business, comprising production, administration, selling and distribution overheads.

owners' equity: amounts owed by the accounting entity (business) to the owners and comprising contributed capital (called share capital in a company) and retained earnings.

pari passu: on an equal basis.

per se: of itself.

period, accounting: see accounting period.

plaintiff: person initiating civil proceedings.

pleadings: formal documents to be served by the parties to proceedings on each other and filed in court.

plenary summons: the document used to commence most High Court proceedings except where a summary summons, a special summons, a petition or an originating notice of motion is required or authorised. Plenary proceedings usually involve pleadings, including a statement of claim, and oral evidence.

policies, accounting: see accounting policies.

precedent: previous decision of a court that is binding on another court.

prepayments: income paid in advance and shown as a liability (the service or product is owed by the accounting entity) or expenses paid in advance and shown in the financial statements as an asset (the service or product is owed to the accounting entity).

present value: see net present value.

principles, accounting: see accounting principles.

profit: excess of the revenue or income of an accounting period over the expenses incurred in generating that revenue.

profit and loss account: a financial statement summarising the revenues and expenses of a business for a specified accounting period.

prosecution on indictment: prosecution by means of a written accusation of a crime.

prudence: a basic accounting concept whereby: (i) revenues are not anticipated but are recognised in the financial statements when they are earned or realised; and (ii) expenses and losses are recognised in the financial statements as soon as they are foreseeable.

punitive damages: see exemplary damages.

QC: Queen's Counsel – equivalent in England and Wales of a senior counsel.
quia timet: in fear of.
quantum meruit: value of service provided under a contract.

ratio decidendi: reasons for court's decision on an issue in the proceedings.
realisation: revenues are realised when they are received in the form of cash or some other asset the ultimate cash realisation of which is reasonably certain.
receivables: amounts due to the accounting entity, including debtors, rent due, interest earned and due, prepayments, etc.
receiver: person appointed by a creditor to sell company assets to allow for repayment of the debt (secured on those company assets) owed by the company to the creditor.
reckless trading: where a person knowingly carries on business in a reckless manner or with intent to defraud creditors. That person may be found personally liable for debts of the company.
recognition in accounting: recording of transactions, assets and liabilities in the accounts.
recognizance: an obligation made to a court binding a person to perform a specified act.
re-examination: questions posed by counsel for one party to witnesses called by that party; follows cross-examination, may not include leading questions and is limited to matters raised in cross-examination.
registrar: court official. Responsibilities include making the formal record of orders made by the court.
related company: see associated companies – related company is the equivalent term used in the Companies Acts.
replies to particulars: the written replies to a notice for particulars.
reply: a pleading used by a party to respond to a defence or a later pleading delivered by another party.
res ipsa loquitur: the facts speak for themselves.
res judicata: a matter adjudicated.
reserves: profits and surpluses of the accounting entity retained in the business. There are two types of reserves: (i) distributable reserves which may be paid out to the owners/shareholders (as dividends) and (ii) non-distributable reserves which may not be paid to owners. Examples of non-distributable reserves are surpluses on revaluation of assets (which are not distributable until the asset is sold and the surplus is realised), and reserves restricted under a legal agreement.
respondent: party against whom a motion or appeal is brought in court; party against whom a claim is made in arbitration.
restitutio in integrum: plaintiff to be restored to the position he would have been in had the wrongful act not been done.
retained earnings (reserves): retained earnings or retained reserves are profits and surpluses not paid out to owners or shareholders (in the form of dividends) which are kept for use in the business.

revenue: inflows of assets in the form of cash or other assets, the ultimate cash realisation of which is reasonably certain, arising from sale of goods and services, or other activities of the business. *see also* **income**.

revenue expenditure: expenditure which is expensed in the profit and loss account (the opposite of capital expenditure).

revenue reserve: profits of the accounting entity distributable to the owners/shareholders.

security for costs: relief sought by a defendant where there is a doubt that, in the event that the defendant is successful in his defence and is awarded his costs by the court, the plaintiff will be in a position to meet the defendant's costs or that the order for costs can be enforced successfully. If granted the plaintiff is ordered to lodge a specified amount in court.

SC: *see* **senior counsel**.

senior counsel: a barrister who has been called to the inner bar and who takes precedence over other barristers, called junior counsel. *see also* **silk**.

settlement: resolution of a dispute by the parties before it is determined by a court or arbitrator.

shareholders' funds: a collective term for the share capital and retained reserves of a company. In a company balance sheet it would include the share capital, share premium, capital reserves and revenue reserves.

silk: senior counsel.

special damages: damages which are capable of substantially exact calculation.

special summons: a document that may be used to commence proceedings falling within certain classes of claims, including several aspects of the administration of the estate of a deceased person, and in a wide variety of specified situations, including a number of applications under the Companies Acts.

specific performance: a court order compelling a party to perform his obligations under an agreement.

standard of proof: in criminal cases – "beyond a reasonable doubt"; in civil cases – "on the balance of probabilities"; the standard to be attained in order for the party initiating the proceedings to succeed.

stare decisis: doctrine by which previous decisions bind courts in future proceedings.

statement of claim: The document in which the plaintiff in High Court proceedings sets out all relevant particulars of his claim, distinguishing between the damage he alleges he has suffered and the grounds on which he alleges that the defendant is liable to him for that damage.

status quo ante: the same state as before.

statute-barred: where a claim cannot be pursued in court because it is initiated too late.

Statute of Limitations: period prescribed by statute within which a civil claim must be initiated.

stay of proceedings: suspension of proceedings.

step costs: costs that increase or decrease abruptly at intervals of activity because their acquisition comes in indivisible chunks.

stock: the term used in Ireland and the United Kingdom in place of the United States equivalent "Inventory" to refer to products of the business not yet sold and therefore still owned by the business and shown in the balance sheet as an asset.

subpoena: a document on foot of which an individual must attend court, with or without documents.

subsidiary: a company over which the parent company can exercise control – generally presumed when more than 50 per cent of the voting shares are held by the parent, although control may be exercise even where less than 50 per cent of voting shares are held.

substance over form: the principle of substance over form is required by accounting standards. Transactions should be accounted for in accordance with their business and economic substance rather than in compliance with their strict legal form.

summary offence: offence triable by summary proceedings.

summary proceedings: proceedings without a jury in the District Court.

summary summons: the document used to commence certain High Court proceedings, including claims for the recovery of a debt or for the recovery by the landlord of possession of land against a tenant in certain circumstances. The procedure by summary summons, which is governed by Order 2 of the Rules of the Superior Courts 1986, is designed to allow for speedy and relatively inexpensive recourse to the court where the plaintiff's case is clear and there is no apparent defence.

summary trial: see summary proceedings.

summons: in criminal proceedings, a written command issued to a defendant for the purpose of getting him to attend court on a specific date to answer a specified complaint. In civil proceedings, the document that, when issued by the appropriate authority and subsequently served on behalf of one party on another party within a specified period, marks the beginning of a set of legal proceedings between those parties.

surplus: the term used in place of "profit" in a non-profit making organisation. Also used to refer to unrealised gains (*e.g.* surplus on revaluation).

suspense accounts: under double entry bookkeeping the accounts should balance. Differences arising when the accounts do not balance are recorded temporarily in suspense accounts until the reasons for the differences are discovered and the transactions can be accounted for correctly.

tangibles: assets other than intangible assets.

taxation of costs: process of measuring reasonable costs where, following the making of an order for costs requiring one party to pay the costs of the other, the parties are unable to agree an appropriate level of costs between them. The matter is sent for adjudication to a Taxing Master in the High Court, or the County Registrar in the Circuit Court.

Taxing Master: court official who determines recoverable costs of High Court cases where these are not agreed between the parties.

testimony: evidence.

third party notice: document prepared by a defendant joining to the proceedings an additional party against whom the defendant believes he has a cause of action arising out of the same circumstances as those giving rise to the plaintiff's claim.

tort: a private or civil wrong or injury, other than a breach of contract, inflicted by one person on another, compensable by damages.

trial balance: a list of balances extracted from the accounts of the accounting entity, organised into two columns, the debit and the credit column. One of the functions of the trial balance is to check whether it (and the company accounts) balances, *i.e.* whether the total of the debit balances agrees with the total of the credit balances.

trial on indictment: see prosecution on indictment.

tribunal: a body appointed to adjudicate on a matter.

true and fair view: company law requires directors to prepare financial statements that give a true and fair view, and auditors to express an opinion as to whether the financial statements give a true and fair view. The term is not defined and, in practice, is interpreted subjectively. If the financial statements comply with professional accounting standards there is prima facie evidence that they give a true and fair view.

ultra vires: outside the powers of a company as expressed in its memorandum of association. Ultra vires actions by companies are null and void.

unamortised: fixed assets which have not been charged to the profit and loss account.

variable costs: costs that vary with level of activity such as sales (expressed in units or sales value) or production in units, etc.

venditioni exponas: order to compel a sheriff to sell assets seized under an order of *fieri facias* and remaining in his possession unsold.

voire dire: a trial within a trial to facilitate consideration of legal points in the absence of a jury.

volenti non fit injuria: a defence saying that the plaintiff took the risk on himself of the damage he actually suffered.

without prejudice: settlement proposals or other communications between parties to proceedings that, if the matter is not settled and proceeds to trial, may not be admitted in evidence without the express agreement of both parties.

witness: person giving sworn evidence to a court.

working capital: net current liabilities, *i.e.* current assets less current liabilities.

writ: a formal written command issued from a court commanding a person to do, or to refrain from doing, some act.

APPENDIX 4

BIBLIOGRAPHY

Ashe, M.T., *International Tracing of Assets* (FT Law & Tax, London, 1997).

Ashe, M.T., and Murphy, Y., *Insider Dealing* (Round Hall Press, Dublin, 1992).

Ashe, M.T. and Reid, P., *Money Laundering* (Round Hall Sweet & Maxwell, Dublin, 2000).

Barson, K.A., *Investigative Accounting in Divorce* (Wiley Law, New York, 1996).

Berenblut, M.L. and Rosen, H.N., *Litigation Accounting: The Quantification of Economic Damages* (Carswell Thomson Professional Publishing, Ontario, 1995).

Bologna, G.J. and Lindquist, R.J., *Fraud Auditing and Forensic Accounting: New Tools and Techniques* (2nd ed., John Wiley & Sons Inc, New York, 1995).

Buckley, A.J., *Insurance Law in Ireland* (Oak Tree Press, Dublin, 1997).

Byrne, R. and McCutcheon, J.P., *Irish Legal System* (Butterworths, Dublin 1996).

Cahill, D., *Corporate Finance Law* (Round Hall Sweet & Maxwell, Dublin, 1999).

Cahill, E., *Discovery in Ireland* (Round Hall Sweet & Maxwell, Dublin, 1996).

Central Statistics Office Ireland, *Statistical Abstract* (Stationery Office, Dublin, Annual).

Charleton, P., McDermott, P.A. and Bolger, M., *Criminal Law* (Butterworths, Dublin, 1999).

Chase, G., *Taxation Treatment of Compensation and Damages* (Butterworths, London, 1994).

Clark, R., *Contract Law in Ireland* (4th ed., Round Hall Sweet & Maxwell, Dublin, 1998).

Clark, R. and Clarke, B., *Contract Cases and Materials* (2nd ed., Gill & Macmillan, Dublin, 2000).

Clark, R. and Smyth, S., *Intellectual Property Law in Ireland* (Butterworths, Dublin, 1997).

Clarke, B., *Takeovers and Mergers Law in Ireland* (Round Hall Sweet & Maxwell, Dublin, 1999).

Cloughton, D., *Riley on Business Interruption and Consequential Loss Insurance* (8th ed., Sweet & Maxwell, London, 1999).

Coggans, S. and Jackson, N., *Family Law (Divorce) Act 1996* (Round Hall Sweet & Maxwell, Dublin, 1998).

897

Collins, A.M. and O'Reilly, J., *Civil Proceedings and the State in Ireland: A Practitioner's Guide* (Round Hall Press, Dublin, 1990).

Comer, M.J., *Corporate Fraud* (3rd ed., Gower Publishing Ltd, Aldershot, 1998).

Cook, C.J. and Kerse, C.S., *EC Merger Control* (3rd ed., Sweet & Maxwell, London, 1996).

Corrigan, M. and Campbell, J.A., *A Casebook of Irish Insurance Law* (Oak Tree Press, Dublin, 1995).

Corrigan, K., *Revenue Law* (Round Hall Sweet & Maxwell, Dublin, 2000).

Courtney, T.B., *Mareva Injunctions and Related Interlocutory Orders* (Butterworths, Dublin, 1998).

Courtney, T.B., *The Law of Private Companies* (Butterworths, Dublin, 1994).

Courts Service, *The Courts System in Ireland – An Introduction* (Courts Service, Dublin, 2000).

Cregan, B.J., *Competition Law in Ireland: Digest and Commenary* (Gill & Macmillan, Dublin, 1997).

Cross, R. and Tapper, C., *Cross on Evidence* (7th ed., Butterworths, London, 1990).

Davies, D., *Fraud Watch – A Guide for Business* (2nd ed., Accountancy Books, London, 1999).

Delany, H., *Equity and the Law of Trusts in Ireland* (2nd ed., Round Hall Sweet & Maxwell, Dublin, 1999).

Delany, V.T.H. and Lysaght, C. (ed), *The Administration of Justice in Ireland* (4th ed., Institute of Public Administration, Dublin, 1975).

Doolan, B., *Principles of Irish Law* (5th ed., Gill & Macmillan, Dublin, 1999).

Duncan, W.R. and Scully, P.E., *Marriage Breakdown in Ireland: Law and Practice* (Butterworths (Ireland) Ltd, Dublin, 1990).

Eastaway, N.A., Booth H. and Eamer, K., *Practical Share Valuation* (4th ed., Butterworths, London, 1998).

Ellis, H., *Irish Company Law for Business* (Jordans, Bristol, 1998).

Ernst & Young, *Fraud: The Unmanaged Risk – An International Survey of the Effects of Fraud on Business* (Ernst & Young, London, 2000).

Fennell, C., *Law of Evidence in Ireland* (2nd ed., Butterworths, Dublin, 2000).

Finucane, F. and Buggy, B., *Irish Pensions Law and Practice* (Oak Tree Press, Dublin, 1996).

Flynn, J. and Halpin, A., *Taxation of Costs* (Blackhall Publishing, Dublin, 1999).

Forde, M., *The Law of Company Insolvency* (The Round Hall Press, Dublin, 1993).

Forde, M., *Arbitration Law and Procedure* (The Round Hall Press, Dublin, 1994).

Forde, M., *Commercial Law* (2nd ed., Butterworths, Dublin, 1997).

Forde, M., *Company Law* (3rd ed., Round Hall Sweet & Maxwell, Dublin, 1999).

Forde, M., *Employment Law* (2nd ed., Round Hall Sweet & Maxwell, Dublin, 2000).

Foy, A., *The Capital Markets: Irish and International Laws and Regulations* (Round Hall Sweet & Maxwell, Dublin, 1998).

Fraud Advisory Panel, *Study of Published Literature on the Nature and Extent of Fraud in the Public and Private Sector* (Institute of Chartered Accountants in England and Wales, London, 1999).

Friel, R., *The Law of Contract* (2nd ed, Round Hall Sweet & Maxwell, Dublin, 2000).

Freckleton, I. and Selby, H., *The Law of Expert Evidence* (LBC Information Services, Sydney, 1999).

Gamlen, E. and Philips, J., *Business Interruption Insurance* (Buckley Press, London, 1992).

Gaughan, P.A. and Thornton, R.J. (eds), *Litigation Economics* (JAI Press, Greenwich, Connecticut, 1993).

Giblin, B.H., *Valuation of Shares in Private Companies* (3rd ed., Institute of Taxation in Ireland, Dublin, 1999).

Haigh, S.P., *Contract Law in an E-commerce Age* (Round Hall Sweet & Maxwell, Dublin, 2001).

Hickmott, G.J.R., *Interruption Insurance: Proximate Loss Issues* (Witherby & Co Ltd, London, 1990).

Hickmott, G.J.R., *Interruption Insurance: Practical Issues* (Witherby & Co Ltd, London, 1999).

Hollington, R., *Minority Shareholders' Rights* (Sweet & Maxwell, London, 1990).

Hogan, G. and Morgan, D.G., *Administrative Law in Ireland* (3rd ed., Round Hall Sweet & Maxwell, Dublin, 1998).

Hogan, G. and Whyte, G. in *Kelly: The Irish Constitution* (3rd ed., Butterworths, Dublin, 1994).

Government Advisory Committee on Fraud, *Report of the Government Advisory Committee on Fraud* (Government Publications, Dublin, 1992).

Irish Law Times, *Expert Witness Directory 1999* (Round Hall Sweet & Maxwell, Dublin, 1999).

Jackson, R.M. and Powell, J.L. (eds), *Jackson & Powell on Professional Negligence* (especially Chapter 8 "Accountants") (Sweet & Maxwell, London, 1992).

Keane, D., *Building and the Law* (3rd ed., Royal Institute of Architects in Ireland, Dublin, 1998).

Keane, D., *The RIAI Contracts: A Working Guide* (3rd ed., Royal Institute of Architects in Ireland, Dublin, 1997).

Keane, R., *Company Law* (3rd ed., Butterworths, Dublin, 2000).

Kelleher, D. and Murray, K., *Information Technology Law in Ireland* (Butterworths, Dublin, 1997).

Kemp, D., *Damages for Personal Injury and Death* (7th ed., Sweet & Maxwell, London, 1998).

Kirk, D.N. and Woodcock, A.J.J., *Serious Fraud: Investigation and Trial* (2nd ed., Butterworths, London, 1992).

KPMG, *Fraud Awareness Survey* (KPMG, Dublin, 1995).

KPMG, *The Complete Fraud Investigation: Suspicion to Recovery* (KPMG, London, 1996).

Lemar, C.J. and Mainz, A.J. (eds), *Litigation Support* (4th ed., Butterworths, London, 1999).

Lynch, I., Marshall, J. and O'Ferrall, R., *Corporate Insolvency and Rescue Law and Practice* (Butterworths, Dublin, 1996).

MacCann, L., *A Casebook on Company Law* (Butterworths, Dublin, 1991).

McCormack, G., *The New Companies Legislation* (The Round Hall Press, Dublin, 1991).

McDermott, S. and Woulfe, R., *Compulsory Purchase and Compensation: Law and Practice in Ireland* (Butterworth (Ireland) Ltd., Dublin, 1992).

McGahon, D., *Irish Company Law Index* (Dublin, Gill & Macmillan, 1991).

MacGregor, G. and Hobbs, I., *Expert Accounting Evidence: A Guide for Litigation Support* (Accountancy Books, London, 1998).

McGregor, H., *McGregor on Damages* (16th ed., Sweet & Maxwell, London, 1997).

McMahon, B.M.E. and Binchy, W., *Law of Torts* (3rd ed., Butterworths, Dublin, 2000).

Madden, D. and Kerr, T., *Unfair Dismissal: Cases and Commentary* (Irish Business and Employers Federation, Dublin, 1996).

Maher, I., *Competition Law Alignment and Reform* (Round Hall Sweet & Maxwell, Dublin, 1999).

Martin, G.D. and Vavoulis, T., *Determining Economic Damages* (James Publishing Inc, California, 1999).

Massey, P. and O'Hare, P., *Competition Law and Policy in Ireland* (Oak Tree Press, Dublin, 1996).

Munkman, J., *Damages for Personal Injuries and Death* (10th ed., Butterworths, London, 1996).

Murdoch, H., *Murdoch's Dictionary of Irish Law* (3rd ed., Topaz Publications, Dublin, 2000).

Mustill, M.J. and Boyd, S.C., *The Law and Practice of Commercial Arbitration in England* (2nd ed., Butterworths, 1989).

Mustill, M.J. and Boyd, S.C., *Commercial Arbitration – 2000 Companion Volume* (Butterworths, London, 2000).

Ó'Floinn, *Practice and Procedure in the Superior Courts* (Butterworths, Dublin, 1996).

O'Reilly, P., *Commercial and Consumer Law* (Butterworths, Dublin, 1999).

O'Regan Cazabon, A., *Irish Insurance Law* (Round Hall Sweet & Maxwell, Dublin, 1999).

Peelo, D., *Valuations, Mergers and Sales of Professional Practices* (Peelo & Partners, Dublin, 1998).

Pierse, R., *Quantum of Damages for Personal Injuries* (2nd ed., Round Hall Sweet & Maxwell, Dublin, 1999).

Powell-Smith, V. and Sims, J., *Building Contract Claims* (3rd ed., Blackwells, London, 1997).

Powell-Smith, V., Stephenson, D. and Redmond, J., *Civil Engineering Claims* (3rd ed., Blackwells, London, 1999).

Power, V.J.G., *Competition Law and Practice* (Butterworths, Dublin, 1999).

Redmond, M., *Dismissal Law in Ireland* (Dublin, Butterworths (Ireland) Ltd, Dublin, 1999).

Review Group on Auditing, *Report of the Review Group on Auditing* (Government Publications, Dublin, 2000). Also available at www.entemp.ie/publications.htm

Shannon (ed.), *Family Law Practitioner* (Round Hall Sweet & Maxwell, 2000).

Shatter, A.J., *Shatter's Family Law* (4th ed., Butterworths, Dublin, 1997).

Spollen, A.L., *Corporate Fraud: The Danger from Within* (Oak Tree Press, Dublin, 1997).

Taub, M., Rapazzini, A., Bond, C., Solon, M., Brown, A., Murrie, A., Linnell, K. and Burn, S., *Tolley's Accountancy Litigation Support* (Butterworths, London, looseleaf).

Trickey, G. and Hackett, M., *The Presentation and Settlement of Contractors' Claims* (2nd ed., Spon Press, London, 2001).

Twomey, M.J., *Partnership Law* (Butterworths, Dublin, 2000).

Von Prondzynski, F., *Von Prondzynski and McCarthy on Employment Law in Ireland* (2nd ed., Sweet & Maxwell, London, 1989).

Wallace, I.D., *Hudson's Building and Engineering Contracts* (11th ed., Sweet & Maxwell, London, 1994).

Walmsley, R.M., *Business Interruption Insurance* (Witherby & Co Ltd, London, 1999).

Walton, A. and Vitoria, M. *Russell on the Law of Arbitration* (20th ed., Stevans & Sons, London, 1982).

Weil, R.L., Wagner M.J. and Frank, P.B. (eds), *Litigation Services Handbook: The Role of the Accountant as Expert* (2nd ed., John Wiley & Sons, Inc, New York, 1995).

White, J.P.M., *Irish Law of Damages for Personal Injuries and Death* (Butterworths (Ireland) Ltd, Dublin, 1989).

White, J.P.M., *Civil Liability for Industrial Accidents* (Oak Tree Press, Dublin, 1994).

Wood, K. and O'Shea, P., *Divorce in Ireland: the Options, the Issues, the Law* (The O'Brien Press Ltd, Dublin, 1997).

JOURNALS AND NEWSLETTERS ON FORENSIC ACCOUNTING

Dispatches
Society of Expert Witnesses
PO Box 345
Newmarket
Suffolk CB8 7TU
Tel: +44-845-702 3014
Fax: +44-1638-668 656
e-mail: Helpline@sew.org.uk
Website: www.sew.org.uk

The Expert
Journal of the Academy of Experts
Academy of Experts
2, South Square
Grays Inn
London WC1R 5HT
Tel: +44-20-7637 0333
Fax: +44-20-7637 1893
e-mail: admin@academy-experts.org
Website: www.academy-experts.org

The Expert
Blum Shapiro Litigation Consulting
Group, LLC
29 South Main Street
PO Box 272000
West Hartford
CT 06127-2000
USA
Tel: +1-860-561 4000
Fax: +1-860-521 9241
e-mail: info@blumshapiro.com
Website:
www.forensic.blumshapiro.com

The Expert Witness Newsletter
Economics Limited
1190, 700 - 4th Avenue SW
Calgary, Alberta, Canada, T2P 3J4
Tel: +1-403-297 0012
Fax: +1-403-2625458
E-mail: experts@economica.ca
Website: www.economica.ca

Fighting Fraud
KPMG Forensic Accounting
20, Farringdon Street
London EC4A 4PP
Tel: +44-20-7311 3964
Fax: +44-20-7311 3630
e-mail: Paul.Tombleson@kpmg.com
Website: www.kpmg.co.uk

The Forensic Accountant
KPMG Forensic Accounting
20, Farringdon Street
London EC4A 4PP
Tel: +44-20-7311 3964
Fax: +44-20-7311 3630
e-mail: Paul.Tombleson@kpmg.com
Website: www.kpmg.co.uk

Forensic Brief
H.L.B. Kidsons
Spectrum House
20-26 Cursitor Street
London EC4A 1HY
Tel: +44-20-7405 2088
Fax: +44-20-7831 2206

e-mail: rlewi@kilondon.co.uk
Website: www.kidsons.co.uk

Forensic Group News
Institute of Chartered Accountants in
England and Wales
Chartered Accountants' House
PO Box 433
Moorgate Place
London EC2P 2BJ
Tel: +44-20-7920 8798
Fax: +44-20-7920 8547
e-mail:
charmaine.d'souzo@icaew.co.uk
Website: www.icaew.co.uk

Fraud Detective
The Forensic Group LLC
15, John Street
Red Bank
New Jersey 07701-2337
USA
Tel: +1-732-319 6502
Fax: +1-732-842 2403
e-mail: info@frauddetectives.com
Website: www.frauddetectives.com

Inside Fraud Bulletin
Maxima Group plc
29 Queen Anne's Gate
London SW1H 9BU
Tel: +44-1825-712 069
Fax: +44-20-7227 3311
e-mail:
ifbulletin@maxima-group.com
Website: www.insidefraud.com

Journal of Forensic Accounting:
Auditing, Fraud, and Taxation
R.T. Edwards, Inc
116 Azalea Way
Flourtown
PA 19031
USA

Tel: +1-215-233 5046
Fax: +1-215-233 2421
e-mail: info@edwardspub.com
Website: www.rtedwards.com

Journal of Forensic Economics
Litigation Economics Review
National Association of Forensic
Economists
PO Box 30067
Kansas City
MO 64112
USA
Tel: +1-816-235 2833
Fax: +1-816-235 5263
e-mail: nancy.eldredge@nafe.net
Website: www.nafe.net

The Smoking Gun
Vogon International Ltd
Talisman Business Centre
Talisman Road
Bicester OX26 6HR
Tel: +44-1869-355 255
Fax: +44-1869-355 256
e-mail:
investigate@vogon-
international.com
Website:
www.vogon-international.com

Valuation Concepts
Blum Shapiro Litigation Consulting
Group, LLC
29 South Main Street
PO Box 272000
West Hartford
CT 06127-2000
USA
Tel: +1-860-561 4000
Fax: +1-860-521 0035
e-mail: info@blumshapiro.com
Website:
www.forensic.blumshapiro.com

Vogon News
Vogon International Ltd
Talisman Business Centre
Talisman Road
Bicester OX26 6JX
Tel: +44-1869-355 255
Fax: +44-1869-355 256
e-mail: info@vogon-
international.com
Website: www.vogon-
international.com

Vogon Vision
Vogon International Ltd
Talisman Business Centre
Talisman Road
Bicester OX26 6JX
Tel: +44-1869-355 255
Fax: +44-1869-355 256
e-mail: info@vogon-
international.com
Website: www.vogon-
international.com

APPENDIX 6

USEFUL ORGANISATIONS

Academy of Experts
2, South Square
Grays Inn
London WC1R 5HP
Tel: +44-20-7637 0333
Fax: +44-20-7637 1893
e-mail: admin@academy-experts.org
Website: www.academy-experts.org

Alliance for Excellence in
Investigative and Forensic
Accounting
Canadian Institute of Chartered
Accountants
277 Wellington Street West
Toronto, Ontario, M5V 3H2
Canada
Tel: +1-416-204 3344
Fax: +1-416-204 3414
e-mail: ifa.alliance@cica.ca
Website: www.cica.ca

American College of Forensic
Examiners
2750 East Sunshine
Springfield
Missouri 65804
USA
Tel: +1-417-881-3818
Fax: +1-417-881-4702
e-mail: info@acfe.com
Website: www.acfe.com

Association of Certified Fraud
Examiners
The Gregor Building
716 West Avenue
Austin
Texas 78701
USA
Tel: +1-512-478 9070
Fax: +1-512-478 9297
e-mail: info@cfenet.com
Website: www.cfenet.com

Association of Chartered Certified
Accountants – Irish Region
9, Leeson Park
Dublin 6
Tel: +353-1-498 8900
Fax: +353-1-496 3615
e-mail: not available
Website: www.acca.ie

Bar Council of Ireland
PO Box 4460
Law Library
158/9 Church Street
Dublin 7
Tel: +353-1-817 5000
Fax: +353-1-817 5150
e-mail: barcouncil@lawlibrary.ie
Website: www.lawlibrary.ie

Chartered Institute of Arbitrators
8, Merrion Square
Dublin 2
Tel: +353-1-662 7867
Fax: +353-1-662 7891
e-mail: ciarb@arbitration.ie
Website: www.arbitration.ie

Chartered Institute of Management
Accountants
44, Upper Mount Street
Dublin 2
Tel: +353-1-676 1721; 678 5133
Fax: +353-1-676 1796
e-mail: dublin@cimaglobal.com
Website: www.cimaireland.com

Courts Service
Green Street Courthouse
Halston Street
Dublin 7
Tel: +353-1-888 6431
Fax: +353-1-873 5242
e-mail: not available
Website: www.courts.ie

Expert Witness Institute
Africa House
64-78 Kingsway
London WC2B 6BD
Tel: +44-20-7405 5854
Fax: +44-20-7405 5850
e-mail: info@ewi.org.uk
Website: www.ewi.org.uk

The Law Society of Ireland
Blackhall Place
Dublin 7
Tel: +353-1-672 4800
Fax: +353-1-672 4801

e-mail: general@lawsociety.ie
Website: www.lawsociety.ie

London Court of International
Arbitration (LCIA)
The International Dispute Resolution
Centre
8, Breams Buildings
Chancery Lane
EC4A 1HP
Tel: +44-20-7405 8008
Fax: +44-20-7405 8009
e-mail: kia@icia-arbitration.com
Website: www.icia-arbitration.com

Institute of Chartered Accountants in
Ireland
Chartered Accountants House
87-89 Pembroke Road
Ballsbridge
Dublin 4
Tel: +353-1-637 7200
Fax: +353-1-668 0842
e-mail: ca@icai.ie
Website: www.icai.ie

Institute of Certified Public
Accountants in Ireland
9, Ely Place
Dublin 2
Tel: +353-1-676 7353
Fax: +353-1-661 2367
e-mail: cpa@cpaireland.ie
Website: www.cpaireland.ie

National Association of Forensic
Economists
PO Box 30067
Kansas City
MO 64112
USA

Tel: +1-816-235 2833
Fax: +1-816-235 5263
e-mail: nancy.eldredge@nafe.net
Website: www.nafe.net

National Litigation Support Services
Association
111 East Wacker Drive
Suite #990
Chicago
Illinois 60601
USA
Tel: +1-800-869-0491
Fax: +1-312-729 9800
e-mail: info@nlssa.com
Website: www.nlssa.com

Society of Expert Witnesses
PO Box 345
Newmarket
Suffolk CB8 7TU
Tel: +44-845-702 3014
Fax: +44-1638-668 656
e-mail: Helpline@sew.org.uk
Website: www.sew.org.uk

USEFUL WEBSITES

Economica
Canadian site which contains articles on the economics of personal injury damages and an electronic newsletter
www.economica.ca

Expert Search
Site contains sample case summaries
www.expertsearch.com

Forensic Accountant
Contains basic information about forensic accounting
www.forensicaccountant.com

Forensic Economics Sites
Information on all aspects of forensic economics, including bibliography, consultants and links to other forensic economics websites
www.willyancey.com/forensic.htm

Internet for Investigations
Contains information on forensic accounting including links to other forensic accounting sites
www.webinvestigator.ca

Kruglick's Forensic Accounting Bibliographic References
Contains some forensic accounting bibliography and links to other forensic accounting sites
www.kruglaw.com

Murdoch University Forensic Accounting Website
Contains bibliography on forensic accounting and links to other forensic accounting sites
wwwscience.murdoch.edu.au/teaching/m235/forensicaccount.htm

INDEX

This index is to paragraph number.

913

conditions 9.13
generally 9.06
remedy dependent on term 9.15
warranties 9.14
forensic accountants, role of
forensic accountants, role of
case histories 9.25-9.27
generally 9.23-9.24
generally 2.29, 9.03, 9.04
illegality 2.29, 15.05
implied terms
business custom 9.08
common law, implied by 9.09
fundamental rights of individuals 9.11
generally 9.06
"officious bystander" test 9.07
statute, implied by 9.10
legal context 9.16-9.22
limitation of actions 2.29, 20.09
misrepresentation 2.29, 15.05
mistake 2.29, 15.05
non-compete covenants 9.22
remedies 9.15, 15.06
rescission for 15.06
restitution 9.29, 15.98
sellers, by 9.17-9.20
specific performance 9.29, 15.16
types of dispute 9.05
Breach of duty 7.08
Breach of statutory duty 7.08
damages 15.09
Breach of warranty
accounting calculations
generally 9.42
mergers and acquisitions 9.43-9.44
damages 9.38, 9.42-9.44, 15.06
definition of "warranty" 9.14, 9.35
express warranty 9.42
forensic accountants, role of 9.38-9.41
generally 9.34
implied warranty 9.42
legal context 9.35-9.37
mergers and acquisitions 9.34, 9.36-
9.37, 9.43-9.44
purpose of 9.34
Bribery 3.46
Building contracts *see* Construction
claims
Bunreacht na hÉireann *see* Irish
Constitution

Business valuations
adjustments to accounting records
18.87-18.88
assets of company, and 18.84
auditors, by 18.139
closely held businesses
difficulties in valuation 18.102
discounts 18.108
lack of marketability of shares, for
18.110-18.112
minority interests, for 18.113
portfolio discount 18.116-18.117
Quantitative Marketability Discount
Model 18.115
traditional approach 18.114
fair market value 18.104
generally 18.102-18.107
premium for controlling interest
18.108, 18.109
compulsory acquisition 9.168-9.169,
18.100
date of
matrimonial assets 18.137-18.138
shares 18.132-18.136
discounting in 19.58-19.60
divorce, for
closely held businesses 7.109-7.111
generally 1.22, 7.70, 7.94-7.95,
18.89-18.90
goodwill 18.94-18.98
method of valuation 18.91
unrecorded assets, liabilities, earnings
and expenses 18.92-18.93
economic factors 18.84
fair value under articles of association or
by agreement between parties 18.124
financial information 18.84
financial statements 18.18-18.21
firm-specific factors 18.84
forensic accountants, role of 7.94-7.95,
18.09-18.14
generally 18.01-18.03
going-concern valuation
net assets basis of valuation 18.122-
18.123
non-assets basis of valuation 18.121
goodwill
compulsory acquisition 18.100
divorce, valuation for 18.94-18.98
net assets approach 18.45

breach of policy conditions 9.60
business interruption insurance 9.68
consequential loss insurance 9.68
fire and property insurance 9.64-9.67,
9.72
forensic accountants, role of 1.25,
9.69-9.70
fraudulent claims 9.60
generally 9.59-9.60
legal context 9.61-9.62
loss of profits claims 9.73
nature of insurance contract 9.61
non-disclosure of material facts 9.60
preparation of claim 9.70
professional indemnity claim 9.70
rejection of claim 9.60
stock claims 9.65-9.67
types of claims 9.63-9.68
unvalued policies 9.60
valued policies 9.60
Intellectual property rights
accounting calculations 9.107-9.120
copyright infringement 9.95-9.99
computer copyright 9.158-9.161,
9.164, 9.165
damages
account of profits approach 9.113-
9.115, 17.57-17.58
Entire Market Value Rule 9.111
generally 9.107-9.108, 9.109-9.111
lost profit calculations 9.108, 9.112,
17.56-17.50
parasitic damages 9.111
price depression 9.111
reasonable royalty approach 9.111,
9.116-9.120, 17.59
springboard damages 9.111
forensic accountants, role of 9.121-9.122
patent infringement 9.91-9.94, 9.110,
9.111
reasonable royalty 9.111, 9.116-9.120,
17.59
trade mark infringement 9.100-9.104
passing off 9.105-9.106
Interrogatories 22.53-22.57
forensic accountants, role of 22.58-22.63
Investigative accounting 1.12-1.15
see also Forensic accounting
investigations

Investment business firms
failure to keep books of account 8.70
Investment fraud 8.101
Irish Constitution 2.05-2.06, 2.09-2.10,
2.18, 2.21
Irish legal system *see* Legal system in
Ireland

Judicial review
tax issues 11.29-11.30
tribunal decisions 13.03
Judicial separation *see* Matrimonial
disputes

Kiting 3.53

Lapping 3.52
Larceny
clerk or servant, by 8.11
definition 3.08
embezzlement distinguished 8.12-8.13
false pretences, by *see* Obtaining by
false pretences
forensic accountants, role of 8.18-8.19
fraud, and 3.17
generally 3.17, 8.10
simple larceny 8.11
Legal aid
civil 2.60-2.65
criminal 2.52-2.54, 20.78
generally 2.48, 6.92
Legal profession
barristers 2.16-2.17
solicitors 2.15
Legal professional privilege 22.03, 23.36,
23.52-23.59
Legal system in Ireland
adversarial system 2.12-2.13
alternative dispute resolution 2.45
An Bord Pleanála 2.46
barristers 2.16
civil cases
breach of contract 2.29
costs
civil legal aid 2.60-2.65
generally 2.58-2.59
legal aid and advice, access to
2.66-2.66
taxation of 2.67-2.72
generally 2.27-2.29

THOMA

CH00661287

RELIQUES

OF

ANCIENT ENGLISH POETRY

CONSISTING OF

Old Heroic Ballads, Songs,

AND OTHER PIECES OF OUR EARLIER POETS;

TOGETHER

WITH SOME FEW OF LATER DATE

Volume 2

Elibron Classics
www.elibron.com

COLLECTION

OF

BRITISH AUTHORS.

VOL. 848.

RELIQUES OF ANCIENT ENGLISH POETRY
BY
THOMAS PERCY.

IN THREE VOLUMES.

VOL. II.

RELIQUES

OF

ANCIENT ENGLISH POETRY:

CONSISTING OF

𝔒𝔩𝔡 𝔥𝔢𝔯𝔬𝔦𝔠 𝔅𝔞𝔩𝔩𝔞𝔡𝔰, 𝔖𝔬𝔫𝔤𝔰,

AND OTHER PIECES OF OUR EARLIER POETS;

TOGETHER

WITH SOME FEW OF LATER DATE.

BY

THOMAS PERCY,

LORD BISHOP OF DROMORE.

IN THREE VOLUMES.

VOL. II.

LEIPZIG

BERNHARD TAUCHNITZ

1866.

CONTENTS

OF VOLUME THE SECOND.

BOOK THE FIRST.

BOOK THE SECOND.

BOOK THE THIRD.

CONTENTS OF VOLUME THE SECOND.   VII

Though some make slight of LIBELS, yet you may see by them how the wind sits: as, take a straw and throw it up into the air, you may see by that which way the wind is, which you shall not do by casting up a stone. More solid things do not show the complection of the times so well as BALLADS and Libels.

SELDEN'S TABLE-TALK.

RELIQUES

OF

ANCIENT POETRY.

&c.

SERIES THE SECOND.

BOOK I.

I.

Richard of Almaigne,

"A BALLAD made by one of the adherents to Simon de
Montfort, Earl of Leicester, soon after the battle of Lewes,
which was fought May 14, 1264,"—affords a curious specimen
of ancient satire, and shows that the liberty, assumed by the
good people of this realm, of abusing their kings and princes
at pleasure, is a privilege of very long standing.

To render this antique libel intelligible, the reader is to
understand that just before the battle of Lewes, which proved
so fatal to the interests of Henry III., the barons had offered
his brother Richard, king of the Romans, 30,000*l.* to procure
a peace upon such terms as would have divested Henry of all
his regal power, and therefore the treaty proved abortive.
The consequences of that battle are well known: the king,
prince Edward his son, his brother Richard, and many of his
friends, fell into the hands of their enemies; while two great
barons of the king's party, John, Earl of Warren, and Hugh
Bigot, the king's Justiciary, had been glad to escape into
France.

In the 1st stanza, the aforesaid sum of 30,000*l.* is alluded to; but, with the usual misrepresentation of party malevolence, is asserted to have been the exorbitant demand of the king's brother.

With regard to the 2nd stanza, the reader is to note that Richard, along with the earldom of Cornwall, had the honours of Wallingford and Eyre confirmed to him on his marriage, with Sanchia, daughter of the Count of Provence, in 1243. Windsor Castle was the chief fortress belonging to the king, and had been garrisoned by foreigners; a circumstance which furnishes out the burthen of each stanza.

The 3rd stanza alludes to a remarkable circumstance which happened on the day of the battle of Lewes. After the battle was lost, Richard, king of the Romans, took refuge in a windmill, which he barricadoed, and maintained for some time against the barons, but in the evening was obliged to surrender. See a very full account of this in the *Chronicle of Mailros.* Oxon. 1684. p. 229.

The 4th stanza is of obvious interpretation: Richard, who had been elected king of the Romans in 1256, and had afterwards gone over to take possession of his dignity, was in the year 1259 about to return into England, when the barons raised a popular clamour, that he was bringing with him foreigners to overrun the kingdom: upon which he was forced to dismiss almost all his followers, otherwise the barons would have opposed his landing.

In the 5th stanza, the writer regrets the escape of the Earl of Warren; and in the 6th and 7th stanzas, insinuates that, if he and Sir Hugh Bigot once fell into the hands of their adversaries, they should never more return home; a circumstance which fixes the date of this ballad; for, in the year 1265, both these noblemen landed in South Wales, and the royal party soon after gained the ascendant. See Holinshed, Rapin, &c.

The following is copied from a very ancient MS. in the British Museum. [Harl. MSS. 2253. s. 23.] This MS. is judged, from the peculiarities of the writing, to be not later than the

time of Richard II.; *th* being every where expressed by the
character þ; the ẏ is pointed, after the Saxon manner, and
the *í* hath an oblique stroke over it.

Prefixed to this ancient libel on government was a small
design, which the engraver intended should correspond with
the subject. On the one side a Satyr, (emblem of Petulance
and Ridicule,) is trampling on the ensigns of Royalty; on
the other, Faction, under the mask of Liberty, is exciting
Ignorance and Popular Rage to deface the royal image,
which stands on a pedestal inscribed MAGNA CHARTA, to denote that the rights of the king, as well as those of the
people, are founded on the laws; and that to attack one,
is in effect to demolish both.

SITTETH alle stille, ant herkneth to me;
The kyng of Alemaigne, bi mi leaute,
Thritti thousent pound askede he
For te make the pees in the countre,
        Ant so he dude more.   5
    Richard, thah thou be ever trichard,
        Trichen shalt thou never more.

Richard of Alemaigne, whil that he wes kying,
He spende al is tresour opon swyvyng,
Haveth he nout of Walingford oferlẏng,   10
Let him habbe, ase he brew, bale to dryng,
        Maugre Wyndesore.
    Richard, thah thou be ever, &c.

The kyng of Alemaigne wende do ful wel,
He saisede the mulne for a castel,   15
With hare sharpe swerdes he grounde the stel,
He wende that the sayles were mangonel
        To helpe Wyndesore.
    Richard, thah thou be ever, &c.

Ver. 2, kyn. MS.

The kyng of Alemaigne gederede ys host,   20
Makede him a castel of a mulne post,
Wende with is prude, ant is muchele bost,
Brohte from Alemayne monẏ sori gost
       To store Wyndesore.
    Richard, thah thou be ever, &c.   25

By God, that is aboven ous, he dude muche sẏnne,
That lette passen over see the erl of Warynne:
He hath robbed Engelond, the mores, ant th fenne,
The gold, ant the selver, and ẏ-boren henne,
       For love of Wyndesore.   30
    Richard, thah thou be ever, &c.

Sire Simond de Mountfort hath suore bi ẏs chyn,
Hevede he nou here the erl of Warẏn,
Shuld he never more come to is ẏn,
Ne with sheld, ne with spere, ne with other gyn,   35
       To help of Wyndesore.
    Richard, thah thou be ever, &c.

Sire Simond de Montfort hath suore bi ys cop,
Hevede he nou here Sire Hue de Bigot:
Al he shulde grante here twelfmoneth scot   40
Shulde he never more with his sot pot
       To helpe Wyndesore.
    Richard, thah thou be ever, &c.

Be the luef, be the loht, sire Edward,
Thou shalt ride sporeles o thy lyard   45
Al the ryhte way to Dovere-ward,
Shalt thou never more breke foreward;
       Ant that reweth sore
    Edward, thou dudest as a shreward,
       Forsoke thyn emes lore.   50
    Richard, &c.

V. 40, g'te here. MS. *i. e.* grant their. Vide Glos.
V. 44, this stanza was omitted in the former editions.

⁎ This ballad will rise in its importance with the reader, when he finds that it is even believed to have occasioned a law in our Statute-Book, viz. "Against slanderous reports or tales, to cause discord betwixt king and people." (*Westm. Primer*, c. xxxiv. anno 3 Edw. I.) That it had this effect, is the opinion of an eminent writer. See *Observations upon the Statutes*, &c. 4to. 2nd edit. 1766, p. 71.

However, in the Harl. Collection may be found other satirical and defamatory rhymes of the same age, that might have their share in contributing to this first law against libels.

II.

On the Death of K. Edward the First.

We have here an early attempt at Elegy. Edward I. died July 7, 1307, in the 35th year of his reign, and 69th of his age. This poem appears to have been composed soon after his death. According to the modes of thinking peculiar to those times, the writer dwells more upon his devotion, than his skill in government; and pays less attention to the martial and political abilities of this great monarch, in which he had no equal, than to some little weaknesses of superstition, which he had in common with all his contemporaries. The king had in the decline of life vowed an expedition to the Holy Land; but finding his end approach, he dedicated the sum of 32,000*l.* to the maintenance of a large body of knights, (140 say historians, 80 says our poet,) who were to carry his heart with them into Palestine. This dying command of the king was never performed. Our poet, with the honest prejudices of an Englishman, attributes this failure to the advice of the king of France, whose daughter Isabel, the young monarch, who succeeded, immediately married. But the truth is, Edward and his destructive favourite, Piers Gaveston, spent the money upon their pleasures. To do the greater honour to the memory of his hero, our poet puts his eloge in the mouth of the Pope, with the

same poetic licence as a more modern bard would have introduced Britannia, or the Genius of Europe, pouring forth
his praises.

This antique elegy is extracted from the same MS. volume
as the preceding article; is found with the same peculiarities
of writing and orthography; and, though written at near the
distance of half a century, contains little or no variation of
idiom: whereas the next following poem, by Chaucer, which
was probably written not more than 50 or 60 years after this,
exhibits almost a new language. This seems to countenance
the opinion of some antiquaries, that this great poet made
considerable innovations in his mother tongue, and introduced
many terms and new modes of speech from other languages.

ALLE, that beoth of huerte trewe,
   A stounde herkneth to my song
Of duel, that Deth hath diht us newe,
   That maketh me syke, ant sorewe among;
Of a knyht, that wes so strong,   5
   Of wham God hath don ys wille;
Me-thuncheth that deth hath don us wrong,
   That he so sone shall ligge stille.

Al Englond ahte for te knowe
   Of wham that song is, that y synge;   10
Of Edward kyng, that lith so lowe,
   Zent al this world is nome con springe:
Trewest mon of alle thinge,
   Ant in werre war ant wys,
For him we ahte oure honden wrynge,   15
   Of Christendome he ber the prys.

Byfore that oure kyng was ded,
   He spek ase mon that wes in care,
"Clerkes, knyhtes, barons, he sayde,
   Y charge ou by oure sware,   20

That ye to Engelonde be trewe.
   Y deze, y ne may lyven na more;
Helpeth mi sone, ant crouneth him newe,
   For he is nest to buen y-core.

"Ich biqueth myn herte arhyt,   25
   That hit be write at my devys,
Over the see that Hue[1] be diht,
   With fourscore knyhtes al of prys,
In werre that buen war ant wys,
   Azein the hethene for te fyhte,   30
To wynne the croiz that lowe lys,
   Myself ycholde zef that y myhte."

Kyng of Fraunce, thou hevedest 'sinne,'
   That thou the counsail woldest fonde,
To latte the wille of 'Edward kyng'   35
   To wende to the holy londe:
That oure kynge hede take on honde
   All Engelond to zeme ant wysse,
To wenden in to the holy londe
   To wynnen us heveriche blisse.   40

The messager to the pope com,
   And seyde that our kynge was ded:
Ys oune hond the lettre he nom,
   Ywis his herte was full gret:
The Pope him self the lettre redde,   45
   Ant spec a word of gret honour.
"Alas! he seid, is Edward ded?
   Of Christendome he ber the flour."

The Pope to is chaumbre wende,
   For dol ne mihte he speke na more;   50

Ver. 33, sunne. MS.   V. 35, kyng Edward. MS.   V. 43. ys is probably a contraction of *in hys*, or *yn his*.

[1] This is probably the name of the person who was to preside over this
business.

Ant after cardinals he sende,
   That muche couthen of Cristes lore,
Bothe the lasse, ant eke the more,
   Bed hem bothe rede ant synge:
Gret deol me myhte se thore,   55
   Mony mon is honde wrynge.

The Pope of Peyters stod at is masse
   With ful gret solempnetè,
Ther me con the soule blesse:
   "Kyng Edward honoured thou be: 60
God love thi sone come after the,
   Bringe to ende that thou hast bygonne,
The holy crois y-mad of tree,
   So fain thou woldest hit hav y-wonne.

"Jerusalem, thou hast i-lore   65
   The flour of al chivalrie
Now kyng Edward liveth na more:
   Alas! that he zet shulde deye!
He wolde ha rered up ful heyze
   Oure banners, that bueth broht to grounde; 70
Wel! longe we mowe clepe and crie
   Er we a such kyng han y-founde."

Nou is Edward of Carnarvan
   King of Engelond al aplyht,
God lete him ner be worse man   75
   Then his fader, ne lasse of myht,
To holden is pore men to ryht,
   And understonde good counsail,
Al Engelong for to wysse ant dyht;
   Of gode knyhtes darh him nout fail.   80

Thah mi tonge were mad of stel,
   Ant min herte yzote of bras,
The godness myht y never telle,
   That with kyng Edward was:

V. 55, 59, me, *i. e.* men; so in Robert of Gloucester, passim.

Kyng, as thou art cleped conquerour,   85
   In uch bataille thou hadest prys;
God bringe thi soule to the honour,
   That ever wes, ant ever ys[2].

[2] Here follow in the original three lines more, which, as seemingly redundant, are thus appended, viz.

     That lasteth ay withouten ende,
      Bidde we God, ant oure Ledy to thilke blisse
     Jesus us sende. Amen.

III.

An original Ballad by Chaucer.

THIS little sonnet, which hath escaped all the editors of Chaucer's works, is now printed for the first time from an ancient MS. in the Pepysian library, that contains many other poems of its venerable author. The versification is of that species which the French call *Rondeau*, very naturally Englished by our honest countrymen *Round O*. Though so early adopted by them, our ancestors had not the honour of inventing it: Chaucer picked it up, along with other better things, among the neighbouring nations. A fondness for laborious trifles hath always prevailed in the dark ages of literature. The Greek poets have had their *wings* and *axes:* the great father of English poesy may therefore be pardoned one poor solitary *rondeau.* Geofrey Chaucer died Oct. 25, 1400, aged 72.

I. 1.

YOURE two eyn will sle me sodenly
I may the beaute of them not sustene,
So wendeth it thorowout my herte kene.

2.

And but your words will helen hastely
My hertis wound, while that it is grene,
Youre two eyn will sle me sodenly.

3.

Upon my trouth I sey yow feithfully,
That ye ben of my liffe and deth the quene;
For with my deth the trouth shal be sene.
    Youre two eyn, &c.

II. 1.

So hath youre beauty fro your herte chased
Pitee, that me n' availeth not to pleyn:
For daunger halt your mercy in his cheyne.

2.

Giltless my deth thus have ye purchased;
I sey yow soth, me nedeth not to fayn:
So hath your beaute fro your herte chased.

3.

Alas, that nature hath in yow compassed
So grete beaute, that no man may atteyn
To mercy, though he sterve for the peyn.
    So hath youre beaute, &c.

III. 1.

Syn I fro love escaped am so fat,
I nere thinke to ben in his prison lene;
Syn I am fre, I counte hym not a bene.

2.

He may answere, and sey this and that,
I do no fors, I speak ryght as I mene;
Syn I fro love escaped am so fat.

3.

Love hath my name i-strike out of his sclat,
And he is strike out of my bokes clene:
For ever mo 'ther[1]' is non other mene,
    Syn I fro love escaped, &c.

[1] This, MS.

IV.

𝕿𝖍𝖊 𝕿𝖚𝖗𝖓𝖆𝖒𝖊𝖓𝖙 𝖔𝖋 𝕿𝖔𝖙𝖙𝖊𝖓𝖍𝖆𝖒.

OR, THE WOOEING, WINNING, AND WEDDING OF TIBBE, THE REEV'S
DAVGHTER THERE.

It does honour to the good sense of this nation, that while
all Europe was captivated with the bewitching charms of
chivalry and romance, two of our writers in the rudest times
could see through the false glare that surrounded them, and
discover whatever was absurd in them both. Chaucer wrote
his Rhyme of Sir Thopas in ridicule of the latter; and in the
following poem we have a humorous burlesque of the former.
Without pretending to decide whether the institution of
chivalry was upon the whole useful or pernicious in the rude
ages, a question that has lately employed many good writers[1],
it evidently encouraged a vindictive spirit, and gave such
force to the custom of duelling, that there is little hope of
its being abolished. This, together with the fatal consequences which often attended the diversion of the Turnament, was sufficient to render it obnoxious to the graver part
of mankind. Accordingly the Church early denounced its
censures against it, and the State was often prevailed on to
attempt its suppression. But fashion and opinion are superior
to authority: and the proclamations against tilting were as
little regarded in those times, as the laws against duelling
are in these. This did not escape the discernment of our
poet, who easily perceived that inveterate opinions must be
attacked by other weapons besides proclamations and censures; he accordingly made use of the keen one of RIDICULE.
With this view he has here introduced with admirable humour
a parcel of clowns, imitating all the solemnities of the
Tourney. Here we have the regular challenge — the appointed day — the lady for the prize — the formal preparations — the display of armour — the scutcheons and devices

---

[1] See [Mr. Hurd's] Letters on Chivalry, 8vo. 1762. Mémoire de la Che-
valerie, par M. de la Curne des Palais, 1759, 2 tom. 12mo, &c.

— the oaths taken on entering the lists — the various accidents
of the encounter — the victor leading off the prize — and the
magnificent feasting — with all the other solemn fopperies
that usually attended the pompous turnament. And how
acutely the sharpness of the author's humour must have been
felt in those days, we may learn from what we can perceive
of its keenness now, when time has so much blunted the edge
of his ridicule.

The Turnament of Tottenham was first printed from an
ancient MS. in 1631, 4to., by the Rev. Whilhem Bedwell,
rector of Tottenham, who was one of the translators of the
Bible. He tells us it was written by Gilbert Pilkington,
thought to have been some time parson of the same parish,
and author of another piece, entitled *Passio Domini Jesu
Christi*. Bedwell, who was eminently skilled in the oriental
and other languages, appears to have been but little con-
versant with the ancient writers in his own; and he so little
entered into the spirit of the poem he was publishing, that
he contends for its being a serious narrative of a real event,
and thinks it must have been written before the time of
Edward III., because turnaments were prohibited in that
reign. "I do verily believe," says he, "that this Turnament
was acted before this proclamation of King Edward. For
how durst any to attempt to do that, although in sport, which
was so straightly forbidden, both by the civill and ec-
clesiasticall power? For although they fought not with
lances, yet, as our author sayth, 'It was no children's game.'
And what would have become of him, thinke you, which
should have slayne another in this manner of jeasting?
Would he not, trow you, have been *hang'd for it in earnest?
yea, and have bene buried like a dogge?*" It is, however, well
known that turnaments were in use down to the reign of
Elizabeth.

In the former editions of this work, Bedwell's copy was
reprinted here, with some few conjectural emendations; but
as Bedwell seemed to have reduced the orthography at least,
if not the phraseology, to the standard of his own time, it

was with great pleasure that the Editor was informed of an ancient MS. copy preserved in the Museum, [Harl. MSS. 5396,] which appeared to have been transcribed in the reign of King Henry VI., about 1456. This obliging information the Editor owed to the friendship of Thomas Tyrwhitt, Esq., and he has chiefly followed that more authentic transcript, improved however by some readings from Bedwell's book.

Of all thes kene conquerours to carpe it were kynde;
Of fele feyztyng folk ferly we fynde,
The Turnament of Totenham have we in mynde;
It were harme sych hardynes were holden byhynde,
 In story as we rede   5
  Of Hawkyn, of Herry,
  Of Tomkyn, of Terry,
  Of them that were dughty
   And stalworth in dede.

It befel in Totenham on a dere day,   10
Ther was mad a shurtyng be the hy-way:
Theder com al the men of the contray,
Of Hyssylton, of Hy-gate, and of Hakenay,
 And all the swete swynkers.
  Ther hopped Hawkyn,   15
  Ther daunsed Dawkyn,
  Ther trumped Tomkyn,
   And all were trewe drynkers.

Tyl the day was gon and evyn-song past,
That they schuld reckyn ther scot and ther counts cast;   20
Perkyn the potter into the press past,
And sayd Randol the refe, a dozter thou hast,
 Tyb the dere:
  Therfor faine wyt wold I,

Ver. 20. It is not very clear in the MS. whether it should be *conts* or *conters.*

> Whych of all thys bachelery   25
> Were best worthye
>   To wed hur to hys fere.

Upstyrt thos gadelyngys wyth ther lang staves,
And sayd, Randol the refe, lo! thys lad raves;
Boldely amang us thy dozter he craves;   30
We er rycher men than he, and mor gode haves
   Of cattell and corn;
      Then sayd Perkyn, To Tybbe I have hyzt
      That I schal be alway redy in my ryzt,
      If that it schuld be thys day sevenyzt,   35
        Or elles zet to morn.

Then sayd Randolfe the refe, Ever be he waryd,
That about thys carpyng lenger wold be taryd:
I wold not my dozter, that scho were miscaryd,
But at hur most worschip I wold scho were maryd;   40
   Therfor a Turnament schal begynne
      Thys day sevenyzt, —
      Wyth a flayl for to fyzt:
      And 'he' that is most of myght
        Schal brouke hur wyth wynne.   45

Whoso berys hym best in the turnament,
Hym schal be granted the gre be the comon assent,
For to wynne my dozter wyth 'dughtynesse' of dent,
And 'coppell' my brode-henne 'that' was brozt out of Kent:
   And my dunnyd kowe,   51
      For no spens wyl I spare,
      For no cattell wyl I care,
      He schal have my gray mare,
        And my spottyd sowe.

Ther was many 'a' bold lad ther bodyes to bede: 55
Than thay toke thayr leve, and homward they zede;

V. 48, dozty. MS.   V. 49, coppeld.   We still use the phrase "a copple.
crowned hen."

And all the weke afterward graythed ther wede,
Tyll it come to the day, that thay suld do ther dede.
   They armed tham in matts;
      Thay set on ther nollys,   60
      For to kepe ther pollys,
      Gode blake bollys,
        For batryng of bats.

Thay sowed tham in schepeskynnes, for thay schuld not
     brest:
Ilk-on toke a blak hat, insted of a crest: 65
'A basket or a panyer before on ther brest,'
And a flayle in ther hande; for to fyght prest,
   Furth gon thay fare:
      Ther was kyd mekyl fors,
      Who schuld best fend hys cors: 70
      He that had no gode hors,
        He gat hym a mare.

Sych another gadryng have I not sene oft,
When all the gret company com rydand to the croft:
Tyb on a gray mare was set up on loft   75
On a sek ful of fedyrs, for scho schuld syt soft,
   And led 'till the gap.'
      For cryeng of the men
      Forther wold not Tyb then,
      Tyl scho had hur brode hen   80
      Set in hur Lap.

A gay gyrdyl Tyb had on, borowed for the nonys,
And a garland on hur hed ful of rounde bonys,
And a broche on hur brest ful of 'sapphyre' stonys,
Wyth the holy-rode tokenyng, was wrotyn for the nonys; 85

V. 57, gayed. P.C.   V. 66 is wanting in MS. and supplied from P.C.
V. 72, he borrowed him. P.C.   V. 76, the MS. had once *sedys*, i. e. *seeds*,
which appears to have been altered to *fedyrs*, or feathers. Bedwell's copy
has *senvy*, i. e. *mustard-seed*.   V. 77, And led hur to cap. MS.   V. 83,
Bedwell's P.C. has *ruel-bones*.   V. 84, safer stones. MS.   V. 85, wrotyn,
i. e. wrought. P.C. reads *written*.

For no 'spendings' thay had spared.
   When joly Gyb saw hur thare,
   He gyrd so hys gray mare,
   'That scho lete a fowkin' fare
      At the rereward.   90

I wow to God, quoth Herry, I schal not lefe behynde,
May I mete wyth Bernard on Bayard the blynde,
Ich man kepe hym out of my wynde,
For whatsoever that he be, before me I fynde,
   I wot I schall hym greve.   95
      Wele sayd, quoth Hawkyn,
      And I wow, quoth Dawkyn,
      May I mete wyth Tomkyn,
        Hys flayle I schal hym reve.

I make a vow, quoth Hud, Tyb, son schal thou se,   100
Whych of all thys bachelery 'granted' is the gre:
I schal scomfet thaym all, for the love of the;
In what place so I come thay schal have dout of me,
   Myn armes ar so clere:
      I bere a reddyl, and a rake,   105
      Poudred wyth a brenand drake,
      And three cantells of a cake
        In ycha cornere.

I vow to God, quoth Hawkyn, yf 'I' have the gowt,
Al that I fynde in the felde 'thrustand' here aboute,   110
Have I twyes or thryes redyn thurgh the route,
In ycha stede ther thay me se, of me thay schal have doute,
   When I begyn to play.
      I make avowe that I ne schall,
      But yf Tybbe wyl me call,   115
      Or I be thryes don fall,
        Ryzt onys com away.

V. 86, no catel [perhaps *chatel*] they had spared. MS.   V. 89, Then ...
fan.con. MS.   V. 101, grant. MS.   V. 109, yf he have. MS.   V. 110,
the MS. literally has *th*^{r}. *sand* here.

Then sayd Terry, and swore be hys crede;
Saw thou never yong boy forther hys body bede,
For when thay fyzt fastest and most ar in drede,   120
I schall take Tyb by the hand, and hur away lede:
 I am armed at the full;
  In myn armys I bere wele
  A doz trogh, and a pele,
  A sadyll wythout a panell,   125
   Wyth a fles of woll.

I make a vow, quoth Dudman, and swor be the stra,
Whyls me ys left my 'mare,' thou gets hurr not swa;
For scho ys wele schapen, and lizt as the rae,
Ther is no capul in thys myle befor hur schal ga;   130
 Sche wul ne nozt begyle:
  Sche wyl me bere, I dar say,
  On a lang somerys day,
  Fro Hyssylton to Hakenay,
   Nozt other half myle.   135

I make a vow, quoth Perkyn, thow speks of cold rost,
I schal wyrch 'wyselyer' without any bost:
Five of the best capulys, that ar in thys ost,
I wot I schal thaym wynne, and bryng thaym to my cost,
 And here I grant thaym Tybbe.   140
  Wele boyes here ys he,
  That wyl fyzt, and not fle,
  For I am in my jolyte,
   Wyth so forth, Gybbe.

When thay had ther vowes made, furth can thay hie,   145
Wyth flayles, and hornes, and trumpes mad of tre:
Ther were all the bachelerys of that contre;
Thay were dyzt in aray, as thaymselfes wold be:
 Thayr baners were ful bryzt
  Of an old rotten fell;   150

V. 128, merth. MS. V. 137, swyselior. MS. V. 146, flailes, and harnisse. P. C.

Percy. II.   2

The cheveron of a plow-mell;
And the schadow of a bell,
    'Quartred' wyth the mone lyzt.

I wot yt 'was' no chylder game, whan thay togedyr met,
When icha freke in the feld on hys feloy bet,   155
And layd on styfly, for nothyng wold thay let,
And foght ferly fast, tyll ther horses swet,
    And few wordys spoken.
        Ther were flayles al to slatred,
        Ther were scheldys al to flatred,   160
        Bollys and dysches al to schatred,
           And many hedys brokyn.

Ther was clynkyng of cart-sadelys, and clatteryng of cannes;
Of fele frekys in the feld brokyn were their fannes;
Of sum were the hedys brokyn, of sum the brayn-pannes, 165
And yll were thay besene, or thay went thanns,
    Wyth swyppyng of swepyls:
        Thay were so wery for-foght,
        Thay myzt not fyzt mare oloft,
        But creped about in the 'croft,'   170
           As thay were croked crepyls.

Perkyn was so wery, that he began to loute;
Help, Hud, I am ded in thys ylk rowte:
An hors for forty pens, a gode and a stoute!
That I may lyztly come of my noye oute,   175
    For no cost wyl I spare.
        He styrt up as a snayle,
        And hent a capul be the tayle,
        And 'reft' Dawkin hys flayle,
           And wan there a mare.   180

V. 151, The chiefe, P. C.   V. 153, Poundred. MS.   V. 154, yt ys. MS.
V. 168, The boyes were. MS.   V. 170, creped then about in the croft. MS.
V. 179, razt. MS.

Perkyn wan five, and Hud wan twa:
Glad and blythe thay ware, that thay had don sa;
Thay wold have tham to Tyb, and present hur with tha:
The Capulls were so wery, that thay myzt not ga,
    But styl gon thay stond.   185
        Alas! quoth Hudde, my joye I lese:
        Mee had lever then a ston of chese,
        That dere Tyb had al these,
        And wyst it were my sond.

Perkyn turnyd hym about in that ych thrang,   190
Among those wery boyes he wrest and he wrang;
He threw tham doun to the erth, and thrast tham amang,
When he saw Tyrry away wyth Tyb fang,
    And after hym ran;
        Off his horse he hym drogh,   195
        And gaf hym of hys flayl inogh:
        We te he! quoth Tyb, and lugh,
        Ye er a dughty man.

'Thus' thay tugged, and rugged, tyl yt was nere nyzt:
All the wyves of Totenham came to see that syzt   200
Wyth wyspes, and kexis, and ryschys there lyzt,
To fetch hom ther husbandes, that were tham trouth plyzt;
    And some brozt gret harwos,
        Ther husbandes hom to fetch,
        Som on dores, and sum on hech,   205
        Sum on hyrdyllys, and som on crech,
        And sum on whele-barows.

Thay gaderyd Perkyn about, 'on' everych syde,
And grant hym ther 'the gre,' the more was hys pryde:
Tyb and he, wyth gret 'mirth,' homeward con thay ryde, 210
And were al nyzt togedyr, tyl the morn tyde:

V. 185, stand. MS.   V. 189, sand. MS.   V. 190, ilk throng. P. C.
V. 199, Thys. MS.   V. 204, hom for to fetch. MS.   V. 208, about everych
side. MS.   V. 209, the *gre*, is wanting in MS.   V. 210, mothe. MS.
                           2*

And thay 'to church went:'
   So wele hys nedys he has sped,
   That dere Tyb he 'hath' wed;
   The prayse-folk, that hur led,   215
     Were of the Turnament.

To that ylk fest com many for the nones;
Some come hyphalte, and some trippand 'thither' on the
   stonys:
Sum a staf in hys hand, and sum two at onys;
Of sum where the hedes broken, of some the schulder
   bonys: 220
   With sorrow come thay thedyr.
     Wo was Hawkyn, wo was Herry,
     Wo was Tomkyn, wo was Terry,
     And so was all the bachelary,
      When thay met togedyr.   225

2 At that fest thay wer servyd with a ryche aray,
Every fyve and fyve had a cokenay;
And so thay sat in jolyte al the lung day;
And at the last thay went to bed with ful gret deray:
   Mekyl myrth was them among;   230
     In every corner of the hous
     Was melody delycyous
     For to here precyus
      Of six menys song 3.

V. 212, And thay ifere assent. MS.   V. 214, had wed. MS.   V. 215,
The cheefemen. P. C.   V. 218, trippand on. MS.

2 In the former impressions, this concluding stanza was only given from
Bedwell's printed edition; but it is here copied from the old MS. wherein it
has been since found separated from the rest of the poem, by several pages
of a money-account, and other heterogeneous matter.

3 Six-men's song, *i. e.* a song for six Voices. So Shakspeare uses Three-
man song-men, in his *Winter's Tale*, act iii. sc. 3, to denote men that could
sing Catches composed for three Voices. Of this sort are Weelkes's Madrigals mentioned below, book ii. song 9. So again Shakspeare has Three-
men beetle; *i. e.* a beetle or rammer worked by three men, 2 *Hen. IV.* act i.
sc. 3.

Musical Notes for the Victory at Agincourt.

Deo gratias Anglia   redde pro victoria.

Owre Kynge went forth to Normandy with grace and

myzt of chivalry; the God for him wrouzt marvelously,

Wherefore Englonde may calle, and cry *Deo Gratias*,

CHORUS.

Deo Gratias, Anglia redde   pro   Victoria.

V.

𝔉or t̸e 𝔐ictory at 𝔄gincourt.

THAT our plain and martial ancestors could wield their
swords much better than their pens, will appear from the
following homely rhymes, which were drawn up by some
poet-laureate of those days to celebrate the immortal victory
gained at Agincourt, Oct. 25, 1415. This song or hymn is
given merely as a curiosity, and is printed from a MS. copy
in the Pepys collection, vol. i. fol. It is there accompanied
with the musical notes, which are here copied.

   Deo gratias Anglia redde pro victoria!
OWRE kynge went forth to Normandy,
With grace and myzt of chivalry;
The God for him wrouzt marvelously,
Wherefore Englonde may calle, and cry   5
     Deo gratias:
  Deo gratias Anglia redde pro victoria.

He sette a sege, the sothe for to say,
To Harflue toune with ryal aray;
That toune he wan, and made a fray,   10
That Fraunce shall rywe tyl domes day.
     Deo gratias, &c.

Then went owre kynge, with alle his oste,
Thorowe Fraunce for all the Frenshe boste;
He spared 'for' drede of leste, ne most,   15
Tyl he come to Agincourt coste
     Deo gratias, &c.

Than for sothe that knyzt comely
In Agincourt feld he fauzt manly,
Thorow grace of God most myzty   20
He had both the felde, and the victory:
     Deo Gratias, &c.

Ther dukys, and erlys, lorde and barone,
Were take, and slayne, and that wel sone,
And some were ledde in to Lundone   25
With joye, and merthe, and grete renone.
Deo gratias, &c.

Now gracious God he save owre kynge.
His peple, and all his wel wyllynge,
Gef him gode lyfe, and gode endynge,   30
That we with merth mowe savely synge
Deo gratias:
Deo gratias Anglia redde pro victoria.

VI.

Ϲђe Ποt-Brohne Ϻaγd.

THE sentimental beauties of this ancient ballad have always recommended it to readers of taste, notwithstanding
the rust of antiquity which obscures the style and expression.
Indeed, if it had no other merit than the having afforded the
ground-work to Prior's *Henry and Emma*, this ought to preserve it from oblivion. That we are able to give it in so
correct a manner, is owing to the great care and exactness
of the accurate editor of the *Prolusions*, 8vo. 1760; who has
formed the text from two copies found in two different editions of *Arnolde's Chronicle*, a book supposed to be first
printed about 1521. From the copy in the Prolusions the
following is printed, with a few additional improvements
gathered from another edition of Arnolde's book[1], preserved
in the public library at Cambridge. All the various readings
of this copy will be found here, either received into the text,
or noted in the margin. The references to the Prolusions

[1] This (which my friend Mr. Farmer supposes to be the first edition) is
in folio: the folios are numbered at the bottom of the leaf: the song begins
at folio 75. The poem has since been collated with a very fine copy that
was in the collection of the late James West, Esq.; the readings extracted
thence are denoted thus, 'Mr. W.'

will show where they occur. In our ancient folio MS. described in the preface, is a very corrupt and defective copy of this ballad, which yet afforded a great improvement in one passage. See v. 310.

It has been a much easier task to settle the text of this poem, than to ascertain its date. The ballad of the *Not Browne Mayd* was first revived in *The Muses Mercury* for June 1707, 4to., being prefaced with a little "Essay on the old English Poets and Poetry:" in which this poem is concluded to be "near 300 years old," upon reasons which, though they appear inconclusive to us now, were sufficient to determine Prior, who there first met with it. However, this opinion had the approbation of the learned Wanley, an excellent judge of ancient books. For that whatever related to the reprinting of this old piece was referred to Wanley, appears from two letters of Prior's preserved in the British Museum [Harl. MSS. No. 3777]. The editor of the Prolusions thinks it cannot be older than the year 1500, because in Sir Thomas More's tale of *The Serjeant*, &c., which was written about that time, there appears a sameness of rhythmus and orthography, and a very near affinity of words and phrases, with those of this ballad. But this reasoning is not conclusive; for if Sir Thomas More made this ballad his model, as is very likely, that will account for the sameness of measure, and in some respect for that of words and phrases, even though this had been written long before; and, as for the orthography, it is well known that the old printers reduced that of most books to the standard of their own times. Indeed it is hardly probable that an antiquary like Arnolde would have inserted it among his historical Collections, if it had been then a modern piece; at least, he would have been apt to have named its author. But to show how little can be inferred from a resemblance of rhythmus or style, the Editor of these volumes has in his ancient folio MS. a poem on the victory of Flodden-field, written in the same numbers, with the same alliterations, and in orthography, phraseology, and style nearly resembling the *Visions of*

Pierce Plowman, which are yet known to have been composed above 160 years before that battle. As this poem is a great curiosity, we shall give a few of the introductory lines:

> "Grant gracious God, grant me this time,
> That I may 'say, or I cease, thy selven to please;
> And Mary his mother, that maketh this world;
> And all the seemlie saints, that sitten in heaven;
> I will carpe of kings, that conquered full wide.
> That dwelled in this land, that was alyes noble;
> Henry the seventh, that soveraigne lord," &c.

With regard to the date of the following ballad, we have taken a middle course, neither placed it so high as Wanley and Prior, nor quite so low as the editor of the Prolusions: we should have followed the latter in dividing every other line into two, but that the whole would then have taken up more room than could be allowed it in this volume.

Be it ryght, or wrong, these men among
    On women do complayne[1];
Affyrmynge this, how that it is
    A labour spent in vayne,
To love them wele; for never a dele   5
    They love a man agayne:
For late a man do what he can,
    Theyr favour to attayne,
Yet, yf a newe do them persue,
    Theyr first true lover than   10
Laboureth for nought; for from her thought
    He is a banyshed man.

I say nat nay, but that all day
    It is bothe writ and sayd

Ver. 2, woman. Prolusions, and Mr. West's copy.   V. 11, her, *i. e.* their.

[1] My friend, Mr. Farmer, proposes to read the first lines thus, as a Latinism:

> Be it right or wrong, 'tis men among,
> On women to complayne.

That womans faith is, as who sayth   15
  All utterly decayd;
But, neverthelesse, ryght good wytnèsse
  In this case might be layd,
That they love true, and continùe:
  Recorde the Not-browne Mayde: 20
Which, when her love came, her to prove,
  To her to make his mone,
Wolde nat depart: for in her hart
  She loved but hym alone.

Than betwaine us late us dyscus   25
  What was all the manere
Betwayne them two: we wyll also
  Tell all the payne, and fere,
That she was in. Nowe I begyn,
  So that ye me answère;   30
Wherefore, all ye, that present be
  I pray you, gyve an ere.
"I am the knyght; I come by nyght,
  As secret as I can;
Sayinge, Alas! thus standeth the case,   35
  I am a banyshed man."

SHE.

And I your wyll for to fulfyll
  In this wyll nat refuse;
Trustying to shewe, in wordès fewe,
  That men have an yll use   40
(To theyr own shame) women to blame,
  And causelesse them accuse;
Therfore to you I answere nowe,
  All women to excuse,—
Myne owne hart dere, with you what chere?   45
  I pray you tell anone;
For, in my mynde, of all mankynde
  I love but you alone.

HE.

It standeth so; a dede is do
    Wherof grete harme shall growe: 50
My destiny is for to dy
    A shamefull deth, I trowe;
Or elles to fle: the one must be.
    None other way I knowe,
But to withdrawe as an outlawe,   55
    And take me to my bowe.
Wherfore, adue, my owne hart true!
    None other rede I can:
For I must to the grene wode go,
    Alone, a banyshed man.   60

SHE.

O Lord, what is thys worldys blysse,
    That changeth as the mone!
My somers day in lusty may
    Is derked before the none.
I here you say, farewell: Nay, nay,   65
    We dèpart nat so sone.
Why say ye so? wheder wyll ye go?
    Alas! what have ye done?
All my welfàre to sorrowe and care
    Sholde chaunge, yf ye were gone;   70
For, in my mynde, of all mankynde
    I love but you alone.

HE.

I can beleve, it shall you greve,
    And somewhat you dystrayne;
But, aftyrwarde, your paynes harde   75
    Within a day or twayne
Shall sone aslake; and ye shall take
    Comfort to you agayne.

V. 63, The somers. Prol.

Why sholde ye ought? for, to make thought,
 Your labour were in vayne.   80
And thus I do; and pray you to,
 As hartely as I can;
For I must to the grene wode go,
 Alone, a banyshed man.

SHE.

Now, syth that ye have shewed to me   85
 The secret of your mynde,
I shall be playne to you agayne,
 Lyke as ye shall me fynde.
Syth it is so, that ye wyll go,
 I wolle not leve behynde;   90
Shall never be sayd, the Not-browne Mayd
 Was to her love unkynde:
Make you redy, for so am I,
 Allthough it were anone;
For, in my mynde, of all mankynde   95
 I love but you alone.

HE.

Yet I you rede to take good hede
 What men wyll thynke, and say:
Of yonge and olde it shall be tolde,
 That ye be gone away,   100
Your wanton wyll for to fulfill,
 In grene wode you to play;
And that ye myght from your delyght
 No lenger make delay.
Rather than ye sholde thus for me   105
 Be called an yll womàn,
Yet wolde I to the grene wode go,
 Alone, a banyshed man.

SHE.

Though it be songe of old and yonge,
 That I sholde be to blame,   110

V. 91, Shall it never. Prol. and Mr. W. V. 94, Althought. Mr. W.

Theyrs be the charge, that speke so large
  In hurtynge of my name:
For I wyll prove, that faythfulle love
  It is devoyd of shame;
In your dystresse, and hevynesse,   115
  To part with you, the same:
And sure all tho, that do not so,
  True lovers are they none;
For, in my mynde, of all mankynde
  I love but you alone.   120

HE.

I counceyle you, remember howe,
  It is no maydens lawe,
Nothynge to dout, but to renne out
  To wode with an outlàwe:
For ye must there in your hand bere   125
  A bowe, redy to drawe;
And, as a thefe, thus must you lyve,
  Ever in drede and awe;
Wherby to you grete harme myght growe:
  Yet had I lever than,   130
That I had to the grene wode go,
  Alone, a banyshed man.

SHE.

I thinke nat nay, but as ye say,
  It is no maydens lore:
But love may make me for your sake,   135
  As I have sayd before
To come on fote, to hunt, and shote
  To gete us mete in store;
For so that I your company
  May have, I aske no more: 140
From which to part, it maketh my hart
  As colde as ony stone;

V. 117, To shewe all. Prol. and Mr. W.   V. 133, I say nat. Prol. and
Mr. W.   V. 138, and store. Camb. copy.

For, in my mynde, of all mankynde
  I love but you alone.

HE.

For an outlawe this is the lawe,   145
  That men hym take and bynde;
Without pytè, hanged to be,
  And waver with the wynde.
If I had nede, (as God forbede!)
  What rescous coud ye fynde?   150
Forsoth, I trowe, ye and your bowe
  For fere wolde drawe behynde:
And no mervayle; for lytell avayle
  Were in your counceyle than:
Wherefore I wyll to the grene wode go,   155
  Alone, a banyshed man.

SHE.

Ryght wele knowe ye, that women be
  But feble for to fyght;
No womanhede it is indede
  To be bolde as a knyght: 160
Yet, in such fere yf that ye were
  With enemyes day or nyght,
I wolde withstande, with bowe in hande,
  To greve them as I myght,
And you to save; as women have   165
  From deth 'men' many one:
For, in my mynde, of all mankynde
  I love but you alone.

HE.

Yet take good hede; for ever I drede
  That ye coude nat sustayne   170

The thornie wayes, the depe valèies,
  The snowe, the frost, the rayne,
The colde, the hete: for dry, or wete,
  We must lodge on the playne;
And, us above, none other rofe   175
  But a brake bush, or twayne:
Which sone sholde greve you, I beleve;
  And ye wolde gladly than
That I had to the grene wode go,
  Alone, a banyshed man.   180

SHE.

Syth I have here bene partynère
  With you of joy and blysse,
I must also parte of your wo
  Endure, as reson is:
Yet am I sure of one plesùre;   185
  And, shortely, it is this:
That, where ye be, me semeth, pardè,
  I coude nat fare amysse.
Without more speche, I you beseche
  That we were sone agone;
For, in my mynde, of all mankynde   190
  I love but you alone.

HE.

If ye go thyder, ye must consyder,
  Whan ye have lust to dyne,
There shall no mete be for you gete,   195
  Nor drinke, bere, ale, ne wyne.
Ne shetès clene, to lye betwene,
  Made of threde and twyne;
None other house, but leves and bowes,
  To cover your hed and myne,   200
O myne harte swete, this evyll dyète
  Sholde make you pale and wan;

V. 172, frost and rayne. Mr. W.   V. 174, Ye must. Prol.   V. 189,
shortley gone. Prol. and Mr. W.   V. 196, Neyther bere. Prol. and Mr. W.
V. 201, Lo myn. Mr. W.

Wherfore I wyll to the grene wode go,
    Alone, a banyshed man.

SHE.

Among the wylde dere, such an archère,   205
    As men say that ye be,
Ne may nat fayle of good vitayle,
    Where is so grete plentè:
And water clere of the ryvère
    Shall be full swete to me;   210
With which in hele I shall ryght wele
    Endure, as ye shall see;
And, or we go, a bedde or two
    I can provyde anone;
For, in my mynde, of all mankynde   215
    I love but you alone.

HE.

Lo yet, before, ye must do more,
    Yf ye wyll go with me:
As cut your here up by your ere,
    Your kyrtel by the kne;   220
With bowe in hande, for to withstande
    Your enemyes, yf nede be:
And this same nyght before day-lyght,
    To wode-warde wyll I fle.
Yf that ye wyll all this fulfill,   225
    Do it shortely as ye can:
Els wyll I to the grene wode go,
    Alone, a banyshed man.

SHE.

I shall as nowe do more for you
    Than longeth to womanhede;   230
To shorte my here, a bow to bere,
    To shote in tyme of nede.

V. 207, May *ye* nat fayle. Prol.   Ib. May nat fayle. Mr. W.   V. 219,
above your ere. Prol.   V. 220, above the kne. Prol. and Mr. W.   V. 223,
the same. Prol. and Mr. W.

O my swete mother, before all other
    For you I have most drede:
But nowe, adue! I must ensue,   235
    Where fortune doth me lede.
All this mark ye: Now let us fle;
    The day cometh fast upon;
For, in my mynde, of all mankynde
    I love but you alone.   240

HE.

Nay, nay, nat so; ye shall nat go,
    And I shall tell ye why, ——
Your appetyght is to be lyght
    Of love, I wele espy:
For, lyke as ye have sayed to me,   245
    In lyke wyse hardely
Ye wolde answère whosoever it were,
    In way of company.
It is sayd of olde, Sone hote, sone colde;
    And so is a womàn.   250
Wherfore I to the wode wyll go,
    Alone, a banyshed man.

SHE.

Yf ye take hede, it is no nede
    Such wordes to say by me;
For oft ye prayed, and longe assayed,   255
    Or I you loved, pardè:
And though that I of auncestry
    A barons daughter be,
Yet have you proved howe I you loved
    A squyer of lowe degrè;   260
And ever shall, whatso befall;
    To dy therfore[1] anone;

V. 251, For I must to the grene wode go. Prol. and Mr. W.   V. 253,
yet is. Camb. copy: perhaps for *yt is*.

[1] *i. e.* for this cause; though I were to die for having loved you.

For, in my mynde, of all mankynde
    I love but you alone.

HE.

A barons chylde to be begylde!   265
    It were a cursed dede;
To be felàwe with an outlawe!
    Almighty God forbede!
Yet beter were, the pore squyère
    Alone to forest yede,   270
Than ye sholde say another day,
    That, by my cursed dede,
Ye were betray'd: Wherfore, good mayd,
    The best rede that I can,
Is, that I to the grene wode go,   275
    Alone, a banyshed man.

SHE.

Whatever befall, I never shall
    Of this thyng you upbrayd;
But yf ye go, and leve me so,
    Than have ye me betrayd.   280
Remember you wele, howe that ye dele;
    For, yf ye, as ye sayd,
Be so unkynde, to leve behynde,
    Your love, the Not-browne Mayd,
Trust me truly, that I shall dy   285
    Sone after ye be gone;
For, in my mynde, of all mankynde
    I love but you alone.

HE.

Yf that ye went, ye sholde repent;
    For in the forest nowe   290
I have purvayed me of a mayd,
    Whom I love more than you;

V. 262, dy with him. Editor's MS.   V. 278, outbrayd, Prol. and Mr. W.
V. 282, ye be as. Prol. and Mr. W.   V. 283, Ye were unkynde to lev me
behynde. Prol. and Mr. W.

Another fayrère, than ever ye were,
   I dare it wele avowe;
And of you bothe eche sholde be wrothe   295
   With other, as I trowe:
It were myne ese, to lyve in pese;
   So wyll I, yf I can;
Wherfore I to the wode wyll go,
   Alone, a banyshed man.   300

SHE.

Though in the wode I undyrstode
   Ye had a paramour,
All this may nought remove my thought,
   But that I wyll be your:
And she shall fynde me soft, and kynde,   305
   And courteys every hour;
Glad to fulfyll all that she wyll
   Commaunde me to my power:
For had ye, lo, an hundred mo,
   'Of them I wolde be one;'   310
For, in my mynde, of all mankynde
   I love but you alone.

HE.

Myne own dere love, I se the prove
   That ye be kynde, and true;
Of mayde, and wyfe, in all my lyfe,   315
   The best that ever I knewe.
Be mery and glad, be no more sad,
   The case is chaunged newe;
For it were ruthe, that, for your truthe,
   Ye sholde have cause to rewe.   320
Be nat dismayed; whatsoever I sayd
   To you, whan I began;

V. 310, So the Editor's MS. All the printed copies read,
         Yet wold I be that one.
     V. 315, of all. Prol. and Mr. W.

I wyll nat to the grene wode go,
    I am no banyshed man.

SHE.

These tydings be more gladd to me,   325
    Than to be made a quene,
Yf I were sure they sholde endure:
    But it is often sene,
Whan men wyll breke promyse, they speke
    The wordès on the splene.   330
Ye shape some wyle me to begyle,
    And stele from me, I wene:
Than were the case worse than it was,
    And I more wo-begone:
For, in my mynde, of all mankynde   335
    I love but you alone.

HE.

Ye shall nat nede further to drede;
    I wyll nat dysparàge
You, (God defend!) syth ye descend
    Of so grete a lynàge.   340
Now undyrstande; to Westmarlande,
    Which is myne herytage,
I wyll you brynge; and with a rynge,
    By way of maryage
I wyll you take, and lady make,   345
    As shortely as I can:
Thus have you won an erlys son,
    And not a banyshed man.

AUTHOR.

Here may ye se, that women be
    In love, meke, kynde, and stable: 350
Late never man reprove them than,
    Or call them variable;

V. 325, gladder. Prol. and Mr. W.   V. 340, grete lynyage. Prol. and Mr.
W.   V. 347, Then have. Prol.   V. 348, And no banyshed. Prol. and Mr.
W.   V. 352, This line wanting in Prol. and Mr. W.

But, rather, pray God, that we may
    To them be comfortable;
Which sometyme proveth such, as he loveth,   355
    Yf they be charytable.
For syth men wolde that women sholde
    Be meke to them each one;
Moche more ought they to God obey,
    And serve but hym alone.   360

V. 355, proved — loved. Prol. and Mr. W.   Ib. as loveth. Camb.
V. 357, Forsoth. Prol. and Mr. W.

VII.

A Balet by the Earl Rivers.

THE amiable light in which the character of Anthony
Widville, the gallant Earl Rivers, has been placed by the
elegant author of the *Catalogue of Noble Writers*, interests us
in whatever fell from his pen. It is presumed, therefore,
that the insertion of this little sonnet will be pardoned,
though it should not be found to have much poetical merit.
It is the only original poem known of that nobleman's; his
more voluminous works being only translations. And if we
consider that it was written during his cruel confinement in
Pomfret Castle, a short time before his execution in 1483, it
gives us a fine picture of the composure and steadiness with
which this stout earl beheld his approaching fate.

This ballad we owe to Rouse, a contemporary historian,
who seems to have copied it from the earl's own hand-writing.
In tempore, says this writer, *incarcerationis apud Pontem-
fractum edidit unum* BALET *in anglicis, ut mihi monstratum est,
quod subsequitur sub his verbis:* **Sum what musyng,** &c. *Rossi
Hist.* 8vo. 2d'edit. p. 213. In Rouse the second stanza, &c. is
imperfect, but the defects are here supplied from a more
perfect copy, printed in "Ancient Songs, from the Time of
K. Henry III. to the Revolution," p. 87.

This little piece, which perhaps ought rather to have been printed in stanzas of eight short lines, is written in imitation of a poem of Chaucer's, that will be found in Urry's edit. 1721, p. 555, beginning thus:

> "Alone walkyng, In thought plainyng,
>   And sore sighying, All desolate.
> My remembryïng Of my lyving
>   My death wishyng Both erly and late.

> "Infortunate Is so my fate
>   That wote ye what, Out of mesure
> My life I hate; Thus desperate
>   In such pore estate, Doe I endure," &c.

———

Sumwhat musyng, And more mornyng
 In remembring The unstydfastnes;
This world being Of such whelyng,
 Me contrarieng, What may I gesse?

I fere dowtles, Remediles,   5
 Is now to sese My wofull chaunce.
[For unkyndness, Withouten less,
 And no redress, Me doth avaunce,

With displesaunce, To my grevaunce,
 And no suraunce Of remedy.]   10
Lo in this traunce, Now in substaunce,
 Such is my dawnce, Wyllyng to dye.

Me thynkys truly, Bowndyn am I,
 And that gretly, To be content:
Seyng playnly, Fortune doth wry   15
 All contrary From myn entent.

My lyff was lent Me to on intent,
 Hytt is ny spent. Welcome fortune!
But I ne went Thus to be shent,
 But sho hit ment; such is hur won.   20

Ver. 15, That fortune. Rossi Hist. V. 19, went, *i. e.* weened.

———

VIII.

Cupid's Assault; by Lord Vaux.

THE reader will think that infant Poetry grew apace between the times of Rivers and Vaux, though nearly contemporaries; if the following song is the composition of that Sir Nicholas (afterwards Lord) Vaux, who was the shining ornament of the court of Henry VII., and died in the year 1523.

And yet to this lord it is attributed by Puttenham, in his *Art of Eng. Poesie*, 1589, 4to., a writer commonly well informed: take the passage at large. "In this figure [Counterfait Action] the Lord Nicholas Vaux, a noble gentleman and much delighted in vulgar making, and a man otherwise of no great learning, but having herein a marvelous facilitie, made a dittie representing the Battayle and Assault of Cupide, so excellently well, as for the gallant and propre application of his fiction in every part, I cannot choose but set downe the greatest part of his ditty, for in truth it cannot be amended, 'When Cupid scaled,' &c." p. 200. For a farther account of Nicholas Lord Vaux, see Mr. Walpole's *Noble Authors*, vol. i.

The following copy is printed from the first edit. of *Surrey's Poems*, 1557, 4to. See another song of Lord Vaux's in the preceding volume, book ii. no. 2.

———————

WHEN Cupide scaled first the fort,
   Wherein my hart lay wounded sore;
The batry was of such a sort,
   That I must yelde or die therfore.

There sawe I Love upon the wall,   5
   How he his banner did display:
Alarme, alarme, he gan to call:
   And bad his souldiours kepe aray.

The armes, the which that Cupide bare,
  Were pearced hartes with teares besprent,   10
In silver and sable to declare
  The stedfast love, he alwayes ment.

There might you se his band all drest
  In colours like to white and blacke,
With powder and with pelletes prest   15
  To bring the fort to spoile and sacke.

Good-wyll, the maister of the shot,
  Stode in the rampire brave and proude,
For spence of pouder he spared not
  Assault! assault! to crye aloude.   20

There might you heare the cannons rore;
  Eche pece discharged a lover's loke;
Which had the power to rent, and tore
  In any place whereas they toke.

And even with the trumpettes sowne;   25
  The scaling ladders were up set,
And Beautie walked up and downe,
  With bow in hand, and arrowes whet.

Then first Desire began to scale,
  And shrouded him under 'his' targe;   30
As one the worthiest of them all,
  And aptest for to geve the charge.

Then pushed souldiers with their pikes,
  And halberdes with handy strokes;
The argabushe in fleshe it lightes,   35
  And duns the ayre with misty smokes.

And, as it is the souldiers use
  When shot and powder gins to want,
I hanged up my flagge of truce,
  And pleaded up for my lives grant.   40

Ver. 30, her. ed. 1557: so ed. 1585.

When Fansy thus had made her breche,
   And Beauty entred with her band,
With bagge and baggage, sely wretch,
   I yelded into Beauties hand.

Then Beautie bad to blow retrete,   45
   And every souldier to retire,
And mercy wyll'd with spede to fet
   Me captive bound as prisoner.

Madame, quoth I, sith that this day
   Hath served you at all assayes,   50
I yeld to you without delay
   Here of the fortresse all the kayes

And sith that I have ben the marke,
   At whom you shot at with your eye;
Nedes must you with your handy warke,   55
   Or salve my sore, or let me die.

*** Since the foregoing song was first printed off, reasons have occurred, which incline me to believe that Lord Vaux, the poet, was not the Lord Nicholas Vaux who died in 1523, but rather a successor of his in the title. For, in the first place, it is remarkable that all the old writers mention Lord Vaux, the poet, as contemporary or rather posterior to Sir Thomas Wyat and the Earl of Surrey, neither of which made any figure till long after the death of the first Lord Nicholas Vaux. Thus Puttenham, in his *Art of English Poesie*, 1589, in p. 48, having named Skelton, adds, "In the latter end of the same kings raigne, [Henry VIII.] sprong up a new company of courtly Makers, [poets,] of whom Sir Thomas Wyat th' elder, and Henry Earl of Surrey, were the two chieftaines, who having travailed into Italie, and there tasted the sweet and stately measures and stile of the Italian poesie ... greatly polished our rude and homely manner of vulgar

42   CUPID'S ASSAULT.

poesie . . . . . In the *same time*, or *not long after*, was the Lord
Nicholas Vaux, a man of much facilitie in vulgar making[1]."
— Webbe, in his *Discourse of English Poetrie*, 1586, ranges
them in the following order, — "The Earl of Surrey, the
Lord Vaux, Norton, Bristow." And Gascoigne, in the place
quoted in the first volume of this work, [b. ii. no. 2,] mentions Lord Vaux after Surrey. — Again, the style and measure
of Lord Vaux's pieces seem too refined and polished for the
age of Henry VII., and rather resemble the smoothness and
harmony of Surrey and Wyat, than the rude metre of Skelton
and Hawes: but what puts the matter out of all doubt, in the
British Museum is a copy of his poem, *I lothe that I did love*,
[vid. vol. i. ubi supra,] with this title, "A dyttye or sonet
made by the Lord Vaus, in the time of the noble Quene
Marye, representing the image of Death." Harl. MSS.
No. 1703, §. 25.

It is evident, then, that Lord Vaux the poet was not he
that flourished in the reign of Henry VII., but either his son,
or grandson: and yet, according to Dugdale's *Baronage*, the
former was named Thomas, and the latter William: but this
difficulty is not great, for none of the old writers mention the
Christian name of the poetic Lord Vaux[2], except Puttenham;
and it is more likely that he might be mistaken in that lord's
name, than in the time in which he lived, who was so nearly
his contemporary.

Thomas Lord Vaux, of Harrowden in Northamptonshire,
was summoned to parliament in 1531. When he died does
not appear; but he probably lived till the latter end of Queen
Mary's reign, since his son

William was not summoned to parliament till the last
year of that reign, in 1558. This lord died in 1595. See
Dugdale, vol. ii. p. 304. — Upon the whole, I am inclined to
believe that Lord Thomas was the poet.

[1] *i. e.* Compositions in English.
[2] In the *Paradise of Dainty Devises*, 1596, he is called simply "Lord Vaux
the elder."

IX.

Sir Aldingar.

THIS old fabulous legend is given from the Editor's folio MS. with conjectural emendations, and the insertion of some additional stanzas to supply and complete the story.

It has been suggested to the Editor, that the author of this poem seems to have had in his eye the story of Gunhilda, who is sometimes called Eleanor, and was married to the Emperor (here called King) Henry.

OUR king he kept a false stewàrde,
  Sir Aldingar they him call;
A falser steward than he was one,
  Servde not in bower nor hall.

He wolde have layne by our comelye queene,   5
  Her deere worshippe to betraye:
Our queene she was a good womàn,
  And evermore said him naye.

Sir Aldingar was wrothe in his mind,
  With her hee was never content,   10
Till traiterous meanes he colde devyse,
  In a fyer to have her brent.

There came a lazar to the kings gate,
  A lazar both blinde and lame:
He tooke the lazar upon his backe,   15
  Him on the queenes bed has layne.

"Lye still, lazàr, wheras thou lyest,
  Looke thou goe not hence away;
Ile make thee a whole man and a sound
  In two howers of the day[1]."   20

[1] He probably insinuates that the king should heal him by his power of touching for the King's Evil.

Then went him forth sir Aldingar,
    And hyed him to our king:
"If I might have grace, as I have space,
    Sad tydings I could bring."

Say on, say on, sir Aldingar,   25
    Saye on the soothe to mee.
"Our queene hath chosen a new new love,
    And shee will have none of thee.

If shee had chosen a right good knight,
    The lesse had beene her shame;   30
But she hath chose her a lazar man,
    A lazar both blinde and lame."

If this be true, thou Aldingar,
    The tyding thou tellest to me,
Then will I make thee a rich rich knight,   35
    Rich both of golde and fee.

But if it be false, sir Aldingar,
    As God nowe grant it bee!
Thy body, I sweare by the holye rood,
    Shall hang on the gallows tree.   40

He brought our king to the queenes chambèr,
    And opend to him the dore.
A lodlye love, king Harry says,
    For our queene dame Elinore!

If thou were a man, as thou art none,   45
    Here on my sword thoust dye;
But a payre of new gallowes shall be built,
    And there shalt thou hang on hye.

Forth then hyed our king, I wysse,
    And an angry man was hee;   50
And soone he found queene Elinore,
    That bride so bright of blee.

Now God you save, our queene, madame,
  And Christ you save and see;
Here you have chosen a newe newe love,   55
  And you will have none of mee.

If you had chosen a right good knight,
  The lesse had been your shame:
But you have chose you a lazar man,
  A lazar both blinde and lame.   60

Therfore a fyer there shall be built,
  And brent all shalt thou bee. —
"Now out alacke! sayd our comlye queene,
  Sir Aldingar's false to mee.

Now out alacke! sayd our comlye queene,   65
  My heart with griefe will brast.
I have thought swevens had never been true;
  I have proved them true at last.

I dreamt in my sweven on thursday eve,
  In my bed wheras I laye,   70
I dreamt a grype and a grimlie beast,
  Had carryed my crowne awaye;

My gorgett and my kirtle of golde,
  And all my faire head-geere:
And he wold worrye me with his tush   75
  And to his nest y-beare:

Saving there came a little 'gray' hawke,
  A merlin him they call,
Which untill the grounde did strike the grype,
  That dead he downe did fall.   80

Giffe I were a man, as now I am none,
  A battell wold I prove,

Ver. 77, see below, ver. 137.

To fight with that traitor Aldingar;
    Att him I cast my glove.

But seeing Ime able noe battell to make,   85
    My liege, grant me a knight
To fight with that traitor, sir Aldingar,
    To maintaine me in my right."

"Now forty dayes I will give thee
    To seeke thee a knight therin: 90
If thou find not a knight in forty dayes
    Thy bodye it must brenn."

Then shee sent east, and shee sent west,
    By north and south bedeene:
But never a champion colde she find,   95
    Wolde fight with that knight soe keene.

Now twenty dayes were spent and gone,
    Noe helpe there might be had;
Many a teare shed our comelye queene
    And aye her hart was sad.   100

Then came one of the queenes damsèlles,
    And knelt upon her knee,
"Cheare up, cheare up, my gracious dame,
    I trust yet helpe may be.

And here I will make mine avowe,   105
    And with the same me binde;
That never will I return to thee,
    Till I some helpe may finde."

Then forth she rode on a faire palfràye
    Oer hill and dale about: 110
But never a champion colde she finde,
    Wolde fighte with that knight so stout.

And nowe the daye drewe on a pace,
  When our good queene must dye;
All woe-begone was that faire damsèlle,   115
  When she found no helpe was nye.

All woe-begone was that faire damsèlle,
  And the salt teares fell from her eye:
When lo! as she rode by a rivers side,
  She met with a tinye boye.   120

A tinye boye she mette, God wot,
  All clad in mantle of golde;
He seemed noe more in mans likenèsse,
  Then a childe of four yeere olde.

Why grieve you, damselle faire, he sayd,   125
  And what doth cause you moane?
The damsell scant wolde deigne a looke,
  But fast she pricked on.

Yet turne againe, thou faïre damsèlle,
  And greete thy queene from mee;   130
When bale is att hyest, boote is nyest,
  Nowe helpe enoughe may bee.

Bid her remember what she dreamt
  In her bedd, wheras shee laye;
How when the grype and the grimly beast   135
  Wolde have carried her crowne awaye.

Even then there came the little gray hawke,
  And saved her from his clawes:
Then bidd the queene be merry at hart,
  For heaven will fende her cause.   140

Back then rode that faire damsèlle,
  And her hart it lept for glee:
And when she told her gracious dame
  A gladd woman then was shee.

But when the appointed day was come,   145
   No helpe appeared nye:
Then woeful, woeful was her hart,
   And the teares stood in her eye.

And nowe a fyer was built of wood;
   And a stake was made of tree;   150
And now queene Elinor forth was led,
   A sorrowful sight to see.

Three times the herault he waved his hand,
   And three times spake on hye:
Giff any good knight will fende this dame,   155
   Come forth, or shee must dye.

No knight stood forth, no knight there came,
   No helpe appeared nye:
And now the fyer was lighted up,
   Queen Elinor she must dye.   160

And now the fyer was lighted up,
   As hot as hot might bee;
When riding upon a little white steed,
   The tinye boy they see.

"Away with that stake, away with those brands,   165
   And loose our comelye queene:
I am come to fight with sir Aldingar,
   And prove him a traitor keene."

Forthe then stood sir Aldingar,
   But when he saw the chylde,   170
He laughed, and scoffed, and turned his backe,
   And weened he had been beguylde.

"Now turne, now turne thee, Aldingar,
   And eyther fighte or flee;
I trust that I shall avenge the wronge,   175
   Thoughe I am so small to see."

The boye pulld forth a well good sworde,
   So gilt it dazzled the ee;
The first stroke stricken at Aldingar
   Smote off his leggs by the knee.   180

"Stand up, stand up, thou false traitòr,
   And fight upon thy feete,
For and thou thrive, as thou begin'st,
   Of height wee shall be meete."

A priest, a priest, sayes Aldingàr,   185
   While I am a man alive.
A priest, a priest, sayes Aldingàr,
   Me for to houzle and shrive.

I wolde have laine by our comlie queene,
   But shee wolde never consent;   190
Then I thought to betraye her unto our kinge
   In a fyer to have her brent.

There came a lazar to the kings gates,
   A lazar both blind and lame:
I tooke the lazar upon my backe,   195
   And on her bedd had him layne.

Then ranne I to our comlye king,
   These tidings sore to tell.
But ever alacke! sayes Aldingar,
   Falsing never doth well.   200

Forgive, forgive me, queene, madame,
   The short time I must live.
"Nowe Christ forgive thee, Aldingar,
   As freely I forgive."

Here take thy queene, our king Harryè,   205
   And love her as thy life,
For never had a king in Christentye,
   A truer and fairer wife.

King Henrye ran to claspe his queene,
   And loosed her full sone: 210
Then turnd to look for the tinye boye;
   —— The boye was vanisht and gone.

But first he had touchd the lazar man,
   And stroakt him with his hand:
The lazar under the gallowes tree   215
   All whole and sounde did stand.

The lazar under the gallowes tree
   Was comelye, straight and tall;
King Henrye made him his head stewàrde
   To wayte withinn his hall.   220

                                  *_**

X.

The Gaberlunzie Man.

A SCOTTISH SONG.

TRADITION informs us that the author of this song was
King James V. of Scotland. This prince (whose character
for wit and libertinism bears a great resemblance to that of
his gay successor Charles II.) was noted for strolling about
his dominions in disguise[1], and for his frequent gallantries
with country girls. Two adventures of this kind he hath
celebrated with his own pen, viz. in this ballad of *The Gaberlunzie Man;* and in another entitled *The Jolly Beggar*, beginning thus:

        · Thair was a jollie beggar, and a begging he was boun,
         And he tuik up his quarters into a land'art toun.
                         Fa, la, la, &c.

It seems to be the latter of these ballads (which was too
licentious to be admitted into this collection) that is meant
in the *Catalogue of Royal and Noble Authors*[2], where the in-

---

[1] Sc. of a tinker, beggar, &c. Thus he used to visit a smith's daughter
at Niddry, near Edinburgh.
[2] Vol. ii. p. 203.

gènious writer remarks, that there is something very ludicrous in the young woman's distress when she thought her
first favour had been thrown away upon a beggar.

Bishop Tanner has attributed to James V. the celebrated
ballad of *Christ's Kirk on the Green*, which is ascribed to
King James I. in Bannatyne's MS., written in 1568. And
notwithstanding that authority, the Editor of this book is of
opinion that Bishop Tanner was right.

King James V. died Dec. 13th, 1542, aged 33.

THE pauky auld Carle came ovir the lee
Wi' mony good-eens and days to mee,
Saying, Goodwife, for zour courtesie,
 Will ze lodge a silly poor man?
The night was cauld, the carle was wat,   5
And down azont the ingle he sat;
My dochters shoulders he gan to clap,
 And cadgily ranted and sang.

O wow! quo he, were I as free,
As first when I saw this countrie,   10
How blyth and merry wad I bee!
 And I wad nevir think lang.
He grew canty, and she grew fain;
But little did her auld minny ken
What thir slee twa togither were say'n,   15
 When wooing they were sa thrang.

And O! quo he, ann ze were as black,
As evir the crown of your dadyes hat,
Tis I wad lay thee by my back,
 And awa wi' me thou sould gang.   20
And O! quoth she, ann I were as white,
As evir the snaw lay on the dike,
Ild clead me braw, and lady-like,
 And awa with thee Ild gang.

Between the twa was made a plot;   25
They raise a wee before the cock,
And wyliely they shot the lock,
    And fast to the bent are they gane.
Up the morn the auld wife raise,
And at her leisure put on her claiths,   30
Syne to the servants bed she gaes
    To speir for the silly poor man.

She gaed to the bed, whair the beggar lay,
The strae was cauld, he was away,
She clapt her hands, cryd, Dulefu' day!   35
    For some of our geir will be gane.
Some ran to coffer, and some to kist,
But nought was stown that could be mist.
She dancid her lane, cryd, Praise be blest,
    I have lodgd a leal poor man.   40

Since naithings awa, as we can learn,
The kirns to kirn, and milk to earn,
Gae butt the house, lass, and waken my bairn,
    And bid her come quickly ben.
The servant gaed where the dochter lay,   45
The sheets was cauld, she was away,
And fast to her goodwife can say,
    Shes aff with the gaberlunzie man.

O fy gar ride, and fy gar rin,
And hast ze, find these traitors agen;   50
For shees be burnt, and hees be slein,
    The wearyfou gaberlunzie man.
Some rade upo horse, some ran a fit,
The wife was wood, and out o' her wit;
She could na gang, nor yet could she sit,   55
    But ay did curse and did ban.

Mean time far hind out owre the lee,
For snug in a glen, where nane could see,

Ver. 29, the carline, other copies.

The twa, with kindlie sport and glee,
   Cut frae a new cheese a whang.   60
The priving was gude, it pleas'd them baith,
To lo'e her for ay, he gae her his aith.
Quo she, to leave thee, I will be laith,
   My winsome gaberlunzie man.

O kend my minny I were wi' zou,   65
Illfardly wad she crook her mou,
Sic a poor man sheld nevir trow,
   Aftir the gaberlunzie mon.
My dear, quo he, zee're zet owre zonge;
And hae na learnt the beggars tonge,   70
To follow me frae toun to toun,
   And carrie the gaberlunzie on.

Wi' kauk and keel, Ill win zour bread,
And spindles and whorles for them wha need,
Whilk is a gentil trade indeed   75
   The gaberlunzie to carrie—o.
Ill bow my leg and crook my knee,
And draw a black clout owre my ee,
A criple or blind they will cau me:
   While we sall sing and be merrie—o.   80

XI.
On Thomas Lord Cromwell.

It is ever the fate of a disgraced minister to be forsaken by his friends, and insulted by his enemies, always reckoning among the latter the giddy, inconstant multitude. We have here a spurn at fallen greatness from some angry partisan of declining Popery, who could never forgive the downfall of their Diana, and loss of their craft. The ballad seems to have been composed between the time of Cromwell's commitment to the Tower, June 11, 1540, and that of his being beheaded, July 28, following. A short interval!

but Henry's passion for Catherine Howard would admit of no delay. Notwithstanding our libeller, Cromwell had many excellent qualities: his great fault was too much obsequiousness to the arbitrary will of his master; but let it be considered that this master had raised him from obscurity, and that the high-born nobility had shown him the way in every kind of mean and servile compliance. The original copy, printed at London in 1540, is entitled "A newe ballade made of Thomas Crumwel, called *Trolle on Away*." To it is prefixed this distich by way of burthen,

> Trolle on away, trolle on awaye.
> Synge heave and howe rombelowe trolle on away.

Both man and chylde is glad to here tell
Of that false traytoure Thomas Crumwell,
Now that he is set to learn to spell.
Synge trolle on away.

When fortune lokyd the in thy face,
Thou haddyst fayre tyme, but thou lackydyst grace;   5
Thy cofers with golde thou fyllydst a pace.
Synge, &c.

Both plate and chalys came to thy fyst,
Thou lockydst them vp where no man wyst,
Tyll in the kynges treasoure suche thinges were myst.
Synge, &c.

Both crust and crumme came thorowe thy handes,   10
Thy marchaundyse sayled over the sandes,
Therfore nowe thou art layde fast in bandes.
Synge, &c.

Fyrste when kynge Henry, God saue his grace!
Perceyud myschefe kyndlyd in thy face,
Then it was tyme to purchase the a place.   15
Synge, &c.

Hys grace was euer of gentyll nature,
Mouyd with petye, and made the hys seruyture:
But thou, as a wretche, suche thinges dyd procure.
Synge, &c.

Thou dyd not remembre, false heretyke,
One God, one fayth, and one kynge catholyke,   20
For thou hast bene so long a scysmatyke.
Synge, &c.

Thou woldyst not learne to knowe these thre;
But euer was full of iniquite:
Wherfore all this lande hathe ben troubled with the.
Synge, &c.

All they, that were of the new trycke,   25
Agaynst the churche thou baddest them stycke;
Wherfore nowe thou hast touchyd the quycke.
Synge, &c.

Both sacramentes and sacramentalles
Thou woldyst not suffre within thy walles;
Nor let vs praye for all chrysten soules.   30
Synge, &c.

Of what generacyon thou were no tonge can tell,
Whyther of Chayme, or Syschemell,
Or else sent vs frome the deuyll of hell.
Synge, &c.

Thou woldest neuer to vertue applye,
But couetyd euer to clymme to hye,   35
And nowe haste thou trodden thy shoo awrye.
Synge, &c.

Who-so-euer dyd winne thou wolde not lose;
Wherfore all Englande doth hate the, as I suppose,
Bycause thou wast false to the redolent rose.
Synge, &c.

Ver. 32, *i. e.* Cain, or Ishmael. See below, the note, book ii. no. iii.
stanza 3d.

Thou myghtest have learned thy cloth to flocke   40
Upon thy gresy fullers stocke;
Wherfore lay downe thy heade vpon this blocke.
                                Synge, &c.

Yet saue that soule, that God hath bought,
And for thy carcas care thou nought,
Let it suffre payne, as it hath wrought.   45
                                Synge, &c.

God saue kyng Henry with all his power,
And prynce Edwarde that goodly flower,
With al hys lordes of great honoure.
        Synge trolle on awaye, syng trolle on away.
        Hevye and how rombelowe trolle on awaye.

V. 41, Cromwell's father is generally said to have been a blacksmith at
Putney: but the author of this ballad would insinuate that either he himself, or some of his ancestors, were fullers by trade.

*** The foregoing piece gave rise to a poetic controversy,
which was carried on through a succession of seven or eight
ballads, written for and against Lord Cromwell. These are
all preserved in the archives of the Antiquarian Society, in
a large folio Collection of Proclamations, &c., made in the
reigns of King Henry VIII., King Edward VI., Queen Mary,
Queen Elizabeth, King James I., &c.

XII.

Harpalus.

AN ANCIENT ENGLISH PASTORAL.

THIS beautiful poem, which is perhaps the first attempt
at pastoral writing in our language, is preserved among the
"Songs and Sonnettes" of the Earl of Surrey, &c. 4to. in
that part of the collection which consists of pieces by "uncertain Auctours." These poems were first published in

1557, ten years after that accomplished nobleman fell a victim to the tyranny of Henry VIII.: but it is presumed most of them were composed before the death of Sir Thomas Wyat, in 1541. See Surrey's Poems, 4to. folios 19, 49.

Though written perhaps near half a century before the *Shepherd's Calendar*[1], this will be found far superior to any of those Eclogues, in natural unaffected sentiments, in simplicity of style, in easy flow of versification, and all other beauties of pastoral poetry. Spenser ought to have profited more by so excellent a model.

    PHYLIDA was a faire mayde,
      As fresh as any flowre;
    Whom Harpalus the herdman prayde
      To be his paramour.

    Harpalus, and eke Corin,   5
      Were herdmen both yfere:
    And Phylida could twist and spinne,
      And thereto sing full clere.

    But Phylida was all tò coye,
      For Harpalus to winne: 10
    For Corin was her onely joye,
      Who forst her not a pinne.

    How often would she flowers twine?
      How often garlandes make
    Of couslips and of colombine?   15
      And al for Corin's sake.

    But Corin, he had haukes to lure,
      And forced more the field:
    Of lovers lawe he toke no cure;
      For once he was begilde.   20

[1] First published in 1579.

Harpalus prevailed nought,
   His labour all was lost:
For he was fardest from her thought,
   And yet he loved her most.

Therefore waxt he both pale and leane,   25
   And drye as clot of clay:
His fleshe it was consumed cleane;
   His colour gone away.

His beard it had not long be shave;
   His heare hong all unkempt;   30
A man most fit even for the grave,
   Whom spitefull love had spent.

His eyes were red, and all 'forewacht;'
   His face besprent with teares:
It semde unhap had him long 'hatcht,'   35
   In mids of his dispaires.

His clothes were blacke, and also bare;
   As one forlorne was he;
Upon his head alwayes he ware
   A wreath of wyllow tree.   40

His beastes he kept upon the hyll,
   And he sate in the dale;
And thus with sighes and sorrowes shril,
   He gan to tell his tale.

Oh Harpalus! (thus would he say)   45
   Unhappiest under sunne!
The cause of thine unhappy day,
   By love was first begunne.

For thou wentest first by sute to seeke
   A tigre to make tame,   50
That settes not by thy love a leeke;
   But makes thy griefe her game.

Ver. 33, &c.   The corrections are from ed. 1574.

As easy it were for to convert
   The frost into 'a' flame;
As for to turne a frowarde hert,   55
   Whom thou so faine wouldst frame.

Corin he liveth carèlesse:
   He leapes among the leaves:
He eats the frutes of thy redresse:
   Thou 'reapst,' he takes the sheaves.   60

My beastes, a whyle your foode refraine,
   And harke your herdmans sounde:
Whom spitefull love, alas! hath slaine,
   Through-girt with many a wounde.

O happy be·ye, beastès wilde,   65
   That here your pasture takes:
I se that ye be not begilde
   Of these your faithfull makes.

The hart he feedeth by the hinde:
   The bucke harde by the do: 70
The turtle dove is not unkinde
   To him that loves her so.

The ewe she hath by her the ramme:
   The young cow hath the bull:
The calfe with many a lusty lambe   75
   Do fede their hunger full.

But, wel-away! that nature wrought
   The, Phylida, so faire:
For I may say that I have bought
   Thy beauty all tò deare.   80

What reason is that crueltie
   With beautie should have part?
Or els that such great tyranny
   Should dwell in womans hart?

I see therefore to shape my death   85
   She cruelly is prest;
To th' ende that I may want my breath:
   My dayes been at the best.

O Cupide, graunt this my request,
   And do not stoppe thine eares,   90
That she may feele within her brest
   The paines of my dispaires:

Of Corin, 'who' is carèlesse,
   That she may crave her fee:
As I have done in great distresse,   95
   That loved her faithfully.

But since that I shal die her slave;
   Her slave, and eke her thrall:
Write you, my frendes, upon my grave
   This chaunce that is befall.   100

"Here lieth unhappy Harpalus
   By cruell love now slaine:
Whom Phylida unjustly thus
   Hath murdred with disdaine."

XIII.

Robin and Makyne.

AN ANCIENT SCOTTISH PASTORAL.

THE palm of pastoral poesy is here contested by a contemporary writer with the author of the foregoing. The
critics will judge of their respective merits; but must make
some allowance for the preceding ballad, which is given
simply as it stands in the old editions: whereas this which
follows has been revised and amended throughout by Allan
Ramsay, from whose *Ever-Green*, vol. i., it is here chiefly
printed. The curious reader may however compare it with

the more original copy, printed among "Ancient Scottish
Poems, from the MS. of George Bannatyne, 1568, Edinb.
1770, 12mo." Mr. Robert Henryson (to whom we are indebted for this poem) appears to so much advantage among
the writers of eclogue, that we are sorry we can give little
other account of him besides what is [contained in the following eloge, written by W. Dunbar, a Scottish poet, who
lived about the middle of the 16th century:

> "In Dumferling, he [Death] hath tane Broun,
> With gude Mr. Robert Henryson."

Indeed, some little further insight into the history of the
Scottish bard is gained from the title prefixed to some of his
poems preserved in the British Museum; viz. "The morall
Fabillis of Esop compylit be Maister Robert Henrisoun, scol-
maister of Dumfermling, 1571." Harleian MSS. 3865, § 1.

In Ramsay's *Ever-Green*, vol. i., whence the above distich
is extracted, are preserved two other little Doric pieces by
Henryson; the one entitled *The Lyon and the Mouse;* the
other, *The garment of gude Ladyis.* Some other of his poems
may be seen in the "Ancient Scottish Poems, printed from
Bannatyne's MS." above referred to.

> Robin sat on the gude grene hill,
> Keipand a flock of fie,
> Quhen mirry Makyne said him till,
> "O Robin rew on me:
> I haif thee luivt baith loud and still,   5
> Thir towmonds twa or thre;
> My dule in dern bot giff thou dill,
> Doubtless but dreid Ill die."
>
> Robin replied, Now by the rude,
> Naithing of luve I knaw,   10
> But keip my sheip undir yon wod:
> Lo quhair they raik on raw.
> Quhat can have mart thee in thy mude,
> Thou Makyne to me schaw;

Or quhat is luve, or to be lude?   15
    Fain wald I leir that law.

"The law of luve gin thou wald leir,
    Tak thair an A, B, C;
Be heynd, courtas, and fair of feir,
    Wyse, hardy, kind and frie,   20
Sae that nae danger do the deir,
    Quhat dule in dern thou drie;
Press ay to pleis, and blyth appeir,
    Be patient and privie."

Robin, he answert her againe,   25
    I wat not quhat is luve;
But I haif marvel in certaine
    Quhat makes thee thus wanrufe.
The wedder is fair, and I am fain;
    My sheep gais hail abuve;   30
And sould we pley us on the plain,
    They wald us baith repruve.

"Robin, tak tent unto my tale,
    And wirk all as I reid;
And thou sall haif my heart all hale,   35
    Eik and my maiden-heid:
Sen God, he sendis bute for bale,
    And for murning remeid,
I'dern with thee bot gif I dale,
    Doubtless I am but deid."   40

Makyne, to-morn be this ilk tyde,
    Gif ye will meit me heir,
Maybe my sheip may gang besyde,
    Quhyle we have liggd full neir;
But maugre haif I, gif I byde,   45
    Frae thay begin to steir,

Quhat lyes on heart I will nocht hyd,
  Then Makyne mak gude cheir.

"Robin, thou reivs me of my rest;
  I luve bot thee alane."   50
Makyne, adieu! the sun goes west,
  The day is neir-hand gane.
"Robin, in dule I am so drest,
  That luve will be my bane."
Makyn, gae luv quhair-eir ye list,   55
  For leman I luid nane.

"Robin, I stand in sic a style,
  I sich and that full sair."
Makyne, I have bene here this quyle;
  At hame I wish I ware.   60
"Robin, my hinny, talk and smyle,
  Gif thou will do nae mair."
Makyne, som other man beguyle,
  For hameward I will fare.

Syne Robin on his ways he went,   65
  As light as leif on tree;
But Makyne murnt and made lament,
  Scho trow'd him neir to see.
Robin he brayd attowre the bent:
  Then Makyne cried on hie,   70
"Now may thou sing, for I am shent!
  Quhat ailis luve at me?"

Makyne went hame withouten fail,
  And weirylie could weip;
Then Robin in a full fair dale   75
  Assemblit all his sheip.
Be that some part of Makyne's ail,
  Out-throw his heart could creip;
Hir fast he followt to assail,
  And till her tuke gude keip.   80

Abyd, abyd, thou fair Makyne,
  A word for ony thing;
For all my luve, it sall be thyne,
  Withouten departing.
All hale thy heart for till have myne,   85
  Is all my coveting;
My sheip to morn quhyle houris nyne,
  Will need of nae keiping.

"Robin, thou hast heard sung and say,
  In gests and storys auld   90
The man that will not when he may,
  Sall have nocht when he wald.
I pray to heaven baith nicht and day,
  Be eiked their cares sae cauld,
That presses first with thee to play   95
  Be forrest, firth, or fauld."

Makyne, the nicht is soft and dry,
  The wether warm and fair,
And the grene wod richt neir-hand by,
  To walk attowre all where: 100
There may nae janglers us espy,
  That is in luve contrair;
Therin, Makyne, baith you and I
  Unseen may mak repair.

"Robin, that warld is now away,   105
  And quyt brocht till an end:
And nevir again thereto, perfay,
  Sall it be as thou wend;
For of my pain thou made but play;
  I words in vain did spend: 110
As thou hast done, sae sall I say,
  Murn on, I think to mend."

Makyne, the hope of all my heil,
  My heart on thee is set;

V. 99, Bannatyne's MS. has *woid*, not *woud*, as in ed. 1770.

I'll evermair to thee be leil,   115
　Quhyle I may live butt lett,
Never to fail as uthers feill,
　Quhat grace so eir I get.
"Robin, with thee I will not deill;
　Adieu, for this we met."   120

Makyne went hameward blyth enough,
　Outowre the holtis hair;
Pure Robin murnd, and Makyne leugh;
　Scho sang, and he sicht sair:
And so left him bayth wo and wreuch,   125
　In dolor and in care,
Keipand his herd under a heuch,
　Amang the rushy gair.

V. 117, Bannatyne's MS. reads as above *feill*, not *faill*, as in ed. 1770.

XIV.

Gentle Herdsman, tell to Me.

DIALOGUE BETWEEN A PILGRIM AND HERDSMAN.

THE scene of this beautiful old ballad is laid near Walsingham in Norfolk, where was anciently an image of the
Virgin Mary, famous over all Europe for the numerous
pilgrimages made to it, and the great riches it possessed.
Erasmus has given a very exact and humorous description of
the superstitions practised there in his time. See his account
of the Virgo Parathalassia, in his colloquy, entitled, *Pere-
grinatio Religionis Ergo*. He tells us, the rich offerings in
silver, gold, and precious stones, that were there shown him,
were incredible, there being scarce a person of any note in
England but what some time or other paid a visit, or sent a
present, to Our Lady of Walsingham[1]. At the dissolution
of the monasteries in 1538, this splendid image, with another

[1] See at the end of this ballad an account of the annual offerings of the
Earls of Northumberland.

from Ipswich, was carried to Chelsea, and there burnt in the presence of commissioners, who, we trust, did not burn the jewels and the finery.

This poem is printed from a copy in the Editor's folio MS., which had greatly suffered by the hand of time; but vestiges of several of the lines remaining, some conjectural supplements have been attempted, which, for greater exactness, are in this one ballad distinguished by italics.

GENTLE heardsman, tell to me,
   Of curtesy I thee pray,
Unto the towne of Walsingham
   Which is the right and ready way.

"Unto the towne of Walsingham   5
   The way is hard for to be gon;
And verry crooked are those pathes
   For you to find out all alone."

Weere the miles doubled thrise,
   And the way never soe ill,   10
Itt were not enough for mine offence;
   Itt is soe grievous and soe ill.

"Thy yeeares are young, thy face is faire,
   Thy witts are weake, thy thoughts are greene;
Time hath not given thee leave, as yett,   15
   For to committ so great a sinne."

Yes, heardsman, yes, soe woldest thou say,
   If thou knewest soe much as I;
My witts, and thoughts, and all the rest,
   Have well deserved for to dye.   20

I am not what I seeme to bee,
   My clothes and sexe doe differ farr:
I am a woman, woe is me!
   Born to greeffe and irksome care.

For my beloved, and well-beloved,   25
   My wayward cruelty could kill:
And though my teares will nought avail,
   Most dearely I bewail him still.

*He was the flower of n*oble wights,
   *None ever more since*re *colde* bee;   30
Of comely mien and shape hee was,
   *And tenderlye he*e loved mee.

*When thus 1 saw he l*oved me well,
   *I grewe so proud his p*aine to see,
That I, who did not know myselfe,   35
   Thought scorne of such a youth as hee.

[2] And grew soe coy and nice to please,
   As women's lookes are often soe,
He might not kisse, nor hand forsooth,
   Unlesse I willed him soe to doe.   40

Thus being wearyed with delayes
   To see I pittyed not his greeffe,

---

[2] Three of the following stanzas have been finely paraphrased by Dr. Goldsmith, in his charming ballad of *Edwin and Angelina;* the reader of taste will have a pleasure in comparing them with the original.

      'And' still I try'd each fickle art,
        Importunate and vain;
      And while his passion touch'd my heart,
        I triumph'd in his pain.

      'Till quite dejected with my scorn,
        He left me to my pride;
      And sought a solitude forlorn,
        In secret, where he dy'd.

      But mine the sorrow, mine the fault,
        And well my life shall pay;
      I'll seek the solitude he sought,
        And stretch me where he lay.

      And there forlorn despairing hid,
        I'll lay me down and die:
      'Twas so for me that Edwin did,
        And so for him will I.

He gott him to a secrett place,
　　And there he dyed without releeffe.

And for his sake these weeds I weare,　　　　　　45
　　And sacriffice my tender age;
And every day Ile begg my bread,
　　To undergoe this pilgrimage.

Thus every day I fast and pray,
　　And ever will doe till I dye;　　　　　　　　50
And gett me to some secrett place,
　　For soe did hee, and soe will I.

Now, gentle heardsman, aske no more,
　　But keepe my secretts I thee pray;
Unto the towne of Walsingham　　　　　　　　55
　　Show me the right and readye way.

"Now goe thy wayes, and God before!
　　For he must ever guide thee still:
Turne downe that dale, the right hand path,
　　And soe, faire pilgrim, fare thee well!"　　　60

－－－－

*** To show what constant tribute was paid to OUR LADY
OF WALSINGHAM, I shall give a few extracts from the "House-
hold-Book of Henry Algernon Percy, 5th Earl of Northumberland." Printed 1770, 8vo.
　　　　　Sect. XLIII. page 337, &c.
ITEM, My Lorde usith yerly to send afor Michaelmas for
　　his Lordschip's Offerynge to our Lady of Walsyngeham,
　　—iiij d.
ITEM, My Lorde usith ande accustumyth to sende yerely for
　　the upholdynge of the Light of Wax which his Lordschip
　　fyndith birnynge yerly befor our Lady of Walsyngham,
　　contenynge xj lb. of Wax in it after vij d. ob. for the
　　fyndynge of every lb. redy wrought by a covenaunt maid
　　with the Channon by great, for the hole yere, for the
　　fyndinge of the said Lyght byrning, —vi s. viiij d.

ITEM, My Lord useth and accustomith to syende yerely to the Channon that kepith the Light before our Lady of Walsyngham, for his reward for the hole yere, for kepynge of the said Light, lightynge of it at all service tymes daily thorowt the yere, — *xij* d.

ITEM, My Lord usith and accustomyth yerely to send to the Prest that kepith the Light, lyghtynge of it at all service tymes daily thorowt the yere, — *iij* s. *iiij* d.

XV.

K. Edward IV. and the Tanner of Tamworth

WAS a story of great fame among our ancestors. The author of the *Art of English Poesie*, 1589, 4to, seems to speak of it as a real fact. Describing that vicious mode of speech, which the Greeks called *Acyron, i. e.* "When we use a dark and obscure word, utterly repugnant to that we should express;" he adds, "Such manner of uncouth speech did the Tanner of Tamworth use to King Edward the fourth; which Tanner, having a great while mistaken him, and used very broad talke with him, at length perceiving by his traine that it was the king, was afraide he should be punished for it, [and] said thus, with a certain rude repentance,

'I hope I shall be hanged to-morrow,'

for [*I feare me*] *I shall be hanged;* whereat the king laughed a good[1], not only to see the Tanner's vaine feare, but also to heare his illshapen terme: and gave him for recompence of his good sport, the inheritance of Plumpton-parke. *I am afraid,*" concludes this sagacious writer, "*the poets of our times that speake more finely and correctly, will come too short of such a reward,*" p. 214. The phrase here referred to is not found in this ballad at present[2], but occurs with some variation in another old poem, entitled, *John the Reeve*, described in the following volume. (See the Preface to *The King and the Miller*,) viz.

[1] Vide Gloss. [2] Nor in that of the Barker mentioned below.

"Nay, sayd John, by Gods grace
And Edward wer in this place,
    Hee shold not touch this tonne:
He wold be wroth with John I HOPE,
Thereffore I beshrew the soupe,
    That in his mouth shold come." Pt. ii. st. 24.

The following text is selected (with such other corrections
as occurred) from two copies in black letter. The one in the
Bodleian library, entitled, "A merrie, pleasant, and de-
lectable historie betweene King Edward the Fourth, and a
Tanner of Tamworth, &c., printed at London, by John
Danter, 1596." This copy, ancient as it now is, appears to have
been modernised and altered at the time it was published;
and many vestiges of the more ancient readings were recovered from another copy, (though more recently printed,)
in one sheet folio, without date, in the Pepys collection.

But these are both very inferior in point of antiquity to
the old ballad of *The King and the Barker*, reprinted with
other "Pieces of Ancient Popular Poetry from Authentic
Manuscripts, and old Printed Copies, edited by Ritson,"
Lond. 1791, 8vo. As that very antique poem had never occurred to the Editor of the *Reliques*, till he saw it in the above
collection, he now refers the curious reader to it, as an imperfect and incorrect copy of the old original ballad.

————

In summer time, when leaves grow greene,
    And blossoms bedecke the tree,
King Edward wolde a hunting ryde,
    Some pastime for to see.

With hawke and hounde he made him bowne,   5
    With horne, and eke with bowe;
To Drayton Basset he tooke his waye,
    With all his lordes a rowe.

And he had ridden ore dale and downe
    By eight of clocke in the day,   10
When he was ware of a bold tannèr,
    Come ryding along the waye.

A fayre russet coat the tanner had on
    Fast buttoned under his chin,
And under him a good cow-hide,   15
    And a mare of four shilling[3].

Nowe stand you still, my good lordes all,
    Under the grene wood spraye;
And I will wend to yonder fellowe,
    To weet what he will saye.   20

God speede, God speede thee, said our king.
    Thou art welcome, sir, sayd hee.
"The readyest waye to Drayton Basset
    I praye thee to shewe to mee."

"To Drayton Basset woldst thou goe,   25
    Fro the place where thou dost stand?
The next payre of gallowes thou comest unto,
    Turne in upon thy right hand."

That is an unreadye waye, sayd our king,
    Thou doest but jest I see;   30
Nowe shewe me out the nearest waye,
    And I pray thee wend with mee.

Awaye with a vengeance! quoth the tanner:
    I hold thee out of thy witt:
All day have I rydden on Brocke my mare,   35
    And I am fasting yett.

"Go with me downe to Drayton Basset,
    No daynties we will spare;
All daye shalt thou eate and drinke of the best,
    And I will paye thy fare."   40

[3] In the reign of Edward IV., Dame Cecill, lady of Torboke, in her will dated March 7, A.D. 1466, among many other bequests has this, "Also I will that my sonne Thomas of Torboke have 13s. 4d. to buy him an horse." Vide Harleian Catalogue, 2176. 27. Now if 13s. 4d. would purchase a steed fit for a person of quality, a tanner's horse might reasonably be valued at four or five shillings.

Gramercye for nothing, the tanner replyde,
    Thou payest no fare of mine:
I trowe I've more nobles in my purse,
    Than thou hast pence in thine.

God give thee joy of them, sayd the king,   45
    And send them well to priefe.
The tanner wolde faine have beene away,
    For he weende he had beene a thiefe.

What art thou, he sayde, thou fine fellòwe,
    Of thee I am in great feare,   50
For the cloathes, thou wearest upon thy backe,
    Might beseeme a lord to weare.

I never stole them, quoth our king,
    I tell you, sir, by the roode.
"Then thou playest, as many an unthrift doth,   55
    And standest in midds of thy goode[4]."

What tydinges heare you, sayd the kynge,
    As you ryde farre and neare?
"I heare no tydinges, sir, by the masse,
    But that cowe-hides are deare."   60

"Cowe-hides! cow-hides! what things are those?
    I marvell what they bee?"
What art thou a foole? the tanner reply'd;
    I carry one under mee.

What craftsman art thou, said the king,   65
    I praye thee tell me trowe.
"I am a barker[5], sir, by my trade;
    Nowe tell me what art thou?"

I am a poore courtier, sir, quoth he,
    That am forth of service worne;   70
And faine I wolde thy prentise bee,
    Thy cunninge for to learne.

[4] i. e. hast no other wealth but what thou carriest about thee.
[5] i. e. a dealer in bark.

Marrye heaven forfend, the tanner replyde,
  That thou my prentise were:
Thou woldst spend more good than I shold winne   75
  By fortye shilling a yere.

Yet one thinge wolde I, sayd our king,
  If thou wilt not seeme strange:
Thoughe my horse be better than thy mare,
  Yet with thee I faine wold change.   80

"Why if with me thou faine wilt change,
  As change full well maye wee,
By the faith of my bodye, thou proude fellòwe,
  I will have some boot of thee."

That were against reason, sayd the king,   85
  I sweare, so mote I thee:
My horse is better than thy mare,
  And that thou well mayst see.

"Yea, sir, but Brocke is gentle and mild,
  And softly she will fare: 90
Thy horse is unrulye and wild, I wiss;
  Aye skipping here and theare."

What boote wilt thou have? our king reply'd;
  Now tell me in this stound.
"Noe pence, nor half pence, by my faye,   95
  But a noble in gold so round."

"Here's twentye groates of white moneyè,
  Sith thou will have it of mee."
I would have sworne now, quoth the tanner,
  Thou hadst not had one penniè.   100

But since we two have made a change,
  A change we must abide,
Although thou hast gotten Brocke my mare,
  Thou gettest not my cowe-hide.

I will not have it, sayd the kinge,   105
   I sweare, so mought I thee;
Thy foule cowe-hide I wolde not beare,
   If thou woldst give it to mee.

The tanner hee tooke his good cowe-hide,
   That of the cow was hilt;   110
And threwe it upon the king's sadèlle,
   That was soe fayrelye gilte.

"Now help me up, thou fine fellòwe,
   'Tis time that I were gone;
When I come home to Gyllian my wife,   115
   Sheel say I am a gentilmon."

The king he tooke him up by the legge;
   The tanner a f** lett fall.
Nowe marrye, good fellowe, sayd the kyng,
   Thy courtesye is but small.   120

When the tanner he was in the kinges sadèlle,
   And his foote in the stirrup was;
He marvelled greatlye in his minde,
   Whether it were golde or brass.

But when his steede saw the cows taile wagge,   125
   And eke the blacke cowe-horne;
He stamped, and stared, and awaye he ranne,
   As the devill had him borne.

The tanner he pulld, the tanner he sweat,
   And held by the pummil fast: 130
At length the tanner came tumbling downe;
   His necke he had well-nye brast.

Take thy horse again with a vengeance, he sayd,
   With mee he shall not byde.
"My horse wolde have borne thee well enoughe,   135
   But he knewe not of thy cowe-hide.

Yet if agayne thou faine woldst change,
    As change full well may wee,
By the faith of my bodye, thou jolly tannèr,
    I will have some boote of thee."   140

What boote wilt thou have, the tanner replyd,
    Nowe tell me in this stounde?
"No pence nor half-pence, sir, by my faye,
    But I will have twentye pound."

"Here's twentye groates out of my purse;   145
    And twentye I have of thine:
And I have one more, which we will spend
    Together at the wine."

The king set a bugle horne to his mouthe,
    And blewe both loude and shrille: 150
And soone came lords, and soone came knights,
    Fast ryding over the hille.

Nowe, out alas! the tanner he cryde,
    That ever I sawe this daye!
Thou art a strong thiefe, yon come thy fellowes   155
    Will beare my cowe-hide away.

They are no thieves, the king replyde,
    I sweare, soe mote I thee:
But they are the lords of the north countrèy,
    Here come to hunt with mee.   160

And soone before our king they came,
    And knelt downe on the grounde:
Then might the tanner have beene awaye,
    He had lever than twentye pounde.

A coller, a coller, here: sayd the king,   165
    A coller he loud gan crye:
Then woulde he lever then twentye pound,
    He had not beene so nighe.

A coller, a coller, the tanner he sayd,
  I trowe it will breed sorrowe: 170
After a coller commeth a halter,
  I trowe I shall be hang'd to-morrowe.

Be not afraid tanner, said our king;
  I tell thee, so mought I thee,
Lo here I make thee the best esquire   175
  That is in the north countrie[6].

For Plumpton-parke I will give thee,
  With tenements faire beside:
'Tis worth three hundred markes by the yeare,
  To maintaine thy good cowe-hide.   180

Gramercye, my liege, the tanner replyde,
  For the favour thou hast me showne;
If ever thou comest to merry Tamwòrth,
  Neates leather shall clout thy shoen.

⁎

XVI.

As Ye came from the Holy Land.

DIALOGUE BETWEEN A PILGRIM AND A TRAVELLER.

THE scene of this song is the same as in No. xiv. The
pilgrimage to Walsingham suggested the plan of many popular pieces. In the Pepys collection, vol. i. p. 226, is a

---

[6] This stanza is restored from a quotation of this ballad in Selden's *Titles
of Honour*, who produces it as a good authority to prove, that one mode of
creating *Esquires* at that time was by the imposition of a *collar*. His words
are, "Nor is that old pamphlet of the *Tanner of Tamworth* and *King Edward
the Fourth* so contemptible, but that wee may thence note also an observable
passage, wherein the use of making Esquires, by giving Collars, is expressed."—(Sub. Tit. Esquire; and vide in Spelmanni Glossar. Armiger.)
This form of creating Esquires actually exists at this day among the Ser-
geants at Arms, who are invested with a Collar (which they wear on Collar
days) by the king himself.

This information I owe to Samuel Pegge, Esq., to whom the public is
indebted for that curious work the *Curialia*, 4to.

kind of Interlude in the old ballad style, of which the first stanza alone is worth reprinting.

As I went to Walsingham,
  To the shrine with speede,
Met I with a jolly palmer
  In a pilgrimes weede.
Now God you save, you jolly palmer;
  "Welcome, lady gay,
Oft have I sued to thee for love"
  —Oft have I said you nay.

The pilgrimages undertaken on pretence of religion were often productive of affairs of gallantry, and led the votaries to no other shrine than that of Venus[1].

The following ballad was once very popular; it is quoted in Fletcher's *Knight of the burning Pestle*, act ii. sc. ult., and in another old play, called *Hans Beer-pot, his invisible Comedy*, &c. 4to, 1618, act i. The copy below was communicated to the Editor by the late Mr. Shenstone, as corrected by him from an ancient copy, and supplied with a concluding stanza.

We have placed this, and *Gentle Herdsman*, &c., thus early in the volume, upon a presumption that they must have been written, if not before the dissolution of the monasteries, yet while the remembrance of them was fresh in the minds of the people.

Hermets on a heape, with hoked staves,
Wenten to Walsingham, and her[2] wenches after.

As ye came from the holy land
  Of blessed Walsingham,
O met you not with my true love
  As by the way ye came?

[1] Even in the time of Langland, pilgrimages to Walsingham were not unfavourable to the rites of Venus. Thus, in his *Visions of Pierce Plowman*, fo. 1.

[2] *i. e.* their.

"How should I know your true love,   5
    That have met many a one,
As I came from the holy land,
    That have both come, and gone?"

My love is neither white[3], nor browne,
    But as the heavens faire;   10
There is none hath her form divine,
    Either in earth, or ayre.

"Such an one did I meet, good sir,
    With an angelicke face;
Who like a nymphe, a queene appeard   15
    Both in her gait, her grace."

Yes: she hath cleane forsaken me,
    And left me all alone;
Who some time loved me as her life,
    And called me her owne.   20

"What is the cause she leaves thee thus,
    And a new way doth take,
That some times loved thee as her life,
    And thee her joy did make?"

I that loved her all my youth,   25
    Growe old now as you see;
Love liketh not the falling fruite,
    Nor yet the withered tree.

For love is like a carelesse childe,
    Forgetting promise past: 30
He is blind, or deaf, whenere he list;
    His faith is never fast.

His fond desire is fickle found,
    And yieldes a trustlesse joye;
Wonne with a world of toil and care,   35
    And lost ev'n with a toye.

[3] Sc. pale.

Such is the love of womankinde,
　　Or Loves faire name abusde,
Beneathe which many vaine desires,
　　And follyes are excusde.　　　　　　　　　40

But true love is a lasting fire,
　　Which viewless vestals[4] tend;
That burnes for ever in the soule,
　　And knowes nor change, nor end.'

　　　　[4] Sc. angels.

XVII.

Hardyknute.

A SCOTTISH FRAGMENT.

As this fine morsel of heroic poetry hath generally passed
for ancient, it is here thrown to the end of our earliest pieces;
that such as doubt of its age may the better compare it with
other pieces of genuine antiquity.　For after all, there is
more than reason to suspect, that it owes most of its beauties
(if not its own existence) to the pen of a lady, within the
present century.　The following particulars may be depended
on.　One Mrs. Wardlaw, whose maiden name was Halket,
(aunt to the late Sir Peter Halket, of Pitferran, in Scotland,
who was killed in America, along with General Braddock,
in 1755,) pretended she had found this poem, written on
shreds of paper, employed for what is called the bottoms of
clues.　A suspicion arose that it was her own composition.
Some able judges asserted it to be modern.　The lady did
in a manner acknowledge it to be so.　Being desired to show
an additional stanza, as a proof of this, she produced the
two last, beginning with "There's nae light," &c., which
were not in the copy that was first printed.　The late Lord
President Forbes, and Sir Gilbert Elliot, of Minto, (late
Lord Justice Clerk for Scotland,) who had believed it ancient,
contributed to the expense of publishing the first edition, in

folio, 1719. This account was transmitted from Scotland,
by Sir David Dalrymple, the late Lord Hailes, who yet was
of opinion, that part of the ballad may be ancient, but re-
touched and much enlarged by the lady above mentioned.
Indeed he had been informed, that the late William Thompson, the Scottish musician, who published the *Orpheus Cale-
donius*, 1733, 2 vols. 8vo, declared he had heard fragments
of it repeated in his infancy, before Mrs. Wardlaw's copy
was heard of.

The poem is here printed from the original edition, as it
was prepared for the press, with the additional improvements. (See below, page 91.)

———

I.

STATELY stept he east the wa',
    And stately stept he west,
Full seventy years he now had seen,
    Wi' scarce seven years of rest.
He liv'd when Britons breach of faith   5
    Wrought Scotland mickle wae:
And ay his sword tauld to their cost,
    He was their deadlye fae.

II.

High on a hill his castle stood,
    With ha's and tow'rs a height,   10
And goodly chambers fair to se,
    Where he lodged mony a knight.
His dame sae peerless anes and fair,
    For chast and beauty deem'd,
Nae marrow had in all the land,   15
    Save ELENOR the queen.

III.

Full thirteen sons to him she bare,
    All men of valour stout:

In bloody fight with sword in hand
   Nine lost their lives bot doubt: 20
Four yet remain, lang may they live
   To stand by liege and land:
High was their fame, high was their might,
   And high was their command.

IV.

Great love they bare to FAIRLY fair,   25
   Their sister saft and dear,
Her girdle shaw'd her middle gimp,
   And gowden glist her hair.
What waefu' wae her beauty bred!
   Waefu' to young and auld,   30
Waefu' I trow to kyth and kin,
   As story ever tauld.

V.

The king of Norse in summer tyde,
   Puff'd up with pow'r and might,
Landed in fair Scotland the isle   35
   With mony a hardy knight.
The tydings to our good Scots king
   Came, as he sat at dine,
With noble chiefs in brave aray,
   Drinking the blood-red wine.   40

VI.

"To horse, to horse, my royal liege,
   Your faes stand on the strand,
Full twenty thousand glittering spears
   The king of Norse commands."
Bring me my steed Mage dapple gray,   45
   Our good king rose and cry'd,
A trustier beast in a' the land
   A Scots king nevir try'd.

VII.

Go little page, tell Hardyknute,
  That lives on hill sae hie,   50
To draw his sword, the dread of faes,
  And haste and follow me.
The little page flew swift as dart
  Flung by his master's arm,
"Come down, come down, lord Hardyknute, 55
  And rid your king frae harm."

VIII.

Then red red grew his dark-brown cheeks,
  Sae did his dark-brown brow;
His looks grew keen, as they were wont
  In dangers great to do;   60
He's ta'en a horn as green as glass,
  And gi'en five sounds sae shrill,
That trees in green wood shook thereat,
  Sae loud rang ilka hill.

IX.

His sons in manly sport and glee,   65
  Had past that summer's morn,
When low down in a grassy dale
  They heard their father's horn.
That horn, quo' they, ne'er sounds in peace,
  We've other sport to bide,   70
And soon they hy'd them up the hill,
  And soon were at his side.

X.

"Late late the yestreen I ween'd in peace
  To end my lengthened life,
My age might well excuse my arm   75
  Frae manly feats of strife;

But now that Norse do's proudly boast
  Fair Scotland to inthrall,
It's ne'er be said of Hardyknute,
  He fear'd to fight or fall.   80

XI.
"Robin of Rothsay, bend thy bow,
  Thy arrows shoot sae leel,
That mony a comely countenance
  They've turned to deadly pale.
Brade Thomas take you but your lance 85
  You need nae weapons mair,
If you fight wi't as you did anes
  'Gainst Westmoreland's fierce heir.

XII.
"And Malcolm, light of foot as stag
  That runs in forest wild,   90
Get me my thousands three of men
  Well bred to sword and shield:
Bring me my horse and harnisine,
  My blade of mettal clear:
If faes but ken'd the hand it bare, 95
  They soon had fled for fear.

XIII.
"Farewell my dame sae peerless good,
  (And took her by the hand,)
Fairer to me in age you seem,
  Than maids for beauty fam'd. 100
My youngest son shall here remain
  To guard these stately towers,
And shut the silver bolt that keeps
  Sae fast your painted bowers."

XIV.
And first she wet her comely cheiks, 105
  And then her boddice green,

6*

Her silken cords of twirtle twist,
   Well plett with silver sheen;
And apron set with mony a dice
   Of needle-wark sae rare,   110
Wove by nae hand, as ye may guess,
   Save that of Fairly fair.

XV.

And he has ridden o'er muir and moss,
   O'er hills and mony a glen,
When he came to a wounded knight   115
   Making a heavy mane;
"Here maun I lye, here maun I dye,
   By treacherie's false guiles;
Witless I was that e'er ga faith
   To wicked woman's smiles."   120

XVI.

"Sir knight, gin you were in my bower,
   To lean on silken seat,
My lady's kindly care you'd prove,
   Who ne'er knew deadly hate:
Herself wou'd watch you a' the day,   125
   Her maids a dead of night;
And Fairly fair your heart wou'd chear,
   As she stands in your sight.

XVII.

"Arise young knight, and mount your stead,
   Full lowns the shynand day: 130
Choose frae my menzie whom ye please
   To lead you on the way."
With smileless look and visage wan
   The wounded knight reply'd,
"Kind chieftain, your intent pursue,   135
   For here I maun abyde.

XVIII.

To me nae after day nor night
 Can e're be sweet or fair,
But soon beneath some draping tree,
 Cauld death shall end my care."   140
With him nae pleading might prevail;
 Brave Hardyknute to gain
With fairest words, and reason strong,
 Strave courteously in vain.

XIX.

Syne he has gane far hynd out o'er   145
 Lord Chattan's land sae wide;
That lord a worthy wight was ay,
 When faes his courage sey'd:
Of Pictish race by mother's side,
 When Picts rul'd Caledon,   150
Lord Chattan claim'd the princely maid,
 When he sav'd Pictish crown.

XX.

Now with his fierce and stalwart train,
 He reach'd a rising hight,
Quhair braid encampit on the dale,   155
 Norss menzie lay in sicht.
"Yonder my valiant sons and feirs
 Our raging revers wait,
On the unconquert Scottish sward
 To try with us their fate.   160

XXI.

Make orisons to him that sav'd
 Our sauls upon the rude;
Syne bravely shaw your veins are fill'd
 With Caledonian blude."

Then furth he drew his trusty glave,   165
    While thousands all around
Drawn frae their sheaths glanc'd in the sun;
    And loud the bougles sound.

XXII.

To joyn his king adoun the hill
    In hast his merch he made,   170
While, playand pibrochs, minstralls meit
    Afore him stately strade.
"Thrice welcome valiant stoup of weir,
    Thy nations shield and pride;
Thy king nae reason has to fear   175
    When thou art by his side."

XXIII.

When bows were bent and darts were thrawn;
    For thrang scarce cou'd they flee;
The darts clove arrows as they met,
    The arrows dart the tree.   180
Lang did they rage and fight fu' fierce,
    With little skaith to mon,
But bloody bloody was the field,
    Ere that lang day was done.

XXIV.

The king of Scots, that sindle brook'd   185
    The war that look'd like play,
Drew his braid sword, and brake his bow,
    Sin bows seem'd but delay.
Quoth noble Rothsay, "Mine I'll keep,
    I wat it's bled a score."   190
Haste up my merry men, cry'd the king,
    As he rode on before.

XXV.

The king of Norse he sought to find,
    With him to mense the faught,

But on his forehead there did light 195
   A sharp unsonsie shaft;
As he his hand put up to feel
   The wound, an arrow keen,
O waefu' chance! there pinn'd his hand
   In midst between his een. 200

XXVI.

"Revenge, revenge, cry'd Rothsay's heir,
   Your mail-coat sha' na bide
The strength and sharpness of my dart:"
   Then sent it through his side.
Another arrow well he mark'd, 205
   It pierc'd his neck in twa,
His hands then quat the silver reins,
   He low as earth did fa'.

XXVII.

"Sair bleids my liege, sair, sair he bleeds!"
   Again wi' might he drew 210
And gesture dread his sturdy bow,
   Fast the braid arrow flew:
Wae to the knight he ettled at;
   Lament now queen Elgreed;
High dames too wail your darling's fall, 215
   His youth and comely meed.

XXVIII.

"Take aff, take aff his costly jupe
   (Of gold well was it twin'd,
Knit like the fowler's net, through quhilk,
   His steelly harness shin'd,) 220
Take, Norse, that gift frae me, and bid
   Him venge the blood it bears;
Say, if he face my bended bow,
   He sure nae weapon fears."

XXIX.

Proud Norse with giant body tall,   225
  Braid shoulders and arms strong,
Cry'd, "Where is Hardyknute sae fam'd,
  And fear'd at Britain's throne:
Tho' Britons tremble at his name,
  I soon shall make him wail,   230
That e'er my sword was made sae sharp,
  Sae saft his coat of mail."

XXX.

That brag his stout heart cou'd na bide,
  It lent him youthfu' micht:
"I'm Hardyknute; this day, he cry'd,   235
  To Scotland's king I heght
To lay thee low, as horses hoof;
  My word I mean to keep."
Syne with the first stroke e'er he strake,
  He garr'd his body bleed.   240

XXXI.

Norss' een like gray gosehawk's stair'd wyld,
  He sigh'd wi' shame and spite;
"Disgrac'd is now my far-fam'd arm
  That left thee power to strike:"
Then ga' his head a blow sae fell,   245
  It made him doun to stoup,
As laigh as he to ladies us'd
  In courtly guise to lout.

XXXII.

Fu' soon he rais'd his bent body,
  His bow he marvell'd sair,   250
Sin blows till then on him but darr'd
  As touch of FAIRLY fair:

Norse marvell'd too as sair as he
  To see his stately look;
Sae soon as e'er he strake a fae,   255
  Sae soon his life he took.

XXXIII.
Where like a fire to heather set,
  Bauld Thomas did advance,
Ane sturdy fae with look enrag'd
  Up toward him did prance;   260
He spurr'd his steid through thickest ranks
  The hardy youth to quell,
Wha stood unmov'd at his approach
  His fury to repell.

XXXIV.
"That short brown shaft sae meanly trimm'd, 265
  Looks like poor Scotlands gear,
But dreadfull seems the rusty point!"
  And loud he leugh in jear.
"Oft Britons blood has dimm'd its shine;
  This point cut short their vaunt:"   270
Syne pierc'd the boaster's bearded cheek;
  Nae time he took to taunt.

XXXV.
Short while he in his saddle swang,
  His stirrup was nae stay,
Sae feeble hang his unbent knee   275
  Sure taiken he was fey:
Swith on the harden't clay he fell,
  Right far was heard the thud:
But Thomas look't nae as he lay
  All waltering in his blud: 280

XXXVI.
With careless gesture, mind unmov't,
  On rode he north the plain;

His seem in throng of fiercest strife,
   When winner ay the same:
Nor yet his heart dames dimplet cheek   285
   Could mease soft love to bruik,
Till vengefu' Ann return'd his scorn,
   Then languid grew his luik.

XXXVII.

In thraws of death with walowit cheik
   All panting on the plain,   290
The fainting corps of warriours lay,
   Ne're to arise again;
Ne're to return to native land,
   Nae mair with blithsome sounds
To boast the glories of the day,   295
   And shaw their shining wounds.

XXXVIII.

On Norways coast the widowit dame
   May wash the rocks with tears,
May lang luik ow'r the shipless seas
   Befor her mate appears.   300
Cease, Emma, cease to hope in vain;
   Thy lord lyes in the clay;
The valiant Scots nae revers thole
   To carry life away

XXXIX.

Here on a lee, where stands a cross   305
   Set up for monument,
Thousands fu' fierce that summer's day
   Fill'd keen war's black intent.
Let Scots, while Scots, praise Hardyknute,
   Let Norse the name ay dread,   310
Ay how he faught, aft how he spar'd,
   Shall latest ages read.

XL.

Now loud and chill blew th' westlin wind,
   Sair beat the heavy shower,
Mirk grew the night ere Hardyknute   315
   Wan near his stately tower.
His tow'r that us'd wi' torches blaze
   To shine sae far at night,
Seem'd now as black as mourning weed,
   Nae marvel sair he sigh'd.   320

XLI.

"There's nae light in my lady's bower,
   There's nae light in my ha';
Nae blink shines round my FAIRLY fair,
   Nor ward stands on my wa'.
What bodes it? Robert, Thomas, say;"   325
   Nae answer fitts their dread.
"Stand back, my sons, I'le be your guide:"
   But by they past with speed.

XLII.

"As fast I've sped owre Scotlands faes,"
   There ceas'd his brag of weir,   330
Sair sham'd to mind ought but his dame,
   And maiden FAIRLY fair.
Black fear he felt, but what to fear
   He wist nae yet; wi' dread
Sair shook his body, sair his limbs,   335
   And a' the warrior fled.
        *   *   *   *   *

*** In an elegant publication, entitled *Scottish Tragic Ballads*, printed by and for J. Nichols, 1781, 8vo, may be seen a continuation of the ballad of *Hardyknute*, by the addition of a Second Part, which hath since been acknowledged to be his own composition by the ingenious editor: to whom the late Sir D. Dalrymple communicated (subsequent to the account drawn up above in p. 79), extracts of a letter from Sir John Bruce, of Kinross, to Lord Binning, which plainly proves the pretended discoverer of the fragment of *Hardyknute* to have been Sir John Bruce himself. His words are, "To perform my promise, I send you a true copy of the manuscript I found some weeks ago in a vault at Dumferline. It is written on vellum, in a fair Gothic character, but so much defaced by time, as you'll find that the tenth part is not legible." He then gives the whole fragment as it was first published in 1719, save one or two stanzas, marking several passages as having perished by being illegible in the old MS. Hence it appears that Sir John was the author of *Hardyknute*, but afterwards used Mrs. Wardlaw to be the midwife of his poetry, and suppressed the story of the vault; as is well observed by the editor of the *Tragic Ballads*, and of Maitland's *Scot. Poets*, vol. i. p. cxxvii.

To this gentleman we are indebted for the use of the copy, whence the second edition was afterwards printed, as the same was prepared for the press by John Clerk, M. D., of Edinburgh, an intimate companion of Lord President Forbes.

The title of the first edition was, "Hardyknute, a fragment, Edinburgh, printed for James Watson, &c. 1719," folio, twelve pages.

Stanzas not in the first edition are Nos. 17, 18, 20, 21, 22, 23, 34, 35, 36, 37, 41, 42.

In the present impression the orthography of Dr. Clerk's copy has been preserved, and his readings carefully followed, except in a few instances, wherein the common edition appeared preferable: viz. He had in ver. 20, *but* — v. 56, *of harm.* — v. 64, *every.* — v. 67, *lo down.* — v. 83, *That* omitted. — v. 89, *And* omitted. — v. 143, *With argument but vainly strave Lang.* — v. 148, *say'd.* — v. 155, *incampit on the plain.* — v. 156, *Norse squadrons.* — v. 158, *regand revers.* — v. 170, *his strides he bent.* — v. 171, *minstrals playand Pibrochs fine.* — v. 172, *stately went.* — v. 182, *mon.* — v. 196, *sharp and fatal.* — v. 219,

which. — v. 241, *stood wyld.* — stanza 39 preceded stanza 38. —
v. 305, *There.* — v. 313, *blew wrestling.* — v. 336 had originally
been, *He fear'd a' cou'd be fear'd.*

The Editor was also informed, on the authority of Dr.
David Clerk, M.D., of Edinburgh, (son of the aforesaid Dr.
John Clerk,) that between the present stanzas 36 and 37, the
two following had been intended, but were on maturer consideration omitted, and do not now appear among the MS.
additions.

> Now darts flew wavering through slaw speed,
> Scarce could they reach their aim;
> Or reach'd, scarce blood the round point drew,
> 'Twas all but shot in vain:
> Right strengthy arms forefeebled grew,
> Sair wreck'd wi' that day's toils:
> E'en fierce-born minds now lang'd for peace,
> And curs'd war's cruel broils.
>
> Yet still wars horns sounded to charge,
> Swords clash'd and harness rang;
> But saftly sae ilk blaster blew
> The hills and dales fraemang.
> Nae echo heard in double dints,
> Nor the lang-winding horn
> Nae mair she blew out brade as she
> Did eir that summers morn.

END OF THE FIRST BOOK.

RELIQUES

OF

ANCIENT POETRY.

&c.

SERIES THE SECOND.
BOOK II.

I.

𝔄 𝔅allaꝺ of 𝔏utȝer, tȝe 𝔓ope, a 𝔆arꝺinal, anꝺ a 𝔥us=banꝺman.

In the former book we brought down this second series of poems as low as about the middle of the sixteenth century. We now find the Muses deeply engaged in religious controversy. The sudden revolution wrought in the opinions of mankind by the Reformation, is one of the most striking events in the history of the human mind. It could not but engross the attention of every individual in that age, and therefore no other writings would have any chance to be read, but such as related to this grand topic. The alterations made in the established religion by Henry VIII., the sudden changes it underwent in the three succeeding reigns within so short a space as eleven or twelve years, and the violent struggles between expiring Popery and growing Protestantism, could not but interest all mankind. Accordingly every pen was engaged in the dispute. The followers of the Old and New Profession (as they were called) had their respective ballad-makers; and every day produced

some popular sonnet for or against the Reformation. The
following ballad, and that entitled *Little John Nobody*, may
serve for specimens of the writings of each party. Both
were written in the time of Edward VI.; and are not the
worst that were composed upon the occasion. Controversial
divinity is no friend to poetic flights. Yet this ballad of
"Luther and the Pope," is not altogether devoid of spirit; it
is of the dramatic kind, and the characters are tolerably
well sustained: especially that of Luther, which is made to
speak in a manner not unbecoming the spirit and courage
of that vigorous Reformer. It is printed from the original
black-letter copy, (in the Pepys collection, vol. i. folio,) to
which is prefixed a large wooden cut, designed and executed
by some eminent master.

We are not to wonder that the ballad-writers of that age
should be inspired with the zeal of controversy, when the
very stage teemed with polemic divinity. I have now before me two very ancient quarto black-letter Plays: — the
one published in the time of Henry VIII., entitled 𝕰𝖛𝖊𝖗𝖞
𝕸𝖆𝖓; the other called 𝕷𝖚𝖘𝖙𝖞 𝕵𝖚𝖛𝖊𝖓𝖙𝖚𝖘, printed in the reign
of Edward VI. In the former of these, occasion is taken to
inculcate great reverence for old mother church and her
superstitions[1]: in the other, the poet, (one R. Wever,) with

---

[1] Take a specimen from his high encomiums on the priesthood.

> "There is no emperour, kyng, duke, ne baron
> That of God hath commissyon,
> As hath the leest preest in the world beynge.
>   *   *   *   *   *
> God hath to them more power gyven,
> Than to any aungell, that is in heven;
> With v. words he may consecrate
> Goddes body in flesshe and blode to take,
> And handeleth his maker bytwene his handes.
> The preest byndeth and unbindeth all bandes,
> Both in erthe and in heven. —
> Thou ministers all the sacramentes seven.
> Though we kyst thy feete thou were worthy;
> Thou art the surgyan that cureth synne dedly:
> No remedy may we fynde under God,
> But alone on preesthode.

great success, attacks both. So that the stage in those days literally was, what wise men have always wished it, — a supplement to the pulpit. This was so much the case, that in the play of "Lusty Juventus," chapter and verse are every where quoted as formally as in a sermon: take an instance:

"The Lord by his prophet Ezechiel sayeth in this wise playnlye,
 As in the xxxiij chapter it doth appere:
 Be converted, O ye children," &c.

From this Play we learn that most of the young people were new Gospellers, or friends to the Reformation, and that the old were tenacious of the doctrines imbibed in their youth: for thus the Devil is introduced lamenting the downfal of superstition: —

"The olde people would believe stil in my lawes,
 But the yonger sort leade them a contrary way,
 They wyl not beleve, they playnly say,
 In olde traditions, and made by men," &c.

And in another place Hypocrisy urges,

"The worlde was never meri
 Since chyldren were so boulde:
 Now evry boy will be a teacher,
 The father a foole, the chyld a preacher."

Of the plays above mentioned, to the first is subjoined the following printer's colophon, ¶ Thus endeth this moral playe of Every Man. ¶ Imprynted at London in Powles chyrche yarde by me John Skot. In Mr. Garrick's collection is an imperfect copy of the same play, printed by Richarde Pynson.

The other is entitled, An enterlude called Lusty Juventus: and is thus distinguished at the end: Finis. quod R. Weber. Imprynted at London in Paules churche yeard by Abraham Dele at the signe of the Lambe. Of this too Mr. Garrick has an imperfect copy of a different edition.

—— God gave preest that dignitè,
And letteth them in his stede amonge us be,
Thus be they above aungels in degre."
          See Hawkins's Orig. of Eng. Drama, vol. i. p. 61.

Of these two plays the reader may find some further particulars in the former volume, book ii. See "The Essay on
the Origin of the English Stage;" and the curious reader
will find the plays themselves printed at large in Hawkins's
"Origin of the English Drama," 3 vols. Oxford, 1773, 12mo.

THE HUSBANDMAN.

Let us lift up our hartes all,
　And prayse the Lordes magnificence,
Which hath given the wolues a fall,
　And is become our strong defence:
　For they thorowe a false pretens　　　　　5
From Christes bloude dyd all us leade[2],
　Gettynge from every man his pence,
As satisfactours for the deade.

For what we with our FLAYLES coulde get
　To kepe our house, and servauntes;　　　10
That did the Freers from us fet,
　And with our soules played the merchauntes:
　And thus they with theyr false warrantes
Of our sweate have easelye lyved,
　That for fatnesse theyr belyes pantes,　　15
So greatlye have they us deceaued.

They spared not the fatherlesse,
　The carefull, nor the pore wydowe;
They wolde have somewhat more or lesse,
　If it above the ground did growe:　　　　20
　But now we Husbandmen do knowe
Al their subteltye, and their false caste;
　For the Lorde hath them overthrowe
With his swete word now at the laste.

DOCTOR MARTIN LUTHER.

Thou antichrist, with thy thre crownes,　　25
　Hast usurped kynges powers,

[2] i. e. denied us the cup, see below, ver. 94.

As having power over realmes and townes,
　　Whom thou oughtest to serve all houres:
　　Thou thinkest by thy jugglyng colours
Thou maist lykewise Gods word oppresse;   30
　　As do the deceatful foulers,
When they theyr nettes craftelye dresse.

Thou flatterest every prince, and lord,
　　Threatening poore men with swearde and fyre;
All those, that do followe Gods worde,   35
　　To make them cleve to thy desire,
　　Theyr bokes thou burnest in flaming fire;
Cursing with boke, bell, and candell,
　　Such as to reade them have desyre,
Or with them are wyllynge to meddell.   40

Thy false power wyl I bryng down,
　　Thou shalt not raygne many a yere,
I shall dryve the from citye and towne,
　　Even with this PEN that thou seyste here:
　　Thou fyghtest with swerd, shylde, and speare,   45
But I wyll fyght with Gods worde;
　　Which is now so open and cleare,
That it shall brynge the under the borde[3].

THE POPE.

Though I brought never so many to hel,
　　And to utter dampnacion,   50
Throughe myne ensample, and consel,
　　Or thorow any abhominacion,
　　Yet doth our lawe excuse my fashion.
And thou, Luther, arte accursed;
　　For blamynge me, and my condicion,   55
The holy decres have the condempned.

Thou stryvest against my purgatory,
　　Because thou findest it not in scripture;

_____
[3] i. e. make thee knock under the table.

As though I by myne auctorite
   Myght not make one for myne honoure.   60
   Knowest thou not, that I have power
To make, and mar, in heaven and hell,
   In erth, and every creature?
Whatsoever I do it must be well.

As for scripture, I am above it;   65
   Am not I Gods hye vicare?
Shulde I be bounde to folowe it,
   As the carpenter his ruler[4]?
   Nay, nay, hereticks ye are,
That will not obey my auctoritie.   70
   With this sworde I wyll declare,
That ye shal al accursed be.

THE CARDINAL.

I am a Cardinall of Rome,
   Sent from Christes hye vicary,
To graunt pardon to more, and sume,   75
   That wil Luther resist strongly:
   He is a greate hereticke treuly,
And regardeth to much the scripture;
   For he thinketh onely thereby
To subdue the popes high honoure.   80

Receive ye this pardon devoutely.
   And loke that ye agaynst him fight;
Plucke up youre herts, and be manlye,
   For the pope sayth ye do but ryght:
   And this be sure, that at one flyghte,   85
Allthough ye be overcome by chaunce,
   Ye shall to heaven go with greate myghte;
God can make you no resistaunce.

But these heretikes for their medlynge
   Shall go down to hel every one;   90

[4] i. e. his rule.

For they have not the popes blessynge,
   Nor regarde his holy pardòn:
   They thinke from all destruction
By Christes bloud to be saved,
   Fearynge not our excommunicacion,   95
Therefore shall they al be dampned.

II.

John Anderson my Jo.

A SCOTTISH SONG.

WHILE in England verse was made the vehicle of controversy, and Popery was attacked in it by logical argument, or stinging satire, we may be sure the zeal of the Scottish Reformers would not suffer their pens to be idle, but many a pasquil was discharged at the Romish priests, and their enormous encroachments on property. Of this kind perhaps is the following, (preserved in Maitland's MS. Collection of Scottish poems in the Pepysian library):

"Tak a Wobster, that is leill,
   And a Miller, that will not steill,
   With ane Priest, that is not gredy,
   And lay ane deid corpse thame by,
   And throw virtue of thame three,
   That deid corpse sall qwyknit be."

Thus far all was fair: but the furious hatred of Popery led them to employ their rhymes in a still more licentious manner. It is a received tradition in Scotland, that at the time of the Reformation, ridiculous and obscene songs were composed to be sung by the rabble to the tunes of the most favourite hymns in the Latin Service. *Green Sleeves and Pudding Pies*, (designed to ridicule the Popish Clergy,) is said to have been one of these metamorphosed hymns: *Maggy Lauder* was another: *John Anderson my Jo* was a third. The original music of all these burlesque sonnets was very fine. To give a specimen of their manner, we have inserted one of the least offensive. The reader will pardon the meanness of the composition for the sake of the anecdote, which strongly marks the spirit of the times.

In the present edition this song is much improved by some new readings communicated by a friend, who thinks by the "seven bairns," in stanza 2d, are meant the Seven Sacraments; five of which were the spurious offspring of mother Church, as the first stanza contains a satirical allusion to the luxury of the Popish Clergy.

The adaptation of solemn church music to these ludicrous pieces, and the jumble of ideas thereby occasioned, will account for the following fact. — From the Records of the General Assembly in Scotland, called *The Book of the Universal Kirk*, p. 90, 7th July, 1568, it appears, that Thomas Bassendyne, printer in Edinburgh, printed "a psalme buik, in the end whereof was found printit ane baudy song, called *Welcome Fortunes*[1]."

WOMAN.

John Anderson my jo, cum in as ze gae bye,
And ze sall get a sheips heid weel baken in a pye;
Weel baken in a pye, and the haggis in a pat;
John Anderson my jo, cum in, and ze's get that.

MAN.

And how doe ze, Cummer? and how hae ze threven?
And how mony bairns hae ze? Wom. Cummer, I hae seven.
Man. Are they to zour awin gude man? Wom. Na, Cummer, na;
For five of tham were gotten, quhan he was awa'.

[1] See also Biograph. Britan. 1st. edit. vol. i. p. 177.

III.

Little John Nobody.

WE have here a witty libel on the Reformation under
King Edward VI., written about the year 1550, and preserved in the Pepys collection, British Museum, and Strype's
Memoirs of Cranmer. The author artfully declines entering
into the merits of the cause, and wholly reflects on the lives
and actions of many of the reformed. It is so easy to find
flaws and imperfections in the conduct of men, even the best
of them, and still easier to make general exclamations about
the profligacy of the present times, that no great point is
gained by arguments of that sort, unless the author could
have proved that the principles of the reformed Religion had
a natural tendency to produce a corruption of manners;
whereas he indirectly owns, that their Reverend Father
[Archbishop Cranmer] had used the most proper means to
stem the torrent, by giving the people access to the Scriptures, by teaching them to pray with understanding, and by
publishing homilies, and other religious tracts. It must,
however, be acknowledged, that our libeller had at that time
sufficient room for just satire. For under the banners of the
reformed had enlisted themselves many concealed papists
who had private ends to gratify; many that were of no religion; many greedy courtiers, who thirsted after the possessions of the church; and many dissolute persons, who
wanted to be exempt from all ecclesiastical censures: and as
these men were loudest of all others in their cries for Reformation, so in effect none obstructed the regular progress
of it so much, or by their vicious lives brought vexation and
shame more on the truly venerable and pious Reformers.

The reader will remark the fondness of our satirist for
alliteration: in this he was guilty of no affectation or singu-
larity; his versification is that of *Pierce Plowman's Visions*,
in which a recurrence of similar letters is essential: to this
he has only superadded rhyme, which in his time began to

be the general practice.　See an Essay on this very peculiar
kind of metre, prefixed to book iii. in this volume.

———

In december, when the dayes draw to be short,
After november, when the nights wax noysome and long;
As I past by a place privily at a port,
I saw one sit by himself making a song:
His last[1] talk of trifles, who told with his tongue
That few were fast i' th' faith.　I 'freyned[2]' that freake,
Whether he wanted wit, or some had done him wrong.
　　He said, he was little John Nobody, that durst not speake.

John Nobody, quoth I, what news? thou soon note and tell
What maner men thou meane, that are so mad.
He said, These gay gallants, that wil construe the gospel,
As Solomon the sage, with semblance full sad;
To discusse divinity they nought adread;
More meet it were for them to milk kye at a fleyke.
Thou lyest, quoth I, thou losel, like a leud lad.
　　He said he was little John Nobody, that durst not speake.

Its meet for every man on this matter to talk,
And the glorious gospel ghostly to have in mind;
It is sothe said, that sect but much unseemly skalk;
As boyes babble in books, that in scripture are blind:
Yet to their fancy soon a cause will find;
As to live in lust, in lechery to leyke:
Such caitives count to be come of Cains kind[3];
　　But that I little John Nobody durst not speake.

For our reverend father hath set forth an order,
Our service to be said in our seignours tongue;
As Solomon the sage set forth the scripture;

[1] Perhaps He left talk.　　　　　[2] feyned, MSS. and P.C.
[3] Cain's kind.]　So in Pierce the Plowman's Creed, the proud friars are
said to be
　　—"Of Caymes kind." Vide sig. C ij. b.

Our suffrages, and services, with many a sweet song,
With homilies, and godly books us among,
That no stiff, stubborn stomacks we should freyke:
But wretches nere worse to do poor men wrong;
   But that I little John Nobody dare not speake.

For bribery was never so great, since born was our Lord,
And whoredom was never les hated, sith Christ harrowed hel
And poor men are so sore punished commonly through the
      world,
That it would grieve any one, that good is, to hear tel.
For al the homilies and good books, yet their hearts be so
      quel,
That if a man do amisse, with mischiefe they wil him
      wreake;
The fashion of these new fellows it is so vile and fell:
   But that I little John Nobody dare not speake.

Thus to live after their lust, that life would they have,
And in lechery to leyke al their long life;
For al the preaching of Paul, yet many a proud knave
Wil move mischiefe in their mind both to maid and wife
To bring them in advoutry, or else they wil strife
And in brawling about baudery, Gods commandments breake:
But of these frantic il fellowes, few of them do thrife;
   Though I little John Nobody dare not speake.

If thou company with them, they wil currishly carp, and
      not care
According to their foolish fantacy; but fast wil they naught:
Prayer with them is but prating; therefore they it forbear:
Both almes deeds, and holiness, they hate it in their
      thought:
Therefore pray we to that prince, that with his bloud us
      bought,
That he wil mend that is amiss: for many a manful freyke
Is sorry for these sects, though they say little or nought;
   And that I little John Nobody dare not once speake.

Thus in NO place, this NOBODY, in NO time I met,
Where NO man, 'ne[4]' NOUGHT was, nor NOTHING did appear;
Through the sound of a synagogue for sorrow I swett,
That 'Aeolus[5]' through the eccho did cause me to hear.
Then I drew me down into a dale whereas the dumb deer
Did shiver for a shower; but I shunted from a freyke:
For I would no wight in this world wist who I were,
But little John Nobody, that dare not once speake.

[4] then, MSS. and P.C.   [5] Hercules, MSS. and P.C.

IV.

Q. Elizabeth's Verses while Prisoner at Woodstock,

WRIT WITH CHARCOAL ON A SHUTTER,

ARE preserved by Hentzner, in that part of his Travels
which has been reprinted in so elegant a manner at Straw-
berry-Hill. In Hentzner's book they were wretchedly corrupted, but are here given as amended by his ingenious
editor. The old orthography, and one or two ancient readings
of Hentzner's copy, are here restored.

Oh, Fortune! how thy restlesse wavering state
    Hath fraught with cares my troubled witt!
Witnes this present prisonn, whither fate
    Could beare me, and the joys I quit.
Thou causedest the guiltie to be losed   5
From bandes, wherein are innocents inclosed:
    Causing the guiltles to be straite reserved,
    And freeing those that death hath well deserved.
But by her envie can be nothing wroughte,
So God send to my foes all they have thoughte.   10

A.D. MDLV.   ELIZABETHE, PRISONNEE.

Ver. 4, *Could beare*, is an ancient idiom, equivalent to *did bear*, or *hath borne*. See below, the *Beggar of Bednal Green*, ver. 57, Could say.

V.

The Heir of Linne.

THE original of this ballad is found in the Editor's folio
MS., the breaches and defects in which rendered the insertion of supplemental stanzas necessary. These it is hoped
the reader will pardon, as indeed the completion of the story
was suggested by a modern ballad on a similar subject.

From the Scottish phrases here and there discernible in
this poem, it should seem to have been originally composed
beyond the Tweed.

The Heir of Linne appears not to have been a lord of
parliament, but a laird, whose title went along with his
estate.

PART THE FIRST.

LITHE and listen, gentlemen,
    To sing a song I will beginne:
It is of a lord of faire Scotland,
    Which was the unthrifty heire of Linne.

His father was a right good lord,   5
    His mother a lady of high degree;
But they, alas! were dead, him froe,
    And he lov'd keeping companie.

To spend the daye with merry cheare,
    To drinke and revell every night,   10
To card and dice from eve to morne,
    It was, I ween, his hearts delighte.

To ride, to runne, to rant, to roare,
    To alwaye spend and never spare,
I wott, an' it were the king himselfe,   15
    Of gold and fee he mote be bare.

Soe fares the unthrifty lord of Linne
   Till all his gold is gone and spent;
And he maun selle his landes so broad,
   His house, and landes, and all his rent.   20

His father had a keen stewàrde,
   And John o' the Scales was called hee:
But John is become a gentel-man,
   And John has gott both gold and fee.

Sayes, Welcome, welcome, lord of Linne,   25
   Let nought disturb thy merry cheere;
Iff thou wilt sell thy landes soe broad,
   Good store of gold Ile give thee heere.

My gold is gone, my money is spent;
   My lande nowe take it unto thee: 30
Give me the golde, good John o' the Scales,
   And thine for aye my lande shall bee.

Then John he did him to record draw,
   And John he cast him a gods-pennie[1];
But for every pounde that John agreed,   35
   The lande, I wis, was well worth three.

He told him the gold upon the borde,
   He was right glad his land to winne;
The gold is thine, the land is mine,
   And now Ile be the lord of Linne.   40

Thus he hath sold his land soe broad,
   Both hill and holt, and moore and fenne,
All but a poore and lonesome lodge,
   That stood far off in a lonely glenne.

---

[1] *i. e.* earnest-money; from the French 'denier à Dieu.' At this day, when application is made to the Dean and Chapter of Carlisle to accept an exchange of the tenant under one of their leases, a piece of silver is presented by the new tenant, which is still called a *God's-penny.*

For soe he to his father hight.   45
   My sonne, when I am gonne, sayd hee,
Then thou wilt spend thy lande so broad,
   And thou wilt spend thy gold so free:

But sweare me nowe upon the roode,
   That lonesome lodge thou'lt never spend;   50
For when all the world doth frown on thee,
   Thou there shalt find a faithful friend.

The heire of Linne is full of golde:
   And come with me, my friends, sayd hee,
Let's drinke, and rant, and merry make,   55
   And he that spares, ne'er mote he thee.

They ranted, drank, and merry made,
   Till all his gold it waxed thinne;
And then his friendes they slunk away;
   They left the unthrifty heire of Linne.   60

He had never a penny left in his purse,
   Never a penny left but three,
And one was brass, another was lead,
   And another it was white money.

Nowe well-aday, sayd the heire of Linne,   65
   Nowe well-aday, and woe is mee,
For when I was the lord of Linne,
   I never wanted gold nor fee.

But many a trustye friend have I,
   And why shold I feel dole or care?   70
Ile borrow of them all by turnes,
   Soe need I not be never bare.

But one, I wis, was not at home;
   Another had payd his gold away;

Ver. 63, 64, 65, &c. Sic MSS.

Another call'd him thriftless loone,   75
   And bade him sharpely wend his way.

Now well-aday, said the heire of Linne,
   Now well-aday, and woe is me;
For when I had my landes so broad,
   On me they liv'd right merrilee.   80

To beg my bread from door to door
   I wis, it were a brenning shame:
To rob and steal it were a sinne:
   To worke my limbs I cannot frame.

Now Ile away to lonesome lodge,   85
   For there my father bade me wend;
When all the world should frown on mee
   I there shold find a trusty friend.

PART THE SECOND.

AWAY then hyed the heire of Linne
   Oer hill and holt, and moor and fenne,
Untill he came to lonesome lodge,
   That stood so lowe in a lonely glenne.

He looked up, he looked downe,   5
   In hope some comfort for to winne:
But bare and lothly were the walles.
   Here's sorry cheare, quo' the heire of Linne.

The little windowe dim and darke
   Was hung with ivy, brere, and yewe;   10
No shimmering sunn here ever shone;
   No halesome breeze here ever blew.

No chair, ne table he mote spye,
   No chearful hearth, ne welcome bed,
Nought save a rope with renning noose,   15
   That dangling hung up o'er his head.

And over it in broad lettèrs,
  These words were written so plain to see:
"Ah! gracelesse wretch, hast spent thine all,
  And brought thyselfe to penurie?   20

"All this my boding mind misgave,
  I therefore left this trusty friend:
Let it now sheeld thy foule disgrace,
  And all thy shame and sorrows end."

Sorely shent wi' this rebuke,   25
  Sorely shent was the heire of Linne;
His heart, I wis, was near to brast
  With guilt and sorrowe, shame and sinne.

Never a word spake the heire of Linne,
  Never a word he spake but three: 30
"This is a trusty friend indeed,
  And is right welcome unto mee."

Then round his necke the corde he drewe,
  And sprang aloft with his bodìe:
When lo! the ceiling burst in twaine,   35
  And to the ground came tumbling hee.

Astonyed lay the heire of Linne,
  Ne knewe if he were live or dead:
At length he looked, and sawe a bille,
  And in it a key of gold so redd.   40

He took the bill, and lookt it on,
  Strait good comfort found he there:
Itt told him of a hole in the wall,
  In which there stood three chests in-fere[2].

Two were full of the beaten golde,   45
  The third was full of white monèy;

[2] In-fere, *i. e.* together.

And over them in broad lettèrs
 These words were written so plaine to see:

"Once more, my sonne, I sette thee clere;
 Amend thy life and follies past;   50
For but thou amend thee of thy life,
 That rope must be thy end at last."

And let it bee, sayd the heire of Linne;
 And let it bee, but if I amend[3]:
For here I will make mine avow,   55
 This reade[4] shall guide me to the end.

Away then went with a merry cheare,
 Away then went the heire of Linne
I wis, he neither ceas'd ne blanne,
 Till John o' the Scales house he did winne. 60

And when he came to John o' the Scales,
 Upp at the speere[5] then looked hee;
There sate three lords upon a rowe,
 Were drinking of the wine so free.

And John himself sate at the bord-head,   65
 Because now lord of Linne was hee.
I pray thee, he said, good John o' the Scales,
 One forty pence for to lend mee.

Away, away, thou thriftless loone;
 Away, away, this may not bee;   70
For Christs curse on my head, he sayd,
 If ever l trust thee one pennìe.

V. 60, an old northern phrase.

[3] *i. e.* unless I amend.   [4] *i. e.* advice, counsel.
[5] Perhaps the hole in the door or window, by which it was *speered, i. e.* sparred, fastened, or shut. In Bale's 2d part of the *Acts of Eng. Votaries*, we have this phrase (fol. 38), "The dore thereof oft tymes opened and *speared* agayne."

Then bespake the heire of Linne,
  To John o' the Scales wife then spake he:
Madame, some almes on me bestowe,   75
  I pray for sweet saint Charitie.

Away, away, thou thriftless loone,
  I swear thou gettest no almes of mee;
For if we shold hang any losel heere,
  The first we wold begin with thee.   80

Then bespake a good fellòwe,
  Which sat at John o' the Scales his bord;
Sayd, Turn againe, thou heire of Linne;
  Some time thou wast a well good lord:

Some time a good fellow thou hast been,   85
  And sparedst not thy gold and fee;
Therefore Ile lend thee forty pence,
  And other forty if need bee.

And ever, I pray thee, John o' the Scales,
  To let him sit in thy companie: 90
For well I wot thou hadst his land,
  And a good bargain it was to thee.

Up then spake him John o' the Scales,
  All wood he answer'd him againe:
Now Christs curse on my head, he sayd,   95
  But I did lose by that bargàine.

And here I proffer thee, heire of Linne,
  Before these lords so faire and free,
Thou shalt have it backe again better cheape,
  By a hundred markes, than I had it of thee.   100

I drawe you to record, lords, he said.
  With that he cast him a gods pennie:
Now by my fay, sayd the heire of Linne,
  And here, good John, is thy monèy.

V. 34. of part i., and 102 of part ii., *cast* is the reading of the MS.

And he pull'd forth three bagges of gold,   105
    And layd them down upon the bord:
All woe begone was John o' the Scales,
    Soe shent he cold say never a word.

He told him forth the good red gold,
    He told it forth [with] mickle dinne.   110
The gold is thine, the land is mine,
    And now Ime againe the lord of Linne.

Sayes, Have thou here, thou good fellòwe,
    Forty pence thou didst lend mee:
Now I am againe the lord of Linne,   115
    And forty pounds I will give thee.

Ile make thee keeper of my forrest,
    Both of the wild deere and the tame;
For but I reward thy bounteous heart,
    I wis, good fellowe, I were to blame.   120

Now well-aday! sayth Joan o' the Scales:
    Now well-aday! and woe is my life!
Yesterday I was lady of Linne,
    Now Ime but John o' the Scales his wife.

Now fare thee well, sayd the heire of Linne;   125
    Farewell now, John o' the Scales, said hee:
Christs curse light on me, if ever again
    I bring my lands in jeopardy.
                                    ⁎

⁎ In the present edition of this ballad, several ancient
readings are restored from the folio MS.

VI.

Gascoigne's Praise of the Fair Bridges, afterwards Lady Sandes,

ON HER HAVING A SCAR IN HER FOREHEAD.

GEORGE GASCOIGNE was a celebrated poet in the early part of Queen Elizabeth's reign, and appears to great advantage among the miscellaneous writers of that age. He was author of three or four plays, and of many smaller poems; one of the most remarkable of which is a satire in blank verse, called the *Steele-glass*, 1576, 4to.

Gascoigne was born in Essex, educated in both universities, whence he removed to Gray's-inn; but, disliking the study of the law, became first a dangler at court, and afterwards a soldier in the wars of the Low Countries. He had no great success in any of these pursuits, as appears from a poem of his, entitled, "Gascoigne's Wodmanship, written to Lord Gray of Wilton." Many of his epistles dedicatory, are dated in 1575, 1576, from "his poore house in Walthamstoe:" where he died a middle-aged man in 1578, according to Anth. Wood; or rather in 1577, if he is the person meant in an old tract, entitled, "A Remembrance of the well employed Life and Godly End of George Gascoigne, Esq. who deceased at Stamford in Lincolnshire, Oct. 7. 1577, by Geo. Whetstone, gent. an eye-witness of his godly and charitable end in this world," 4to. no date. — [From a MS. of Oldys.]

Mr. Thomas Warton thinks "Gascoigne has much exceeded all the poets of his age in smoothness and harmony of versification[1]." But the truth is, scarce any of the earlier poets of Queen Elizabeth's time are found deficient in harmony and smoothness, though those qualities appear so rare in the writings of their successors. In the *Paradise of dainty Devises*[2], (the Dodsley's Miscellany of those times,)

---

[1] Observations on the *Faerie Queen*, vol. ii. p. 168.
[2] Printed in 1578, 1596, and perhaps oftener, in 4to., black-letter.

will hardly be found one rough or inharmonious line[3]:
whereas the numbers of Jonson, Donne, and most of their
contemporaries, frequently offend the ear, like the filing of
a saw. — Perhaps this is in some measure to be accounted
for from the growing pedantry of that age, and from the
writers affecting to run their lines into one another, after the
manner of the Latin and Greek poets.

The following poem (which the elegant writer above
quoted hath recommended to notice, as possessed of a de-
licacy rarely to be seen in that early state of our poetry)
properly consists of Alexandrines of twelve and fourteen
syllables, and is printed from two quarto black-letter collections of Gascoigne's pieces; the first entitled, "A hun-
dreth sundrie flowres, bounde up in one small posie, &c.
London, imprinted for Richarde Smith:" without date, but
from a letter of H. W. (p. 202), compared with the printer's
epist. to the reader, it appears to have been published in
1572, or 3. The other is entitled, "The Posies of George
Gascoigne, Esq. corrected, perfected, and augmented by the
author, 1575. — Printed at London, for Richard Smith," &c.
No year, but the epist. dedicat. is dated 1576.

In the title-page of this last (by way of printer's[4], or
bookseller's device) is an ornamental wooden cut, tolerably
well executed, wherein Time is represented drawing the
figure of Truth out of a pit or cavern, with this legend,
Occulta Veritas Tempore patet, [R. S.] This is mentioned, because it is not improbable but the accidental sight of this,
or some other title-page containing the same device, suggested to Rubens that well-known design of a similar kind,
which he has introduced into the Luxemburg Gallery[5], and
which has been so justly censured for the unnatural manner
of its execution.

---

[3] The same is true of most of the poems in the *Mirrour of Magistrates,*
1563, 4to., and also of Surrey's Poems, 1557.

[4] Henrie Binneman.

[5] Le Tems découvre la Vérité.

In court whoso demaundes
    What dame doth most excell;
For my conceit I must needes say,
    Faire Bridges beares the bel.

Upon whose lively cheeke,   5
    To prove my judgment true,
The rose and lillie seeme to strive
    For equall change of hewe:

And therewithall so well
    Hir graces all agree;   10
No frowning cheere dare once presume
    In hir sweet face to bee.

Although some lavishe lippes,
    Which like some other best,
Will say, the blemishe on hir browe   15
    Disgraceth all the rest.

Thereto I thus replie;
    God wotte, they little knowe
The hidden cause of that mishap,
    Nor how the harm did growe: 20

For when dame Nature first
    Had framde hir heavenly face,
And thoroughly bedecked it
    With goodly gleames of grace;

It lyked hir so well: 25
    Lo here, quod she, a peece
For perfect shape, that passeth all
    Appelles' worke in Greece.

This bayt may chaunce to catche
    The greatest God of love,   30
Or mightie thundring Jove himself,
    That rules the roast above.

But out, alas! those wordes
    Were vaunted all in vayne:
And some unseen were present there,   35
    Pore Bridges, to thy pain.

For Cupide, crafty boy,
    Close in a corner stoode,
Not blyndfold then, to gaze on hir:
    I gesse it did him good.   40

Yet when he felte the flame
    Gan kindle in his brest,
And herd dame Nature boast by hir
    To break him of his rest,

His hot newe-chosen love   45
    He chaunged into hate,
And sodeynly with mightie mace
    Gan rap hir on the pate.

It greeved Nature muche
    To see the cruell deede: 50
Mee seemes I see hir, how she wept
    To see hir dearling bleede.

Wel yet, quod she, this hurt
    Shal have some helpe I trowe:
And quick with skin she coverd it,   55
    That whiter is than snowe.

Wherwith Dan Cupide fled,
    For feare of further flame,
When angel-like he saw hir shine,
    Whome he had smit with shame.   60

Lo, thus was Bridges hurt
    In cradel of hir kind.
The coward Cupide brake hir browe
    To wreke his wounded mynd.

V. 62, In cradel of hir kind: *i. e.* in the cradle of her family. See Warton's *Observations*, vol. ii. p. 137.

    The skar still there remains;   65
       No force, there let it bee:
    There is no cloude that can eclipse
       So bright a sunne, as she.

*** The lady here celebrated was Catharine, daughter
of Edmond second Lord Chandos, wife of William Lord
Sands. See Collins's *Peerage*, vol. ii. p. 133, ed. 1779.

VII.

Fair Rosamond.

MOST of the circumstances in this popular story of King
Henry II. and the beautiful Rosamond, have been taken for
fact by our English historians, who, unable to account for
the unnatural conduct of Queen Eleanor in stimulating her
sons to rebellion, have attributed it to jealousy, and supposed that Henry's amour with Rosamond was the object of
that passion.

Our old English annalists seem, most of them, to have
followed Higden, the monk of Chester, whose account, with
some enlargements, is thus given by Stow. "Rosamond the
fayre daughter of Walter lord Clifford, concubine to Henry II.
(poisoned by queen Elianor, as some thought), dyed at
Woodstocke [A.D. 1177], where king Henry had made for
her a house of wonderfull working; so that no man or woman
might come to her, but he that was instructed by the king,
or such as were right secret with him touching the matter.
This house after some was named Labyrinthus, or Dedalus
worke, which was wrought like unto a knot in a garden,
called a Maze[1]; but it was commonly said, that lastly the
queene came to her by a clue of thridde, or silke, and so
dealt with her, that she lived not long after: but when she

---

[1] Consisting of vaults under ground, arched and walled with brick and
stone, according to Drayton. See note on his *Epistle of Rosamond*.

was dead, she was buried at Godstow in an house of nunnes, beside Oxford, with these verses upon her tombe:

HIC JACET IN TUMBA, ROSA MUNDI, NON ROSA MUNDA:
NON REDOLET, SED OLET, QUÆ REDOLERE SOLET.

In English thus:

"The rose of the world, but not the cleane flowre,
    Is now here graven; to whom beauty was lent:
In this grave full darke nowe is her bowre,
    That by her life was sweete and redolent:
    But now that she is from this life blent,
Though she were sweete, now foully doth she stinke.
A mirrour good for all men, that on her thinke."
                              Stow's Annals, ed. 1631, p. 154.

How the queen gained admittance into Rosamond's bower is differently related. Holinshed speaks of it, as "the common report of the people, that the queene . . . founde hir out by a silken thread, which the king had drawne after him out of hir chamber with his foot, and dealt with hir in such sharpe and cruell wise, that she lived not long after." Vol. iii. p. 115. On the other hand, in Speed's Hist., we are told that the jealous queen found her out "by a clew of silke, fallen from Rosamund's lappe as shee sate to take ayre, and suddenly fleeing from the sight of the searcher, the end of her silke fastened to her foot, and the clew still unwinding, remained behinde: which the queene followed, till shee had found what she sought, and upon Rosamund so vented her spleene, as the lady lived not long after." 3d edit. p. 509. Our ballad-maker with more ingenuity, and probably as much truth, tells us the clue was gained by surprise, from the knight who was left to guard her bower.

It is observable, that none of the old writers attribute Rosamond's death to poison (Stowe, above, mentions it merely as a slight conjecture); they only give us to understand, that the queen treated her harshly; with furious menaces, we may suppose, and sharp expostulations, which had such effect on her spirits, that she did not long survive it. Indeed, on her tomb-stone, as we learn from a person of

credit[2], among other fine sculptures, was engraven the figure
of a *cup*. This, which, perhaps, at first was an accidental
ornament, (perhaps only the chalice,) might in after-times
suggest the notion that she was poisoned; at least this construction was put upon it when the stone came to be demolished after the nunnery was dissolved. The account is
that "the tombstone of Rosamund Clifford was taken up at
Godstow, and broken in pieces, and that upon it were interchangeable weavings drawn out and decked with roses red
and green, and the picture of the *cup*, out of which she drank
the poison given her by the queen, carved in stone."

Rosamond's father having been a great benefactor to the
nunnery of Godstow, where she had also resided herself in
the innocent part of her life, her body was conveyed there,
and buried in the middle of the choir; in which place it
remained till the year 1191, when Hugh, bishop of Lincoln,
caused it to be removed. The fact is recorded by Hoveden,
a contemporary writer, whose words are thus translated by
Stow: "Hugh, bishop of Lincolne, came to the abbey of
nunnes, called Godstow, ... and when he had entred the
church to pray, he saw a tombe in the middle of the quire,
covered with a pall of silke, and set about with lights of
waxe: and demanding whose tomb it was, he was answered
that it was the tombe of Rosamond, that was some time
lemman to Henry II. ...... who for the love of her had
done much good to that church. Then, quoth the bishop,
take out of this place the harlot, and bury her without the
church, lest Christian religion should grow in contempt; and
to the end that, through example of her, other women being
made afraid, may beware, and keepe themselves from un-
lawfull and advouterous company with men." — Annals,
p. 159.

History further informs us, that King John repaired
Godstow nunnery, and endowed it with yearly revenues,

---

[2] Tho. Allen, of Glouc. Hall, Oxon, who died in 1632, aged 90. See
Hearne's rambling discourse concerning Rosamond, at the end of *Gul.
Neubrig. Hist.* vol. iii. p. 739.

"that these holy virgins might releeve with their prayers the soules of his father king Henrie, and of lady Rosamund, there interred[3]." ... In what situation her remains were found at the dissolution of the nunnery, we learn from Leland: "Rosamundes tumbe at Godstowe nunnery was taken up [of] late; it is a stone with this inscription, *Tumba Rosamundæ*. Her bones were closid in lede, and withyn that bones were closyd yn lether. When it was opened, a very swete smell came owt of it[4]." See Hearne's discourse above quoted, written in 1718; at which time, he tells us, were still seen by the pool at Woodstock the foundations of a very large building, which were believed to be the remains of Rosamond's labyrinth.

To conclude this (perhaps too prolix) account, Henry had two sons by Rosamond, from a computation of whose ages, a modern historian has endeavoured to invalidate the received story. These were William Longue-espé, (or Long-sword,) Earl of Salisbury, and Geoffrey, Bishop of Lincolne[5]. Geoffrey was the younger of Rosamond's sons, and yet is said to have been twenty years old at the time of his election to that see in 1173. Hence this writer concludes, that King Henry fell in love with Rosamond in 1149, when in King Stephen's reign he came over to be knighted by the King of Scots; he also thinks it probable that Henry's commerce with this lady "broke off upon his marriage with Eleanor, [in 1152,] and that the young lady, by a natural effect of grief and resentment at the defection of her lover, entered on that occasion into the nunnery of Godstowe, where she died, probably before the rebellion of Henry's sons in 1173." [Carte's Hist. vol. i. p. 652.] But let it be observed, that Henry was but sixteen years old when he came over to be knighted; that he stayed but eight months in this island,

---

[3] Vide reign of Henry II. in Speed's History, writ by Dr. Barcham, Dean of Bocking.

[4] This would have passed for miraculous, if it had happened in the tomb of any clerical person, and a proof of his being a saint.

[5] Afterwards Archbishop of York, temp. Rich. I.

and was almost all the time with the King of Scots; that he
did not return back to England till 1153, the year after his
marriage with Eleanor; and that no writer drops the least
hint of Rosamond's having ever been abroad with her lover,
nor indeed is it probable that a boy of sixteen should venture
to carry over a mistress to his mother's court. If all these
circumstances are considered, Mr. Carte's account will be
found more incoherent and improbable than that of the old
ballad; which is also countenanced by most of our old
historians.

Indeed, the true date of Geoffrey's birth, and consequently of Henry's commerce with Rosamond, seems to be
best ascertained from an ancient manuscript in the Cotton
library; wherein it is thus registered of Geoffrey Plantagenet,
"Natus est 5⁰ Henry II. [1159.] Factus est miles 25⁰ Henry II.
[1179.]   Elect. in Episcop. Lincoln. 28⁰ Henry II. [1182]."
Vide Chron. de Kirkstall, (Domitian XII.) Drake's Hist. of
York, p. 422.

The ballad of *Fair Rosamond* appears to have been first
published in "Strange Histories or Songs and Sonnets of
Kinges, Princes, Dukes, Lords, Ladyes, Knights, and
Gentlemen, &c. By Thomas Delone. Lond. 1612," 4to. It
is now printed (with conjectural emendations) from four
ancient copies in black-letter; two of them in the Pepys
library.

WHEN as king Henry rulde this land,
  The second of that name,
Besides the queene, he dearly lovde
  A faire and comely dame.

Most peerlesse was her beautye founde,   5
  Her favour, and her face;
A sweeter creature in this worlde
  Could never prince embrace.

Her crisped lockes like threads of golde
  Appeard to each mans sight;   10

Her sparkling eyes, like Orient pearles,
  Did cast a heavenlye light.

The blood within her crystal cheekes
  Did such a colour drive,
As though the lillye and the rose   15
  For mastership did strive.

Yea Rosamonde, fair Rosamonde,
  Her name was called so,
To whom our queene, dame Ellinor,
  Was known a deadlye foe.   20

The king therefore, for her defence,
  Against the furious queene,
At Woodstocke builded such a bower,
  The like was never seene.

Most curiously that bower was built   25
  Of stone and timber strong,
An hundered and fifty doors
  Did to this bower belong:

And they so cunninglye contriv'd
  With turnings round about,   30
That none but with a clue of thread,
  Could enter in or out.

And for his love and ladyes sake,
  That was so faire and brighte,
The keeping of this bower he gave   35
  Unto a valiant knighte.

But fortune, that doth often frowne
  Where she before did smile,
The kinges delighte and ladyes joy
  Full soon shee did beguile: 40

For why, the kinges ungracious sonne,
　Whom he did high advance,
Against his father raised warres
　Within the realme of France.

But yet before our comelye king　　　　45
　The English land forsooke,
Of Rosamond, his lady faire,
　His farewelle thus he tooke:

"My Rosamonde, my only Rose,
　That pleasest best mine eye:　　　　50
The fairest flower in all the worlde
　To feed my fantasye:

The flower of mine affected heart,
　Whose sweetness doth excelle:
My royal Rose, a thousand times　　　55
　I bid thee nowe farwelle!

For I must leave my fairest flower,
　My sweetest Rose, a space,
And cross the seas to famous France,
　Proud rebelles to abase.　　　　60

But yet, my Rose, be sure thou shalt
　My coming shortlye see,
And in my heart, when hence I am,
　Ile beare my Rose with mee."

When Rosamond, that ladye brighte,　65
　Did heare the king saye soe,
The sorrowe of her grieved heart
　Her outward lookes did showe;

And from her cleare and crystall eyes
　The teares gusht out apace,　　　　70
Which like the silver-pearled dewe
　Ranne downe her comely face.

Her lippes, erst like the corall redde,
    Did waxe both wan and pale,
And for the sorrow she conceivde   75
    Her vitall spirits faile;

And falling downe all in a swoone
    Before king Henryes face,
Full oft he in his princelye armes
    Her bodye did embrace: 80

And twentye times, with watery eyes,
    He kist her tender cheeke,
Untill he had revivde againe
    Her senses milde and meeke.

Why grieves my Rose, my sweetest Rose?   85
    The king did often say.
Because, quoth shee, to bloodye warres
    My lord must part awaye.

But since your grace on forrayne coastes
    Amonge your foes unkinde   90
Must goe to hazard life and limbe,
    Why should I staye behinde?

Nay rather, let me, like a page,
    Your sworde and target beare;
That on my breast the blowes may lighte,   95
    Which would offend you there.

Or lett mee, in your royal tent,
    Prepare your bed at nighte,
And with sweete baths refresh your grace,
    At your returne from fighte.   100

So I your presence may enjoye
    No toil I will refuse:
But wanting you, my life is death;
    Nay, death Ild rather chuse.

"Content thy self, my dearest love;   105
    Thy rest at home shall bee
In Englandes sweet and pleasant isle;
    For travell fits not thee.

Faire ladies brooke not bloodye warres:
    Soft peace their sexe delightes;   110
'Not rugged campes, but courtlye bowers;
    Gay feastes, not cruell fightes.'

My Rose shall safely here abide,
    With musicke passe the daye;
Whilst I, amonge the piercing pikes,   115
    My foes seeke far awaye.

My Rose shall shine in pearle, and golde,
    Whilst Ime in armour dighte;
Gay galliards here my love shall dance,
    Whilst I my foes goe fighte.   120

And you, sir Thomas, whom I truste
    To bee my loves defence;
Be carefull of my gallant Rose
    When I am parted hence."

And therewithall he fetcht a sigh,   125
    As though his heart would breake:
And Rosamonde, for very griefe,
    Not one plaine word could speake.

And at their parting well they mighte
    In heart be grieved sore: 130
After that daye faire Rosamonde
    The king did see no more.

For when his grace had past the seas,
    And into France was gone;
With envious heart, queene Ellinor,   135
    To Woodstocke came anone.

And forth she calls this trustye knighte,
   In an unhappy houre;
Who with his clue of twined thread,
   Came from this famous bower.   140

And when that they had wounded him,
   The queene this thread did gette,
And wente where ladye Rosamonde
   Was like an angell sette.

But when the queene with stedfast eye   145
   Beheld her beauteous face,
She was amazed in her minde
   At her exceeding grace.

Cast off from thee those robes, she said,
   That riche and costlye bee;   150
And drinke thou up this deadlye draught,
   Which I have brought to thee.

Then presentlye upon her knees
   Sweet Rosamonde did falle;
And pardon of the queene she crav'd   155
   For her offences all.

"Take pitty on my youthfull yeares,
   Faire Rosamonde did crye;
And lett mee not with poison stronge
   Enforced bee to dye.   160

I will renounce my sinfull life,
   And in some cloyster bide;
Or else be banisht, if you please,
   To range the world soe wide.

And for the fault which I have done,   165
   Though I was forc'd theretoe,
Preserve my life, and punish mee
   As you thinke meet to doe."

And with these words, her lillie handes
  She wrunge full often there;   170
And downe along her lovely face
  Did trickle many a teare.

But nothing could this furious queene
  Therewith appeased bee;
The cup of deadlye poyson stronge,   175
  As she knelt on her knee,

She gave this comelye dame to drinke;
  Who tooke it in her hand,
And from her bended knee arose,
  And on her feet did stand: 180

And casting up her eyes to heaven,
  Shee did for mercye calle;
And drinking up the poison stronge,
  Her life she lost withalle.

And when that death through everye limbe   185
  Had showde its greatest spite,
Her chiefest foes did plaine confesse
  Shee was a glorious wight.

Her body then they did entomb,
  When life was fled away,   190
At Godstowe, neare to Oxford towne,
  As may be seene this day.

VIII.

Queen Eleanor's Confession.

"ELEANOR, the daughter and heiress of William Duke of
Guienne, and Count of Poictou, had been married sixteen
years to Louis VII. King of France, and had attended him
in a croisade, which that monarch commanded against the
infidels; but having lost the affections of her husband, and

even fallen under some suspicions of gallantry with a hand-some Saracen, Louis, more delicate than politic, procured a divorce from her, and restored her those rich provinces which, by her marriage, she had annexed to the crown of France. The young Count of Anjou, afterwards Henry II. King of England, though at that time but in his nineteenth year, neither discouraged by the disparity of age, nor by the reports of Eleanor's gallantry, made such successful court-ship to that princess, that he married her six weeks after her divorce, and got possession of all her dominions as a dowry. A marriage thus founded upon interest was not likely to be very happy: it happened accordingly. Eleanor, who had disgusted her first husband by her gallantries, was no less offensive to her second by her jealousy: thus carrying to extremity, in the different parts of her life, every circum-stance of female weakness. She had several sons by Henry, whom she spirited up to rebel against him; and endeavour-ing to escape to them disguised in man's apparel in 1173, she was discovered and thrown into a confinement, which seems to have continued till the death of her husband in 1189. She however survived him many years: dying in 1204, in the sixth year of the reign of her youngest son, John." See Hume's History, 4to, vol. i. pp. 260. 307. Speed, Stow, &c.

It is needless to observe, that the following ballad (given, with some corrections, from an old printed copy) is altogether fabulous: whatever gallantries Eleanor encouraged in the time of her first husband, none are imputed to her in that of her second.

QUEENE Elianor was a sicke womàn,
    And afraid that she should dye:
Then she sent for two fryars of France
    To speke with her speedilye.

The king calld downe his nobles all,   5
    By one, by two, by three;

"Earl marshall, Ile go shrive the queene,
  And thou shalt wend with mee."

A boone, a boone; quoth earl marshàll;
  And fell on his bended knee;   10
That whatsoever queene Elianor saye,
  No harme therof may bee.

Ile pawne my landes, the king then cryd,
  My sceptre, crowne, and all,
That whatsoere queen Elianor sayes   15
  No harme thereof shall fall.

Do thou put on a fryars coat,
  And Ile put on another;
And we will to queen Elianor goe
  Like fryar and his brother.   20

Thus both attired then they goe:
  When they came to Whitehall,
The bells did ring, and the quiristers sing,
  And the torches did lighte them all.

When that they came before the queene 25
  They fell on their bended knee;
A boone, a boone, our gracious queene,
  That you sent so hastilee.

Are you two fryars of France, she sayd,
  As I suppose you bee?   30
But if you are two Englishe fryars,
  You shall hang on the gallowes tree.

We are two fryars of France, they sayd,
  As you suppose we bee,
We have not been at any masse   35
  Sith we came from the sea.

The first vile thing that ever I did
  I will to you unfolde;

Earl marshall had my maidenhed,
   Beneath this cloth of golde.   40

Thats a vile sinne, then sayd the king;
   May God forgive it thee!
Amen, amen, quoth earl marshall;
   With a heavye heart spake hee.

The next vile thing that ever I did,   45
   To you Ile not denye,
I made a boxe of poyson strong,
   To poison king Henrye.

Thats a vile sinne, then sayd the king,
   May God forgive it thee!   50
Amen, amen, quoth earl marshall;
   And I wish it so may bee.

The next vile thing that ever I did,
   To you I will discover;
I poysoned fair Rosamonde,   55
   All in fair Woodstocke bower.

Thats a vile sinne, then sayd the king;
   May God forgive it thee!
Amen, amen, quoth earl marshall;
   And I wish it so may bee.   60

Do you see yonders little boye,
   A tossing of the balle?
That is earl marshalls eldest sonne,
   And I love him the best of all.

Do you see yonders little boye,   65
   A catching of the balle?
That is king Henryes youngest sonne,
   And I love him the worst of all.

Ver. 63, 67. She means that the eldest of these two was by the earl
marshall, the youngest by the king.

His head is fashyon'd like a bull;
  His nose is like a boare.   70
No matter for that, king Henrye cryd,
  I love him the better therfore.

The king pulled off his fryars coate,
  And appeared all in redde:
She shrieked, and cryd, and wrung her hands,   75
  And sayd she was betrayde.

The king lookt over his left shoulder,
  And a grimme look looked hee,
Earl marshall, he sayd, but for my oathe,
  Or hanged thou shouldst bee.   80

IX.

The Sturdy Rock.

THIS poem, subscribed M. T. [perhaps invertedly for T. Marshall[1]] is preserved in *The Paradise of daintie Devises.* The two first stanzas may be found accompanied with musical notes in "An howres recreation in musicke, &c. by Richard Alison, Lond. 1606, 4to:" usually bound up with three or four sets of "Madrigals set to music by Tho. Weelkes, Lond. 1597, 1600, 1608, 4to." One of these madrigals is so complete an example of the Bathos, that I cannot forbear presenting it to the reader.

> Thule, the period of cosmographie,
>   Doth vaunt of Hecla, whose sulphureous fire
> Doth melt the frozen clime, and thaw the skie,
>   Trinacrian Ætna's flames ascend not hier:
> These things seeme wondrous, yet more wondrous I,
> Whose heart with feare doth freeze, with love doth fry.
>
> The Andelusian merchant, that returnes
>   Laden with cutchinele and china dishes,
> Reports in Spaine, how strangely Fogo burnes
>   Amidst an ocean full of flying fishes:
> These things seeme wondrous, yet more wondrous I,
> Whose heart with feare doth freeze, with love doth fry.

[1] Vide Athen. Ox. pp. 152. 316.

Mr. Weelkes seems to have been of opinion, with many of his brethren of later times, that nonsense was best adapted to display the powers of musical composure.

THE sturdy rock for all his strength
  By raging seas is rent in twaine:
The marble stone is pearst at length,
  With little drops of drizling rain:
The oxe doth yeeld unto the yoke,   5
The steele obeyeth the hammer stroke.

The stately stagge, that seemes so stout,
  By yalping hounds at bay is set:
The swiftest bird, that flies about,
  Is caught at length in fowlers net: 10
The greatest fish, in deepest brooke,
Is soon deceived by subtill hooke.

Yea man himselfe, unto whose will
  All things are bounden to obey,
For all his wit and worthie skill,   15
  Doth fade at length, and fall away.
There is nothing but time doeth waste;
The heavens, the earth consume at last.

But vertue sits triumphing still
  Upon the throne of glorious fame: 20
Though spiteful death mans body kill,
  Yet hurts he not his vertuous name:
By life or death what so betides,
The state of vertue never slides.

X.

The Beggar's Daughter of Bednall-Green.

THIS popular old ballad was written in the reign of Elizabeth, as appears not only from ver. 23, where the arms of England are called the "Queenes armes," but from its tunes being quoted in other old pieces, written in her time. See the ballad on Mary Ambree in this volume. The late Mr. Guthrie assured the Editor, that he had formerly seen another old song on the same subject, composed in a different measure from this; which was truly beautiful, if we may judge from the only stanza he remembered. In this it was said of the old beggar, that "down his neck

> ——his reverend lockes
> In comelye curles did wave;
> And on his aged temples grewe
> The blossomes of the grave."

The following ballad is chiefly given from the Editor's folio MS. compared with two ancient printed copies: the concluding stanzas, which contain the old beggar's discovery of himself, are not, however, given from any of these, being very different from those of the vulgar ballad. Nor yet does the Editor offer them as genuine, but as a modern attempt to remove the absurdities and inconsistencies which so remarkably prevailed in this part of the song as it stood before: whereas, by the alteration of a few lines, the story is rendered much more affecting, and is reconciled to probability and true history. For this informs us, that at the decisive battle of Evesham, (fought August 4, 1265,) when Simon de Montfort, the great Earl of Leicester, was slain at the head of the barons, his eldest son Henry fell by his side, and, in consequence of that defeat, his whole family sunk for ever, the king bestowing their great honours and possessions on his second son, Edmund Earl of Lancaster.

PART THE FIRST.

ITT was a blind beggar, had long lost his sight,
He had a faire daughter of bewty most bright;
And many a gallant brave suiter had shee,
For none was soe comelye as pretty Bessee.

And though shee was of favor most faire,   5
Yett seeing shee was but a poor beggars heyre,
Of ancyent housekeepers despised was shee,
Whose sonnes came as suitors to prettye Bessee.

Wherefore in great sorrow faire Bessy did say,
Good father, and mother, let me goe away   10
To seeke out my fortune, whatever itt bee.
This suite then they granted to prettye Bessee.

Then Bessy, that was of bewtye so bright,
All cladd in gray russett, and late in the night
From father and mother alone parted shee;   15
Who sighed and sobbed for prettye Bessee.

Shee went till shee came to Stratford-le-Bow;
Then knew shee not whither, nor which way to goe:
With teares shee lamented her hard destinie,
Soe sadd and soe heavy was pretty Bessee.   20

Shee kept on her journey untill it was day,
And went unto Rumford along the hye way;
Where at the Queenes armes entertained was shee:
Soe faire and wel favoured was pretty Bessee.

Shee had not been there a month to an end,   25
But master and mistres and all was her friend:
And every brave gallant, that once did her see,
Was straight-way enamourd of pretty Bessee.

Great gifts they did send her of silver and gold,
And in their songs daylye her love was extold;   30
Her beawtye was blazed in every degree;
Soe faire and soe comelye was pretty Bessee.

The young men of Rumford in her had their joy;
Shee shewed herself curteous, and modestlye coye;
And at her commandment still wold they bee;   35
Soe fayre and so comelye was pretty Bessee.

Foure suitors att once unto her did goe;
They craved her favor, but still she sayd noe;
I wold not wish gentles to marry with mee.
Yett ever they honored prettye Bessee.   40

The first of them was a gallant young knight,
And he came unto her disguisde in the night,
The second a gentleman of good degree,
Who wooed and sued for prettye Bessee.

A merchant of London, whose wealth was not small,   45
He was the third suiter, and proper withall:
Her masters owne sonne the fourth man must bee,
Who swore he would dye for pretty Bessee.

And, if thou wilt marry with mee, quoth the knight,
Ile make thee a ladye with joy and delight;   50
My hart's so inthralled by thy bewtie,
That soone I shall dye for prettye Bessee.

The gentleman sayd, Come, marry with mee,
As fine as a ladye my Bessy shal bee:
My life is distressed: O heare me, quoth hee;   55
And grant me thy love, my prettye Bessee.

Let me bee thy husband, the merchant cold say,
Thou shalt live in London both gallant and gay;
My shippes shall bring home rych jewells for thee,
And I will for ever love pretty Bessee.   60

Then Bessy shee sighed, and thus shee did say,
My father and mother I meane to obey;
First gett their good will, and be faithfull to mee,
And you shall enjoye your prettye Bessee.

To every one this answer shee made,   65
Wherfore unto her they joyfullye sayd,
This thing to fulfill we all doe agree;
But where dwells thy father, my prettye Bessee?

My father, shee said, is soone to be seene:
The seely blind beggar of Bednall-greene,   70
That daylye sits begging for charitie,
He is the good father of pretty Bessee.

His markes and his tokens are knowen very well;
He always is led with a dogg and a bell:
A seely olde man, God knoweth, is hee,   75
Yet hee is the father of pretty Bessee.

Nay then, quoth the merchant, thou art not for mee:
Nor, quoth the innholder, my wiffe thou shalt bee:
I lothe, sayd the gentle, a beggars degree,
And therefore, adewe, my pretty Bessee!   80

Why then, quoth the knight, hap better or worse,
I waighe not true love by the waight of the pursse,
And bewtye is bewtye in every degree;
Then welcome unto me, my pretty Bessee.

With thee to thy father forthwith I will goe.   85
Nay soft, quoth his kinsmen, it must not be soe;
A poor beggars daughter noe ladye shal bee,
Then take thy adew of pretty Bessee.

But soone after this, by breake of the day
The knight had from Rumford stole Bessy away.   90
The younge men of Rumford, as thicke might bee,
Rode after to feitch againe pretty Bessee.

As swifte as the winde to ryde they were seene,
Until they came neare unto Bednall-greene;
And as the knight lighted most courteouslie,   95
They all fought against him for pretty Bessee.

But rescew came speedilye over the plaine,
Or else the young knight for his love had been slaine.
This fray being ended, then straitway he see
His kinsmen come rayling at pretty Bessee.   100

Then spake the blind beggar, Although I bee poore,
Yett rayle not against my child at my own doore:
Though shee be not decked in velvett and pearle,
Yet will I dropp angells with you for my girle.

And then, if my gold may better her birthe,   105
And equall the gold that you lay on the earth,
Then neyther rayle nor grudge you to see
The blind beggars daughter a lady to bee.

But first you shall promise, and have itt well knowne,
The gold that you drop shall all be your owne.   110
With that they replyed, Contented bee wee.
Then here's, quoth the beggar, for pretty Bessee.

With that an angell he cast on the ground,
And dropped in angels full three thousand[1] pound;
And oftentimes itt was proved most plaine,   115
For the gentlemens one the beggar droppt twayne:

Soe that the place, wherin they did sitt,
With gold it was covered every whitt.
The gentlemen then having dropt all their store,
Sayd, Now, beggar, hold, for wee have noe more.   120

Thou hast fulfilled thy promise arright.
Then marry, quoth he, my girle to this knight;
And heere, added hee, I will now throwe you downe
A hundred pounds more to buy her a gowne.

The gentlemen all, that this treasure had seene,   125
Admired the beggar of Bednall-greene:

[1] In the Editor's folio MS. it is 500 l.

And all those, that were her suitors before,
Their fleshe for very anger they tore.

Thus was faire Bessey matched to the knight,
And then made a ladye in others despite: 130
A fairer ladye there never was seene,
Than the blind beggars daughter of Bednall-greene.

But of their sumptuous marriage and feast,
What brave lords and knights thither were prest,
The SECOND FITT[2] shall set forth to your sight 135
With marveilous pleasure, and wished delight.

PART THE SECOND.

OFF a blind beggars daughter most bright,
That late was betrothed unto a younge knight;
All the discourse therof you did see;
But now comes the wedding of pretty Bessee.

Within a gorgeous palace most brave, 5
Adorned with all the cost they cold have,
This wedding was kept most sumptuouslie,
And all for the creditt of pretty Bessee.

All kind of dainties, and delicates sweete
Were bought for the banquet, as it was most meete; 10
Partridge, and plover, and venison most free,
Against the brave wedding of pretty Bessee.

This marriage through England was spread by report,
Soe that a great number thereto did resort
Of nobles and gentles in every degree; 15
And all for the fame of prettye Bessee.

To church then went this gallant younge knight;
His bride followed after, an angell most bright,

[2] See an Essay on the word FIT at the end of the Second Part.

With troopes of ladyes, the like nere was seene
As went with sweete Bessy of Bednall-greene.   20

This marryage being solempnized then,
With musicke performed by the skilfullest men,
The nobles and gentles sate downe at that tyde,
Each one admiring the beautifull bryde.

Now, after the sumptuous dinner was done,   25
To talke and to reason a number begunn:
They talkt of the blind beggars daughter most bright,
And what with his daughter he gave to the knight.

Then spake the nobles, "Much marveil have wee,
This jolly blind beggar wee cannot here see."   30
My lords, quoth the bride, my father's so base,
He is loth with his presence these states to disgrace.

"The prayse of a woman in questyon to bringe
Before her own face, were a flattering thinge;
But wee thinke thy father's baseness, quoth they,   35
Might by thy bewtye be cleane put awaye."

They had noe sooner these pleasant words spoke,
But in comes the beggar cladd in a silke cloke;
A faire velvet capp, and a fether had hee,
And now a musicyan forsooth he wold bee.   40

He had a daintye lute under his arme,
He touched the strings, which made such a charme,
Saies, Please you to heare any musicke of mee,
Ile sing you a song of pretty Bessee.

With that his lute he twanged straightway,   45
And thereon begann most sweetlye to play;
And after that lessons were playd two or three,
He strayn'd out this song most delicatelie.

"A poore beggars daughter did dwell on a greene,
Who for her fairenesse might well be a queene: 50

A blithe bonny lasse, and a daintye was shee,
And many one called her pretty Bessee.

"Her father hee had noe goods, nor noe land,
But beggd for a penny all day with his hand;
And yett to her marriage hee gave thousands three[3],⁣   55
And still he hath somewhat for pretty Bessee.

"And if any one here her berth doe disdaine,
Her father is ready, with might and with maine,
To proove shee is come of noble degree:
Therfore never flout att prettye Bessee."   60

With that the lords and the companye round
With harty laughter were readye to swound;
Att last said the lords, Full well wee may see,
The bride and the beggar's behoulden to thee.

On this the bride all blushing did rise,   65
The pearlie dropps standing within her faire eyes,
O pardon my father, grave nobles, quoth shee,
That throughe blind affection thus doteth on mee.

If this be thy father, the nobles did say,
Well may he be proud of this happy day;   70
Yett by his countenance well may wee see,
His birth and his fortune did never agree:

And therfore, blind man, we pray thee bewray,
(And looke that the truth thou to us doe say)
Thy birth and thy parentage, what itt may bee;   75
For the love that thou bearest to pretty Bessee.

"Then give me leave, nobles and gentles, each one,
One song more to sing, and then I have done;
And if that itt may not winn good report,
Then doe not give me a GROAT for my sport.   80

[3] So the folio MS.

"[Sir Simon de Montfort my subject shal bee;
Once chiefe of all the great barons was hee,
Yet fortune so cruelle this lorde did abase,
Now loste and forgotten are hee and his race.

" When the barons in armes did king Henrye oppose,   85
Sir Simon de Montfort their leader they chose;
A leader of courage undaunted was hee,
And oft-times he made their enemyes flee.

"At length in the battle on Eveshame plaine
The barons were routed, and Montfort was slaine;   90
Moste fatall that battel did prove unto thee,
Thoughe thou wast not borne then, my prettye Bessee!

"Along with the nobles, that fell at that tyde,
His eldest son Henrye, who fought by his side,
Was fellde by a blowe, he receivde in the fight!   95
A blowe that deprivde him for ever of sight.

"Among the dead bodyes all lifelesse he laye,
Till evening drewe on of the following daye,
When by a yong ladye discoverd was hee;
And this was thy mother, my prettye Bessee!   100

"A barons faire daughter stept forth in the nighte
To search for her father, who fell in the fight,
And seeing yong Montfort, where gasping he laye,
Was moved with pitye, and brought him awaye.

"In secrette she nurst him, and swaged his paine,   105
While he throughe the realme was beleevd to be slaine:
At lengthe his faire bride she consented to bee,
And made him glad father of prettye Bessee.

"And nowe lest oure foes our lives sholde betraye,
We clothed ourselves in beggars arraye;   110
Her jewelles shee solde, and hither came wee:
All our comfort and care was our prettye Bessee.]

"And here have wee lived in fortunes despite,
Thoughe poore, yet contented with humble delighte:
Full forty winters thus have I beene   115
A silly blind beggar of Bednall-greene.

"And here, noble lordes, is ended the song
Of one, that once to your own ranke did belong:
And thus have you learned a secrette from mee,
That ne'er had beene knowne, but for prettye Bessee." 120

Now when the faire companye everye one,
Had heard the strange tale in the song he had showne,
They all were amazed, as well they might bee,
Both at the blinde beggar, and pretty Bessee.

With that the faire bride they all did embrace,   125
Saying, Sure thou art come of an honourable race,
Thy father likewise is of noble degree,
And thou art well worthy a lady to bee.

Thus was the feast ended with joye and delighte,
A bridegroome most happy then was the young knighte, 130
In joy and felicitie long lived hee,
All with his faire ladye, the pretty Bessee.

*_**

_{*} The word FIT, for *part*, often occurs in our ancient
ballads and metrical romances; which, being divided into
several parts for the convenience of singing them at public
entertainments, were in the intervals of the feast sung by
fits, or intermissions. So Puttenham, in his *Art of English
Poesie*, 1589, says, "the Epithalamie was divided by breaches
into three partes to serve for three several FITS, or times to
be sung." — p. 41.

From the same writer we learn some curious particulars
relative to the state of ballad-singing in that age, that will

throw light on the present subject: speaking of the quick
returns of one manner of tune in the short measures used by
common rhymers; these, he says, "glut the eare, unless it
be in small and popular musickes, sung by these Cantabanqui,
upon benches and barrels heads, where they have none other
audience then boys or countrey fellowes, that passe by them
in the streete; or else by *blind harpers*, or such like taverne
Minstrels, that give a FIT of mirth for a *groat*, ... their matter
being for the most part stories of old time, as the tale of Sir
Topas, the reportes of Bevis of Southampton, Guy of Warwicke, Adam Bell and Clymme of the Clough, and such
other old romances or historical rimes, made purposely for
recreation of the common people at Christmasse dinners and
brideales, and in tavernes and alehouses, and such other
places of base resorte."—p. 69.

This species of entertainment, which seems to have been
handed down from the ancient bards, was in the time of
Puttenham falling into neglect; but that it was not, even
then, wholly excluded more genteel assemblies, he gives us
room to infer from another passage. "We ourselves," says
this courtly writer[4], "have written for pleasure a little brief
romance, or historical ditty, in the English tong, of the Isle
of Great Britaine, in short and long meetres, and by breaches
or divisions [*i. e.* FITS,] to be more commodiously sung to the
harpe in places of assembly, where the company shal be
desirous to heare of old adventures, and valiaunces of noble
knights in times past, as are those of king Arthur and his
knights of the round table, Sir Bevys of Southampton, Guy
of Warwicke, and others like."—p. 33.

In more ancient times, no grand scene of festivity was
complete without one of these reciters to entertain the company with feats of arms and tales of knighthood, or, as one
of these old minstrels says, in the beginning of an ancient
romance on *Guy and Colbronde*, in the Editor's folio MS.

---

[4] He was one of Q. Elizabeth's gent. pensioners, at a time when the
whole band consisted of men of distinguished birth and fortune. Vide
Ath. Ox.

"When meate and drinke is great plentyè,
  And lords and ladyes still wil bee,
    And sitt and solace lythe[5];
  Then itt is time for mee to speake,
  Of keene knightes, and kempès great,
    Such carping for to kythe."

If we consider that a groat in the age of Elizabeth was more than equivalent to a shilling now, we shall find that the old harpers were even then, when their art was on the decline, upon a far more reputable footing than the ballad-singers of our time. The reciting of one such ballad as this of the *Beggar of Bednall-green*, in two parts, was rewarded with half a crown of our money. And that they made a very respectable appearance, we may learn from the dress of the old beggar, in the preceding ballad, p. 140, where he comes into company in the habit and character of one of these minstrels, being not known to be the bride's father till after her speech, ver. 68. The exordium of his song, and his claiming a groat for his reward, ver. 80, are peculiarly characteristic of that profession. Most of the old ballads begin in a pompous manner, in order to captivate the attention of the audience, and induce them to purchase a recital of the song: and they seldom conclude the first part without large promises of still greater entertainment in the second. This was a necessary piece of art to incline the hearers to be at the expense of a second groat's-worth. Many of the old romances extend to eight or nine FITS, which would afford a considerable profit to the reciter.

To return to the word FIT; it seems at one time to have peculiarly signified the pause, or breathing-time, between the several parts (answering to PASSUS in the *Visions of Pierce Plowman*): thus in the ancient ballad of *Chevy-Chase*, vol. i. p. 8, the first part ends with this line,

"The first FIT here I fynde:"

i. e. here I come to the first pause or intermission. (See also vol. i. p. 22.) By degrees it came to signify the whole part

[5] Perhaps "blythe."

or division preceding the pause. (See the concluding verses
of the First and Second Parts of "Adam Bell, Clym of the
Clough, and William of Cloudsly," in vol. i.) This sense it
had obtained so early as the time of Chaucer; who thus concludes the first part of his rhyme of Sir Thopas (writ in
ridicule of the old ballad romances):

> "Lo! lordis mine, here is a FITT;
> If ye woll any more of it,
> 　To tell it woll I fonde."

The word FIT indeed appears originally to have signified
a poetic strain, verse, or poem; for in these senses it is used
by the Anglo-Saxon writers. Thus king Ælfred in his *Boetius*,
having given a version of lib. 3, metr. 5, adds, þaɼe pıɼðom
tha thaɼ ɼıcce aɼungen hæɼðe, page 65, *i. e.* "when wisdom had
sung these [FITTS] verses." And in the Proem to the same
book ɼon on ɼıcce, "put into [FITT] verse." So in Cedmon,
p. 45, ɼeonð on ɼıcce, seems to mean "composed a song," or
"poem." The reader will trace this old Saxon phrase in the
application of the word *fond*, in the foregoing passage of
Chaucer. See Glossary.

Spenser has used the word *fit* to denote "a strain of
music." See his poem entitled, "Collin Clout's come home
again," where he says,

> "The Shepherd of the ocean [Sir Walt. Raleigh]
> Provoked me to play some pleasant FIT.
> 　And when he heard the music which I made
> 　He found himself full greatlye pleas'd at it," &c.

It is also used in the old ballad of *King Estmere*, vol. i. p. 61,
v. 243.

From being applied to music, this word was easily transferred to dancing; thus in the old play of Lusty Juventus,
(described in p. 96, and vol. i. p. 115,) Juventus says,

> "By the masse I would fayne go daunce a FITTE."

And from being used as a part or division in a ballad,
poem, &c., it is applied by Bale to a section or chapter in a
book, though I believe in a sense of ridicule or sarcasm; for
thus he entitles two chapters of his English Dotaryes, part ii.

viz. — fol. 49, "The fyrst Fʏᴛᴛ of Anselme with Kynge Wyllyam Rufus."— fol. 50, "An other Fʏᴛᴛ of Anselme with kynge Wyllyam Rufus."

XI.

Fancy and Desire.

BY THE EARL OF OXFORD.

Edward Vere, Earl of Oxford, was in high fame for his poetical talents in the reign of Elizabeth: perhaps it is no injury to his reputation, that few of his compositions are preserved for the inspection of impartial posterity. To gratify curiosity, we have inserted a sonnet of his, which is quoted with great encomiums for its "excellencie and wit," in Puttenham's *Arte of Eng. Poesie*,[1] and found entire in the *Garland of Good-will*. A few more of his sonnets (distinguished by the initial letters E. O.) may be seen in the *Paradise of daintie Devises*. One of these is entitled "The Complaint of a Lover, wearing blacke and tawnie." The only lines in it worth notice are these:

> A crowne of baies shall that man 'beare'
> Who triumphs over me;
> For black and tawnie will I weare,
> Which mourning colours be.

We find in Hall's *Chronicle*, that when Queen Catharine of Arragon died, Jan. 8, 1536, "Queen Anne [Bullen] ware ʏᴇʟʟᴏᴡᴇ for the mourning." And when this unfortunate princess lost her head, May 19, the same year, "on the ascension day following, the kyng for mourning ware ᴡʜʏᴛᴇ," fol. 227, 228.

Edward, who was the 17th Earl of Oxford, of the family of Vere, succeeded his father in his title and honours in 1562, and died an aged man in 1604. See Mr. Walpole's *Noble Authors*. Athen. Oxon, &c.

[1] Lond. 1589, p. 172.

10*

Come hither shepherd's swayne:
  "Sir, what do you require?"
I praye thee, shewe to me thy name.
  "My name is Fond Desire."

When wert thou borne, Desire?   5
  "In pompe and pryme of may."
By whom, sweet boy, wert thou begot?
  "By fond Conceit, men say."

Tell me, who was thy nurse?
  "Fresh Youth in sugred joy."   10
What was thy meate and dayly foode?
  "Sad sighes with great annoy."

What hadst thou then to drinke?
  "Unsavoury lovers teares."
What cradle wert thou rocked in?   15
  "In hope devoyde of feares."

What lulld thee then asleepe?
  "Sweete speech, which likes me best."
Tell me, where is thy dwelling place?
  "In gentle hartes I rest."   20

What thing doth please thee most?
  "To gaze on beautye stille."
Whom dost thou thinke to be thy foe?
  "Disdayn of my good wille."

Doth companye displease?   25
  "Yes, surelye, many one."
Where doth Desire delighte to live?
  "He loves to live alone."

Doth either tyme or age
  Bringe him unto decaye?   30
"No, no, Desire both lives and dyes
  Ten thousand times a daye."

Then, fond Desire, farewelle,
  Thou art no mate for mee;
I sholde be lothe, methinkes, to dwelle   35
  With such a one as thee.

XII.

Sir Andrew Barton.

I CANNOT give a better relation of the fact, which is the subject of the following ballad, than in an extract from the late Mr. Guthrie's *Peerage;* which was begun upon a very elegant plan, but never finished. Vol. i. 4to. p. 22.

"The transactions which did the greatest honour to the earl of Surrey[1] and his family at this time, [A. D. 1511,] was their behaviour in the case of Barton, a Scotch sea-officer. This gentleman's father having suffered by sea from the Portuguese, he had obtained letters of marque for his two sons to make reprisals upon the subjects of Portugal. It is extremely probable, that the court of Scotland granted these letters with no very honest intention. The council-board of England, at which the earl of Surrey held the chief place, was daily pestered with complaints from the sailors and merchants, that Barton, who was called Sir Andrew Barton, under pretence of searching for Portuguese goods, interrupted the English navigation. Henry's situation at that time rendered him backward from breaking with Scotland, so that their complaints were but coldly received. The earl of Surrey, however, could not smother his indignation, but gallantly declared at the council-board, that while he had an estate that could furnish out a ship, or a son that was capable of commanding one, the narrow seas should not be infested.

"Sir Andrew Barton, who commanded the two Scotch ships, had the reputation of being one of the ablest sea-officers of his time. By his depredations, he had amassed

---

[1] Thomas Howard, afterwards created Duke of Norfolk.

great wealth, and his ships were very richly laden. Henry, notwithstanding his situation, could not refuse the generous offer made by the earl of Surrey. Two ships were immediately fitted out, and put to sea with letters of marque, under his two sons, Sir Thomas[2] and Sir Edward Howard. After encountering a great deal of foul weather, Sir Thomas came up with the Lion, which was commanded by Sir Andrew Barton in person; and Sir Edward came up with the Union, Barton's other ship [called by Hall the Bark of Scotland]. The engagement which ensued was extremely obstinate on both sides; but at last the fortune of the Howards prevailed. Sir Andrew was killed fighting bravely, and encouraging his men with his whistle, to hold out to the last; and the two Scotch ships with their crews were carried into the river Thames. [Aug. 2, 1511.]

"This exploit had the more merit, as the two English commanders were in a manner volunteers in the service, by their father's order. But it seems to have laid the foundation of Sir Edward's fortune; for, on the 7th of April, 1512, the king constituted him (according to Dugdale) admiral of England, Wales, &c.

"King James 'insisted' upon satisfaction for the death of Barton, and capture of his ship: 'though' Henry had generously dismissed the crews, and even agreed that the parties accused might appear in his courts of admiralty by their attornies, to vindicate themselves." This affair was in a great measure the cause of the battle of Flodden, in which James IV. lost his life.

In the following ballad will be found perhaps some few deviations from the truth of history: to atone for which, it has probably recorded many lesser facts, which history hath not condescended to relate. I take many of the little circumstances of the story to be real, because I find one of the most unlikely to be not very remote from the truth. In

---

[2] Called by old historians Lord Howard, afterwards created Earl of Surrey in his father's lifetime. He was father of the poetical Earl of Surrey.

part ii. v. 156, it is said, that England had before "but two ships of war." Now the Great Harry had been built only seven years before, viz. in 1504; which "was properly speaking the first ship in the English navy. Before this period, when a prince wanted a fleet, he had no other expedient but hiring ships from the merchants." — Hume.

This ballad, which appears to have been written in the reign of Elizabeth, has received great improvements from the Editor's folio MS. wherein was an ancient copy, which, though very incorrect, seemed in many respects superior to the common ballad; the latter being evidently modernized and abridged from it. The following text is however in some places amended and improved by the latter, (chiefly from a black-letter copy in the Pepys collection,) as also by conjecture.

THE FIRST PART.

" When Flora with her fragrant flowers
　　Bedeckt the earth so trim and gaye,
And Neptune with his daintye showers
　　Came to present the monthe of Maye[3];"
King Henrye rode to take the ayre,　　　　　　　　5
　　Over the river of Thames past hee;
When eighty merchants of London came,
　　And downe they knelt upon their knee.

"O yee are welcome, rich merchànts;
　　Good saylors, welcome unto mee."　　　　　　　10
They swore by the rood, they were saylors good,
　　But rich merchànts they cold not bee:
"To France nor Flanders dare we pass:
　　Nor Bordeaux voyage dare we fare;
And all for a rover that lyes on the seas,　　　　15
　　Who robbs us of our merchant ware."

Ver. 15, 83, robber. MS.

[3] From the pr. copy.

King Henrye frownd, and turned him rounde,
    And swore by the Lord, that was mickle of might,
"I thought he had not beene in the world,
    Durst have wrought England such unright."   20
The merchants sighed, and said, alas!
    And thus they did their answer frame,
He is a proud Scott, that robbs on the seas,
    And Sir Andrewe Barton is his name.

The king lookt over his left shouldèr,   25
    And an angrye look then looked hee:
"Have I never a lorde in all my realme,
    Will feitch yond traytor unto mee?"
Yea, that dare I; lord Howard sayes;
    Yea, that dare I with heart and hand;   30
If it please your grace to give me leave,
    Myselfe wil be the only man.

Thou art but yong; the kyng replyed:
    Yond Scott hath numbred manye a yeare.
"Trust me, my liege, Ile make him quail,   35
    Or before my prince I will never appeare."
Then bowemen and gunners thou shalt have,
    And chuse them over my realme so free;
Besides good mariners, and shipp-boyes,
    To guide the great shipp on the sea.   40

The first man, that lord Howard chose,
    Was the ablest gunner in all the realm,
Thoughe he was threescore yeeres and ten;
    Good Peter Simon was his name.
Peter, sais hee, I must to the sea,   45
    To bring home a traytor live or dead:
Before all others I have chosen thee;
    Of a hundred gunners to be the head.

V. 29, lord Charles Howard. MS.

If you, my lord, have chosen mee
  Of a hundred gunners to be the head,   50
Then hang me up on your maine-mast tree,
  If I misse my marke one shilling bread[4].
My lord then chose a boweman rare,
  "Whose active hands had gained fame[5],"
In Yorkshire was this gentleman borne,   55
  And William Horseley was his name[6].

Horseley, sayd he, I must with speede
  Go seeke a traytor on the sea,
And now of a hundred bowemen brave
  To be the head I have chosen thee.   60
If you, quoth hee, have chosen mee
  Of a hundred bowemen to be the head;
On your main-màst Ile hanged bee,
  If I miss twelvescore one penny bread.

With pikes and gunnes, and bowemen bold,   65
  This noble Howard is gone to the sea;
With a valyant heart and a pleasant cheare,
  Out at Thames mouth sayled he.
And days he scant had sayled three,
  Upon the 'voyage' he tooke in hand,   70
But there he mett with a noble shipp,
  And stoutely made itt stay and stand.

Thou must tell me, lord Howard said,
  Now who thou art, and what's thy name;
And shewe me where thy dwelling is: 75
  And whither bound, and whence thou came.

V. 70, journey. MS.

[4] An old English word for breadth.
[5] Pr. copy.
[6] Mr. Lambe, in his notes to the poem on the *Battle of Flodden Field*, contends that this expert bowman's name was not *Horseley*, but *Hustler*, of a family long seated near Stockton, in Cleveland, Yorkshire. Vide p. 5.

My name is Henry Hunt, quoth hee
  With a heavye heart, and a carefull mind;
I and my shipp doe both belong
  To the Newcastle, that stands upon Tyne.   80

Hast thou not heard, nowe, Henrye Hunt,
  As thou hast sayled by daye and by night,
Of a Scottish rover on the seas;
  Men call him Sir Andrew Barton, knight?
Then ever he sighed, and sayd alas!   85
  With a grieved mind, and well away!
But over-well I knowe that wight,
  I was his prisoner yesterday.

As I was sayling uppon the sea,
  A Burdeaux voyage for to fare;   90
To his hach-borde he claspcd me,
  And robd me of all my merchant ware:
And mickle debts, God wot, I owe,
  And every man will have his owne;
And I am nowe to London bounde,   95
  Of our gracious king to beg a boone.

That shall not need, lord Howard sais;
  Lett me but once that robber see,
For every penny tane thee froe
  It shall be doubled shillings three.   100
Nowe God forefend, the merchant said,
  That you shold seek soe far amisse!
God keepe you out of that traitors hands!
  Full litle ye wott what a man hee is.

Hee is brasse within, and steele without,   105
  With beames on his topcastle stronge;
And eighteen pieces of ordinance
  He carries on each side along:

V. 91, The MS. has here *archborde*, but in part ii. ver. 5, *hachebard*

And he hath a pinnace deerlye dight,
   St. Andrewes crosse that is his guide;   110
His pinnace beareth ninescore men,
   And fifteen canons on each side.

Were ye twentye shippes, and he but one;
   I sweare by kirke, and bower, and hall;
He wold overcome them everye one,   115
   If once his beames they doe downe fall[7].
This is cold comfort, sais my lord,
   To wellcome a stranger thus to the sea:
Yet Ile bring him and his shipp to shore,
   Or to Scottland hee shall carrye mee.   120

Then a noble gunner you must have,
   And he must aim well with his ee,
And sinke his pinnace into the sea,
   Or else hee never orecome will bee:
And if you chance his shipp to borde,   125
   This counsel I must give withall,
Let no man to his topcastle goe
   To strive to let his beames downe fall.

And seven pieces of ordinance,
   I pray your honour lend to mee,   130
On each side of my shipp along,
   And I will lead you on the sea.

---

[7] It should seem from hence, that before our marine artillery was brought to its present perfection, some naval commanders had recourse to instruments or machines, similar in use, though perhaps unlike in construction, to the heavy *Dolphins*, made of lead or iron, used by the ancient Greeks; which they suspended from beams or yards fastened to the mast, and which they precipitately let fall on the enemy's ships, in order to sink them, by beating holes through the bottoms of their undecked Triremes, or otherwise damaging them. These are mentioned by Thucydides, lib. vii. p. 256, ed. 1564, folio, and are more fully explained in *Scheffer de Militiâ Navali*, lib. ii. cap. v. p. 136, ed. 1653, 4to.

N B. It every where in the MS. seems to be written *beanes*.

A glasse Ile sett, that may be seene,
    Whether you sayle by day or night;
And to-morrowe, I sweare, by nine of the clocke   135
    You shall meet with Sir Andrewe Barton knight.

THE SECOND PART.

THE merchant sett my lorde a glasse
    Soe well apparent in his sight,
And on the morrowe, by nine of the clocke,
    He shewed him Sir Andrewe Barton knight.
His hachebord it was 'gilt' with gold,   5
    Soe deerlye dight it dazzled the ee:
Nowe by my faith, lord Howarde sais,
    This is a gallant sight to see.

Take in your ancyents, standards eke,
    So close that no man may them see;   10
And put me forth a white willowe wand,
    As merchants use to sayle the sea.
But they stirred neither top, nor mast[8];
    Stoutly they past Sir Andrew by.
What English churles are yonder, he sayd,   15
    That can soe litle curtesye?

Now by the roode, three yeares and more
    I have been admirall over the sea;
And never an English nor Portingall
    Without my leave can passe this way.   20
Then called he forth his stout pinnàce;
    "Fetch backe yond pedlars nowe to mee:
I sweare by the masse, yon English churles
    Shall all hang att my maine-mast tree."

With that the pinnace itt shott off,   25
    Full well Lord Howard might it ken;

V. 5, 'hached with gold.' MS.   8 *i. e.* did not salute.

For itt stroke down my lord's fore mast,
    And killed fourteen of his men.
Come hither, Simon, sayes my lord,
    Looke that thy word be true, thou said;   30
For at my maine-mast thou shalt hang,
    If thou misse thy marke one shilling bread.

Simon was old, but his heart itt was bold,
    His ordinance he laid right lowe;
He put in chaine full nine yardes long,   35
    With other great shott lesse, and moe;
And he lette goe his great gunnes shott:
    Soe well he settled itt with his ee,
The first sight that Sir Andrew sawe,
    He see his pinnace sunke in the sea.   40

And when he saw his pinnace sunke,
    Lord, how his heart with rage did swell!
"Nowe cutt my ropes, itt is time to be gon;
    Ile fetch yond pedlars backe mysell."
When my Lord sawe Sir Andrewe loose,   45
    Within his heart hee was full faine:
"Nowe spread your ancyents, strike up drummes,
    Sound all your trumpetts out amaine."

Fight on, my men, Sir Andrewe sais,
    Weale howsoever this geere will sway;   50
Itt is my lord admirall of Englànd,
    Is come to seeke mee on the sea.
Simon had a sonne, who shott right well,
    That did Sir Andrew mickle scare;
In att his decke he gave a shott,   55
    Killed threescore of his men of warre.

Then Henrye Hunt with rigour hott
    Came bravely on the other side,

V. 35, *i. e.* discharged chain-shot.

Soone he drove downe his fore-mast tree,
    And killed fourscore men beside.   60
Nowe, out alas! Sir Andrewe cryed,
    What may a man now thinke, or say?
Yonder merchant theefe, that pierceth mee,
    He was my prisoner yesterday.

Come hither to me, thou Gordon good,   65
    That aye wast ready att my call;
I will give thee three hundred markes,
    If thou wilt let my beames downe fall.
Lord Howard hee then calld in haste,
    "Horseley see thou be true in stead;   70
For thou shalt at the maine-mast hang,
    If thou misse twelvescore one penny bread.

Then Gordon swarved the maine-mast tree,
    He swarved it with might and maine;
But Horseley with a bearing arrowe,   75
    Stroke the Gordon through the braine;
And he fell unto the haches again,
    And sore his deadlye wounde did bleed:
Then word went through Sir Andrews men,
    How that the Gordon hee was dead.   80

Come hither to mee, James Hambilton,
    Thou art my only sisters sonne,
If thou wilt let my beames downe fall,
    Six hundred nobles thou hast wonne.
With that he swarved the maine-mast tree,   85
    He swarved it with nimble art;
But Horseley with a broad arrowe
    Pierced the Hambilton thorough the heart:

And downe he fell upon the deck,
    That with his blood did streame amaine: 90

V. 67, 84, pounds. MS.   V. 75, bearinge, sc. that carries well, &c. But
see Gloss. vol. i.

Then every Scott cryed, Well-away!
  Alas a comelye youth is slaine!
All woe begone was Sir Andrew then,
  With griefe and rage his heart did swell:
"Go fetch me forth my armour of proofe,   95
  For I will to the topcastle mysell."

"Goe fetch me forth my armour of proofe;
  That gilded is with gold soe cleare:
God be with my brother John of Barton!
  Against the Portingalls hee it ware;   100
And when he had on this armour of proofe,
  He was a gallant sight to see:
Ah! nere didst thou meet with living wight,
  My deere brother, could cope with thee."

Come hither Horseley, sayes my lord,   105
  And looke your shaft that itt goe right,
Shoot a goode shoote in time of need,
  And for it thou shalt be made a knight.
Ile shoot my best, quoth Horseley then,
  Your honour shall see, with might and maine;   110
But if I were hanged at your maine-mast,
  I have now left but arrowes twaine.

Sir Andrew he did swarve the tree,
  With right good will he swarved then:
Upon his breast did Horseley hitt,   115
  But the arrow bounded back agen.
Then Horseley spyed a privye place
  With a perfect eye in a secrette part;
Under the spole of his right arme
  He smote Sir Andrew to the heart.   120

"Fight on, my men, Sir Andrew sayes,
  A little Ime hurt, but yett not slaine;
Ile but lye downe and bleede a while,
  And then Ile rise and fight againe.

Fight on, my men, Sir Andrew sayes,   125
   And never flinche before the foe;
And stand fast by St. Andrewes crosse
   Untill you hear my whistle blowe."

They never heard his whistle blow, —
   Which made their hearts waxe sore adread: 130
Then Horseley sayd, Aboard, my lord,
   For well I wott, Sir Andrew's dead.
They boarded then his noble shipp,
   They boarded it with might and maine;
Eighteen score Scots alive they found,   135
   The rest were either maimed or slaine.

Lord Howard tooke a sword in hand,
   And off he smote Sir Andrewes head,
"I must have left England many a daye,
   If thou wert alive as thou art dead."   140
He caused his body to be cast
   Over the hatchbord into the sea,
And about his middle three hundred crownes:
   "Wherever thou land this will bury thee."

Thus from the warres lord Howard came,   145
   And backe he sayled ore the maine,
With mickle joy and triumphìng
   Into Thames mouth he came againe.
Lord Howard then a letter wrote,
   And sealed it with seale and ring;   150
"Such a noble prize have I brought to your grace,
   As never did subject to a king:

"Sir Andrewes shipp I bring with mee;
   A braver shipp was never none:
Nowe hath your grace two shipps of warr,   155
   Before in England was but one."
King Henryes grace with royall cheere
   Welcomed the noble Howard home,

And where, said he, is this rover stout,
   That I myselfe may give the doome?   160

"The rover, he is safe, my leige,
   Full many a fadom in the sea;
If he were alive as he is dead,
   I must have left England many a day;
And your grace may thank four men i'the ship   165
   For the victory wee have wonne,
These are William Horseley, Henry Hunt,
   And Peter Simon, and his sonne."

To Henry Hunt, the king then sayd,
   In lieu of what was from thee tane,   170
A noble a day now thou shalt have,
   Sir Andrewes jewels and his chayne.
And Horseley thou shalt be a knight,
   And lands and livings shalt have store;
Howard shall be erle Surrye hight,   175
   As Howards erst have beene before.

Nowe, Peter Simon, thou art old,
   I will maintaine thee and thy sonne:
And the men shall have five hundred markes
   For the good service they have done.   180
Then in came the queene with ladyes fair
   To see Sir Andrewe Barton knight:
They weend that hee were brought on shore,
   And thought to have seen a gallant sight.

But when they see his deadlye face,   185
   And eyes soe hollow in his head,
I wold give, quoth the king, a thousand markes,
   This man were alive as hee is dead:
Yett for the manfull part hee playd,
   Which fought soe well with heart and hand,   190

V. 175, 6, ... Erle of Nottingham, And soe was never, &c. MS.

His men shall have twelvepence a day,
  Till they come to my brother kings high land.

*_**

XIII.

Lady Anne Bothwell's Lament.

A SCOTTISH SONG.

THE subject of this pathetic ballad the Editor once thought might possibly relate to the Earl of Bothwell, and his desertion of his wife, Lady Jean Gordon, to make room for his marriage with the Queen of Scots: but this opinion he now believes to be groundless; indeed Earl Bothwell's age, who was upwards of 60 at the time of that marriage, renders it unlikely that he should be the object of so warm a passion as this elegy supposes. He has been since informed, that it entirely refers to a private story: A young lady of the name of Bothwell, or rather Boswell, having been, together with her child, deserted by her husband or lover, composed these affecting lines herself, which here are given from a copy in the Editor's folio MS., corrected by another in Allan Ramsay's *Miscellany*.

BALOW, my babe, lye still and sleipe!
It grieves me sair to see thee weipe:
If thoust be silent, Ise be glad,
Thy maining maks my heart ful sad.
Balow, my boy, thy mothers joy,   5
Thy father breides me great annoy.
  Balow, my babe, ly stil and sleipe,
  It grieves me sair to see thee weepe.

Whan he began to court my luve,
And with his sugred wordes[1] to muve,   10

---

[1] When sugar was first imported into Europe, it was a very great dainty; and therefore the epithet *sugred* is used by all our old writers metaphori-

His faynings fals, and flattering cheire
To me that time did not appeire:
But now I see, most cruell hee
Cares neither for my babe nor mee.
              Balow, &c.

Lye still, my darling, sleipe a while,   15
And when thou wakest, sweitly smile:
But smile not, as thy father did,
To cozen maids: nay God forbid!
But yett I feire, thou wilt gae neire
Thy fatheris hart, and face to beire.   20
              Balow, &c.

I cannae chuse, but ever will
Be luving to thy father still:
Whair-eir he gae, whair-eir he ryde,
My luve with him doth still abyde:
In weil or wae, whair-eir he gae,   25
Mine hart can neire depart him frae.
              Balow, &c.

But doe not, doe not, prettie mine,
To faynings fals thine hart incline;
Be loyal to thy luver trew,
And nevir change hir for a new: 30
If gude or faire, of hir have care,
For womens banning's wonderous sair.
              Balow, &c.

Bairne, sin thy cruel father is gane,
Thy winsome smiles maun eise my paine;
My babe and I'll together live,   35
He'll comfort me when cares doe grieve:

cally, to express extreme and delicate sweetness. (See above p. 148, v. 10.) Sugar at present is cheap and common; and therefore suggests now a coarse and vulgar idea.

My babe and I right saft will ly,
And quite forgeit man's cruelty.
                              Balow, &c.

Fareweil, fareweil, thou falsest youth
That evir kist a womans mouth!   40
I wish all maides be warnd by mee
Nevir to trust man's curtesy;
For if we doe bot chance to bow,
They'le use us then they care not how.
          Balow, my babe, ly stil, and sleipe,   45
          It grives me sair to see thee weipe.

XIV.

The Murder of the King of Scots.

THE catastrophe of Henry Stewart, Lord Darnley, the
unfortunate husband of Mary Queen of Scots, is the subject
of this ballad. It is here related in that partial, imperfect
manner, in which such an event would naturally strike the
subjects of another kingdom, of which he was a native.
Henry appears to have been a vain, capricious, worthless
young man, of weak understanding and dissolute morals.
But the beauty of his person, and the inexperience of his
youth, would dispose mankind to treat him with an in-
dulgence, which the cruelty of his murder would afterwards
convert into the most tender pity and regret; and then
imagination would not fail to adorn his memory with all
those virtues he ought to have possessed. This will account
for the extravagant eulogium bestowed upon him in the first
stanza, &c.

Henry Lord Darnley was the eldest son of the Earl of
Lennox, by the Lady Margaret Douglas, niece of Henry VIII.
and daughter of Margaret Queen of Scotland, by the Earl of
Angus, whom that princess married after the death of
James IV. Darnley, who had been born and educated in

England, was but in his 21st year when he was murdered,
Feb. 9, 1567-8. This crime was perpetrated by the Earl of
Bothwell, not out of respect to the memory of Riccio, but in
order to pave the way for his own marriage with the queen.

This ballad (printed, with a few corrections, from the
Editor's folio MS.) seems to have been written soon after
Mary's escape into England in 1568, see v. 65. It will be
remembered at v. 5, that this princess was Queen-dowager of
France, having been first married to Francis II., who died
Dec. 4, 1560.

Woe worth, woe worth thee, false Scotlànde!
  For thou hast ever wrought by sleight;
The worthyest prince that ever was borne,
  You hanged under a cloud by night.

The queene of France a letter wrote,   5
  And sealed itt with harte and ringe;
And bade him come Scotland within,
  And shee wold marry and crowne him kinge.

To be a king is a pleasant thing,
  To bee a prince unto a peere: 10
But you have heard, and soe have I too,
  A man may well buy gold too deare.

There was an Italyan in that place,
  Was as well beloved as ever was hee,
Lord David was his name,   15
  Chamberlaine to the queene was hee.

If the king had risen forth of his place,
  He wold have sate him downe in the cheare,
And tho itt beseemed him not so well,
  Altho the kinge had beene present there.   20

Ver. 15, sic MS.

Some lords in Scotlande waxed wroth,
 And quarrelled with him for the nonce;
I shall you tell how it befell,
 Twelve daggers were in him att once.

When the queene saw her chamberlaine was slaine,   25
 For him her faire cheeks shee did weete,
And made a vowe for a yeare and a day
 The king and shee wold not come in one sheete

Then some of the lords they waxed wrothe,
 And made their vow all vehementlye;   30
For the death of the queenes chamberlaine,
 The king himselfe, how he shall dye.

With gun-powder they strewed his roome,
 And layd greene rushes in his way:
For the traitors thought that very night   35
 This worthye king for to betray.

To bedd the king he made him bowne;
 To take his rest was his desire;
He was noe sooner cast on sleepe,
 But his chamber was on a blasing fire.   40

Up he lope, and the window brake,
 And hee had thirtye foote to fall;
Lord Bodwell kept a privy watch,
 Underneath his castle wall.

Who have wee here? lord Bodwell sayd: 45
 Now answer me, that I may know.
"King Henry the eighth my uncle was;
 For his sweete sake some pitty show."

Who have we here? lord Bodwell sayd,
 Now answer me when I doe speake.   50
"Ah, lord Bodwell, I know thee well;
 Some pitty on me I pray thee take."

Ile pitty thee as much, he sayd,
   And as much favor show to thee,
As thou didst to the queenes chamberlaine,   55
   That day thou deemedst him to die[1].

Through halls and towers the king they ledd,
   Through towers and castles that were nye,
Through an arbor into an orchàrd,
   There on a peare-tree hanged him hye.   60

When the governor of Scotland heard
   How that the worthye king was slaine;
He pursued the queen so bitterlye,
   That in Scotland shee dare not remaine.

But she is fledd into merry England,   65
   And here her residence hath taine;
And through the queene of Englands grace,
   In England now shee doth remaine.

       [1] Pronounced after the northern manner *dee.*

XV.

A Sonnet by Q. Elizabeth.

The following lines, if they display no rich vein of poetry,
are yet so strongly characteristic of their great and spirited
authoress, that the insertion of them will be pardoned. They
are preserved in Puttenham's *Arte of English Pœsie:* a book
in which are many sly addresses to the queen's foible of
shining as a poetess. The extraordinary manner in which
these verses are introduced, shows what kind of homage was
exacted from the courtly writers of that age, viz.

"I find," says this antiquated critic, "none example in
English metre, so well maintaining this figure [*Exargasia,* or
the Gorgeous, Lat. *Expolitio*] as that dittie of her majesties
owne making, passing sweete and harmonicall; which figure

beyng, as his very originall name purporteth, the most bewtifull and gorgious of all others, it asketh in reason to be reserved for a last complement, and desciphred by a ladies
penne, herselfe beyng the most bewtifull, or rather bewtie of
queenes[1]. And this was the occasion; our soveraigne lady
perceiving how the Scottish queenes residence within this
realme at so great libertie and ease (as were skarce meete
for so great and dangerous a prysoner) bred secret factions
among her people, and made many of the nobilitie incline to
favour her partie: some of them desirous of innovation in
the state: others aspiring to greater fortunes by her libertie
and life: the queene our soveraigne ladie, to declare that
she was nothing ignorant of those secret practizes, though
she had long with great wisdome and pacience dissembled
it, writeth this dittie most sweet and sententious, not hiding
from all such aspiring minds the danger of their ambition
and disloyaltie: which afterwards fell out most truly by th'
exemplary chastisement of sundry persons, who in favour of
the said Scot. Qu. declining from her majestie, sought to
interrupt the quiet of the realme by many evill and unduti-
full practizes."

This sonnet seems to have been composed in 1569, not
long before the Duke of Norfolk, the Earls of Pembroke and
Arundel, the Lord Lumley, Sir Nich. Throcmorton, and
others, were taken into custody. See Hume, Rapin, &c. It
was originally written in long lines, or Alexandrines, each
of which is here divided into two.

The present edition is improved by some readings adopted
from a copy printed in a collection from the papers of Sir
John Harrington, intituled, *Nugæ Antiquæ*, Lond. 1769, 12mo,
where the verses are accompanied with a very curious letter,
in which this sonnet is said to be "of her Highness own in-
diting . . . . My Lady Willoughby did covertly get it on her
Majesties tablet, and had much hazzard in so doing; for the
Queen did find out the thief, and chid for her spreading evil
bruit of her writing such toyes, when other matters did so

[1] She was at this time near threescore.

occupy her employment at this time; and was fearful of being thought too lightly of for so doing." * * *

THE doubt of future foes
 Exiles my present joy;
And wit me warnes to shun such snares,
 As threaten mine annoy.

For falshood now doth flow,   5
 And subjects faith doth ebbe:
Which would not be, if reason rul'd,
 Or wisdome wove the webbe.

But clowdes of joyes untried
 Do cloake aspiring mindes;   10
Which turn to raine of late repent,
 By course of changed windes.

The toppe of hope supposed
 The roote of ruthe will be;
And frutelesse all their graffed guiles, 15
 As shortly all shall see.

Then dazeld eyes with pride,
 Which great ambition blindes,
Shal be unseeld by worthy wights,
 Whose foresight falshood finds.   20

The daughter of debate[2],
 That discord ay doth sowe,
Shall reape no gaine where former rule
 Hath taught stil peace to growe.

No forreine bannisht wight   25
 Shall ancre in this port;

Ver. 1, dread. al. ed.   V. 9, toyes. al. ed.
[2] She evidently means here the Queen of Scots.

Our realme it brookes no strangers force,
    Let them elsewhere resort.

Our rusty sworde with rest
    Shall first his edge employ,   30
To poll the toppes, that seeke such change,
    Or gape for such like joy.

                                        † ┴ †

———

₊ I cannot help subjoining to the above sonnet another
distich of Elizabeth's, preserved by Puttenham, (page 197,)
"which (says he) our soveraigne lady wrote in defiance of
fortune."

    Never thinke you, Fortune can beare the sway,
    Where Vertue's force can cause her to obay.

The slightest effusion of such a mind deserves attention.

———

XVI.

King of Scots and Andrew Browne.

This ballad is a proof of the little intercourse that sub-
sisted between the Scots and English before the accession
of James I. to the crown of England.   The tale which is
here so circumstantially related, does not appear to have had
the least foundation in history, but was probably built upon
some confused hearsay report of the tumults in Scotland
during the minority of that prince, and of the conspiracies
formed by different factions to get possession of his person.
It should seem, from ver. 97, to have been written during the
regency, or at least before the death, of the Earl of Morton,
who was condemned and executed, June 2, 1581, when James
was in his 15th year.

The original copy (preserved in the Archives of the
Antiquarian Society, London,) is entitled, "A new Ballad,
declaring the great treason conspired against the young
King of Scots, and how one Andrew Browne, an English-

man, which was the king's chamberlaine, prevented the same. To the tune of *Milfield*, or els to *Green Sleeves*." At the end is subjoined the name of the author, W. Elderton. "Imprinted at London for Yarathe James, dwelling in Newgate Market, over against Ch. Church," in black-letter, folio.

This Elderton, who had been originally an attorney in the sheriffs' courts of London, and afterwards (if we may believe Oldys) a comedian, was a facetious fuddling companion, whose tippling and rhymes rendered him famous among his contemporaries. He was author of many popular songs and ballads; and probably other pieces in these volumes, besides the following, are of his composing. He is believed to have fallen a victim to his bottle before the year 1592. His epitaph has been recorded by Camden, and translated by Oldys.

HIC SITUS EST SITIENS, ATQUE EBRIUS ELDERTONUS,
QUID DICO HIC SITUS EST? HIC POTIUS SITIS EST.

> Dead drunk here Elderton doth lie;
> Dead as he is, he still is dry:
> So of him it may well be said,
> Here he, but not his thirst, is laid.

See Stow's Lond. [Guild-hall.]—Biogr. Brit. [Drayton, by Oldys, Note B.]—Ath. Ox.—Camden's Remains.—The Exale-tation of Ale, among Beaumont's Poems, 8vo, 1653.

"Out alas!" what a griefe is this
   That princes subjects cannot be true,
But still the devill hath some of his,
   Will play their parts whatsoever ensue;
Forgetting what a grievous thing   5
It is to offend the anointed king?
     Alas for woe, why should it be so,
     This makes a sorrowful heigh ho.

In Scotland is a bonnie kinge,
   As proper a youth as neede to be,   10

Well given to every happy thing,
   That can be in a kinge to see:
Yet that unluckie country still,
   Hath people given to craftie will.
     Alas for woe, &c.   15

On Whitsun eve it so befell,
   A posset was made to give the king,
Whereof his ladie nurse hard tell,
   And that it was a poysoned thing:
She cryed, and called piteouslie;   20
Now help, or els the king shall die!
     Alas for woe, &c.

One Browne, that was an English man,
   And hard the ladies piteous crye,
Out with his sword, and bestir'd him than,   25
   Out of the doores in haste to flie;
But all the doores were made so fast,
Out of a window he got at last.
     Alas for woe, &c.

He met the bishop coming fast,   30
   Having the posset in his hande:
The sight of Browne made him aghast,
   Who bad him stoutly staie and stand.
With him were two that ranne awa,
For feare that Browne would make a fray.   35
     Alas for woe, &c.

Bishop, quoth Browne, what hast thou there?
   Nothing at all, my friend, sayde he;
But a posset to make the king good cheere.
   Is it so? sayd Browne, that will I see.   40
First I will have thyself begin,
Before thou go any further in;
     Be it weale or woe, it shall be so,
     This makes a sorrowful heigh ho.

The Bishop sayde, Browne I doo know,   45
  Thou art a young man poore and bare;
Livings on thee I will bestowe:
  Let me go on, take thou no care.
No, no, quoth Browne, I will not be
A traitour for all Christiantie: 50
    Happe well or woe, it shall be so,
    Drink now with a sorrowfull, &c.

The bishop dranke, and by and by
  His belly burst and he fell downe:
A just rewarde for his traitery.   55
  This was a posset indeed, quoth Brown!
He serched the bishop, and found the keyes,
To come to the kinge when he did please.
    Alas for woe, &c.

As soon as the king got word of this,   60
  He humbly fell uppon his knee,
And praysed God that he did misse
  To tast of that extremity:
For that he did perceive and know,
His clergie would betray him so: 65
    Alas for woe, &c.

Alas, he said, unhappie realme,
  My father, and grandfather slaine:
My mother banished, O extreame!
  Unhappy fate, and bitter bayne!   70
And now like treason wrought for me,
What more unhappie realme can be!
    Alas for woe, &c.

The king did call his nurse to his grace,
  And gave her twenty poundes a yeere;   75

Ver. 67. His father was Henry Lord Darnley. His grandfather, the old Earl of Lenox, regent of Scotland, and father of Lord Darnley, was murdered at Stirling, Sept. 5, 1571.

And trustie Browne too in like case,
 He knighted him with gallant geere:
And gave him 'lands and livings great,'
For dooing such a manly feat,
  As he did showe, to the bishop's woe, 80
  Which made, &c.

When all this treason done and past,
 Tooke not effect of traytery;
Another treason at the last,
 They sought against his majestie: 85
How they might make their kinge away,
By a privie banket on a daye.
  Alas for woe, &c.

'Another time' to sell the king
 Beyonde the seas they had decreede: 90
Three noble Earles heard of this thing,
 And did prevent the same with speede.
For a letter came, with such a charme,
That they should doo their king no harme:
  For further woe, if they did soe, 95
  Would make a sorrowful heigh hoe.

The Earle Mourton told the Douglas then,
 Take heede you do not offend the king;
But shew yourselves like honest men
 Obediently in every thing: 100
For his godmother[1] will not see
Her noble childe misus'd to be
  With any woe; for if it be so,
  She will make, &c.

God graunt all subjects may be true, 105
 In England, Scotland, every where:
That no such daunger may ensue,
 To put the prince or state in feare:

    [1] Queen Elizabeth.

That God the highest king may see
Obedience as it ought to be, 110
    In wealth or woe, God graunt it be so
    To avoide the sorrowful heigh ho.

XVII.

The Bonny Earl of Murray.

A SCOTTISH SONG.

In December, 1591, Francis Stewart, Earl of Bothwell, had made an attempt to seize on the person of his sovereign, James VI., but being disappointed, had retired towards the north. The king unadvisedly gave a commission to George Gordon, Earl of Huntley, to pursue Bothwell and his followers with fire and sword. Huntley, under cover of executing that commission, took occasion to revenge a private quarrel he had against James Stewart, Earl of Murray, a relation of Bothwell's. In the night of Feb. 7, 1592, he beset Murray's house, burnt it to the ground, and slew Murray himself; a young nobleman of the most promising virtues, and the very darling of the people. See Robertson's History.

The present Lord Murray hath now in his possession a picture of his ancestor naked and covered with wounds, which had been carried about, according to the custom of that age, in order to inflame the populace to revenge his death. If this picture did not flatter, he well deserved the name of the BONNY EARL, for he is there represented as a tall and comely personage. It is a tradition in the family, that Gordon of Bucky gave him a wound in the face: Murray half expiring, said, "You hae spilt a better face than your awin." Upon this, Bucky, pointing his dagger at Huntley's breast, swore, "You shall be as deep as I;" and forced him to pierce the poor defenceless body.

King James, who took no care to punish the murderers, is said by some to have privately countenanced and abetted them, being stimulated by jealousy for some indiscreet praises which his queen had too lavishly bestowed on this unfortunate youth. See the preface to the next ballad. See also Mr. Walpole's *Catalogue of Royal Authors*, vol. i. p. 42.

Yᴇ highlands, and ye lawlands,
    Oh! quhair hae ye been?
They hae slaine the Earl of Murray,
    And hae laid him on the green.

Now wae be to thee, Huntley!   5
    And quhairfore did you sae!
I bade you bring him wi' you,
    But forbade you him to slay.

He was a braw gallant,
    And he rid at the ring;   10
And the bonny Earl of Murray,
    Oh! he might hae been a king.

He was a braw gallant,
    And he playd at the ba';
And the bonny Earl of Murray   15
    Was the flower among them a.

He was a braw gallant,
    And he playd at the gluve;
And the bonny Earl of Murray,
    Oh! he was the Queenes luve.   20

Oh! lang will his lady
    Luke owre the castle downe[1],
Ere she see the Earl of Murray
    Cum sounding throw the towne.

[1] *Castle downe* here has been thought to mean the *Castle of Downe,* a seat belonging to the family of Murray.

XVIII.

Young Waters.

A SCOTTISH BALLAD.

IT has been suggested to the Editor, that this ballad covertly alludes to the indiscreet partiality which Queen Anne of Denmark is said to have shown for the bonny Earl of Murray; and which is supposed to have influenced the fate of that unhappy nobleman. Let the reader judge for himself.

The following account of the murder is given by a contemporary writer, and a person of credit,—Sir James Balfour, knight, Lyon King of Arms, whose MS. of the Annals of Scotland is in the Advocates' library at Edinburgh.

"The seventh of Febry, this zeire, 1592, the Earle of Murray was cruelly murthered by the Earle of Huntley at his house in Dunibrissel in Fyffe-shyre, and with him Dunbar, sheriffe of Murray. It was given out and publickly talkt, that the Earle of Huntley was only the instrument of perpetrating this facte, to satisfie the King's jealousie of Murray, quhum the Queene, more rashely than wisely, some few days before had commendit in the King's hearing, with too many epithets of a proper and gallant man. The reasons of these surmises proceedit from a proclamatione of the Kings, the 13 of Marche following; inhibiteine the zoung Earle of Murray to persue the Earle of Huntley, for his father's slaughter, in respect he being wardeit [imprisoned] in the castell of Blacknesse for the same murther, was willing to abide a tryall, averring that he had done nothing but by the King's majesties commissione; and was neither airt nor part in the murther[1]."

The following ballad is here given from a copy printed not long since at Glasgow, in one sheet, 8vo. The world was indebted for its publication to the Lady Jean Hume, sister to the Earl of Hume, who died at Gibraltar.

[1] This extract is copied from the *Critical Review*.

Abоut Zule, quhen the wind blew cule,
  And the round tables began,
A'! there is cum to our kings court
  Mony a well-favoured man.

The queen luikt owre the castle wa,   5
  Beheld baith dale and down,
And then she saw zoung Waters
  Cum riding to the town.

His footmen they did rin before,
  His horsemen rade behind,   10
Ane mantel of the burning gowd
  Did keip him frae the wind.

Gowden graith'd his horse before
  And siller shod behind,
The horse zong Waters rade upon   15
  Was fleeter than the wind.

But than spake a wylie lord,
  Unto the queen said he,
O tell me qhua's the fairest face
  Rides in the company.   20

I've sene lord, and I've sene laird,
  And knights of high degree;
Bot a fairer face than zoung Watèrs
  Mine eyne did never see.

Out then spack the jealous king,   25
  (And an angry man was he)
O, if he had been twice as fair,
  Zou micht have excepted me.

Zou're neither laird nor lord, she says,
  Bot the king that wears the crown;   30
Theris not a knight in fair Scotland
  Bot to thee maun bow down .

For a' that she could do or say,
  Appeasd he wad nae bee;
Bot for the words which she had said   35
  Zoung Waters he maun dee.

They hae taen zoung Waters, and
  Put fetters to his feet;
They hae taen zoung Waters, and
  Thrown him in dungeon deep.   40

Aft I have ridden thro' Stirling town
  In the wind both and the weit;
Bot I neir rade thro' Stirling town
  Wi fetters at my feet.

Aft have I ridden thro' Stirling town   45
  In the wind both and the rain;
Bot I neir rade thro' Stirling town
  Neir to return again.

They hae taen to the heiding-hill[2]
  His zoung son in his craddle,   50
And they hae taen to the heiding-hill,
  His horse both and his saddle.

They hae taen to the heiding-hill
  His lady fair to see.
And for the words the Queen had spoke   55
  Zoung Waters he did dee.

[2] *Heiding-hill*; *i. e.* heading [beheading] hill. The place of execution was anciently an artificial hillock.

XIX.

Mary Ambree.

In the year 1584, the Spaniards, under the command of Alexander Farnese, Prince of Parma, began to gain great advantages in Flanders and Brabant, by recovering many strong-holds and cities from the Hollanders, as Ghent, (called then by the English Gaunt,) Antwerp, Mechlin, &c. See Stow's Annals, p. 711. Some attempt made, with the assistance of English volunteers, to retrieve the former of those places, probably gave occasion to this ballad. I can find no mention of our heroine in history, but the following rhymes rendered her famous among our poets. Ben Jonson often mentions her, and calls any remarkable virago by her name. See his *Epicœne*, first acted in 1609, act 4, sc. 2: his *Tale of a Tub*, act 1, sc. 4: and his masque entitled the *Fortunate Isles*, 1626, where he quotes the very words of the ballad.

> —— Mary Ambree,
> (Who marched so free
> To the siege of Gaunt,
> And death could not daunt,
> As the ballad doth vaunt)
> Were a braver wight, &c.

She is also mentioned in Fletcher's *Scornful Lady*, act 5, *sub finem*.

"—— My large gentlewoman, my Mary Ambree, had I but seen into you, you should have had another bed-fellow. ——"

It is likewise evident, that she is the virago intended by Butler in *Hudibras*, (p. i. c. iii. v. 365,) by her being coupled with Joan d'Arc, the celebrated Pucelle d'Orléans.

> A bold virago stout and tall
> As *Joan* of France, or English *Mall*.

This ballad is printed from a black-letter copy in the Pepys collection, improved from the Editor's folio MS. and by conjecture. The full title is, "the valorous acts performed at Gaunt by the brave bonnie lass Mary Ambree, who in revenge of her lovers death did play her part most gallantly. The tune is *The Blind Beggar*, &c."

WHEN captaines couragious, whom death cold not daunte,
Did march to the siege of the citty of Gaunt,
They mustred their souldiers by two and by three,
And the formost in battle was Mary Ambree.

When brave Sir John Major[1] was slaine in her sight,   5
Who was her true lover, her joy, and delight,
Because he was slaine most treacherouslie,
Then vowd to revenge him Mary Ambree.

She clothed herselfe from the top to the toe
In buffe of the bravest, most seemelye to showe;   10
A faire shirt of male[2] then slipped on shee;
Was not this a brave bonny lass, Mary Ambree?

A helmett of proofe shee strait did provide,
A strong arminge sword shee girt by her side,
On her hand a goodly faire gauntlett put shee;   15
Was not this a brave bonny lass, Mary Ambree?

Then tooke shee her sworde and her targett in hand,
Bidding all such, as wold, bee of her band;
To wayte on her person came thousand and three:
Was not this a brave bonny lass, Mary Ambree?   20

My soldiers, she saith, soe valiant and bold,
Nowe followe your captaine, whom you doe beholde;
Still formost in battel myselfe will I bee:
Was not this a brave bonny lasse, Mary Ambree?

Then cryed out her souldiers, and loude they did say,   25
Soe well thou becomest this gallant array,
Thy harte and thy weapons soe well do agree,
Noe mayden was ever like Mary Ambree.

[1] So MS. Serjeant Major, in P. C.
[2] A peculiar kind of armour, composed of small rings of iron, and worn
under the clothes. It is mentioned by Spenser, who speaks of the Irish
gallowglass, or foot-soldier, as "armed in a long shirt of mayl." (View of
the State of Ireland.)

Shee cheared her souldiers, that foughten for life,
With ancyent and standard, with drum and with fife,   30
With brave clanging trumpetts, that sounded so free;
Was not this a brave bonny lasse, Mary Ambree?

Before I will see the worst of you all
To come into danger of death, or of thrall,
This hand and this life I will venture so free: 35
Was not this a brave bonny lasse, Mary Ambree?

Shee led upp her souldiers in battaile array,
Gainst three times theyr number by breake of the daye;
Seven howers in skirmish continued shee:
Was not this a brave bonny lasse, Mary Ambree?   40

She filled the skyes with the smoke of her shott,
And her enemyes bodyes with bullets soe hott;
For one of her owne men a score killed shee:
Was not this a brave bonny lasse, Mary Ambree?

And when her false gunner, to spoyle her intent,   45
Away all her pellets and powder had sent,
Straight with her keen weapon shee slasht him in three:
Was not this a brave bonny lasse, Mary Ambree?

Being falselye betrayed for lucre of hyre,
At length she was forced to make a retyre;   50
Then her souldiers into a strong castle drew shee:
Was not this a brave bonny lasse, Mary Ambree?

Her foes they besett her on everye side,
As thinking close siege shee cold never abide;
To beate down the walles they all did decree: 55
But stoutlye deffyd them brave Mary Ambree.

Then tooke shee her sword and her targett in hand,
And mounting the walls all undaunted did stand,
There daring their captaines to match any three:
O what a brave captaine was Mary Ambree!   60

Now saye, English captaine, what woldest thou give
To ransome thy selfe, which else must not live?
Come yield thy selfe quicklye, or slaine thou must bee.
Then smiled sweetlye brave Mary Ambree.

Ye captaines couragious, of valour so bold,   65
Whom thinke you before you now you doe behold?
A knight, sir, of England, and captaine soe free,
Who shortelye with us a prisoner must bee.

No captaine of England; behold in your sight
Two brests in my bosome, and therfore no knight;   70
Noe knight, sirs, of England, nor captaine you see,
But a poor simple mayden, called Mary Ambree.

But art thou a woman, as thou dost declare,
Whose valor hath proved so undaunted in warre?
If England doth yield such brave maydens as thee,   75
Full well may they conquer, fair Mary Ambree.

The prince of Great Parma heard of her renowne
Who long had advanced for Englands faire crowne;
Hee wooed her and sued her his mistress to bee,
And offerd rich presents to Mary Ambree.   80

But this virtuous mayden despised them all,
Ile nere sell my honour for purple nor pall:
A mayden of England, sir, never will bee
The whore of a monarcke, quoth Mary Ambree.

Then to her owne country shee backe did returne,   85
Still holding the foes of faire England in scorne:
Therfore English captaines of every degree
Sing forth the brave valours of Mary Ambree.

XX.

Brave Lord Willoughbey.

PEREGRINE BERTIE, Lord Willoughby of Eresby, had, in the year 1586, distinguished himself at the siege of Zutphen, in the Low Countries. He was, the year after, made general of the English forces in the United Provinces, in room of the Earl of Leicester, who was recalled. This gave him an opportunity of signalizing his courage and military skill in several actions against the Spaniards. One of these, greatly exaggerated by popular report, is probably the subject of this old ballad, which, on account of its flattering encomiums on English valour, hath always been a favourite with the people.

"My lord Willoughbie (says a contemporary writer) was one of the queenes best swordsmen: . . . . . he was a great master of the art military . . . . I have heard it spoken, that had he not slighted the court, but applied himself to the queene, he might have enjoyed a plentifull portion of her grace; and it was his saying, and it did him no good, that he was none of the *Reptilia;* intimating, that he could not creepe on the ground, and that the court was not his element; for, indeed, as he was a great souldier, so he was of suitable magnanimitie, and could not brooke the obsequiousnesse and assiduitie of the court."—(Naunton.)

Lord Willoughbie died in 1601. Both Norris and Turner were famous among the military men of that age.

The subject of this ballad (which is printed from an old black-letter copy, with some conjectural emendations,) may possibly receive illustration from what Chapman says, in the dedication to his version of Homer's *Frogs and Mice,* concerning the brave and memorable retreat of Sir John Norris, with only 1000 men, through the whole Spanish army under the Duke of Parma, for three miles together.

Tʜᴇ fifteenth day of July,
  With glistering spear and shield,
A famous fight in Flanders
  Was foughten in the field.:
The most couragious officers   5
  Were English captains three;
But the bravest man in battel
  Was brave lord Willoughbèy.

The next was captain Norris,
  A valiant man was hee: 10
The other captain Turner,
  From field would never flee.
With fifteen hundred fighting men,
  Alas! there were no more,
They fought with fourteen thousand then,   15
  Upon the bloody shore.

Stand to it noble pikemen,
  And look you round about:
And shoot you right you bow-men,
  And we will keep them out: 20
You musquet and calliver men,
  Do you prove true to me,
I'le be the formost man in fight,
  Says brave lord Willoughbèy.

And then the bloody enemy   25
  They fiercely did assail,
And fought it out most furiously,
  Not doubting to prevail:
The wounded men on both sides fell
  Most pitious for to see,   30
Yet nothing could the courage quell
  Of brave lord Willoughbèy.

For seven hours to all mens view
  This fight endured sore,

Until our men so feeble grew   35
   That they could fight no more;
And then upon dead horses
   Full savoury they eat,
And drank the puddle water,
   They could no better get.   40

When they had fed so freely,
   They kneeled on the ground,
And praised God devoutly
   For the favour they had found;
And beating up their colours,   45
   The fight they did renew,
And turning tow'rds the Spaniard,
   A thousand more they slew.

The sharp steel-pointed arrows,
   And bullets thick did fly;   50
Then did our valiant soldiers
   Charge on most furiously;
Which made the Spaniards waver,
   They thought it best to flee,
They fear'd the stout behaviour   55
   Of brave lord Willoughbèy.

Then quoth the Spanish general,
   Come let us march away,
I fear we shall be spoiled all
   If here we longer stay;   60
For yonder comes lord Willoughbèy
   With courage fierce and fell,
He will not give one inch of way
   For all the devils in hell.

And then the fearful enemy   65
   Was quickly put to flight,
Our men persued couragiously,
   And caught their forces quite;

But at last they gave a shout,
   Which ecchoed through the sky,
God, and St. George for England!   70
   The conquerers did cry.

This news was brought to England
   With all the speed might be,
And soon our gracious queen was told   75
   Of this same victory.
O this is brave lord Willoughbey,
   My love that ever won,
Of all the lords of honour,
   'Tis he great deeds hath done.   80

To the souldiers that were maimed,
   And wounded in the fray,
The queen allowed a pension
   Of fifteen pence a day;
And from all costs and charges   85
   She quit and set them free:
And this she did all for the sake
   Of brave lord Willoughbèy.

Then courage, noble Englishmen,
   And never be dismaid: 90
If that we be but one to ten,
   We will not be afraid
To fight with foraign enemies,
   And set our nation free,
And thus I end the bloody bout   95
   Of brave lord Willoughbèy.

XXI.

Victorious Men of Earth.

THIS little moral sonnet hath such a pointed application
to the heroes of the foregoing and following ballads, that I

cannot help placing it here, though the date of its composition is of a much later period. It is extracted from "Cupid and Death, a masque by J. S. [James Shirley] presented Mar. 26, 1653." London, printed 1653, 4to.

VICTORIOUS men of earth, no more
    Proclaim how wide your empires are;
Though you binde in every shore,
    And your triumphs reach as far
        As night or day;   5
    Yet you proud monarchs must obey,
And mingle with forgotten ashes, when
Death calls yee to the crowd of common men.

Devouring famine, plague, and war,
    Each able to undo mankind,   10
Death's servile emissaries are,
    Nor to these alone confin'd,
        He hath at will
    More quaint and subtle wayes to kill;
A smile or kiss, as he will use the art,   15
Shall have the cunning skill to break a heart.

XXII.

The Winning of Cales.

THE subject of this ballad is the taking of the city of Cadiz, (called by our sailors corruptly *Cales*,) on June 21, 1596, in a descent made on the coast of Spain, under the command of the Lord Howard, admiral, and the Earl of Essex, general.

The valour of Essex was not more distinguished on this occasion than his generosity: the town was carried sword in hand, but he stopped the slaughter as soon as possible, and treated his prisoners with the greatest humanity, and even

affability and kindness. The English made a rich plunder
in the city, but missed of a much richer, by the resolution
which the duke of Medina, the Spanish admiral, took, of
setting fire to the ships, in order to prevent their falling into
the hands of the enemy. It was computed, that the loss which
the Spaniards sustained from this enterprise, amounted to
twenty millions of ducats. See Hume's History.

The Earl of Essex knighted on this occasion not fewer
than sixty persons, which gave rise to the following sarcasm:

> A gentleman of Wales, a knight of Cales,
>   And a laird of the North country;
> But a yeoman of Kent with his yearly rent
>   Will buy them out all three.

The ballad is printed, with some corrections, from the
Editor's folio MS., and seems to have been composed by some
person who was concerned in the expedition. Most of the circumstances related in it will be found supported by history.

———

Long the proud Spaniards had vaunted to conquer us,
  Threatning our country with fyer and sword;
Often preparing their navy most sumptuous
  With as great plenty as Spain could afford.
    Dub a dub, dub a dub, thus strike their drums: 5
    Tantara, tantara, the Englishman comes.

To the seas presentlye went our lord admiral,
  With knights couragious and captains full good;
The brave Earl of Essex, a prosperous general,
  With him prepared to pass the salt flood.   10
    Dub a dub, &c.

At Plymouth speedilye, took they ship valiantlye,
  Braver ships never were seen under sayle,
With their fair colours spread, and streamers ore their head,
  Now bragging Spaniards, take heed of your tayle,   15
    Dub a dub, &c.

Unto Cales cunninglye, came we most speediiye,
   Where the kinges navy securelye did ryde;
Being upon their backs, piercing their butts of sacks,
   Ere any Spaniards our coming descryde.   20
     Dub a dub, &c.

Great was the crying, the running, and ryding,
   Which at that season was made in that place;
The beacons were fyred, as need then required;
   To hyde their great treasure they had little space.   25
     Dub a dub, &c.

There you might see their ships, how they were fyred fast,
   And how their men drowned themselves in the sea;
There might you hear them cry, wayle and weep piteously,
   When they saw no shift to scape thence away.   30
     Dub a dub, &c.

The great St. Phillip, the pryde of the Spaniards,
   Was burnt to the bottom, and sunk in the sea;
But the St. Andrew, and eke the St. Matthew,
   Wee took in fight manfullye and brought away.   35
     Dub a dub, &c.

The Earl of Essex most valiant and hardye,
   With horsemen and footmen marched up to the town;
The Spanyards, which saw them, were greatly alarmed,
   Did fly for their savegard, and durst not come down. 40
     Dub a dub, &c.

Now, quoth the noble Earl, courage my soldiers all,
   Fight and be valiant, the spoil you shall have;
And be well rewarded all from the great to the small;
   But looke that the women and children you save.   45
     Dub a dub, &c.

The Spaniards at that sight, thinking it vain to fight,
   Hung upp flags of truce and yielded the towne;

Wee marched in presentlye, decking the walls on hye,
  With English colours which purchased renowne.		50
    Dub a dub, &c.

Entering the houses then, of the most richest men,
  For gold and treasure we searched eche day;
In some places we did find, pyes baking left behind,
  Meate at fire rosting, and folkes run away.		55
    Dub a dub, &c.

Full of rich merchandize, every shop catched our eyes,
  Damasks and sattens and velvets full fayre;
Which soldiers measur'd out by the length of their swords;
  Of all commodities eche had a share.			60
    Dub a dub, &c.

Thus Cales was taken, and our brave general
  March'd to the market-place, where he did stand:
There many prisoners fell to our several shares,
  Many crav'd mercye, and mercye they fannd.		65
    Dub a dub, &c.

When our brave General saw they delayed all,
  And wold not ransome their towne as they said,
With their fair wanscots, their presses and bedsteds,
  Their joint-stools and tables a fire we made;		70
    And when the town burned all in flame,
    With tara, tantara, away wee all came.

XXIII.

The Spanish Lady's Love.

This beautiful old ballad most probably took its rise from one of these descents made on the Spanish coasts in the time of Queen Elizabeth; and in all likelihood from that which is celebrated in the foregoing ballad.

It was a tradition in the West of England, that the person

admired by the Spanish lady was a gentleman of the Popham family, and that her picture, with the pearl neck-lace mentioned in the ballad, was not many years ago preserved at Littlecot, near Hungerford, Wilts, the seat of that respectable family.

Another tradition hath pointed out Sir Richard Levison, of Trentham, in Staffordshire, as the subject of this ballad; who married Margaret, daughter of Charles Earl of Nottingham, and was eminently distinguished as a naval officer and commander in all the expeditions against the Spaniards in the latter end of Queen Elizabeth's reign, particularly in that to Cadiz in 1596, when he was aged 27. He died in 1605, and has a monument, with his effigy in brass, in Wolverhampton church.

It is printed from an ancient black-letter copy, corrected in part by the Editor's folio MS.

WILL you hear a Spanish lady,
    How shee wooed an English man?
Garments gay as rich as may be
    Decked with jewels she had on.
Of a comely countenance and grace was she,   5
And by birth and parentage of high degree.

As his prisoner there he kept her,
    In his hands her life did lye;
Cupid's bands did tye them faster
    By the liking of an eye.   10
In his courteous company was all her joy,
To favour him in any thing she was not coy.

But at last there came commandment
    For to set the ladies free,
With their jewels still adorned,   15
    None to do them injury.
Then said this lady mild, Full woe is me;
O let me still sustain this kind captivity!

Gallant captain, shew some pity
  To a ladye in distresse;   20
Leave me not within this city,
  For to dye in heavinesse:
Thou hast set this present day my body free,
But my heart in prison still remains with thee.

"How should'st thou, fair lady, love me,   25
  Whom thou knowst thy country's foe?
Thy faire wordes make me suspect thee:
  Serpents lie where flowers grow."
All the harm I wishe to thee, most courteous knight,
God grant the same upon my head may fully light.   30

Blessed be the time and season,
  That you came on Spanish ground;
If our foes you may be termed,
  Gentle foes we have you found:
With our city, you have won our hearts eche one,   35
Then to your country bear away, that is your owne.

"Rest you still, most gallant lady;
  Rest you still, and weep no more;
Of fair lovers there is plenty,
  Spain doth yield a wonderous store."   40
Spaniards fraught with jealousy we often find,
But Englishmen through all the world are counted kind.

Leave me not unto a Spaniard,
  You alone enjoy my heart;
I am lovely, young, and tender,   45
  Love is likewise my desert:
Still to serve thee day and night my mind is prest;
The wife of every Englishman is counted blest.

"It wold be a shame, fair lady,
  For to bear a woman hence;   50

Percy. II.   13

English soldiers never carry
  Any such without offence."
I'll quickly change myself, if it be so,
And like a page Ile follow thee, where'er thou go.

"I have neither gold nor silver   55
  To maintain thee in this case,
And to travel is great charges,
  As you know in every place."
My chains and jewels every one shal be thy own,
And eke five hundred pounds[1] in gold that lies unknown. 60

"On the seas are many dangers,
  Many storms do there arise,
Which wil be to ladies dreadful,
  And force tears from watery eyes."
Well in troth I shall endure extremity,   65
For I could find in heart to lose my life for thee.

"Courteous ladye, leave this fancy,
  Here comes all that breeds the strife;
I in England have already
  A sweet woman to my wife: 70
I will not falsify my vow for gold nor gain,
Nor yet for all the fairest dames that live in Spain."

O how happy is that woman
  That enjoys so true a friend!
Many happy days God send her;   75
  Of my suit I make an end:
On my knees I pardon crave for my offence,
Which did from love and true affection first commence.

Commend me to thy lovely lady,
  Bear to her this chain of gold;   80

Ver. 65, Well in worth. MS.

[1] So the MS.—10,000*l*. P. C.

And these bracelets for a token;
 Grieving that I was so bold:
All my jewels in like sort take thou with thee,
For they are fitting for thy wife, but not for me.

I will spend my days in prayer,   85
 Love and all her laws defye;
In a nunnery will I shroud mee
 Far from any companye:
But ere my prayers have an end, be sure of this,
To pray for thee and for thy love I will not miss.   90

Thus farewell, most gallant captain!
 Farewell too my heart's content!
Count not Spanish ladies wanton,
 Though to thee my love was bent:
Joy and true prosperity goe still with thee!   95
"The like fall ever to thy share, most fair ladie."

V. 86, So the folio MS. Other editions read *his laws*.

XXIV.

Argentile and Curan

Is extracted from an ancient historical poem in thirteen
books, entitled *Albion's England*, by William Warner; "An
author (says a former editor) only unhappy in the choice of
his subject, and measure of his verse. His poem is an
epitome of the British history, and written with great learning,
sense, and spirit; in some places fine to an extraordinary
degree, as I think will eminently appear in the ensuing
episode [of *Argentile and Curan*,] — a tale full of beautiful
incidents in the romantic taste, extremely affecting, rich in
ornament, wonderfully various in style; and in short, one of
the most beautiful pastorals I ever met with." — [Muses'
Library, 1738, 8vo.] To his merit nothing can be objected,
unless perhaps an affected quaintness in some of his expressions, and an indelicacy in some of his pastoral images.

13*

Warner is said, by A. Wood[1], to have been a Warwick-
shire man, and to have been educated in Oxford, at Mag-
dalene-hall: as also in the latter part of his life to have been
retained in the service of Henry Cary, Lord Hunsdon, to
whom he dedicates his poem. However that may have been,
new light is thrown upon his history, and the time and
manner of his death are now ascertained by the following
extract from the parish register-book of Amwell, in Hertford-
shire, which was obligingly communicated to the editor by
Mr. Hoole, the very ingenious translator of Tasso, &c.

[1608—1609.] "Master William Warner, a man of good
yeares and of honest reputation; by his profession an
Atturnye of the Common Pleas; author of Albions England,
diynge suddenly in the night in his bedde, without any
former complaynt or sicknesse, on thursday night beeinge
the 9th daye of March, was buried the satturday following,
and lyeth in the church at the corner under the stone of
Walter Ffader."

"*Signed* Tho. Hassall Vicarius."

Though now Warner is so seldom mentioned, his contemporaries ranked him on a level with Spenser, and called
them the Homer and Virgil of their age[2]. But Warner rather
resembled Ovid, whose Metamorphoses he seems to have
taken for his model, having deduced a perpetual poem from
the Deluge down to the era of Elizabeth, full of lively di-
gressions and entertaining episodes. And though he is
sometimes harsh, affected, and obscure, he often displays a
most charming and pathetic simplicity: as where he describes
Eleanor's harsh treatment of Rosamond:

> With that she dasht her on the lippes
> So dyed double red:
> Hard was the heart that gave the blow,
> Soft were those lippes that bled.

The edition of *Albion's England* here followed, was printed
in 4to, 1602; said in the title-page to have been "first penned

[1] Athen. Oxon.   [2] Ibid.

and published by William Warner, and now revised and newly enlarged by the same author." The story of *Argentile and Curan* is, I believe, the poet's own invention; it is not mentioned in any of our chronicles. It was, however, so much admired, that not many years after he published it, came out a larger poem on the same subject in stanzas of six lines, entitled "The most pleasant and delightful historie of Curan a prince of Danske, and the fayre princesse Argentile, daughter and heyre to Adelbright, sometime king of Northumberland, &c. by William Webster, London, 1617," in 8 sheets, 4to. An indifferent paraphrase of the following poem. This episode of Warner's has also been altered into the common ballad of "the two young Princes on Salisbury Plain," which is chiefly composed of Warner's lines, with a few contractions and interpolations, but all greatly for the worse. See the collection of *Historical Ballads*, 1727, 3 vols. 12mo.

Though here subdivided into stanzas, Warner's metre is the old-fashioned Alexandrine of fourteen syllables. The reader therefore must not expect to find the close of the stanzas consulted in the pauses.

THE Bruton's 'being' departed hence
  Seaven kingdoms here begonne,
Where diversly in divers broyles
  The Saxons lost and wonne.

King Edel and king Adelbright   5
  In Diria jointly raigne;
In loyal concorde during life
  These kingly friends remaine.

When Adelbright should leave his life,
  To Edel thus he sayes;   10
By those same bondes of happie love,
  That held us friends alwaies;

By our by-parted crowne, of which
  The moyetie is mine;
By God, to whom my soule must passe,   15
  And so in time may thine;

I pray thee, nay I cònjure thee,
  To nourish, as thine owne,
Thy neece, my daughter Argentile,
  Till she to age be growne;   20
And then, as thou receivest it,
  Resigne to her my throne.

A promise had for his bequest,
  The testatòr he dies:
But all that Edel undertooke,   25
  He afterwards denies.

Yet well he 'fosters for' a time
  The damsell that was growne
The fairest lady under heaven;
  Whose beautie being knowne,   30

A many princes seeke her love;
  But none might her obtaine;
For grippell Edel to himselfe
  Her kingdome sought to gaine;
And for that cause from sight of such   35
  He did his ward restraine.

By chance one Curan, sonne unto
  A prince in Danske, did see
The maid, with whom he fell in love,
  As much as man might bee.   40

Unhappie youth, what should he doe?
  His saint was kept in mewe;
Nor he, nor any noble-man
  Admitted to her vewe.

One while in melancholy fits　45
　He pines himselfe awaye;
Anon he thought by force of arms
　To win her if he maye:

And still against the kings restraint
　Did secretly invay.　50
At length the high controller Love,
　Whom none may disobay,

Imbased him from lordlines
　Into a kitchen drudge,
That so at least of life or death　55
　She might become his judge.

Accesse so had to see and speake,
　He did his love bewray,
And tells his birth: her answer was,
　She husbandles would stay.　60

Meane while the king did beate his braines,
　His booty to atcheive,
Nor caring what became of her,
　So he by her might thrive;
At last his resolution was　65
　Some pessant should her wive.

And (which was working to his wish)
　He did observe with joye
How Curan, whom he thought a drudge,
　Scapt many an amorous toye[3].　70

The king, perceiving such his veine,
　Promotes his vassal still,
Lest that the basenesse of the man
　Should lett, perhaps, his will.

[3] The construction is, "How that many an amorous toy, or foolery of love, 'scaped Curan;" i. e. escaped from him, being off his guard.

Assured therefore of his love,   75
　But not suspecting who
The lover was, the king himselfe
　In his behalf did woe.

The lady resolute from love,
　Unkindly takes that he   80
Should barre the noble, and unto
　So base a match agree:

And therefore shifting out of doores,
　Departed thence by stealth;
Preferring povertie before   85
　A dangerous life in wealth.

When Curan heard of her escape,
　The anguish in his hart
Was more than much, and after her
　From court he did depart;   90

Forgetfull of himselfe, his birth,
　His country, friends, and all,
And only minding (whom he mist)
　The foundresse of his thrall.

Nor meanes he after to frequent   95
　Or court, or stately townes,
But solitarily to live
　Amongst the country grownes.

A brace of years he lived thus
　Well pleased so to live,   100
And shepherd-like to feed a flocke
　Himselfe did wholly give.

So wasting, love, by worke, and want,
　Grew almost to the waine:
But then began a second love,   105
　The worser of the twaine.

A country wench, a neatherds maid,
  Where Curan kept his sheepe,
Did feed her drove: and now on her
  Was all the shepherds keepe. 110

He borrowed on the working daies
  His holy russets oft,
And of the bacon's fat, to make
  His startops blacke and soft.

And least his tarbox should offend, 115
  He left it at the folde:
Sweete growte, or whig, his bottle had,
  As much as it might holde.

A sheeve of bread as browne as nut,
  And cheese as white as snow, 120
And wildings, or the seasons fruit
  He did in scrip bestow.

And whilst his py-bald curre did sleepe,
  And sheep-hooke lay him by,
On hollow quilles of oten straw 125
  He piped melody.

But when he spyed her his saint,
  He wip'd his greasie shooes,
And clear'd the drivell from his beard,
  And thus the shepheard wooes. 130

"I have, sweet wench, a peece of cheese,
  As good as tooth may chawe,
And bread and wildings souling well,
  (And therewithall did drawe

"His lardrie) and in 'yeaning' see 135
  Yon crumpling ewe, quoth he,

Ver. 112, *i. e.* holy-day russets.   V. 135, eating. P. CC.

Did twinne this fall, and twin shouldst thou,
    If I might tup with thee.

"Thou art too elvish, faith thou art,
    Too elvish and too coy: 140
Am I, I pray thee, beggarly,
    That suche a flocke enjoy?

"I wis I am not: yet that thou
    Doest hold me in disdaine
Is brimme abroad, and made a gybe   145
    To all that keepe this plaine.

"There be as quaint (at least that thinke
    Themselves as quaint) that crave
The match, that thou, I wot not why,
    Maist, but mislik'st to have.   150

"How wouldst thou match? (for well I wot,
    Thou art a female) I,
Her know not here that willingly
    With maiden-head would die.

"The plowmans labour hath no end,   155
    And he a churle will prove:
The craftsman hath more worke in hand
    Then fitteth unto love:

"The merchant, traffiquing abroad,
    Suspects his wife at home: 160
A youth will play the wanton; and
    An old man prove a mome.

"Then chuse a shepheard: with the sun
    He doth his flocke unfold,
And all the day on hill or plaine,   165
    He merrie chat can hold;

V. 153, Her know I not her that. ed. 1602.

"And with the sun doth folde againe;
   Then jogging home betime,
He turnes a crab, or turnes a round,
   Or sings some merry ryme.   170

"Nor lacks he gleefull tales, whilst round
   The nut-brown bowl doth trot;
And sitteth singing care away,
   Till he to bed be got:

"Theare sleepes he soundly all the night,   175
   Forgetting morrow-cares:
Nor feares he blasting of his corne,
   Nor uttering of his wares;

"Or stormes by seas, or stirres on land,
   Or cracke of credit lost: 180
Not spending franklier than his flocke
   Shall still defray the cost.

"Well wot I, sooth they say, that say
   More quiet nights and daies
The shepheard sleeps and wakes, than he   185
   Whose cattel he doth graize.

"Beleeve me, lasse, a king is but
   A man, and so am I:
Content is worth a monarchie,
   And mischiefs hit the hie;   190

"As late it did a king and his
   Not dwelling far from hence,
Who left a daughter, save thyselfe,
   For fair a matchless wench." ——
Here did he pause, as if his tongue   195
   Had done his heart offence.

V. 169, *i. e.* roasts a crab, or apple.   V. 171, to tell, whilst round the
bole doth trot. ed. 1597.

The neatresse, longing for the rest,
  Did egge him on to tell
How faire she was, and who she was.
  "She bore, quoth he, the bell   200

"For beautie: though I clownish am,
  I know what beautie is;
Or did I not, at seeing thee,
  I senceles were to mis.
      *   *   *   *

"Her stature comely, tall; her gate   205
  Well graced; and her wit
To marvell at, not meddle with,
  As matchless I omit.

"A globe-like head, a gold-like haire,
  A forehead smooth, and hie,   210
An even nose; on either side
  Did shine a grayish eie:

"Two rosie cheeks, round ruddy lips,
  White just-set teeth within;
A mouth in meane; and underneathe   215
  A round and dimpled chin.

"Her snowie necke, with blewish veines,
  Stood bolt upright upon
Her portly shoulders: beating balles
  Her veined breasts, anon   220

"Adde more to beautie. Wand-like was
  Her middle falling still,
And rising whereas women rise: * * *
  — Imagine nothing ill.

"And more, her long, and limber armes   225
  Had white and azure wrists;
And slender fingers aunswere to
  Her smooth and lillie fists.

"A legge in print, a pretie foot;
   Conjecture of the rest: 230
For amorous eies, observing forme,
   Think parts obscured best.

"With these O raretie! with these
   Her tong of speech was spare;
But speaking, Venus seem'd to speake,   235
   The balle from Ide to bear.

"With Phœbe, Juno, and with both
   Herselfe contends in face:
Wheare equall mixture did not want
   Of milde and stately grace.   240

"Her smiles were sober, and her lookes
   Were chearefull unto all:
Even such as neither wanton seeme,
   Nor waiward; mell, nor gall.

"A quiet minde, a patient moode,   245
   And not disdaining any;
Not gybing, gadding, gawdy: and
   Sweete faculties had many.

"A nimph, no tong, no heart, no eie,
   Might praise, might wish, might see; 250
For life, for love, for forme; more good,
   More worth, more faire than shee.

"Yea such an one, as such was none,
   Save only she was such:
Of Argentile to say the most,   255
   Were to be silent much."

I knew the lady very well,
   But worthles of such praise,
The neatresse said: and muse I do,
   A shepheard thus should blaze   260

The 'coate' of beautie[1].   Credit me,
  Thy latter speech bewraies

Thy clownish shape a coined shew.
  But wherefore dost thou weepe?
The shepheard wept, and she was woe,   265
  And both doe silence keepe.

"In troth, quoth he, I am not such,
  As seeming I professe:
But then for her, and now for thee,
  I from myselfe digresse.   270

"Her loved I (wretch that I am
  A recreant to be)
I loved her, that hated love,
  But now I die for thee.

"At Kirkland is my fathers court,   275
  And Curan is my name,
In Edels court sometimes in pompe,
  Till love countrould the same:

"But now—what now?—deare heart, how now?
  What ailest thou to weepe?"   280
The damsell wept, and he was woe,
  And both did silence keepe.

I graunt, quoth she, it was too much,
  That you did love so much:
But whom your former could not move,   285
  Your second love doth touch.

Thy twice-beloved Argentile
  Submitteth her to thee,
And for thy double love presents
  Herself a single fee,   290

---

[1] *i. e.* emblazon beauty's coat. Ed. 1597, 1602, 1612, read *coote.*

In passion not in person chang'd,
    And I, my lord, am she.

They sweetly surfeiting in joy,
    And silent for a space,
When as the extasie had end,   295
    Did tenderly imbrace;
And for their wedding, and their wish
    Got fitting time and place.

Not England (for of Hengist then
    Was named so this land)   300
Then Curan had an hardier knight;
    His force could none withstand:
Whose sheep-hooke laid apart, he then
    Had higher things in hand.

First, making knowne his lawfull claime   305
    In Argentile her right,
He warr'd in Diria², and he wonne
    Bernicia² too in fight:

And so from trecherous Edel tooke
    At once his life and crowne,   310
And of Northumberland was king,
    Long raigning in renowne.

---

² During the Saxon heptarchy, the kingdom of Northumberland (consisting of six northern counties, besides part of Scotland) was for a long
time divided into two lesser sovereignties, viz. Deira (called here Diria)
which contained the southern parts, and Bernicia, comprehending those
which lay north.

XXV.

Corin's Fate.

ONLY the three first stanzas of this song are ancient:
these are extracted from a small quarto MS. in the Editor's

possession, written in the time of Queen Elizabeth. As they seemed to want application, this has been attempted by a modern hand.

———————

Corin, most unhappie swaine,
 Whither wilt thou drive thy flocke?
Little foode is on the plaine;
 Full of danger is the rocke:

Wolfes and beares doe kepe the woodes;   5
 Forests tangled are with brakes:
Meadowes subject are to floodes;
 Moores are full of miry lakes.

Yet to shun all plaine, and hill,
 Forest, moore, and meadow-ground,   10
Hunger will as surely kill:
 How may then reliefe be found?

Such is hapless Corins fate:
 Since my waywarde love begunne,
Equall doubts begett debate   15
 What to seeke, and what to shunne.

Spare to speke, and spare to speed;
 Yet to speke will move disdaine:
If I see her not I bleed,
 Yet her sight augments my paine.   20

What may then poor Corin doe?
 Tell me, shepherdes, quicklye tell;
For to linger thus in woe
 Is the lover's sharpest hell.

*_**

———————

XXVI.

Jane Shore.

THOUGH so many vulgar errors have prevailed concerning this celebrated courtesan, no character in history has been more perfectly handed down to us. We have her portrait drawn by two masterly pens; the one has delineated the features of her person, the other those of her character and story. Sir Thomas More drew from the life, and Drayton has copied an original picture of her. The reader will pardon the length of the quotations, as they serve to correct many popular mistakes relating to her catastrophe. The first is from Sir Thomas More's history of Richard III., written in 1513, about thirty years after the death of Edward IV.

"Now then by and by, as it wer for anger, not for covetise, the protector sent into the house of Shores wife (for her husband dwelled not with her) and spoiled her of al that ever she had, (above the value of two or three thousand marks,) and sent her body to prison. And when he had a while laide unto her, for the maner sake, that she went about to bewitch him, and that she was of counsel with the lord chamberlein to destroy him: in conclusion, when that no colour could fasten upon these matters, then he layd heinously to her charge the thing that herselfe could not deny, that al the world wist was true, and that natheles every man laughed at to here it then so sodainly so highly taken, — that she was naught of her body. And for thys cause, (as a goodly continent prince, clene and fautless of himself, sent oute of heaven into this vicious world for the amendment of mens maners,) he caused the bishop of London to put her to open pennance, going before the crosse in procession upon a sonday with a taper in her hand. In which she went in countenance and pace demure so womanly; and albeit she was out of al array save her kyrtle only, yet went she so fair and lovely, namelye, while the wondering of the people caste a comly rud in her chekes, (of which she before had most misse,) thàt her great shame wan her much praise among those that were more amorous of her body, then curious of her soule. And many good folke also, that hated her living, and glad wer to se sin corrected, yet pittied thei more her penance then rejoiced therin, when thei considred that the protector procured it more of a corrupt intent, then any virtuous affeccion.

"This woman was born in London, worshipfully frended, honestly brought up, and very wel maryed, saving somewhat to soone; her husbande an honest citizen, yonge, and goodly, and of good substance. But forasmuche as they were coupled ere she wer wel ripe, she not very fervently loved, for whom she never longed. Which was happely the thinge, that the more easily made her encline unto the king's appetite, when he required her. Howbeit the respect of his royaltie, the hope of gay apparel, ease, plesure, and other wanton welth, was abl soone to perse a soft tender hearte. But when the king had abused her, anon her husband (as he was an honest man, ar l one that could his good, not presuming to touch a kinį es concubine) left her up to him al together. When the k ıg died, the lord chamberlen [Hastings] toke her[1]: whicl in the kinges daies, albeit he was sore enamoured upon h r, yet he forbare her, either for reverence, or for a certai frendly faithfulness.

"Proper she was, nd faire: nothing in her body that you wold have changed, but if you would have wished her somewhat higher. Thus say thei that knew her in her youthe.

---

[1] After the death of Hastings she was kept by the Marquis of Dorset, son to Edward IV.'s queen. In Rymer's Fœdera is a proclamation of Richard's, dated at Leicester, October 23, 1483, wherein a reward of 1000 marks in money, or 100 a-year in land, is offered for taking "Thomas late marquis of Dorset," who, "not having the fear of God, nor the salvation of his own soul, before his eyes, has damnably debauched and defiled many maids, widows, and wives, and *lived in actual adultery with the wife of Shore.*" —Buckingham was at that time in rebellion, but as Dorset was not with him, Richard could not accuse him of treason, and therefore made a handle of these pretended debaucheries to get him apprehended. Vide Rym. Fœd. tom. xij. p. 204.

Albeit some that *now see her*, *(for yet she liveth,)* deme her never to have been wel visaged. Whose jugement seemeth me somewhat like as though men should gesse the bewty of one longe before departed, by her scalpe taken out of the charnel-house; for now is she old, lene, withered, and dried up, nothing left but ryvilde skin, and hard bone. And yet being even such, whoso wel advise her visage, might gesse and devise which partes how filled, wold make it a fair face.

"Yet delited not men so much in her bewty, as in her pleasant behaviour. For a proper wit had she, and could both rede wel and write; mery in company, redy and quick of aunswer, neither mute nor ful of bable; sometime taunting without displeasure, and not without disport. The king would say, That he had three concubines, which in three divers properties diversly excelled. One the meriest, another the wiliest, the thirde the holiest harlot in his realme, as one whom no man could get out of the church lightly to any place, but it wer to his bed. The other two wer somewhat greater personages, and natheles of their humilite content to be nameles, and to forbere the praise of those properties; but the meriest was the Shoris wife, in whom the king therfore toke special pleasure. For many he had, but her he loved, whose favour, to sai the trouth (for sinne it wer to belie the devil) she never abused to any mans hurt, but to many a mans comfort and relief. Where the king toke displeasure, she would mitigate and appease his mind: where men were out of favour, she wold bring them in his grace: for many, that had highly offended, shee obtained pardon: of great forfeitures she gate men remission: and finally in many weighty sutes she stode many men in gret stede, either for none or very smal rewardes, and those rather gay than rich: either for that she was content with the dede selfe well done, or for that she delited to be sued unto, and to show what she was able to do wyth the king, or for that wanton women and welthy be not alway covetous.

"I doubt not some shal think this woman too sleight a thing to be written of, and set amonge the remembraunces of

14*

great matters: which thei shal specially think, that happely
shal esteme her only by that thei *now see her*. But me semeth
the chaunce so much the more worthy to be remembred, in
how much she is *now* in the more beggarly condicion, un-
frended and worne out of acquaintance, after good substance,
after as grete favour with the prince, after as grete sute and
seeking to with al those, that in those days had busynes to
spede, as many other men were of their times, which be now
famouse only by the infamy in their il dedes. Her doinges
were not much lesse, albeit thei be muche lesse remembred
because thei were not so evil. For men use, if they have an
evil turne, to write it in marble: and whoso doth us a good
tourne, we write it in duste[2]. Which is not worst proved by
her; for *at this daye* shee beggeth of many at this daye living,
that at this day had begged, if shee had not bene." See
More's Works, folio, black letter, 1557, pp. 56, 57.

Drayton has written a poetical epistle from this lady to
her royal lover, and in his notes thereto he thus draws her
portrait: "Her stature was meane, her haire of a dark
yellow, her face round and full, her eye gray, delicate harmony being betwixt each part's proportion, and each proportion's colour, her body fat, white, and smooth, her
countenance cheerfull and like to her condition. The picture
which I have seen of hers was such as she rose out of her
bed in the morning, having nothing on but a rich mantle
cast under one arme over her shoulder, and sitting on a
chaire, on which her naked arm did lie. What her father's
name was, or where she was borne, is not certainly knowne:
but Shore, a young man of right goodly person, wealth, and
behaviour, abandoned her bed after the king had made her
his concubine. Richard III. causing her to do open penance

---

[2] The words of Sir Thomas More probably suggested to Shakspeare that
proverbial reflection in Henry VIII. act iv. sc. 2.

　　"Men's evil manners live in brass: their virtues
　　　We write in water."

Shakspeare, in his play of Richard III., follows More's history of that reign,
and therefore could not but see this passage.

in Paul's church-yard, *commanded that no man should relieve her*, which the tyrant did, not so much for his hatred to sinne, but that by making his brother's life odious, he might cover his horrible treasons the more cunningly." See *England's Heroical Epistles*, by Michael Drayton, Esq., London, 1637, 12mo.

The history of Jane Shore receives new illustration from the following letter of King Richard III., which is preserved in the Harl. MSS. number 433, article 2378, but of which the copy transmitted to the Editor has been reduced to modern orthography, &c. It is said to have been addressed to Russel, bishop of Lincoln, lord chancellor, anno 1484.

By the KING.

"Right Reverend Father in God, &c. signifying unto you, that it is shewed unto us, that our Servant and Solicitor Thomas Lynom, marvellously blinded and abused with the late Wife of William Shore, now living in Ludgate by our commandment, hath made Contract of Matrimony with her, as it is said, and intendeth to our full great marvel, to effect the same. WE, for many causes, would be sorry that he should be so disposed; pray you therefore to send for him, and in that ye goodly may, exhort, and stir him to the contrary: And if ye find him utterly set for to marry her, and none otherwise would be advertised, then, if it may stand with the laws of the church, we be content the time of marriage be deferred to our coming next to London; that upon sufficient Surety found of her good abearing, ye do so send for her Keeper, and discharge him of our said commandment, by Warrant of these, committing her to the rule, and guiding of her Father, or any other, by your direction, in the mean season. Given, &c. "RIC. Rex."

It appears from two articles in the same MS. that King Richard had granted to the said Thomas Linom the office of King's Solicitor, (Article 134,) and also the manor of Colmeworth, com. Bedf. to him, his heirs male. (Article 596.)

An original picture of Jane Shore, almost naked, is preserved in the Provost's lodgings at Eton; and another picture
of her is in the Provost's Lodge at King's College, Cambridge,
to both which foundations she is supposed to have done
friendly offices with Edward IV. A small 4to mezzotinto
print was taken from the former of these by J. Faber.

The following ballad is printed (with some corrections)
from an old black-letter copy in the Pepys collection. Its
full title is, "The woefull lamentation of Jane Shore, a
goldsmith's wife in London, sometime king Edward IV. his
concubine. To the tune of '*Live with me*, &c.'" [See the first
volume.] To every stanza is annexed the following burthen:

> Then maids and wives in time amend,
> For love and beauty will have end.

> If Rosamonde that was so faire,
> Had cause her sorrowes to declare,
> Then let Jane Shore with sorrowe sing,
> That was beloved of a king.

> In maiden yeares my beautye bright   5
> Was loved dear of lord and knight;
> But yet the love that they requir'd,
> It was not as my friends desir'd.

> My parents they, for thirst of gaine,
> A husband for me did obtaine;   10
> And I, their pleasure to fulfille,
> Was forc'd to wedd against my wille.

> To Matthew Shore I was a wife,
> Till lust brought ruine to my life;
> And then my life I lewdlye spent,   15
> Which makes my soul for to lament.

> In Lombard-street I once did dwelle,
> As London yet can witness welle;

Where many gallants did beholde
My beautye in a shop of golde.   20

I spred my plumes, as wantons doe,
Some sweet and secret friende to wooe,
Because chast love I did not finde
Agreeing to my wanton minde.

At last my name in court did ring   25
Into the eares of Englandes king, ,
Who came and lik'd, and love requir'd,
But I made coye what he desir'd:

Yet Mistress Blague, a neighbour neare,
Whose friendship I esteemed deare,   30
Did saye, It was a gallant thing
To be beloved of a king.

By her persuasions I was led,
For to defile my marriage-bed,
And wronge my wedded husband Shore,   35
Whom I had married yeares before.

In heart and mind I did rejoyce,
That I had made so sweet a choice;
And therefore did my state resigne,
To be king Edward's concubine.   40

From city then to court I went,
To reape the pleasures of content;
There had the joyes that love could bring,
And knew the secrets of a king.

When I was thus advanc'd on highe   45
Commanding Edward with mine eye,
For Mrs. Blague I in short space
Obtainde a livinge from his grace.

No friende I had but in short time
I made unto promotion climbe;   50

But yet for all this costlye pride,
My husbande could not mee abide.

His bed, though wronged by a king,
His heart with deadlye griefe did sting;
From England then he goes away   55
To end his life beyond the sea.

He could not live to see his name
Impaired by my wanton shame;
Although a prince of peerlesse might
Did reape the pleasure of his right.   60

Long time I lived in the courte,
With lords and ladies of great sorte;
And when I smil'd all men were glad,
But when I frown'd my prince grewe sad.

But yet a gentle minde I bore   65
To helplesse people, that were poore;
I still redrest the orphans crye,
And sav'd their lives condemnd to dye.

I still had ruth on widowes tears,
I succour'd babes of tender yeares;   70
And never look'd for other gaine
But love and thankes for all my paine.

At last my royall king did dye,
And then my dayes of woe grew nighe;
When crook-back Richard got the crowne,   75
King Edwards friends were soon put downe.

I then was punisht for my sin,
That I so long had lived in;
Yea, every one that was his friend,
This tyrant brought to shameful end.   80

Then for my lewd and wanton life,
That made a strumpet of a wife,

I penance did in Lombard-street,
In shamefull manner in a sheet.

Where many thousands did me viewe, 85
Who late in court my credit knewe;
Which made the teares run down my face,
To thinke upon my foul disgrace.

Not thus content, they took from mee
My goodes, my livings, and my fee, 90
And charg'd that none should me relieve,
Nor any succour to me give.

Then unto Mrs. Blague I went,
To whom my jewels I had sent,
In hope therebye to ease my want, 95
When riches fail'd, and love grew scant:

But she denyed to me the same
When in my need for them I came;
To recompence my former love,
Out of her doores shee did me shove. 100

So love did vanish with my state,
Which now my soul repents too late;
Therefore example take by mee,
For friendship parts in povertie.

But yet one friend among the rest, 105
Whom I before had seen distrest,
And sav'd his life, condemn'd to die,
Did give me food to succour me:

For which, by lawe, it was decreed
That he was hanged for that deed; 110
His death did grieve me so much more,
Than had I dyed myself therefore.

Then those to whom I had done good,
Durst not afford mee any food;

Whereby I begged all the day,   115
And still in streets by night I lay.

My gowns beset with pearl and gold,
Were turn'd to simple garments old;
My chains and gems and golden rings,
To filthy rags and loathsome things.   120

Thus was I scorn'd of maid and wife,
For leading such a wicked life;
Both sucking babes and children small,
Did make their pastime at my fall.

I could not get one bit of bread,   125
Whereby my hunger might be fed:
Nor drink, but such as channels yield,
Or stinking ditches in the field.

Thus, weary of my life, at lengthe
I yielded up my vital strength   130
Within a ditch of loathsome scent,
Where carrion dogs did much frequent:

The which now since my dying daye,
Is Shoreditch call'd, as writers saye[3];
Which is a witness of my sinne,   135
For being concubine to a king.

You wanton wives, that fall to lust,
Be you assur'd that God is just;
Whoredome shall not escape his hand,
Nor pride unpunish'd in this land.   140

If God to me such shame did bring,
That yielded only to a king,
How shall they scape that daily run
To practise sin with every one?

---

[3] But it had this name long before; being so called from its being a common *Sewer* (vulgarly *Shore*) or drain. See Stow.

You husbands, match not but for love,   145
Lest some disliking after prove;
Women, be warn'd when you are wives,
What plagues are due to sinful lives:
    Then, maids and wives, in time amend,
    For love and beauty will have end.

XXVII.

Corydon's Doleful Knell.

THIS little simple elegy is given, with some corrections, from two copies, one of which is in *The golden Garland of Princely Delights.*

The burthen of the song, DING DONG, &c. is at present appropriated to burlesque subjects, and therefore may excite only ludicrous ideas in a modern reader; but in the time of our poet, it usually accompanied the most solemn and mournful strains. Of this kind is that fine aërial dirge in Shakspeare's *Tempest:*

"Full fadom five thy father lies,
    Of his bones are corrall made;
Those are pearles that were his eyes;
    Nothing of him, that doth fade,
But doth suffer a sea-change
Into something rich and strange:
Sea-nymphs hourly ring his knell,
Harke now I heare them, Ding dong bell."
              "Burthen, Ding dong."

I make no doubt but the poet intended to conclude the above air in a manner the most solemn, and expressive of melancholy.

My Phillida, adieu love!
For evermore farewel!
Ay me! I've lost my true love,
    And thus I ring her knell,

Ding dong, ding dong, ding dong,   5
    My Phillida is dead!
I'll stick a branch of willow
    At my fair Phillis' head.

For my fair Phillida
    Our bridal bed was made: 10
But 'stead of silkes so gay,
    She in her shroud is laid.
        Ding, &c.

Her corpse shall be attended
    By maides in fair array,
Till the obsequies are ended,   15
    And she is wrapt in clay.
        Ding, &c.

Her herse it shall be carried
    By youths that do excell;
And when that she is buried,
    I thus will ring her knell.   20
        Ding, &c.

A garland shall be framed
    By art and natures skill,
Of sundry-colour'd flowers,
    In token of good-will[1].
        Ding, &c.

And sundry-colour'd ribbands   25
    On it I will bestow;
But chiefly black and yellowe[2]:
    With her to grave shall go.
        Ding, &c.

[1] It is a custom in many parts of England, to carry a flowery garland before the corpse of a woman who dies unmarried.
[2] See above, preface to no. xi. book ii. p. 147.

I'll decke her tomb with flowers,
  The rarest ever seen,
And with my tears, as showers,
  I'll keepe them fresh and green.
    Ding, &c.

Instead of fairest colours,
  Set forth with curious art[3],
Her image shall be painted
  On my distressed heart.
    Ding, &c.

And thereon shall be graven,
  Her epitaph so faire,
"Here lies the loveliest maiden,
  That e'er gave shepheard care."
    Ding, &c.

In sable will I mourne;
  Blacke shall be all my weede:
Ay me! I am forlorne,
  Now Phillida is dead!
    Ding dong, ding dong, ding dong,
      My Phillida is dead!
    I'll stick a branch of willow
      At my fair Phillis' head.

[3] This alludes to the painted effigies of alabaster, anciently erected upon tombs and monuments.

END OF THE SECOND BOOK.

30

35

40

45

RELIQUES

OF

ANCIENT POETRY.

&c.

SERIES THE SECOND.

BOOK III.

I.

𝕿𝖍𝖊 𝕮𝖔𝖒𝖕𝖑𝖆𝖎𝖓𝖙 𝖔𝖋 𝕮𝖔𝖓𝖘𝖈𝖎𝖊𝖓𝖈𝖊.

I SHALL begin this Third Book with an old allegoric Satire: a manner of moralizing, which, if it was not first introduced by the author of *Pierce Plowman's Visions*, was at least chiefly brought into repute by that ancient satirist. It is not so generally known that the kind of verse used in this ballad hath any affinity with the peculiar metre of that writer, for which reason I shall throw together some cursory remarks on that very singular species of versification, the nature of which has been so little understood.

ON THE ALLITERATIVE METRE, WITHOUT RHYME,
IN PIERCE PLOWMAN'S VISIONS.

We learn from Wormius[1], that the ancient Islandic poets used a great variety of measures: he mentions 136 different kinds, without including *rhyme*, or a correspondence of final

---

[1] Literatura Runica. Hafniæ, 1636, 4to.—1651, fol. The Islandic language is of the same origin as our Anglo-Saxon, being both dialects of the ancient Gothic or Teutonic. Vide Hickesii Præfat. in Grammat. Anglo-Saxon. & Moeso-Goth. 4to. 1689.

syllables: yet this was occasionally used, as appears from the *Ode of Egil*, which Wormius hath inserted in his book.

He hath analyzed the structure of one of these kinds of verse, the harmony of which neither depended on the quantity of the syllables, like that of the ancient Greeks and Romans, nor on the rhymes at the end, as in modern poetry, but consisted altogether in alliteration, or a certain artful repetition of the sounds in the middle of the verses. This was adjusted according to certain rules of their prosody, one of which was, that every distich should contain at least three words beginning with the same letter or sound. Two of these correspondent sounds might be placed either in the first or second line of the distich, and one in the other: but all three were not regularly to be crowded into one line. This will be best understood by the following examples[2].

> "*M*eire og *M*inne   " *G*ab *G*inunga
> *M*ogu heimdaller."   " Enn *G*ras huerge."

There were many other little niceties observed by the Islandic poets, who, as they retained their original language and peculiarities longer than the other nations of Gothic race, had time to cultivate their native poetry more, and to carry it to a higher pitch of refinement, than any of the rest.

Their brethren, the Anglo-Saxon poets, occasionally used the same kind of alliteration, and it is common to meet in their writings with similar examples of the foregoing rules. Take an instance or two in modern characters[3]:

> "*Sk*eop tha and *Sk*yrede   "*H*am and *H*eahsetl
> *Sk*yppend ure."   *H*eofena rikes."

I know not, however, that there is any where extant an entire Saxon poem all in this measure. But distichs of this sort perpetually occur in all their poems of any length.

Now, if we examine the versification of *Pierce Plowman's Visions*, we shall find it constructed exactly by these rules; and therefore each line, as printed, is in reality a distich of two verses, and will, I believe, be found distin-

[2] Vide Hickes, Antiq. Literatur. Septentrional. tom. l. p. 217.
[3] Ibid.

guished as such, by some mark or other in all the ancient
MSS. viz.

> "In a *S*omer *S*eason, | when 'hot'[4] was the *S*unne,
> I *Sh*ope me into *Sh*roubs, | as I a *Sh*epe were ;
> In *H*abite as an *H*armet | un*H*oly of werkes,
> Went *W*yde in thys world | *W*onders to heare," &c.

So that the author of this poem will not be found to have
invented any new mode of versification, as some have supposed, but only to have retained that of the Old Saxon and
Gothic poets: which was probably never wholly laid aside,
but occasionally used at different intervals: though the
ravages of time will not suffer us now to produce a regular
series of poems entirely written in it.

There are some readers whom it may gratify to mention,
that these *Visions of Pierce* [*i. e.* Peter] *the Plowman*, are
attributed to Robert Langland, a secular priest, born at
Mortimer's Cleobury in Shropshire, and Fellow of Oriel
College in Oxford, who flourished in the reigns of Edward III.
and Richard II., and published his poem a few years after
1350. It consists of xx Passus or Breaks[5], exhibiting a series
of visions, which he pretends happened to him on Malvern
hills in Worcestershire. The author excels in strong allegoric
painting, and has with great humour, spirit, and fancy, censured most of the vices incident to the several professions of
life; but he particularly inveighs against the corruption of
the clergy, and the absurdities of superstition. Of this work
I have now before me four different editions in black-letter
quarto. Three of them are printed in 1550 by 𝕽obert 𝕮rowley
𝖉welling in 𝕰lye rentes in 𝕳olburne. It is remarkable that
two of these are mentioned in the title-page as both of the
second impression, though they contain evident variations in

---

4 So I would read with Mr. Warton, rather than either 'soft,' as in MS.
or 'set,' as in P. CC.

5 The poem properly contains xxi. parts: the word *Passus,* adopted by
the author, seems only to denote the break or division between two parts,
though by the ignorance of the printer applied to the parts themselves. See
vol. iii. preface to ballad iii. where *Passus* seems to signify *Pause.*

every page[6]. The other is said to be *newlye imprynted after the authors olde copy . . . by Owen Rogers*, Feb. 21, 1561.

As Langland was not the first, so neither was he the last that used this alliterative species of versification. To Rogers's edition of the *Visions* is subjoined a poem, which was probably writ in imitation of them, entitled *Pierce the Plowman's Crede.* It begins thus:

> "*C*ros, and *C*urteis *C*hrist, this beginning spede
> For the *F*aders *F*rendshipe, that *F*ourmed heaven,
> And through the *Sp*ecial *Sp*irit, that *Sp*rong of hem tweyne,
> And al in one godhed endles dwelleth."

The author feigns himself ignorant of his Creed, to be instructed in which he applies to the four religious orders, viz. the gray friers of St. Francis, the black friers of St. Dominic, the Carmelites or white friers, and the Augustines. This affords him occasion to describe, in very lively colours, the sloth, ignorance, and immorality of those reverend drones. At length he meets with Pierce, a poor ploughman, who resolves his doubts, and instructs him in the principles of true religion. The author was evidently a follower of Wiccliff, whom he mentions (with honour) as no longer living[7]. Now that reformer died in 1384. How long after his death this poem was written, does not appear.

In the Cotton Library is a volume of ancient English poems[8], two of which are written in this alliterative metre, and have the division of the lines into distichs distinctly marked by a point, as is usual in old poetical MSS. That which stands first of the two (though perhaps the latest written) is entitled *The Sege of I Erlam* [*i. e.* Jerusalem], being an old fabulous legend composed by some monk, and

---

[6] That which seems the first of the two, is thus distinguished in the title-page, *nowe the seconde tyme imprinted by Roberte Crowlye:* the other thus, *nowe the seconde time imprinted by Robert Crowley.* In the former, the folios are thus erroneously numbered, 39, 39, 41, 63, 43, 42, 45, &c. The booksellers of those days were not ostentatious of multiplying editions.

[7] Signature *T ii.*   [8] Caligula A. ij. fol. 109, 123.

Percy. II.   15

stuffed with marvellous figments concerning the destruction
of the holy city and temple.   It begins thus:

> "In *T*yberius *T*yme . the *T*rewe emperour
> *S*yr *S*esar himself . be*S*ted in Rome
> Whyll *P*ylat was *P*rovoste . under that *P*rynce ryche
> And *J*ewes *J*ustice also . of *J*udeas londe
> *H*erode under empere . as *H*erytage wolde
> *K*yng," &c.

The other is entitled *Chevalere Assigne* [or De Cigne], that is,
"The Knight of the Swan," being an ancient romance, beginning thus:

> "*A*ll-*W*eldynge God . *W*hene it is his *W*ylle
> *W*ele he *W*ereth his *W*erke . *W*ith his owene honde
> For ofte *H*armes were *H*ente . that *H*elpe we ne myzte
> Nere the *H*yznes of *H*ym . that lengeth in *H*evene
> For this," &c.

Among Mr. Garrick's collection of old Plays[9] is a prose
narrative of the adventures of this same Knight of the Swan,
"newly translated out of Frenshe into Englyshe, at thin-
stigacion of the puyssaunt and illustryous prynce, lorde Edward duke of Buckynghame." This lord, it seems, had a
peculiar interest in the book, for in the preface the translator tells us, that this "highe dygne and illustryous prynce
my lorde Edwarde by the grace of god Duke of Buckyngham,
erle of Hereforde, Stafforde, and Northampton, desyrynge
cotydyally to encrease and augment the name and fame of
such as were relucent in vertuous feates and triumphaunt
actes of chyvalry, and to encourage and styre every lusty
and gentell herte by the exemplyficacyon of the same,
havyng a goodli booke of the highe and miraculous histori
of a famous and puyssaunt kynge, named Oryant, sometime
reynynge in the parties of beyonde the sea, havynge to his
wife a noble lady; of whome she conceyved sixe sonnes and
a daughter, and chylded of them at one only time; at whose
byrthe echone of them had a chayne of sylver at their
neckes, the whiche were all tourned by the provydence of
god into whyte swannes, save one, of the whiche this present

hystory is compyled, named Helyas, the knight of the swanne, *of whome linially is dyscended my sayde lorde.* The whiche ententifly to have the sayde hystory more amply and unyversally knowen in thys hys natif countrie, as it is in other, hath of hys hie bountie by some of his faithful and trusti servauntes cohorted mi mayster Wynkin de Worde [10] to put the said vertuous hystori in prynte . . . at whose instigacion and stiring I (Roberte Copland) have me applied, moiening the helpe of god, to reduce and translate it into our maternal and vulgare english tonge after the capacitè and rudenesse of my weke entendement." —— A curious picture of the times! While in Italy literature and the fine arts were ready to burst forth with classical splendour under Leo X., the first peer of this realm was proud to derive his pedigree from a fabulous knight of the swan [1].

To return to the metre of Pierce Plowman: In the folio MS. so often quoted in these volumes, are two poems written in that species of versification. One of these is an ancient allegorical poem entitled *Death and Life* (in two fitts or parts, containing 458 distichs), which, for aught that appears, may have been written as early, if not before, the time of Langland. The first forty lines are broke, as they should be, into distichs, a distinction that is neglected in the remaining part of the transcript, in order, I suppose, to save room. It begins,

> "*Ch*rist *Ch*risten king,
>   that on the *Cr*osse tholed;
> Hadd *P*aines and *P*assyons
>   to defend our soules;
> *G*ive us *G*race on the *G*round
>   the *G*reatlye to serve,
> For that *R*oyall *R*ed blood
>   that *R*ann from thy side."

---

[10] W. de Worde's edit. is in 1512. See Ames, p. 92. Mr. G.'s copy is "¶ Imprinteð at Lonðon by me Ꝯꭑyllïam Coplanð."

[1] He is said in the story-book to be the grandfather of Godfrey of Boulogne, through whom I suppose the duke made out his relation to him. This duke was beheaded May 17, 1521, 13 Henry VIII.

The subject of this piece is a vision, wherein the poet sees a contest for superiority between "our lady Dame LIFE," and the "ugly fiend Dame DEATH;" who, with their several attributes and concomitants, are personified in a fine vein of allegoric painting. Part of the description of Dame LIFE is,

> "Shee was *B*righter of her *B*lee,
>   then was the *B*right sonn:
> Her *R*udd *R*edder then the *R*ose,
>   that on the *R*ise hangeth:
> *M*eekely smiling with her *M*outh,
>   and *M*erry in her lookes;
> Ever *L*aughing for *L*ove,
>   as shee *L*ike would.
> And as shee came by the *B*ankes,
>   the *B*oughes eche one
> They *L*owted to that *L*adye.
>   and *L*ayd forth their branches;
> *B*lossomes and *B*urgens
>   *B*reathed full sweete;
> *F*lowers *F*lourished in the *F*rith,
>   where shee *F*orth stepped;
> And the *G*rasse, that was *G*ray,
>   *G*reened belive."

DEATH is afterwards sketched out with a no less bold and original pencil.

The other poem is that which is quoted in page 25 of this volume, and which was probably the last that was ever written in this kind of metre in its original simplicity, unaccompanied with rhyme. It should have been observed above, in page 25, that in this poem the lines are throughout divided into distichs, thus:

> "*G*rant *G*racious God,
>   *G*rant me this time," &c.

It is entitled *Scottish Fielde*, (in 2 FITTS, 420 distichs,) containing a very circumstantial narrative of the battle of Flodden, fought Sept. 9, 1513: at which the author seems to have been present, from his speaking in the first person plural:

> "Then WE *T*ild downe OUR *T*ents,
>   that *T*old were a thousand."

In the conclusion of the poem he gives this account of himself:

"He was a *G*entleman by *J*esu,
   that this *G*est[2] made:
Which *S*ay but as he *S*ayd[3]
   for *S*ooth and noe other.
At *B*agily that *B*earne
   his *B*iding place had;
And his ancestors of old time
   have yearded[4] theire longe,
Before William *C*onquerour
   this *C*untry did inhabitt.
*J*esus *B*ring 'them'[5] to *B*lisse,
   that *B*rought us forth of *B*ALE,
That hath *H*earkned me *H*eare
   or *H*eard my TALE."

The village of Bagily or Baguleigh is in Cheshire, and had belonged to the ancient family of Legh for two centuries before the battle of Flodden. Indeed, that the author was of that country, appears from other passages in the body of the poem, particularly from the pains he takes to wipe off a stain from the Cheshiremen, who, it seems, ran away in that battle; and from his encomiums on the Stanleys, Earls of Derby, who usually headed that county. He laments the death of James Stanley, bishop of Ely, as what had recently happened when this poem was written; which serves to ascertain its date, for that prelate died March 22, 1514-5.

Thus have we traced the Alliterative Measure so low as the sixteenth century. It is remarkable, that all such poets as used this kind of metre, retained along with it many peculiar Saxon idioms, particularly such as were appropriated to poetry: this deserves the attention of those who are desirous to recover the laws of the ancient Saxon Poesy, usually given up as inexplicable: I am of opinion that they will find what they seek in the metre of Pierce Plowman[6].

[2] Jest. MS.   [3] Probably corrupted for—"Says but as he Saw."
[4] Yearded, *i. e. buried, earthed,* earded. It is common to pronounce "earth," in some parts of England, "yearth," particularly in the North.— Pitscottie, speaking of James III., slain at Bannockburn, says, "Nae man wot whar they *yearded* him."
[5] 'us.' MS. In the second line above, the MS. has 'bidding.'
[6] And in that of Robert of Gloucester. See the next note.

About the beginning of the sixteenth century, this kind of versification began to change its form: the author of *Scottish Field*, we see, concludes his poem with a couplet in rhyme: this was an innovation that did but prepare the way for the general admission of that more modish ornament: till at length the old uncouth verse of the ancient writers would no longer go down without it. Yet when rhyme began to be superadded, all the niceties of alliteration were at first retained along with it; and the song of *Little John Nobody* exhibits this union very clearly. By degrees the correspondence of final sounds engrossing the whole attention of the poet, and fully satisfying the reader, the internal embellishment of alliteration was no longer studied, and thus was this kind of metre at length swallowed up and lost in our common Burlesque Alexandrine, or Anapestic verse[7], now never used but in ballads and pieces of light humour, as in the following song of *Conscience*, and in that well-known doggrel,

"A cobler there was, and he lived in a stall."

But although this kind of measure hath with us been thus degraded, it still retains among the French its ancient

---

[7] Consisting of four anapests, ($\smile \smile -$) in which the accent rests upon every third syllable. This kind of verse, which I also call the Burlesque Alexandrine, (to distinguish it from the other Alexandrines of eleven and fourteen syllables, the parents of our lyric measure: see examples, page 114, 115 &c.) was early applied by Robert of Gloucester to serious subjects. That writer's metre, like this of Langland's, is formed on the Saxon models (each verse of his containing a Saxon distich); only instead of the internal alliterations adopted by Langland, he rather chose final rhymes, as the French poets have done since. Take a specimen.

"The Saxons tho in ther power, tho thii were so rive,
Seve kingdoms made in Engelonde, and sutlie but vive:
The king of Northomberlond, and of Eastangle also,
Of Kent, and of Westsex, and of the March, therto."

Robert of Gloucester wrote in the western dialect, and his language differs exceedingly from that of other contemporary writers, who resided in the metropolis, or in the midland counties. Had the Heptarchy continued, our English language would probably have been as much distinguished for its different dialects as the Greek; or at least as that of the several independent states of Italy.

dignity; their grand heroic verse of twelve syllables [8] is the same genuine offspring of the old alliterative metre of the ancient Gothic and Francic poets, stript like our Anapestic of its alliteration, and ornamented with rhyme; but with this difference, that whereas this kind of verse hath been applied by us only to light and trivial subjects, to which, by its quick and lively measure, it seemed best adapted, our poets have let it remain in a more lax unconfined state [9], as a greater degree of severity and strictness would have been inconsistent with the light and airy subjects to which they have applied it. On the other hand, the French having retained this verse as the vehicle of their epic and tragic flights, in order to give it a stateliness and dignity, were obliged to confine it to more exact laws of scansion; they have therefore limited it to the number of twelve syllables; and by making the cæsura or pause as full and distinct as possible, and by other severe restrictions, have given it all the solemnity of which it was capable. The harmony of both, however, depends so much on the same flow of cadence and disposal of the pause, that they appear plainly to be of the same original; and every French heroic verse evidently

[8] Or of thirteen syllables, in what they call a feminine verse. It is remarkable that the French alone have retained this old Gothic metre for their serious poems; while the English, Spaniards, &c., have adopted the Italic verse of ten syllables, although the Spaniards, as well as we, anciently used a short-lined metre. I believe the success with which Petrarch, and perhaps one or two others, first used the heroic verse of ten syllables in Italian poesy, recommended it to the Spanish writers; as it also did to our Chaucer, who first attempted it in English; and to his successors Lord Surrey, Sir Thomas Wyat, &c.; who afterwards improved it and brought it to perfection. To Lord Surrey we also owe the first introduction of blank verse in his versions of the second and fourth Books of the Æneid, 1557, 4to.

[9] Thus our poets use this verse indifferently with twelve, eleven, and even ten syllables. For though regularly it consists of four anapests ($\smile \smile$ —) or twelve syllables, yet they frequently retrench a syllable from the first or third anapest, and sometimes from both; as in these instances from Prior, and from the following song of *Conscience;*

> Whŏ hăs eēr beĕn ăt Pārĭs, mŭst nēeds knŏw thĕ Grēve,
> Thĕ fātăl rĕtrēat ŏf th' ŭnfŏrtŭnăte brāve.
> Hĕ stēpt tŏ hĭm strāight, ănd dīd hĭm rĕquīre.

consists of the ancient distich of their Francic ancestors:
which, by the way, will account to us why this verse of the
French so naturally resolves itself into two complete hemistichs. And, indeed, by making the cæsura or pause always to rest on the last syllable of a word, and by making a
kind of pause in the sense, the French poets do in effect reduce their hemistichs to two distinct and independent verses:
and some of their old poets have gone so far as to make the
two hemistichs rhyme to each other[10].

After all, the old alliterative and anapestic metre of the
English poets, being chiefly used in a barbarous age and
in a rude unpolished language, abounds with verses defective in length, proportion, and harmony, and therefore cannot
enter into a comparison with the correct versification of the
best modern French writers; but making allowances for
these defects, that sort of metre runs with a cadence so
exactly resembling the French heroic Alexandrine, that I
believe no peculiarities of their versification can be produced which cannot be exactly matched in the alliterative
metre. I shall give, by way of example, a few lines from
the modern French poets, accommodated with parallels from
the ancient poem of *Life and Death*; in these I shall denote
the cæsura or pause by a perpendicular line, and the cadence
by the marks of the Latin quantity.

Lĕ sŭccēs fŭt toŭjoŭrs | ŭn ĕnfănt dĕ l'ăudăce;
All shăll drўe wĭth thĕ dīnts | thăt Ĭ dēal wĭth mў hānds.

L' hŏmmĕ prŭdĕnt vŏit trŏp | l'ĭllūsĭon lĕ sŭit,
Yŏndĕr dāmsĕl ĭs dēath | thăt drĕssĕth hĕr tŏ smīte.

L' ĭntrĕpīdĕ vŏit mĭeux | ĕt lĕ făntŏmĕ fŭit[1],
Whĕn shĕ dōlefŭllў sāw | hŏw shĕ dāng dŏwne hĭr fŏlke.

Mĕme aŭx yeŭx dĕ l'ĭnjŭste | ŭn ĭnjŭste ĕst hŏrrĭblĕ[2].
Thĕn shĕ cāst ŭp ă crўe | tŏ thĕ hīgh kĭng of hēaven.

Dŭ mĕnsŏngĕ toŭjoŭrs | lĕ vrăi dĕmĕurĕ măitrĕ,
Thŏu shălt bĭttĕrlўe bўe | ŏr ēlse thĕ bōokĕ făilĕth.

Poŭr părŏitre hŏnnĕte hŏmme | ĕn ŭn mŏt, ĭl făut l' ētre[3].
Thŭs Ĭ fāred thrŏughe ă frўthe | whĕre thĕ flōwĕrs wĕre mănўe.

[10] See instances in *L'Hist. de la Poésie Françoise* par Massieu, &c.   In the
same book are also specimens of alliterative French verses.

[1] Catalina, A. 3.   [2] Boileau Sat.   [3] Boil. Sat. 11.

To conclude; the metre of *Pierce Plowman's Visions* has no kind of affinity with what is commonly called blank verse; yet has it a sort of harmony of its own, proceeding not so much from its alliteration, as from the artful disposal of its cadence, and the contrivance of its pause; so that when the ear is a little accustomed to it it is by no means unpleasing; but claims all the merit of the French heroic numbers, only far less polished; being sweetened, instead of their final rhymes, with the internal recurrence of similar sounds.

This Essay will receive illustration from another specimen in Warton's *History of English Poetry*, vol. i. page 309, being the fragment of a MS. poem on the subject of Alexander the Great, in the Bodleian Library, which he supposes to be the same with number 44, in the Ashmol. MS. containing 27 passus, and beginning thus:

> Whener folk fastid [feasted, *qu.*] and fed,
>> fayne wolde thei her [i. e. *hear*]
> Some farand thing, &c.

It is well observed by Mr. Tyrwhitt, on Chaucer's sneer at this old alliterative metre, (vol. iii. p. 305,) viz.

> ——I am a Sotherne [i. e. *Southern*] man,
> I cannot geste, rom, ram, raf, by my letter,

that the fondness for this species of versification, &c. was retained longest in the Northern provinces; and that the author of *Pierce Plowman's Visions* is, in the best MSS., called William, without any surname. See vol. iv. p. 74.

ADDITIONS TO THE ESSAY ON THE ALLITERATIVE METRE.

Since the foregoing Essay was first printed, the Editor hath met with some additional examples of the old alliterative metre.

The first is in MS.[4], which begins thus:

> "*C*rist *C*rowned *K*yng, that on *C*ros didest[5],
> And art *C*omfort of all *C*are, thow[6] kind go out of *C*ours,
> With thi *H*alwes in *H*even *H*eried mote thu be,

---

[4] In a small 4to. MS. containing 38 leaves, in private hands.
[5] Didst dye.   [6] Though.

> And thy *W*orshipful *W*erkes *W*orshiped evre,
> That suche *S*ondry *S*ignes *S*hewest unto man,
> In *D*remyng, in *D*recchyng[7], and in *D*erke swevenes."

The author, from this proemium, takes occasion to give an account of a dream that happened to himself; which he introduces with the following circumstances:

> "*O*nes y me *O*rdayned, as y have *O*fte doon,
> With *F*rendes, and *F*elawes, *F*rendemen, and other;
> And *C*aught me in a *C*ompany on *C*orpus *C*hristi even,
> *S*ix, other[8] *S*even myle, oute of *S*uthampton,
> To take *M*elodye, and *M*irthes, among my *M*akes;
> With *R*edyng of *R*O*M*A*U*N*C*E*S*, and *R*evelyng among,
> The *D*ym of the *D*erknesse *D*rewe me into the west;
> And be*G*on for to spryng in the *G*rey day.
> Than *L*ift y up my *L*yddes, and *L*oked in the sky,
> And *K*newe by the *K*ende *C*ours, hit clered in the est:
> *B*lyve y *B*usked me down, and to *B*ed went,
> For to *C*omforte my *K*ynde, and *C*acche a slepe."

He then describes his dream:

> "*M*ethought that y *H*oved on *H*igh on an *H*ill.
> And loked *D*oun on a *D*ale *D*epest of othre;
> Ther y *S*awe in my *S*ighte a *S*elcouthe peple;
> The *M*ultitude was so *M*oche, it *M*ighte not be nombred.
> *M*ethoughte y herd a *C*rowned *K*yng, of his *C*omunes axe
> A *S*oleyne[9] *S*ubsidie, to *S*usteyne his werres.
>   *   *   *   *   *
> With that a *C*lerk *K*neled adowne and *C*arped these wordes,
> *L*iege *L*ord, yif it you *L*ike to *L*isten a while,
> *S*om *S*awes of *S*alomon y shall you shewe *S*one."

The writer then gives a solemn lecture to kings on the art of governing. From the demand of subsidies 'to susteyne his werres,' I am inclined to believe this poem was composed in the reign of King Henry V., as the MS. appears from a subsequent entry to have been written before the 9th of Henry VI. The whole poem contains but 146 lines

The Alliterative Metre was no less popular among the old Scottish poets, than with their brethren on this side the Tweed. In Maitland's Collection of ancient Scottish Poems, MS. in the Pepysian library, is a very long poem in this species of versification, thus inscribed:

---

[7] **Being overpowered.**   [8] *i. e.* either, or.   [9] **Solemn.**

HEIR begins the Tretis of the Twa Marriit Wemen, and the Wedo compylit
be Maister William Dunbar[10].

"Upon the *M*idsummer evven *M*irriest of nichtis
I *M*uvit furth alane quhen as *M*idnight was past
Besyd ane *G*udlie *G*rene *G*arth[1], full of *G*ay flouris
*H*egeit[2] of ane *H*uge *H*icht with *H*awthorne treeis
Quairon ane *B*ird on ane *B*ransche so *B*irst out hir notis
That nevir ane *B*lythfuller *B*ird was on the *B*euche[3] hard," &c.

The author pretends to overhear three gossips sitting in
an arbour, and revealing all their secret methods of alluring
and governing the other sex: it is a severe and humorous
satire on bad women, and nothing inferior to Chaucer's Pro-
logue to his *Wife of Bath's* Tale. As Dunbar lived till about
the middle of the sixteenth century, this poem was probably
composed after *Scottish Field*, (described above in p. 228,)
which is the latest specimen I have met with written in England. This poem contains about 500 lines.

But the current use of the Alliterative Metre in Scotland,
appears more particularly from those popular vulgar pro-
phecies, which are still printed for the use of the lower
people in Scotland, under the names of Thomas the Rymer,
Marvellous Merling, &c. This collection seems to have been
put together after the accession of James I. to the crown of
England, and most of the pieces in it are in the metre of
Pierce Plowman's Visions. The first of them begins thus:

"Merling sayes in his book, who will *R*ead *R*ight,
Although his *S*ayings be uncouth, they *S*hall be true found.
In the seventh chapter, read *W*hoso *W*ill,
One thousand and more after Christ's birth," &c.

And the *Prophesie of Beid:*

"Betwixt the chief of *S*ummer and the *S*ad winter;
Before the *H*eat of summer *H*appen shall a war
That *E*urop's lands *E*arnestly shall be wrought
And *E*arnest *E*nvy shall last but a while," &c.

[10] Since the above was written, this poem hath been printed in "Ancient
Scottish Poems, &c., from the MS. Collection of Sir R. Maitland, of Leth-
ington, knight, of London, 1786," 2 vols. 12mo. The two first lines are here
corrected by that edition.
[1] Garden.　　　[2] Hedged.　　　[3] Bough.

So again the *Prophesie of Berlington:*

> "When the *R*uby is *R*aised, *R*est is there none,
> But much *R*ancour shall *R*ise in *R*iver and plain,
> Much *S*orrow is *S*een through a *S*uth-hound
> That beares *H*ornes in his *H*ead like a wyld *H*art," &c.

In like metre is the *Prophesie of Waldhave:*

> "Upon *L*owdon *L*aw alone as I *L*ay,
> *L*ooking to the *L*ennox, as me *L*ief thought,
> The first *M*orning of *M*ay, *M*edicine to seek
> For *M*alice and *M*elody that *M*oved me sore," &c.

And lastly, that entitled the *Prophesie of Gildas:*

> "When holy kirk is *W*racked and *W*ill has no *W*it
> And *P*astors are *P*luckt, and *P*il'd without *P*ity
> When *I*dolatry *I*s *I*n ENS and RE
> And spiritual pastours are vexed away," &c.

It will be observed in the foregoing specimens, that the alliteration is extremely neglected, except in the third and fourth instances, although all the rest are written in imitation of the cadence used in this kind of metre. It may perhaps appear from an attentive perusal, that the poems ascribed to Berlington and Waldhave are more ancient than the others: indeed, the first and fifth appear evidently to have been new modelled, if not entirely composed, about the beginning of the last century, and are probably the latest attempts ever made in this species of verse.

In this and the foregoing Essay are mentioned all the specimens I have met with of the Alliterative Metre without rhyme; but instances occur sometimes in old manuscripts, of poems written both with final rhymes and the internal cadence and alliterations of the metre of Pierce Plowman.

END OF THE ESSAY.

THE following Song, entitled *The Complaint of Conscience*, is printed from the Editor's folio manuscript. Some corruptions in the old copy are here corrected; but with notice to the reader wherever it was judged necessary, by inclosing the corrections between inverted 'commas.'

As I walked of late by 'an' wood side,
To God for to meditate was my entent;
Where under a hawthorne I suddenlye spyed
A silly poore creature ragged and rent,
With bloody teares his face was besprent,   5
  His fleshe and his color consumed away,
   And his garments they were all mire, mucke, and clay.

This made me muse, and much 'to' desire
To know what kind of man hee shold bee;
I stept to him straight, and did him require   10
His name and his secretts to shew unto mee.
His head he cast up, and wooful was hee,
  My name, quoth he, is the cause of my care,
   And makes me scorned, and left here so bare.

Then straightway he turnd him, and prayd 'me' sit downe,
And I will, saithe he, declare my whole greefe;   16
My name is called CONSCIENCE:—wheratt he did frowne,
He pined to repeate it, and grinded his teethe,
'Thoughe now, silly wretche, I'm denyed all releef,'
  'Yet' while I was young, and tender of yeeres,   20
   I was entertained with kinges, and with peeres.

There was none in the court that lived in such fame,
For with the kings councell 'I' sate in commission;
Dukes, earles, and barrons esteem'd of my name;
And how that I liv'd there needs no repetition: 25

Ver. 1, one. MS.   V. 15, him. MS.   V. 19, not in MS.   V. 23, he sate. MS.

I was ever holden in honest condition,
　For howsoever the lawes went in Westminster-hall,
　When sentence was given, for me they wold call.

No incomes at all the landlords wold take,
But one pore peny, that was their fine;　　　　　　　30
And that they acknowledged to be for my sake.
The poore wold doe nothing without councell mine:
I ruled the world with the right line:
　For nothing was passed betweene foe and friend,
　But Conscience was called to bee at 'the' end.　　35

Noe bargaines, nor merchandize merchants wold make
But I was called a wittenesse therto:
No use for noe money, nor forfett wold take,
But I wold controule them, if that they did soe·:
'And' that makes me live now in great woe,　　　　40
　For then came in Pride, Sathan's disciple,
　That is now entertained with all kind of people.

He brought with him three, whose names, 'thus they call,'
That is Covetousnes, Lecherye, Usury, beside:
They never prevail'd, till they had wrought my downe-fall:
Soe Pride was entertained, but Conscience decried,　　46
And 'now ever since' abroad have I tryed
　To have had entertainment with some one or other;
　But I am rejected, and scorned of my brother.

Then went I to the Court the gallants to winn,　　50
But the porter kept me out of the gate:
To Bartlemew Spittle to pray for my sinne,
They bade me goe packe, it was fitt for my state;
Goe, goe, threed-bare Conscience, and seeke thee a mate.
　Good Lord, long preserve my king, prince, and queene,
　With whom evermore I esteemed have been.　　　56

V. 35, an end. MS.　　V. 43, they be these. MS.　　V. 46, was derided.
MS.　　V. 53, packe me. MS.

Then went I to London, where once I did 'dwell:'
But they bade away with me, when they knew my name;
For he will undoe us to bye and to sell!
They bade me goe pack me, and hye me for shame: 60
They lought at my raggs, and there had good game;
   This is old threed-bare Conscience, that dwelt with saint
      Peter:
   But they wold not admitt me to be a chimney-sweeper.

Not one wold receive me, the Lord 'he' doth know:
I having but one poor pennye in my purse,   65
On an awle and some patches I did it bestow;
'For' I thought better cobble shooes than doe worse.
Straight then all the coblers began for to curse,
   And by statute wold prove me a rogue, and forlorne,
   And whipp me out of towne to 'seeke' where I was borne.

Then did I remember, and call to my minde,   71
The Court of Conscience where once I did sit:
Not doubting but there I some favor shold find,
For my name and the place agreed soe fit;
But there of my purpose I fayled a whit,   75
   For 'thoughe' the judge us'd my name in everye 'com-
      mission,
   The lawyers with their quillets wold get 'my' dismission.

Then Westminster-hall was noe place for me:
Good lord! how the lawyers began to assemble,
And fearfull they were, lest there I shold bee!   80
The silly poore clarkes began for to tremble;
I showed them my cause, and did not dissemble;
   Soe they gave me some money my charges to beare,
   But swore me on a booke I must never come there.

Next the Merchants said, Counterfeite, get thee away,   85
Dost thou remember how wee thee fond?

V. 57, wonne. MS.   V. 70, see. MS.   V. 76, condicion. MS.   V. 77, get a. MS.

We banisht thee the country beyond the salt sea,
And sett thee on shore in the New-found land;
And there thou and wee most friendly shook hand,
    And we were right glad when thou didst refuse us;   90
    For when we wold reape profitt here thou woldst accuse us.

Then had I noe way, but for to goe on
To Gentlemens houses of an ancyent name;
Declaring my greeffes, and there I made moane,
'Telling' how their forefathers held me in fame: 95
And at letting their farmes 'how always I came.'
    They sayd, Fye upon thee! we may thee curse:
    'Theire' leases continue, and we fare the worse.

And then I was forced a begging to goe
To husbandmens houses, who greeved right sore,   100
And sware that their landlords had plagued them so,
That they were not able to keepe open doore,
Nor nothing had left to give to the poore:
    Therefore to this wood I doe me repayre,
    Where hepps and hawes, that is my best fare.   105

Yet within this same desert some comfort I have
Of Mercy, of Pittye, and of Almes-deeds;
Who have vowed to company me to my grave.
Wee are 'all' put to silence, and live upon weeds,
'And hence such cold house-keeping proceeds;'   110
    Our banishment is its utter decay,
    The which the riche glutton will answer one day.

Why then, I said to him, me-thinks it were best
To goe to the Clergie; for dailye they preach
Eche man to love you above all the rest;   115
Of Mercye, and Pittie, and Almes-'deeds,' they teach.

V. 95, And how. MS.   V. 101, so sore. MS.   V. 109, ill. MS.
V. 110, not in MS.

O, said he, noe matter of a pin what they preach,
  For their wives and their children soe hange them upon,
  That whosoever gives almes they will⁶ give none.

Then laid he him down, and turned him away,   120
And prayd me to goe, and leave him to rest.
I told him, I haplie might yet see the day
For him and his fellowes to live with the best.
First, said he, banish Pride, then all England were blest:
  For then those wold love us, that now sell their land,   125
  And then good 'house-keeping wold revive' out of hand.

V. 119, almes-deeds. MS.   V. 126, houses every where wold be kept. MS.
       ⁶ We ought in justice and truth to read 'can.'

II.

Plain Truth, and Blind Ignorance.

THIS excellent old ballad is preserved in the little ancient
Miscellany, entitled, *The Garland of Goodwill.* Ignorance is
here made to speak in the broad Somersetshire dialect. The
scene we may suppose to be Glastonbury Abbey.

TRUTH.

GOD speed you, ancient father,
  And give you a good daye;
What is the cause, I praye you,
  So sadly here you staye?
And that you keep such gazing   5
  On this decayed place,
The which, for superstition,
  Good princes down did raze?

IGNORANCE.

Chill tell thee, by my vazen¹,
  That zometimes che have knowne   10

¹ *i. e.* faithen: as in the midland counties they say housen, closen, for
houses, closes. A.

A vair and goodly abbey
  Stand here of bricke and stone;
And many a holy vrier,
  As ich may say to thee,
Within these goodly cloysters   15
  Che did full often zee.

TRUTH.

Then I must tell thee, father,
  In truthe and veritiè,
A sorte of greater hypocrites
  Thou couldst not likely see;   20
Deceiving of the simple
  With false and feigned lies:
But such an order truly
  Christ never did devise.

IGNORANCE.

Ah! ah! che zmell thee now, man;   25
  Che know well what thou art;
A vellow of mean learning,
  Thee was not worth a vart:
Vor when we had the old lawe,
  A merry world was then;   30
And every thing was plenty
  Among all zorts of men.

TRUTH.

Thou givest me an answer,
  As did the Jewes sometimes
Unto the prophet Jeremye,   35
  When he accus'd their crimes:
'Twas merry, sayd the people,
  And joyfull in our rea'me,
When we did offer spice-cakes
  Unto the queen of heav'n.   40

IGNORANCE.

Chill tell thee what, good vellowe,
  Before the vriers went hence,

A bushell of the best wheate
  Was zold vor vourteen pence;
And vorty egges a penny,   45
  That were both good and newe;
And this che zay my zelf have zeene,
  And yet ich am no Jewe.

TRUTH.

Within the sacred bible
  We find it written plain,   50
The latter days should troublesome
  And dangerous be, certaine;
That we should be self-lovers,
  And charity wax colde;
Then 'tis not true religion   55
  That makes thee grief to holde.

IGNORANCE.

Chill tell thee my opinion plaine,
  And choul'd that well ye knewe,
Ich care not for the bible booke;
  Tis too big to be true.   60
Our blessed ladyes psalter
  Zhall for my money goe;
Zuch pretty prayers, as there bee[2],
  The bible cannot zhowe.

TRUTH.

Nowe hast thou spoken trulye,   65
  For in that book indeede
No mention of our lady,
  Or Romish saint we read:
For by the blessed Spirit
  That book indited was,   70
And not by simple persons,
  As was the foolish masse.

[2] Probably alluding to the illuminated Psalters, Missals, &c.

IGNORANCE.

Cham zure they were not voolishe
   That made the masse, che trowe;
Why, man, 'tis all in Latine,   75
   And vooles no Latine knowe.
Were not our fathers wise men,
   And they did like it well;
Who very much rejoyced
   To heare the zacring bell?   80

TRUTH.

But many kinges and prophets,
   As I may say to thee,
Have wisht the light that you have,
   And could it never see:
For what art thou the better   85
   A Latin song to heare,
And understandest nothing,
   That they sing in the quiere?

IGNORANCE.

O hold thy peace, che pray thee,
   The noise was passing trim   90
To heare the vriers zinging,
   As we did enter in:
And then to zee the rood-loft
   Zo bravely zet with saints;—
But now to zee them wandring   95
   My heart with zorrow vaints.

TRUTH.

The Lord did give commandment,
   No image thou shouldst make,
Nor that unto idolatry
   You should your self betake: 100
The golden calf of Israel
   Moses did therefore spoile;

And Baal's priests and temple
  Were brought to utter foile.

IGNORANCE.

But our lady of Walsinghame   105
  Was a pure and holy zaint,
And many men in pilgrimage
  Did shew to her complaint.
Yea with zweet Thomas Becket,
  And many other moe;   110
The holy maid of Kent[3] likewise
  Did many wonders zhowe.

TRUTH.

Such saints are well agreeing
  To your profession sure;
And to the men that made them   115
  So precious and so pure;
The one for being a traytoure,
  Met an untimely death;
The other eke for treason
  Did end her hateful breath.   120

IGNORANCE.

Yea, yea, it is no matter,
  Dispraise them how you wille:
But zure they did much goodnesse;
  Would they were with us stille!
We had our holy water,   125
  And holy bread likewise,
And many holy reliques
  We zaw before our eyes.

TRUTH.

And all this while they fed you
  With vaine and empty showe,   130

[3] By name Eliz. Barton, executed April 21, 1534. Stow, p. 570.

Which never Christ commanded,
  As learned doctors knowe:
Search then the holy scriptures,
  And thou shalt plainly see
That headlong to damnation   135
  They alway trained thee.

IGNORANCE.

If it be true, good vellowe,
  As thou dost zay to mee,
Unto my heavenly Fader
  Alone then will I flee: 140
Believing in the Gospel,
  And passion of his Zon,
And with the zubtil papistes
  Ich have for ever done.

III.

The Wandering Jew.

THE story of the Wandering Jew is of considerable antiquity: it had obtained full credit in this part of the world
before the year 1228, as we learn from Matthew Paris. For
in that year, it seems, there came an Armenian archbishop
into England, to visit the shrines and reliques preserved in
our churches, who, being entertained at the monastery of
St. Alban's, was asked several questions relating to his
country, &c. Among the rest, a monk, who sat near him,
inquired, "If he had ever seen or heard of the famous person
named Joseph, that was so much talked of; who was present
at our Lord's crucifixion and conversed with him, and who
was still alive in confirmation of the Christian faith." The
archbishop answered, That the fact was true. And afterwards one of his train, who was well known to a servant of
the abbot's, interpreting his master's words, told them in
French, "That his lord knew the person they spoke of very

well: that he had dined at his table but a little while before he left the East: that he had been Pontius Pilate's porter, by name Cartaphilus; who, when they were dragging Jesus out of the door of the Judgment-hall, struck him with his fist on the back, saying, "Go faster, Jesus, go faster, why dost thou linger?" Upon which Jesus looked at him with a frown, and said, "I indeed am going, but thou shalt tarry till I come." Soon after he was converted, and baptized by the name of Joseph. He lives for ever, but at the end of every hundred years falls into an incurable illness, and at length into a fit or ecstasy, out of which, when he recovers, he returns to the same state of youth he was in when Jesus suffered, being then about thirty years of age. He remembers all the circumstances of the death and resurrection of Christ, the saints that arose with him, the composing of the Apostles' creed, their preaching and dispersion; and is himself a very grave and holy person." This is the substance of Matthew Paris's account, who was himself a monk of St. Alban's, and was living at the time when this Armenian archbishop made the above relation.

Since his time, several impostors have appeared at intervals under the name and character of the *Wandering Jew;* whose several histories may be seen in Calmet's *Dictionary of the Bible.* See also the *Turkish Spy,* vol. ii. book iii. let. 1. The story that is copied in the following ballad is of one who appeared at Hamburgh in 1547, and pretended he had been a Jewish shoemaker at the time of Christ's crucifixion. The ballad, however, seems to be of later date. It is preserved in black-letter in the Pepys collection.

WHEN as in faire Jerusalem
　Our Saviour Christ did live,
And for the sins of all the worlde
　His own deare life did give;
The wicked Jewes with scoffes and scornes
　Did dailye him molest,

　　　　5

That never till he left his life,
  Our Saviour could not rest.

When they had crown'd his head with thornes,
  And scourg'd him to disgrace,   10
In scornfull sort they led him forthe
  Unto his dying place,
Where thousand thousands in the streete
  Beheld him passe along,
Yet not one gentle heart was there,   15
  That pityed this his wrong.

Both old and young reviled him,
  As in the streete he wente,
And nought he found but churlish tauntes,
  By every ones consente: 20
His owne deare crosse he bore himselfe,
  A burthen far too great,
Which made him in the streete to fainte,
  With blood and water sweat.

Being weary thus, he sought for rest,   25
  To ease his burthened soule,
Upon a stone; the which a wretch
  Did churlishly controule;
And sayd, Awaye, thou king of Jewes,
  Thou shalt not rest thee here;   30
Pass on; thy execution place
  Thou seest nowe draweth neare.

And thereupon he thrust him thence;
  At which our Saviour sayd,
I sure will rest, but thou shalt walke,   35
  And have no journey stayed.
With that this cursed shoemaker,
  For offering Christ this wrong,
Left wife and children, house and all,
  And went from thence along.   40

Where after he had seene the bloude
  Of Jesus Christ thus shed,
And to the crosse his bodye nail'd,
  Awaye with speed he fled
Without returning backe againe   45
  Unto his dwelling place,
And wandred up and downe the worlde,
  A runnagate most base.

No resting could he finde at all,
  No ease, nor hearts content;   50
No house, nor home, nor biding place:
  But wandring forth he went
From towne to towne in foreigne landes,
  With grieved conscience still,
Repenting for the heinous guilt   55
  Of his fore-passed ill.

Thus after some fewe ages past
  In wandring up and downe;
He much again desired to see
  Jerusalems renowne,   60
But finding it all quite destroyd
  He wandred thence with woe,
Our Saviours wordes, which he had spoke,
  To verifie and showe.

"I'll rest, sayd hee, but thou shalt walke,"   65
  So doth this wandring Jew
From place to place, but cannot rest
  For seeing countries newe;
Declaring still the power of him,
  Whereas he comes or goes,   70
And of all things done in the east,
  Since Christ his death, he showes.

The world he hath still compast round
  And seene those nations strange,

That hearing of the name of Christ,   75
    Their idol gods doe change:
To whom he hath told wondrous thinges
    Of time forepast, and gone,
And to the princes of the worlde
    Declares his cause of moane: 80

Desiring still to be dissolv'd,
    And yeild his mortal breath;
But, if the Lord hath thus decreed,
    He shall not yet see death.
For neither lookes he old nor young,   85
    But as he did those times,
When Christ did suffer on the crosse
    For mortall sinners crimes.

He hath past throughe many a foreigne place,
    Arabia, Egypt, Africa,   90
Grecia, Syria, and great Thrace,
    And throughout all Hungaria.
Where Paul and Peter preached Christ,
    Those blest apostles deare;
There he hath told our Saviours wordes,   95
    In countries far and neare

And lately in Bohemia,
    With many a German towne;
And now in Flanders, as tis thought,
    He wandreth up and downe: 100
Where learned men with him conferre
    Of those his lingering dayes,
And wonder much to heare him tell
    His journeyes, and his wayes.

If people give this Jew an almes,   105
    The most that he will take
Is not above a groat a time:
    Which he, for Jesus' sake,

Will kindlye give unto the poore,
   And thereof make no spare,
Affirming still that Jesus Christ
   Of him hath dailye care.   110

He ne'er was seene to laugh nor smile,
   But weepe and make great moane;
Lamenting still his miseries,   115
   And dayes forepast and gone:
If he heare any one blaspheme,
   Or take God's name in vaine,
He telles them that they crucifie
   Their Saviour Christe againe.   120

If you had seene his death, saith he,
   As these mine eyes have done,
Ten thousand thousand times would yee
   His torments think upon:
And suffer for his sake all paine   125
   Of torments, and all woes.
These are his wordes and eke his life
   Whereas he comes or goes.

IV.

The Lye,

BY SIR WALTER RALEIGH,

Is found in a very scarce miscellany, entitled "Davison's Poems, or a poeticall Rapsodie, divided into sixe books. . . . The 4th impression newly corrected and augmented, and put into a forme more pleasing to the reader. Lond. 1621, 12mo." This poem is reported to have been written by its celebrated author the night before his execution, Oct. 29, 1618. But this must be a mistake, for there were at least two editions of Davison's Poems before that time, one in

1608[1], the other in 1611[2]. So that unless this poem was an
after-insertion in the fourth edit. it must have been written
long before the death of Sir Walter: perhaps it was composed soon after his condemnation in 1603. — See Oldys's
Life of Sir Walter Raleigh, p. 173, fol.

————

Goe, soule, the bodies guest,
  Upon a thankelesse arrant;
Feare not to touche the best,
  The truth shall be thy warrant:
    Goe, since I needs must dye,   5
    And give the world the lye.

Goe tell the court, it glowes
  And shines like rotten wood;
Goe tell the church it showes
  What's good, and doth no good: 10
    If church and court reply,
    Then give them both the lye.

Tell potentates they live,
  Acting by others actions;
Not lov'd unlesse they give,   15
  Not strong but by their factions;
    If potentates reply,
    Give potentates the lye.

Tell men of high condition,
  That rule affairs of state,   20
Their purpose is ambition,
  Their practise onely hate;
    And if they once reply,
    Then give them all the lye.

[1] Catalogue of T. Rawlinson, 1727.
[2] Catalogue of Sion Coll. library. This is either lost or mislaid.

Tell them that brave it most,   25
   They beg for more by spending,
Who in their greatest cost
   Seek nothing but commending;
     And if they make reply,
     Spare not to give the lye.   30

Tell zeale, it lacks devotion;
   Tell love, it is but lust;
Tell time, it is but motion;
   Tell flesh, it is but dust;
     And wish them not reply,   35
     For thou must give the lye.

Tell age, it daily wasteth;
   Tell honour, how it alters;
Tell beauty, how she blasteth;
   Tell favour, how she falters;   40
     And as they shall reply,
     Give each of them the lye.

Tell wit, how much it wrangles
   In tickle points of nicenesse:
Tell wisedome, she entangles   45
   Herselfe in over-wisenesse;
     And if they do reply,
     Straight give them both the lye.

Tell physicke of her boldnesse;
   Tell skill, it is pretension;   50
Tell charity of coldness;
   Tell law, it is contention;
     And as they yield reply,
     So give them still the lye.

Tell fortune of her blindnesse;   55
   Tell nature of decay;

Tell friendship of unkindnesse;
  Tell justice of delay:
    And if they dare reply,
    Then give them all the lye.   60

Tell arts, they have no soundnesse,
  But vary by esteeming;
Tell schooles, they want profoundnesse,
  And stand too much on seeming:
    If arts and schooles reply,   65
    Give arts and schooles the lye.

Tell faith, it's fled the citie;
  Tell how the countrey erreth;
Tell, manhood shakes off pitie;
  Tell, vertue least preferreth: 70
    And, if they doe reply,
    Spare not to give the lye.

So, when thou hast, as I
  Commanded thee, done blabbing,
Although to give the lye   75
  Deserves no less than stabbing,
    Yet stab at thee who will,
    No stab the soule can kill.

V.

Verses by King James I.

In the first edition of this book were inserted, by way of
specimen of His Majesty's poetic talents, some Punning
Verses made on the disputations at Stirling: but it having
been suggested to the Editor, that the king only gave the
quibbling commendations in prose, and that some obsequious
court-rhymer put them into metre[1], it was thought proper

---

[1] See a folio entitled *The Muses Welcome to King James*.

to exchange them for two sonnets of King James's own composition. James was a great versifier, and therefore out of the multitude of his poems, we have here selected two, which (to show our impartiality) are written in his best and his worst manner. The first would not dishonour any writer of that time; the second is a most complete example of the Bathos.

A SONNET ADDRESSED BY KING JAMES TO HIS SON PRINCE HENRY.

FROM King James's Works in folio: where is also printed another, called His Majesty's own Sonnet: it would perhaps be too cruel to infer from thence that this was NOT His Majesty's own Sonnet.

> GOD gives not kings the stile of Gods in vaine,
>   For on his throne his scepter do they swey:
>   And as their subjects ought them to obey,
> So kings should feare and serve their God againe.
>
> If then ye would enjoy a happie reigne,   5
>   Observe the statutes of our heavenly King;
>   And from his law make all your laws to spring;
> Since his lieutenant here ye should remaine.
>
> Rewarde the just, be stedfast, true and plaine;
>   Represse the proud, maintayning aye the right;   10
>   Walke always so, as ever in HIS sight,
> Who guardes the godly, plaguing the prophane.
>   And so ye shall in princely vertues shine,
>   Resembling right your mightie King divine.

A SONNET OCCASIONED BY THE BAD WEATHER WHICH HINDERED THE SPORTS AT NEW-MARKET IN JANUARY, 1616.

THIS is printed from Drummond of Hawthornden's Works, folio: where also may be seen some verses of Lord Stirling's

upon this Sonnet, which concludes with the finest anti-climax
I remember to have seen.

How cruelly these catives do conspire?
  What loathsome love breeds such a baleful band
  Betwixt the cankred king of Creta land[2],
That melancholy old and angry sire,

And him, who wont to quench debate and ire   5
  Among the Romans, when his ports were clos'd[3]?
  But now his double face is still dispos'd,
With Saturn's help, to freeze us at the fire.

The earth ore-covered with a sheet of snow,
Refuses food to fowl, to bird, and beast: 10
  The chilling cold lets every thing to grow,
And surfeits cattle with a starving feast.
  Curs'd be that love and mought[4] continue short,
  Which kills all creatures, and doth spoil our sport.

    [2] Saturn.   [3] Janus.   [4] *i. e.* may it.

VI.

𝕂ing 𝕁ohn and the 𝔸bbot of ℂanterbury.

THE common popular ballad of *King John and the Abbot*
seems to have been abridged and modernised about the time
of James I. from one much older, entitled *King John and the
Bishop of Canterbury*. The Editor's folio MS. contains a
copy of this last, but in too corrupt a state to be reprinted;
it however afforded many lines worth reviving, which will be
found inserted in the ensuing stanzas.

    The archness of the following questions and answers hath
been much admired by our old ballad-makers; for besides
the two copies above mentioned, there is extant another
ballad on the same subject, (but of no great antiquity or

merit.) entitled, *King Olfrey and the Abbot*[1]. Lastly, about
the time of the civil wars, when the cry ran against the bi-
shops, some Puritan worked up the same story into a very
doleful ditty, to a solemn tune, concerning "King Henry and
a Bishop;" with this stinging moral:

> "Unlearned men hard matters out can find,
> When learned bishops princes eyes do blind."

The following is chiefly printed from an ancient black-
letter copy, to "The tune of Derry down."

An ancient story Ile tell you anon
Of a notable prince, that was called king John;
And he ruled England with maine and with might,
For he did great wrong, and maintein'd little right.

And Ile tell you a story, a story so merrye,   5
Concerning the Abbot of Canterbùrye;
How for his house-keeping, and high renowne,
They rode poste for him to fair London towne.

An hundred men, the king did heare say,
The abbot kept in his house every day;   10
And fifty golde chaynes, without any doubt,
In velvet coates waited the abbot about.

How now, father abbot, I heare it of thee,
Thou keepest a farre better house than mee,
And for thy house-keeping and high renowne,   15
I feare thou work'st treason against my crown.

My liege, quo' the abbot, I would it were knowne,
I never spend nothing, but what is my owne;
And I trust, your grace will doe me no deere,
For spending of my owne true-gotten geere.   20

----

[1] See the collection of Historical Ballads, 3 vols., 1727. Mr. Wise supposes Olfrey to be a corruption of Alfred, in his pamphlet concerning the
WHITE HORSE in Berkshire, p. 15.

Yes, yes, father abbot, thy fault it is highe,
And now for the same thou needest must dye;
For except thou canst answer me questions three,
Thy head shall be smitten from thy bodìe.

And first, quo' the king, when I'm in this stead,   25
With my crowne of golde so faire on my head,
Among all my liege-men so noble of birthe,
Thou must tell me to one penny what I am worthe

Secondlye, tell me, without any doubt,
How soone I may ride the whole world about.   30
And at the third question thou must not shrink,
But tell me here truly what I do think.

O, these are hard questions for my shallow witt,
Nor I cannot answer your grace as yet:
But if you will give me but three weekes space,   35
Ile do my endeavour to answer your grace.

Now three weeks space to thee will I give,
And this is the longest time thou hast to live;
For if thou dost not answer my questions three,
Thy lands and thy livings are forfeit to mee.   40

Away rode the abbot all sad at that word,
And he rode to Cambridge, and Oxenford;
But never a doctor there was so wise,
That could with his learning an answer devise.

Then home rode the abbot of comfort so cold,   45
And he mett his shepheard a going to fold:
How now, my lord abbot, you are welcome home;
What newes do you bring us from good king John?

"Sad newes, sad newes, shepheard, I must give;
That I have but three days more to live: 50
For if I do not answer him questions three,
My head will be smitten from my bodìe

The first is to tell him there in that stead,
With his crowne of golde so fair on his head,
Among all his liege men so noble of birth,   55
To within one penny of what he is worth.

The seconde, to tell him, without any doubt,
How soone he may ride this whole world about:
And at the third question I must not shrinke,
But tell him there truly what he does thinke."   60

Now cheare up, sire abbot, did you never hear yet,
That a fool he may learn a wise man witt?
Lend me horse, and serving men, and your apparel,
And I'll ride to London to answere your quarrel.

Nay frowne not, if it hath bin told unto mee,   65
I am like your lordship, as ever may bee:
And if you will but lend me your gowne,
There is none shall knowe us at fair London towne.

Now horses, and serving-men thou shalt have,
With sumptuous array most gallant and brave;   70
With crozier, and miter, and rochet, and cope,
Fit to appeare 'fore our fader the pope.

Now welcome, sire abbot, the king he did say,
Tis well thou'rt come back to keepe thy day;
For and if thou canst answer my questions three,   75
Thy life and thy living both saved shall bee.

And first, when thou seest me here in this stead,
With my crown of golde so fair on my head,
Among all my liege-men so noble of birthe,
Tell me to one penny what I am worth.   80

"For thirty pence our Saviour was sold
Amonge the false Jewes, as I have bin told;
And twenty-nine is the worth of thee,
For I thinke, thou art one penny worser than hee."

17*

The king he laughed, and swore by St. Bittel[2],   85
I did not think I had been worth so littel!
—Now secondly tell mee, without any doubt,
How soone I may ride this whole world about.

"You must rise with the sun, and ride with the same,
Until the next morning he riseth againe;   90
And then your grace need not make any doubt,
But in twenty-four hours you'll ride it about."

The king he laughed, and swore by St. Jone,
I did not think, it could be gone so soone!
—Now from the third question thou must not shrinke,   95
But tell me here truly what I do thinke.

"Yea, that shall I do, and make your grace merry:
You thinke I'm the abbot of Canterbùry;
But I'm his poor shepheard, as plain you may see,
That am come to beg pardon for him and for mee."   100

The king he laughed, and swore by the masse,
Ile make thee lord abbot this day in his place!
"Now naye, my liege, be not in such speede,
For alacke I can neither write, ne reade."

Four nobles a weeke, then I will give thee,   105
For this merry jest thou hast showne unto mee;
And tell the old abbot when thou comest home,
Thou hast brought him a pardon from good king John.

***

[2] Meaning probably St. Botolph.

VII.

Pou Weaner Beauties.

THIS little sonnet was written by Sir Henry Wotton,
Knight, on that amiable princess, Elizabeth, daughter of

James I. and wife of the Elector Palatine, who was chosen
King of Bohemia, Sept. 5, 1619. The consequences of this
fatal election are well known: Sir Henry Wotton, who in
that and the following year was employed in several em-
bassies in Germany on behalf of this unfortunate lady,
seems to have had an uncommon attachment to her merit
and fortunes, for he gave away a jewel worth a thousand
pounds, that was presented to him by the emperor, "because
it came from an enemy to his royal mistress the Queen of
Bohemia." See Biogr. Britan.

This song is printed from the *Reliquiæ Wottonianæ* 1651,
with some corrections from an old MS. copy.

<pre>
You meaner beauties of the night,
    That poorly satisfie our eies
More by your number, than your light;
    You common people of the skies,
    What are you when the Moon shall rise?   5

Ye violets that first appeare,
    By your pure purple mantles known
Like the proud virgins of the yeare,
    As if the Spring were all your own;
    What are you when the Rose is blown?   10

Ye curious chaunters of the wood,
    That warble forth dame Nature's layes,
Thinking your passions understood
    By your weak accents: what's your praise,
    When Philomell her voyce shall raise?   15

So when my mistris shal be seene
    In sweetnesse of her looks and minde;
By virtue first, then choyce a queen;
    Tell me, if she was not design'd
    Th' eclipse and glory of her kind?   20
</pre>

VIII.

The Old and Young Courtier.

THIS excellent old song, the subject of which is a comparison between the manners of the old gentry, as still subsisting in the times of Elizabeth, and the modern refinements affected by their sons in the reigns of her successors, is given, with corrections, from an ancient black-letter copy in the Pepys collection, compared with another printed among some miscellaneous "poems and songs" in a book entitled *Le Prince d'Amour*, 1660, 8vo.

———

An old song made by an aged old pate,
Of an old worshipful gentleman, who had a greate estate,
That kept a brave old house at a bountiful rate,
And an old porter to relieve the poor at his gate;
      Like an old courtier of the queen's,
      And the queen's old courtier.

With an old lady, whose anger one word asswages;
They every quarter paid their old servants their wages,
And never knew what belong'd to coachmen, footmen, nor
      pages,
But kept twenty old fellows with blue coats and badges;
      Like an old courtier, &c.

With an old study fill'd full of learned old books,
With an old reverend chaplain, you might know him by his
      looks.
With an old buttery hatch worn quite off the hooks,
And an old kitchen, that maintain'd half a dozen old cooks:
      Like an old courtier, &c.

With an old hall, hüng about with pikes, guns, and bows,
With old swords, and bucklers, that had borne many
      shrewde blows,

And an old frize coat, to cover his worship's trunk hose,
And a cup of old sherry, to comfort his copper nose;
    Like an old courtier, &c.

With a good old fashion, when Christmasse was come,
To call in all his old neighbours with bagpipe and drum,
With good chear enough to furnish every old room,
And old liquor able to make a cat speak, and man dumb,
    Like an old courtier, &c.

With an old falconer, huntsman, and a kennel of hounds,
That never hawked, nor hunted, but in his own grounds,
Who, like a wise man, kept himself within his own bounds,
And when he dyed gave every child a thousand good pounds;
    Like an old courtier, &c.

But to his eldest son his house and land he assign'd,
Charging him in his will to keep the old bountifull mind,
To be good to his old tenants, and to his neighbours be kind:
But in the ensuing ditty you shall hear how he was inclin'd;
    Like a young courtier of the king's,
    And the king's young courtier.

Like a flourishing young gallant, newly come to his land,
Who keeps a brace of painted madams at his command,
And takes up a thousand pound upon his father's land,
And gets drunk in a tavern, till he can neither go nor stand;
    Like a young courtier, &c.

With a new-fangled lady, that is dainty, nice, and spare,
Who never knew what belong'd to good house-keeping, or
    care,
Who buyes gaudy-color'd fans to play with wanton air,
And seven or eight different dressings of other womens hair;
    Like a young courtier, &c.

With a new-fashion'd hall, built where the old one stood,
Hung round with new pictures, that do the poor no good,

With a fine marble chimney, wherein burns neither coal
          nor wood,
And a new smooth shovelboard, whereon no victuals ne'er
          stood;
          Like a young courtier, &c.

With a new study, stuft full of pamphlets, and plays,
And a new chaplain, that swears faster than he prays,
With a new buttery hatch, that opens once in four or five
          days,
And a new French cook, to devise fine kickshaws. and toys;
          Like a young courtier, &c.

With a new fashion, when Christmas is drawing on,
On a new journey to London straight we all must begone,
And leave none to keep house, but our new porter John,
Who relieves the poor with a thump on the back with a
          stone;
          Like a young courtier, &c.

With a new gentleman-usher, whose carriage is compleat,
With a new coachman, footman, and pages to carry up the
          meat,
With a waiting-gentlewoman, whose dressing is very neat,
Who when her lady has din'd, lets the servants not eat;
          Like a young courtier, &c.

With new titles of honour bought with his father's old gold,
For which sundry of his ancestors old manors are sold;
And this is the course most of our new gallants hold,
Which makes that good house-keeping is now grown so cold,
          Among the young courtiers of the king,
          Or the king's young courtiers.

                                                    ₊

IX.

Sir John Suckling's Campaigne.

WHEN the Scottish covenanters rose up in arms, and advanced to the English borders in 1639, many of the courtiers complimented the king by raising forces at their own expense. Among these, none were more distinguished than the gallant Sir John Suckling, who raised a troop of horse, so richly accoutred, that it cost him 12,000*l*. The like expensive equipment of other parts of the army made the king remark, that "the Scots would fight stoutly, if it were but for the Englishmen's fine cloaths." [Lloyd's Memoirs.] When they came to action, the rugged Scots proved more than a match for the fine showy English: many of whom behaved remarkably ill, and among the rest this splendid troop of Sir John Suckling's.

This humorous pasquil has been generally supposed to have been written by Sir John, as a banter upon himself. Some of his contemporaries, however, attributed it to Sir John Mennis, a wit of those times, among whose poems it is printed in a small poetical miscellany, entitled, "Musarum deliciæ: or the Muses recreation, containing several pieces of poetique wit, 2nd edition. By Sir J. M. [Sir John Mennis] and Ja. S. [James Smith.] London, 1656, 12mo." [See Wood's *Athenæ*, ii. 397, 418.] In that copy is subjoined an additional stanza, which probably was written by this Sir John Mennis, viz.

> "But now there is peace, he's return'd to increase
> His money, which lately he spent-a
> But his lost honour must lye still in the dust;
> At Barwick away it went-a."

SIR JOHN he got him an ambling nag,
    To Scotland for to ride-a,
With a hundred horse more, all his own he swore,
    To guard him on every side-a.

No Errant-knight ever went to fight   5
  With halfe so gay a bravada,
Had you seen but his look, you'ld have sworn on a book,
  Hee'ld have conquer'd a whole armada.

The ladies ran all to the windows to see
  So gallant and warlike a sight-a,   10
And as he pass'd by, they said with a sigh,
  Sir John, why will you go fight-a?

But he, like a cruel knight, spurr'd on;
  His heart would not relent-a,
For, till he came there, what had he to fear?   15
  Or why should he repent-a?

The king (God bless him!) had singular hopes
  Of him and all his troop-a:
The borderers they, as they met him on the way,
  For joy did hollow and whoop-a.   20

None lik'd him so well, as his own colonell,
  Who took him for John de Wert-a;
But when there were shows of gunning and blows,
  My gallant was nothing so pert-a.

For when the Scots army came within sight,   25
  And all prepared to fight-a,
He ran to his tent, they ask'd what he meant,
  He swore he must needs goe sh*te-a.

The colonell sent for him back agen,
  To quarter him in the van-a,   30
But Sir John did swear, he would not come there,
  To be kill'd the very first man-a.

Ver. 22. John de Wert was a German general of great reputation, and
the terror of the French in the reign of Louis XIII. Hence his name became
proverbial in France, where he was called De Vert. See Bayle's Dictionary.

To cure his fear, he was sent to the reare,
  Some ten miles back, and more-a;
Where Sir John did play at trip and away,   35
  And ne'er saw the enemy more-a.

X.
To Althea from Prison.

THIS excellent sonnet, which possessed a high degree of fame among the old Cavaliers, was written by Colonel Richard Lovelace, during his confinement in the Gatehouse, Westminster: to which he was committed by the House of Commons, in April, 1642, for presenting a petition from the county of Kent, requesting them to restore the king to his rights, and to settle the government. See Wood's *Athenæ*, vol. ii. p. 228, and Lysons' *Environs of London*, vol. i. p. 109; where may be seen at large the affecting story of this elegant writer, who, after having been distinguished for every gallant and polite accomplishment, the pattern of his own sex, and the darling of the ladies, died in the lowest wretchedness, obscurity, and want, in 1658.

This song is printed from a scarce volume of his poems, entitled *Lucasta*, 1649, 12mo, collated with a copy in the Editor's folio MS.

    WHEN love with unconfined wings
      Hovers within my gates,
    And my divine Althea brings
      To whisper at my grates;
    When I lye tangled in her haire,   5
      And fetter'd with her eye,
    The birds that wanton in the aire,
      Know no such libertye.

    When flowing cups run swiftly round
      With no allaying Thames,   10

Ver. 10, With woe-allaying themes. MS. Thames is here used for water in general.

Our carelesse heads with roses crown'd,
  Our hearts with loyal flames;
When thirsty griefe in wine we steepe,
  When healths and draughts goe free,
Fishes, that tipple in the deepe,   15
  Know no such libertie.

When, linnet-like, confined I
  With shriller note shall sing
The mercye, sweetness, majestye,
  And glories of my king;   20
When I shall voyce aloud how good
  He is, how great should be,
Th' enlarged windes, that curle the flood,
  Know no such libertie.

Stone walls doe not a prison make,   25
  Nor iron barres a cage,
Mindes, innocent and quiet, take
  That for an hermitage:
If I have freedom in my love,
  And in my soule am free,   30
Angels alone, that soare above,
  Enjoy such libertie.

XI.

The Downfall of Charing-Cross.

CHARING-CROSS, as it stood before the civil wars, was one of those beautiful Gothic obelisks erected to conjugal affection by Edward I., who built such an one wherever the hearse of his beloved Eleanor rested in its way from Lincolnshire to Westminster. But neither its ornamental situation, the beauty of its structure, nor the noble design of its erection, (which did honour to humanity,) could preserve it from the merciless zeal of the times: for, in 1647, it was demolished by order of the House of Commons, as popish and superstitious. This occasioned the following not unhumorous sarcasm, which has been often printed among the popular sonnets of those times.

The plot referred to in ver. 17, was that entered into by Mr. Waller the poet, and others, with a view to reduce the city and tower to the service of the king, for which two of them, Nathaniel Tomkins and Richard Chaloner, suffered death, July 5, 1643. Vide Athen. Ox. ii. 24.

UNDONE, undone the lawyers are,
   They wander about the towne,
Nor can find the way to Westminster,
   Now Charing-cross is downe:
At the end of the Strand, they make a stand,   5
   Swearing they are at a loss,
And chaffing say, that's not the way,
   They must go by Charing-cross.

The parliament to vote it down
   Conceived it very fitting,   10
For fear it should fall, and kill them all,
   In the house, as they were sitting.
They were told, god-wot, it had a plot,
   Which made them so hard-hearted,
To give command, it should not stand,   15
   But be taken down and carted.

Men talk of plots, this might have been worse
   For any thing I know,
Than that Tomkins, and Chaloner,
   Were hang'd for long agoe.   20
Our parliament did that prevent,
   And wisely them defended,
For plots they will discover still,
   Before they were intended.

But neither man, woman, nor child,   25
    Will say, I'm confident,
They ever heard it speak one word
    Against the parliament.
An informer swore, it letters bore,
    Or else it had been freed: 30
I'll take, in troth, my Bible oath,
    It could neither write, nor read.

The committee said, that verily
    To popery it was bent;
For ought I know, it might be so,   35
    For to church it never went,
What with excise, and such device,
    The kingdom doth begin
To think you'll leave them ne'er a cross,
    Without doors nor within.   40

Methinks the common-council shou'd
    Of it have taken pity,
'Cause, good old cross, it always stood
    So firmly to the city.
Since crosses you so much disdain   45
    Faith, if I were as you,
For fear the king should rule again,
    I'd pull down Tiburn too.

*** Whitelocke says, "May 7, 1643, Cheapside-cross and other crosses were voted down," &c. But this vote was not put in execution with regard to Charing-cross till four years after, as appears from Lilly's 'Observations on the Life, &c. of King Charles,' viz. "Charing-cross, we know, was pulled down, 1647, in June, July, and August. Part of the stones were converted to pave before Whitehall. I have seen knife-hafts made of some of the stones, which, being well polished, looked like marble." Ed. 1715, p. 18, 12mo.

See an account of the pulling down Cheapside-cross, in the Supplement to *Gent. Mag.* 1764.

XII.

Loyalty Confined.

Tᴴɪꜱ excellent old song is preserved in David Lloyd's "Memoires of those that suffered in the cause of Charles I." London, 1668, fol. p. 96. He speaks of it as the composition of a worthy personage, who suffered deeply in those times, and was still living with no other reward than the conscience of having suffered. The author's name he has not mentioned, but if tradition may be credited, this song was written by Sir Roger L'Estrange. Some mistakes in Lloyd's copy are corrected by two others, one in MS., the other in the "Westminster Drollery, or a choice Collection of Songs and Poems, 1671," 12mo.

Bᴇᴀᴛ on, proud billows; Boreas blow;
    Swell, curled waves, high as Jove's roof;
Your incivility doth show,
    That innocence is tempest proof;
Though surly Nereus frown, my thoughts are calm;   5
Then strike, Affliction, for thy wounds are balm.

That which the world miscalls a jail,
    A private closet is to me:
Whilst a good conscience is my bail,
    And innocence my liberty: 10
Locks, bars, and solitude, together met,
Make me no prisoner, but an anchoret.

I, whilst I wisht to be retir'd,
    Into this private room was turn'd:
As if their wisdoms had conspir'd   15
    The salamander should be burn'd;

Or like those sophists, that would drown a fish.
I am constrain'd to suffer what I wish.

The cynick loves his poverty;
　　The pelican her wilderness;　　　　　　　　　　20
And 'tis the Indian's pride to be
　　Naked on frozen Caucasus:
Contentment cannot smart, Stoicks we see
Make torments easie to their apathy.

These manacles upon my arm　　　　　　　　　　25
　　I, as my mistress' favours, wear;
And for to keep my ancles warm,
　　I have some iron shackles there:
These walls are but my garrison; this cell,
Which men call jail, doth prove my citadel.　　　30

I'm in the cabinet lockt up,
　　Like some high-prized margarite,
Or, like the great mogul or pope,
　　Am cloyster'd up from publick sight:
Retiredness is a piece of majesty,　　　　　　　　35
And thus, proud sultan, I'm as great as thee.

Here sin for want of food must starve,
　　Where tempting objects are not seen;
And these strong walls do only serve
　　To keep vice out, and keep me in:　　　　　　40
Malice of late's grown charitable sure,
I'm not committed, but am kept secure

So he that struck at Jason's life [1],
　　Thinking t' have made his purpose sure,
By a malicious friendly knife　　　　　　　　　　45
　　Did only wound him to a cure:
Malice, I see, wants wit; for what is meant
Mischief, oft-times proves favour by th' event.

[1] See this remarkable story in Cicero de Nat. Deorum, lib. iii. c. xxviii.;
Cic. de Offic. l. i. c. xxx.; see also Val. Max. i. viii.

When once my prince affliction hath,
   Prosperity doth treason seem;   50
And to make smooth so rough a path,
   I can learn patience from him:
Now not to suffer shews no loyal heart,
When kings want ease subjects must bear a part.

What though I cannot see my king   55
   Neither in person or in coin;
Yet contemplation is a thing
   That renders what I have not, mine:
My king from me what adamant can part,
Whom I do wear engraven on my heart?   60

Have you not seen the nightingale,
   A prisoner like, coopt in a cage,
How doth she chaunt her wonted tale
   In that her narrow hermitage?
Even then her charming melody doth prove,   65
That all her bars are trees, her cage a grove.

I am that bird, whom they combine
   Thus to deprive of liberty;
But though they do my corps confine,
   Yet maugre hate, my soul is free: 70
And though immur'd, yet can I chirp, and sing
Disgrace to rebels, glory to my king.

My soul is free, as ambient air,
   Although my baser part's immew'd,
Whilst loyal thoughts do still repair   75
   T" accompany my solitude:
Although rebellion do my body binde,
My king alone can captivate my minde.

XIII.

𝔙𝔢𝔯𝔰𝔢𝔰 𝔟𝔶 𝔎𝔦𝔫𝔤 ℭ𝔥𝔞𝔯𝔩𝔢𝔰 𝔍.

"This prince, like his father, did not confine himself to prose: Bishop Burnet has given us a pathetic elegy, said to be written by Charles in Carisbrooke Castle [in 1648]. The poetry is most uncouth and unharmonious, but there are strong thoughts in it, some good sense, and a strain of majestic piety." — Walpole's *Royal and Noble Authors*, v. i.

It is in his *Memoirs of the Duke of Hamilton*, p. 379, that Burnet hath preserved this elegy, which he tells us he had from a gentleman, who waited on the king at the time when it was written, and copied it out from the original. It is there entitled, "MAJESTY IN MISERY: OR AN IMPLORATION TO THE KING OF KINGS."

Hume hath remarked of these stanzas, "that the truth of the sentiment, rather than the elegance of the expression, renders them very pathetic." See his History, 1763, 4to, vol. v. pp. 437, 442, which is no bad comment upon them. — These are almost the only verses known of Charles's composition. Indeed, a little poem, *On a Quiet Conscience*, printed in the Poetical Calendar, 1763, vol. viii., is attributed to King Charles I.; being reprinted from a thin 8vo, published by Nahum Tate, called "Miscellanea Sacra, or Poems on Divine and Moral Subjects."

GREAT monarch of the world, from whose power springs
The potency and power of kings,
Record the royal woe my suffering sings;

And teach my tongue, that ever did confine
Its faculties in truth's seraphick line,   5
To track the treasons of thy foes and mine.

Nature and law, by thy divine decree,
(The only root of righteous royaltie)
With this dim diadem invested me:

With it, the sacred scepter, purple robe,   10
The holy unction, and the royal globe:
Yet am I levell'd with the life of Job.

The fiercest furies, that do daily tread
Upon my grief, my grey discrowned head,
Are those that owe my bounty for their bread.   15

They raise a war, and christen it THE CAUSE,
While sacrilegious hands have best applause,
Plunder and murder are the kingdom's laws;

Tyranny bears the title of taxation,
Revenge and robbery are reformation,   20
Oppression gains the name of sequestration.

My loyal subjects, who in this bad season
Attend me (by the law of God and reason,)
They dare impeach, and punish for high treason.

Next at the clergy do their furies frown,   25
Pious episcopacy must go down,
They will destroy the crosier and the crown.

Churchmen are chain'd, and schismaticks are freed,
Mechanicks preach, and holy fathers bleed,
The crown is crucified with the creed.   30

The church of England doth all factions foster,
The pulpit is usurpt by each impostor,
Extempore excludes the *Paternoster.*

The Presbyter, and Independent seed
Springs with broad blades.   To make religion bleed   35
Herod and Pontius Pilate are agreed.

The corner stone's misplac'd by every pavier:
With such a bloody method and behaviour
Their ancestors did crucifie our Saviour

18*

My royal consort, from whose fruitful womb   40
So many princes legally have come,
Is forc'd in pilgrimage to seek a tomb.

Great Britain's heir is forced into France,
Whilst on his father's head his foes advance:
Poor child! he weeps out his inheritance.   45

With my own power my majesty they wound,
In the king's name the king himself's uncrown'd:
So doth the dust destroy the diamond.

With propositions daily they enchant
My people's ears, such as do reason daunt,   50
And the Almighty will not let me grant.

They promise to erect my royal stem,
To make me great, t' advance my diadem,
If I will first fall down, and worship them!

But for refusal, they devour my thrones,   55
Distress my children, and destroy my bones;
I fear they'll force me to make bread of stones

My life they prize at such a slender rate,
That in my absence they draw bills of hate,
To prove the king a traytor to the state.   60

Felons obtain more privilege than I,
They are allow'd to answer ere they die;
'Tis death for me to ask the reason, why.

But, sacred Saviour, with thy words I woo
Thee to forgive, and not be bitter to   65
Such, as thou know'st do not know what they do.

For since they from their Lord are so disjointed,
As to contemn those edicts he appointed,
How can they prize the power of his anointed?

Augment my patience, nullifie my hate,   70
  Preserve my issue, and inspire my mate;
Yet, though we perish, BLESS THIS CHURCH and STATE.

XIV.

𝕿𝖍𝖊 𝕾𝖆𝖑𝖊 𝖔𝖋 𝕽𝖊𝖇𝖊𝖑𝖑𝖎𝖔𝖚𝖘 𝕳𝖔𝖚𝖘𝖍𝖔𝖑𝖉-𝖘𝖙𝖚𝖋𝖋.

THIS sarcastic exultation of triumphant loyalty is printed
from an old black-letter copy in the Pepys collection, corrected by two others, one of which is preserved in "A choice
collection of 120 loyal songs, &c." 1684, 12mo. — To the
tune of *Old Simon the king.*

REBELLION hath broken up house,
  And hath left me old lumber to sell;
Come hither, and take your choice,
  I'll promise to use you well:
Will you buy the old speaker's chair?   5
  Which was warm and easie to sit in,
And oft hath been clean'd I declare,
  When as it was fouler than fitting.
      Says old Simon the king, &c.

Will you buy any bacon-flitches,   10
  The fattest, that ever were spent?
They're the sides of the old committees,
  Fed up in the long parliament.
Here's a pair of bellows, and tongs,
  And for a small matter I'll sell ye 'um;   15
They are made of the presbyters lungs,
  To blow up the coals of rebellion.
      Says old Simon, &c.

I had thought to have given them once
  To some black-smith for his forge;   20

But now I have considered on't,
   They are consecrate to the church:
So I'll give them unto some quire,
   They will make the big organs roar,
And the little pipes to squeeke higher,   25
   Than ever they could before
      Says old Simon, &c.

Here's a couple of stools for sale,
   One's square, and t'other is round;
Betwixt them both the tail   30
   Of the Rump fell down to the ground.
Will you buy the states council-table,
   Which was made of the good wain Scot?
The frame was a tottering Babel
   To uphold the Independent plot.   35
      Says old Simon, &c.

Here's the beesom of Reformation,
   Which should have made clean the floor,
But it swept out the wealth of the nation,
   And left us dirt good store.   40
Will you buy the states spinning-wheel,
   Which spun for the roper's trade?
But better it had stood still,
   For now it has spun a fair thread.
      Says old Simon, &c.   45

Here's a glyster-pipe well try'd,
   Which was made of a butcher's stump [1],
And has been safely apply'd,
   To cure the colds of the rump.
Here's a lump of Pilgrims-Salve,   50
   Which once was a justice of peace,

---

[1] Alluding probably to Major-General Harrison, a butcher's son, who assisted Cromwell in turning out the long parliament, April 20, 1653.

Who Noll and the Devil did serve;
   But now it is come to this.
      Says old Simon, &c.

Here's a roll of the states tobacco,   55
   If any good fellow will take it;
No Virginia had e'er such a smack-o,
   And I'll tell you how they did make it:
'Tis th' Engagement, and Covenant cookt
   Up with the Abjuration oath;   60
And many of them, that have took't,
   Complain it was foul in the mouth.
      Says old Simon, &c.

Yet the ashes may happily serve
   To cure the scab of the nation,   65
Whene'er 't has an itch to swerve
   To Rebellion by innovation.
A Lanthorn here is to be bought,
   The like was scarce ever gotten,
For many plots it has found out   70
   Before they ever were thought on.
      Says old Simon, &c.

Will you buy the RUMP's great saddle,
   With which it jocky'd the nation?
And here is the bitt, and the bridle,   75
   And curb of Dissimulation:
And here's the trunk-hose of the RUMP,
   And their fair dissembling cloak,
And a Presbyterian jump,
   With an Independent smock.   80
      Says old Simon, &c.

Will you buy a Conscience oft turn'd,
   Which serv'd the high-court of justice,
And stretch'd until England it mourn'd:
   But Hell will buy that if the worst is.   85

Here's Joan[2] Cromwell's kitchen-stuff tub,
    Wherein is the fat of the Rumpers,
With which old Noll's horns she did rub,
    When he was got drunk with false bumpers.
        Says old Simon, &c.   90

Here's the purse of the public faith;
    Here's the model of the Sequestration,
When the old wives upon their good troth,
    Lent thimbles to ruine the nation.
Here's Dick Cromwell's Protectorship,   95
    And here are Lambert's commissions,
And here is Hugh Peters his scrip
    Cramm'd with the tumultuous Petitions.
        Says old Simon, &c.

And here are old Noll's brewing vessels,   100
    And here are his dray, and his slings;
Here are Hewson's awl, and his bristles;
    With diverse other odd things:
And what is the price doth belong
    To all these matters before ye?   105
I'll sell them all for an old song,
    And so I do end my story.
        Says old Simon, &c.

Ver. 94.   See Grey's *Hudibras*, pt. i. cant. ii. v. 570, &c.
V. 100, 102.   Cromwell had in his younger years followed the brewing
trade at Huntingdon. Col. Hewson is said to have been originally a cobbler.

[2] This was a cant name given to Cromwell's wife by the Royalists,
though her name was Elizabeth. She was taxed with exchanging the kitchen-
stuff for the candles used in the Protector's household, &c.   See *Gent. Mag.*
for March, 1788, p. 242.

XV.

𝕿𝖍𝖊 𝕭𝖆𝖋𝖋𝖑𝖊𝖉 𝕶𝖓𝖎𝖌𝖍𝖙, 𝖔𝖗 𝕷𝖆𝖉𝖞'𝖘 𝕻𝖔𝖑𝖎𝖈𝖞.

GIVEN (with some corrections) from a MS. copy, and collated with two printed ones in Roman character in the Pepys collection.

THERE was a knight was drunk with wine,
    A riding along the way, sir;
And there he met with a lady fine,
    Among the cocks of hay, sir.

Shall you and I, O lady faire,   5
    Among the grass lye down-a:
And I will have a special care
    Of rumpling of your gowne-a.

Upon the grass there is a dewe,
    Will spoil my damask gowne, sir: 10
My gowne and kirtle they are newe,
    And cost me many a crowne, sir.

I have a cloak of scarlet red,
    Upon the ground I'll throwe it;
Then, lady faire, come lay thy head;   15
    We'll play, and none shall knowe it.

O yonder stands my steed so free
    Among the cocks of hay, sir;
And if the pinner should chance to see,
    He'll take my steed away, sir.   20

Upon my finger I have a ring,
    Its made of finest gold-a,
And, lady, it thy steed shall bring
    Out of the pinner's fold-a.

O go with me to my father's hall;   25
  Fair chambers there are three, sir:
And you shall have the best of all,
  And I'll your chamberlaine bee, sir.

He mounted himself on his steed so tall,
  And her on her dapple gray, sir: 30
And there they rode to her father's hall,
  Fast pricking along the way, sir.

To her father's hall they arrived strait;
  'Twas moated round about-a;
She slipped herself within the gate,   35
  And lockt the knight without-a.

Here is a silver penny to spend,
  And take it for your pain, sir;
And two of my father's men I'll send
  To wait on you back again, sir.   40

He from his scabbard drew his brand,
  And wiped it upon his sleeve-a:
And cursed, he said, be every man,
  That will a maid believe-a!

She drew a bodkin from her haire,   45
  And whip'd it upon her gown-a;
And curs'd be every maiden faire,
  That will with men lye down-a!

A herb there is, that lowly grows,
  And some do call it rue, sir: 50
The smallest dunghill cock that crows,
  Would make a capon of you, sir.

A flower there is, that shineth bright,
  Some call it mary-gold-a:
He that wold not when he might,   55
  He shall not when he wold-a.

The knight was riding another day,
   With cloak and hat and feather:
He met again with that lady gay,
   Who was angling in the river.   60

Now, lady faire, I've met with you,
   You shall no more escape me;
Remember, how not long agoe
   You falsely did intrap me.

The lady blushed scarlet red,   65
   And trembled at the stranger:
How shall I guard my maidenhead
   From this approaching danger?

He from his saddle down did light,
   In all his riche attyer;   70
And cryed, As I am a noble knight,
   I do thy charms admyer.

He took the lady by the hand,
   Who seemingly consented;
And would no more disputing stand: 75
   She had a plot invented.

Looke yonder, good sir knight, I pray,
   Methinks I now discover
A riding upon his dapple gray,
   My former constant lover.   80

On tip-toe peering stood the knight,
   Fast by the rivers brink-a;
The lady pusht with all her might:
   Sir knight, now swim or sink-a.

O'er head and ears he plunged in,   85
   The bottom faire he sounded;
Then rising up, he cried amain,
   Help, helpe, or else I'm drownded!

Now, fare-you-well, sir knight, adieu!
   You see what comes of fooling: 90
That is the fittest place for you;
   Your courage wanted cooling.

Ere many days, in her fathers park,
   Just at the close of eve-a,
Again she met with her angry sparke;   95
   Which made this lady grieve-a.

False lady, here thou'rt in my powre,
   And no one now can hear thee:
And thou shalt sorely rue the hour,
   That e'er thou dar'dst to jeer me.   100

I pray, sir knight, be not so warm
   With a young silly maid-a:
I vow and swear I thought no harm,
   'Twas a gentle jest I playd-a.

A gentle jest, in soothe, he cry'd,   105
   To tumble me in and leave me!
What if I had in the river dy'd?——
   That fetch will not deceive me.

Once more I'll pardon thee this day,
   Tho' injur'd out of measure;   110
But then prepare without delay
   To yield thee to my pleasure.

Well then, if I must grant your suit,
   Yet think of your boots and spurs, sir:
Let me pull off both spur and boot,   115
   Or else you cannot stir, sir.

He set him down upon the grass,
   And begg'd her kind assistance;
Now, smiling thought this lovely lass,
   I'll make you keep your distance.   120

Then pulling off his boots half-way;
　Sir knight, now I'm your betters:
You shall not make of me your prey;
　Sit there like a knave in fetters.

The knight when she had served him soe,　125
　He fretted, fum'd, and grumbled:
For he could neither stand nor goe,
　But like a cripple tumbled.

Farewell, sir knight, the clock strikes ten,
　Yet do not move nor stir, sir:　130
I'll send you my father's serving men,
　To pull off your boots and spurs, sir.

This merry jest you must excuse,
　You are but a stingless nettle:
You'd never have stood for boots or shoes,　135
　Had you been a man of mettle.

All night in grievous rage he lay,
　Rolling upon the plain-a;
Next morning a shepherd past that way,
　Who set him right again-a.　140

Then mounting upon his steed so tall,
　By hill and dale he swore-a:
I'll ride at once to her father's hall;
　She shall escape no more-a.

I'll take her father by the beard,　145
　I'll challenge all her kindred;
Each dastard soul shall stand affeard;
　My wrath shall no more be hindred.

He rode unto her father's house,
　Which every side was moated:　150
The lady heard his furious vows,
　And all his vengeance noted.

Thought shee, sir knight, to quench your rage,
   Once more I will endeavour:
This water shall your fury 'swage,   155
   Or else it shall burn for ever.

Then faining penitence and feare,
   She did invite a parley:
Sir knight, if you'll forgive me heare,
   Henceforth I'll love you dearly.   160

My father he is now from home,
   And I am all alone, sir:
Therefore a-cross the water come;
   And I am all your own, sir.

False maid, thou canst no more deceive;   165
   I scorn the treacherous bait-a:
If thou would'st have me thee believe,
   Now open me the gate-a.

The bridge is drawn, the gate is barr'd,
   My father he has the keys, sir;   170
But I have for my love prepar'd
   A shorter way and easier.

Over the moate I've laid a plank
   Full seventeen feet in measure:
Then step a-cross to the other bank,   175
   And there we'll take our pleasure.

These words she had no sooner spoke,
   But strait he came tripping over:
The plank was saw'd, it snapping broke;
   And sous'd the unhappy lover.   180

⁎

XVI.

Why so Pale?

FROM Sir John Suckling's Poems. This sprightly knight was born in 1613, and cut off by a fever about the 29th year of his age. See above, Song ix. of this book.

WHY so pale and wan, fond lover?
  Prethee, why so pale?
Will, when looking well can't move her,
  Looking ill prevail?
  Prethee why so pale?   5

Why so dull and mute, young sinner?
  Prethee why so mute?
Will, when speaking well can't win her,
  Saying nothing doe't?
  Prethee why so mute?   10

Quit, quit for shame; this will not move,
  This cannot take her;
If of herself she will not love,
  Nothing can make her.
  The devil take her!   15

XVII.

Old Tom of Bedlam.

MAD SONG THE FIRST.

IT is worth attention, that the English have more songs and ballads on the subject of madness, than any of their neighbours. Whether there be any truth in the insinuation, that we are more liable to this calamity than other nations, or that our native gloominess hath peculiarly recommended

subjects of this cast to our writers, we certainly do not
find the same in the printed collections of French, Italian
songs, &c.

Out of a much larger quantity, we have selected half a
dozen MAD SONGS for these volumes. The three first are
originals in their respective kinds: the merit of the three
last is chiefly that of imitation. They were written at considerable intervals of time; but we have here grouped them
together, that the reader may the better examine their com-
parative merits. He may consider them as so many trials of
skill in a very peculiar subject, as the contest of so many
rivals to shoot in the bow of Ulysses. The two first were
probably written about the beginning of the last century;
the third about the middle of it; the fourth and sixth towards
the end; and the fifth within the eighteenth century.

This is given from the Editor's folio MS. compared with
two or three old printed copies. — With regard to the author
of this old rhapsody, in Walton's *Complete Angler*, cap. 3, is
a song in praise of angling, which the author says was made
at his request "by Mr. William Basse, one that has made
the choice songs of the *Hunter in his Career*, and of *Tom of
Bedlam*, and many others of note," p. 84. See Sir John
Hawkins's curious edition, 8vo, of that excellent old book.

FORTH from my sad and darksome cell,
Or from the deepe abysse of hell,
Mad Tom is come into the world againe
To see if he can cure his distempered braine.

Feares and cares oppresse my soule;   5
Harke, howe the angrye Fureys houle!
Pluto laughes, and Proserpine is gladd
To see poore naked Tom of Bedlam madd.

Through the world I wander night and day
To seeke my straggling senses,   10

In an angrye moode I mett old Time,
  With his pentarchye of tenses:

  When me he spyed,
  Away he hyed,
For time will stay for no man: 15
  In vaine with cryes
  I rent the skyes,
For pity is not common.

  Cold and comfortless I lye:
  Helpe, oh helpe! or else I dye!   20
Harke! I heare Apollo's teame,
  The carman 'gins to whistle;
Chast Diana bends her bowe,
  The boare begins to bristle.

Come, Vulcan, with tools and with tackles,   25
To knocke off my troublesome shackles;
Bid Charles make ready his waine
To fetch me my senses againe.

  Last night I heard the dog-star bark;
Mars met Venus in the darke;   30
Limping Vulcan het an iron barr,
And furiouslye made at the god of war.

  Mars with his weapon laid about,
But Vulcan's temples had the gout,
For his broad horns did so hang in his light,   35
He could not see to aim his blowes aright:

Mercurye, the nimble post of heaven,
  Stood still to see the quarrell;
Gorrel-bellyed Bacchus, gyant-like,
  Bestryd a strong-beere barrell.   40

  To mee he dranke,
  I did him thanke,

But I could get no cyder;
  He dranke whole butts
  Till he burst his gutts,   45
But mine were ne'er the wyder.

Poore naked Tom is very drye:
A little drinke for charitye!
Harke, I hear Acteon's horne!
  The huntsmen whoop and hallowe;   50
Ringwood, Royster, Bowman, Jowler,
  All the chase do followe.

The man in the moone drinkes clarret,
Eates powder'd beef, turnip, and carret,
But a cup of old Malaga sack   55
Will fire the bushe at his backe.

XVIII.

The Distracted Puritan,

MAD SONG THE SECOND,

WAS written about the beginning of the seventeenth century by the witty bishop Corbet, and is printed from the third edition of his Poems, 12mo, 1672, compared with a more ancient copy in the Editor's folio MS.

AM I mad, O noble Festus,
When zeal and godly knowledge
  Have put me in hope
  To deal with the pope,
As well as the best in the college?   5
  Boldly I preach, hate a cross, hate a surplice,
    Mitres, copes, and rochets:
  Come hear me pray nine times a day,
    And fill your heads with crotchets.

In the house of pure Emanuel[1]   10
I had my education,
   Where my friends surmise
   I dazel'd my eyes
With the sight of revelation.
   Boldly I preach, &c.

They bound me like a bedlam,   15
They lash'd my four poor quarters;
   Whilst this I endure,
   Faith makes me sure
To be one of Foxes martyrs.
   Boldly I preach, &c.

These injuries I suffer   20
Through antichrist's perswasion:
   Take off this chain,
   Neither Rome nor Spain
Can resist my strong invasion.
   Boldly I preach, &c.

Of the beast's ten horns (God bless us!)   25
I have knock'd off three already;
   If they let me alone
   I'll leave him none:
But they say I am too heady.
   Boldly I preach, &c.

When I sack'd the seven-hill'd city,   30
I met the great red dragon;
   I kept him aloof
   With the armour of proof,
Though here I have never a rag on.
   Boldly I preach, &c.

With a fiery sword and target,   35
There fought I with this monster:

[1] Emanuel College, Cambridge, was originally a seminary of Puritans.

But the sons of pride
My zeal deride,
And all my deeds misconster.
    Boldly I preach, &c.

I un-hors'd the Whore of Babel,   40
With the lance of Inspiration;
    I made her stink,
    And spill the drink
In her cup of abomination.
    Boldly I preach, &c.

I have seen two in a vision   45
With a flying book[2] between them.
    I have been in despair
    Five times in a year,
And been cur'd by reading Greenham[3].
    Boldly I preach, &c.

I observ'd in Perkins' tables[4]   50
The black line of damnation;
    Those crooked veins
    So stuck in my brains,
That I fear'd my reprobation.
    Boldly I preach, &c.

In the holy tongue of Canaan   55
I plac'd my chiefest pleasure:

---

[2] Alluding to some visionary exposition of Zech. ch. v. ver. 1; or, if the date of this song would permit, one might suppose it aimed at one Coppe, a strange enthusiast, whose life may be seen in Wood's Athen. vol. ii. p. 501. He was author of a book entitled *The Fiery Flying Roll*; and afterwards published a recantation, part of whose title is, *The Fiery Flying Roll's Wings clipt*, &c.

[3] See Greenham's Works, fol. 1605, particularly the tract entitled *A sweet Comfort for an Afflicted Conscience*.

[4] See Perkins's Works, fol. 1616, vol. i. p. 11; where is a large half sheet folded, containing, "A survey, or table, declaring the order of the causes of salvation and damnation, &c.," the pedigree of damnation being distinguished by a broad black zig-zag line.

Till I prick'd my foot
With an Hebrew root,
That I bled beyond all measure.
  Boldly I preach, &c.

I appear'd before the archbishop[5],   60
And all the high commission:
  I gave him no grace,
  But told him to his face,
That he favour'd superstition.
  Boldly I preach, hate a cross, hate a surplice, 65
    Mitres, copes, and rochets:
  Come hear me pray nine times a day,
    And fill your heads with crotchets.

[5] Abp. Laud.

XIX.

The Lunatic Lover,

MAD SONG THE THIRD,

Is given from an old printed copy in the British Museum,
compared with another in the Pepys collection: both in
black letter.

GRIM king of the ghosts, make haste,
  And bring hither all your train;
See how the pale moon does waste,
  And just now is in the wane.
Come, you night-hags, with all your charms, 5
  And revelling witches away,
And hug me close in your arms;
  To you my respects I'll pay.

I'll court you, and think you fair,
  Since love does distract my brain: 10

I'll go, I'll wed the night-mare,
   And kiss her, and kiss her again:
But if she prove peevish and proud,
   Then, a pise on her love! let her go:
I'll seek me a winding shroud,   15
   And down to the shades below.

A lunacy sad I endure,
   Since reason departs away;
I call to those hags for a cure,
   As knowing not what I say.   20
The beauty, whom I do adore,
   Now slights me with scorn and disdain;
I never shall see her more:
   Ah! how shall I bear my pain?

I ramble, and range about   25
   To find out my charming saint;
While she at my grief does flout,
   And smiles at my loud complaint.
Distraction I see is my doom,
   Of this I am now too sure;   30
A rival is got in my room,
   While torments I do endure.

Strange fancies do fill my head,
   While wandering in despair,
I am to the desarts lead,   35
   Expecting to find her there.
Methinks in a spangled cloud
   I see her enthroned on high;
Then to her I crie aloud,
   And labour to reach the sky.   40

When thus I have raved awhile,
   And wearyed myself in vain,
I lye on the barren soil,
   And bitterly do complain.

Till slumber hath quieted me,   45
  In sorrow I sigh and weep:
The clouds are my canopy
  To cover me while I sleep.

I dream that my charming fair
  Is then in my rival's bed,   50
Whose tresses of golden hair
  Are on the fair pillow bespread.
Then this doth my passion inflame,
  I start, and no longer can lie:
Ah! Sylvia, art thou not to blame   55
  To ruin a lover? I cry.

Grim king of the ghosts, be true,
  And hurry me hence away,
My languishing life to you
  A tribute I freely pay.   60
To the Elysian shades I post
  In hopes to be freed from care,
Where many a bleeding ghost
  Is hovering in the air.

XX.

The Lady distracted with Love,

MAD SONG THE FOURTH,

Was originally sung in one of Tom D'Urfey's comedies of
Don Quixote, acted in 1694 and 1696; and probably composed
by himself. In the several stanzas, the author represents his
pretty Mad-woman as, 1, sullenly mad; 2, mirthfully mad;
3, melancholy mad; 4, fantastically mad; and 5, stark mad.
But this and No. xxii. are printed from D'Urfey's *Pills to
purge Melancholy*, 1719, vol. i.

FROM rosie bowers, where sleeps the god of love,
   Hither ye little wanton cupids fly;
Teach me in soft melodious strains to move
   With tender passion my heart's darling joy:
Ah! let the soul of musick tune my voice,   5
To win dear Strephon, who my soul enjoys.

      Or, if more influencing
         Is to be brisk and airy,
      With a step and a bound,
      With a frisk from the ground,   10
         I'll trip like any fairy.

      As once on Ida dancing
         Were three celestial bodies:
      With an air, and a face,
      And a shape and a grace,   15
         I'll charm, like beauty's goddess.

Ah! 'tis in vain! 'tis all, 'tis all in vain!
Death and despair must end the fatal pain:
Cold, cold despair, disguis'd like snow and rain,
Falls on my breast; bleak winds in tempests blow;   20
My veins all shiver, and my fingers glow;
My pulse beats a dead march for lost repose,
And to a solid lump of ice my poor fond heart is froze.

      Or say, ye powers, my peace to crown,
      Shall I thaw myself, and drown   25
         Among the foaming billows?
      Increasing all with tears I shed,
         On beds of ooze, and crystal pillows,
      Lay down, lay down my love-sick head?

      No, no, I'll strait run mad, mad, mad;   30
         That soon my heart will warm;
      When once the sense is fled, is fled,
         Love has no power to charm.

Wild thro' the woods I'll fly, I'll fly,
   Robes, locks — shall thus — be tore!   35
A thousand, thousand times I'll dye
Ere thus, thus, in vain, — ere thus in vain adore.

XXI.

The Distracted Lover,

MAD SONG THE FIFTH,

WAS written by Henry Carey, a celebrated composer of
music at the beginning of the eighteenth century, and author
of several little theatrical Entertainments, which the reader
may find enumerated in the *Companion to the Play-house*, &c.
The sprightliness of this songster's fancy could not preserve
him from a very melancholy catastrophe, which was effected
by his own hand. In his Poems, 4to, Lond. 1729, may be
seen another Mad Song of this author, beginning thus:

> "Gods! I can never this endure,
> Death alone must be my cure," &c.

I GO to the Elysian shade,
   Where sorrow ne'er shall wound me;
Where nothing shall my rest invade,
   But joy shall still surround me.

I fly from Celia's cold disdain,   5
   From her disdain I fly;
She is the cause of all my pain,
   For her alone I die.

Her eyes are brighter than the mid-day sun,
When he but half his radiant course has run,   10
When his meridian glories gaily shine,
And gild all nature with a warmth divine.

See yonder river's flowing tide,
   Which now so full appears;
Those streams, that do so swiftly glide,   15
   Are nothing but my tears.

There I have wept till I could weep no more,
And curst mine eyes, when they have wept their store:
Then, like the clouds, that rob the azure main,
I've drain'd the flood to weep it back again.   20

      Pity my pains,
      Ye gentle swains!
   Cover me with ice and snow,
   I scorch, I burn, I flame, I glow!

      Furies, tear me,   25
      Quickly bear me
   To the dismal shades below!
      Where yelling, and howling,
      And grumbling, and growling,
   Strike the ear with horrid woe.   30

      Hissing snakes,
      Fiery lakes
   Would be a pleasure, and a cure:
      Not all the hells,
      Where Pluto dwells,   35
   Can give such pain as I endure.

   To some peaceful plain convey me,
   On a mossey carpet lay me,
   Fan me with ambrosial breeze,
   Let me die, and so have ease!   40

XXII.

The Frantic Lady.

MAD SONG THE SIXTH.

This, like number XX., was originally sung in one of D'Urfey's Comedies of *Don Quixote*, (first acted about the year 1694,) and was probably composed by that popular songster, who died Feb. 26, 1723.

This is printed in the "Hive, a Collection of Songs," 4 vols. 1721, 12mo, where may be found two or three other Mad Songs not admitted into these volumes.

I BURN, my brain consumes to ashes!
Each eye-ball too like lightning flashes!
Within my breast there glows a solid fire,
Which in a thousand ages can't expire!

Blow, blow, the winds' great ruler!   5
   Bring the Po, and the Ganges hither,
     'Tis sultry weather;
   Pour them all on my soul,
   It will hiss like a coal,
But be never the cooler.   10

   'Twas pride hot as hell,
   That first made me rebell,
From love's awful throne a curst angel I fell;
   And mourn now my fate,
   Which myself did create: 15
Fool, fool, that consider'd not when I was well!

   Adieu! ye vain transporting joys!
   Off ye vain fantastic toys!
That dress this face—this body—to allure!
   Bring me daggers, poison, fire!   20
   Since scorn is turn'd into desire.
All hell feels not the rage, which I, poor I, endure.

XXIII.

Lilli Burlero.

The following rhymes, slight and insignificant as they may now seem, had once a more powerful effect than either the Philippics of Demosthenes or Cicero, and contributed not a little towards the great revolution in 1688. Let us hear a contemporary writer.

"A foolish ballad was made at that time, treating the Papists, and chiefly the Irish, in a very ridiculous manner, which had a burden said to be Irish words, 'Lero, lero, lilliburlero,' that made an impression on the [king's] army, that cannot be imagined by those that saw it not. The whole army, and at last the people, both in city and country, were singing it perpetually. And perhaps never had so slight a thing so great an effect."—Burnet.

It was written, or at least republished, on the Earl of Tyrconnel's going a second time to Ireland in October, 1688. Perhaps it is unnecessary to mention, that General Richard Talbot, newly created Earl of Tyrconnel, had been nominated by King James II. to the lieutenancy of Ireland in 1686, on account of his being a furious papist, who had recommended himself to his bigoted master by his arbitrary treatment of the Protestants in the preceding year, when only lieutenant-general, and whose subsequent conduct fully justified his expectations and their fears. The violence of his administration may be seen in any of the histories of those times: particularly in Bishop King's "State of the Protestants in Ireland," 1691, 4to.

Lilliburlero and *Bullen-a-lah* are said to have been the words of distinction used among the Irish Papists in their massacre of the Protestants in 1641.

Ho! broder Teague, dost hear de decree?
Lilli burlero, bullen a-la.

Dat we shall have a new deputie,
    Lilli burlero, bullen a-la.
        Lero lero, lilli burlero, lero lero, bullen a-la,   5
        Lero lero, lilli burlero, lero lero, bullen a-la.

Ho! by shaint Tyburn, it is de Talbote:
    Lilli, &c.
And he will cut all de English troate.
    Lilli, &c.   10

Dough by my shoul de English do praat,
    Lilli, &c.
De law's on dare side, and Creish knows what.
    Lilli, &c.

But if dispence do come from de pope,   15
    Lilli, &c.
We'll hang Magna Charta and dem in a rope.
    Lilli, &c.

For de good Talbot is made a lord,
    Lilli, &c.   20
And with brave lads is coming aboard:
    Lilli, &c.

Who all in France have taken a sware,
    Lilli, &c.
Dat dey will have no protestant heir.   25
    Lilli, &c.

Ara! but why does he stay behind?
    Lilli, &c.
Ho! by my shoul 'tis a protestant wind.
    Lilli, &c.   30

But see de Tyrconnel is now come ashore,
    Lilli, &c.

Ver. 7, Ho by my shoul. al. ed.

And we shall have commissions gillore.
  Lilli, &c.

And he dat will not go to de mass,   35
  Lilli, &c.
Shall be turn out, and look like an ass.
  Lilli, &c.

Now, now de hereticks all go down,
  Lilli, &c.   40
By Chrish and shaint Patrick, de nation's our own.
  Lilli, &c.

Dare was an old prophesy found in a bog,
  Lilli, &c.
"Ireland shall be rul'd by an ass and a dog."   45
  Lilli, &c.

And now dis prophesy is come to pass,
  Lilli, &c.
For Talbot's de dog, and Ja**s is de ass.
  Lilli, &c.   50

*** The foregoing song is attributed to Lord Wharton in a small pamphlet, entitled, "A true relation of the several facts and circumstances of the intended riot and tumult on Queen Elizabeth's birth-day," &c. third edition, London, 1712, price 2d. See p. 5, viz. "A late Viceroy, [of Ireland,] who has so often boasted himself upon his talent for mischief, invention, lying, and for making a certain *Lilliburlero Song;* with which, if you will believe himself, he sung a deluded Prince out of three Kingdoms."

V. 43. What follows is not in some copies.

XXIV.

The Braes of Yarrow,

IN IMITATION OF THE ANCIENT SCOTS MANNER,

WAS written by William Hamilton, of Bangour, Esq., who died March 25, 1754, aged 50. It is printed from an elegant edition of his Poems, published at Edinburgh, 1760, 12mo. This song was written in imitation of an old Scottish ballad on a similar subject, with the same burden to each stanza.

———————

A. Busk ye, busk ye, my bonny bonny bride,
    Busk ye, busk ye, my winsome marrow,
  Busk ye, busk ye, my bonny bonny bride,
    And think nae mair on the Braes of Yarrow.

B. Where gat ye that bonny bonny bride?   5
    Where gat ye that winsome marrow?
A. I gat her where I dare na weil be seen,
    Puing the birks on the Braes of Yarrow.

  Weep not, weep not, my bonny bonny bride,
    Weep not, weep not, my winsome marrow;   10
  Nor let thy heart lament to leive
    Puing the birks on the Braes of Yarrow.

B. Why does she weep, thy bonny bonny bride?
    Why does she weep, thy winsome marrow?
  And why dare ye nae mair weil be seen   15
    Puing the birks on the Braes of Yarrow?

A. Lang maun she weep, lang maun she, maun she weep,
    Lang maun she weep with dule and sorrow;
  And lang maun I nae mair weil be seen
    Puing the birks on the Braes of Yarrow.   20

For she has tint her luver, luver dear,
   Her luver dear, the cause of sorrow;
And I hae slain the comliest swain
   That eir pu'd birks on the Braes of Yarrow.

Why rins thy stream, O Yarrow, Yarrow, reid?   25
   Why on thy braes heard the voice of sorrow?
And why yon melancholious weids
   Hung on the bonny birks of Yarrow?

What's yonder floats on the rueful rueful flude?
   What's yonder floats? O dule and sorrow!   30
O 'tis he the comely swain I slew
   Upon the duleful Braes of Yarrow.

Wash, O wash his wounds, his wounds in tears,
   His wounds in tears with dule and sorrow;
And wrap his limbs in mourning weids,   35
   And lay him on the Braes of Yarrow.

Then build, then build, ye sisters, sisters sad,
   Ye sisters sad, his tomb with sorrow;
And weep around in waeful wise
   His hapless fate on the Braes of Yarrow.   40

Curse ye, curse ye, his useless, useless shield,
   My arm that wrought the deed of sorrow,
The fatal spear that pierc'd his breast,
   His comely breast on the Braes of Yarrow.

Did I not warn thee, not to, not to luve?   45
   And warn from fight? but to my sorrow
Too rashly bauld a stronger arm
   Thou mett'st, and fell'st on the Braes of Yarrow.

Sweet smells the birk, green grows, green grows the
      grass,
   Yellow on Yarrow's bank the gowan,   50

Fair hangs the apple frae the rock,
  Sweet the wave of Yarrow flowan.

Flows Yarrow sweet? as sweet, as sweet flows Tweed,
  As green its grass, its gowan as yellow,
As sweet smells on its braes the birk,   55
  The apple frae its rock as mellow.

Fair was thy luve, fair fair indeed thy luve,
  In flow'ry bands thou didst him fetter;
Tho' he was fair, and weil beluv'd again
  Than me he never luv'd thee better.   60

Busk ye, then busk, my bonny bonny bride,
  Busk ye, busk ye, my winsome marrow;
Busk ye, and luve me on the banks of Tweed,
  And think nae mair on the Braes of Yarrow.

C. How can I busk a bonny bonny bride?   65
  How can I busk a winsome marrow?
How luve him upon the banks of Tweed,
  That slew my luve on the Braes of Yarrow?

O Yarrow fields, may never never rain
  Nor dew thy tender blossoms cover,   70
For there was basely slain my luve,
  My luve, as he had not been a lover.

The boy put on his robes, his robes of green,
  His purple vest, 'twas my awn sewing:
Ah! wretched me! I little, little kenn'd   75
  He was in these to meet his ruin.

The boy took out his milk-white, milk-white steed,
  Unheedful of my dule and sorrow.
But ere the toofall of the night
  He lay a corps on the Braes of Yarrow.   80

Much I rejoyc'd that waeful waeful day;
   I sang, my voice the woods returning:
But lang ere night the spear was flown,
   That slew my luve, and left me mourning.

What can my barbarous barbarous father do,   85
   But with his cruel rage pursue me?
My luver's blood is on thy spear,
   How canst thou, barbarous man, then wooe me?

My happy sisters may be, may be proud
   With cruel and ungentle scoffin',   90
May bid me seek on Yarrow's Braes
   My luver nailed in his coffin.

My brother Douglas may upbraid, upbraid,
   And strive with threatning words to muve me:
My luver's blood is on thy spear,   95
   How canst thou ever bid me luve thee?

Yes, yes, prepare the bed, the bed of luve,
   With bridal sheets my body cover,
Unbar, ye bridal maids, the door,
   Let in the expected husband lover.   100

But who the expected husband husband is?
   His hands, methinks, are bath'd in slaughter:
Ah me! what ghastly spectre's yon
   Comes in his pale shroud, bleeding after?

Pale as he is, here lay him, lay him down,   105
   O lay his cold head on my pillow;
Take aff, take aff these bridal weids,
   And crown my careful head with willow.

Pale tho' thou art, yet best, yet best beluv'd,
   O could my warmth to life restore thee!   110
Yet lye all night between my breists,
   No youth lay ever there before thee.

Pale, pale indeed, O luvely luvely youth!
  Forgive, forgive so foul a slaughter:
And lye all night between my breists;   115
  No youth shall ever lye there after.

A. Return, return, O mournful, mournful bride,
  Return, and dry thy useless sorrow:
Thy luver heeds none of thy sighs,
  He lyes a corps in the Braes of Yarrow.   120

XXV.

Admiral Hosier's Ghost,

Was a party song written by the ingenious author of *Leonidas*[1], on the taking of Porto Bello from the Spaniards by Admiral Vernon, Nov. 22, 1739. The case of Hosier, which is here so pathetically represented, was briefly this. In April, 1726, that commander was sent with a strong fleet into the Spanish West Indies, to block up the galleons in the ports of that country; or, should they presume to come out, to seize and carry them into England: he accordingly arrived at the Bastimentos, near Porto Bello, but being employed rather to overawe than to attack the Spaniards, with whom it was probably not our interest to go to war, he continued long inactive on that station, to his own great regret. He afterwards removed to Carthagena, and remained cruising in these seas, till far the greater part of his men perished deplorably by the diseases of that unhealthy climate. This brave man, seeing his best officers and men thus daily swept away, his ships exposed to inevitable destruction, and himself made the sport of the enemy, is said to have died of a broken heart. Such is the account of Smollett, compared with that of other less partial writers.

The following song is commonly accompanied with a

[1] An ingenious correspondent informs the Editor, that this ballad hath also been attributed to the late Lord Bath.

20*

Second Part, or Answer, which being of inferior merit, and
apparently written by another hand, hath been rejected.

————

As near Porto-Bello lying
   On the gently swelling flood,
At midnight with streamers flying
   Our triumphant navy rode;
There while Vernon sate all-glorious   5
   From the Spaniards' late defeat:
And his crews, with shouts victorious,
   Drank success to England's fleet:

On a sudden shrilly sounding,
   Hideous yells and shrieks were heard;   10
Then each heart with fear confounding,
   A sad troop of ghosts appear'd,
All in dreary hammocks shrouded,
   Which for winding-sheets they wore,
And with looks by sorrow clouded   15
   Frowning on that hostile shore.

On them gleam'd the moon's wan lustre,
   When the shade of Hosier brave
His pale bands was seen to muster
   Rising from their wat'ry grave.   20
O'er the glimmering wave he hy'd him,
   Where the Burford[2] rear'd her sail,
With three thousand ghosts beside him,
   And in groans did Vernon hail.

Heed, oh heed our fatal story,   25
   I am Hosier's injur'd ghost,
You who now have purchas'd glory
   At this place where I was lost!
Tho' in Porto-Bello's ruin
   You now triumph free from fears,   30

        [2] Admiral Vernon's ship.

When you think on our undoing,
   You will mix your joy with tears.

See these mournful spectres sweeping
   Ghastly o'er this hated wave,
Whose wan cheeks are stain'd with weeping;   35
   These were English captains brave.
Mark those numbers pale and horrid,
   Those were once my sailors bold:
Lo, each hangs his drooping forehead,
   While his dismal tale is told.   40

I, by twenty sail attended,
   Did this Spanish town affright;
Nothing then its wealth defended
   But my orders not to fight.
Oh! that in this rolling ocean   45
   I had cast them with disdain,
And obey'd my heart's warm motion
   To have quell'd the pride of Spain!

For resistance I could fear none,
   But with twenty ships had done   50
What thou, brave and happy Vernon,
   Hast atchiev'd with six alone.
Then the bastimentos never
   Had our foul dishonour seen,
Nor the sea the sad receiver   55
   Of this gallant train had been.

Thus, like thee, proud Spain dismaying,
   And her galleons leading home,
Though condemn'd for disobeying,
   I had met a traitor's doom,   60
To have fallen, my country crying
   He has play'd an English part,
Had been better far than dying
   Of a griev'd and broken heart.

Unrepining at thy glory,   65
  Thy successful arms we hail;
But remember our sad story,
  And let Hosier's wrongs prevail.
Sent in this foul clime to languish,
  Think what thousands fell in vain,   70
Wasted with disease and anguish,
  Not in glorious battle slain.

Hence with all my train attending
  From their oozy tombs below,
Thro' the hoary foam ascending,   75
  Here I feed my constant woe:
Here the bastimentos viewing,
  We recal our shameful doom,
And our plaintive cries renewing,
  Wander thro' the midnight gloom.   80

O'er these waves for ever mourning
  Shall we roam depriv'd of rest,
If to Britain's shores returning
  You neglect my just request;
After this proud foe subduing,   85
  When your patriot friends you see,
Think on vengeance for my ruin,
  And for England sham'd in me.

XXVI.

Jemmy Dawson.

JAMES DAWSON was one of the Manchester rebels, who was
hanged, drawn, and quartered, on Kennington-common, in
the county of Surrey, July 30, 1746.—This ballad is founded
on a remarkable fact, which was reported to have happened
at his execution. It was written by the late William
Shenstone, Esq., soon after the event, and has been printed

amongst his posthumous works, 2 vols. 8vo. It is here given
from a MS. which contained some small variations from that
printed copy.

COME listen to my mournful tale,
   Ye tender hearts, and lovers dear;
Nor will you scorn to heave a sigh,
   Nor will you blush to shed a tear.

And thou, dear Kitty, peerless maid,   5
   Do thou a pensive ear incline;
For thou canst weep at every woe,
   And pity every plaint, but mine.

Young Dawson was a gallant youth,
   A brighter never trod the plain;   10
And well he lov'd one charming maid,
   And dearly was he lov'd again.

One tender maid she lov'd him dear,
   Of gentle blood the damsel came,
And faultless was her beauteous form,   15
   And spotless was her virgin fame.

But curse on party's hateful strife,
   That led the faithful youth astray
The day the rebel clans appear'd:
   O had he never seen that day!   20

Their colours and their sash he wore,
   And in the fatal dress was found;
And now he must that death endure,
   Which gives the brave the keenest wound.

How pale was then his true love's cheek,   25
   When Jemmy's sentence reach'd her ear!
For never yet did Alpine snows
   So pale, nor yet so chill appear.

With faltering voice, she weeping said,
    Oh, Dawson, monarch of my heart,   30
Think not thy death shall end our loves,
    For thou and I will never part.

Yet might sweet mercy find a place,
    And bring relief to Jemmy's woes,
O GEORGE, without a prayer for thee   35
    My orisons should never close.

The gracious prince that gives him life
    Would crown a never-dying flame,
And every tender babe I bore
    Should learn to lisp the giver's name.   40

But though, dear youth, thou should'st be dragg'd
    To yonder ignominious tree,
Thou shalt not want a faithful friend
    To share thy bitter fate with thee.

O then her mourning-coach was call'd,   45
    The sledge mov'd slowly on before;
Tho' borne in a triumphal car,
    She had not lov'd her favourite more.

She follow'd him, prepar'd to view
    The terrible behests of law;   50
And the last scene of Jemmy's woes
    With calm and stedfast eye she saw.

Distorted was that blooming face,
    Which she had fondly lov'd so long:
And stifled was that tuneful breath,   55
    Which in her praise had sweetly sung:

And sever'd was that beauteous neck,
    Round which her arms had fondly clos'd:
And mangled was that beauteous breast,
    On which her love-sick head repos'd: 60

And ravish'd was that constant heart,
   She did to every heart prefer;
For though it could his king forget,
   'Twas true and loyal still to her.

Amid those unrelenting flames   65
   She bore this constant heart to see;
But when 'twas moulder'd into dust,
   Now, now, she cried, I'll follow thee.

My death, my death alone can show
   The pure and lasting love I bore: 70
Accept, O heaven, of woes like ours,
   And let us, let us weep no more.

The dismal scene was o'er and past,
   The lover's mournful hearse retir'd;
The maid drew back her languid head,   75
   And sighing forth his name expir'd.

Tho' justice ever must prevail,
   The tear my Kitty sheds is due;
For seldom shall she hear a tale
   So sad, so tender, and so true.   80

END OF THE THIRD BOOK.

A GLOSSARY

OF

THE OBSOLETE AND SCOTTISH WORDS IN THE SECOND VOLUME.

Such words as the reader cannot find here, he is desired to look for in the Glossaries to the other volumes.

A deid of nicht, s. *in dead of night.*
Aboven ous, *above us.*
Advoutry, Advouterous, *adultery, adulterous.*
Aff, s. *off.*
Ahte, *ought.*
Aith, s. *oath.*
Al, p. 4, albeit, *although.*
Alemaigne, f. *Germany.*
Alyes, p. 25, probably corrupted for algates, *always.*
Ancient, *a flag, banner.*
Angel, *a gold coin worth 10 s.*
Ant, *and.*
Aplyht, al aplyht, p. 8, *quite complete.*
Argabushe, *harquebusse, an old-fashioned kind of musket.*
Ase, *as.*
Attowre, s. *out over, over and above.*
Azein, agein, *against.*
Azont the ingle, s. p. 51, *beyond the fire. The fire was in the middle of the room* [1].

B.

Bairded, s. *bearded.*
Bairn, s. *child.*
Bale, *evil, mischief, misery*
Balow, s. a nursery term, *hush! lullaby! &c.*
Ban, *curse,* banning, *cursing.*
Battes, *heavy sticks, clubs.*
Bayard, *a noted blind horse, in the old romances.* The horse on which the four sons of Aymon rode, is called *Bayard Montalbon,* by Skelton, in his *Phillip Sparrow.*
Be, s. *by;* be that, *by that time.*
Bearn, bairn, s. *child;* also, *human creature.*
Bed, p. 8, *bade.*
Bede, p. 14, *offer, engage.*
Befall, p. 60, *befallen.*
Befoir, s. *before.*
Belive, *immediately, presently.*
Ben, s. *within, the inner room,* p. 52 [2].

[1] In the west of Scotland, at this present time, in many cottages they pile their peats and turfs upon stones in the middle of the room. There is a hole above the fire in the ridge of the house to let the smoke out at. In some places are cottage-houses, from the front of which a very wide chimney projects like a bow window: the fire is in a grate, like a malt-kiln grate, round which the people sit: sometimes they draw this grate into the middle of the room. — (Mr. Lambe.)

[2] "BUT o' house" means the outer part of the house, outer room, viz. that part of the house into which you first enter, suppose, from the street. "BEN o' house" is the inner room, or more retired part of the house. The daughter did not lie out of doors. The cottagers often desire their landlords to build them a BUT, and a BEN. (Vide Gloss. to vol. iii.) — Mr. Lambe.

Ben, p. 10, *be, are.*

Bene, p. 10, *bean,* an expression of contempt.

Beoth, p. 6, *be, are.*

Ber the prys, p. 6, *bear the prize.*

Berys, *beareth.*

Besprent, *besprinkled.*

Bested, p. 226, *abode.*

Bet, *better.* Bett, *did beat.*

Bewraies, *discovers, betrays.*

Bi mi leautè, *by my loyalty, honesty.*

Birk, s. *birch-tree.*

Blan, blanne, *did* blin, *i. e. linger, stop.*

Blee, *complexion.*

Blent, p. 119, *ceased.*

Blink, s. *a glimpse of light; the sudden light of a candle seen in the night at a distance.*

Boist, boisteris, s. *boast, boasters.*

Bollys, p. 15, *bowls.*

Bonny, s. *handsome, comely.*

Boote, *gain, advantage.*

Bot, s. *but;* sometimes it seems to be used for *both,* or *besides, moreover.*

Bot, s. *without.* Bot dreid, *without dread,* i. e. *certainly.*

Bougils, s. *bugle horns.*

Bowne, *ready.*

Brade, braid, s. *broad.*

Braes of Yarrow, s. *the hilly banks of the river Yarrow.*

Braifly, s. *bravely.*

Braw, s. *brave.*

Brayd, s. *arose, hastened.*

Brayd attowre the bent, s. *hasted over the field.*

Brede, *breadth.* So Chaucer.

Brenand drake, p. 16, may perhaps be the same as a *fire-drake,* or *fiery serpent,* a meteor or fire-work so called: here it seems to signify *burning embers,* or *fire-brands.*

Brimme, *public, universally known.* A. S. bryme, *idem.*

Brouch, *an ornamental trinket: a stone-buckle for a woman's breast, &c.* Vid. Brooche, Gloss. vol. iii.

Brouke hur wyth wynne, *enjoy her with pleasure,* p. 14, A. S. brok.

Brozt, *brought.*

Buen, bueth, *been, be, are.*

Buik, s. *book.*

Burgens, *buds, young shoots.*

Busk ye, s. *dress ye.*

But, *without,* but let, *without hindrance.*

Bute, s. *boot, advantage, good.*

Butt, s. *out, the outer room* (cf. Ben).

C.

Cadgily, s. *merrily, cheerfully.*

Caliver, *a kind of musket.*

Can curtesye, *know, understand, good manners.*

Cannes, p. 18, *wooden cups, bowls.*

Cantabanqui, Ital. *ballad - singers, singers on benches.*

Cantles, *pieces, corners.*

Canty, s. *cheerful, chatty.*

Capul, *a poor horse.*

Carle, *churl, clown.* It is also used in the north for a strong hale old man.

Carline, s. the feminine of *carle.*

Carpe, *to speak, recite:* also, *to censure.*

Carping, *reciting.*

Chayme, p. 55, *Cain.*

Che (Somerset dialect), *I.*

Cheis, s. *choose.*

Cheveron, p. 18, *the upper part of the scutcheon in heraldry.*

Chill (Som. dial.), *I will.*

Chould (ditto), *I would.*

Chylded, *brought forth, was delivered.*

Chylder, *children, children's.*

Clattered, *beat so as to rattle.*

Clead, s. *clad, clothe.*

Clepe, *call.*

Clynking, *clinking, jingling.*

Cohorted, *incited, exhorted.*

Cokenay, p. 20, seems to be a diminutive for *cook;* from the Latin *coquinator,* or *coquinarius.* The meaning seems to be, that "Every five and five had a cook, or scullion to attend them." Chaucer's Cant. Tales, 8vo. vol. iv. p. 253.

Cold rost (a phrase), *nothing to the purpose.*

Com, p. 7, *came.*

Con, can, *gan, began.* Item, conspringe (a phrase), *sprung;* con fare, *went, passed.*

Coote, p. 206 (note), *coat*

Cop, *head, the top of any thing,* Sax.

Cost, *coast, side.*

Cotydyallye, *daily, every day.*

Covetise, *covetousness.*

Could bear, a phrase for *bare.* Could creip, s. *crept.* Could say, *said.* Could weip, s. *wept.*

Could his good, p. 210, *knew what was good for him;* or perhaps, *could live upon his own.*
Couthen, p. 8, *knew.*
Croft, *an inclosure near a house.*
Crolz, *cross.*
Crompling, *crooked;* or perhaps, *with crooked knotty horns.*
Crook my knee, p. 53, *make lame my knee.* They say in the north, "The horse is crookit," *i. e.* lame. "The horse crooks," *i. e.* goes lame.
Crouneth, p. 7, *crown ye.*
Cule, s. *cool.*
Cummer, s. *gossip, friend,* fr. Commere, compere.
Cure, *care, heed, regard.*

D.

Dale, s. *deal,* p. 63; bot gif I dale, *unless I deal,* p. 62.
Dampned, *damned.*
Dan, p. 117, *an ancient title of respect;* from Lat. Dominus.
Danske, p. 198, *Denmark.*
Darh, p. 8, perhaps for *Thar, there.*
Darr'd, s. *hit.*
Dart the trie, s. *hit the tree.*
Daukin, *diminutive of David.*
Daunger hault, *coyness holdeth.*
Deare day, *charming, pleasant day.*
Dede is do, p. 27, *deed is done.*
Deere, *hurt, mischief.*
Deerlye dight, *richly fitted out.*
Deimpt, s. *deem'd, esteem'd.*
Deir, s. *dear.* Item, *hurt, trouble, disturb.*
Dele, *deal.*
Deme, deemed, *judge, doomed.*
Dent, p. 14, *a dint, blow.*
Deol, *dole, grief.*
Dere, deere, *dear;* also, *hurt.*
Derked, *darkened.*
Dern, s. *secret,* p. 62. I' dern, *in secret.*
Devys, *devise, the act of bequeathing by will.*
Deze, deye, *die.*
Dight, dicht, s. *decked, dressed, prepared, fitted out, done.*
Dill, *still, calm, mitigate.*
Dine, s. p. 81, *dinner.*
Dol. *See* Deol, Dule.
Don, p. 16, *down.*
Doughtiness of dent, *sturdiness of blows.*

Dozter, *daughter.*
Doz trogh, *a dough-trough, a kneading-trough,* p. 17.
Drake. *See* Brenand drake.
Dric, s. *suffer.*
Drowe, *drew.*
Dryng, *drink.*
Dude, *did.* Dudest, *didst.*
Dule, s. *duel, dol, dole, grief.*
Dyce, s. *dice, chequer-work.*
Dyht, p. 8, *to dispose, order.*
Dyzt. Vid. Dight.

E.

Eard, s. *earth.*
Earn, s. *to curdle, make cheese.*
Eiked, s. p. 65, *added, enlarged.*
Elvish, *peevish, fantastical.*
Eme, *kinsman, uncle.*
Ene, s. eyn, *eyes.* Ene, s. *even.*
Ensue, *follow.*
Entendement, f. *understanding.*
Ententifly, *to the intent, purposely.*
Er, ere, *before;* p. 14, *are.* Ere, *ear.*
Ettled, *aimed.*

F.

Fader, Fatheris, s. *father, fathers.*
Fair of feir, s. *of a fair and healthful look* (Ramsay). Perhaps, *far off (free from) fear.*
Falsing, *dealing in falsehood.*
Fang, p. 19, *seize, carry off.*
Fannes, p. 18, *instruments for winnowing corn.*
Fare, *go, pass, travel.*
Fare, *the price of a passage;* p. 71, *shot, reckoning.*
Fauzt, faucht, s. *fought.* Item, *fight.*
Feill, s. p. 65, *fele, many.*
Feiztyng, *fighting.*
Felay, feloy, p. 18, *fellow.*
Fele, fell, *furious;* p. 18, *skin.*
Fend, *defend.*
Fere, *fear.* Item, *companion, wife.*
Ferliet, s. *wondered.*
Ferly, *wonder;* also, *wonderful.*
Fey, s. *predestinated to death, or some misfortune: under a fatality.*
Fie, s. *beasts, cattle.*
Firth, Frith, s. p. 64, *a wood.* Item, *an arm of the sea,* l. fretum.
Fit, s. *foot.*

Fitt, *division, part.* See p. 143 & seq. [3].

Fles, p. 17, *fleece.*

Fleyke, p. 103, *a large kind of hurdle.* Cows are frequently milked in hovels made of Fleyks.

Flowan, s. *flowing.*

Fond, *contrive;* also, *endeavour, try.*

Force, no force, p. 118, *no matter.*

Forced, *regarded, heeded.*

Forfend, *avert, hinder.*

For-foght, p. 18, *over-fought.*

Fors. I do no fors, p. 10, *I don't care.*

Forst, p. 57, *heeded, regarded.*

Forwatcht, *over-watched, kept awake.*

Fowkin, *a cant word for a fart.*

Fox't, *drunk.*

Frae thay begin, p. 62, *from their beginning, from the time they begin.*

Freake, freeke, freyke, *man, human creature.*

Freers, fryars, *friars, monks.*

Freyke, p. 103, *humour, indulge freakishly, capriciously.*

Freyned, *asked.*

Frie, s. *fre, free.*

G.

Ga, gais, s. *go, goes.*

Gaberlunzie, gaberlunyo, s. *a wallet.*

Gaberlunzie-man, s. *a wallet-man,* i. e. *tinker, beggar.*

Gadlings, *gaddlers, idle fellows.*

Gadryng, *gathering.*

Galliard, *a sprightly kind of dance.*

Gar, s. *to make, cause, &c.*

Gayed, *made gay (their clothes).*

Gear, geire, geir, gair, s. *goods, effects, stuff.*

Gederede ys host, *gathered his host.*

Geere will sway, p. 157, *this matter will turn out; affair terminate.*

Gef, geve, *give.*

Gest, p. 229, *act, feat, story, history.* (It is *Jest* in MS.)

Gie, gien, s. *give, given.*

Gif, giff, s. p. 62, *if.*

Gillore (Irish), *plenty.*

Gimp, jimp, s. *neat, slender.*

Girt, s. *pierced.* Through-girt, p. 59, *pierced through.*

Give, s. *if.*

Glaive, f. *sword.*

Glen, s. *a narrow valley.*

Glie, s. glee, *merriment, joy.*

Glist, s. *glistered.*

God before, p. 68, i. e. *God be thy guide:* a form of blessing [4].

Gode, godness, *good, goodness.*

Good, p. 69, sc. *a good deal.*

Good-e'ens, *good-s'enings.*

Gorget, *the dress of the neck.*

Gowan, s. *the common yellow crow-foot, or goldcup.*

Graithed (gowden), s. *was caparisoned with gold.*

Graythed, p. 15, s. *decked, put on.*

Gree, s. *prize, victory.*

Greened, s. *grew green.*

Gret, p. 7, *great; grieved, swoln, ready to burst.*

Grippel, *griping, tenacious, miserly.*

Grownes, *grounds,* p. 200 (rhythmi gratia). Vid. Sowne.

Growte, p. 201, in Northamptonshire, is a kind of small beer, extracted from the malt after the strength has been drawn off. In Devon, it is a kind of sweet ale, medicated with eggs, said to be a Danish liquor [5].

Grype, *a griffin.*

Gybe, *jest, joke.*

Gyles, s. *guiles.*

Gyn, *engine, contrivance.*

Gyrd, p. 16, *girded, lashed, &c.*

Gyse, s. *guise, form, fashion.*

H.

Ha, *have;* ha, s. *hall.*

---

[3] FITTS, *i. e.* "divisions or parts in music," are alluded to in *Troilus and Cressida,* act 3, sc. 1. See Mr. Steevens's note.

[4] So in Shakspeare's *King Henry* V. (act 3, sc. viii.) the King says,

"My army's but a weak and sickly guard; Yet, GOD BEFORE, tell him we will come on."

[5] GROWTE is a kind of fare much used by Danish sailors, being boiled groats (*i. e.* hulled oats), or else shelled barley, served up very thick, and butter added to it. — (Mr. Lambe.)

Habbe, ase he brew, p. 3, *have as he brews*.

Haggis, s. *a sheep's stomach, stuffed with a pudding made of mincemeat, &c.*

Hail, hale, s. *whole, altogether*.

Halt, *holdeth*.

Hame, hamward, *home, homeward*.

Hare .. swerdes, p. 3, *their .. swords*.

Harnisine, *harness, armour*.

Harrowed, harassed, *disturbed*.

Harwos, *harrows*.

Hav, *have*.

Haves (of), *effects, substance, riches*.

Hawkin, synonymous to *Halkin*, dimin. of *Harry*.

He, p. 17, hie, *hasten*.

Heare, here; p. 58, *hari*.

Hech, p. 19, *hatch, small door*.

Hecht to lay thee law, s. *promised, engaged to lay thee low*.

Hed, *head*.

Hede, p. 7, he'd, *he would*; p. 33, *heed*.

Heicht, s. *height*.

Heiding-hill, s. *the 'heading [i. e. beheading] hill*. The place of execution was anciently an artificial hillock.

Heil, s. hele, *health*.

Helen, *heal*.

Helpeth, *help ye*.

Hem, *them*.

Henne, *hence*.

Hent, hente, *held, laid hold of*; also, *received*.

Her, p. 25, *their*.

Here, p. 4, *their*; p. 54, *hear*; p. 32, *hair*.

Herkneth, *hearken ye*.

Herte, hertis, *heart, hearts*.

Hes, s. *has*.

Het, *hot*.

Hether, heather, s. *heath, a low shrub, that grows upon the moor, &c., so luxuriantly as to choke the grass; to prevent which the inhabitants set whole acres of it on fire; the rapidity of which gave the poet that apt and noble simile in p. 89.* (Mr. Hutchinson.)

Heuch, s. *a rock or steep hill*.

Hevede, hevedest, *had, hadst*.

Heveriche, hevenrich, *heavenly*, p. 7.

Heynd, hend, *gentle, obliging*.

Heyze, *high*; heyd, s. *hied*.

Hicht; a-hicht, s. *on height*.

High dames too wail, s. p. 87, *high [or great] ladies to wail*; or, *hasten ladies to wail, &c.*

Hight, *promised, engaged*; also, *named*.

Hilt, *taken off, flayed*. Sax. hyldan.

Hinch-boys, hench- (properly haunch-) men, *pages of honour; pages attending on persons of office*.

Hind, s. *behind*.

Hinny, s. *honey*.

Hit, *it*; hit be write, p. 7, *it be written*.

Holden, *hold*.

Holtis hair, s. p. 65, *hoar hills*.

Holy-roode, *holy cross*.

Honden wrynge, *hands wring*.

Hop-halt, *limping; hopping and halting*.

Houzle, *give the sacrament*.

Howeres, howers, *hours*.

Huerte, *heart*.

Hye, hyest, *high, highest*.

Hynd attowre, s. *behind, over*, or *about*.

Hyp-halte, *lame in the hip*.

Hys, *his*; also, *is*.

Hyt, hytt, *it*.

Hyznes, *highness*.

I.

Janglers, *talkative persons, tell-tales;* also, *wranglers*.

I-fere, *together*.

I-lore, *lost*. I-strike, *stricken*.

I-trowe [*I believe*], *verily*.

Ich, *I*. Ich biqueth, *I bequeath*.

Jenkin, diminutive of *John*.

Ilk; this ilk, s. *this same*.

Ilke; every ilke, *every one*.

Ilk one, *each one*.

Illfardly, s. *ill-favour'dly, uglily*.

Inogh, *enough*.

Into, s. *in*.

Jo, s. *sweet-heart, friend. Jo* is properly the contraction of *Joy;* so *rejoice* is written *rejoce* in old Scottish MSS., particularly Bannatyne's, *passim*.

Io forth, corruptly printed *so*, should probably be *loo*, i. e. *halloo*.

Is, p. 3, *his*.

Ise, s. *I shall*.

It's ne'er, s. p. 83, *it shall ne'er*.

Jupe, s. p. 87, *an upper garment;* fr. *a petticoat*.

K.

Kauk, s. *chalk.*
Keel, p. 53, s. *raddle.*
Keipand, s. *keeping.*
Kempes, *soldiers, warriors.*
Kend, s. *knew.*
Kene, *keen.*
Kid, kyd, kithed, *made known, shown.*
Kind, kynde, *nature,* p. 13. To carp
  is our kind, *it is natural for us to*
  talk of.
Kirm, s. *churn.*
Kists, s. *chests.*
Kith and Kin, *acquaintance and*
  kindred.
Kowe, p. 14, *cow.*
Kye, *kine, cows.*
Kyrtel, kirtle, *petticoat.*
Kythe, *appear;* also, *make appear,*
  show, declare.
Kythed, s. *appeared.*

L.

Laide unto her, p. 209, *imputed to her.*
Lane, lain, s. *lone;* her lane, *alone,*
  by herself.
Lasse, *less.*
Layne, *lien:* also, *laid.*
Leal, leil, s. *loyal, honest, true;* f. loyal.
Leeke, p. 58, *phrase of contempt.*
Leiman, leman, *lover, mistress.*
Leir, s. lere, *learn.*
Lenger, *longer.*
Lengeth in, p. 226, *resideth in.*
Let, latte, *hinder;* p. 18, *slacken,*
  leave off; late, *let.*
Lever, *rather.*
Leves and bowes, *leaves and boughs.*
Leuch, leugh, s. *laughed.*
Leyke, like, *play,* pp. 103. 228.
Lie, s. lee, p. 90, *field, plain.*
Liege-men, *vassals, subjects.*
Lightly, *easily.*
Lire, *flesh, complexion.*
Lodlye, p. 44, *loathsome.* Vid. Gloss.
  vol. iii. lothly.

Lo'e, s. *love.*
Loht, ... (ballad i. ver. 44.)
Loo, *halloo!*
Lore, *lesson, doctrine, learning.*
Lore, *lost.*
Lorrel, *a sorry, worthless person.*
Losel, *ditto.*
Loud and still, phr. *at all times.*
Lought, lowe, lugh, p. 19, *laughed.*
Lowns, s. p. 84, *blazes.* Rather op-
  posed to *windy, boisterous.*
Lowte, lout, *bow, stoop.*
Lude, luid, luivt, s. *loved.*
Luef, *love.*
Luiks, s. *looks.*
Lyard, *grey:* a name given to a horse
  from its grey colour, as *Bayard*
  from bay.
Lys, *lies.*
Lythe, p. 145, *easy, gentle.*
Lyven na more, *live no more, no longer.*
Lyzt, *light.*

M.

Maden, *made.*
Making, p. 39, sc. *verses; versifying.*
Mane, maining, s. *moan, moaning.*
Mangonel, *an engine used for dis-*
  charging great stones, arrows, &c.
  before the invention of gunpowder.
Margarite, *a pearl,* lat.
Marrow, s. *equal.*
Mart, s. *marred, hurt, damaged.*
Maugre, p. 3, *spite of;* p. 62, *ill-will*
  (*I incur*).
Maze, *a labyrinth* [6], *any thing entangled*
  or intricate.
Me, p. 8, *men.* Me con, *men gan.*
Me-thuncketh, *methinks.*
Mean, *moderate, middle-sized.*
Mease, s. *soften, reduce, mitigate,*
  p. 90.
Meed, s. p. 87, *mood.*
Meit, s. meet, *fit, proper.*
Mell, *honey;* also, *meddle, mingle.*
Mense the faught, s. p. 86, *measure*
  the battle. To give to the mense, is,
  to give above the measure. Twelve

[6] On the top of Catharine-hill, Winchester (the usual play-place of the
school), was a very perplexed and winding path, running in a very small
space over a great deal of ground, called a MIZ-MAZE. The senior boys
obliged the juniors to tread it, to prevent the figure from being lost, as I am
informed by an ingenious correspondent.

and one to the mense, is common with children in their play.

Menzie, s. meaney, *retinue, company.*

Messager, f. *messenger.*

Minny, s. *mother.*

Mirk, s. *dark, black.*

Mirry, s. meri, *merry.*

Miskaryed, miscarried.

Mister, s. *to need.*

Mo, moe, *more.*

Moiening, *by means of,* fr.

Mome, *a dull, stupid person.*

Mone, *moon.*

More, mure, s. *moor, heath, marshy ground;* also, *wild hill;* p. 4, mores, ant the fenne, *q. d. hill and dale.*

Morne, to-morn, p. 62, *to-morrow, in the morning.*

Mornyng, p. 38, *mourning.*

Mote I thee, *might I thrive.*

Mowe, *may;* mou, s. *mouth.*

Muchele bost, p. 4, *mickle boast, great boast.*

Mude, s. *mood.*

Mulne, *mill.*

Murne, murnt, murning, s. *mourn, mourned, mourning.*

Myzt, myzty, *might, mighty.*

N.

Natheless, *nevertheless.*

Near, s. ner, nere, *ne'er, never.*

Neat, *oxen, cows, large cattle.*

Neatherd, *a keeper of cattle.*

Neatresse, *a female ditto.*

Nere, p. 226, *ne were; were it not for.*

Nest, nyest, *next, nearest.*

Noble, *a gold coin, in value 20 groats, or 6s. 8d.*

Nollys, p. 15, *noddles, heads.*

Nom, p. 7, *took.* Nome, *name.*

Non, *none.* None, *noon.*

Nonce, *purpose;* for the nonce, *for the occasion.*

Norse, s. *Norway.*

Nou, *now.*

Nout, nocht, s. *nought;* also, *not.* Nout, p. 8, *seems for* 'ne mought.'

Nowght, *nought.*

Nowls, *noddles, heads.*

Noye, p. 18, v. 175, *annoy;* query.

Nozt, p. 17, *nought, not.*

Nyzt, *night.*

O.

Ocht, s. *ought.*

Oferlyng, *superior, paramount;* opposed to *underling,* p. 3.

On, p. 38, *one, an.*

On loft, p. 15, *aloft.*

Onys, *once.*

Or, *ere, before.*

Orisons, s. *prayers,* f. oraisons.

Ou, oure, p. 6, *you, your;* ibid. *our.*

Out alas! *exclamation of grief.*

Outowre, s. *out over.*

Owene, awen, ain, s. *own.*

Owre, s. *over.*

P.

Pardè, perdie, *verily;* f. par dieu.

Pauky, s. *shrewd, cunning, sly;* or, *saucy, insolent.*

Pece, *piece, sc. of cannon.*

Pees, pese, *peace.*

Pele, *a baker's peel.*

Pentarchye of tenses, *five tenses.*

Perchmine, f. *parchment.*

Perfay, s. *verily;* f. par foy.

Perkin, diminutive of *Peter.*

Persit, s. pearced, *pierced.*

Petye, *pity.*

Peyn, *pain.*

Pibrochs, s. *Highland war-tunes.*

Playand, s. *playing.*

Plett, s. *platted.*

Plow-mell, p. 18, *a small wooden hammer occasionally fixed to the plow,* still used in the north: in the midland counties in its stead is used a plow-hatchet.

Plyzt, *plight.*

Poll-cat, *a cant word for a whore.*

Pollys, powlls, polls, *head.*

Poudred, p. 16, a term in heraldry, for *sprinkled over.*

Powlls, polls, *heads.*

Prest, f. *ready.*

Priefe, p. 72, *prove.*

Priving, s. *proving, tasting.*

Prove, p. 35, *proof.*

Prude, p. 4, *pride.* It. *proud.*

Puing, s. *pulling.*

Purchased, p. 10, *procured.*

Purvayed, *provided.*

Q.

Quaint, p. 188, *cunning*; p. 202, *nice, fantastical.*

Quat, s. *quitted.*

Quel, p. 104, *cruel, murderous.*

Quillets, *quibbles*, 1. quidlibet.

Quyle, s. *while.*

Quyt, s. *quite.*

Qwyknit, s. *quickened, restored to life.*

R.

Rae, *a roe.*

Raik, s. *to go apace.* Raik on raw. *go fast in a row.*

Ranted, s. p. 51, *were merry.* Vid. Gl. to Gent. Shepherd.

Raught, *reached, gained, obtained.*

Razt, *raught;* or p. 18, reft, *bereft.*

Rea'me, reaume, *realm.*

Rede, redde, p. 8, *read.*

Rede, read, p. 27, *advise, advice.*

Redresse, p. 59, *care, labour.*

Refe, reve, reeve, *bailiff.*

Rofe, *bereave;* or perhaps, *rive, split.*

Reid, s. *advise.*

Remeid, s. *remedy.*

Rescous, *rescues.*

Reve, p. 16, *bereave, deprive.*

Revers, s. *robbers, pirates, rovers.*

Rew, s. *take pity.*

Reweth, *regrets, has reason to repent.*

Rin, s. *run.*

Rise, p. 228, *shoot, bush, shrub.*

Rive, p. 230, *rife, abounding.*

Rood-loft, *the place in the church where the images were set up.*

Rudd, *ruddiness, complexion.*

Rude, s. rood, *cross.*

Ruel-bones, p. 15, *note,* perhaps *bones diversely coloured,* f. riolé; or perhaps, *small bone-rings,* from the fr. rouelle, *a small ring or hoop.* Cotgrave's Diction.

Rugged, p. 19, *pulled with violence.*

Rushy, s. p. 65, should be, rashy gair, *rushy stuff; ground covered with rushes.*

Ruthe, p. 35, *pity;* p. 169, *woe.*

Ryschys, p. 19, *rushes.*

Rywe, *rue.*

Ryzt, *right.*

S.

Safer, p. 15 (*note*), *sapphire.*

Saif, s. *save.* Savely, *safely.*

Saisede, *seized.*

'Say, p. 25, *essay, attempt.*

Scant, *scarce.*

Schal, *shall.*

Schatred, *shattered.*

Schaw, s. *show.*

Schene, s. *sheen, shining;* also, *brightness.*

Schiples, s. *shipless*

Scho, s. *she.*

Schuke, s. *shook.*

Sclat, p. 10, *slate; little table-book of slates to write upon.*

Scomfit, *discomfit.*

Scot, *tax, revenue;* p. 4, *a year's tax of the kingdom;* also, *shot, reckoning.*

Se, sene, seying, *see, seen, seeing.*

Se, sees, s. *sea, seas.*

Sek, *sack,* p. 15.

Selven, *self.*

Selver, siller, s. *silver.*

Sely, seely, *silly, simple.*

Sen, s. *since.*

Seavy, *mustard-seed;* f. senvie.

Seve, p. 230, *seven.*

Sey yow, p. 10, *say to, tell you.*

Seyd, s. *saw.*

Shave, p. 58, be shave, *been shaven.*

Sheeve, shive, *a great slice or luncheon of bread,* p. 201.

Shirt of male, or mail, *a garment for defence, made all of rings of iron, worn under the coat.* According to some, the *hawberk* was so formed.

Sho, s. *she.*

Shope, p. 224, *betook me, shaped my course.*

Shorte, s. *shorten.*

Shrew, *a bad, an ill-tempered person.*

Shreward, *a male shrew.*

Shrive, *confess.* Item, *hear confession.*

Shunted, *shunned.*

Shurtyng, *recreation, diversion, pastime,* p. 13. Vid. Gaw. Dougl. Gloss.

Shynand, s. *shining.*

Sich, sic, s. *such;* sich, s. *sigh.*

Side, s. *long.*

Sindle, s. *seldom.*

Sitteth, p. 3, *sit ye.*

Skaith, *scath, harm, mischief.*

Skalk, p. 103, perhaps from the Germ. Schalck, *malicious, perverse.* (Sic Dan. Skalck, *Nequitia, malicia, &c.* Sheringham de Angl. Orig. p. 318.)

— Or perhaps from the Germ. Schalchen, *to squint*. Hence our northern word *skelly*, to squint.

Skinker, *one that serves drink*.

Skomfit, *discomfit*.

Skott, *shot, reckoning*.

Slatred, *slit, broke into splinters*.

Sle, slea, sley, slo, *slay*.

Slee, s. *slay; also sly*.

Sond, *a present, a sending*.

Sone, p. 8, soon, *soon*.

Sonn, p. 228, son, *sun*.

Soth, sooth, *truth; also, true*.

Soothly, *truly*.

Sould, s. schuld (p. 15), *should*.

Souling, p. 201, *victualling*. Sowle is still used in the north for any thing eaten with bread. A. S. Sᵹuƚe, Suƚle. *Joh.* xxi. 5 (or *to sowle*, may be from the French word *saouler*, "to stuff and cram, to glut." Vide Cotgrave).

Sowne, *sound*, p. 40 (rhythmi gratia).

Spec, spak, spack, s. *spake*.

Speere, p. 111, vide locum.

Speered, sparred, *i. e. fastened, shut⁷*, vide p. 111.

Speir, s. speer, *spear*.

Speir, s. (p. 52,) speer, speare, *ask, inquire*. Vide Gloss. vol. iii.

Spence, spens, *expense*.

Spilt, s. *spoilt*.

Spindles and whorles, *the instruments used for spinning in Scotland, instead of spinning-wheels⁸*.

Spole, *shoulder*, f. espaule; p. 159, it seems to mean *armpit*.

Sporeles, *spurless, without spurs*.

Stalwart, stalworth, *stout*.

Startopes, *buskins*, or *half-boots*, worn by rustics, laced down before.

Stead, stede, *place*.

Steir, s. *stir*.

Stel, *steel*, steilly, s. *steely*.

Stound, *time*, a stounde, *a while*

Stoup of weir, p. 86, *a pillar of war*.

Stown, s. *stolen*.

Stra, strae, s. *straw*.

Strike, p. 10, *stricken*.

Styrt, *start*.

Suore bi ys chin, *sworn by his chin*.

Suthe, swith, *soon, quickly*.

Swa, sa, *so*.

Swaird, *the grassy surface of the ground*.

Swarvde, swarved, *climbed; or*, as it is now expressed in the midland counties, *swarmed;* to *swarm*, is to draw oneself up a tree, or any other thing, clinging to it with the legs and arms; as hath been suggested by an ingenious correspondent.

Swearde, swerd, *sword*.

Sweare, *swearing, oath*.

Swepyls, p. 18, a swepyl is that part of the flail with which the corn is beaten out, vulg. *a supple* (called in the midland counties a *swindgell*; where the other part is termed the *hand-staff*).

Swevens, *dreams*.

Swyke, *sigh*.

Swynkers, *labourers*.

Swyppyng, p. 18, *striking fast*. [Cimb. suipan, *cito agere*, or rather *scourging*, from *volvere, rupture*.] Scot. Sweap, *to scourge*. Vid. Gloss. to Gawin Douglas.

Swyving, *whoring*.

Sych, *such*.

Syns, *since;* syne, s. *then*.

Syschemell, p. 55, *Ishmael*.

Syth, *since*.

Syzt, *sight*.

T.

Taiken, s. p. 89, *token, sign*.

Take, p. 23, *taken*.

Targe, *target, shield*.

---

⁷ So in an old "Treatyse agaynst Pestilence, &c. 4to, emprynted by Wynkyn de Worde:" we are exhorted to "SPERE (*i. e.* shut or bar) the wyndowes ayenst the south." fol. 5.

⁸ The ROCK, SPINDLES, and WHORLES, are very much used in Scotland and the northern parts of Northumberland at this time. The thread for shoe-makers, and even some linen-webs, and all the twine of which the Tweed salmon-nets are made, are spun upon SPINDLES. They are said to make a more even and smooth thread than spinning-wheels.

Te, *to;* te make, p. 3, *to make.*
Te he! *interjection of laughing.*
Tent, s. *heed.*
Terry, diminutive of Thierry. *Theodoricus, Didericus.* Lat. also of Terence.
Tha, p. 19, *them;* thah, *though.*
Thare, theire, ther, thore, *there.*
The, *thee.*
The God, p. 22, seems contracted for The he, i. e. *high God.*
The, thee, *thrive.* So mote I thee, p. 73, *so may I thrive* [9].
Thii, p. 230, *they.*
Thi sone, p. 8, *thy son.*
Thilke, *this.*
Thir, s. *this, these.*
Thir' towmonds, s. *these twelve months.*
Thirtti thousent, *thirty thousand.*
Tho, *then,* p. 29, *those, the.*
Thole, tholed, *suffer, suffered.*
Thoust, *thou shalt* or *shouldest.*
Thrang, s. *throng, close.*
Thrawis, s. *throes.*
Thrie, s. thre, *three.*
Thrif, *thrive.*
Thruch, throuch, s. *through.*
Thud, p. 89, *noise of a fall.*
Tibbe. In Scotland *Tibbe* is the diminutive of *Isabel.*
Tild downe, p. 228, *pitched, qt.*
Till, s. *to.*
Timkin, diminutive of *Timothy.*
Tint, s. *lost.*
To, *too.*
Too-fall [10], s. *twilight.*
Traiterye, *treason.*
Trichard, *treacherous;* f. tricheur. *Vid.* p. 3.
Tricthen, *trick, deceive. Ibid.*
Trie, s. tre, *tree.*
Trough, trouth, *troth.*
Trow, *think, believe, trust.*
Trumped, p. 13, *boasted, told bragging lies, lying stories.* So in the north they say, *that's a* trump, i. e. *a lie.* "She goes about trumping," *i. e.* telling lies.
Trumpes, made of a tree, p. 17, perhaps *wooden trumpets: musical*

instruments *fit enough for a mock tournament.*
Tuke gude keip, s. *kept a close eye upon her.*
Turnes a crab, sc. *at the fire; roasts a crab.*
Twirtle twist, s. p. 84, *thoroughly twisted,* "*twisted:*" "*twirled twist.*" f. tortille.
Tyl, s. *to;* p. 13, *when* (query?).

V.

Vair, Somersetsh. dialect, *fair.*
Valzient, s. *valiant.*
Vazen, Som. probably for *faithen,* i. e. *faiths;* as *housen, closen, &c.*
Uch, *each.*
Vive, p. 230, Somerset. *five.*
Unmutit, s. *undisturbed, unconfounded, perhaps* unmuvit.
Unseeled, *opened;* a term in falconry.
Unsonsie, s. *unlucky, unfortunate.*
Vriers, p. 244, Som. *friers* (it is *Vicars,* in rcc.).
Uthers, s. *others.*

W.

Wa, s. p. 80, *way;* p. 178, *wall.*
Wad, s. *would.*
Waine, *waggon.*
Wallowit, s. *faded, withered.*
Wame, s. *womb.*
Wan neir, s. *drew near.*
Wanrufe, s. *uneasy.*
War ant wys, p. 6, *wary and wise.*
Ward, s. *watch, sentinel.*
Warke, s. *work.*
Warld, s. *world.*
Waryd, s. *accursed.*
Wate, s. weete, wete, witte, wot, wote, wotte, *know.*
Weale, weel, weil, wele, s. *well.*
Wearifou', *wearisome, tiresome, disturbing.*
Wee, s. *little.*
Weet, s. *wet.*
Weid, s. wede, weed, *clothes, clothing.*
Weinde, s. wende, went, weende, *weened, thought.*

---

[9] So in Chaucer, passim. Canterb. Tales, vol. i. p. 308.
"God let him never THE."
[10] "Tofall of the night," seems to be an image drawn from a suspended canopy, so let fall as to cover what is below. — (Mr. Lambe.)

Weldyngo, *ruling.*
Wend, wenden, *go.*
Wende, p. 7, *went,* wendeth, *goeth.*
Wene, weenest, *ween,* weenest.
Wer, *were.*
Wereth, p. 226, *defendeth.*
Werre, weir, s. *war;* warris, s. *war's.*
Wes, *was.*
Wesilin, s. *western.*
Whang, s. *a large slice.*
Wheder, *whither.*
Whelyng, *wheeling.*
Whig, *sour whey,* or *buttermilk.*
Whorles. *See* Spindles.
Wildings, *wild apples.*
Win, s. *get, gain.*
Winsome, s. *agreeable, engaging.*
Wirke wislier, *work more wisely.*
Wiss, wist, *know, knew.*
Withouten, *without.*
Wobster, s. webster, *weaver.*
Wode-warde, p. 32, *towards the wood.*
Woe worth, *woe be to* [*thee*].
Won, wont, *usage.*
Wonders, *wonderous.*
Wood, *mad, furious.*
Worshipfully frended, p. 210, *of worshipful friends.*
Wote, wot, *know;* I wote, *verily.*
Wow, *an exclamation of wonder;* also, *vow,* Lond. dialect.
Wreake, *pursue revengefully.*
Wreuch, *wretchedness.*
Wrouzt, *wrought.*
Wynnen, *win, gain.*
Wysse, p. 7, *direct, govern, take care of.* A. S. pıɲɲıan.

Y.

Y, *I.* Y singe, *I sing.*
Yae, s. *euch.*
Y-beare, *beare.* Y-boren, *borne. So* Y-founde, *found.* Y-mad, *made.* Y-wonne, *won.*
Y-core, *chosen.*
Y-was, [I know] *verily.*
Y-zote, *molten, melted.*
Yalping, s. *yelping.*
Ycha, ilka, *each, every.*
Ycholde, yef, *I should, if.*
Ychon, *each one.*
Yearded, p. 229, *buried.*
Yede, yode, *went.*
Yf, *if.*
Yfere, *together.*
Yll, *ill.*
Yu, *house, home.*
Ys, p. 9, *is;* p. 4, *his;* p. 7. in his.

Z.

Zacring bell, Som. Sacring bell, *a little bell rung to give notice of the elevation of the Host.* (It is *Zeering* in PCC. p. 244.)
Zede, yede, *went.*
Zee, zeene, Som. *see, seen.*
Zof, yef, *if.*
Zeirs, s. *years.*
Zeme, *take care of.* A. S. ʒeman.
Zent, *through.* A. S. ʒeonð.
Zestrene, s. *yester-e'en.*
Zit, s. zet, *yet.*
Zoud, s. *you'd, you would.*
Zule, s. yule, *Christmas.*
Zung, zonge, s. *young.*

END OF VOL. II.

PRINTING OFFICE OF THE PUBLISHER.

Printed in Great Britain
by Amazon

45537483R00190